GOVERNMENT IN AMERICA

GOVERNMENT IN AMERICA

PEOPLE, POLITICS, AND POLICY

2014 ELECTIONS AND UPDATES SIXTEENTH EDITION

George C.
EDWARDS III

Texas A&M University

Martin P.
WATTENBERG

University of California - Irvine

PEARSON

Boston   Columbus   Indianapolis   New York   San Francisco   Amsterdam   Cape Town
Dubai   London   Madrid   Milan   Munich   Paris   Montréal   Toronto   Delhi
Mexico City   São Paulo   Sydney   Hong Kong   Seoul   Singapore   Taipei   Tokyo

PEARSON

10 9 8 7 6 5 4 3 2
V011

VP, Product Development: Dickson Musslewhite
Acquisitions Editor: Jeff Marshall
Editorial Assistant: Kieran Marshall
Program Team Lead: Maureen Richardson
Project Team Lead: Melissa Feimer
Program Manager: Beverly Fong
Project Manager: Cheryl Keenan
Development Editor: Jennifer Jacobson, Ohlinger
   Publishing Services
Field Marketing Manager: Brittany Pongue-Mohammed
Product Marketing Manager: Tricia Murphy
Procurement Manager: Mary Fischer

Procurement Specialist: Mary Ann Gloriande
Associate Director of Design: Blair Brown
Cover Design Manager: Maria Lange
Cover Design: Pentagram
Cover Credit: Lauren Metcalfe/Getty Images
Digital Media Project Manager: Tina Gagliostro
Full-Service Project Management: Jenna Vittorioso /
   Lumina Datamatics
Cover Printer: Courier/Kendallville
Printer/Binder: Courier/Kendallville
Text Font: Adobe Caslon Pro 10/13.5

Library of Congress Cataloging-in-Publication Data
Edwards, George C.
Government in america : people, politics, and policy / George C. Edwards III, Martin P Wattenberg. — 2014 elections and updates edition.
      pages cm
Includes bibliographical references and index.
ISBN 978-0-205-86561-1 — ISBN 0-205-86561-5
1. United States—Politics and government. I. Wattenberg, Martin P., 1956- II. Title.
JK276.E39 2014
320.473—dc23

                                2014043385

PEARSON
Education

This book is not for sale or distribution in the U.S.A. or Canada

2709873

Student Edition:
ISBN 10: 0-13-390504-7
ISBN 13: 978-0-13-390504-5
Books à la Carte Edition:
ISBN 10: 0-13-391372-4
ISBN 13: 978-0-13-391372-9

BRIEF CONTENTS

Contents vi • To the Student xvi • To the Instructor xvii

PART I CONSTITUTIONAL FOUNDATIONS

1 Introducing Government in America 2

2 The Constitution 30

3 Federalism 68

4 Civil Liberties and Public Policy 98

5 Civil Rights and Public Policy 144

PART II PEOPLE AND POLITICS

6 Public Opinion and Political Action 180

7 The Mass Media and the Political Agenda 214

8 Political Parties 244

9 Campaigns and Voting Behavior 272

10 Interest Groups 312

PART III THE POLICYMAKERS

11 Congress 340

12 The Presidency 376

13 The Budget: The Politics of Taxing and Spending 420

14 The Federal Bureaucracy 450

15 The Federal Courts 484

PART IV POLICIES

16 Economic and Social Welfare Policymaking 522

17 Policymaking for Health Care, the Environment, and Energy 552

18 National Security Policymaking 582

Appendices 619 • Glossary 641 • Key Terms in Spanish 655 • Notes 661 • Credits 683 • Index 691 • Answer Key 717

CONTENTS

To the Student xvi • To the Instructor xvii

PART I CONSTITUTIONAL FOUNDATIONS

1 Introducing Government in America 2

1.1 Government 8

1.2 Politics 10

1.3 The Policymaking System 11

People Shape Policy 12

Policies Impact People 13

1.4 Democracy in America 14

Traditional Democratic Theory 14

Three Contemporary Theories of American Democracy 15

Challenges to Democracy 17

American Political Culture and Democracy 19

A Culture War? 21

■ POINT TO PONDER 22

1.5 The Scope of Government in America 23

How Active Is American Government? 24

2 The Constitution 30

2.1 The Origins of the Constitution 32

The Road to Revolution 33

Declaring Independence 33

The English Heritage: The Power of Ideas 34

The American Creed 35

Winning Independence 36

The "Conservative" Revolution 37

2.2 The Government That Failed: 1776–1787 37

The Articles of Confederation 37

■ WHY IT MATTERS TO YOU: A STRONG NATIONAL GOVERNMENT 38

Changes in the States 38

Economic Turmoil 39

The Aborted Annapolis Meeting 40

2.3 Making a Constitution: The Philadelphia Convention 41

Gentlemen in Philadelphia 41

Philosophy into Action 41

2.4 Critical Issues at the Convention 42

The Equality Issues 42

■ WHY IT MATTERS TO YOU: REPRESENTATION IN THE SENATE 43

■ POINT TO PONDER 44

The Economic Issues 44

The Individual Rights Issues 46

2.5 The Madisonian System 47

Thwarting Tyranny of the Majority 47

■ WHY IT MATTERS TO YOU: CHECKS AND BALANCES 49

The Constitutional Republic 49

The End of the Beginning 50

2.6 Ratifying the Constitution 51

Federalists and Anti-Federalists 51

Ratification 52

vi

2.7 Changing the Constitution 53

The Formal Amending Process 54

AMERICA IN PERSPECTIVE: THE UNUSUAL RIGIDITY OF THE U.S. CONSTITUTION 55

The Informal Processes of Constitutional Change 56

YOU ARE THE POLICYMAKER: HOW FREQUENTLY SHOULD WE AMEND THE CONSTITUTION? 56

The Importance of Flexibility 59

2.8 Understanding the Constitution 60

The Constitution and Democracy 60

YOUNG PEOPLE & POLITICS: LOWERING THE VOTING AGE 61

The Constitution and the Scope of Government 61

3 Federalism 68

3.1 Defining Federalism 70

AMERICA IN PERSPECTIVE: WHY FEDERALISM? 71

3.2 The Constitutional Basis of Federalism 72

The Division of Power 72

WHY IT MATTERS TO YOU: PROTECTING RIGHTS 73

National Supremacy 73

WHY IT MATTERS TO YOU: COMMERCE POWER 77

States' Obligations to Each Other 78

3.3 Intergovernmental Relations 79

From Dual to Cooperative Federalism 80

YOUNG PEOPLE & POLITICS: FEDERAL SUPPORT FOR COLLEGES AND UNIVERSITIES 81

Devolution? 82

Fiscal Federalism 83

WHY IT MATTERS TO YOU: GRANTS-IN-AID 83

POINT TO PONDER 86

3.4 Diversity in Policy 88

YOU ARE THE POLICYMAKER: SHOULD *WHETHER* YOU LIVE DEPEND ON *WHERE* YOU LIVE? 89

3.5 Understanding Federalism 89

Federalism and Democracy 90

Federalism and the Scope of the National Government 92

4 Civil Liberties and Public Policy 98

4.1 The Bill of Rights 100

The Bill of Rights—Then and Now 101

The Bill of Rights and the States 102

4.2 Freedom of Religion 102

The Establishment Clause 103

WHY IT MATTERS TO YOU: THE ESTABLISHMENT CLAUSE 106

The Free Exercise Clause 107

AMERICA IN PERSPECTIVE: TOLERANCE FOR THE FREE SPEECH RIGHTS OF RELIGIOUS EXTREMISTS 107

4.3 Freedom of Expression 109

YOU ARE THE JUDGE: THE CASE OF ANIMAL SACRIFICES 109

Prior Restraint 110

Free Speech and Public Order 111

YOU ARE THE JUDGE: THE CASE OF THE PURLOINED PENTAGON PAPERS 111

Obscenity 112

YOU ARE THE JUDGE: THE CASE OF THE DRIVE-IN THEATER 113

Libel and Slander 115

WHY IT MATTERS TO YOU: LIBEL LAW 115

Symbolic Speech 116

Free Press and Fair Trials 116

Commercial Speech 117

Regulation of the Public Airwaves 117

Campaigning 119

4.4 Freedom of Assembly 119

Right to Assemble 119

Right to Associate 120

YOU ARE THE JUDGE: THE CASE OF THE NAZIS' MARCH IN SKOKIE 121

4.5 Right to Bear Arms 121

POINT TO PONDER 122

4.6 Defendants' Rights 123

Searches and Seizures 125

WHY IT MATTERS TO YOU: THE EXCLUSIONARY RULE 126

YOU ARE THE JUDGE: THE CASE OF MS. MONTOYA 126

Self-Incrimination 127

The Right to Counsel 129

Trials 129

YOU ARE THE JUDGE: THE CASE OF THE ENTICED FARMER 129

Cruel and Unusual Punishment 132

YOU ARE THE JUDGE: THE CASE OF THE FIRST OFFENDER 132

YOUNG PEOPLE & POLITICS: COLLEGE STUDENTS HELP PREVENT WRONGFUL DEATHS 134

4.7 The Right to Privacy 135

Is There a Right to Privacy? 135

Controversy over Abortion 135

4.8 Understanding Civil Liberties 137

Civil Liberties and Democracy 138

Civil Liberties and the Scope of Government 138

5 Civil Rights and Public Policy 144

5.1 The Struggle for Equality 146

Conceptions of Equality 147

The Constitution and Inequality 147

Equal Education 150

WHY IT MATTERS TO YOU: BROWN V. BOARD OF EDUCATION 151

5.2 African Americans' Civil Rights 149

Slavery 149

Reconstruction and Segregation 149

The Civil Rights Movement and Public Policy 152

YOUNG PEOPLE & POLITICS: FREEDOM RIDERS 153

Voting Rights 154

WHY IT MATTERS TO YOU: THE VOTING RIGHTS ACT 155

5.3 The Rights of Other Minority Groups 156

Native Americans 156

Hispanic Americans 158

Asian Americans 159

Arab Americans and Muslims 160

5.4 The Rights of Women 161

The Battle for the Vote 161

The "Doldrums": 1920–1960 161

The Second Feminist Wave 162

Women in the Workplace 163

WHY IT MATTERS TO YOU: CHANGES IN THE WORKPLACE 164

YOU ARE THE JUDGE: IS MALE-ONLY DRAFT REGISTRATION GENDER DISCRIMINATION? 165

Sexual Harassment 166

5.5 Other Groups Active Under the Civil Rights Umbrella 166

Civil Rights and the Graying of America 167

Civil Rights and People with Disabilities 167

LGBT Rights 168

5.6 Affirmative Action 170

POINT TO PONDER 170

YOU ARE THE JUDGE: THE CASE OF THE NEW HAVEN FIREFIGHTERS 172

5.7 Understanding Civil Rights and Public Policy 173

Civil Rights and Democracy 173

AMERICA IN PERSPECTIVE: RESPECT FOR MINORITY RIGHTS 174

Civil Rights and the Scope of Government 174

PART II PEOPLE AND POLITICS

6 Public Opinion and Political Action 180

6.1 The American People 182

The Immigrant Society 183

The American Melting Pot 184

YOU ARE THE POLICYMAKER: SHOULD IMMIGRATION BE BASED MORE ON SKILLS THAN BLOOD TIES? 185

The Regional Shift 188

The Graying of America 188

6.2 How Americans Learn About Politics: Political Socialization 189

The Process of Political Socialization 189

Political Learning over a Lifetime 191

6.3 Measuring Public Opinion and Political Information 191

How Polls Are Conducted 192

The Role of Polls in American Democracy 193

What Polls Reveal About Americans' Political Information 195

■ POINT TO PONDER 196

■ WHY IT MATTERS TO YOU: POLITICAL KNOWLEDGE OF THE ELECTORATE 196

The Decline of Trust in Government 197

6.4 What Americans Value: Political Ideologies 199

Who Are the Liberals and Conservatives? 200

■ YOUNG PEOPLE & POLITICS: HOW YOUNGER AND OLDER AMERICANS COMPARE ON THE ISSUES 200

Do People Think in Ideological Terms? 201

6.5 How Americans Participate in Politics 203

Conventional Participation 204

Protest as Participation 204

■ AMERICA IN PERSPECTIVE: CONVENTIONAL AND UNCONVENTIONAL POLITICAL PARTICIPATION 206

Class, Inequality, and Participation 207

■ WHY IT MATTERS TO YOU: POLITICAL PARTICIPATION 207

6.6 Understanding Public Opinion and Political Action 208

Public Attitudes Toward the Scope of Government 208

Democracy, Public Opinion, and Political Action 208

7 The Mass Media and the Political Agenda 214

7.1 The Mass Media Today 216

The Mass Media 219

7.2 The Development of Media Politics 218

The Print Media 219

The Emergence of Radio and Television 220

■ YOU ARE THE POLICYMAKER: SHOULD NEWSPAPERS BE ALLOWED TO BE NONPROFIT ORGANIZATIONS? 221

Government Regulation of Electronic Media 222

From Broadcasting to Narrowcasting: The Rise of Cable and Cable News 222

■ YOUNG PEOPLE & POLITICS: LEARNING FROM COMEDY SHOWS? 223

The Impact of the Internet 226

Private Control of the Media 228

■ WHY IT MATTERS TO YOU: MEDIA AS A BUSINESS 229

7.3 Reporting the News 230

Finding the News 230

Presenting the News 231

■ WHY IT MATTERS TO YOU: THE INCREASING SPEED OF NEWS DISSEMINATION 232

■ AMERICA IN PERSPECTIVE: THE LENGTH OF CANDIDATE SOUND BITES IN FOUR COUNTRIES 233

Bias in the News 234

7.4 The News and Public Opinion 236

7.5 Policy Entrepreneurs and Agenda Setting 237

7.6 Understanding the Mass Media 238

The Media and the Scope of Government 238

Individualism and the Media 238

■ POINT TO PONDER 239

Democracy and the Media 239

8 Political Parties 244

8.1 The Meaning of Party 246

Tasks of the Parties 247

■ WHY IT MATTERS TO YOU: POLITICAL PARTIES 248

Parties, Voters, and Policy: The Downs Model 248

8.2 The Party in the Electorate 250

■ YOUNG PEOPLE & POLITICS: THE PARTIES FACE AN INDEPENDENT YOUTH 252

8.3 The Party Organizations: From the Grass Roots to Washington 252

Local Parties 253

The 50 State Party Systems 254

8.4 The Party in Government: Promises and Policy 255

The National Party Organizations 255

■ YOU ARE THE POLICYMAKER: SHOULD POLITICAL PARTIES CHOOSE THEIR NOMINEES IN OPEN OR CLOSED PRIMARIES? 254

8.5 Party Eras in American History 256

1796–1824: The First Party System 258

1828–1856: Jackson and the Democrats Versus the Whigs 258

1860–1928: The Two Republican Eras 259

1932–1964: The New Deal Coalition 259

1968–Present: Southern Realignment and the Era of Divided Party Government 261

■ WHY IT MATTERS TO YOU: DIVIDED PARTY GOVERNMENT 262

8.6 Third Parties: Their Impact on American Politics 263

■ AMERICA IN PERSPECTIVE: MULTIPARTY SYSTEMS IN OTHER COUNTRIES 264

8.7 Understanding Political Parties 265

Democracy and Responsible Party Government: How Should We Govern? 265

■ POINT TO PONDER 267

American Political Parties and the Scope of Government 267

9 Campaigns and Voting Behavior 272

9.1 The Nomination Game 275

Competing for Delegates 275

■ POINT TO PONDER 279

■ WHY IT MATTERS TO YOU: EARLY DELEGATE CONTESTS 280

The Convention Send-Off 282

9.2 The Campaign Game 283

The High-Tech Media Campaign 283

■ YOUNG PEOPLE & POLITICS: WILL THE INTERNET REVOLUTIONIZE POLITICAL CAMPAIGNS? 284

Organizing the Campaign 285

9.3 Money and Campaigning 286

Regulations on Campaign Contributions 287

Regulations on Independent Political Expenditures 289

Does Money Buy Victory? 291

■ WHY IT MATTERS TO YOU: MONEY AND ELECTIONS 291

Are Campaigns Too Expensive? 291

9.4 The Impact of Campaigns 292

9.5 Whether to Vote: A Citizen's First Choice 292

Deciding Whether to Vote 293

Registering to Vote 294

■ AMERICA IN PERSPECTIVE: WHY TURNOUT IN THE UNITED STATES IS SO LOW COMPARED TO TURNOUT IN OTHER COUNTRIES 295

Who Votes? 296

■ WHY IT MATTERS TO YOU: YOUTH TURNOUT 297

9.6 How Americans Vote: Explaining Citizens' Decisions 298

Party Identification 299

Candidate Evaluations: How Americans See the Candidates 299

Policy Voting 300

2012: A Battle for the Middle-Class Vote 301

9.7 The Last Battle: The Electoral College 303

■ YOU ARE THE POLICYMAKER: SHOULD WE MAKE EVERY STATE A BATTLEGROUND BY ELECTING THE PRESIDENT BY A NATIONAL POPULAR VOTE? 305

9.8 Understanding Campaigns and Voting Behavior 305

Are Nominations and Campaigns Too Democratic? 306

Do Elections Affect Public Policy? 307

Do Campaigns Lead to Increases in the Scope of Government? 307

10 Interest Groups 312

10.1 The Role of Interest Groups 315

■ AMERICA IN PERSPECTIVE: INTEREST GROUP PARTICIPATION 315

10.2 Theories of Interest Group Politics 316

Pluralism 316

Elitism 317

Hyperpluralism 317

■ POINT TO PONDER 318

■ WHY IT MATTERS TO YOU: THEORIES OF INTEREST GROUP POLITICS 319

10.3 What Makes an Interest Group Successful? 319

The Surprising Ineffectiveness of Large Groups 319

Intensity 321

■ YOUNG PEOPLE & POLITICS: THE VIRGINIA 21 COALITION 321

Financial Resources 322

10.4 How Groups Try to Shape Policy 322

Lobbying 323

Electioneering 325

■ WHY IT MATTERS TO YOU: PACs 326

■ YOU ARE THE POLICYMAKER: SHOULD PACs BE ELIMINATED? 327

Litigation 327

Going Public 328

10.5 Types of Interest Groups 329

Economic Interests 330

Environmental Interests 332

Equality Interests 333

Consumer and Other Public Interest Lobbies 334

10.6 Understanding Interest Groups 334

Interest Groups and Democracy 334

Interest Groups and the Scope of Government 335

PART III THE POLICYMAKERS

11 Congress 340

11.1 The Representatives and Senators 342

The Members 342

Why Aren't There More Women in Congress? 344

11.2 Congressional Elections 345

Who Wins Elections? 345

■ WHY IT MATTERS TO YOU: INCUMBENT SUCCESS 345

The Advantages of Incumbency 346

The Role of Party Identification 349

Defeating Incumbents 349

Open Seats 350

Stability and Change 350

■ YOU ARE THE POLICYMAKER: SHOULD WE IMPOSE TERM LIMITS ON MEMBERS OF CONGRESS? 350

11.3 How Congress Is Organized to Make Policy 351

American Bicameralism 351

■ WHY IT MATTERS TO YOU: THE FILIBUSTER 353

Congressional Leadership 353

■ WHY IT MATTERS TO YOU: PARTY STRENGTH 355

The Committees and Subcommittees 355

■ WHY IT MATTERS TO YOU: INCONSISTENT OVERSIGHT 358

■ WHY IT MATTERS TO YOU: THE COMMITTEE SYSTEM 359

Caucuses: The Informal Organization of Congress 360

Congressional Staff 360

■ YOUNG PEOPLE & POLITICS: ARE OPPORTUNITIES TO INTERN BIASED IN FAVOR OF THE WEALTHY? 361

11.4 The Congressional Process and Decision Making 362

Presidents and Congress: Partners and Protagonists 364

Party, Ideology, and Constituency 365

Lobbyists and Interest Groups 367

■ POINT TO PONDER 368

11.5 Understanding Congress 369

Congress and Democracy 369

■ AMERICA IN PERSPECTIVE: MALAPPORTIONMENT IN THE UPPER HOUSE 370

Congress and the Scope of Government 371

12 The Presidency 376

12.1 The Presidents 378

Great Expectations 379

Who They Are 379

■ POINT TO PONDER 379

How They Got There 380

■ WHY IT MATTERS TO YOU: STANDARDS OF
IMPEACHMENT 382

■ YOU ARE THE POLICYMAKER: WHAT SHOULD
BE THE CRITERIA FOR IMPEACHING THE
PRESIDENT? 384

12.2 Presidential Powers 384

Constitutional Powers 384

■ AMERICA IN PERSPECTIVE: PRESIDENT OR
PRIME MINISTER? 385

The Expansion of Power 386

Perspectives on Presidential Power 386

**12.3 Running the Government: The Chief
Executive 387**

The Vice President 388

The Cabinet 388

The Executive Office 389

The White House Staff 391

The First Lady 392

**12.4 Presidential Leadership of Congress:
The Politics of Shared Powers 393**

Chief Legislator 394

■ WHY IT MATTERS TO YOU: THE PRESIDENT'S
VETO 394

Party Leadership 395

Public Support 398

Legislative Skills 399

**12.5 The President and National Security
Policy 401**

Chief Diplomat 401

Commander in Chief 402

War Powers 403

■ WHY IT MATTERS TO YOU: WAR
POWERS 404

Crisis Manager 404

Working with Congress 406

**12.6 Power from the People: The Public
Presidency 407**

Going Public 407

Presidential Approval 408

Policy Support 409

■ YOUNG PEOPLE & POLITICS:
THE GENERATION GAP IN PRESIDENTIAL
APPROVAL 410

Mobilizing the Public 411

12.7 The President and the Press 412

Nature of News Coverage 413

The Presidency and Democracy 415

The Presidency and the Scope of Government 415

**12.8 Understanding the American
Presidency 414**

**13 The Budget: The Politics of
Taxing and Spending 420**

13.1 Federal Revenue and Borrowing 423

Personal and Corporate Income Tax 423

■ WHY IT MATTERS TO YOU: THE PROGRESSIVE
INCOME TAX 424

Social Insurance Taxes 425

Borrowing 425

■ WHY IT MATTERS TO YOU: DEFICIT
SPENDING 427

Taxes and Public Policy 427

■ YOUNG PEOPLE & POLITICS: EDUCATION AND
THE FEDERAL TAX CODE 429

■ AMERICA IN PERSPECTIVE: HOW BIG IS THE
TAX BURDEN? 430

13.2 Federal Expenditures 430

Big Governments, Big Budgets 431

The Rise of the National Security State 431

The Rise of the Social Service State 433

Incrementalism 435

"Uncontrollable" Expenditures 436

■ WHY IT MATTERS TO YOU:
"UNCONTROLLABLE" SPENDING 436

■ POINT TO PONDER 437

13.3 The Budgetary Process 437

Budgetary Politics 437

The President's Budget 440

Congress and the Budget 440

■ YOU ARE THE POLICYMAKER: BALANCING
THE BUDGET 443

13.4 **Understanding Budgeting 443**

Democracy and Budgeting 443

The Budget and the Scope of Government 445

14 **The Federal Bureaucracy 450**

14.1 **The Bureaucrats 452**

Some Bureaucratic Myths and Realities 453

Civil Servants 455

WHY IT MATTERS TO YOU: THE MERIT SYSTEM 456

Political Appointees 456

14.2 **How the Federal Bureaucracy Is Organized 457**

Cabinet Departments 457

Independent Regulatory Commissions 459

WHY IT MATTERS TO YOU: INDEPENDENT REGULATORY COMMISSIONS 459

Government Corporations 460

The Independent Executive Agencies 461

14.3 **Bureaucracies as Implementors 461**

What Implementation Means 461

Why the Best-Laid Plans Sometimes Flunk the Implementation Test 461

YOUNG PEOPLE & POLITICS: DRUG OFFENSES AND FINANCIAL AID 462

WHY IT MATTERS TO YOU: BUREAUCRATIC RESOURCES 465

POINT TO PONDER 467

A Case Study of Successful Implementation: The Voting Rights Act of 1965 469

Privatization 470

14.4 **Bureaucracies as Regulators 471**

Regulation in the Economy and in Everyday Life 471

Deregulation 472

YOU ARE THE POLICYMAKER: HOW SHOULD WE REGULATE? 473

14.5 **Controlling the Bureaucracy 473**

Presidents Try to Control the Bureaucracy 474

AMERICA IN PERSPECTIVE: INFLUENCING INDEPENDENT AGENCIES 474

Congress Tries to Control the Bureaucracy 475

Iron Triangles and Issue Networks 476

14.6 **Understanding Bureaucracies 478**

Bureaucracy and Democracy 478

Bureaucracy and the Scope of Government 478

15 **The Federal Courts 484**

15.1 **The Nature of the Judicial System 486**

Participants in the Judicial System 487

15.2 **The Structure of the Federal Judicial System 488**

District Courts 489

Courts of Appeals 490

The Supreme Court 491

15.3 **The Politics of Judicial Selection 493**

WHY IT MATTERS TO YOU: JUDICIAL ELECTION 493

The Lower Courts 494

WHY IT MATTERS TO YOU: SENATORIAL COURTESY 494

The Supreme Court 495

15.4 **The Backgrounds of Judges and Justices 498**

Backgrounds 499

Criteria for Selection 500

Background Characteristics and Policymaking 501

15.5 **The Courts as Policymakers 502**

Accepting Cases 502

The Process of Decision Making 504

The Basis of Decisions 505

POINT TO PONDER 507

Implementing Court Decisions 507

WHY IT MATTERS TO YOU: THE LACK OF A JUDICIAL BUREAUCRACY 509

15.6 **The Courts and Public Policy: A Historical Review 509**

John Marshall and the Growth of Judicial Review 509

■ YOUNG PEOPLE & POLITICS: THE SUPREME COURT IS CLOSER THAN YOU THINK 510

The "Nine Old Men" 511

The Warren Court 512

The Burger Court 512

■ AMERICA IN PERSPECTIVE: THE TENURE OF SUPREME COURT JUDGES 512

The Rehnquist and Roberts Courts 513

15.7 Understanding the Courts 513

The Courts and Democracy 513

The Scope of Judicial Power 515

■ YOU ARE THE POLICYMAKER: THE DEBATE OVER JUDICIAL ACTIVISM 516

PART IV POLICIES

16 Economic and Social Welfare Policymaking 522

16.1 Economic Policymaking 525

Two Major Worries: Unemployment and Inflation 525

■ YOUNG PEOPLE & POLITICS: UNEMPLOYMENT RATES BY AGE AND RACE/ETHNICITY, 2011 526

Policies for Controlling the Economy 527

■ WHY IT MATTERS TO YOU: INTEREST RATES 528

■ WHY IT MATTERS TO YOU: KEYNESIAN VERSUS SUPPLY-SIDE ECONOMICS 531

■ POINT TO PONDER 531

Why It Is Hard to Control the Economy 532

16.2 Types of Social Welfare Policies 532

■ WHY IT MATTERS TO YOU: PERCEPTIONS OF POVERTY 533

16.3 Income, Poverty, and Public Policy 533

Who's Getting What? 534

Who's Poor in America? 535

How Public Policy Affects Income 537

16.4 Helping the Poor? Social Policy and the Needy 540

"Welfare" as We Knew It 540

Ending Welfare as We Knew It: The Welfare Reforms of 1996 541

■ WHY IT MATTERS TO YOU: THE 1996 REFORM OF WELFARE 542

■ YOU ARE THE POLICYMAKER: SHOULD GOVERNMENT BENEFITS BE DENIED TO ILLEGAL IMMIGRANTS? 543

16.5 Social Security: Living on Borrowed Time 543

The Growth of Social Security 544

Reforming Social Security 544

16.6 Social Welfare Policy Elsewhere 545

■ AMERICA IN PERSPECTIVE: PARENTAL LEAVE POLICIES 546

16.7 Understanding Economic and Social Welfare Policymaking 546

Democracy and Economic and Social Welfare Policies 547

Economic and Social Welfare Policies and the Scope of Government 548

17 Policymaking for Health Care, the Environment, and Energy 552

17.1 Health Care Policy 554

The Cost of Health Care 554

■ AMERICA IN PERSPECTIVE: THE COSTS AND BENEFITS OF HEALTH CARE 555

Access to Health Care 556

■ YOUNG PEOPLE & POLITICS: HEALTH INSURANCE, EMERGENCY ROOMS, AND YOUNG AMERICANS 559

The Role of Government in Health Care 560

Reform Efforts 561

■ WHY IT MATTERS TO YOU: NATIONAL HEALTH INSURANCE 562

17.2 Environmental Policy 564

Economic Growth and the Environment 564

Environmental Policies in America 566

■ YOU ARE THE POLICYMAKER: HOW MUCH SHOULD WE DO TO SAVE A SPECIES? THE FLORIDA MANATEE 568

■ WHY IT MATTERS TO YOU: "NIMBY" 570

Global Warming 570

WHY IT MATTERS TO YOU: GLOBAL WARMING 571

17.3 Energy Policy 572

Coal 572

Petroleum and Natural Gas 572

Nuclear Energy 574

■ POINT TO PONDER 574

Renewable Sources of Energy 575

17.4 Understanding Health Care, Environmental, and Energy Policy 575

Democracy, Health Care, and Environmental Policy 575

The Scope of Government and Health Care, Environmental, and Energy Policy 576

18 National Security Policymaking 582

18.1 American Foreign Policy: Instruments, Actors, and Policymakers 584

Instruments of Foreign Policy 584

Actors on the World Stage 585

The Policymakers 587

■ POINT TO PONDER 588

18.2 American Foreign Policy Through the Cold War 591

Isolationism 592

The Cold War 593

18.3 American Foreign Policy and the War on Terrorism 597

The Spread of Terrorism 597

Afghanistan and Iraq 598

18.4 Defense Policy 600

Defense Spending 600

■ WHY IT MATTERS TO YOU: THE DEFENSE BUDGET 601

Personnel 601

Weapons 602

Reforming Defense Policy 603

18.5 The New National Security Agenda 603

The Changing Role of Military Power 604

■ WHY IT MATTERS TO YOU: THE ONLY SUPERPOWER 604

Nuclear Proliferation 605

The International Economy 606

■ YOU ARE THE POLICYMAKER: DEFANGING A NUCLEAR THREAT 607

■ WHY IT MATTERS TO YOU: ECONOMIC INTERDEPENDENCE 607

■ YOUNG PEOPLE & POLITICS: EMBRACING GLOBALIZATION 608

Energy 610

Foreign Aid 610

■ AMERICA IN PERSPECTIVE: RANKING LARGESSE 611

18.6 Understanding National Security Policymaking 612

National Security Policymaking and Democracy 612

National Security Policymaking and the Scope of Government 613

Appendices

The Declaration of Independence 619

The Federalist No. 10 621

The Federalist No. 51 624

The Constitution of the United States of America 626

Presidents of the United States 636

Party Control of the Presidency, Senate, and House of Representatives in the Twentieth and Twenty-first Centuries 639

Supreme Court Justices Serving in the Twentieth and Twenty-first Centuries 640

Glossary 641 • Key Terms in Spanish 655 • Notes 661 • Credits 683 • Index 691 • Answer Key 717

TO THE STUDENT

In 2012, American voters reelected President

Barack Obama, a Democrat. In 2014, voters elected Republican majorities to both the House and the Senate. You may be puzzled about why voters divide political power in Washington. And you might also wonder why our political system permits, and even encourages, such mixed verdicts. We have found that election results like these lead many students to conclude that government in America is incredibly complex and hard to make sense of. We are not going to make false promises and tell you that American government is easy to understand. However, we do intend to provide you with a clear roadmap to understanding our complex political system.

The framers of our Constitution could have designed a much simpler system, but they purposely built in complexities as insurance against the concentration of power. Despite these complexities, many of the founders, such as Jefferson, were confident that the American people would be able to navigate their constitutional system and effectively govern themselves within it. In writing this book, we are similarly confident that young adults in the twenty-first century can participate effectively in our democracy.

The major message that we convey in this book is that politics and government matter to everyone. *Government in America* explains how policy choices make a difference and shape the kind of country in which we live. We will show you how these choices affect the taxes we pay, the wars we fight, the quality of our environment, and many other critical aspects of our lives.

Students often ask us whether we are trying to convey a liberal or conservative message in this book. The answer is that our goal is to explain the major viewpoints, how they differ, and how such differences matter. We wish to give you the tools to understand American politics and government. Once you have these tools, you can make your own judgment about policy choices and become a well-informed participant in our democratic process. In the twenty-first century, it is often said that "knowledge is power." We sincerely hope that the knowledge conveyed in this book will help you exercise your fair share of political power in the years to come.

Meet Your Authors

GEORGE C. EDWARDS III

is University Distinguished Professor of Political Science at Texas A&M University and the Jordan Chair in Presidential Studies. He is also a Distinguished Fellow at the University of Oxford. When he determined that he was unlikely to become shortstop for the New York Yankees, he turned to political science. Today, he is one of the country's leading scholars of the presidency and has written or edited 26 books on American politics.

MARTIN P. WATTENBERG

teaches courses on American politics at the University of California, Irvine. His first regular paying job was with the Washington Redskins, from which he moved on to receive a Ph.D. at the University of Michigan. He is the author of *Is Voting for Young People?*, which examines the role of young people in elections today. His research also encompasses how elections in the United States compare to those in other established democracies.

TO THE INSTRUCTOR

In 2008, the United States elected Barack Obama as

president in the hope of making progress on a host of issues, including the wars in Iraq and Afghanistan, the worst economic crisis since the Great Depression, immigration, climate change, and health care. Some changes did occur: health care reform expanded health insurance coverage to millions of Americans and protected millions of others against abuses by insurance companies; new regulations on Wall Street were put in place in the wake of the financial crisis of 2008; and immigration policy limited the deportation of young illegal immigrants.

More generally, however, the nation faced gridlock, especially following the substantial Republican gains in the 2010 congressional elections. The national government even came close to defaulting on its debt. Democrats and Republicans have been further apart in their thinking about the role of government than at any time since Reconstruction, and Republicans have pledged to undo the Democrats' health care reform.

The 2014 Elections and Updates Edition of Government in America explains the reasons we have such a difficult time resolving differences over public policy and the stakes we all have in finding solutions to the challenges facing our nation. We frame its content with a public policy approach to government in the United States and continually ask—and answer—the question, "What difference does politics make to the policies that governments produce?" It is one thing to describe the Madisonian system of checks and balances and separation of powers or the elaborate and unusual federal system of government in the United States; it is something else to ask how these features of our constitutional structure affect the policies that governments generate.

The essence of our approach to American government and politics is that *politics matters*. The national government provides important services, ranging from retirement security and health care to recreation facilities and weather forecasts. The government may also send us to war or negotiate peace with our adversaries, expand or restrict our freedom, raise or lower our taxes, and increase or decrease aid to education. In the twenty-first century, decision makers of both political parties are facing difficult questions regarding American democracy and the scope of our government. Students need a framework for understanding these questions.

We do not discuss policy at the expense of politics, however. We provide extensive coverage of four core subject areas: constitutional foundations, patterns of political behavior, political institutions, and public policy outputs; but we try to do so in a more analytically significant—and interesting—manner. We take special pride in introducing students to relevant work from current political scientists, for example, on the role of PACs and SuperPACs or the impact of divided party government—something we have found instructors to appreciate.

New to This Update

Government in America, 2014 Elections and Updates Edition, has been revised and updated to reflect recent changes—often of a historic magnitude—in politics, policy, and participation. The revisions focus on updates in the following areas:

- The 2014 congressional elections
- Recent Supreme Court decisions, ranging from searches and seizures to same-sex marriage.
- The Obama administration
- Current policies, including health care reform and conflict in the Middle East
- Recent events with significant political implications
- The 2012 presidential election, incorporating additional data and the most recent scholarly studies

Naturally, we have full up-to-the-minute coverage of the **2014 congressional elections** and of the **latest Supreme Court decisions** on civil liberties, civil rights, federalism, and congressional and presidential powers. The updating of Supreme Court decisions includes recent key decisions such as those on the conflict between religious views and insurance mandates, searches and seizures, and same-sex marriage.

In addition, we have devoted attention to **recent events with significant political implications** such as Edward Snowden and leaked national security documents; changes in the rules on women in combat, the Senate filibuster, and on campaign contributions; and the clash over the legalization of marijuana. The historic struggles over the budget and national debt, health care reform, economic policy, and the wars in Iraq and Afghanistan also receive significant coverage.

In our chapter on the presidency and throughout the book, we have **broad coverage of the Obama administration and current policies**, in areas ranging from budgetary policy and relations with Congress in this era of polarization to foreign policy challenges such as the upheaval in the Middle East. The entire chapter on the core issue of the budget has been thoroughly updated to reflect the central importance of taxing and spending in American government and the core issues of the fiscal and debt crises. We have the latest on all the policies we cover, from health care reform and Medicare to the war in Afghanistan and relations with Iran.

All of the **figures and tables reflect the latest available data.** Since the last edition, we have been able to incorporate **updated data related to the 2012 presidential election, and the most recent scholarly studies.** We take pride in continuously improving our graphical presentations of this data.

REVEL™
Educational technology designed for the way today's students read, think, and learn

When students are engaged deeply, they learn more effectively and perform better in their courses. This simple fact inspired the creation of REVEL: an immersive learning experience designed for the way today's students read, think, and learn. Built in collaboration with educators and students nationwide, REVEL is the newest, fully digital way to deliver respected Pearson content.

REVEL enlivens course content with media interactives and assessments—integrated directly within the authors' narrative—that provide opportunities for students to read about and practice course material in tandem. This immersive educational technology boosts student engagement, which leads to better understanding of concepts and improved performance throughout the course.

Learn more about REVEL <http://www.pearsonhighered.com/revel/>

Themes and Features

Government in America follows two central themes. The first great question central to governing, a question every nation must answer, is, *How should we govern?* In the United States, our answer is "by democracy." Yet democracy is an evolving and somewhat ambiguous concept. The first theme, then, is the nature of our democracy. In Chapter 1, we define democracy as a means of selecting policymakers and of organizing government so that policy represents and responds to citizens' preferences. As with previous editions, we incorporate theoretical issues in our discussions of different models of American democracy. We try to encourage students to think analytically about the theories and to develop independent assessments of how well the American system lives up to citizens' expectations of democratic government. To help them do this, in every chapter we raise questions about democracy. For example, does Congress give the American people the policies they want? Is a strong presidency good for democracy? Does our mass media make us more democratic? Are powerful courts that make policy decisions compatible with democracy?

The second theme, the scope of government, focuses on another great question of governing: *What should government do?* Here we discuss alternative views concerning the proper role and size for American government and how the workings of institutions and politics influence this scope. The government's scope is the core question around which politics revolves in contemporary America, pervading many crucial issues: To what degree should Washington impose national standards for health care or speed limits on state policies? How high should taxes be? Do elections encourage politicians to promise more governmental services? Questions about the scope of government are policy questions and thus obviously directly related to our policy approach. Since the scope of government is the pervasive question in American politics today, students will have little problem finding it relevant to their lives and interests.

Each chapter begins with a preview of the relevancy of our two themes to the chapter's subject matter, refers to the themes at points within the chapter, and ends with an "Understanding" section that discusses how the themes illuminate that subject matter.

Our coverage of American government and politics is comprehensive. First, we present an introductory chapter that lays out the dimensions of our policymaking system and introduces our themes of democracy and the scope of government. Next, we provide four chapters on the constitutional foundations of American government, including the Constitution, federalism, civil liberties, and civil rights. We then offer five chapters focusing on influences on government, including public opinion, the media, interest groups, political parties, and elections and voting behavior.

Our next five chapters focus on the workings of the national government. These chapters include Congress, the president, budgeting (at the core of many issues before policymakers), the federal courts, and the federal bureaucracy. Finally, we present three chapters on the decisions policymakers take and the issues they face. First are economic and social welfare policies, then

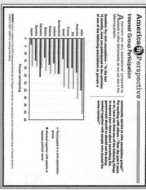

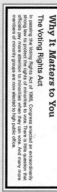

come health care, environmental protection, and energy policies, and finally, we focus on national security policy.

Our features support our fundamental idea that politics matters and engage students in important political and policy issues.

- **Chapter-opening vignettes** make the subject matter of each chapter as relevant as possible to current concerns and pique student interest. From the first chapter, we emphasize the significance of government to young people and the importance of their participation.

- The classic **You Are the Policymaker** asks students to read arguments on both sides of a current issue—such as whether we should prohibit PACs—and then to make a policy decision. In Chapters 4 and 5 (Civil Liberties and Civil Rights), this feature is titled **You Are the Judge** and presents the student with an actual court case.

- The **America in Perspective** feature examines how the United States compares to other countries on topics such as tax rates, voter turnout, and the delivery of public services. By reading these boxes and comparing the United States to other nations, students can obtain a better perspective on the size of our government and the nature of democracy. Instructors report that this feature provides them with especially useful teaching points.

- Several times in each chapter, **Why It Matters to You** insets encourage students to think critically about an aspect of government, politics, or policy and to consider the repercussions—including for themselves—if things worked differently. Each Why It Matters to You feature extends the book's policy emphasis to situate it directly within the context of students' daily lives.

- The popular **Young People & Politics** feature illustrates how policies specifically impact young adults, how their political behavior patterns are unique and important, and how public officials are meeting or ignoring their particular policy desires.

Every chapter includes a **marginal glossary** to support students' understanding of new and important concepts at first encounter. For easy reference, key terms from the marginal glossary are repeated at the end of each chapter and in the end-of-book glossary. Unique to *Government in America*, we also include a key term glossary in Spanish.

We hope that students—long after reading *Government in America*—will employ these perennial questions about the nature of our democracy and the scope of our government when they examine political events. The specifics of policy issues will change, but questions about whether the government is responsive to the people or whether it should expand or contract its scope will always be with us.

Supplements

Make more time for your students with instructor resources that offer effective learning assessments and classroom engagement. Pearson's partnership with educators does not end with the delivery of course materials; Pearson is there with you on the first day of class and beyond. A dedicated team of local Pearson representatives will work with you to not only choose course materials but also integrate them into your class and assess their effectiveness. Our goal is your goal—to improve instruction with each semester.

Pearson is pleased to offer the following resources to qualified adopters of *Government in America*. Several of these supplements are available to instantly download on the Instructor Resource Center (IRC); please visit the IRC at **www.pearsonhighered.com/irc** to register for access.

TEST BANK. Evaluate learning at every level. Reviewed for clarity and accuracy, the Test Bank measures this book's learning objectives with multiple choice, true/false, fill-in-the-blank, short answer, and essay questions. You can easily customize the assessment to work in any major learning management system and to match what is covered in your course. Word, Blackboard, and WebCT versions available on the IRC and Respondus versions available upon request from **www.respondus.com.**

PEARSON MYTEST. This powerful assessment generation program includes all of the questions in the Test Bank. Quizzes and exams can be easily authored and saved online and then printed for classroom use, giving you ultimate flexibility to manage assessments anytime and anywhere. To learn more, visit **www.pearsonhighered.com/mytest.**

INSTRUCTOR'S MANUAL. Create a comprehensive roadmap for teaching classroom, online, or hybrid courses. Designed for new and experienced instructors, the Instructor's Manual includes a sample syllabus, lecture and discussion suggestions, activities for in or out of class and essays on teaching American Government. Available on the IRC.

POWERPOINT PRESENTATION WITH CLASSROOM RESPONSE SYSTEM (CRS). Make lectures more enriching for students. The PowerPoint Presentation includes a full lecture script, discussion questions, and photos and figures from the book. With integrated clicker questions, get immediate feedback on what your students are learning during a lecture. Available on the IRC.

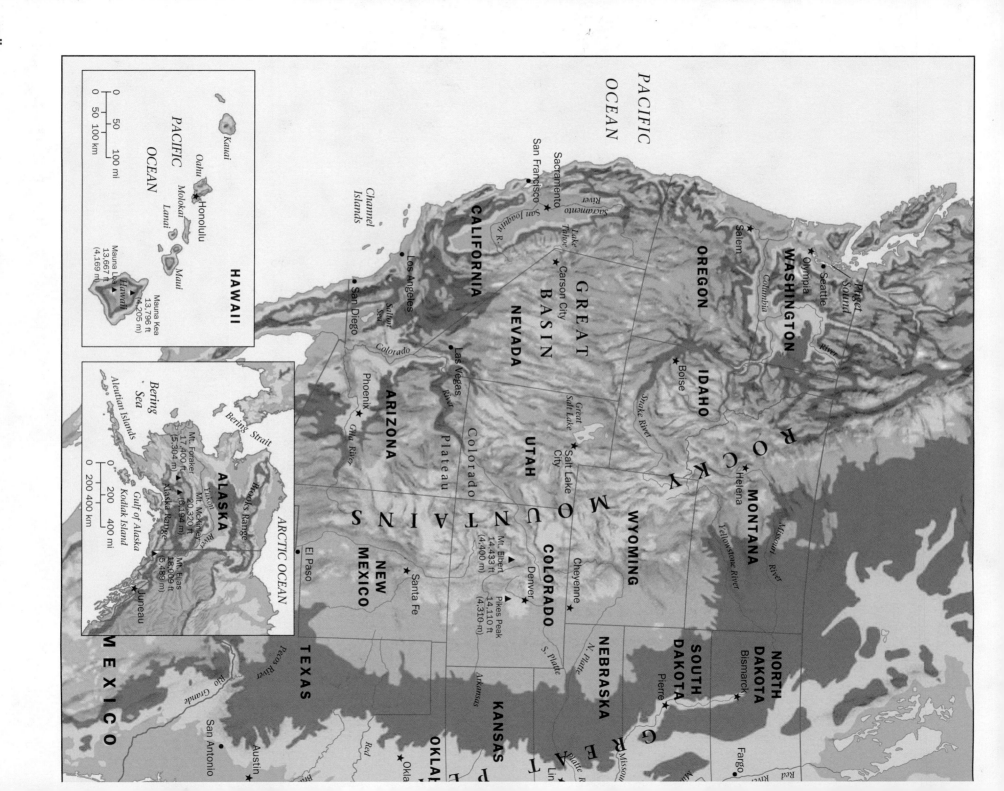

PACIFIC OCEAN

PACIFIC OCEAN

HAWAII

Kauai

Oahu

Honolulu

Molokai

Lanai

Maui

Mauna Loa
13,667 ft
(4,169 m)

Hawaii

Mauna Kea
13,796 ft
(4,205 m)

0   50   100 km
0   50   100 mi

Bering Sea

Aleutian Islands

Bering Strait

Brooks Range

ARCTIC OCEAN

ALASKA

Yukon River

Mt. Foraker
17,400 ft
(5,304 m)

Mt. McKinley
20,320 ft
(6,194 m)

Alaska Range

Gulf of Alaska

Kodiak Island

Mt. Elias
18,009 ft
(5,489 m)

Juneau

0   200   400 km
0   200   400 mi

PACIFIC OCEAN

San Francisco

Sacramento

Sacramento River

San Joaquin R.

Channel Islands

CALIFORNIA

Lake Tahoe

Carson City

Los Angeles

San Diego

Salton Sea

Colorado

Phoenix

ARIZONA

Gila River

Las Vegas

NEVADA

GREAT BASIN

Salt River

Colorado Plateau

Colorado

OREGON

Salem

WASHINGTON

Olympia

Seattle

Columbia

Puget Sound

River

IDAHO

Boise

Snake River

Great Salt Lake

UTAH

Salt Lake City

WYOMING

Cheyenne

COLORADO

Denver

Mt. Elbert
14,433 ft
(4,400 m)

Pikes Peak
14,110 ft
(4,310 m)

S. Platte

N. Platte

ROCKY MOUNTAINS

MONTANA

Helena

Yellowstone River

Missouri River

NEBRASKA

Lin

SOUTH DAKOTA

Pierre

NORTH DAKOTA

Bismarck

Fargo

Red River

Missouri

MEXICO

El Paso

NEW MEXICO

Santa Fe

TEXAS

Pecos River

Rio Grande

San Antonio

Austin

San Diego

KANSAS

OKLAHOMA

Okla

Arkansas

Red

Platte R

Missouri R

GREAT

PLA

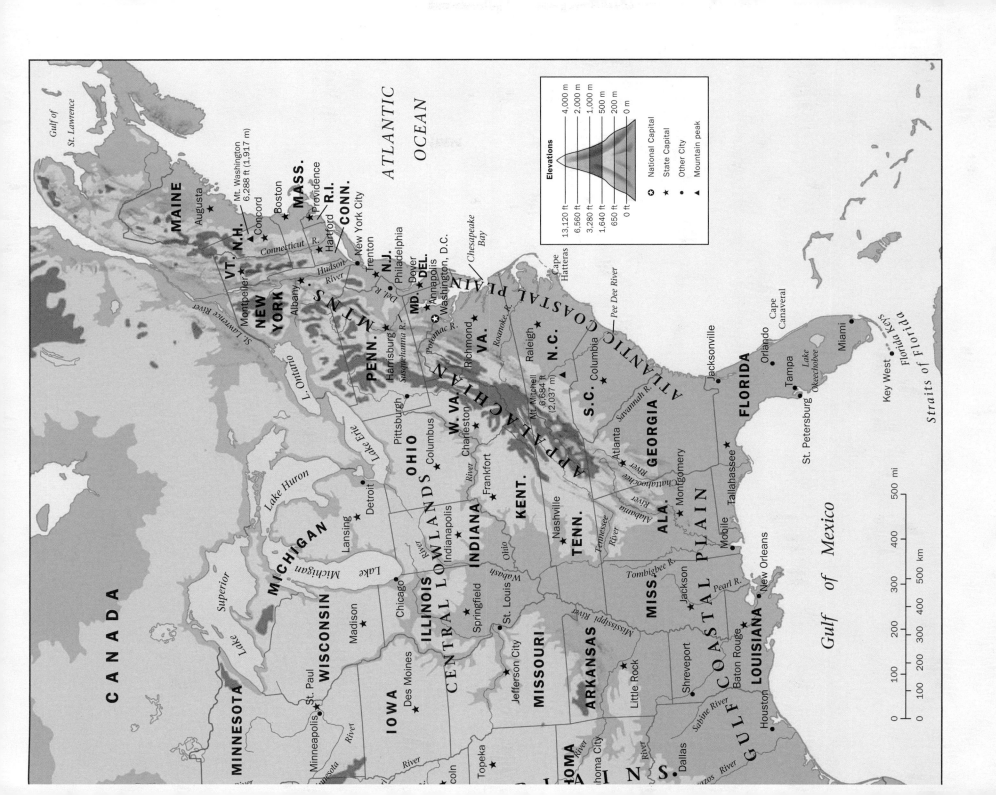

GOVERNMENT IN AMERICA

1

Introducing Government in America

P OLITICS AND GOVERNMENT MATTER—that is the single most important message of this book. Consider, for example, the following list of ways that government and politics may have already impacted your life:

- Chances are pretty good that you or someone in your family has recently been the recipient of one of the 80 million payments made to individuals by the federal government every month. In 2014, nearly 20 percent of the money that went into Americans' wallets was from government payments like jobless benefits, food stamps, Social Security payments, veterans' benefits, and so on.

- Any public schools you attended were prohibited by the federal government from discriminating against females and minorities and from holding prayer sessions led by school officials. Municipal school boards regulated your education, and the state certified and paid your teachers.

- The ages at which you could get your driver's license, drink alcohol, and vote were all determined by state and federal governments.

- Before you could get a job, the federal government had to issue you a Social Security number, and you have been paying Social Security taxes every month that you have been employed. If you worked at a low-paying job, your starting wages were likely determined by state and federal minimum-wage laws.

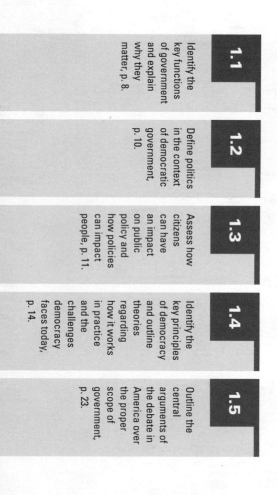

1.1 Identify the key functions of government and explain why they matter, p. 8.

1.2 Define politics in the context of democratic government, p. 10.

1.3 Assess how citizens can have an impact on public policy and how policies can impact people, p. 11.

1.4 Identify the key principles of democracy and outline theories regarding how it works in practice and the challenges democracy faces today, p. 14.

1.5 Outline the central arguments of the debate in America over the proper scope of government, p. 23.

Our political leaders play a symbolic role in representing our nation—one that transcends partisan affiliation. Here, Democrats Barack Obama and Hillary Clinton and Republicans George W. and Laura Bush are shown arriving in South Africa to represent the United States at Nelson Mandela's funeral in December 2013.

3

- As a college student, you may be drawing student loans financed by the government. The government even dictates certain school holidays.

- Even though gasoline prices have risen substantially in recent years, federal policy continues to make it possible for you to drive long distances relatively cheaply compared to citizens in most other countries. In many other advanced industrialized nations, such as England and Japan, gasoline is twice as expensive as in the United States because of the high taxes their governments impose on fuel.

- If you apply to rent an apartment, by federal law landlords cannot discriminate against you because of your race or religion.

This list could, of course, be greatly extended. And it helps explain the importance of politics and government. As Barack Obama said when he first ran for public office in 1993, "Politics does matter. It can make the difference in terms of a benefits check. It can make the difference in terms of school funding. Citizens can't just remove themselves from that process. They actually have to engage themselves and not just leave it to the professionals."[1]

More than any other recent presidential campaign, Obama's 2008 run for the White House was widely viewed as having turned many young Americans on to politics. *Time* magazine even labeled 2008 as the "Year of the Youth Vote," noting that Obama was "tapping into a broad audience of energized young voters hungry for change."[2] And young people did more than display enthusiasm at massive rallies for Obama. By supporting Obama by a two-to-one margin, they provided him with a key edge in the election. Many observers proclaimed that the stereotype of politically apathetic American youth should finally be put to rest.

Stereotypes can be outdated or even off the mark; unfortunately, the perception that young Americans are less engaged in politics than older people has been and continues to be supported by solid evidence. Whether because they think that politicians don't listen to them, that they can't make a difference, that the political system is corrupt, or they just don't care, many young Americans are clearly apathetic about public affairs. And while political apathy isn't restricted to young people, a tremendous gap has opened up between young adults and the elderly on measures of political interest, knowledge, and participation. It cannot be emphasized enough that such a gap has not always existed. Consider some data from the National Election Study, a nationally representative survey conducted each presidential election year since 1952.

In 2012, when the National Election Study asked a nationwide sample of people about their general level of interest in politics, roughly half of Americans under the age of 30 said they paid infrequent attention to politics and elections compared to just 17 percent among those over the age of 65. One might think that this is a normal pattern, with young people always expressing less interest in politics than older people. But notice in Figure 1.1 that in the 1970s there was no generation gap in political interest. Something has happened in the years since that has resulted in young adults being substantially less interested in politics than the elderly.

Lack of interest often leads to lack of information. The National Election Study asks a number of political knowledge questions. Figure 1.2 shows the average percentage of correct answers for age groups in 1972 and 2012. In 2012 young people were correct only 37 percent of the time, whereas people over 65 were correct 57 percent of the time. Whether the question concerned identifying partisan control of the House and Senate, or accurately estimating the unemployment rate, or identifying prominent politicians, the result was the same in 2012: Young people were less knowledgeable than the elderly. This pattern of age differences in political knowledge has been found time and time again in surveys in recent years.[3] By contrast, Figure 1.2 shows that in 1972 there was virtually no pattern by age, with those under 30 scoring 4 percent higher than those over 65.[4]

Thomas Jefferson once said that there has never been, nor ever will be, a people who are politically ignorant and free. If this is indeed the case, write Stephen Bennett and Eric Rademacher, then "we can legitimately wonder what the future holds," if young people "remain as uninformed as they are about government and public affairs."[5] While this may well be an overreaction, there definitely are important consequences when citizens lack

FIGURE 1.1 POLITICAL APATHY AMONG YOUNG AND OLD AMERICANS, 1972–2012

In every presidential election from 1972 to 2012, the American National Election Studies has asked a cross-section of the public how often they follow what's going on in government and public affairs. Below we have graphed the percentage who said they followed politics on an infrequent basis. Lack of political interest among young people hit a record high during the 2000 campaign between Bush and Gore, when over two-thirds said they rarely followed public affairs. Since then, political interest among young people has recovered somewhat; however, compared to senior citizens, they are still much more likely to report low political interest.

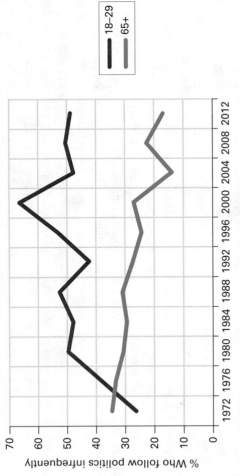

18–29
65+

% Who follow politics infrequently

1972 1976 1980 1984 1988 1992 1996 2000 2004 2008 2012

SOURCE: Authors' analysis of 1972–2012 American National Election Studies data.

political information. In *What Americans Know About Politics and Why It Matters*, Michael Delli Carpini and Scott Keeter make a strong case for the importance of staying informed about public affairs. Political knowledge, they argue, (1) fosters civic virtues, such as political tolerance; (2) helps citizens to identify what policies would truly benefit them and then incorporate this information in their voting behavior; and (3) promotes active participation in politics.[6] If you've been reading about the debate on immigration reform, for example,

FIGURE 1.2 AGE AND POLITICAL KNOWLEDGE, 1972 AND 2012

This figure shows the percentage of correct answers to five questions in 1972 and twelve questions in 2012 by age group. In 1972, the relationship between age and political knowledge was basically flat: each age group displayed roughly the same level of information about basic political facts, such as which party currently had more seats in the House of Representatives. By 2012, the picture had changed quite dramatically, with young people being substantially less likely to know the answer to such questions than older people.

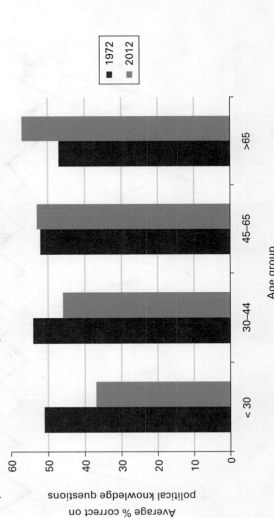

1972
2012

Average % correct on political knowledge questions

< 30   30–44   45–65   >65

Age group

SOURCE: Authors' analysis of 1972 and 2012 National Election Studies data.

you'll be able to understand the proposed legislation, and that knowledge will then help you identify and vote for candidates whose views agree with yours.

As you will see throughout this book, those who participate in the political process are more likely to benefit from government programs and policies. Young people often complain that the elderly have far more political clout than they do—turnout statistics make clear why this is the case. As shown in Figure 1.3, in recent decades the voter turnout rate for people under 25 has consistently been much lower than that for senior citizens, particularly for midterm elections. Whereas turnout rates for the young have generally been going down, turnout among people over 65 years of age has actually gone up slightly since 1972. Political scientists used to write that the frailties of old age led to a decline in turnout after age 60; now such a decline occurs only after 80 years of age. Greater access to medical care because of the passage of Medicare in 1965 must surely be given some of the credit for this change. Who says politics doesn't make a difference?

More than any other age group, the elderly know that they have much at stake in every election, with much of the federal budget now devoted to programs that help them, such as Medicare and Social Security. In recent decades these programs have consumed more and more of the federal domestic (non-military) budget as the population has aged and the costs of medical care have skyrocketed. Furthermore, they are projected to continue to grow as the baby boom generation retires. In contrast, the share of domestic federal spending that benefits children, though substantial, has generally declined. Julia Isaacs et al. estimate that in 2020 spending on Social Security benefits and health care for the elderly will make up 51 percent of domestic federal spending, as compared to just 11 percent for programs that benefit children.[7]

FIGURE 1.3 ELECTION TURNOUT RATES OF YOUNG AND OLD AMERICANS, 1972–2012

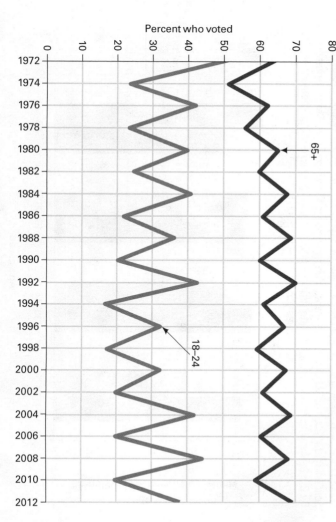

This graph shows the turnout gap between young and old Americans in all presidential and midterm elections from 1972 through 2012. The sawtooth pattern of both lines illustrates how turnout always drops off between a presidential election and a midterm congressional election (e.g., from 2008 to 2010). The ups and downs in the graph are much more evident among young people because they are less interested in politics and hence less likely to be regular voters. In 2008, turnout among young people rose to the highest level since 1972, spurred by a surge of participation by minority youth. Record rates of turnout were set by young African Americans, who for the first time had a higher turnout rate than young whites, and by young Hispanics and Asian Americans. The 2010 election, however, saw a sharp drop-off in youth turnout. Some, but not all, of these young voters came back to the polls in 2012. If the normal pattern holds, young people's turnout in 2014 will be quite low—probably only about 20 percent—whereas turnout among senior citizens is likely to be roughly three times that high.

SOURCE: U.S. Census Bureau Current Population Surveys.

Of course, today's youth have not had any policy impact them in the way that, say, the introduction of Medicare or the military draft and the Vietnam War affected previous generations. However, the causes of young people's political apathy probably run deeper. Today's young adults have grown up in an environment in which news about political events has been increasingly more avoidable than in the past. When CBS, NBC, and ABC dominated the airwaves, in the 1960s and 1970s, their extensive coverage of presidential speeches, political conventions, and presidential debates frequently left little else to watch on TV. As channels proliferated over subsequent decades, it became much easier to avoid exposure to politics by switching the channel—and of course the Internet has exponentially broadened the choices. Major political events were once shared national experiences. But for many young adults today, September 11, 2001, represents the only time that they closely followed a major national event along with everyone else.

Consider some contrasting statistics about audiences for presidential speeches. Presidents Nixon, Ford, and Carter all got an average Nielsen rating of 50 for their televised addresses, meaning that half the population was watching. In contrast, President Obama averaged only about 23 for his nationally televised appearances from 2009 to 2014, despite the public's anxiety about the economy.[8] Political conventions, which once received more TV coverage than the Summer Olympics, have been relegated to an hour per night and draw abysmal ratings. The 2008 and 2012 presidential debates averaged a respectable Nielsen rating of 37, but this was only about three-fifths of the size of the typical audience from 1960 to 1980.

In sum, young people today have never known a time when most citizens paid attention to major political events. As a result, most of them have yet to get into the habit of following and participating in politics. In a 2012 Pew Research Center survey, 24 percent of young adults said they enjoyed keeping up with the news, compared to 58 percent of senior citizens. And young people have grown up in a fragmented media environment in which hundreds of TV channels and millions of Internet sites have provided them with a rich and varied socialization experience but have also enabled them to easily avoid political events. It has become particularly difficult to convince a generation that has channel and Internet surfed all their lives that politics really does matter.

How will further expansion of channels and, especially, blogs and other Web sites, affect youth interest in and knowledge of politics? Political scientists see both opportunities and

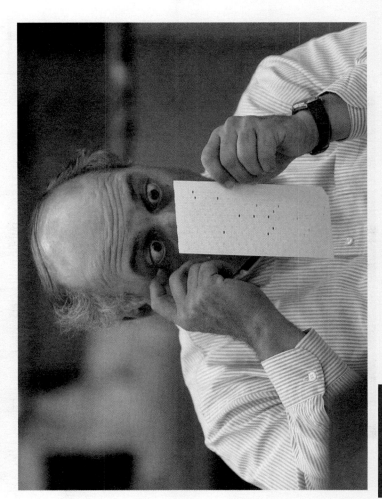

The narrow 537-vote margin by which George W. Bush carried the state of Florida in 2000 proved the old adage that "every vote counts." Here, an election official strains to figure out how to interpret a voter's punch in the tedious process of recounting ballots by hand.

government
The institutions through which public policies are made for a society.

Government

Identify the key functions of government and explain why they matter.

The institutions that make public policy decisions for a society are collectively known as **government**. In the case of our own national government, these institutions are Congress, the president, the courts, and federal administrative agencies ("the bureaucracy"). Thousands of state and local governments also decide on policies that influence our lives. There are about 500,000 elected officials in the United States. Thus, policies that affect you are being made almost constantly.

When elections result in a change of party control, power is transferred peacefully in the United States. In 2011, the outgoing Speaker of the House, Democrat Nancy Pelosi, symbolically passed the gavel to the incoming Speaker, Republican John Boehner.

challenges. Some optimistic observers see these developments as offering "the prospect of a revitalized democracy characterized by a more active and informed citizenry."[9] Political junkies will certainly find more political information available than ever before, and electronic communications will make it easier for people to express their political views in various forums and directly to public officials. However, with so many media choices for so many specific interests, it will also be easy to avoid the subject of public affairs. It may also be easier to avoid a range of opinions. Political scientist Jeremy Mayer argues that "if we all get to select exactly how much campaign news we will receive, and the depth of that coverage, it may be that too many Americans will choose shallow, biased sources of news on the Internet."[10]

Groups that are concerned about low youth turnout are focusing on innovative ways of reaching out to young people via new technologies, such as social networking sites like Facebook, to make them more aware of politics. In doing so, they are encouraged and spurred by the fact that young people are far from inactive in American society and in recent years have been doing volunteer community service at record rates. As Harvard students Ganesh Sitaraman and Previn Warren write in *Invisible Citizens: Youth Politics After September 11,* "Young people are some of the most active members of their communities and are devoting increasing amounts of their time to direct service work and volunteerism."[11] It is only when it comes to politics that young people seem to express indifference about getting involved.

It is our hope that after reading this book, you will be persuaded that paying attention to politics and government is important. Government has a substantial impact on all our lives. But it is also true that we have the opportunity to have a substantial impact on government. Involvement in public affairs can take many forms, ranging from simply becoming better informed by browsing through political Web sites to running for elected office. In between are countless opportunities for everyone to make a difference.

Because government shapes how we live, it is important to understand the process by which decisions are made as well as what is actually decided. Two fundamental questions about governing will serve as themes throughout this book:

- **How should we govern?** Americans take great pride in calling their government democratic. This chapter examines the workings of democratic government; the chapters that follow will evaluate the way American government actually works compared to the standards of an "ideal" democracy. We will continually ask, "Who holds power and who influences the policies adopted by government?"

- **What should government do?** This text explores the relationship between *how* American government works and *what* it does. In other words, it addresses the question, "Does our government do what we want it to do?" Debates over the scope of governmental power are among the most important in American political life today. Some people would like to see the government take on more responsibilities; others believe it already takes on too much.

While citizens often disagree about what their government should do for them, all governments have certain functions in common. National governments throughout the world perform the following functions:

- **Maintain a national defense.** A government protects its national sovereignty, usually by maintaining armed forces. In the nuclear age, some governments possess awesome power to make war through highly sophisticated weapons. The United States currently spends over $600 billion a year on national defense. Since September 11, 2001, the defense budget has been substantially increased in order to cope with the threat of terrorism on U.S. soil.

- **Provide public goods and services.** Governments in this country spend billions of dollars on schools, libraries, hospitals, highways, and many other public goods

Governments provide a wide range of public services, including providing a national defense. Because of the threat from Al Qaeda, U.S. troops have been in Afghanistan since 2001. Here, an Afghan farmer walks by while U.S. troops work to secure the road against improvised explosive devices planted by Taliban insurgents.

collective goods
Goods and services, such as clean air and clean water, that by their nature cannot be denied to anyone.

politics
The process determining the leaders we select and the policies they pursue. Politics produces authoritative decisions about public issues.

political participation
All the activities by which citizens attempt to influence the selection of political leaders and the policies they pursue. Voting is the most common means of political participation in a democracy. Other means include contacting public officials, protest, and civil disobedience.

and services. These goods and services are of two types. Some are what is called **collective goods**; if they exist, by their very nature they cannot be denied to anyone and therefore must be shared by everyone. Access to highways, for example, cannot be denied. As the private sector would have no incentive to provide goods and services that everyone automatically has access to, these can be provided only by government. Other public goods and services, such as college or medical care, can be provided to some individuals without being provided to all; these are widely provided by the private sector as well as by government.

- **Preserve order.** Every government has some means of maintaining order. When people protest in large numbers, governments may resort to extreme measures to restore order. For example, the National Guard was called in to stop the looting and arson after rioting broke out in Los Angeles following the 1992 Rodney King verdict.

- **Socialize the young.** Governments politically socialize the young—that is, instill in children knowledge of and pride in the nation and its political system and values. Most modern governments pay for education, and school curricula typically include a course on the theory and practice of the country's government. Rituals like the daily Pledge of Allegiance seek to foster patriotism and love of country.

- **Collect taxes.** Approximately one out of every three dollars earned by American citizens goes to national, state, and local taxes—money that pays for the public goods and services the government provides.

All these governmental tasks add up to weighty decisions that our political leaders must make. For example, how much should we spend on national defense as opposed to education? How high should taxes for Medicare and Social Security be? We answer such questions through politics.

Politics

1.2 Define politics in the context of democratic government.

Politics determines whom we select as our governmental leaders and what policies these leaders pursue. Political scientists often cite Harold D. Lasswell's famous definition of politics: "Who gets what, when, and how."[12] It is one of the briefest and most useful definitions of politics ever penned. Admittedly, this broad definition covers a lot of ground (office politics, sorority politics, and so on) in which political scientists are generally not interested. They are interested primarily in politics related to governmental decision making.

The media usually focus on the *who* of politics. At a minimum, this includes voters, candidates, groups, and parties. *What* refers to the substance of politics and government—benefits, such as medical care for the elderly, and burdens, such as new taxes. *How* refers to the ways in which people participate in politics. People get what they want through voting, supporting, compromising, lobbying, and so forth. In this sense, government and politics involve winners and losers. Behind every arcane tax provision or item in an appropriations bill, there are real people getting something or getting something taken away.

The ways in which people get involved in politics make up their **political participation.** Many people judge the health of a government by how widespread political participation is. America does quite poorly when judged by its voter turnout, which is one of the lowest in the world. Low voter turnout has an effect on who

Pro-life and pro-choice groups are single-minded and usually uncompromising. Few issues stir up as much passion as whether abortion should be permitted and, if so, under what conditions.

holds political power. Because so many people do not show up at the polls, voters are a distorted sample of the public as a whole. Groups with a high turnout rate, such as the elderly, benefit, whereas those with a low turnout rate, such as young people, lack political clout.

Voting is only one form of political participation, as you'll see in later chapters. For a few Americans, politics is a vocation: they run for office, and some even earn their live-lihood from holding political office. In addition, there are many Americans who treat politics as critical to their interests. Many of these people are members of **single-issue groups**—groups so concerned with one issue that members often cast their votes on the basis of that issue only, ignoring a politician's stand on everything else. Groups of activists dedicated either to outlawing abortion or to preserving abortion rights are good examples of single-issue groups.

Individual citizens and organized groups get involved in politics because they understand that public policy choices made by governments affect them in significant ways. Will all those who need student loans receive them? Will everyone have access to medical care? Will people be taken care of in their old age? Is the water safe to drink? These and other questions tie politics to policymaking.

single-issue groups
Groups that have a narrow interest on which their members tend to take an uncompromising stance.

policymaking system
The process by which policy comes into being and evolves. People's inter-ests, problems, and concerns create political issues for government policy-makers. These issues shape policy, which in turn impacts people, gen-erating more interests, problems, and concerns.

The Policymaking System

1.3 Assess how citizens can have an impact on public policy and how policies can impact people.

mericans frequently expect the government to do something about their problems. For example, the president and members of Congress are expected to keep the economy humming along; voters will penalize them at the polls if they do not. It is through the **policymaking system** that our government responds to the priorities of its people. Figure 1.4 shows a skeletal model of this system, in which people shape policies and in turn are impacted by them. The rest of this book will flesh out this model, but for now it will help you understand how government policy comes into being and evolves over time.

linkage institutions
The political channels through which people's concerns become political issues on the policy agenda. In the United States, linkage institutions include elections, political parties, interest groups, and the media.

policy agenda
The issues that attract the serious attention of public officials and other people involved in politics at a point in time.

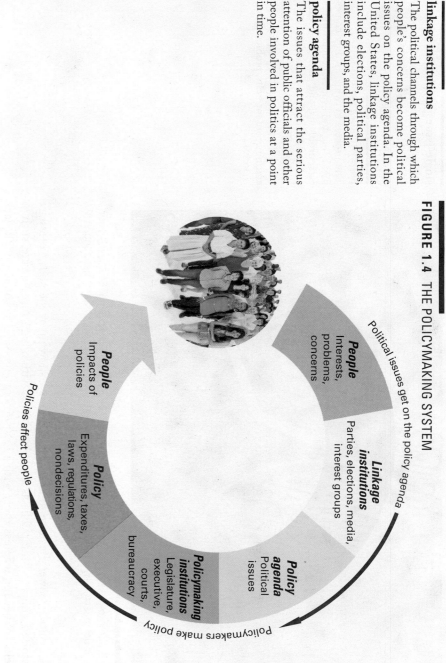

FIGURE 1.4 THE POLICYMAKING SYSTEM

Political issues get on the policy agenda

People
Interests, problems, concerns

Linkage institutions
Parties, elections, media, interest groups

Policy agenda
Political issues

Policymakers make policy

Policymaking institutions
Legislature, executive, courts, bureaucracy

Policy
Expenditures, taxes, laws, regulations, nondecisions

Policies affect people

People
Impacts of policies

People Shape Policy

The policymaking system begins with people. All Americans have interests, problems, and concerns that are touched on by public policy. Some people think the government should spend more to train people for jobs in today's increasingly technology-oriented economy; others think that the government is already spending too much, resulting in high taxes that discourage business investments. Some citizens expect government to do something to curb domestic violence; others are concerned about prospects that the government may make it much harder to buy a handgun.

What do people do to express their opinions in a democracy? As mentioned, people have numerous avenues for participation, such as voting for candidates who represent their opinions, joining political parties, posting messages to Internet chat groups, and forming *interest groups*—organized groups of people with a common interest. In this way, people's concerns enter the linkage institutions of the policymaking system. **Linkage institutions**—parties, elections, interest groups, and the media—transmit Americans' preferences to the policymakers in government. Parties and interest groups strive to ensure that their members' concerns receive appropriate political attention. The media investigate social problems and inform people about them. Elections provide citizens with the chance to make their opinions heard by choosing their public officials.

All these institutions help to shape the government's **policy agenda**, the issues that attract the serious attention of public officials and other people actively involved in politics at a given time. Some issues will be considered, and others will not. If politicians want to get elected, they must pay attention to the problems that concern voters. When you vote, you are partly looking at whether a candidate shares your agenda. If you are worried about rising health care costs and a certain candidate talks only about America's moral decay and ending legalized abortions, you will probably support another candidate.

A government's policy agenda changes regularly. When jobs are scarce and business productivity is falling, economic problems occupy a high position on the government's agenda. If the economy is doing well and trouble spots around the world occupy the headlines, foreign policy questions are bound to dominate the agenda. In general, bad news—particularly about a crisis situation—is more likely than good news to draw sufficient media attention to put a subject on the policy agenda. As the old saying goes, "Good news is no news." When unemployment rises sharply, it leads the news; when jobs are plentiful, the latest unemployment report is much less of a news story. Thus, the policy agenda responds more to societal failures than successes. The question politicians constantly ask is, "How can we as a people do better?"

People, of course, do not always agree on what government should do. Indeed, one group's positions and interests are often at odds with those of another group. A **political issue** is the result of people disagreeing about a problem or about the public policy needed to fix it. There is never a shortage of political issues; government, however, will not act on any issue until it is high on the policy agenda.

Policymakers stand at the core of the system, working within the three **policymaking institutions** established by the U.S. Constitution: Congress, the presidency, and the courts. Policymakers scan the issues on the policy agenda, select those they consider important, and make policies to address them. Today, the power of the bureaucracy is so great that most political scientists consider it a fourth policymaking institution.

Very few policies are made by a single policymaking institution. Environmental policy is a good example. Some presidents have used their influence with Congress to urge clean-air and clean-water policies. When Congress responds by passing legislation to clean up the environment, bureaucracies have to implement the new policies. The bureaucracies, in turn, create extensive volumes of rules and regulations that define how policies are to be implemented. In addition, every law passed and every rule made can be challenged in the courts. Courts make decisions about what policies mean and whether they conflict with the Constitution.

☐ Policies Impact People

Every decision that government makes—every law it passes, budget it establishes, and ruling it hands down—is **public policy**. Public policies are of various types, depending in part on which policymaking institution they originated with. Some of the most important types—*statute, presidential action, court decision, budgetary choice,* and *regulation*—are defined and exemplified in Table 1.1.

Once policies are made and implemented, they affect people. **Policy impacts** are the effects that a policy has on people and on society's problems. People want policy

political issue
An issue that arises when people disagree about a problem and how to fix it.

policymaking institutions
The branches of government charged with taking action on political issues. The U.S. Constitution established three policymaking institutions—Congress, the presidency, and the courts. Today, the power of the bureaucracy is so great that most political scientists consider it a fourth policymaking institution.

public policy
A choice that government makes in response to a political issue. A policy is a course of action taken with regard to some problem.

policy impacts
The effects a policy has on people and problems. Impacts are analyzed to see how well a policy has met its goal and at what cost.

TABLE 1.1 TYPES OF PUBLIC POLICIES

Type	Definition	Example
Congressional statute	Law passed by Congress	The $787 billion American Recovery and Reinvestment Act of 2009 is enacted.
Presidential action	Decision by president	American jets bomb ISIS targets in Syria.
Court decision	Opinion by Supreme Court or other court	Supreme Court rules that individuals have a constitutional right to own a gun.
Budgetary choices	Legislative enactment of taxes and expenditures	The federal budget resolution is enacted.
Regulation	Agency adoption of regulation	The Department of Education issues guidelines for qualifying for the federal student loan forgiveness program.

democracy
A system of selecting policymakers and of organizing government so that policy represents and responds to the public's preferences.

that effectively addresses their interests, problems, and concerns; clearly, a new law, executive order, bureaucratic regulation, or court judgment doesn't mean much if it doesn't work. Environmentalists want an industrial emissions policy that not only claims to prevent air pollution but also does so. Minority groups want a civil rights policy that not only promises them equal treatment but also ensures it.

Having a policy implies having a goal. Whether we want to reduce poverty, cut crime, clean the water, or hold down inflation, we have a goal in mind. Policy impact analysts ask how well a policy achieves its goal—and at what cost. The analysis of policy impacts carries the policymaking system back to its point of origin: the interests, problems, and concerns of the people. Translating people's desires into effective public policy is crucial to the workings of democracy.

Democracy in America

Identify the key principles of democracy and outline theories regarding how it works in practice and the challenges democracy faces today.

D emocracy is a system of selecting policymakers and of organizing government so that policy reflects citizens' preferences. Today, the term *democracy* takes its place among terms like *freedom, justice,* and *peace* as a word that seemingly has only positive connotations; surveys around the world routinely show that most people in most democracies believe that democracy is the best form of government. Yet the writers of the U.S. Constitution had no fondness for democracy, as many of them doubted the ability of ordinary Americans to make informed judgments about what government should do. Roger Sherman, a delegate to the Constitutional Convention, said, "The people should have as little to do as may be about the government." Only much later did Americans come to cherish democracy and believe that all citizens should actively participate in choosing their leaders.

Most Americans would probably say that democracy is "government by the people." These words are, of course, part of the famous phrase by which Abraham Lincoln defined democracy in his Gettysburg Address: "government of the people, by the people, and for the people." The extent to which each of these three aspects of democracy holds true is a matter crucial to evaluating how well our government is working. Certainly, government has always been "of the people" in the United States, for the Constitution forbids the granting of titles of nobility—a status of privilege within the government, usually passed down from generation to generation. On the other hand, it is a physical impossibility for government to be "by the people" in a nation of over 300 million people. Therefore, our democracy involves choosing people from among our midst to govern. Where the serious debate begins is whether political leaders govern "for the people," as there are always significant biases in how the system works. Democratic theorists have elaborated a set of goals to use in evaluating this crucial question.

☐ Traditional Democratic Theory

Traditional democratic theory rests on a number of key principles that specify how governmental decisions are made in a democracy. Robert Dahl, one of America's leading theorists, suggests that an ideal democratic process should satisfy the following five criteria:

- *Equality in voting.* The principle of "one person, one vote" is basic to democracy. No one's vote should count more than anyone else's.

- *Effective participation.* Citizens must have adequate and equal opportunities to express their preferences throughout the decision-making process.

- *Enlightened understanding.* A democratic society must be a marketplace of ideas. A free press and free speech are essential to civic understanding. If one group monopolizes and distorts information, citizens cannot truly understand issues.

- *Citizen control of the agenda.* Citizens should have the collective right to control the government's policy agenda. If particular groups, such as the wealthy, have influence far exceeding what would be expected based on their numbers, then the agenda will be distorted—the government will not be addressing the issues that the public as a whole feels are most important.

- *Inclusion.* The government must include, and extend rights to, all those subject to its laws. Citizenship must be open to all within a nation if the nation is to call itself democratic.[13]

Ideally, only if it satisfies these criteria can a political system be called democratic. Furthermore, democracies must practice **majority rule**, meaning that policies made should reflect the will of over half the voters. At the same time, most Americans would not want to give the majority free rein to do anything they can agree on. Restraints on the majority are built into the American system of government in order to protect the minority. Thus, the majority cannot infringe on **minority rights**; freedom of speech, freedom of assembly, and so on are freedoms for those in a minority as well as the majority. In a society too large to make its decisions in open meetings, a few must look after the concerns of the many. The relationship between the few leaders and the many citizens is one of **representation**. The literal meaning of representation is to "make present once again." In politics, this means that the desires of the people should be replicated in government through the choices of elected officials. The closer the correspondence between representatives and their constituents, the closer the approximation to an ideal democracy. As might be expected for such a crucial question, theorists disagree widely about the extent to which this actually occurs in America.

☐ Three Contemporary Theories of American Democracy

Theories of American democracy are essentially theories about who has power and influence. All, in one way or another, ask the question, "Who really governs in our nation?" Each focuses on a key aspect of politics and government, and each reaches a somewhat different conclusion about the state of American democracy.

PLURALISM One important theory of American democracy, **pluralism**, states that groups with shared interests influence public policy by pressing their concerns through organized efforts. The National Rifle Association (NRA), the National Organization for Women (NOW), and the American Council on Education (ACE) are contemporary examples of such interest groups.

According to pluralist theory, because of open access to various institutions of government and public officials, organized groups can compete with one another for control over policy and no one group or set of groups dominates. Given that power is dispersed in the American form of government, groups that lose in one arena can take their case to another. For example, civil rights groups faced congressional roadblocks in the 1950s but were able to win the action they were seeking from the courts.

Pluralists are generally optimistic that the public interest will eventually prevail in the making of public policy through a complex process of bargaining and compromise. They believe that, rather than speaking of majority rule, we should speak of groups of minorities working together. Robert Dahl expresses this view well when he writes that in America "all active and legitimate groups in the population can make themselves heard at some crucial stage in the process."[14]

Group politics is certainly as American as apple pie. Writing in the 1830s, Alexis de Tocqueville called us a "nation of joiners" and pointed to the high level of associational activities as one of the crucial reasons for the success of American democracy.

majority rule
A fundamental principle of traditional democratic theory. In a democracy, choosing among alternatives requires that the majority's desire be respected.

minority rights
A principle of traditional democratic theory that guarantees rights to those who do not belong to majorities.

representation
A basic principle of traditional democratic theory that describes the relationship between the few leaders and the many followers.

pluralism
A theory of American democracy emphasizing that the policymaking process is very open to the participation of all groups with shared interests, with no single group usually dominating. Pluralists tend to believe that as a result, public interest generally prevails.

elitism
A theory of American democracy contending that an upper-class elite holds the power and makes policy, regardless of the formal governmental organization.

The recent explosion of interest group activity can therefore be seen as a very positive development from the perspective of pluralist theory. Interest groups and their lobbyists—the groups' representatives in Washington—have become masters of the technology of politics. Computers, mass mailing lists, sophisticated media advertising, and hard-sell techniques are their stock-in-trade. As a result, some observers believe that Dahl's pluralist vision of all groups as being heard through the American political process is more true now than ever before.

On the other hand, Robert Putnam argues that many of the problems of American democracy today stem from a decline in group-based participation.[15] Putnam theorizes that advanced technology, particularly television, has served to increasingly isolate Americans from one another. He shows that membership in a variety of civic associations, such as parent–teacher associations, the League of Women Voters, and the Elks, Shriners, and Jaycees, has been declining for decades. Interestingly, Putnam does not interpret the decline of participation in civic groups as meaning that people have become "couch potatoes." Rather, he argues that Americans' activities are becoming less tied to institutions and more self-defined. The most famous example he gives to illustrate this trend is the fact that membership in bowling leagues has dropped sharply at the same time that more people are bowling—indicating that more and more people must be bowling alone. Putnam believes that participation in interest groups today is often like bowling alone. Groups that have mushroomed lately, such as the AARP, typically just ask their members to participate by writing a check from the comfort of their own home. If people are indeed participating in politics alone rather than in groups, then pluralist theory is becoming less descriptive of American politics today.

ELITISM

Critics of pluralism believe that it paints too rosy a picture of American political life. By arguing that almost every group can get a piece of the pie, they say, pluralists miss the larger question of how the pie is distributed. The poor may get their food stamps, but businesses get massive tax deductions worth far more. Some governmental programs may help minorities, but the income gap between whites and blacks remains wide.

Elitism contends that our society, like all societies, is divided along class lines and that an upper-class elite pulls the strings of government. Wealth—the holding of assets such as property, stocks, and bonds—is the basis of this power. Over a third of the nation's wealth is currently held by just 1 percent of the population. Elite and class theorists believe that this 1 percent of Americans controls most policy decisions because they can afford to finance election campaigns and control key institutions, such as large corporations. According to elite and class theory, a few powerful Americans do not merely influence policymakers—they *are* the policymakers.

At the center of all theories of elite dominance is big business, whose dominance may have grown in recent decades. Thus, political scientists Jacob Hacker and Paul Pierson write that "America's political market no longer looks like the effectively functioning market that economics textbooks laud. Rather, it increasingly resembles the sort of market that gave us the Enron scandal, in which corporate bigwigs with privileged information got rich at the expense of ordinary shareholders, workers, and consumers."[16] With the increasing dominance of big business, elite theorists point out that income and wealth have become more concentrated. After the government bailout of large financial firms in 2008, public resentment about this concentration of income and wealth escalated notably. Recently, the "Occupy Wall Street" movement emerged to visibly protest the rising disparities. Its slogan "We are the 99 percent" referred to the vast concentration of wealth among the top 1 percent of income earners, among them Wall Street executives.

The most extreme proponents of elite theory maintain that who holds office in Washington is of marginal consequence; the corporate giants always have the power. Clearly, most people in politics would disagree with this view, noting that, for example, it made a difference that Bush was elected in 2000 rather than Gore. According to

hyperpluralism
A theory of American democracy contending that groups are so strong that government, which gives in to the many different groups, is thereby weakened.

Gore's promises in 2000, the wealthiest Americans would have received no tax cuts had he become president; under President Bush, all taxpayers, including the wealthiest Americans, saw their taxes cut.

HYPERPLURALISM A third theory, **hyperpluralism**, offers a different critique of pluralism. Hyperpluralism is pluralism gone sour. In this view, the many competing groups are so strong that government is weakened, as the influence of so many groups cripples government's ability to make policy. The problem is not that a few groups excessively influence government action but that many groups together render government unable to act.

Whereas pluralism maintains that input from groups is a good thing for the political decision-making process, hyperpluralist theory asserts that there are *too* many ways for groups to control policy. Our fragmented political system made up of governments with overlapping jurisdictions is one major factor that contributes to hyperpluralism. Too many governments can make it hard to coordinate policy implementation. Any policy requiring the cooperation of the national, state, and local levels of government can be hampered by the reluctance of any one of them. Furthermore, groups use the fragmented system to their advantage. As groups that lose policymaking battles in Congress increasingly carry the battle to the courts, the number of cases brought to state and federal courts has soared. Ecologists use legal procedures to delay construction projects they feel will damage the environment, businesses take federal agencies to court to fight the implementation of regulations that will cost them money, labor unions go to court to secure injunctions against policies they fear will cost them jobs, and civil liberties groups go to court to defend the rights of people who are under investigation for possible terrorist activities. The courts have become one more battleground in which policies can be effectively opposed as each group tries to bend policy to suit its own purposes.

Hyperpluralist theory holds that government gives in to every conceivable interest and single-issue group. Groups have become sovereign, and government is merely their servant. When politicians try to placate every group, the result is confusing, contradictory, and muddled policy—if the politicians manage to make policy at all. Like elite and class theorists, hyperpluralist theorists suggest that the public interest is rarely translated into public policy.

☐ Challenges to Democracy

Regardless of which theory is most convincing, there are a number of continuing challenges to democracy. Many of these challenges apply to American democracy as well as to other democracies around the world.

INCREASED COMPLEXITY OF ISSUES Traditional democratic theory holds that ordinary citizens have the good sense to reach political judgments and that government has the capacity to act on those judgments. Today, however, we live in a society with complex issues and experts whose technical knowledge of those issues vastly exceeds the knowledge of the general population. What, after all, does the average citizen—however conscientious—know about eligibility criteria for welfare, agricultural price supports, foreign competition, and the hundreds of other issues that confront government each year? Even the most rigorous democratic theory does not demand that citizens be experts on everything, but as human knowledge has expanded, it has become increasingly difficult for individual citizens to make well-informed decisions.

LIMITED PARTICIPATION IN GOVERNMENT When citizens do not seem to take their citizenship seriously, democracy's defenders worry. There is plenty of evidence that Americans know relatively little about who their leaders are, much less about their policy decisions. Furthermore, Americans do not take full advantage of

policy gridlock
A condition that occurs when interests conflict and no coalition is strong enough to form a majority and establish policy, so nothing gets done.

their opportunities to shape government or select its leaders. Limited participation in government challenges the foundation of democracy. In particular, because young people represent the country's future, their low voting turnout rates point to an even more serious challenge to democracy on the horizon.

ESCALATING CAMPAIGN COSTS Many political observers worry about the close connection between money and politics, especially in congressional elections. Winning a House seat these days usually requires a campaign war chest of *at least* a million dollars, and Senate races are even more costly. Congressional candidates have become increasingly dependent on political action committees (PACs) to fund their campaigns because of the escalation of campaign costs. These PACs often represent specific economic interests, and they care little about how members of Congress vote on most issues—just the issues that particularly affect them. Critics charge that when it comes to the issues PACs care about, the members of Congress listen, lest they be denied the money they need for their reelection. When democracy confronts the might of money, the gap between democratic theory and reality widens further.

DIVERSE POLITICAL INTERESTS The diversity of the American people is reflected in the diversity of interests represented in the political system. As will be shown in this book, this system is so open that interests find it easy to gain access to policymakers. When interests conflict, which they often do, no coalition may be strong enough to form a majority and establish policy. But each interest may use its influence to thwart those whose policy proposals they oppose. In effect, they have a veto over policy, creating what is often referred to as **policy gridlock**. In a big city, gridlock occurs when there are so many cars on the road that no one can move; in politics, it occurs when each policy coalition finds its way blocked by others.

Democracy is not necessarily an end in itself. For many, evaluations of democracy depend on what democratic government produces. Thus, a major challenge to democracy in America is to overcome the diversity of interests and fragmentation of power in order to deliver policies that are responsive to citizens' needs.

The influence of the wealthy on politics drew increased public attention in 2012, as billionaires like Sheldon and Miriam Adelson (shown here) made multimillion-dollar contributions to Super PACs that supported particular presidential candidates. With their net worth of over $25 billion, the Adelsons' announced intention of spending $100 million on the presidential campaign was equivalent to the average family with a net worth of $7,000 committing to spend $308.

☐ American Political Culture and Democracy

The key factor that holds American democracy together, in the view of many scholars, is its **political culture**—the overall set of values widely shared within American society. As Ronald Inglehart and Christian Welzel argue in their book on cultural change and democracy, "Democracy is not simply the result of clever elite bargaining and constitutional engineering. It depends on deep-rooted orientations among the people themselves. These orientations motivate them to demand freedom and responsive government. . . . Genuine democracy is not simply a machine that, once set up, functions by itself. It depends on the people."[17]

Because Americans are so diverse in terms of ancestry, religion, and heritage, the political culture of the United States is especially crucial to understanding its government. What unites Americans more than anything else is a set of shared beliefs and values. As G. K. Chesterton, the noted British observer of American politics, wrote in 1922, "America is the only nation in the world that is founded on a creed. That creed is set forth with dogmatic and even theological lucidity in the Declaration of Independence."[18] Arguing along the same lines, Seymour Martin Lipset writes that "the United States is a country organized around an ideology which includes a set of dogmas about the nature of good society."[19] Lipset argues that the American creed can be summarized by five elements: liberty, egalitarianism, individualism, laissez-faire, and populism.[20]

LIBERTY One of the most famous statements of the American Revolution was Patrick Henry's "Give me liberty or give me death." During the Cold War, a common bumper sticker was "Better Dead Than Red," reflecting many Americans' view that they would prefer to fight to the bitter end than submit to the oppression of communist rule. To this day, New Hampshire's official state motto is "Live Free or Die." When immigrants are asked why they came to America, by far the most common response is to live in freedom.

Freedom of speech and religion are fundamental to the American way of life. In the Declaration of Independence, Thomas Jefferson placed liberty right along with life and the pursuit of happiness as an "unalienable right" (that is, a right not awarded by human power, not transferable to another power, and not revocable).

One of the fundamental values that most Americans cherish is that of liberty. The state of New Hampshire has even gone so far to place a slogan to this effect on all the automobile license plates in the state.

EGALITARIANISM The most famous phrase in the history of democracy is the Declaration of Independence's statement "We hold these truths to be self-evident, that all men are created equal. . . ." As the French observer Alexis de Tocqueville noted long ago, egalitarianism in the United States involves equality of opportunity and respect in the absence of a monarchy and aristocracy. Americans have never been equal in terms of condition. What is most critical to this part of the American creed is that everyone have a chance to succeed in life.

Tocqueville accurately foresaw that the social equality he observed in American life in the 1830s would eventually lead to political equality. Although relatively few Americans then had the right to vote, he predicted that all Americans would be given this right because, in order to guarantee equality of opportunity, everyone must have an equal chance to participate in democratic governance. Thus, another key aspect of egalitarianism is equal voting rights for all adult American citizens.

The ideal of egalitarianism extends also to equality of opportunity for members of all groups. In a recent survey, about three out of four Americans said they were proud of the fair and equal treatment of all groups in the United States. As you can see in Figure 1.5, this level of pride in the country's egalitarianism is extremely high compared to that in other democracies.

INDIVIDUALISM One of the aspects of American political culture that has shaped the development of American democracy has been individualism—the belief that people can and should get ahead on their own. The immigrants who founded American society may have been diverse, but many shared a common dream of America as a place where one could make it on one's own without interference from government. Louis Hartz's *The Liberal Tradition in America* is a classic analysis of the dominant political beliefs during America's formative years. Hartz argues that the major force behind limited government in America is that it was settled by people who fled from the feudal and clerical oppressions of the Old World. Once in the New World, they wanted little from government other than for it to leave them alone.[21]

FIGURE 1.5 PRIDE IN EQUAL TREATMENT OF GROUPS IN THE UNITED STATES AND OTHER ESTABLISHED DEMOCRACIES

Americans rank very high in terms of being proud of their country's fair and equal treatment of all groups. This figure shows the percentages who said "very proud" or "somewhat proud" in response to the question, "How proud are you of [country] in . . . its fair and equal treatment of all groups—very proud, somewhat proud, not very proud, not proud at all?"

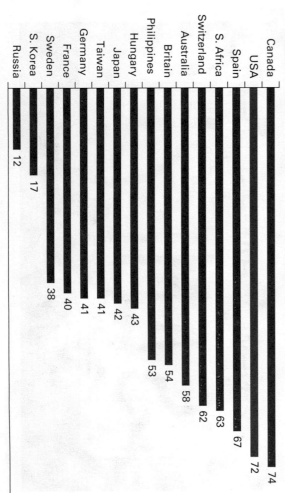

Country	Percent
Canada	74
USA	72
Spain	67
S. Africa	63
Switzerland	62
Australia	58
Britain	54
Philippines	53
Hungary	43
Japan	42
Taiwan	41
Germany	41
France	40
Sweden	38
S. Korea	17
Russia	12

Percent proud of equal treatment of all groups in their country

SOURCE: Authors' analysis of 2003 International Social Survey Program surveys.

Another explanation for American individualism is the existence of a bountiful frontier, at least up until the start of the twentieth century. Not only did many people come to America to escape from governmental interference, but the frontier allowed them to get away from government almost entirely once they arrived. Frederick Jackson Turner's famous work on the significance of the frontier in American history argues that "the frontier is productive of individualism."22 According to Turner, being in the wilderness and having to survive on one's own left settlers with an aversion to any control from the outside world—particularly from the government.

LAISSEZ-FAIRE An important result of American individualism has been a clear tendency to prefer laissez-faire economic policies, which promote free markets and limited government. As John Kingdon writes in his book *America the Unusual*, "Government in the United States is much more limited and much smaller than government in virtually every other advanced industrialized country on earth."23 Compared to most other economically developed nations, the United States devotes a smaller percentage of its resources to government. Americans have a lighter tax burden than citizens of other democratic nations.

Further, all of the other advanced industrial democracies have long had a system of national health insurance that guarantees care to all their citizens; it wasn't until 2014 that the United States implemented a system to guarantee most Americans health insurance via the Patient Protection and Affordable Care Act that President Obama signed into law. In other countries, national governments have taken it on themselves to start up airline, telephone, and communications companies. Governments have built much housing in most Western nations, compared to only a small fraction of the housing in America. Thus, in terms of its impact on citizens' everyday lives, government in the United States actually does less than the governments of these other democracies.

POPULISM Abraham Lincoln summarized American democracy as "government of the people, for the people, and by the people." Such an emphasis on *the people* is at the heart of populism, which can best be defined as a political philosophy supporting the rights of average citizens in their struggle against privileged elites. As Lipset writes, American populist thought holds that the people at large "are possessed of some kind of sacred mystique, and proximity to them endows the politician with esteem—and with legitimacy."24

In America, being on the side of the ordinary people against big interests is so valued that liberal and conservative politicians alike frequently claim this mantle. Liberals are inclined to argue that they will stand up to big multinational corporations and protect the interests of ordinary Americans. Conservatives, on the other hand, are likely to repeat Ronald Reagan's famous promise to get big government off the backs of the American people. A populist pledge to "put the people first" is always a safe strategy in the American political culture.

☐ A Culture War?

Although Americans are widely supportive of cultural values like liberty and egalitarianism, some scholars are concerned that a sharp polarization into rival liberal versus conservative political cultures has taken place in recent years. James Q. Wilson defines such a polarization as "an intense commitment to a candidate, a culture, or an ideology that sets people in one group definitively apart from people in another, rival group."25 Wilson maintains that America is a more polarized nation today than at any time in living memory. He argues that the intensity of political divisions in twenty-first-century America is a major problem, writing that "a divided America encourages our enemies, disheartens our allies, and saps our resolve—potentially to fatal effect."26

Point to Ponder

In his first major political speech, Barack Obama proclaimed that there was no such thing as red or blue states—only the United States. For Obama, the social and political stereotypes portrayed in this Pulitzer Prize-winning cartoon are exaggerations.

What do you think—is there a cultural war going on in America?

SOURCE: David Horsey, *Seattle-Post Intelligencer*, 2002.

Other scholars, however, believe that there is relatively little evidence of a so-called culture war going on among ordinary American citizens. Morris Fiorina concludes, "There is little indication that voters are polarized now or that they are becoming more polarized—even when we look specifically at issues such as abortion that supposedly are touchstone issues in the culture war. If anything, public opinion has grown more centrist on such issues and more tolerant of the divergent views, values, and behavior of other Americans."[27] Wayne Baker outlines three ways in which America might be experiencing a crisis of cultural values: (1) a loss over time of traditional values, such as the importance of religion and family life; (2) an unfavorable comparison with the citizens of other countries in terms of key values such as patriotism; and (3) the division of society into opposed groups with irreconcilable moral differences. Baker tests each of these three possibilities thoroughly with recent survey data from the United States and other countries and finds little evidence of cultural division or an ongoing crisis of values in America.[28]

The Scope of Government in America

1.5 Outline the central arguments of the debate in America over the proper scope of government.

I n proposing a massive $787 billion economic stimulus package to deal with the nation's economic woes in 2009, President Obama stated, "It is true that we cannot depend on government alone to create jobs or long-term growth, but at this particular moment, only government can provide the short-term boost necessary to lift us from a recession this deep and severe." In response, Republican House Leader John Boehner countered, "This bill makes clear that the era of Big Government is back, and the Democrats expect you to pay for it." He and other conservatives opposed the stimulus bill, arguing that such increases in the scope of the federal government would result in less freedom and prosperity. Had they been in the majority in 2009, they would have focused instead on tax cuts that would have had the effect of reducing the scope of government.

Those who are inclined to support an active role for government argue that its intervention is sometimes the only means of achieving important goals in American society. How else, they ask, can we ensure that people have enough to eat, clean air and water, and affordable health care? How else can we ensure that the disadvantaged

The Women, Infants, and Children (WIC) program is just one of many federal programs that provides support for individuals with low income. Here, a worker in Los Angeles organizes WIC vouchers, which currently go to about 9 million women, infants, and children under the age of 5. Supporters of such programs argue that they provide a much-needed safety net, enabling people to get by during hard times. Critics see these programs as expanding the scope of government too much and as often encouraging a dependency that actually perpetuates poverty.

gross domestic product (GDP)
The sum total of the value of all the goods and services produced in a year in a nation.

are given opportunities for education and jobs and are not discriminated against? Opponents of widening the scope of government agree that these are worthwhile goals but challenge whether involving the federal government is an effective way to pursue them. Dick Armey, who was one of the key figures in the establishment of the conservative Tea Party movement, expressed this view well when he wrote, "There is more wisdom in millions of individuals making decisions in their own self-interest than there is in even the most enlightened bureaucrat (or congressman) making decisions on their behalf."[29] Or, as Ronald Reagan argued in his farewell presidential address, "As government expands, liberty contracts."

To understand the dimensions of this debate, it is important first to get some sense of the current scope of the federal government's activities.

How Active Is American Government?

In terms of dollars spent, government in America is vast. Altogether, our governments—national, state, and local—spend about a third of our **gross domestic product (GDP)**, the total value of all goods and services produced annually by the United States. Government not only spends large sums of money but also employs large numbers of people. About 24 million Americans work for our government, mostly at the state and local level as teachers, police officers, university professors, and so on. Consider some facts about the size of our national government:

- It spends about $3.5 trillion annually (printed as a number, that's $3,500,000,000,000 a year).
- It employs about 2.7 million civilians, as well as 1.4 million in the military.
- It owns about one-third of the land in the United States.
- It occupies over 3.2 billion square feet of office space.

How does the American national government spend $3.6 trillion a year? National defense takes about one-sixth of the federal budget, a smaller percentage than it did three decades ago—even with the increase after September 11. Social Security consumes more than one-fifth of the budget. Medicare is another big-ticket item, requiring over one-tenth of the budget. State and local governments also get important parts of the federal government's budget, totaling over $600 billion in recent years. The federal government helps fund highway construction, police departments, school districts, and other state and local functions.

When expenditures grow, tax revenues must grow to pay the additional costs. When taxes do not grow as fast as spending, a budget deficit results. The federal government ran a budget deficit every year from 1969 through 1997. The last few Clinton budgets showed surpluses, but soon after George W. Bush took over, the government was running a deficit once again due to the combination of reduced taxes and of increased expenditures on national security following the events of September 11. The severe economic recession at the end of Bush's presidency led to his running up further red ink in 2008 to bail out the financial system and to Obama's doing the same in 2009 with an economic stimulus package to combat unemployment. The net result was that in each fiscal year from 2009 through 2012 the annual deficit exceeded one trillion dollars. The deficit fell to $680 billion in 2013 and $486 billion in 2014. All this deficit spending has left the country with a national debt of over $17 trillion, which will pose a problem for policymakers for decades to come.

The sheer size of federal government expenditures should hardly be surprising in light of the many issues that Americans have come to expect their government to deal with. Whatever the national problem—unemployment, terrorism, illegal immigration, energy, education, lack of access to health care—many people expect Congress and the president to work to solve it through legislation. In short, the American government is vast on any measure—whether dollars spent, persons employed, or laws passed. Our concern, however, is not so much about the absolute size of government as about whether the level of government activity is what we want it to be.

Review the Chapter

Government

1.1 Identify the key functions of government and explain why they matter, p. 8.

The functions that all governments perform include maintaining a national defense, providing public services, preserving order, socializing the young, and collecting taxes. By performing these functions, governments regularly shape the way in which we live.

Politics

1.2 Define politics in the context of democratic government, p. 10.

Politics determines what leaders we select and what policies they pursue. The *who* of politics is the voters, candidates, parties, and groups; the *what* is the benefits and burdens of government; the *how* is the various ways in which people participate in politics.

The Policymaking System

1.3 Assess how citizens can have an impact on public policy and how policies can impact people, p. 11.

The policymaking system is in effect a cycle. Citizens' interests and concerns are transmitted through linkage institutions (parties and elections, interest groups, the media). These concerns shape the government's policy agenda, from which those in policymaking institutions (Congress, the presidency, the courts) choose issues to address. The policies that are made (laws, executive orders, regulations, and court judgments) then influence people's lives.

Democracy in America

1.4 Identify the key principles of democracy and outline theories regarding how it works in practice and the challenges democracy faces today, p. 14.

According to traditional democratic theory, the ideal democracy is characterized by "one person, one vote," equal opportunities to participate, freedom of speech and the press, citizen control of the policy agenda, and inclusion. Pluralist theory holds that American democracy works well, as competition among many organized groups means that the public interest becomes public policy. This view is disputed by elitist theory, which claims that the powerful few dominate, and by hyperpluralist theory, which sees the excessive influence of many competing groups as leading to muddled policy or inaction. Contemporary challenges to American and other democracies include the complexity of issues today, citizens' limited participation, escalating campaign costs, and the policy gridlock resulting from diverse political interests.

Government in America

1.5 Outline the central arguments of the debate in America over the proper scope of government, p. 23.

One of the most important issues facing modern American democracy is the proper scope of government. Politicians constantly debate whether the scope of government responsibilities is too vast, just about right, or not comprehensive enough. This debate concerns whether the goals that are agreed to be important are best achieved through government action or rather through means other than government.

Learn the Terms

government, p. 8
collective goods, p. 10
politics, p. 10
political participation, p. 10
single-issue groups, p. 11
policymaking system, p. 11
linkage institutions, p. 12
policy agenda, p. 12
political issue, p. 13
policymaking institutions, p. 13
public policy, p. 13
policy impacts, p. 13
democracy, p. 14
majority rule, p. 15
minority rights, p. 15
representation, p. 15
pluralism, p. 15
elitism, p. 16
hyperpluralism, p. 17
policy gridlock, p. 18
political culture, p. 19
gross domestic product, p. 24

Test Yourself

1. Which of the following functions does the national government perform?

a. determining teachers' salaries

b. organizing interest groups

c. providing educational opportunities

d. socializing the young

e. trying to get citizens involved in politics

2. Clean water is considered a _____ and must be shared by everyone.

a. collective good

b. collective liberty

c. collective right

d. government right

e. political good

3. What is the difference between the National Guard and the rest of the armed forces?

a. The National Guard exists for defense of the country against foreign attack. The rest of the armed forces exist to help the Central Intelligence Agency and Federal Bureau of Investigation in investigations.

b. The National Guard is another name for the U.S. armed forces.

c. The National Guard is used by the government to assist Federal Emergency Management Agency and disaster relief, whereas the rest of the armed forces are used in violent situations, such as riots or war defense.

d. The National Guard is used by the government to keep law and order within the country during times of disaster or upheaval. The rest of the armed forces exist for defense of the country against foreign attack.

e. The National Guard patrols the U.S. coasts, whereas the rest of the armed forces work on the ground or in other countries.

4. Why do young voters have less "political clout" than seniors do?

a. Young voters are discriminated against by the government because they are young.

b. Young voters are too busy with school and work to get involved, whereas seniors are retired and have more free time.

c. Young voters are too focused on single issues and not enough on benefiting society as a whole.

d. Young voters have a lower voter turnout and therefore less influence on election results.

e. Young voters have less experience, and therefore their opinions have less value than those of the seniors.

5. What is politics mainly about?

a. how each generation interprets the Constitution

b. individual candidates' campaign promises

c. the system of checks and balances

d. voter confidence in government

e. who gets what, when, and how

6. Compared to other modern democracies, why do many consider the health of the American government to be poor?

a. America has some of the lowest voter turnout in the world.

b. Americans are limited in the ways they can criticize the government.

c. Among developed nations, America is seen as one of the most corrupt.

d. Political participation is limited to a select few in America.

e. There are few ways in America to change the course of government.

7. Differentiate between a political issue and the policy agenda.

a. A political issue arises when people disagree about how to fix a problem. The policy agenda contains the issues that attract the most attention from the politicians and the people at a specific point in time.

b. A political issue is an issue of a magazine or newspaper that deals exclusively with politics. A policy agenda is the list of political topics a news company is going to discuss that day.

c. A political issue is created by the media to be a talking point for candidates on a campaign. The policy agenda is what the representatives actively work on once elected.

d. A political issue is something that politicians discuss during debates. A policy agenda is determined by the leaders of the military.

e. Policy agenda is simply another way of saying political issue.

8. Which of the following is a linkage institution that a citizen might employ to get an issue on the policy agenda?

a. an interest group

b. e-mail

c. public education

d. the Internal Revenue Service

e. the military

9. Due to its immense power, the _____ is often considered the fourth policymaking institution of America.

a. bureaucracy
b. defense industry
c. Federal Reserve
d. higher education community
e. media

10. What are the differences among pluralism, elitism, and hyperpluralism?

a. Pluralism is the form of government that the Founders of America thought was best for our country. Elitism is the government the American Revolution sought to overthrow. Hyperpluralism is what we call our modified form of the Founders' original government.

b. Pluralism states that government should be "for the people, by the people, of the people." Elitism states that government is really ruled by the bureaucracy. Hyperpluralism states that the federal government should be disbanded and we should rely on the 50 state governments instead.

c. Pluralism states that government should be run on the concept of majority rule. Elitism states that only a select few upper-class individuals should have the right to vote. Hyperpluralism states that government should be a combination of the two.

d. Pluralism states that groups compete and check one another's power and influence. Elitism states that a small group of upper-class people have the most influence on government. Hyperpluralism states that interest groups are the real power and that government itself has been weakened by them.

e. Pluralism states that representative democracy is the best form of government. Elitism states that any form of democracy is best, provided there are limits on who can vote. Hyperpluralism states that direct democracy is the best form of government.

11. Which of the following illustrates Dahl's concept of enlightened understanding?

a. distorting news coverage to intentionally mislead and influence people
b. lobbying Congress
c. the freedom to participate in the stock market
d. the freedom to read or write opinion pieces in a newspaper
e. the right to vote

12. What is the one fundamental question that any theory of democracy should answer?

a. Can the United States compete with other democracies?
b. Is great wealth necessary to succeed in the United States?
c. Is the bureaucracy of the United States necessary?
d. Which part of the population will vote?
e. Who really governs our nation?

13. The federal government has usually run a budget deficit since 1969, except for during part of the administration of which president?

a. Bill Clinton
b. George W. Bush
c. Jimmy Carter
d. Richard Nixon
e. Ronald Reagan

14. Which of the following best explains why a budget deficit develops?

a. Economic recession causes an increase in the number of Americans without jobs.
b. Taxes do not increase at the same rate as government expenditures do.
c. Taxes increase faster than government spending does.
d. The government does not make proper use of a stimulus package.
e. The government takes more than its fair share of the gross domestic product.

15. The role of government changes over time. What is the most likely reason for such change?

a. a crisis such as a war occurs
b. a natural disaster such as a hurricane wreaks havoc on an area of the country
c. citizens' attitudes about government's role changes
d. new technologies are introduced that cause fundamental changes in business
e. rising sea levels occur due to rising global temperatures

Explore Further

WEB SITES

www.policyalmanac.org
Contains a discussion of major policy issues of the day and links to resources about them.

www.bowlingalone.com
A site designed to accompany Robert Putnam's work, which contains information concerning the data he used and projects he is working on to reinvigorate American communities.

www.politicalwire.com
A good daily guide to some of the most interesting political stories of the day, as seen from a liberal's perspective.

www.realclearpolitics.com
A good daily guide to some of the most interesting political stories of the day, as seen from a conservative's perspective.

FURTHER READING

Alesina, Alberto and Edward L. Glaeser. *Fighting Poverty in the US and Europe: A World of Difference.* New York: Oxford, 2004. A comprehensive analysis of how and why the scope of government is smaller in the United States than in Europe.

Bok, Derek. *The State of the Nation: Government and the Quest for a Better Society.* Cambridge, MA: Harvard University Press, 1996. An excellent analysis of how America is doing, compared to other major democracies, on a wide variety of policy aspects.

Dahl, Robert A. *Democracy and Its Critics.* New Haven, CT: Yale University Press, 1982. A very thoughtful work by one of the world's most articulate advocates of pluralist theory.

de Tocqueville, Alexis. *Democracy in America.* New York: Mentor Books, 1956. This classic by a nineteenth-century French aristocrat remains one of the most insightful works on the nature of American society and government.

Hartz, Louis. *The Liberal Tradition in America.* New York: Harcourt, Brace, 1955. A classic analysis of why the scope of American government has been more limited than in other democracies.

Kingdon, John W. *Agendas, Alternatives, and Public Policies.* 2nd ed. New York: HarperCollins, 1995. One of the best efforts by a political scientist to examine the political agenda.

Macedo, Stephen, et al. *Democracy at Risk: How Political Choices Undermine Citizen Participation, and What We Can Do About It.* Washington, DC: Brookings, 2005. An insightful review of many aspects of political participation in America.

Putnam, Robert. *Bowling Alone: The Collapse and Revival of American Community.* New York: Simon & Schuster, 2000. Putnam's highly influential work shows how Americans have become increasingly disconnected from one another since the early 1960s.

Sitaraman, Ganesh and Previn Warren. *Invisible Citizens: Youth Politics After September 11.* New York: iUniverse, Inc., 2003. Two Harvard students examine why today's youth demonstrate a commitment to community service while at the same time largely neglect involvement in politics.

Stanley, Harold W., and Richard G. Niemi. *Vital Statistics on American Politics, 2011–2012.* Washington, DC: CQ Press, 2012. Useful data on government, politics, and policy in the United States.

Wolfe, Alan. *Does American Democracy Still Work?* New Haven: Yale University Press, 2006. An influential critique of the problems of democracy in America today.

2
The Constitution

Politics in Action: Amending the Constitution

2.1
Describe the ideas behind the American Revolution and their role in shaping the Constitution, p. 32.

2.2
Analyze how the weaknesses of the Articles of Confederation led to its failure, p. 37.

2.3
Describe the delegates to the Constitutional Convention and the core ideas they shared, p. 41.

2.4
Categorize the issues at the Constitutional Convention and outline the resolutions reached on each type of issue, p. 42.

2.5
Analyze how the components of the Madisonian system addressed the dilemma of reconciling majority rule with the protection of minority interests, p. 47.

2.6
Compare and contrast the Federalists and Anti-Federalists in terms of their background and their positions regarding government, p. 51.

2.7
Explain how the Constitution can be formally amended and how it changes informally, p. 53.

2.8
Assess whether the Constitution establishes a majoritarian democracy and how it limits the scope of government, p. 60.

G regory Lee Johnson knew little about the Constitution, but he knew that he was upset. He felt that the buildup of nuclear weapons in the world threatened the planet's survival, and he wanted to protest presidential and corporate policies concerning nuclear weapons. Yet he had no money to hire a lobbyist or to purchase an ad in a newspaper. So he and some other demonstrators marched through the streets of Dallas, chanting political slogans and stopping at several corporate locations to stage "die-ins" intended to dramatize the consequences of nuclear war. The demonstration ended in front of Dallas City Hall, where Gregory doused an American flag with kerosene and set it on fire.

Burning the flag violated the law, and Gregory was convicted of "desecration of a venerated object," sentenced to one year in prison, and fined $2,000. He appealed his conviction, claiming that the law that prohibited burning the flag violated his freedom of speech. In the case of *Texas v. Gregory Lee Johnson* the U.S. Supreme Court agreed.

Gregory was pleased with the Court's decision, but he was nearly alone. The public howled its opposition to the decision, and President George H. W. Bush called for a constitutional amendment authorizing punishment of flag desecraters. Many public officials vowed to support the amendment, and organized opposition to it was scarce. However, an amendment to prohibit burning the American flag did not obtain the two-thirds vote in each house of Congress necessary to send it to the states for ratification.

The Constitution guarantees rights, even in the face of widespread public opposition. Thus, protestors, like those pictured here, can engage in the unpopular act of burning the flag to make a political point.

31

constitution
A nation's basic law. It creates political institutions, assigns or divides powers in government, and often provides certain guarantees to citizens. Constitutions can be either written or unwritten.

2.1

2.2

2.3

2.4

2.5

2.6

2.7

2.8

Instead, Congress passed a law—the Flag Protection Act—that outlawed the desecration of the American flag. The next year, however, in *United States v. Eichman*, the Supreme Court found the act an impermissible infringement on free speech.

After years of political posturing, legislation, and litigation, little has changed. Burning the flag remains a legally protected form of political expression despite the objections of the overwhelming majority of the American public. Gregory Johnson did not prevail because he was especially articulate, nor did he win because he had access to political resources, such as money or powerful supporters. He won because of the nature of the Constitution.

Understanding how an unpopular protestor like Gregory Lee Johnson could triumph over the combined forces of the public and its elected officials is central to understanding the American system of government. The Constitution supersedes statutory law, even when the law represents the wishes of a majority of citizens. The Constitution not only guarantees individual rights but also decentralizes power. Even the president cannot force Congress to start the process of amending the Constitution. Power is not concentrated efficiently in the hands of one person, such as the president. Instead, there are numerous checks on the exercise of power and many obstacles to change. Some complain that this system is inefficient and too often produces stalemate, while others praise the way in which it protects minority views. Both positions are correct.

Gregory Johnson's case raises some important questions about government in America. What does democracy mean if the majority does not always get its way? Is this how we should be governed? And is it appropriate that the many limits on the scope of government action, both direct and indirect, sometimes prevent action most citizens desire?

Our theme of the scope of government runs throughout this chapter, which focuses on what the national government can and cannot do. A nation that prides itself on being "democratic" must evaluate the Constitution according to democratic standards, the core of our other theme. To understand government and to answer questions about how we are governed and what government does, we must first understand the Constitution.

A **constitution** is a nation's basic law. It creates political institutions, assigns the powers of government, and provides guarantees to citizens. A constitution is also an unwritten accumulation of traditions and precedents that have established acceptable means of governing. As the body of rules that govern our nation, the U.S. Constitution has an impact on many aspects of our everyday lives, such as the rights we enjoy, the health care we receive, and the taxes we pay.

The Origins of the Constitution

2.1 Describe the ideas behind the American Revolution and their role in shaping the Constitution.

I

n the summer of 1776, a small group of men met in Philadelphia and passed a resolution that began an armed rebellion against the government of what was then the most powerful nation on Earth. The resolution was, of course, the Declaration of Independence, and the armed rebellion, the American Revolution.

The attempt to overthrow a government forcibly is a serious and unusual act. All countries, including the United States, consider it treasonous and levy serious punishments for it. A set of compelling ideas drove our forefathers to take such drastic and risky action. Understanding the Constitution requires an understanding of these ideas.

FIGURE 2.1 EUROPEAN CLAIMS IN NORTH AMERICA

Following its victory in the French and Indian War in 1763, Britain obtained from the French an enormous new territory to govern. (Britain also gained Florida from Spain.) To raise revenues to defend and administer the new territory, it raised taxes on the colonists and tightened enforcement of trade regulations.

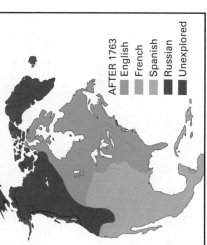

BEFORE 1754
English
French
Spanish
Russian
Unexplored

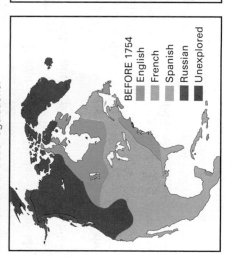

AFTER 1763
English
French
Spanish
Russian
Unexplored

The Road to Revolution

By eighteenth-century standards, life was not bad for most people in America at the time of the Revolution, slaves and indentured servants being major exceptions. In fact, white colonists "were freer, more equal, more prosperous, and less burdened with cumbersome feudal and monarchical restraints than any other part of mankind."[1] Although the colonies were part of the British Empire, the king and Parliament generally confined themselves to governing America's foreign policy and trade. They left almost everything else to the discretion of individual colonial governments. Although commercial regulations irritated colonial shippers, planters, land speculators, and merchants, these rules had little influence on the vast bulk of the population, who were self-employed farmers or artisans.

As you can see in Figure 2.1, Britain obtained an enormous new territory in North America after the French and Indian War (also known as the Seven Years' War) ended in 1763. The cost of defending this territory against foreign adversaries was large, and Parliament reasoned that it was only fair that those who were the primary beneficiaries—the colonists—should contribute to their own defense. In order to raise revenue to defend the new territory, the British Parliament passed a series of taxes on official documents, publications like newspapers, and imported paper, glass, paint, and tea. Britain also began tightening enforcement of its trade regulations, which were designed to benefit the mother country, not the colonists.

The colonists lacked direct representation in Parliament and resented its imposing taxes on them without their consent. They protested, boycotted the taxed goods, and, as a symbolic act of disobedience, even threw 342 chests of tea into Boston Harbor. Britain reacted by applying economic pressure through a naval blockade of the harbor, further fueling the colonists' anger. The colonists responded by forming the First Continental Congress in September 1774, sending delegates from each colony to Philadelphia to discuss the future of relations with Britain.

Declaring Independence

Talk of independence was common among the delegates. Thomas Paine's fiery tract *Common Sense* appeared in January 1776 and fanned the already hot flames of revolution. In May and June 1776, the Continental Congress began debating resolutions about independence. On June 7, Richard Henry Lee of Virginia moved "that these United States are and of right ought to be free and independent states." A committee composed of Thomas Jefferson of Virginia, John Adams of Massachusetts, Benjamin Franklin of

2.1
2.2
2.3
2.4
2.5
2.6
2.7
2.8

Declaration of Independence

The document approved by representatives of the American colonies in 1776 that stated their grievances against the British monarch and declared their independence.

COMMON SENSE;

ADDRESSED TO THE

INHABITANTS

OF

A M E R I C A,

On the following interesting

S U B J E C T S.

I. Of the Origin and Design of Government in general, with concise Remarks on the English Constitution.

II. Of Monarchy and Hereditary Succession.

III. Thoughts on the present State of American Affairs.

IV. Of the present Ability of America, with some miscellaneous Reflections.

Man knows no Master save creating HEAVEN,
Or those whom choice and common good ordain.
THOMSON.

PHILADELPHIA;
Printed, and Sold, by R. BELL, in Third-Street.
MDCCLXXVI.

Thomas Paine's *Common Sense* encouraged the colonists to declare independence from Britain.

Pennsylvania, Roger Sherman of Connecticut, and Robert Livingston of New York was formed to draft a document to justify the inevitable declaration. On July 2, Congress formally approved Lee's motion to declare independence from England. Congress adopted the **Declaration of Independence** two days later, on July 4.

The primary author of the Declaration of Independence was Thomas Jefferson, a 33-year-old, well-educated Virginia lawmaker who was a talented author steeped in the philosophical writings of European moral philosophers.[2] The Declaration quickly became one of the most widely quoted and revered documents in America. Filled with fine principles and bold language, it can be read as both a political tract and a philosophical treatise.

Much of the Declaration was a polemic, a political argument, announcing the Revolution to the citizens of the colonies and justifying it. Most of the document—27 of its 32 paragraphs—listed the ways in which the king had abused the colonies. The delegates accused George III of all sorts of evil deeds, including inciting the "merciless Indian savages" to make war on the colonists. The delegates focused blame on the king because they held that only he, not Parliament, had authority over the colonies.

The Declaration's polemical aspects were also important because the colonists needed foreign assistance to take on Britain, the most powerful nation in the world. France, which was engaged in a war with Britain, was a prime target for the delegates' diplomacy and eventually provided aid that was critical to the success of the Revolution.

Today, we study the Declaration of Independence more as a statement of philosophy than as a political call to arms. In just a few sentences, Jefferson set forth the American democratic creed, the most important and succinct statement of the philosophy underlying American government—as applicable today as it was in 1776.

☐ The English Heritage: The Power of Ideas

The Declaration articulates ideas that were by then common knowledge on both sides of the Atlantic, especially among those people who wished to challenge the power of kings. Franklin, Jefferson, James Madison of Virginia, Robert Morris of Pennsylvania, Alexander Hamilton of New York, and other intellectual leaders in the colonies were

John Adams (from right), Roger Sherman, Robert R. Livingston, Thomas Jefferson, and Benjamin Franklin submit the Declaration of Independence to Continental Congress President John Hancock. Legend has it that Hancock remarked, "We must be unanimous; there must be no pulling different ways; we must hang together," to which Franklin replied, "We must indeed all hang together, or, most assuredly, we shall hang separately."

natural rights

Rights inherent in human beings, not dependent on governments, which include life, liberty, and property. The concept of natural rights was central to English philosopher John Locke's theories about government and was widely accepted among America's Founders.

consent of the governed

The idea that government derives its authority from the people.

limited government

The idea that certain restrictions should be placed on government to protect the natural rights of citizens.

learned and widely read men, familiar with the works of English, French, and Scottish political philosophers. These leaders corresponded about the ideas they encountered in their reading, quoted philosophers in their debates over the Revolution, and applied the philosopher's ideas to the new government they would form with the Constitution.

John Locke was one of the most influential philosophers the Founders read. His writings, especially *The Second Treatise of Civil Government* (1689), profoundly influenced American political leaders. His work was "the dominant political faith of the American colonies in the second quarter of the eighteenth century."[3]

The foundation on which Locke built his powerful philosophy was a belief in **natural rights**—rights inherent in human beings, not dependent on governments. Before governments arose, Locke held, people existed in a state of nature, in which they were governed not by formal laws but by the laws of nature—laws determined by people's innate moral sense. This natural law provided natural rights, including life, liberty, and property. Natural law could even justify a challenge to the rule of a tyrannical king because it was superior to manmade law. Government, Locke argued, must be built on the **consent of the governed**; in other words, the people must agree on who their rulers will be. It should also be a **limited government**; that is, there must be clear restrictions on what rulers can do. Indeed, the sole purpose of government, according to Locke, was to protect natural rights. The idea that certain things were beyond the realm of government contrasted sharply with the traditional notion that kings possessed divinely granted, absolute rights over their subjects.

Two limits on government were particularly important to Locke. First, governments must provide standing laws so that people know in advance whether their acts will be acceptable. Second, and Locke was very forceful on this point, "The supreme power cannot take from any man any part of his property without his consent." To Locke, the preservation of property was the principle purpose of government. The sanctity of property was one of the few ideas absent from Jefferson's draft of the Declaration of Independence, which altered Locke's phrase "life, liberty, and property" to "life, liberty, and the pursuit of happiness." We shall soon see, however, how the Lockean idea of the sanctity of property figured prominently at the Constitutional Convention. James Madison, the most influential member of that body, directly echoed Locke's view that the preservation of property is the purpose of government.

Locke argued that in an extreme case people have a right to revolt against a government that no longer has their consent. Anticipating critics' charges that this right would lead to constant civil disturbances, he emphasized that people should not revolt until injustices become deeply felt. The Declaration of Independence accented the same point, declaring that "governments long established should not be changed for light and transient causes." But when matters went beyond "patient sufferance," severing the ties between the people and their government was necessary.[4]

Locke represented only one element of revolutionary thought from which Jefferson and his colleagues borrowed. Another was a tradition well established in the English countryside of opposition to the executive power of the Crown and emphasizing the rights of the people. The American colonists themselves had developed a set of political ideas that stressed moral virtue, patriotism, relations based on merit, and the equality of independent citizens. These American ideas intensified the radicalism of the British "country" ideology and linked it with older currents of European thought, stretching back to antiquity, regarding the rights of citizens and the role of government.

The American Creed

There are some remarkable parallels between Locke's thought and the language in the Declaration of Independence (see Table 2.1). Finessing the issue of how the rebels knew that men had rights, Jefferson simply declared that it was "self-evident" that men were equally "endowed by their Creator with certain unalienable rights," including "life, liberty, and the pursuit of happiness." Because the purpose of government was to "secure" these rights, the people could form a new government if the existing one failed to do so.

TABLE 2.1 LOCKE AND THE DECLARATION OF INDEPENDENCE: SOME PARALLELS

Locke	Declaration of Independence
Natural Rights "The state of nature has a law to govern it" "life, liberty, and property"	"Laws of Nature and Nature's God" "life, liberty, and the pursuit of happiness"
Purpose of Government "to preserve himself, his liberty, and property"	"to secure these rights"
Equality "men being by nature all free, equal and independent"	"all men are created equal"
Consent of the Governed "for when any number of men have, by the consent of every individual, made a community, with a power to act as one body, which is only by the will and determination of the majority"	"Governments are instituted among men, deriving their just powers from the consent of the governed."
Limited Government "Absolute arbitrary power, or governing without settled laws, can neither of them consist with the ends of society and government." "As usurpation is the exercise of power which another has a right to, so tyranny is the exercise of power beyond right, which nobody can have a right to."	"The history of the present King of Great Britain is a history of repeated injuries and usurpations."
Right to Revolt "The people shall be the judge. . . . Oppression raises ferments and makes men struggle to cast off an uneasy and tyrannical yoke."	"Prudence, indeed, will dictate that Governments long established should not be changed for light and transient causes. . . . But when a long train of abuses and usurpations, pursuing invariably the same Object evinces a design to reduce them under absolute Despotism, it is their right, it is their duty, to throw off such Government."

It was in the American colonies that the powerful ideas of European political thinkers took root and grew into what Seymour Martin Lipset termed the "first new nation."[5] With these revolutionary ideas in mind, Jefferson claimed in the Declaration of Independence that people should have primacy over governments, that they should rule instead of being ruled. Moreover, each person was important as an individual, "created equal," and endowed with "unalienable rights." Consent of the governed, not divine rights or tradition, made the exercise of political power legitimate.

No government had ever been based on these principles. Ever since 1776, Americans have been concerned about fulfilling the high aspirations of the Declaration of Independence.

☐ Winning Independence

Declaring independence did not win the Revolution—it merely announced its beginning. John Adams wrote to his wife, Abigail, "You will think me transported with enthusiasm, but I am not. I am well aware of the toil, blood, and treasure that it will cost us to maintain this Declaration, and support and defend these states." Adams was right. The colonists seemed little match for the finest army in the world, whose size was nearly quadrupled by hired guns from the German state of Hesse and elsewhere. In 1775, the British had 8,500 men stationed in the colonies and had hired nearly 30,000 mercenaries. Initially, the colonists had only 5,000 men in uniform in the Continental Army, and their number waxed and waned as the war progressed. How they won is a story best left to history books. In the following sections we will explore how they formed a new government.

The "Conservative" Revolution

Revolutions such as the 1789 French Revolution, the 1917 Russian Revolution, and the 1978–1979 Iranian Revolution produced great societal change—as well as plenty of bloodshed. The American Revolution was different. Despite the revolutionary ideas behind it, the Revolution was essentially a conservative movement that did not drastically alter the colonists' way of life. Its primary goal was to restore rights that the colonists felt were theirs as British subjects and to enable them to live as they had before Britain tightened its regulations following the Seven Years' War.

American colonists did not feel the need for great social, economic, or political upheavals. Despite their opposition to British rule, they "were not oppressed people; they had no crushing imperial shackles to throw off."[6] As a result, the Revolution did not create class conflicts that would split society for generations to come. The colonial leaders' belief that they needed the consent of the governed blessed the new nation with a crucial element of stability—a stability the nation would need.

The Government That Failed: 1776–1787

2.2 Analyze how the weaknesses of the Articles of Confederation led to its failure.

The Continental Congress that adopted the Declaration of Independence was only a voluntary association of the states. In 1776, Congress appointed a committee to draw up a plan for a permanent union of the states. That plan, our first constitution, was the **Articles of Confederation**.[7]

The Articles of Confederation

The Articles established a government dominated by the states. The United States, according to the Articles, was a confederation, a "league of friendship and perpetual union" among 13 states. The Articles established a national legislature with one house; states could send as many as seven delegates or as few as two, but each state had only one vote. There was no president and no national court, and the powers of the national legislature were strictly limited. Most authority rested with the state legislatures because many leaders feared that a strong central government would become as tyrannical as British rule. Table 2.2 summarizes the key provisions of the Articles.

Articles of Confederation

The first constitution of the United States, adopted by Congress in 1777 and ratified in 1781. The Articles established the Continental Congress as the national legislature, but left most authority with the state legislatures.

TABLE 2.2 KEY PROVISIONS OF THE ARTICLES OF CONFEDERATION

Feature of National Government	Provision
Central government	Weak
Executive	None
Legislature	One chamber with one vote per state
Courts	None
Regulation of commerce	None
Taxation	No power of direct taxation
Amendment of Articles	Required unanimous consent
National defense	Could raise and maintain an army and navy
Power over states	None

38

2.1
2.2
2.3
2.4
2.5
2.6
2.7
2.8

Because unanimous consent of the states was needed to put the Articles into operation, the Articles adopted by the Continental Congress in 1777 did not go into effect until 1781, when laggard Maryland finally ratified them. In the meantime, the Continental Congress barely survived, lurching from crisis to crisis. At one point during the war, some of Washington's troops threatened to create a monarchy and make him king unless Congress paid their overdue wages.

Even after the states ratified the Articles of Confederation, many logistical and political problems plagued Congress. State delegations attended haphazardly. Congress had few powers outside maintaining an army and navy—and little money to do even that. It had to request money from the states because it had no power to tax. If states refused to send money (which they often did), Congress did without. In desperation, Congress sold off western lands (land east of the Mississippi and west of the states) to speculators, issued securities that sold for less than their face value, or used its own presses to print money that was virtually worthless. Congress also voted to disband the army despite continued threats from Britain and Spain.

Under the Articles, Congress lacked the power to regulate commerce, which inhibited foreign trade and the development of a strong national economy. It did, however, manage to develop sound policies for the management of the western frontiers, passing the Northwest Ordinance of 1787 that encouraged the development of the Great Lakes region.

In general, the weak and ineffective national government could take little independent action. Most governing power rested in the states. The national government could not compel the states to do anything, and it had no power to deal directly with individual citizens. The weakness of the national government prevented it from dealing with the hard times that faced the new nation. There was one benefit of the Articles, however: when the nation's leaders began to write a new constitution, they could look at the provisions of the Articles of Confederation and know some of the things they should avoid.

Why It Matters to You
A Strong National Government

One of the most important features of the Constitution is the creation of a strong national government. If the Framers had retained a weak national government, as under the Articles of Confederation, Congress could not create a great national economic market through regulating interstate commerce, no president could conduct a vigorous foreign policy, federal courts could not issue orders to protect civil rights, and the federal government could not raise the funds to pay for Social Security benefits or grants and loans for college students.

☐ Changes in the States

What was happening in the states was as important as what was happening in Congress. The most significant change was a dramatic increase in democracy and liberty, at least for white males. Many states adopted bills of rights to protect freedoms, abolished religious qualifications for holding office, and liberalized requirements for voting.

Expanded political participation brought to power a new middle class, which included artisans and farmers who owned small homesteads. Before the Revolution, almost all members of New York's assembly had been wealthy urban merchants, large landowners, or lawyers. In the 1769 assembly, for example, only 25 percent of the legislators were farmers, even though nearly 95 percent of New Yorkers were farmers. After the Revolution, a major power shift occurred. With expanded voting privileges, farmers and artisans became a decisive majority in the New York assembly, and the old

FIGURE 2.2 POWER SHIFT: ECONOMIC STATUS OF STATE LEGISLATORS BEFORE AND AFTER THE REVOLUTIONARY WAR

After the Revolution, power in the state legislatures shifted from the hands of the wealthy to those with more moderate incomes and from merchants and lawyers to farmers. This trend was especially evident in the northern states.

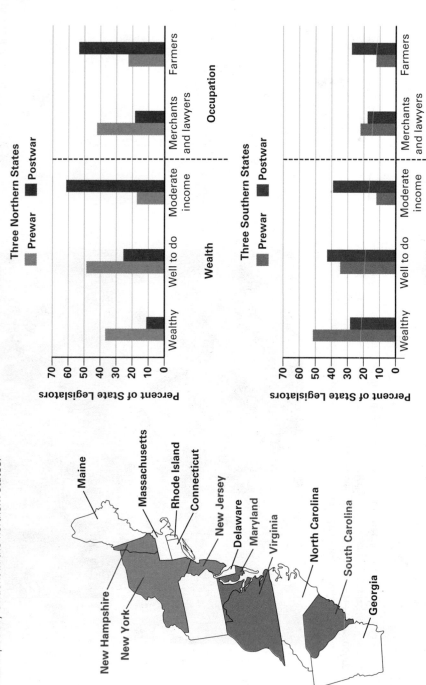

elite saw its power shrink. The same change occurred in other states as power shifted from a handful of wealthy individuals to a more broad-based group (see Figure 2.2). Democracy was taking hold everywhere.

The structure of government in the states also became more responsive to the people. State constitutions concentrated power in the legislatures because most people considered legislators to be closer to the voters than governors or judges. Many legislatures selected the governors and kept them on a short leash, with brief tenures and limited veto and appointment powers. Legislatures also overruled court decisions and criticized judges for unpopular decisions.

The idea of equality, at least among white males, was driving change throughout the nation. Although the Revolutionary War itself did not transform American society, it unleashed the egalitarian tendencies in American life. Americans were in the process of becoming "the most liberal, the most democratic, and the most modern people in the world."[8] Members of the old colonial elite found this turn of affairs quite troublesome because it challenged their hold on power.

☐ Economic Turmoil

Economic issues were at the top of the political agenda. A postwar depression had left many small farmers unable to pay their debts; creditors threatened them with mortgage foreclosures. Now under control of people more sympathetic to debtors, the state legislatures often listened to the demands of small farmers. A few states, notably Rhode

Shays's Rebellion
A series of attacks on courthouses by a small band of farmers led by Revolutionary War captain Daniel Shays to block foreclosure proceedings.

Shays's Rebellion, in which farmers physically prevented judges from foreclosing on farms, helped spur the birth of the Constitution. News of the small rebellion spread quickly around the country, and some of the Philadelphia delegates thought a full-fledged revolution would result. The event reaffirmed the Framers' belief that the new federal government needed to be a strong one.

Island, passed laws that favored debtors over creditors. Some states printed tons of paper money and passed "force acts" requiring reluctant creditors to accept the almost worthless money. Debtors could thus pay big debts with cheap currency.

Policies favoring debtors over creditors did not please the economic elite, who had once controlled nearly all the state legislatures. They were further shaken when, in 1786, a small band of farmers in western Massachusetts rebelled at losing their land to creditors. Led by Revolutionary War captain Daniel Shays, this rebellion, called **Shays's Rebellion**, was a series of armed attacks on courthouses to prevent judges from foreclosing on farms. Farmers in other states were also unruly—although never in large numbers. The economic elite were scared by rebels like Shays who took the law into their own hands and violated the property rights of others. Neither Congress nor the state was able to raise a militia to stop Shays and his followers, so elites assembled a privately paid force to do the job. This necessity further fueled dissatisfaction with the weakness of the Articles of Confederation system.

☐ The Aborted Annapolis Meeting

In September 1786, a handful of leaders assembled in Annapolis, Maryland, to consider commercial conflicts that had arisen among the states under the Articles of Confederation. Only five states—New York, New Jersey, Delaware, Pennsylvania, and Virginia—were represented at the meeting. The delegates decided that a larger meeting and a broader proposal were needed. They therefore issued a call for a full-scale meeting of the states in Philadelphia the following May—in retrospect, a rather bold move for so small a group. The Continental Congress granted their request, however, and called for a meeting of all the states. In May 1787, what we now term the Constitutional Convention got down to business in Philadelphia.

Making a Constitution: The Philadelphia Convention

2.3　Describe the delegates to the Constitutional Convention and the core ideas they shared.

epresentatives from 12 states came to Philadelphia to heed the Continental Congress's call to "take into consideration the situation in the United States." Only Rhode Island, a stronghold of paper-money interests and thus skeptical of reforms favoring creditors, refused to send delegates. Virginia's Patrick Henry (the colonial firebrand who had declared, "Give me liberty or give me death!") feared a centralization of power and also did not attend.

The delegates were ordered to meet "for the sole and express purpose of revising the Articles of Confederation." The Philadelphia delegates did not pay much attention to this order, however, because amending the Articles required the unanimous consent of the states, which they knew would be impossible. Thus, the 55 delegates ignored their instructions and began writing what was to become the **U.S. Constitution.**

☐ Gentlemen in Philadelphia

Who were these 55 men? They may not have been "demigods," as Jefferson, perhaps sarcastically, called them, but they were certainly an elite group of economic and political notables. They were mostly wealthy planters, successful (or once-successful) lawyers and merchants, and men of independent wealth. Many were college graduates, and most had practical political experience. Most were coastal residents rather than residents of the expanding western frontiers, and a significant number were urbanites rather than part of the primarily rural American population.

☐ Philosophy into Action

The delegates in Philadelphia were an uncommon combination of philosophers and shrewd political architects. Their debates ranged from high principles on the big issues to self-interest on the small ones.⁹ The delegates devoted the first two weeks mainly to general debates about the nature of republican government (government in which ultimate power rests with the voters). After that, practical and divisive issues sometimes threatened to dissolve the meeting.

Obviously, the 55 delegates did not share the same political philosophy. For example, democratic Benjamin Franklin held very different views from those delegates who were wary of democracy. Yet the Founders shared a common core of ideas. The group agreed on the critical questions of (1) human nature, (2) the causes of political conflict, (3) the objects of government, and (4) the nature of a republican government.

HUMAN NATURE In his famous work titled *Leviathan*, written in 1651, Thomas Hobbes argued that man's natural state was war and that a strong absolute ruler was necessary to restrain man's bestial tendencies. Without a strong government, Hobbes wrote, life would be "solitary, poor, nasty, brutish, and short." The delegates agreed with Hobbes that people were naturally self-interested and that government should play a key role in restraining selfish impulses. However, the Framers opposed a powerful monarch; they sided with Locke's argument that government should be limited.¹⁰

POLITICAL CONFLICT Of all the words written by and about the delegates, none have been more widely quoted than these by James Madison from Federalist 10: "The most common and durable source of factions has been the various and unequal distribution of property." In other words, *the distribution of wealth* (land was the main form of

U.S. Constitution

The document written in 1787 and ratified in 1788 that sets forth the institutional structure of U.S. government, the tasks these institutions perform, and the relationships among them. It replaced the Articles of Confederation.

factions
Groups such as interest groups, that arise according to James Madison, from the unequal distribution of property or wealth and have the potential to cause instability in government.

wealth in those days) *is the source of political conflict.* "Those who hold and those who are without property," Madison went on, "have ever formed distinct interests in society." Other sources of conflict: included religion, views of governing, and attachment to various leaders.[11]

Arising from these sources of conflict are **factions**, what today we might call interest groups. A majority faction might well be composed of those who have little or no property; a minority faction, of those with property. The delegates thought that if one of these factions went unchecked it would eventually tyrannize the other. The majority would try to seize the government to reduce the wealth of the minority; the minority would try to seize the government to secure its own gains. Governments run by factions, the Founders (also called the Framers) believed, are prone to instability, tyranny, and even violence. The Framers intended to check the effects of factions.

PURPOSE OF GOVERNMENT To Gouverneur Morris of Pennsylvania, the preservation of property was the "principal object of government." Morris plainly overlooked some other purposes of government, including providing security from invasion, ensuring domestic peace, and promoting the public's health and welfare. However, Morris's remark typifies the philosophy of many of the delegates. As property holders themselves, these delegates could not imagine a government that did not make its principal objective an economic one: the preservation of individual rights to acquire and hold wealth. A few (like Morris) were intent on shutting out the propertyless altogether. "Give the votes to people who have no property," Morris claimed, "and they will sell them to the rich who will be able to buy them."

NATURE OF GOVERNMENT Given their beliefs about human nature, the causes of political conflict, the need to protect property, and the threat of tyranny by a faction, what sort of government did the delegates believe would work? They answered this question in different ways, but the message was always the same. Power should be set against power so that no one faction would overwhelm the others. The secret of good government is "balanced" government. They were influenced by the writings of a French aristocrat, Baron Montesquieu, who advocated separate branches of government, each of which had distinct powers and the ability to check the other branches. The Framers agreed, concluding that a limited government would have to involve checks on its own power. So long as no faction could seize the whole of government at once, tyranny could be avoided. A balanced government required a complex network of checks and balances, and a separation of powers.

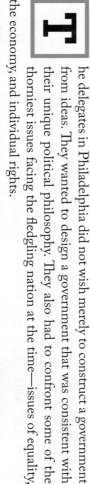

Critical Issues at the Convention

2.4 Categorize the issues at the Constitutional Convention and outline the resolutions reached on each type of issue.

he delegates in Philadelphia did not wish merely to construct a government from ideas. They wanted to design a government that was consistent with their unique political philosophy. They also had to confront some of the thorniest issues facing the fledgling nation at the time—issues of equality, the economy, and individual rights.

☐ The Equality Issues

The Declaration of Independence states that all men are created equal; the Constitution, however, is silent on equality. Nevertheless, some of the most important issues on the Framers' policy agenda concerned equality. Three issues occupied much of their attention: whether the states were to be equally represented, what to do about slavery, and whether to ensure equality in voting.

REPRESENTATION OF THE STATES One crucial policy issue was how to constitute the new Congress. The **New Jersey Plan**, proposed by William Paterson of New Jersey, called for each state to be equally represented in the new Congress. The opposing strategy, suggested by Edmund Randolph of Virginia, is usually termed the **Virginia Plan**. It called for giving each state representation in Congress based on the state's share of the American population.

The delegates resolved this conflict with a compromise devised by Roger Sherman and William Johnson of Connecticut. The solution, proposed in what is known as the **Connecticut Compromise**, was to create two houses of Congress. One body, the Senate, would have two members from each state (the New Jersey Plan), and the second body, the House of Representatives, would have representation based on population (the Virginia Plan). The U.S. Congress is still organized in exactly this way. Each state has two senators, and a state's population determines its representation in the House.

Although the Connecticut Compromise was intended to maximize equality among the states, it actually gives more power to people who live in states with small populations than to those who live in more heavily populated states. Every state has two senators and at least one member of the House, no matter how small its population. To take the most extreme case, Wyoming and California have the same number of votes in the Senate (two), although Wyoming has less than 2 percent of California's population. Thus, a citizen of Wyoming has about *70 times* the representation in the Senate as does a citizen of California.[12]

Because it is the Senate, not the House, that ratifies treaties, confirms presidential nominations, and hears trials of impeachment, citizens in less populated states have a greater say in these key tasks. In addition, in presidential elections the electoral college (the body that actually elects the president) gives small states greater weight. And if no presidential candidate receives a majority in the electoral college, the House of Representatives makes the final decision—with each state having one vote. In such a case (which has not occurred since 1824), the votes of citizens of Wyoming would again carry about 70 times as much weight as those of Californians.

Whether representation in the Senate is "fair" is a matter of debate. What is not open to question is that the Framers had to accommodate various interests and viewpoints in order to convince all the states to join an untested union.

New Jersey Plan
The proposal at the Constitutional Convention that called for equal representation of each state in Congress regardless of the size of the state's population.

Virginia Plan
The proposal at the Constitutional Convention that called for representation of each state in Congress to be proportional to its population.

Connecticut Compromise
The compromise reached at the Constitutional Convention that established two houses of Congress: the House of Representatives, in which representation is based on a state's population; and the Senate, in which each state has two representatives.

Why It *Matters* to You

Representation in the Senate

The Senate both creates a check on the House and overrepresents states with small populations. If there were only one house of Congress, governance would be more efficient. If representation were based solely on population, interests centered in states with small populations would lose an advantage and there might be a closer correspondence between public opinion and public policy. At the same time, there would be one fewer important check on government action. Which do you prefer?

SLAVERY The second equality issue was slavery. The contradictions between slavery and the sentiments of the Declaration of Independence are obvious, but in 1787 slavery was legal in every state except Massachusetts. It was concentrated in the South, however, where slave labor was commonplace in agriculture. Some delegates, like Gouverneur Morris, denounced slavery in no uncertain terms. But the Convention could not accept Morris's position in the face of powerful Southern opposition led by Charles C. Pinckney of South Carolina. The delegates did agree that Congress could limit the *importing* of slaves in the future—they allowed it to be outlawed after 1808—but they did not forbid slavery itself. The Constitution, in fact, inclines toward recognizing slavery, referring to slaves it states that persons legally "held to service or labour," who escaped to free states had to be returned to their owners.

Point to Ponder

The Framers could not reach agreement regarding slavery. As a result, it persisted for several generations until the Civil War resolved the issue. Yet one could argue that leaving difficult decisions to future generations is a primary reason for the survival of the nation.

What do you think—were the Framers copping out, or smartly trying not to take on too much conflict at once and leaving flexibility for future generations?

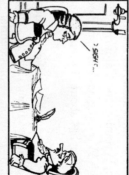

DOONESBURY   Garry Trudeau

How should slaves be counted regarding representation in the House? Southerners wanted slaves counted as part of the population since doing so would increase their representation. However, they were reluctant to count slaves in determining each state's apportionment of taxation. Northerners held the opposite positions. The result was the famous *three-fifths compromise*. Representation in the House and taxation were to be based on the "number of free persons" in a state plus three-fifths of the number of "all other persons." Everyone, of course, knew who those other persons were.

EQUALITY IN VOTING The delegates dodged one other issue of equality. A handful of delegates, led by Benjamin Franklin, suggested that all free adult males should be able to vote in national elections. This still would have left a majority of the population disenfranchised, but for those still smarting from Shays's Rebellion and the fear of mob rule, the suggestion was too democratic. Many delegates wanted to include property ownership as a qualification for voting. Ultimately, they decided to leave the rules on voting to the states. People qualified to vote in state elections could also vote in national elections. Table 2.3 summarizes how the Founders dealt with the three issues of equality.

☐ The Economic Issues

The Philadelphia delegates were deeply concerned about the state of the American economy and wanted to strengthen it. Americans generally disagreed (in fact, historians still disagree) as to whether the postcolonial economy was a shambles.[13] But there was a consensus among the writers of the Constitution that the economy was indeed in disarray and that they needed to address the following problems:

- States had imposed tariffs on products from other states.
- Paper money was virtually worthless in some states; however, many state governments that were controlled by debtors forced it on creditors anyway.
- Congress was having trouble raising money because the economy was in a recession.

TABLE 2.3 HOW THE CONSTITUTION RESOLVED THREE ISSUES OF EQUALITY

Problem	Solution
Representation of the States	
Should states be represented equally (the New Jersey Plan) or in proportion to their population (the Virginia Plan)?	Both, according to the Connecticut Compromise. States have equal representation in the Senate, but representation in the House is proportionate to population.
Slavery	
Should slavery be abolished?	No. Congress was permitted to stop the importing of slaves after 1808. States were required to return runaway slaves from other states.
How should slaves be counted in determining representation in the House of Representatives?	Three-fifths of slaves in a state should be counted.
Voting	
Should the right to vote be based on universal manhood suffrage, or should it be restricted?	Let the states decide qualifications for voting.

Understanding something about the delegates and their economic interests gives us insight into their views on the role of government in the economy. They were members of the nation's economic elite. Some were budding capitalists. Others were creditors whose loans were being wiped out by cheap paper money. Many were merchants who, on account of tariffs, could not carry on trade with neighboring states. Virtually all of them thought a strong national government was needed to bring economic stability to the chaotic union of states that existed under the Articles of Confederation.[14]

It is not surprising, then, that the Framers of the Constitution would seek to strengthen the economic powers (and thus the scope) of the new national government. One famous historian, Charles A. Beard, claimed that their principal motivation for doing so was to increase their personal wealth. The Framers, he said, were propertied, upper-class men protecting their interests; they held bonds and investments whose value would increase if the Constitution were adopted. The best evidence, however, indicates that although the Framers were concerned about protecting property rights, they were motivated primarily by a desire to build a strong economy rather than to the narrow one of increasing their own personal wealth.[15]

The delegates made sure that the Constitution clearly spelled out the economic powers of Congress (see Table 2.4). Consistent with the general allocation of power in the Constitution, Congress was to be the chief economic policymaker. It could obtain revenues through taxing and borrowing. These tools, along with the power to appropriate funds, became crucial instruments for influencing the economy. By maintaining sound money and guaranteeing payment for the national debt, Congress was to encourage economic enterprise and investment in the United States. The Constitution also allocates to Congress power to build the nation's infrastructure by constructing post offices and roads and establishing standard weights and measures. To protect property rights, Congress was charged with punishing counterfeiters and pirates, ensuring patents and copyrights, and legislating rules for bankruptcy. Equally important (and now a key congressional power, with a wide range of implications for the economy) was Congress's new ability to regulate interstate and foreign commerce. In sum, the Constitution granted Congress the power to create the conditions within which markets could flourish.

In addition, the Framers prohibited practices in the states that they viewed as inhibiting economic development, such as maintaining individual state monetary systems, placing duties on imports from other states, and interfering with lawfully contracted debts. Moreover, the states were to respect civil judgments and contracts made in other states, and they were to return runaway slaves to their owners. To help the states, the national government guaranteed them "a republican form of government" to prevent a recurrence of Shays's Rebellion, in which some people used violence instead of legislation and the courts to resolve commercial disputes.

46

2.1

2.2

2.3

2.4

2.5

2.6

2.7

2.8

writ of habeas corpus
A court order requiring authorities to explain to a judge what lawful reason they have for are holding a prisoner in custody.

TABLE 2.4 ECONOMICS IN THE CONSTITUTION

Powers of Congress

1. Levy taxes.

2. Pay debts.

3. Borrow money.

4. Coin money and regulate its value.

5. Regulate interstate and foreign commerce.

6. Establish uniform laws of bankruptcy.

7. Punish piracy.

8. Punish counterfeiting.

9. Create standard weights and measures.

10. Establish post offices and post roads.

11. Protect copyrights and patents.

Prohibitions on and Obligations of the States

States could not …

1. Coin money or issue paper money.

2. Tax imports or exports from abroad or from other states.

3. Pass laws impairing the obligations of contract.

4. Require payment of debts in paper money.

States were to …

1. Respect civil court judgments and contracts made in other states.

2. Return runaway slaves from other states.

Other Key Provisions

1. The new government assumed the national debt contracted under the Articles of Confederation.

2. A republican form of government was guaranteed.

The Constitution also obligated the new government to repay all the public debts incurred under the governments of the Continental Congress and the Articles of Confederation—debts that totaled $54 million. Paying off the debts would restore the confidence of investors in the young nation and ensure from the outset that money would flow into the American economy.

☐ The Individual Rights Issues

Another major agenda item at the Constitutional Convention was designing a system that would preserve individual rights. There was no dispute about the importance of safeguarding individual rights and liberties, and the Framers believed that doing this would be relatively easy. After all, they were constructing a limited government that, by design, could not threaten personal freedoms. In addition, they dispersed power among the three branches of the national government and between the national and state governments so that each branch or level could restrain the other. Also, most of the delegates believed that the states were already doing a sufficient job of protecting individual rights.

As a result, the Constitution they drafted says little about personal freedoms. The protections it does offer are the following:

- It prohibits suspension of the **writ of habeas corpus** (except during invasion or rebellion). Such a court order enables persons detained by authorities to secure an immediate inquiry into the causes of their detention. If no lawful explanation is offered, a judge may order their release. (Article I, Section 9)

- It prohibits Congress or the states from passing bills of attainder (which punish people without a judicial trial). (Article I, Section 9)

- It prohibits Congress or the states from passing *ex post facto* laws (which punish people for acts that were not illegal when they were done or retroactively increase the penalties for illegal acts). (Article I, Section 9)

- It prohibits the imposition of religious qualifications for holding office in the national government. (Article VI)

- It narrowly defines and outlines strict rules of evidence for conviction of treason. To be convicted, a person must levy war against the United States or adhere to and aid its enemies during war. Conviction requires confession in open court or the testimony of *two* witnesses to the *same* overt act. The Founders would have been executed as traitors if the Revolution had failed, and they were therefore sensitive to treason laws. (Article III, Section 3)

- It upholds the right to trial by jury in criminal cases. (Article III, Section 2)

The delegates were content with their document. When it came time to ratify the Constitution, however, there was widespread criticism of the absence of specific protections of individual rights, such as free expression and various rights of the accused.

The Madisonian System

2.5 Analyze how the components of the Madisonian system addressed the dilemma of reconciling majority rule with the protection of minority interests.

The Framers believed that human nature was self-interested and that inequalities of wealth were the principal source of political conflict. Yet they had no desire to eliminate the economic divisions in society by converting private property to common ownership; they also believed that protecting private property was a key purpose of government. Their experience with state governments under the Articles of Confederation reinforced their view that democracy was a threat to property. Many of them felt that, if given political power, the nonwealthy majority—an unruly mob—would tyrannize the wealthy minority. Thus, the delegates to the Constitutional Convention faced the dilemma of reconciling economic inequality with political freedom. How could they devise a government that was responsive to the majority while protecting private property?

□ Thwarting Tyranny of the Majority

James Madison was neither wealthy nor a great orator. He was, however, a careful student of politics and government and became the principal architect of the government's final structure, which we sometimes refer to as the *Madisonian system*.[16] He and his colleagues feared both majority and minority factions. Either could take control of the government and use it to their own advantage. Factions of the minority, however, were easy to handle; the majority could simply outvote them. Factions of the majority were harder to handle. If the majority united around some policy issue, such as the redistribution of wealth, they could oppress the minority, violating the latter's basic rights.[17]

As Madison would later explain in Federalist 51:

> Ambition must be made to counteract ambition. . . . If men were angels, no government would be necessary. If angels were to govern men, neither external nor internal controls would be necessary. In framing a government which is to be administered by men over men, the great difficulty lies in this: you must first enable the government to control the governed; and then in the next place oblige it to control itself.[18]

To prevent the possibility of a tyranny of the majority, Madison proposed the following:

1. Place as much of the government as possible beyond the direct control of the majority.
2. Separate the powers of different institutions.
3. Construct a system of checks and balances.

James Madison was the key figure in writing the Constitution. His views on checking power remain at the core of the structure of American government.

separation of powers
A feature of the Constitution that requires each of the three branches of government—executive, legislative, and judicial—to be relatively independent of the others so that one cannot control the others. Power is shared among these three institutions.

LIMITING MAJORITY CONTROL
Madison believed that to thwart tyranny by the majority, it was essential to keep most of the government beyond their power. His plan, as shown in Figure 2.3, placed only one element of government, the House of Representatives—elected every two years, within direct control of the votes of the majority. In contrast, state legislatures were to elect senators and special electors were to choose the president; in other words, a small minority, not the people themselves, would elect most government officials. The president was to nominate federal judges. Even if the majority seized control of the House of Representatives, they still could not enact policies without the agreement of the Senate and the president. To further insulate government officials from public opinion, the Constitution gives judges lifetime tenure and senators terms of six years, with only one-third of the Senate elected every two years.

SEPARATING POWERS The Madisonian scheme also provided for a **separation of powers.** Each of the three branches of government—executive (the president), legislative (Congress), and judicial (the courts)—would be relatively independent of one another so that no single branch could control the others. The Framers gave the

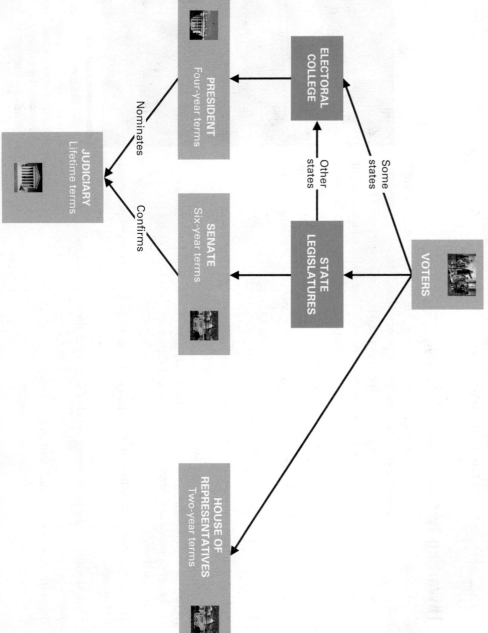

FIGURE 2.3 THE CONSTITUTION AND THE ELECTORAL PROCESS: THE ORIGINAL PLAN

Under Madison's plan, which was incorporated in the Constitution, voters' electoral influence was limited. Voters directly elected only the House of Representatives. Senators and presidents were indirectly elected—senators by state legislatures, and presidents by the electoral college, whose members, depending on the state, were chosen by state legislatures or by voters; the president nominated judges. Over the years, Madison's original model has been substantially democratized. The Seventeenth Amendment (1913) established direct election of senators by popular majorities. Today, the electoral college has become largely a rubber stamp, voting the way the popular majority in each state votes.

president, Congress, and the courts independent elements of power. The Constitution does not divide power absolutely, however. Instead, it *shares* it among the three institutions.

CREATING CHECKS AND BALANCES Because powers were not completely separate, each branch required the consent of the others for many of its actions. This created a system of **checks and balances** that reflected Madison's goal of setting power against power to constrain government actions. He reasoned that if a faction seized one institution, it still could not damage the whole system. The system of checks and balances was an elaborate and delicate creation. The president checks Congress by holding veto power; Congress, in turn, holds the purse strings of government and the Senate must approve presidential nominations.

The courts also were central to the system of checks and balances. Presidents can nominate judges, but these nominees must be confirmed by the Senate. In *Marbury v. Madison* (1803), the Supreme court asserted its power to check the other branches through judicial review: the power to hold actions of the other two branches unconstitutional. This capacity, which is not specifically outlined in the Constitution, considerably strengthens the Court's ability to restrain the other branches of government. For a summary of the separation of powers and the checks and balances system, see Figure 2.4.

Why It Matters to You
Checks and Balances

People often complain about gridlock in government, but gridlock is a product of checks and balances. Making it difficult for either a minority or a majority to dominate easily also makes it difficult to pass legislation over which there is disagreement.

ESTABLISHING A FEDERAL SYSTEM The Framers also established a federal system of government that divides the power to govern between the national and state governments. Most government activity in the late eighteenth century occurred in the states. The Framers thus saw the federal system as an additional check on the national government.

☐ The Constitutional Republic

When asked what kind of government the delegates had produced, Benjamin Franklin is said to have replied, "A republic … if you can keep it." Because the Framers did not wish to have the people directly make all decisions (as in a town meeting where everyone has one vote), and because even in 1787 the country was far too large for such a proposal to be feasible, they did not choose to create a direct democracy. Their solution was to establish a **republic**: a system based on the consent of the governed in which representatives of the public exercise power. This deliberative democracy encourages these officials to reflect and refine the public's views through a complex decision-making process.

The system of checks and balances and the separation of powers favors the status quo. Those opposed to change need only win at one point in the policymaking process—say in obtaining a presidential veto—whereas those who favor change must win *every* battle along the way. To win all these battles usually requires the support of a sizable majority of the country, not just a simple majority of 51 percent. Change usually comes slowly, if at all. As a result, the Madisonian system encourages moderation and

---

checks and balances
Features of the Constitution that require each branch of the federal government to obtain the consent of the others for its actions; they limit the power of each branch.

republic
A form of government in which the people select representatives to govern them and make laws.

50

2.1
2.2
2.3
2.4
2.5
2.6
2.7
2.8

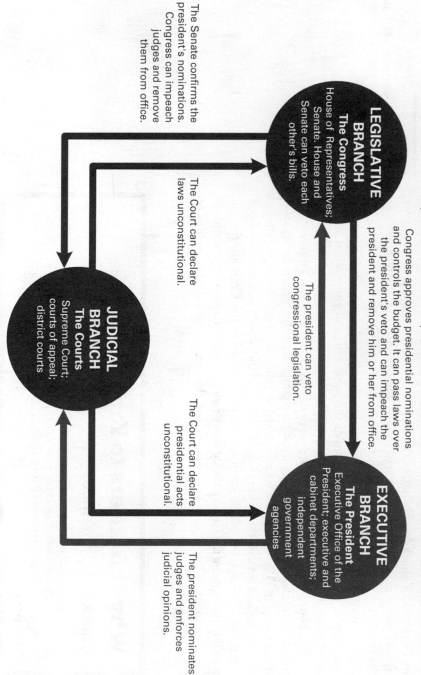

FIGURE 2.4 SEPARATION OF POWERS AND CHECKS AND BALANCES IN THE CONSTITUTION

The doctrine of separation of powers allows the three branches of government to check and balance one another. Judicial review—the power of courts to hold executive and congressional policies unconstitutional—was not explicit in the Constitution but was soon asserted by the Supreme Court in *Marbury v. Madison*.

LEGISLATIVE BRANCH
The Congress
House of Representatives; Senate. House and Senate can veto each other's bills.

EXECUTIVE BRANCH
The President
Executive Office of the President; executive and cabinet departments; independent government agencies

JUDICIAL BRANCH
The Courts
Supreme Court; courts of appeal; district courts

The Senate confirms the president's nominations. Congress can impeach judges and remove them from office.

Congress approves presidential nominations and controls the budget. It can pass laws over the president's veto and can impeach the president and remove him or her from office.

The president can veto congressional legislation.

The Court can declare laws unconstitutional.

The Court can declare presidential acts unconstitutional.

The president nominates judges and enforces judicial opinions.

compromise and slows change. It is difficult for either a minority or a majority to tyrannize, and both property rights and personal freedoms have survived with only occasional lapses.

Franklin was correct that our system is not easy to maintain. It requires careful nurturing and balancing of diverse interests. Some critics argue that the policymaking process lacks efficiency, preventing effective responses to pressing matters. We will examine this issue closely throughout *Government in America*.

☐ The End of the Beginning

On the 109th day of the meetings, in stifling heat made worse because the windows of the Pennsylvania statehouse were closed to ensure secrecy, the final version of the Constitution was read aloud. Then Benjamin Franklin rose to deliver a speech he had written; however, he was so enfeebled that he had to ask James Wilson to deliver it. Franklin noted, "There are several parts of this Constitution of which I do not at present approve, but I am not sure that I shall never approve them." Then he asked for a vote. Ten states voted yes, and none voted no, although South Carolina's delegates were divided. After all but three of the delegates who had remained at the convention signed the document (Elbridge Gerry of Massachusetts and Edmund Randolph and George Mason of Virginia refused to sign), they adjourned to a tavern. The experience of the last few hours, when conflict intermingled with consensus, reminded them that implementing this new document would be no small feat.

George Washington presides over the signing of the Constitution. "The business being closed," he wrote, "the members adjourned to the City Tavern, dined together and took cordial leave of each other."

Ratifying the Constitution

2.6 Compare and contrast the Federalists and Anti-Federalists in terms of their background and their positions regarding government.

he Constitution did not go into effect once the Constitutional Convention was over. The states first had to ratify it. There is no way of determining precisely the public's feelings about the new document, but as John Marshall (who later became chief justice) suggested, "It is scarcely to be doubted that *in some of the adopting states, a majority of the people were in opposition*" (emphasis added).[19] The Constitution itself required that only 9 of the 13 states approve the document before it could be implemented. Thus the Framers eased the path to ratification by ignoring the requirement that the Articles of Confederation be amended only by unanimous consent.

☐ Federalists and Anti-Federalists

Throughout the states, a fierce battle erupted between the **Federalists**, who supported the Constitution, and the **Anti-Federalists**, who opposed it. Newspapers were filled with letters and articles, many written under pseudonyms, praising or condemning the document. In praise of the Constitution, three men—James Madison, Alexander Hamilton, and John Jay—wrote a series of 85 essays under the name Publius. These essays, known as the **Federalist Papers**, are second only to the Constitution itself in reflecting the thinking of the Framers.

On October 27, 1787, barely a month after the Convention ended, the first of the 85 *Federalist Papers* appeared in New York newspapers as part of the ratification debate in New York. They not only defended the Constitution detail by detail but also represented an important statement of political philosophy. (The essays influenced few of the New York delegates, however, who voted to ratify the Constitution only after New York City threatened to secede from the state if they did not.)

Federalists

Supporters of the U.S. Constitution at the time the states were contemplating its adoption.

Anti-Federalists

Opponents of the U.S. Constitution at the time when the states were contemplating its adoption.

Federalist Papers

The *Federalist Papers* are a set of 85 essays that advocate ratification of the Constitution and provide insightful commentary on the nature of the new system of government.

| 2.1 | 2.2 | 2.3 | 2.4 | 2.5 | 2.6 | 2.7 | 2.8 |

Bill of Rights
The first 10 amendments to the U.S. Constitution, drafted in response to some of the Anti-Federalists' concerns. These amendments define such basic liberties as freedom of religion, speech, and press, and they guarantee defendants' rights.

TABLE 2.5 FEDERALISTS AND ANTI-FEDERALISTS COMPARED

	Anti-Federalists	Federalists
Backgrounds	Small farmers, shopkeepers, laborers	Large landowners, wealthy merchants, professionals
Government Preferred		
	Strong state government	Weaker state governments
	Weak national government	Strong national government
	Direct election of officials	Indirect election of officials
	Shorter terms	Longer terms
	Rule by the common man	Government by the elite
	Strengthened protections for individual liberties	Expected few violations of individual liberties

Far from being unpatriotic or un-American, the Anti-Federalists sincerely believed that the new government was an enemy of freedom, the very freedom they had just fought a war to ensure. They launched bitter, biting, even brilliant attacks on the work of delegates such as Washington, Madison, Franklin, and Hamilton, and frankly questioned the motives of the Constitution's authors.

One objection was that the new Constitution was a class-based document, intended to ensure that the economic elite controlled the public policies of the national government.[20] Another fear of the Anti-Federalists was that the new government would erode fundamental liberties. Why, they asked, was there no list of rights in the Constitution? You can compare the views of the Federalists and Anti-Federalists in Table 2.5.

To allay fears that the Constitution would restrict personal freedoms, the Federalists promised to add amendments to the document specifically protecting individual liberties. They kept their word; James Madison introduced 12 constitutional amendments during the First Congress in 1789. Ten were ratified by the states and took effect in 1791. These first 10 amendments to the Constitution, which restrain the national government from limiting personal freedoms, have come to be known as the **Bill of Rights** (see Table 2.6). Another of Madison's original 12 amendments, one dealing with congressional salaries, was ratified 201 years later as the Twenty-seventh Amendment.

Opponents also feared that the Constitution would weaken the power of the states (which it did). Patrick Henry railed against strengthening the federal government at the expense of the states. "We are come hither," he told his fellow delegates to the Virginia ratifying convention, "to preserve the poor commonwealth of Virginia."[21] Many state political leaders feared that the Constitution would diminish their own power as well.

Finally, not everyone supported the new government's economic powers. Creditors opposed the power to issue paper money because it might produce inflation and make the money they received as payment on their loans decline in value. Debtors favored paper money, however. Their debts (such as the mortgages on their farms) would remain constant, but if money became more plentiful, it would be easier for them to pay off their debts.

Ratification

Federalists may not have had the support of the majority, but they made up for it in shrewd politicking. They knew that many members of the legislatures of some states were skeptical of the Constitution and that state legislatures were filled with political leaders who would lose power under the Constitution. Thus, the Federalists specified that the Constitution be ratified by special conventions in each of the states—not by state legislatures.

TABLE 2.6 THE BILL OF RIGHTS (ARRANGED BY FUNCTION)

Protection of Free Expression

Amendment 1:	Freedom of speech, press, and assembly
	Freedom to petition government

Protection of Personal Beliefs

Amendment 1:	No government establishment of religion
	Freedom to exercise religion

Protection of Privacy

Amendment 3:	No forced quartering of troops in homes during peacetime
Amendment 4:	No unreasonable searches and seizures

Protection of Defendants' Rights

Amendment 5:	Grand jury indictment required for prosecution of serious crime
	No second prosecution for the same offense
	No compulsion to testify against oneself
	No loss of life, liberty, or property without due process of law
Amendment 6:	Right to a speedy and public trial by a local, impartial jury
	Right to be informed of charges against oneself
	Right to legal counsel
	Right to compel the attendance of favorable witnesses
	Right to cross-examine witnesses
Amendment 7:	Right to jury trial in civil suit where the value of controversy exceeds $20
Amendment 8:	No excessive bail or fines
	No cruel and unusual punishments

Protection of Other Rights

Amendment 2:	Right to bear arms
Amendment 5:	No taking of private property for public use without just compensation
Amendment 9:	Unlisted rights are not necessarily denied
Amendment 10:	Powers not delegated to the national government or denied to the states are reserved for the states or the people

Delaware was the first to approve, on December 7, 1787. Only six months passed before New Hampshire's approval (the ninth) made the Constitution official. Virginia and New York then voted to join the new union. Two states were holdouts: North Carolina and Rhode Island made the promise of the Bill of Rights their price for joining the other states.

With the Constitution ratified, it was time to select officeholders. The Framers of the Constitution assumed that George Washington would be elected the first president of the new government—even giving him the Convention's papers for safekeeping—and they were right. The general was the unanimous choice of the electoral college. He took office on April 30, 1789, in New York City, the first national capital. New Englander John Adams became the vice president—or, as Franklin called him, "His Superfluous Excellence."

Changing the Constitution

2.7 Explain how the Constitution can be formally amended and how it changes informally.

"**T**he Constitution," said Jefferson, "belongs to the living and not to the dead." The U.S. Constitution is frequently—and rightly—referred to as a living document. It is constantly being tested and altered.

Constitutional changes are made either by formal amendments or by a number of informal processes. Formal amendments change the text of the Constitution. Informal processes, by changing an unwritten body of tradition, practice, and procedure related to the Constitution, may change the way the constitutional system functions.

☐ The Formal Amending Process

The most explicit means of changing the Constitution is through the formal process of amendment. Article V of the Constitution outlines procedures for formal amendment. There are two stages to the amendment process—proposal and ratification—and each stage has two possible avenues (see Figure 2.5). An amendment may be proposed either by a two-thirds vote in each house of Congress or by a national convention called by Congress at the request of two-thirds of the state legislatures. An amendment may be ratified either by the legislatures of three-fourths of the states or by special state conventions called in three-fourths of the states. The president has no formal role in amending the Constitution, although the chief executive may influence the success of proposed amendments. In general, it is difficult to formally amend the Constitution (see "America in Perspective: The Unusual Rigidity of the U.S. Constitution").

All but one of the successful amendments to the Constitution have been proposed by Congress and ratified by the state legislatures. The exception was the Twenty-first Amendment, which repealed the short-lived Eighteenth Amendment—the prohibition amendment that outlawed the sale and consumption of alcohol. The Twenty-first Amendment was ratified by special state conventions rather than by state legislatures. Because proponents of repeal doubted that they could win in conservative state legislatures, they persuaded Congress to require that conventions be called in each state.

FIGURE 2.5 HOW THE CONSTITUTION CAN BE AMENDED

The Constitution sets up two alternative routes for proposing amendments and two for ratifying them. One of the four combinations has been used in every case but one.

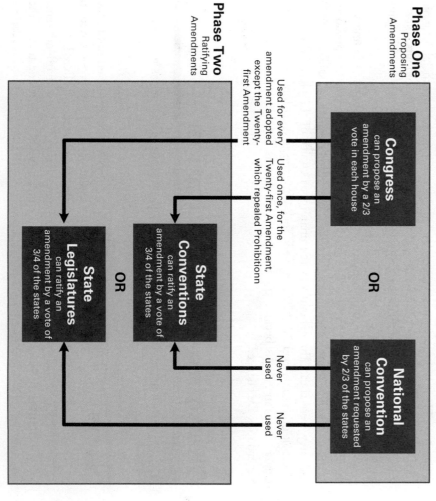

Phase One
Proposing
Amendments

Congress
can propose an
amendment by a 2/3
vote in each house

OR

National Convention
can propose an
amendment requested
by 2/3 of the states

Never used

Never used

Phase Two
Ratifying
Amendments

Used for every
amendment adopted
except the Twenty-
first Amendment

Used once, for the
Twenty-first Amendment,
which repealed Prohibition

State Conventions
can ratify an
amendment by a vote of
3/4 of the states

OR

State Legislatures
can ratify an
amendment by a vote of
3/4 of the states

Overall, the most important effect of constitutional amendments has been to expand liberty, democracy, and equality in the United States. Amendments that emphasize equality and increase the ability of a popular majority to affect government now provide a balance to the emphasis on economic issues in the original document. The Bill of Rights, discussed in detail in the civil liberties chapter, heads the amendments (see Table 2.6). Later amendments, including the Thirteenth Amendment, which abolished slavery, forbid certain types of political, social, and economic discrimination based on race, gender, and age. Yet other amendments, discussed later in this chapter, have democratized the political system, making it easier for voters to influence the government. Only one existing amendment specifically addresses the economy—the Sixteenth, or "income tax," Amendment.

Some amendments proposed by Congress have not been ratified by the states. The best known of these is the **Equal Rights Amendment (ERA)**. The ERA stated simply, "Equality of rights under the law shall not be denied or abridged by the United States or by any State on account of sex." This seemingly benign amendment sailed through Congress and the first few state legislatures.[22] Despite clear public support,[23] however, it failed, in part because many conservative Southern

Equal Rights Amendment (ERA)
A constitutional amendment passed by Congress in 1972 stating that "equality of rights under the law shall not be denied or abridged by the United States or by any state on account of sex." The amendment failed to acquire the necessary support from three-fourths of the state legislatures.

America in Perspective

The Unusual Rigidity of the U.S. Constitution

In the Federalist 43, James Madison wrote that the Founders designed a process for adopting amendments to the U.S. Constitution that "guards equally against that extreme facility, which would render the Constitution too mutable; and that extreme difficulty, which might perpetuate its discovered faults." In other words, Madison felt that the American Constitution was rigid enough to provide stability in government yet also flexible enough to allow adaptation over time.

Most other democracies have a procedure for adopting constitutional amendments, but few of the world's established democracies have made it as difficult as it is in the United States. We can measure constitutional rigidity based on the percentage vote required at the most demanding stage of the amending process.

In the United States, this would be 75 percent because at least three-quarters of the state legislatures or of conventions in the states must approve constitutional amendments. As you can see in the following table, only 4 of 22 other established democracies require a majority of greater than two-thirds to amend their national constitution. In this regard, then, the U.S. Constitution is unusually rigid.

CRITICAL THINKING QUESTIONS
1. Would it be better if it were easier to change the U.S. Constitution?
2. Does the difficulty of changing the Constitution make it too rigid?

Requirements for Constitutional Amendments in Developed Democracies, 2012

Simple Majority (50% Plus 1)	Between a Simple Majority and Two-Thirds Majority	Two-Thirds Majority	Supermajority (Greater Than Two-Thirds)
Great Britain	Denmark	Austria	Australia
Iceland	France	Belgium	Canada
Israel	Greece	Finland	Japan
New Zealand	Ireland	Germany	Switzerland
	Italy	Netherlands	United States
	Sweden	Norway	
		Portugal	
		Spain	

56

2.1
2.2
2.3
2.4
2.5
2.6
2.7
2.8

states opposed it, so that it fell a few states short of the three-fourths of states required. In response to this failure, more than 20 states have amended their own constitutions by adding versions of the ERA.

Proponents of other constitutional amendments have been active in recent years. You can consider the issue of amending the Constitution in "You Are the Policymaker: How Frequently Should We Amend the Constitution?"

☐ The Informal Processes of Constitutional Change

Think for a moment about all of the changes that have taken place in the United States without anyone changing a word or a letter of the Constitution. For example, there is nothing in the Constitution related to any of the following developments:

- The United States has a two-party system (the oldest party system in the world).
- Abortions through the second trimester of pregnancy (when the fetus cannot live outside the mother's womb) are legal in the United States.
- Members of the electoral college almost always follow the preference of their state's electorate.
- Television influences our political agenda and influences our assessments of candidates and issues.
- The president has become the driving force in national policymaking.

None of these developments is "unconstitutional." The political parties emerged, the law permitted abortions, parties named as electors loyalists who would support

---

You Are the Policymaker
How Frequently Should We Amend the Constitution?

Since the ratification of the Bill of Rights in 1791, there have been only 17 amendments to the Constitution—an average of 1 amendment every 13 years. It is now common, however, for political activists—and even political party platforms—to call for amendments. Some recent examples include prohibiting gay marriage, the burning of the American flag, and abortion; permitting prayer in public schools; requiring a balanced national budget; limiting the number of congressional terms; guaranteeing women's rights (the ERA); and protecting victims' rights.

Conservatives have been in the forefront of most recent calls for amendments (the ERA being an exception); many of the proposals for constitutional change are designed to overcome liberal Supreme Court decisions. Liberals, quite naturally, have opposed these amendments. There is a larger question here than just the particular changes that advocates of amending the Constitution support, however. The central question is "How frequently should we change the fundamental law of the land?"

Those who support amending the Constitution argue that it should reflect the will of the people. If the overwhelming majority of the public wants to prohibit burning the American flag, for example, why shouldn't the Constitution reflect its preference? There is little possibility that a minority or even a narrow majority will be able to impose its will on the people, they argue, because the Constitution requires an extraordinary majority to ratify an amendment. So why should we be reluctant to test the waters of change?

Opponents of more frequent changes to the Constitution have their own arguments. It is ironic, they say, that conservatives, who typically wish to preserve the status quo, should be in the forefront of fundamental change. They argue that the Constitution has served the United States very well for more than two centuries with few changes. Why should we risk altering the fundamentals of the political system? And if we do, will we be setting a dangerous precedent that will encourage yet more change in the future? Will such changes undermine the very nature of a constitution that is designed to set the basic rules of the game and be above the political fray?

What do you think? Are the arguments simply a reflection of ideologies? Should the Constitution reflect the current sentiment of the public and be changed when public opinion changes? Or should we show more caution in amending the Constitution no matter how we feel about a specific amendment?

their candidates if they won the popular vote, television came to prominence in American life—and none of this required any tinkering with the Framers' handiwork. These developments could occur because the Constitution changes *informally* as well as formally. There are several ways in which the Constitution changes informally: through judicial interpretation, through political practice, and as a result of changes in technology and changes in the demands on policymakers.

JUDICIAL INTERPRETATION Disputes often arise about the meaning of the Constitution. If it is the "supreme law of the land," then someone has to decide how to interpret the Constitution when disputes arise. In 1803, in the famous case of *Marbury v. Madison*, the Supreme Court decided it would be the one to resolve differences of opinion. It claimed for itself the power of **judicial review**. Implied but never explicitly stated in the Constitution,[24] this power gives courts the right to decide whether the actions of the legislative and executive branches of state and national governments are in accord with the Constitution.

Judicial interpretation can profoundly affect how the Constitution is understood. For example, in 1896 the Supreme Court decided that the Constitution allowed racial discrimination in public accommodations. Fifty-eight years later, the Court overruled itself and concluded that segregation by law violated the Constitution. In 1973, the Supreme Court decided that the Constitution protected privacy and thus a woman's right to an abortion during the first two trimesters of pregnancy when the fetus is not viable outside the womb—an issue the Founders never imagined.

CHANGING POLITICAL PRACTICE Current political practices also give new meaning to the Constitution. Probably no changes are more important to American politics than those related to parties and presidential elections.

Marbury v. Madison
The 1803 case in which the Supreme Court asserted its power to determine the meaning of the U.S. Constitution. The decision established the Court's power of judicial review over acts of Congress.

judicial review
The power of the courts to determine whether acts of Congress and those of the executive branch are in accord with the U.S. Constitution. Judicial review was established by *Marbury v. Madison*.

Amending the Constitution to give women the right to vote was an important step in the women's rights movement. Here suffragettes march for the right to vote, in New York City in 1913.

58

2.1
2.2
2.3
2.4
2.5
2.6
2.7
2.8

Political parties as we know them did not exist when the Constitution was written. In fact, its authors would have disliked the idea of parties, which are a type of faction. Regardless, by 1800 a party system had developed, and parties play a key role in making policy today. American government would be radically different if there were no political parties, even though the Constitution is silent about them.

Changing political practice has also changed the role of the electoral college in selecting the president. The writers of the Constitution intended that there be no popular vote for the president; instead, state legislatures or the voters (depending on the state) would select wise electors who would then choose a "distinguished character of continental reputation" (as the *Federalist Papers* put it) to be president. These electors formed the electoral college.

In 1796, the first election in which George Washington was not a candidate, electors scattered their votes among 13 candidates. By the election of 1800, domestic and foreign policy issues had divided the country between two political parties. To increase their chances of achieving a majority of the electoral vote, the parties required electors to pledge in advance to vote for the candidate who won their state's popular vote, leaving electors with a largely clerical role. Nothing in the Constitution prohibits an elector from voting for any candidate he or she wants to (occasionally this happens). Nevertheless, the idea of electors exercising independent judgments is a constitutional anachronism, changed not by formal amendment but by political practice.

TECHNOLOGY Technology has also greatly changed the Constitution. The media have always played an important role in politics—questioning governmental policies, supporting candidates, and helping shape citizens' opinions. In the nineteenth century, modern technology spurred the development of a *mass* media that could rapidly reach huge audiences. With the rise of the Internet, mass media have dramatically increased their reach. Technology has fundamentally changed the way in which we select elected officials. The government bureaucracy has grown in importance with the development of computers, which create new potential for officials to serve the public (for example, by writing over 64 million Social Security checks each month)—and, at times, create mischief. Electronic communications and the development of atomic weapons have given the president's role as commander in chief added significance, increasing the power of the chief executive in the constitutional system.

INCREASED DEMANDS FOR NEW POLICIES
The significance of the presidency has also grown as a result of increased demands for new policies. The evolution of the United States in the realm of international affairs—from an insignificant country that kept to itself to a superpower with an extraordinary range of international obligations—has concentrated additional power in the hands of the chief executive, whom the Constitution designates to take the lead in foreign affairs. Similarly, the increased demands of domestic policy have positioned the president in a more prominent role in preparing the federal budget and a legislative program.

Consider, as an example, the war on terrorism. Wars increase presidential power because they place additional demands on the commander in chief. Congress of necessity delegates to the president the authority to prosecute a war, which involves a multitude of decisions, ranging from military strategy to logistics. The war on terrorism has taken delegation of authority one step further, however. Because the enemy may be not a country but, rather, an amorphous group of people who employ the weapons of terrorism as political instruments, it is more difficult for Congress to specify the president's authority.

Thus, following the attacks of September 2001, Congress passed a broad resolution authorizing the president to use force against those nations, organizations, or persons that he alone determined were involved in the attacks. This resolution served as the legal basis for the war in Afghanistan that began that year. In addition, several weeks

MIKE LUCKOVICH
Country Times-Picayune (New Orleans)

Takes a licking and keeps on ticking.

The Constitution is a short document that has survived for more than 200 years, in large part because of its adaptability to the needs of new generations.

after the attacks, Congress passed the USA Patriot Act, giving the executive branch broad new powers for the wiretapping, surveillance, and investigation of terrorism suspects. The invasion of Iraq in March 2003, similarly, followed a congressional resolution authorizing the president to use "all means necessary and appropriate," including the use of military force, to defend the United States against Iraq—a broad grant of power delegating to the president the right to determine if and when the United States would go to war.

☐ The Importance of Flexibility

The Constitution, even with all 27 amendments, is a short document containing fewer than 8,000 words. It does not prescribe in detail the structure and functioning of the national government. Regarding the judiciary, the Constitution simply tells Congress to create a court system as it sees fit. The Supreme Court is the only court required by the Constitution, and even here the Constitution leaves the number of justices and their qualifications up to Congress. Similarly, many of the governing units we have today—such as the executive departments, the various offices in the White House, the independent regulatory commissions, and the committees of Congress, to name only a few examples—are not mentioned at all in the Constitution.

There is little question that the document the Framers produced over 200 years ago was not meant to be static, written in stone. Instead, the Constitution's authors created a flexible system of government, one that could adapt to the needs of the times without sacrificing personal freedom. The Framers allowed future generations to determine their own needs and to interpret the Constitution accordingly. (The constitutions of the various states tend to be much longer and much more detailed. As a result, they have to be amended frequently.) This flexibility has helped ensure the survival of the Constitution—and the nation. Although the United States is young compared to most other Western nations, it has the oldest functioning constitution. France, which experienced a revolution in 1789, the same year the Constitution took effect, has had 12 constitutions over the past 2 centuries. Despite the great diversity of the American population, the enormous size of the country, and the extraordinary changes that have taken place over the course of the nation's history, the U.S. Constitution is still going strong.

60

2.1

2.2

2.3

2.4

2.5

2.6

2.7

2.8

Understanding the Constitution

he Constitution sets the broad rules for government and politics in America. As we will see, *these rules are never neutral.* Instead, they give some participants and some policy options advantages over others in the policymaking process.

☐ The Constitution and Democracy

Although the United States is often said to be one of the most democratic societies in the world, few would describe the original Constitution as democratic. This paradox is hardly surprising, considering the political philosophies of the men who wrote it. Members of eighteenth-century, upper-class society generally despised democratic government. If democracy was a way of permitting the majority's preference to become policy, the Constitution's authors wanted no part of it. The American government was to be a government by the "rich and well-born," as Hamilton said, a government in which John Jay's wish that "the people who own the country ought to govern it" would be a reality. Almost no one today would consider these thoughts to be democratic.

The Constitution did not, however, create a monarchy or a feudal aristocracy. It created a republic, a representative form of democracy modeled after the Lockean tradition of limited government. Thus, the undemocratic—even antidemocratic—Constitution established a government that permitted substantial movement toward democracy.

One of the central themes of American history is the gradual democratization of the Constitution. What began as a document characterized by numerous restrictions on direct voter participation has slowly become much more democratic. Today, few people share the Founders' fear of democracy. The expansion of voting rights has moved the American political system away from the elitist model of democracy and toward the pluralist model.

The Constitution itself offered no guidelines on voter eligibility, leaving it to each state to decide. In the early republic only a small percentage of adults could vote; states excluded women and slaves entirely. Of the 17 constitutional amendments passed since the Bill of Rights, 5 focus on the expansion of the electorate. The Fifteenth Amendment (1870) prohibited discrimination on the basis of race in determining voter eligibility. (It took the Voting Rights Act of 1965 to make the amendment effective, however.) The Nineteenth Amendment (1920) gave women the right to vote. (Some states had already done so.) The Twenty-third Amendment (1961) accorded the residents of Washington, D.C., the right to vote in presidential elections. Three years later, the Twenty-fourth Amendment prohibited poll taxes (which discriminated against the poor). Finally, the Twenty-sixth Amendment (1971) lowered the voter eligibility age to 18 (see "Young People and Politics: Lowering the Voting Age").

Not only are more people eligible to vote, but voters now have more officials to elect. The Seventeenth Amendment (1913) provided for direct election of senators. The development of political parties has fundamentally altered presidential elections. By placing the same candidate on the ballot in all the states and requiring members of the electoral college to support the candidate who receives the most votes, parties have increased the probability that the candidate for whom most Americans vote will also receive a majority of the electoral college vote. Nevertheless, it is possible for the

Young People & Politics

Lowering the Voting Age

The 1960s were a tumultuous era, and massive protests by students and other young people regarding the war in Vietnam were common in the last half of the decade. Many young people felt that protesting was the best they could do because the voting age was 21 in most states—even though 18-year-olds were old enough to marry, work, and pay taxes as other adults did. In the Vietnam War, the average age of U.S. soldiers was 19, and young citizens often asserted, "If we're old enough to fight, we're old enough to vote." (Imagine the response today if soldiers fighting overseas could not vote.)

Agreeing that the voting age was unfair, Congress passed the Voting Rights Act of 1970, which lowered the voting age to 18 in both federal and state elections. The Supreme Court, however, held that Congress had exceeded its authority and could set voting ages only in national elections. Changing the voting age in state elections would require a constitutional amendment.

In 1971, Senator Jennings Randolph, a Democrat from West Virginia, proposed an amendment to lower the voting age to 18 years: "The right of citizens of the United States, who are eighteen years of age or older, to vote shall not be denied or abridged by the United States or by any State on account of age." Randolph was a warrior for peace and had great faith in young people, arguing, "They possess a great social conscience, are

perplexed by the injustices in the world, and are anxious to rectify those ills."

Aided by appreciation of the sacrifices of young soldiers in Vietnam, the amendment passed the Senate unanimously and the House of Representatives by a vote of 400 to 19. It was then sent to the states for ratification. No state wanted to maintain two sets of voter registration books and go to the expense of running separate election systems for federal elections and for all other elections. Thus, the states were receptive to the proposed amendment, and in just 100 days three-fourths of the states ratified it.

On July 5, the Twenty-sixth Amendment was formally adopted into the Constitution, adding 11 million potential voters to the electorate. Half of these young voters cast their ballots in the 1972 presidential election.

CRITICAL THINKING QUESTIONS

1. There are proposals in some states to lower the voting age below 18. What is the appropriate age for voting?

2. Would it be appropriate for different states to have different ages for voting in either national or state and local elections?

---

candidate who receives the most popular votes to lose the election, as occurred in 1824, 1876, 1888, and 2000.

Technology has diminished the separation of the people from those who exercise power. Officeholders communicate directly with the public through television, radio, targeted mailings, e-mail, and social media. Air travel makes it easy for members of Congress to commute regularly between Washington and their districts. Similarly, public opinion polls, the telephone, e-mail, and the Internet enable officials to stay apprised of citizens' opinions on important issues. Even though the American population has grown since the census of 1790 from fewer than 4 million to more than 325 million people, the national government has never been closer to those it serves.

☐ The Constitution and the Scope of Government

The Constitution created the U.S. system of government—its political institutions and the rules for politics and policymaking. Many of these rules limit government action, protecting liberty and opening the system to a broad range of participants.

62

2.1

2.2

2.3

2.4

2.5

2.6

2.7

2.8

Because the Constitution decentralizes power, officials usually must negotiate to pass legislation. Here President Barack Obama, a Democrat, meets the Republican Speaker of the House, John Boehner.

This limiting function is what the Bill of Rights and related provisions in the Constitution are all about. Thus, for example, it would be unconstitutional for the government to establish a state-supported church.

Even with these limits, the potential range of action for the government is quite wide. Thus, it would be constitutionally permissible, although highly unlikely, for the national government to, say, abolish Social Security payments to the elderly or take over ownership of the oil industry or the nation's airlines.

Nonetheless, the separation of powers and checks and balances—crucial aspects of the constitutional system—have profound implications for what the government does and does not do.

On one hand, the system of separation of powers and checks and balances allows almost all groups some place in the political system where their demands for public policy can be heard. Because many institutions share power, groups can usually find at least one sympathetic ear in government. Even if the president opposes the policies a particular group favors, Congress, the courts, or some other institution can help the group achieve its policy goals. In the early days of the civil rights movement, for example, African Americans found Congress and the president unsympathetic, so they turned to the Supreme Court. Getting their interests on the political agenda would have been much more difficult if the Court had not had important constitutional power.

On the other hand, the system encourages stalemate. By designing a decentralized system that provides effective access for so many interests, the Framers created a system of policymaking that makes it difficult for the government to act. By allowing institutions to check each other, the separation of powers and the system of checks and balances promote the politics of bargaining, compromise, and playing one institution against another.

Some scholars suggest that so much checking was built into the American political system that effective government is almost impossible.[25] If the president, Congress, and the courts all pull in different directions on policy, the result may be either no policy at all (gridlock) or an inadequate, makeshift policy. The outcome may be nondecisions when the country requires that difficult decisions be made. If government cannot respond effectively because its policymaking processes are too fragmented, then its performance will be inadequate. Perhaps the Constitution limits the ability of government to reach effective policy decisions, thus in effect reducing the scope of government. Certainly, radical departures from the status quo are atypical in American politics.

Review the Chapter

The Origins of the Constitution

2.1
Describe the ideas behind the American Revolution and their role in shaping the Constitution, p. 32.

The American Revolution was built on the foundation of belief in natural rights, consent of the governed, limited government, the responsibility of government to protect private property, and the equality of citizens. The Constitution would reflect all these ideas.

The Government That Failed: 1776–1787

2.2
Analyze how the weaknesses of the Articles of Confederation led to its failure, p. 37.

The Articles of Confederation established a government dominated by the states, without a permanent executive or national judiciary. A weak central government could not raise sufficient funds to support a national defense, regulate commerce to encourage trade, protect property rights, or take action without the unanimous consent of the states.

Making a Constitution: The Philadelphia Convention

2.3
Describe the delegates to the Constitutional Convention and the core ideas they shared, p. 41.

The Framers of the Constitution were more educated, wealthy, and urban than most Americans. They shared some core ideas, including that people were self-interested, that the distribution of wealth was the principal source of political conflict, that the main object of government was protecting private property, and that power should be set against power to balance government.

Critical Issues at the Convention

2.4
Categorize the issues at the Constitutional Convention and outline the resolutions reached on each type of issue, p. 42.

Conflicts over equality led to the Connecticut Compromise, the three-fifths compromise on slavery, and the decision to leave the issue of voting rights to the states. The greatest inequality of all—that of slavery—was so contentious an issue that the Framers simply avoided addressing it.

The Framers, many of whom belonged to the economic elite, believed that the American economy was in shambles and intended to make the national government an economic

stabilizer. They also knew that a strong national government would be better able to ensure the nation's security. The specificity of the powers assigned to Congress left no doubt that Congress was to forge national economic policy.

Because they believed that the limited government they had constructed would protect freedom, the Framers said little about individual rights in the Constitution. They did, however, take a number of specific steps, including substantially limiting the suspension of the writ of habeas corpus.

The Madisonian System

2.5
Analyze how the components of the Madisonian system addressed the dilemma of reconciling majority rule with the protection of minority interests, p. 47.

The Founders reconciled majority rule with minority interests by constraining both the majority and the minority. The Madisonian system did this primarily by dispersing power among separate branches of government, each with a somewhat different constituency, and giving them shared powers so that each branch had a check on the others.

Ratifying the Constitution

2.6
Compare and contrast the Federalists and Anti-Federalists in terms of their background and their positions regarding government, p. 51.

Ratification of the Constitution was not a foregone conclusion. The Federalists, who were largely from the economic elite, supported a strong national government and preferred to insulate public officials from public opinion. Anti-Federalists, largely from the middle class, supported a weaker national government and direct forms of democracy, and they wanted stronger protection of individual liberties than the original Constitution offered. As a result, the Federalists promised to propose what became the Bill of Rights.

Changing the Constitution

2.7
Explain how the Constitution can be formally amended and how it changes informally, p. 53.

Constitutional change—both formal and informal—continues to shape and alter the letter and the spirit of the Madisonian system. The formal amendment process, requiring supermajorities in both houses of Congress and among the states, poses difficult hurdles to overcome. However, judicial interpretation, changing political practices, technology, and the increasing demands on policymakers have also changed the constitutional system in fundamental ways, providing a valuable flexibility.

Understanding the Constitution

2.8 Assess whether the Constitution establishes a majoritarian democracy and how it limits the scope of government, p. 60.

The Constitution did not create a majoritarian democracy. Majorities do not always rule in America. Nevertheless, there has been a gradual democratization of the Constitution as the right to vote has expanded, direct election of senators has

been instituted, electors have become agents of political parties, and technology has facilitated direct, two-way communication between office holders and the public.

By protecting individual rights, and thus limiting the ability of officials to restrict them, the Constitution limits the scope of government. By dispersing power among institutions, it increases the access of interests to government but also allows these interests to check each other and produce a stalemate.

Learn the Terms

constitution, p. 32
Declaration of Independence, p. 34
natural rights, p. 35
consent of the governed, p. 35
limited government, p. 35
Articles of Confederation, p. 37
Shays's Rebellion, p. 40
U.S. Constitution, p. 41

factions, p. 42
New Jersey Plan, p. 43
Virginia Plan, p. 43
Connecticut Compromise, p. 43
writ of habeas corpus, p. 46
separation of powers, p. 48
checks and balances, p. 49
republic, p. 49

Federalists, p. 51
Anti-Federalists, p. 51
Federalist Papers, p. 51
Bill of Rights, p. 52
Equal Rights Amendment, p. 55
Marbury v. Madison, p. 57
judicial review, p. 57

Test Yourself

1. The notion that the people must agree on who their rulers will be is referred to as _____.
a. consent of the governed
b. direct democracy
c. limited government
d. natural rights
e. sanctity of property rights

2. How did Thomas Jefferson's language in the Declaration of Independence make the colonies feel they had the right to revolt?
a. Jefferson argued that the tactics of the British government so oppressed the colonists that their only choice was to revolt.
b. Jefferson argued that when the government did not do its job by protecting individual rights, the people could form a new government.
c. Jefferson made the argument that the colonies were not being fairly represented in the British Parliament.
d. Jefferson used the example of the Seven Years' War to convince the colonists they needed to revolt.
e. Jefferson's language argued convincingly that the excessive taxes being imposed by the British justified the colonists' revolt.

3. Which of the following occurred under the Articles of Confederation?
a. Funding for the national government was reliable.
b. The government effectively enforced law and order.
c. The middle class came to power.
d. The national government had no policy success.
e. The states narrowed the qualifications for voting.

4. According to James Madison, which of the following is the primary source of political conflict?
a. different religious views
b. differing political ideologies
c. self-interested human nature
d. the distribution of wealth
e. the lack of education

5. Among the powers the Constitution delegates to the national government is the power to _____.
a. acquire territory by exploration
b. administer grants-in-aid
c. buy jet fighters
d. establish a national bank
e. fix standard weights and measures

6. A person who does not confess may be convicted of treason _____.
a. by a court closed to the public
b. for making a speech favoring Iraq
c. for running for office as a Communist
d. only if several witnesses testify to a series of treasonous actions
e. only if two witnesses testify to the same overt act

7. The U.S. Constitution in its original form, prior to amendment, _____.

a. dealt more thoroughly with economic issues than with issues of equality

b. dealt more thoroughly with issues of equality than with economic issues

c. dealt with neither economic nor equality issues

d. emphasized both economic and equality issues to a large degree

e. mentioned both economic and equality issues only in passing

8. The system of governance set up in the U.S. tends to do which of the following?

a. be relatively efficient in producing political results

b. centralize power

c. encourage direct democracy

d. encourage the speedy resolution of disputes

e. favor the status quo and limit political change

9. When the Framers constructed a federal government in which each branch has specific powers that are checked by the other two branches, what was one advantage they intended?

a. It ensured that only the most qualified officials would serve in office.

b. It ensured that the federal government was less powerful than state governments in all situations.

c. It gave citizens a strong voice in elections.

d. It promoted a more effective national government.

e. It protected against government tyranny by one branch or by all three acting together.

10. What was one objection the Anti-Federalists made to the Constitution?

a. It did not list rights, thereby restricting personal freedoms.

b. It limited the role of the central government.

c. It provided for a government that would tax the citizens heavily.

d. It provided for a weak central government.

e. It would strengthen the power of the states.

11. Which of the following processes has never been used to amend the Constitution?

a. proposal by the Supreme Court

b. proposal by two-thirds support in both houses of Congress

c. proposal through a national convention called by Congress

d. ratification by three-fourths of state conventions

e. ratification by three-fourths of state legislatures

12. The Constitution has much language that is vague and often hard to interpret for exact meaning. The problems created by such language have been solved by the application of which practice?

a. Congress immediately amending the Constitution to clarify discrepancies in language

b. the attorney general making a ruling about the language

c. the issues created by the vague language being processed through state and federal courts and being settled by judicial interpretation

d. the states calling for a constitutional convention to define the language in question

e. the states dealing with the issues through action by their own legislatures

13. Which of the following best describes the view of the Constitution as a living document?

a. One should adhere to the original intent of the Constitution.

b. One should be willing to adapt the Constitution to changing societal needs.

c. One should pay attention to the institutional role the Constitution plays.

d. One should read the Constitution based on the intent of the founding authors.

e. One should view the Constitution as an instrument of government.

14. Why did the Framers create the electoral college?

a. because they did not trust the masses to elect the president directly

b. so that ordinary Americans could influence the selection of the president

c. to ensure that the public could fully evaluate all presidential and vice presidential candidates

d. to placate the British Parliament

e. to prevent partisan bickering about who would be president

15. Which of the following is generally true about the effect of constitutional amendments on the American political system?

a. Amendments have dramatically expanded the power of the states over the national government.

b. Amendments have made the country more democratic and expanded rights to excluded groups.

c. Amendments have reinforced the power of elites over most governmental institutions.

d. Amendments have reinforced the power of the legislative branch over domestic and international politics.

e. Amendments have sometimes restricted individual rights and reinforced tyranny of the minority.

Explore Further

WEB SITES

http://www.earlyamerica.com/earlyamerica/milestones/commonsense/
Thomas Paine's *Common Sense*

http://www.usconstitution.net/articles.html
The Articles of Confederation

http://thomas.loc.gov/home/histdox/fedpapers.html
Federalist Papers in support of the ratification of the Constitution

http://www.constitution.org/afp/afp.htm
Anti-Federalist writings opposing the ratification of the Constitution

http://www.usconstitution.net/constframedata.html
Background of the Framers

FURTHER READING

Bailyn, Bernard. *The Ideological Origins of the American Revolution.* Cambridge, MA: Harvard University Press, 1967. A leading work on the ideas that spawned the American Revolution.

Becker, Carl L. *The Declaration of Independence: A Study in the History of Political Ideas.* New York: Random House, 1942. Classic work on the meaning of the Declaration.

Dahl, Robert A. *How Democratic Is the American Constitution?* 2nd ed. New Haven, CT: Yale University Press, 2003. Questions the extent to which the Constitution furthers democratic goals.

Hamilton, Alexander, James Madison, and John Jay. *The Federalist Papers.* 2nd ed. Edited by Roy P. Fairfield. Baltimore: Johns Hopkins University Press, 1981. Key tracts in the campaign for the Constitution and cornerstones of American political thought.

Higginbotham, A. Leon, Jr. *In the Matter of Color: Race and the American Legal Process, the Colonial Period.* New York: Oxford University Press, 1978. Chronicles how colonial governments established the legal foundations for the enslavement of African Americans.

Jensen, Merrill. *The Articles of Confederation.* Madison: University of Wisconsin Press, 1940. Definitive and balanced treatment of the Articles.

Norton, Mary Beth. *Liberty's Daughters.* Boston: Little, Brown, 1980. Examines the role of women during the era of the Revolution and concludes that the Revolution transformed gender roles, setting women on the course to equality.

Rakove, Jack N. *Original Meanings: Politics and Ideas in the Making of the Constitution.* New York: Alfred A. Knopf, 1996. Shows the difficulty of divining the original intentions of the Framers.

Rossiter, Clinton. *1787: The Grand Convention.* New York: Macmillan, 1966. A well-written study of the making of the Constitution.

Storing, Herbert J. *What the Anti-Federalists Were For.* Chicago: University of Chicago Press, 1981. Analysis of the political views of those opposed to ratification of the Constitution.

Wood, Gordon S. *The Creation of the American Republic.* Chapel Hill: University of North Carolina Press, 1969. In-depth study of American political thought prior to the Constitutional Convention.

Wood, Gordon S. *Empire of Liberty: A History of the Early Republic, 1789–1815.* New York: Oxford University Press, 2009. Excellent account of America's pivotal first quarter-century.

Wood, Gordon S. *The Radicalism of the American Revolution.* New York: Vintage, 1993. Shows how American society and politics were thoroughly transformed in the decades following the Revolution.

3

Federalism

Politics in Action: Conflict Between Levels of Government

he Controlled Substances Act of 1970 prohibits the possession, use, or sale of marijuana. In 1996, California voters passed the Compassionate Use Act, legalizing the medical use of marijuana. Nineteen other states and Washington, D.C., have followed California's lead in legalizing medical marijuana. In 2013, Colorado and Washington states decriminalized personal recreational use of small amounts of marijuana. National and many state laws are clearly in conflict.

In California there emerged a thriving industry of marijuana growers and storefront dispensaries that paid substantial sums in state and local taxes but that national drug officials saw as largely illegal. Operating under the principle that national law preempts state law, the Drug Enforcement Administration routinely arrested medical marijuana patients and seized the business assets of growers and dispensaries. The Internal Revenue Service also began a crackdown, denying some sellers the right to deduct marijuana-related business expenses.

Medical marijuana users argued the national law exceeded the power granted to Congress by the Constitution to regulate interstate commerce, because the marijuana they used was grown, transported, and consumed entirely within the state in which they lived and thus did not implicate interstate commerce. In *Gonzales v. Raich* (2005), however, the U.S. Supreme Court disagreed. It ruled that under the Constitution's commerce clause, Congress may criminalize the production and use of marijuana even if these occur within states that have approved its use for medicinal purposes. Marijuana grown for medical purposes is indistinguishable from illicit marijuana, the Court reasoned, and local use affected supply and demand in the national marijuana market, making the regulation of within-state use essential to regulating the drug's national market.

National prosecutors and drug agents say much of California's burgeoning marijuana industry hides behind the mask of meeting medical needs while engaging, in large-scale illegal sales. Although the Department of Justice has issued guidelines making it a low priority to prosecute patients with serious illnesses or their caregivers who are complying with state laws on medical

3.1
Define federalism and contrast it with alternative ways of organizing a nation, p. 70.

3.2
Outline the constitutional basis for the division of power between national and state governments, the establishment of national supremacy, and states' obligations to each other, p. 72.

3.3
Characterize the shift from dual to cooperative federalism and the role of fiscal federalism in intergovernmental relations today, p. 79.

3.4
Explain the consequences of federalism for diversity in public policies among the states, p. 88.

3.5
Assess the impact of federalism on democratic government and the scope of government, p. 89.

Federalism can put the national and state governments in conflict. Here a California man compares the aroma of various varieties of marijuana on the final day of business of a medical marijuana dispensary, legal in California but put out of business by the national government.

federalism

A way of organizing a nation so that two or more levels of government share formal authority over the same area and people.

unitary governments

A central government that holds supreme power in a nation. Most national governments today are unitary governments, and has this growth been at the expense of the states?

Defining Federalism

3.1

Define federalism and contrast it with alternative ways of organizing a nation.

 ederalism is a way of organizing a nation so that two or more levels of government share formal authority over the same area and people. For example, the state of Texas has formal authority over its inhabitants, but the national government (often referred to as the *federal government*) can also pass laws and establish policies, such as Social Security, Medicare, and aid to college students, that affect Texans. Americans are subject to the formal authority of both state and national governments.

Although federalism is not unique to the United States, it is not a common method of governing. Only 11 of the 190 or so nations of the world have federal systems, and these countries—including, for example, Germany, Mexico, Argentina, Canada, Australia, and India—share little else as a group (see "America in Perspective: Why Federalism?").

Most nations instead have a **unitary government**, in which supreme power resides in the central government. If the French Assembly, for instance, wants to redraw the boundaries of local governments or change their forms of government, it can, and, in fact, it has. The U.S. Congress, by contrast, cannot, say, abolish Alabama or redraw its boundary with Georgia.

American states are unitary governments with respect to their local governments. That is, local governments derive their authority from the states, which can create or abolish local governments and can make rules for them; for example, by telling them how they will be organized, how they can tax people, on what they can spend money, and even what their speed limits will be. In contrast, states receive their authority not from the national government but *directly* from the Constitution.

There is a third form of governmental structure, a *confederation*. The United States began as a confederation under the Articles of Confederation. In a confederation, the national government is weak, and most or all power is in the hands of the country's components—for example, the individual states. Today, confederations are rare and mainly take the form of international organizations such as the United Nations. Table 3.1 summarizes the authority relations in the three systems of government.

In exploring American federalism, we will be especially attentive to our themes of democracy and the scope of government. Does federalism, the vertical division of power, enhance democracy in the United States? Does the additional layer of policymakers at the state level make government more responsive to public opinion or merely more complicated? Does it enhance the prospects that a majority of Americans will have their way in public policy? And what are the implications of federalism for the scope of the national government's activities? Why has the national government grown so much relative to state governments, and has this growth been at the expense of the states?

marijuana, it has nonetheless cracked down on growers and on dispensaries and their landlords. State and national laws remain in conflict, creating ongoing issues and illustrating the importance of understanding American federalism, the complex relationships between different levels of government in the United States.

TABLE 3.1 AUTHORITY RELATIONS IN THREE SYSTEMS OF GOVERNMENT

	Unitary	Confederate	Federal
Central government	Holds primary authority	Limited powers to coordinate state activities	Shares power with states
State government	Few or no powers; Duties regulated by central government	Sovereign; Allocates some duties to central government	Shares power with central government
Citizens	Vote for central government officials	Vote for state government officials	Vote for both state and central government officials

The workings of the federal system are sometimes called **intergovernmental relations**. This term refers to the entire set of interactions among national, state, and local governments, including regulations, the transfers of funds, and the sharing of information.

intergovernmental relations
The entire set of interactions among national, state, and local governments—including regulations, transfers of funds, and the sharing of information—that constitute the workings of the federal system.

America in Perspective

Why Federalism?

Only 11 countries, shown in the following table, have federal systems. All three North American nations have federal systems, but the trend does not continue in South America, where only two nations have federal systems.

Countries large in size—such as Canada and Australia—or large in both size and population—such as India, the United States, Brazil, and Mexico—tend to have federal systems, which decentralize the administration of governmental services. Nevertheless, China and Indonesia—two large and populous countries—have unitary governments, and tiny Malaysia and Switzerland have federal systems.

A nation's diversity may also play a role in the development of a federal system. Brazil, Canada, India, Malaysia, Switzerland, and the United States have large minority ethnic groups, often distinct in language and religion. Many nations with unitary systems, however, ranging from Belgium to most African countries, are also replete with ethnic diversity.

Most federal systems are democracies, although most democracies are not federal systems. Authoritarian regimes generally do not wish to disperse power away from the central government. However, both the former Soviet Union and the former Yugoslavia, perhaps reflecting the extraordinary diversity of their populations, had federal systems—of a sort: in both countries, the central government retained ultimate power. As democracy swept through these countries, their national governments dissolved, and multiple smaller nations were formed.

CRITICAL THINKING QUESTIONS

1. Why might a federal system be useful for a country with a large area or population or for a country with large ethnic minority groups?

2. How might the United States be different if it had a unitary system rather than a federal system?

Nation	Population	Area (Thousands Square Miles)	Diversity (Ethnic, Linguistic, and Religious)
Argentina	43,024,374	1,068	Low
Australia	22,507,617	2,968	Low
Austria	8,223,062	32	Low
Brazil	202,656,788	3,286	Medium
Canada	34,834,841	3,852	High
Germany	80,996,685	138	Low
India	1,236,344,631	1,269	High
Malaysia	30,073,353	127	High
Mexico	120,286,655	762	Low
Switzerland	8,061,516	16	Medium
United States	318,892,103	3,718	Medium

SOURCE: Central Intelligence Agency, *The World Factbook, 2014.*

The Constitutional Basis of Federalism

Outline the constitutional basis for the division of power between national and state government, the establishment of national supremacy, and states' obligations to each other.

T he word *federalism* does not occur in the Constitution. Not much was said about federalism at the Constitutional Convention. Eighteenth-century Americans had little experience in thinking of themselves as Americans first and state citizens second. In fact, loyalty to state governments was so strong that the Constitution would have been resoundingly defeated had it tried to abolish them. In addition, a central government, working alone, would have had difficulty trying to govern eighteenth-century Americans. The people were too widely dispersed and the country's transportation and communication systems too primitive to allow governing from a central location. There was no other practical choice in 1787 but to create a federal system of government.

☐ The Division of Power

Although they favored a stronger national government, the Framers still made states vital components in the machinery of government. Indeed, as a result of the necessity of relying on the states to provide public services, the Constitution does not carefully define the powers of state governments. In general, states have responsibility for a wide range of policies and may largely organize themselves and their local governments as they wish. The Constitution makes states responsible for both state and national elections—an important power—and it also gives the states the power to ratify constitutional amendments.

The Constitution guarantees states equal representation in the Senate, and in Article V even makes this provision unamendable. Furthermore, the Constitution virtually guarantees the continuation of each state; Congress is forbidden to create new states by chopping up old ones, unless a state's legislature approves (an unlikely event). Congress is also forbidden to tax articles exported from one state to another.

The Constitution also creates obligations of the national government toward the states. For example, the national government is to protect states against violence and invasion.

The Constitution is more specific about the powers that states do *not* possess than about those they do. As you can see in Table 3.2, limits on the states focus on foreign policy, economic matters, and basic rights, including voting rights. The limitations related to basic rights are the results of constitutional amendments that also restrict the national government.

TABLE 3.2 SOME POWERS DENIED TO STATES BY THE CONSTITUTION

Economic	Individual Rights	Foreign Affairs
Tax imports or exports	Grant titles of nobility	Enter into treaties
Coin money or issue paper money	Pass bills of attainder	Declare war
Impair obligations of contract	Pass ex post facto laws	
	Permit slavery	
	Abridge citizens' privileges or immunities	
	Deny due process of law	
	Raise or maintain military forces	
	Deny equal protection of law	
	Impose poll taxes	
	Deny right to vote because of race, gender, or age	

supremacy clause
The clause in Article VI of the Constitution that makes the Constitution, national laws, and treaties supreme over state laws as long as the national government is acting within its constitutional limits.

Why It Matters to You

Protecting Rights

State constitutions guarantee many basic rights. However, few Americans would feel comfortable with only state protections for their liberties. The Bill of Rights in the U.S. Constitution is the ultimate legal defense of freedom.

The states and the national government have overlapping responsibilities for important matters, such as establishing courts, maintaining law and order, protecting citizens' health and safety, and regulating financial institutions. Both levels of government can raise revenues through taxes, borrow money, and spend for the general welfare of their citizens. They may even take private property for public purposes, with just compensation to the owners.

☐ National Supremacy

Shared power and responsibilities to govern between states and the national government inevitably lead to disputes between them. In the past, people debated whether the states or the national government should regulate the railroads, pass child labor laws, or adopt minimum-wage legislation. Today, people debate whether the states or the national government should regulate abortions, set standards for public schools, determine speed limits on highways, protect the environment, or provide health care for the poor. Many of our policy debates are debates about federalism.

When the national government places prohibitions or requirements on the states—whether through acts of Congress or agency regulations—inevitably issues arise for the courts to decide. In a dispute between the states and the national government, which prevails? The second paragraph of Article VI of the Constitution, often referred to as the **supremacy clause**, provides the answer. It states that the following three items are the supreme law of the land:

1. The Constitution
2. Laws of the national government, as long as they are consistent with the Constitution
3. Treaties (which can be made only by the national government)

Emphasizing the supremacy of the Constitution, the Framers mandated that all state executives, legislators, and judges are bound by oath to support the Constitution, even if their state constitutions or state laws directly contradict it.

Occasionally, issues arise in which states challenge the authority of the national government. Several states have challenged federal education regulations resulting from the 2002 No Child Left Behind Act. Some states began a challenge of the requirement that every American purchase health insurance even before the 2010 health care reform bill passed Congress. In such cases, the federal government usually wins.

Over the years, the federal government has gained power relative to the states. The Civil War and the struggle for racial equality were key events in settling the issue of how national and state powers are related. Equally important were the Supreme Court's interpretation of the Tenth and Eleventh Amendments, implied powers, and the commerce clause.

THE CIVIL WAR We typically think of the Civil War (1861–1865) as mainly a struggle over slavery, but it was also a struggle between states and the national government. (In fact, Abraham Lincoln announced in his 1861 inaugural address that he

Tenth Amendment
The constitutional amendment stating, "The powers not delegated to the United States by the Constitution, nor prohibited by it to the states, are reserved to the states respectively, or to the people."

In 1963, Alabama governor George Wallace made a dramatic stand at the University of Alabama to resist integration of the all-white school. Federal marshals won this confrontation, and since then the federal government in general has been able to impose national standards of equal opportunity on the states.

would support a constitutional amendment guaranteeing slavery if it would save the Union.) As a result of the North's victory, the national government asserted its power over the Southern states' claim of sovereignty.

THE STRUGGLE FOR RACIAL EQUALITY

A century later, conflict between the states and the national government again erupted over states' rights and national power. In 1954, in *Brown v. Board of Education*, the Supreme Court held that school segregation was unconstitutional. Southern politicians responded with what they called "massive resistance" to the decision. When a federal judge ordered the admission of two African American students to the University of Alabama in 1963, Governor George Wallace literally blocked the school entrance to prevent federal marshals and the students from entering the admissions office; the students were nonetheless admitted. And throughout the 1960s the federal government enacted laws and policies to end segregation in schools, housing, public accommodations, voting, and jobs. The conflict between states and the national government over racial equality was decided in favor of the national government. National standards of racial equality prevailed.

THE TENTH AMENDMENT

Although supreme, the national government can operate only within its appropriate sphere. It cannot usurp the states' powers. But what are the boundaries of the national government's powers?

According to some commentators, the **Tenth Amendment** provides part of the answer. It states that the "powers not delegated to the United States by the Constitution, nor prohibited by it to the states, are reserved to the states respectively, or to the people." To those advocating *states' rights*, the amendment clearly means that the national government has only those powers that the Constitution explicitly assigns to it. The states or people have supreme power over any activity not mentioned there. Despite this interpretation, in 1941 the Supreme Court (in *United States v. Darby*) called the Tenth Amendment a constitutional truism—that is, a mere assertion that the states have independent powers of their own, and not a declaration that state powers are superior to those of the national government.

The Court seemed to backtrack on this ruling in a 1976 case, *National League of Cities v. Usery*, in which it held that extending national minimum-wage and maximum-hours standards to employees of state and local governments was an unconstitutional intrusion of the national government into the domain of the states. In 1985, however, in *Garcia v. San Antonio Metro*, the Court overturned the *National League of Cities* decision. The Court held, in essence, that it was up to Congress to decide which actions of the states should be regulated by the national government.

Thus, once again, the Court ruled that the Tenth Amendment did not give states power superior to that of the national government for activities not mentioned in the Constitution. Nevertheless, in *Bond v. United States* (2011), the Court held that a person indicted under a federal statute may challenge the statute on the Tenth Amendment grounds that, in enacting the statute, the federal government invaded state powers under the Constitution.

THE ELEVENTH AMENDMENT   There is a more specific constraint on the national government. Federal courts can order states to obey the Constitution or federal laws and treaties.[1] However, in deference to the states the Eleventh Amendment gives them immunity from certain prosecution: it prohibits federal courts, state courts,[2] or federal administrative agencies from hearing cases in which a private party names a state as a defendant or seeks monetary relief from a state officer in his or her official capacity (for example, a police officer for violating one's rights) unless the state gives its consent to the hearing. That is why, for example, the Supreme Court voided a provision of the Americans with Disabilities Act that allowed citizens to sue states for damages: the provision violated state immunity as established by the Eleventh Amendment.[3]

There are limits to state immunity. Federal courts do have the jurisdiction to hear cases in which a private party names a state officer acting in an official capacity as a defendant when what is at issue are basic, constitutional rights. In these circumstances the courts may grant injunctive relief, that is, require the officer to do or refrain from doing certain acts. Cases arising under the Fourteenth Amendment (usually cases involving racial discrimination) also make for exceptions to the provisions regarding state immunity.[4] Congress may deny states immunity from suits that concern bankruptcy cases.[5] Moreover, unlike private parties, both the federal government and other states may sue a state in federal court. In 2011, the Supreme Court held that it was permissible for an independent state agency to sue a state in federal court in order to enforce federal law.[6]

The Supreme Court has also made it easier for citizens to control the behavior of local officials. The Court ruled that an 1871 federal law passed to protect newly freed slaves permits individuals to sue local governments for damages or seek injunctions against any local official acting in an official capacity who they believe has deprived them of any right secured by the Constitution or by federal law.[7] Such suits are now common in the federal courts.

IMPLIED POWERS   As early as 1819, the issue of state versus national power came before the Supreme Court. The case that landed it there was *McCulloch v. Maryland*, which involved the Second Bank of the United States.

The new American government had moved quickly on many economic policies. In 1791, it had created a national bank, a government agency empowered to print money, make loans, and engage in many other banking tasks. A darling of Alexander Hamilton and his allies, the bank had numerous opponents—including Thomas Jefferson, farmers, and state legislatures—who opposed strengthening the national government's role in the economy and who saw the bank as an instrument of the elite. Congress allowed the First Bank of the United States to expire. However, during James Madison's presidency it created the Second Bank, and so fueled a great national debate.

Railing against the "Monster Bank," the state of Maryland passed a law in 1818 taxing the national bank's Baltimore branch $15,000 a year. The Baltimore branch refused to pay, whereupon the state of Maryland sued the cashier, James McCulloch, for payment. When the state courts upheld Maryland's law and its tax, the bank appealed to the U.S. Supreme Court. John Marshall was chief justice, and two of the country's most capable lawyers argued the case before the Court. Daniel Webster, widely regarded as one of the greatest senators in U.S. history, argued for the national bank, and Luther Martin, a delegate to the Constitutional Convention, argued for Maryland.

Martin maintained that the Constitution was very clear about the powers of Congress (outlined in its Article I). The power to create a national bank was not among them. Thus, Martin concluded, Congress had exceeded its powers, and Maryland had

McCulloch v. Maryland
An 1819 Supreme Court decision that established the supremacy of the national government over state governments. The Court, led by Chief Justice John Marshall, held that Congress had certain implied powers in addition to the powers enumerated in the Constitution.

enumerated powers
Powers of the federal government that are listed explicitly in the Constitution. For example, Article I, Section 8, specifically gives Congress the power to coin money and regulate its value and impose taxes.

implied powers
Powers of the federal government that go beyond those enumerated in the Constitution, in accordance with the statement in the Constitution that Congress has the power to "make all laws necessary and proper for carrying into execution" the powers enumerated in Article I.

elastic clause
The final paragraph of Article I, Section 8, of the Constitution, which authorizes Congress to pass all laws "necessary and proper" to carry out the enumerated powers.

a right to tax the bank. On behalf of the bank, Webster argued for a broader interpretation of the powers of the national government. The Constitution was not meant to stifle congressional powers, he said, but rather to permit Congress to use all means "necessary and proper" to fulfill its responsibilities.

In their decision, Marshall and his colleagues set forth two great constitutional principles. The first was the *supremacy of the national government over the states.* Marshall wrote, "The government of the United States, though limited in its power, is supreme within its sphere of action." As long as the national government behaved in accordance with the Constitution, its policies took precedence over state policies, as the Constitution's supremacy clause said. Because of this principle, federal laws or regulations—for example, civil rights acts, rules regulating hazardous substances, water quality, and clean-air standards—*preempt* state or local laws or regulations and thus preclude their enforcement.

For example, in *Arizona et al. v. United States* (2012) the Court held that federal law preempted the state of Arizona from making it a crime for immigrants to fail to register under a federal law or for illegal immigrants to work or to try find work; federal law also preempted the state from allowing police to arrest people without warrants simply because they believed people had done things that would make them deportable under federal law. However, the Court did uphold the state requirement that state law enforcement officials determine the immigration status of anyone they stop or arrest if there is reason to suspect that the individual is an illegal immigrant.

The other key principle of *McCulloch* is that *the national government has certain implied powers that go beyond its enumerated powers.* For this reason, the Court held that Congress was behaving consistently with the Constitution when it created the national bank. Congress had certain **enumerated powers**, powers *specifically* listed in Article I of the Constitution. These included coining money and regulating its value, imposing taxes, and so forth. The Constitution did not enumerate creating a bank, but Article I, Section 8, concludes by stating that Congress has the power to "make all laws necessary and proper for carrying into execution the foregoing powers." That final clause, said Marshall, gave Congress certain **implied powers**, which it can exercise as long as it does so in terms consistent with the Constitution.

Commentators often refer to the "necessary and proper" clause of the Constitution as the **elastic clause.** Hundreds of congressional policies, especially in the economic

The supremacy clause allows the national government to preempt state laws if it is acting within its legal sphere. Immigration policy is one example. Here, undocumented immigrants are being repatriated to their home country.

domain, involve powers not specifically mentioned in the Constitution. Federal policies to regulate food and drugs, build interstate highways, protect consumers, clean up dirty air and water, and do many other things are all justified as implied powers of Congress.

COMMERCE POWER The Constitution gives Congress the power to regulate interstate and international commerce. American courts have spent many years trying to define "commerce." In 1824, the Supreme Court, in deciding the case of **Gibbons v. Ogden**, defined commerce very broadly to encompass virtually every form of commercial activity. Today, commerce covers not only the movement of goods but also radio signals, electricity, telephone messages, the Internet, insurance transactions, and much more.

The Supreme Court's decisions establishing the national government's implied powers (*McCulloch v. Maryland*) and a broad definition of interstate commerce (*Gibbons v. Ogden*) established the power of Congress to *promote economic development* through subsidies and services for business interests. In the latter part of the nineteenth century, however, Congress sought in addition to use its interstate commerce power to *regulate the economy*, for example, by requiring safer working conditions for laborers and protecting children from working long hours. The Court then ruled that the interstate commerce power did not give Congress the right to regulate local commercial activities.

The Great Depression placed new demands on the national government. Beginning in 1933, the New Deal of President Franklin D. Roosevelt produced an avalanche of regulatory and social welfare legislation. Although initially the Supreme Court voided much of this legislation, after 1937 the Court began to loosen restrictions on the national government's regulation of commerce. In 1964, when Congress prohibited racial discrimination in places of public accommodation, it did so on the basis of its power to regulate interstate commerce. Thus, regulating commerce became one of the national government's most important sources of power, used by Congress for policies ranging from protecting the environment to providing health care for the elderly.

In recent years, the Supreme Court has scrutinized some uses of the commerce power with a skeptical eye, however. In 1995, the Court held in *United States v. Lopez* that the federal Gun-Free School Zones Act of 1990, which forbade the possession of firearms in public schools, exceeded Congress's constitutional authority to regulate commerce. Guns in a school zone, the majority said, have nothing to do with commerce. Similarly, in 2000, the Court ruled in *United States v. Morrison* that the power to regulate interstate commerce did not give Congress the authority to enact the 1994 Violence Against Women Act, which provided a federal civil remedy for the victims of gender-motivated violence. Gender-motivated crimes of violence are not, the Court said, in any sense economic activity.

Several other recent cases have had important implications for federalism. In *Printz v. United States* (1997) and *Mack v. United States* (1997), the Supreme Court voided the congressional mandate in the Brady Handgun Violence Prevention Act that the chief law enforcement officer in each local community conduct background checks on prospective gun purchasers. According to the Court, "The federal government may neither issue directives requiring the states to address particular problems, nor commend the states' officers, or those of their political subdivision, to administer or enforce a federal regulatory program."

Gibbons v. Ogden
A landmark case decided in 1824 in which the Supreme Court interpreted very broadly the clause in Article I, Section 8, of the Constitution and defined the power of Congress to regulate interstate commerce as encompassing virtually every form of commercial activity.

full faith and credit
A clause in Article IV of the Constitution requiring each state to recognize the public acts, records, and judicial proceedings of all other states.

extradition
A legal process whereby a state surrenders a person charged with a crime to the state in which the crime is alleged to have been committed.

privileges and immunities
The provision of the Constitution according citizens of each state the privileges of citizens of any state in which they happen to be.

In 2012, the Supreme Court heard challenges to the Affordable Care Act, which Congress passed in 2010. Critics contended that the mandate that everyone purchase health insurance exceeded the reach of the commerce clause and was thus unconstitutional. The Supreme Court agreed but nevertheless upheld the mandate on the basis of Congress's tax power.[8]

☐ States' Obligations to Each Other

Federalism involves more than relationships between the national government and state and local governments. The states must deal with each other as well, and the Constitution outlines certain obligations that each state has to every other state.

FULL FAITH AND CREDIT Suppose that, like millions of other Americans, a person divorces and then remarries. This person purchases a marriage license, which registers the marriage with a state. On the honeymoon, the person travels across the country. Is this person married in each state he or she passes through, even though the marriage license is with only one state? Can the person be arrested for bigamy because the divorce occurred in only one state?

The answer, of course, is that a marriage license and a divorce, like a driver's license and a birth certificate, are valid in all states. Article IV of the Constitution requires that states give **full faith and credit** to the public acts, records, and civil judicial proceedings of every other state. This reciprocity is essential to the functioning of society and the economy. Without the full faith and credit clause, people could avoid their obligations, say, to make payments on automobile loans simply by crossing a state boundary. In addition, because courts can enforce contracts between business firms across state boundaries, firms incorporated in one state can do business in another.

Usually, the full faith and credit provision in the Constitution poses little controversy. An exception involves the issue of same-sex marriages, which we discuss in more detail in Chapter 5. Several states have legalized same-sex marriages while others prohibit them. What would happen in states that do not recognize marriages between same-sex partners? In 1996, Congress answered with the Defense of Marriage Act, which permitted states to disregard same-sex marriages, even if they were legal elsewhere in the United States. In 2013, the Supreme Court struck down the law down as an unconstitutional violation of equal rights.[9] It remains to be seen how individual states will deal with the issue, but opponents of gay marriage propose amending the Constitution to allow states not to recognize same-sex marriages. They are unlikely to succeed, however, because public opinion is rapidly changing in favor of same-sex marriage.

EXTRADITION What about criminal penalties? Almost all criminal law is state law. If someone robs a store, steals a car, or commits a murder, the chances are that this person is breaking a state, not a federal, law. The Constitution says that states are required to return a person charged with a crime in another state to that state for trial or imprisonment, a legal process called **extradition**. There is no way to force states to comply, but they usually are happy to do so, not wishing to harbor criminals and hoping that other states will reciprocate. Thus, a lawbreaker cannot avoid punishment by simply escaping to another state.

PRIVILEGES AND IMMUNITIES The most complicated obligation among the states is the requirement that citizens receive all the **privileges and immunities** of any state in which they happen to be. The goal of this constitutional provision is to prohibit states from discriminating against citizens of other states. If, for example, a New Yorker visits Florida, the New Yorker will pay the same sales tax and receive the same police protection as residents of Florida.

There are many exceptions to the privileges and immunities clause, however. For example, consider tuition at public universities. If you reside in the state in which your

Because of the full faith and credit clause of the Constitution, marriage certificates issued by one state are valid in every state. People are also entitled to most of the benefits—and subject to most of the obligations—of citizenship in any state they visit, thanks to the privileges and immunities clause. Gay marriage is straining these principles, however, as some states refuse to recognize marriages between same-sex partners.

university is located, you generally pay a tuition substantially lower than that paid by your fellow students from out of state. Only residents of a state can vote in state elections. States often attempt to pass some of the burdens of financing the state government to those outside the state, for example, through taxes on minerals mined in the state but consumed elsewhere or special taxes on hotel rooms rented by tourists.

The Supreme Court has never clarified just which privileges a state must make available to all Americans except that the clause only applies to activities that bear "on the vitality of the Nation as a single entity."[10] In general, the more fundamental the right, the less likely it is that a state can discriminate against citizens of another state. Relying on the privileges and immunities clause of the Fourteenth Amendment (which prohibits states from denying the privileges and immunities of citizens of the United States), in 1999 the Supreme Court held in *Saenz v. Roe* that California could not require a new resident to wait a year before becoming eligible for welfare.

Intergovernmental Relations

3.3 Characterize the shift from dual to cooperative federalism and the role of fiscal federalism in intergovernmental relations today.

ntergovernmental relations reflect two major changes in American federalism, both related to the shift toward national dominance discussed earlier. The first major change has been a gradual shift in the nature of power sharing between the national and state governments.[11] The second has been the rise of *fiscal federalism*, an elaborate array of federal grants-in-aid to the states and localities.

dual federalism
A system of government in which the states and the national government each remain supreme within their own spheres, each with different powers and policy responsibilities.

cooperative federalism
A system of government in which states and the national government share powers and policy assignments.

From Dual to Cooperative Federalism

One way to understand the changes in American federalism is to contrast two types of federalism. Dual and cooperative federalism are two different ways of dividing power and responsibility.

In **dual federalism**, the national government and the states remain supreme within their own spheres. The national government is responsible for some policies, the states for others. For example, the national government has exclusive control over foreign and military policy, the postal system, and monetary policy. States have exclusive control over schools, law enforcement, and road building. In dual federalism, then, the powers and policy assignments of the two layers of government are distinct, as in a layer cake. Proponents of dual federalism generally believe that the powers of the national government should be interpreted narrowly.

In **cooperative federalism**, the national government and the states share powers and policy assignments.[12] This type of federalism is like a marble cake, with responsibilities of the two levels of government mingled and clear distinctions between them blurred. Thus, for example, after the terrorist attacks on September 11, 2001, the national government asked state and local governments to investigate suspected terrorists, and both national and state public health officials dealt with the threat caused by anthrax in the mail in Florida, New York, and Washington, D.C.

Initially, before the national government began to assert its dominance, the U.S. federal system leaned toward dual federalism. Today, however, most politicians and political scientists would describe the system as one of cooperative federalism.

From the beginning a neat separation into purely state and purely national responsibilities did not characterize American federalism. A look at the area of education, which is usually thought of as being mainly a state and local responsibility, illustrates this point and also shows the movement toward cooperative federalism.

Even under the Articles of Confederation, Congress set aside land in the Northwest Territory to be used for public schools. During the Civil War, the national government adopted a policy to create land grant colleges. Important American universities such as Wisconsin, Texas A&M, Illinois, Ohio State, North Carolina State, and Iowa State owe their origins to this policy.

In the 1950s and 1960s, the national government began supporting public elementary and secondary education. In 1958, Congress passed the National Defense Education Act, largely in response to Soviet success in the space race. The act provided federal grants and loans for college students as well as financial support for elementary and secondary education in science and foreign languages. In 1965, Congress passed the Elementary and Secondary Education Act, which provided federal aid to numerous schools. Although these policies expanded the national government's role in education, they were not a sharp break with the past.

Today, the federal government's presence is felt in every schoolhouse. Almost all school districts receive some federal assistance. To do so, they must comply with federal rules and regulations; for example, they must maintain desegregated and nondiscriminatory programs. The No Child Left Behind Act established standards of performance along with sanctions, including loss of federal aid, for schools failing to meet its standards. In addition, federal courts have ordered local schools to implement elaborate desegregation plans and have placed constraints on school prayers. The federal government also plays a crucial role in higher education (see Young People and Politics: Federal Support for Colleges and Universities).

Highways are another example of the movement toward cooperative federalism. In an earlier era, states and cities were largely responsible for building roads, although the Constitution does authorize Congress to construct "post roads." In 1956, Congress initiated the building of the interstate highway system, a joint federal-state project, and specified the cost and sharing of funds. In this and many other areas, the federal system has promoted a partnership between the national and state governments.

Young People & Politics

Federal Support for Colleges and Universities

Because most colleges and universities are public institutions created by state and local governments, federalism has direct consequences for the students who attend them. State and local governments provide most of the funding for public colleges and universities, but almost everyone agrees that this funding is inadequate. In response to this problem, the national government has stepped in to support postsecondary education programs.

One could argue that the federal government makes it possible for many students to attend college at all because it is the primary source of financial aid. The federal government provides about $160 billion in financial assistance (including grants, loans, and work-study assistance) to more than 50 million postsecondary students each year. Nearly two-thirds of all full-time undergraduates receive some form of financial aid from the federal government.

The federal government also provides several billion dollars of direct grants to colleges and universities across the nation. Billions more in federal funds support research and training in certain areas, especially science and engineering—which receive about $32 billion a year. The libraries, laboratories, and the buildings in most colleges and universities have benefitted from federal government grants.

Each year the federal government provides about 10 percent of the revenue for public universities and 15 percent for private, not-for-profit colleges and universities. Few colleges and universities could withstand a 10 or 15 percent budget cut and the loss of most of the financial assistance for their students. Federalism, then, matters quite a lot to college students.

CRITICAL THINKING QUESTIONS

1. Why do state institutions of higher education require aid from the federal government? Why don't the states provide adequate funds to run their own colleges and universities?

2. The federal government is experiencing huge budget deficits. Would it be better to rely completely on state support to fund higher education?

SOURCE: U.S. Department of Education, National Center for Education Statistics, *Digest of Education Statistics, 2014.*

The principal basis for cooperative federalism is shared programs such as education and transportation that are mainly state responsibilities. For hundreds of programs, cooperative federalism involves the following:

- *Shared costs*. Cities and states can receive federal money for airport construction, sewage treatment plants, youth programs, and many other programs, but only if they pay part of the bill.

- *Federal guidelines*. Most federal grants to states and cities come with strings attached. For example, Congress spends billions of dollars to support state highway construction, but to get their share, states must adopt and enforce limits on the legal drinking age.

- *Shared administration*. State and local officials implement federal policies, but they have administrative powers of their own. The U.S. Department of Labor, for example, gives billions of dollars to states for implementing job training, but states administer the money and have considerable latitude in spending it.

The cooperation between the national government and state governments is such an established feature of American federalism that it persists even when the two levels of government are in conflict on certain matters. For example, officials in a number of states challenged in court the health care bill Congress passed in 2010. Nevertheless, most implemented the act and cooperated well with Washington on other policies.

States are responsible for most public policies dealing with social, family, and moral issues. The Constitution does not give the national government the power to pass laws that *directly* regulate drinking ages, marriage and divorce, or speed limits.

devolution
Transferring responsibility for policies from the federal government to state and local governments.

Cooperative federalism began during the Great Depression of the 1930s and continues into the twenty-first century. The federal government provides much of the funding for interstate highways, for example, but also attaches requirements that states must meet.

These policy prerogatives belong to the states. They become national issues, however, when aggrieved or angry groups take their cases to Congress or the federal courts in an attempt to use the power of the national government to *influence* states or to convince federal courts to find a state's policy unconstitutional.

A good example of this process is the federal requirement that states raise their drinking age to 21 in order to receive highway funds. Candy Lightner, a Californian whose 13-year-old daughter was killed by a drunk driver, formed Mothers Against Drunk Driving (MADD) in 1980. After an intense lobbying campaign by MADD, Congress passed a law withholding federal highway funds from any state that did not raise its drinking age to 21. Today, 21 is the legal drinking age in every state.

☐ Devolution?

The shift toward greater power and responsibility for the national government has not gone unchallenged. Party goals have played a role in the debate.

For most of the twentieth century, Democrats supported increasing the power of the federal government in order to advance national policies in areas ranging from child labor laws and education to Social Security and health care. Republicans, in contrast, generally opposed these policies and favored states taking responsibility for such issues. They often articulated their opposition to increased federal power in terms of a defense of state authority in a federal system. However, when Republican Ronald Reagan tried to reduce the role of the national government in domestic programs and return responsibility to the states, few officials at either the state or national levels agreed with him. Despite their objections, Reagan's opposition to federal spending on domestic programs, together with the huge federal deficits of the 1980s, forced Congress to reduce federal funds for state and local governments.

In the 1994 elections, Republicans captured Congress, the first time in 40 years that they had majorities in both houses. Their rhetoric centered on **devolution**, the transferring of responsibility for policies from the federal government to state and local

fiscal federalism

The pattern of spending, taxing, and providing grants in the federal system; it is the cornerstone of the national government's relations with state and local governments.

governments. They followed their rhetoric with action by, for example, repealing federal speed limits, allowing states more latitude in dealing with welfare policy, and making it more difficult for state prisoners to seek relief in federal courts.

Soon, however, Republicans became less concerned with abstract principles and more with adopting a pragmatic approach to federalism to achieving their goals. They found turning to the federal government—and *restricting* state power—the most effective way to achieve a wide range of policy objectives, including loosening economic and environmental regulations, controlling immigration, setting health insurance standards, restricting the expansion of government-financed health care coverage, stiffening penalties for criminals, extending federal criminal penalties, and tracking child-support violators.[13]

Continuing with this more practical approach, during the presidency of George W. Bush, Republicans passed a law removing most class-action lawsuits from state courts. Most significantly, they passed the No Child Left Behind Act, the largest expansion of the federal role in education since Lyndon Johnson's Great Society and a policy that has allowed more federal intrusion into a state domain than almost any other in U.S. history. Many states have complained loudly about the problems and the cost of implementing the legislation.

In this decade, some political leaders, especially those associated with the Tea Party movement, have called not only for a smaller national government in general but also for devolving the principal responsibility for policies such as health care and income security to the states. Most Americans, however, embrace a pragmatic view of governmental responsibilities: They see the national government as more capable than the states of handling some matters—for example, managing the economy, ensuring access to health care and the safety of food and drugs, preserving the environment, and providing income security for the elderly. They see state and local governments as better at handling others like crime and education.[14] In any event, both levels of government are, of necessity, involved in most policy areas.

☐ Fiscal Federalism

As you have already seen, shared program costs are a key element of cooperative federalism. Indeed, the second major change in American federalism has been the rise of **fiscal federalism**, in which *grants-in-aid*, federal funds appropriated by Congress for distribution to state and local governments, serve as instruments through which the national government both aids and influences states and localities.

Why It *Matters to* You
Grants-in-Aid

The federal system of grants-in-aid sends revenues derived from federal taxes to state and local governments. This spending transfers the burden of paying for services from those who pay state and local taxes, such as taxes on sales and property, to those who pay national taxes, especially the federal income tax.

The amount of money spent on federal grants has grown rapidly since the 1960s and especially since the 1990s, as you can see in Figure 3.1. For 2015, federal grants-in-aid (including loan subsidies, such as cases in which the federal government pays the interest on student loans until a student graduates) totals more than $640 billion. Federal aid, covering a wide range of policy areas, accounts for about one-fourth of all the funds spent by state and local governments and for about 16 percent of all federal government expenditures.[15]

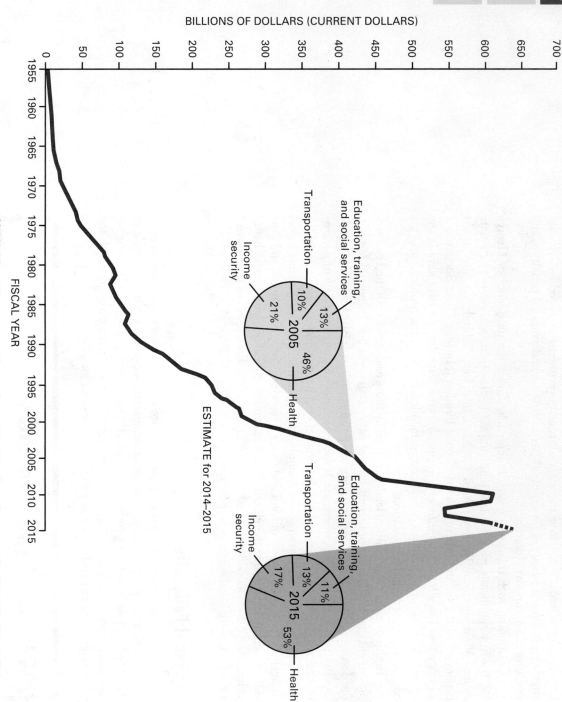

FIGURE 3.1 FISCAL FEDERALISM: FEDERAL GRANTS TO STATE AND LOCAL GOVERNMENTS

Federal grants to state and local governments have grown rapidly in recent decades and now amount to more than $640 billion per year. The sharp increase in grants for 2010 and 2011 was the result of the stimulus package designed to counter the country's financial crisis. The distribution of grants is not static. The percentage of grants devoted to health care, especially Medicaid, has increased substantially, mostly at the expense of income security programs.

BILLIONS OF DOLLARS (CURRENT DOLLARS)

FISCAL YEAR

ESTIMATE for 2014–2015

2005: Education, training, and social services 13%; Transportation 10%; Income security 21%; Health 46%

2015: Education, training, and social services 13%; Transportation 11%; Income security 17%; Health 53%

SOURCE: Office of Management and Budget, *Budget of the United States Government, Fiscal Year 2015: Historical Tables* (Washington, DC: U.S. Government Printing Office, 2014), Tables 12.1 and 12.2.

THE GRANT SYSTEM There are two major types of federal grants-in-aid for states and localities: *categorical grants* and *block grants.* **Categorical grants** are the main source of federal aid to state and local governments. These grants can be used only for specific purposes, or categories, of state and local spending.

Because direct orders from the federal government to the states are rare (an exception is the Equal Opportunity Act of 1982, which bars job discrimination by state and local governments), most federal regulation is accomplished in a more indirect manner: as you have already seen, Congress attaches conditions to the grants that states receive. Such restrictions on grants have been especially common since the 1970s.

categorical grants
Federal grants that can be used only for specific purposes, or categories, of state and local spending. They come with strings attached, such as nondiscrimination provisions.

project grants
Federal **categorical grant** given for specific purposes and awarded on the basis of the merits of applications.

formula grants
Federal **categorical grants** distributed according to a formula specified in legislation or in administrative regulations.

block grants
Federal grants given more or less automatically to states or communities to support broad programs in areas such as community development and social services.

One string commonly attached to categorical and other federal grants is a nondiscrimination provision, stating that aid may not be used for purposes that discriminate against minorities, women, or other groups. Another string, a favorite of labor unions, is that federal funds may not support construction projects that pay below the local union wage. Other restrictions may require an environmental impact statement for a federally supported construction project or provisions for community involvement in the planning of the project.

The federal government may also employ *crossover sanctions*—using federal dollars in one program to influence state and local policy in another. Crossover sanctions are applied when, for example, funds for highway construction are withheld unless states raise the drinking age to 21 or establish highway beautification programs.

Crosscutting requirements occur when a condition on one federal grant is extended to all activities supported by federal funds, regardless of their source. The grandfather of these requirements is Title VI of the 1964 Civil Rights Act, which bars discrimination in the use of federal funds on account of race, color, national origin, gender, or physical disability. For example, if a university discriminates illegally in one program—such as athletics—it may lose the federal aid it receives for all of its programs. There are also crosscutting requirements dealing with environmental protection, historic preservation, contract wage rates, access to government information, the care of experimental animals, the treatment of human subjects in research projects, and a host of other policies.

Categorical grants are of two types:

- **Project grants**, the more common type, are awarded on the basis of competitive applications. National Science Foundation grants obtained by university professors are an example.
- **Formula grants**, as their name implies, are distributed according to formulas. These formulas vary from grant to grant and may be computed on the basis of population, per capita income, percentage of rural population, or some other factor. A state or local government does not apply for a formula grant; a formula determines how much money the particular government will receive. Vigorous political battles are fought in Congress over formulas. The most common formula grants are those for Medicaid, child nutrition programs, sewage treatment plant construction, public housing, community development programs, and training and employment programs.

Complaints about the cumbersome paperwork and the many strings attached to categorical grants led to the adoption of the second major type of federal aid, **block grants**. These grants are given more or less automatically to states or communities, which then have discretion within broad areas in deciding how to spend the money. First adopted in 1966, block grants support programs in areas like community development that can be used for programs like housing and expanding employment opportunities for persons with lower incomes.

THE SCRAMBLE FOR FEDERAL DOLLARS With $640 billion in federal grants at stake, most states and many cities have established full-time staffs in Washington.[16] Their task is to identify what federal funds are available and to help their state or city obtain some of it. There are many Washington organizations of governments—the US Conference of Mayors and the National League of Cities, for example—that act like other interest groups in lobbying Congress. Senators and representatives regularly go to the voters with stories of their influence in securing federal funds for their constituencies. They need continued support at the polls, they say, so that they will rise in seniority and get key posts to help "bring home the bacon."

Despite some variations, on the whole federal grant distribution follows the principle of *universalism*: something for everybody. The vigilance of senators and representatives keeps federal aid reasonably well spread among the states. This rough parity makes good politics, but it also may undermine public policy. Title I of the 1965 Elementary and Secondary Education Act is the federal government's principal endeavor to assist public schools. The primary intent of Title I was to give extra help to poor children. Yet the funds are allocated to 95 percent of all the school districts in the country, President Bill Clinton's proposal to concentrate Chapter I funds on the poorest students failed when it ran into predictable opposition in Congress.

THE MANDATE BLUES States and localities are usually pleased to receive aid from the national government, but there are times when they would just as soon not have it. For example, say Congress decides to expand a program administered by the states and funded, in part, by the national government. It passes a law requiring the states to expand the program if they want to keep receiving aid, which most states do. Requirements that direct states or local governments to provide additional services under threat of penalties or as a condition of receiving a federal grant are a type of *mandate*. Congress usually appropriates some funds to help pay for the new policy, but whether it does or does not, the states suddenly have to budget more funds for the program just to receive federal grant money.

Medicaid, which provides health care for poor people, is a prime example of a federal grant program that puts states in a difficult situation. Administered by the states, Medicaid receives wide support from both political parties. The national government pays the majority of the bill, and the states pick up the rest. In the past two decades, Congress has moved aggressively to expand Medicaid to specific populations, requiring the states to extend coverage to children, pregnant women, and elderly poor under certain income levels. Congress has also increased its funding for the program, but the new

Point to Ponder

States usually are pleased to accept federal funds, revenue they do not have to raise themselves. The states are not always happy with the strings that come attached with federal funds, however.

Would it be better if states raised their own funds rather than depending on federal aid? Are there obstacles to states raising their own revenues?

"In Two Words, Yes And No"

A 1949 Herblock Cartoon, ©The Herb Block Foundation

requirements have meant huge new demands on state budgets. In effect, Congress has set priorities for the states. In 2012, the Supreme Court held that the Affordable Care Act of 2010 had gone too far. Congress can offer money to the states to expand Medicaid and can attach conditions to such grants, but it cannot penalize states that choose not to participate in the new program by reducing their existing Medicaid funding.[17]

A related problem arises when Congress passes a law creating financial obligations for the states but provides no funds to meet these obligations. For example, in 1990 Congress passed the Americans with Disabilities Act, requiring states to make facilities, such as state colleges and universities, accessible to individuals with disabilities, but it did not allocate funds to implement this policy. Similarly, the Clean Air Act of 1970 established national air quality standards but required states to implement them and to appropriate funds for that purpose.

In an attempt to deal with this problem, in 1995, Congress passed a law requiring the Congressional Budget Office to estimate the costs of all bills that impose such mandates. This requirement does not apply to antidiscrimination legislation or to most legislation requiring state and local governments to take various actions in exchange for continued federal funding (such as grants for transportation). The law also ordered federal agencies to design new processes to allow for greater input by state and local officials into the development of regulations imposing mandates.

Mandates coupled with insufficient federal funds continue to pose problems for state and local governments. Such governments are the first responders in most emergencies: their police forces provide most of the nation's internal security, they maintain most of the country's transportation infrastructure, and they are responsible for protecting the public's health and providing emergency health care. The heightened concern for homeland security since September 11, 2001, led Congress to impose sizable new mandates on the states to increase their ability to deal with acts of terrorism, but Congress has not provided all the resources necessary to increase state and local capabilities. Similarly, as we saw, the No Child Left Behind Act threatens school systems with the loss of federal funds if their schools do not improve student performance, but many local officials complain that the federal government has not provided a sufficient increase in funding to help their school systems bring about required improvements.

Policies of the federal government may have major impacts on core policies of state and local governments, like elementary and secondary education, and determine how much is spent on these policies.

Diversity in Policy

3.4

Explain the consequences of federalism for diversity in public policies among the states.

s you have seen, the federal system assigns states important responsibilities for public policies. An important effect is diversity in policy among the states.

One implication is that it is possible for the diversity of opinion within the country to be reflected in different public policies among the states. If the citizens of Texas wish to have a death penalty, for example, they can vote for politicians who support it, even if other states move to abolish the death penalty (see "You Are the Policymaker: Should *Whether* You Live Depend on *Where* You Live?").

Another effect of the federal system is facilitating policy innovation. The American states have always been policy innovators.[18] They overflow with reforms. From clean-air legislation to health care, the states constitute a national laboratory to develop and test public policies, and they share the results with other states and the national government. Almost every policy that the national government has adopted had its beginnings in the states. One or more states pioneered child labor laws, minimum-wage legislation, unemployment compensation, antipollution legislation, civil rights protections, and the income tax. More recently, states have been active in reforming health care, education, and welfare—and the national government has been paying close attention to their efforts.

States may also take initiatives on what most people view as national policies when the federal government acts contrary to the views of people within those states. Many states raised the minimum wage when Congress did not. Some states funded stem cell research after George W. Bush severely restricted it on the federal level. Similarly, many states have taken the lead in raising the standards for environmental protection after they concluded that the national government was too lenient. Other states have enacted strict immigration laws to deter illegal immigration.

Yet another implication of diversity is that states, responsible for supplying public services, differ in the resources they can or will devote to services like public education.

The federal government may also unintentionally create financial obligations for the states. California, New York, Texas, Florida, and other states have sued the federal government for reimbursement for the cost of health care, education, prisons, and other public services that the states provide to illegal residents. The states charged that the federal government's failure to control its borders was the source of huge new demands on their treasuries and that Washington, not the states, should pay for the problem. Although the states have not won their cases, their point is a valid one.

A combination of federal regulations and inadequate resources may also put the states in a bind. The national government requires that a local housing authority build or acquire a new low-income housing facility for each one it demolishes. But for years Congress has provided little money for the construction of public housing. As a result, a provision intended to help the poor by ensuring a stable supply of housing actually hurts them because it discourages local governments from demolishing unsafe and inadequate housing. Similarly, a few states have recently rejected some short-term federal aid for unemployment benefits because they did not want to accept the requirements to maintain the benefits in the long term.

Federal courts, too, create unfunded mandates for the states. In recent years, federal judges have issued states orders in areas such as prison construction and management, school desegregation, and facilities in mental health hospitals. These court orders often require states to spend funds to meet standards imposed by a judge.

You Are the Policymaker

Should *Whether* You Live Depend on *Where* You Live?

Because the federal system allocates major responsibilities for public policy to the states, policies among the states often vary, in keeping with the views of the citizens of the states. The differences among public policies on the criminal justice system are especially dramatic.

In 32 states, a conviction for first-degree murder may well mean the death penalty for the convicted murderer. In 18 other states and the District of Columbia, first-degree murderers are subject to a maximum penalty of life behind bars.

What do you think? Some people see diversity in public policy as one of the advantages of federalism. Others argue that citizens of the same country ought to be subject to uniform penalties. Should *whether* you live depend on *where you live?*

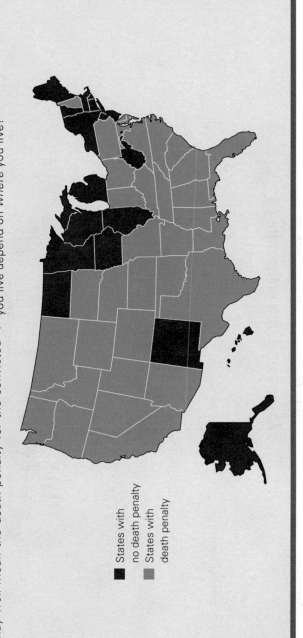

States with
no death penalty

States with
death penalty

Thus, the quality of education a child receives is heavily influenced by the state in which the child's parents happen to reside. In 2011, New York spent $19,076 per student while Utah spent only $6,212 (see Figure 3.2).

Diversity in policy can also discourage states from providing services that they might otherwise provide. Political scientists have found that generous welfare benefits can strain a state's treasury by attracting poor people from states with lower benefits. As a result, states may be deterred from providing generous benefits to those in need. A national program with uniform welfare benefits would provide no incentive for welfare recipients to move from one state to another in search of higher benefits.[19]

Understanding Federalism

3.5 Assess the impact of federalism on democratic government and the scope of government.

T he federal system is central to politics, government, and policy in America. The division of powers and responsibilities between the states and the national government has implications for the themes of both democracy and the scope of government.

FIGURE 3.2 STATE AND LOCAL SPENDING ON PUBLIC EDUCATION

A downside of the public policy diversity fostered by federalism is that the resources for public services vary widely from state to state. This map shows the great variation among the states in the money spent on children in the public schools.

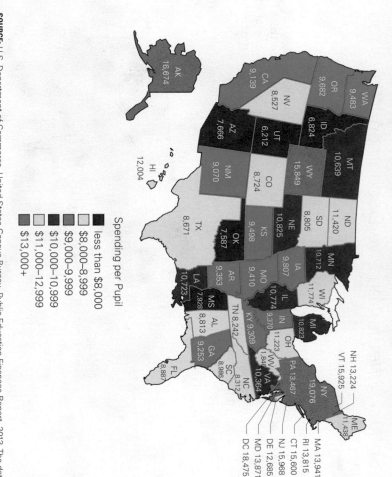

Spending per Pupil

- less than $8,000
- $8,000–8,999
- $9,000–9,999
- $10,000–10,999
- $11,000–12,999
- $13,000+

SOURCE: U.S. Department of Commerce, United States Census Bureau, Public Education Finances Report, 2013. The data are for 2011.

☐ Federalism and Democracy

One of the reasons that the Framers established a federal system was to allay the fears of those who believed that a powerful and distant central government would tyrannize the states and limit their voice in government. By decentralizing the political system, federalism was designed to contribute to democracy—or at least to the limited form of democracy supported by the Framers.

Has the federal system in fact contributed to democracy? In many ways, the answer appears to be yes.

The federal system in America decentralizes our politics. Voters elect senators as representatives of individual states, not of the entire nation. Different interests are concentrated in different states: energy in Texas, citrus growing in Florida and California, and copper mining in Montana, for example. The federal system allows an interest concentrated in a state to exercise substantial influence in the election of that state's officials, both local and national. In turn, these officials promote policies advantageous to the interest in both the state capital and Washington. This is a pluralism of interests that James Madison, among others, valued within a large republic.

Moreover, by ensuring that most disputes over policy are handled at the state and local levels, federalism reduces conflict at the national level, making democracy more effective. If every issue had to be resolved in Washington, the national government would be overwhelmed.

In providing for decision making at the state level, federalism allows for a diversity of policy choices among the states. Thus states can better reflect the preferences of majorities of their citizens. If the citizens of Texas wish to have a death penalty, for example, they can vote for politicians who support it, even if other states move to abolish the death penalty.

In addition, the more levels of government, the more opportunities there are for people to participate in politics. State and local governments provide thousands of elected offices for which citizens may vote and/or run.

Additional levels of government also contribute to democracy by increasing access to government. Some citizens and interest groups are likely to have better access to state-level governments and others to the national government, so the two levels increase the opportunities for government to be responsive to demands for policies.[20] For example, in the 1950s and 1960s, when advocates of civil rights found themselves stymied in Southern states, they turned to the national government for help in achieving racial equality. Business interests, on the other hand, have traditionally found state governments to be more responsive than the national government to their demands. Organized labor is not well established in some states, but it can usually depend on some sympathetic officials at the national level to champion its proposals.

Another advantage of federalism for democracy is that even if a party loses at the national level, it can rebuild in its areas of strength and develop leaders under its banner at the state and local levels. As a result, losing an election becomes more acceptable, and the peaceful transfer of power is more probable. The ability to rebuild politically at the state and local level was especially important in the early years of the nation before our political norms had become firmly established.

Despite these advantages, sometimes the decentralization of politics can be a detriment to democracy. Even the presidential election, choosing a leader for the national government, is actually 51 presidential elections, one in each state and one in Washington, D.C. It is possible—as happened in 2000—for a candidate who receives the most popular votes in the country to lose the election because of the way in which the Constitution distributes electoral votes by state. Such a result is a questionable contribution to democracy.[21]

Federalism may also have a negative effect on democracy insofar as local interests are able to thwart national majority support of certain policies. As we discussed earlier in this chapter, in the 1960s, the states—especially those in the South—became battlegrounds when the national government tried to enforce national civil rights laws and court decisions. Federalism complicated and delayed efforts to end racial discrimination because state and local governments were responsible for public education and voting eligibility, for example, and because they had passed most of the laws supporting racial segregation.

At last count there were an astonishing 89,055 American governments (see Table 3.3). The sheer number of governments in the United States is, at times, as much a burden as a boon to democracy. The relationships between governments at the local, state, and national levels often confuse Americans. These confusions stem from the complexities

TABLE 3.3 THE NUMBER OF GOVERNMENTS IN AMERICA

Government Level	Number of Governments
U.S. government	1
States	50
Counties	3,031
Municipalities	19,519
Townships or towns	16,360
School districts	12,880
Special districts	38,266
Total	89,055

SOURCE: U.S. Department of Commerce, U.S. Census Bureau, *Census of Governments*, 2014.

of the relationships. Locally elected school boards run neighborhood schools, but the schools also receive state and national funds, and with those funds come state and national rules and regulations. Local airports, sewage systems, pollution control systems, and police departments also receive a mix of local, state, and national funds, so they operate under a complex web of rules and regulations imposed by each level of government.

Americans often speak eloquently about their state and local governments as grassroots governments, close to the people. Yet having so many governments makes it difficult to know which levels are doing what. Exercising democratic control over them is even more difficult; voter turnout in local elections is often less than 20 percent.

Federalism and the Scope of the National Government

One of the most persistent questions in American politics has been the question of the appropriate scope of the national government relative to that of state governments. To address this question, we must first understand why the national government grew and then ask whether this growth was at the expense of the states or occurred because of the unique capabilities and responsibilities of the national government.

Consider first the economic domain, and a few examples of the national government's interventions to help American businesses. Ronald Reagan negotiated quotas on imports of Japanese cars in order to give advantages to the American auto industry. He placed quotas on the amount of steel that could be imported. After airplanes were grounded because of the terrorist attacks of September 11, 2001, Congress approved $15 billion in subsidies and loan guarantees to the faltering airlines. In 2008, George W. Bush obtained extensive authority for the federal government to intervene in and subsidize financial institutions and automakers—policies Barack Obama continued.

In each of these cases and dozens of others, the national government has involved itself (some might say interfered) in the economic marketplace with quotas, subsidies, and regulations intended to help American businesses. From the very founding of the republic, the national government took a direct interest in economic affairs. As the United States industrialized, new problems arose and, with them, new demands for governmental action. The national government responded with a national banking system, subsidies for railroads and airlines, and a host of other policies that dramatically increased its role in the economy.

The industrialization of the country raised other issues as well. For example, with the formation of large corporations in the late nineteenth century came the potential for such abuses as monopoly pricing. If there is only one railroad in town, it can charge farmers inflated prices to ship their grain to market. If a single company distributes most of the gasoline in the country, it can set the price at which gasoline sells. Thus many interests asked the national government to restrain monopolies and to encourage open competition.

There were additional demands on the national government for new public policies. Farmers sought services such as agricultural research, rural electrification, and price supports. Unions wanted the national government to protect their rights to organize and bargain collectively and to help provide safer working conditions, a minimum wage, and pension protection. Together with other groups, they pushed for a wide range of social welfare policies, from education to health care, that would benefit the average worker. And urbanization brought new problems in the areas of housing, welfare, the environment, and transportation. In each case, the relevant interests turned to the national government for help.

Why not turn to the state governments instead? The answer in most cases is simple: a problem or policy requires the authority and resources of the national government; to deal with it otherwise would be at best inefficient. The Constitution forbids states from having independent defense policies, but even if it did not, how many states would want to take on a responsibility that represents more than half the federal workforce and about one-fifth of federal expenditures? It would not be sensible for Louisiana to pass strict controls on polluting the Mississippi River if most of the river's pollution occurs upstream, where Louisiana has no jurisdiction. Rhode Island has no incentive to create an energy policy because it has no natural energy reserves.

Similarly, how effectively can any state regulate an international conglomerate such as General Motors? How can each state, acting individually, manage the nation's money supply? Although states could in theory have their own space programs, it is much more efficient to have one national program. The largest category of federal expenditures is that for economic security, including the Social Security program. If each state had its own retirement program, would retirees who moved to Florida or Arizona be paid by their new state or the state they moved from? A national program is the only feasible method of ensuring the incomes of the mobile elderly of today's society.

Figure 3.3 shows that the national government's share of American governmental expenditures has grown considerably since 1929. The period of rapid growth was the 1930s and 1940s, a period that included the Great Depression and World War II. Before that time, the national government spent an amount equal to only 2.5 percent of the size of the economy, the gross domestic product (GDP). Today, it spends nearly a fourth of our GDP, if we include grants to states and localities. The proportion of our GDP spent by state and local governments has grown far less. States and localities spent 7.4 percent of our GDP in 1929; they spend about 12 percent today, not including federal grants.[22]

To return to our initial question, Figure 3.3 strongly suggests that the federal government has not supplanted the states. The states carry out virtually all the functions they always have. What has occurred instead is that, with the support of the American people, the national government, possessing unique capacities, has taken on new responsibilities. In addition, the national government has added programs to help the states meet their own responsibilities.

FIGURE 3.3 FISCAL FEDERALISM: THE SIZE OF THE PUBLIC SECTOR

The federal government's spending as a percentage of GDP increased rapidly during the Great Depression and World War II. Recent decades have not seen much increase in spending as a percentage of GDP on the part of either the federal government or state governments. In 2009, however, federal spending increased substantially in response to the economic crisis.

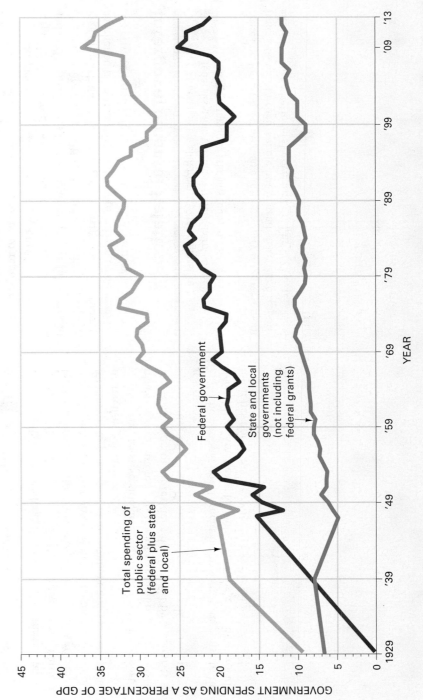

SOURCE: Office of Management and Budget, *Budget of the United States Government, Fiscal Year 2015: Historical Tables* (Washington, DC: U.S. Government Printing Office, 2014), Table 15.3.

Review the Chapter

Defining Federalism

3.1 Define federalism and contrast it with alternative ways of organizing a nation, p. 70.

Federalism is a way of organizing a nation so that two or more levels of government have formal authority over the same area and people. Federal systems are more decentralized than unitary systems but less so than confederations.

The Constitutional Basis of Federalism

3.2 Outline the constitutional basis for the division of power between national and state governments, the establishment of national supremacy, and states' obligations to each other, p. 72.

The Constitution divides power between the national (federal) government and state governments and makes the national government supreme within its sphere. The national government has implied as well as enumerated powers, as *McCulloch v. Maryland* made clear. The Civil War also helped establish the preeminence of the national government, and over the years the Supreme Court has interpreted these powers—particularly Congress's power to regulate interstate commerce—broadly, as Washington has taken on more responsibilities to deal with matters such as the economy and civil rights. States have obligations to give full faith and credit to the public acts, records, and civil judicial proceedings of other states, return a person charged with a crime in another state to that state, and accord citizens of other states the privileges and immunities enjoyed by their own citizens.

Intergovernmental Relations

3.3 Characterize the shift from dual to cooperative federalism and the role of fiscal federalism in intergovernmental relations today, p. 79.

States no longer have exclusive responsibility for government functions within their sphere but instead share these responsibilities with the federal government. Through categorical and block grants, the federal government provides state and local governments with substantial portions of their budgets, and it uses this leverage to influence policy by attaching conditions to receiving the grants. Sometimes Washington mandates state policy without providing the resources to implement the policy.

Diversity in Policy

3.4 Explain the consequences of federalism for diversity in public policies among the states, p. 88.

Federalism allows for considerable diversity among the states in their policies. This constitutional arrangement facilitates state innovations in policy, and it allows states to move beyond the limits of national policy. However, federalism also leaves states dependent upon the resources within their borders to finance public services, and it may discourage states from providing some services.

Understanding Federalism

3.5 Assess the impact of federalism on democratic government and the scope of government, p. 89.

On the positive side, federalism provides for effective representation of local interests, reduces conflict at the national level, encourages politicians and political parties to peacefully accept losing elections, and increases the opportunities for citizens to participate in government and see their policy preferences reflected in law.

On the negative side, federalism increases the opportunities for local interests to thwart national policy, can result in the election of a president not favored by a majority of the public, and complicates efforts to make government responsive.

The national government has grown in response to the demands of Americans for public services it can best provide, but it has not in any way supplanted the states.

Learn the Terms

federalism, p. 70
unitary governments, p. 70
intergovernmental relations, p. 71
supremacy clause, p. 73
Tenth Amendment, p. 74
McCulloch v. Maryland, p. 75
enumerated powers, p. 76

implied powers, p. 76
elastic clause, p. 76
Gibbons v. Ogden, p. 77
full faith and credit, p. 78
extradition, p. 78
privileges and immunities, p. 78
dual federalism, p. 80

cooperative federalism, p. 80
devolution, p. 82
fiscal federalism, p. 83
categorical grants, p. 84
project grants, p. 85
formula grants, p. 85
block grants, p. 85

Test Yourself

1. What principle did the landmark *McCulloch v. Maryland* case establish?

a. A national bank was unconstitutional.
b. Congress may use all means "necessary and proper" to fulfill its duties.
c. Federal laws may not preempt state laws.
d. National government's policies always take precedence over state policies.
e. The national government is limited to powers enumerated in the Constitution.

2. A person is suspected of murder in one state and is captured in another state. What is the procedure whereby he is returned to the state in which the crime was allegedly committed called?

a. ex post facto
b. extradition
c. full faith and credit
d. habeas corpus
e. privileges and immunities

3. How does federalism allow unity without uniformity?

a. If states adopt programs that fail, the negative effects are limited; if programs succeed, they can be adopted by other states and the national government.
b. It encourages experiments in public policy, and provides a training ground for state and local politicians to gain experience before moving to the national stage.
c. It provides numerous arenas for decision making and engages many people in the process of government, which helps keep government closer to the people.
d. National politicians and parties do not have to resolve all divisive issues; instead, these issues are debated at state, county, and municipal levels.
e. When one political party loses control of the national government, it may still hold a number of state offices and continue to challenge the party in power at the national level.

4. The Framers intended to create which type of national government?

a. confederal
b. decentralized
c. independent
d. subordinate
e. unitary

5. Which of the following is an example of cooperative federalism?

a. a public policy created by the federal government and imposed on a city
b. a public policy program funded by the national government and administered by a state government
c. a public policy program jointly funded, administered, and determined by both the national government and a state government
d. a public policy program that is funded, administered, and determined by a state government
e. a public policy program that is funded, administered, and determined by the national government

6. What can American federalism be seen as a response to?

a. concerns about the potential abuses by a strong central government
b. desire of the Founders to establish a system of government responsive to the will of the people
c. popularity of the British federal system in the colonies
d. strength of the state governments under the Articles of Confederation
e. weakness of state governments under the Articles of Confederation

7. Congress's so-called "implied powers" are directly derived from _____.

a. enumerated powers
b. habit
c. legal precedent
d. the Constitution
e. tradition

8. What was one of the major arguments in favor of devolution?

a. A large portion of Americans said that they wanted state governments to do less and the national government to take over most of the states' roles.

b. A substantial majority of Americans believed that state governments were more effective and more trustworthy than the national government.

c. Americans during the Great Depression no longer believed that the government in Washington could manage the entire nation.

d. The Articles of Confederation could not control the country, so they needed to be reviewed and rewritten.

e. The Civil War Amendments were not strong enough, so the Civil Rights Act of 1965 was created to replace them.

9. Together the states are sometimes referred to as a national laboratory. What does this refer to?

a. the competitive grants to the states for addressing major scientific and technological problems

b. the danger of political reform driven by the national government

c. the electoral system established under the Constitution

d. the fact that the multi-layered government structure in the United States represents a system that allows for a consensus of domestic affairs among the separate governing units

e. the fact that, working independently, the states have a high likelihood of developing innovative solutions

10. The largest category of federal grant-in-aid expenditures is in what area?

a. economic security
b. education
c. defense
d. health
e. homeland security

11. In practical terms, what was the most important result of the court cases *Gibbons v. Ogden* and *McCullough v. Maryland*?

a. They allowed Congress to directly affect national economic development and regulate the economy.

b. They allowed Congress to subvert the rights of states.

c. They allowed the states to create New Deal programs to combat the Great Depression.

d. They allowed the states to place tariffs on goods shipped from other states.

e. They gave regulation power over railroads and other forms of interstate commerce to the states.

12. Why might the federal government pay attention when the states work toward reforming public issues such as health care and education?

a. because the federal government is responsible for making sure states obey their own constitutions

b. because the federal government may wish to quash those reforms before they are enacted

c. because the federal government must make sure any reforms passed by one state are adopted by other states

d. because the states are much more willing to innovate when it comes to public policy than the federal government

e. because the states offer a laboratory in which public policies may be tested for future adoption by the nation as a whole

13. In contrast with federalism, the United Nations has no strong central governing body, and its power is derived from its individual member states. It most closely follows which type of government?

a. confederation
b. direct democracy
c. monarchy
d. republic
e. secretaryship

14. Political scientists have devised terms to explain various kinds of federalism. Which of these forms of federalism works to aid and to influence states and localities?

a. competitive federalism
b. cooperative federalism
c. dual federalism
d. fiscal federalism
e. marble-cake federalism

15. The Constitution grants citizens of one state comparable services to citizens of other states through the _____ provision.

a. Article IV assessment
b. faith and credit
c. privileges and immunity
d. separate but equal
e. Title I Code

16. Why did the Framers insert the interstate commerce clause into the Constitution?

a. to create virtual business arrangements with the states

b. to make it more difficult for states to work together

c. to prevent any state from changing its commercial boundaries

d. to prevent states from abusing their fiscal authority

e. to regulate all commercial activity between states

Explore Further

WEB SITES

www.cfda.gov/index?cck=1&au=&ck=
The Catalog of Federal Domestic Assistance allows you to search through hundreds of federal grants.

www.ncsl.org/statefed/StateFederalCommittees/tabid/773/Default.aspx
Information and discussion of issues on federal–state relations from the National Conference of State Legislatures.

www.csg.org
Council of State Governments Web site offers information on states and state public policies.

usgovinfo.about.com/od/rightsandfreedoms/a/federalism.htm
The powers of the national and state governments.

www.aei.org/outlook/11716
Original research on American federalism, sponsored by the American Enterprise Institute.

www.cas.umt.edu/polsci/faculty/greene/federalismhistory.htm
The history of U.S. federalism.

FURTHER READING

Bednar, Jenna. *The Robust Federation: Principles of Design.* New York: Cambridge University Press, 2009. Shows how complementary institutions maintain and adjust the distribution of authority between national and state governments.

Beer, Samuel H. *To Make a Nation: The Rediscovery of American Federalism.* Cambridge, MA: Harvard University Press, 1993. An excellent study of the philosophical bases of American federalism.

Chemerinsky, Erwin. *Enhancing Government: Federalism for the 21st Century.* Stanford, CA: Stanford Law Books, 2008. Argues that federalism allows government to solve problems and to enhance individual liberties.

Feeley, Malcolm, and Edward Rubin. *Federalism: Political Identity and Tragic Compromise.* Ann Arbor: University of Michigan Press, 2011. Overview of key aspects of federalism.

Gerston, Larry N. *American Federalism.* New York: M. E. Sharpe, 2007. A concise introduction to federalism.

Miller, Lisa L. *The Perils of Federalism: Race, Poverty, and the Politics of Crime Control.* New York: Oxford University Press, 2008. How federalism affects the making and implementation of policy regarding crime.

O'Toole, Laurence. *American Intergovernmental Relations,* 4th ed. Washington, DC: CQ Press, 2006. Essays on many aspects of federalism.

Peterson, Paul E. *The Price of Federalism.* Washington, DC: Brookings Institution, 1995. A good assessment of the costs and benefits of federalism.

Posner, Paul L., and Timothy J. Conlan. *Intergovernmental Management for the 21st Century.* Washington, DC: Brookings Institution, 2007. Assesses the state of intergovernmental relations in the United States and an agenda for improving them.

Schapiro, Robert A. *Polyphonic Federalism: Toward the Protection of Fundamental Rights.* Chicago: University of Chicago Press, 2009. Argues that the multiple perspectives on policy provided by federalism are a great advantage for the United States.

4

Civil Liberties and Public Policy

Politics in Action: Free Speech on Campus

T he Board of Regents of the University of Wisconsin System requires students at the university's Madison campus to pay an activity fee that supports various campus services and extracurricular student activities. In the university's view, such fees enhance students' educational experiences by promoting extracurricular activities, stimulating advocacy and debate on diverse points of view, enabling participation in campus administrative activity, and providing opportunities to develop social skills—all consistent with the university's broad educational mission. Registered student organizations (RSOs) expressing a wide range of views are eligible to receive a portion of the fees, which the student government administers subject to the university's approval.

There has been broad agreement that the process for approving RSO applications for funding is administered in a viewpoint-neutral fashion. RSOs may also obtain funding through a student referendum. Some students, however, sued the university, alleging that the activity fee violated their First Amendment rights because it forced them to support expressions of views they did not share. They argued that the university must grant them the choice not to fund RSOs that engage in political and ideological expression offensive to their personal beliefs.

The Supreme Court held in a unanimous decision in *Board of Regents of University of Wisconsin System v. Southworth* that, if a university determines that its mission is well served when students have the means to engage in dynamic discussion on a broad range of issues, it

4.1
Trace the process by which the Bill of Rights has been applied to the states, p. 100.

4.2
Distinguish the two types of religious rights protected by the First Amendment and determine the boundaries of those rights, p. 102.

4.3
Differentiate the rights of free expression protected by the First Amendment and determine the boundaries of those rights, p. 109.

4.4
Describe the rights to assemble and associate protected by the First Amendment and their limitations, p. 119.

4.5
Describe the right to bear arms protected by the Second Amendment and its limitation, p. 121.

4.6
Characterize defendants' rights and identify issues that arise in their implementation, p. 123.

4.7
Outline the evolution of a right to privacy and its application to the issue of abortion, p. 135.

4.8
Assess how civil liberties affect democratic government and how they both limit and expand the scope of government, p. 137.

These UCLA students are exercising their right to protest, an important civil liberty. Determining the boundaries of civil liberties often raises complex questions and may involve balancing competing values.

100

4.1
4.2
4.3
4.4
4.5
4.6
4.7
4.8

The Bill of Rights

Trace the process by which the Bill of Rights has been applied to the states.

B y 1787, all state constitutions had bills of rights, some of which survive, intact, to this day. Although the new U.S. Constitution had no bill of rights, the state ratifying conventions made its inclusion a condition of ratification. The First Congress passed the Bill of Rights in 1789 and sent it to the states for ratification. In 1791, these amendments became part of the Constitution.

Civil liberties are constitutional and other legal protections of individuals against government actions. Americans' civil liberties are set down in the **Bill of Rights**, the first 10 amendments to the Constitution. At first glance, many questions about civil liberties issues may seem straightforward. For example, the Bill of Rights' guarantee of a free press appears to mean that Americans can write what they choose. In the real world of American law, however, these issues are subtle and complex.

Disputes about civil liberties often end up in court. The Supreme Court of the United States is the final interpreter of the content and scope of our liberties; this ultimate power to interpret the Constitution accounts for the ferocious debate over presidential appointments to the Supreme Court.

Throughout this chapter you will find special features titled "You Are the Judge." Each feature describes an actual case heard by the Supreme Court and asks you to decide the case and then compare your decision with that of the Court.

To understand the specifics of American civil liberties, we must first understand the Bill of Rights.

Civil liberties

The constitutional and other legal protections against government actions. Our civil liberties are formally set down in the Bill of Rights.

Bill of Rights

The first 10 amendments to the U.S. Constitution, which define such basic liberties as freedom of religion, speech, and the press, and they guarantee defendants' rights.

- Issues of civil liberties present many vexing problems for the courts to resolve.
- For example, *is a display of the Ten Commandments on a government site simply a recognition of their historic importance to the development of law or an impermissible use of government power to establish religion?*

may impose a mandatory fee to sustain such dialogue. The Court recognized that inevitably such a fee will subsidize speech that some students find objectionable or offensive. Thus, the Court held that a university must protect students' First Amendment rights by requiring viewpoint neutrality in the allocation of funding support.

The University of Wisconsin case represents the sort of complex controversy that shapes American civil liberties. Debates about the right to abortion, the right to bear arms, the separation of church and state, and similar issues are constantly in the news. Some of these issues arise from conflicting interests. The need to protect society against crime often conflicts with society's need to protect the rights of people accused of crime. Other conflicts derive from strong differences of opinion about what is ethical, moral, or right. To some Americans, abortion is murder, the taking of a human life. To others, a woman's choice of whether to bear a child, free of governmental intrusion, is a fundamental right. Everyone, however, is affected by the extent of our civil liberties.

Deciding complex questions about civil liberties requires balancing competing values, such as maintaining an open system of expression while protecting individuals from the excesses such a system may produce. Civil liberties are essential to democracy. How could we have free elections without free speech, for example? But does it follow that critics of officials should be able to say whatever they want, no matter how untrue? And who should decide the extent of our liberty? Should it be a representative institution such as Congress or a judicial elite such as the Supreme Court?

The role of the government in resolving civil liberties controversies is also the subject of much debate. Conservatives usually advocate narrowing the scope of government, yet many conservatives strongly support government-imposed limits on abortion and government-sanctioned prayers in public schools. They also want government to be less hindered by concern for defendants' rights. Liberals, who typically support a broader scope of government, usually want to limit government's role in prohibiting abortion and encouraging religious activities and to place greater constraints on government's freedom of action in the criminal justice system.

4.1

4.2

4.3

4.4

4.5

4.6

4.7

4.8

101

☐ The Bill of Rights—Then and Now

The Bill of Rights ensures Americans' basic liberties, such as freedom of speech and religion and protection against arbitrary searches and being held for long periods without trial (see Table 4.1). When the Bill of Rights was ratified, British abuses of the colonists' civil liberties were still a fresh and bitter memory. Colonial officials had jailed newspaper editors, arrested citizens without cause, and detained people and forced them to confess at gunpoint or worse. Thus, the first 10 amendments enjoyed great popular support.

Political scientists have discovered that Americans are devotees of rights in theory; their support often wavers when it comes time to put those rights into practice, however.[1] For example, Americans in general believe in freedom of speech, but many citizens oppose letting the Ku Klux Klan speak in their neighborhood or allowing public schools to teach about atheism or homosexuality. In addition, Americans seem willing to trade civil liberties for security when they feel that the nation is threatened, as in the case of terrorism.[2] Because few rights are absolute, we cannot avoid the difficult questions of how to balance civil liberties with other individual and societal values.

TABLE 4.1 THE BILL OF RIGHTS

These amendments were passed by Congress on September 25, 1789, and ratified by the states on December 15, 1791.

Amendment I—Religion, Speech, the Press, Assembly, Petition

Congress shall make no law respecting an establishment of religion, or prohibiting the free exercise thereof; or abridging the freedom of speech, or of the press; or the right of the people peaceably to assemble, and to petition the Government for a redress of grievances.

Amendment II—Right to Bear Arms

A well regulated Militia, being necessary to the security of a free State, the right of the people to keep and bear Arms, shall not be infringed.

Amendment III—Quartering of Soldiers

No Soldier shall, in time of peace be quartered in any house, without the consent of the Owner, nor in time of war, but in a manner to be prescribed by law.

Amendment IV—Searches and Seizures

The right of the people to be secure in their persons, houses, papers, and effects, against unreasonable searches and seizures, shall not be violated, and no Warrants shall issue, but upon probable cause, supported by Oath or affirmation, and particularly describing the place to be searched, and the persons or things to be seized.

Amendment V—Grand Juries, Double Jeopardy, Self-Incrimination, Due Process, Eminent Domain

No person shall be held to answer to a capital, or otherwise infamous crime, unless on a presentment or indictment of a Grand Jury, except in cases arising in the land or naval forces, or in the Militia, when in actual service in time of war or public danger; nor shall any person be subject for the same offense to be twice put in jeopardy of life or limb; nor shall be compelled in any criminal case to be a witness against himself, nor be deprived of life, liberty, or property, without due process of law; nor shall private property be taken for public use, without just compensation.

Amendment VI—Criminal Court Procedures

In all criminal prosecutions, the accused shall enjoy the right to a speedy and public trial, by an impartial jury of the State and district wherein the crime shall have been committed, which district shall have been previously ascertained by law, and to be informed of the nature and cause of the accusation; to be confronted with the witnesses against him; to have compulsory process for obtaining witnesses in his favor, and to have the Assistance of Counsel for his defence.

Amendment VII—Trial by Jury in Common-Law Cases

In Suits at common law, where the value in controversy shall exceed twenty dollars, the right of trial by jury shall be preserved, and no fact tried by a jury, shall be otherwise re-examined in any Court of the United States, than according to the rules of the common law.

Amendment VIII—Bails, Fines, and Punishment

Excessive bail shall not be required, nor excessive fines imposed, nor cruel and unusual punishments inflicted.

Amendment IX—Rights Retained by the People

The enumeration in the Constitution, of certain rights, shall not be construed to deny or disparage others retained by the people.

Amendment X—Rights Reserved to the States

The powers not delegated to the United States by the Constitution, nor prohibited by it to the States, are reserved to the States respectively, or to the people.

SOURCE: U.S Constitution, The Ten Amendments

102

4.1
4.2
4.3
4.4
4.5
4.6
4.7
4.8

☐ The Bill of Rights and the States

Take another look at the **First Amendment**. Note the first words: "Congress shall make no law. . . ." The Founders wrote the Bill of Rights to restrict the powers of the new national government. In 1791, Americans were comfortable with their state governments; after all, every state constitution had its own bill of rights. But a literal reading of the First Amendment suggests that it does not prohibit a state government from passing a law prohibiting the free exercise of religion, free speech, or freedom of the press.

What happens if a state passes a law that violates one of the rights protected by the federal Bill of Rights and the state's constitution does not prohibit this abridgment of freedom? In 1833, the answer to that question was "nothing." The Bill of Rights, said the Supreme Court in *Barron v. Baltimore*, restrained only the national government, not states or cities.

An opening toward a different answer was provided by the **Fourteenth Amendment**, one of the three "Civil War amendments," which was ratified in 1868. The Fourteenth Amendment declares,

> No State shall make or enforce any law which shall abridge the privileges or immunities of citizens of the United States nor shall any State deprive any person of life, liberty, or property, without due process of law; nor deny to any person within its jurisdiction the equal protection of the laws.

Nonetheless, in the Slaughterhouse Cases (1873), the Supreme Court gave a narrow interpretation of the Fourteenth Amendment's *privileges or immunities clause*, concluding that it applied only to national citizenship and not state citizenship and thus did little to protect citizens against state actions.

In 1925, in *Gitlow v. New York*, however, the Court relied on the Fourteenth Amendment to rule that a state government must respect some First Amendment rights. Specifically, the Court said that freedoms of speech and press "were fundamental personal rights and liberties protected by the **due process clause** of the Fourteenth Amendment from impairment by the states." In effect, the Court interpreted the Fourteenth Amendment to say that states could not abridge the freedoms of expression protected by the First Amendment.

This decision began the development of the **incorporation doctrine**, the legal concept under which the Supreme Court has nationalized the Bill of Rights by making most of its provisions applicable to the states through the Fourteenth Amendment. In *Gitlow*, the Supreme Court held only parts of the First Amendment to be binding on the states. Gradually, and especially during the 1960s, the Court applied most of the Bill of Rights to the states (see Table 4.2). Many of the decisions that nationalized provisions of the Bill of Rights were controversial. Nevertheless, today the Bill of Rights guarantees individual freedoms against infringement by state and local governments as well as by the national government. Only the Third and Seventh Amendments, the grand jury requirement of the Fifth Amendment, and the prohibition against excessive fines and bail in the Eighth Amendment have not been applied specifically to the states.

Freedom of Religion

4.2
Distinguish the two types of religious rights protected by the First Amendment and determine the boundaries of those rights.

The First Amendment contains two elements regarding religion and government. These elements are commonly referred to as the establishment clause and the free exercise clause. The **establishment clause** states that "Congress shall make no law respecting an establishment of religion."

TABLE 4.2 THE INCORPORATION OF THE BILL OF RIGHTS

Date	Amendment	Right	Case
1925	First	Freedom of speech	Gitlow v. New York
1931	First	Freedom of the press	Near v. Minnesota
1937	First	Freedom of assembly	De Jonge v. Oregon
1940	First	Free exercise of religion	Cantwell v. Connecticut
1947	First	Establishment of religion	Everson v. Board of Education
1958	First	Freedom of association	NAACP v. Alabama
1963	First	Right to petition government	NAACP v. Button
2010	Second	Right to bear arms	McDonald v. Chicago
	Third	No quartering of soldiers	Not incorporated[a]
1949	Fourth	No unreasonable searches and seizures	Wolf v. Colorado
1961	Fourth	Exclusionary rule	Mapp v. Ohio
1897	Fifth	Guarantee of just compensation	Chicago, Burlington, and Quincy RR v. Chicago
1964	Fifth	Immunity from self-incrimination	Mallory v. Hogan
1969	Fifth	Immunity from double jeopardy	Benton v. Maryland
	Fifth	Right to grand jury indictment	Not incorporated
1932	Sixth	Right to counsel in capital cases	Powell v. Alabama
1948	Sixth	Right to public trial	In re Oliver
1963	Sixth	Right to counsel in felony cases	Gideon v. Wainwright
1965	Sixth	Right to confrontation of witnesses	Pointer v. Texas
1966	Sixth	Right to impartial jury	Parker v. Gladden
1967	Sixth	Right to speedy trial	Klopfer v. North Carolina
1967	Sixth	Right to compulsory process for obtaining witnesses	Washington v. Texas
1968	Sixth	Right to jury trial for serious crimes	Duncan v. Louisiana
1972	Sixth	Right to counsel for all crimes involving jail terms	Argersinger v. Hamlin
	Seventh	Right to jury trial in civil cases	Not incorporated
1962	Eighth	Freedom from cruel and unusual punishment	Robinson v. California
	Eighth	Freedom from excessive fines or bail	Not incorporated
1965	Ninth	Right of privacy	Griswold v. Connecticut

[a]The quartering of soldiers has not occurred under the Constitution.

The **free exercise clause** prohibits the abridgment of citizens' freedom to worship or not to worship as they please. Sometimes these freedoms conflict. The government's practice of providing chaplains on military bases is one example of this conflict; some accuse the government of establishing religion in order to ensure that members of the armed forces can freely practice their religion. Usually, however, the establishment clause and the free exercise clause cases raise different kinds of conflicts. Religious issues and controversies have assumed importance in political debate in recent years,[3] so it is not surprising that interpretations of the Constitution are intertwined with partisan politics.

free exercise clause
A First Amendment provision that prohibits government from interfering with the practice of religion.

☐ The Establishment Clause

Some nations, such as Great Britain, have an established church that is officially supported by the government and recognized as a national institution. Some American colonies at one time had official churches, but the religious persecutions that incited many colonists to move to America discouraged the First Congress from establishing

Lemon v. Kurtzman
The 1971 Supreme Court decision that established that aid to church-related schools must (1) have a secular legislative purpose; (2) have a primary effect that neither advances nor inhibits religion; and (3) not foster excessive government entanglement with religion.

Zelman v. Simmons-Harris
The 2002 Supreme Court decision that upheld a state vouchers program providing families with vouchers that could be used to pay for tuition at religious schools.

a national church in the United States. Thus, the First Amendment prohibits an established national religion.

It is much less clear, however, what else the First Congress intended to include in the establishment clause. Some people argued that it meant only that the government could not favor one religion over another. In contrast, Thomas Jefferson argued that the First Amendment created a "wall of separation" between church and state, forbidding not just favoritism but also any support for religion at all. These interpretations continue to provoke argument, especially when religion is mixed with education, as occurs with such issues as government aid to church-related schools and prayer in public schools.

EDUCATION Proponents of aid to church-related schools argue that it does not favor any specific religion. Some opponents reply that the Roman Catholic Church has by far the largest religious school system in the country and gets most of the aid. It was Lyndon B. Johnson, a Protestant, who in 1965 obtained the passage of the first substantial aid to parochial elementary and secondary schools. He argued that the aid went to students, not schools, and thus should go wherever the students were, including church-related schools.

In **Lemon v. Kurtzman** (1971), the Supreme Court declared that laws that provide aid to church-related schools must do the following:

1. Have a secular legislative purpose
2. Have a primary effect that neither advances nor inhibits religion
3. Not foster an excessive government "entanglement" with religion

Since *Lemon*, the Court has had to draw a fine line between aid that is permissible and aid that is not. For instance, the Court has allowed religiously affiliated colleges and universities to use public funds to construct buildings. Public funds may also be used to provide students in parochial schools with textbooks, computers and other instructional equipment, lunches, and transportation to and from school, and to administer standardized testing services. However, schools may not use public funds to pay teacher salaries or to provide transportation for students on field trips. The theory underlying these decisions is that it is possible to determine that buildings, textbooks, lunches, school buses, and standardized tests are not used to support sectarian education. However, determining how teachers handle a subject in class or focus a field trip may require complex and constitutionally impermissible regulation of religion.

In an important loosening of its constraints on aid to parochial schools, the Supreme Court decided in 1997 in *Agostini v. Felton* that public school systems could send teachers into parochial schools to teach remedial and supplemental classes to needy children. In a landmark decision in 2002, the Court in **Zelman v. Simmons-Harris** upheld a program that provided some families in Cleveland, Ohio, with vouchers they could use to pay tuition at religious schools.

RELIGIOUS ACTIVITIES IN PUBLIC SCHOOLS In recent decades, the Supreme Court has also been opening public schools to religious activities. The Court decided that public universities that permit student groups to use their facilities must allow student religious groups on campus to use the facilities for religious worship.[4] In the 1984 Equal Access Act, Congress made it unlawful for any public high school receiving federal funds (almost all of them do) to keep student groups from using school facilities for religious worship if the school opens its facilities for other student meetings.[5] In 2001 the Supreme Court extended this principle to public elementary schools.[6] Similarly, in 1993, the Court required public schools that rent facilities to secular organizations to do the same for religious groups.[7]

Beyond the use of school facilities there is the question of the use of public funds for religious activities in public school contexts. In 1995 the Court held that the University of Virginia was constitutionally required to subsidize a student religious magazine on the same basis as other student publications.[8] However, in 2004 the Court held that the state of Washington could exclude students pursuing a devotional theology degree from its general scholarship program.[9]

The threshold of constitutional acceptability becomes higher when public funds are used more directly for education. Thus school authorities may not permit religious instructors to come into public school buildings during the school day to provide religious education,[10] although they may release students from part of the compulsory school day to receive religious instruction elsewhere.[11] In 1980 the Court prohibited the posting of the Ten Commandments on the walls of public classrooms.[12]

Two particularly contentious topics related to religion in public schools are school prayer and the teaching of "alternatives" to the theory of evolution.

SCHOOL PRAYER In *Engel v. Vitale* (1962) and *School District of Abington Township, Pennsylvania v. Schempp* (1963), the Supreme Court aroused the wrath of many Americans by ruling that requiring public school students to recite a prayer violates the establishment clause; in the second case, it made a similar ruling about requiring students to recite passages from the Bible. In the 1963 decision, the justices observed that "the place of religion in our society is an exalted one . . . [but] in the relationship between man and religion, the State is firmly committed to a position of neutrality."

It is *not* unconstitutional, of course, to pray in public schools. Students may pray silently as much as they wish. What the Constitution forbids is the sponsorship or encouragement of prayer, directly or indirectly, by public school authorities. Thus the Court has ruled that school-sponsored prayer at a public school graduation[13] and student-led prayer at football games are unconstitutional.[14] When several Alabama laws authorized public schools to hold one-minute periods of silence for "meditation or voluntary prayer," the Court rejected its approach because the state made it clear that the purpose of the statute was to return prayer to public schools. The Court indicated that a less clumsy approach would pass its scrutiny.[15]

One of the most controversial issues regarding the First Amendment's prohibition of the establishment of religion is prayer in public schools. Although students may pray on their own, school authorities may not sponsor or encourage prayer. Some schools violate the law, however.

• *What was your experience with prayer in school?*

Many school districts have simply ignored the Supreme Court's ban on school prayer and continue to allow prayers in their classrooms. Some religious groups and many members of Congress, especially conservative Republicans, have pushed for a constitutional amendment permitting prayer in school. A majority of the public consistently supports school prayer.[16]

EVOLUTION Fundamentalist and evangelical Christian groups have pressed some state legislatures to mandate the teaching of "creation science"—their alternative to Darwin's theory of evolution—in public schools. Louisiana, for example, passed a law requiring schools that taught Darwinian theory to teach creation science too. In 1987 the Supreme Court ruled that this law violated the establishment clause.[17] The Court had already held, in a 1968 case, that states cannot prohibit Darwin's theory of evolution from being taught in the public schools.[18] More recently, some groups have advocated, as an alternative to evolution, "intelligent design," the view that living things are too complicated to have resulted from natural selection and thus must be the result of an intelligent cause. Although they claim that their belief has no religious implications, lower courts have begun to rule that requiring teachers to present intelligent design as an alternative to evolution is a constitutionally unacceptable promotion of religion in the classroom.

PUBLIC DISPLAYS The Supreme Court has also struggled to interpret the establishment clause in other areas. In 2005 the Court found that two Kentucky counties violated the establishment clause when they posted large, readily visible copies of the Ten Commandments in their courthouses, concluding that the counties' primary purpose was to advance religion.[19] However, the Court did not hold that it is never constitutional for a governmental body to integrate a sacred text constitutionally into a governmental display on law or history. Thus in 2005, the Court held that Texas could include a monolith inscribed with the Ten Commandments among the 21 historical markers and 17 monuments surrounding the Texas State Capitol. The Court argued that a display that simply has religious content or promotes a message consistent with a religious doctrine does not run afoul of the establishment clause. Texas's placement of the Commandments monument on its capitol grounds was a far more passive use of those texts than their posting in elementary school classrooms and also served a legitimate historical purpose.[20] The Court has also upheld saying a prayer to open a legislative session.[21]

Displays of religious symbols during the holidays have prompted considerable controversy. In 1984 the Court found that Pawtucket, Rhode Island, could set up a Christmas nativity scene on public property—along with Santa's house and sleigh, Christmas trees, and other symbols of the Christmas season.[22] Five years later, the Court extended the principle to a Hanukkah menorah placed next to a Christmas tree. The Court concluded that these displays had a secular purpose and provided little or no benefit to religion. At the same time, the Court invalidated the display of the nativity scene in a courthouse because it was not accompanied by secular symbols and thus gave the impression of endorsing a religious message.[23]

Why It Matters to You
The Establishment Clause

What if the Constitution did not prohibit the establishment of religion? If a dominant religion received public funds and was in a position to control health care, public education, and other important aspects of public policy, public policies might well reflect the values and beliefs of that religion. In addition, the potential for conflict between followers of the established religion and adherents of other religions would be substantial.

The Court's basic position is that the Constitution does not require complete separation of church and state; it mandates accommodation of all religions and forbids hostility toward any. At the same time, the Constitution forbids government endorsement of religious beliefs. Drawing the line between neutrality toward religion and promotion of it is not easy; this dilemma ensures that cases involving the establishment of religion will continue to come before the Court.

☐ The Free Exercise Clause

The First Amendment also guarantees the free exercise of religion. This guarantee seems simple enough. Whether people hold no religious beliefs, practice voodoo, or go to a church, a temple, or a mosque, they should have the right to practice religion as they choose. In general, Americans are tolerant of those with religious views outside the mainstream, as you can see in "America in Perspective: Tolerance for the Free Speech Rights of Religious Extremists."[24]

The matter is, of course, more complicated. Religions sometimes forbid actions that society thinks are necessary; conversely, religions may require actions that society finds unacceptable. For example, what if a religion justifies multiple marriages or the use of illegal drugs? Muhammad Ali, the boxing champion, refused induction into the armed services during the Vietnam War because, he said, military service would violate his Muslim faith. Amish parents often refuse to send their children to public schools. Jehovah's Witnesses and Christian Scientists may refuse to accept blood transfusions and certain other kinds of medical treatment for themselves or their children.

America in Perspective

Tolerance for the Free Speech Rights of Religious Extremists

Despite 9/11, Americans are more tolerant of the free speech rights of religious extremists than are people in other democracies with developed economies.

Question: There are some people whose views are considered extreme by the majority. Consider religious extremists, that is, people who believe that their religion is the only true faith and all other religions should be considered enemies. Do you think such people should be allowed to hold public meetings to express their views?

CRITICAL THINKING QUESTION

Why do you think Americans are so tolerant?

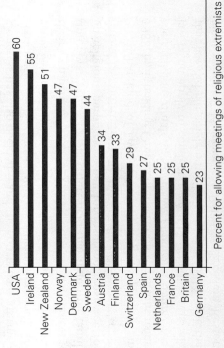

	Percent for allowing meetings of religious extremists
USA	60
Ireland	55
New Zealand	51
Norway	47
Denmark	47
Sweden	44
Austria	34
Finland	33
Switzerland	29
Spain	27
Netherlands	25
France	25
Britain	25
Germany	23

SOURCE: Authors' analysis of 2008 International Social Survey Program data.

Cassius Clay was the world heavyweight boxing champion before he converted to Islam, changed his name to Muhammad Ali, and was drafted during the war in Vietnam. Arguing that he opposed war on religious grounds, he refused to join the army. The federal government prosecuted him for draft dodging, and he was stripped of his title. In 1971, the Supreme Court overturned his conviction for draft evasion. He is pictured here at the Houston induction center in 1967.

Consistently maintaining that people have an inviolable right to *believe* whatever they want, the courts have been more cautious about the right to *practice* a belief. What if, the Supreme Court once asked, a person "believed that human sacrifices were a necessary part of religious worship?" Not all religious practices receive constitutional protection. Thus, over the years, the Court has upheld laws and regulations forbidding polygamy, prohibiting business activities on Sunday (restricting the commerce of Orthodox Jews, for whom Sunday is a workday), denying tax exemptions to religious schools that discriminate on the basis of race,[25] allowing the building of a road through ground sacred to some Native Americans, and even prohibiting a Jewish air force captain from wearing his yarmulke while on duty. (Congress later intervened to permit military personnel to wear yarmulkes.)

At the same time, Congress and the Supreme Court have granted protection to a range of religiously motivated practices. The Court has allowed Amish parents to take their children out of school after the eighth grade, reasoning that the Amish community is well established and that its children will not burden the state.[26] More broadly, parents have a right to send their children to accredited religious schools rather than public schools. A state may not require Jehovah's Witnesses or members of other religions to participate in public school flag-saluting ceremonies. Congress has also decided—and the courts have affirmed—that people can become conscientious objectors to war on religious grounds. The free exercise clause prevents government from interfering with the freedom of religious groups to select their own personnel, so religious groups are not subject to employment discrimination laws.[27] In 2014 the Court held that requiring family-owned corporations run on religious purposes to pay for insurance coverage for contraception violated a federal law protecting religious freedom.[28]

What kind of laws restricting religious practices might be constitutional? In 1988, in upholding Oregon's prosecution of persons using the drug peyote as part of their religious rituals (*Employment Division v. Smith*), the Court decided that a state law could apply to conduct, even if the conduct was religiously inspired, as long as that law did not single out religious practices because they were engaged in for religious reasons.[29] However, the Religious Freedom Restoration Act, which Congress passed in 1993 and which applies only to the national government,[30] requires laws to meet a more restrictive standard: a law or regulation cannot interfere with religious practices unless the government can show that it is narrowly tailored and in pursuit of a "compelling interest." The Court in a 2006 decision allowed a small religious sect to use a hallucinogenic tea in its rituals despite the federal government's attempts to bar its use.[31]

In 2000, Congress passed legislation that, in accordance with the "compelling interest" standard, made it more difficult for local governments to enforce zoning or other regulations on religious groups and required governments to allow those institutionalized in state facilities (such as prisons) to practice their faith. The Supreme Court upheld this law in 2005.[32] For a case involving a city's ban on ritual animal sacrifices, see "You Are the Judge: The Case of Animal Sacrifices."

Freedom of Expression

> 4.3 Differentiate the rights of free expression protected by the First Amendment and determine the boundaries of those rights.

 democracy depends on the free expression of ideas. Thoughts that are muffled, speech that is forbidden, and meetings that cannot be held are the enemies of the democratic process. Totalitarian governments know this, which is why they go to enormous trouble to limit expression.

Americans pride themselves on their free and open society. Freedom of conscience is absolute; Americans can *believe* whatever they want. The First Amendment plainly forbids the national government from limiting freedom of *expression*—that is, the right to say or publish what one believes. Is freedom of expression, then, like freedom of conscience, *absolute*? Most experts answer "no." Supreme Court justice Oliver Wendell Holmes offered a classic example of impermissible speech in 1919: "The most stringent protection of free speech would not protect a man in falsely shouting 'fire' in a theater and causing a panic."

You Are the Judge
The Case of Animal Sacrifices

The church of Lukumi Babalu Aye, in Hialeah, Florida, practiced Santeria, a Caribbean-based mix of African ritual, voodoo, and Catholicism. Central to Santeria is the ritual sacrifice of animals—at birth, marriage, and death rites as well as at ceremonies to cure the sick and initiate new members.

Offended by these rituals, the city of Hialeah passed ordinances prohibiting animal sacrifices in religious ceremonies. The church challenged the constitutionality of these laws, claiming they violated the free exercise clause of the First Amendment because the ordinances essentially barred the practice of Santeria. The city, the Santerians claimed, was discriminating against a religious minority. Besides, many other forms of killing animals were legal, including fishing, using animals in medical research, selling lobsters to be boiled alive, and feeding live rats to snakes.

YOU BE THE JUDGE:

Do the Santerians have a constitutional right to sacrifice animals in their religious rituals? Does the city's interest in protecting animals outweigh the Santerians' requirement for animal sacrifice?

DECISION:

In 1993, the Court overturned the Hialeah ordinances that prohibited the use of animal sacrifice in religious ritual. In *Church of the Lukumi Babalu Aye, Inc. v. City of Hialeah*, the justices concluded that governments that permit other forms of killing animals may not then ban sacrifices or ritual killings. In this instance, the Court found no compelling state interest that justified the abridgment of the freedom of religion.

prior restraint
Government actions that prevent material from being published. As confirmed in *Near v. Minnesota*, prior restraint is usually prohibited by the First Amendment.

Near v. Minnesota
The 1931 Supreme Court decision holding that the First Amendment protects newspapers from prior restraint.

Given that not all speech is permissible, the courts have had to address two questions in deciding where to draw the line separating permissible from impermissible speech. First, can the government censor speech that it thinks will violate the law? Second, what constitutes *speech* (or press) within the meaning of the First Amendment and thus deserves constitutional protection, and what does not?

Holding a political rally to attack an opposing candidate's stand receives First Amendment protection. Obscenity and libel and incitements to violence and overthrow of the government do not. But just how do we know, for example, what is obscene? To complicate matters further, certain forms of nonverbal speech, such as picketing, are considered symbolic speech and receive First Amendment protection. Judges also have had to balance freedom of expression against competing values, such as public order, national security, and the right to a fair trial. Then there are questions regarding commercial speech. Does it receive the same protection as religious and political speech? Regulating the publicly owned airwaves raises yet another set of difficult questions.

One controversial freedom of expression issue involves so-called hate speech. Advocates of regulating hate speech forcefully argue that, for example, racial insults, like fighting words, are "undeserving of First Amendment protection because the perpetrator's intent is not to discover the truth or invite dialogue, but to injure the victim."[33] In contrast, critics of hate speech policy argue that "sacrificing free speech rights is too high a price to pay to advance the cause of equality."[34] In 1992, the Supreme Court ruled that legislatures and universities may not single out racial, religious, or sexual insults or threats for prosecution as "hate speech" or "bias crimes."[35]

Prior Restraint

In the United States, the First Amendment ensures that even if the government frowns on some material, a person's right to publish it is all but inviolable. That is, it ensures that there will not be **prior restraint**, government actions that prevent material from being published—or, in a word, censorship. A landmark case involving prior restraint is *Near v. Minnesota* (1931). A blunt newspaper editor called local officials a string of names including "grafters" and "Jewish gangsters." The state closed down his business, preventing him from publishing, but the Supreme Court ordered the paper reopened.[36] Of course, the newspaper editor could later be punished for violating a law or someone's rights (such as not to be libeled) *after* publication.

The extent of an individual's or group's freedom from prior restraint does depend in part, however, on who that individual or group is. Expressions of students in public school may be limited more than those of adults in other settings. In 1988 the Supreme Court ruled that a high school newspaper was not a public forum and could be regulated in "any reasonable manner" by school officials.[37] In 2007, the Court held that the special characteristics of the school environment and the governmental interest in stopping student drug abuse allow schools to restrict student expressions that they reasonably regard as promoting such abuse.[38]

In the name of national security, the Supreme Court has also upheld restrictions on the right to publish. Wartime often brings widely supported censorship to protect classified information. Few want to publish troop movement plans during a war. The constitutional restrictions have not been limited to wartime censorship. Former CIA officials have to meet their contractual obligations to submit books about their work to the agency for censorship, even though the books revealed no classified information.[39] In recent years, WikiLeaks has published hundreds of thousands of classified government documents covering a wide range of foreign policy issues. The U.S. Department of Justice has opened a criminal probe of WikiLeaks founder Julian Assange. The government is similarly pursuing Edward Snowden for divulging documents related to electronic surveillance.

Nevertheless, the courts are reluctant to issue injunctions prohibiting the publication of material, even on the grounds of national security. The most famous case regarding prior restraint and national security involved stolen papers concerning the war in Vietnam. You can examine this case in "You Are the Judge: The Case of the Purloined Pentagon Papers."

☐ Free Speech and Public Order

In wartime and peacetime, considerable conflict has arisen over the tradeoff between free speech and the need for public order. During World War I, Charles T. Schenck, the secretary of the American Socialist Party, distributed thousands of leaflets urging young men to resist the draft. Schenck was convicted of impeding the war effort. In *Schenck v. United States* (1919) the Supreme Court upheld his conviction. Justice Holmes declared that government could limit speech if it provokes a clear and present danger of substantive evils. But only when such danger exists can government restrain speech. It is difficult to say, of course, when speech becomes dangerous rather than simply inconvenient for the government.

The courts confronted the issue of free speech and public order in the late 1940s and early 1950s, when there was widespread fear that communists had infiltrated the government. American anticommunism was a powerful force, and the national government was determined to jail the leaders of the Communist Party. On the basis of the Smith Act of 1940, which forbade advocating the violent overthrow of the American government, Senator Joseph McCarthy and others in Congress persecuted people whom they thought were subversive. In *Dennis v. United States* (1951), the Supreme Court upheld prison sentences for several Communist Party leaders for conspiring to advocate the violent overthrow of the government—even in the absence of evidence that they actually urged people to commit specific acts of violence.

Schenck v. United States
A 1919 Supreme Court decision upholding the conviction of a socialist who had urged resistance to the draft during World War I. Justice Holmes declared that government can limit speech if the speech provokes a "clear and present danger" of substantive evils.

You Are the Judge
The Case of the Purloined Pentagon Papers

During the Johnson administration, the Department of Defense amassed an elaborate secret history of American involvement in the Vietnam War that included hundreds of documents, many of them classified cables, memos, and war plans. Many documented American ineptitude and South Vietnamese duplicity. One former Pentagon official, Daniel Ellsberg, had become disillusioned with the Vietnam War and retained a copy of these Pentagon papers. Hoping that revelations of the Vietnam quagmire would help end American involvement, Ellsberg decided to leak the Pentagon papers to the *New York Times*.

The Nixon administration pulled out all the stops in its effort to embarrass Ellsberg and prevent publication of the Pentagon papers. Nixon's chief domestic affairs adviser, John Ehrlichman, approved a burglary of Ellsberg's psychiatrist's office, hoping to find damaging information on Ellsberg. (The burglary was bungled, and it eventually led to Ehrlichman's conviction and imprisonment.) In the courts, Nixon administration lawyers sought an injunction against the *Times* that would have

ordered it to cease publication of the secret documents. Government lawyers argued that national security was being breached and that Ellsberg had stolen the documents from the government. The *Times* argued that its freedom to publish would be violated if an injunction were granted. In 1971, the case of *New York Times v. United States* was decided by the Supreme Court.

YOU BE THE JUDGE:

Did the *Times* have a right to publish secret, stolen Department of Defense documents?

DECISION:

In a 6-to-3 decision, a majority of the justices agreed that the "no prior restraint" rule prohibited prosecution before the papers were published. The justices also made it clear that if the government brought prosecution for theft, the Court might be sympathetic. No such charges were filed.

Roth v. United States
A 1957 Supreme Court decision ruling that "obscenity is not within the area of constitutionally protected speech or press."

The prevailing political climate often determines what limits the government will place on free speech. During the early 1950s, Senator Joseph McCarthy's persuasive—if unproven—accusations that many public officials were communists created an atmosphere in which the courts placed restrictions on freedom of expression—restrictions that would be unacceptable today.

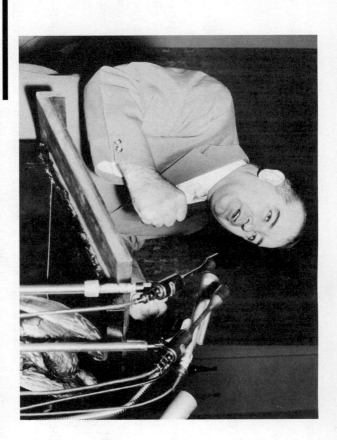

Although the activities of this tiny, unpopular group resembled yelling "Fire!" in an *empty* theater rather than a crowded one, the Court ruled that a communist takeover was so grave a danger that the government could squelch the threat. Thus, the Court concluded that protecting national security outweighed First Amendment rights.

Soon the political climate changed, however, and the Court narrowed the interpretation of the Smith Act, making it more difficult to prosecute dissenters. In later years, the Court has found that it is permissible to advocate the violent overthrow of the government in the abstract but not actually to incite anyone to imminent lawless action (*Yates v. United States* [1957]; *Brandenburg v. Ohio* [1969]).

The 1960s brought waves of protest over political, economic, racial, and social issues, and, especially, the Vietnam War. Many people in more recent times have engaged in public demonstrations, such as those opposing the war in Iraq or protesting against Wall Street. Courts have been quite supportive of the right to protest, pass out leaflets, or gather signatures on petitions—as long as it is done in public places. People may even distribute campaign literature anonymously.[40] First Amendment free speech guarantees do not apply when a person is on private property,[41] however, although a state may include within its own free speech guarantee politicking in shopping centers.[42] Moreover, cities cannot bar residents from posting signs on their own property.[43]

☐ Obscenity

Obscenity is one of the more perplexing of free speech issues. In 1957, in *Roth v. United States*, the Supreme Court held that "obscenity is not within the area of constitutionally protected speech or press." Deciding what is obscene, however, has never been an easy matter. Obviously, public standards vary from time to time, place to place, and person to person. Many of today's music videos would have been banned only a few decades ago. What might be acceptable in Manhattan's Greenwich Village would shock residents of some other areas of the country. Works that some people call obscene might be good entertainment or even great art to others. At one time or another, the works of Aristophanes, Mark Twain, and even the "Tarzan" stories by Edgar Rice Burroughs were banned. The state of Georgia banned the acclaimed film *Carnal Knowledge* (the Supreme Court struck down the ban in 1974).[44]

The Court tried to clarify its doctrine by spelling out what what could be classified as obscene and thus outside First Amendment protection in the 1973 case of *Miller v. California.* Warren Burger, chief justice at the time, wrote that a work was obscene under the following circumstances:

1. The work, taken as a whole, appealed "to a prurient interest in sex."

2. The work showed "patently offensive" sexual conduct that was specifically defined by an obscenity law.

3. The work, taken as a whole, lacked "serious literary, artistic, political, or scientific value."

Decisions regarding whether material is obscene, said the Court, should be based on how average people (in other words, juries) apply the contemporary standards of local—not national—communities.

The Court did provide "a few plain examples" of what sort of material might fall within this definition of obscenity. Among these examples were "patently offensive representations of ultimate sexual acts … actual or simulated," "patently offensive representations of masturbation or excretory functions," or "lewd exhibition of the genitals." Cities throughout the country duplicated the language of *Miller* in their obscenity ordinances. The qualifying adjectives *lewd* and *offensive* prevent communities from banning anatomy texts, for example, as obscene. The difficulty remains in determining what is *lewd* or *offensive.*

The difficulty of defining obscenity makes it difficult to obtain an obscenity conviction. So does the absence of a nationwide consensus that offensive material should be banned—at least not when it is restricted to adults. In many communities the laws on pornography are lenient; prosecutors know that they may not get a jury to convict, even when the disputed material is obscene as defined by *Miller.* Thus obscene material is widely available in adult bookstores, video stores, and movie theaters.

Miller v. California

A 1973 Supreme Court decision holding that community standards be used to determine whether material is obscene, defined as appealing to a "prurient interest," being "patently offensive," and lacking in "serious literary, artistic, political, or scientific value."

You Are the Judge
The Case of the Drive-in Theater

Almost everyone concedes that *sometimes* obscenity should be banned by public authorities. One instance might be when a person's right to show pornographic movies clashes with another's right to be shielded from pornography. Watching dirty movies in an enclosed theater or in the privacy of your own home is one thing. Showing them in public places where anyone, including schoolchildren, might inadvertently see them is something else. Or is it?

The city of Jacksonville, Florida, wanted to limit the screening of certain kinds of movies at drive-in theaters. Its city council reasoned that drive-ins were public places and that drivers passing by would be involuntarily exposed to movies they might prefer not to see. Some members of the council argued that drivers distracted by steamy scenes might even cause accidents. So the council passed a local ordinance forbidding movies showing nudity (defined in the ordinance as "bare buttocks … female bare breasts, or human bare pubic areas") at drive-in theaters.

Arrested for violating the ordinance, a Mr. Erznoznik challenged the constitutionality of the ordinance. He claimed that the law was overly broad and banned nudity, not obscenity. The lawyers for the city insisted that the law was acceptable under the First Amendment. The government, they claimed, had a responsibility to forbid a "public nuisance," especially one that might cause a traffic hazard.

YOU BE THE JUDGE:

Did Jacksonville's ban on nudity in drive-in movies go too far, or was it a constitutional limit on free speech?

DECISION:

In *Erznoznik v. Jacksonville* (1975), the Supreme Court held that Jacksonville's ordinance was unconstitutionally broad. The city council had gone too far; it could end up banning movies that might not be obscene. The ordinance would, said the Court, ban a film "containing a picture of a baby's buttocks, the nude body of a war victim or scenes from a culture where nudity is indignous." Said Justice Powell for the Court, "Clearly, all nudity cannot be deemed obscene."

114

4.1
4.2
4.3
4.4
4.5
4.6
4.7
4.8

Despite the Court's best efforts to define obscenity and determine when it can be banned, state and local governments continue to struggle with the application of these rulings. In one famous case, a small New Jersey town tried to get rid of a nude dancing parlor by using its zoning power to ban all live entertainment. The Court held that the measure was too broad, restricting too much expression, and was thus unlawful.[45] However, the Court has upheld laws specifically banning nude dancing when their effect on overall expression was minimal.[46] Jacksonville, Florida, tried to ban drive-in movies containing nudity. You can examine the Court's reaction in "You Are the Judge: The Case of the Drive-in Theater."

Regulations such as rating systems for movies and television that are aimed at keeping obscene material away from the young, who are considered more vulnerable to harmful influences, have wide public support; courts have consistently ruled that states may protect children from obscenity. The public and the courts also strongly support laws designed to protect the young from being exploited in pornography. It is a violation of federal law to send or receive sexually explicit photographs of children through the mail or over the Internet, and in 1990 the Supreme Court upheld Ohio's law forbidding the possession of child pornography.[47]

Advances in technology have created a new wrinkle in the obscenity issue. The Internet and the World Wide Web make it easier to distribute obscene material rapidly, and a number of online information services have taken advantage of this opportunity. In 1996 Congress passed the Communications Decency Act, banning obscene material online and criminalizing the electronic transmission of indecent speech or images to anyone under 18 years of age. This law made no exception for material that has serious literary, artistic, political, or scientific merit as outlined in *Miller v. California*. In 1997, the Supreme Court overturned it as being overly broad and vague and thus a violation of free speech.[48] In 2002, the Court overturned a law banning virtual child pornography on similar grounds.[49] (Apparently the Supreme Court views the Internet similarly to print media, with similar protections against government regulation.) In 1999, however, the Court upheld prohibitions on obscene e-mail and faxes.

In 2011 the Court ruled that a California law banning the sale or rental of violent video games to minors violated the First Amendment because the games communicate ideas.[50] Depictions of violence, the Court added, have never been subject to government regulation and thus do not qualify for the same exceptional treatment afforded to obscene materials. The California law imposed a restriction on the content of protected speech and was invalid because the state could not show that it served a compelling government interest and was narrowly tailored to serve that interest.

Many people are concerned about the impact of violent video games on children. Although government can regulate depictions of some sexual material, it cannot regulate depictions of violence.

☐ Libel and Slander

Another type of expression not protected by the First Amendment is defamation, false statements that are malicious and may damage a person's reputation. **Libel** refers to written defamation, *slander* to spoken defamation.

Of course, if politicians could collect damages for every untrue thing said about them, the right to criticize the government—which the Supreme Court termed "the central meaning of the First Amendment"—would be stifled. No one would dare be critical for fear of making a factual error. To encourage public debate, the Supreme Court has held in cases such as *New York Times v. Sullivan* (1964) that statements about public figures are libelous only if made with malice and reckless disregard for the truth. Public figures have to prove to a jury, in effect, that whoever wrote or said untrue statements about them knew that the statements were untrue and intended to harm them. This standard makes libel cases difficult for public figures to win because it is difficult to prove that a publication was intentionally malicious.[51]

Why It *Matters* to You
Libel Law

It is difficult for public figures to win libel cases. Public figures are likely to lose even when they can show that a defendant made defamatory falsehoods about them. This may not be fair, but it is essential for people to feel free to criticize public officials. Fear of losing a lawsuit would have a chilling effect on democratic dialogue.

To win libel lawsuits, *private individuals* have a lower standard to meet than public figures do. They need to show only that statements about them are defamatory falsehoods and that those who made the statements were negligent. Nevertheless, it is unusual for someone to pursue a libel case; most people do not wish to draw attention to critical statements about themselves.

If public debate is not free, there can be no democracy; yet in the process of free debate some reputations will be damaged (or at least bruised), sometimes unfairly. Libel cases must thus balance freedom of expression with respect for individual reputations. In one widely publicized case, General William Westmoreland, once the commander of American troops in South Vietnam, sued CBS over a documentary it broadcast called *The Uncounted Enemy*. It claimed that American military leaders in Vietnam, including Westmoreland, systematically lied to Washington to make it appear that the United States was winning the war. The evidence, including CBS's own internal memoranda, showed that the documentary made errors of fact. Westmoreland sued CBS for libel. Ultimately, the power of the press—in this case, a sloppy, arrogant press—prevailed. Fearing defeat at the trial, Westmoreland settled for a mild apology from CBS.[52]

An unusual case that explored the line between parody and libel came before the Supreme Court in 1988, when Reverend Jerry Falwell sued *Hustler* magazine. *Hustler* had printed a parody of a Campari Liquor ad about various celebrities called "First Time," in which celebrities related the first time they drank Campari; the phrase "first time" had an intentional double meaning. When *Hustler* depicted the Reverend Jerry Falwell having had his "first time" in an outhouse with his mother, Falwell sued. He alleged that the ad subjected him to great emotional distress and mental anguish. The case tested the limits to which a publication could go to parody or lampoon a public figure. The Supreme Court ruled that they can go pretty far—all nine justices ruled in favor of the magazine.[53]

libel
The publication of false and malicious statements that may damage someone's reputation.

New York Times v. Sullivan
A 1964 Supreme Court decision establishing that, to win damage suits for libel, public figures must prove that the defamatory statements about them were made with "actual malice" and reckless disregard for the truth.

Texas v. Johnson
A 1989 case in which the Supreme Court struck down a law banning the burning of the American flag on the grounds that such action was symbolic speech protected by the First Amendment.

symbolic speech
Nonverbal communication, such as burning a flag or wearing an armband. The Supreme Court has accorded some symbolic speech protection under the First Amendment.

Symbolic Speech

Freedom of speech, broadly interpreted, is a guarantee of freedom of expression. In 1965, school authorities in Des Moines, Iowa, suspended Mary Beth Tinker and her brother John when they wore black armbands to school to protest the Vietnam War. The Supreme Court held that the suspension violated the Tinkers' First Amendment rights. The right to freedom of speech, said the Court, went beyond the spoken word.[54]

As discussed in Chapter 2, when Gregory Lee Johnson set a flag on fire at the 1984 Republican National Convention in Dallas to protest nuclear weapons, the Supreme Court decided that the state law prohibiting flag desecration violated the First Amendment (**Texas v. Johnson** [1989]). Burning the flag, the Court said, constituted symbolic speech and not just dramatic action.[55] When Massachusetts courts ordered the organizers of the annual St. Patrick's Day parade to include the Irish-American Gay, Lesbian, and Bisexual Group of Boston, the Supreme Court declared that a parade is a form of protected speech and thus that the organizers are free to include or exclude whomever they want.

Wearing an armband, burning a flag, and marching in a parade are examples of **symbolic speech**: actions that do not consist of speaking or writing but that express an opinion. Court decisions have classified these activities somewhere between pure speech and pure action. The doctrine of symbolic speech is not precise; for example, although burning a flag is protected speech, burning a draft card is not.[56] In 2003 the Court held that states may make it a crime to burn a cross with a purpose to intimidate, as long as the law clearly gives prosecutors the burden of proving that the act was intended as a threat and not as a form of symbolic expression.[57] Despite the imprecisions, these cases make it clear that First Amendment rights are not limited by a rigid definition of what constitutes speech.

Free Press and Fair Trials

The Bill of Rights is an inexhaustible source of potential conflicts among different types of freedoms. One is the conflict between the right of the press to print what it wants and the right to a fair trial. The quantity of press coverage given to the trial of Michael Jackson on charges of child sexual abuse was extraordinary, and little of it was sympathetic to Jackson. Defense attorneys argue that such publicity can inflame the community—and potential jurors—against defendants and compromise the fairness of a trial. It very well may.

Nevertheless, the Court has *never* upheld a restriction on the press in the interest of a fair trial. The constitutional guarantee of freedom of the press entitles journalists to cover every trial. When a Nebraska judge issued a gag order forbidding the press to report any details of a particularly gory murder (or even to report the gag order itself), the outraged Nebraska Press Association took the case to the Supreme Court. The Court sided with the editors and revoked the gag order.[58] In 1980 the Court reversed a Virginia judge's order to close a murder trial to the public and the press. "The trial of a criminal case," said the Court, "must be open to the public."[59] A pretrial hearing, though, is a different matter. In a 1979 case, the Supreme Court permitted a closed hearing on the grounds that pretrial publicity might compromise the defendant's right to fairness. Ultimately, the only feasible measure that the judicial system can take against the influence of publicity in high-profile cases is to sequester the jury, thereby isolating it from the media and public opinion.

Occasionally a reporter withholds some critical evidence that either the prosecution or the defense wants in a criminal case, information that may be essential for a fair trial. Reporters argue that "protecting their sources" should exempt them from revealing notes from confidential informants. Some states have passed *shield laws* to protect reporters in these situations. In most states, however, reporters have no more rights than other citizens once a case has come to trial. The Supreme Court ruled in *Branzburg v. Hayes* (1972) that in the absence of a shield law, the right to a fair trial preempts the reporter's right to protect his or her sources. After a violent confrontation with student protestors at Stanford University, the police got a search warrant and marched off to the *Stanford Daily* for photographs of the scene they could use to make arrests. The paper argued that its files were protected by the First Amendment, but the decision in *Zurcher v. Stanford Daily* (1978) sided with the police.

☐ Commercial Speech

As we have seen, not all forms of communication receive the full protection of the First Amendment. Laws restrict **commercial speech**, such as advertising, far more extensively than expressions of opinion on religious, political, or other matters. The Federal Trade Commission (FTC) decides what kinds of goods may be advertised on radio and television and regulates the content of such advertising. These regulations have responded to changes in social mores and priorities. At one time, for example, tampons could not be advertised on TV but cigarettes could; today, the situation is the reverse.

The FTC attempts to ensure that advertisers do not make false claims for their products, but "truth" in advertising does not prevent misleading promises. For example, when ads imply that the right mouthwash or deodorant will improve one's love life, that dubious message is perfectly legal.

Nevertheless, laws may regulate commercial speech on the airwaves in ways that would clearly be impossible in the political or religious realm. Laws may actually require manufacturers to include certain words in their advertising. For example, the makers of Excedrin pain reliever were required to add to their commercials the words "on pain other than headache." (The claim of superior effectiveness was based on tests of how Excedrin relieved pain that many women experience after giving birth.)

Although commercial speech is regulated more rigidly than other types of speech, the courts have been broadening its protection under the Constitution. For years, many states had laws that prohibited advertising for professional services—such as legal and engineering services—and for certain products ranging from eyeglasses and prescription drugs to condoms and abortions. Advocates of these laws claimed that they were designed to protect consumers against misleading claims, while critics charged that the laws prevented price competition. The courts have struck down many such restrictions—including restrictions on advertising casino gambling where such gambling is legal—as violations of freedom of speech.[60] In general, the Supreme Court has allowed the regulation of commercial speech when the speech concerns unlawful activity or is misleading, but otherwise regulations must advance a substantial government interest and be no more extensive than necessary to serve that interest.[61]

☐ Regulation of the Public Airwaves

The Federal Communications Commission (FCC) regulates the content, nature, and very existence of radio and television broadcasting. Although newspapers do not need licenses, radio and television stations do. A licensed station must comply with regulations, including a requirement that it devote a certain percentage of broadcast time to public service, news, children's programming, political candidates, or views other than those its owners support. The rules are more relaxed for cable channels, which can specialize in a particular type of broadcasting because consumers pay for, and thus have more choice about, the service.

Miami Herald Publishing Company v. Tornillo

A 1974 case in which the Supreme Court held that a state could not force a newspaper to print replies from candidates it had criticized. The case illustrates the limited power of government to restrict the print media.

Red Lion Broadcasting Company v. Federal Communications Commission

A 1969 case in which the Supreme Court upheld restrictions on radio and television broadcasting similar to those it had overturned in *Miami Herald Publishing Company v. Tornillo*. The Court reasoned that regulating radio and television broadcasting is justified because there are only a limited number of broadcasting frequencies available.

Licensing would clearly violate the First Amendment if it were imposed on the print media. For example, Florida passed a law requiring newspapers in the state to provide space for political candidates to reply to newspaper criticisms. In *Miami Herald Publishing Company v. Tornillo*. In this case, the Supreme Court, without hesitation, voided this law. In contrast, in *Red Lion Broadcasting Company v. Federal Communications Commission* (1969), the Court upheld similar restrictions on radio and television stations, reasoning that such laws were justified because only a limited number of broadcast frequencies were available.

One FCC rule regulating the content of programs restricts the use of obscene words. Comedian George Carlin had a famous routine called "Filthy Words" that could never be said over the airwaves. A New York City radio station tested the FCC rule by airing his routine. The ensuing events proved Carlin right. In 1978 the Supreme Court upheld the commission's policy of barring obscene words from radio or television when children might hear them.[62] Similarly, the FCC twice fined New York radio personality Howard Stern $600,000 for indecency. Had Stern's commentaries been carried by cable or satellite instead of the airwaves, he could have expressed himself with impunity because cable is viewed as private communication between individuals. (In 2006, Stern made the move to satellite radio.)

The Supreme Court has held that government has a legitimate right to regulate sexually oriented programming on cable television but that any regulation designed to do that must be narrowly tailored to serve a compelling government interest in the least restrictive way. In 1996 Congress had passed a law banning transmission of such programming for most of the day so that children would not be exposed to it. The Court concluded that targeted blocking, which allows subscribers to ask their cable companies to block specific channels, is less restrictive and a feasible and effective means of furthering the government's compelling interest, so banning transmission could not be justified.[63]

Although the Supreme Court ruled in *Roth v. United States* that obscenity is not protected by the First Amendment, determining just what is obscene has proven difficult. Popular radio personality Howard Stern pressed the limits of obscenity rules when he worked for radio stations using the public airwaves. Ultimately, he moved to satellite radio, where the rules are much less restrictive.

Campaigning

A relatively recent dimension of free speech relates to the effort of both the national and state governments to limit the role of money in political campaigns. The Federal Election Campaign Act of 1971 included limits on campaign contributions to candidates for the presidency and Congress, disclosure and reporting requirements, and public financing of presidential elections. In *Buckley v. Valeo* (1976) the Court upheld these provisions. However, it also ruled that spending money to influence elections is a form of constitutionally protected speech. Thus, the Court voided those parts of the law that limited total campaign expenditures, independent expenditures by individuals and groups, and expenditures by candidates from their personal or family funds.

In 2002, Congress passed the Bipartisan Campaign Reform Act, often referred to as the McCain-Feingold Act. It banned unrestricted ("soft money") donations made directly to political parties (often by corporations, unions, or wealthy individuals) and the solicitation of those donations by elected officials. It also limited advertising that unions, corporations, and nonprofit organizations could engage in up to 60 days prior to an election, and it restricted political parties' use of their funds for advertising on behalf of candidates in the form of "issue ads" or "coordinated expenditures". The Supreme Court upheld most of the law in 2003,[64] but in 2007 it held that issue ads that do not urge the support or defeat of a candidate may not be banned in the months preceding a primary or general election.[65]

In *Citizens United v. Federal Election Commission* (2010), the Supreme Court made a broader decision, striking down provisions of McCain-Feingold in holding that the First Amendment prohibits government from restricting political broadcasts in candidate elections when those broadcasts are funded by corporations or unions. Further limiting the reach of campaign finance laws, in 2014 the Court struck down as violating the First Amendment the overall limits that an individual could contribute to all federal candidates and the limit that an individual could contribute to political party committees every two years.[66]

The Supreme Court also found that Arizona's public finance system for state candidates violated the First Amendment rights of candidates who raise private money because they may be inhibited from spending money to speak if they know that it will give rise to counter-speech paid for by the government.[67]

Freedom of Assembly

 4.4 Describe the rights to assemble and associate protected by the First Amendment and their limitations.

he last of the great rights guaranteed by the First Amendment is the freedom to "peaceably assemble." Commentators often neglect this freedom in favor of the more trumpeted freedoms of speech, press, and religion, yet it is the basis for forming interest groups, political parties, and professional associations as well as for picketing and protesting. There are two facets to the freedom of assembly.

Right to Assemble

The first facet is the literal right to assemble—that is, to gather together in order to make a statement. This freedom can conflict with other societal values when it disrupts public order, traffic flow, peace and quiet, or bystanders' freedom to go about their business without interference. Within reasonable limits, called *time, place, and manner restrictions*, freedom of assembly includes the rights to parade, picket, and protest.

White supremacists and people opposing them square off. The Supreme Court has generally upheld the right of any group, no matter how controversial or offensive, to peaceably assemble, as long as the group's demonstrations remain on public property.

Whatever a group's cause, it has the right to demonstrate. For example, in 2011 the Supreme Court upheld the right of the congregation of a small church to picket military funerals to communicate its belief that God hates the United States for its tolerance of homosexuality, particularly in America's military.[68]

However, no group can simply hold a spontaneous demonstration anytime, anywhere, and in any way it chooses. Usually, a group must apply to the local city government for a permit and post a bond of a few hundred dollars as a sort of security deposit. The governing body must grant a permit as long as the group pledges to hold its demonstration at a time and in a place that allows the police to prevent major disruptions. There are virtually no limitations on the content of a group's message. One important case arose when the American Nazi Party applied to march in the streets of Skokie, Illinois, a Chicago suburb with a sizable Jewish population, including many survivors of Hitler's death camps. You can examine the Court's decision in "You Are the Judge: The Case of the Nazis' March in Skokie."

Protest that verges on harassment tests the balance between freedom and order. Pro-life advocates protest abortion outside abortion clinics and seek to shame or even harass clients into staying away. Thus, rights are in conflict: a woman has the right to obtain an abortion; the demonstrators have the right to protest the very existence of the clinic. The courts have acted to restrain these demonstrators, setting limits on how close they may come to clinics and upholding clinic clients' damage claims, and Congress has enacted broad penalties against abortion protestors. In 2014, however, the Supreme Court ruled that a buffer zone around a Massachusetts clinic restricted access to public space and was not narrowly tailored to balance rights.[69] Pro-life demonstrators in a Milwaukee, Wisconsin, suburb paraded outside the home of a physician who performed abortions. The town board forbade future picketing in residential neighborhoods. The Supreme Court agreed that the right to residential privacy is a legitimate local concern and upheld the ordinance.[70]

☐ Right to Associate

The second facet to freedom of assembly is the right to associate with people who share a common interest, including an interest in political change. In a famous case at the height of the civil rights movement, Alabama tried to harass the state chapter of the

You Are the Judge

The Case of the Nazis' March in Skokie

Hitler's Nazis slaughtered 6 million Jews in death camps like Auschwitz. Many of the survivors migrated to the United States, and thousands settled in Skokie, Illinois, a suburb just north of Chicago, eventually establishing a large Jewish community there.

The American Nazi Party in the Skokie area was a ragtag group of perhaps 25 to 30 members. Its headquarters was a storefront building on the West Side of Chicago, near an area with an expanding African American population. After Chicago denied them a permit to march in an African American neighborhood, the American Nazis announced their intention to march in Skokie. Skokie's city government required that they post a $300,000 bond to obtain a parade permit. The Nazis claimed that the high bond was set in order to prevent their march and that it infringed on their freedoms of speech and assembly. The American Civil Liberties Union (ACLU), despite its loathing of the Nazis, defended the Nazis' claim and their right to march. The ACLU lost half its Illinois membership because it took this position.

YOU BE THE JUDGE:

Do Nazis have the right to parade, preach anti-Jewish propaganda, and perhaps provoke violence in a community peopled with survivors of the Holocaust? What rights or obligations does a community have to maintain order?

DECISION:

A federal district court ruled that Skokie's ordinance did restrict freedom of assembly and association. No community could use its power to grant parade permits to stifle free expression. In *Collins v. Smith* (Collins was the Nazi leader, and Smith was the mayor of Skokie), the Supreme Court let the lower-court decision stand. In fact, the Nazis did not march in Skokie, settling instead for Chicago, where their demonstrations were poorly attended.

National Association for the Advancement of Colored People (NAACP) by requiring it to turn over its membership list. In *NAACP v. Alabama* (1958), the Supreme Court found this demand an unconstitutional restriction on freedom of association.

In 2006 some law schools argued that a law that required them to grant military recruiters access to their students violated the schools' freedoms of speech and association. Siding with the government, the Supreme Court concluded that the law regulated conduct, not speech. In addition, it argued, nothing about recruiting suggests that law schools must agree with any speech by recruiters, and nothing in the law restricts what law schools may say about the military's policies. Nor does the law force law schools to accept students and faculty it does not desire, and students and faculty are free to voice their disapproval of the military's message.[71]

NAACP v. Alabama

The 1958 Supreme Court decision that the right to assemble meant that Alabama could not require the state chapter of NAACP to reveal its membership list.

Right to Bear Arms

4.5 Describe the right to bear arms protected by the Second Amendment and its limitations.

Few issues generate as much controversy as gun control. In an attempt to control gun violence, many communities have passed restrictions on owning and carrying handguns. National, state and local laws have also mandated background checks for gun buyers and limited the sale of certain types of weapons altogether. Yet other laws have required that guns be stored so as to prevent their being stolen or used by children. Some groups, most notably the National Rifle Association, have invested millions of dollars to fight almost all gun control efforts, arguing that they violate the Second Amendment's guarantee of a right to bear arms. Many advocates of gun control argue that the Second Amendment applies only

Point to Ponder

In its humorous way, this cartoon shows that constitutional rights are sometimes in conflict.

Is there any way to prioritize our basic rights?

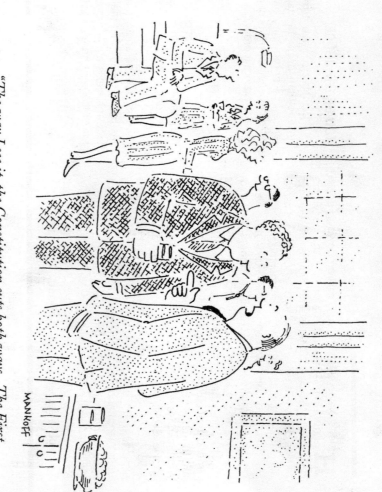

"The way I see it, the Constitution cuts both ways. The First Amendment gives you the right to say what you want, but the Second Amendment gives me the right to shoot you for it."

to the right of states to create militias. Surprisingly, the Supreme Court has rarely dealt with gun control.

In 2008, however, the Court directly faced the issue. A District of Columbia law restricted most residents from owning handguns. The law also required that, when not in use, all lawfully owned firearms, including rifles and shotguns, be unloaded and disassembled or bound by a trigger lock or similar device. In *District of Columbia v. Heller* (2008), the Supreme Court held that the Second Amendment protects an individual right to possess a firearm, that the right is unconnected with service in a militia, and that an individual may use a firearm for lawful purposes, such as self-defense within the home. Similarly, the requirement that any lawful firearm be disassembled or bound by a trigger lock when not in use is unconstitutional because it makes it impossible for citizens to use arms for self-defense. In 2010 in *McDonald v. Chicago*, the Court extended the Second Amendment's limits on restricting an individual's right to bear arms to state and local gun control laws.

Nevertheless, like most rights, the right to bear arms is not unlimited. It is not a right to keep and carry any weapon whatsoever in any manner whatsoever and for whatever purpose. For example, prohibitions on concealed weapons are permissible, as are limits on the possession of firearms by felons and the mentally ill, laws forbidding the carrying of firearms in sensitive places such as schools and government buildings, laws imposing conditions and qualifications on the commercial sale of arms, and laws restricting "dangerous and unusual weapons" that are not typically used for self-defense or recreation.

This mother and daughter attending the annual meeting of the National Rifle Association are enjoying the right to bear arms. This right is not absolute, however.

Defendants' Rights

4.6 Characterize defendants' rights and identify issues that arise in their implementation.

T he Bill of Rights contains only 45 words that guarantee the freedoms of religion, speech, press, and assembly. Most of the remaining words concern the rights of people accused of crimes. The Founders intended these rights to protect the accused in *political* arrests and trials; the British abuse of colonial political leaders was still fresh in the memory of American citizens. Today the courts apply the protections in the Fourth, Fifth, Sixth, Seventh, and Eighth Amendments mostly in criminal justice cases.

It is useful to think of the criminal justice system as a funnel. Following a *crime* there is (sometimes) an *arrest*, which is (sometimes) followed by a *prosecution*, which is (sometimes) followed by a *trial*, which (usually) results in a *verdict* of innocence or guilt. The funnel gets smaller and smaller. For example, the ratio of crimes reported to arrests made is about five to one. At each stage of the process, the Constitution protects the rights of the accused (see Figure 4.1).

The language of the Bill of Rights comes from the late 1700s and is often vague. For example, just how speedy is a "speedy trial"? How "cruel and unusual" does a punishment have to be in order to violate the Eighth Amendment? The courts continually must rule on the constitutionality of actions by police, prosecutors, judges, and legislatures—actions that a citizen or group could claim violate certain rights. Defendants' rights, just like those rights protected by the First Amendment, are not clearly defined in the Bill of Rights.

One thing is clear, however. The Supreme Court's decisions have extended specific provisions of the Bill of Rights—one by one—to the states as part of the general process

4.1 4.2 4.3 4.4 4.5 4.6 4.7 4.8

of incorporation we discussed earlier. Virtually all the rights we discuss in the following sections affect the actions of both national and state authorities. Incorporation is especially important because most cases involving defendants' rights originate in the states.

FIGURE 4.1 THE CONSTITUTION AND THE STAGES OF THE CRIMINAL JUSTICE SYSTEM

Although our criminal justice system is complex, it can be broken down into stages. The Constitution protects the rights of the accused at every stage.

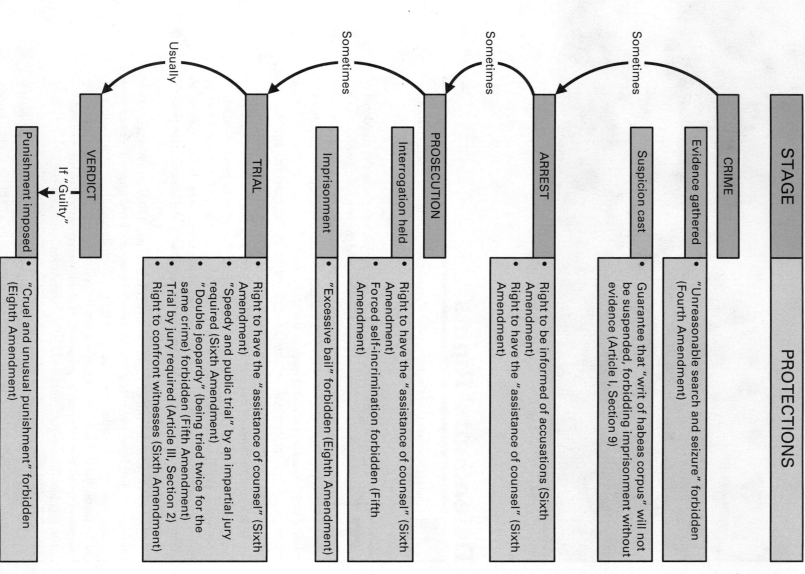

STAGE	PROTECTIONS
CRIME	
Evidence gathered	• "Unreasonable search and seizure" forbidden (Fourth Amendment)
Suspicion cast	• Guarantee that "writ of habeas corpus" will not be suspended, forbidding imprisonment without evidence (Article I, Section 9)
ARREST	• Right to be informed of accusations (Sixth Amendment) • Right to have the "assistance of counsel" (Sixth Amendment)
PROSECUTION	
Interrogation held	• Right to have the "assistance of counsel" (Sixth Amendment) • Forced self-incrimination forbidden (Fifth Amendment)
Imprisonment	• "Excessive bail" forbidden (Eighth Amendment)
TRIAL	• Right to have the "assistance of counsel" (Sixth Amendment) • "Speedy and public trial" by an impartial jury required (Sixth Amendment) • "Double jeopardy" (being tried twice for the same crime) forbidden (Fifth Amendment) • Trial by jury required (Article III, Section 2) • Right to confront witnesses (Sixth Amendment)
VERDICT	
Punishment imposed	• "Cruel and unusual punishment" forbidden (Eighth Amendment)

Sometimes

Sometimes

Sometimes

Sometimes

Usually

If "Guilty"

Searches and Seizures

Police cannot arrest a citizen without reason. Before making an arrest, police need what the courts call **probable cause**, reasonable grounds to believe that someone is guilty of a crime.

Police often need to get physical evidence—a car thief's fingerprints, a snatched purse—to use in court. To prevent the abuse of police power, the Fourth Amendment forbids **unreasonable search and seizure**. It requires police to meet certain conditions.

A search can occur if a court has issued a **search warrant**. Courts can issue a warrant only if there is probable cause to believe that a crime has occurred or is about to occur. A warrant, which must be in writing, must specify the area to be searched and the material sought in the police search.

A search can take place without a warrant (as most do) if probable cause of a crime exists, if the search is necessary to protect an officer's safety, if the search is limited to material relevant to a suspected crime or within the suspect's immediate control, or if there is a need to prevent the imminent destruction of evidence.[72] The Supreme Court has also held that police may enter a home without a warrant when they have an objectively reasonable basis for believing that an occupant is seriously injured or imminently threatened with serious injury.[73]

In various rulings, the Supreme Court has upheld a wide range of warrantless searches, including aerial searches to secure key evidence in cases involving marijuana growing and environmental violations, roadside checkpoints in which police randomly examine drivers for signs of intoxication,[74] the use of narcotics-detecting dogs at a routine stop for speeding,[75] and the search of a passenger and car following a routine check of the car's registration.[76] The Court also has approved warrantless "hot pursuit" of criminal suspects; warrantless car stops and "stop-and-frisk" encounters with passengers and pedestrians when they are based on reasonable suspicion of criminal activity, rather than the higher standard of probable cause; and mandatory drug testing of transportation workers and high school athletes, even those who are not suspected of using drugs. Searches of K–12 students require only that there be a reasonable chance of finding evidence of wrongdoing, rather than probable cause.[77] Officials may strip-search anyone arrested for any offense before admitting them to jails, even if the officials do not suspect the presence of contraband,[78] and taking and analyzing a cheek swab of an arrestee's DNA is a legitimate police booking procedure.[79]

However, some decisions have offered more protection against searches. The Court has held that, although an officer may order a driver and passengers out of a car while issuing a traffic citation and may search for weapons to protect himself from danger, he cannot search a car if there is no threat to his safety.[80] In 2009 the Court decided that the police may search a vehicle incident to an arrest only if it is reasonable to believe the arrestee might access the vehicle at the time of the search (to obtain a weapon or destroy evidence, for example) or that the vehicle contains evidence of the specific offense of an arrest. They cannot search vehicles for evidence of other crimes.[81] Similarly, the Supreme Court prohibited highway checkpoints designed to detect ordinary criminal wrongdoing, such as possessing illegal drugs,[82] and it ruled that an anonymous tip that a person is carrying a gun is not sufficient justification for a police officer to stop and frisk that person.[83] In addition, the Court found that police use of a thermal imaging device to detect abnormal heat (needed for growing marijuana) in a home violated the Fourth Amendment.[84] In 2012, the Court held that the government's installation of a GPS device on a target's vehicle, and its use of that device to monitor the vehicle's movements, constituted a "search" and required a warrant.[85] In 2014, the Court held that the police must usually have a warrant to search a cell phone.[86]

What happens if evidence used in court was obtained through unreasonable search and seizure? In a 1914 decision, the Supreme Court established the **exclusionary rule**, which prevents prosecutors from introducing illegally seized evidence in court. Until 1961, however, the exclusionary rule applied only to the federal government. The Court broadened its application in the case of a Cleveland woman named Dollree Mapp. The local police had broken into Mapp's home looking for a suspected bombing fugitive, and while there, they searched it and found a cache of obscene materials. Mapp was convicted of possessing them. She appealed her case to the federal courts, claiming that since the

probable cause
Reasonable grounds for believing that a person is guilty of a crime. In order to make a lawful arrest, the police must have probable cause.

unreasonable searches and seizures
Obtaining evidence in an unlawful manner, a practice prohibited by the Fourth Amendment. The police must have probable cause and/or a search warrant in order to make a legal and proper search for and seizure of incriminating evidence and seize such evidence.

search warrant
A written authorization from a court specifying the area to be searched and what the police may search for.

exclusionary rule
The rule that evidence cannot be introduced into a trial if it was not obtained in a constitutional manner. The rule prohibits use of evidence obtained through unreasonable search and seizure.

4.1

4.2

4.3

4.4

4.5

4.6

4.7

4.8

Mapp v. Ohio

The 1961 Supreme Court decision ruling that the Fourth Amendment's protection against unreasonable searches and seizures must be extended to the states.

The 1961 Supreme Court decision ruling that the Fourth Amendment's protection against unreasonable searches and seizures must be extended to the states.

police had no probable cause to search for obscene materials, the evidence should not have been used against her. In an important decision, *Mapp v. Ohio*, the Supreme Court ruled that the evidence had been seized illegally and reversed Mapp's conviction. Since then, the exclusionary rule, treated as part of the Fourth Amendment, has been incorporated within the rights that restrict the states as well as the federal government.

Why It *Matters* to You

The Exclusionary Rule

The exclusionary rule, which requires courts to disregard evidence obtained illegally, has been controversial. Although critics view the rule as a technicality that helps criminals to avoid justice, this rule protects defendants (who have not been proven guilty) from abuses of police power.

Critics of the exclusionary rule, including some Supreme Court justices, argue that its strict application may permit guilty persons to go free because of police carelessness or innocent errors. The guilty, they say, should not go free because of a "technicality." Supporters of the exclusionary rule respond that the Constitution is not a technicality and that—because everyone is presumed innocent until proven guilty—defendants' rights protect the *accused*, not the guilty. You can examine one contemporary search-and-seizure case in "You Are the Judge: The Case of Ms. Montoya."

You Are the Judge

The Case of Ms. Montoya

Rosa Elvira Montoya de Hernandez arrived at the Los Angeles International Airport on Avianca Flight 080 from Bogotá, Colombia. Her first official encounter was with U.S. Customs Inspector Talamantes, who noticed that she spoke no English. Interestingly, Montoya's passport indicated eight recent quick trips from Bogotá to Los Angeles. She was carrying $5,000 in cash but no pocketbook or credit cards.

Talamantes and his fellow customs officers were suspicious. Stationed in Los Angeles, they were hardly unaware of the fact that Colombia was a major drug supplier. They questioned Montoya, who explained that her husband had a store in Bogotá and that she planned to spend the $5,000 at Kmart and JC Penney, stocking up on items for the store.

The inspector, somewhat wary, handed Montoya over to female customs inspectors for a search. These agents noticed what the Supreme Court later referred to delicately as a "firm fullness" in Montoya's abdomen. Suspicions, already high, increased. The agents applied for a court order to conduct pregnancy tests, X-rays, and other types of examinations; eventually they found 88 balloons containing 80 percent pure cocaine in Montoya's alimentary canal.

Montoya's lawyer argued that the tests constituted unreasonable search and seizure and that her arrest and

conviction should be set aside. There was, he said, no direct evidence that would have led the officials to suspect cocaine smuggling. The government argued that the arrest had followed from a set of odd facts leading to a reasonable suspicion that something was amiss.

YOU BE THE JUDGE:

Did Montoya's arrest violate the Fourth Amendment protection against unreasonable search and seizure?

DECISION:

The Supreme Court held that US Customs agents were well within their constitutional authority to search Montoya. Even though the collection of evidence took the better part of two days, Justice William Rehnquist, the author of the Court's opinion, remarked wryly that "the rudimentary knowledge of the human body which judges possess in common with the rest of mankind tells us that alimentary canal smuggling cannot be detected in the amount of time in which other illegal activities may be investigated through brief ... stops."

Since the 1980s, the Supreme Court has made some exceptions to the exclusionary rule, including allowing the use of illegally obtained evidence when this evidence leads police to a discovery that they eventually would have made without it.[87] The justices also have decided to establish a good-faith exception to the rule; evidence can be used in court if the police who seized it mistakenly thought they were operating under a constitutionally valid warrant.[88] In 1995 the Court held that the exclusionary rule does not bar evidence obtained illegally as the result of clerical errors.[89] In 2006 it held that a police failure to abide by the rule requiring them to knock and announce themselves before entering a home was not a justification for suppressing the evidence they found upon entry with a warrant.[90] The Court has even allowed evidence illegally obtained from a banker to be used to convict one of his customers.[91] In a 2009 decision, *Herring v. United States*, the Court held that the exclusionary rule does not apply when there is isolated police negligence rather than systematic error or reckless disregard of constitutional requirements.

THE WAR ON TERRORISM The *USA Patriot Act*, passed just six weeks after the September 11, 2001, terrorist attacks, gave the government broad new powers to engage in wiretapping and surveillance when investigating terrorism suspects. Attorney General John Ashcroft also eased restrictions on domestic spying in counterterrorism operations, allowing agents to monitor political or religious groups without any connection to a criminal investigation. The Patriot Act gave the federal government the power to examine a terrorist suspect's records held by third parties, such as doctors, libraries, bookstores, universities, and Internet service providers. It also allowed the government to search private property without probable cause and without notifying the owner until after the search had been executed, limiting the owner's opportunities to challenge the search. Congress reauthorized the law in 2006 with few changes.

Without the court-approved warrants ordinarily required for domestic spying, President George W. Bush in 2001 ordered the National Security Agency (NSA) to monitor the international telephone calls and e-mail messages of people inside the United States. In 2008 Congress overhauled the nation's surveillance law, the Foreign Intelligence Surveillance Act (FISA), allowing officials to use broad warrants to eavesdrop on large groups of foreign suspects and ending the requirement that officials obtain a warrant for each individual suspect, as long as they wiretapped only communications (phone calls, e-mail messages, and texts) to and from foreigners that happened to pass through American telecommunications switches. In order to wiretap Americans, however, officials must obtain individual warrants from the special FISA court—although in an emergency they are permitted to wiretap an American suspect for up to seven days without a court order.

The NSA tracked Americans' calls using numbers that had not been vetted in accordance with court-ordered procedures. Intelligence court judges ruled that under the "special needs" doctrine the NSA's collection and examination of Americans' communications data to track possible terrorists does not violate the Fourth Amendment. The NSA also collected and stored all phone records of American citizens and tracked their use of the Internet and their financial transactions. President Obama has proposed ending the systematic collection of data about Americans' calling, storing the bulk records at phone companies, and requiring the NSA to receive judicial permission before obtaining specific records.

☐ Self-Incrimination

Suppose that evidence has been gathered and the police are ready to make an arrest. In the American system, the burden of proof rests on the police and the prosecutors. The **Fifth Amendment** forbids forced **self-incrimination**, stating that no person "shall be compelled to be a witness against himself." Whether in a congressional hearing, a courtroom, or a police station, the accused need not provide evidence that can later be used against them. However, the government may guarantee

Fifth Amendment
A constitutional amendment designed to protect the rights of persons accused of crimes. It provides protection against double jeopardy, self-incrimination, and punishment without due process of law.

self-incrimination
Being a witness against oneself. The Fifth Amendment forbids involuntary self-incrimination.

Miranda v. Arizona
The 1966 Supreme Court decision that set guidelines for police questioning of accused persons to protect them against self-incrimination and to protect their right to counsel.

One of the most important principles of constitutional law is that defendants in criminal cases have rights. Probable cause and/or a search warrant are required for a legal search for and seizure of incriminating evidence. Here, as required by *Miranda v. Arizona*, police officers read a suspect his rights.

suspects *immunity*—exemption from prosecution in exchange for suspects' testimony regarding their own and others' misdeeds.

You have probably seen television shows in which an arrest is made and the arresting officers recite, often from memory, a set of rights to the arrestee. The recitation of these rights is authentic and originated from a famous court decision—perhaps the most important modern decision in criminal law—involving an Arizona man named Ernesto Miranda.[92]

Miranda was picked up as a prime suspect in the rape and kidnapping of an 18-year-old girl. Identified by the girl from a police lineup, he was questioned by police for two hours. During this time, they did not tell him of either his constitutional right against self-incrimination or his right to counsel. Miranda said enough to lead eventually to a conviction. The Supreme Court reversed his conviction on appeal, however. In *Miranda v. Arizona* (1966), the Court established guidelines for police questioning. Suspects must be told the following:

- They have a constitutional right to remain silent and may stop answering questions at any time.

- What they say can be used against them in a court of law.

- They have a right to have a lawyer present during questioning, and the court will provide them with a lawyer if they cannot afford their own.

Ironically, when Ernesto Miranda himself was murdered, police read the suspect in his murder his "Miranda rights."

In the decades since the *Miranda* decision, the Supreme Court has made a number of exceptions to its requirements. In 1991, for example, the Court held that a coerced confession introduced in a trial does not automatically taint a conviction. If other evidence is enough for a conviction, then the coerced confession is a "harmless error" that does not necessitate a new trial.[93] The Court has also declared that criminal suspects seeking to protect their right to remain silent must clearly state they are invoking it.[94] Nevertheless, in 2000 in *Dickerson v. U.S.*, the Court made it clear that it supported the *Miranda* decision and that Congress was not empowered to change it. In 2010 the Court held that police may take a second run at questioning a suspect who has invoked his or her Miranda rights, but they must wait until 14 days after the suspect has been released from custody.[95] In 2011 the Court declared that officials must take greater care to explain rights to children when they question them.[96]

The Fifth Amendment prohibits not only coerced confessions but also coerced crimes. The courts have overturned convictions based on *entrapment*, in which law enforcement officials encouraged persons to commit crimes (such as accepting bribes or purchasing illicit drugs) that they otherwise would not have committed. "You Are the Judge: The Case of the Enticed Farmer" addresses this issue.

☐ The Right to Counsel

A crucial *Miranda* right is the right to counsel. The **Sixth Amendment** has always guaranteed right to counsel in federal courts. In state courts a guaranteed right to counsel traces back only to 1932, when the Supreme Court, in *Powell v. Alabama*, ordered the states to provide an attorney for poor defendants in capital crime cases (cases in which the death penalty could be imposed). Most crimes are not capital crimes, however, and most crimes are tried in state courts. It was not until 1963, in *Gideon v. Wainwright*,[97] that the Supreme Court extended the right to an attorney for everyone accused of a felony in a state court. Subsequently, the Court went a step further, holding that whenever imprisonment can be imposed, a lawyer must be provided for the accused (*Argersinger v. Hamlin* [1972]). In addition, the Supreme Court has found that a trial court's erroneous deprivation of a criminal defendant's right to *choose* a counsel entitles him or her to reversal of his conviction.[98] In 2011, however, the Court held that in civil contempt cases carrying the potential for imprisonment states are not obligated to provide counsel.[99]

☐ Trials

The Sixth Amendment (and the Constitution's protection against the suspension of the writ of *habeas corpus*) guarantees that anyone who is arrested has a right to be brought before a judge. This guarantee applies at two stages of the judicial process. First, those

Sixth Amendment

A constitutional amendment designed to protect individuals accused of crimes. It includes the right to counsel, the right to confront witnesses, and the right to a speedy and public trial.

Gideon v. Wainwright

The 1963 Supreme Court decision holding that anyone accused of a felony where imprisonment may be imposed has a right to a lawyer. The decision requires the government to provide a lawyer to anyone so accused who is too poor to afford one.

You Are the Judge
The Case of the Enticed Farmer

In 1984 Keith Jacobson, a 56-year-old farmer who supported his elderly father in Nebraska, ordered two magazines and a brochure from a California adult bookstore. He expected to receive nude photographs of adult males but instead found that he had been sent photographs of nude boys. He ordered no other magazines.

Three months later, Congress changed federal law to make the receipt of such materials illegal. Finding his name on the mailing list of the California bookstore, two government agencies repeatedly enticed Jacobson to send away for sexually explicit photographs of children. (They did so by creating five fictitious organizations and a bogus pen pal who solicited Jacobson to order the photographs.) After 26 months of enticement, Jacobson finally ordered a magazine. He was then arrested for violating the Child Protection Act.

He was convicted of receiving child pornography through the mail, which he undoubtedly did. Jacobson claimed, however, that he had been entrapped into committing the crime.

YOU BE THE JUDGE:

Was Jacobson an innocent victim of police entrapment? Would he have sought child pornography if he had not been enticed to do so?

DECISION:

The Court agreed with Jacobson. In *Jacobson v. United States* (1992), it ruled that the government had overstepped the line between setting a trap for the "unwary innocent" and the "unwary criminal" and failed to establish that Jacobson was independently predisposed to commit the crime for which he was arrested. Jacobson's conviction was overturned.

plea bargaining
A bargain struck between a defendant's lawyer and a prosecutor to the effect that the defendant will plead guilty to a lesser crime (or fewer crimes) in exchange for the state's promise not to prosecute the defendant for a more serious crime or for additional crimes.

detained have a right to be informed of the accusations against them. Second, they have a right to a *speedy and public trial, by an impartial jury*.

Despite the drama of highly publicized trials, trials are in fact relatively rare. In American courts, 90 percent of all criminal cases begin and end with a guilty plea. Most of these cases are settled through a process called **plea bargaining**. A plea bargain results from a bargain struck between a defendant's lawyer and a prosecutor to the effect that a defendant will plead guilty to a lesser crime (or fewer crimes) in exchange for a state not prosecuting that defendant for a more serious (or additional) crime.

Critics of the plea-bargaining system believe that it permits many criminals to avoid the full punishment they deserve. After decades of new laws to toughen sentencing for criminals, however, prosecutors have gained greater leverage to extract guilty pleas from defendants, often by using the threat of more serious charges with mandatory sentences or other harsher penalties.

The plea-bargaining process works to the advantage of both sides; it saves the state the time and money that would be spent on a trial, and it permits defendants who think they might be convicted of a serious charge to plead guilty to a lesser one. A study of sentencing patterns in three California counties discovered that a larger proportion of defendants who went to trial ended up going to prison compared with those who pleaded guilty and had no trial. In answer to their question "Does it pay to plead guilty?" the researchers gave a qualified yes.[100] Good or bad, plea bargaining is a practical necessity. Only a vast increase in resources would allow the court system to cope with a trial for every defendant. In 2012 the Supreme Court recognized the dominant role plea bargaining plays in criminal law when it held in two cases that defendants have a right to an effective lawyer during pretrial negotiations.[101]

The defendants in the 300,000 cases per year that actually go to trial are entitled to many rights, including the right to a speedy trial by an impartial jury, which is guaranteed by the Sixth Amendment. An impartial jury includes one that is not racially biased (one from which potential jurors of the defendant's race have been excluded).[102] Lawyers for both sides spend hours questioning prospective jurors in a major case. Defendants, of course, prefer a jury that is biased toward them, and those who can afford it do not leave jury selection to chance. A sophisticated technology of jury selection has developed. Jury consultants—often psychologists or other social scientists—develop profiles of jurors likely to be sympathetic or hostile to a defendant.

The Constitution does not specify the size of a jury; in principle, it could be anywhere from 1 to 100 people. Tradition in England and America has set jury size at 12, although in petty cases 6 jurors are sometimes used. Traditionally, too, a jury had to be unanimous in order to convict. The Supreme Court has eroded both traditions, permitting states to use fewer than 12 jurors and to convict with a less-than-unanimous vote. Federal courts still employ juries of 12 persons and require unanimous votes for a criminal conviction.

In recent years, the Supreme Court has aggressively defended the jury's role in the criminal justice process—and limited the discretion of judges in sentencing. In several cases, the Court has held that, other than a previous conviction, any fact that might increase the penalty for a convicted defendant beyond what the law usually allows or what such defendants usually receive must be submitted to a jury and proved beyond a reasonable doubt.[103] These decisions ensure that the judge's authority to sentence derives wholly from the jury's verdict.

The Sixth Amendment also gives defendants the right to confront the witnesses against them. The Supreme Court has held that prosecutors cannot introduce testimony into a trial unless the accused can cross-examine the witness.[104] This is so even if the witness is providing facts such as lab reports.[105] Moreover, defendants have the right to question those who prepare such reports.[106]

Defendants also have a right to know about evidence that may exonerate them. In 2010 the Supreme Court held that due process prohibits a state from withholding evidence that is favorable to a defendant's defense and key to determining a defendant's guilt or punishment.[107]

DETENTIONS AND THE WAR ON TERRORISM Normally, Sixth Amendment guarantees present few issues. However, in the aftermath of the September 11, 2001, terrorist attacks, the FBI detained more than 1,200 persons as possible dangers to national security. Of these persons, 762 were illegal aliens (mostly Arabs and Muslims); and many of them languished in jail for months until cleared by the FBI. For the first time in U.S. history, the federal government withheld the names of detainees, reducing their opportunities to exercise their rights for access to the courts and to counsel. The government argued that releasing the names and information about those arrested would give terrorists a window on its investigation of terrorism. In 2004 the Supreme Court refused to consider whether the government properly withheld names and other details about these prisoners. However, in other cases, the Court found that detainees, both in the United States and at the naval base at Guantánamo Bay, Cuba, have the right to challenge their detention before a judge or other neutral decision maker (*Hamdi v. Rumsfeld* and *Rasul v. Bush* [2004]).

In a historic decision in 2006 (*Hamdan v. Rumsfeld*), the Supreme Court held that the procedures President Bush had approved for trying prisoners at Guantánamo Bay lacked congressional authorization and violated both the Uniform Code of Military Justice and the Geneva Conventions. The flaws the Court cited were (1) the failure to guarantee defendants the right to attend their trial and (2) the prosecution's ability under the rules to introduce hearsay evidence, unsworn testimony, and evidence obtained through coercion. Equally important, the Court declared, the Constitution did not empower the president to establish judicial procedures on his own.

Later that year, Congress passed the Military Commissions Act (MCA), which specifically authorized military commissions to try alien, unlawful enemy combatants and denied such combatants access to the courts. It also denied access for those alien detainees who were waiting for the government to determine whether they were enemy combatants. The MCA allowed the U.S. government to detain such aliens indefinitely without prosecuting them in any manner.

However, in 2008, the Supreme Court held in *Boumediene v. Bush* that foreign terrorism suspects held at Guantánamo Bay have constitutional rights to challenge their detention in U.S. courts. "The laws and Constitution are designed to survive, and remain in force, in extraordinary times," the Court proclaimed as it declared unconstitutional the provision of the MCA that stripped the federal courts of jurisdiction

Prisoners held at the U.S. naval base at Guantánamo Bay, Cuba, present difficult issues of prisoners' rights.

Eighth Amendment

The constitutional amendment that forbids cruel and unusual punishment.

cruel and unusual punishment

Court sentences prohibited by the Eighth Amendment.

tion as enemy combatants. The Court also found that the procedure established for reviewing enemy combatant status failed to offer the fundamental procedural protections of habeas corpus.

☐ Cruel and Unusual Punishment

Punishments for citizens convicted of a crime range from probation to the death penalty. The **Eighth Amendment** forbids **cruel and unusual punishment**, although it does not define the phrase. Since 1962 this provision of the Bill of Rights has been applied to the states.

What constitutes cruel and unusual punishment? In 2011 the Supreme Court upheld a lower court order that found that conditions in California's overcrowded prisons were so bad that they violated the ban on cruel and unusual punishment and thus the state had to release some of the prisoners.[108] The Court has also held that it is a violation of the cruel and unusual punishment clause to sentence a juvenile offender to life in prison without parole for a crime.[109] (For another case related to cruel and unusual punishment, see "You Are the Judge: The Case of the First Offender.") Almost the entire constitutional debate over cruel and unusual punishment, however, has centered on the death penalty. More than 3,300 people are currently on death row, nearly half of them in California, Texas, and Florida.

The Supreme Court first confronted the question of whether the death penalty is inherently cruel and unusual punishment in *Furman v. Georgia* (1972), when it overturned Georgia's death penalty law because the state imposed the penalty in a "freakish" and "random" manner. Following this decision, 35 states passed new death penalty laws to address the Court's concerns. Thus some states, to prevent arbitrariness in punishment, mandated death penalties for some crimes. In *Woodson v. North Carolina* (1976), the Supreme Court ruled against mandatory death penalties. The Court has upheld the death penalty itself, however, concluding in ***Gregg v. Georgia*** (1976), that capital punishment is "an expression of society's outrage at particularly offensive conduct.... It is an extreme sanction, suitable to the most extreme of crimes."

Gregg v. Georgia

The 1976 Supreme Court decision that upheld the constitutionality of the death penalty, as "an extreme sanction, suitable to the most extreme of crimes."

You Are the Judge

The Case of the First Offender

R onald Harmelin of Detroit was convicted of possessing 672 grams of cocaine (a gram is about one-thirtieth of an ounce). Michigan's mandatory sentencing law required the trial judge to sentence Harmelin, a first-time offender, to life imprisonment without possibility of parole. Harmelin argued that this was cruel and unusual punishment because it was "significantly disproportionate," meaning that, as we might say, the punishment did not fit the crime. Harmelin's lawyers argued that many other crimes more serious than cocaine possession would net similar sentences.

YOU BE THE JUDGE:

Was Harmelin's sentence cruel and unusual punishment?

DECISION:

The Court upheld Harmelin's conviction in *Harmelin v. Michigan* (1991), spending many pages to explain that severe punishments were quite commonplace, especially when the Bill of Rights was written. Severity alone does not qualify a punishment as "cruel and unusual." The severity of punishment was up to the legislature of Michigan, which, the justices observed, knew better than they the conditions on the streets of Detroit. Later, Michigan reduced the penalty for possession of small amounts of cocaine and released Harmelin from jail.

Shortly before retiring from the bench in 1994, Supreme Court justice Harry Blackmun denounced the death penalty, declaring that its administration "fails to deliver the fair, consistent and reliable sentences of death required by the Constitution" (*Callins v. Collins* [1994]). Social scientists have shown that minority murderers whose victims are white are more likely to receive death sentences than are white murderers or those whose victims are not white. Nevertheless, in *McCleskey v. Kemp* (1987), the Supreme Court concluded that the death penalty does not violate the equal protection of the law guaranteed by the Fourteenth Amendment. The Court insisted that the unequal distribution of death penalty sentences was constitutionally acceptable because there was no evidence that juries intended to discriminate on the basis of race.

Today, the death penalty remains a part of the American criminal justice system. About 1,100 persons have been executed since the Court's decision in *Gregg*. The Court has also made it more difficult for death row prisoners to file petitions that would force legal delays and appeals to stave off execution; it has made it easier for prosecutors to exclude jurors opposed to the death penalty (*Wainwright v. Witt*, 1985); and it has allowed "victim impact" statements detailing the character of murder victims and their families' suffering to be used against a defendant. Most Americans support the death penalty, although there is evidence that racism plays a role in the opinions of whites.[110] It is interesting to note that the European Union prohibits the death penalty in member countries.

In recent years evidence that courts have sentenced innocent people to be executed has reinvigorated the debate over the death penalty. Attorneys have employed the new technology of DNA evidence in a number of states to obtain the release of dozens of death row prisoners. In 1999 Governor George Ryan of Illinois declared a moratorium on executions in his state after researchers proved that 13 people on death row were innocent. Later, he commuted the death sentences of all prisoners in the state. In general, there has been a decline in executions, as you can see in Figure 4.2.

McCleskey v. Kemp

The 1987 Supreme Court decision that upheld the constitutionality of the death penalty against charges that it violated the Fourteenth Amendment because minority defendants were more likely to receive the death penalty than were white defendants.

FIGURE 4.2 THE DECLINE OF EXECUTIONS

Supreme Court decisions, new DNA technology, and perhaps a growing public concern about the fairness of the death penalty have resulted in a dramatic drop in the number of death sentences—from 98 in 1999 to 39 in 2013. Texas leads the nation in executions, representing 41 percent of the national total in 2013. Texas prosecutors and juries are no more apt to seek and impose death sentences than those in other states that have the death penalty. However, once a death sentence is imposed there, prosecutors, the courts, the pardon board, and the governor are united in moving the process along.

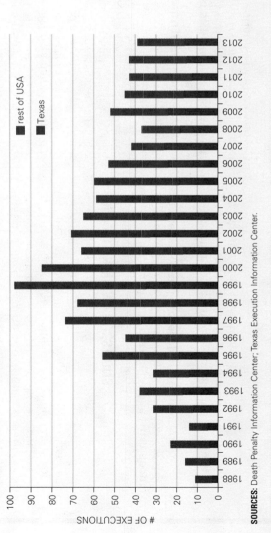

SOURCES: Death Penalty Information Center; Texas Execution Information Center.

Young People & Politics

College Students Help Prevent Wrongful Deaths

The Center on Wrongful Convictions at Northwestern University investigates possible wrongful convictions and represents imprisoned clients with claims of actual innocence. The young staff, including faculty, cooperating outside attorneys, and Northwestern University law students, pioneered the investigation and litigation of wrongful convictions—including the cases of nine innocent men sentenced to death in Illinois.

Undergraduates as well as law students have been involved in establishing the innocence of men who had been condemned to die. One instance involved the case of a man with an IQ of 51. The Illinois Supreme Court stayed his execution, just 48 hours before it was due to be carried out, because of questions about his mental fitness. This stay provided a professor and students from a Northwestern University investigative journalism class with an opportunity to investigate the man's guilt.

They tracked down and re-interviewed witnesses. One eyewitness recanted his testimony, saying that investigators had pressured him into implicating the man. The students found a woman who pointed to her ex-husband as the killer. Then a private investigator interviewed the ex-husband, who made a videotaped statement claiming he killed in self-defense. The students literally helped to save the life of an innocent man.

On January 11, 2003, Governor George H. Ryan of Illinois chose Lincoln Hall at Northwestern University's

School of Law to make a historic announcement. He commuted the death sentences of all 167 death row prisoners in Illinois (he also pardoned 4 others based on innocence the previous day). The governor felt it was fitting to make the announcement there, before "the students, teachers, lawyers, and investigators who first shed light on the sorrowful conditions of Illinois' death penalty system."

In addition to saving the lives of wrongfully convicted individuals in Illinois, the Northwestern investigations have also helped trigger a nationwide reexamination of the capital punishment system. To learn more about the Center on Wrongful Convictions, visit its Web site at http://www.law.northwestern.edu /wrongfulconvictions/.

CRITICAL THINKING QUESTIONS

1. Why do you think college students and others were better able to determine the truth about the innocence of condemned men than were the police and prosecutors at the original trial?

2. Are there other areas of public life in which students can make important contributions through their investigations?

In addition, the Supreme Court has placed constraints on the application of the death penalty, holding that the Constitution bars the execution of the mentally ill (*Ford v. Wainwright*, 1986); mentally retarded persons (*Atkins v. Virginia*, 2002) or the intellectually disabled (*Hall v. Florida*, 2014); those under the age of 18 when they commit their crimes (*Roper v. Simmons*, 2005); and those convicted of raping women (*Coker v. Georgia*, 1977) and children (*Kennedy v. Louisiana*, 2008) where the crime did not result, and was not intended to result, in the victim's death. In *Kennedy*, the Court ruled out the death penalty where the victim is an individual—as opposed to offenses against the state, like treason or espionage—where the victim's life was not taken. In addition, the Court has required that a jury, not just a judge, find that an aggravating circumstance is associated with a murder when a state requires such a circumstance for imposing the death penalty (*Ring v. Arizona*, 2002). The Court has also required lawyers for defendants in death penalty cases to make reasonable efforts to fight for their clients at a trial's sentencing phase (*Rompilla v. Beard* [2005]).

Debate over the death penalty continues. In 2008 the Supreme Court upheld the use of lethal injection, concluding that those who challenge this method of execution must show not only that a state's method "creates a demonstrated risk of severe pain," but also that there are alternatives that are "feasible" and "readily implemented" that would "significantly" reduce that risk.[111] You can see what some students are doing about the injustices they perceive in the death penalty system in "Young People and Politics: College Students Help Prevent Wrongful Deaths."

The Right to Privacy

4.7 Outline the evolution of a right to privacy and its application to the issue of abortion.

he members of the First Congress who drafted the Bill of Rights and enshrined in it the most basic American civil liberties would never have imagined that Americans would go to court to argue about wiretapping, surrogate motherhood, abortion, or pornography. New technologies have raised ethical issues unimaginable in the eighteenth century and focused attention on the question of privacy rights.

☐ Is There a Right to Privacy?

Nowhere does the Bill of Rights explicitly say that Americans have a **right to privacy**. Clearly, however, the First Congress had a concept of privacy in mind when it crafted the first ten amendments. Freedom of religion implies the right to exercise private beliefs. The Third Amendment prohibits the government from forcing citizens to quarter soldiers in their homes during times of peace. Protections against "unreasonable searches and seizures" make persons secure in their homes. Private property cannot be seized without "due process of law." In 1928 Justice Louis Brandeis hailed privacy as "the right to be left alone—the most comprehensive of the rights and the most valued by civilized men."

The idea that the Constitution guarantees a right to privacy was first enunciated in a 1965 case involving a Connecticut law forbidding the use of contraceptives. It was a little-used law, but a doctor and a family planning specialist were arrested for disseminating birth control devices. The state reluctantly brought them to court, and they were convicted. The Supreme Court, in the case of *Griswold v. Connecticut*, wrestled with the privacy issue. Seven justices finally decided that the explicitly stated rights in the Constitution implied a right to privacy, including a right to family planning between husband and wife. Supporters of privacy rights argued that this ruling was reasonable enough, for what could be the purpose of the Fourth Amendment, for example, if not to protect privacy? Critics of the ruling—and there were many of them—claimed that the Supreme Court was inventing protections not specified by the Constitution.

There are other areas of privacy rights, including the sexual behavior of gays and lesbians, as discussed in the chapter on civil rights. The most important application of privacy rights, however, came in the area of abortion. The Supreme Court unleashed a constitutional firestorm in 1973 that has not yet abated.

☐ Controversy over Abortion

In 1972 the Supreme Court heard one of the most controversial cases ever to come before the Court. Under the pseudonym of "Jane Roe," a Texas woman named Norma McCorvey sought an abortion. She argued that the state law allowing the procedure only to save the life of a mother was unconstitutional. Texas argued that states have the power to regulate moral behavior, including abortions. The Court ruled in *Roe v. Wade* (1973) that a right to privacy extends to a woman's decision to have an abortion under the due process clause in the Fourteenth Amendment. However, that right must be balanced against the state's two legitimate interests in regulating abortions: protecting prenatal life and protecting the woman's health. Saying that these state interests become stronger over the course of a pregnancy, the Court resolved this balancing test by tying state regulation of abortion to a woman's current trimester of pregnancy. *Roe* forbade any state control of abortions during the first trimester. It permitted states to regulate abortion procedures in the second trimester, but only for the sake of protecting a mother's health. It allowed states to ban abortion during the third trimester, except when the mother's life or health was in danger. This decision unleashed a storm of protest.

Since *Roe v. Wade*, there have been more than 50 million legal abortions in the United States, more than a million in 2011. Abortion is a common experience; 22 percent of all

right to privacy
The right to a private personal life free from the intrusion of government.

Roe v. Wade
The 1973 Supreme Court decision holding that a Texas state ban on abortions was unconstitutional. The decision forbade state control over abortions during the first trimester of pregnancy, permitted states to limit abortions to protect a mother's health in the second trimester, and permitted states to ban abortion during the third trimester.

136

4.1 4.2 4.3 4.4 4.5 4.6 4.7 4.8

Planned Parenthood v. Casey
A 1992 case in which the Supreme Court loosened its standard for evaluating restrictions on abortion from one of "strict scrutiny" of any restraints on a "fundamental right" to abortion to one in which regulations not impose an "undue burden" on women.

Abortion is perhaps the nation's most divisive issue, raising strong emotions on both sides of the debate. Here pro-life activists pray across the street from the Washington, D.C., offices of Planned Parenthood.

pregnancies (excluding miscarriages) end in abortion. At current rates, about 3 in 10 American women will have had an abortion by the time they reach age 45. Moreover, a broad cross section has abortions. Fifty-seven percent of women having abortions are in their twenties; 61 percent have one or more children; 45 percent have never married; 42 percent have incomes below the federal poverty level; and 78 percent report a religious affiliation. No racial or ethnic group makes up a majority: 36 percent of women obtaining abortions are white non-Hispanic, 30 percent are black non-Hispanic, 25 percent are Hispanic, and 9 percent are of other racial backgrounds.[112]

The furor over *Roe* has never subsided. Congress has passed numerous statutes forbidding the use of federal funds for abortions. Many states have passed similar restrictions. For example, Missouri forbade the use of state funds or state employees to perform abortions. The Supreme Court upheld this law in *Webster v. Reproductive Health Services* (1989).

In 1992, in *Planned Parenthood v. Casey*, the Court changed its standard for evaluating restrictions on abortion from one of "strict scrutiny" of any restraints on a "fundamental right" to one of "undue burden," which permits considerably more regulation. The Court upheld a 24-hour waiting period, a parental or judicial consent requirement for minors, and a requirement that doctors present women with information on the risks of the operation. The Court struck down a provision requiring a married woman to tell her husband of her intent to have an abortion; however, the majority of the justices also affirmed their commitment to the basic right to abortion.

One area of controversy has involved a procedure termed by its opponents as "partial birth" abortion. In 2000, the Court held in *Sternberg v. Carhart* that Nebraska's prohibition of partial birth abortions was unconstitutional, first, because the law placed an undue burden on women seeking an abortion by limiting their options to less safe procedures; second, because the law provided no exception for cases where the health of the mother was at risk; and, third, because the law did not clearly specify prohibited procedures. In 2003 Congress passed a law banning partial birth abortions, providing an exception to the ban in order to save the life of a mother but no exception to preserve a mother's health, on the grounds that the procedure was never necessary for a woman's health. In *Gonzales v. Carhart* (2007),

FIGURE 4.3   THE ABORTION DEBATE

In few areas of public opinion research do scholars find more divided opinion than abortion. Some people feel very strongly about the matter, enough so that they are "single-issue voters" unwilling to support any candidate who disagrees with them. The largest group takes a middle position, supporting the principle of abortion but also accepting restrictions on it.

Question: Do you think abortions should be legal under any circumstances, legal only under certain circumstances, or illegal in all circumstances?

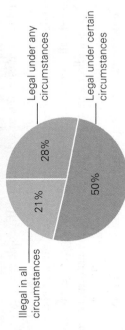

Illegal in all circumstances

Legal under any circumstances

Legal under certain circumstances

28%

21%

50%

SOURCE: Gallup Poll, May 8–11, 2014.

the Supreme Court upheld that law, finding it was specific and did not subject women to significant health risks or impose an undue burden on women. The Court also took pains to point out that the law would not affect most abortions, which are performed early in a pregnancy, and that safe alternatives to the prohibited procedure are available.

Americans are deeply divided on the issue of abortion (see Figure 4.3). Proponents of choice believe that access to legal abortions is essential if women are to be fully autonomous human beings and are to be protected from the dangers of illegal abortions. Opponents call themselves pro-life because they believe that the fetus is fully human and that an abortion therefore deprives a human of the right to life. These positions are irreconcilable; wherever a politician stands on this divisive issue, a large number of voters will be enraged.

With passions running so strongly on the issue, some pro-life advocates have taken extreme action. In the last two decades, abortion opponents have bombed a number of abortion clinics and murdered several physicians who performed abortions.

As mentioned earlier in the section on the right to assemble, women's right to obtain an abortion has clashed with protesters' rights to free speech and assembly. The Supreme Court has consolidated the right to abortion established in *Roe* with the protection of a woman's right to enter an abortion clinic to exercise that right and the government's interest in preserving order by upholding buffer zones around abortion clinics.[113] In 1994 Congress passed the Freedom of Access to Clinic Entrances Act, which makes it a federal crime to intimidate abortion providers or women seeking abortions. The Supreme Court also decided that abortion clinics could sue violent antiabortion protest groups for damages.[114]

Recently many state legislatures have passed laws restricting abortion providers, limiting medication abortion, increasing abortion reporting requirements, restricting acceptable reasons for abortions, limiting insurance coverage of abortion, and banning abortions after 20 weeks post-fertilization. As a result of these laws it is difficult for women to obtain an abortion in some parts of the country.

Understanding Civil Liberties

4.8   Assess how civil liberties affect democratic government and how they both limit and expand the scope of government.

 merican government is both democratic and constitutional. America is democratic because it is governed by officials who are elected by the people and, as such, are accountable for their actions. The American government is constitutional because it has a fundamental organic law, the Constitution, that limits the things that government may do. By restricting the

138

4.1
4.2
4.3
4.4
4.5
4.6
4.7
4.8

government, the Constitution limits what the people can empower the government to do. The democratic and constitutional components of government can produce conflicts, but they also reinforce one another.

Civil Liberties and Democracy

The rights ensured by the First Amendment—particularly the freedoms of speech, press, and assembly—are essential to a democracy. If people are to govern themselves, they need access to all available information and opinions in order to make intelligent and responsible decisions. If the right to participate in public life is to be open to all, then Americans—in all their diversity—must have the right to express their opinions.

Individual participation and the expression of ideas are crucial components of democracy, but so is majority rule, which can conflict with individual rights. The majority does not have the freedom to decide that there are some ideas it would rather not hear, although at times the majority tries to enforce its will on the minority. The conflict is even sharper in relation to the rights guaranteed by the Fourth, Fifth, Sixth, Seventh, and Eighth Amendments. These rights protect all Americans, but they also make it more difficult to punish criminals. It is easy—although misleading—for the majority to view these guarantees as benefits for criminals at the expense of society.

With some notable exceptions, the United States has done a good job of protecting the rights of diverse interests to express themselves. There is little danger that a political or economic elite will muffle dissent. Similarly, the history of the past five decades is one of increased protections for defendants' rights, and defendants are typically not among the elite. Ultimately, the courts have decided what constitutional guarantees mean in practice. Although federal judges, appointed for life, are not directly accountable to popular will,[115] "elitist" courts have often protected civil liberties from the excesses of majority rule.

Civil Liberties and the Scope of Government

Civil liberties in America are both the foundation for and a reflection of our emphasis on individualism. When there is a conflict between an individual or a group attempting to express themselves or worship as they please and an effort by a government to constrain them in some fashion, the individual or group usually wins. If protecting the freedom of an individual or group to express themselves results in inconvenience or even injustice for the public officials they criticize or the populace they wish to reach, so be it. Every nation must choose where to draw the line between freedom and order. In the United States, we generally choose liberty.

Today's government is huge and commands vast, powerful technologies. Americans' Social Security numbers, credit card numbers, driver's licenses, and school records are all on giant computers to which the government has immediate access. It is virtually impossible to hide from the police, the FBI, the Internal Revenue Service, or any governmental agency. Because Americans can no longer avoid the attention of government, strict limitations on governmental power are essential. The Bill of Rights provides these vital limitations.

Thus, in general, civil liberties limit the scope of government. Yet substantial government efforts are often required to protect the expansion of rights that we have discussed in this chapter. Those seeking abortions may need help reaching a clinic, defendants may demand that lawyers be provided to them at public expense, advocates of unpopular causes may require police protection, and litigants in complex lawsuits over matters of birth or death may rely on judges to resolve their conflicts. It is ironic—but true—that an expansion of freedom may require a simultaneous expansion of government.

Review the Chapter

The Bill of Rights

4.1 Trace the process by which the Bill of Rights has been applied to the states, p. 100.

In accordance with the incorporation doctrine, most of the freedoms outlined in the Bill of Rights limit the states as well as the national government. The due process clause of the Fourteenth Amendment provides the basis for this protection of rights.

Freedom of Religion

4.2 Distinguish the two types of religious rights protected by the First Amendment and determine the boundaries of those rights, p. 102.

The establishment clause of the First Amendment prohibits government sponsorship of religion, religious exercises, or religious doctrine, but government may support religious activities that have a secular purpose if doing so does not foster its excessive entanglement with religion. The free exercise clause guarantees that people may hold any religious views they like, but government may at times limit practices related to those views.

Freedom of Expression

4.3 Differentiate the rights of free expression protected by the First Amendment and determine the boundaries of those rights, p. 109.

Americans enjoy wide protections for expression, both spoken and written, including symbolic and commercial speech. Free expression is protected even when it conflicts with other rights, such as the right to a fair trial. However, the First Amendment does not protect some expression, such as libel, fraud, obscenity, and incitement to violence, and government has more leeway to regulate expression on the public airwaves.

Freedom of Assembly

4.4 Describe the rights to assemble and associate protected by the First Amendment and their limitations, p. 119.

The First Amendment protects the right of Americans to assemble to make a statement, although time, place, and manner restrictions on parades, picketing, and protests are permissible. Citizens also have the right to associate with others who share a common interest.

Right to Bear Arms

4.5 Describe the right to bear arms protected by the Second Amendment and its limitations, p. 121.

Most people have a right to possess firearms and use them for traditionally lawful purposes. However, government may limit this right to certain classes of people, certain areas, and certain weapons, and may require qualifications for purchasing firearms.

Defendants' Rights

4.6 Characterize defendants' rights and identify issues that arise in their implementation, p. 123.

The Bill of Rights provides defendants with many rights, including protections against unreasonable searches and seizures, self-incrimination, entrapment, and cruel and unusual punishment. (The Supreme Court has not found the death penalty unconstitutional.) Defendants also have a right to be brought before a judicial officer when arrested, to have the services of a lawyer, to receive a speedy and fair trial by an impartial jury, and to confront witnesses who testify against them. When arrested, suspects must be told of their rights. Nevertheless, the implementation of each of these rights requires judges to make nuanced decisions about the meaning of relevant provisions of the Constitution.

The Right to Privacy

4.7 Outline the evolution of a right to privacy and its application to the issue of abortion, p. 135.

Beginning in the 1960s, the Supreme Court articulated a right to privacy, as implied by the Bill of Rights. This right has been applied in various domains and is the basis for a woman's right to an abortion under most, but not all, circumstances.

Understanding Civil Liberties

4.8 Assess how civil liberties affect democratic government and how they both limit and expand the scope of government, p. 137.

The rights of speech, press, and assembly are essential to democracy. So is majority rule. When any of the rights protected by the Bill of Rights conflicts with majority rule, rights prevail.

There is a paradox about civil liberties and the scope of government. Civil liberties, by definition, limit the scope of government action, yet substantial government efforts may be necessary to protect the exercise of rights.

Learn the Terms

civil liberties, p. 100
Bill of Rights, p. 100
First Amendment, p. 100
Fourteenth Amendment, p. 102
due process clause, p. 102
incorporation doctrine, p. 102
establishment clause, p. 102
free exercise clause, p. 103

prior restraint, p. 110
libel, p. 115
symbolic speech, p. 116
commercial speech, p. 117
probable cause, p. 125
unreasonable searches and
  seizures, p. 125
search warrant, p. 125

exclusionary rule, p. 125
Fifth Amendment, p. 127
self-incrimination, p. 127
Sixth Amendment, p. 129
plea bargaining, p. 130
Eighth Amendment, p. 132
cruel and unusual punishment, p. 132
right to privacy, p. 135

Key Cases

Barron v. Baltimore (1833)
Gitlow v. New York (1925)
Lemon v. Kurtzman (1971)
Zelman v. Simmons-Harris (2002)
Engel v. Vitale (1962)
*School District of Abington Township,
  Pennsylvania v. Schempp* (1963)
Near v. Minnesota (1931)
Schenck v. United States (1919)

Roth v. United States (1957)
Miller v. California (1973)
New York Times v. Sullivan (1964)
Texas v. Johnson (1989)
Zurcher v. Stanford Daily (1978)
*Miami Herald Publishing Company
  v. Tornillo* (1974)
*Red Lion Broadcasting Company v. Federal
  Communications Commission* (1969)

NAACP v. Alabama (1958)
Mapp v. Ohio (1961)
Miranda v. Arizona (1966)
Gideon v. Wainwright (1963)
Gregg v. Georgia (1976)
McCleskey v. Kemp (1987)
Roe v. Wade (1973)
Planned Parenthood v. Casey (1992)

Test Yourself

1. In the 1780s, why did state ratifying conventions insist on the inclusion of a Bill of Rights?

a. They believed that the national government did not have enough power.

b. They distrusted states with the power given to them by the Constitution.

c. They remembered the abuses of civil liberties levied on colonists by the British Empire.

d. They wanted to give the president more power relative to the Congress.

e. They were pressured to do so by their local governments.

2. Prior to the Supreme Court ruling in *Gitlow v. New York*, how were state governments restricted by the Bill of Rights?

a. Only the First Amendment restricted state governments, with the Bill of Rights in its entirety applying just to the national government.

b. The Bill of Rights restricted state governments just as it did the national government.

c. The Bill of Rights did not restrict state governments but did restrict the national government.

d. The Bill of Rights restricted state governments on a case-by-case basis as it did the national government.

e. The Bill of Rights restricted state action only on a case-by-case basis while restricting the national government generally.

3. What is the legal concept under which the Supreme Court has nationalized the Bill of Rights?

   a. the due process clause

   b. the establishment doctrine

   c. the inclusion doctrine

   d. the incorporation doctrine

   e. the privileges and immunities clause

4. Which of the following statements best explains the Supreme Court's interpretation of what the government may do to regulate religion?

   a. It can prohibit religious beliefs and practices it considers inappropriate.

   b. It can prohibit religious beliefs and practices so long as it does not specifically target a religion.

   c. It can prohibit some religious practices but not religious beliefs.

   d. It can prohibit neither religious beliefs nor religious practices.

   e. It can prohibit religious practices and beliefs for only certain religions.

5. Imagine that you are an administrator at a public university and the Christian Fellowship has petitioned to use university facilities. According to Supreme Court decisions on the matter of religion and public schools, you

   a. can deny the Christian Fellowship the use of the university facilities

   b. must allow the Christian Fellowship to use the facilities, just like the Political Science Club and other student organizations

   c. must allow the Christian Fellowship to use the facilities as long as its activities there do not include worship

   d. must put the question to a vote of your student body

   e. must require the Christian Fellowship group to file a religious exemption before you grant its request

6. Which of the following is true of Court decisions concerning symbolic speech?

   a. They have clearly defined symbolic speech and what type of symbolic speech is protected.

   b. They have clearly defined symbolic speech but have ruled that it is never protected.

   c. They have extended protections to only some forms of symbolic speech.

   d. They have ruled that symbolic speech is always protected.

   e. They have not directly addressed the matter of symbolic speech.

7. What measures can a court take in order to guarantee the right to a fair trial in the face of media scrutiny?

   a. The court can limit journalists' access to particularly sensitive trials.

   b. The court can exercise prior restraint against the publication of information that might influence the jury.

   c. The court can force journalists to hold back sensitive information until after the trial has ended.

   d. The court can threaten journalists with fines and imprisonment for revealing sensitive information.

   e. The Supreme Court has never upheld a restriction on the press in the interest of a fair trial.

8. Which of the following is a result of the First Amendment's right to assembly?

   a. Governments can restrict political associations.

   b. There can be no restrictions on assembling to express opposition to government action.

   c. There are virtually no limitations on the content of a protest group's message.

   d. States can demand the names of members of a group interested in political change.

   e. Governments do not have to protect protestors from violence by onlookers.

9. Which of the following court decisions restricted the ability of public officials to sue the press for libel?

   a. *New York Times v. Sullivan*, 1964

   b. *New York Times v. United States*, 1974

   c. *United States v. Nixon*, 1974

   d. *Nebraska Press Association v. Stuart*, 1976

   e. *Collin v. Smith*, 1978

10. What is the primary complication involved in the free speech issue of obscenity?

   a. banning minors from playing violent games

   b. choosing appropriate rating systems for movies

   c. deciding what type of material should be banned

   d. determining what does and does not qualify as obscene

   e. understanding how to restrict the Internet

11. The purpose of the Second Amendment

   a. can by interpreted by the states

   b. is limited to protect the rights of non-citizens

   c. is limited to the use of handguns and rifles

   d. is to ensure that all guns are obtained legally

   e. is to guarantee the right for citizens to bear arms

12. If a judge rules that a prosecutor cannot use improperly obtained evidence, the judge is applying ————.

a. Miranda rights

b. probable cause

c. protection against self-incrimination

d. the exclusionary rule

e. the right to be represented by counsel

13. What was the significance of the decision in *McCleskey v. Kemp* (1987)?

a. The Court decided that the Second Amendment did not extend to owning any firearm sold from one individual to another.

b. The Court denied equal protection to African Americans because they were once considered private property.

c. The Court declared that the death penalty does not violate the Fourteenth Amendment because juries did not convict unduly on the basis of race.

d. Georgia's death penalty law was deemed unconstitutional because it targeted women more than men.

e. "Victim statements" were deemed unconstitutional because they violated the Fifth Amendment's protection against self-incrimination.

14. According to a 2008 decision, the Supreme Court said terrorism suspects held at Guantánamo Bay have the right to challenge their detention in a court because

a. citizens accused of terrorism must be detained at Guantánamo Bay, and citizens are guaranteed *habeas corpus*

b. detainees have no right to legal representation

c. the government cannot hold closed-door deportation hearings

d. the laws of the Constitution are enforceable by states only, except where enemy combatants are concerned

e. the laws of the Constitution cannot be set aside, even during extraordinary times

15. What did the landmark *Roe v. Wade* Supreme Court decision force states to do?

a. make abortions legal throughout all three trimesters of pregnancy

b. make abortions illegal in cases of rape, incest, and the health of the mother

c. grant paid maternity leave to women who decided not to have abortions

d. find a balance between a woman's right to privacy and the state's interest in the life of the child and health of the mother

e. balance *habeas corpus* with a woman's right to privacy

16. Why can the Fourth, Fifth, Sixth, Seventh, and Eighth Amendments be incongruent with majority rule?

a. because they ensure minority rule in certain cases

b. because they limit the power of Congress in declaring war

c. because they limit the scope of civil liberties

d. because they prevent dissent against the government

e. because they protect rights of the accused even if the public disagrees

---

Explore Further

WEB SITES

www.freedomforum.org
Background information and recent news on First Amendment issues.

www.eff.org
Web site concerned with protecting online civil liberties.

www.aclu.org
Home page of the American Civil Liberties Union, offering information and commentary on a wide range of civil liberties issues.

www.firstamendmentcenter.org/category/religion
Background on freedom of religion in the United States and discussion of major church–state cases.

www.firstamendmentcenter.org/category/speech
Background on freedom of speech in the United States and discussion of major free speech issues.

www.firstamendmentcenter.org/category/press
Background on freedom of the press in the United States and discussion of major free press issues.

Explains changes in public support for the death penalty and the number of executions.

Garrow, David J. *Liberty and Sexuality.* New York: Macmillan, 1994. The most thorough treatment of the development of the law on the right to privacy and abortion.

Heymann, Philip B. *Terrorism, Freedom, and Security.* Cambridge, MA: MIT Press, 2004. Thoughtfully balances concerns for freedom with those of safety from terrorism.

Irons, Peter. *The Courage of Their Convictions: Sixteen Americans Who Fought Their Way to the Supreme Court.* New York: Penguin Books, 1990. Accounts of 16 Americans over a period of 50 years who took their cases to the Supreme Court in defense of civil liberties.

Levy, Leonard W. *The Emergence of a Free Press.* New York: Oxford University Press, 1985. A major work on the Framers' intentions regarding freedom of expression.

Levy, Leonard W. *The Establishment Clause: Religion and the First Amendment.* New York: Macmillan, 1986. The author argues that it is unconstitutional for government to provide aid to any religion.

Lewis, Anthony. *Make No Law: The Sullivan Case and the First Amendment.* New York: Random House, 1991. A well-written story of the key case regarding American libel law and an excellent case study of a Supreme Court case.

Rose, Melody. *Safe, Legal, and Unavailable: Abortion Politics in the United States.* Washington, DC: CQ Press, 2007. Explores how many women do not have the ability to exercise their constitutional right to an abortion.

www.cc.org
Christian Coalition home page, containing background information and discussion of current events.

www.deathpenaltyinfo.org
The Death Penalty Information Center, providing data on all aspects of the death penalty.

www.guttmacher.org
The Guttmacher Institute, a nonpartisan source of information on all aspects of abortion.

reproductiverights.org/en
Center for Reproductive Rights Web site.

www.nrlc.org
National Right to Life Web site.

FURTHER READING

Adler, Renata. *Reckless Disregard.* New York: Knopf, 1986. The story of two monumental conflicts between free press and individual reputations.

Baker, Liva. *Miranda: The Crime, the Law, the Politics.* New York: Atheneum, 1983. An excellent book-length treatment of one of the major criminal cases of our time.

Baumgartner, Frank R., Suzanne L. De Boef, and Amber E. Boydstun. *The Decline of the Death Penalty and the Discovery of Innocence.* New York: Cambridge University Press, 2008.

5

Civil Rights and Public Policy

Politics in Action: Launching the Civil Rights Movement

A 42-year-old seamstress named Rosa Parks was riding in the "colored" section of a Montgomery, Alabama, city bus on December 1, 1955. A white man got on the bus and found that all the seats in the front, which were reserved for whites, were taken. He moved on to the equally crowded colored section. J. F. Blake, the bus driver, then ordered all four passengers in the first row of the colored section to surrender their seats because the law prohibited whites and blacks from sitting next to or even across from one another.

Three of the African Americans hesitated and then complied with the driver's order. But Rosa Parks, a politically active member of the National Association for the Advancement of Colored People, said no. The driver threatened to have her arrested, but she refused to move. He then called the police, and a few minutes later two officers boarded the bus and arrested her.

At that moment the civil rights movement went into high gear. There had been substantial efforts to use the courts to end racial segregation, some of which had yielded significant successes. But Rosa Parks's refusal to give up her seat led to extensive mobilization of African

5.1 Differentiate the Supreme Court's three standards of review for classifying people under the equal protection clause, p. 146.

5.2 Trace the evolution of civil rights protections of the rights of African Americans and explain the application of nondiscrimination principles to issues of race, p. 149.

5.3 Relate civil rights principles to the evolution of women's rights and explain how civil rights principles apply to gender issues, p. 156.

5.4 Trace the evolution of the struggles for civil rights of older Americans, persons with disabilities, and LGBT Americans, p. 161.

5.5 Summarize the struggles for civil rights of older Americans, persons with disabilities, and LGBT Americans, p. 166.

5.6 Trace the evolution of affirmative action policy and assess the arguments for and against it, p. 170.

5.7 Establish how civil rights policy advances democracy and increases the scope of government, p. 173.

The struggle for equality has been a long one. The civil rights movement, led by African Americans such as Dr. Martin Luther King, Jr., pictured here addressing the March on Washington in August 1963, played a critical role in winning more equal treatment for African Americans and, eventually, for other minority groups in America.

civil rights
Policies designed to protect people against arbitrary or discriminatory treatment by government officials or individuals.

5.1

5.2

5.3

5.4

5.5

5.6

5.7

The Struggle for Equality

Differentiate the Supreme Court's three standards of review for classifying people under the equal protection clause.

he struggle for equality has been a persistent theme in our nation's history. Slaves sought freedom, free African Americans fought for the right to vote and to be treated as equals, women pursued equal participation in society and politics, and the economically disadvantaged called for better treatment and economic opportunities. The fight for equality has affected all Americans. Philosophically, the struggle has involved defining the term *equality*. Constitutionally, it has involved interpreting laws. Politically, it has often involved power.

The phrase "All men are created equal" is at the heart of American political culture, yet implementing this principle has proved to be one of our nation's most enduring struggles. Throughout our history, a host of constitutional questions have been raised by issues involving African Americans, other racial and ethnic minorities, women, the elderly, persons with disabilities, and gays and lesbians—issues ranging from slavery and segregation to unequal pay and discrimination in hiring. The rallying cry of minority groups has been **civil rights**, which are policies designed to protect people against arbitrary or discriminatory treatment by government officials or individuals.

Individual liberty is central to democracy. So is a broad notion of equality, such as that implied by the concept of "one person, one vote." Sometimes these values conflict, as when individuals or a majority of the people want to act in a discriminatory fashion. How should we resolve such conflicts between liberty and equality? Can we have a democracy if some citizens do not enjoy basic rights to political participation or suffer discrimination in employment? Can we or should we try to remedy past discrimination against minorities and women?

Many people have called on government to protect the rights of minorities and women, increasing the scope and power of government in the process. Ironically, this increase in government power is often used to *check* government, as when the federal courts restrict the actions of state legislatures. It is equally ironic that society's collective efforts to use government to protect civil rights are designed not to limit individualism but to enhance it, freeing people from suffering and from prejudice. But how far should government go in these efforts? Is an increase in the scope of government to protect some people's rights an unacceptable threat to the rights of other citizens?

Americans have never fully come to terms with equality. Most Americans favor equality in the abstract—a politician who advocated inequality would not attract many votes—yet the concrete struggle for equal rights under the Constitution has been our nation's most bitter battle. It pits person against person, as in the case of Rosa Parks and the nameless white passenger, and group against group. Those people who enjoy privileged positions in American society have been reluctant to give them up.

On December 21, 1956, Rosa Parks boarded a Montgomery city bus for the first time in over a year. She could sit wherever she liked and chose a seat near the front.

It took the U.S. Supreme Court to end the boycott. On November 13, 1956, the Court declared that Alabama's state and local laws requiring segregation on buses were illegal. On December 20, federal injunctions were served on the city and bus company officials, forcing them to follow the Supreme Court's ruling.

It took a year. She could sit wherever she liked and chose a seat near the front.

even riding mules, they persisted in boycotting the buses.

were harassed by the police and went without motor transportation, instead walking or almost killed, but neither he nor the African American community wavered. Although they buses. He was jailed, his house was bombed, and his wife and infant daughter were tance. A new preacher in town, Martin Luther King, Jr., organized a boycott of the city Americans. Protestors employed a wide range of methods, including nonviolent resis-

5.1
5.2
5.3
5.4
5.5
5.6
5.7

147

Conceptions of Equality

What does *equality* mean? Jefferson's statement in the Declaration of Independence that "all men are created equal" did not mean that he believed everybody was exactly alike or that there were no differences among human beings. The Declaration went on to speak, however, of "unalienable rights" to which all are equally entitled. American society does not emphasize *equal results* or *equal rewards*; few Americans argue that everyone should earn the same salary or have the same amount of property. Instead, a belief in *equal rights* has led to a belief in *equality of opportunity*; in other words, everyone should have the same chance to succeed.

The Constitution and Inequality

The Constitution creates a plan for government, not guarantees of individual rights. Although the Bill of Rights guarantees individual rights, it does not mention equality. It does, however, have implications for equality in that it does not limit the scope of its guarantees to specified groups within society. It does not say, for example, that only whites have freedom from compulsory self-incrimination or that only men are entitled to freedom of speech. The First Amendment guarantees of freedom of expression, in particular, are important because they allow all those who are discriminated against to work toward achieving equality. As we will see, this kind of political activism has proven effective for groups fighting for civil rights.

The first and only place in which the idea of equality appears in the Constitution is in the **Fourteenth Amendment**, one of the three amendments passed after the Civil War. (The Thirteenth Amendment abolished slavery. The Fifteenth Amendment extended the right to vote to African Americans.) Ratified in 1868, the Fourteenth Amendment forbids the states from denying to anyone "**equal protection of the laws.**" This *equal protection clause* became the principal tool for waging struggles for equality. Laws, rules, and regulations inevitably classify people. For example, some people are eligible to vote while others are not; some people are eligible to attend a state university while others are denied admission. Such classifications cannot violate the equal protection of the law.

How do the courts determine whether a classification in a law or regulation is permissible or violates the equal protection clause? For this purpose, the Supreme Court developed three levels of scrutiny, or analysis, called *standards of review* (see Table 5.1). The Court has ruled that to pass constitutional muster, most classifications must only be *reasonable*. In practice, this means that a classification must bear a rational relationship to some legitimate governmental purpose, for example, to educating

Fourteenth Amendment

The constitutional amendment adopted after the Civil War that states, "No State shall make or enforce any law which shall abridge the privileges or immunities of citizens of the United States; nor shall any state deprive any person of life, liberty, or property, without due process of law, nor deny to any person within its jurisdiction the equal protection of the laws." It is the first and only part of the Constitution to invoke the idea of equality.

equal protection of the laws

Part of the Fourteenth Amendment emphasizing that the laws must provide equivalent "protection" to all people.

TABLE 5.1 SUPREME COURT'S STANDARDS FOR CLASSIFICATIONS UNDER THE EQUAL PROTECTION CLAUSE OF THE FOURTEENTH AMENDMENT

The Supreme Court has three standards of review for evaluating whether a classification in a law or regulation is constitutionally permissible. Most classifications must bear only a rational relationship to some legitimate governmental purpose. The burden of proof is on anyone challenging such classifications to show that they are not reasonable, but arbitrary. At the other extreme, the burden of proof is on the rule maker. Racial and ethnic classifications are inherently suspect, and courts presume that they are invalid and uphold them only if they serve a compelling public interest and there is no other way to accomplish the purpose of the law. The courts make no presumptions about classifications based on gender. They must bear a substantial relationship to an important governmental purpose, a lower threshold than serving a compelling public interest.

Basis of Classification	Standard of Review	Applying the Test
Race and ethnicity	Inherently suspect *difficult to meet*	Is the classification necessary to accomplish a compelling governmental goal? Is it the least restrictive way to achieve that goal?
Gender	Intermediate scrutiny *moderately difficult to meet*	Does the classification bear a substantial relationship to an important governmental goal?
Other (age, wealth, etc.)	Reasonableness *easy to meet*	Does the classification have a rational relationship to a legitimate governmental goal?

148

5.1

5.2

5.3

5.4

5.5

5.6

5.7

students in colleges. The courts defer to rule makers, typically legislatures. Anyone who challenges classifications has the burden of proving that they are not reasonable but arbitrary. (A classification that is arbitrary—a law singling out, say, people with red hair or blue eyes for inferior treatment—is unconstitutional.) Thus, for example, the states can restrict the right to vote to people over the age of 18; age is a reasonable classification and hence a permissible basis for determining who may vote.

With some classifications, however, the burden of proof is on the rule maker. The Court has ruled that racial and ethnic classifications, such as those that would prohibit African Americans from attending school with whites or that would deny a racial or ethnic group access to public services such as a park or swimming pool, are *inherently suspect*. Courts presume that these classifications are invalid and uphold them only if they serve a "compelling public interest" and there is no other way to accomplish the purpose of the law. In the case of a racial or ethnic classification, the burden of proof is on the government that created the classification to prove that it meets these criteria. It is virtually impossible to show that a classification by race or ethnicity that serves to disadvantage a minority group serves a compelling public interest. What about classifications by race and ethnicity, such as for college admissions, that are designed to *remedy* previous discrimination? As we will see in our discussion of affirmative action, the Court is reluctant to approve even these laws.

Classifications based on gender receive *intermediate scrutiny*; the courts presume them to be neither constitutional nor unconstitutional. A law that classifies people by gender, such as one that makes men but not women eligible for a military draft, must bear a substantial relationship to an important governmental purpose, a lower threshold than serving a "compelling public interest."

Conditions for women and minorities would be radically different if it were not for the "equal protection" clause.[1] The following sections show how equal protection litigation has worked to the advantage of minorities, women, and other groups seeking protection under the civil rights umbrella.

The African American struggle for equality paved the way for women and other minorities to organize movements for their civil rights. Here, civil rights leaders Roy Wilkins, James Farmer, Dr. Martin Luther King Jr., and Whitney Young meet with President Lyndon B. Johnson.

African Americans' Civil Rights

5.1
5.2
5.3
5.4
5.5
5.6
5.7

149

5.2 Trace the evolution of protections of the rights of African Americans and explain the application of nondiscrimination principles to issues of race.

frican Americans have always been the most visible minority group in the United States. They have blazed the constitutional trail for securing equal rights for all Americans. They made very little progress, however, until well into the twentieth century.

Slavery

For the first 250 years of American settlement, most African Americans lived in slavery. Slaves were the property of their masters. They could be bought and sold; they could neither vote nor own property. The Southern states, whose plantations relied on large numbers of unpaid workers, were the primary market for slave labor. Policies of the slave states and the federal government accommodated the property interests of slave owners, who were often wealthy and enjoyed substantial political influence.

In 1857 the Supreme Court bluntly announced in *Dred Scott v. Sandford* that a black man, slave or free, was "chattel" and had no rights under a white man's government. The Court declared that Congress had no power to ban slavery in the western territories. Thus it invalidated the hard-won Missouri Compromise (1820), which had allowed Missouri to become a slave state on the condition that northern territories would remain free of slavery. As a result, the *Dred Scott* decision was an important milestone on the road to the Civil War.

The Union victory in the Civil War and the ratification of the **Thirteenth Amendment** ended slavery. The promises implicit in this amendment and the other two Civil War amendments, The Fourteenth and Fifteenth Amendments, introduced the era of reconstruction and segregation, in which the promises were first honored and then broken.

Reconstruction and Segregation

After the Civil War ended, Congress imposed strict conditions on the former Confederate states before it would seat their representatives and senators. No one who had served in secessionist state governments or in the Confederate army could hold state office, the legislatures had to ratify the new amendments to the Constitution, and the U.S. military would govern the states like "conquered provinces" until they complied with the tough federal plans for reconstruction. Many African American men held state and federal offices during the 10 years following the war. Some government agencies, such as the Freedmen's Bureau, provided assistance to former slaves who were making the difficult transition from slavery to freedom.

To ensure his election in 1876, Rutherford B. Hayes promised to pull federal troops out of the South and let the Southern states do as they pleased. Southerners lost little time reclaiming power and imposing a code of *Jim Crow laws*, or segregationist laws, on African Americans. ("Jim Crow" was the name of a stereotypical African American in a nineteenth-century minstrel song.) These laws relegated African Americans to separate public facilities, separate school systems, and even separate restrooms. Not only had most whites lost interest in helping former slaves, but much of what the Jim Crow laws mandated in the South was also common practice in the North. Indeed, the national government practiced segregation in the armed forces, employment, housing programs, and prisons.[2] At the time, racial segregation affected every part of life, from the cradle to the grave. African Americans were delivered by African American physicians or midwives and buried in African American cemeteries. Groups such as the Ku Klux Klan terrorized African Americans who violated the norms of segregation, lynching hundreds of people.

Scott v. Sandford
The 1857 Supreme Court decision ruling that a slave who had escaped to a free state enjoyed no rights as a citizen and that Congress had no authority to ban slavery in the territories.

Thirteenth Amendment
The constitutional amendment ratified after the Civil War that forbade slavery and involuntary servitude.

5.1

5.2

5.3

5.4

5.5

5.6

5.7

Plessy v. Ferguson
An 1896 Supreme Court decision that provided a constitutional justification for segregation by ruling that a Louisiana law requiring "equal but separate accommodations for the white and colored races" was constitutional.

In the era of segregation, Jim Crow laws, such as those requiring separate drinking fountains for African Americans and whites, governed much of life in the South.

The Supreme Court was of little help. Although it voided a law barring African Americans from serving on juries (*Strauder v. West Virginia* [1880]), in the *Civil Rights Cases* (1883), it held that the Fourteenth Amendment did not prohibit racial discrimination by private businesses and individuals.

The Court then provided a constitutional justification for segregation in the 1896 case of *Plessy v. Ferguson*. The Louisiana legislature had required "equal but separate accommodations for the white and colored races" in railroad transportation. Although Homer Plessy was seven-eighths white, he had been arrested for refusing to leave a railway car reserved for whites. The Court upheld the law, saying that segregation in public facilities was not unconstitutional as long as the separate facilities were substantially equal. Moreover, the Court subsequently paid more attention to the "separate" than to the "equal" part of this ruling, allowing Southern states to maintain high schools and professional schools for whites even where there were no such schools for blacks. Significantly, until the 1960s, nearly all the African American physicians in the United States were graduates of two medical schools, Howard University in Washington, D.C., and Meharry Medical College in Tennessee.

Nevertheless, some progress on the long road to racial equality was made in the first half of the twentieth century. The Niagara Movement was an early civil rights organization, founded in 1905. It folded into the National Association for the Advancement of Colored People (NAACP), which was formed in 1908, partly in response to the continuing practice of lynching and a race riot that year in Springfield, Illinois. The Brotherhood of Sleeping Car Porters, the first labor organization led by African Americans, was founded in 1928.

In the meantime, the Supreme Court voided some of the most egregious practices limiting the right to vote (discussed later in this chapter). In 1941 President Franklin D. Roosevelt issued an executive order forbidding racial discrimination in defense industries, and in 1948, President Harry S. Truman ordered the desegregation of the armed services. The leading edge of change, however, was in education.

☐ Equal Education

Education is at the core of Americans' beliefs in equal opportunity. It is not surprising, then, that civil rights advocates focused many of their early efforts on desegregating schools. To avoid the worst of backlashes, they started with higher education.

5.1
5.2
5.3
5.4
5.5
5.6
5.7

151

Brown v. Board of Education

The 1954 Supreme Court decision holding that school segregation is inherently unconstitutional because it violates the Fourteenth Amendment's guarantee of equal protection. This case marked the end of legal segregation in the United States.

The University of Oklahoma admitted George McLaurin, an African American, as a graduate student but forced him to use separate facilities, including a special table in the cafeteria, a designated desk in the library, and a desk just outside the classroom doorway. In *McLaurin v. Oklahoma State Regents* (1950), the Supreme Court ruled that a public institution of higher learning may not provide different treatment to a student solely because of his or her race. In the same year, in *Sweatt v. Painter*, the Court found the "separate but equal" formula generally unacceptable for professional schools.

At this point, civil rights leaders turned to elementary and secondary education. After searching carefully for the perfect opportunity to challenge legal public school segregation, the Legal Defense Fund of the NAACP selected the case of Linda Brown. Brown was an African American student in Topeka, Kansas, required by Kansas law to attend a segregated school. In Topeka, African American schools were fairly equivalent to white schools with regard to the visible signs of educational quality—teacher qualifications, facilities, and so on. The NAACP chose the case in order to test the *Plessy v. Ferguson* doctrine of "separate but equal." It wanted to force the Supreme Court to rule directly on whether school segregation was inherently unequal and thereby violated the requirement in the Fourteenth Amendment that states guarantee "equal protection of the laws."

President Dwight D. Eisenhower had just appointed Chief Justice Earl Warren. So important was the case that the Court heard two rounds of arguments, one before Warren joined the Court, one afterward. The justices, after hearing the oral arguments, met in the Supreme Court's conference room. Believing that a unanimous decision would have the most impact, the justices negotiated a broad agreement and then determined that Warren himself should write the opinion.

In ***Brown v. Board of Education*** (1954), the Supreme Court set aside its precedent in *Plessy* and held that school segregation was inherently unconstitutional because it violates the Fourteenth Amendment's guarantee of equal protection. Legal segregation had come to an end.

A year after its decision in *Brown*, the Court ordered lower courts to proceed with "all deliberate speed" to desegregate public schools. Desegregation proceeded slowly in the South, however. A few counties threatened to close their public schools; white enrollment in private schools soared. In 1957 President Eisenhower had to send troops to desegregate Central High School in Little Rock, Arkansas. In 1969, 15 years after its first ruling that school segregation was unconstitutional, and in the face of continued massive resistance, the Supreme Court withdrew its earlier grant of time to school authorities and declared, "Delays in desegregating school systems are no longer tolerable" (*Alexander v. Holmes County Board of Education*). Thus, after nearly a generation of modest progress, Southern schools were suddenly integrated (see Figure 5.1).

Why It Matters to You
Brown v. Board of Education

In *Brown v. Board of Education*, the Supreme Court overturned its decision in *Plessy v. Ferguson*. The decision in *Brown* represents a major step in changing the face of America. Just imagine what the United States would be like today if we still had segregated public facilities and services like universities and restaurants.

In general, the Court has found that if schools have been legally segregated, authorities have an obligation to overcome past discrimination. They could do this by, for example, assigning students to schools in a way that would promote racial balance. Some federal judges ordered the busing of students to achieve racially balanced schools, a practice upheld (but not required) by the Supreme Court in *Swann v. Charlotte–Mecklenberg County Schools* (1971).

FIGURE 5.1 PERCENTAGE OF BLACK STUDENTS ATTENDING SCHOOL WITH ANY WHITES IN SOUTHERN STATES

Despite the Supreme Court's decision in *Brown v. Board of Education* in 1954, school integration proceeded at a snail's pace in the South for a decade. Most Southern African American children entering the first grade in 1955 never attended school with white children. Things picked up considerably in the late 1960s, however, when the Supreme Court insisted that obstruction of implementation of its decision in *Brown* must come to an end.

The figure is based on elementary and secondary students in 11 Southern states—Virginia, North Carolina, South Carolina, Georgia, Alabama, Mississippi, Louisiana, Texas, Arkansas, Tennessee, and Florida.

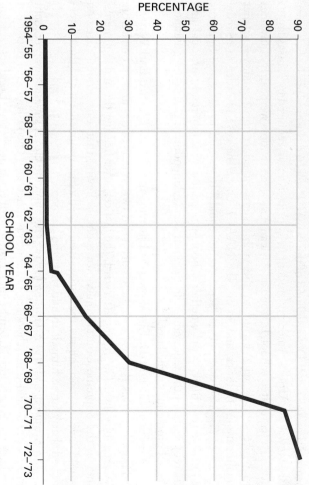

SOURCE: Data from Lawrence Baum.

Not all racial segregation is what is called *de jure* ("by law") segregation. *De facto* ("in reality") segregation results, for example, when children are assigned to schools near their homes and those homes are in neighborhoods that are racially segregated for social and economic reasons. Sometimes the distinction between *de jure* and *de facto* segregation has been blurred by past official practices. Because minority groups and federal lawyers demonstrated that Northern schools, too, had purposely drawn school district lines to promote segregation, school busing came to the North as well. Denver, Boston, and other cities instituted busing for racial balance, just as Southern cities did.

Majorities of both whites and blacks have opposed busing, which is one of the least popular remedies for discrimination. In recent years, it has become less prominent as a judicial instrument. Courts do not have the power to order busing between school districts; thus, school districts that are composed largely of minorities must rely on other means to integrate.

The Civil Rights Movement and Public Policy

The civil rights movement organized both African Americans and whites. Using tactics such as sit-ins, marches, and civil disobedience, movement leaders sought to establish equal opportunities in the political and economic sectors and to end the policies and practices of segregation (see "Young People and Politics: Freedom Riders"). The movement's trail was long and sometimes bloody. Police turned their dogs on nonviolent marchers in Birmingham, Alabama. Racists murdered civil rights activists in Meridian, Mississippi, and Selma, Alabama. Fortunately, the goals of the civil rights movement appealed to the national conscience. By the 1970s, overwhelming majorities of white Americans supported racial integration.[3] Today, the principles established in *Brown*

Young People & Politics

Freedom Riders

Most political activity is quite safe. There have been occasions, however, when young adults have risked bodily harm and even death to fight for their beliefs. Years after *Brown v. Board of Education* (1954), segregated transportation was still the law in some parts of the Deep South. To change this system, the Congress of Racial Equality (CORE) organized freedom rides in 1961. Young black and white volunteers in their teens and early twenties traveled on buses through the Deep South. In Anniston, Alabama, segregationists destroyed one bus, and men armed with clubs, bricks, iron pipes, and knives attacked riders on another. In Birmingham, the passengers were greeted by members of the Ku Klux Klan with further acts of violence. At Montgomery, the state capital, a white mob beat the riders with chains and ax handles.

The Ku Klux Klan hoped that this violent treatment would stop other young people from taking part in freedom rides. It did not. Over the next six months, more than a thousand people took part in freedom rides. A young white man from Madison, Wisconsin, James Zwerg, was badly injured by a mob and left in the road for over an hour. White-run ambulances refused to take him to the hospital. In an interview afterward, he reflected the grim determination of the freedom riders: "Segregation must be stopped. It must be broken down. Those of us on the Freedom Ride will continue. No matter what happens we are dedicated to this. We will take the beatings. We are willing to accept death."

As with the Montgomery bus boycott and the conflict at Little Rock, the freedom riders gave worldwide publicity to the racial discrimination suffered by African Americans, and in doing so they helped to bring about change. Attorney General Robert Kennedy petitioned the Interstate Commerce Commission (ICC) to draft regulations to end racial segregation in bus terminals. The ICC was reluctant, but in September 1961 it issued the necessary orders.

The freedom riders did not limit themselves to desegregating buses. During the summer of 1961, they also sat together in segregated restaurants, lunch counters, and hotels. Typically they were refused service, and they were often threatened and sometimes attacked. The sit-in tactic was especially effective when it focused on large companies that feared boycotts in the North and that began to desegregate their businesses.

In the end, the courage of young people committed to racial equality prevailed. They helped to change the face of America.

CRITICAL THINKING QUESTIONS

1. What are young adults doing to fight racism today?
2. Does civil disobedience have a role in contemporary America?

It was the courts as much as the national conscience that put civil rights goals on the nation's policy agenda. *Brown v. Board of Education* was the beginning of a string of Supreme Court decisions holding various forms of discrimination—not only in education but in other areas—unconstitutional. *Brown* and these other cases gave the civil rights movement momentum that would grow in the years that followed.

As a result of national conscience, the courts, the civil rights movement, and the increased importance of African American voters, the 1950s and 1960s saw a marked increase in public policies seeking to foster racial equality. These innovations included policies to promote voting rights, access to public accommodations, open housing, and nondiscrimination in many other areas of social and economic life. The **Civil Rights Act of 1964** was the most important civil rights law in nearly a century. It did the following:

- Made racial discrimination illegal in hotels, motels, restaurants, and other places of public accommodation
- Forbade discrimination in employment on the basis of race, color, national origin, religion, or gender[4]
- Created the Equal Employment Opportunity Commission (EEOC) to monitor and enforce protections against job discrimination
- Provided for withholding federal grants from state and local governments and other institutions that practiced racial discrimination

Civil Rights Act of 1964

The law making racial discrimination in public accommodations illegal. It forbade many forms of job discrimination. It also strengthened voting rights.

154

5.1

5.2

5.3

5.4

5.5

5.6

5.7

- Strengthened voting rights legislation
- Authorized the U.S. Justice Department to initiate lawsuits to desegregate public schools and facilities

The Voting Rights Act of 1965 (discussed next) was the most extensive federal effort to crack century-old barriers to African Americans voting in the South. The Supreme Court decided in *Jones v. Mayer* (1968) that to prevent racial discrimination Congress could regulate the sale of private property, and Congress passed the *Open Housing Act of 1968* to forbid discrimination in the sale or rental of housing.

In short, in the years following *Brown*, congressional and judicial policies attacked virtually every type of segregation. By the 1980s there were few, if any, forms of racial discrimination in the law left to legislate against. Efforts to pass civil rights legislation were successful, in part, because by the mid-1960s federal laws effectively protected the right to vote. Members of minority groups thus had some power to hold their legislators accountable.

☐ Voting Rights

The early Republic limited **suffrage**, the legal right to vote, to a handful of the population—mostly property-holding white males. The **Fifteenth Amendment**, adopted in 1870, guaranteed African Americans the right to vote—at least in principle. It said, "The right of citizens to vote shall not be abridged by the United States or by any state on account of race, color, or previous condition of servitude." The gap between these words and their implementation, however, remained wide for a full century. States seemed to outdo one another in developing ingenious methods of circumventing the Fifteenth Amendment.

Many states required potential voters to complete literacy tests before registering to vote. Typically the requirement was that they read, write, and show that they understood the state constitution or the U.S. Constitution. In practice, however, registrars rarely administered the literacy tests to whites, while the standard of literacy they required of blacks was so high that few were ever able to pass the test. In addition, Oklahoma and other Southern states used a *grandfather clause* that exempted persons whose grandfathers were eligible to vote in 1860 from taking these tests. This exemption did not apply, of course, to the grandchildren of slaves, but it did allow illiterate whites to vote. The law was blatantly unfair; it was also unconstitutional, said the Supreme Court in the 1915 decision *Guinn v. United States*.

To exclude African Americans from registering to vote, most Southern states also relied on **poll taxes**, which were small taxes levied on the right to vote that often fell due at a time of year when poor sharecroppers had the least cash on hand. To render African American votes ineffective, most Southern states also used the **white primary**, a device that permitted political parties to exclude African Americans from voting in primary elections. Because the South was so heavily Democratic, white primaries had the effect of depriving African Americans of a voice in the most important contests and letting them vote only when it mattered least, in the general election. The Supreme Court declared white primaries unconstitutional in 1944 in *Smith v. Allwright*.

The civil rights movement put suffrage high on its political agenda; one by one, the barriers to African American voting fell during the 1960s. The **Twenty-fourth Amendment**, which was ratified in 1964, prohibited poll taxes in federal elections. Two years later, the Supreme Court voided poll taxes in state elections in *Harper v. Virginia State Board of Elections*.

To combat the use of discriminatory voter registration tests the **Voting Rights Act of 1965** prohibited any government from using voting procedures that denied a person the vote on the basis of race or color; it also abolished the use of literacy requirements for anyone who had completed the sixth grade. The federal government sent election registrars to areas with long histories of discrimination. These same areas had to submit all proposed changes in their voting laws or practices to a federal official for approval[5] (the Supreme Court held

---

suffrage
The legal right to vote, extended to African Americans by the Fifteenth Amendment, to women by the Nineteenth Amendment, and to 18- to 20-year-olds by the Twenty-sixth Amendment.

Fifteenth Amendment
The constitutional amendment adopted in 1870 to extend suffrage to African Americans.

poll taxes
Small taxes levied on the right to vote. Poll taxes were used by most Southern states to exclude African Americans from voting.

white primary
Primary elections from which African Americans were excluded, an exclusion that, in the heavily Democratic South, deprived African Americans of a voice in the real contests. The Supreme Court declared white primaries unconstitutional in 1944.

Twenty-fourth Amendment
The constitutional amendment passed in 1964 that declared poll taxes void in federal elections.

Voting Rights Act of 1965
A law designed to help end formal and informal barriers to African American suffrage. Under the law, hundreds of thousands of African Americans registered to vote, and the number of African American elected officials increased dramatically.

The Voting Rights Act of 1965 produced a major increase in the number of African Americans registered to vote in Southern states. Voting also translated into increased political clout for African Americans.

in 2013, however, that the most recent formula Congress had used to determine whether jurisdictions had to seek federal preclearance was unconstitutional because it was based on 1975 data[6].)

As a result of these changes, hundreds of thousands of African Americans registered to vote in Southern states. In 1965 only 70 African Americans held public office in the 11 former Confederate states. By the early 1980s, more than 2,500 African Americans held elected offices in those states, and the number has continued to grow. There are currently more than 9,400 African American elected officials in the United States.[7]

The Voting Rights Act of 1965 not only secured the right to vote for African Americans but also attempted to ensure that their votes would not be diluted through racial gerrymandering (drawing district boundaries to advantage a specific group). For example, in many cases, the residences of minorities were clustered in one part of a city. If members of the city council were elected from districts within the city, minority candidates had a better chance to win some seats. In order to reduce the chance that a geographically concentrated minority would elect a minority council member, some cities chose to elect their council members to at-large seats, meaning that voters from any part of the city could elect council members. When Congress amended the Voting Rights Act in 1982, it insisted that minorities be able to "elect representatives of their choice" when their numbers and configuration permitted. Thus, governments at all levels had to draw district boundaries to avoid discriminatory *results* and not just discriminatory *intent*. In 1986, in *Thornburg v. Gingles*, the Supreme Court upheld this principle.

Why It Matters to You
The Voting Rights Act

In passing the Voting Rights Act of 1965, Congress enacted an extraordinarily strong law to protect the rights of minorities to vote. There is little question that officials pay more attention to minorities when they can vote. And many more members of minority groups are now elected to high public office.

5.1
5.2
5.3
5.4
5.5
5.6
5.7

The Rights of Other Minority Groups

Relate civil rights principles to progress made by other ethnic groups in the United States.

merica is heading toward a *minority majority*, a situation in which Americans who are members of minority groups will outnumber Americans of European descent, a number of states already have minority majorities (see Figure 5.2). African Americans are not the only minority group that has suffered legally imposed discrimination. Even before the civil rights struggle, Native Americans, Hispanics, and Asians learned how powerless they could be in a society dominated by whites. The civil rights laws for which African Americans fought have benefited members of these groups as well. In addition, social movements tend to beget new social movements; thus the African American civil rights movement of the 1960s spurred other minorities to mobilize to protect their rights.

□ Native Americans

The earliest inhabitants of the continent, American Indians, are, of course, the oldest minority group. About 6.3 million people identify themselves as at least part Native American or Native Alaskan, including 11 percent of New Mexicans and Oklahomans, and 19 percent of Alaskans.[13]

The history of poverty, discrimination, and exploitation experienced by American Indians is a long one. For generations, U.S. policy promoted westward expansion at the expense of Native Americans' lands. The government isolated Native Americans on reservations, depriving them of their lands and their rights. Then, with the Dawes Act of 1887, the federal government turned to a strategy of forced assimilation, sending children to boarding schools off the reservations, often against the will of their families, and banning tribal rituals and languages.

Officials in the Justice Department, which is responsible for enforcing the Voting Rights Act, and state legislatures that drew new district lines interpreted the amendment of the Voting Rights Act and the *Thornburg* decision as a mandate to create minority-majority districts, districts in which a minority group accounted for a majority of the voters. However, in 1993 the Supreme Court decried the abandonment of traditional redistricting standards such as compactness and contiguity.[8] In 1994 the Court ruled that a state legislative redistricting plan that does not create the greatest possible number of minority-majority districts is not in violation of the Voting Rights Act,[9] and in 1995 the Court rejected the efforts of the Justice Department to achieve the maximum possible number of minority districts. It held that the use of race as a "predominant factor" in drawing district lines should be presumed to be unconstitutional.[10] The next year, the Supreme Court voided several convoluted congressional districts on the grounds that race had been the primary reason for abandoning compact district lines and that the state legislatures had crossed the line into unconstitutional racial gerrymandering.[11]

In yet another turn, in 1999 the Court declared in *Hunt v. Cromartie* that conscious consideration of race is not automatically unconstitutional if the state's primary motivation is potentially political rather than racial. (For example, in drawing district lines, a state may consider the fact that African Americans tend to be Democrats.) The Court has also decided that state legislatures may redraw district boundaries at any time and not only after a census.[12]

FIGURE 5.2 MINORITY POPULATION BY STATE

The country's minority population has now reached over 115 million, including about 53 million Hispanic Americans and 39 million African Americans. Minorities make up approximately 37 percent of all Americans. Forty-six percent of all the children under 18 are from minority families. This map shows minorities as a percentage of each state's population. Hawaii has the largest minority population at 77 percent, followed by the District of Columbia (64 percent), California (60 percent), New Mexico (60 percent), and Texas (55 percent). In eight other states—Arizona, Florida, Georgia, Maryland, Mississippi, Nevada, New Jersey, and New York—minorities make up at least 40 percent of the population.

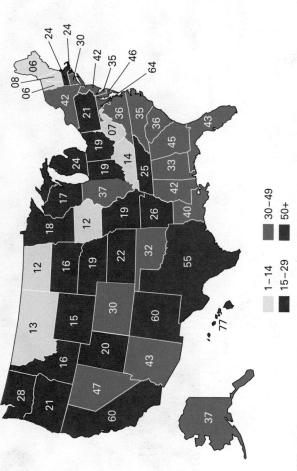

1–14   30–49
15–29   50+

SOURCE: U.S. Census Bureau, 2014.

Finally, in 1924 Congress made American Indians citizens of the United States and gave them the right to vote, a status that African Americans had achieved a half century before. Not until 1946 did Congress establish the Indian Claims Act to settle Indians' claims against the government related to land that had been taken from them.[14]

Today, Native Americans still have high rates of poverty and ill health, and almost half live on or near a reservation. Native Americans know, perhaps better than any other group, the significance of the gap between public policy regarding discrimination and the realization of that policy.

But progress is being made. The civil rights movement of the 1960s created a more favorable climate for Native Americans to secure guaranteed access to the polls, to housing, and to jobs and to reassert their treaty rights. The Indian Bill of Rights was adopted as Title II of the Civil Rights Act of 1968, applying most of the provisions of the Constitution's Bill of Rights to tribal governments. In *Santa Clara Pueblo v. Martinez* (1978), the Supreme Court strengthened the tribal power of individual tribe members and furthered self-government by Indian tribes.

Progress came in part through the activism of Indians such as Dennis Means of the American Indian Movement (AIM), Vine Deloria, and Dee Brown, who drew attention to the plight of American Indian tribes. In 1969, for example, some Native Americans seized Alcatraz Island in San Francisco Bay to protest the loss of Indian lands. In 1973 armed members of AIM seized 11 hostages at Wounded Knee, South Dakota—the site of an 1890 massacre of 200 Sioux (Lakota) by U.S. cavalry—and remained there for 71 days until the federal government agreed to examine Indian treaty rights.

Equally important, Indians began to use the courts to protect their rights. The Native American Rights Fund (NARF), founded in 1970, has won important victories concerning hunting, fishing, and land rights. Native Americans are also retaining access to their sacred places and have had some success in stopping the building of roads and buildings on ancient burial grounds and other sacred spots. Several tribes have won court cases protecting them from taxation of tribal profits.

Despite some progress, many Native Americans, such as these grandparents and their grandchildren, continue to suffer poverty and ill health.

As in other areas of civil rights, the preservation of Native American culture and the exercise of Native American rights sometimes conflict with the interests of the majority. For example, some tribes have gained special rights to fish and even to hunt whales. Anglers concerned with the depletion of fishing stock and environmentalists worried about loss of the whale population have voiced protests. Similarly, Native American rights to run businesses denied to others by state law and to avoid taxation on tribal lands have made running gambling casinos a lucrative option for Indians. This has irritated both those who oppose gambling and those who are offended by the tax-free competition.

☐ Hispanic Americans

Hispanic Americans (or Latinos, as some prefer to be called)—chiefly from Mexico, Puerto Rico, and Cuba but also from El Salvador, Honduras, and other countries in Central and South America—have displaced African Americans as the largest minority group. Today they number more than 53 million and account for 17 percent of the U.S. population. Hispanics make up 47 percent of the population of New Mexico and about 40 percent of both California and Texas.[15]

In Texas and throughout much of the southwestern United States in the first half of the twentieth century, people of Mexican origin were subjected to discrimination and worse. They were forced to use segregated public restrooms and attend segregated schools. Hundreds were killed in lynchings. Approximately 500,000 Latinos served in the U.S. armed forces in World War II, but many of these veterans faced discrimination upon their return. Dr. Hector P. Garcia founded the American GI Forum, the country's first Latino veterans' advocacy group, in 1948 after he saw the Naval Station at Corpus Christi refusing to treat sick Latino veterans. Garcia's organization received national attention when the remains of Felix Longoria, a Mexican American soldier killed while on a mission in the Pacific, were returned to his relatives in Three Rivers, Texas, for final burial. The only funeral parlor in Longoria's hometown would not allow his family to hold services for him there because of his Mexican heritage. Soon the incident became the subject of outrage across the country. With the help of the Forum and the sponsorship of then Senator Lyndon B. Johnson, Longoria was buried in Arlington National Cemetery.

In the early 1950s, in Jackson County, Texas, where Mexican Americans made up 14 percent of the population, not a single person with a Spanish surname had been allowed to serve on a jury in 25 years. Some 70 Texas counties had similar records of exclusion. When an all-Anglo jury convicted Pete Hernandez, a migrant cotton picker, of murder in Jackson County, a team of Hispanic civil rights lawyers from the American GI Forum and the League of United Latin American Citizens (LULAC) filed suit, arguing that the jury that convicted him of murder could not be impartial because of the exclusion of Hispanics from the jury. This case eventually reached the Supreme Court; for the first time Hispanic lawyers argued before the Court. In *Hernandez v. Texas* (1954), the Supreme Court unanimously ruled in Hernandez's favor, holding that in excluding Hispanics from jury duty, Texas had unreasonably singled out a class of people for discriminatory treatment. The defendant had been deprived of the equal protection guaranteed by the Fourteenth Amendment, a guarantee "not directed solely against discrimination between whites and Negroes." This landmark decision, which protects Hispanics and the right to fair trials, helped widen the definition of discrimination beyond race.

Hispanic leaders drew from the tactics of the African American civil rights movement, using sit-ins, boycotts, marches, and related activities to draw attention to their cause. In 1968, inspired by the NAACP's Legal Defense Fund, they also created the Mexican American Legal Defense and Education Fund (MALDEF) to help argue their civil rights cases in court. In the 1970s, MALDEF established the Chicana Rights Project to challenge sex-discrimination against Mexican American women. Hispanic groups began mobilizing in other ways to protect their interests, too. An early prominent example was the United Farm Workers, led by César Chávez, who in the 1960s publicized the plight of migrant workers, a large proportion of whom were and are Hispanic.

The rights of illegal immigrants have been a matter of controversy for decades. In 1975 Texas revised its education laws to withhold state funds for educating children who had not been legally admitted to the United States; it authorized local school districts to deny enrollment to such students. In *Plyler v. Doe* (1982), the Supreme Court struck down the law as a violation of the Fourteenth Amendment, arguing that illegal immigrant children are entitled to protection from discrimination unless a substantial state interest can be shown to justify it. The Court found no substantial state interest that would be served by denying an education to students who had no control over being brought to the United States. The Court observed that denying them an education would likely contribute to "the creation and perpetuation of a subclass of illiterates within our boundaries, surely adding to the problems and costs of unemployment, welfare, and crime."

A major concern of Latinos has been discrimination in employment hiring and promotion. Using the leverage of discrimination suits, MALDEF has won a number of consent decrees with employers to increase the opportunities for employment for Latinos.

Like Native Americans, Hispanic Americans benefit from the nondiscrimination policies originally established to protect African Americans. There are now more than 5,200 elected Hispanic officials in the United States,[16] and Hispanic Americans play a prominent role in the politics of such major cities as Houston, Miami, Los Angeles, and San Diego. In 1973 Hispanics won a victory when the Supreme Court found that multimember electoral districts (in which more than one person represents a single district) in Texas discriminated against minority groups because they decreased the probability of a minority being elected.[17] Nevertheless, poverty, discrimination, and language barriers continue to depress Hispanic voter registration and turnout.

☐ Asian Americans

Asian Americans are the fastest-growing minority group: more than 19 million persons who are at least part Asian make up about 6 percent of the U.S. population.[18] For more than one hundred years prior to the civil rights acts of the 1960s, Asian Americans suffered discrimination in education, jobs, and housing as well as restrictions

Hernandez v. Texas
A 1954 Supreme Court decision that extended protection against discrimination to Hispanics.

Their growing numbers have made Hispanic Americans the largest minority group in the United States. Their political power is reflected in the two dozen Hispanic members of the U.S. House of Representatives, such as Loretta and Linda Sanchez of California, the first set of sisters to serve simultaneously in Congress.

5.1
5.2
5.3
5.4
5.5
5.6
5.7

Korematsu v. United States
A 1944 Supreme Court decision that upheld as constitutional the internment of more than 100,000 Americans of Japanese descent in encampments during World War II.

on immigration and naturalization. Discrimination was especially egregious during World War II when the U.S. government, beset by fears of a Japanese invasion of the Pacific Coast, rounded up more than 100,000 Americans of Japanese descent and herded them into encampments. These internment camps were, critics claimed, America's concentration camps. The Supreme Court, however, in *Korematsu v. United States* (1944), upheld the internment as constitutional. Congress has since authorized reparation payments to the former internees and their families. The policy changes we associate with the civil rights movement have led to changes in status and in political strength for Asian Americans. Today, Americans of Chinese, Japanese, Indian, Korean, Vietnamese, and other Asian ethnicities have assumed prominent positions in U.S. society.

☐ Arab Americans and Muslims

There are about 3.5 million persons of Arab ancestry in the United States, and about 6 million Muslims of various ethnicities.[19] Since the terrorist attacks of September 11, 2001, Arabs, Muslims, Sikhs, South Asian Americans, and those perceived to be members of these groups have been the victims of increased numbers of bias-related assaults, threats, vandalism, and arson. The incidents have consisted of telephone, Internet, mail, and face-to-face threats; minor assaults as well as assaults with dangerous weapons and assaults resulting in serious injury and death; and vandalism, shootings, arson, and bombings directed at homes, businesses, and places of worship. Members of these groups have also experienced discrimination in employment, housing, education, and access to public accommodations and facilities.

One of the low points in the protection of civil rights in the United States occurred during World War II when more than 100,000 Americans of Japanese descent were moved to internment camps.

Nineteenth Amendment
The constitutional amendment adopted in 1920 that guarantees women the right to vote.

In the wake of the September 11, 2001, terrorist attacks, the FBI detained more than 1,200 persons as possible threats to national security. About two-thirds of these persons—mostly Arabs and Muslims—were illegal aliens, and many of them languished in jail for months until cleared by the FBI. Their detention seemed to violate the Sixth Amendment right of detainees to be informed of accusations against them, as well as the constitutional protection against the suspension of the writ of habeas corpus. As we have seen, in 2004 the Supreme Court declared that detainees in the United States had the right to challenge their detention before a judge or other neutral decision maker.

The Rights of Women

5.4 Trace the evolution of women's rights and explain how civil rights principles apply to gender issues.

he first women's rights activists were products of the abolitionist movement, in which they had often encountered sexist attitudes. Noting that the status of women shared much in common with that of slaves, some leaders resolved to fight for women's rights. Two of these women, Lucretia Mott and Elizabeth Cady Stanton, organized a meeting at Seneca Falls in upstate New York. They had much to discuss. Not only were women denied the vote, but they were also subjected to patriarchal (male-dominated) family law and denied educational and career opportunities. The legal doctrine known as *coverture* deprived married women of any legal identity separate from that of their husbands; wives could not sign contracts or own or dispose of property. Divorce law was heavily biased in favor of husbands. Even abused women found it almost impossible to end their marriages; men had the legal advantage in securing custody of the children.

☐ The Battle for the Vote

On July 19, 1848, 100 men and women signed the Seneca Falls Declaration of Sentiments and Resolutions. Patterned after the Declaration of Independence, it proclaimed, "The history of mankind is a history of repeated injuries and usurpations on the part of man toward woman, having in direct object the establishment of an absolute tyranny over her." Thus began the movement that would culminate, 72 years later, in the ratification of the **Nineteenth Amendment**, giving women the vote. Charlotte Woodward, 19 years old in 1848, was the only signer of the Seneca Falls Declaration who lived to vote for the president in 1920.

Although advocates of women's suffrage had hoped that the Fifteenth Amendment would extend the vote to women as well as to newly freed slaves, they were disappointed. As it turned out, the battle for women's suffrage was fought mostly in the late nineteenth and early twentieth centuries. Leaders like Stanton and Susan B. Anthony were prominent in the cause, which emphasized the vote but also addressed women's other grievances. The suffragists had considerable success in the states, especially in the West. Several states allowed women to vote before the constitutional amendment passed. The feminists lobbied, marched, protested, and even engaged in civil disobedience.[20]

☐ The "Doldrums": 1920–1960

Winning the right to vote did not automatically win equal status for women. In fact, the feminist movement seemed to lose rather than gain momentum after women won the vote, perhaps because in the early twentieth century the vote was about the only goal on which all feminists agreed. There was considerable division within the movement on other priorities.

Many suffragists accepted the traditional model of the family. Fathers were breadwinners, mothers bread bakers. Although most suffragists thought that women should have the opportunity to pursue any occupation they chose, many also believed

Equal Rights Amendment

Equal Rights Amendment
A constitutional amendment originally introduced in Congress in 1923 and passed by Congress in 1972, stating that "equality of rights under the law shall not be denied or abridged by the United States or by any state on account of sex." Despite public support, the amendment fell short of the three-fourths of state legislatures required for passage.

Reed v. Reed
The landmark case in 1971 in which the Supreme Court for the first time upheld a claim of gender discrimination.

Craig v. Boren
The 1976 ruling in which the Supreme Court established the "intermediate scrutiny" standard for determining gender discrimination.

that women's primary obligations revolved around the roles of wife and mother. Many suffragists had defended the vote as basically an extension of the maternal role into public life, arguing that a new era of public morality would emerge when women could vote. These *social feminists* were in tune with prevailing attitudes.

Public policy toward women continued to be dominated by protectionism rather than by the principle of equality. Laws protected working women from the burdens of overtime work, long hours on the job, and heavy lifting. The fact that these laws also protected male workers from female competition received little attention. State laws tended to reflect—and reinforce—traditional family roles. These laws concentrated on limiting women's work opportunities outside the home so they could concentrate on their duties within it. The laws in most states required husbands to support their families (even after a divorce) and to pay child support, though divorced fathers did not always pay. When a marriage ended, mothers almost always got custody of the children, although husbands had the legal advantage in custody battles. Public policy was designed to preserve traditional motherhood and hence, supporters claimed, to protect the family and the country's moral fabric.[21]

Only a minority of feminists challenged the traditional views that shaped public policy. Alice Paul, the author of the original **Equal Rights Amendment** (ERA), was one activist who claimed that the real result of protectionist law was to perpetuate gender inequality. Simply worded, the ERA reads, "Equality of rights under the law shall not be denied or abridged by the United States or by any state on account of sex." Most people saw the ERA as a threat to the family when it was introduced in Congress in 1923. It gained little support. In fact, women were less likely to support the amendment than men were.

The Second Feminist Wave

The civil rights movement of the 1950s and 1960s attracted many female activists, some of whom also joined student and antiwar movements. These women often met with the same prejudices as had women abolitionists. Betty Friedan's book *The Feminine Mystique*, published in 1963, encouraged women to question traditional assumptions and to assert their own rights. Groups such as the National Organization for Women (NOW) and the National Women's Political Caucus were organized in the 1960s and 1970s.

Before the advent of the contemporary feminist movement, the Supreme Court upheld virtually every instance of gender-based discrimination. The state and federal governments could discriminate against women—and, indeed, men—as they chose. In the 1970s the Court began to take a closer look at gender discrimination. In **Reed v. Reed** (1971), the Court ruled that any "arbitrary" gender-based classification violated the equal protection clause of the Fourteenth Amendment. This was the first time the Court declared any law unconstitutional on the basis of gender discrimination.

Five years later, the Court heard a case regarding an Oklahoma law that prohibited the sale of 3.2 percent beer to males under the age of 21 but allowed females over the age of 18 to purchase it. In **Craig v. Boren** (1976), the Court voided the statute and established an "intermediate scrutiny" standard (see Table 5.1): the Court would not presume gender discrimination to be either valid or invalid. The courts were to show less deference to gender classifications than to more routine classifications but more deference than to racial classifications. Nevertheless, the Court has repeatedly said that there must be an "exceedingly persuasive justification" for any government to classify people by gender.

The Supreme Court has struck down many laws and rules for discriminating on the basis of gender. For example, the Court voided laws giving husbands exclusive control over family property.[22] The Court also voided employers' rules that denied women equal monthly retirement benefits because they live longer than men.[23]

Despite *Craig v. Boren*, men have been less successful than women in challenging gender classifications. The Court upheld a statutory rape law applying only to men[24] and the male-only draft, which we will discuss shortly. The Court also allowed a Florida law giving property tax exemptions only to widows, not to widowers.[25]

Contemporary feminists have suffered defeats as well as victories. The ERA was revived when Congress passed it in 1972 and extended the deadline for ratification

5.1 5.2 5.3 5.4 5.5 5.6 5.7

until 1982. Nevertheless, the ERA was three states short of ratification when time ran out. Paradoxically, whereas the 1920 suffrage victory weakened feminism, losing the ERA battle stimulated the movement.

Women in the Workplace

One reason why feminist activism persists has nothing to do with ideology or other social movements. The family pattern that traditionalists sought to preserve—father at work, mother at home—is becoming a thing of the past. There are 72 million women in the civilian labor force (compared to 82 million males), representing 58 percent of adult women. Fifty percent of these women are married and living with their spouse. There are also 36 million female-headed households (more than 8 million of which include children), and about 64 percent of American mothers who have children below school age are in the labor force.[26] As conditions have changed, public opinion and public policy demands have changed, too.

WAGE DISCRIMINATION AND COMPARABLE WORTH Traditionally female jobs often pay much less than traditionally male jobs that demand comparable skill; for example, a secretary may earn far less than an accounts clerk with comparable qualifications. Median weekly earnings for women working full time are only 81 percent of those for men working full time.[27] In other words, although the wage gap has narrowed, women still earn only $0.81 for every $1.00 men make. There are many explanations for this disparity, but wage discrimination is one of them.

The Equal Pay Act of 1963 makes it illegal to pay different wages to men and women if they perform equal work in the same workplace. The law also makes it illegal to retaliate against a person because the person complained about discrimination, filed a charge of discrimination, or participated in an employment discrimination investigation or lawsuit. The first significant legislation that Barack Obama signed as president was a 2009 bill outlawing "discrimination in compensation," which is broadly defined to include wages and employee benefits. The law also makes it easier for workers to win lawsuits claiming pay discrimination based on gender, race, religion, national origin, age, or disability.

EMPLOYMENT Congress has made some important progress, especially in the area of employment. The Civil Rights Act of 1964 banned gender discrimination in employment. The protection this law offered has been expanded several times.

In recent years, women have entered many traditionally male-dominated occupations. Here astronauts Peggy Wilson and Pam Melroy meet in the International Space Station.

164

5.1
5.2
5.3
5.4
5.5
5.6
5.7

For example, in 1972 Congress gave the EEOC the power to sue employers suspected of illegal discrimination. The Pregnancy Discrimination Act of 1978 made it illegal for employers to exclude pregnancy and childbirth from their sick leave and health benefits plans. The Civil Rights and Women's Equity in Employment Act of 1991 shifted the burden of proof in justifying hiring and promotion practices to employers, who must show that a gender requirement is necessary for a particular job.

The Supreme Court has also weighed in against gender discrimination in employment and business activity. In 1977 it voided laws and rules barring women from jobs through arbitrary height and weight requirements (*Dothard v. Rawlinson*). Any such prerequisites must be directly related to the duties required in a particular position. Women have also been protected from being required to take mandatory pregnancy leaves from their jobs[28] and from being denied a job because of an employer's concern for harming a developing fetus.[29] Many commercial contacts are made in private business and service clubs, which often have excluded women from membership. The Court has upheld state and city laws that prohibit such discrimination.[30]

Why It Matters to You
Changes in the Workplace

Laws and Supreme Court decisions striking down barriers to employment for women are not just words. They have had important consequences for employment opportunities for many millions of women and have helped women make substantial gains in entering careers formerly occupied almost entirely by men.

EDUCATION Education is closely related to employment. Title IX of the Education Act of 1972 forbids gender discrimination in federally subsidized education programs (which include almost all colleges and universities), including athletics. But what about single-gender schooling? In 1996 the Supreme Court declared that Virginia's categorical exclusion of women from education opportunities at the state-funded Virginia Military Institute (VMI) violated women's rights to equal protection of the law.[31] A few days later, the Citadel, the nation's only other state-supported all-male college, announced that it would also admit women.

MILITARY SERVICE Military service has raised controversial questions about gender equality. Women have served in every branch of the armed services since World War II. Originally, they served in separate units such as the WACS (Women's Army Corps), the WAVES (Women Accepted for Volunteer Emergency Service in the navy), and the Nurse Corps. Until the 1970s, the military had a 2 percent quota for women (which was never filled). Now women are part of the regular armed services. They make up about 15 percent of the active duty forces[32] and compete directly with men for promotions. Congress opened all the service academies to women in 1975. Women have done well, sometimes graduating at the top of their class.

In 2013 Defense Secretary Leon E. Panetta lifted the ban on women in combat. Women are now permitted to serve in the most intense and physically hazardous combat positions in the military, including the Navy SEALs and the Army Rangers. Even before the change in policy, women were flying jets, piloting helicopters at the front, operating antimissile systems, patrolling streets with machine guns, disposing of explosives, and providing unit and convoy security. They were also serving as combat pilots in the navy and air force and stationed on navy warships, including submarines. Some women have been taken as prisoners of war, and more than 100 have been killed in combat in Iraq and Afghanistan. Nevertheless, the Supreme Court held in 1981 that it is permissible to require only men register for the military draft when they turn 18.[33] (See "You Are the Judge: Is Male-Only Draft Registration Gender Discrimination?")

Women, such as this soldier patrolling the streets in Afghanistan, are playing increasingly important roles in the military.

You Are the Judge

Is Male-Only Draft Registration Gender Discrimination?

Since 1973 the United States has had a volunteer force, and in 1975, registration for the draft was suspended. However, in 1979, after the Soviet Union invaded Afghanistan, President Jimmy Carter asked Congress to require both men and women to register for the draft. Registration was designed to facilitate any eventual conscription. Congress reinstated registration in 1980, but, as before, for men only. In response, several young men filed a suit. They contended that the registration requirement was gender-based discrimination that violated the due process clause of the Fifth Amendment.

YOU BE THE JUDGE:

Does requiring only males to register for the draft unconstitutionally discriminate against them?

DECISION:

The Supreme Court displayed its typical deference to the elected branches in the area of national security when it ruled in 1981 in *Rostker v. Goldberg* that male-only registration did not violate the Fifth Amendment. The Court found that male-only registration bore a substantial relationship to Congress's goal of ensuring combat readiness and that Congress acted well within its constitutional authority to raise and regulate armies and navies when it authorized the registration of men and not women. Congress, the Court said, was allowed to focus on the question of military need rather than "equity."

5.1
5.2
5.3
5.4
5.5
5.6
5.7

Sexual Harassment

Whether in schools,[34] in the military, on the assembly line, or in the office, women for years have voiced concern about sexual harassment, which, of course, does not affect only women. The U.S. Equal Employment Opportunity Commission defines sexual harassment as "unwelcome sexual advances, requests for sexual favors, and other verbal or physical conduct of a sexual nature ... when this conduct explicitly or implicitly affects an individual's employment, unreasonably interferes with an individual's work performance, or creates an intimidating, hostile, or offensive work environment."[35]

In 1986 the Supreme Court articulated this broad principle: sexual harassment that is so pervasive as to create a hostile or abusive work environment is a form of gender discrimination, which is forbidden by the 1964 Civil Rights Act. In 1993, in *Harris v. Forklift Systems*, the Court reinforced its decision. No single factor, the Court said, is required to win a sexual harassment case under Title VII of the 1964 Civil Rights Act. The law is violated when the workplace environment "would reasonably be perceived, and is perceived, as hostile or abusive." Thus workers are not required to prove that the workplace environment is so hostile as to cause them "severe psychological injury" or that they are unable to perform their jobs. The protection of federal law comes into play before the harassing conduct leads to psychological difficulty.[36] The Court has also made it clear that employers are responsible for preventing and eliminating harassment at work,[37] and they cannot retaliate against someone filing a complaint about sexual harassment,[38] although plaintiffs must prove that retaliation was the determinative factor in a negative action.[39] The Court has also ruled that school districts can be held liable for sexual harassment in cases of student-on-student harassment.[40]

Sexual harassment may be especially prevalent in male-dominated occupations such as the military. A 1991 convention of the Tailhook Association, an organization of naval aviators, made the news after reports surfaced of drunken sailors sexually assaulting female guests, including naval officers, as they stepped off the elevator. After the much-criticized initial failure of the navy to identify the officers responsible for the assault, heads rolled, including those of several admirals and the secretary of the navy. In 1996 and 1997, a number of army officers and noncommissioned officers were discharged—and some went to prison—for sexual harassment of female soldiers in training situations. Behavior that was once viewed as simply male high jinks is now recognized as intolerable. The Pentagon removed top officials at the Air Force Academy in 2003 following charges that many female cadets had been sexually assaulted by male cadets. With more women serving in the military, the issue of protecting female military personnel from sexual harassment becomes ever more pressing.

Other Groups Active Under the Civil Rights Umbrella

Summarize the struggles for civil rights of older Americans, persons with disabilities, and LGBT Americans.

olicies enacted to protect one or two groups can be applied to other groups as well. Three recent entrants into the civil rights arena are aging Americans, people with disabilities, and gays and lesbians. All of these groups claim equal rights, as racial and ethnic minorities and women do, but they each face and pose different challenges.

☐ Civil Rights and the Graying of America

America is aging rapidly. More than 40 million people are 65 or older, accounting for 13 percent of the total population. About 5.5 million people are 85 or older.[41] People in their eighties are the fastest-growing age group in the country.

When the Social Security program began in the 1930s, 65 was chosen as the retirement age for the purpose of benefits. The choice was apparently arbitrary, but 65 soon became the usual age for mandatory retirement. Although many workers prefer to retire while they are still healthy and active enough to enjoy leisure, not everyone wants or can afford to do so. Nevertheless, employers routinely refused to hire people over a certain age. In the past, age discrimination was not limited to older workers. Graduate and professional schools often rejected applicants in their thirties on the grounds that their professions would get fewer years—and thus less return—out of them. In the 1950s and 1960s, age-related policies had a severe impact on housewives and veterans who wanted to return to school.

As early as 1967 in the Age Discrimination in Employment Act, Congress banned some kinds of age discrimination. In 1975 Congress passed a law denying federal funds to any institution that discriminates against people over the age of 40 because of their age. Today, for most workers there can be no compulsory retirement. In 1976 the Supreme Court, however, declared that it would not place age in the inherently suspect classification category, when it upheld a state law requiring police officers to retire at the age of 50. Age classifications still fall under the reasonableness standard of review,[42] and employers need only show that age is related to the ability to do a job to require workers to retire.

Job bias is often hidden, and proving it depends on inference and circumstantial evidence. The Supreme Court made it easier to win cases of job bias in 2000 when it held in *Reeves v. Sanderson* that a plaintiff's evidence of an employer's bias, combined with sufficient evidence to find that the employer's asserted justification is false, may permit juries and judges to conclude that an employer unlawfully discriminated. Five years later, the Court found that employers can be held liable for discrimination even if they never intended any harm. Older employees need only show an employer's policies disproportionately harmed them—and that there was no reasonable basis for the employer's policy.[43] Thus employees can win lawsuits without direct evidence of an employer's illegal intent. In 2008 the Supreme Court ruled that it is up to the employer to show that action against a worker stems from reasonable factors other than age (*Meacham v. Knolls Atomic Power Laboratory*). The impact of these decisions is likely to extend beyond questions of age discrimination to the litigation of race and gender discrimination cases brought under Title VII of the Civil Rights Act of 1964 as well as cases brought under the Americans with Disabilities Act.

☐ Civil Rights and People with Disabilities

Americans with disabilities have suffered from both direct and indirect discrimination. Governments and employers have often denied them rehabilitation services, education, and jobs. And even when there has been no overt discrimination, many people with disabilities have been excluded from the workforce and isolated. Throughout most of American history, public and private buildings have been hostile to the blind, deaf, and mobility impaired. Stairs, buses, telephones, and other necessities of modern life have been designed in ways that keep the disabled out of offices, stores, and restaurants. As one slogan said, "Once, blacks had to ride at the back of the bus. We can't even get on the bus."

The first rehabilitation laws were passed in the late 1920s, mostly to help veterans of World War I. Accessibility laws had to wait another 50 years. The Rehabilitation Act of 1973 added people with disabilities to the list of Americans protected from discrimination. Because the law defines an inaccessible environment as a form of discrimination, wheelchair ramps, grab bars on toilets, and Braille signs have become

Americans with Disabilities Act of 1990

A law passed in 1990 that requires employers and public facilities to make "reasonable accommodations" for people with disabilities and prohibits discrimination against these individuals in employment.

LGBT Rights

common features of American life. The Education of All Handicapped Children Act of 1975 entitled all children to a free public education appropriate to their needs. The **Americans with Disabilities Act of 1990** (ADA) strengthened these protections, requiring employers and administrators of public facilities to make "reasonable accommodations" and prohibiting employment discrimination against people with disabilities. The Supreme Court has ruled that the law also affirms the right of individuals with disabilities if at all possible to live in their communities rather than be institutionalized.[44]

Determining who is "disabled" has generated some controversy. Are people with AIDS entitled to protections? In 1998 the Supreme Court answered "yes." It ruled that the ADA offered protection against discrimination to people with AIDS.[45] In 2008, Congress expanded the definition of disability, making it easier for workers to prove discrimination. Accordingly, in deciding whether a person is disabled, courts are not to consider the effects of "mitigating measures" like prescription drugs, hearing aids, and artificial limbs. Moreover, "an impairment that is episodic or in remission is a disability if it would substantially limit a major life activity when active." Otherwise, the more successful a person is at coping with a disability, the more likely it is that a court would find that he or she is no longer disabled and therefore no longer covered under the ADA.

Nobody wants to oppose policies beneficial to people with disabilities. Nevertheless, laws designed to protect the rights of these individuals have met with opposition and, once passed, have only been sluggishly enforced. The source of the resistance is concern about the cost of accommodations. Such concern is often shortsighted, however. Changes allowing people with disabilities to become wage earners, spenders, and taxpayers are a gain rather than a drain on the economy.

☐ LGBT Rights

Even by conservative estimates, several million Americans are homosexual, representing every social stratum and ethnic group. Yet gays and lesbians have often faced

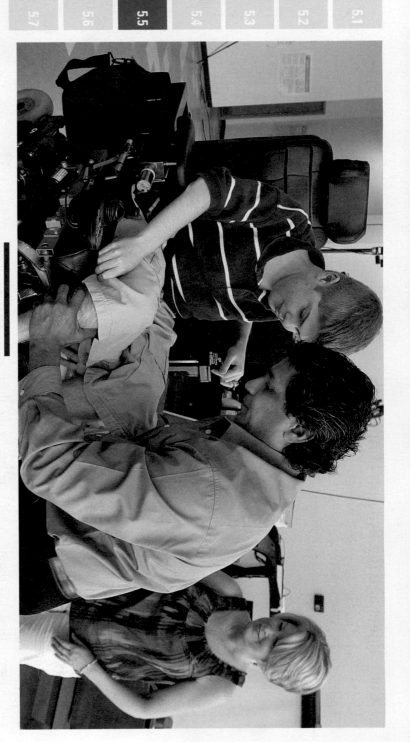

In recent decades, public policy has focused on integrating the disabled, such as this college student being fitted with an all-terrain wheelchair, to participate more fully in society.

discrimination in hiring, education, access to public accommodations, and housing, and they may face the toughest battle for equality.

Homophobia—fear and hatred of homosexuals—has many causes. Some of these causes are deep-rooted, relating, for example, to the fact that certain religious groups condemn homosexuality. Homophobia has even led to killings, including the brutal 1998 killing of Matthew Shepard, a 21-year-old political science freshman at the University of Wyoming. Shepard was found tied to a fence, having been hit in the head with a pistol 18 times and repeatedly kicked in the groin.

The growth of the gay rights movement was stimulated by a notorious incident in a New York City bar in 1969. Police raided the Stonewall Inn, a bar frequented by gay men. Such raids were then common. This time, customers at the bar resisted the police. Unwarranted violence, arrests, and injury to persons and property resulted. In the aftermath of Stonewall, gays and lesbians organized in an effort to protect their civil rights, in the process developing political skills and forming effective interest groups. Significantly, most colleges and universities now have gay rights organizations on campus.

The record on gay rights is mixed. In an early defeat, the Supreme Court, in 1986 ruled in *Bowers v. Hardwick* that states could ban homosexual relations. More recently, in 2000 the Court held that the Boy Scouts could exclude a gay man from being an adult member because homosexuality violates the organization's principles.[46] But in 1996, in *Romer v. Evans*, the Supreme Court voided a state constitutional amendment approved by the voters of Colorado that denied homosexuals protection against discrimination, finding the Colorado amendment violated the U.S. Constitution's guarantee of equal protection of the law. In 2003, in *Lawrence v. Texas*, the Supreme Court overturned *Bowers v. Hardwick* when it voided a Texas anti-sodomy law on the grounds that such laws are unconstitutional intrusions on the right to privacy. Gay activists have won other important victories. Several states, including California, and more than a hundred communities have passed laws protecting homosexuals against some forms of discrimination.[47]

Few Americans oppose equal employment opportunities for homosexuals, and majorities support the legality of homosexual relations and the acceptability of homosexuality as a lifestyle. A clear majority of the public views homosexual relations as moral.[48] In a reflection of Americans' changed attitudes toward homosexuality, in 2011, with the support of Congress and the president, the Pentagon ended the "don't ask, don't tell" policy in the military and allowed gays to serve openly.

Today the most prominent issue concerning gay rights may be same-sex marriage. Most states have laws banning such marriages and the recognition of same-sex marriages that occur in other states. In 1996 Congress passed the Defense of Marriage Act (DOMA), which permits states to disregard same-sex marriages even if they are legal elsewhere in the United States. Section 3 of the act required the federal government to interpret "marriage" and "spouse" to apply only to heterosexual unions when applying federal law. In 2013, however, the Supreme Court struck down Section 3 of DOMA as unconstitutional because it discriminated against those in gay marriages and had no legitimate purpose.[49]

Since then, actions by state legislatures to change the law and by courts to void laws prohibiting it have resulted in same-sex marriage being legal in 32 states and Washington, D.C. A majority of the public now support legalizing same-sex marriage.[50] When given the opportunity, gay and lesbian couples have rushed to the altar, provoking a strong backlash from social conservatives. President George W. Bush called for a constitutional amendment to ban same-sex marriage, but Congress has yet to pass such an amendment. With the prospects for gay marriage remaining uncertain, gays also continue to push for benefits associated with marriage, including health insurance, taxes, Social Security payments, hospital visitation rights, and much else that most people take for granted.

5.1
5.2
5.3
5.4
5.5
5.6
5.7

affirmative action
A policy designed to give special attention to or compensatory treatment for members of some previously disadvantaged group.

Affirmative Action

5.6
Trace the evolution of affirmative action policy and assess the arguments for and against it.

Some people argue that groups that have suffered invidious discrimination require special efforts to provide them with access to education and jobs. In 1965 President Lyndon Johnson signed Executive Order 11246, prohibiting federal contractors and federally assisted construction contractors and subcontractors from discriminating in employment decisions on the basis of race, color, religion, sex, or national origin. The order also required contractors to take "affirmative action" against employment discrimination in hiring by devising and implementing plans to increase the participation of minorities and women in the workplace.

Affirmative action involves efforts to bring about increased employment, promotion, or admission for members of groups who have suffered from discrimination. The goal is to move beyond *equal opportunity* (in which everyone has the same chance of obtaining good jobs, for example) toward *equal results* (in which different groups have the same percentage of success in obtaining those jobs). This goal may be accomplished through special rules in the public and private sectors that recruit or otherwise give preferential treatment to previously disadvantaged groups. Numerical quotas that ensure that a certain portion of government contracts, law school admissions, or police department promotions go to minorities and women are the strongest and most controversial form of affirmative action. At present, the constitutional status of affirmative action is in doubt.

At one point, the federal government mandated that all state and local governments, as well as each institution receiving aid from or contracting with the federal government, adopt an affirmative action program. The University of California at Davis (UC–Davis) introduced one such program. Eager to produce more minority physicians in California, the medical school set aside 16 of 100 places in the

Point to Ponder

While supporters see affirmative action as a policy designed to provide greater opportunities for minorities to excel, opponents see it as a violation of the merit principle.

Is it possible to design a policy that addresses both our concern for equality and the principle of merit as the basis of advancement?

Regents of the University of California v. Bakke

A 1978 Supreme Court decision holding that a state university may weigh race or ethnic background as one element in admissions but may not set aside places for members of particular racial groups.

Adarand Constructors v. Pena

A 1995 Supreme Court decision holding that federal programs that classify people by race, even for an ostensibly benign purpose such as expanding opportunities for minorities, should be presumed to be unconstitutional.

entering class for "disadvantaged groups." One white applicant who did not make the freshman class was Allan Bakke. After receiving a rejection letter from Davis two years in a row, Bakke learned that the mean scores on the Medical College Admissions Test of students admitted under the university's affirmative action program were in the 46th percentile on verbal tests and the 35th on science tests. Bakke's scores on the same tests were in the 96th and 97th percentiles, respectively. He sued UC–Davis, claiming that it had denied him equal protection of the laws by discriminating against him because of his race.

The result was an important Supreme Court decision in Bakke's favor, *Regents of the University of California v. Bakke* (1978).[51] The Court ordered Bakke admitted, holding that the UC–Davis Special Admissions Program did discriminate against him because of his race. Yet the Court refused to order UC–Davis never to use race as a criterion for admission. A university could, said the Court, adopt an "admissions program in which race or ethnic background is simply one element—to be weighed fairly against other elements—in the selection process." It could *not*, as the UC–Davis Special Admissions Program did, set aside a quota of spots for particular groups.

Over the next 18 years, the Supreme Court upheld voluntary union- and management-sponsored quotas in a training program,[52] as well as preferential treatment of minorities in promotions,[53] and it ordered quotas for minority union memberships.[54] It also approved a federal rule setting aside 10 percent of all federal construction contracts for minority-owned firms[55] and a requirement for preferential treatment for minorities to increase their ownership of broadcast licenses.[56] It did, however, find a Richmond, Virginia, plan that reserved 30 percent of city subcontracts for minority firms to be unconstitutional.[57]

Things changed in 1995, however. In *Adarand Constructors v. Pena*, the Court overturned the decision regarding broadcast licenses and cast grave doubt on its holding regarding contracts set aside for minority-owned firms. It held that federal programs that classify people by race, even for an ostensibly benign purpose such as expanding opportunities for members of minorities, should be presumed to be unconstitutional. Such programs must be subject to the most searching judicial inquiry and can survive only if they are "narrowly tailored" to accomplish a "compelling governmental interest." In other words, the Court applied criteria for evaluating affirmative action programs similar to those it applies to other racial classifications, the suspect standard we discussed earlier in the chapter. Although *Adarand* did not void federal affirmative action programs in general, it certainly limited their potential impact.

In addition, in 1984 the Court ruled that affirmative action does not exempt recently hired minorities from traditional work rules specifying the "last hired, first fired" order of layoffs.[58] And in 1986, it found unconstitutional an effort to give preference to African American public school teachers in layoffs because this policy punished innocent white teachers and the African American teachers in question had not been actual victims of past discrimination.[59] We examine a more recent case of a public employer using affirmative action promotions to counter underrepresentation of minorities in the workplace in "You Are the Judge: The Case of the New Haven Firefighters."

Opposition to affirmative action comes also from the general public. Such opposition is especially strong when affirmative action is seen as *reverse discrimination*—in which, as in the case of Allan Bakke, individuals are discriminated against when people who are less qualified are hired or admitted to programs because of their minority status. Several states have banned state affirmative action programs based on race, ethnicity, or gender in public hiring, contracting, and educational admissions.

In 2003, the Supreme Court made two important decisions on affirmative action in university admissions. In the first, the Court agreed that there was a compelling interest in promoting racial diversity on campus. In *Grutter v. Bollinger* (2003), the

5.1
5.2
5.3
5.4
5.5
5.6
5.7

You Are the Judge

The Case of the New Haven Firefighters

New Haven, Connecticut, used objective examinations to identify those firefighters best qualified for promotion. When the results of such an exam to fill vacant lieutenant and captain positions showed that white candidates had outperformed minority candidates, the city threw out the results based on the statistical racial disparity. White and Hispanic firefighters who passed the exams but were denied a chance at promotions by the city's refusal to certify the test results sued the city alleging that discarding the test results was tantamount to using a quota, which it outlawed in *Bakke*, because it made the factor of race decisive for virtually every minimally qualified, underrepresented minority applicant. The 20 points awarded to minorities were more than the school awarded for some measures of academic excellence, writing ability, or leadership skills.

In 2007 the Supreme Court addressed the use of racial classification to promote racial balance in public schools in Seattle, Washington, and Jefferson County, Kentucky. Some parents had filed lawsuits contending that using race as a tiebreaker to decide which students would be admitted to popular schools violated the Fourteenth Amendment's equal protection guarantee. In *Parents Involved in Community Schools v. Seattle School District No. 1* (2007), the Court agreed that the school districts' use of race in their voluntary integration plans, even for the purpose of preventing resegregation, violated the equal protection guarantee and therefore was unconstitutional. Using the inherently suspect standard related to racial classifications, the Court found that the school districts lacked the compelling interest of remedying the effects of past intentional discrimination and concluded that racial balancing by itself was not a compelling state interest. The Court did indicate that school authorities might use a "race conscious" means to achieve diversity but that the school districts must be sensitive to other aspects of diversity besides race and narrowly tailor their programs to achieve diversity.

Court upheld the University of Michigan law school's use of race as one of many factors in admission. The Court found that the law school's use of race as a plus in the admissions process was narrowly tailored and that the school made individualistic, holistic reviews of applicants in a nonmechanical fashion.

However, in its second decision, *Gratz v. Bollinger* (2003), the Court struck down the University of Michigan's system of undergraduate admissions in which every applicant from an underrepresented racial or ethnic minority group was automatically awarded 20 points of the 100 needed to guarantee admission. The Court said that the system was tantamount to using a quota, which it outlawed in *Bakke*, because it made the factor of race decisive for virtually every minimally qualified, underrepresented minority applicant. The 20 points awarded to minorities were more than the school awarded for some measures of academic excellence, writing ability, or leadership skills.

YOU BE THE JUDGE:

Did New Haven discriminate against white and Hispanic firefighters?

DECISION:

In *Ricci v. DeStefano* (2009), the Court held that if an employer uses a hiring or promotion test, it generally has to accept the test results unless the employer has strong evidence that the test was flawed and improperly favored a particular group. New Haven could not reject the test results simply because the higher-scoring candidates were white.

Whatever the Court may rule in the future with regard to affirmative action, the issue is clearly a complex and difficult one. Opponents of affirmative action argue that merit is the only fair basis for distributing benefits and that any race or gender discrimination is wrong, even when its purpose is to rectify past injustices rather than to reinforce them. Proponents of affirmative action argue in response that what constitutes merit is highly subjective and can embody prejudices of which the decision maker may be quite unaware. For example, experts suggest, a man might "look more like" a road dispatcher than a woman and thus get a higher rating from interviewers. Many affirmative action advocates also believe that increasing the number of women and minorities in desirable jobs is such an important social goal that it should be considered when looking at individuals' qualifications. They claim that what white males lose from affirmative action programs are privileges to which they were never entitled in the first place; after all, nobody has the right to be a doctor or a road dispatcher. Moreover, research suggests that affirmative action offers significant benefits to women and minorities and involves relatively small costs for white males.[60]

Understanding Civil Rights and Public Policy

5.7 Establish how civil rights policy advances democracy and increases the scope of government.

 he Constitution is silent on the issue of equality, except in the Fourteenth Amendment, which forbids the states to deny "equal protection of the laws." Those five words have been the basis for major civil rights statutes and scores of judicial rulings protecting the rights of minorities and women. These laws and decisions granting people new rights have empowered minority groups to seek and gain still more victories. The implications of their success for democracy and the scope of government are substantial.

☐ Civil Rights and Democracy

Equality is a basic principle of democracy. Every citizen has one vote because democratic government presumes that each person's needs, interests, and preferences are neither any more nor any less important than the needs, interests, and preferences of every other person. Individual liberty is an equally important democratic principle, one that can conflict with equality.

Equality tends to favor majority rule. Because under simple majority rule everyone's wishes rank equally, the policy outcome that most people prefer seems to be the fairest choice in cases of conflict. What happens, however, if the majority wants to deprive the minority of certain rights? In situations like these, the principle of equality can invite the denial of minority rights, whereas the principle of liberty condemns such action.[61] In general, Americans today strongly believe in protecting minority rights against majority restrictions, as you can see in "America in Perspective: Respect for Minority Rights."

Majority rule is not the only threat to liberty. Politically and socially powerful minorities have suppressed majorities as well as other minorities. Women have long outnumbered men in America, about 51 percent to 49 percent. In the era of segregation, African Americans outnumbered whites in many Southern states. Inequality persisted, however, because of entrenched customs and because inequality served the interests of the dominant groups. When slavery and segregation existed in an agrarian economy, whites could get cheap agricultural labor. When men were breadwinners and women were homemakers, married men had a source of cheap domestic labor.

174

5.1
5.2
5.3
5.4
5.5
5.6
5.7

America in Perspective

Respect for Minority Rights

Americans rate the importance of protection of minority rights relatively highly compared to other democracies.

Question: There are different opinions about people's rights in a democracy. On a scale of 1 to 7, where 1 is not at all important and 7 is very important, how

important is it that government authorities respect and protect rights of minorities?

CRITICAL THINKING QUESTION

Why do you think that Americans tend to strongly believe in protection of minority rights?

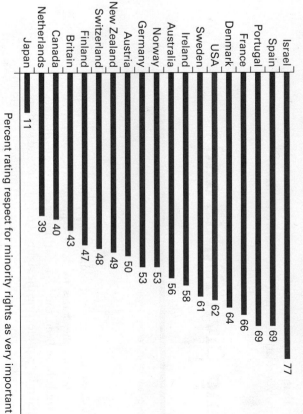

Country	Percent
Israel	77
Spain	69
Portugal	69
France	66
Denmark	64
USA	62
Sweden	61
Ireland	58
Australia	56
Norway	53
Germany	53
Austria	50
New Zealand	49
Switzerland	48
Finland	47
Britain	43
Canada	40
Netherlands	39
Japan	11

Percent rating respect for minority rights as very important

SOURCE: Authors' analysis of 2004 International Society Survey Program data.

Both African Americans and women made many gains even when they lacked one essential component of democratic power: the vote. They used other rights—such as their First Amendment freedoms—to fight for equality. When in the 1960s Congress protected the right of African Americans to vote, the nature of Southern politics changed dramatically. The democratic process is a powerful vehicle for disadvantaged groups to press their claims.

☐ Civil Rights and the Scope of Government

The Founders might be greatly perturbed if they knew about all the civil rights laws the government has enacted; these laws do not conform to the eighteenth-century idea of limited government. But the Founders would expect the national government to do whatever is necessary to hold the nation together. The Civil War showed that the Constitution of 1787 did not adequately deal with issues like slavery that could destroy the society the Framers had struggled to secure.

Civil rights laws increase the scope and power of government. These laws regulate the behavior of individuals and institutions. Restaurant owners must serve all patrons, regardless of race. Professional schools must admit women. Employers must accommodate people with disabilities and make an effort to find minority workers, whether they want to or not.

However, civil rights, like civil liberties, is an area in which increased government activity in protecting basic rights also represents limits on government and the protection of individualism. Remember that much of segregation was *de jure*, established by governments. Moreover, basic to the notion of civil rights is that individuals are not to be judged according to characteristics they share with a group. Thus civil rights protect the individual against collective discrimination.

The question of where to draw the line in the government's efforts to protect civil rights has received different answers at different points in American history, but few Americans want to turn back the clock to the days of *Plessy v. Ferguson* and Jim Crow laws or to once again exclude women from the workplace.

Review the Chapter

The Struggle for Equality

5.1 Differentiate the Supreme Court's three standards of review for classifying people under the equal protection clause, p. 146.

Americans have emphasized equal rights and opportunities rather than equal results. In the Constitution, only the Fourteenth Amendment mentions equality. To determine whether classifications in laws and regulations are in keeping with the amendment's equal protection clause, the Supreme Court developed three standards of review: most classifications need only be reasonable, racial or ethnic classifications are inherently suspect, and classifications based on gender receive intermediate scrutiny.

African Americans' Civil Rights

5.2 Trace the evolution of protections of the rights of African Americans and explain the application of nondiscrimination principles to issues of race, p. 149.

Racial discrimination is rooted in the era of slavery, which lasted about 250 years and persisted in an era of segregation, especially in the South, into the 1950s. The civil rights movement achieved victories through civil disobedience and through the Court rulings, beginning with *Brown v. the Board of Education*, voiding discrimination in education, transportation, and other areas of life. In the 1960s, Congress prohibited discrimination in public accommodations, employment, housing, and voting through legislation such as the 1964 Civil Rights Act and the 1965 Voting Rights Act. Through their struggle for civil rights, African Americans blazed the constitutional trail for securing equal rights for all Americans.

The Rights of Women

5.3 Relate civil rights principles to progress made by other ethnic groups in the United States, p. 156.

Native Americans, Hispanic Americans, Asian Americans, and Arab Americans and Muslims have suffered discriminatory treatment. Yet each group has benefited from the application of Court decisions and legislation of the civil rights era. These groups have also engaged in political action to defend their rights.

5.4 Trace the evolution of women's rights, and explain how civil rights principles apply to gender issues, p. 161.

After a long battle, women won the vote, with the passage of the Nineteenth Amendment, in 1920. Beginning in the 1960s, a second feminist wave successfully challenged gender-based classifications regarding employment, property, and other economic issues. Despite increased equality, issues remain, including lack of parity in wages, participation in the military, and combating sexual harassment.

Other Groups Active Under the Civil Rights Umbrella

5.5 Summarize the struggles for civil rights of older Americans, persons with disabilities, and LGBT Americans, p. 166.

Seniors and people with disabilities have successfully fought bias in employment, and the latter have gained greater access to education and public facilities. Gays and lesbians have faced more obstacles to overcoming discrimination and have been more successful in areas such as employment and privacy than in obtaining the right to marry.

Affirmative Action

5.6 Trace the evolution of affirmative action policy and assess the arguments for and against it, p. 170.

Affirmative action policies, which began in the 1960s, are designed to bring about increased employment, promotion, or admission for members of groups that have suffered from discrimination. In recent years, the Supreme Court has applied the inherently suspect standard to affirmative action policies and prohibited quotas and other means of achieving more equal results.

Understanding Civil Rights and Public Policy

5.7 Establish how civil rights policy advances democracy and increases the scope of government, p. 173.

Civil rights policies advance democracy because equality is a basic principle of democratic government. When majority rule threatens civil rights, the latter must prevail. Civil rights policies limit government discrimination but also require an active government effort to protect the rights of minorities.

The Rights of Other Minority Groups

Learn the Terms

civil rights, p. 146
Fourteenth Amendment, p. 147
equal protection of the laws, p. 147
Thirteenth Amendment, p. 149
Civil Rights Act of 1964, p. 153
suffrage, p. 154

Fifteenth Amendment, p. 154
poll taxes, p. 154
white primary, p. 154
Twenty-fourth Amendment, p. 154
Voting Rights Act of 1965, p. 154
Nineteenth Amendment, p. 161

Equal Rights Amendment, p. 162
Americans with Disabilities Act
   of 1990, p. 168
affirmative action, p. 170

Key Cases

Scott v. Sandford (1857)
Plessy v. Ferguson (1896)
Brown v. Board of Education (1954)
Hernandez v. Texas (1954)

Koremastu v. United States (1944)
Reed v. Reed (1971)
Craig v. Boren (1976)

*Regents of the University of California
   v. Bakke* (1978)
Adarand Constructors v. Pena (1995)

Test Yourself

1. Which of the following best characterizes the original Constitution's treatment of equality?

a. The Constitution does not address equality in its original form.

b. The Constitution treats equality as corresponding with equal representation in Congress.

c. The Constitution treats equality as corresponding with equal results and equal rewards.

d. The Constitution treats equality as corresponding with the equal protection of the laws.

e. The Constitution treats equality as corresponding with the phrase "all men are created equal."

2. What do courts presume classifications based on race to be?

a. constitutional
b. offensive
c. reasonable
d. remedial
e. suspect

3. Why is the Fourteenth Amendment to the U.S. Constitution especially significant?

a. because it applied the federal Bill of Rights to the individual states, protecting citizens from infringement of their rights under the federal constitution by state governments

b. because it effectively gave African Americans full rights following the Civil War

c. because it explicitly prohibited discrimination on account of gender, thus assuring the equal rights of women

d. because it made it possible for the federal government to engage in revenue sharing with the several states

e. because it prohibited discrimination on grounds of age, securing the right to vote for Americans 18 years of age or older

4. Which of the following statements best characterizes post-reconstruction developments for African Americans?

a. African Americans held seats in Congress and in state legislatures.

b. African Americans increasingly sought employment in the federal government, which did not segregate by race.

c. African Americans slowly gained a foothold on power.

d. The departure of federal troops from Southern states led to a surge of segregationist laws.

e. The Supreme Court continued to strike down anti-discriminatory laws.

5. Which of the following was one of the provisions of the Civil Rights Act of 1964?

a. It authorized the U.S. Justice Department to win women equal wages.

b. It created the Affirmative Action Commission.

c. It prohibited discrimination in employment on the basis of race and gender.

d. It prohibited discrimination in the sale or rental of housing.

e. It strengthened the states' power over voting rules.

6. What was the immediate response of the South to the Supreme Court's decision in *Brown v. Board of Education?*

a. The South avoided implementing the Court's decision.

b. The South complied with both the letter and the spirit of the Supreme Court's decision.

c. The South erupted in jubilation due to their victory at the Supreme Court.

d. The South immediately complied with the spirit of the Court decision because they were eager to put the whole affair behind them.

e. The South reluctantly complied with the Court's mandate, although they did not agree with the decision.

7. Which of the following statements is true regarding the civil rights of minority groups?

a. Arab Americans may be denied the right to attend mosques.

b. Asian Americans are a group that has not suffered racial discrimination.

c. Children not legally admitted to the United States are not protected by the Fourteenth Amendment.

d. Native Americans were always considered U.S. citizens.

e. The landmark *Hernandez v. Texas* case helped widen the definition of discrimination beyond race.

8. Which of the following was an effect of the federal government's strategy to assimilate Native Americans in 1887?

a. Native Americans were forced to disperse throughout the country.

b. Native Americans were sent to teach their language to neighboring towns.

c. Reservations received grants for economic reconstruction.

d. The government issued additional land to Native American reservations.

e. Tribal rituals and languages were banned.

9. Following the ratification of the Nineteenth Amendment, which gave women the right to vote, what happened?

a. A backlash led to more restricted social conditions for women.

b. New state laws began to expand opportunities for women in the workplace.

c. The feminist movement continued to gain strength as women were able to vote for officials who supported their goals.

d. The feminist movement lost momentum as it lacked unified support for its goals.

e. The movement for women's rights turned to promoting equality through public policy.

10. Which of the following was true prior to the start of the women's rights movement in the nineteenth century?

a. Abused women usually found it easy to end marriages due to the patriarchal structure of society.

b. Coverture deprived married women of a legal identity separate from their husbands.

c. Divorce law heavily favored women.

d. Women were always accepted by abolitionist organizations.

e. Women were only allowed to vote in primary elections.

11. Which of the following is the standard for evaluating age discrimination claims?

a. the employer's bias standard

b. the medium scrutiny standard

c. the reasonableness standard

d. the strict scrutiny standard

e. The Supreme Court has yet to rule on a proper classification for age discrimination.

12. Opposition to civil rights laws for the disabled has been justified primarily on the basis of the _____.

a. fear that a new, special, protected status would further stigmatize the disabled

b. fear that laws will lead to a quota system to hire disabled persons

c. fear that the disabled will take jobs away from able-bodied persons

d. high cost of programs to help the disabled

e. inability of disabled persons to handle most employment requirements

13. Which statement about affirmative action best reflects current Supreme Court precedent?

a. Affirmative action in any form is reverse discrimination and is therefore unconstitutional under the Civil Rights Act of 1964.

b. Although racial set-asides are unconstitutional, race may be considered as one among many factors in determining college admissions.

c. Racial set-asides can be used by universities and colleges in order to promote diversity.

d. Quotas or set-asides may be used in both employment and education to redress past discrimination.

e. Quotas or set-asides may be used only in employment to redress past discrimination.

14. Which of these statements expresses the sentiments of those who support affirmative action?

a. Affirmative action is intended to achieve equal results, not just equal opportunities.

b. Any form of quota system is unjust.

c. Merit is the least fair basis for distributing benefits.

d. Once affirmative action policies are in place, discrimination in schools and the workplace will be eliminated.

e. The Supreme Court has been clear and unequivocal in the constitutionality of affirmative action.

15. Which of the following most often conflicts with the demand for greater civil rights?

a. affirmative action

b. democracy

c. equality

d. individual liberty

e. minority rule

Explore Further

WEB SITES

www.justice.gov/crt/
Home page of the Civil Rights Division of the U.S. Department of Justice, containing background information and discussion of current events.

www.ada.gov
Home page of the Americans with Disabilities Act of the U.S. Department of Justice, containing background information and discussion of current events.

www.naacp.org
Home page of the NAACP, containing background information and discussion of current events.

www.lulac.org
League of United Latin American Citizens home page, with information on Latino rights and policy goals.

civilrightsproject.ucla.edu/
Home page of the Civil Rights Project at UCLA, with background information and other resources on civil rights.

www.now.org
Home page of the National Organization of Women, containing material on issues dealing with women's rights.

www.hrc.org
Human Rights Campaign home page, with information on lesbian, gay, bisexual, and transgender rights.

www.usccr.gov/
U.S. Commission on Civil Rights home page, with news of civil rights issues around the country.

FURTHER READING

Anderson, Terry H. *The Pursuit of Fairness.* New York: Oxford University Press, 2005. A history of affirmative action.

Baer, Judith A. *Women in American Law: The Struggle Toward Equality from the New Deal to the Present,* 3rd rev. ed. New York: Holmes and Meier, 2003. An excellent analysis of women's changing legal status.

Garcia, John A. *Latino Politics in America: Community, Culture, and Interests.* Lanham, MD: Rowman & Littlefield, 2003. An insightful view of Latino politics.

Mansbridge, Jane. *Why We Lost the ERA.* Chicago: University of Chicago Press, 1986. The politics of women's rights.

McClain, Paula D., and Joseph Stewart. *Can We All Get Along?* 5th ed. Boulder, CO: Westview, 2009. Racial and ethnic minorities in American politics.

Nakanishi, Don T., and James S. Lai, eds. *Asian American Politics: Law, Participation, and Policy.* Lanham, MD: Rowman & Littlefield, 2003. Essays focusing on Asian American politics.

Pinello, Daniel R. *America's Struggle for Same-Sex Marriage.* New York: Cambridge University Press, 2006. The social movement for same-sex marriage and the political controversies surrounding it.

Rimmerman, Craig A. *The Lesbian and Gay Movements.* Boulder, CO: Westview, 2008. Examines the strategies and issues of gay and lesbian politics.

Wilkins, David E. *American Indian Politics and the American Political System,* rev. ed. Lanham, MD: Rowman & Littlefield, 2003. Excellent treatment of Native American issues and politics.

Woodward, C. Vann. *The Strange Career of Jim Crow,* 2nd ed. New York: Oxford University Press, 1966. Examines the evolution of Jim Crow laws in the South.

6

Public Opinion and Political Action

Politics in Action: The Limits of Public Understanding of Health Care Reform

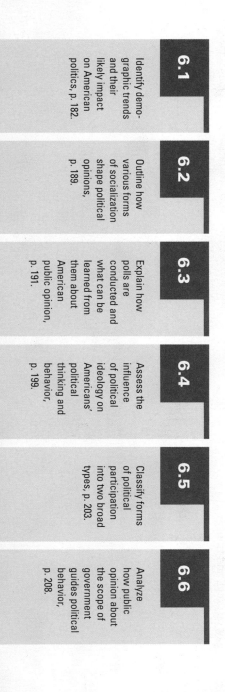

The Affordable Care Act stands out as President Obama's major legislative achievement. No other recent public policy issue has been debated in as much detail. Yet, as people started to sign up for coverage in 2013, the public's knowledge about the legislation remained sketchy. The Kaiser tracking poll asked a nationally representative sample whether they thought a variety of provisions were included in the Affordable Care Act. They found that accurate perceptions of what it was designed to do were only slightly more common than misperceptions about the legislation.

On the positive side, 60 percent of the sample thought that the Affordable Care Act provided for three things that were based on fact: (1) providing financial help for Americans who don't get insurance through their jobs to help them purchase coverage; (2) prohibiting insurance companies from denying coverage because of a person's medical history; and (3) giving states the option of expanding their Medicaid program to cover more people with low incomes. On the negative side, though, more than 40 percent wrongly believed that Obamacare: (1) established a government

6.1 Identify demographic trends and their likely impact on American politics, p. 182.

6.2 Outline how various forms of socialization shape political opinions, p. 189.

6.3 Explain how polls are conducted and what can be learned from them about American public opinion, p. 191.

6.4 Assess the influence of political ideology on Americans' political thinking and behavior, p. 199.

6.5 Classify forms of political participation into two broad types, p. 203.

6.6 Analyze how public opinion about the scope of government guides political behavior, p. 208.

Protestors against President Obama's health care reforms react in front of the Supreme Court after the Court upheld its constitutionality in June 2012. The general public was less interested in this case than were these protestors. A week after this historic ruling, the Pew Research Center found that only 55 percent of Americans knew which way the Court had ruled.

6.1
6.2
6.3
6.4
6.5
6.6

public opinion
The distribution of the population's beliefs about politics and policy issues.

demography
The science of population changes.

census
An "actual enumeration" of the population, which the Constitution requires that the government conduct every 10 years. The census is a valuable tool for understanding demographic changes.

The American People

6.1

Identify demographic trends and their likely impact on American politics.

O
ne way of looking at the American public is through **demography**— the science of human populations. The most valuable tool for understanding demographic changes in America is the **census**. The U.S. Constitution requires that the government conduct an "actual enumeration" of the population every 10 years. The first census was conducted in 1790; the most recent census was done in 2010.

The Census Bureau tries to conduct the most accurate count of the population possible. It isn't an easy job, even with the allocation of billions of federal dollars to the task. In 2010, a census form was mailed out to all 134 million residential addresses in the United States. Despite the fact that federal law requires a response from every household—a fact that is noted on the mailing envelope—only 72 percent of households responded, ranging from a high of 81 percent in Wisconsin to a low of 62 percent in Alaska. Thus, 800,000 people were hired to follow up with the remaining 28 percent through door-to-door canvassing. In explaining on its Web site why participation was so important, the Census Bureau noted that "the information the census collects helps to determine how more than $400 billion of federal funding each year is spent

panel to make decisions about end-of-life care; (2) cut benefits to Medicare; and (3) allowed undocumented immigrants to receive financial help to buy health insurance.[1]

Public opinion polling has become a major growth industry in recent years. The media seem to love to report on the latest polls. If there is nothing new in their findings, journalists can always fall back on one sure pattern: the lack of public attention to matters of public policy. Whether it's health care reform, cap-and-trade policy, or the question of immigration reform, the safest prediction that a public opinion analyst can make is that many people will be unaware of the major elements of the legislative debate going on in Washington.

In a democracy, the people are expected to guide public policy. But do people pay enough attention to public affairs to fulfill their duty as citizens? As we shall see in this chapter, there is much reason to be concerned about how little the American public knows about policy issues; however, a case can also be made that most people know *enough* for democracy to work reasonably well. Like public opinion itself, evaluating the state of public knowledge of public policy is complex.

Politicians and columnists commonly intone the words "the American people" and then claim their view as that of the citizenry. Yet it would be hard to find a statement about the American people—who they are and what they believe—that is either entirely right or entirely wrong. The American people are wondrously diverse. There are over 300 million Americans, forming a mosaic of racial, ethnic, and cultural groups. America was founded on the principle of tolerating diversity and individualism, and it remains one of the most diverse countries in the world. Most Americans view this diversity as among the most appealing aspects of their society.

The study of American **public opinion** aims to understand the distribution of the population's beliefs about politics and policy issues. Because there are many groups and a great variety of opinions in the United States, this is an especially complex task. This is not to say that public opinion would be easy to study even if America were a more homogeneous society; as you will see, measuring public opinion involves painstaking interviewing procedures and careful wording of questions.

For American government to work efficiently and effectively, the diversity of the American public and its opinions must be faithfully channeled through the political process. This chapter reveals just how difficult this task is.

In an attempt to get more people to fill out their Census form, the Census Bureau advertised heavily in 2010 to try to increase public awareness of the Census and its importance. One controversial allocation of money was $1.2 million to sponsor NASCAR driver Greg Biffle during three auto races in March. Critics derided this as an absurd use of taxpayer money. In response, Census director Robert Groves argued that millions of Americans followed NASCAR races and that an increase in the initial response to the Census of just 0.1 percent could cut the cost of conducting the Census by $8.5 million.

on infrastructure and services like (1) hospitals; (2) job training centers; (3) schools; (4) senior centers; (5) bridges, tunnels and other public works projects; and (6) emergency services."[2] Communities that are usually undercounted in the census—primarily those with high concentrations of minorities, people with low incomes, and children—end up getting less from the federal government than they should.

Changes in the U.S. population, which census figures reflect, also impact our culture and political system in numerous ways, as will be examined in the next few sections.

The Immigrant Society

The United States has always been a nation of immigrants. As John F. Kennedy said, America is "not merely a nation but a nation of nations."[3] All Americans except Native Americans are descended from immigrants or are immigrants themselves. Today, federal law allows for about 1 million new immigrants a year, and in recent years about 500,000 illegal immigrants a year have also entered the United States. Combined, this is equivalent to adding roughly the population of Phoenix every year. The Census Bureau estimates that currently 11 percent of the nation's population are immigrants and that 45 percent of this group have already become U.S. citizens. States vary substantially in the percentage of their residents who are foreign born—from a high of 27 percent in California to a low of 1 percent in West Virginia.

There have been three great waves of immigration to the United States:

- In the first wave, in the early and mid-nineteenth century, immigrants were mainly northwestern Europeans (English, Irish, Germans, and Scandinavians).

- In the second wave, in the late nineteenth and early twentieth centuries, many immigrants were southern and eastern Europeans (Italians, Jews, Poles, Russians, and others). Most came through Ellis Island in New York (now a popular museum).

- In the most recent wave, since the 1960s, immigrants have been especially Hispanics (particularly from Cuba, Central America, and Mexico) and Asians (from Vietnam, Korea, the Philippines, and elsewhere).

6.1
6.2
6.3
6.4
6.5
6.6

melting pot
A term often used to characterize the United States, with its history of immigration and mixing of cultures, ideas, and peoples.

minority majority
The situation, likely beginning in the mid-twenty-first century, in which the non-Hispanic whites will represent a minority of the U.S. population and minority groups together will represent a majority.

For the first century of U.S. history, America had an open door policy for anyone who wanted to come to fill up its vast unexplored territory. The first restrictions on immigration, in 1875, limited criminals and prostitutes from staying in the United States, and soon lunatics and people with serious diseases were banned also. The first geographically based restrictions were imposed in 1882 when the Chinese Exclusion Act was passed. As concern grew about the flood of new immigrants from southern and eastern Europe, the Johnson-Reid Immigration Act was passed in 1924, establishing official quotas for immigrants based on national origins. These quotas were based on the number of people from each particular country living in the United States at the time of the 1890 census. By tying the quotas to a time when most Americans were from northwestern Europe, this law greatly cut down on the flow of immigrants from elsewhere.

It wasn't until the Hart-Celler Immigration and Nationality Act of 1965 that these quotas were abolished. This 1965 law made family integration the prevailing goal for U.S. immigration policy. As historian Steven Gillon argues, this law produced an unanticipated chain of immigration under the auspices of family unification. For example, he writes,

> An engineering student from India could come to the United States to study, find a job after graduating, get labor certification, and become a legal resident alien. His new status would then entitle him to bring over his wife, and six years later, after being naturalized, his brothers and sisters. They in turn could begin the process all over again by sponsoring their wives, husbands, children, and siblings.[4]

Today, some politicians believe that America's competitiveness in the globalized economy would be better served by reducing the emphasis on family unification in our immigration policy and reallocating a substantial percentage of immigrant visas to people with special talents. You can read about this issue in "You Are the Policymaker: Should Immigration Be Based More on Skills Than Blood Ties?"

☐ The American Melting Pot

With its long history of immigration, the United States has often been called a **melting pot**, in which cultures, ideas, and peoples blend into one. As the third wave of immigration continues, policymakers have begun to speak of a new **minority majority**, meaning that America will eventually cease to have a non-Hispanic white majority. As of 2012, the Census Bureau reported an all-time low in the percentage of non-Hispanic white Americans—just 63 percent of the population. Hispanics made up the largest minority group, accounting for 17 percent of the U.S. population, with African Americans making up 13 percent, Asian Americans 6 percent, and Native Americans 1 percent. In recent years, minority populations have been growing at a much faster rate than the white non-Hispanic population. As you can see in Figure 6.1, the Census Bureau estimates that by the middle of the twenty-first century, non-Hispanic whites will represent less than half of the population. The projected increases are based on two trends that are likely to continue for decades to come. First, immigration into the United States has been and will probably continue to be concentrated among Hispanics and Asian Americans. Second, birth rates have been consistently higher among minorities. Indeed, the Census Bureau reported that among the babies it counted in the 2010 census less than 50 percent were non-Hispanic whites.

For most of American history, African Americans were the largest minority group in the country. Most African Americans are descended from reluctant immigrants—Africans brought to America by force as slaves. A legacy of centuries of racism and discrimination is that a relatively high proportion of African Americans are economically disadvantaged—in 2013, according to Census Bureau data, 27 percent of African Americans lived below the poverty line compared to 10 percent of non-Hispanic whites. Although this economic disadvantage persists, African Americans have been exercising more political power, and the number of African Americans serving in

You Are the Policymaker

Should Immigration Be Based More on Skills Than Blood Ties?

In today's interconnected world, migration from one country to another is easier than ever before, and countries that attract immigrants with valuable skills can improve their economic status. Thus, a country's immigration policy, which sets criteria for admitting people from abroad for permanent residence, can be a valuable economic tool—if a country so chooses. Some people think the United States needs to put economic factors further up on its list of priorities for immigrants.

Immigrants to the United States can be roughly classified into three categories: (1) family sponsored, (2) employment sponsored, and (3) refugees and political asylum. In the figure below you can see the distribution of American immigrants in a typical recent year — 2013.

In his 2011 book titled *Brain Gain: Rethinking U.S. Immigration Policy,* Darrell M. West argues that America needs to reorient its immigration policy toward enhancing economic development and attracting more of the world's best-educated people. He criticizes immigration policy in the United States as being based too much on *who* one knows and not enough on *what* one knows.

West points out that other countries, such as Canada and Australia, allocate a much larger percentage of their entry visas to people with special skills who can make substantial contributions to their new country's economic development. He proposes changing U.S. policy to narrow the definition of which family members are eligible for immigration under the auspices of family reunification, eliminating aunts, uncles, cousins, and other distant relatives. This simple change would allow the number of visas granted for employment purposes to be doubled.

Of course, whenever there is a substantial change in policy, there are losers as well as winners. West's proposed change would certainly lead to a more educated crop of immigrants. But immigration rates from lands with relatively low rates of higher education would likely be cut. Hence, representatives in Congress who have many constituents who trace their roots to such countries would likely be opposed to such a change from the status quo.

What do you think? Would you support the proposal to reallocate a substantial number of entry visas from those who have family ties in the United States to those who have special skills? Why or why not?

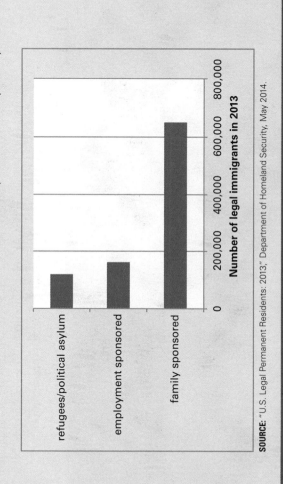

SOURCE: "U.S. Legal Permanent Residents: 2013," Department of Homeland Security, May 2014.

an elected office has increased by over 600 percent since 1970.[5] African Americans have been elected as mayors of many of the country's biggest cities, including Los Angeles, New York, and Chicago. Under George W. Bush, two African Americans, Colin Powell and Condoleezza Rice, served as secretary of state. And the biggest African American political breakthrough of all occurred when Barack Obama was elected president in 2008.

In the 2000 census, the Hispanic population outnumbered the African American population for the first time. Like African Americans, Hispanics are concentrated in

FIGURE 6.1 THE COMING MINORITY MAJORITY

Based on current birthrates and immigration rates, the Census Bureau estimates that the demographics of the United States should change as shown in the accompanying graph. As of 2012, the census estimated that minority groups should be in the majority for the nation as a whole sometime between 2040 and 2045. Of course, should rates of birth and immigration change, so would these estimates.

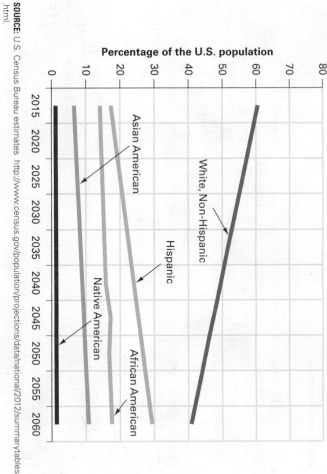

Percentage of the U.S. population

White, Non-Hispanic

Hispanic

Asian American

African American

Native American

SOURCE: U.S. Census Bureau estimates. http://www.census.gov/population/projections/data/national/2012/summarytables.html.

cities. Hispanics are rapidly gaining political power in the Southwest, and cities such as San Antonio and Los Angeles have elected mayors of Hispanic heritage. As of 2014, the state legislatures of Arizona, California, Florida, Nevada, New Mexico, New York, and Texas had at least 10 percent Hispanic representation.[6]

As of 2012, the Department of Homeland Security estimated that the number of illegal immigrants in the United States stood at 11.5 million, 59 percent of whom were from Mexico. Here, a border patrol car (at the upper right) patrols along the fence between Nogales, Arizona, and Mexico.

An issue of particular relevance to the Hispanic community is that of illegal immigration. According to the Department of Homeland Security, there were about 11.5 million unauthorized persons residing in the United States in 2011, 74 percent of whom were from Mexico and other Central American countries.[7] Although Presidents Bush and Obama both pledged to address the problems of illegal immigration, no significant reform has been enacted since the 1986 Simpson–Mazzoli Act. This law requires that employers document the citizenship of their employees. Whether people are born in Canton, Ohio, or Canton, China, they must prove that they are either U.S. citizens or legal immigrants in order to work. Civil and criminal penalties can be assessed against employers who knowingly employ undocumented immigrants. However, it has proved difficult for authorities to establish that employers have knowingly accepted false social security cards and other forged identity documents, and, as a result, the Simpson–Mazzoli Act has not significantly slowed illegal immigration.

Whereas many Hispanics have come to America to escape poverty, the recent influx of Asians has involved a substantial number of professional workers looking for greater opportunity. Indeed, the new Asian immigrants are the most highly skilled immigrant group in American history,[8] and Asian Americans have often been called the superachievers of the emerging minority majority. Significantly, over half of Asian Americans over the age of 25 hold a college degree, almost twice the national average.[9] As a result, their median family income has already surpassed that of non-Hispanic whites. Although still a very small minority group, Asian Americans have had some notable political successes. For example, in 1996 Gary Locke (a Chinese American) was elected governor of Washington, in 2001 Norman Mineta (a Japanese American) was appointed secretary of transportation, and Nikki Haley and Bobby Jindal (both of whom are the children of immigrants from India) currently serve as the governors of South Carolina and Louisiana, respectively.

By the time this little Chinese-American girl (born in China but now an American citizen) graduates from college, Asian Americans will represent 8 percent of the U.S. population. As the most highly educated segment of the coming "minority majority," it is likely that they will be exercising a good deal of political power by then.

6.1
6.2
6.3
6.4
6.5
6.6

political culture
An overall set of values widely shared within a society.

reapportionment
The process of reallocating seats in the House of Representatives every 10 years on the basis of the results of the census.

Americans live in an increasingly multicultural and multilingual society. Yet, regardless of ethnic background, Americans have a common **political culture**—an overall set of values widely shared within the society. For example, there is much agreement across ethnic groups about such basic American values as the principle of treating all equally. Debra Schildkraut's recent study of immigrants finds that the longer one's family has had to integrate into American society, the greater the likelihood that one will identify oneself primarily as American. Thus, integration is a simple matter of time for most immigrants. She therefore concludes that "there is not much validity to concerns that American national identity is disintegrating or that the newest Americans are more likely than anyone else to reject their own American identity or American institutions."[10]

However, not all observers view this most recent wave of immigration without concern. Ellis Cose, a prominent journalist, has written that "racial animosity has proven to be both an enduring American phenomenon and an invaluable political tool." Because America has entered a period of rapid ethnic change, Cose predicts immigration "will be a magnet for conflict and hostility."[11] For Robert Putnam, the concern takes a different form, as he finds that "diversity does *not* produce 'bad race relations' or ethnically defined group hostility" but, rather, that "inhabitants of diverse communities tend to withdraw from collective life" and to distrust their neighbors.[12] Putnam thus recommends a renewed emphasis on the motto on our one dollar bill—*e pluribus unum* (out of many, one) to deal with the challenge created by the growing diversity within American communities.

The emergence of the minority majority is just one of several major demographic changes that are altering the face of American politics. In addition, the population has been moving and aging.

☐ The Regional Shift

For most of American history, the most populous states were concentrated north of the Mason–Dixon Line and east of the Mississippi River. However, much of America's population growth since World War II has been centered in the West and South. In particular, the populations of Arizona, Texas, and Florida have grown rapidly as people moved to the Sun Belt. From 2000 to 2010, the rate of population growth was 29 percent in Arizona, 19 percent in Texas, and 16 percent in Florida. In contrast, population growth in the Northeast was a scant 3 percent.

Demographic changes are associated with political changes. States gain or lose congressional representation as their population changes, and thus power shifts as well. This **reapportionment** process occurs once a decade, after each census, when the 435 seats in the House of Representatives are reallocated to reflect each state's proportion of the population. If the census finds that a state has 5 percent of the population, then it receives 5 percent of the seats in the House for the next 10 years. Thus, as the percentage of Americans residing in Texas grew with the movement to the Sun Belt, its representation in the House increased from 22 for the 1962–1972 elections to 35 for the 2012–2020 elections. During this same time period, in contrast, New York lost over one-third of its delegation.

☐ The Graying of America

Florida, currently the nation's fourth most populous state, has grown in large part as a result of its attractiveness to senior citizens. Nationwide, citizens over 65 are the fastest-growing age group in America. Not only are people living longer as a result of medical advances, but in addition the fertility rate has dropped substantially—from 3.6 children per woman in 1960 to about 2.1 today.

The aging of the population has enormous implications for Social Security. Social Security is structured as a pay-as-you-go system, which means that today's workers pay the benefits for today's retirees. In 1960, there were 5.7 workers per retiree; today there are 3. By 2040, there will be only about 2 workers per retiree. This ratio will put

political socialization
The process through which individuals in a society acquire political attitudes, views, and knowledge, based on inputs from family, schools, the media, and others.

tremendous pressure on the Social Security system, which, even today, is exceeded only by national defense as America's most costly public policy. The current group of older Americans and those soon to follow can lay claim to trillions of dollars guaranteed by Social Security. People who have been promised benefits naturally expect to collect them, especially benefits for which they have made monthly contributions. Thus, both political parties have long treated Social Security benefits as sacrosanct. For example, Republican representative Paul Ryan's recent proposal for reshaping the Social Security system carefully promised to keep the system unchanged for anyone over the age of 55.

How Americans Learn About Politics: Political Socialization

6.2 Outline how various forms of socialization shape political opinions.

C entral to the formation of public opinion is **political socialization**, or "the process through which an individual acquires his or her particular political orientations—his or her knowledge, feelings, and evaluations regarding his or her political world."[13] As people become more socialized with age, their political orientations grow firmer. Thus, governments typically aim their socialization efforts largely at the young. Authoritarian regimes are particularly concerned with indoctrinating their citizens at an early age. For example, youth in the former Soviet Union were organized into the Komsomol—the Young Communist League. Membership in these groups was helpful in gaining admission to college and entering certain occupations. In the Komsomol, Soviet youth were taught their government's view of the advantages of communism (though apparently not well enough to keep the system going). Political socialization is a much more subtle process in the United States.

The Process of Political Socialization

Only a small portion of Americans' political learning is formal. Civics or government classes in high school teach citizens some of the nuts and bolts of government—how many senators each state has, what presidents do, and so on. But such formal socialization is only the tip of the iceberg. Americans do most of their political learning without teachers or classes.

Informal learning is really much more important than formal, in-class learning about politics. Most of this informal socialization is almost accidental. Few parents sit down with their children and say, "Johnny, let us tell you why we're Republicans." Instead, the informal socialization process might be best described by words like *pick up* and *absorb*.

The family, the media, and the schools all serve as important agents of political socialization. We look at each in turn.

THE FAMILY The family's role in socialization is central because of its monopoly on two crucial resources in the early years: time and emotional commitment. If your parents are interested in politics, chances are you will be also, as your regular interactions with them will expose you to the world of politics as you are growing up. Furthermore, children often pick up their political leanings from the attitudes of their parents. Most students in an American government class like to think of themselves as independent thinkers, especially when it comes to politics. Yet one can predict how the majority of young people will vote simply by knowing the party identification of their parents.[14]

Some degree of adolescent rebellion against parents and their beliefs does take place. Witnessing the outpouring of youthful rebellion in the late 1960s and early 1970s, many people thought a generation gap was opening up. Supposedly, radical youth condemned their backward-thinking parents. Although such a gap occurred in some families, the

190

6.1
6.2
6.3
6.4
6.5
6.6

overall evidence for it was slim. For example, eight years after Jennings and Niemi first interviewed a sample of high school seniors and their parents in the mid-1960s, they still found far more agreement than disagreement across the generational divide.[15] Recent research has demonstrated that one of the reasons for the long-lasting impact of parental influence on political attitudes is simply genetics. In one study, Alford, Funk, and Hibbing compared the political opinions of identical twins and nonidentical twins.[16] If the political similarity between parents and children is due just to environmental factors, then the identical twins should agree on political issues to about the same extent the nonidentical twins do, as in both cases the twins are raised in the same environment. However, if genetics are an important factor, then identical twins, who are genetically the same, should agree with one another more often than nonidentical twins, who are not. On all the political questions they examined, there was substantially more agreement between the identical twins—clearly demonstrating that genetics play an important role in shaping political attitudes.

THE MASS MEDIA

The mass media are the "new parent," according to many observers. Average grade-school youngsters spend more time each week watching television than they spend at school. And television displaces parents as the chief source of information as children get older.

Unfortunately, today's generation of young adults is significantly less likely to watch television news and read newspapers than their elders. Many studies have attributed the relative lack of political knowledge of today's youth to their media consumption or, more appropriately, to their lack of it.[17] In 1965, Gallup found virtually no difference between age groups in frequency of following politics through the media. In recent years, however, a considerable age gap has opened up, with older people paying the most attention to the news and young adults the least. The median age of viewers of CBS, ABC, and NBC news programs in 2012 was 63—18 years older than the audience for a typical prime-time program. If you have ever turned on the TV news and wondered why so many of the commercials seem to be for various prescription drugs, now you know why.

SCHOOL

Political socialization is as important to a government as it is to an individual. Governments, including our own, often use schools to promote national loyalty and support for their basic values. In most American schools, the day begins with the Pledge of Allegiance. As part of promoting support for the basic values of the system, American children have long been successfully educated about the virtues of free enterprise and democracy.

Any democracy has a vested interest in students' learning the positive features of their political system because this helps ensure that youth will grow up to be supportive citizens. David Easton and Jack Dennis have argued that "those children who begin to develop positive feelings toward the political authorities will grow into adults who will be less easily disenchanted with the system than those children who early acquire negative, hostile sentiments."[18] Of course, this is not always the case. Well-socialized youths of the 1960s led the opposition to the American regime and the war in Vietnam. It could be argued, however, that even these protestors had been positively shaped by the socialization process, for the goal of most activists was to make the system more democratically responsive rather than to change American government radically. Most American schools are public schools, financed by the government. Their textbooks are often chosen by the local and state boards, and teachers are certified by the state government. Schooling is perhaps the most obvious intrusion of the government into Americans' socialization. And education does exert a profound influence on a variety of political attitudes and behavior. Better-educated citizens are more likely to vote in elections, they exhibit more knowledge about politics and public policy, and they are more tolerant of opposing (even radical) opinions.

The payoffs of schooling thus extend beyond better jobs and better pay. Educated citizens also more closely approximate the model of a democratic citizen. A formal civics course may not make much difference, but the whole context of education does.

FIGURE 6.2 TURNOUT INCREASES WITH AGE

In the 2010 congressional elections, as in most midterm elections, the relationship between age and turnout was particularly pronounced, as you can see in this figure. Because today's young adults lean in the liberal direction, political analysts concluded that the low turnout rate of young people cost the Democrats a substantial number of seats in the House and Senate in 2010.

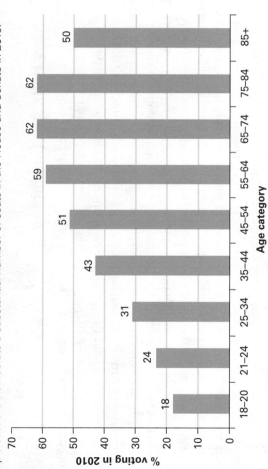

SOURCE: Authors' analysis of 2010 Census Bureau data.

As Albert Einstein once said, "Schools need not preach political doctrine to defend democracy. If they shape men and women capable of critical thought and trained in social attitudes, that is all that is necessary."

☐ Political Learning over a Lifetime

Political learning does not, of course, end when one reaches 18 or even when one graduates from college. Politics is a lifelong activity. Because America is an aging society, it is important to consider the effects of growing older on political learning and behavior.

Aging increases political participation as well as strength of party attachment. Young adults lack experience with politics. Because political behavior is to some degree learned behavior, there is some learning yet to do. Political participation rises steadily with age until the infirmities of old age make it harder to participate, as can be seen in Figure 6.2. Similarly, strength of party identification increases as people often develop a pattern of usually voting for one party or the other.

Politics, like most other things, is thus a learned behavior. Americans learn to vote, to pick a political party, and to evaluate political events in the world around them. One of the products of all this learning is what is known as public opinion.

Measuring Public Opinion and Political Information

6.3 Explain how polls are conducted and what can be learned from them about American public opinion.

 efore examining the role that public opinion plays in American politics, it is essential to learn about the science of public opinion measurement. How do we really know the approximate answers to questions such as "what percentage of young people favor abortion rights," "how many Hispanics supported Barack Obama's 2012 reelection campaign," or "what percentage of the

sample
A relatively small proportion of people who are chosen in a survey so as to be representative of the whole.

random sampling
The key technique employed by survey researchers, which operates on the principle that everyone should have an equal probability of being selected for the sample.

sampling error
The level of confidence in the findings of a public opinion poll. The more people interviewed, the more confident one can be of the results.

public is looking for a job but cannot find one?" Polls provide these answers, but there is much skepticism about polls. Many people wonder how accurately public opinion can be measured by interviewing only 1,000 or 1,500 people around the country.[19] This section provides an explanation of how polling works; it is hoped that this will enable you to become a well-informed consumer of polls.

☐ How Polls Are Conducted

Public opinion polling is a relatively new science. It was first developed by a young man named George Gallup, who initially did some polling for his mother-in-law, a long-shot candidate for secretary of state in Iowa in 1932. With the Democratic landslide of that year, she won a stunning victory, thereby further stimulating Gallup's interest in politics. From that little acorn the mighty oak of public opinion polling has grown. The firm that Gallup founded spread throughout the democratic world, and in some languages *Gallup* is actually the word used for an opinion poll.[20]

It would be prohibitively expensive and time-consuming to ask every citizen his or her opinion on a whole range of issues. Instead, polls rely on a **sample** of the population—a relatively small proportion of people who are chosen to represent the whole. Herbert Asher draws an analogy to a blood test to illustrate the principle of sampling.[21] Your doctor does not need to drain a gallon of blood from you to determine whether you have mononucleosis, AIDS, or any other disease. Rather, a small sample of blood will reveal its properties.

In public opinion polling, a random sample of about 1,000 to 1,500 people can accurately represent the "universe" of potential voters. The key to the accuracy of opinion polls is the technique of **random sampling**, which operates on the principle that everyone should have an equal probability of being selected as part of the sample. Your chance of being asked to be in the poll should therefore be as good as that of anyone else—rich or poor, black or white, young or old, male or female. If the sample is randomly drawn, about 13 percent of those interviewed will be African American, slightly over 50 percent female, and so forth, matching the population as a whole.

Remember that the science of polling involves estimation; a sample can represent the population with only a certain degree of confidence. The level of confidence is known as the **sampling error**, which depends on the size of the sample. The more people that are randomly interviewed for a poll, the more confident one can be of the results. A typical poll of about 1,500 to 2,000 respondents has a sampling error of ±3 percent. What this means is that 95 percent of the time the poll results are within 3 percent of what the entire population thinks. If 40 percent of the sample say they approve of the job the president is doing, one can be pretty certain that the true figure is between 37 and 43 percent.

In order to obtain results that will usually be within sampling error, researchers must follow proper sampling techniques. In perhaps the most infamous survey ever, a 1936 *Literary Digest* poll underestimated the vote for President Franklin Roosevelt by 19 percent, erroneously predicting a big victory for Republican Alf Landon. The well-established magazine suddenly became a laughingstock and soon went out of business. Although the number of responses the magazine obtained for its poll was a staggering 2,376,000, its polling methods were badly flawed. Trying to reach as many people as possible, the magazine drew names from the biggest lists they could find: telephone books and motor vehicle records. In the midst of the Great Depression, the people on these lists were above the average income level (only 40 percent of the public had telephones then; fewer still owned cars) and were more likely to vote Republican. The moral of the story is this: accurate representation, not the number of responses, is the most important feature of a public opinion survey. Indeed, as polling techniques have advanced over the past 80 years, typical sample sizes have been getting smaller, not larger.

Computer and telephone technology has made surveying less expensive and more commonplace. In the early days of polling, pollsters needed a national network of interviewers to traipse door-to-door in their localities with a clipboard of questions.

Now most polling is done on the telephone with samples selected through **random-digit dialing.** Calls are placed to phone numbers within randomly chosen exchanges (for example, 512-471-XXXX) around the country. In this manner, both listed and unlisted numbers are reached at a cost of about one-fifth that of person-to-person interviewing. There are a couple of disadvantages, however. A small percentage of the population does not have a phone, and people are substantially less willing to participate over the telephone than in person—it is easier to hang up than to slam the door in someone's face. These are small trade-offs for political candidates running for minor offices, for whom telephone polls are the only affordable method of gauging public opinion.

However, in this era of cell phones, many pollsters are starting to worry whether this methodology will continue to be affordable. As of 2014, government studies showed that over a quarter of the population had cell phone service only. This percentage is significantly higher among young adults, minorities, and people who are transient. Because federal law prohibits use of automated dialing programs to cell phones, pollsters have to use the far more expensive procedure of dialing cell phones numbers manually. In addition, studies have shown that people are much less likely to agree to be interviewed when they are reached on a cell phone as compared to a landline. All told, Mark Mellman, one of America's top political pollsters, estimates that it is 5 to 15 times as expensive to gather interviews from the cell-phone-only segment of the population as from landline users.[22] Although big firms like Gallup have successfully made the adjustment so far, the costs of conducting phone polls are likely to further escalate as more people give up their landlines.

As with many other aspects of commerce in America, the future of polling may lie with the Internet. Internet pollsters, such as Knowledge Networks, assemble representative panels of the population by first contacting people on the phone and asking them whether they are willing to participate in Web-based surveys on a variety of topics. If they agree, they are paid a small sum every time they participate. And if they don't have Internet access, they are provided with it as part of their compensation. Once someone agrees to participate, he or she is then contacted exclusively by e-mail. As Knowledge Networks proclaims, "This permits surveys to be fielded very quickly and economically. In addition, this approach reduces the burden placed on respondents, since e-mail notification is less obtrusive than telephone calls, and most respondents find answering Web questionnaires to be more interesting and engaging than being questioned by a telephone interviewer."[23]

From its modest beginning, with George Gallup's 1932 polls for his mother-in-law in Iowa, polling has become a big business. That it has grown so much and spread throughout the world is no surprise: from Manhattan to Moscow, from Tulsa to Tokyo, people want to know what other people think.

The Role of Polls in American Democracy

Polls help political candidates detect public preferences. Supporters of polling insist that it is a tool for democracy. With it, they say, policymakers can keep in touch with changing opinions on the issues. No longer do politicians have to wait until the next election to see whether the public approves or disapproves of the government's course. If the poll results shift, then government officials can make corresponding midcourse corrections. Indeed, it was George Gallup's fondest hope that polling could contribute to the democratic process by providing a way for public desires to be heard at times other than elections. His son, George Gallup, Jr., argued that this hope had been realized in practice, that polling had "removed power out of the hands of special interest groups," and "given people who wouldn't normally have a voice a voice."[24]

Critics of polling, by contrast, say it makes politicians more concerned with following than leading. Polls might have told the Constitutional Convention delegates that the Constitution was unpopular or might have told President Thomas Jefferson that people did not want the Louisiana Purchase. Certainly they would have told William Seward

---

random-digit dialing
A technique used by pollsters to place telephone calls randomly to both listed and unlisted numbers when conducting a survey.

6.1
6.2
6.3
6.4
6.5
6.6

exit poll
Public opinion surveys used by major media pollsters to predict electoral winners with speed and precision.

> Nothing is more dangerous than to live in the temperamental atmosphere of a Gallup poll, always taking one's pulse and taking one's temperature.... There is only one duty, only one safe course, and that is to try to be right and not to fear to do or say what you believe.[25]

Based on their research, Jacobs and Shapiro argue that the common perception of politicians pandering to the results of public opinion polls may be mistaken. Their examination of major recent debates finds that political leaders "track public opinion not to make policy but rather to determine how to craft their public presentations and win public support for the policies they and their supporters favor."[26] Staff members in both the White House and Congress repeatedly remarked that their purpose in conducting polls was not to set policies but rather to find the key words and phrases with which to promote policies already in place. Thus, rather than using polls to identify centrist approaches that will have the broadest popular appeal, Jacobs and Shapiro argue, elites use them to formulate strategies that enable them to avoid compromising on what they want to do. As President Obama's chief pollster, Joel Benenson, said in 2009 about his team's work for the president: "Our job isn't to tell him what to do. Our job is to help him figure out if he can strengthen his message and persuade more people to his side. The starting point is where he is and then you try to help strengthen the message and his reasons for doing something."[27]

Yet, polls might weaken democracy in another way—they may distort the election process by creating a *bandwagon effect*. The wagon carrying the band was the centerpiece of nineteenth-century political parades, and enthusiastic supporters would literally jump on it. Today, the term refers to voters who support a candidate merely because they see that others are doing so. Although only 2 percent of people in a recent CBS/*New York Times* poll said that poll results had influenced them, 26 percent said they thought others had been influenced (showing that Americans feel that "it's the other person who's susceptible"). Beyond this, polls play to the media's interest in who's ahead in the race. The issues of recent presidential campaigns have sometimes been drowned out by a steady flood of poll results.

Probably the most widely criticized type of poll is the Election Day **exit poll**. For this type of poll, voting places are randomly selected around the country. Workers are then sent to these places and told to ask every tenth person how he or she voted. The results are accumulated toward the end of the day, enabling the television networks to project the outcomes of all but very close races before hardly any votes are actually counted. In some presidential elections, such as 1984 and 1996, the networks declared a national winner while millions on the West Coast still had hours to vote. Critics have charged that this practice discourages many people from voting and thereby affects the outcome of some state and local races.

Perhaps the most pervasive criticism of polling is that by altering the wording of a question, pollsters can manipulate the results. Small changes in question wording can sometimes produce significantly different results. For example, in February 2010, the *New York Times*/CBS News poll found that 70 percent favored permitting "gay men and lesbians" to serve in the military whereas only 44 percent favored military service by "homosexuals" who "openly announce their sexual orientation." Thus, proponents of gays and lesbians in the armed forces could rightly say that a solid public majority favored their military service while opponents could rightly counter that only a minority favored lifting the ban on open military service by homosexuals. This example illustrates why, in evaluating public opinion data, it is crucial to carefully evaluate how questions are posed. Fortunately, most major polling organizations now post their questionnaires online, thereby making it much easier than ever before for everyone to scrutinize their work.

A nuts-and-bolts knowledge of how polls are conducted will help you avoid the common mistake of taking poll results for solid fact. But being an informed consumer

not to buy Alaska, a transaction known widely at the time as "Seward's Folly." Polls may thus discourage bold leadership, like that of Winston Churchill, who once said,

In exit polls, voters are interviewed just after they have voted. These polls are used by the media to project election results as soon as the polls are closed, as well as to help the media understand what sorts of people have supported particular candidates.

of polls also requires that you think about whether the questions are fair and unbiased. The good—or the harm—that polls do depends on how well the data are collected and how thoughtfully the data are interpreted.

What Polls Reveal About Americans' Political Information

Thomas Jefferson and Alexander Hamilton had very different views about the wisdom of common people. Jefferson trusted people's good sense and believed that education would enable them to take the tasks of citizenship ever more seriously. Toward that end, he founded the University of Virginia. In contrast, Hamilton lacked confidence in people's capacity for self-government. His response to Jefferson was the infamous phrase, "Your people, sir, is a great beast."

If there had been polling data in the early days of the American republic, Hamilton would probably have delighted in throwing some of the results in Jefferson's face. If public opinion analysts agree about anything, it is that the level of public knowledge about politics is dismally low. This is particularly true for young people, but the level of knowledge for the public overall is not particularly encouraging either. For example, in October 2008, the National Annenberg Election Survey asked a set of factual questions about some prominent policy stands taken by Obama and McCain during the campaign. The results were as follows:

- 63 percent knew that Obama supported more middle-class tax cuts.
- 47 percent knew McCain favored overturning *Roe v. Wade.*
- 30 percent knew McCain was more likely to support free trade agreements.
- 8 percent knew that both candidates supported stem cell research funding.

If so many voters did not know about the candidates' stands on these hotly debated issues, then there is little doubt that most were also unaware of the detailed policy platforms the candidates were running on.

No amount of Jeffersonian faith in the wisdom of the common people can erase the fact that Americans are not well informed about politics. Polls have regularly found

196

6.1
6.2
6.3
6.4
6.5
6.6

Point to Ponder

Pollsters sometimes ask people about policy issues with which they are largely unfamiliar.

What do you think—should one take the findings from such polls with a big grain of salt?

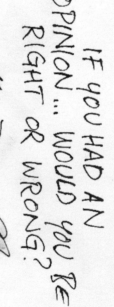

IF YOU HAD AN OPINION... WOULD YOU BE RIGHT OR WRONG?

that less than half the public can name their representative in the House. Asking people to explain their opinion on whether trade policy toward China should be liberalized, or whether research on the proposed "Star Wars" missile defense system should be continued, or whether the strategic oil reserve should be tapped when gasoline prices skyrocket often elicits blank looks. When trouble flares in a far-off country, polls regularly find that people have no idea where that country is. In fact, surveys show that many Americans lack a basic awareness of the world around them; you can see one such example in Figure 6.3.

As Lance Bennett points out, these findings provide "a source of almost bitter humor in light of what the polls tell us about public information on other subjects."[28] For example, slogans from TV commercials are better recognized than famous political figures. And in a Zogby national poll in 2006, 74 percent of respondents were able to name each of the "Three Stooges"—Larry, Curly, and Moe—whereas just 42 percent could name each of the three branches of the U.S. government—judicial, executive, and legislative.

Why It Matters to You

Political Knowledge of the Electorate

The average American clearly has less political information than most analysts consider to be desirable. While this level of information is surely adequate to maintain our democracy, survey data plainly show that citizens with above-average levels of political knowledge are more likely to vote and to have stable and consistent opinions on policy issues. If political knowledge were to increase overall, it would in all likelihood be good for American democracy.

FIGURE 6.3 MANY AMERICANS SHOW LITTLE KNOWLEDGE OF WORLD GEOGRAPHY

In 2002, a major study sponsored by *National Geographic* interviewed a representative sample of 18- to 24-year-old Americans to assess their knowledge of world geography. The average respondent got 46 percent of the questions right. Believe it or not, 11 percent of young Americans could not even find their own country on the map. Despite the American military campaign in Afghanistan after September 11, only 17 percent could correctly place that country on the map. You can take the test yourself in this figure.

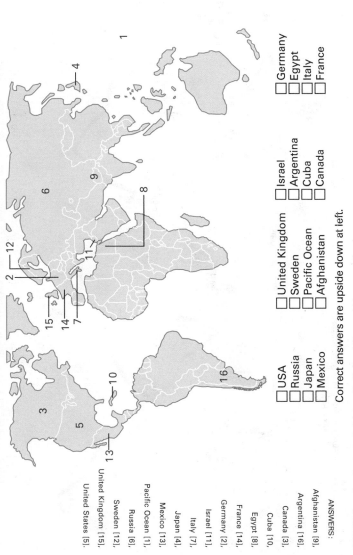

USA □ United Kingdom □ Germany
Russia □ Sweden □ Egypt
Japan □ Pacific Ocean □ Italy
Mexico □ Afghanistan □ France
Israel □ Argentina
□ Cuba
□ Canada

Correct answers are upside down at left.

ANSWERS:
United States [5].
United Kingdom [15],
Sweden [12],
Russia [6],
Pacific Ocean [1],
Mexico [13],
Japan [4],
Italy [7],
Israel [11],
Germany [2],
France [14],
Egypt [8],
Cuba [10,
Canada [3],
Argentina [16],
Afghanistan [6]',

SOURCE: Based on the test administered in *National Geographic's* cross-national survey.

How can Americans, who live in the most information-rich society in the world, be so ill informed about politics? Some blame the schools. E. D. Hirsch, Jr., criticizes schools for a failure to teach "cultural literacy."[29] People, he says, often lack the basic contextual knowledge—for example, where Afghanistan is, or what the provisions of the Affordable Care Act are—necessary to understand and use the information they receive from the news media or from listening to political candidates. Nevertheless, it has been found that increased levels of education over the past five decades have scarcely raised public knowledge about politics.[30] Despite the apparent glut of information provided by the media, Americans do not remember much about what they are exposed to through the media. (Of course, there are many critics who say that the media fail to provide much meaningful information.)

The "paradox of mass politics," says Russell Neuman, is that the American political system works as well as it does given the discomforting lack of public knowledge about politics.[31] Scholars have suggested numerous ways that this paradox can be resolved. Although many people may not know the ins and outs of most policy questions, some will base their political behavior on knowledge of just one issue that they really care about, such as abortion or environmental protection. Others will rely on simple information regarding which groups (Democrats, big business, environmentalists, Christian fundamentalists, etc.) are for and against a proposal, siding with the group or groups they trust the most.[32] And finally, some people will simply vote for or against incumbent officeholders based on how satisfied they are with the job the government is doing.

□ The Decline of Trust in Government

Sadly, the American public has become increasingly dissatisfied with government in recent decades, as shown in Figure 6.4. In the late 1950s and early 1960s, nearly three-quarters of Americans said that they trusted the government in Washington to do the

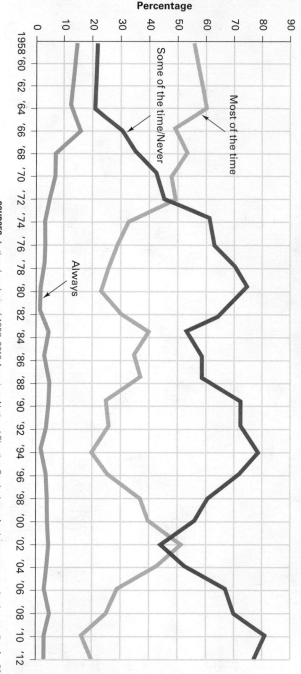

6.1
6.2
6.3
6.4
6.5
6.6

Percentage

90
80
70
60
50
40
30
20
10
0

1958 '60 '62 '64 '66 '68 '70 '72 '74 '76 '78 '80 '82 '84 '86 '88 '90 '92 '94 '96 '98 '00 '02 '04 '06 '08 '10 '12

Some of the time/Never

Most of the time

Always

FIGURE 6.4 THE DECLINE OF TRUST IN GOVERNMENT, 1958–2012

This graph shows how people have responded over time to the following question: how much of the time do you think you can trust the government in Washington to do what is right—just about always, most of the time, or only some of the time? When this question was written in 1958, survey researchers could not imagine that anyone would respond "never," so the traditional wording of the trust in government question omits this option. In 2012, about 5 percent of respondents volunteered that they never trusted the government. Some pollsters have experimented with including the option of "never" and have found that as much as 10 percent of their sample will choose it.

SOURCES: Authors' analysis of 1958–2012 American National Election Study data. As there were no election studies for 2006 and 2010 we have used the following sources for those years: December 2006 Pew Research Center poll; February 5–10, 2010 New York Times/CBS News Poll.

right thing always or mostly. By the late 1960s, however, researchers started to see a precipitous drop in public trust in government. First Vietnam and then Watergate shook people's confidence in the federal government. The economic troubles of the Carter years and the Iran hostage crisis helped continue the slide; by 1980, only one-quarter of the public thought the government could be trusted most of the time or always. Since then, trust in government has occasionally risen for a while, but the only time a majority said they could trust the government most of the time was in 2002, after the events of September 11.

Some analysts have noted that a healthy dose of public cynicism helps to keep politicians on their toes. Others, however, note that a democracy is based on the consent of the governed and that a lack of public trust in the government is a reflection of their belief that the system is not serving them well. These more pessimistic analysts have frequently wondered whether such a cynical population would unite behind their government in a national emergency. Although the drop in political cynicism after September 11 was not too great, the fact that it occurred at all indicates that cynicism will not stop Americans from rallying behind their government in times of national crisis. Widespread political cynicism about government apparently applies only to "normal" times; it has not eroded Americans' fundamental faith in our democracy.

Perhaps the greatest impact of declining trust in government since the 1960s has been to drain public support for policies that address the problems of poverty and racial inequality. Mark Hetherington argues, "People need to trust the government when they pay the costs but do not receive the benefits, which is exactly what antipoverty and race-targeted programs require of most Americans. When government programs require people to make sacrifices, they need to trust that the result will be a better future for everyone."[33] Hetherington's careful data analysis shows that declining trust in government has caused many Americans to believe that "big government" solutions to social problems are wasteful and impractical, thereby draining public support from them. Indeed, during the debate over health care reform, President Obama's advisers argued that the primary obstacle they faced was not persuading the public of the need for health care reform but, rather, convincing them to put sufficient trust in the government's ability to carry out the reform.[34] Obama acknowledged the problem in his 2010 State of the Union address, saying, "We have to recognize that we face more than a deficit of dollars right now. We face a deficit of trust—deep and corrosive doubts about how Washington works that have been growing for years." In the 2012 election, Republicans tried to exploit such doubts about the trustworthiness of the federal government, arguing that their values favoring free enterprise solutions over governmental programs were more in tune with Americans' basic values.

What Americans Value: Political Ideologies

6.4 Assess the influence of political ideology on Americans' political thinking and behavior.

A coherent set of values and beliefs about public policy is a **political ideology**. Liberal ideology, for example, supports a wide scope for the central government, often involving policies that aim to promote equality. Conservative ideology, in contrast, supports a less active scope of government that gives freer rein to the private sector. Table 6.1 attempts to summarize some of the key differences between liberals and conservatives.

political ideology
A coherent set of beliefs about politics, public policy, and public purpose, which helps give meaning to political events.

TABLE 6.1 HOW TO TELL A LIBERAL FROM A CONSERVATIVE

Liberal and *conservative*—these labels are thrown around in American politics as though everyone knows what they mean. Here are some of the political beliefs likely to be preferred by liberals and conservatives. This table, to be sure, is oversimplified.

	Liberals	Conservatives
Foreign Policy		
Military spending	Believe we should spend less	Believe we should maintain peace through strength
Use of force	Less willing to commit American troops to action overseas	More likely to support American military intervention around the world
Social Policy		
Abortion	Support "freedom of choice"	Support "right to life"
Prayer in schools	Are opposed	Are supportive
Affirmative action	Favor	Oppose
Economic Policy		
Scope of government	View government as a regulator in the public interest	Favor free-market solutions
Taxes	Want to tax the rich more	Want to keep taxes low
Spending	Want to spend more on the poor	Want to keep spending low
Crime		
How to cut crime	Believe we should solve the problems that cause crime	Believe we should stop "coddling criminals"
Defendants' rights	Believe we should guard them carefully	Believe we should stop letting criminals hide behind laws

200

6.6

6.5

6.4

6.3

6.2

6.1

☐ Who Are the Liberals and Conservatives?

Decades of survey data have consistently shown that more Americans choose the ideological label of *conservative* over *liberal*. In 2012, the Gallup poll reported that of those who labeled themselves, 38 percent were conservatives, 36 percent were moderates, and just 23 percent were liberals. The predominance of conservative thinking in America is one of the most important reasons for the relatively restrained scope of government activities compared to most European nations.

Yet there are some groups that are more liberal than others and thus would generally like to see the government do more. Among people under the age of 30, there are slightly more liberals than conservatives, as shown in "Young People and Politics: How Younger and Older Americans Compare on the Issues." The younger the individual, the less likely that person is to be a conservative. The fact that younger people are also less likely to vote means that conservatives are overrepresented at the polls.

In general, groups with political clout tend to be more conservative than groups whose members have often been shut out from the halls of political power.

Young People & Politics

How Younger and Older Americans Compare on the Issues

The following table compares young adults and senior citizens on a variety of issues. Because younger citizens are much less likely to vote than older people, the differences between the two groups give us some indication of how public opinion is not accurately reflected at the polls. As you can see, younger people are substantially more likely to call themselves liberal than are senior citizens. Befitting their greater liberalism, they are more supportive of government spending on health care and environmental protection, and they are less inclined than seniors to spend more on the military. Younger voters are also more supportive of abortion rights and gay rights.

However, younger people are not always more likely to take the liberal side of an issue. Younger people are more supportive of investing Social Security funds

in the stock market—a reform proposal that has been primarily championed by conservative politicians such as George W. Bush.

CRITICAL THINKING QUESTIONS

1. Only a few issues could be covered in this table because of space limitations. On what other issues do you think there are likely to be differences of opinion between young and old people?

2. Do you think the differences shown in the table are important? If so, what difference might it make to the American political agenda if young people were to vote at the same rate as the elderly?

	18–29	65+
Liberal	29	13
Moderate or don't know	47	43
Conservative	25	44
Believe abortion should be a matter of personal choice	48	26
Believe same sex couples should be allowed to marry	60	19
Favor government paying for all necessary medical care for all Americans	60	34
Believe the environment must be protected even if it costs some jobs	47	23
Favor the federal government making it more difficult to buy guns	53	43
Favor spending more spending on the military	31	59
Oppose investing Social Security funds in stocks and bonds	24	55

SOURCE: Authors' analysis of the 2008 American National Election Study.

gender gap
The regular pattern in which women are more likely to support Democratic candidates, in part because they tend to be less conservative than men and more likely to support spending on social services and to oppose higher levels of military spending.

This is in large part because excluded groups have often looked to the government to rectify the inequalities they have faced. For example, government activism in the form of the major civil rights bills of the 1960s was crucial in bringing African Americans into the mainstream of American life. Many African American leaders currently place a high priority on retaining social welfare and affirmative action programs in order to assist African Americans' progress. It should come as little surprise, then, that African Americans are more liberal than the national average. Similarly, Hispanics also are less conservative than non-Hispanic whites, and the influx of more Hispanics into the electorate may well move the country in a slightly more liberal direction.

Women are not a minority group—making up, as they do, about 54 percent of the population—but they have been politically and economically disadvantaged. Compared to men, women are more likely to support spending on social services and to oppose the higher levels of military spending, which conservatives typically advocate. These issues concerning the priorities of government (rather than the issue of abortion, on which men and women actually differ very little) lead women to be significantly less conservative than men. This ideological difference between men and women has resulted in the **gender gap**, a regular pattern in which women are more likely to support Democratic candidates. In his 1996 reelection, for example, Bill Clinton carried the women's vote, whereas Bob Dole won more support from men. In 2012, surveys showed that women were about 10 percent more likely to support Barack Obama than men.

The gender gap is a relatively new predictor of ideological positions, dating back only to 1980, when Ronald Reagan was first elected. A more traditional source of division between liberals and conservatives has been financial status, or what is often known as social class. But in actuality, the relationship between family income and ideology is now relatively weak; social class has become much less predictive of political behavior than it used to be.[35] Even among the much-talked-about wealthiest 1 percent of Americans, Gallup has found that conservatism is not much more prevalent than in the population as a whole.[36]

The role of religion in influencing political ideology has also changed greatly in recent years. Catholics and Jews, as minority groups who struggled for equality, have long been more liberal than Protestants. Today, Jews remain by far the most liberal demographic group in the country.[37] However, the ideological gap between Catholics and Protestants is now smaller than the gender gap. Ideology is now determined more by religiosity—that is, the degree to which religion is important in one's life—than by religious denomination. What is known as the new Christian Right consists of Catholics and Protestants who consider themselves fundamentalists or "born again." The influx of new policy issues dealing with matters of morality and traditional family values has recently tied this aspect of religious beliefs to political ideology. Those who identify themselves as born-again Christians are currently the most conservative demographic group. On the other hand, people who say they have no religious affiliation (roughly 15 percent of the population) are more liberal than conservative.

Political ideology doesn't necessarily guide political behavior. It would probably be a mistake to assume that when conservative candidates do better than they have in the past, this necessarily means people want more conservative policies, for not everyone thinks in ideological terms.

Do People Think in Ideological Terms?

The authors of the classic study *The American Voter* first examined how much people rely on ideology to guide their political thinking.[38] They divided the public into four groups, according to ideological sophistication. Their portrait of the American electorate was not flattering. Only 12 percent of people showed evidence of thinking in

202

6.1
6.2
6.3
6.4
6.5
6.6

ideological terms. These people, classified as *ideologues*, could connect their opinions and beliefs with broad policy positions taken by parties or candidates. They might say, for example, that they liked the Democrats because they were more liberal or the Republicans because they favored a smaller government. Forty-two percent of Americans were classified as *group benefits* voters. These people thought of politics mainly in terms of the groups they liked or disliked; for example, "Republicans support small business owners like me" or "Democrats are the party of the working person." Twenty-four percent of the population was limited to whether the times seemed good or bad to them; they might vaguely link the party in power with the country's fortune or misfortune. Finally, 22 percent of the voters expressed no ideological or issue content in making their political evaluations. They were called the *no issue content* group. Most of them simply voted routinely for a party or judged the candidates solely by their personalities. Overall, at least during the 1950s, Americans seemed to care little about the differences between liberal and conservative politics.

There has been much debate about whether this portrayal has been and continues to be an accurate characterization of the public. In the 1970s, Nie, Verba, and Petrocik argued that voters were more sophisticated than they had been in the 1950s.[39] Others, though, have concluded that people have seemed more informed and ideological only because the wording of the questions changed.[40] Recently, the authors of *The American Voter Revisited* updated the analysis of *The American Voter* using survey data from the 2000 election. They found that just 20 percent of the population met the criteria for being classified as an ideologue in 2000—not that much more than the 12 percent in 1956. Echoing the analysts of the 1950s, they conclude that "it is problematic to attribute ideological meaning to aggregate voting patterns when most of the individuals making their decisions about the candidates are not motivated by ideological concepts."[41]

These findings do not mean that the vast majority of the population does not have a political ideology. Rather, for most people the terms *liberal* and *conservative* are just not as important as they are for members of the political elite, such as politicians, activists, and journalists. Relatively few people have ideologies that organize their political beliefs as clearly as in the columns of Table 6.1. Thus, the authors of *The American Voter* concluded that "the views of the American citizenry look indicating a movement of the public either left (to more liberal policies) or right (to more conservative policies) is not justified because most voters do not think in such terms. Furthermore, those who do are actually the least likely to shift from one election to the next.

Morris Fiorina makes a similar argument with regard to the question of whether America is in the midst of a political culture war. In the media these days, one frequently hears claims that Americans are deeply divided on fundamental political issues, making it seem like there are two different nations—the liberal blue states versus the conservative red states. After a thorough examination of public opinion data, Fiorina concludes that "the views of the American citizenry look moderate, centrist, nuanced, ambivalent—choose your term—rather than extreme, polarized, unconditional, dogmatic."[42] He argues that the small groups of liberal and conservative activists who act as if they are at war with one another have led most Americans in a position analogous to "unfortunate citizens of some third-world countries who try to stay out of the crossfire while Maoist guerrillas and right-wing death squads shoot at each other."[43]

One of the issues that many commentators believe have led to a political culture war is that of gay rights. However, as illustrated in Figure 6.5, the survey data over the past two decades show a growing acceptance of homosexuals among liberals, moderates, and conservatives alike. Rather than reflect an ideological culture war, this example shows how all ideological groups have changed with the changing social mores of the times.

FIGURE 6.5 CHANGING ATTITUDES TOWARD GAYS AND LESBIANS

It is often said that public opinion surveys are merely "snapshots in time." Thus, public opinion can change from one time point to the next, as people's attitudes are subject to change.

The American National Election Studies have regularly asked respondents to rate gays and lesbians on a "feeling thermometer" scale ranging from 0 to 100. They are told that 0 represents very cool feelings, whereas 100 represents very warm feelings, with 50 being the neutral point. This graph displays the average ratings that liberals, moderates, and conservatives gave gays and lesbians from 1988 to 2008. During these two decades, the average rating given to gays and lesbians had risen by roughly 20 points among all three ideological groups. Thus, societal attitudes have changed across the political spectrum.

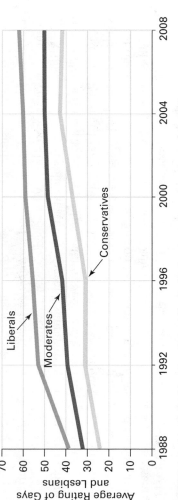

SOURCE: Authors' analysis of American National Election Studies data.

How Americans Participate in Politics

6.5 Classify forms of political participation into two broad types.

I n politics, as in many other aspects of life, the squeaky wheel gets the grease. The way citizens "squeak" in politics is to participate. Americans have many avenues of political participation open to them:

- Mrs. Jones of Iowa City goes to a neighbor's living room to attend her local precinct's presidential caucus.

- Demonstrators against abortion protest at the Supreme Court on the anniversary of the *Roe v. Wade* decision.

- Parents in Alabama file a lawsuit to oppose textbooks that, in their opinion, promote "secular humanism."

- Mr. Smith, a Social Security recipient, writes to his senator to express his concern about a possible cut in his cost-of-living benefits.

- Over 120 million people vote in a presidential election.

All these activities are types of **political participation**, which encompasses the many activities in which citizens engage to influence the selection of political leaders or the policies they pursue.[44] Participation can be overt or subtle. The mass protests against communist rule throughout Eastern Europe in the fall of 1989 represented an avalanche of political participation, yet quietly writing a letter to your congressperson also represents political participation. Political participation can be violent or peaceful, organized or individual, casual or consuming.

Generally, the United States has a culture that values political participation. Americans express very high levels of pride in their democracy: the General Social Survey has consistently found that over 80 percent of Americans say they are proud of how democracy works in the United States. Nevertheless, just 59 percent of adult

political participation
All the activities used by citizens to influence the selection of political leaders or the policies they pursue. The most common means of political participation in a democracy is voting; other means include protest and civil disobedience.

204

6.1

6.2

6.3

6.4

6.5

6.6

protest
A form of political participation designed to achieve policy change through dramatic and unconventional tactics.

American citizens voted in the presidential election of 2012, and only about 36 percent turned out for the 2014 midterm elections. At the local level, the situation is even worse, with elections for city council and school board often drawing less than 10 percent of the eligible voters.

☐ Conventional Participation

Although the line is hard to draw, political scientists generally distinguish between two broad types of participation: conventional and unconventional. *Conventional participation* includes many widely accepted modes of influencing government—voting, trying to persuade others, ringing doorbells for a petition, running for office, and so on. In contrast, *unconventional participation* includes activities that are often dramatic, such as protesting, civil disobedience, and even violence.

Millions take part in political activities beyond simply voting. In two comprehensive studies of American political participation conducted by Sidney Verba and his colleagues in 1967 and 1987, samples of Americans were asked about their role in various kinds of political activities, such as voting, working in campaigns, contacting government officials, signing petitions, working on local community issues, and participating in political protests.[45] Recently, Russell Dalton has extended the time series for some of these dimensions of political participation into the twenty-first century.[46] All told, voting is the only aspect of political participation that a majority of the population reported engaging in but also the only political activity for which there is evidence of a decline in participation in recent years. Substantial increases in participation have been found on the dimensions of giving money to candidates and contacting public officials, and small increases are evident for all the other activities. Thus, although the disappointing election turnout rates in the United States are something Americans should rightly be concerned about, a broader look at political participation reveals some positive developments for participatory democracy.

☐ Protest as Participation

From the Boston Tea Party to burning draft cards to demonstrating against abortion, Americans have engaged in countless political protests. **Protest** is a form of political participation designed to achieve policy change through dramatic and unconventional

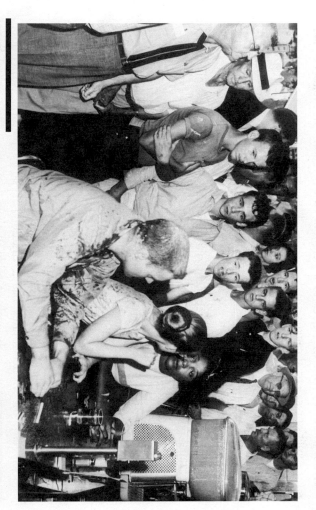

Nonviolent civil disobedience was one of the most effective techniques of the civil rights movement in the American South. Young African Americans sat at "whites only" lunch counters to protest segregation. Photos such as this drew national attention to the injustice of racial discrimination.

tactics. The media's willingness to cover the unusual can make protests worthwhile, drawing attention to a point of view that many Americans might otherwise never encounter. For example, when an 89-year-old woman walked across the country to draw attention to the need for campaign finance reform, she put this issue onto the front page of newspapers most everywhere she traveled. Using more flamboyant means, the Occupy Wall Street activists attracted a good deal of attention to the issue of economic inequality by camping out in prominent public places. The liberal Occupy movement and the conservative Tea Party movement may not share many political values, but they have both followed the now-standard playbook for demonstrations—orchestrating their activities so as to provide television cameras with vivid images. Demonstration coordinators steer participants to prearranged staging areas and provide facilities for press coverage.

Throughout American history, individuals and groups have sometimes used **civil disobedience** as a form of protest; that is, they have consciously broken a law that they thought was unjust. In the 1840s, Henry David Thoreau refused to pay his taxes as a protest against the Mexican War and went to jail; he stayed only overnight because his friend Ralph Waldo Emerson paid the taxes. Influenced by India's Mahatma Gandhi, the Reverend Martin Luther King, Jr., and others in the civil rights movement engaged in civil disobedience in the 1950s and 1960s to bring an end to segregationist laws. King's "Letter from a Birmingham Jail" is a classic defense of civil disobedience.[47] In 1964, King was awarded a Nobel Peace Prize at the age of 35—the youngest person ever to receive this honor.

Sometimes political participation can be violent. The history of violence in American politics is a long one—not surprising, perhaps, for a nation born in rebellion. The turbulent 1960s included many outbreaks of violence. African American neighborhoods in American cities were torn by riots. College campuses sometimes turned into battle zones as protestors against the Vietnam War fought police and National Guard units; students were killed at Kent State and Jackson State in 1970. At various points throughout American history, violence has been resorted to as a means of pressuring the government to change its policies.

Although the history of American political protest includes many well-known incidents, Americans today are less likely to report that they have participated in

civil disobedience
A form of political participation based on a conscious decision to break a law believed to be unjust and to suffer the consequences.

Perhaps the best-known image of American political violence from the Vietnam War era: A student lies dead on the Kent State campus, one of four killed when members of the Ohio National Guard opened fire on anti–Vietnam War demonstrators.

America in Perspective

Conventional and Unconventional Political Participation

In a cross-national survey of political behavior in 20 established democracies, citizens were asked whether they had engaged in a variety of forms of political participation over the past 5 years. Whereas Americans were among the most likely to engage in the conventional mode of contacting politicians, they were among the least likely to engage in protest demonstrations.

CRITICAL THINKING QUESTIONS

1. Do you think the fact that Americans are more likely to contact politicians than protest is a good sign for American democracy, showing that people are largely content with conventional channels of transmitting public opinion to policymakers?

2. Do you think that when many people engage in political protest, this indicates that citizens are frustrated and discontented with their government, or is it likely just a reflection of political passion and involvement?

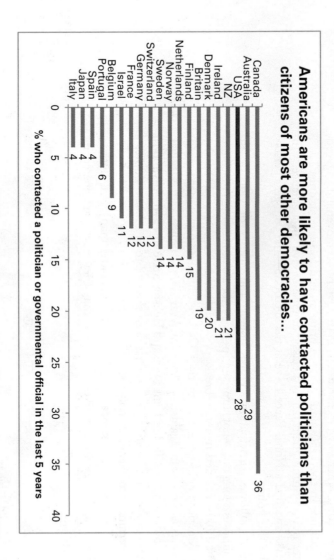

Americans are more likely to have contacted politicians than citizens of most other democracies...

% who contacted a politician or governmental official in the last 5 years

Canada	36
Australia	29
USA	28
NZ	21
Denmark	20
Ireland	19
Britain	15
Finland	14
Netherlands	14
Norway	14
Sweden	12
Switzerland	12
Germany	12
France	11
Israel	11
Belgium	9
Portugal	6
Spain	4
Japan	4
Italy	4

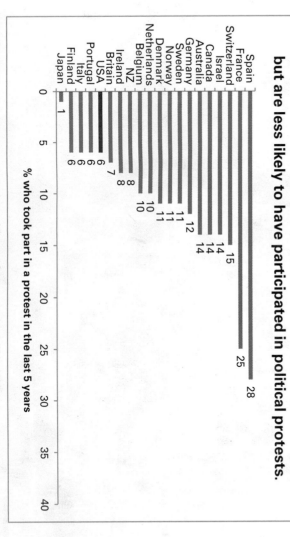

but are less likely to have participated in political protests.

% who took part in a protest in the last 5 years

Spain	28
France	25
Switzerland	15
Israel	14
Canada	14
Australia	14
Germany	12
Sweden	11
Norway	11
Denmark	11
Netherlands	10
Belgium	10
NZ	8
Britain	8
Ireland	7
USA	6
Portugal	6
Italy	6
Finland	6
Japan	1

SOURCE: Authors' analysis of the Comparative Study of Electoral Systems, module 2 (2001–2006).

protests than citizens of most other established democracies around the world. As you can see in "America in Perspective: Rates of Conventional and Unconventional Political Participation," the relative lack of protest activity in the United States is not because Americans are "couch potatoes" when it comes to political participation. Rather, Americans are just more likely to employ conventional political participation—contacting politicians and/or governmental officials—than they are to engage in protests.

☐ Class, Inequality, and Participation

Rates of political participation are unequal among Americans. Virtually every study of political participation has come to the conclusion that "citizens of higher social economic status participate more in politics. This generalization ... holds true whether one uses level of education, income, or occupation as the measure of social status."[48] People with higher incomes and levels of education are not only more likely to donate money to campaigns but also to participate in other ways that do not require financial resources, such as contacting governmental officials and signing petitions. Theorists who believe that America is ruled by a small, wealthy elite make much of this fact to support their view.

To what extent does race affect participation? When the scenes of despair among poor African Americans in New Orleans during the aftermath of Hurricane Katrina refocused attention on racial inequalities, some commentators speculated that one reason that the federal government was so slow in coming to the aid of African Americans is that they are less likely to vote. But in actuality, the difference in turnout rates between whites and blacks in Louisiana has been minimal to nonexistent in recent years; in 2012, for example, 57.6 percent of whites voted compared to 57.8 percent of blacks.[49] (Notably, in the area that encompasses the poverty-stricken lower Ninth Ward, the turnout rate of African Americans was exactly the same as it was statewide.)

One reason for this relatively small participation gap is that minorities have a group consciousness that gives them an extra incentive to vote. Political scientists have long recognized that when blacks and whites with equal levels of education are compared, the former actually participate more in politics.[50] For example, the Census Bureau's 2008 nationwide survey on turnout found that among people without a high school diploma, blacks were 11 percent more likely to vote than were whites.

People who believe in the promise of democracy should definitely be concerned with the inequalities of political participation in America. Those who participate are easy to listen to; nonparticipants are easy to ignore. Just as the makers of denture cream do not worry too much about people with healthy teeth, many politicians don't concern themselves much with the views of groups with low participation rates, such as the young and people with low incomes. Who gets what in politics therefore depends in part on who participates.

Why It Matters to You
Political Participation

Inequality in political participation is a problem in a representative democracy. Public policy debates and outcomes would probably be substantially different if people of all age groups and income groups participated equally. If young adults participated more, politicians might be more inclined to seek ways by which the government could help young people get the training necessary to obtain good jobs in a changing economy. And if the poor participated at higher levels, government programs to alleviate poverty would likely be higher on the political agenda.

Understanding Public Opinion and Political Action

6.6

Analyze how public opinion about the scope of government guides political behavior.

I n many third world countries, there have been calls for more democracy in recent years. One often hears that citizens of developing nations want their political system to be like America's in the sense that ordinary people's opinions determine how the government is run. However, as this chapter has shown, there are many limits on how public opinion plays in the American political system. The average person is not very well informed about political issues, including the crucial issue of the scope of government.

☐ Public Attitudes Toward the Scope of Government

Central to the ideology of the Republican Party is the belief that the scope of American government has become too wide. According to Ronald Reagan, probably the most admired Republican in recent history, government was not the solution to society's problems—it was the problem. He called for the government to "get off the backs of the American people."

Because of Americans' long history of favoring limited government, taking a general stand about the need to streamline the federal establishment is appealing to the majority of the public more often than not. Since 1992, the Gallup Poll has regularly asked samples the following question: "Some people think the government is trying to do too many things that should be left to individuals and businesses. Others think that government should do more to solve our country's problems. Which comes closer to your own view?" On average, 52 percent have said the government is doing too much, whereas just 40 percent have said the government should do more, with the rest saying it depends or they don't know. The only time Gallup found that at least 50 percent said that the government should do more was in the month after the terrorist attacks of September 11.[51]

However, public opinion on the scope of government, as with most issues, is often complex and inconsistent. Although more people today think that overall the government is too big, a plurality has consistently called for more spending on such programs as education, health care, aid to cities, protecting the environment, and fighting crime.[52] Many political scientists have looked at these contradictory findings and concluded that Americans are ideological conservatives but operational liberals—meaning that they oppose the idea of big government in principle but favor it in practice. The fact that public opinion is contradictory on these important aspects of the scope of the government contributes to policy gridlock, as both liberal and conservative politicians can make a plausible case that the public is on their side.

☐ Democracy, Public Opinion, and Political Action

Remember, though, that American democracy is representative rather than direct. As *The American Voter* stated many years ago, "The public's explicit task is to decide not what government shall do but rather who shall decide what government shall do."[53] When individuals under communist rule protested for democracy, what they wanted most was the right to have a say in choosing their leaders. Americans can—and often do—take for granted the opportunity to replace their leaders at the next election. Protest is thus directed at making the government listen to specific demands, not overthrowing it. In this sense, it can be said that American citizens have become well socialized to democracy.

If the public's task in democracy is to choose who is to lead, we must still ask whether it can do so wisely. If people know little about where candidates stand on issues, how can they make rational choices? Most choose performance criteria over policy criteria. As Morris Fiorina has written, citizens typically have one hard bit of data to go on: "They know what life has been like during the incumbent's administration. They need not know the precise economic or foreign policies of the incumbent administration in order to see or feel the results of those policies."[54] Thus, even if they are voting only based on a general sense of whether the country is moving in the right or wrong direction, their voices are clearly being heard—holding public officials accountable for their actions.

Review the Chapter

The American People

6.1 Identify demographic trends and their likely impact on American politics, p. 182.

Immigration—both legal and illegal—has accelerated in America in recent decades. Largely as a consequence, the size of the minority population has increased greatly. If current trends continue, by the middle of the twenty-first century non-Hispanic whites will represent less than half of the population. The American population has also been aging and moving to Sunbelt states such as California, Texas, and Florida.

How Americans Learn About Politics: Political Socialization

6.2 Outline how various forms of socialization shape political opinions, p. 189.

Much of the process of political socialization is informal. People pick up and absorb political orientations from major actors in their everyday environment. The principal actors in the socialization process are the family, the media, and schools. As people age, the firmness with which they hold political attitudes, such as party identification, tends to increase.

Measuring Public Opinion and Political Information

6.3 Explain how polls are conducted and what can be learned from them about American public opinion, p. 191.

Polls are conducted through the technique of random sampling, in which every member of the population has an equal probability of being selected for an interview. A random sample of about 1,000 Americans will yield results that are normally within plus or minus three percentage points of what would be found if everyone were interviewed. The responses from such samples can be important tools for democracy, measuring what the public thinks about political matters between elections. Polls also help analysts assess the age-old question of how well informed people are about political issues.

What Americans Value: Political Ideologies

6.4 Assess the influence of political ideology on Americans' political thinking and behavior, p. 199.

A political ideology is a coherent set of values and beliefs about public policy. The two most prominent ideologies in American politics are conservatism and liberalism. These ideologies guide people's thinking on policy issues. Although roughly 60 percent of the American public call themselves either conservatives or liberals, even many of these individuals are not necessarily ideologically consistent in their political attitudes. Often they are conservative in principle but liberal in practice; that is, they are against big government but favor more spending on a wide variety of programs.

How Americans Participate in Politics

6.5 Classify forms of political participation into two broad types, p. 203.

Conventional forms of political participation include voting, writing letters or e-mails to public officials, attending political meetings, signing petitions, and donating money to campaigns and political groups. Unconventional participation involves activities such as attending protest demonstrations and acts of civil disobedience. Many studies have found that citizens of higher social economic status participate more in American politics.

Understanding Public Opinion and Political Action

6.6 Analyze how public opinion about the scope of government guides political behavior, p. 208.

Conservatives typically believe that the scope of American government has become too wide in recent decades. They look to Ronald Reagan's pledge to get the government "off the backs of the American people" as inspiration. In contrast, liberals believe the scope of government should be further increased, and they support policies like the Obama administration's health care reform law.

Learn the Terms

public opinion, p. 182
demography, p. 182
census, p. 182
melting pot, p. 184
minority majority, p. 184
political culture, p. 188

reapportionment, p. 188
political socialization, p. 189
sample, p. 192
random sampling, p. 192
sampling error, p. 192
random-digit dialing, p. 193

exit poll, p. 194
political ideology, p. 199
gender gap, p. 201
political participation, p. 203
protest, p. 204
civil disobedience, p. 205

Test Yourself

1. Based on the regional shift, which of these states would have been expected to gain representation following the 2010 census?

a. Arizona
b. Illinois
c. Michigan
d. New York
e. Tennessee

2. When does reapportionment of congressional representation take place?

a. at the end of each calendar year
b. every two years after a midterm election
c. every four years after the presidential election
d. every 10 years after each census
e. on a rotational basis declared by the government

3. Hispanic voters are a growing force in American politics because of _____.

a. the popularity of Latin music
b. the proximity of Mexico
c. the signing of the North American Free Trade Agreement
d. the Summit of the Americas
e. their projected population increase

4. As people grow older, what happens to their rate of political participation and strength of their party attachment?

a. turnout increases but strength of party identification decreases
b. turnout decreases but strength of party identification increases
c. turnout and strength of party identification increase
d. turnout and strength of party identification decrease
e. turnout and strength of party identification remain stable

5. Currently the mass media has been called the _____ by observers because of the way grade school children gather information.

a. core curriculum
b. mass consumption
c. new parent
d. political reporter
e. sole informant

6. What is a possible negative effect of the media's use of exit polls on a national election?

a. Most polls are inaccurate.
b. Polling data can inadvertently support a separatist political party.
c. Polling firms use the results to increase their influence over the national dialogue on important issues.
d. Voters in states where polling places have not closed might be inclined not to vote.
e. Voters in states where polling places have not closed might be more inclined to vote.

7. Computer and telephone technology have made polling _____ expensive and _____ common place

a. less; less
b. less; more
c. more; less
d. more; more
e. steadily; just as

8. Which of these would most influence the accuracy of a poll?

a. day of week the poll is conducted
b. number of people being sampled
c. political position of pollsters
d. time of day the poll is conducted
e. unbiased wording

9. Male and female political opinions are the most divergent on _____.

a. a balanced budget
b. abortion rights
c. government regulation of corporations
d. religion
e. social services

Explore Further

10. Liberals, more than conservatives, tend to believe which of the following?

a. Government should reduce services to the public.
b. Gun purchases should be easier or at least no more difficult.
c. The death penalty should be an available option.
d. The United States should spend as much or more on defense.
e. Women should have the freedom of choice.

11. Which type of voters think of politics in terms of the groups they like or dislike?

a. centrist
b. group benefits
c. ideologue
d. liberal
e. nature of the times

12. In the classic study *The American Voter*, the "no issue content group" _____.

a. based their political views on whether the times seem good or bad
b. could connect their opinions with broad policy positions
c. simply voted routinely for a party or judged the candidates by their personalities
d. thought of politics mainly in terms of groups they liked or disliked
e. were ideologues

13. Some theorists believe that America is ruled by a small group of wealthy elite. Which of these facts best supports that theory?

a. A higher proportion of white Americans vote than African Americans.
b. Citizens of higher socioeconomic status participate more in politics.
c. Most people who run for office, even in local elections, are wealthy.
d. One must pay massive fees to run for office.
e. Political participation on all levels can be prohibitively expensive.

14. When comparing blacks and whites who have the same education level, blacks _____.

a. and whites have the same political activity
b. participate less politically
c. participate more politically
d. vote less
e. vote more

15. What is the main purpose of protests?

a. to cause social unrest
b. to disproportionately increase the importance of an issue
c. to make the government listen to specific demands
d. to overthrow the current government
e. to skew polling data

WEB SITES

www.census.gov
The census is the best source of information on America's demography. Go to the list of topics to find out the range of materials that are available.

www.gallup.com
The Gallup Poll regularly posts reports about its political surveys at this site.

www.census.gov/compendia/statab/
The *Statistical Abstract of the United States* contains a wealth of demographic and political information that can be downloaded in Adobe Acrobat format from this site.

www.pollster.com
A good source of information about current polls and the polling business.

FURTHER READING

Abrajano, Marisa A., and R. Michael Alvarez. *New Faces, New Voices: The Hispanic Electorate in America.* Princeton, NJ: Princeton University Press, 2010. An examination of the current state of Latino public opinion and how more Latinos could be politically mobilized in the future.

Asher, Herbert. *Polling and the Public: What Every Citizen Should Know,* 7th ed. Washington, DC: Congressional Quarterly Press, 2007. A highly readable introduction to the perils and possibilities of polling and surveys.

Campbell, Angus, et al. *The American Voter.* New York: Wiley, 1960. The classic study of the American voter, based on data from the 1950s.

Delli Carpini, Michael X., and Scott Keeter. *What Americans Know About Politics and Why It Matters.* New Haven, CT: Yale University Press, 1996. The best study of the state of political knowledge in the electorate.

Fiorina, Morris P. *Culture War? The Myth of a Polarized America,* 3rd ed. New York: Longman, 2010. This book argues that the so-called culture war between the red and blue states is highly exaggerated, as most Americans possess relatively moderate and nuanced opinions on political issues.

Hetherington, Marc J. *Why Trust Matters.* Princeton, NJ: Princeton University Press, 2005. The author argues that the decline of trust in government in recent decades has weakened support for progressive policies to address problems of poverty and racial inequality.

Jacobs, Lawrence R., and Robert Y. Shapiro. *Politicians Don't Pander.* Chicago: University of Chicago Press, 2000. Contrary to popular notions that politicians hold their fingers to the wind and try to follow the polls, Jacobs and Shapiro argue that politicians use polls to figure out how to best persuade the public to support their preferred policies.

Jennings, M. Kent, and Richard G. Niemi. *Generations and Politics: A Panel Study of Young Adults and Their Parents.* Princeton, NJ: Princeton University Press, 1981. A highly influential study of the class of 1965, their parents, and how both generations changed over the course of eight years.

Lewis-Beck, Michael S., et al. *The American Voter Revisited.* Ann Arbor, MI: University of Michigan Press, 2008. A replication of the classic analysis in *The American Voter* employing data from the 2000 and 2004 American National Election Studies.

Persily, Nathaniel, Jack Citrin, and Patrick J. Egan. *Public Opinion and Constitutional Controversy.* New York: Oxford University Press, 2008. A review of public opinion data on major issues that have recently come before the Supreme Court, such as abortion, the death penalty, and affirmative action.

Schildkraut, Deborah J. *Americanism in the Twenty-First Century: Public Opinion in the Age of Immigration.* New York: Cambridge University Press, 2011. An insightful analysis of what it means to be, or become, an American.

Tate, Katherine. *What's Going On? Political Incorporation and the Transformation of Black Public Opinion.* Washington, DC: Georgetown University Press, 2010. An excellent examination of public opinion and participation among the African American community.

Verba, Sidney, and Norman H. Nie. *Participation in America.* New York: Harper & Row, 1972. A landmark study of American political participation.

West, Darrell M. *Brain Gain: Rethinking U.S. Immigration Policy.* Washington, DC: Brookings Institution Press, 2011. An excellent analysis of some of the issues involved in immigration reform.

7

The Mass Media and the Political Agenda

Politics in Action: The Increasing Difficulty of Getting Out a Presidential Message

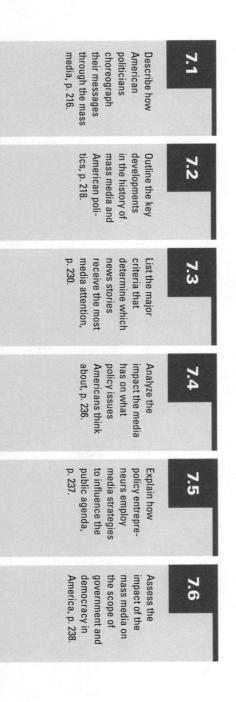

Because policymaking often depends upon politicians' power to persuade, the ability to communicate with the American public is a key tool for policymakers.

When presidents speak to the nation, they expect a large viewing audience and anticipate that their message will continue to reach the public through news reports for days afterward. But a series of changes in the mass media environment has made it much less likely that these expectations will be fulfilled today compared to just several decades ago. A tale of the initial speeches given to Congress by President Reagan in 1981 and President Obama in 2009 provides a good illustration of the profound changes in the presidential media environment discussed in this chapter.

President Ronald Reagan addressed Congress during prime time on February 18, 1981, to outline his proposed policies for economic recovery. Reagan's speech was covered live on CBS, NBC, and ABC and garnered a Nielsen rating of 60, meaning that three-fifths of the American public watched it. Beyond reaching this enormous live audience, Reagan knew he could communicate his message

7.1
Describe how American politicians choreograph their messages through the mass media, p. 216.

7.2
Outline the key developments in the history of mass media and American politics, p. 218.

7.3
List the major criteria that determine which news stories receive the most media attention, p. 230.

7.4
Analyze the impact the media has on what policy issues Americans think about, p. 236.

7.5
Explain how policy entrepreneurs employ media strategies to influence the public agenda, p. 237.

7.6
Assess the impact of the mass media on the scope of government and democracy in America, p. 238.

Presidential addresses to Congress were once shared national experiences, as TV audiences had nothing else to watch when three networks dominated the airwaves. With the proliferation of channels, however, the ability of presidents to reach a mass audience has declined, as evidenced by the lack of interest at this New Orleans bar during President Obama's 2011 State of the Union speech.

high-tech politics
A politics in which the behavior of citizens and policymakers and the political agenda itself are increasingly shaped by technology.

mass media
Television, radio, newspapers, magazines, the Internet, and other means of popular communication.

The Mass Media Today

7.1 Describe how American politicians choreograph their messages through the mass media.

W hether one is promoting a candidate, drawing attention to a social issue, or proposing a government program, political success depends on effectively communicating a message. The key is gaining control over the political agenda, which today, as throughout the period of high-tech politics, involves getting one's priorities presented at the top of the daily news.

Politicians have learned that one way to guide the media's focus successfully is to give the media carefully staged events to report on. A recent study of TV news coverage of the last four weeks of a presidential campaign found that 80 percent of the stories involved to the many people who would soon read and view news about his remarks. The next day, at least 55 percent of the public—the percentage that said they read a newspaper every day in surveys at that time—could be expected to pick up a newspaper containing stories about the president's speech. Later that evening, roughly 38 percent could be expected to view some coverage of the president's speech on the highly rated national newscasts at dinnertime.

The situation was markedly different when President Barack Obama went to Capitol Hill on February 24, 2009, to set forth his proposals for dealing with the economic crisis. Obama's speech, too, was covered live on CBS, NBC, and ABC—and on Fox, Fox News, CNN, MSNBC, CNBC, Telemundo, and Univision. Yet, whereas Reagan received a rating of 60 on the 3 networks, Obama achieved a rating of just 32 on 10 channels. In this age of narrowcasting, in which a plethora of channels appeal to specialized audiences, large audiences are increasingly rare—and even presidents usually do not achieve them. Not only was the audience rating for Obama's speech about half of Reagan's, but he also could not count on a regular audience of news consumers learning about his remarks the next day. By the time Obama assumed office, the percentage of the public who read the newspaper daily had fallen from the 55 percent of the early 1980s to only about 32 percent. And the typical ratings of the nightly newscasts on the three traditional broadcast networks had plummeted from 38 to just 16. (Of course, there are now also cable news shows available to most viewers. But these shows, which typically get ratings of less than 2, scarcely make up for the lost audience of the network broadcasts.)

The diminishing audience for presidential messages, as well as for national news, means that the president now faces a significantly more difficult task in getting messages through to the entire public than was the case a few decades ago. For politicians other than the president, of course, this problem is even more acute. Moreover, the problem is one that may have considerable consequences. Democracy depends upon an informed citizenry, and the citizenry depends on the mass media for its information. If only a fraction of the public is paying attention to political events, then democracy may well suffer. As with many areas of American life, the future of the mass media may lie with the Internet. Yet, so far, the promise of the Internet for broadening political discourse remains unfulfilled.

Since the latter part of the twentieth century, the American political system has been in a period of **high-tech politics**—a politics in which the behavior of citizens and policymakers, as well as the political agenda itself, is increasingly shaped by technology. A key part of this evolving technology is the **mass media**, including television, radio, newspapers, magazines, and the Internet. These and other means of popular communication are called *mass media* because they reach and profoundly influence not only the elites but also the masses.

This chapter examines media politics, focusing on the rise of modern media in America's advanced technological society, the making of the news and its presentation through the media, biases in the news, and the impact of the media on policymakers and the public. It also reintroduces the concept of the policy agenda, in which the media play an important role.

7.1
7.2
7.3
7.4
7.5
7.6

tightly scripted appearances by the candidates.[1] Such **media events** are staged primarily for the purpose of being covered; if the media were not there, the event would probably not happen or would have little significance. Getting the right image on the TV news for just 30 seconds can have a much greater payoff than a whole day's worth of handshaking. Whereas once a candidate's G.O.T.V. program stood for "Get Out the Vote," today it is more likely to mean "Get on TV."

Slickly produced TV commercials are another important tool in high-tech politics. For example, approximately 60 percent of presidential campaign spending is now devoted to TV ads. Moreover, in this case, the message being communicated is largely a negative one: In recent presidential elections, about two-thirds of the prominently aired ads were negative ads.[2] Some political scientists have expressed concern that the tirade of accusations, innuendoes, and countercharges in political advertising may be poisoning the American political process.[3]

Media events and TV commercials are largely about image making. Such image making does not stop with the campaign; it is also a critical element in day-to-day governing. Politicians' images in the press are seen as good indicators of their clout. Image is especially important for presidents, who in recent decades have devoted much attention to maintaining a well-honed public image. Few, if any, administrations devoted so much effort and energy to the president's media appearance as did Ronald Reagan's. It has often been said that Reagan played to the media as he had played to the cameras in Hollywood, with his aides choreographing his public appearances. According to journalist Mark Hertsgaard, news management in the Reagan White House operated on the following seven principles: (1) plan ahead, (2) stay on the offensive, (3) control the flow of information, (4) limit reporters' access to the president, (5) talk about the issues you want to talk about, (6) speak in one voice, and (7) repeat the same message many times.[4]

If Reagan was exceptional in his ability to handle the media, he was far from alone in his realization of its importance to the presidency. In today's high-tech age, presidents can hardly lead the country if they cannot communicate effectively with it. President Clinton once reflected on *Larry King Live:* "The thing that has surprised me most is

7.1
7.2
7.3
7.4
7.5
7.6

217

media events

Events that are purposely staged for the media and that are significant just because the media are there.

Politicians often stage activities primarily for the benefit of TV cameras. The sight of a major presidential candidate walking the streets asking ordinary people for their support is something that the media finds difficult to pass up. In this swing down a street in Clinton, Iowa, Mitt Romney met perhaps 30 of the 30,000 people who voted for him in the 2012 Iowa caucuses. But the number of people who saw pictures like this in their newspaper or viewed the video footage on TV was far, far greater.

how difficult it is . . . to really keep communicating what you're about to the American people. That to me has been the most frustrating thing." According to journalist Bob Woodward, Clinton confided to a friend that "I did not realize the importance of communications and the overriding importance of what is on the evening television news. If I am not on, or there with a message, someone else is, with their message."[5]

7.1

7.2

7.3

7.4

7.5

7.6

press conferences
Meetings of public officials with reporters.

investigative journalism
The use of in-depth reporting to unearth scandals, scams, and schemes, at times putting reporters in adversarial relationships with political leaders.

The Development of Media Politics

7.2   Outline the key developments in the history of mass media and American politics.

T here was virtually no daily press when the U.S. Constitution was written. The daily newspaper is largely a product of the mid-nineteenth century; radio and television have been around only since the first half of the twentieth century. As recently as the presidency of Herbert Hoover (1929–1933), reporters submitted their questions to the president in writing, and he responded in writing—if at all. As Hoover put it, "The President of the United States will not stand and be questioned like a chicken thief by men whose names he does not even know."[6]

Hoover's successor, Franklin D. Roosevelt (1933–1945), practically invented media politics. To Roosevelt, the media were a potential ally. Roosevelt promised reporters two presidential **press conferences**—meetings with reporters—a week, resulting in about 1,000 press conferences during his 12 years in the White House. He used presidential wrath to warn reporters off material he did not want covered, and he chastised news reports he deemed inaccurate. His wrath was rarely invoked, however, and the press revered him, never even reporting to the American public that the president was confined to a wheelchair. The idea that a political leader's health status might be public business was alien to journalists in FDR's day.

This relatively cozy relationship between politicians and the press lasted through the early 1960s. ABC's Sam Donaldson said that when he first came to Washington in 1961, "many reporters saw themselves as an extension of the government, accepting, with very little skepticism, what government officials told them."[7] And coverage of a politician's personal life was generally off limits. For example, as a young reporter, R. W. Apple, Jr., of the *New York Times* once observed a beautiful woman being escorted to President Kennedy's suite. Thinking he had a major scoop, he rushed to tell his editor. But he was quickly told, "Apple, you're supposed to report on political and diplomatic policies, not girlfriends. No story."[8]

With the events of the Vietnam War and the Watergate scandal, though, unquestioning acceptance soon gave way to skepticism and even cynicism. Newspeople have come to assume that politicians rarely tell the whole story and that their own job is to ferret out the truth. As Sam Donaldson of ABC News wrote in his book *Hold On, Mr. President!*,

If you send me to cover a pie-baking contest on Mother's Day, I'm going to ask dear old Mom whether she used artificial sweetener in violation of the rules, and while she's at it, could I see the receipt for the apples to prove she didn't steal them. I maintain that if Mom has nothing to hide, no harm will have been done. But the questions should be asked.[9]

Thus, for example, when the Clinton–Lewinsky scandal broke, so strong was the desire to find out what the president had to hide in his personal life that 75 percent of the questions asked during the daily White House press briefings that week concerned the scandal.[10] Many political scientists, however, are critical of such **investigative journalism**—the use of detective-like reporting methods to check up on the statements of governmental officials. They see the adversarial role of the media, in which reporters pit themselves against political leaders, as contributing to public cynicism and negativity about politics.[11]

The White House press secretary battles daily with the press corps, as correspondents attempt to obtain ever more information while the president's spokesperson tries to control the news agenda and spin stories in the administration's favor. Symbolizing this conflict, Obama's press secretary Robert Gibbs offered to give members of the press a chance to dunk him in a tank at the annual White House luau one year. Four reporters stepped up to take a shot at dunking Gibbs and two succeeded in dunking him in the tank.

In his analysis of media coverage of presidential campaigns since 1960, Thomas Patterson found that news coverage of presidential candidates has become increasingly less favorable. Patterson's careful analysis uncovers two major aspects of this trend toward more negative coverage: The emphasis of campaign reporting has changed dramatically from "what" to "why," and whereas the "what" was primarily candidates' policy statements, today's "why" focuses on the campaign as a horse race. This emphasis on hard-biting analysis of political maneuvering and campaign controversies naturally leads to unfavorable impressions of the candidates. Clearly, little favorable could come of coverage of such issues as how much Barack Obama knew about the incendiary comments of Reverend Wright or why Mitt Romney had a Swiss bank account. Those who run campaigns naturally complain about such coverage. As Karl Rove, one of George W. Bush's top political advisers, said after the 2000 election,

> The general nature of the tone of the coverage was very much in keeping with what Patterson suggests, that it is process oriented, highly cynical, negative, dismissive of issue positions, focused on the internals of the campaign and not on the big messages and really serves to trivialize the whole contest.[12]

Whether or not such media coverage is ultimately in the public's best interest is much debated. The press maintains that the public is now able to get a complete, accurate, and unvarnished look at the candidates. Critics of the media charge the controversial aspects of the campaign are emphasized at the expense of an examination of the major issues.

To explore the development of media politics, we need to distinguish between two kinds of media: the **print media**, which include newspapers and magazines, and the **electronic media**, which include radio, television, and the Internet. Newspapers, radio, and television have each reshaped political communication at some point in American history. It is difficult to assess the likely impact of the Internet at this point, but there is at least some reason to believe that political communication is being reshaped once again.

□ The Print Media

The first American daily newspaper was printed in Philadelphia in 1783, but such papers did not proliferate until the technological advances of the mid-nineteenth

print media
Newspapers and magazines, as compared with electronic media.

electronic media
Television, radio, and the Internet, as compared with print media.

220

7.1
7.2
7.3
7.4
7.5
7.6

century. The ratification of the First Amendment in 1791, guaranteeing freedom of speech, gave even the earliest American newspapers freedom to print whatever they saw fit. In so doing, it gave the media a unique ability to display the government's dirty linen, an ability that, as we've seen, the American press today makes ample use of.

Thomas Jefferson famously said, "If I had to choose between government without newspapers, and newspapers without government, I wouldn't hesitate to choose the latter." Our first mass medium, newspapers, have continued to play a crucial role down through the centuries. Even in recent decades, with the emergence of other media, most political scientists who have researched media and politics agree on the value of newspapers as a source of information. Studies invariably find that regular newspaper readers are better informed and more likely to vote.[13] For example, Robert Putnam, in his highly influential book titled *Bowling Alone*, finds that "those who *read* the news are more engaged and knowledgeable about the world than those who only *watch* the news." Putnam concludes that "newspaper reading and good citizenship go together."[14] All of this should hardly be surprising given that newspapers have so much more information than TV. A major metropolitan newspaper averages roughly 100,000 words daily, whereas a typical broadcast of the nightly news on TV amounts to only about 3,600 words.[15]

Despite the continued value of newspapers, ever since the rise of TV and TV news, American newspaper circulation rates have been declining. And with the rise of the Internet, this trend has been greatly accelerated. Whereas in 1960 one newspaper was sold for every two adults, by 2012 this ratio had plummeted to one paper for every five adults. With young adults reading newspapers at record low rates, the accelerated decline in readership is likely to continue.

Many people believe the future of the newspaper business lies with the Internet. For most major newspapers, online editions have become a source of advertising revenue. However, this advertising revenue falls far short of what newspapers need to maintain a full staff of reporters and editors; as of 2012, it represented only about 11 percent of newspapers' total take from advertising.[16] Some newspapers have tried charging for access to their reporting. But this strategy of selling Internet subscriptions has thus far generated substantial revenues mostly for papers that focus on business news, such as the *Wall Street Journal* and the *Financial Times*. As Howard Kurtz writes, most newspapers are facing the problem that "in a world of Twitter feeds and gigabytes of gossip and a thousand other distractions, most people will see no need to pay for news. There will always be enough aggregators out there for them to cherry-pick the latest headlines, photos and video."[17] The financial situation of many major city newspapers is now so tenuous that some policymakers have proposed making it possible for newspapers to become tax-exempt nonprofit organizations, as you can read about in "You Are the Policymaker: Should Newspapers Be Allowed to Be Nonprofit Organizations?"

Magazines, the other component of the print media, are also struggling in the Internet age. For the few magazines that focus on political events, this struggle is especially dire, since their circulation levels are not among the industry's highest. The so-called newsweeklies, intended for a wide audience—*Time*, *Newsweek*, and *U.S. News & World Report*—rank well behind such popular favorites as *Reader's Digest*, *Better Homes and Gardens*, and *National Geographic*. More serious magazines of political news and opinion—for example, the *New Republic*, *National Review*, and the *Atlantic Monthly*—tend to be read only by the educated elite, and they are outsold by other magazines meant for specific audiences, such as *Hot Rod*, *Weightwatchers Magazine*, and *Organic Gardening*.

□ The Emergence of Radio and Television

Gradually, electronic media—beginning with radio and then television—have displaced the print media as Americans' principal source of news and information. By the middle of the 1930s, radio ownership had become almost universal in America, and during World War II, radio went into the news business in earnest, taking the nation to the

You Are the Policymaker

Should Newspapers Be Allowed to Be Nonprofit Organizations?

The newspaper business is clearly in financial trouble. Long-established newspapers in Denver, Oakland, and Seattle have recently gone out of business, and papers in Philadelphia, Chicago, Los Angeles, Minneapolis, and Baltimore, among others, have recently filed for Chapter 11 bankruptcy. The red ink that the newspaper business is facing is of concern to many policymakers today. President Obama, a self-proclaimed "big newspaper junkie," has said that "it's something that I think is absolutely critical to the health of our democracy."

One plan to help out the struggling newspaper industry is a bill proposed by Senator Benjamin Cardin, called the Newspaper Revitalization Act. This bill would offer newspapers the option of operating as nonprofit organizations for educational purposes. Such a classification would give them a tax status similar to public broadcasting companies. With this tax status, newspapers would no longer have to pay taxes on any advertising or subscription revenue they generate. In addition, much like PBS radio and TV stations, they could receive tax-deductible contributions.

Although most policymakers are supportive of the goal of keeping newspapers in operation, many have raised serious questions about the wisdom of this bill. Some are concerned that, if newspapers were to receive a tax break, they would become beholden to politicians and thus less likely to pursue critical stories and investigations. Others are troubled by the fact that newspapers operating as nonprofits could no longer speak out with commentaries or endorsements. Any nonprofit newspaper would also have to be wary of seeming to support a particular point of view lest it risk its tax-exempt status. Proponents of the bill acknowledge these drawbacks, but reply that any newspaper in a community is better than none at all.

What do you think? Would you favor allowing newspapers to operate as nonprofit entities?

---

war in Europe and the Pacific. A decade later, the public was getting its news from television as well. Then, in 1960, John Kennedy faced off against Richard Nixon in the first-ever televised presidential debate. Haggard from a week in the hospital, and with his five-o'clock shadow and perspiration clearly visible, Nixon looked awful compared to the crisp, clean, attractive Kennedy. The poll results from this debate illustrate the visual power of television in American politics: people listening on the radio gave the edge to Nixon, but those who saw the debate on television thought Kennedy had won. Russell Baker, who covered the event for the *New York Times*, writes in his memoirs that "television replaced newspapers as the most important communications medium in American politics" that very night.[18] Nixon blamed his poor appearance in this debate for his narrow defeat in the election.[19]

Much like radio and World War II in the 1940s, television took the nation to the war in Vietnam in the 1960s. Television exposed governmental naïveté—and sometimes outright lying—about the progress of the war. Every night, Americans watched the horrors of war in living color on television. President Johnson soon had two wars on his hands, one in faraway Vietnam and the other at home with antiwar protesters—both covered in detail by the media. In 1968, CBS anchor Walter Cronkite journeyed to Vietnam for a firsthand look at the state of the war. In an extraordinary TV special, Cronkite reported that the war was not being won nor was it likely to be. Watching from the White House, Johnson sadly remarked that if he had lost Cronkite, he had lost the support of the American people.[20]

Walter Cronkite on CBS, and his counterparts on ABC and NBC, highly trusted and influential, brought about and symbolized the golden era of network news. That era is clearly coming to an end, as cable news and the Internet have increasingly supplanted the nightly news shows. As *New York Times* media critic Frank Rich wrote, "The No. 1 cliché among media critics is that we're watching the 'last hurrah' of network news anchors as we have known them for nearly half a century."[21] Today, these shows attract an audience of about 15 percent of the population every weeknight during the

7.1
7.2
7.3
7.4
7.5
7.6

narrowcasting
Media programming on cable TV (e.g., on MTV, ESPN, or C-SPAN) or the Internet that is focused on a particular interest and aimed at a particular audience, in contrast to broadcasting.

☐ Government Regulation of Electronic Media

With the invention of radio, a number of problems that the government could help with—such as overlapping use of the same frequency—soon became apparent. In 1934, Congress created the Federal Communications Commission (FCC) to regulate the use of airwaves. Today, the FCC regulates communications via radio, television, telephone, cable, and satellite. The FCC is an independent regulatory body, although, like other such bodies, it is subject to political pressures, including through Congress's control over its budget and the president's appointing its members.

The FCC's regulation takes several important forms. First, to prevent near monopolies of control over a broadcast market, the FCC has instituted rules to limit the number of stations owned or controlled by one company. Since a simplification in 1996, the rule has been just that no single owner can control more than 35 percent of the broadcast market. Second, the FCC conducts periodic examinations of the goals and performance of stations as part of its licensing authority. Congress long ago stipulated that in order to receive a broadcasting license, a station must serve the public interest. The FCC has on only rare occasion withdrawn licenses for failing to do so, as when a Chicago station lost its license for neglecting informational programs and for presenting obscene movies. Third, the FCC has issued a number of fair treatment rules concerning access to the airwaves for political candidates and officeholders. The equal time rule stipulates that if a station sells advertising time to one candidate, it must be willing to sell equal time to other candidates for the same office. And the right-of-reply rule states if a person is attacked on a broadcast other than the news, then that person has a right to reply via the same station. For many years, the fairness doctrine required broadcasters to give time to opposing views if they broadcast a program slanted to one side of a controversial issue. But with the development of so many TV channels via cable, by the late 1980s this rule was seen as unnecessary and was abolished. This change opened up the way for today's highly partisan news shows, such as the conservative *O'Reilly Factor* on Fox News and the liberal *Rachel Maddow Show* on MSNBC.

☐ From Broadcasting to Narrowcasting: The Rise of Cable and Cable News

The first major networks—ABC, NBC, and CBS—included the term "broadcasting" in their name because their signal was being sent out to a broad audience. Each of these networks dealt with various subjects that had widespread public appeal, including politics and government. But with the development of cable TV, market segmentation took hold. Sports buffs can watch ESPN all day, music buffs can tune in to MTV or VH1, history buffs can stay glued to the History Channel, and so forth. If you are interested in politics, you can switch between C-SPAN, C-SPAN2, CNN, MSNBC, Fox News Channel, and others. Rather than appealing to a general audience, channels such as ESPN, MTV, and C-SPAN focus on a narrow, particular interest. Hence, their mission can be termed **narrowcasting**, as opposed to the traditional broadcasting.

Narrowcasting has significantly affected media usage patterns, especially for young adults. Having grown up with narrowcasting alternatives, young adults are less likely than other age groups to be using newspapers and broadcast media as news and information sources. Interestingly, one source of information about politics that young people are more likely than other age groups to rely on is humorous shows that cover current events, or "infotainment," as you can see in "Young People and Politics: Learning from Comedy Shows?"

dinner hour, as compared to about 40 percent during their heyday in the period from the mid-1960s to the mid-1980s. In this era of 24-hour cable news channels and the Internet, turning on the television to get the news at a set time early in the evening seems like a quaint remnant of the past to many Americans, especially young adults.

Young People & Politics

Learning from Comedy Shows?

In January 2012, the Pew Research Center asked a representative sample of Americans how they learned about the presidential campaign. One of its most interesting findings was that young people were much more likely than older people to say they regularly or sometimes learned about the campaign from comedy programs like *The Daily Show* or *Saturday Night Live*, as you can see in the following figure. When an earlier Pew survey first showed this pattern, Jon Stewart of *The Daily Show* initially dismissed the notion that young people were turning to his comedy show to learn about political events. Subsequently, his show adopted the slogan of "Keeping America Informed—Unintentionally." Is this slogan in fact accurate? How much do comedy shows contribute to their viewers' store of political information?

Scholars have found that by wrapping bits of political content into an amusing package, entertainment shows that cover current events can make politics more appealing to viewers who might otherwise ignore the subject, and thereby add to their political knowledge. Barry A. Hollander specifically examined what young adults take away from infotainment shows and concluded that they glean "at least modest amounts of campaign information from such content."[a] Matthew Baum found that exposure to entertainment-oriented TV talk shows among voters with lower-than-average political interest had a significant impact on how they evaluated the candidates.[b]

Although infotainment programs are clearly an element of political discourse today, some academic studies have revealed their limitations in terms of actually helping viewers understand the political world. Kim and Vishak conducted an experimental study to compare learning from traditional news and infotainment coverage of the same political events. They found that subjects who were shown Jon Stewart's coverage of the Supreme Court nomination process then in progress learned less factual information than those who were shown a similar amount of coverage of this topic culled from the nightly news. The title of their article—"Just Laugh! You Don't Need to Remember"—nicely summarizes their most important finding with regard to infotainment shows.[c]

Ironically, it is the fact that infotainment shows are not designed to convey political information that makes them desirable as shows for politicians to appear on in person. As the old saying goes, "If you want to go duck hunting, you need to go where the ducks are." People who are not much interested in politics can often only be reached by appearing on shows that don't normally do politics.

CRITICAL THINKING QUESTIONS

1. How much do you think can really be learned about politics from the comedy shows that so many young people say they learn from?
2. Do you think presidential candidates should go on these shows in order to reach people who do not watch traditional news shows, or do you think the nature of comedy shows demeans politicians who appear on them?

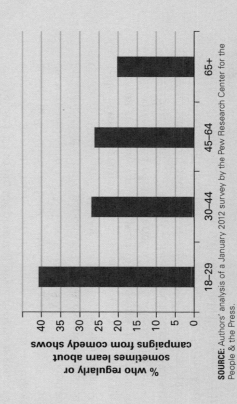

% who regularly or sometimes learn about campaigns from comedy shows

SOURCE: Authors' analysis of a January 2012 survey by the Pew Research Center for the People & the Press.

[a]Barry A. Hollander, "Late-Night Learning: Do Entertainment Programs Increase Political Campaign Knowledge for Young Viewers?" *Journal of Broadcasting and Electronic Media* (December 2005): 412.

[b]Matthew A. Baum, "Talking the Vote: Why Presidential Candidates Hit the Talk Show Circuit," *American Journal of Political Science* (April 2005): 213-34.

[c]Young Mie Kim and John Vishak, "Just Laugh! You Don't Need to Remember: The Effects of Entertainment Media on Political Information Acquisition and Information Processing in Political Judgment," *Journal of Communication* June 2008): 338-60.

224

7.1
7.2
7.3
7.4
7.5
7.6

With so many channels to choose from in the narrowcasting age, major politicians now often agree to interviews on entertainment shows in order to reach people who don't frequently watch the news. Here, Mitt Romney can be seen chatting with Jay Leno on the *Tonight Show*.

Narrowcasting clearly has great potential for disseminating news to the American public. With the growth of cable TV news channels, television can be said to have entered a new era of bringing the news to people—and to political leaders, as it happens. Michael Bohn, a former high-ranking government intelligence officer, writes that during the George W. Bush administration cable news became a valuable source of breaking information in the White House Situation Room.[22] President Bush and his aides regularly turned to cable news stations when major terrorist incidents grabbed worldwide attention.

Currently, about two-thirds of the American public subscribe to cable television and thereby have access to dozens of channels. Sometime in the not-too-distant future it is expected that most cable systems will offer 500 channels. As the number of channels increases, anyone who is really interested in politics will find political information readily available.

Yet, at least so far, the potential of cable news is generally not realized in practice. One common criticism is that cable news channels fail to systematically cover political events and issues, perhaps because their resources are far from up to the task. A content analysis of CNN, Fox News, and MSNBC programming confirms just how little substantive information cable news channels tend to convey. In this analysis, Columbia University's Project for Excellence in Journalism looked at 240 hours of cable news programming. Its report provides a telling indictment of the medium. Among the many findings were that (1) only 11 percent of the time was taken up with written and edited stories; (2) the role of the reporter was primarily to talk extemporaneously; (3) stories were repeated frequently, usually without any important new information; and (4) coverage of the news was spotty, ignoring many important topics. All in all, this comprehensive study paints a very unflattering portrait of what is shown on cable news networks, labeling much of it as simply "talk radio on television."[23]

Like talk radio, cable TV news has become more and more ideologically charged in recent years. Sarah Sobieraj and Jeffrey Berry have recently studied the prevalence of "outrage" on such shows. They define "outrage discourse" as involving "efforts to provoke emotional responses (e.g., anger, fear, moral indignation) from the audience through the use of overgeneralizations, sensationalism, misleading or patently

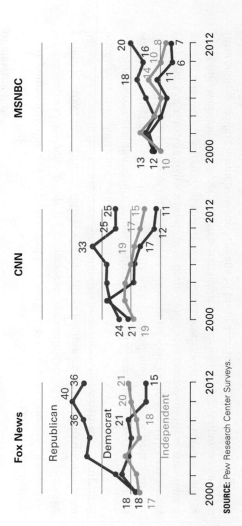

selective exposure
The process through which people consciously choose to get the news from information sources that have viewpoints compatible with their own.

inaccurate information, ad hominenm attacks, and belitting ridicule of opponents."[24] They estimate that such rhetoric is used on average once every 90 seconds on cable TV shows and even more frequently on talk radio. The most common mode of outrage according to their content analysis was mockery/sarcasm, followed by misrepresentative exaggeration, name calling, and insulting language.[25]

Given such highly charged content, it is no surprise that Americans' viewing habits for news are falling more and more into line with their own political predispositions. The basic principle of **selective exposure** in politics is that people tend to choose information sources that have similar points of view to their own and avoid those that present discordant information. In a set of carefully controlled experiments, Shanto Iyengar and Kyu Hahn took a set of news stories and randomly assigned whether they were presented to subjects as originating from Fox, CNN, or NPR. They found that conservatives chose to view stories that they had been told had come from Fox, regardless of what the subject heading of the story was. On the other side of the coin, liberals tended to avoid stories from Fox, preferring CNN or NPR instead.[26] In other words, the subjects selectively exposed themselves to sources of information that they thought conformed with their political leanings. Such a pattern mirrors what has actually happened to the news audience over the past decade or so. As you can see in Figure 7.1, the regular audiences for the cable news networks have become increasingly segmented by political party, with Fox being the channel that appeals to Republicans whereas MSNBC and CNN appeal more to Democrats.

Whether the evolution of narrowcasting and the segmentation of the news audience into opposing camps is good or bad for democracy is a matter of much debate. On the positive side, it can be said that the new, more ideologically tinged presentation of the news stimulates political involvement for many viewers. It also often helps to clarify what is at stake in policy decisions. On the negative side, the increasingly strident tone in the news has turned some people off from politics and contributed to a generalized decline in trust of the mass media. It has also made it harder for those who are politically involved to see the other side of political arguments and to be willing to compromise.[27]

FIGURE 7.1 HOW THE AUDIENCES OF CABLE NEWS CHANNELS HAVE POLARIZED INTO RIVAL PARTISAN CAMPS

In 2000, the Pew Research Center found that the regular audiences of each of the three major cable news channels were roughly equally divided between Democrats and Republicans. By 2012, Fox News viewers were much more likely to be Republicans than Democrats whereas CNN and MSNBC viewers were much more likely to be Democrats than Republicans.

Percent who regularly watch...

SOURCE: Pew Research Center Surveys.

Two other common criticisms of cable news channels are that too much of the time they show people yelling at one another and that when a story breaks they tend to sensationalize it. President Obama once remarked that he doesn't watch the cable news channels because "it feels like WWF wrestling." Softening this derogatory remark, the president went on to say that "it's not even necessarily that there's not good reporting on it; it's just that everyone is having to accelerate to get the next story; the new story, and if there's a story that people think is going to sell, then they overdo it."[28]

In view of these issues, it is not surprising that many scholars of the media feel that the shift from network news to cable news has reduced the overall quality of political journalism. As media critic Thomas Rosensteil writes, "Network journalism originally was designed not to make a profit but to create prestige. Cable is all about profit and keeping costs low. What is disappearing is an idealism about the potential of TV as a medium to better our politics and society."[29]

☐ The Impact of the Internet

Some scholars have optimistically predicted that the Internet will be a boon for American democracy by enabling citizens to become well informed about politics. Indeed, as any college student knows, the Internet is the ultimate research tool. Want to know something specific? The answer can usually be found by searching the Internet using a few key words. If you want to know how presidential candidates stand on federal support for higher education, an Internet search should quickly reveal the answers. Or if you want to know how your two U.S. senators voted on Medicaid appropriations, the records of the Senate roll calls can be found on the Internet. In short, for anyone with basic computing skills, gaining information about political issues is now easier than ever before.

Yet the fact that so much political information is at one's fingertips via the Internet doesn't necessarily mean that people will take advantage of this unprecedented opportunity to become well informed about politics. To a far greater extent than TV, the Internet is purposive—that is, what people see is the product of their own intentional choices. Politics is only one of a myriad of subjects that one can find out about on the Internet. Most Americans' interest in politics is fairly limited. People with limited political interest will probably not be motivated to use the Internet to look up detailed information about politics very often, let alone to follow politics on a regular basis. Indeed, the data on Lycos searches displayed in Table 7.1 indicate that even during the week of the first 2008 presidential election debate, Americans were more likely to be looking for information on pop culture than politics. In the most comprehensive study of the Internet and politics to date, Matthew Hindman finds that traffic to political sites accounts for just 0.12 percent of all Web traffic, with the most frequently visited political site—HuffingtonPost.com—ranking 796th in terms of viewing hits.[30]

So far, the Internet has had its main impact on politics largely by facilitating more communication in every conceivable direction. Through the Internet, journalists, politicians, and interest group organizers can communicate more readily with the public at large, and ordinary citizens can respond far more easily and frequently than before. As a result, there have been some important changes in the nature of campaigning as well as in political communication.

For campaigns, the ability to post information and communicate with supporters via the Internet appears to help somewhat with political mobilization. Bruce Bimber and Richard Davis's study of campaigning online found that "campaign web sites attract supporters of the candidates who display them, and the messages of these sites have a modest tendency to strengthen and reinforce voters' predispositions."[31] As these authors point out, with the decline of traditional neighborhood-based party organizations, the Internet is providing a much-needed means to bring activists together, employing such vehicles as Meetup and Facebook.

TABLE 7.1 THE TOP 25 LYCOS SEARCHES FOR THE WEEK OF THE FIRST 2008 PRESIDENTIAL DEBATE

Every week, the search engine Lycos lists the search terms that its users have most frequently used to seek information on the Internet. Here you can find the top 25 searches for the week ending September 30, 2008—the week of the first Obama–McCain presidential debate. As you can see, only 2 of the top 25 search items reflect an interest in the election or news events. More people used the Internet to get information about pop culture figures such as Clay Aiken and Paris Hilton than to learn about the stunning news of Lehman Brothers' bankruptcy or about the presidential candidates.

The rankings reflect what Internet users are most interested in. Political scientists have long argued that politics are only a peripheral part of most people's lives, and these rankings clearly reflect that fact.

Rank	Search Term
1.	Clay Aiken
2.	Paris Hilton
3.	YOUTUBE
4.	Travis Barker
5.	Pamela Anderson
6.	Kim Kardashian
7.	Facebook
8.	DJ AM
9.	Britney Spears
10.	Dragonball
11.	Lindsay Lohan
12.	Sarah Palin
13.	Megan Fox
14.	Naruto
15.	WWE
16.	Kanye West
17.	Lance Armstrong
18.	Biggest Loser
19.	Bristol Palin
20.	Lehman Brothers Bankruptcy
21.	RUNESCAPE
22.	Kendra Wilkinson
23.	Carmen Electra
24.	Jennifer Hudson
25.	Eva Mendes

SOURCE: http://50.lycos.com.

Blogs in particular have provided political activists with a means to make their concerns heard to an extent that was previously possible only for professional journalists. Indeed, Brian Williams of NBC News remarks that because of blogs, the news media now faces competition from "people who have an opinion, a modem, and a bathrobe." He further laments, "All of my life, developing credentials to cover my field of work, and now I'm up against a guy named Vinny in an efficiency apartment in the Bronx who hasn't left the efficiency apartment in two years."[32] His lament appears to be somewhat exaggerated, however. In theory, anyone can challenge Brian Williams in the blogosphere, but in practice few bloggers are ever going to be able to reach as many people as a network anchor. Posting a blog entry is easy, but getting it national attention is difficult. Matthew Hindman analyzed the most successful political bloggers and found that in their credentials they are far more similar to the leading

Blogs are playing an increasing important role in the reporting of political news. In 2005, 23-year-old Garrett Graff, who was writing a blog about the news media in Washington, became the first person to receive a White House press pass for the specific purpose of writing a blog. Here, bloggers cover a candidate speech during the 2012 presidential primary campaign.

traditional journalists than to Brian Williams' "Vinny." In particular, the major political bloggers like Markos Moulitsas Zuniga and Hugh Hewitt all have strong analytic training, excellent writing skills, and an encyclopedic knowledge of politics. Hindman concludes that, in fact, blogs have "given a small group of educational, professional, and technical elites new influence in U.S. politics" but "have done far less to amplify the political voice of average citizens."[33]

Even if blogs remain largely a tool of elites, they have on occasion made it possible for citizens without journalistic credentials to get the media to pay attention to stories that might otherwise be ignored and to serve as watchdogs over the media. For example, when Dan Rather and CBS News ran a story in 2004 about documents that allegedly showed that George W. Bush had shirked his duties with the National Guard in the 1970s, a number of bloggers quickly raised questions concerning their authenticity. The bloggers were ultimately proven right, and CBS News apologized for running the story.

☐ Private Control of the Media

As we have seen, America has a rich diversity of media sources. One of the main reasons that this has long been the case is that journalism has long been big business in the United States, with control of virtually all media outlets being in private hands. Only a relatively small number of TV stations are publicly owned in America,

chains

Groups of newspapers published by media conglomerates and today accounting for over four-fifths of the nation's daily newspaper circulation.

and these PBS stations play a minimal role in the news business, attracting very low ratings. In contrast, in many other countries major TV networks are owned by the government. In Canada, the most prominent stations are part of the state-run network (the Canadian Broadcasting Company); this is the case in most European countries as well.

Because of private ownership of the media and the First Amendment right to free speech, American journalists have long had an unfettered capacity to criticize government leaders and policies. In established democracies where major networks are government owned, government ownership is not supposed to inhibit journalists from criticizing the government because the journalists are assured autonomy. However, in some countries, like China, that do not have democratic systems, the media—newspapers as well as television—are typically government enterprises and have to carefully avoid any criticism of the government. In countries where freedom of the press is restricted, journalists may work in fear of physical threats, imprisonment, and even being murdered. Their offices can be searched at any time or their work confiscated, and their stories must be cleared by government censors.

Although the American media are independent when it comes to journalistic content, they are totally dependent on advertising revenues to keep their businesses going. Public ownership means that the media can serve the public interest without worrying about the size of their audience; private ownership means that getting the biggest possible audience is the primary—indeed, sometimes the only—objective. This focus on audience is exacerbated by the fact that media in America today tend to be part of large conglomerates. Consider, for example, the major television networks. The Disney Corporation bought ABC, General Electric acquired NBC, Viacom (a conglomerate that owns many entertainment companies, including Blockbuster, Paramount Pictures, MTV, and Simon & Schuster) took over CBS, and CNN became part of Time Warner. In the newspaper business, **chains**, such as Gannett, Knight-Ridder, and Newhouse, control newspapers that together represent over 80 percent of the nation's daily circulation.[34] This increasing profit orientation has had repercussions for American journalism and, specifically, political reporting. For example, the major television networks once had bureaus all over the world; however, these foreign bureaus became a target for cost cutting, as they were expensive to operate and surveys showed that the public was not much interested in news from overseas (except for periods when American troops are involved in major combat, such as in Iraq in 2003). Similarly, foreign coverage in newspapers has been dropped off precipitously as newspapers have to cut their costs in light of declining revenues. Priya Kumar's study of a set of major newspapers found that the total number of foreign news stories in these newspapers declined by over 50 percent between 1985 and 2010.[35] As we shall see in the following section, striving for profits greatly shapes how the news is reported in America.

Why It *Matters* to You
Media as a Business

In his classic book *Understanding Media*, Marshall McLuhan coined the famous phrase "The medium is the message." By this, McLuhan meant that the way we communicate information can be more influential than the information itself. In the United States, news is a commodity controlled by the media, not a public service. Therefore, the news media have far more incentive to make their reports interesting than informative about policy issues. The public would probably be exposed to more policy information were it not for this incentive system.

Reporting the News

7.1
7.2
7.3
7.4
7.5
7.6

7.3 List the major criteria that determine which news stories receive the most media attention.

A s journalism students will quickly tell you, news is what is timely and different. It is a man biting a dog, not a dog biting a man. An often-repeated speech on foreign policy or a well-worn statement on the need for immigration reform is less newsworthy than an odd episode. The public rarely hears about the routine ceremonies at state dinners, but when President George H. W. Bush threw up all over the Japanese prime minister in 1992, the world's media jumped on the story. Similarly, when Howard Dean screamed wildly to a crowd of supporters after the 2004 Iowa caucuses, the major networks and cable news channels played the clip over 600 times in the following four days, virtually obliterating any serious discussion of the issues. In its search for the unusual, the news media can give its audience a peculiar, distorted view of events and policymakers.

Millions of new and different events happen every day; journalists must decide which of them are newsworthy. A classic look into how the news is produced can be found in Edward J. Epstein's *News from Nowhere*,[36] which summarizes his insights from a year of observing NBC's news department from inside the organization. Epstein found that in the pursuit of high ratings, news shows are tailored to a fairly low level of audience sophistication. To a large extent, TV networks define news as what is entertaining to the average viewer. A dull and complicated story would have to be of enormous importance to get on the air; in contrast, relatively trivial stories can make the cut if they are interesting enough. Leonard Downie, Jr. and Robert Kaiser of the *Washington Post* argue that entertainment has increasingly pushed out information in the TV news business. They write that the history of TV news can be summarized in a couple sentences:

> As audiences declined, network executives decreed that news had to become more profitable. So news divisions sharply reduced their costs, and tried to raise the entertainment value of their broadcasts.[37]

Regardless of the medium, it cannot be emphasized enough that news reporting is a business in America. The quest for profits shapes how journalists define what is newsworthy, where they get their information, and how they present it. And the pursuit of types of news stories that will attract more viewers or readers also leads to certain biases in what the American public sees and reads.

☐ Finding the News

Americans' popular image of correspondents or reporters somehow uncovering the news is accurate in some cases, yet most news stories come from well-established sources. Major news organizations assign their best reporters to particular **beats**—specific locations from which news often emanates, such as Congress. For example, in covering military conflicts, the majority of TV news stories usually originate from correspondents posted at the White House, Pentagon, and State Department beats.

Politicians depend on the media to spread certain information and ideas to the general public. Sometimes they feed stories to reporters in the form of **trial balloons,** information leaked to see what the political reaction will be. For example, a few days prior to President Clinton's admission that he had had an "inappropriate relationship" with Monica Lewinsky, top aides to the president leaked the story to Richard Berke of the *New York Times*. The timing of the leak was obvious; the story appeared just before Clinton had to decide how to testify before Kenneth Starr's grand jury. When the public's reaction was that it was about time he admitted this relationship, it was probably easier for him to do so—at least politically.

Journalists and politicians have a symbiotic relationship, with politicians relying on journalists to get their message out and journalists relying on politicians to keep them in the know. When reporters feel that their access to information is being impeded, complaints of censorship become widespread. During the Gulf War in 1991, reporters' freedom of movement and observation was severely restricted. After the fighting was over, 15 influential news organizations sent a letter to the secretary of defense complaining that the rules for reporting the war were designed more to control the news than to facilitate it.[38] Largely because of such complaints, during the 2003 military campaign to oust Saddam Hussein the Pentagon "embedded" about 500 reporters with coalition fighting forces, thus enabling them to report on combat activity as it happened. The result was an increased ability to transmit combat footage. A content analysis by Farnsworth and Lichter found that 35 percent of major TV network stories contained combat scenes compared to just 20 percent in 1991.[39] The public response to this new form of war reporting was largely positive.[40]

Although journalists are typically dependent on familiar sources, an enterprising reporter occasionally has an opportunity to live up to the image of the crusading truth seeker. Local reporters Carl Bernstein and Bob Woodward of the *Washington Post* uncovered important evidence about the Watergate break-in and cover-up in the early 1970s. Ever since the Watergate scandal, news organizations have regularly sent reporters on beats to expose the uglier side of government corruption and inefficiency, and, as discussed earlier, journalists have seen such reporting as among their important roles.

There are many cases of good investigative reporting making an important impact on the conduct of government as well as business. For example, in 1997, the *New York Times* won a Pulitzer Prize for its reports on how a proposed gold-mining operation threatened the environment of part of Yellowstone National Park. After these stories drew President Clinton's attention, he made sure that the project was stopped. In 1999, the *Chicago Tribune* documented the experiences of numerous Illinois men sentenced to death who had been convicted on questionable evidence or coerced into confessing. Soon after the series was published, the governor of Illinois suspended executions in the state. In 2007, a reporter with the *Birmingham News* won a Pulitzer Prize for his exposure of cronyism and corruption in Alabama's two-year college system, resulting in the dismissal of the chancellor and other corrective action. And in 2013 two reporters from the *New York Times* won a Pulitzer for their reports on how Wal-Mart used widespread bribery to dominate the market in Mexico, resulting in changes in company practices.

Presenting the News

Once the news has been "found," it has to be neatly compressed into a 30-second news segment or fit in among other stories and advertisements in a newspaper. If you had to pick a single word to describe news coverage by the news media, it would be *superficial*. "The name of the game," says former White House Press Secretary Jody Powell, "is skimming off the cream, seizing on the most interesting, controversial, and unusual aspects of an issue."[41] Editors do not want to bore or confuse their audience. TV news, in particular, is little more than a headline service. According to former CBS anchor Dan Rather, "You simply cannot be a well-informed citizen by just watching the news on television."[42]

Except for the little-watched but highly regarded *NewsHour* on PBS and ABC's late-night *Nightline*, analysis of news events rarely lasts more than a minute. Patterson's study of campaign coverage found that only skimpy attention was given to the issues during a presidential campaign. Clearly, if coverage of political events

sound bites
Short video clips of approximately 10 seconds. Typically, they are all that is shown from a politician's speech on the nightly television news.

during the height of an election campaign is thin, coverage of day-to-day policy questions is even thinner. Issues such as reforming the Medicare system, adjusting eligibility levels for food stamps, and regulating the financial services industry are highly complex and difficult to treat in a short news clip. A careful study of media coverage of Bill and Hillary Clinton's comprehensive health care proposal in 1993–1994 found that the media focused much more on strategy and who was winning the political game than on the specific policy issues involved.[43] President Obama faced exactly the same problem in his battle to reform America's health care system in 2009–2010, frequently admonishing the press, "This isn't about me. This isn't about politics."

Ironically, as technology has enabled the media to pass along information with greater speed, news coverage has become less thorough.[44] High-tech communication has helped reporters do their job faster but not necessarily better. Newspapers once routinely reprinted the entire text of important political speeches. Now that speech transcripts can be found via Google, newspapers rarely print them, and only the most interested people search for them. In place of speeches, Americans now usually hear **sound bites** of about 10 seconds on TV. The average length of time that a presidential candidate was given to talk uninterrupted on the TV news has declined precipitously from 43 seconds in 1968 to just 9 seconds in 2008.[45] As you can see in "America in Perspective: The Length of Candidate Sound Bites in Four Countries," sound bites are not that much longer in other established democracies.

Many politicians have expressed frustration with sound-bite journalism. Even in the 1970s, for example, President Jimmy Carter told a reporter that

it's a strange thing that you can go through your campaign for president, and you have a basic theme that you express in a 15- or 20-minute standard speech . . . but the traveling press—sometimes exceeding 100 people—will never report that speech to the public. The peripheral aspects become the headlines, but the basic essence of what you stand for and what you hope to accomplish is never reported.[46]

Sound-bite journalism has meant both that politicians are unable to present the issues and that they are able to avoid the issues. Why should politicians work to build a carefully crafted case for their point of view when a catchy line will do just as well? And as Walter Cronkite wrote, "Naturally, nothing of any significance is going to be said in seven seconds, but this seems to work to the advantage of many politicians. They are not required to say anything of significance, and issues can be avoided rather than confronted."[47]

Indeed, a series of studies of TV news reporting of presidential elections over the last two decades has found the coverage wanting in both quantity and quality. Farnsworth and Lichter's content analysis of the 1988 to 2008 campaigns concludes that "the networks consistently focused on the horse race, shortchanged matters of substance, and accentuated the most negative aspects of the campaign trail, and in so doing failed to provide an accurate and fair reflection of the presidential campaigns."[48] Notably, Farnsworth and Lichter absolve the candidates from any blame

Why It Matters to You
The Increasing Speed of News Dissemination

When Samuel Morse sent the first telegraph message from the U.S. Capitol building, he tapped out a question, "What hath God wrought?" The answer back was "What is the news from Washington?" Ever since, the transmission of news via electronic means has become faster and faster. As a result, over time there has been less and less time for deliberative action to deal with long-term problems, and the political agenda has come to focus more on the here and now.

America in Perspective

The Length of Candidate Sound Bites in Four Countries

During the period from 2000 to 2007, media researchers in four countries conducted a cross-national study of TV coverage of the final four weeks of national election campaigns. Among the topics they looked at was the average length of uninterrupted time that a party's national leader was given to speak on the newscasts. One might think that in European countries with public ownership of the networks, as in Britain with the BBC, major politicians would be given longer to make their case than in the strictly commercial-driven media in the United States. However, as you can see in the figure, the sound bites for politicians in Germany, France, and Great Britain are not that much longer than those for American politicians.

Thus, two factors appear to be at work in advanced industrialized democracies. First, technological advancements in editing have made it quite easy to cut political statements into small tidbits. And, second, networks usually feel that, to keep their audience, brief sound bites are best—lest people change to another channel.

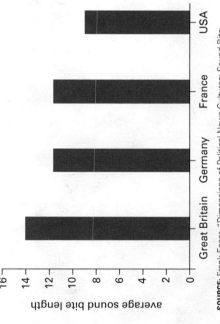

SOURCE: Frank Esser, "Dimensions of Political News Cultures: Sound Bite and Image Bite News in France, Germany, Great Britain, and the United States." *The International Journal of Press/Politics* (2008): 401–428.

CRITICAL THINKING QUESTIONS

1. Do you think the difference between 15 seconds and sound bites in Great Britain and 10 seconds in the United States is significant? Try timing a political statement into 15 seconds and then cutting it down to 10 seconds to see if crucial information is lost by such a cut.

2. Do you think the TV networks in these countries are shortchanging the voters by presenting them with such short sound bites? Why or why not?

for this state of affairs. Their careful analysis of what candidates present in their speeches, campaign ads, and Web sites finds plenty of in-depth discussion of policy issues; the problem they point to is that the media all too frequently fail to pass this on to the public, or at best present only small morsels of what the candidates are trying to get across.

The problem of getting the networks to cover serious issues in-depth scarcely goes away once a president assumes office. During the Cold War, presidents could routinely obtain coverage for their speeches on the three major networks anytime they requested it. Now, with the networks able to shunt the coverage to CNN and other cable news outlets, it is easy for them to say "no" to even the president. In May 2000, for example, Bill Clinton was rebuffed when he asked for time on ABC, NBC, and CBS to address U.S.–China relations. "Are you crazy? It's sweeps month!" was one of the responses.[49] In September 2009, Fox opted to show an episode of *So You Think You Can Dance* instead of Obama's address to Congress about health care.

234

7.1

7.2

7.3

7.4

7.5

7.6

☐ Bias in the News

Some have argued that political reporting is biased in favor of one point of view—most often that the media have a liberal bias. There is limited evidence to support this charge of a liberal bias. In four comprehensive surveys of American journalists conducted between 1971 and 2002, David Weaver and his colleagues consistently found that reporters were more likely to classify themselves as liberal than the general public. For example, in 2002, 40 percent of journalists surveyed said they leaned to the left compared to only 25 percent who leaned to the right.[50] However, the vast majority of studies have found that most reporting is not systematically biased toward a particular ideology or party.

That reporting typically reflects little explicit ideological bias does not mean that it is uninfluenced by reporters' backgrounds and assumptions. Thus, former CBS News reporter Bernard Goldberg argued in his best-selling book *Bias* that "real media bias comes not so much from what party they attack. Liberal bias is the result of how they see the world."[51] According to Goldberg (who, it should be noted, is an outspoken conservative), on social issues like feminism, gay rights, and welfare the nightly news clearly leans to the left, shaped by the big-city environment in which network reporters live. He asks, "Do we really think that if the media elites worked out of Nebraska instead of New York; and if they were overwhelmingly social conservatives instead of liberals ... do we really think that would make no difference?"[52]

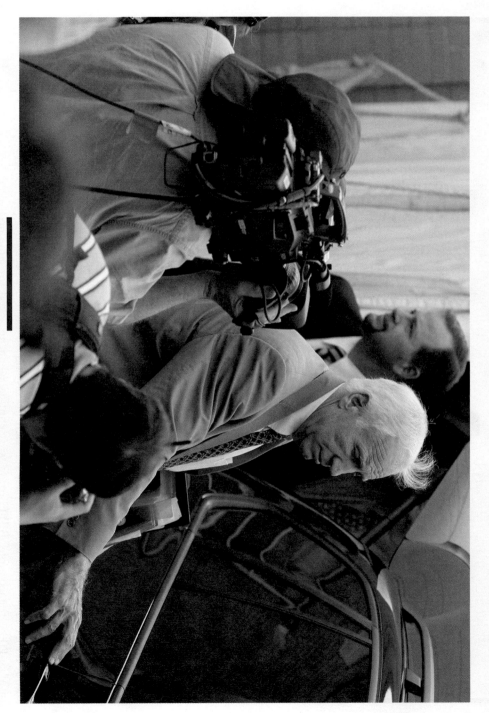

The clearest and most consistent bias in the news is the focus on sensational stories. When Jerry Sandusky (a former Penn State assistant football coach, shown here) was arrested on sex abuse charges, the media gave far more coverage to this story than to stories going on at the time that involved complex issues, such as the European debt crisis, the debate over health care, or unrest in the Middle East.

talking head

A shot of a person's face talking directly to the camera. Because such shots are visually unstimulating, the major networks rarely show politicians talking for very long.

The overriding bias, however, is not an ideological bias but, rather, as we have seen, a bias toward stories that will draw the largest audience. Bernard Goldberg also writes, "In the United States of Entertainment there is no greater sin than to bore the audience. A TV reporter could get it wrong from time to time. He could be snippy and snooty. But he could not be boring."[53] Surveys show that people are most fascinated by, and most likely to follow, stories involving conflict, violence, disaster, or scandal, as is reflected in the data in Table 7.2. Such stories have the drama that brings in big audiences.

Television is particularly biased toward stories that generate good pictures. Seeing a **talking head** (a shot of a person's face talking directly to the camera) is boring; viewers will switch channels in search of more interesting visual stimulation. For example, during an unusually contentious and lengthy interview of George H. W. Bush by Dan Rather concerning the Iran-Contra scandal in the 1980s, CBS's ratings actually went down as people tired of watching two talking heads argue.[54] In contrast, ratings can be increased by, say, ambassadors squaring off in a fistfight at the United Nations, a scene CBS showed

---

TABLE 7.2 STORIES CITIZENS HAVE TUNED IN AND TUNED OUT

Since 1986, the monthly survey of the Pew Research Center for the People & the Press has asked Americans how closely they have followed major news stories. As one would expect, stories involving disaster or human drama have drawn more attention than have complicated issues of public policy. A representative selection of their findings is presented here. The percentage in each case is the proportion who reported following the story "very closely."

Story	Percentage
The explosion of the space shuttle Challenger in 1986	80%
Terrorist attacks on the World Trade Center and Pentagon	74%
Impacts of hurricanes Katrina and Rita	73%
Los Angeles riots in 1992	70%
1987 rescue of baby Jessica McClure from a well	69%
School shootings at Columbine High School in Colorado	68%
Iraq's invasion of Kuwait in 1990	66%
2010 earthquake in Haiti	60%
Start of hostilities against Iraq in 2003	57%
Supreme Court decision on flag burning	51%
Killing of Osama bin Laden in a raid by U.S. forces	50%
Passage of Obama's health care reform bill in 2010	49%
Arrest of O. J. Simpson	48%
Obama's decision to send 30,000 additional troops to Afghanistan	43%
The partial shutdown of the federal government in 2013	43%
2000 presidential election outcome	38%
A sex abuse scandal involving Penn State football coach Joe Paterno	34%
Impeachment trial of President Clinton in the Senate	31%
How the rollout of Obamacare was going in December 2013	26%
Confirmation of Sonia Sotomayor to the Supreme Court	22%
Obama's decision to reject the Keystone oil pipeline	22%
2010 Supreme Court decision allowing corporations and unions to pay for ads about political candidates	18%
Ethnic violence in the Darfur region of Sudan	16%
Passage of the Communications Deregulation Bill	12%
FDA's 2013 proposal to severely restrict trans fats in foods	10%

SOURCE: Pew Research Center for the People & the Press.

The News and Public Opinion

7.4 Analyze the impact the media has on what policy issues Americans think about.

H ow does the news media's depiction of a threatening, hostile, and corrupt world shape Americans' political opinions and behaviors? This question is difficult to answer, as the effects of the news media can be difficult to accurately assess. One reason is that it is hard to separate the media from other influences. When presidents, legislators, and interest groups—as well as news organizations—are all discussing an issue, it is not easy to isolate the opinion changes that come from political leadership from those that come from the news. Moreover, the effect of one news story on public opinion may be trivial but the cumulative effect of dozens of news stories may be important.

For many years, students of the subject tended to doubt that the media had more than a marginal effect on public opinion. The "minimal effects hypothesis" stemmed from the fact that early scholars were looking for direct impacts—for example, whether the media affected how people voted.[57] When the focus turned to how the media affect *what Americans think about*, the effects began to appear more significant. In a series of controlled laboratory experiments, Shanto Iyengar and Donald Kinder subtly manipulated the stories participants saw on the TV news.[58] They found that they could significantly affect the importance people attached to a given problem by splicing a few stories about it into the news over the course of a week. Iyengar and Kinder do not maintain that the networks can make something out of nothing or conceal problems that actually exist. But they do conclude that "what television news does, instead, is alter the priorities Americans attach to a circumscribed set of problems, all of which are plausible contenders for public concern."[59] Subsequent research by Miller and Krosnick has revealed that agenda-setting effects are particularly strong among politically knowledgeable citizens who trust the media. Thus, rather than the media manipulating the public, they argue that agenda setting reflects a deliberate and thoughtful process on the part of sophisticated citizens who rely on what they consider a credible institutional source of information.[60]

Nonetheless, this agenda-setting effect can have a range of far-reaching consequences. First, by increasing public attention to specific problems, the media influence the criteria by which the public evaluates political leaders. When unemployment goes up but inflation goes down, does public support for the president increase or decrease? The answer could depend in large part on which story the media emphasized. The fact that the media emphasized the country's slow economic growth in 1992 rather than the good news of low inflation and interest rates was clearly instrumental in setting the stage for Bill Clinton's ousting the incumbent president, George H. W. Bush, that year. Similarly, the emphasis on the slowly improving American economic situation in 2012 rather than the bad news about the record number of long-term unemployed Americans was clearly an advantage for Barack Obama and a disadvantage for Mitt Romney.

The media can even have a dramatic effect on how the public evaluates specific events by emphasizing one event over others. When, during a 1976 presidential debate, President Ford incorrectly stated that the Soviet Union did not dominate Eastern Europe, the press gave substantial coverage to Ford's misstatement, and this coverage had an impact on the public. Polls showed that most people did not realize the president had made an error until the press told them so. Afterward, the initial assessment that Ford had won the debate shifted, as voters expressed increased concern about his competence in foreign policymaking.[61] Similarly, the media's focus on misstatements by Al

three times in one day—without once discussing the cause of the fight.[55] The result of this kind of bias, political scientist Lance Bennett points out, is that "the public is exposed to a world driven into chaos by seemingly arbitrary and mysterious forces."[56]

policy agenda
The issues that attract the serious attention of public officials and other people actively involved in politics at the time.

policy entrepreneurs
People who invest their political "capital" in an issue. According to John Kingdon, a policy entrepreneur "could be in or out of government, in elected or appointed positions, in interest groups or research organizations."

Gore during the first presidential debate of 2000 had an impact on public opinion. In the days immediately following this debate, the percentage who thought that Gore had beaten Bush declined markedly.[62]

Much remains unknown about the effects of the media and the news on American political opinion and behavior. Enough is known, however, to conclude that the media are a key political institution. The media control much of the technology that in turn controls much of what Americans believe about politics and government. For this reason, it is important to look at the American policy agenda and the media's role in shaping it.

Policy Entrepreneurs and Agenda Setting

7.5 Explain how policy entrepreneurs employ media strategies to influence the public agenda.

omeone who asks you "What's your agenda?" wants to know something about your priorities. Governments, too, have agendas. John Kingdon defines **policy agenda** as "the list of subjects or problems to which government officials, and people outside of government closely associated with those officials, are paying some serious attention at any given time."[63] Interest groups, political parties, individual politicians, public relations firms, bureaucratic agencies—and, of course, the president and Congress—are all pushing for their priorities to take precedence over others. Health care, education, unemployment, and immigration reform—these and scores of other issues compete for attention from the government.

Political activists depend heavily on the media to get their ideas placed high on the governmental agenda. Political activists are often called **policy entrepreneurs**—people who invest their political "capital" in an issue (as an economic entrepreneur invests capital in an idea for making money). Kingdon says that policy entrepreneurs can "be in or out of government, in elected or appointed positions, in interest groups or research organizations."[64] Policy entrepreneurs' arsenal of weapons includes press releases, press conferences, and letter writing; convincing reporters and columnists to tell their side; trading on personal contacts; and, in cases of desperation, resorting to staging dramatic events. Such activities are often shrugged off as self-serving and mere public relations ploys. Political scientist Patrick Sellers firmly disagrees with this view in his study of strategic communication in Congress. He concludes, "Promotional campaigns are a way to discursively organize public deliberation, allowing political actors to present their arguments and for others to understand and evaluate these arguments."[65]

The media are not always monopolized by political elites; the poor and downtrodden have access to them too. Civil rights groups in the 1960s relied heavily on the media to tell their stories of unjust treatment. Many believe that the introduction of television helped to accelerate the movement by showing Americans—in the North and South alike—just what the situation was.[66] Protest groups have learned that if they can stage an interesting event that attracts the media's attention, at least their point of view will be heard. Radical activist Saul Alinsky once dramatized the plight of one neighborhood by having its residents collect rats and dump them on the mayor's front lawn. The story was one that local reporters could hardly resist. In 2002, graduate students at the University of California, Irvine, camped out in tents in the campus park to protest the lack of investment in on-campus housing. The prime organizer, a teaching assistant for an introduction to American government course, issued press releases and made calls to news directors urging them to come down and take a look. Soon after several stations put the sorry scene on TV, the university administration gave in to the graduate students' demands.

Conveying a long-term, positive image through the media is more important than gaining media coverage of a few dramatic events. Policy entrepreneurs, in or out of

238

7.1
7.2
7.3
7.4
7.5
7.6

Understanding the Mass Media

Assess the impact of the mass media on the scope of government and democracy in America.

he media act as key linkage institutions between the people and the policymakers and have a profound impact on the political policy agenda. Bernard Cohen goes so far as to say, "No major act of the American Congress, no foreign adventure, no act of diplomacy, no great social reform can succeed unless the press prepares the public mind."[68] If Cohen is right, then the growth of government in America would have been impossible without the media having established the need for it.

☐ The Media and the Scope of Government

The media's watchdog function helps to keep politicians in check. Notably, this is one aspect of the media's job performance that Americans consistently evaluate positively. For over two decades, the Pew Research Center for People & the Press has consistently found that a clear majority of the public has said that press criticism of political leaders does more good than harm. In 2013, a Pew Research Center poll found that 68 percent said that press criticism of political leaders is worth it because it keeps leaders from doing things that should not be done, while 21 percent believed criticism keeps political leaders from doing their jobs.[69] Reporters themselves consider exposing officeholders to be an essential role of the press in a free society. They often hold disparaging views of public officials, seeing them as self-serving, hypocritical, lacking in integrity, and preoccupied with reelection. Thus, it is not surprising that journalists frequently see a need to debunk public officials and their policy proposals.

As every new policy proposal is met with media skepticism, constraints are placed on the scope of what government can do. The watchdog orientation of the press can be characterized as neither liberal nor conservative but reformist. Reporters often see their job as crusading against foul play and unfairness in government and society. This focus on injustice in society inevitably encourages enlarging the scope of government. Once the media identify a problem in society—such as poverty, inadequate medical care for the elderly, or poor education for certain children—reporters usually begin to ask what the government is doing about it. Could it be acting more effectively to solve the problem? What do people in the White House and Congress (as well as state and local government) have to say about it? In this way, the media portray government as responsible for handling almost every major problem. Although skeptical of what politicians say and do, the media report on America's social problems in a manner that often also encourages government to take on more and more tasks.

☐ Individualism and the Media

More than any other development in the past century, the rise of television broadcasting has reinforced and furthered individualism in the American political process. Candidates are now much more capable of running for office on their own by appealing to people directly through television. Individual voters can see the candidates "up close and personal" for themselves, and they have much less need for political parties or social groups to help them make their decisions.

Television finds it easier to focus on individuals than on groups. As a result, candidate personality is more important than ever. In part because of this focus on individuals, TV has also affected the relative amount of coverage accorded to the three

government, depend on goodwill and good images. Thus, groups, individuals, and even countries sometimes turn to public relations firms to improve their image and their ability to peddle their issue positions.[67]

Point to Ponder

Studies have found that the focus of television news in recent years has shifted toward more human interest stories, with the result being less coverage of national and international politics.

Do you think TV news producers are just responding to what Americans want? And, if so, do you think that is what TV news *should* be doing?

A. BACALL

"Responding to viewer sentiment, we have eliminated world news and expanded our entertainment and sports news."

branches of government. Whereas there are 535 members of Congress, there is only one president. Doris Graber's study of nightly news broadcasts in 2008–2009 found that 65 percent of the coverage devoted to the three branches was devoted to the president as compared to 29 percent for Congress. The Supreme Court, which does not allow TV cameras to cover its proceedings and whose members rarely give interviews, is almost invisible on TV newscasts, receiving a mere 6 percent of the coverage.[70]

☐ Democracy and the Media

As Ronald Berkman and Laura Kitch remark, "Information is the fuel of democracy."[71] Widespread access to information could be the greatest boon to democracy since the secret ballot, yet most observers think that the great potential of today's high-tech media has yet to be realized. Noting the vast increase in information available through the news media, Berkman and Kitch state, "If the sheer quantity of news produced greater competency in the citizenry, then we would have a society of political masters."[72] Yet, this is clearly not the case. The rise of the "information society" has not brought about the rise of the "informed society."

Whenever the media are criticized for being superficial, their defense is to say that this is what people want. Network executives remark that if people suddenly started to watch in-depth shows such as PBS's *NewsHour*, then they would gladly imitate them—if people wanted serious coverage of the issues, they would be happy to provide it. They point out that they are in business to make a profit and that, to do so, they must appeal to the maximum number of people. As Matthew Kerbel observes, "The people who bring you the evening news would like it to be informative *and* entertaining, but when these two values collide, the shared orientations of the television news world push the product inexorably toward the latter."[73] It is not their fault if the resulting news coverage is superficial, network executives argue; blame capitalism or blame the people—most of whom like news to be more entertaining than educational. Thus, if people are not better informed in the high-tech age, it is largely because they do not care to hear about complicated political issues. In this sense, one can say that the people really do rule through the media.

Review the Chapter

The Mass Media Today

7.1 Describe how American politicians choreograph their messages through the mass media, p. 216.

Politicians stage media events for the primary purpose of getting attention from the media. These events are artfully stage-managed to present the intended message. Campaign commercials are also carefully crafted to convey specific images and information.

The Development of Media Politics

7.2 Outline the key developments in the history of mass media and American politics, p. 218.

Newspapers were long the dominant media through which Americans got their news. But ever since the emergence of television they have been on the decline. The Internet has further accelerated the decline of newspaper reading; newspapers have thus far failed to establish profitability for their online editions. The nightly network news broadcasts on CBS, NBC, and ABC were the #1 means by which Americans got their news from the 1960s through the 1980s. But ever since the emergence of cable and cable news they have seen their audiences shrink, as American television has moved from the broadcasting to the narrowcasting era. The Internet provides more access to political information than ever possible before. How much typical citizens will take advantage of these opportunities remains to be seen. But certainly campaigns and political activists have been able to use the Internet to organize for political action and to get specially targeted messages out.

Reporting the News

7.3 List the major criteria that determine which news stories receive the most media attention, p. 230.

The media define "news" largely as events that are unusual and out of the ordinary. Because of economic pressures, the media are biased in favor of stories with high drama that will attract people's interest instead of extended analyses of complex issues.

The News and Public Opinion

7.4 Analyze the impact the media has on what policy issues Americans think about, p. 236.

The media are instrumental in setting the American political agenda—that is, the issues that get seriously addressed by politicians. What issues Americans think about is much influenced by which issues the media choose to cover. It has often been said that the media are like a searchlight, bringing one episode and then another out of darkness and into the public eye.

Policy Entrepreneurs and Agenda Setting

7.5 Explain how policy entrepreneurs employ media strategies to influence the public agenda, p. 237.

Policy entrepreneurs seek to influence the policy agenda by getting the media to pay attention to the issues that they are particularly concerned with. They employ a variety of strategies to obtain media coverage, including press releases, press conferences, and letter writing. Sometimes they will resort to staging dramatic events that are so interesting and unusual that reporters can hardly resist covering them.

Understanding the Mass Media

7.6 Assess the impact of the mass media on the scope of government and democracy in America, p. 238.

The media's role as a watchdog over government sometimes constrains expansions of the scope of government by fomenting skepticism about what government can accomplish. On the other hand, media crusades against injustices sometimes serve to encourage government to take on increased responsibilities. The media's superficial coverage of policy issues is criticized by many democratic theorists. Yet, members of the media argue in their own defense that they are only providing the sort of coverage of politics that draws the biggest audiences.

Learn the Terms

high-tech politics, p. 216
mass media, p. 216
media event, p. 217
press conferences, p. 218
investigative journalism, p. 218
print media, p. 219

electronic media, p. 219
narrowcasting, p. 222
selective exposure, p. 225
chains, p. 229
beats, p. 230
trial balloons, p. 230

sound bites, p. 232
talking head, p. 235
policy agenda, p. 237
policy entrepreneurs, p. 237

Test Yourself

1. What is one reason that media outlets might be considered subjective rather than objective?

a. They can only cover stories that are considered important by the federal government.

b. They can only cover stories that are considered important by the state government.

c. They follow trends on social media and report the most often discussed topics.

d. They tend to sensationalize news to capture an audience.

e. Opinion pieces are becoming the most common type of story.

2. Which of the following statements best describes the final month of TV news coverage of a presidential campaign?

a. Most events shown on TV are unscripted so as to increase viewer interest.

b. Most of the events are carefully prepared by the candidates, with only about 20 percent being unscripted.

c. The candidates thoughtfully control all appearances with a carefully prepared script and audience.

d. The candidates try to control many appearances, but when they do so the media refuse to pay much attention to such events.

e. The balance between scripted and unscripted events has varied in recent years, as some candidates choose far different mixtures than other candidates.

3. When did the trend toward more negative and cynical news coverage begin?

a. during the Great Depression of the 1930s

b. during World War II

c. during the Korean War

d. during the Vietnam War

e. during the Iraq War

4. The relationship between politicians and the press was _____ during the 20th century until the 1960s.

a. antagonistic

b. barely existent

c. competitive

d. cozy

e. weak

5. Even though the Federal Communications Commission (FCC) is an independent body, what is a reason it is subject to political pressure?

a. Congress appoints its members.

b. Congress exerts control over its budget.

c. The broadcast industry gives financial rewards to members.

d. The president can fire any member.

e. The Supreme Court approves its appointees.

6. In recent years, how has the Constitution been interpreted as it applies to government and the media?

a. The government can prevent the publication of sensitive political news.

b. The government can restrict certain kinds of news with an anonymous source.

c. The government cannot prevent the publication of most news, but it can punish those who publish it.

d. The government cannot prevent the publication of most news or punish those who publish it.

e. The government cannot restrict publication of anything whatsoever.

7. Many analysts believe that media coverage of American politics in recent years has led to _____.

a. an increase in negative feelings about the political system

b. better informed Americans

c. greater public trust in governmental institutions

d. increased respect for the media

e. more analysis instead of sensationalism

8. Which is the most persistent media bias?

a. against policy makers
b. conservative
c. liberal
d. toward a compelling story
e. toward policy makers

9. After the Gulf War was over, 15 influential news organizations sent a letter to the secretary of defense complaining that the rules for reporting the war were designed more to control the news than to facilitate it. How did this affect access to covering the next war?

a. Nothing really changed.
b. Reporters were given greater access to cover combat.
c. Reporters were given greater access to the enemy.
d. Reporters were given less access to cover combat.
e. The president agreed to hold more press conferences.

10. When you look at which story the media emphasized in covering issues, you are examining the _____ of the media.

a. agenda-setting effect
b. news making
c. persuasiveness
d. political socialization
e. whistle blowing

11. Which is an example of how the poor and downtrodden, in addition to the political elites, can use the media?

a. civil rights groups in the 1960s
b. fans following the World Cup
c. NBC coverage of the Olympics
d. sit-coms set in the future
e. students in Moscow watching MTV

12. Which of the following roles describes the media when they dig up facts and reports about corrupt public officials?

a. They are acting as gatekeepers.
b. They are acting as watchdogs.
c. They are creating the template.
d. They are helping voters distinguish among candidates.
e. They are providing views concerning public policy.

13. What appears to be a huge expansion in the amount of political news can often actually be attributed to what?

a. an expansion in the number of elections
b. an expansion in the number of mainstream news organizations
c. an expansion in the number of policy programs
d. an expansion in the number of politicians
e. an expansion in the number of ways the same news is being distributed

14. George W. Bush's "mission accomplished" announcement regarding the Iraq war from the deck of the aircraft carrier USS *Lincoln* was best described as what?

a. a spontaneous decision during his sightseeing tour of New York
b. an attempt to manage public perception by staging an event that conveyed a strong symbolic message
c. an effort at giving a commencement speech
d. an indication of his strong personal identification with the military
e. the result of a reunion with his friends on the West Point faculty

15. How does selective exposure minimize the media's influence on the public?

a. People choose not to listen to candidates who have different opinions from them.
b. People tend to distrust information that they see on television.
c. When people have so many differing opinions, they cancel out each other.
d. When people receive too much information, they cannot process it all.
e. Using selective exposure, people screen out information or opinions with which they disagree.

16. How can agenda setting affect public policy?

a. The public prefers that the media emphasize local issues over national ones.
b. The public tends to assume that the items emphasized by the media will be addressed by politicians.
c. The public tends to distrust media coverage of political topics.
d. The public tends to evaluate programs and policy based on the items emphasized by the media.
e. The public tends to ignore news items emphasized by the media.

17. How have sound bites minimized the depth of news coverage?

a. It is hard for viewers to find coverage similar to their point of view in the mainstream media.
b. Reporters can manipulate stories to support their personal views.
c. The media plays a larger than intended role in the formation of news.
d. Viewers are not able to learn as much about a particular issue just by watching a typical news program.
e. Viewers turn to Twitter and Facebook for news.

18. Why would an administration float a trial balloon?

a. to build political consensus
b. to discredit a member of their political party
c. to gain support for an unpopular policy
d. to gauge the public's reaction to something they are considering doing
e. to welcome a foreign leader to a meeting

Explore Further

WEB SITES

www.journalism.org
The Pew Research Center's Project for Excellence in Journalism regularly posts studies about the mass media at this site.

www.appcpenn.org
The Annenberg Public Policy Center conducts studies that analyze the content of TV coverage of politics.

www.usnpl.com
Listings for newspapers all over the country, including Web links, where available.

www.cmpa.com
The Center for Media and Public Affairs posts its studies of the content of media coverage of politics at this site.

www.livingroomcandidate.org
A great collection of classic and recent political commercials from 1952 through 2012.

FURTHER READING

Davis, Richard. *Typing Political: The Role of Blogs in American Politics.* New York: Oxford University Press, 2009. A comprehensive assessment of the growing role played by political blogs and their relationship with the mainstream media.

Farnsworth, Stephen J., and S. Robert Lichter. *The Nightly News Nightmare: Media Coverage of U.S. Presidential Elections, 1988–2008.* Lanham, MD: Rowman & Littlefield, 2011. An in-depth content analysis of how the news media covered recent presidential elections.

Goldberg, Bernard. *Bias: A CBS Insider Exposes How the Media Distort the News.* Washington, DC: Regnery, 2002. A best-selling account of the network news that argues there is a liberal bias on many issues, especially social policies.

Graber, Doris A. *Mass Media and American Politics,* 8th ed. Washington, DC: Congressional Quarterly Press, 2010. The standard textbook on the subject.

Hindman, Matthew. *The Myth of Digital Democracy.* Princeton, NJ: Princeton University Press, 2009. Hindman presents much evidence to argue that rather than broadening political discourse, the Internet has empowered a small set of elites—some new, but most familiar.

Iyengar, Shanto, and Donald R. Kinder. *News That Matters.* Chicago: University of Chicago Press, 1987. Two political psychologists show how the media can affect the public agenda.

Kingdon, John W. *Agendas, Alternatives, and Public Policy,* 2nd ed. New York: HarperCollins, 1995. The best overall study of the formation of policy agendas.

Ladd, Jonathan M. *Why Americans Hate the Media and How It Matters.* Princeton, NJ: Princeton University Press, 2012. A good analysis of the causes and consequences of declining public confidence in the news media.

Patterson, Thomas E. *Out of Order.* New York: Knopf, 1993. A highly critical and well-documented examination of how the media cover election campaigns.

Prior, Markus. *Post-Broadcast Democracy: How Media Choice Increases Inequality in Political Involvement and Polarizes Elections.* New York: Cambridge University Press, 2007. The best book so far on how the transition from broadcasting to narrowcasting has impacted American politics.

Stroud, Natalie Jomini. *Niche News: The Politics of News Choice.* New York: Oxford University Press, 2011. An examination of how people often deliberately select news sources to match their own views, and what difference such choices make to the workings of American democracy.

West, Darrell M. *Air Wars: Television Advertising in Election Campaigns, 1952–2008.* Washington, DC: Congressional Quarterly Press, 2009. An analysis of how TV campaign ads have evolved over the past four decades and what impact they have had on elections.

8

Political Parties

Politics in Action: How Political Parties Can Make Elections User-Friendly for Voters

I n the 2010 elections, the Republicans gained control of the House of Representatives just two years after Barack Obama's historic election to the presidency. One of the strategies they pursued was to compile a list of proposals that most Republicans supported entitled "A Pledge to America." With unemployment hovering near 10 percent, the Republican proposals concentrated on specific agenda items that they argued would be better suited to revive the nation's economy than the agenda of Obama and the Democrats. Among the items in this list were extending the tax cuts passed under President Bush, providing for new tax deductions for small businesses, and repealing newly enacted health care mandates on business.

"A Pledge to America" was sometimes referred to in the media as the "Contract with America, Part II." In 1994, the original Contract with America was credited by many with helping the Republicans gain control of the House of Representatives after 40 years of Democratic majorities. It outlined 10 bills that the Republicans promised to focus on during the first 100 days of a Republican-controlled House of Representatives. The contract was the brainchild of Newt Gingrich and Richard Armey (both of whom were college professors before being elected to Congress). Gingrich and Armey thought the Republicans needed a stronger message in 1994 than a simple statement of opposition to President Clinton's policies. The contract was an attempt to offer voters a positive program for reshaping American public policy and reforming how Congress works. Without actually knowing much about the individual candidates themselves, voters would know what to expect of the signers of the contract and would be able to hold them accountable for these promises in the future. In this sense, the contract endeavored to make politics user-friendly for the voters.

8.1	8.2	8.3	8.4	8.5	8.6	8.7
Identify the functions that political parties perform in American democracy, p. 246.	Determine the significance of party identification in America today, p. 250.	Describe how political parties are organized in the United States, p. 252.	Evaluate how well political cal parties generally do in carrying out their promises, p. 255.	Differentiate the various party eras in American politics and their limitations, p. 256.	Assess both the impact of third parties on American politics and their limitations, p. 263.	Evaluate the advantages and disadvantages of responsible party government, p. 265.

Political party conventions are where the parties formalize their platforms, presenting their plan for governing the nation to the voters. Here, the Texas delegates to the 2012 Republican National Convention cheer after the national anthem was sung at the beginning of the day's proceedings.

246

8.1

8.2

8.3

8.4

8.5

8.6

8.7

political party

According to Anthony Downs, a "team of men [and women] seeking to control the governing apparatus by gaining office in a duly constituted election."

The Meaning of Party

Identify the functions that political parties perform in American democracy.

lmost all definitions of political parties have one thing in common: parties try to win elections. This is their core function and the key to their definition. By contrast, interest groups do not nominate candidates for office, though they may try to influence elections. For example, no one has ever been elected to Congress as the nominee of the National Rifle Association, though many nominees have received the NRA's endorsement. Thus, Anthony Downs defined a **political party** as a "team of men [and women] seeking to control the governing apparatus by gaining office in a duly constituted election."[2]

The word *team* is the slippery part of this definition. Party teams may not be as well disciplined and single-minded as teams fielded by top football coaches. Individuals on a party's team often run every which way and are difficult to lead. So who are the members of these teams? A widely adopted way of thinking about parties in political science is as "three-headed political giants." The three heads are (1) the party in the electorate, (2) the party as an organization, and (3) the party in government.[3]

The *party in the electorate* is by far the largest component of an American political party. Unlike many European political parties, American parties do not require dues or membership cards to distinguish members from nonmembers. Americans may register as Democrats, Republicans, Libertarians, or whatever, but registration is not legally binding and is easily changed. To be a member of a party, you need only claim to be a member. If you call yourself a Democrat, you are one—even if you never talk to a party official, never work in a campaign, and often vote for Republicans.

The *party as an organization* has a national office, a full-time staff, rules and bylaws, and budgets. In addition to its national office, each party maintains state and local headquarters. The party organization includes precinct leaders, county chairpersons, state chairpersons, state delegates to the national committee, and officials in the party's Washington office. These are the people who keep the party running between elections and make its rules. From the party's national chairperson to its local precinct captain, the party organization pursues electoral victory.

America's Founding Fathers were more concerned with their fear that political parties could be forums for corruption and national divisiveness than they were with the role that parties could play in making politics user-friendly for ordinary voters. Thomas Jefferson spoke for many when he said, "If I could not go to heaven but with a party, I would not go there at all." In his farewell address, George Washington also warned of the dangers of parties.

Today, most observers would agree that political parties have contributed greatly to American democracy. In one of the most frequently—and rightly—quoted observations about American politics, E. E. Schattschneider said that "political parties created democracy . . . and democracy is unthinkable save in terms of the parties."[1] Political scientists and politicians alike believe that a strong party system is desirable.

The strength of the parties has an impact not only on how we are governed but also on what government does. Major expansions or contractions of the scope of government have generally been accomplished through the implementation of one party's platform. Currently, the Democrats and Republicans differ greatly on the issue of the scope of government. Which party controls the presidency and whether the same party also controls the Congress make a big difference.

The *party in government* consists of elected officials who call themselves members of the party. Although presidents, members of Congress, governors, and lesser officeholders may share a common party label, they do not necessarily agree on policy. Presidents and governors may have to wheedle and cajole their own party members into voting for their policies. In the United States, it is not uncommon to put personal principle—or ambition—above loyalty to the party's leaders. These leaders are the main spokespersons for the party, however. Their words and actions personify the party to millions of Americans. If the party is to translate its promises into policy, the job must be done by the party in government.

Political parties are everywhere in American politics—present in the electorate's mind, as an organization, and in government offices—and one of their major tasks is to link the people of the United States to their government and its policies.

☐ Tasks of the Parties

The road from public opinion to public policy is long and winding. Millions of Americans cannot raise their voices in unison. In a large democracy, **linkage institutions** translate inputs from the public into outputs from the policymakers. Linkage institutions sift through all the issues, identify the most pressing concerns, and put these onto the governmental agenda. In other words, linkage institutions help ensure that public preferences are heard loud and clear. In the United States, there are four main linkage institutions: parties, elections, interest groups, and the media.

Kay Lawson writes that "parties are seen, both by the members and by others, as agencies for forging links between citizens and policymakers."[4] Here is a checklist of the tasks that parties perform—or should perform—if they are to serve as effective linkage institutions:

PARTIES PICK CANDIDATES Almost no one above the local level gets elected to a public office without winning a party's endorsement.[5] A party's official endorsement is called a *nomination*; it entitles the nominee to be listed on the general election ballot as that party's candidate for a particular office. Up until the early twentieth century, American parties chose their candidates with little or no input from voters. Progressive reformers led the charge for primary elections, in which citizens would have the power to choose their nominees for office. The innovation of primary elections spread rapidly, transferring the nominating function from the party organization to the party identifiers.

PARTIES RUN CAMPAIGNS Through their national, state, and local organizations, parties coordinate political campaigns. However, television and the Internet have made it easier for candidates to build their own personal campaign organization, and thus take their case directly to the people without the aid of the party organization.

PARTIES GIVE CUES TO VOTERS Just knowing whether a candidate is a Democrat or a Republican provides crucial information to many voters. Voters can reasonably assume that if a candidate is a Democrat, chances are good that he or she favors progressive principles and a broader scope of government. On the other side of the coin, it can be reasonably assumed that a Republican favors conservative principles and a more limited scope of government. A voter therefore need not do extensive research on the individual candidates but rather can rely on the informational shortcut provided by their party affiliations.

PARTIES ARTICULATE POLICIES Each political party advocates specific policy alternatives. For example, the Democratic Party platform has for many years advocated support for a woman's right to an abortion, whereas the Republican Party platform has repeatedly called for restrictions on abortion.

linkage institutions
The channels through which people's concerns become political issues on the government's policy agenda. In the United States, linkage institutions include elections, political parties, interest groups, and the media.

248

8.1

8.2

8.3

8.4

8.5

8.6

8.7

rational-choice theory
A popular theory in political science to explain the actions of voters as well as politicians. It assumes that individuals act in their own best interest, carefully weighing the costs and benefits of possible alternatives.

PARTIES COORDINATE POLICYMAKING When a president commits himself to a major policy goal, the first place he usually looks for support is from members of his own party. In America's fragmented government, parties are essential for coordinating policymaking between the executive and legislative branches.

The importance of these tasks makes it easy to see why most political scientists accept Schattschneider's famous assertion that modern democracy is unthinkable without competition between political parties.

Why It Matters to You

Political Parties

Parties perform many important tasks in American politics. Among the most important are generating symbols of identification and loyalty, mobilizing majorities in the electorate and in government, recruiting political leaders, implementing policies, and fostering stability in government. Hence, it has often been argued that the party system has to work well for the government to work well.

☐ Parties, Voters, and Policy: The Downs Model

The parties compete, at least in theory, as in a marketplace. A party competes for voters' support; its products are its candidates and policies. Anthony Downs has provided a working model of the relationship among citizens, parties, and policy, employing a rational-choice perspective.[6] **Rational-choice theory** "seeks to explain political processes and outcomes as consequences of purposive behavior. Political actors are assumed to have goals and to pursue those goals sensibly and efficiently."[7] Downs argues that (1) voters want to maximize the chance that policies they favor will be adopted by government and that (2) parties want to win office. Thus, in order to win office, the wise party selects policies that are widely favored. If Party A figures out what the voters want more accurately than does Party B, then Party A should be more successful. Governor Chris Christie spoke for many pragmatists in government when he told the Republican National Committee that, "For our ideas to matter we have to win. And if we don't govern all we do is shout to the wind, and so I am going to do anything I need to do to win."[8]

The long history of the American party system has shown that successful parties rarely stray too far from the midpoint of public opinion. In the American electorate, a few voters are extremely liberal and a few extremely conservative, but the majority are in the middle or lean just slightly one way or the other (see the first part of Figure 8.1). This pattern is even more evident if we examine the key swing voters, namely, those who identify themselves as being independent of party affiliation. As you can see in the second part of Figure 8.1, Independents are very much concentrated near the middle of the liberal–conservative spectrum. Thus, if Downs's theory is right, then parties must stay fairly near the center in order to broaden their appeal.

Downs also notes, though, that from a rational-choice perspective, one should expect the parties to significantly differentiate themselves in order to win over loyal adherents, who will participate in party activities and provide a core of regular supporters. Just as Ford tries to offer something different from and better than Toyota in order to build buyer loyalty, so Democrats and Republicans have to forge substantially different identities to build voter loyalty. As you can see in third and fourth parts of Figure 8.1, those who identify with the two parties do indeed have distinct ideological profiles. Democrats lean to the left of center (toward liberalism), and Republicans clearly lean to the right of center (conservatism).

8.1

8.2

8.3

8.4

8.5

8.6

8.7

249

FIGURE 8.1 THE DOWNS MODEL: HOW RATIONAL PARTIES POSITION THEMSELVES NEAR (BUT NOT AT) THE CENTER OF PUBLIC OPINION

The General Social Survey regularly asks a sample of the American population to classify themselves on a 7-point scale from extremely liberal to extremely conservative. As illustrated in the four graphs below, both political parties regularly face the challenge of positioning themselves relatively close to the median voter, in particular to appeal to Independents, while at the same time being responsive to the position of their own base of supporters.

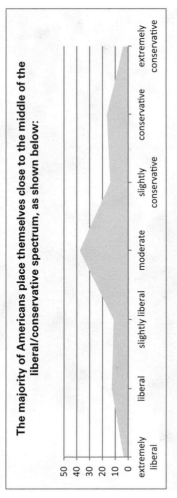

The majority of Americans place themselves close to the middle of the liberal/conservative spectrum, as shown below:

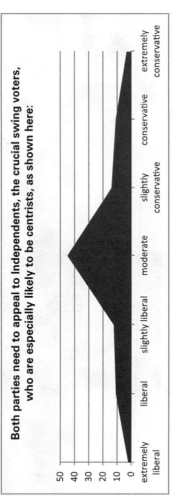

Both parties need to appeal to Independents, the crucial swing voters, who are especially likely to be centrists, as shown here:

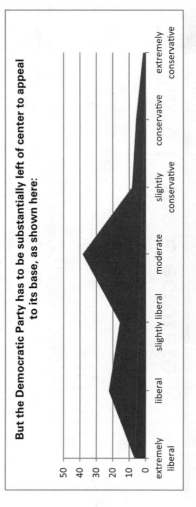

But the Democratic Party has to be substantially left of center to appeal to its base, as shown here:

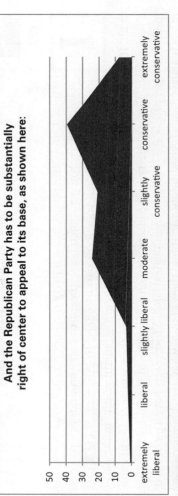

And the Republican Party has to be substantially right of center to appeal to its base, as shown here:

SOURCE: Author's analysis of combined 2008 and 2010 General Social Survey data.

In order to win party nominations, politicians need the support of the median voter within their own party—namely, people who are substantially to the left or right of center. But they need to balance satisfying their own party's core supporters with

8.1

8.2

8.3

8.4

8.5

8.6

8.7

party image
The voter's perception of what the Republicans or Democrats stand for, such as conservatism or liberalism.

party identification
A citizen's self-proclaimed preference for one party or the other.

The Party in the Electorate

8.2   Determine the significance of party identification in America today.

I n most European nations, being a party member means formally joining a political party. You get a membership card to carry around, you pay dues, and you vote to pick your local party leaders. In America, being a party member takes far less work. There is no formal "membership" in the parties at all. If you believe you are a Democrat or a Republican, then you are a Democrat or a Republican. Thus, the party in the electorate consists largely of symbolic images and ideas. For most people the party is a psychological label. Most voters have a **party image** of each party; that is, they know (or think they know) what the Democrats and Republicans stand for. Liberal or conservative, pro-labor or pro-business, pro-choice or pro-life—these are some of the elements of each party's images.

Party images help shape people's **party identification**, the self-proclaimed preference for one party or the other. Because many people routinely vote for the party they identify with (all else being equal), even a shift of a few percentage points

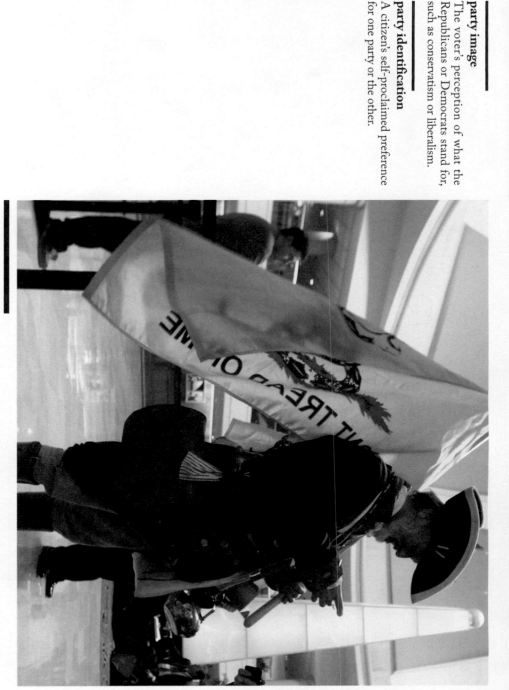

Political parties have to cater to their most enthusiastic and active supporters—liberals for the Democrats and conservatives for the Republicans. Tea Party activists, who advocate a strict adherence to the U.S. Constitution, have been quite visible among conservatives in recent years. Here, a member of the Tea Party dresses as a eighteenth-century patriot at the annual Conservative Political Action Conference.

not moving too far away from the center of national opinion, and in particular from Independent swing voters.

in the distribution of party identification is important. Since 1952, the American National Election Study surveys have asked a sample of citizens, "Generally speaking, do you usually think of yourself as a Republican, a Democrat, or an Independent?" Repeatedly asking this question permits political scientists to trace party identification over time (see Figure 8.2). In recent presidential elections, two clear patterns have been evident. First, in contrast to the 1952–1980 period when Democrats greatly outnumbered Republicans, the Democratic Party's edge in terms of identifiers in the electorate has lately been quite modest. In 1964, there were more than twice as many Democrats as Republicans, whereas in 2012 Republicans trailed Democrats by just 9 percentage points. Second, in most recent elections the most frequent response to the party identification question has been the Independent option. In 2012, 44 percent of the population called themselves Independents. Over the years, surveys have repeatedly shown that the younger one is, the more likely he or she is to be a political independent; in 2012, 52 percent of respondents under the age of 30 were independents (see "Young People and Politics: The Parties Face an Independent Youth").

Voters who call themselves Independents are the most likely to engage in the practice of **ticket splitting**—voting with one party for one office and the other party for another office. Independents overwhelmingly agree that they vote for the person, not the party. And in practice they sometimes do just that, voting for some Democrats and some Republicans. The result of many voters being open to splitting their tickets is that even when one party has a big edge in a state, the other party always has a decent shot at winning at least some important offices. In other words, despite media labels of red and blue states, the practice of ticket splitting means that no state is ever completely safe for a given party. Thus, Massachusetts, Maryland, and Illinois lean heavily toward the Democrats in national elections, but as of 2015 all the governors of these states were Republicans. On the other side of the coin, Democrats were serving as governors in heavily Republican states such as West Virginia and Montana.

ticket splitting
Voting with one party for one office and with another party for other offices.

FIGURE 8.2 PARTY IDENTIFICATION IN THE UNITED STATES, 1952–2012[a]

Political analysts and scholars carefully monitor changes in the distribution of party identification. Below, you can see the percentage of the population that has identified itself as Democrats, Independents, and Republicans during each presidential election year from 1952 to 2012.

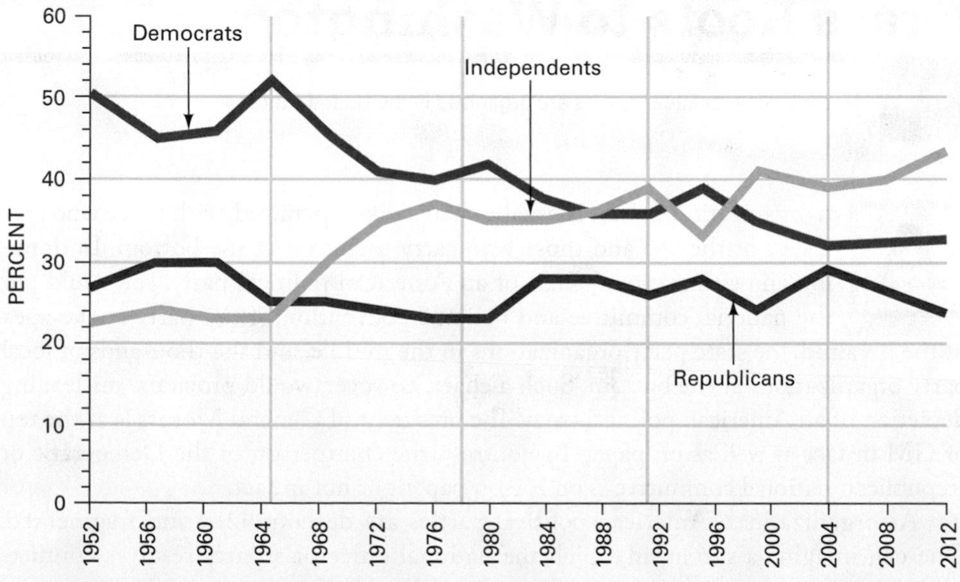

[a]In percentage of people; the small percentage who identify with a minor party or who cannot answer the question are excluded.

SOURCE: American National Election Studies, 1952–2012.

Young People & Politics

The Parties Face an Independent Youth

Younger people have always had a tendency to be more independent of the major political parties than older people. But this has rarely been as evident in survey data as it is now. As you can see from the 2008 national survey data displayed here, 54 percent of people between the ages of 18 and 24 said they were political independents. In contrast, only 31 percent of people over 65 called themselves Independents. Data over time indicate that as people get older, they become more likely to identify with one of the major parties. But whether this will be true for the current generation of youth remains to be seen.

Age	Democrat	Independent	Republican
18–24	29	54	17
25–34	30	49	21
35–44	32	40	28
45–54	35	33	33
55–64	37	38	25
65+	36	31	33

SOURCE: Authors' analysis of the 2008 American National Election Study.

CRITICAL THINKING QUESTIONS

1. Do you think that as the current generation of young people ages they will become more likely to identify with the major political parties?

2. Because younger people are so likely to be independent, does this mean that many young voters are particularly open to persuasion during campaigns? If so, why don't the Democrats and Republicans pay special attention to getting them on their side?

8.3

Describe how political parties are organized in the United States.

The Party Organizations: From the Grass Roots to Washington

An organizational chart is usually shaped like a pyramid, with those who give orders at the top and those who carry them out at the bottom. In drawing an organizational chart of an American political party, you could put the national committee and national convention of the party at the apex of the pyramid, the state party organizations in the middle, and the thousands of local party organizations at the bottom. Such a chart, however, would provide a misleading depiction of an American political party. The president of General Motors is at the top of GM in fact as well as on paper. By contrast, the chairperson of the Democratic or Republican national committee is on top on paper but not in fact.

As organizations, American political parties are decentralized and fragmented. One can imagine a system in which the national office of a party resolves conflicts among its state and local branches, determines the party's position on the issues, and then passes orders down through the hierarchy. One can even imagine a system in which the party leaders have the power to enforce their decisions by offering greater influence and resources to officeholders who follow the party line and by punishing—even expelling—those who do not. Many European parties work just that way, but in America the formal party organizations have little such power. Candidates in the United States can get elected on their own. They do not need the help of the party most of the time, and hence the party organization is relegated to a comparatively limited role.

Local Parties

The urban political party was once the main political party organization in America. From the late nineteenth century through the New Deal of the 1930s, scores of cities were dominated by **party machines**. A machine is a kind of party organization, very different from the typical fragmented and disorganized political party in America today. It can be defined as a party organization that depends on rewarding its members in some material fashion.

Patronage is one of the key inducements used by party machines. A patronage job is one that is awarded for political reasons rather than for merit or competence alone. In the late nineteenth century, political parties routinely sold some patronage jobs to the highest bidder. Party leaders made no secret of their corruption, openly selling government positions to raise money for the party. Some of this money was used to buy votes, but a good deal went to line the pockets of the politicians themselves. The most notable case was that of New York City's Democratic leader William Tweed, widely known as "Boss Tweed," whose ring reportedly made between $40 million and $200 million from tax receipts, payoffs, and kickbacks.

At one time, urban machines in Albany, Chicago, Philadelphia, Kansas City, and elsewhere depended heavily on ethnic group support. Some of the most fabled machine leaders were Irish politicians, including New York's George Washington Plunkett, Boston's James Michael Curley, and Chicago's Richard J. Daley. Daley's Chicago machine was the last survivor, steamrolling its opposition amid charges of racism and corruption. Even today there are remnants of Daley's machine in Chicago. Machine politics in Chicago survived through its ability to limit the scope of reform legislation. A large proportion of city jobs were classified as "temporary" even though they had been held by the same person for decades, and these positions were exempted from the merit system of hiring. At its height, the Democratic political machine in Chicago dispensed 40,000 patronage jobs, the recipients of which were expected to deliver at least 10 votes each on Election Day and to kick back 5 percent of their salary in the form of a donation to the local Democratic Party.[9]

Urban party organizations are also no longer very active as a rule. Progressive reforms that placed jobs under the merit system rather than at the machine's discretion weakened the machines' power. Regulations concerning fair bidding on government contracts also took away much of their ability to reward the party faithful. As ethnic integration occurred in big cities, the group loyalties that the machines often relied on no longer seemed very relevant to many people.

Partly filling in the void created by the decline of the inner-city machines has been a revitalization of party organization at the county level—particularly in affluent suburbs. These county organizations distribute yard signs and campaign literature, register voters, get out the vote on Election Day, and help state and local candidates any way they can. Traditionally, local organizations relied on personal knowledge of individuals in the neighborhood who could be persuaded to support the party. Today, these organizations have access to computerized lists with all sorts of details about registered voters that they use to try to tailor their appeals to each individual.

A 2008 survey of county party leaders by Melody Crowder-Meyer found that county parties play an important role in many elections, especially lower profile elections such as those for county commissioner, sheriff, mayor, and school board members. She

party machines
A type of political party organization that relies heavily on material inducements, such as patronage, to win votes and to govern.

patronage
One of the key inducements used by party machines. A patronage job, promotion, or contract is one that is given for political reasons rather than for merit or competence alone.

Mayor Richard J. Daley ruled the city of Chicago from 1955 until his death in 1976. His Cook County Democratic Party organization was highly organized at the precinct level. Members of the organization kept people in their neighborhoods happy by providing for their local needs, such as street maintenance, new stoplights, no-parking zones, and so on, and the people reciprocated on Election Day by supporting the organization's candidates.

254

8.1
8.2
8.3
8.4
8.5
8.6
8.7

closed primaries
Elections to select party nominees in which only people who have registered in advance with the party can vote for that party's candidates, thus encouraging greater party loyalty.

open primaries
Elections to select party nominees in which voters can decide on Election Day whether they want to participate in the Democratic or Republican contests.

☐ The 50 State Party Systems

American national parties are a loose aggregation of state parties, which are themselves a fluid association of individuals, groups, and local organizations. There are 50 state party systems, and no two are exactly alike. In a few states, the parties are well organized, have sizable staffs, and spend a lot of money. Pennsylvania is one such state. In other states, such as California, party organizations are weak and underfunded.

The states are allowed wide discretion in the regulation of party activities, and how they choose to organize elections substantially influences the strength of the parties. In particular, the choice between holding open versus closed primaries is a crucial one, as you can read about in "You Are the Policymaker: Should Political Parties Choose Their Nominees in Open or Closed Primaries?" When it comes to the general election, some states promote voting according to party by listing the candidates of each party down a single column, whereas others place the names in

concludes that "county parties have the potential to significantly affect who is recruited to run for office, who receives party support, who gains assistance from community and interest groups, and who is eventually elected to public office."[10]

You Are the Policymaker

Should Political Parties Choose Their Nominees in Open or Closed Primaries?

Some states restrict who can participate in party nomination contests far more than others. In **closed primaries** only people who have registered in advance with a party can vote in its primary. In contrast, **open primaries** allow voters to decide on Election Day whether they want to participate in the Democratic or Republican contests. Each state legislature is faced with making the choice between an open or closed primary, and the pros and cons of these two basic options are often hotly debated.

Closed primaries are generally favored by the party organizations themselves because they encourage voters to officially declare a partisan preference when they register to vote. By requiring voters to sign up in advance in order to participate in its primary, a party can be reasonably assured that most people who participate in their nomination decisions will be reasonably committed to its platform. In other words, closed primaries favor ideological purity and help to keep the policy distinctions between Democrats and Republicans clear. A further advantage for the party organizations is that a closed primary system requires the state's election authority to maintain a record of the party registration of each voter. It is, of course, a secret who you vote for, but anything you put down on your voter registration form is public information. Hence, a closed primary provides each party with invaluable information identifying voters who consider themselves to be party members. Imagine running a business and having the government collect information for you regarding who likes your product. It's no

wonder that if the decision were left up to the leaders of the party organizations most would choose a closed primary.

Despite these advantages, the trend among the states in recent years has been toward more open primaries. The main advantage of open primaries is that they allow for more voters to participate in party nomination decisions. Because independents can vote in either party's primary and partisans can readily switch sides, the two major parties are faced with the task of competing for voter support in the primary round as well as the general election. In particular, young people, whose independent streak often leaves them on the sidelines in closed primaries, can be brought into the parties' fold in an open primary. For many policymakers, the chance to widen participation in one's own party via an open primary outweighs the advantage of limiting participation to loyal party members in a closed primary. However, even advocates of open primaries acknowledge that they come with some risk for mischief. There is always a possibility that the partisans of one side will "raid" the other party's primary in order to give a boost to its least viable candidate. This would be akin to letting UCLA students participate in the choice of the quarterback for USC's football team. Though raiding is always a theoretical possibility, scholars have found that when voters cast a ballot in the other party's primary, it is usually for candidates whom they genuinely support.

What do you think? Would you choose an open or closed primary?

random order. About a third of the states currently have a provision on their ballots that enables a voter to cast a vote for all of one party's candidates with a single act. This option clearly encourages straight-ticket voting and makes the support of the party organization more important to candidates in these states.

Organizationally, state parties are on the upswing throughout the country. In the 1960s, half the state party organizations did not even maintain a permanent headquarters; when the state party elected a new chairperson, the party organization simply shifted its office to his or her hometown.[11] In contrast, almost all state parties today have a permanent physical headquarters, typically in the capital city or the largest city. State party budgets have also increased greatly, as parties have acquired professional staffs and high-tech equipment. Nevertheless, as John Bibby points out, they mostly serve to supplement the candidates' own personal campaign organizations; thus, state party organizations rarely manage campaigns. The job of the state party, writes Bibby, is merely "to provide technical services" within the context of a candidate-centered campaign.[12]

☐ The National Party Organizations

The supreme power within each of the parties is its **national convention**. The convention meets every four years, and its main task is to write the party's platform and then nominate its candidates for president and vice president. Keeping the party operating between conventions is the job of the **national committee**, composed of representatives from the states and territories. Typically, each state has a national committeeman and a national committeewoman as delegates to the party's national committee. The Democratic committee also includes assorted governors, members of Congress, and other party officials.

Day-to-day activities of the national party are the responsibility of the party's **national chairperson**. The national party chairperson hires the staff, raises the money, pays the bills, and attends to the daily duties of the party. When asked, at a joint appearance, what their biggest organizational challenge was, the chairs of the Democratic and Republican parties both promptly responded "money."[13] Together, the Democratic and Republican national committees spent $723 million in 2012, thereby plunging a tremendous amount of funds into the presidential campaign.

The chairperson of the party that controls the White House is normally selected by the president himself (subject to routine ratification by the national committee), whereas the contest for chair of the party out of power is often a hotly fought battle. In the early 1970s, two of the people who served for a while as chair of the Republican Party at the request of President Nixon were Bob Dole and George H. W. Bush, both of whom used this position as a means of political advancement. Other notables to have served as chair of their party's national committee include former governors Ed Rendell (D-PA), Howard Dean (D-VT), Haley Barbour (R-MS), and Tim Kaine (D-VA).

national convention
The meeting of party delegates every four years to choose a presidential ticket and write the party's platform.

national committee
One of the institutions that keeps the party operating between conventions. The national committee is composed of representatives from the states and territories.

national chairperson
The person responsible for the day-to-day activities of the party.

The Party in Government: Promises and Policy

8.4 Evaluate how well political parties generally do in carrying out their promises.

W hich party controls each of America's many elected offices matters because both parties and the elected officials who represent them usually try to turn campaign promises into action. As a result, the party that has control over the most government offices will have the most influence in determining who gets what, where, when, and how.

8.1

8.2

8.3

8.4

8.5

8.6

8.7

coalition
A group of individuals with a common interest on which every political party depends.

Voters are attracted to a party in government by its performance and policies. What a party has done in office—and what it promises to do—greatly influences it. Sometimes voters suspect that political promises are made to be broken. To be sure, there are notable instances in which politicians have turned—sometimes 180 degrees—from their policy promises. Lyndon Johnson repeatedly promised in the 1964 presidential campaign that he would not "send American boys to do an Asian boy's job" and involve the United States in the Vietnam War, but he did. In the 1980 campaign, Ronald Reagan asserted that he would balance the budget by 1984, yet his administration quickly ran up the largest deficit in American history. Throughout the 1988 campaign George H. W. Bush proclaimed, "Read my lips—no new taxes," but he reluctantly changed course two years later when pressured on the issue by the Democratic majority in Congress. Barack Obama promised to cut income tax rates for the middle class and raise them for the wealthiest Americans, but he backed off these promises after he was elected in 2008.

It is all too easy to forget how often parties and presidents do exactly what they say they will do. For every broken promise, many more are kept. Ronald Reagan promised to step up defense spending and cut back on social welfare expenditures, and his administration quickly delivered on these pledges. Bill Clinton promised to support bills providing for family leave, easing voting registration procedures, and tightening gun control that had been vetoed by his predecessor. He lobbied hard to get these measures through Congress again and proudly signed them into law once they arrived on his desk. George W. Bush promised a major tax cut for every taxpayer in America, and he delivered just that in 2001. Barack Obama pledged to get American troops out of Iraq and accomplished this feat by the end of 2011. In sum, the impression that politicians and parties never produce policy out of promises is off the mark.

Indeed, two projects that have monitored President Obama's actions on his campaign promises found far more promises that were followed through on than broken. The *National Journal's* "Promise Audit" (http://promises.nationaljournal.com/) identified about 200 of Obama's most important promises and found at least some progress made on keeping 84 percent of them. Similarly, PolitiFact, a Pulitzer Prize–winning feature of the *St. Petersburg Times* (http://www.politifact.com/truth-o-meter/promises/) reported at least some progress on 76 percent of a broader selection of over 500 promises made by Obama. In both studies, unfulfilled promises usually fell in the category of proposals that had been shelved for one reason or other; relatively few promises were broken outright.

If parties generally do what they say they will, then the party platforms adopted at the national conventions represent blueprints, however vague, for action. In their study of party platforms and voter attitudes over three decades, Elizabeth Simas and Kevin Evans find that "voters are in fact picking up on the parties' objective policy positions."[14] Consider what the two major parties promised the voters in their 2012 platforms (see Table 8.1). There is little doubt that the choice between Democratic and Republican policies in 2012 was clear on many important issues facing the country. When voters selected Barack Obama over Mitt Romney, the country was poised to move in a direction that was significantly different than had the election gone the other way.

Party Eras in American History

Differentiate the various party eras in American history.

hile studying political parties, remember the following: *America is a two-party system and always has been.* Of course, there are many minor parties around—Libertarians, Socialists, Reform, Greens—but they rarely have a chance of winning a major office. In contrast, most

TABLE 8.1 PARTY PLATFORMS, 2012

Although few people actually read party platforms, they are one of the best-written sources for what the parties believe in. A brief summary of some of the contrasting positions in the Democratic and Republican platforms of 2012 illustrates major differences in beliefs between the two parties.

Republicans

The War in Afghanistan

Future decisions by a Republican President will never subordinate military necessity to domestic politics or an artificial timetable. … We cannot expect others to remain resolute unless we show the same determination ourselves.

Immigration

We oppose any form of amnesty for those who, by intentionally violating the law, disadvantage those who have obeyed it. … We will create humane procedures to encourage illegal aliens to return home voluntarily, while enforcing the law against those who overstay their visas.

Abortion

We assert the sanctity of human life and affirm that the unborn child has a fundamental individual right to life which cannot be infringed. We support a human life amendment to the Constitution.

Same-Sex Marriage

We reaffirm our support for a Constitutional amendment defining marriage as the union of one man and one woman.

Health Care

Obamacare is falling by the weight of its own confusing, unworkable, budget-busting, and conflicting provisions. … Republicans are committed to its repeal. … Then the American people, through the free market, can advance affordable and responsible health care reform.

Taxes

Taxes, by their very nature, reduce a citizen's freedom. … We propose to extend the 2001 and 2003 tax relief packages—commonly known as the Bush tax cuts.

Rising college costs

New systems of learning are needed to compete with traditional four-year colleges: expanded community colleges and technical institutions, private colleges, online universities, life-long learning, and work-based training schools. New models for acquiring advanced skills will be ever more important in the rapidly changing economy.

Campaign finance

We support repeal of the remaining sections of McCain-Feingold, support either raising or repealing contribution limits, and oppose passage of the DISLCOSE Act or any similar legislation designed to vitiate the Supreme Court's recent decisions protecting political speech.

Democrats

The War in Afghanistan

We have begun the process of bringing our troops home from Afghanistan, including removing 33,000 by September 2012. And, with the support of our allies, the President has outlined a plan to end the war in Afghanistan in 2014.

Immigration

The country urgently needs comprehensive immigration reform that brings undocumented immigrants out of the shadows and requires them to get right with the law, learn English, and pay taxes in order to get on a path to earn citizenship.

Abortion

The Democratic Party strongly and unequivocally supports *Roe v. Wade* and a woman's right to decisions regarding her pregnancy, including a safe and legal abortion, regardless of ability to pay.

Same-Sex Marriage

We support marriage equality and support the movement to secure equal treatment under law for same-sex couples.

Health Care

We believe that accessible, affordable, high quality health care is part of the American promise… We refuse to go back to the days when health insurance companies had unchecked power to cancel your health policy, deny you coverage, or charge women more than men.

Taxes

We support allowing the Bush tax cuts for wealthiest to expire and closing loopholes and deductions for the largest corporations and the highest-earning taxpayers.

Rising college costs

President Obama has pledged to encourage colleges to keep their costs down by reducing federal aid for those that do not, investing in colleges that keep tuition affordable and provide good value, doubling the number of work-study jobs available to students, and continuing to ensure that students have access to federal loans at reasonable rates.

Campaign finance

We support campaign finance reform, by constitutional amendment if necessary. We support legislation to close loopholes and require greater disclosure of campaign spending. … We support requiring groups trying to influence elections to reveal their donors.

SOURCE: Excerpts from party platforms as posted on the Web sites of each organization.

democratic nations have more than two parties represented in their national legislature. Throughout American history, one party has been the dominant majority party for long periods of time. A majority of voters identify with the party in power; thus, this party tends to win a majority of the elections. Political scientists call these periods **party eras.**

party eras

Historical periods in which a majority of voters cling to the party in power, which tends to win a majority of the elections.

critical election
An electoral "earthquake," where new issues emerge, new coalitions replace old ones, and the majority party is often displaced by the minority party. Critical election periods are sometimes marked by a national crisis and may require more than one election to bring about a new party era.

party realignment
The displacement of the majority party by the minority party, usually during a critical election period.

Punctuating each party era is a **critical election**.[15] A critical election is an electoral earthquake: fissures appear in each party's coalition, which begins to fracture; new issues appear, dividing the electorate. Each party forms a new coalition—one that endures for years. A critical election period may require more than one election before change is apparent, but in the end, the party system will be transformed.

This process is called **party realignment**—a rare event in American political life that is akin to a political revolution. Realignments are typically associated with a major crisis or trauma in the nation's history. One of the major realignments, when the Republican Party emerged, was connected to the Civil War. Another was linked to the Great Depression of the 1930s, when the majority Republicans were displaced by the Democrats. The following sections look more closely at the various party eras in American history.

1796–1824: The First Party System

In the *Federalist Papers*, James Madison warned strongly against the dangers of "factions," or parties. But Alexander Hamilton, one of the coauthors of the *Federalist Papers*, did as much as anyone to inaugurate our party system.[16] Hamilton was the nation's first secretary of the treasury, for which service his picture appears on today's $10 bill. To garner congressional support for his pet policies, particularly a national bank, he needed votes. From this politicking and coalition building came the rudiments of the Federalist Party, America's first political party. The Federalists were also America's shortest-lived major party. After Federalist candidate John Adams was defeated in his reelection bid in 1800, the party quickly faded. The Federalists were poorly organized, and by 1820 they no longer bothered to offer up a candidate for president. In this early period of American history, most party leaders did not regard themselves as professional politicians. Those who lost often withdrew completely from the political arena. The ideas of a loyal opposition and rotation of power in government had not yet taken hold.[17] Each party wanted to destroy the other party, not just defeat it—and such was the fate of the Federalists.

The party that crushed the Federalists was led by Virginians Jefferson, Madison, and Monroe, each of whom was elected president for two terms in succession. They were known as the Democratic-Republicans, or sometimes as the Jeffersonians. The Democratic-Republican Party derived its coalition from agrarian interests rather than from the growing number of capitalists who supported the Federalists. This made the party particularly popular in the largely rural South. As the Federalists disappeared, however, the old Jeffersonian coalition was torn apart by factionalism as it tried to be all things to all people.

1828–1856: Jackson and the Democrats Versus the Whigs

More than anyone else, General Andrew Jackson founded the modern American political party. In the election of 1828, he forged a new coalition that included Westerners as well as Southerners, new immigrants as well as settled Americans. Like most successful politicians of his day, Jackson was initially a Democratic-Republican, but soon after his ascension to the presidency, his party became known as simply the Democratic Party, which continues to this day. The "Democratic" label was particularly appropriate for Jackson's supporters because their cause was to broaden political opportunity by eliminating many vestiges of elitism and mobilizing the masses.

Whereas Jackson was the charismatic leader, the Democrats' behind-the-scenes architect was Martin Van Buren, who succeeded Jackson as president. Van Buren's one term in office was relatively undistinguished, but his view of party competition left a lasting mark. He "sought to make Democrats see that their only hope for maintaining the purity of their own principles was to admit the existence of an opposing party."[18] A realist, Van Buren argued that a party could not aspire to pleasing all the people all the time. He argued that a governing party needed a loyal opposition to represent parts of society that it could not. This opposition was provided by the Whigs. The Whig Party included such notable statesmen as Henry Clay and Daniel Webster, but it was able to win the presidency only when it nominated military heroes such as William Henry Harrison (1840) and Zachary Taylor (1848). The Whigs had two distinct wings—Northern industrialists and Southern planters—who were brought together more by the Democratic policies they opposed than by the issues on which they agreed.

1860–1928: The Two Republican Eras

In the 1850s, the issue of slavery dominated American politics and split both the Whigs and the Democrats. Slavery, said Senator Charles Sumner, an ardent abolitionist, "is the only subject within the field of national politics which excites any real interest." In *Dred Scott v. Sandford*, the Supreme Court of 1857 held that slaves could not be citizens and that former slaves could not be protected by the Constitution. This decision further sharpened the divisions in public opinion, making civil war increasingly likely.

The Republicans rose in the late 1850s as the antislavery party. Folding in the remnants of several minor parties, in 1860 the Republicans forged a coalition strong enough to elect Abraham Lincoln president and to ignite the Civil War. The "War Between the States" was one of those political earthquakes that realigned the parties. After the war, the Republican Party thrived for more than 60 years. The Democrats controlled the South, though, and the Republican label remained a dirty word in the old Confederacy.

A second Republican era was initiated with the watershed election of 1896, perhaps the bitterest battle in American electoral history. The Democrats nominated William Jennings Bryan, populist proponent of "free silver" (linking money with silver, which was more plentiful than gold, and thus devaluing money to help debtors). The Republican Party made clear its positions in favor of the gold standard, industrialization, the banks, high tariffs, and the industrial working classes as well as its positions against the "radical" Western farmers and "silverites." "Bryan and his program were greeted by the country's conservatives with something akin to terror." The *New York Tribune* howled that Bryan's Democrats were "in league with the Devil." On the other side, novelist Frank Baum lampooned the Republicans in his classic novel *The Wizard of Oz*. Dorothy follows the yellow brick road (symbolizing the gold standard) to the Emerald City (representing Washington), only to find that the Wizard (whose figure resembles McKinley) is powerless. But by clicking on her *silver* slippers (the color was changed to ruby for Technicolor effect in the movie), she finds that she can return home.

Political scientists call the 1896 election a realigning one because it shifted the party coalitions and entrenched the Republicans for another generation. For the next three decades the Republicans continued as the nation's majority party, until the stock market crashed in 1929. The ensuing Great Depression brought about another fissure in the crust of the American party system.

1932–1964: The New Deal Coalition

President Herbert Hoover's handling of the Depression turned out to be disastrous for the Republicans. He solemnly pronounced that economic depression could not be cured by legislative action. Americans, however, obviously disagreed and voted for Franklin D. Roosevelt, who promised the country a *New Deal*. In his first 100 days as president, Roosevelt prodded Congress into passing scores of anti-Depression measures. Party realignment began in earnest after the Roosevelt administration got the country moving again. First-time voters flocked to the polls, pumping new blood into the Democratic ranks and providing much of the margin for Roosevelt's four presidential victories. Immigrant groups in Boston and other cities had been initially attracted to the Democrats by the 1928 campaign of Al Smith, the first Catholic to be nominated by a major party for the presidency. Roosevelt reinforced the partisanship of these groups, and the Democrats forged the **New Deal coalition**.

CARRY ON with ROOSEVELT

Franklin Roosevelt reshaped the Democratic Party, bringing together a diverse array of groups that had long been marginalized in American political life. Many of the key features of the Democratic Party today, such as support from labor unions, can be traced to the FDR era.

New Deal coalition
A coalition forged by the Democrats, who dominated American politics from the 1930s to the 1960s. Its basic elements were the urban working class, ethnic groups, Catholics and Jews, the poor, Southerners, African Americans, and intellectuals.

The basic elements of the New Deal coalition were the following:

- *Urban dwellers.* Big cities such as Chicago and Philadelphia were staunchly Republican before the New Deal realignment; afterward, they were Democratic bastions.

- *Labor unions.* FDR became the first president to support unions enthusiastically, and they returned the favor.

- *Catholics and Jews.* During and after the Roosevelt period, Catholics and Jews were strongly Democratic.

- *The poor.* Although the poor had low turnout rates, their votes went overwhelmingly to the party of Roosevelt and his successors.

- *Southerners.* Ever since pre–Civil War days, white Southerners had been Democratic loyalists. This alignment continued unabated during the New Deal. For example, Mississippi voted over 90 percent Democratic in each of FDR's four presidential election victories.

- *African Americans.* The Republicans freed the slaves, but under FDR the Democrats attracted the majority of African Americans.

As you can see in Figure 8.3, many of the same groups that supported FDR's New Deal continue to be part of the Democratic Party's coalition today.

The New Deal coalition made the Democratic Party the clear majority party for decades. Harry S Truman, who succeeded Roosevelt in 1945, promised a Fair Deal. World War II hero and Republican Dwight D. Eisenhower broke the Democrats'

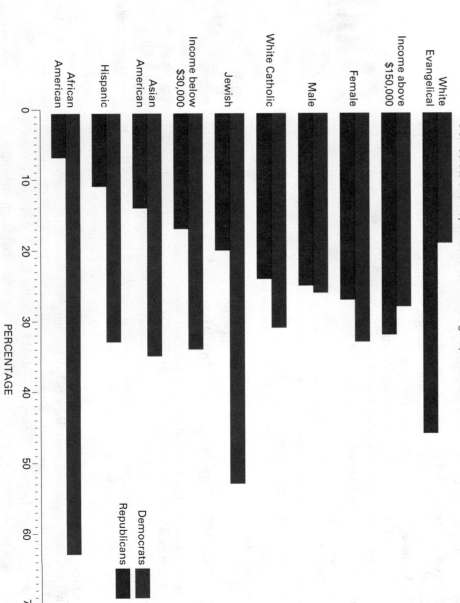

FIGURE 8.3 PARTY COALITIONS TODAY

The two parties continue to draw support from very different social groups, many of which have existed since the New Deal era. This figure shows the percentage identifying as Democrats and Republicans for various groups in 2012.

SOURCE: Authors' analysis of two Pew Research Center polls conducted in January 2012.

grip on power by being elected president twice during the 1950s, but the Democrats regained the presidency in 1960 with the election of John F. Kennedy. His New Frontier was in the New Deal tradition, with platforms and policies designed to help labor, the working classes, and minorities. Lyndon B. Johnson became president after Kennedy's assassination and was overwhelmingly elected to a term of his own in 1964. His Great Society programs vastly increased the scope of government in America, and his War on Poverty was reminiscent of Roosevelt's activism in dealing with the Depression. Johnson's Vietnam War policies, however, tore the Democratic Party apart in 1968, leaving the door to the presidency wide open for Republican candidate Richard M. Nixon.

□ 1968–Present: Southern Realignment and the Era of Divided Party Government

When Richard Nixon was first elected to the presidency in 1968, he formulated what became widely known as his "Southern strategy." Emphasizing his support for states' rights, law and order, and a strong military posture, Nixon hoped to win over Southern conservatives to the Republican Party, thereby breaking the Democratic Party's long dominance in the former Confederacy. Party realignment in the South did not happen as quickly as Nixon would have liked, but it has taken place gradually over the four decades since 1968.[22] As you can see in Figure 8.4, whereas the Democrats held the vast majority of the South's Senate seats in the late 1960s and the 1970s, ever since the Congress of 1995–1996 the Republicans have been the dominant party in the South. This trend is evident in representation in the House of Representatives as well. In 1969, the Republicans were outnumbered 24 to 77 by the Democrats in the South. By 2015, the balance of Southern seats in the House had changed dramatically, with the Republicans holding 101 seats to just 37 for the Democrats.

FIGURE 8.4 REALIGNMENT IN THE SOUTH

One of the most significant political changes over the past four decades has been the partisan realignment in the Southern states that has transformed this region from a solid Democratic base of support to a solid Republican area.

Without strong Southern support for the Republicans in recent elections, it is doubtful that the GOP would have been able to attain majority party status in the Congress for the majority of the period from 1995 to 2016. The crucial role of the South in Republican politics has lately been reflected in the makeup of the GOP congressional leadership. Mitch McConnell of Kentucky and Trent Lott of Mississippi have served as the Republicans' leader in the Senate. Georgia's Newt Gingrich served as Speaker of the House for three terms, and Louisiana's Stephen Scalise currently holds the position of House Majority Whip.

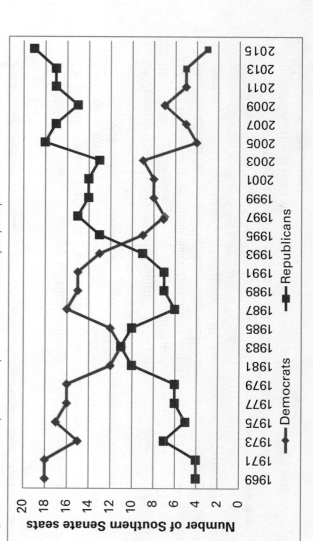

Number of Southern Senate seats

Democrats ◆   Republicans ■

1969 1971 1973 1975 1977 1979 1981 1983 1985 1987 1989 1991 1993 1995 1997 1999 2001 2003 2005 2007 2009 2011 2013 2015

party dealignment
The gradual disengagement of people from the parties, as seen in part by having his party in control of both houses of Congress. Prior to 1968, most newly shrinking party identification.

Another noteworthy aspect of Nixon's 1968 election was that for the first time in the twentieth century, a newly elected president moved into the White House without having his party in control of both houses of Congress. Prior to 1968, most newly elected presidents had swept a wave of their fellow partisans into office with them. For example, the Democrats gained 62 seats in the House when Woodrow Wilson was elected in 1912 and 97 when FDR was elected in 1932. Nixon's inability to bring in congressional majorities with him was not to be an exception, however, but rather the beginning of a new pattern—repeated in the presidential elections won by Ronald Reagan and George Bush. For a time, it seemed that the normal state of affairs in Washington was for American government to be divided with a Republican president and a Democratic Congress.

Bill Clinton's election in 1992 briefly restored united party government until the Republicans won both houses of Congress in the 1994 elections. For the remaining six years of his presidency, Clinton was forced to battle with Republican majorities in both houses who generally opposed his most cherished policy priorities. During the eight years of George W. Bush's presidency, the Republicans maintained control of the Congress for just the middle four years, from 2003 through 2006. Barack Obama enjoyed Democratic majorities in Congress during his first two years as president, but divided government returned to Washington when the Republicans gained control of the House in 2010. After the Republicans' gains in the 2010 elections, their leaders were optimistic that they were at last on the verge of a new era of Republican dominance. On the other side, Democratic leaders were hopeful that voters would not like the actions of the new Republican House majority and would restore unified Democratic control of the government. In the end, the ambitions of both sides were frustrated as voters opted to continue divided government by reelecting President Obama along with a Republican majority in the House.

Why It Matters to You
Divided Party Government

When one party controls the White House and the other party controls one or both houses of Congress, divided party government exists. Given that one party can check the other's agenda, it is virtually impossible for a party to say what it is going to do and then actually put these policies into effect. This situation is bad if you want clear lines of accountability on policy, but it is good if you prefer that the two parties be forced to work out compromises.

With only about 60 percent of the electorate currently identifying with the Democrats or Republicans, it may well be difficult for either one to gain a strong enough foothold to maintain simultaneous control of both ends of Pennsylvania Avenue for very long. All told, both houses of Congress and the presidency have been simultaneously controlled by the same party for just 12 of the 48 years from 1969 to 2016. The regularity with which partisan control of the presidency and Congress has been divided during this period is unprecedented in American political history. The recent pattern of divided government has caused many political scientists to believe that the party system has dealigned rather than realigned. Whereas realignment involves people changing from one party to another, **party dealignment** means that many people are gradually moving away from both parties. When your car is realigned, it is adjusted in one direction or another to improve its steering. Imagine if your car would be useless and remove the steering mechanism instead of adjusting it—your car would be useless and ineffective. This is what many scholars fear has been happening to the parties, hence the federal government.

Third Parties: Their Impact on American Politics

third parties

Electoral contenders other than the two major parties. American third parties are not unusual, but they rarely win elections.

8.6 Assess both the impact of third parties on American politics and their limitations.

T he story of American party struggle is primarily the story of two major parties, but **third parties** are a regular feature of American politics and occasionally attract the public's attention. Third parties in the United States come in three basic varieties:

- Parties that promote certain causes—for example, a controversial single issue such as prohibition of alcoholic beverages—or that take a relatively extreme ideological position such as socialism or libertarianism.

- Splinter parties, or offshoots of a major party. Teddy Roosevelt's Progressives in 1912, Strom Thurmond's States' Righters in 1948, and George Wallace's American Independents in 1968 all claimed they did not get a fair hearing from Republicans or Democrats and thus formed their own new parties.

- Parties that are merely an extension of a popular individual with presidential aspirations. Both John Anderson in 1980 and Ross Perot in 1992 and 1996 offered voters who were dissatisfied with the Democratic and Republican nominees another option.

Although third-party candidates almost never win office in the United States, scholars believe they are often quite important.[23] They have brought new groups into the electorate and have served as "safety valves" for popular discontent. The Free Soilers of the 1850s were the first true antislavery party; the Progressives and the Populists put many social reforms on the political agenda. George Wallace told his supporters in

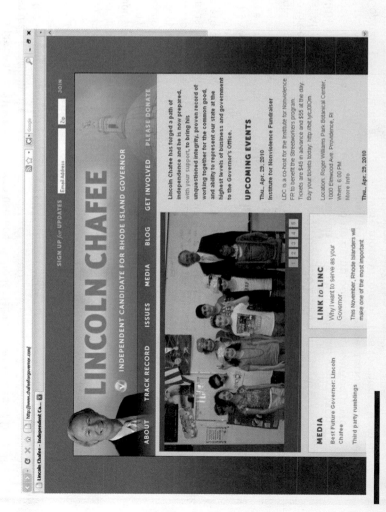

Third party candidates usually struggle to get noticed in the United States, as almost all major elected officials are affiliated with either the Democrats or Republicans. But occasionally a third-party candidate will become a serious contender, as did Lincoln Chafee when he ran successfully for governor of Rhode Island in 2010.

winner-take-all system
An electoral system in which legislative seats are awarded only to the candidates who come in first in their constituencies.

proportional representation
An electoral system used throughout most of Europe that awards legislative seats to political parties in proportion to the number of votes won in an election.

coalition government
When two or more parties join together to form a majority in a national legislature. This form of government is quite common in the multiparty systems of Europe.

America in Perspective

Multiparty Systems in Other Countries

One of the major reasons why the United States has only two parties represented in government is structural. America has a **winner-take-all system**, in which whoever gets the most votes wins the election. There are no prizes awarded for second or third place. Suppose there are three parties: one receives 45 percent of the vote, another 40 percent, and the third 15 percent. Although it got less than a majority, the party that finished first is declared the winner. The others are left out in the cold. In this way, the American system discourages small parties. Unless a party wins, there is no reward for the votes it gets. Thus, it makes more sense for a small party to merge with one of the major parties than to struggle on its own with little hope. In this example, the second- and third-place parties might merge (if they can reach an agreement on policy) to challenge the governing party in the next election.

In a system that employs **proportional representation**, however, such a merger would not be necessary. Under this system, which is used in most European countries, legislative seats are allocated according to each party's percentage of the nationwide vote. If a party wins 15 percent of the vote, then it receives 15 percent of the seats. Even a small party can use its voice in Parliament to be a thorn in the side of the government, standing up strongly for its principles. Such has often been the role of the Greens in Germany, who are ardent environmentalists. After the 2002 German election they formed a **coalition government** along with Germany's Social Democratic Party. Together the coalition controlled over half the seats in the German parliament for three years. Coalition governments are common in Europe. Italy has regularly been ruled by coalition governments since the end of World War II, for example.

Even with proportional representation, not every party gets represented in the legislature. To be awarded seats, a party must exceed a certain minimal percentage of votes, which varies from country to country. Israel has one of the lowest thresholds at 2 percent. This explains why there are always so many parties represented in the Israeli Knesset—12 as of 2012. The founders of Israel's system wanted to make sure that all points of view were represented, but sometimes this has turned into a nightmare, with small extremist parties holding the balance of power.

Parties have to develop their own unique identities to appeal to voters in a multiparty system. This requires strong stands on the issues, but after the election compromises must be made to form a coalition government. If an agreement cannot be reached on the major issues, the coalition is in trouble. Sometimes a new coalition can be formed; other times the result is the calling of a new election. In either case, it is clear that proportional representation systems are more fluid than the two-party system in the United States.

CRITICAL THINKING QUESTIONS

1. If the United States adopted a form of proportional representation, what new parties do you think would be formed and would become important players?

2. Do you think your political views would end up being better represented if we had proportional representation and there were more viable parties to choose from on Election Day? If so, how?

1968 they had the chance to "send a message" to Washington—a message of support for tougher law and order measures, which is still being felt to this day. Ross Perot used his saturation of the TV airwaves in 1992 to ensure that the issue of the federal deficit was not ignored in the campaign. And in 2000, Green Party candidate Ralph Nader forced more attention on environmental issues and ultimately cost Gore the presidency by drawing away a small percentage of liberal votes.

Despite the regular appearance of third parties, the two-party system is firmly entrenched in American politics. Would it make a difference if America had a multiparty system, as so many European countries have? The answer is clearly yes. The most obvious consequence of two-party governance is the moderation of political conflict. If America had many parties, each would have to make a special appeal in order to stand out from the crowd. It is not hard to imagine what a multiparty system might look like in the United States. Environmentalists could constitute their own specific party, vowing to clean up the rivers, oppose nuclear power, and save the wilderness. America could have religious parties, union-based parties, farmers' parties, and all sorts of others. As in some European countries, there could be half a dozen or more parties represented in Congress (see "America in Perspective: Multiparty Systems in Other Countries").

Understanding Political Parties

8.7 Evaluate the advantages and disadvantages of responsible party government.

P olitical parties are considered essential elements of democratic government. Indeed, one of the first steps taken toward democracy in formerly communist Eastern European countries was the formation of competing political parties to contest elections. After years of one-party totalitarian rule, Eastern Europeans were ecstatic to be able to adopt a multiparty system like those that had proved successful in the West. In contrast, the founding of the world's first party system in the United States was seen as a risky adventure in the then uncharted waters of democracy. Wary of having parties at all, the Founders designed a system that has greatly restrained their political role to this day. Whether American parties should continue to be so loosely organized is at the heart of today's debate about their role in American democracy.

☐ Democracy and Responsible Party Government: How Should We Govern?

Ideally, in a democracy candidates should say what they mean to do if elected and, once they are elected, should be able to do what they promised. Critics of the American party system lament that this is all too often not the case and have called for a "more responsible two-party system."[24] Advocates of the **responsible party model** believe the parties should meet the following conditions:

1. Parties must present distinct, comprehensive programs for governing the nation.

2. Each party's candidates must be committed to its program and have the internal cohesion and discipline to carry out its program.

3. The majority party must implement its programs, and the minority party must state what it would do if it were in power.

4. The majority party must accept responsibility for the performance of the government.

A two-party system operating under these conditions would make it easier to convert party promises into governmental policy. A party's officeholders would have firm control of the government, so they would be collectively rather than individually responsible for their actions. Voters would therefore know whom to blame for what the government does and does not accomplish.

As this chapter has shown, American political parties often fall short of these conditions. They are too decentralized to take a single national position and then enforce it. Most candidates are self-selected, gaining their nomination by their own efforts rather than the party's. Because party primaries are electoral contests for popular support, the party's organization and leaders do not have control over those who run in the general election under their labels. In America's loosely organized party system, there simply is no mechanism for a party to discipline officeholders and thereby ensure cohesion in policymaking. Party leaders can help a candidate raise money,[25] get on to the prestigious committees, and sometimes provide support in their efforts to get special benefits for their constituency. But what they cannot do is even more telling: They cannot deny them the party's nomination at the next election or take away their congressional staff support. Thus, unlike politicians in parliamentary systems who can be told by their party leaders that they must follow the party line or else not be renominated in the next election, American politicians enjoy the freedom to buck the party line. American officeholders try to go along with their parties' platform whenever they can. But when the party line conflicts with their own personal opinion and/or the clear desires of their constituents, then they feel perfectly comfortable in voting against their party's leaders.

responsible party model
A view about how parties should work, held by some political scientists. According to the model, parties should offer clear choices to the voters and once in office, should carry out their campaign promises.

Blue Dog Democrats

Fiscally conservative Democrats who are mostly from the South and/or rural parts of the United States.

In the hit fictional series "House of Cards," Kevin Spacey plays a House Whip who tries to keep his party's members in line. In one scene he puts heavy pressure on two members of his own party, but concludes with the phrase, "Vote Your Conscience, Vote Your District." Ultimately, they vote against the wishes of Spacey's character, reflecting their own doubts with the legislation. Tellingly, the chief writer for "House of Cards" said he got the line of "Vote Your Conscience, Vote Your District" from Republican House Whip, Kevin McCarthy, who told him that this is what he tells members. Hence, when the party line conflicts with their own personal opinion and/or the clear desires of their constituents, members of Congress feel comfortable in voting against their party's leaders. For example, although Republicans usually lined up with President George W. Bush's priorities, when it came to votes such as immigration reform or bailing out the banks in 2008, the majority of congressional Republicans voted against his proposals.

As you can see in Table 8.2, even on the key policy votes in Congress during the presidency of George W. Bush, there were numerous disagreements among members of the same party.

Because American officeholders don't always follow the platform planks of their party, even when Democrats controlled majorities in both the House and Senate in 2009–2010, President Obama could not take for granted that his policy proposals would be enacted into law. In particular, Obama regularly encountered resistance from members of the organized caucus known as "**Blue Dog Democrats.**" Back in the days of the Solid South, Democrats would often say that they would vote for "a yellow dog" if their party wanted them to. Today's Blue Dogs say they have been squeezed so often by the liberals in the Democratic leadership that they have turned blue. Hailing mostly from Southern and/or rural areas of the country, they are more fiscally conservative than most Democrats and are resistant to any domestic policy proposals that

TABLE 8.2 PARTISAN DIVISIONS ON KEY ROLL CALL VOTES DURING THE BUSH PRESIDENCY

	Dems For	Dems Against	Reps For	Reps Against
2008 $700 billion bailout bill	172	63	91	108
2008 $168 billion tax rebate	216	10	169	25
2007 immigration reform*	33	15	12	37
2005 USA Patriot Act reauthorization	43	156	214	14
2003 prescription drug program	16	190	204	25
2002 Iraq War	82	126	215	6
2001 USA Patriot Act	145	62	211	3
2001 No Child Left Behind	198	6	183	33
2001 tax cut	10	197	219	0

*The House of Representatives never voted on this proposal because it failed a key test in the Senate. Hence, we display the Senate vote in this case, whereas the other votes displayed are from "the more numerous House."

During the presidency of George W. Bush, there was much discussion in the press about heightened partisan tensions between Democrats and Republicans in Congress. While it is true that congressional voting was more polarized along party lines than had usually been the case in recent times, a close look at the roll calls on nine key proposals that President Bush favored reveals a variety of patterns. On three issues, colored in orange in Table 8.2, there was bipartisan support for Bush's position. On two others, colored in blue, the majority of Democrats supported Bush's proposals whereas the majority of Republicans decided not to go along with their own party's leader. Just four of the nine key votes, colored in green, fit the very loose American criteria for a party-line vote: a majority of the president's party voting in support of his position and a majority of the opposition party voting the other way. Notably, on all these partisan votes at least some Democrats broke ranks to support President Bush, and on the Republican side there was unanimity only on the issue of cutting taxes in 2001.

Point to Ponder

Many people believe that the gap between the two parties has become so wide that it is hard to get bipartisan agreement about anything.

Based on the data shown in Table 8.2, as well as on partisan behavior during the Obama presidency, how accurate is that view?

would enlarge the scope of government. Thus, on congressional votes like the $787 billion economic stimulus package or the even more expensive health care proposal, many Blue Dog Democrats did not support President Obama's initiatives.

Whenever a president's agenda fails to pass because of his inability to rally his own party, advocates of responsible party government bemoan the lack of centralized political parties in America. However, not everyone thinks that America's decentralized parties are a problem. Critics of the responsible party model argue that the complexity and diversity of American society are too great to be captured by such a simple model of party politics. Local differences need an outlet for expression, they say. One cannot expect Texas Democrats always to want to vote in line with New York Democrats. In the view of those opposed to the responsible party model, America's decentralized parties are appropriate for the type of limited government the Founders sought to create and most Americans wish to maintain.[26]

The Founders were very concerned that political parties would trample on the rights of individuals. They wanted to preserve individual freedom of action by various elected officials. With America's weak party system, this has certainly been the case. Individual members of Congress and other elected officials have great freedom to act as they see fit rather than toeing the party line.

American Political Parties and the Scope of Government

The lack of disciplined and cohesive European-style parties in America goes a long way to explain why the scope of governmental activity in the United States is not as broad as it is in other established democracies. The long struggle to guarantee access to health care for all Americans provides a perfect example. In Britain, the Labour Party had long proposed such a system, and after it won the 1945 election, all its members of Parliament voted to enact national health care into law. On the other side of the Atlantic, President Truman also proposed a national health care bill in the first presidential election after World War II. But even though he won the election and had majorities of his own party in both houses of Congress, his proposal never got very far. The weak party structure in the United States allowed many congressional Democrats to oppose Truman's health care proposal. Over four decades later, President Clinton again proposed a system of universal health care and had a Democratic-controlled Congress to work with. But the Clinton health care bill never even came up for a vote in Congress because of the president's inability to get enough members of his own party to go along with the plan. It wasn't until 2010 that something akin to President Truman's proposal for health care for all Americans was finally enacted into law. Notably, this historic bill only passed by a narrow margin in the Democratic-controlled House of Representatives, with 34 House Democrats opposing it despite the strong urging of President Obama. In short, substantially increasing the scope of government in America is not something that can be accomplished through the disciplined actions of one party's members, as is the case in other democracies.

On the other hand, because it is rarely the case that one single party can ever be said to have firm control over American government, the hard choices necessary to cut back on existing government spending are rarely addressed. A disciplined and cohesive governing party might have the power to say no to various demands on the government. In contrast, America's loose party structure makes it possible for many individual politicians—Democrats and Republicans alike—to focus their efforts on getting more from the government for their own constituents.

Review the Chapter

The Meaning of Party

8.1 Identify the functions that political parties perform in American democracy, p. 246.

Even though political parties are one of Americans' least beloved institutions, political scientists see them as a key linkage between policymakers and the people. Political parties operate at three levels: (1) in the electorate; (2) as organizations; and (3) in government. Among the functions that they perform in our democratic system are to pick candidates, run campaigns, give cues to voters, articulate policies, and coordinate policymaking between the branches of government.

The Party in the Electorate

8.2 Determine the significance of party identification in America today, p. 250.

Party identification—one's self-proclaimed general preference for one party or the other—is the most important factor in explaining the political behavior of American voters. People who do not identify with either party are known as political independents. They are the crucial swing voters who can go either way and are also more likely to split their tickets. Young people are especially likely to be Independents.

The Party Organization: From the Grass Roots to Washington

8.3 Describe how political parties are organized in the United States, p. 252.

American political party organizations are decentralized and fragmented. The national party organization can rarely tell state parties what to do. In particular, the state party organizations have a good deal of discretion as to how to choose their nominees for state and local offices. Some states opt to have closed primaries, which restrict participation to people who have registered with the party, whereas others have open primaries, which allow much broader participation. The supreme power within each of the parties is its national convention, which, every four years, nominates candidates for president and vice president and sets party policy. In between conventions, the activities of the national party are guided by each party's national chairperson.

The Party in Government: Promises and Policy

8.4 Evaluate how well political parties generally do in carrying out their promises, p. 255.

Political parties affect policy through their platforms. Despite much cynicism about party platforms, they serve as important roadmaps for elected officials once they come into office. More promises are generally kept than broken.

Party Eras in American History

8.5 Differentiate the various party eras in American history, p. 256.

Throughout American history, one party has generally been dominant for a substantial period of time. The first party era, from 1796 to 1824, was dominated by the Democratic-Republicans, whose agricultural base defeated the business-oriented Federalists. The newly formed Democratic Party dominated from 1828 to 1856, pushing for more power for ordinary individuals. The newly formed Republican Party came to power in 1860 and dominated American politics through 1928—first standing firm against slavery and then successfully promoting the interests of industrialization. The Great Depression led to a reversal of party fortunes, with the Democrats establishing the New Deal coalition that usually prevailed from 1932 to 1964. Since 1968, neither party has been able to hold the reins of power for long. A frequent result has been for power to be divided, with one party controlling the presidency and the other in control of the Congress.

Third Parties: Their Impact on American Politics

8.6 Assess both the impact of third parties on American politics and their limitations, p. 263.

Third parties in the United States have brought new groups into the electorate and have served as a vehicle for sending a protest message to the two major parties. The American winner-take-all electoral system makes it hard for third parties to win elections. In contrast, most European electoral systems use proportional representation, which guarantees that any party that has at least a certain percentage of the vote receives a proportional share of the legislative seats.

Understanding Political Parties

8.7 Evaluate the advantages and disadvantages of responsible party government, p. 265.

Some scholars of American politics have advocated what is known as "responsible party government," in which parties offer clear policy choices which generate clearly identifiable outcomes. That is, at least in theory, parties say what they plan to do and once in office carry out these plans. The main disadvantage is that the party discipline necessary for a party to carry out its pledges requires members of the party in government to toe the line without regard to constituency preferences. Individualism in American politics would be stifled by a true responsible government.

Learn the Terms

political party, p. 246
linkage institutions, p. 247
rational-choice theory, p. 248
party image, p. 250
party identification, p. 250
ticket splitting, p. 251
party machines, p. 253
patronage, p. 253
closed primaries, p. 254
open primaries, p. 254
national convention, p. 255
national committee, p. 255
national chairperson, p. 255
coalition, p. 256
party eras, p. 257
critical election, p. 257
party realignment, p. 258
New Deal coalition, p. 259
party dealignment, p. 262
third parties, p. 263
winner-take-all system, p. 263
proportional representation, p. 264
coalition government, p. 264
responsible party model, p. 265
Blue Dog Democrats, p. 266

Test Yourself

1. What do officials elected under a party banner collectively represent?

a. the party as a fund-raiser
b. the party as an organization
c. the party in government
d. the party in structure
e. the party in the electorate

2. How do interest groups primarily differ from political parties?

a. They are formed not as a requirement of the Constitution but out of political needs.
b. They are more directly concerned with influencing public policy.
c. They are more directly concerned with organizing the electorate to win public office.
d. They do not have to abide by the same Constitutional rules and restrictions that govern parties.
e. They do not require members to be particularly active to accomplish their goals.

3. What are you engaging in if you cast your ballot for a Democratic candidate for president and a Republican candidate for Congress?

a. checks and balances
b. divided government
c. intelligent partisanship
d. separation of powers
e. ticket splitting

4. Why do party organizations favor closed primaries over open primaries?

a. They allow more voters to take part.
b. They are cheaper to operate.
c. They are not regulated by state election law.
d. They favor ideological purity.
e. They reduce the chances of voter fraud.

5. What has happened to the void created by the decline of urban political machines?

a. It has been filled in part by county party organizations.
b. It has led to a revitalization of national party organizations.
c. It has led to a surge in independent voters.

6. Which of the following is true concerning parties in the United States?

a. Organizationally, state parties are on the upswing throughout the country.
b. Parties are adopting rules to ensure that their members vote along party lines.
c. State parties are abdicating much of their authority to the national party.
d. The national parties are requiring the state parties to take on many new official duties.
e. The national parties are working to make themselves more similar to the strong centralized parties of Europe.

7. Which of the following positions is in line with the 2012 Republican Party platform?

a. support of a human life amendment to the Constitution
b. increase government spending on health care
c. increase the power of the Department of Education
d. favor increasing taxes on the wealthiest Americans
e. support same-sex marriages

8. What are the major American political parties made up of?

a. disgruntled voters
b. largely older voters
c. loose coalitions of individuals and groups
d. organized business groups
e. voters with a strong shared ideology

9. What emerged from the realignment in America following the 1968 election of Richard Nixon?

a. African American voters shifted en masse from the Republican to the Democratic Party.
b. Catholic voters shifted en masse from the Democratic to the Republican Party.
c. Instances of divided government became infrequent with a unified government becoming the norm.
d. The Republican Party was able to gradually break the Democratic Party's dominance in the South.
e. The strength of the Democratic Party was slowly relegated to only Northeastern urban centers.

d. It has limited the scope of government reform
e. It remains to be filled.

270

10. What does the American two-party system promote?

a. broad coalitions of party supporters
b. greater conflict and clear policy choices
c. more competitive elections
d. the organization of political parties around special interests
e. voter alienation

11. Which electoral reform would make it easier to elect third-party candidates to Congress?

a. abolishing the Electoral College
b. proportional representation
c. requiring candidates to list all campaign donations online
d. requiring candidates to live in the district they wish to represent
e. strict ballot-access laws

12. What kinds of governments are more likely to occur in democracies with multiparty systems?

a. coalition governments
b. federalist governments
c. minor-party governments
d. unitary governments
e. winner-take-all governments

13. What system did the Founders create for parties in America?

a. They created a system where parties were meant to represent the people on the national level and affect policy.
b. They created a two-party system to ensure that the rights of state and the national government would be protected.
c. They created a two-party system to ensure the system of checks and balances.
d. They envisioned parties as serving as the essential vehicles for change in government and gave them broad powers.
e. Wary of the existence of parties, they designed a system that greatly restrained them.

14. What is often seen as a major weakness of American political parties?

a. Local party organizations have too much power.
b. Local, state, and national campaigns often work at odds.
c. National conventions set the rules by which the party is governed.
d. Parties are vulnerable to being taken over by splinter groups.
e. Their ability to enforce ideological rigidity among elected officials is limited.

15. Which of the following most ensures that no one group dominates congressional decisions?

a. Incumbents must work outside their party to raise enough money.
b. Members of Congress have differing constituencies.
c. Party caucuses can remove committee chairs that do not follow the party line.
d. Party leaders are often at odds with elected officials.
e. The vice president is also president of the Senate.

Explore Further

WEB SITES

www.rnc.org
The official site of the Republican National Committee.

www.democrats.org
The Democratic Party online.

http://ross.house.gov/BlueDog/
The official site of the fiscally conservative Democratic Blue Dog Coalition.

www.lp.org
Although Libertarians rarely get more than a few percent of the vote, they consistently get many of their candidates on the ballot for many offices. You can learn more about their beliefs at this official site.

www.gp.org
The official Web site for the Green Party, which emphasizes environmental protection over corporate profits.

FURTHER READING

Black, Earl, and Merle Black. *The Rise of Southern Republicanism.* Cambridge, MA: Harvard University Press, 2002. An excellent examination of the transformation of party politics in the South.

Burden, Barry C., and David C. Kimball. *Why Americans Split Their Tickets: Campaigns, Competition and Divided Government.* Ann Arbor: University of Michigan Press, 2002. A good analysis of who splits their ticket and under what conditions they are most likely to do so.

Currinder, Marian. *Money in the House: Campaign Funds and Congressional Party Politics.* Boulder, CO: Westview Press, 2009. Examines how congressional parties define and reward loyalty through campaign contributions.

Downs, Anthony. *An Economic Theory of Democracy.* New York: Harper & Row, 1957. An extremely influential theoretical work that applies rational-choice theory to party politics.

Green, John C., and Daniel M. Shea. *The State of the Parties,* 6th ed. Lanham, MD: Rowman & Littlefield, 2011. A diverse set of articles on numerous aspects of party politics, with an emphasis on how well the party system is working.

Hershey, Marjorie Randon. *Party Politics in America,* 15th ed. New York: Longman, 2012. The standard textbook on political parties.

Levendusky, Matthew. *The Partisan Sort: How Liberals Became Democrats and Conservatives Became Republicans.* Chicago: University of Chicago Press, 2009. An insightful analysis of how the ideological gap between Democrats and Republicans has widened in recent decades.

Mayhew, David R. *Electoral Realignments: A Critique of an American Genre.* New Haven, CT: Yale University Press, 2002. A critical look at the historical evidence concerning realignment theory.

Rosenstone, Steven, Roy Behr, and Edward Lazarus. *Third Parties in America,* 2nd ed. Princeton, NJ: Princeton University Press, 1996. An analytical study of why third parties appear, when they do, and what effect they have.

Sundquist, James L. *Dynamics of the Party System,* rev. ed. Washington, DC: Brookings Institution, 1983. One of the best books ever written on the major realignments in American history.

Wattenberg, Martin P. *The Decline of American Political Parties, 1952–1996.* Cambridge, MA: Harvard University Press, 1998. An account of the decline of parties in the electorate.

9

Campaigns and Voting Behavior

9.1
Evaluate the fairness of our current system of presidential primaries and caucuses, p. 275.

9.2
Explain the key objectives of any political campaign, p. 283.

9.3
Outline how the financing of federal campaigns is regulated by campaign finance laws, p. 286.

9.4
Determine why campaigns have an important yet limited impact on election outcomes, p. 292.

9.5
Identify the factors that influence whether people vote, p. 292.

9.6
Assess the impact of party identification, candidate evaluations, and policy opinions on voting behavior, p. 298.

9.7
Evaluate the fairness of the Electoral College system for choosing the president, p. 303.

9.8
Assess the advantages and disadvantages of the U.S. system of campaigns and elections, p. 305.

Politics in Action: How Running for Office Can Be More Demanding than Governing

C ampaigning for any major office has become a massive undertaking in today's political world. Consider Barack Obama's grueling schedule for March 21, 2008, a day in a relatively low-key period of the presidential campaign:

• The senator arrives at the Benson Hotel in Portland, Oregon, after midnight, following a 2,550-mile plane ride from Charleston, West Virginia, where he had spent the previous day campaigning.

• At 7:00 AM, Obama leaves his hotel for a jog around downtown Portland.

• After returning to the hotel for a change of clothes, Obama meets privately with Governor Bill Richardson of New Mexico, who has just decided to endorse him. The pair then proceed to a scheduled rally at the Portland Memorial Coliseum, where the endorsement is publicly announced to an enthusiastic crowd of 12,800 people.

• Following the morning rally, Obama holds a press conference, taking questions from the corps of reporters traveling with him as well as from members of the Oregon media.

• Obama then hops on his campaign bus for an hour's drive down to Oregon's capital city of Salem, where he responds to questions from ordinary Oregonians at a town-hall meeting attended by about 3,000 people.

Supporters reach out to shake hands with Barack Obama following his speech at the Portland Memorial Coliseum on March 21, 2008—one of a number of events in a long typical day on the campaign trail.

- While in Salem, Obama manages to do six separate interviews with Oregon news organizations before getting back on the campaign bus.

- After another hour on the road, the bus pulls up in front of American Dream Pizza in Corvallis, where the candidate pops in for a slice of pizza and an impromptu chat with some pleasantly surprised fellow diners.

- Obama then reboards his bus for another hour's ride to Eugene to address a crowd of 10,000 people at the University of Oregon's basketball arena.

- Following this evening rally, the candidate goes to the Eugene airport to board his campaign plane for a 200-mile flight to Medford, Oregon. Just after 1:00 AM, Obama walks into his hotel for the night, knowing that he has another day like this to look forward to tomorrow.

It is often said that the presidency is the most difficult job in the world, but getting elected to the position may well be tougher. As Karl Rove, George W. Bush's veteran political adviser, writes, "There are few more demanding physical activities than running for president, other than military training or athletics at a very high level."[1] When asked if he was exhausted by the demands of campaigning in 2008, Barack Obama simply answered, "Sometimes, yes, of course."

The current American style of long and arduous campaigns has evolved from the belief of reformers that the cure for the problems of democracy is more democracy. Whether this approach is helpful or harmful to democracy is a question that provokes much debate with respect to American political campaigns. Some scholars believe it is important that presidential candidates go through a long and difficult trial by fire. Others, however, worry that the system makes it difficult for politicians with other responsibilities—such as incumbent governors and senior senators—to take a run at the White House. This chapter will give you a better understanding of the pros and cons of having a nomination and campaign process that is so open and democratic.

The consequences for the scope of government are also debatable. Anthony King argues that American politicians do too little governing because they are always "running scared" in today's perpetual campaign.[2] From King's perspective, the campaign process does not allow politicians the luxury of trying out solutions to policy problems that might be immediately unpopular but would work well in the long run. The scope of government thus stays pretty much as is, given that politicians are usually too concerned with the next election to risk fundamental change. Of course, many analysts argue that officeholders' constant worry about public opinion is good for democracy and that changes in the scope of government should not be undertaken without extensive public consultation.

As you read this chapter, consider whether today's nomination and campaign process provides too much opportunity for interaction between the public and candidates for office, and consider whether the entire process takes too much time and costs too much money. These are very important topics of debate in American politics today.

With about half a million elected officials in this country, there is always someone somewhere running for office. One of these campaigns is for the world's most powerful office—the presidency of the United States. This chapter will focus mainly on this election campaign, although we will explore some other campaigns as well. The chapter on Congress will specifically discuss the congressional election process.

There are really two types of campaigns in American politics: campaigns for party nominations and campaigns between the two nominees. These are called *nomination campaigns* and *election campaigns*. The prize for the first is garnering a party's nod as its candidate; the prize for the second is winning an office.

9.1
9.2
9.3
9.4
9.5
9.6
9.7
9.8

275

nomination

The official endorsement of a candidate for office by a political party. Generally, success in the nomination game requires momentum, money, and media attention.

campaign strategy

The master game plan candidates lay out to guide their electoral campaign.

national party convention

The supreme power within each of the parties. The convention meets every four years to nominate the party's presidential and vice presidential candidates and to write the party's platform.

The Nomination Game

9.1 Evaluate the fairness of our current system of presidential primaries and caucuses.

 nomination is a party's official endorsement of a candidate for office. Anyone can play the nomination game, but few have any serious chance of victory. Generally, success in the nomination game requires money, media attention, and momentum. **Campaign strategy** is the way in which candidates attempt to manipulate each of these elements to achieve the nomination.

The decision to run for public office is often a difficult one. As Richard Fox and Jennifer Lawless found in their study of political ambition, "Considering a candidacy for public office involves pondering the courageous step of going before an electorate and facing potential examination, scrutiny, and rejection."[3] The higher the office, the greater these challenges, with the consequence being that not every politician wants to run for president. As former Speaker of the House Thomas Foley said, "I know of any number of people who I think would make good presidents, even great presidents, who are deterred from running by the torture candidates are obliged to put themselves through."[4] Running for president is an around-the-clock endurance test for over a year: sleep deprivation and strange hotel beds, countless plane rides, junk food eaten on the run, a lack of regular exercise, and copious amounts of stress.

In most advanced industrialized countries, campaigns last no more than two months according to custom and/or law. In contrast, American campaigns seem endless; a presidential candidacy needs to be either announced or an open secret for at least a year before the election. Whoever gets elected president in November 2016 will almost certainly have begun their presidential campaign by the middle of 2015.

Competing for Delegates

In some ways, the nomination game is tougher than the general election game; it whittles a large number of players down to two. The goal of the nomination game is to win the support of a majority of delegates at the **national party convention**—the supreme power within each of the parties, which functions to formally select presidential and vice presidential candidates and to write the party platform.

At each political party's national convention, state delegations meet to cast their votes. Today, the choices of the delegates are well known in advance, and the real contests involve the selection of the delegates from each state in the first place. However, it was not always that way. From the invention of political party conventions in the 1830s up until the late 1960s, the vast majority of the delegates were the political elite—elected officials and heads of the local party organizations. Frequently, each state had one or two party "bosses" who ran the show, such as the state's governor or the mayor of its largest city. These "bosses" could control who went to the convention and how the state's delegates voted once they got there. They were the kingmakers of presidential politics who met in smoke-filled rooms at the convention to cut deals and form coalitions.

Early in the twentieth century, the presidential primary was promoted by reformers who wanted to take nominations out of the hands of the party bosses. The reformers wanted to let the people vote for the candidate of their choice and then bind the delegates to vote for that candidate at the national convention. Although primary elections caught on quickly as a method for nominating candidates for Congress and state government positions, the presidential primary was less quick to catch on: 35 states left the choice of convention delegates to the party elites through the 1960s. It was not until the Democratic Party's disastrous 1968 convention that pressure mounted to rethink the traditional elite-dominated closed procedures for selecting convention delegates. As the war in Southeast Asia raged, another war of sorts took

McGovern–Fraser Commission

A commission formed at the 1968 Democratic convention in response to demands for reform by minority groups and others who sought better representation.

place in the streets of Chicago during the Democratic convention. Demonstrators against the war battled Mayor Richard Daley's Chicago police in what an official report later called a "police riot." Beaten up in the streets and defeated in the convention hall, the antiwar faction won one concession from the party regulars: a special committee to review the party's delegate selection procedures, which they felt had discriminated against them. Minorities, women, youth, and other groups that had been poorly represented in the party leadership also demanded a more open process of convention delegate selection. The result was a committee of inquiry, which was chaired first by Senator George McGovern and later by Representative Donald Fraser.

After a careful review of the procedures used to select delegates to the 1968 Democratic convention, the **McGovern–Fraser Commission** famously concluded that "meaningful participation of Democratic voters in the choice of their presidential nominee was often difficult or costly, sometimes completely illusory, and, in not a few instances, impossible."[5] In order to correct this situation, they wrote new rules to make Democratic Party conventions more representative and open to input from the public. Under these new rules, party leaders could no longer handpick the convention delegates virtually in secret. All delegate selection procedures were required to be open, so that everyone could participate—either a state-run primary election or an open meeting at the local level. Many states decided that the easiest way to comply with these new Democratic delegate selection procedures was simply to hold a primary to select convention delegates.[6] Because state laws instituting primaries typically apply to both parties' selection of delegates, the Republican Party's nomination process was similarly transformed.

Few developments have changed American politics as much as the opening of the presidential nomination process to broad-based public participation. The elite-dominated game of bargaining for the party's nomination was transformed

Riots at the 1968 Democratic national convention led to the establishment of more open procedures for delegate selection. These reforms have made recent party conventions more representative.

superdelegates
National party leaders who automatically get a delegate slot at the national party convention.

invisible primary
The period before any votes are cast when candidates compete to win early support from the elite of the party and to create a positive first impression of their leadership skills.

caucus
A system for selecting convention delegates used in about a dozen states in which voters must attend an open meeting to express their presidential preference.

into a process in which candidates competed for tens of millions of votes. Delegates who were experienced politicians and knew the candidates were mostly replaced by delegates who had attained their seats due to their preferred candidate's ability to pull in votes.

The only remaining vestige of the old elite-dominated system are the so-called **superdelegates**—people who are awarded automatic slots as delegates based on the office they currently hold, such as being a member of Congress or of their party's national committee. In 2012, these members of the political elite made up 14 percent of the Democratic delegates and 8 percent of the Republican delegates. Theoretically, if two candidates are locked in a tight contest—as occurred in 2008 between Barack Obama and Hillary Clinton—the superdelegates could prove to be decisive and even overturn the people's verdict by giving the nomination to the candidate who received fewer popular votes. However, as political scientist William Mayer notes, the principle that nominations are decided by the voters has become so ingrained in the American psyche that even when the superdelegates have "the theoretical capacity to influence the outcome of a closely contested nomination race, they are reluctant to exercise that power."[7] Thus, in practice the Democratic and Republican nominees are determined by the results of the primaries and caucuses.

THE INVISIBLE PRIMARY Before any votes are cast in primaries or caucuses, however, the candidates are hard at work trying to build up crucial sources of support and form positive first impressions. This stage of the nomination campaign is often referred to as "the invisible primary," as it mostly occurs behind the scenes of public view. The major component of the **invisible primary** is the wooing of support from elected officials (most importantly, governors and members of Congress), top fundraisers, and skilled political aides. Political scientist Marty Cohen and his coauthors argue that during the invisible primary key elected officials in a party often coalesce around the candidate that they find most acceptable and via their endorsements give a crucial boost to this candidate.[8] In this way, Cohen and his coauthors contend, the elite of the party often set the agenda during the nomination process, smoothing the way for candidates to unify a party and influence the votes of the rank and file. The fact that Mitt Romney garnered more endorsements than any other GOP presidential candidate in 2012 clearly helped him sew up the Republican nomination.

During the invisible primary, candidates work carefully to create a positive personal image amongst the media, the political elite, and the attentive portion of the public. Because candidates within the same party generally agree more than they disagree on the issues, the personal qualifications, character, and intelligence of the candidates frequently take center stage, as such factors clearly differentiate the contenders. When candidates who are new on the national stage get scrutinized for the first time, major blunders can sink their campaign in no time flat. In 1967, George Romney (Mitt Romney's father) saw his promising bid for the Republican nomination fall apart quickly after he explained his changed stand on the Vietnam War as the result of his having originally been "brainwashed" by the generals. After all, who would want a president who admitted to having been brainwashed? In 2012, the campaign of Texas Governor Rick Perry saw the air go out of its sails when he said he would eliminate three federal cabinet departments but then could not name them, finishing up the exchange with the expression "oops." Incidents such as these not only leave lasting negative impressions but also make it hard to mount the resources needed to succeed once the voters get to make their choices.

THE CAUCUSES AND PRIMARIES From January through June of the election year, the individual state parties busily choose their delegates to the national convention via either caucuses or primaries.

Since 1972, the Iowa caucuses have been the first test of candidates' vote-getting ability. Iowa is one of about a dozen mostly rural states that hold a set of meetings, known as caucuses, to select convention delegates. In a **caucus** system voters must

278

9.1
9.2
9.3
9.4
9.5
9.6
9.7
9.8

presidential primaries
Elections in which a state's voters go to the polls to express their preference for a party's nominee for president. Most delegates to the national party conventions are chosen this way.

The invisible primary involves building a support base even before a candidate formally announces his or her campaign for the presidency. In this 2013 photo, members of the "I'm Ready for Hillary" group show their support for Hillary Clinton for president.

show up at a fixed time and attend an open meeting lasting one or two hours to express their presidential preference. Because attending a caucus requires a greater time commitment than a primary election, participation in caucuses is much lower than the level of turnout for primaries. As such, caucuses represent a rather different sort of test for a presidential candidate than primaries. As Thomas Mann explains, "Caucuses test candidates' strategic acuity, organizational strength, and intensity of support, qualities not irrelevant to performance in the general election and in the White House."[9] Barack Obama's experience as a community organizer before he entered politics is widely thought to have given him special insight into how to mobilize activists to attend a caucus. David Plouffe, Obama's 2008 campaign manager, proudly proclaimed that their "organization and grassroots supporters understood how to win caucuses."[10] Indeed, starting with a victory in Iowa, the Obama campaign won the majority of delegates at stake in every caucus state in 2008—an edge that proved crucial to Obama's narrow victory over Clinton in the race for the Democratic nomination.

Given that the Iowa caucuses are the first test of the candidates' vote-getting ability, they usually become a full-blown media extravaganza.[11] Well-known candidates have seen their campaigns virtually fall apart as a result of poor showings in Iowa. Most important, some candidates have received tremendous boosts from unexpected strong showings in Iowa. An obscure former Georgia governor named Jimmy Carter took his first big presidential step by winning there in 1976. In 2008, Barack Obama's victory shocked the political world and landed him on the covers of the major weekly magazines, *Time* and *Newsweek*. Because of the impact that Iowa's first-in-the-nation caucus can have, candidates spend far more time during the nomination season there than they do in the big states like California, Texas, and Florida. As the *Des Moines Register* editorialized in 2011, urging Iowans to ask the candidates tough questions, "Iowa is in the unique position to help shape political conversations and force candidates to focus on the issues that really matter to average people."[12] The winner of the Iowa caucus doesn't always go on to win the nomination, but the results from Iowa usually serve to winnow down the number of viable candidates for the primaries to come.

Most of the delegates to the Democratic and Republican national conventions are selected in **presidential primaries**, in which a state's voters go to the polls to express their preference for a party's nominee for president. The primary season begins during

frontloading

The recent tendency of states to hold primaries early in the calendar in order to capitalize on media attention.

Point to Ponder

During the nomination process, far more candidate and media attention is paid to Iowa and New Hampshire than to most other states.

What do you think—is this a serious problem? Why or why not?

the winter in New Hampshire. As with the Iowa caucuses, the importance of the New Hampshire primary is not the number of delegates or how representative the state is but rather that it is traditionally first.[13] At this early stage, the campaign is not for delegates but for images—candidates want the rest of the country to see them as front-runners. The frenzy of political activity in this small state is given lavish attention in the national press. During the week of the primary, half the portable satellite dishes in the country can be found in Manchester, New Hampshire, and the networks move their anchors and top reporters to the scene to broadcast the nightly news. In recent years, over a fifth of TV coverage of the nomination races has been devoted to the New Hampshire primary.[14]

With so much attention paid to the early contests, more states have moved their primaries up in the calendar to capitalize on the media attention. This **frontloading** of the process reached its high point in 2008, when two-thirds of both Democratic and Republican delegates were chosen within six weeks of the Iowa caucus. Frontloading poses two potential problems in the eyes of many commentators. First, there is a concern that with so many delegates being chosen so quickly, there may be a rush to judgment before the public can adequately learn about the candidates. Second, often-times states that have held late primaries have proved to be irrelevant given that one candidate had already secured the nomination by the time their primaries were held. For example, by the time Texas and California voted in 2012, Mitt Romney had already wrapped up the Republican nomination. The razor close race between Hillary Clinton and Barack Obama for the Democratic nomination in 2008 is the only recent instance in which all 50 states mattered.

State laws determine how delegates are allocated, operating within the general guidelines set by the parties. The Democrats require all states to use some form of proportional representation in which a candidate who gets 15 percent or more of a state's vote is awarded a roughly proportional share of the delegates. Republicans employ three basic forms of allocating delegates: some states, like Florida, allocate all Republican delegates to whomever wins the most votes; others, like California, award delegates according to who wins each congressional district; and yet others employ proportional representation. In an attempt to discourage frontloading in 2012, the Republicans adopted a rule eliminating winner-take-all primaries for most states voting prior to April 1.[15]

Week after week, the primaries serve as elimination contests, as the media continually monitor the count of delegates won. The politicians, the press, and the public all love a winner. Candidates who fail to score early wins get labeled as losers and typically drop out of the race. Usually they have little choice since losing quickly inhibits a candidate's ability to raise the money necessary to win in other states. As one veteran fund-raiser put it, "People don't lose campaigns. They run out of money and can't get their planes in the air. That's the reality."[16] For example, when Rick Santorum exited the Republican race in April 2012 he candidly admitted that his campaign was in debt and that his attempts to raise more money had come up empty.

Why It Matters to You
Early Delegate Contests

In baseball, no one would declare a team out of the pennant race after it lost the first two games of the season. But in the race for the presidential nomination, the results of the Iowa caucus and the New Hampshire primary frequently end the campaigns of many candidates after only a handful of national delegates have been selected. These contests are important not because of the number of delegates that are chosen but rather because they are the first indicators of public support. If a candidate does not do well in these first two contests, money and media attention dry up quickly.

In the 1980 delegate chase, a commonly used football term became established in the language of American politics. After George H. W. Bush scored a surprise victory over Ronald Reagan in Iowa, he proudly claimed to possess "the big mo"—momentum. Actually, Bush had only a little "mo" and quickly fell victim to a decisive Reagan victory in New Hampshire. But the term neatly describes what candidates for the nomination are after. Primaries and caucuses are more than an endurance contest, although they are certainly that; they are also proving grounds. Week after week, the challenge is to do better than expected. Learning from his father's experience, George W. Bush jokingly told the reporters on his 2000 campaign plane, "Please stow your expectations securely in your overhead bins, as they may shift during the trip and can fall and hurt someone—especially me."[17]

To get "mo" going, candidates have to beat people they were not expected to beat, collect margins above predictions, and—above all else—never lose to people they were expected to trounce. Momentum is good to have, but it is no guarantee of victory because candidates with a strong base sometimes bounce back. Political scientist Larry Bartels found that "substantive political appeal may overwhelm the impact of momentum."[18] Indeed, after being soundly trounced by John McCain in New Hampshire in 2000, George W. Bush quickly bounced back to win the big states necessary to get the Republican nomination. Eight years later, it was John McCain who bounced back to win after Mike Huckabee scored a victory in the first 2008 Republican contest, in Iowa.

EVALUATING THE PRIMARY AND CAUCUS SYSTEM The primaries and the caucuses are here to stay. However, many political scientists are not particularly happy with the system. Criticisms of the marathon campaign are numerous; here are a few of the most important:

- *Disproportionate attention goes to the early caucuses and primaries.* Take a look at Figure 9.1, which shows that the focus of the two major Democratic candidates

FIGURE 9.1 A COUNT OF CLINTON AND OBAMA EVENTS DURING THE 2008 NOMINATION CAMPAIGN

In 2008, for the first time in many years, the contest for the Democratic nomination turned into a 50-state contest, with Obama and Clinton battling in a close race for every delegate. Yet, as usual, the first caucus in Iowa and the first primary in New Hampshire received far more attention from the candidates than their number of delegates would warrant. Here, you can see a map of the 50 states drawn to scale in terms of the number of events the two major Democratic candidates held in them.

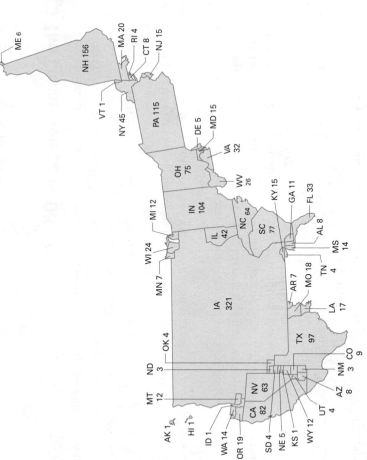

SOURCE: *Washington Post* campaign tracker data for Jan 2007 through May 20, 2008, http://projects.washingtonpost.com/2008-presidential-candidates/tracker/

in 2008 was amazingly concentrated on the early contests for delegates. In particular, Iowa, with the first caucus, and New Hampshire, with the first primary, received far more attention than some of the most heavily populated states, with later contests. Although Iowa and New Hampshire are not always "make-or-break" contests, they play a key—and disproportionate—role in building momentum, by generating money and media attention.

- *Prominent politicians find it difficult to take time out from their duties to run.* Running for the presidency has become a full-time job. It is hard to balance the demands of serving in high public office with running a presidential campaign. This factor sometimes discourages well-qualified politicians from running and forces others to at least partially neglect their elected duties (such as being present for congressional roll call votes) while seeking the presidency.

- *Money plays too big a role in the caucuses and primaries.* Momentum means money—getting more of it than your opponents do. Many people think that money plays too large a role in American presidential elections.

- *Participation in primaries and caucuses is low and unrepresentative.* Although about 60 percent of adult citizens vote in the November presidential election, only about 25 percent cast ballots in presidential primaries. Participation in caucuses is even lower because attending a caucus meeting takes far more time and effort than voting in a primary election. Except for Iowa, where media attention usually boosts the turnout to about 20 percent, only about 5 percent of eligible voters typically show up for caucuses. Moreover, voters in primaries and caucuses are hardly representative of voters at large: they tend to be older and more affluent than average.

9.1
9.2
9.3
9.4
9.5
9.6
9.7
9.8

party platform
A political party's statement of its goals and policies for the next four years. The platform is drafted prior to the party convention by a committee whose members are chosen in rough proportion to each candidate's strength. It is the best formal statement of a party's beliefs.

• *The system gives too much power to the media.* Critics contend that the media have replaced the party bosses as the new kingmakers. The press decides who has momentum at any given moment, and readily labels candidates as winners or losers.

Is this the best way to pick a president? Critics think not, and have come up with ideas for reforming the nomination process, including a national presidential or a series of regional primaries. For the foreseeable future, however, states will continue to select delegates in primaries and caucuses to attend the national conventions, where the nominees are formally chosen.

☐ The Convention Send-Off

Party conventions provided great drama in American politics for more than a century. Great speeches were given, dark-horse candidates suddenly appeared, and ballot after ballot was held as candidates jockeyed to win the nomination. Today, the drama has been drained from the conventions, as the winner is a foregone conclusion. No longer can a powerful governor shift a whole block of votes at the last minute. Delegates selected in primaries and open caucuses have known preferences. The last time there was any doubt as to who would win at the convention was in 1976, when Ford edged out Reagan for the Republican nomination.

Without such drama, the networks have substantially scaled back the number of hours of coverage. In 2012, the Democratic Party responded by cutting their convention from the traditional four days to three for the first time. Even with the condensed TV coverage, the Nielsen ratings have fallen to rather low levels. About 30 million people watched Mitt Romney's speech to the 2012 Republican convention, which was covered by all the major broadcast networks as well as the cable news channels. By contrast, 111 million people tuned in to see the Giants defeat the Patriots in the 2012 Super Bowl, which was broadcast on only one network.

One can hardly blame people for tuning out the conventions when little news is made at them. Today's conventions are carefully scripted to present the party in its best light. As Barack Obama has written, the party convention "serves as a weeklong infomercial for the party and its nominee."[19] The parties carefully orchestrate a massive send-off for the presidential and vice presidential candidates. The party's leaders are there in force, as are many of its most important followers—people whose input will be critical during the general election campaign. As George W. Bush said prior to the Republican convention in 2000, "The convention system provides a system of rewards for hardworking, grass-roots people who end up being delegates. I view it as an opportunity for these people to go back home, energized to help me get elected."[20]

Meeting in an oversized, overstuffed convention hall in a major city, a national party convention has a traditional order of business that has been followed for over a century. The first highlight is usually the keynote speech, in which a dynamic speaker outlines the party's basic principles and touts the nominee-to-be. In 2004, John Kerry chose the little-known Barack Obama for this role at the Democratic convention, and Obama's eloquent speech instantly established him as a rising young political star.

Next, the convention's attention turns to the **party platform**—the party's statement of its goals and policies for the next four years (see the chapter on political parties for some selections from the 2012 party platforms). The platform is drafted prior to the convention by a committee whose members are chosen in rough proportion to each candidate's strength. Any time over 20 percent of the delegates to the platform committee disagree with the majority, they can bring an alternative minority plank to the convention floor for debate. In former times, contests over the platform were key tests of candidates' strength before the actual nomination. These days, party leaders fear any negative publicity that their party might incur by showing open disagreement on a hot issue. Hence, they now maneuver behind the scenes to work out compromises on the platform. This is yet another reason why conventions are no longer very dramatic to watch.

The stage is then set for the main order of business at the convention—formally nominating a candidate for president. One of each candidate's eminent supporters gives a speech extolling the candidate's virtues; a string of seconding speeches then follow. The roll of states is called, and the chair of each state's delegation announces their votes. If no candidate has a majority, then the balloting is repeated as many times as necessary until someone emerges with over 50 percent. For much of American history, multiple-ballot contests involved much behind-the-scenes maneuvering and deal-making; however, the last time a convention took more than one ballot to decide a nomination was in 1952.

Once a presidential candidate is chosen, the convention also has to formally choose a nominee for vice president, though custom dictates that delegates simply vote for whomever the presidential nominee recommends. The vice presidential candidate then comes to the podium to make a brief acceptance speech. This speech is followed by the grand finale—the presidential candidate's acceptance speech, in which the battle lines for the coming campaign are drawn. Afterward, all the party leaders come out to congratulate the party's ticket, raise their hands in unity, and bid the delegates farewell.

The Campaign Game

9.2 Explain the key objectives of any political campaign.

O nce nominated, candidates concentrate on campaigning for the general election. The word *campaign* originated as a military term: generals mounted campaigns, using their limited resources to achieve strategic objectives. Political campaigns proceed in a similar fashion, with candidates allocating their scarce resources of time, money, and energy to achieve their political objectives.

Campaigns involve more than organization and leadership. Artistry also enters the picture, for campaigns deal in images. The campaign is the canvas on which political strategists try to paint portraits of leadership, competence, caring, and other characteristics Americans value in presidents. Campaigning today is an art and a science, heavily dependent—like much else in American politics—on technology.

The High-Tech Media Campaign

Today, television is the most prevalent means used by candidates to reach voters. Thomas Patterson stresses that "today's presidential campaign is essentially a mass media campaign.... It is no exaggeration to say that, for the majority of voters, the campaign has little reality apart from its media version."[21] Barack Obama put this into a candidate's perspective when he wrote, "I—like every politician at the federal level—am almost entirely dependent on the media to reach my constituents. It is the filter through which my votes are interpreted, my statements analyzed, my beliefs examined. For the broad public at least, I am who the media says I am."[22]

The Internet now also plays a major role in political campaigns. Indeed, for young people the Internet rivals TV as a source of information about campaigns, as you can see in "Young People and Politics: Will the Internet Revolutionize Political Campaigns?" Thus, one of the first things presidential candidates now do is establish a Web site with detailed information about their issue stands and background, videos of their key speeches, a schedule of upcoming events, and a form enabling people to donate to the campaign online. A January 2012 survey by the Pew Research Center found that 15 percent of Americans had gone online to read or watch campaign material posted on a candidate's Web site. The same study also found that 16 percent said they regularly receive e-mails with political content and 6 percent had followed a candidate's updates on Facebook or Twitter.[23]

284

9.1
9.2
9.3
9.4
9.5
9.6
9.7
9.8

Young People & Politics

Will the Internet Revolutionize Political Campaigns?

When television first started to play a major role in American campaigns, it was the younger generation who took to it the fastest. Today, as people are relying more and more on the Internet to learn about politics, it is again America's youth that is leading the way. In a 2012 national survey, people were asked, "How have you been getting most of your news about the presidential election campaign?" One or two answers were recorded for each respondent. Below you can see the percentage within each age group who said that TV or the Internet was the main way they got news about the campaign.

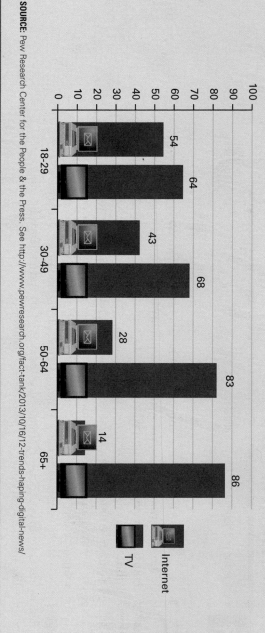

SOURCE: Pew Research Center for the People & the Press. See http://www.pewresearch.org/fact-tank/2013/10/16/12-trends-haping-digital-news/

CRITICAL THINKING QUESTIONS

1. With young people more reliant on the Internet than older people, how will campaigns have to change in order to reach them with their message?

2. Try learning about what's going in politics by first watching about 15 minutes of TV news and then browsing the Internet for the same amount of time. How did your consumption of information change between one format and the other?

---

direct mail

A method of raising money for a political cause or candidate, in which information and requests for money are sent to people whose names appear on lists of those who have supported similar views or candidates in the past.

Nowhere has the impact of the Internet been greater than on political fund-raising. More people are making political donations than ever before because all it takes is a simple submission of a few pieces of information on the Internet. In both 2008 and 2012, the Obama campaign received contributions from over a million people via the Internet. Many donated repeatedly throughout the year in response to occasional e-mail requests from the Obama campaign.

Computer technology has long been used by campaigns in the form of **direct mail**, a technique for locating potential supporters by sending information and a request for money to huge lists of people who have supported candidates with similar views in the past. Conservative fund-raiser Richard Viguerie pioneered the mass mailing list, including in his computerized list the names and addresses of hundreds of thousands of individuals who contributed to conservative causes. The accumulation of mailing lists enables candidates to pick an issue—be it helping the homeless, opposing abortion, aiding Israel, or anything else—and write to a list of people concerned about that issue. The ability to use e-mail has made such targeted fund-raising far easier and more cost effective. Direct mail costs roughly 40 cents for every dollar raised through solicitations sent out via the post office. On the Internet, the main expense is just the staff time to collect addresses and write up the e-mail messages. As Robert Boatright argues, "Candidates who use the Web to raise money can raise larger sums from small donors than has traditionally been the case in campaigns; they can effectively give donors an idea of how their money will be used; and they can more easily resolicit donors throughout the campaign."[24] The e-mail list maintained by the 2012 Obama campaign reportedly exceeded 13 million addresses, to which the campaign e-mailed regularly with strategic updates and requests for further participation. Obama's 2012 campaign even opened a first-of-its-kind campaign office dedicated to high-tech work, such as setting up Twitter feeds, Facebook pages, and other Internet applications. The high-tech campaign is no longer a luxury. Candidates *must* use the media and computer technology just to stay competitive.

The most important goal of any media campaign is simply to get attention. Media coverage is determined by two factors: (1) how candidates use their advertising budget and (2) the "free" attention they get as news makers. The first, obviously, is relatively easy to control; the second is more difficult but not impossible. Almost every logistical decision in a campaign—where to eat breakfast, whom to include on stage, when to announce a major policy proposal—is calculated according to its intended media impact.

The major item in a campaign budget is unquestionably television advertising. At least half the total budget for a presidential or U.S. Senate campaign will be used for campaign commercials. Many observers worry that we have entered a new era of politics in which the slick slogan and the image salesperson dominate. Early in the TV age, one of the first presidential candidates who made a political commercial remarked that "the idea that you can merchandise candidates for high office like breakfast cereal is the ultimate indignity to the democratic process." Ever since, critics of political ads have bemoaned that, like ads for consumer products, political ads tend to emphasize style over substance, image over information. But is this comparison really valid? Most product ads aim to simply create an awareness of the item for sale; political ads are designed in large part to prompt people's thinking. Product ads usually avoid conflict and take a soft-sell approach; political ads tend to heighten conflict and employ a hard-sell approach. These differences between product and political ads help explain why political scientists have found that campaign advertising is an important source of information about policy issues. In a classic study, Thomas Patterson and Robert McClure found that viewers learned a substantial amount about candidates' issue stands from watching their ads on TV.[25] Similarly, a comprehensive study of 230,000 candidate ads that ran in 1998 found that spots that emphasized policy outnumbered those that stressed personal image by a 6-to-1 ratio.[26] Most candidates apparently believe that their policy positions are a crucial part of their campaign, and they are willing to pay substantial sums to communicate them to voters.

Candidates have much less control over the other aspect of the media, news coverage. To be sure, most campaigns have press aides who feed "canned" news releases to reporters. Still, the media largely determine for themselves what is happening in a campaign and what they want to cover. Campaign coverage seems to be a constant interplay between hard news about what candidates say and do and the human interest angle, which most journalists think sells newspapers or interests television viewers. Apparently, news organizations believe that policy issues are of less interest to voters than the campaign itself. The result is that news coverage is disproportionately devoted to campaign strategies, speculation about what will happen next, poll results, and other aspects of the campaign game. Once a candidate has taken a policy position and it has been reported, it becomes old news. The latest poll showing Smith ahead of Jones is thus more newsworthy. Roger Ailes, the president of Fox News, calls this his "orchestra pit" theory of American politics: "If you have two guys on stage and one guy says, 'I have a solution to the Middle East problem,' and the other guy falls in the orchestra pit, who do you think is going to be on the evening news?"[27] A comprehensive study of media coverage of the 2008 campaign found that far more stories dealt with the horse race and strategy than with policy and the candidates' public records.[28]

☐ Organizing the Campaign

In every campaign, there is too much to do and too little time to do it. Every candidate must prepare for a seemingly endless string of speeches, media interviews, fund-raising events, and handshaking. More important, to organize their campaigns effectively, candidates must do the following:

- **Get a campaign manager.** Some candidates try to run their own campaign, but they usually end up regretting it. A professional campaign manager can keep the candidate from getting bogged down in organizational details. This person also bears the day-to-day responsibility for keeping the campaign square on its message and setting its tone.

- **Get a fund-raiser.** Money, as this chapter will soon discuss in detail, is an important key to election victory.

- **Get a campaign counsel.** With all the current federal regulation of campaign financing, legal assistance is essential to ensure compliance with the laws.

- **Hire media and campaign consultants.** Candidates have more important things to do with their time than plan ad campaigns, contract for buttons and bumper stickers, and buy TV time and newspaper space. Professionals can get them the most exposure for their money.

- **Assemble a campaign staff.** It is desirable to hire as many professionals as the campaign budget allows, but it is also important to get a coordinator of volunteers to ensure that envelopes are licked, doorbells rung, and other small but vital tasks addressed. Many campaign volunteers are typically young people, who are the most likely to have the energy and freedom from commitments required for this sort of intensive work.

- **Plan the logistics.** A modern presidential campaign involves jetting around the country at an incredible pace. Aides known as "advance workers" handle the complicated details of candidate scheduling and see to it that events are well publicized and well attended.

- **Get a research staff and policy advisers.** Candidates have little time to master the complex issues reporters will ask about. Policy advisers—often distinguished academics—feed them the information they need to keep up with events.

- **Hire a pollster.** Professional polling firms conduct opinion research to tell candidates how the voters view them and what is on the voters' minds.

- **Get a good press secretary.** Candidates running for major office have reporters dogging them every step of the way. The reporters need news, and a good press secretary can help them make their deadlines with stories that the campaign would like to see reported.

- **Establish a Web site.** A Web site is a relatively inexpensive way of getting a candidate's message out. Candidates generally post position papers, videos of their speeches, and information on how to volunteer and contribute money.

Most of these tasks cost money. Campaigns are not cheap, and the role of money in campaigns is a controversial one.

Money and Campaigning

9.3   Outline how the financing of federal campaigns is regulated by campaign finance laws.

C ampaigns for office are expensive and, in America's high-tech political arena, growing more so. Candidates need money to build a campaign organization and to get their message out. Although many people make small political donations, those who most grease the wheel of political campaigns are hardly representative of middle-class Americans, and there is much concern that wealthy campaign contributors are buying special influence over public policy decisions.

There are two basic ways to contribute money to the dialogue of political campaigns in America:

1. **campaign contributions** to the candidates' campaigns and to the political parties, which go directly into their bank accounts and then can be used in any way they see fit; and

2. donations to groups that make **independent expenditures** to express political views which may aid a candidate's campaign, but that cannot coordinate with the campaign.

We will examine each of these methods in turn and then discuss some fundamental questions about the role of money in campaigns.

☐ Regulations on Campaign Contributions

In the early 1970s, as the costs of campaigning skyrocketed and the Watergate scandal exposed large, illegal campaign contributions, momentum developed for campaign finance reform. Several public interest lobbies led the drive. In 1974, Congress passed the **Federal Election Campaign Act**. The most important consequence of this law was to transform the secretive world of campaign finance into an open book for public scrutiny. It required that all candidates for federal office must disclose: (1) who has contributed money to their campaign; and (2) how the campaign funds have been spent.

In addition to requiring transparency in campaign finance, the historic legislation of 1974 also instituted limits on campaign contributions for the first time. Scandalized to find out that some wealthy individuals had contributed $1 million to the 1972 Nixon campaign, Congress limited individual contributions to presidential and congressional candidates to $1,000 per election. (In 2002, the McCain–Feingold Act, discussed below, increased this limit to $2,000 and provided for it to be indexed to rise with inflation in the future; hence, the limit for 2014 was $2,600.) Interest group donations to campaigns were also limited by the 1974 reforms via regulations on **political action committees** (PACs), which can channel contributions to candidates of up to $5,000 per election.

In order to create a repository for campaign finance reports, as well as to enforce limits on campaign contributions, the 1974 act established the **Federal Election Commission** (FEC). Three spots on the FEC are reserved for Democrats and three for Republicans. The rules of the commission require four votes for any action, and as a result, its critics say, the FEC is all too often locked in partisan stalemate. Nevertheless, it has successfully fulfilled its mission to open up the details of campaign finance for everyone to see. Candidates and parties must file regular detailed contribution and expenditure reports with the commission, which in turn posts them at www.fec.gov. Furthermore, a variety of Web sites have taken on the task of making this information easy to search through. If you want to know how much money a particular candidate for federal office has recently raised for their campaign, you can look up their most recent quarterly statement at www.opensecrets.org. And if you want to know who among your neighbors has donated to federal campaigns, you can also find this information with a simple search at this Web site. As Frank Sorauf writes, detailed reports of American campaign contributions and expenditures have "become a wonder of the democratic political world. Nowhere else do scholars and journalists find so much information about the funding of campaigns, and the openness of Americans about the flow of money stuns many other nationals accustomed to silence and secrecy about such traditionally private matters."[29]

Less successful over the long run has been the system of using taxpayer dollars to pay a substantial part of the cost of presidential campaigns—this portion of the 1974 campaign finance law has withered into irrelevance. Money for public financing of presidential campaigns is still collected from taxpayers via a $3 voluntary check-off box

---

campaign contributions
Donations that are made directly to a candidate or a party and that must be reported to the FEC. As of 2014, individuals were allowed to donate up to $2,600 per election to a candidate and up to $32,400 to a political party.

independent expenditures
Expenses on behalf of a political message that are made by groups that are uncoordinated with any candidate's campaign.

Federal Election Campaign Act
A law passed in 1974 for reforming campaign finances. The act created the Federal Election Commission and provided for limits on and disclosure of campaign contributions.

political action committees
Groups that raise money from individuals and then distribute it in the form of contributions to candidates that the group supports. PACs must register with the FEC and report their donations and contributions to it. Individual contributions to a PAC are limited to $5,000 per year, and a PAC may give up to $5,000 to a candidate for each election.

Federal Election Commission
A six-member bipartisan agency created by the Federal Election Campaign Act of 1974. The Federal Election Commission administers and enforces campaign finance laws.

9.1
9.2
9.3
9.4
9.5
9.6
9.7
9.8

soft money
Political contributions earmarked for party-building expenses at the grassroots level or for generic party advertising. For a time, such contributions were unlimited, until they were banned by the McCain–Feingold Act.

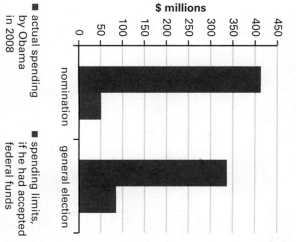

$ millions

- actual spending by Obama in 2008
- spending limits, if he had accepted federal funds

nomination   general election

FIGURE 9.2 HOW OBAMA RAISED MORE CAMPAIGN MONEY BY DECLINING FEDERAL FUNDS

In 2008, Barack Obama became the first presidential candidate to turn down federal funds for the nomination and general election campaigns since the option of public financing was instituted for presidential campaigns in the mid-1970s. The public financing system entitled him to receive matching funds for contributions of up to $250 during the primaries and to completely finance his general election campaign with a check from the FEC. The catch would have been that he would have had limit his total spending to the amount prescribed by Congress in the 1970s, adjusted for inflation. These limits, however, are voluntary—a candidate is free to decline the federal funds. As you can see in the figure, saying "no thanks" to federal financing freed Obama to raise far more money.

SOURCE: Federal Election Commission reports.

on federal income tax returns. But only about 7 percent of taxpayers currently check the box, thereby limiting the amount of money available. More importantly, in order to claim the taxpayer funds, candidates have to agree to restrictions on overall spending, and these restrictions have become an unacceptable condition for any serious presidential campaign. Figure 9.2 compares what Barack Obama actually spent in 2008 to what he would have been limited to spending had he accepted federal funds. One can readily see why he turned down taxpayer dollars to have the freedom to raise as much as possible in individual donations of up to $2,400 (the inflation-indexed contribution limit in 2008). In 2012 no presidential candidate applied for federal funds. And it is unlikely that we'll see any future candidates do so unless the restrictions on overall spending are substantially altered or repealed.

No discussion of campaign donations would be complete without some discussion of the loopholes that have been opened up (and sometimes closed) over the years. Although the 1974 campaign reform act was generally welcomed by both parties, in the 1976 case of *Buckley v. Valeo*, the Supreme Court struck down a portion of the act that had limited the amount individuals could contribute to their own campaigns. The Court reasoned that, while big campaign contributions could corrupt politicians and hence needed to be limited, one could hardly corrupt oneself by donating to one's own campaign. This Court ruling made it possible for Ross Perot to spend over $60 million of his own fortune on his independent presidential candidacy in 1992 and for Mitt Romney to spend $44 million out of his own pocket in pursuit of the Republican presidential nomination in 2008.

Another loophole was opened in 1979 with an amendment to the original act that made it easier for political parties to raise money for voter registration drives, for distributing campaign material at the grassroots level, and for generic party advertising. Money raised for such purposes was known as **soft money** and for a time was not subject to any contribution limits. In 2000, an unprecedented amount of money flowed into the coffers of the national parties through this loophole—a total of nearly half a billion dollars, with many of the contributions coming in increments of hundreds of thousands of dollars. AT&T alone gave over $3 million in soft money, as did the American Federation of State, County, and Municipal Employees. The Democratic Party raised $32 million in soft money donations specifically for its new national headquarters building, including a $7 million donation from Haim Saban, the billionaire creator of the Teenage Mutant Ninja Turtles.

Senators John McCain (R-AZ) and Russell Feingold (D-WI) crusaded for years to remove large soft money campaign contributions from the political system. Their efforts finally came to fruition in 2002 when their bill was passed by the Congress and signed into law by President George W. Bush. The major provision of the McCain–Feingold Act was to ban soft money contributions. Limits on contributions to political parties were set at $25,000 and indexed to rise with inflation; as of 2014, the limit was $32,400. In the 2003 case of *McConnell v. Federal Election Commission*, the Supreme Court ruled 5 to 4 in favor of this ban on unlimited contributions directly to the political parties. The majority concluded that this restriction was justified by the government's legitimate interest in preventing "both the actual corruption threatened by large financial contributions and ... the appearance of corruption" that might result from those contributions.

Although the McCain–Feingold's ban on soft money contributions remains in effect, it did not take long for a people who wanted to spend big money to participate in politics to find other ways to do so. Some scholars call this the "hydraulic theory of money and politics," noting that money, like water, inevitably finds its way around any obstacle. In this instance, the way around was through independent political expenditures, which we turn to next.

☐ Regulations on Independent Political Expenditures

If you hear that rich individuals are giving million dollar contributions to candidates or political parties these days, that is technically and legally incorrect. Instead, what they are doing is giving large sums to groups that are independent of a candidate or party, and whose actions cannot be legally coordinated with them.

The authors of the 2002 McCain–Feingold Act intended that by the next presidential election big money would be removed from politics. But wealthy individuals on both sides of the political spectrum soon found that they could make unlimited contributions to what is known as **527 groups**, which are named after the section of the federal tax code that governs these political groups. In a controversial 2004 ruling, the FEC declined to subject 527 groups to contribution restrictions as long as their political messages did not make explicit endorsements of candidates by using phrases like "Vote for" and "Vote against." The result was that many people who had in the past given big soft money contributions to the parties instead gave big donations to 527 groups, such as the anti-Kerry group Swift Boat Veterans for Truth or the anti-Bush group MoveOn.org. Although such donations were unlimited, they still had to be disclosed to the FEC.

Independent expenditures by 527 groups were partially restricted for about eight years by the McCain–Feingold Act. A major provision of this law prohibited

527 groups
Independent political groups that are not subject to contribution restrictions because they do not directly seek the election of particular candidates. Section 527 of the tax code specifies that contributions to such groups must be reported to the IRS.

David Bossie is president of Citizens United, a conservative nonprofit organization, which in 2008 produced *Hillary: The Movie*. When the Federal Election Commission ruled that this movie was unlawful electioneering, Citizens United successfully sued, establishing the right of any group to engage in independent political expenditures.

Citizens United v. Federal Election Commission

A 2010 landmark Supreme Court case that ruled that individuals, corporations, and unions could donate unlimited amounts of money to groups that make independent political expenditures.

501(c) groups

Groups that are exempted from reporting their contributions and can receive unlimited contributions. Section 501c of the tax code specifies that such groups cannot spend more than half their funds on political activities.

Super PACs

Independent expenditure-only PACs are known as Super PACs because they may accept donations of any size and can endorse candidates. Their contributions and expenditures must be periodically reported to the FEC.

corporations and unions from using their general treasury funds to pay for electioneering communications in the last 60 days of federal campaigns. However, in the 2010 case of *Citizens United v. Federal Election Commission*, the Supreme Court ruled 5 to 4 that this was an unconstitutional restriction on free speech. Thus, both corporations and unions can now spend as much as they like to promote their political views, as long as they do so without coordinating their message with any candidate's campaign.

Soon afterward, **501(c) groups** emerged as vehicles for unlimited political donations that could remain anonymous. Such groups are regulated by the IRS rather than the FEC, and donations do not have to be reported unless a donor gives money specifically for a political ad. Thus, even corporations and unions can now give big sums to 501(c) groups without having any public disclosure of these donations. Presently, the only significant restriction on 501(c) groups is that they cannot spend more than half their funds on political activities, though many in Congress would like to change the law to require that donations of $10,000 or more be disclosed.[30]

Many critics of the *Citizens United* decision, including President Obama, argued that the Supreme Court had opened up the floodgates to special interest money (especially that of corporations) to corrupt the electoral process. The majority of the justices did not see it this way, however. The key portion of the majority decision noted that in 100,000 pages of the record reviewing the McCain–Feingold law there were not "any direct examples of votes being exchanged for independent expenditures." These five justices therefore concluded that "independent expenditures do not lead to, or create the appearance of, *quid pro quo* corruption." In fact, they argued, "there is only scant evidence that independent expenditures even ingratiate." Consequently, the Court ruled that such expenditures were protected under the Constitution as free speech.

Employing this reasoning from the *Citizens United* decision, in the case of *SpeechNow.org v. FEC* the D.C. Court of Appeals ruled that donations to a PAC that makes only independent expenditures could not be limited. Whereas a regular PAC can accept donations of no more than $5,000 a year from each individual and can donate no more than $5,000 per election to a candidate, the *SpeechNow* ruling made it possible for a PAC that just expresses its views to collect and spend heretofore unheard of amounts. Journalists soon realized the explosive impact these independent expenditure-only PACs could have, labeling them **Super PACs.**

In 2012, Super PACs arose to support each of the presidential candidates in both parties. Some of the wealthiest people in the country suddenly found that, although they could donate only $2,500 to the candidate of their choice, they could now send a multi-million dollar check to a Super PAC that would run ads on behalf of this candidate. Critics of this new development in campaign finance argued that it represented a threat to the spirit of limits on campaign contributions designed to minimize corruption in politics. Besides the unprecedented large sums, there was also criticism of how the lines between a candidate's campaign and their Super PAC were not quite so independent, what with top aides to both Obama and Romney appearing at Super PAC fundraising events.

The lack of any formal coordination between a SuperPAC and a candidate's campaign might seem to be a technical matter, but it has real world consequences. This lack of coordination often made SuperPAC ads ineffective according to Stuart Stevens, Mitt Romney's 2012 campaign manager. Stevens candidly told an academic audience after the election that he hated SuperPACs, even though their spending had favored his candidate. He likened the support he got from SuperPACs as being like "putting out a daily newspaper and your lead is going to be sent over by somebody else with your story with your lead picture. And you have no idea what it is. They're just going to drop it in. It could be on the new Mars lunar landing or it could be on a murder. You have no idea. It's the most confounding horrible situation."[31]

It remains to be seen how these new free-spending independent political expenditures may change the answer to two perpetual questions on money and politics to which we turn to next: are campaigns too expensive, and does money buy victory?

Are Campaigns Too Expensive?

The Center for Responsive Politics totaled the cost of the 2012 campaigns for presidency and Congress to be $6.3 billion.[32] This seems like a tremendous amount of money. Yet American elections cost, per person, about as much as a DVD movie. Bradley Smith writes that the proportion of the nation's gross domestic product spent on political activity is a mere .05 percent.[33] What bothers politicians most about the rising costs of campaigning is that fund-raising takes up so much of their time. For example, former Senator Tom Daschle said in 2014 that "A typical United States senator spends two-thirds of the last two years of their term raising money."[34]

Public financing of federal campaigns is often suggested as a possible solution to this problem. Some lawmakers support some sort of public financing reform; however, it will be very difficult to get Congress to consent to equal financing for the people who will challenge them for their seats. Incumbents will not readily give up the advantage they have in raising money.

Does Money Buy Victory?

Perhaps the most basic complaint about money and politics is that there may be a direct link between dollars spent and votes received. Few have done more to dispel this charge than political scientist Gary Jacobson. His research has shown that the more congressional incumbents spend, the worse they do.[35] This fact is not as odd as it sounds. It simply means that incumbents who face a tough opponent must raise more money to meet the challenge. When a challenger is not a serious threat, as they all too often are not, incumbents can afford to campaign cheaply.

More important than having "more" money is having "enough" money. Herbert Alexander calls this "the doctrine of sufficiency." As he writes, "Enough money must be spent to get a message across to compete effectively but outspending one's opponent is not always necessary—even an incumbent with a massive ratio of higher spending."[36] One case in point is that of the late Paul Wellstone, a previously obscure political science professor who beat an incumbent senator in 1990 despite being outspent by 5 to 1.[37] Billionaire Meg Whitman spent over $140 million of her own money in her 2010 bid for the governorship of California but was soundly defeated by Jerry Brown, whose campaign had about $100 million less to spend.

292

9.1
9.2
9.3
9.4
9.5
9.6
9.7
9.8

selective perception
The phenomenon that people's beliefs often guide what they pay the most attention to and how they interpret events.

suffrage
The legal right to vote in the United States, gradually extended to virtually all citizens over the age of 18.

The Impact of Campaigns

9.4 Determine why campaigns have an important yet limited impact on election outcomes.

lmost all politicians figure that a good campaign is the key to victory. Many political scientists, however, question the importance of campaigns. Reviewing the evidence, Dan Nimmo concluded, "Political campaigns are less crucial in elections than most politicians believe."[38] For years, research-

ers studying campaigns have stressed that campaigns have three effects on voters: reinforcement, activation, and conversion. Campaigns can *reinforce* voters' preferences for candidates; they can *activate* voters, getting them to contribute money or ring doorbells as opposed to merely voting; and they can *convert*, changing voters' minds.

Many decades of research on political campaigns leads to a single message: campaigns mostly reinforce and activate; only rarely do they convert. The evidence on the impact of campaigns points clearly to the conclusion that the best-laid plans of campaign managers change very few votes. Given the millions of dollars spent on political campaigns, it may be surprising to find that they do not have a great effect. Several factors tend to weaken campaigns' impact on voters:

- Most people pay relatively little attention to campaigns in the first place. People have a remarkable capacity for **selective perception**—paying most attention to things they already agree with and interpreting events according to their own predispositions.

- Long-term factors, such as party identification, influence voting behavior regardless of what happens in the campaign. As John Sides and Lynn Vavreck wrote in their detailed study of the 2012 campaign, "Strengthening people's natural partisan predispositions is one of the most consistent effects of presidential campaigns."[39]

- Incumbents start with a substantial advantage in terms of name recognition and a track record.

Such findings do not mean, of course, that campaigns never change voters' minds or that converting a small percentage is unimportant. In their careful analysis of survey data, Hillygus and Shields find that a substantial number of voters are persuadable because they disagree with their preferred candidate on at least one issue (for example, pro-choice Republicans). They demonstrate how politicians use what are known as "wedge" issues—issues on which the other party's coalition is divided—to attempt to draw supporters from the opponent's camp into their own.[40] In tight races, a good campaign that targets specific constituencies for persuasion can make the difference between winning and losing.

As the campaign nears its end, voters face two key choices: whether to vote and, if they choose to, how to vote. The following sections investigate the ways that voters make these choices.

Whether to Vote: A Citizen's First Choice

9.5 Identify the factors that influence whether people vote.

ver two centuries of American electoral history, federal laws have greatly expanded **suffrage**—the right to vote. Virtually everyone over the age of 18 now has the right to vote. The two major exceptions concern noncitizens and convicted criminals. There is no federal requirement stating that voters must be citizens, and it was quite common in the nineteenth century for immigrants to vote prior to attaining citizenship. However, no state currently permits residents who are not citizens to vote. Some immigrant groups feel that this ought to at least be changed at the local level. State law varies widely when it comes to crime and voting: virtually all states deny prisoners the right to vote, about half extend the ban to people on parole, and 10 states impose a lifetime ban on convicted felons.

Interestingly, as the right to vote has been extended, proportionately fewer of those eligible have chosen to exercise that right. The 80 percent turnout of eligible adults in the 1896 election was the high point of electoral participation. In 2012, 59 percent of adult citizens voted in the presidential election, and only about 36 percent voted in the midterm congressional elections of 2014.

Deciding Whether to Vote

Realistically, when over 125 million people vote in a presidential election, as they did in 2012, the chance of one vote affecting the outcome is very, very slight. Once in a while, of course, an election is decided by a small number of votes, as was the case with George W. Bush being elected president in 2000 by winning the state of Florida by a mere 537 votes. It is more likely, however, that you will be struck by lightning during your lifetime than participate in an election decided by a single vote.

Not only does your vote probably not make much difference to the outcome, but voting is somewhat costly. You have to spend some of your valuable time becoming informed, making up your mind, and getting to the polls. If you carefully calculate your time and energy, you might rationally decide that the costs of voting outweigh the benefits. Indeed, the most frequent reason for nonvoting given by those who were registered but didn't vote has been that they could not take time off from work or school that day.[41] Some scholars have therefore proposed that one of the easiest ways to increase American turnout levels would be to move Election Day to Saturday or to make it a holiday, as in many other countries.[42]

Economist Anthony Downs, in his model of democracy, tries to explain why a rational person would ever bother to vote. He argues that rational people vote if they believe that the policies of one party will bring more benefits than the policies of

Occasionally election outcomes are so close that all the individual ballots have to be carefully recounted. Here, an election official examines a ballot in the 2008 Minnesota Senate race, with representatives from the opposing candidates observing on either side. In the original count, Norm Coleman finished 215 votes ahead, but after the recount Al Franken won the election by 225 votes.

294

9.1
9.2
9.3
9.4
9.5
9.6
9.7
9.8

political efficacy
The belief that one's political participation really matters—that one's vote can actually make a difference.

civic duty
The belief that in order to support democratic government, a citizen should vote.

voter registration
A system adopted by the states that requires voters to register prior to voting. Some states require citizens to register as much as 30 days in advance, whereas others permit Election Day registration.

Motor Voter Act
A 1993 act that requires states to permit people to register to vote when they apply for a driver's license.

the other party.[43] Thus, people who see policy differences between the parties on the key issues that concern them are more likely to join the ranks of voters. If you are an environmentalist and you expect the Democrats to pass more environmental legislation than the Republicans, then you have an additional incentive to go to the polls. On the other hand, if you are truly indifferent—that is, if you see no difference whatsoever between the two parties—you may rationally decide to abstain.

Another reason why many people vote is that they have a high sense of **political efficacy**—the belief that ordinary people can influence the government. Efficacy is measured by asking people to agree or disagree with statements such as "People like me don't have any say about what the government does." Those who lack strong feelings of efficacy are being quite rational in staying home on Election Day because they don't think they can make a difference. Yet even some of these people will vote anyway, simply to support democratic government. In this case, people are impelled to vote by a sense of **civic duty**. The benefit from doing one's civic duty is the long-term contribution made toward preserving democracy.

Registering to Vote

Politicians used to say, "Vote early and often." Largely to prevent corruption associated with stuffing ballot boxes, around 1900 states adopted **voter registration** laws, which require individuals to first place their name on an electoral roll in order to be allowed to vote. Although these laws have made it more difficult to vote more than once, they have also discouraged some people from voting at all. America's registration system is, in part, to blame for why Americans are significantly less likely to go to the polls than citizens of other democratic nations (see "America in Perspective: Why Turnout in the United States Is So Low Compared to Turnout in Other Countries").

Registration procedures currently differ from state to state. In sparsely populated North Dakota, there is no registration at all, and in Minnesota, Wisconsin, Iowa, Wyoming, Idaho, Montana, New Hampshire, and Maine voters could register on Election Day in 2012. Advocates of this user-friendly procedure are quick to point out that these states all ranked near the top in voter turnout in 2012. For many years, some states—particularly in the South—had burdensome registration procedures, such as requiring people to make a trip to their county courthouse during normal business hours. This situation was changed by the 1993 **Motor Voter Act**, which made voter registration easier by requiring states to allow eligible voters to register by simply checking a box on their driver's license application or renewal form. Nevertheless, its impact on turnout has thus far been largely disappointing. Turnout for the presidential election of 2012 was virtually the same as turnout in the 1992 election, before the act was passed.

In recent years, Democratic and Republican-controlled states have moved in opposite directions in terms of state laws pertaining to voter registration. Many states controlled by the Democrats have made it easier to register online, and Democrats in California and Colorado have led the way for these states to put election day registration into effect for the 2016 presidential election. In the view of many Republican legislators, such easy voter registration procedures are an open invitation for voter fraud. Rather than making voter registration easier, Republican-controlled states, such as Texas and Georgia, have focused on combating voter fraud by requiring people to show an official piece of identification, such as a driver's license, when they sign in to vote. Such procedures were pioneered in Indiana and upheld as constitutional by the Supreme Court in the 2008 case of *Crawford v. Marion County Election Board*. As Governor Nikki Haley of South Carolina said when she signed her state's new voter ID law in 2011, "If you can show a picture to buy Sudafed, if you can show a picture to get on an airplane, you should be able to show a picture ID to vote."[44] Opponents of voter ID requirements have charged that such requirements impose an unfair burden on groups such as students, racial minorities, and poor people, all of whom are less likely to have a government-sponsored photo ID.

America in Perspective

Why Turnout in the United States Is So Low Compared to Turnout in Other Countries

Despite living in a culture that encourages participation, Americans have a woefully low turnout rate compared to citizens of other democracies. The graph below displays the most recent election turnout rates in the United States and a variety of other nations.

There are several reasons given for Americans' abysmally low turnout rate. Probably the one most often cited is the American requirement of voter registration. The governments of many (but not all) other democracies take the responsibility of seeing to it that all their eligible citizens are on the voting lists. In America, the responsibility for registration lies solely with the individual. If we were like the Scandinavian countries, where the government registers every eligible citizen, no doubt our turnout rate would be higher.

A second difference between the United States and other countries is that the American government asks citizens to vote far more often. Whereas the typical European voter may cast two or three ballots in a four-year period, many Americans are faced with a dozen or more separate elections in the space of four years. Furthermore, Americans are expected to vote for a much wider range of political offices. With one elected official for roughly every 500 citizens, and elections held somewhere virtually every week, it is no wonder that it is so difficult to get Americans to the polls. It is probably no coincidence that the one European country that has a lower turnout rate—Switzerland—has also overwhelmed its citizens with voting opportunities, typically asking people to vote three or four times every year.

Third, the stimulus to vote is low in the United States because the choices offered Americans are not

as starkly different as in other countries. The United States is quite unusual in that it has always lacked a major left-wing socialist party. When European voters go to the polls, they are deciding on whether their country will be run by parties with socialist goals or by conservative (and in some cases religious) parties. The consequences of their vote for redistribution of income and the scope of government are far greater than the ordinary American voter can imagine.

Finally, the United States is one of the few democracies that still vote midweek, when most people are working. Article I, Section IV of the U.S. Constitution allows Congress to determine the timing of federal elections. Thus, Congress could certainly change the date of Election Day, if it wanted to. Comparative research has shown that countries that hold elections on the weekend have higher turnout.

CRITICAL THINKING QUESTIONS

1. Some people would like the United States to emulate other countries and have the government automatically register everyone who is eligible to vote. Others oppose this European-style system, believing that this would lead to an intrusive big government that would require everyone to have a national identity card. What do you think?

2. Do you think American turnout rates would be better if we followed the lead of most other democracies and held elections on the weekend?

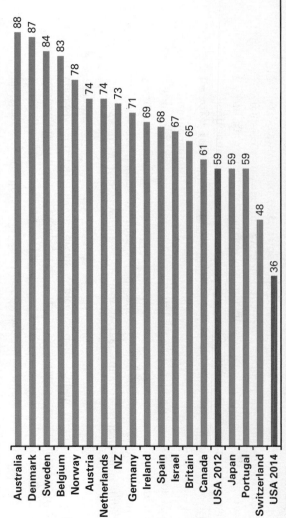

Australia 88
Denmark 87
Sweden 84
Belgium 83
Norway 78
Austria 74
Netherlands 74
NZ 73
Germany 71
Ireland 69
Spain 68
Israel 67
Britain 65
Canada 61
USA 2012 59
Japan 59
Portugal 59
Switzerland 48
USA 2014 36

Percent of citizens (USA) or registered (other countries) voting

SOURCES: In all countries except for the United States, official reports of the percentage of registered voters casting valid votes. For the United States, the percentage of citizens participating was calculated based on Census Bureau reports of the number of citizens of voting age and reports from the states regarding how many people voted.

In recent years, a number of states have adopted laws requiring voters to show a photo ID at the polls. Here, an election judge in Missouri uses a new voter registration computer system to scan a voter's driver's license.

The Department of Justice under President Obama agreed with the opponents of voter IDs, and tried to block implementation of voter ID laws in states covered by the Voting Rights Act.

Who Votes?

Given that turnout among American citizens peaks at about 60 percent in presidential elections and usually runs at about just 40 percent in midterm congressional elections, studying nonvoters becomes especially important. Table 9.1 displays data regarding the turnout rates of various groups in the 2012 presidential election and the 2010 midterm contests. This information reveals numerous demographic factors that are related to turnout:

- **Education.** People with higher-than-average educational levels have a higher rate of voting than people with less education. Highly educated people are more capable of discerning the major differences between the candidates and they are more able to judge how these differences will impact both their own lives and the well-being of the nation.

- **Age.** Young adults are less likely to follow politics regularly and hence often lack sufficient motivation to vote. In addition, younger people have to get themselves on the registration rolls for the first time whereas most older people are already registered to vote. Yet, even just analyzing turnout patterns among people who are registered to vote yields wide turnout differences by age group. In Iowa, for example, the secretary of state reported that among those on the registration rolls, only 24 percent of those under 25 years of age voted in 2010, as compared to 73 percent among those over 65 years of age.[45]

- **Race and ethnicity.** Minorities are usually underrepresented among voters relative to their share of the citizenry. This is clearly evident in the table's turnout

TABLE 9.1 REPORTED TURNOUT RATES FOR GROUPS OF U.S. CITIZENS IN 2012 AND 2010

	% Voting in 2012	% Voting in 2010
18–24	41	21
25–34	54	31
35–44	61	43
45–54	65	51
55–64	71	59
65 and over	72	61
No high school diploma	38	25
High school diploma	53	38
Some college	64	46
College degree	75	58
Advanced degree	81	67
White non-Hispanic	64	49
African American	66	43
Hispanic	48	31
Asian American	48	32
Men	60	45
Women	64	46
Married	69	54
Single	54	36
Government workers	76	60
Self-employed	67	54
Work in private industry	62	43
Unemployed	52	35

SOURCE: Authors' analysis of the 2012 and 2010 U.S. Census Bureau surveys.

Why It Matters to You
Youth Turnout

Young people typically have very low turnout rates in the United States. Who votes matters not only because these individuals decide who wins elections but also because politicians pay attention primarily to voters. The fact that so few young people vote means that politicians are not likely to pay too much attention to their opinions or to promote policies that will particularly help them.

data for Hispanics and Asian Americans. However, for the first time ever, in 2012 the turnout rate for African Americans was higher than for white non-Hispanics.

- **Gender.** In an earlier period many women were discouraged from voting, but today women actually participate in elections at a slightly higher rate than men.
- **Marital status.** People who are married are more likely to vote than those who are not. This pattern is true among all age categories and generally reflects the fact that married people are more tied into their community.
- **Government employment.** Having something at stake (their jobs and the future of the programs they work on) and being in a position to know more about government impels government workers to high levels of participation.

Since the early 1990s, Rock the Vote has sought to engage and build political power for young people in the United States, often using pop music stars to urge young people to vote. Here, DJ Mark Ronson performs at a Rock the Vote event in Chicago.

How Americans Vote: Explaining Citizens' Decisions

9.6
Assess the impact of party identification, candidate evaluations, and policy opinions on voting behavior.

A common explanation of how Americans vote—one favored by journalists and politicians—is that they vote for the candidate whose policy views they prefer. Of course, the candidates have gone to a lot of time and trouble to get those views implanted in the public mind. Starting from the idea that citizens vote for the candidate whose policy views they prefer, many journalists and politicians claim that the election winner has a mandate from the people to carry out the promised policies. This premise is sometimes called the **mandate theory of elections.**

Politicians, of course, are attracted to the mandate theory. It lets them justify what they want to do by claiming public support for their policies. As President Clinton said during the final presidential debate in 1992, "That's why I am trying to be so specific in this campaign—to have a mandate, if elected, so the Congress will know what the American people have voted for."[46] Immediately after declaring victory in the 2004 presidential election, President Bush forcefully asserted that he had a mandate to enact his

mandate theory of elections
The idea that the winning candidate has a mandate from the people to carry out his or her platforms and politics. Politicians like the theory better than political scientists do.

These differences in turnout rates are cumulative. Possessing several of the traits related to higher turnout rates—say, being elderly, well educated, and married—adds significantly to one's likelihood of voting. Conversely, being, say, young, poorly educated, and unmarried is likely to add up to a relatively low probability of voting. If you possess many of the demographic traits of nonvoters, then the interests of people like you are probably not drawing a great deal of attention from politicians—regardless of whether you personally vote or not. Politicians listen far more carefully to groups with high turnout rates, as they know their fate may well be in their hands. Who votes does matter.

proposed policies over the next four years. As Bush stated, "When you win there is a feeling that the people have spoken and embraced your point of view, and that's what I intend to tell the Congress." And following his victory in 2008, President Obama said, "I don't think there's any question that we have a mandate to move the country in a new direction and not continue the same old practices that have gotten us into the fix that we're in."

Political scientists, however, think very little of the mandate theory of elections.[47] Whereas victorious politicians are eager to proclaim "the people have spoken," political scientists know that voters' decisions may involve various elements. Political scientists focus on three major elements of voters' decisions: (1) voters' party identification, (2) voters' evaluation of the candidates, and (3) the match between voters' policy positions and those of the candidates and parties—a factor termed "policy voting."

☐ Party Identification

Party identifications are crucial for many voters because they provide a regular perspective through which voters can view the political world. Once established, party identification is a label that people often adhere to for a long period of time, as they do with other elements of their social identity, such as their religious affiliation, social class, or loyalty to a sports team. Party identification simplifies the political world for many voters and provides a reliable cue as to who is on their side. "Presumably," say Niemi and Weisberg, "people choose to identify with a party with which they generally agree.... As a result they need not concern themselves with every issue that comes along, but can generally rely on their party identification to guide them."[48] For example, some voters in Texas might not know anything about the issues in the race for state comptroller, but if they know which party they usually prefer, then voting based on party would probably lead to the same decision that they would reach if they were to study the issues.

In the 1950s, scholars singled out party affiliation as the best single predictor of a voter's decision. However, following the emergence of television and candidate-centered politics, the parties' hold on voters eroded substantially during the 1960s and 1970s and then stabilized at a new and lower level.[49] Today, many voters agree with the statement that "I choose the best person for the office, regardless of party," in part because modern technology makes it easier for them to evaluate and make their own decisions about the candidates. For these so-called floating voters, election choices have become largely a matter of individual choice; their support is up for grabs in each election. Russell Dalton argues that independent voters have become more numerous because "more Americans approach politics with a greater ability to judge the candidates and issues without reliance on habitual party loyalties."[50] Young people are particularly likely to be independent voters and open to the possibility of voting for candidates who are neither Democrats nor Republicans.

☐ Candidate Evaluations: How Americans See the Candidates

All candidates try to present a favorable personal image. Appearance is a part of personal image, and using laboratory experiments, political psychologists Shawn Rosenberg and Patrick McCafferty showed that it is possible to manipulate a candidate's appearance in a way that affects voters' choices. Holding a candidate's policy views and party identification constant, they find that when good pictures are substituted for bad ones, a candidate's vote-getting ability is significantly increased. Although a laboratory setting may not be representative of the real world, Rosenberg and McCafferty conclude that "with appropriate pretesting and adequate control over a candidate's public appearance, a campaign consultant should be able to significantly manipulate the image projected to the voting public."[51]

To do so, a consultant would need to know what sort of candidate qualities voters are most attuned to. Research by Miller, Wattenberg, and Malanchuk shows that the three most important dimensions of candidate image are integrity, reliability, and

policy voting
Electoral choices that are made on the basis of the voters' policy preferences and where the candidates stand on policy issues.

competence.[52] In 2000, one of the key factors that helped George W. Bush was that he was rated more positively on integrity than was Al Gore, earning better ratings for his perceived honesty and morality. Reliability comprises such traits as being dependable and decisive. When the Bush campaign repeatedly labeled John Kerry a "flip-flopper" during the 2004 campaign, Kerry's image of reliability clearly suffered. The personal traits most often mentioned by voters, though, involve competence. In 2012, competence ratings favored Obama over Romney, as voters rated Obama substantially higher on the specific traits of being knowledgeable and intelligent.[53]

Such evaluations of candidate personality are sometimes seen as superficial and irrational bases for judgments. Miller and his colleagues disagree with this interpretation, arguing that voters rely on their assessments of candidates' personalities to predict how they would perform in office. If a candidate is perceived as too incompetent to carry out policy promises or as too dishonest for those promises to be trusted, it makes perfect sense for a voter to pay more attention to personality than policies. Interestingly, Miller and his colleagues find that college-educated voters are actually the most likely to view the candidates in terms of their personal attributes and to make important issue-oriented inferences from these attributes (for example, that a candidate who is unreliable may not be the right person to be the commander in chief of the armed forces). As Maureen Dowd, a Pulitzer Prize–winning columnist, has remarked, "When I first started writing about politics for the *Times*, I got criticized sometimes for focusing on the persona and not simply the policy. But as a student of Shakespeare, I always saw the person and the policy as inextricably braided. You had to know something about the person to whom you were going to entrust life and death decisions."[54]

☐ Policy Voting

Policy voting occurs when people base their choices in an election on their own issue preferences. True policy voting can only take place when four conditions are met. First, voters must have a clear sense of their own policy positions. Second, voters must know where the candidates stand on policy issues. Third, they must see differences between the candidates on these issues. And finally, they must actually cast a vote for the candidate whose policy positions coincide with their own.

Given these conditions, policy voting is not always easy—even for the educated voter. Abramson, Aldrich, and Rohde analyzed responses to six questions about policy issues in the 2012 National Election Study. They found that on the average issue, 66 percent of the respondents met the first three informational criteria for policy voting. When these criteria were met—when respondents had a position and knew the candidates' stances and saw differences between them—they voted for the candidate closest to their own position 68 percent of the time.[55] Of course, we should never expect all votes to be consistent with policy views, as many people will prefer one candidate on some policies and another candidate on other policies.

One regular obstacle to policy voting is that candidates often decide that the best way to handle a controversial issue is to cloud their positions in rhetoric. For example, in 1968 both major party candidates—Nixon and Humphrey—were deliberately ambiguous about what they would do to end the Vietnam War. This made it extremely difficult for voters to cast their ballots according to how they felt about the war. The media may not be much help, either, as they typically focus more on the "horse race" aspects of the campaign than on the policy stands of the candidates. Voters thus often have to work fairly hard just to be informed enough to potentially engage in policy voting.

In today's political world, it is easier for voters to vote according to policies than it was in the 1960s. The key difference is that candidates are now regularly forced to take clear stands to appeal to their own party's primary voters. As late as 1968, it was still possible to win a nomination by dealing with the party bosses; today's candidates must appeal first to the issue-oriented activists in the primaries. Whatever the major issues are in the next presidential election, it is quite likely that the major contenders for the Democratic and Republican nominations will be taking stands on them in order to gain the support of these activists. Thus, what has changed is not the voters but the electoral process, which now provides much more incentive for candidates to clearly delineate their policy differences. In particular, George W. Bush took strong and clear policy stances on tax cuts, the war on terror, appointing conservative judges, and many other areas. Many scholars feel that as a result, he became a polarizing figure whom voters either loved or hated.[56] Rather than cloud his rhetoric in ambiguity like Presidents Eisenhower or Nixon, George W. Bush took pride in being straightforward and plainspoken. Part of what made Bush such a polarizing figure was stylistic, but also involved was the necessity for any modern candidate to appeal to his or her party's ideologically motivated activists in the primaries. Indeed, President Obama faced these same constraints, and in January 2014 the Gallup Poll reported that his approval ratings were as polarized along party lines in his fifth year as president as were George W. Bush's.[57]

2012: A Battle for the Middle-Class Vote

A year before the election, President Obama's chief political strategist, David Axelrod, was frank in saying the president's reelection was going to be a "titanic struggle" in light of the tough economic circumstances. As he put it, "We don't have the wind at our backs in this election. We have the wind in our face because the American people have the wind in their faces."[58] What informed observers knew long in advance of the election was that the party holding the White House suffers in election returns when the economy suffers. Given the anemic economic growth rate of just 1.8 percent during the first three quarters of 2012, there was no way to run a "feel-good" campaign around a claim that the middle class was much better off than four years before, like the highly successful reelection campaigns of President Reagan in 1984 and President Clinton in 1996. At best, Obama could hope only to replicate the sort of argument that George W. Bush had made before his narrow reelection in 2004—namely, that he had done as well as could be expected under the circumstances and had chosen the best course for public policy.

To challenge President Obama, the Republicans nominated Mitt Romney, the former governor of Massachusetts. A highly successful businessman, Romney was one of the wealthiest individuals ever to be nominated by a major political party for president. He argued that the skills he had honed in business, including taking over companies and making them more profitable, could be applied to fixing the economy and creating millions of new jobs. In keeping with the Republican Party's conservative principles, Romney pledged a smaller and simpler government that would regulate less and foster a climate allowing businesses to increasingly prosper. This approach to the scope of government was received favorably; 51 percent of respondents in the national voter exit poll said the government was doing too much, compared to only 43 percent who said it should do more. Among Romney's specific proposals for reducing the scope of government was his pledge to repeal Obama's health care reforms and replace them with a smaller program that would allocate more responsibility to the states. Again, the exit poll showed that this was a net plus with the voters, as 49 percent wanted to see the 2010 health care law repealed at least in part, compared to 44 percent who wanted to keep it.

In response, President Obama argued that his policies were much more beneficial to middle-class Americans than those of Governor Romney, whom the Obama campaign portrayed as an out-of-touch plutocrat who would favor the interests of the wealthy. The exit poll data confirmed that this was a winning message for Obama; voters were 10 percent more likely to say his policies would favor the middle class than Romney's policies. Furthermore, a majority of the respondents agreed with the claim that Romney would favor the rich. And Obama's proposal to raise taxes on the wealthy met with the approval of 47 percent of respondents, with another 13 percent saying that income tax rates should go up for all taxpayers; only 35 percent agreed with Romney's stance that no income tax rates should be increased.

President Obama, Vice President Biden, and their wives celebrate the reelection of the Obama–Biden ticket at the Democrats' victory party in Chicago.

Among the other major advantages that the exit poll found for President Obama were his immigration policy, his perceived ability to handle an international crisis, and his approach to Medicare. In particular, many political pundits noted that Obama gained crucial support when he issued an executive order allowing young illegal immigrants who had graduated from a U.S. high school to obtain work permits, thereby enabling them to stay in the country legally. In contrast, Mitt Romney famously said that his answer to the immigration problem was "self-deportation," by which people decide to return to their home country when they find they lack legal documentation necessary to obtain work. The national exit poll found that voters preferred Obama's immigration policy by a wide margin, and it helped him earn record levels of support from voters of Hispanic and Asian descent.

The people's verdict in 2012 was to give President Obama four more years in the White House. He carried 51 percent of the popular vote, compared to 48 percent for Romney and 1 percent for third party candidates. As shown in Figure 9.3, this translated into a 332–206 margin in the Electoral College, with the Republicans winning only two states that they had lost in 2008—Indiana and North Carolina. Figure 9.3 also displays some basic data regarding what sort of voters were most likely to cast their ballots for Obama. As you can see, Obama's coalition was heavily reliant on young people, racial minorities, women, Jews, those without a religious affiliation, and people with relatively low incomes.

The results of the 2012 election show how important it is to understand how the Electoral College works. In presidential elections, once voters make their decisions, it is not just a simple matter of counting ballots to see who has won the most support nationwide. Instead, the complicated process of determining Electoral College votes begins.

FIGURE 9.3 ELECTORAL COLLEGE AND EXIT POLL RESULTS FOR 2012

The map shows the number of votes each state had in the Electoral College in 2012 and which states were carried by the Democrats (blue) and Republicans (red). After the map you'll find some selected data from the 2012 national exit poll, which demonstrate some of the individual demographics that were related to voting behavior.

Electoral College

A unique American institution created by the Constitution, providing for the selection of the president by electors chosen by the state parties. Although the Electoral College vote usually reflects a popular majority, less populated states are overrepresented and the winner-take-all rule concentrates campaigns on close states.

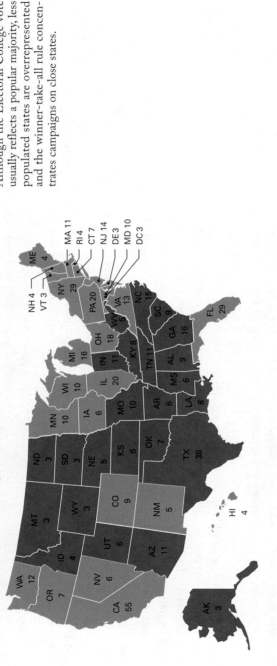

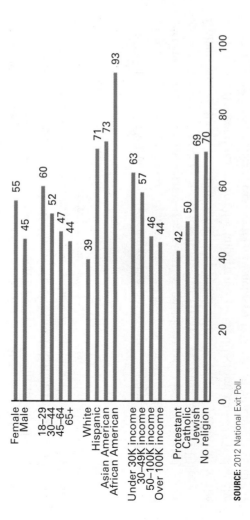

% Voting for Obama in 2012

SOURCE: 2012 National Exit Poll.

The Last Battle: The Electoral College

9.7 Evaluate the fairness of the Electoral College system for choosing the president.

It is the **Electoral College**, not the popular vote, that actually determines who becomes president of the United States. The Electoral College is a unique American institution, created by the Constitution. The American Bar Association once called it "archaic, undemocratic, complex, ambiguous, indirect, and dangerous."[59] Many—but certainly not all—political scientists oppose its continued use, as do most voters.

battleground states
The key states that the presidential campaigns focus on because they are most likely to decide the outcome of the Electoral College vote.

Because the Founders wanted the president to be selected by the nation's elite, not directly by the people, they created the Electoral College, a body of electors who are charged solely with the task of voting for the president and vice president. However, political practice since 1828 has made the vote of members of the Electoral College responsive to popular majorities. Today the electors almost always vote for the candidate who won their state's popular vote.

This is how the Electoral College system works today:

- Each state, according to the Constitution, has as many electoral votes as it has U.S. senators and representatives.[60] The state parties select slates of electors, positions they use as a reward for faithful service to the party.

- Forty-eight out of the fifty states employ a winner-take-all system in which all their electors are awarded to the presidential candidate who wins the most votes statewide.

- In Maine and Nebraska, an elector is allocated for every congressional district won, and whoever wins the state as a whole wins the two electors allotted to the state for its senators. In 2008, Obama won the congressional district around Omaha, Nebraska, whereas McCain won the other two districts and the overall state vote. Therefore, Nebraska's electoral vote ended up being split with four for McCain and one for Obama.

- Electors meet in their states in December, following the November election, and then mail their votes to the vice president (who is also president of the Senate). The vote is counted when the new congressional session opens in January and is reported by the vice president. Thus, Joe Biden had the duty of announcing the reelection of Barack Obama in January 2013.

- If no candidate receives an Electoral College majority, then the election is thrown into the House of Representatives, which must choose from among the top three electoral vote winners. A crucial aspect of the House balloting to note is that each state delegation has one vote, thus giving the one representative from Wyoming an equal say with the 53 representatives from California. Although the Founders envisioned that the House would often have to vote to choose the president, this has not occurred since 1824.

The Electoral College is important to the presidential election for two reasons. First, it introduces a bias into the campaign and electoral process. Because each state gets two electors for its senators regardless of population, the less populated states are overrepresented. One of the key reasons that George W. Bush won the Electoral College vote in 2000 without winning the popular vote was that he did better in the small states. A second reason for the importance of the Electoral College is that the winner-take-all norm means candidates will necessarily focus on winning a relatively small number of **battleground states**, where the polls show that the contest is likely to be closest. The residents of these states are much more likely to see the candidate's ads and to have the candidates and their top surrogates come by to court them during the campaign. As President Obama's 2008 campaign manager wrote:

Most of the country—those who lived in safely red or blue states—did not truly witness the 2008 presidential campaign. The real contest occurred in only about sixteen states, in which swing voters in particular bumped up against the campaign at every turn—at their doors; on their phones; on their local news, TV shows, and radio programs; and on the Internet. In these states, we trotted out the candidate and our surrogates, built large staffs and budgets to support our organizational work, and mounted ferocious and diversified advertising campaigns. They were the canvas on which we sketched the election.[61]

You can see which select states got the vast majority of attention from the Obama and Romney campaigns during the final phase of the 2012 presidential campaign in "You Are the Policymaker: Should We Make Every State a Battleground by Electing the President by a National Popular Vote?"

You Are the Policymaker

Should We Make Every State a Battleground by Electing the President by a National Popular Vote?

Under the Electoral College system it makes no sense for candidates to allocate scarce resources to states they either cannot win or are certain to win. The purple states in the map below were identified by the Obama and/or the Romney campaigns in 2012 as battleground states. All the other states were regarded by both campaigns as safely in the pocket of one candidate or the other.

Direct election of the president via the national popular vote would change the incentives for presidential campaigns. As each extra vote gathered would be of equal importance, candidates would no longer confine their efforts to just a relatively small set of battleground areas. In that sense, direct election of the president would promote political equality. An extra vote in a currently safe state like Texas would count just as much as one in a current battleground state like Florida. It would also give the parties an incentive to organize throughout the country and get the vote out everywhere. Thus, many analysts believe that it would serve to increase the nation's overall level of election turnout.

On the other hand, critics of direct election worry that candidates would jet from one big city to another throughout the campaign, bypassing rural areas and small towns. It is true, they say, that the Electoral College creates an incentive for campaigns to focus on a limited number of battleground states in each election. But under direct popular election of the president, the focus would always be on the *same areas*, whereas battlegrounds change over time. For example, in 1992 some of the most closely fought states were Texas, Georgia, and New Jersey—none of which were battleground states in 2012.

What do you think? Would you favor direct election of the president by popular vote in order to make the whole country a battleground, or would you stick with the Electoral College system?

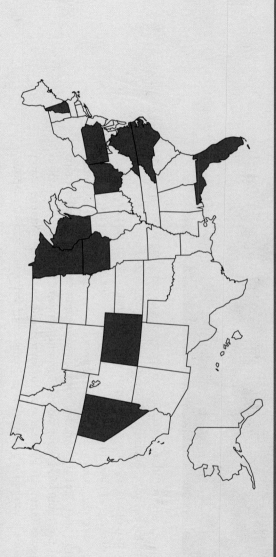

Understanding Campaigns and Voting Behavior

9.8 Assess the advantages and disadvantages of the U.S. system of campaigns and elections.

 lections serve many important functions in American society. They *socialize* and *institutionalize* political activity, making it possible for most political participation to be channeled through the electoral process rather than bubbling up through demonstrations, riots, or revolutions. Because elections provide *regular access to political power*, leaders can be replaced without being overthrown. This feature gives elections *legitimacy* in the eyes of people; that is, elections are accepted as a fair and free method of selecting political leaders.

Throughout the history of American politics, election campaigns have become longer and longer as the system has become increasingly open to public participation. Reformers over the decades have maintained that the solution to the problems of American democracy is yet more democracy—or, as John Lennon sang, "Power to the people." In principle, more democracy always sounds better than less, but in practice it is not such a simple issue.

Are Nominations and Campaigns Too Democratic?

If one judges American campaigns solely by how open they are, then certainly the American system must be viewed favorably. In other countries, the process of leadership nomination occurs within a relatively small circle of party elites. Thus, politicians must work their way up through an apprenticeship system. In contrast, America has an entrepreneurial system in which the people play a crucial role at every stage, from nomination to election. As a result, party outsiders can get elected in a way virtually unknown outside the United States. By appealing directly to the people, a candidate can emerge from nowhere to win the White House. For example, former one-term governor Jimmy Carter was scarcely known outside of his home state a year before his election to the presidency. After serving a number of terms as governor of Arkansas, Bill Clinton was only in a slightly better position than Carter in terms of name recognition when he announced his first campaign for the presidency in 1991. In this sense, the chance to win high office is open to almost any highly skilled politician with even a small electoral base.

There is a price to be paid for all this openness, however. The process of selecting American leaders is a long and convoluted one that has little downtime before it revs up all over again. Barack Obama had scarcely started his second term when potential Republican candidates for 2016 started to schedule visits to Iowa and New Hampshire. Some have even called the American electoral process "the permanent campaign."[62] Many analysts wonder if people would pay more attention to politics if it did not ask so much of them. Given so much democratic opportunity, many Americans are simply overwhelmed by the process and stay on the sidelines. Similarly, the burdens of the modern campaign can discourage good candidates from throwing their hats into the ring. One of the most worrisome burdens candidates face is amassing a sufficient campaign war chest. The system may be open, but it requires a lot of fund-raising to be able to take one's case to the people.

Today's campaigns clearly promote individualism in American politics. The current system of running for office has been labeled by Wattenberg as the "candidate-centered age."[63] It allows for politicians to decide on their own to run, to raise their own campaign

The final chapter of any presidential campaign is the swearing in of the winner at noon on the following January 20. Here, Barack Obama takes the oath in 2009. The original photograph this collage is based on was taken by a *Washington Post* photographer, and the individual pixels that comprise the collage were assembled from thousands of photos taken at the inauguration.

funds, to build their own personal organizations, and to make promises about how they specifically will act in office. The American campaign game is one of individual candidates, by individual candidates, and for individual candidates.

☐ Do Elections Affect Public Policy?

Whether elections in fact make the government pay attention to what the people think is at the center of debate concerning how well democracy works in America. In the hypothetical world of rational-choice theory and the Downs model, elections do in fact guide public policy; however, over a generation of social science research on this question has produced mixed findings. It is more accurate to describe the connection between elections and public policy as a two-way street: elections, to some degree, affect public policy, and public policy decisions partly affect electoral outcomes. There will probably never be a definitive answer to the question of how much elections affect public policy, for it is a somewhat subjective matter. The broad contours of the answer, however, seem reasonably clear: *the greater the policy differences between the candidates, the more likely voters will be able to steer government policies by their choices.*

Of course, the candidates do not always do their best to clarify the issues. One result is that the policy stands are sometimes shaped by what Benjamin Page once called "the art of ambiguity," in which "presidential candidates are skilled at appearing to say much while actually saying little."[64] Occasionally sidestepping controversial questions and hedging answers is indeed part of becoming a professional politician, as you can observe at any presidential press conference. As long as politicians can take refuge in ambiguity (and the skimpy coverage of issues in the media does little to make them clarify their policy stands), the possibility of democratic control of policy is lessened.

☐ Do Campaigns Lead to Increases in the Scope of Government?

Today's long and vigorous campaigns involve much more communication between candidates and voters than America's Founders ever could have imagined. In their view, the presidency was to be an office responsible for tending to the public interest as a whole. They wished to avoid "a contest in which the candidates would have to pose as 'friends' of the people or make specific policy commitments."[65] Thus, the Founders would probably be horrified by the modern practice in which political candidates make numerous promises during nomination and election campaigns.

Because states are the key battlegrounds of presidential campaigns, candidates must tailor their appeals to the particular interests of each major state. In Iowa, for instance, promises are typically made to keep agricultural subsidies high, federal programs to help big cities are usually announced in New York, and oil industry tax breaks are promised in Texas. To secure votes from each region of the country, candidates end up supporting a variety of local interests. Promises mount as the campaign goes on, and these promises usually add up to new government programs and money. The way modern campaigns are conducted is thus one of many reasons why politicians often find it easier to expand the scope of American government than to limit it.

Elections also help to increase generalized support for government and its powers. Because voters know that the government can be replaced at the next election, they are much more likely to feel that it will be responsive to their needs. When people have the power to dole out electoral reward and punishment, they are more likely to see government as their servant instead of their master. As Benjamin Ginsberg writes, "Democratic elections help to persuade citizens that expansion of the state's powers represents an increase in the state's capacity to serve them."[66]

Therefore, rather than wishing to be protected from the state, citizens in a democracy often seek to benefit from it. It is no coincidence that "individuals who believe they can influence the government's actions are also more likely to believe, in turn, that the government should have more power."[67] Voters like to feel that they are sending a message to the government to accomplish something. It should be no surprise that as democracy has spread, government has come to do more and more, and its scope has grown.

308

Review the Chapter

The Nomination Game

9.1 Evaluate the fairness of our current system of presidential primaries and caucuses, p. 275.

The current system of presidential primaries and caucuses, which leads to nomination at the national party conventions, allows tens of millions of Americans to participate in the selection of the Democratic and Republican parties' nominees for president. The system gives some states much greater influence than others. In particular, Iowa, with the first caucus, and New Hampshire, with the first primary, have disproportionate power stemming from the massive media attention devoted to these early contests and the momentum generated by winning them. Some other common criticisms of the nomination process are that money plays too big a role, that turnout rates are lower than in the general election, and that the mass media exercise too much power in determining which candidates are considered to be serious contenders.

The Campaign Game

9.2 Explain the key objectives of any political campaign, p. 283.

Political campaigns involve the allocation of scarce resources of time, money, and energy to achieve the goal of winning elections for political office—an allocation that requires effective organization and effective use of high-tech media. One of the most important goals of any campaign is simply to get attention. Campaigns seek to control the political agenda, getting the media and the public to focus on the issues that they wish to emphasize.

Money and Campaigning

9.3 Outline how the financing of federal campaigns is regulated by campaign finance laws, p. 286.

There are two ways to contribute money to the dialogue of American political campaigns—direct contributions made to candidates and parties, and independent expenditures to express views that may help a campaign. Federal election law restricts direct contributions to federal campaigns to $2,600 for individuals. Groups that make independent expenditures may accept donations of any size (including from corporations and unions) as a result of the Supreme Court's ruling in the 2010 case of *Citizens United v. FEC* and its application in the subsequent case of *SpeechNow v. FEC*. Candidates, parties, and groups that are mainly political in nature must file periodic reports with the Federal Election Commission detailing (1) the donations they have received and (2) how they have spent their funds.

The Impact of Campaigns

9.4 Determine why campaigns have an important yet limited impact on election outcomes, p. 292.

In general, politicians tend to overestimate the impact of campaigns; political scientists have found that campaigning serves primarily to reinforce citizens' views and to activate voters rather than to change views. Factors such as selective perception, party identification, and the incumbency advantage tend to weaken the ability of campaigns to influence voters' decisions.

Whether to Vote: A Citizen's First Choice

9.5 Identify the factors that influence whether people vote, p. 292.

In order to exercise their right to vote, citizens must go through the registration process. Although registration reform has been touted as the answer to America's low turnout problems, the Motor Voter Act of 1993 has yet to produce the benefit of greater voter participation that most people hoped for. Turnout in 2012 was virtually identical to what it was in 1992, and in 2014 only about 36 percent of the eligible electorate voted. Among the factors that make people more likely to vote are being better educated, older, and married.

How Americans Vote: Explaining Citizens' Decisions

9.6 Assess the impact of party identification, candidate evaluations, and policy opinions on voting behavior, p. 298.

Party affiliation is the best predictor of voting behavior as it represents a standing decision to vote with one's party, all else being equal. Candidate evaluations and policy opinions are two factors that can sometimes sway people to defect from their preferred party, and play an especially important role in decision making among Independents (voters do not identify with a party). Candidate evaluations usually involve important performance-relevant factors such as competence, integrity, and reliability. Policy voting often becomes important when voters see clear differences between the candidates and can determine whose stands on the issues best represents their own opinions.

The Last Battle: The Electoral College

9.7 Evaluate the fairness of the Electoral College system for choosing the president, p. 303.

The Electoral College gives voters in the less populated states somewhat greater weight in choosing the president. As a result, the winner of the national popular vote does not always prevail in the Electoral College, as happened most recently in the 2000 contest between Bush and Gore. Because all but two states allocate all their electors in a winner-take-all fashion and because many states lean solidly toward one party or the other, the candidates focus much of their energies on winning about a dozen so-called battleground states. These states, such as Florida and Ohio, receive a lot of attention in the general election campaign, whereas others, such as California and New York, are largely taken for granted by the candidates.

Understanding Campaigns and Voting Behavior

9.8 Assess the advantages and disadvantages of the U.S. system of campaigns and elections, p. 305.

American election campaigns are easily the most open and democratic in the world—some say too open. They are also extraordinarily long, perhaps excessively burdening politicians and leading politicians to make many promises that increase the scope of government. On the other hand, long campaigns give little-known candidates a chance to emerge and provide a strenuous test for all the candidates.

Learn the Terms

nomination, p. 275
campaign strategy, p. 275
national party convention, p. 275
McGovern–Fraser Commission, p. 276
superdelegates, p. 277
invisible primary, p. 277
caucus, p. 277
presidential primaries, p. 278
frontloading, p. 279
party platform, p. 282
direct mail, p. 284

campaign contributions, p. 287
independent expenditures, p. 287
Federal Election Campaign Act, p. 287
political action committee, p. 287
Federal Election Commission, p. 287
soft money, p. 288
527 groups, p. 289
Citizens United v. Federal Election Commission, p. 290
501(c) groups, p. 290
Super PACs, p. 290

selective perception, p. 292
suffrage, p. 292
political efficacy, p. 294
civic duty, p. 294
voter registration, p. 294
Motor Voter Act, p. 294
mandate theory of elections, p. 298
policy voting, p. 300
Electoral College, p. 303
battleground states, p. 304

Test Yourself

1. One major reason states engage in frontloading of primaries and caucuses is because states with early primaries _____.

a. are allotted extra delegates at the parties' national conventions

b. are promised more favorable policies by the candidates

c. become more strategically important to the general election

d. can form powerful political action coalitions to pursue their agendas

e. get more media attention and can have more influence on the nomination

2. Why is it important for candidates to carefully build up a positive public image during the "invisible primary"?

a. to appear the same as the other party candidates

b. to build up a lead before making any embarrassing gaffes in interviews

c. to differentiate themselves from other party candidates

d. to discourage people from contributing financially to candidates' campaigns

e. to prepare for the mudslinging that will occur before the party nominates a candidate

3. Which voters are most likely to get their political information via the Internet?

a. low-income voters

b. undecided voters

c. voters in rural areas

d. voters under age 30

e. voters with strong religious affiliations

4. Most of the major jobs on a campaign staff involve helping the candidate to do which of the following?

a. handle the stress of campaigning

b. meet obligations outside the campaign

c. raise money

d. respond to voter requests

e. work effectively with the media

5. When the soft money loophole was closed, how did money continue to find its way into political campaigns?

a. through 527 groups

b. through buying bulk purchases of books to avoid limits on campaign contributions

c. through dense money

d. through illicit contributions from foreign governments

e. through the McCain–Feingold loophole

6. How can the federal government contribute to presidential campaign funding?

a. Each candidate who receives more than 25 percent of delegate votes at the convention receives a lump sum.

b. Each party's candidate can choose to receive a lump sum of funds to use between the convention and the general election.

c. The House Majority Leader and House Minority Leader are responsible for divvying up public funds.

d. The Treasury Department matches all donations made by individuals and splits them between the two parties.

e. Voters can donate to the campaigns of either party by electing a small donation when submitting property taxes.

7. Which factors weaken political campaigns' effects on voters?

a. campaign expenditures, party identification, and incumbent name recognition

b. negative advertising and incumbent name recognition

c. negative advertising, party identification, and incumbent name recognition

d. party identification and incumbent name recognition

e. party mobilization and character attacks

8. Some political scientists claim that campaigns have minimal effect on the election outcome. How can this be explained?

a. History shows a clear pattern of ineffective political messaging by campaigns.

b. Most eligible voters do not vote but are the target of campaign messaging.

c. Party loyalty of voters is so consistent as to be non-variable.

d. The most predictive factors of the election outcome are in place well before campaigns begin.

e. Voters have become more savvy and are often unmoved by campaign messaging and advertisements.

9. A criticism of state laws requiring voters to show identification has been that the laws _____.

a. allow states to infringe on voters' privacy

b. continue to allow large amounts of voter fraud

c. encourage states to work too closely with the federal government

d. make it unfairly difficult for some groups of people to vote

e. make voting feel less important and more like shopping

10. What is the role of elections in democracy?

a. It is the mechanism through which voters choose a candidate who will enact specific policies.

b. It is the mechanism through which voters choose someone with specialized knowledge about issues to select government officials.

c. It is the mechanism through which voters choose who governs.

d. It is the mechanism through which voters select the party they feel best represents their interests.

e. It is the mechanism through which voters choose the most important issues by selecting a candidate who promises to address those issues.

11. Why do voters pay attention to characteristics such as a candidate's honesty and reliability?

a. Because candidates are vague and noncommittal about policy positions.

b. Because most media reports focus on candidates' personalities.

c. Because most voters lack the education to understand policy issues.

d. Because they believe that personality predicts performance.

e. Because voters prefer to elect someone who resembles their family and friends.

12. Which of the following exemplifies an election propelled by a voter mandate on an issue?

a. Franklin Roosevelt's plans to address the Great Depression

b. Gerald Ford's ideas regarding deficit spending

c. Jimmy Carter's plans for a comprehensive energy policy

d. John Kennedy's involvement in Vietnam

e. Ronald Reagan's theories regarding the Cold War

13. In what situation can the House of Representatives determine the winner of an election?

a. when a candidate does not gain the president's support

b. when a candidate fails to win a majority of the popular vote

c. when a candidate fails to win any of the five states with the most electoral votes

d. when a candidate's support is concentrated in one region

e. when the Electoral College cannot produce a majority

14. Citizen control of the government's agenda is facilitated primarily by which of the following?

a. elections

b. interest groups

c. political parties

d. polling

e. the Electoral College

15. Why has the U.S. election process earned the label "permanent campaign"?

a. Because anything politicians do can be held against them in the next election.

b. Because public participation throughout the election process makes the process very long.

c. Because the growth of social media allows for public votes on policy issues throughout candidates' terms in office.

d. Because the media tends to report all political events in terms of their effect on elections.

e. Because voters have the ability to remove elected officials from office at any moment in their term.

Explore Further

WEB SITES

www.fec.gov
The Federal Election Commission's reports on campaign spending can be found at this site.

www.fundrace.org
This site allows one to look up donations from particular individuals and to map contribution patterns for particular areas.

www.electionstudies.org
The National Election Studies are a standard source of survey data about voting behavior. You can find information about these studies, as well as some of the results from them, at this site.

http://www.census.gov/hhes/www/socdemo/voting/index.html
The Census Bureau's studies of registration and turnout can be found at this address.

FURTHER READING

Abramson, Paul R., et al. *Change and Continuity in the 2012 Elections*. Washington, D.C.: Congressional Quarterly Press, 2014. A good overview of voting behavior in recent elections, which also focuses on recent historical trends.

Cohen, Marty, et al. *The Party Decides: Presidential Nominations Before and After Reform*. Chicago: University of Chicago Press, 2008. A study of how party elites play a crucial role in the nomination process during the invisible primary stage.

Campbell, Angus, et al. *The American Voter*. New York: Wiley, 1960. The classic study of the American electorate in the 1950s, which has shaped scholarly approaches to the subject ever since.

Dalton, Russell J. *The Apartisan American: Dealignment and Changing Electoral Politics*. Washington, D.C.: Congressional Quarterly Press, 2013. An examination of the rise of well-informed independent voters.

Hillygus, D. Sunshine, and Todd G. Shields. *The Persuadable Voter: Wedge Issues in Presidential Campaigns*. Princeton, NJ: Princeton University Press, 2008. An examination of how campaigns use issues to woo swing voters.

Institute of Politics, ed. *Campaign for President: The Managers Look at 2012*. Lanham, MD: Rowman & Littlefield, 2013. The campaign managers for all the 2012 presidential candidates gathered at Harvard to discuss their experiences in the primaries and the general election.

Lewis-Beck, Michael S., et al. *The American Voter Revisited*. Ann Arbor, MI: University of Michigan Press, 2008. A replication of the classic analysis in *The American Voter* employing data from the 2000 and 2004 National Election Studies.

Niemi, Richard G., Herbert F. Weisberg, and David C. Kimball, eds. *Controversies in Voting Behavior*, 5th ed. Washington, D.C.: Congressional Quarterly Press, 2011. An excellent set of readings on some of the most hotly debated facets of voting.

Semiatin, Richard J., ed. *Campaigns on the Cutting Edge*, 2nd ed. Washington, D.C.: Congressional Quarterly Press, 2013. A useful set of articles on how campaigns are taking advantage of innovative new technologies.

Sides, John, and Lynn Vavreck. *The Gamble: Choice and Chance in the 2012 Presidential Election*. Princeton, NJ: Princeton University Press, 2013. A careful academic analysis of the 2012 election that argues that elections aren't decided by game-changing events but rather by economic and international conditions.

Smith, Steven S., and Melanie J. Springer. *Reforming the Presidential Nomination Process*. Washington, D.C.: Brookings Institution Press, 2009. A good set of current readings on the presidential nomination process.

Wattenberg, Martin P. *Where Have All the Voters Gone?* Cambridge, MA: Harvard University Press, 2002. A good review of the reasons for declining voter turnout, as well as what can be done about it.

10

Interest Groups

Politics in Action: How the Beverage Industry Mobilized to Stop a Sugar Tax

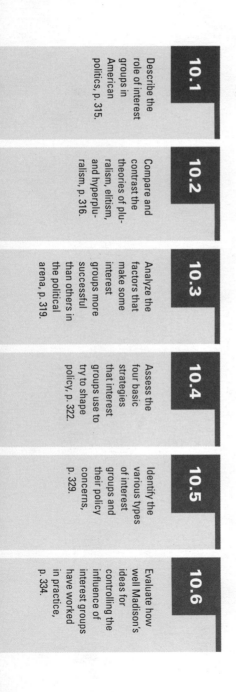

As the debate over health care reform dominated the political agenda in 2009, interest groups mobilized both for and against various policy changes that were under consideration. One of these proposals would have impacted many teenagers every day—namely, a federal tax of a penny an ounce on soft drinks and other highly sugared beverages. The consumption of sugar-sweetened beverages has been linked to risks for obesity, diabetes, and heart disease; therefore, supporters of this tax argued that it made sense to impose a levy on sugary drinks to offset health care costs and to reduce overconsumption of these beverages. They were bolstered by a report in the prestigious *New England Journal of Medicine* in April 2009, which concluded that "a penny-per-ounce excise tax could reduce consumption of sugared beverages by more than 10%." Furthermore, this report argued that such a tax "would generate considerable revenue, and as with the tax on tobacco, it could become a key tool in efforts to improve health."[1] The so-called soda tax proposal got a major boost in July 2009 when President Obama was asked about it by a reporter from *Men's Health* magazine and responded positively, saying, "I actually think it's an idea that we should be exploring. There's no doubt that our kids drink way too much soda."[2] Although Michelle Obama never spoke out about this tax, it was easy for many political observers to see how it would dovetail nicely with her initiative aimed at solving childhood obesity, called "Let's Move." With support from the White House seeming likely, some key members of the tax-writing Ways and Means Committee jumped on the bandwagon in support of this proposal.

In the world of interest groups politics, for every action there is a reaction. With the prospects for enacting a tax on sodas and other sweetened drinks looking up, the producers of such drinks soon mobilized to fight it. A reduction in the consumption of such drinks might have sounded good to

10.1
Describe the role of interest groups in American politics, p. 315.

10.2
Compare and contrast the theories of pluralism, elitism, and hyperpluralism, p. 316.

10.3
Analyze the factors that make some interest groups more successful than others in the political arena, p. 319.

10.4
Assess the four basic strategies that interest groups use to try to shape policy, p. 322.

10.5
Identify the various types of interest groups and their policy concerns, p. 329.

10.6
Evaluate how well Madison's ideas for controlling the influence of interest groups have worked in practice, p. 334.

Michelle Obama has lobbied throughout her time as First Lady to combat child obesity by having schools promote healthy lifestyles. In this 2013 photo, she is shown appearing at a "Let's Move!" event.

public health advocates, but it would mean billions in lost revenue to the companies that make and distribute them. The American Beverage Association, which had been spending about $700,000 per year on lobbying Congress, suddenly spent $18.9 million lobbying Congress in 2009. The two biggest soda producers, Coca-Cola and PepsiCo, together spent $18.6 million on lobbying, up from about $3 million per year.[3] In addition, soft drink producers enlisted a host of allies to work with them in trying to derail any consideration of such a tax. The milk industry quickly signed up, realizing that chocolate milk could well be taxed too. The fast-food industry also joined in, fearing that its sales of soda would suffer. But perhaps most significantly, many Latino groups joined in the alliance, arguing that this tax would disproportionately hurt low-income minority communities. In a $10 million TV and magazine campaign, the coalition known as Americans Against Food Taxes placed ads in English and Spanish that stated, "They say it won't be much, but anything is too much when you're raising a family these days."

With all this lobbying against "the proposed tax on sweetened drinks, members of Congress quickly dropped the idea of a federal tax. It never even came to a vote in a committee of Congress, much less to the floor of either house. Depending upon one's point of view, the success of these groups in derailing this proposal can be interpreted as consistent with any one of the three theories of interest groups that will be reviewed in this chapter. Elitist theorists would clearly focus on the ability of big corporations like PepsiCo to suddenly devote millions of dollars to lobbying. Pluralists would point to the mobilization of potential groups and to the alliance formed between the financially powerful and ethnic minorities, which, although lacking financial resources, brought crucial voting power to the table. Hyperpluralists would argue that this whole episode demonstrates how the government bends over backward to avoid alienating any organized interest group, thereby leading to policy gridlock and the inability to effect policy changes.

Our nation's capital has become a hub of interest group activity. On any given day, it is possible to observe pressure groups in action in many forums. In the morning, you could attend congressional hearings, in which you are sure to see interest groups testifying for and against proposed legislation. At the Supreme Court, you might stop in to watch a public interest lawyer arguing for strict enforcement of environmental regulations. Take a break for lunch at a nice Washington restaurant, and you may see a lobbyist entertaining a member of Congress. In the afternoon, go to any department of the executive branch (such as commerce, labor, or the interior) and you might catch bureaucrats working out rules and regulations with friendly—or sometimes unfriendly—representatives of the interests they are charged with overseeing. You could stroll past the impressive headquarters of the National Rifle Association, the AFL–CIO, or AARP to get a sense of the size of some of the major lobbying organizations. To see some lobbying done on college students' behalf, drop by One Dupont Circle, where you'll find the offices of many of the higher education groups, which lobby for student loans and scholarships, as well as for aid to educational institutions. At dinnertime, if you are able to finagle an invitation to a Georgetown cocktail party, you may see lobbyists trying to get the ear of government officials—both elected and unelected.

Alexis de Tocqueville wrote in the 1830s, "Americans of all ages, all conditions, and all dispositions constantly form associations."[4] Today, this observation still rings true. In cross-national surveys, the United States routinely comes in at, or near, the top in political participation in groups. "America in Perspective: Interest Group Participation" presents results from two such surveys, showing that (1) Americans are more likely than citizens of other countries to participate in a civic association or community-service group and (2) Americans are the more likely than others to have worked with a group to express political views.

In the *Federalist* 10, James Madison defined interest groups as working "adverse" to the interests of the nation as a whole, and he tried to design our constitutional system to prevent such groups from having too much power. Thus, all this interest group activity raises a crucial question: *Do interest groups help or hinder American democracy?* This chapter will explore how interest groups participate in the policymaking process and what they get out of it.

America in Perspective

Interest Group Participation

Americans are very associational compared to people in other democracies, as you can see in the following graphic.

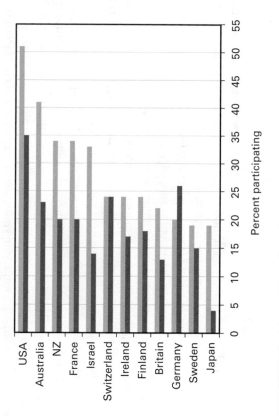

Interest Group Participation

Legend:
- Participated in a civic association group
- Worked together with people to express political views

Countries (top to bottom): USA, Australia, NZ, France, Israel, Switzerland, Ireland, Finland, Britain, Germany, Sweden, Japan

X-axis: Percent participating (0, 5, 10, 15, 20, 25, 30, 35, 40, 45, 50, 55)

QUESTION WORDING: For civic associations – "In the last 12 months, have you participated in the activities of one of the following associations or groups: a community service or civic association group?" For working with others – "Over the past 5 years or so, have you done any of the following things to express your views about something the -government should or should not be doing: worked together with people who shared the same concern?"

SOURCES: Authors' analysis of the 2007 International Social Survey Program survey for civic associations and the Comparative Study of Electoral Systems, module 2 (2001–2006) for working with others.

The Role of Interest Groups

10.1 Describe the role of interest groups in American politics.

All Americans have some interests they want represented. Organizing to promote these interests is an essential part of democracy. The right to organize groups is protected by the Constitution, which guarantees people the right "peaceably to assemble, and to petition the Government for a redress of grievances." This important First Amendment right has been carefully defended by the Supreme Court. The freedom to organize is as fundamental to democratic government as freedom of speech and freedom of the press.

The term *interest group* seems simple enough to define. *Interest* refers to a policy goal; a *group* is a combination of people. An **interest group**, therefore, is an organization of people with similar policy goals who enter the political process to try to achieve those goals. Whatever their goals—outlawing abortion or ensuring the right to one or regulating tax loopholes or creating new ones—interest groups pursue them in many arenas. Every level of government, local t+o federal, is fair game, as is every branch of government. A policy battle lost in Congress may be turned around when it comes to bureaucratic implementation or to the judicial process.

This multiplicity of policy arenas helps distinguish interest groups from political parties. Parties fight their battles through the electoral process; they run candidates for public office. Interest groups may support candidates for office, but American interest

interest group

An organization of people with shared policy goals entering the policy process at several points to try to achieve those goals. Interest groups pursue their goals in many arenas.

10.1
10.2
10.3
10.4
10.5
10.6

pluralism
A theory of government and politics emphasizing that many groups, each pressing for its preferred policies, compete and counterbalance one another in the political marketplace.

elitism
A theory of government and politics contending that an upper-class elite will hold most of the power and thus in effect run the government.

hyperpluralism
A theory of government and politics contending that groups are so strong that government, seeking to please them all, is thereby weakened.

groups do not run their own slate of candidates, as occurs in some other countries. In other words, no serious candidate is ever listed on the ballot as a candidate of the National Rifle Association or Common Cause. It may be well known that a candidate is actively supported by a particular group, but that candidate faces the voters as a Democrat, a Republican, or a third-party candidate.

Another key difference between parties and interest groups is that interest groups are usually policy specialists, whereas parties are policy generalists. Most interest groups have a handful of key policies to push: a farm group cares little about the status of urban transit; an environmental group has its hands full bringing polluters into court without worrying about the minimum wage. Unlike political parties, these groups need not try to appeal to everyone.

The number of interest groups in the United States has been increasing rapidly over the past half century. In 1959, there were about 6,000 groups; by 2014, the *Encyclopedia of Associations* listed over 25,000 groups.[5] There now seems to be an organized group for just about every conceivable interest. Very few occupations or industries go without a group to represent them in Washington. Even lobbyists themselves now have groups to represent their profession, such as the Association of Government Relations Professionals.

One of the major factors behind this explosion in the number of interest groups has been the development of sophisticated technology. A well-organized interest group can deluge members of Congress with tens of thousands of e-mail messages and phone calls in a matter of hours. Technology did not create interest group politics, but it has surely made the process much easier.

Theories of Interest Group Politics

10.2   Compare and contrast the theories of pluralism, elitism, and hyperpluralism.

U nderstanding the debate over whether lobbying and interest groups in general create problems for government in America requires an examination of three important theories. **Pluralism** argues that interest group activity brings representation to all. According to pluralists, groups compete and counterbalance one another in the political marketplace. In contrast, **elitism** argues that a few groups (primarily the wealthy) have most of the power. Finally, **hyperpluralism** asserts that too many groups are getting too much of what they want, resulting in government policy that is often contradictory and lacking in direction. This section looks in turn at each of these three theories' claims with respect to interest groups.

Pluralism

Pluralist theory rests its case on the many centers of power in the American political system. Pluralists consider the extensive organization of competing groups as evidence that influence is widely dispersed among them. They believe that groups win some and lose some but that no group wins or loses all the time. Pluralist theorists offer a *group theory of politics*, which consists of several essential arguments.[6]

- *Groups provide a key link between people and government.* All legitimate interests in the political system can get a hearing from government once they are organized.

- *Groups compete.* Labor, business, farmers, consumers, environmentalists, and other interests constantly make competing claims on the government.

- *No one group is likely to become too dominant.* When one group throws its weight around too much, its opponents are likely to intensify their organization and thus restore balance to the system. For every action, there is a reaction.

- *Groups usually play by the rules of the game.* In the United States, group politics is a fair fight, with few groups lying, cheating, stealing, or engaging in violence to get their way.

- *Groups weak in one resource can use another.* Big business may have money on its side, but labor has numbers. All legitimate groups are able to affect public policy by one means or another.

Pluralists would never deny that some groups are stronger than others or that competing interests do not always get an equal hearing. Still, they can point to many cases in which a potential group organized itself and, once organized, affected policy decisions. African Americans, women, and consumers are all groups who were long ignored by government officials but who, once organized, redirected the course of public policy. In sum, pluralists argue that lobbying is open to all and is therefore not to be regarded as a problem.

☐ Elitism

Whereas pluralists are impressed by the vast number of organized interests, elitists are impressed by how insignificant most of them are. Real power, elitists say, is held by relatively few people, key groups, and institutions. They maintain that the government is run by a few big interests looking out for themselves—a view that the majority of the public has usually agreed with in recent years. In the 2012 American National Election Study, 75 percent of those interviewed said that they thought the government "is pretty much run by a few big interests looking out for themselves" compared to just 25 percent who said that the government "is run for the benefit of all the people."

Elitists critique pluralist theory by pointing to the concentration of power in a few hands. Where pluralists find dispersion of power, elitists find interlocking and concentrated power centers. They note, for example, that about one-third of top institutional positions—corporate boards, foundation boards, university trusteeships, and so on—are occupied by people who hold more than one such position, resulting in so-called interlocking directorates.[7] Elitists see the rise of mighty multinational corporations as further tightening the control of corporate elites. A prime example is America's giant oil companies. Steve Coll has recently documented how ExxonMobil has exercised a great deal of leverage over the U.S. government (as well as those of other countries).[8] According to elitists, the power of multinational corporations regularly prevails over consumer interests.

In sum, the elitist view of the interest group system makes the following assertions:

- The fact that there are numerous groups proves nothing because groups are extremely unequal in power.

- Awesome power is held by the largest corporations.

- The power of a few is fortified by an extensive system of interlocking directorates.

- Other groups may win many minor policy battles, but corporate elites prevail when it comes to the big decisions.

Thus, lobbying is a problem, say elite theorists, because it benefits relatively few at the expense of many.

☐ Hyperpluralism

Hyperpluralists, also critical of pluralism, argue that the interest group system is out of control. For hyperpluralists, the problem is, in a phrase coined by Theodore Lowi, *interest group liberalism*, a situation in which government is excessively deferential to groups, with virtually all pressure group demands seen as legitimate and the job of government to advance them all.[9]

As a result of this effort to please and appease every interest, agencies proliferate, conflicting regulations expand, programs multiply, and, of course, the budget skyrockets.

iron triangles

Subgovernments are composed of interest group leaders interested in a particular policy, the government agency in charge of administering that policy, and the members of congressional committees and subcommittees handling that policy; they exercise a great deal of control over specific policy areas.

Point to Ponder

Hyperpluralists argue that there are too many special interests getting too much of what they want.

In your opinion, what is the effect of a wide range of groups pursuing their interests? Are these self-interests in reality unbridled (i.e., unrestrained)? Looking at the groups in the cartoon, what do you think pluralist and elitist theorists might say?

If environmentalists want clean air, government imposes clean-air rules; if businesses complain that cleaning up pollution is expensive, government gives them a tax write-off for pollution control equipment. If the direct-mail industry wants cheap rates, government gives it to them; if people complain about junk mail, the Postal Service gives them a way to take their names off mailing lists. If cancer researchers convince the government to launch an antismoking campaign, tobacco sales may drop; if they do, government will subsidize tobacco farmers to ease their loss.[10]

According to hyperpluralists, interest group liberalism is promoted by the network of *subgovernments* in the American political system that exercise a great deal of control over specific policy areas. These subgovernments, which are generally known as **iron triangles**, are composed of key interest group leaders interested in policy X, the government agency in charge of administering policy X, and the members of congressional committees and subcommittees handling policy X.

All the elements of the iron triangle have the same goal: protecting their self-interest. The subgovernment in educational policy provides a good example. Education interest groups include the National Education Association, the Coalition for Educational Success, the American Council on Education, and many others. The Department of Education administers a variety of programs to aid education, and these programs look to lobbying by education interest groups to help keep their budgets safe from cuts. Finally, most of the members of the education committees of the House and the Senate are especially committed to promoting education; often they have major concentrations of universities in their constituencies. All these elements want to protect interests related to education. Similar iron triangles of group-agency—committee ties exist in scores of other policy areas.

Hyperpluralists' major criticism of the interest group system is that relations between groups and the government have become too cozy. Hard choices about national policy are rarely made. Instead of making choices between X and Y, the government pretends there is no need to choose and tries to favor both policies. It is a perfect script for policy gridlock. In short, the hyperpluralist position on group politics is as follows:

- Groups have become too powerful in the political process as government tries to appease every conceivable interest.
- Interest group liberalism is aggravated by numerous iron triangles—comfortable relationships among a government agency, the interest group it deals with, and congressional subcommittees.
- Trying to please every group results in contradictory and confusing policy.

Ironically, the recent interest group explosion is seen by some scholars as weakening the power of iron triangles. With so many more interest groups to satisfy, and with many of them competing against one another, a cozy relationship between groups and the government is plainly more difficult to sustain.

Why It Matters to You
Theories of Interest Group Politics

Our conclusions about how well the Madisonian system works to control the power of special interests would depend on whether we used pluralist, elitist, or hyperpluralist interpretations. A pluralist interpretation would suggest that Madison's system has worked as intended. In an elitist interpretation, however, the wealthy hold too much power, and in a hyperpluralist interpretation, too many groups have too much power.

What Makes an Interest Group Successful?

10.3   Analyze the factors that make some interest groups more successful than others in the political arena.

 or a while, *Fortune* magazine issued a list of the 25 most powerful interest groups in politics. Every year the list revealed some surprises. Although such obvious candidates as the National Rifle Association and the American Association of Retired Persons often headed up the list, some of the groups that were considered to be among the most powerful lobbying groups were relatively unknown, such as the National Beer Wholesalers Association and the National Restaurant Association.

Many factors affect the success of an interest group. Among these factors are the size of the group, its intensity, and its financial resources. While greater intensity and more financial resources work to a group's advantage, surprisingly, smaller groups are more likely to achieve their goals than larger groups.

The Surprising Ineffectiveness of Large Groups

In one of the most often quoted statements concerning interest groups, E. E. Schattschneider wrote that "pressure politics is essentially the politics of small groups. . . . Pressure tactics are not remarkably successful in mobilizing general interests."[11] There are perfectly good reasons why consumer groups are less effective than producer groups,

10.1

10.2

10.3

10.4

10.5

10.6

potential group
All the people who might be interest group members because they share some common interest.

actual group
The people in the potential group who actually join.

collective good
Something of value that cannot be withheld from a potential group member.

free-rider problem
For a group, the problem of people not joining because they can benefit from the group's activities without joining.

selective benefits
Goods that a group can restrict to those who actually join.

patients are less effective than doctors, and energy conservationists are less effective than oil companies: Smaller groups have organizational advantages over larger groups.

To shed light on this point, it is important to distinguish between a potential and an actual group. A **potential group** is composed of all people who might be group members because they share some common interest.[12] An **actual group** is composed of those in the potential group who choose to join. Groups vary enormously in the degree to which they enroll their potential membership. Consumer organizations are successful in mobilizing only a small fraction of those who might benefit from their efforts, which is to say almost all Americans. In contrast, organizations such as the National Beer Wholesalers Association, the American Hospital Association, and the Motion Picture Association of America include a good percentage of their potential members. These groups find it easier to get potential members to actually join in and participate.

Economist Mancur Olson explains this phenomenon in *The Logic of Collective Action*.[13] Olson points out that all groups are in the business of providing collective goods. A **collective good** is something of value, such as clean air, that cannot be withheld from anyone. When the AFL-CIO wins a higher minimum wage, all low-paid workers benefit, regardless of whether they are members of the union. In other words, members of the potential group share in benefits that members of the actual group work to secure. If this is the case, an obvious and difficult problem results: Why should potential members work for something if they can get it free? Why join the group, pay dues, and work hard for a goal when a person can benefit from the group's activity without doing anything at all? A perfectly rational response is thus to sit back and let other people do the work. This is commonly known as the **free-rider problem.**

The bigger the potential group, the more serious the free-rider problem. One reason for this is that in a small group, shares of the collective good are more likely to be great enough to give the potential members an incentive to join the group to help it secure its goals. The old saying that "everyone can make a difference" is much more credible in the case of a relatively small group. In the largest groups, in contrast, each member can expect to get only a tiny share of the policy gains. Weighing the costs of participation against the relatively small benefits, the temptation is always to "let somebody else do it." Therefore, as Olson argues, the larger the potential group, the less likely potential members are to contribute.

This distinct advantage of small groups helps explain why consumer groups have a harder time organizing for political action than do businesses. Such groups claim to seek "public interest" goals, but the gains they win are usually spread thin over millions of people. In contrast, the lobbying costs and benefits for business are concentrated. Suppose that, for example, consumer advocates take the airlines to court over charges of price fixing and force the airlines to return $100 million to consumers in the form of lower prices. This $100 million settlement, divided among tens of millions of people who use airlines, amounts to relatively small change for each consumer. Yet, for each of the airline companies it amounts to a substantial sum. One can quickly see which side will be better organized in such a struggle.

In sum, the differences between large and small groups with regard to incentives to participate help explain why interest groups with relatively few members are often so effective. The power of business in the American political system is thus due to more than just money, as proponents of elite theory would have us believe. In addition to their considerable financial strength, multinational corporations have an easier time organizing themselves for political action than larger potential groups, such as consumers. Once well organized, large groups may be very effective, but it is much harder for them to get together in the first place.

The primary way for large potential groups to overcome the free-rider problem is to provide attractive benefits for only those who join the organization. **Selective benefits** are goods that a group can restrict to those who pay their yearly dues, such as information publications, travel discounts, and group insurance rates. AARP has built up a membership list of 38 million Americans over the age of 50 by offering a variety of selective benefits, ranging from insurance to travel discounts.

Intensity

Another way in which a large potential group may be mobilized is through an issue that people feel intensely about. Intensity is a psychological advantage that can be enjoyed by small and large groups alike. When a group shows that it cares deeply about an issue, politicians are more likely to listen; many votes may be won or lost on a single issue. Amy McKay has found that the intensity of lobbying against a proposal is a powerful predictor of whether the proposal is adopted in Congress or by a federal agency.[14] McKay further notes that because groups opposed to a policy change are more likely to feel intensely about their position than groups calling for the change, in practice this often serves to preserve the status quo.

The rise of single-issue groups has been one of the most dramatic political developments in recent years. A **single-issue group** can be defined as a group that has a narrow interest, dislikes compromise, and single-mindedly pursues its goal. Anti–Vietnam War activists may have formed the first modern single-issue group. Opponents of nuclear power plants, of gun control, and of abortion are some of the many such groups that exist today. All these groups deal with issues that evoke the strong emotions characteristic of single-interest groups. Even college students have gotten into the act, forming groups in a number of states to lobby against tuition increases at public universities, as you can read about in "Young People and Politics: The Virginia 21 Coalition."

single-issue groups
Groups that have a narrow interest, tend to dislike compromise, and often draw membership from people new to politics.

Young People & Politics

The Virginia 21 Coalition

As budget crunches have hit most states in recent years, many state legislatures have cut back on funding for higher education and approved sharp increases in tuition at public colleges and universities. In response, college students in some states have started to form interest groups to fight for more state subsidies for higher education and for limiting tuition increases. In Virginia, a group called the "21st Century Virginia Coalition," or simply "Virginia 21" for short, has recently had some success in getting the state's politicians to listen to the opinions of college students regarding funding for higher education.

Virginia 21 first entered the political scene with a campaign to garner support for a bond referendum on the 2002 Virginia ballot to provide over $900 million to state universities for capital improvements. The group raised over $17,000 to support the campaign, made roughly 20,000 telephone calls to round up votes for it, and aired a student-written and student-produced radio commercial on behalf of the referendum, which passed with overwhelming support.

One of the organization's priorities was to push for a 1-cent increase in the state's sales tax that would be dedicated to increasing funds available for education. The organization collected over 10,000 signatures for a petition titled "Fund Virginia's Future" and presented them to the state legislature. But they grabbed more attention when they dropped off over 200,000 pennies at the office of the state treasurer in support of the proposed 1-cent increase in the sales tax. The pennies weighed approximately three-quarters of a ton, and the gesture was designed to show that college students care "a ton" about the funding of higher education. The local media could hardly ignore such a gripping visual image.

In 2006, Virginia 21 successfully lobbied the state legislature to pass a bill designed to cut the costs of textbooks for students in Virginia colleges. The measure required public universities to come up with guidelines mandating that professors acknowledge that they are aware of the exact costs of the books they assign, and to specify whether supplements sold with these books are actually required.

Virginia 21 is committed to lobbying the state legislature to substantially increase funds for higher education. For example, during 2011 and 2012 it conducted a campaign titled "What's Your Number?" which was designed to make legislators more aware of the mounting debt that many students were taking on.

CRITICAL THINKING QUESTIONS

1. Would you give money and/or volunteer for a group in your state like Virginia 21? Why or why not?

2. Which of the strategies of interest group lobbying discussed later in this chapter do you think would be most effective for a group like Virginia 21?

Perhaps the most emotional issue of recent times has been that of abortion. As befits the intensity of the issue, activities have not been limited to conventional means of political participation. Protesting—often in the form of blocking entrances to abortion clinics—has become a common practice for antiabortion activists. Pro-choice activists have organized as well, especially in the wake of the 1989 *Webster v. Reproductive Health Services* case, which allowed states greater freedom to restrict abortions. Both groups' positions are clear, not subject to compromise, and influence their vote.

□ Financial Resources

One of the major indictments of the American interest group system is that it is biased toward the wealthy. When he was the majority leader in the Senate, Bob Dole once remarked that he had never been approached by a Poor People's political action committee. There is no doubt that money talks in the American political system, and those who have it get heard. A big campaign contribution may ensure a phone call, a meeting, or even a favorable vote or action on a particular policy. When Charles Keating, who was eventually convicted of bank fraud and racketeering, was asked whether the $1.3 million he had funneled into the campaigns of five U.S. senators had anything to do with these senators later meeting with federal regulators on his behalf, he candidly responded, "I certainly hope so."

It is important to emphasize, however, that even on some of the most important issues, the big interests do not always win. A recent study of interest group activity on about 100 randomly chosen policy issues by Frank Baumgartner and his colleagues provides the most comprehensive analysis ever of who got what they lobbied for and who did not. The question of how much financial resources mattered was uppermost on the minds of these political scientists, and their results were both definitive and striking. They report, "The usual types of resources that are often assumed to 'buy' policy outcomes—PAC donations, lobbying expenditures, membership size, and organizational budgets—have no observable effect on the outcomes."[15] Based on their analysis, they offer several explanations for why the correlation between big money and lobbying success is so weak. First, they find that lobbying is a very competitive enterprise. Once one side mobilizes its resources, such as money, the other side is almost sure to mobilize whatever resources and allies it has to counter them. In fact, a full 17 percent of the issues they examined involved one of the most powerful 25 interest groups (as rated by *Fortune*) facing off against another. Third, their data revealed a high degree of diversity within sides active in the lobbying game, as groups with substantial financial resources often allied themselves with poor groups with whom they shared a common goal. As Baumgartner and his colleagues explain, "Where the wealthy often ally with the poor ... it is logically impossible to observe a strong correlation between wealth and success."[16] The tale of the wealthy soda industry forming a lobbying alliance with Latino groups recounted at the beginning of this chapter is an excellent example of this phenomenon.

How Groups Try to Shape Policy

10.4 Assess the four basic strategies that interest groups use to try to shape policy.

No interest group has enough staff, money, or time to do everything possible to achieve its policy goals. Interest groups must therefore choose from a variety of tactics. The four basic strategies are lobbying, electioneering, litigation, and appealing to the public. Keep in mind that these are not mutually exclusive strategies; indeed, most groups use multiple tactics to pursue their policy goals.

Lobbying

The term *lobbying* comes from the place where petitioners used to collar legislators. In the early years of politics in Washington, members of Congress had no offices and typically stayed in boardinghouses or hotels while Congress was in session. A person could not call them up on the phone or make an appointment with their secretary; the only sure way of getting in touch with a member of Congress was to wait in the lobby where he was staying to catch him either coming in or going out. These people were dubbed *lobbyists* because they spent so much of their time waiting in lobbies.

Of course, merely loitering in a lobby does not make one a lobbyist; there must be a particular reason for such action. Lester Milbrath has offered a more precise definition of the practice. He writes that **lobbying** is a "communication, by someone other than a citizen acting on his or her own behalf, directed to a governmental decision maker with the hope of influencing his or her decision."[17] Lobbyists, in other words, are political persuaders who represent organized groups. They usually work in Washington, handling groups' legislative business. They are often former legislators themselves. For example, according to a study by Public Citizen's Congress Watch, over 70 former members of Congress lobbied for the financial services sector in 2009—many of them earning sums they only could have dreamed of as lawmakers.[18]

There are two basic types of lobbyists. The first type is a regular, paid employee of a corporation, union, or association. Such lobbyists may hold a title, such as vice president for government relations, but everyone knows that it is for a reason that his or her office is in Washington even if the company headquarters is in Houston. The second type is available for hire on a temporary basis. These lobbyists generally work for groups that are too small to afford a full-time lobbyist or that have a unique, but temporary, need for access to Congress or the executive branch.

The Lobbying Disclosure Act of 1995 established criteria for determining whether an organization or firm should register its employees as lobbyists. Those who fit the criteria must register with the secretary of the U.S. Senate and file a report regarding each of their clients, indicating how much they were paid by them for lobbying services. This information is made public by the Senate's Office of Public Records, and combing through about 20,000 disclosure forms per year has become a substantial business in itself. The spring 2012 edition of *Washington Representatives*, a $270 reference book on participants in the federal lobbying process, advertised that it provided "in-depth profiles on 18,000 lobbyists, 12,000 clients, and 1,700 lobbying firms."[19] Since 1998, the Center for Responsive Politics has been calculating the expenditures on lobbying of each industry. In Figure 10.1 on the next page, you can see the enormous amounts that the top-spending industries doled out for lobbying over the first five years of the Obama administration.

Although lobbyists are primarily out to influence members of Congress, it is important to remember that they can be of help to them as well. Ornstein and Elder list four important ways in which lobbyists can help a member of Congress:[20]

- *They are an important source of information.* Members of Congress have to concern themselves with many policy areas; lobbyists can confine themselves to only one area and can thus provide specialized expertise. If information is power, then lobbyists can often be potent allies. Even the most vociferous critics of our lobbying system acknowledge the informational role that lobbyists play in our democracy. For example, although the president of Common Cause denounced the money that lobbyists funnel to politicians, he also noted, "Most lobbyists are good people who perform a valuable service sharing their expertise on issues with Members of Congress."[21]

- *They can help politicians with political strategy for getting legislation through.* Lobbyists are politically savvy people, and they can be useful consultants. When Leon Panetta served as White House chief of staff in the Clinton administration,

FIGURE 10.1 INDUSTRIES' BIG SPENDERS ON LOBBYING, 2009–2013

This graph presents the total amount spent on lobbying by industries that were the biggest spenders for the first five years of the Obama presidency. Keep in mind that the data are presented in terms of millions of dollars spent. Thus, the pharmaceutical industry spent $1,216,432,546 on lobbying. All told, just these 15 industries spent about $73 billion on lobbying during these five years.

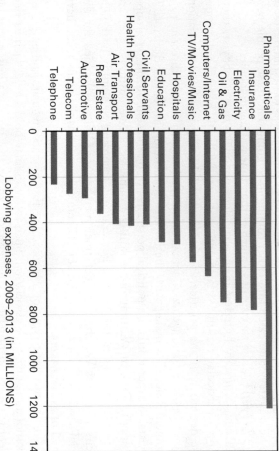

Lobbying expenses, 2009–2013 (in MILLIONS)

SOURCE: Compiled by the author from 2009, 2010, 2011, 2012, and 2013 data from the Center for Responsive Politics. See www.opensecrets.org/lobby/top.php?index.Type=I&showYear=a

he regularly convened a small group of Washington lobbyists to discuss how the administration should present its proposals.[22]

- **They can help formulate campaign strategy and get the group's members behind a politician's reelection campaign.** Labor union leaders, for example, often provide help in how to appeal to typical working people, and they often provide volunteers to help out in campaigns as well.

- **They are a source of ideas and innovations.** Lobbyists cannot introduce bills, but they can peddle their ideas to politicians eager to attach their name to an idea that will bring them political credit.

Like anything else, lobbying can be done crudely or gracefully. Lobbyists can sometimes be heavy handed. They can threaten or cajole a legislator, implying that electoral defeat is a certain result of not "going along." They can even make it clear that money flows to the reelection coffers of those who cooperate. It is often difficult to tell the difference between lobbying and lobbying as a strictly professional representation of legitimate interests.

High-priced lobbyists are often compared to the airline mechanic who is called in to fix the plane, turns just one screw, and submits a bill for a thousand dollars. Asked to justify such a huge fee for such a little bit of work, the mechanic says, "Well it's $10 for turning the screw, and $990 for knowing which screw to turn." Similarly, the skilled lobbyist is paid for knowing whom to contact and with what information. A recent in-depth study of lobbyists and their work by Rogan Kersh concludes that their success depends largely on their ability to deploy information strategically on behalf of their clients. As Kersh writes, "Searching for, analyzing, and presenting information compose the central activity in most lobbyists' daily work."[23] Richard Hall and Alan Deardorff have characterized lobbying as a form of "legislative subsidy," or a "matching grant of costly policy information, political intelligence, and labor to the enterprises of strategically selected legislators,"[24] and have argued that its purpose is not to change anyone's mind but rather simply to help their political allies.

electioneering

Direct group involvement in the electoral process, for example, by helping to fund campaigns, getting members to work for candidates, and forming political action committees.

political action committees (PACs)

Groups that raise money from individuals and then distribute it in the form of contributions to candidates that the group supports. PACs must register with the FEC and report their donations and contributions to it. Individual contributions to a PAC are limited to $5,000 per year and a PAC may give up to $5,000 to a candidate for each election.

For years, the National Rifle Association has successfully lobbied against gun control measures, arguing that the Second Amendment to the Constitution guarantees all citizens the right to bear arms. Here, a shooting instructor fires a high-power pellet rifle in the indoor range at the 2012 annual meeting of the NRA, which was attended by over 70,000 members.

Other evidence, however, suggests that sometimes lobbying can persuade legislators to support a certain policy.[25] The National Rifle Association, which for years kept major gun control policies off the congressional agenda, has long been one of Washington's most effective lobbying groups.[26] In a more specific example, many observers believe that intensive lobbying by the insurance industry derailed the possibility of Congress creating a "public option" to compete against private health insurance providers as part of the landmark 2010 health care bill.

Nailing down the specific effects of lobbying is difficult, partly because it is difficult to isolate its effects from other influences. Lobbying clearly works best on people already committed to the lobbyist's policy position. Thus, like campaigning, lobbying is directed toward primarily activating and reinforcing supporters. For example, antiabortion lobbyists would not think of approaching California's Dianne Feinstein to attempt to convert her to their position, because Feinstein clearly supports the pro-choice position. If Senator Feinstein is lobbied by anyone on the abortion issue, it will be by the pro-choice faction, urging her not to compromise with the opposition.

Electioneering

Because lobbying works best with those already on the same side, getting the right people into office and keeping them there is also a key strategy of interest groups. Many groups therefore get involved in **electioneering**—aiding candidates financially and getting group members out to support them.

A means for interest groups to participate in electioneering is provided by **political action committees (PACs)**. The number of PACs has exploded from 608 in 1974, the year they were created by campaign finance reforms, to 5,680 in 2014, according to the Federal Election Commission (FEC). No major interest group seeking to exert influence on the political process these days can pass up the opportunity to funnel money honestly and openly into the campaign coffers of its supporters. For example, Major League Baseball's PAC made $551,000 in political donations during the 2012 election cycle, mostly to members of congressional committees who were considering legislation that might impact the business of baseball.[27] As economist Roger Noll of Stanford University remarked about the activity of baseball's PAC, "Any industry that has any kind of dependence on government is pretty much forced to do what they're doing," he said. "Unfortunately, this has become the cost of doing business."[28]

A PAC is formed when a business association or some other interest group decides to contribute to candidates whom it believes will support legislation it favors. The group registers as a PAC with the FEC and then puts money into the PAC coffers. The PAC can collect money from stockholders, members, and other interested parties. It then donates the money to candidates, often after careful research on their issue stands and past voting records. During a primary election, a PAC can donate up to $5,000 per candidate, and it can then do the same in the general election. These donations must be reported to the FEC, which makes the records of PAC donations quickly available for public scrutiny. Thus, if PACs are corrupting democracy, as many believe, at least they are doing so openly.

Candidates need PACs because high-tech campaigning is expensive. Tightly contested races for the House of Representatives now frequently cost over $1 million; Senate races can easily cost $1 million for television alone. PACs play a major role in paying for expensive campaigns. Thus, there emerges a symbiotic relationship between the PACs and the candidates: Candidates need money, which they insist can be used without compromising their integrity; PACs want access to officeholders, which they insist can be gained without buying votes. Most any lobbyist will tell his or her clients that politicians will listen to any important interest group but that with a sizable PAC donation they'll listen better.

In recent years, nearly half the candidates running for reelection to the House of Representatives have received the majority of their campaign funds from PACs. These funds often provide incumbents with a major head start in fund-raising, as congressional challengers typically have a hard time attracting PAC donations. For example, during the 2012 election cycle, PACs gave $288 million to congressional incumbents, compared to just $41 million to challengers.[29] Why does PAC money go so overwhelmingly to incumbents? The answer is that PAC contributions are basically investments for the future, and incumbents are the most likely to return the investment. When R. Kenneth Godwin and Barry J. Seldon asked a sample of PAC directors to explain why their PACs gave money to certain candidates, the top five answers were that these candidates were (1) on committees that are important to their interests, (2) very supportive of issues important to them, (3) from a district or state where they had facilities, (4) helping them with executive and regulatory agencies, and (5) in leadership positions that enabled them to influence issues that affect the PAC.[30]

Only a handful of serious congressional candidates have resisted the lure of PAC money in recent years. Critics of the PAC system worry that all this money leads to PAC control over what the winners do once in office. Archibald Cox and Fred Wertheimer write that the role of PACs in campaign finance "is robbing our nation of its democratic ideals and giving us a government of leaders beholden to the moneyed interests who make their election possible."[31] There have been serious calls to do away with PACs altogether, as discussed in "You Are the Policymaker: Should PACs Be Eliminated?"

Why It Matters to You
PACs

The great increase in the number of PACs over the past several decades has enabled far more groups to become involved in electioneering. Insofar as more participation is desirable, the increase of PACs has to be considered a positive development. But given that only groups that can successfully organize and raise substantial sums of money can take advantage of the PAC system, the increased importance of PACs has introduced some obvious biases into the electoral process.

You Are the Policymaker

Should PACs Be Eliminated?

The effect of PAC campaign contributions on congressional votes has become a perennial issue in American politics. Critics of PACs are convinced that they distort the democratic process and corrupt our political system in favor of those who can raise the most money. Many politicians freely admit—once they are out of office—that it is a myth to think that the PACs don't want something in return. They may only want to be remembered on one or two crucial votes or with an occasional intervention with government agencies, but multiply this by the thousands of special interests that are organized today and the worst fears of the hyperpluralists could be realized—a government that constantly yields to every special interest.

Common Cause (www.commoncause.org) has as one of its primary missions exposing what it sees as the evils of the PAC system. It argues that the influence of corporate PACs on Capitol Hill has led to "corporate welfare" and costs taxpayers billions of dollars. For example, Common Cause has attributed the failure of Congress to further regulate tobacco and cigarette advertising to the millions of PAC contributions from tobacco companies. Similarly, they have argued that PAC contributions from the biggest mortgage brokers kept Congress from scrutinizing questionable lending practices that played such a crucial role in bringing on the recession of 2008–2009. More recently, they have accused Verizon Communications of using PAC contributions to influence key members of Congress who are involved in regulating the Internet. Although these contributions were disclosed, they argue that their influence is exercised behind the scenes at committee meetings on technical matters that are hard for journalists to scrutinize.

However, others argue that connection is not causation. They believe that most members of Congress are not affected by PAC contributions, which come largely from groups they already agree with anyway. For instance, labor PACs will not waste their money trying to influence members of Congress who have consistently opposed raising the minimum wage. Defenders of the PAC system also point out that the PAC system further increases participation in the political process. As opposed to individual donations, PACs—which represent groups of people—allow better representation of occupational groups. The PAC system allows people with common professional interests, such as farmers, lawyers, dentists, and college professors, to express their support of candidates jointly through political contributions. Similarly, corporation PACs can represent the interests of stockholders and employees.

If James Madison was right in thinking that the key to controlling the power of interest groups is to expand their sphere of participation, then PACs certainly do this, according to their defenders. Beyond this, the money for today's expensive media campaigns has to come from somewhere. Those who wish to maintain the PAC system typically argue that the alternative of the government providing campaign funds is impractical given that only about 7 percent of taxpayers participate in the $3 voluntary income tax check-off system for financing federal campaigns.

What do you think? Would you consider eliminating PACs? Would you prefer just to leave things as they are? Or, as a middle course, would you favor reducing the amount of money ($5,000 in the primary and another $5,000 in the general election) that PACs can donate directly to candidates?

In addition to their role in financing campaigns, interest groups participate in elections in numerous other ways. Among these are recruiting interest groups members to run as candidates for office, issuing official group endorsements, providing volunteer labor to participate in campaign work, and sending delegates to state and national party conventions to try to influence party platforms.

☐ Litigation

If interest groups fail in Congress or get only a vague piece of legislation, the next step is to go to court in the hope of getting specific rulings. Karen Orren has linked much of the success of environmental interest groups to their use of lawsuits. "Frustrated in Congress," she wrote, "they have made an end run to the courts, where they have skillfully exploited and magnified limited legislative gains."[32] Environmental legislation, such as the Clean Air Act, typically includes provisions allowing ordinary citizens to sue for enforcement. As a result, every federal agency involved in environmental regulation now has hundreds of suits pending against it at any given time. Moreover, the constant threat of a lawsuit increases the likelihood that businesses will consider the environmental impact of what they do.

Perhaps the most famous interest group victories in court were those won by civil rights groups in the 1950s. While civil rights bills remained stalled in Congress, these groups won major victories in court cases concerning school desegregation, equal housing, and employment discrimination. More recently, consumer groups have used suits against businesses and federal agencies as a means of assuring enforcement of consumer regulations.

One tactic that lawyers employ to make the views of interest groups heard by the judiciary is the filing of *amicus curiae* briefs ("friend of the court" briefs), written arguments submitted to the courts in support of one side of a case. Through these written depositions, a group states its collective position as well as how its own welfare will be affected by the outcome of the case. Numerous groups may file *amicus* briefs in highly publicized and emotionally charged cases. For example, in the case of *Regents of the University of California v. Bakke*, which challenged affirmative action programs as reverse discrimination, over 100 different groups filed *amicus* briefs. A study of participation in *amicus* briefs by Caldeira and Wright found that the Supreme Court has been accessible to a wide array of interest groups, both in deciding which cases to hear and in deciding how to rule.[33]

A more direct judicial strategy employed by interest groups is the filing of class action lawsuits, which enable a group of people in a similar situation to combine their common grievances into a single suit. For instance, in 1977 flight attendants won a class action suit against the airline industry's regulation that all stewardesses be unmarried. As one lawyer who specializes in such cases states, "The class action is the greatest, most effective legal engine to remedy mass wrongs."[34]

☐ Going Public

Groups are also interested in the opinions of the public. Because public opinion ultimately makes its way to policymakers, interest groups carefully cultivate their public image and use public opinion to their advantage when they can. As Ken Kollman finds, even the wealthiest and most powerful groups in America appeal to public opinion to help their cause. For example, when the government instituted a requirement for tax-withholding on savings accounts, the American Bankers Association appealed to their customers to protest this to their congressional representatives. After 22 million postcards flooded into Congress, lawmakers quickly reversed the policy.[35]

Interest groups market not only their stand on issues but also their reputations. Business interests want people to see them as "what made America great," not as wealthy Americans trying to ensure large profits. The Teamsters Union likes to be known as a united organization of hardworking men and women, not as an organization that has in the past been influenced by organized crime. Farmers promote the image of a sturdy family working to put bread on the table, not the huge agribusinesses that have largely replaced family farms. In this way, many groups try to create a reservoir of goodwill with the public.

Interest groups' appeals to the public for support have a long tradition in American politics. In 1908, AT&T launched a major magazine advertising campaign to convince people of the need for a telephone monopoly. In 1948, when President Truman proposed a system of national health insurance, the American Medical Association spent millions of dollars on ads attacking "socialized medicine." In both 1994 and 2010, when Congress took up major initiatives to reform health care, many groups placed advertisements in support of and opposition to the proposals made by Presidents

Interest groups spent over $100 million appealing to public opinion during the debate over health care in 1994. In a counter-ad produced by the Democratic National Committee, the argument was made that opponents of the Clinton health care plan were using scare tactics. You can see the tag end of the ad in this photo.

Clinton and Obama. In both cases, so much money was spent (over $100 million) that many observers compared this activity to a national electoral campaign.

Lately, more and more organizations have undertaken expensive public relations (PR) efforts, whether to defend their reputations or to promote their stands on issues. After *60 Minutes* ran a story in 2009 about a lawsuit against Chevron for allegedly contaminating the Ecuadorian Amazon and causing a wave of cancer in the region, Chevron hired former CNN correspondent Gene Randall to produce a video telling its side of the story and posted the video on YouTube. In other recent examples, Toyota ran ads defending itself against charges of negligence after some of its vehicles were found to have acceleration and braking problems, and Microsoft condemned its prosecution by the Justice Department for alleged monopolistic practices. Mobil Oil has long run a visible corporate PR effort to influence the public with its regular editorial-style ads in the *New York Times* and other major publications. These ads typically address issues that affect the oil industry and big business in general. One was even titled "Why Do We Buy This Space?" Mobil answered its rhetorical question by saying that "business needs voices in the media, the same way labor unions, consumers, and other groups in our society do."[36] No one knows just how effective these image-molding efforts are, but many groups seem to believe firmly that advertising pays off.

Types of Interest Groups

10.5 Identify the various types of interest groups and their policy concerns.

W hether they are lobbying, electioneering, litigating, or appealing to the public, interest groups are omnipresent in the American political system. As with other aspects of American politics and policymaking, political scientists loosely categorize interest groups into clusters. Among the most important clusters are those consisting of groups that deal with either economic issues, environmental concerns, equality issues, or the interests of consumers and the public generally. An examination of these four very distinct types of interest groups will give you a good picture of much of the American interest group system.

10.1

10.2

10.3

10.4

10.5

10.6

union shop

A provision found in some collective bargaining agreements requiring all employees of a business to join the union within a short period, usually 30 days, and to remain members as a condition of employment.

right-to-work laws

A state law forbidding requirements that workers must join a union to hold their jobs. State right-to-work laws were specifically permitted by the Taft-Hartley Act of 1947.

☐ Economic Interests

Business, labor, and farmers all fret over the impact of government regulations. Even a minor change in government regulatory policy can cost industries a great deal. Tax policies also affect the livelihood of individuals and firms. How the tax code is written determines whether people and producers pay a lot or a little of their incomes to the government. Government often provides subsidies to farmers, small businesses, railroads, minority businesses, and others, and every economic group wants to get its share of this direct aid and government contracts. In this era of economic global interdependence, economic interests are concerned about such matters as import quotas and tariffs (fees imposed on imports) and the soundness of the dollar. Although labor and business interests both seek to influence government because of the effect of these various aspects of economic policy, the impact on economic policy they seek is considerably different.

LABOR Unions are the main interest groups representing labor. About 10 million workers are members of unions belonging to the AFL-CIO—itself a union of unions. Millions of other workers belong to unions not affiliated with the AFL-CIO, such as the National Education Association, the Teamsters, and the Service Employees International Union.

The major aim of American union organizations is to press for policies to ensure better working conditions and higher wages. Recognizing that many workers would like to enjoy union benefits without actually joining a union and paying dues, unions have fought hard to establish the **union shop**, which requires employees of a business that has a union contract to join the union and stay in it as long as they work there. In contrast, business groups have supported **right-to-work laws**, which outlaw union membership as a condition of employment. They argue that such laws deny a basic freedom—namely, the right not to belong to a group. In 1947, the biggest blow ever to the American labor movement occurred when Congress passed the Taft-Hartley Act, permitting states to adopt right-to-work laws (known within the AFL-CIO as "slave labor laws"). There is little doubt that such laws make a difference. As of 2012, labor union membership averaged 8 percent in the states with right-to-work laws, compared to 16 percent in states that had no such law.

The American labor movement reached its peak in 1956, when 33 percent of the nonagricultural workforce belonged to a union; since then, the percentage has declined to about 11 percent. One factor behind this decline is that low wages in other countries have adversely affected the American job market in a number of key manufacturing sectors. The U.S. steel industry, which once dominated in the domestic market, now has to compete with imports from producers based in Brazil, Korea, and other fast-developing economies. The United Auto Workers found its clout greatly reduced as Detroit faced increasingly heavy competition from Japanese automakers. Some political scientists, however, believe labor's problems result from more than the decline of blue-collar industries. Paul Johnson argues that the biggest factor causing the decline in union membership is the problems unions have in convincing today's workers that they will benefit from unionization. In particular, Johnson argues that this task has become more difficult because of employers' efforts to make nonunion jobs more satisfying.[37]

As labor union membership has declined in traditional blue-collar industries, the labor union movement has expanded in the public sector. In 2013, 35 percent of public sector employees were union members, as compared to only 7 percent of workers in the private sector. With state and local budgets tightening in response to declining revenues in recent years, the collective bargaining rights of public sector employees have become a hot-button issue. Over the vigorous protests of union

Over the vigorous protests of union supporters, shown here, the Wisconsin state legislature passed a law that took away collective bargaining rights from public sector employees. After Governor Walker signed the bill into law, union activists mounted a campaign to recall the governor, which ultimately failed by a 53–47 percent margin in 2012.

members, states such as Wisconsin and Indiana passed controversial measures to limit the power of unions. Supporters of such restrictions argued that they were necessary to bring public sector workers' benefits in line with those in the private sector; opponents charged that they were a power play by conservative forces seeking to break the back of public sector unions.

BUSINESS If elite theorists are correct and there is an American power elite, it certainly must be dominated by leaders of the biggest banks, insurance companies, and multinational corporations. In any event, business is well organized for political action. Most large corporations now have offices in Washington that monitor legislative activity. So do hundreds of trade associations, organizations that bring together businesses that operate in a specific industry. And the Chamber of Commerce has become an imposing lobbying force, spending over $100 million a year lobbying on behalf of its mission to fulfill "the unified interests of American business." Business PACs have increased more dramatically than any other category of PACs over the past several decades.

Many people assume that corporate PAC contributions are always tilted in favor of the Republican Party and its tax-cutting and deregulatory agenda. All else being equal, it is true that corporate PACs are more likely to favor the Republicans. However, as you can see in Figure 10.2, these PACs have also swayed significantly with the political winds over time, with Democrats receiving more business money when they are in the majority than in other years. This pattern indicates that a good part of what business expects to get from PAC contributions is access to the most powerful policymakers.

One should also keep in mind that business interests are far from monolithic, as different business interests compete on many specific issues. Both Microsoft and Google have their lobbyists on Capitol Hill pressing their competing interests. Trucking and construction companies want more highways, but railroads do not.

An increase in international trade will help some businesses expand their markets, but others may be hurt by foreign competition. In short, business interests are generally unified when it comes to promoting greater profits but are often fragmented when policy choices have to be made.

☐ Environmental Interests

Among the newer political interest groups are the environmentalists. A handful of environmental groups, such as the Sierra Club and the Audubon Society, have been around since the nineteenth century, but many others trace their origins to the first Earth Day, April 22, 1970. On that day, ecology-minded people marched on Washington and other places to symbolize their support for environmental protection. Just two decades later, one estimate pegged the number of environmental groups at over 10,000 and their combined revenues at $2.9 billion—demonstrating "how widely and deeply green values had permeated the society."[38] No doubt this figure would be even higher today. Russell Dalton finds that the United States ranks high among democracies in the percentage of its adult population that belongs to a group whose main aim is to protect the environment.[39] Among the environmental groups that can boast at least a million members in the United States are the World Wildlife Fund, the Nature Conservancy, and the National Wildlife Federation.

Environmental groups have promoted policies to control pollution and to combat global warming, wilderness protection, and species preservation. In pursuing their goals, they have opposed a range of policies and practices, including oil drilling in Alaska's Arctic National Wildlife Refuge, strip mining, supersonic aircraft, and nuclear power plants. On these and other issues, environmentalists have exerted a great deal of influence on Congress and state legislatures. In particular, the arguments of environmentalists about radiation risks have had a profound impact on public policy. From 1977, when the nation's worst nuclear accident occurred at Three Mile Island in Pennsylvania, to 2010, no new nuclear plants were approved.[40] More recently, however, Congress appropriated $18 billion in loan guarantees for new reactors built to higher safety standards, and the Obama administration approved new plants for construction in Georgia and South Carolina.

FIGURE 10.2 HOW CORPORATE PACs HAVE SHIFTED TOWARD THE MAJORITY PARTY

This graph shows the percentage of corporate PAC spending in each two-year election cycle that went to Republican candidates for the House of Representatives. In years in which the Republicans were in the majority—those colored in red—they received about two-thirds of corporate PAC donations. In contrast, in years in which the Democrats were in the majority—those colored in blue—the Democrats got a slight majority of corporate PAC donations.

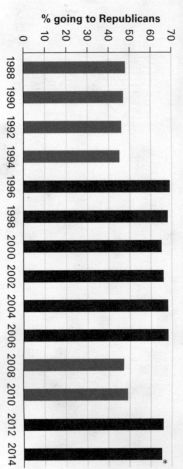

% going to Republicans

*2014 data are through June 30, 2014.

SOURCE: Federal Election Commission.

DEPARTMENT OF THE INTERIOR

GREENPEACE

Secretary Salazar: Save the Polar Bear Now!

A few interest groups use unconventional methods to get attention for their views and demands. The environmental activist group Greenpeace is well known for coming up with activities the media can hardly ignore. Here, Greenpeace activists attract media attention in an attempt to get the secretary of the interior to take regulatory action to combat global warming and help save the polar bear species.

Equality Interests

The Fourteenth Amendment guarantees equal protection under the law. American history, though, shows that this is easier said than done. Two sets of interest groups, representing minorities and women, have made equal rights their main policy goal.

Equality at the polls, in housing, on the job, in education, and in all other facets of American life has long been the dominant goal of African American groups. The oldest and largest of these groups is the National Association for the Advancement of Colored People (NAACP). It argued and won the monumental *Brown v. Board of Education* case, in which the Supreme Court, in 1954, held that segregated schools were unconstitutional. Today, civil rights groups continue to push for equality, for example, through affirmative action programs to ensure that minority groups are given educational and employment opportunities.

Although the work of civil rights interest groups in fighting segregation and discrimination is well known, Dona and Charles Hamilton argue that "much less is known about the 'social welfare agenda'—the fight for social welfare policies to help the poor."[41] They argue that civil rights groups, since their early days, have been concerned with larger and more universal economic problems in American society.

In recent decades, women's rights groups, such as the National Organization for Women (NOW), have lobbied for an end to discrimination against women. One of their top goals has long been the passage of the Equal Rights Amendment (ERA), which states that "equality of rights under the law shall not be abridged on account of sex." Although the ERA fell three states short of ratification, NOW remains committed to achieving the

334

10.1
10.2
10.3
10.4
10.5
10.6

public interest lobbies
According to Jeffrey Berry, organizations that seek "a collective good, the achievement of which will not selectively and materially benefit the membership or activists of the organization."

protection that the amendment would have constitutionally guaranteed by advocating the enactment of many individual statutes. As is often the case with interest group politics, issues are rarely settled once and for all; rather, they shift to different policy arenas.

☐ Consumer and Other Public Interest Lobbies

Today thousands of organized groups are championing various causes or ideas "in the public interest." These **public interest lobbies** are, in Jeffrey Berry's definition, organizations that seek "a collective good, the achievement of which will not selectively and materially benefit the membership or activists of the organization."[42] If products are made safer by the lobbying of consumer protection groups, it is not the members of such groups alone that benefit; rather, everyone should be better off. The benefit that public interest lobbies seek may be for the public as consumers, for the public more broadly defined, or for some sector of the public.

If ever a lobbying effort was spurred by a single person, it was the consumer movement. In the name of consumers, Ralph Nader took on American business almost single-handedly at first. He was propelled to national prominence by his 1965 book, *Unsafe at Any Speed*, which attacked General Motors' Corvair as mechanically deficient and dangerous. General Motors made the mistake of hiring a private detective to look for some dirt they could use to discredit him. Nader eventually learned about the investigation, sued General Motors for invasion of privacy, and won a hefty damage settlement. He used the proceeds to launch the first major consumer group in Washington.

Consumer groups have won many legislative victories. In 1973, for example, Congress responded to consumer advocacy by creating the Consumer Product Safety Commission, which it authorized to regulate all consumer products and to ban products that were dangerous. Products that the commission issued recalls on in 2014 included folding bicycles that broke, infant pacifiers that posed a choking hazard, hockey elbow pads that cracked, and dehumidifiers that overheated and caught on fire.

In addition to consumer groups, the wide range of public interest groups includes groups seeking to protect those who cannot speak for themselves, such as children or the mentally ill; good-government groups such as Common Cause, which push for openness and fairness in government; and religious groups like the Christian Coalition, which pursue what they consider to be moral standards for society.

Understanding Interest Groups

Evaluate how well Madison's ideas for controlling the influence of interest groups have worked in practice.

The problem of interest groups in America is much what it was over 200 years ago when James Madison defined it in speaking of his concerns about factions: A free society must allow for the representation of all groups that seek to influence political decision making, yet groups are usually more concerned with their own self-interest than with the needs of society as a whole; for democracy to work well, it is important that groups not be allowed to assume a dominant position.

☐ Interest Groups and Democracy

Madison's solution to the problems posed by interest groups was to create a wide-open system in which many groups would be able to participate. In a wide-open system, according to Madison, groups with opposing interests would counterbalance one another. Pluralist theorists believe that a rough approximation of the public interest emerges from this competition. Indeed, with the tremendous growth of interest group politics in recent years, for every group with an interest, there now seems to be a competing group to watch over it—not to mention public interest lobbies to watch over them all. Robert Salisbury argues that "the growth in the number, variety, and sophistication of interest groups represented in Washington" has transformed policymaking such that it "is not dominated so often by a relatively small number of powerful interest groups as it may once have been."[43] He concludes that the increase in lobbying activity has actually resulted in less clout overall for interest groups—and in better democracy.

Elite theorists clearly disagree with this conclusion and point to the proliferation of business PACs as evidence of more interest group corruption in American politics than ever. A democratic process requires a free and open exchange of ideas in which candidates and voters can hear one another out, but PACs—the source of so much money in elections—distort the process. Elite theorists particularly note that wealthier interests are greatly advantaged by the PAC system. It is true that there are over 5,000 PACs, but the relatively few big-spending ones dominate the fund-raising game. Rozell, Wilcox, and Madland report that in one recent election cycle a quarter of all PAC contributions came from just 48 PACs, each of which gave over a million dollars. In contrast, the 2,180 smallest PACs (in terms of donations made) accounted for just 10 percent of all PAC contributions.[44]

Hyperpluralist theorists maintain that whenever a major interest group objects strongly to proposed legislation, policymakers will bend over backward to try to accommodate it. With the formation of so many groups in recent years and with so many of them having influence in Washington, hyperpluralists argue that it has been increasingly difficult to accomplish major policy change in Washington. And this policy gridlock, so often evident in American politics today, diminishes democracy.

Interest Groups and the Scope of Government

Although individualistic, Americans are also very associational, as discussed at the start of this chapter. This is not at all contradictory. By joining a number of political associations, Americans are able to politicize a variety of aspects of their own individualism. The multiplicity of the American interest group structure and the openness of American politics to input from interest groups allow individuals many channels for political participation and thus facilitate representation of individual interests.

Although individualism is most often treated in this book as being responsible for the relatively small scope of American government, when it works its way through interest group politics, the result is just the opposite. Individual interest groups fight to sustain government programs that are important to them, thereby making it hard for politicians ever to reduce the scope of government. Many American politicians have found their attempts to cut waste in federal spending frustrated by interest groups. For example, a month before leaving office, President Reagan remarked that "special interest groups, bolstered by campaign contributions, pressure lawmakers into creating and defending spending programs."[45] Above all, most special interest groups strive to maintain established programs that benefit them.

However, one can also argue that the growth in the scope of government in recent decades accounts for a good portion of the proliferation of interest groups. The more areas in which the federal government has become involved, the more interest groups have developed to attempt to influence policy. As William Lunch notes, "A great part of the increase was occasioned by the new government responsibility for civil rights, environmental protection, and greater public health and safety."[46] For example, once the government got actively involved in protecting the environment, many groups sprung up to lobby for strong standards and enforcement. Given the tremendous effects of environmental regulations on many industries, it should come as no surprise that these industries also organized to ensure that their interests were taken into account. As Salisbury writes, many groups have "come to Washington out of need and dependence rather than because they have influence."[47] He argues that interest groups spend much of their time merely monitoring policy developments in order to alert their membership and develop reactive strategies.

Review the Chapter

The Role of Interest Groups

10.1 Describe the role of interest groups in American politics, p. 315.

Interest groups are groups that participate in the political process in order to promote policy goals that members share. They usually focus their efforts on one specific issue area, unlike political parties, which have to address all issues on the public agenda.

Theories of Interest Group Politics

10.2 Compare and contrast the theories of pluralism, elitism, and hyperpluralism, p. 316.

The theory of pluralism asserts that the policymaking process is very open to the participation of all interest groups, with no single group usually dominating. Pluralists tend to believe that as a result the public interest generally prevails. In contrast, elitism contends that an upper-class elite holds the power and makes policy, regardless of the formal governmental organization. Hyperpluralism criticizes pluralism from a different perspective, contending that, with so many groups being so strong, government is weakened and its ability to make effective policy is crippled.

What Makes an Interest Group Successful?

10.3 Analyze the factors that make some interest groups more successful than others in the political arena, p. 319.

Groups that have large numbers of potential members are usually less effective than groups that have a smaller potential membership, because it is easier to mobilize members of a smaller group, who have more incentive to participate. Both large and small groups can benefit from the intensity of their members' beliefs. Money always helps lubricate the wheels of power, though it is hardly a surefire guarantee of success.

How Groups Try to Shape Policy

10.4 Assess the four basic strategies that interest groups use to try to shape policy, p. 322.

Interest groups use four basic strategies to maximize their effectiveness. Lobbying is one well-known group strategy. Although the evidence on its influence is mixed, it is clear that lobbyists are most effective with those legislators already

sympathetic to their side. Thus, electioneering becomes critical because it helps put supportive people in office. Often today, groups operate in the judicial as well as the legislative process, using litigation in the courts when lobbying fails or is not enough. Many also find it important to project a good image, employing public relations techniques to present themselves in the most favorable light.

Types of Interest Groups

10.5 Identify the various types of interest groups and their policy concerns, p. 329.

Economic interest groups involve business and labor, with business focusing on governmental regulations and subsidies, and labor focusing on policies to ensure good working conditions and wages. Environmental interests advocate policies to deal with problems such as global warming and pollution; they are also heavily involved in efforts to protect the wilderness and endangered species. Interest groups that are concerned with equality promote the fair treatment of groups that have been discriminated against in the past, such as African Americans and women. Public interest lobbies pursue policy objectives that they believe will benefit all citizens, such as consumer protection laws.

Understanding Interest Groups

10.6 Evaluate how well Madison's ideas for controlling the influence of interest groups have worked in practice, p. 334.

The issue of controlling interest groups remains as crucial to democracy today as it was in James Madison's time. Some scholars believe that the growth of interest groups has worked to divide political influence, just as Madison hoped it would. Critics of this point of view tend to focus on the PAC system as the new way in which special interests corrupt American democracy or on the problem of too many groups having too much power to block policy change.

Learn the Terms

interest group, p. 315
pluralism, p. 316
elitism, p. 316
hyperpluralism, p. 316
iron triangle, p. 318
potential group, p. 320

actual group, p. 320
collective good, p. 320
free-rider problem, p. 320
selective benefits, p. 320
single-issue group, p. 321
lobbying, p. 323

electioneering, p. 325
political action committees (PACs),
p. 325
union shop, p. 330
right-to-work laws, p. 330
public interest lobbies, p. 334

Test Yourself

1. What distinguishes political parties from interest groups?

a. Interest groups are a vehicle for individual political involvement; political parties are for elected officials' involvement.

b. Interest groups are limited to lobbying legislation, while political parties may sponsor candidates for any branch of government.

c. Interest groups are limited to promoting specific policies relevant to their group; political parties must address all policies as they attempt to govern.

d. Political parties are restricted in how they receive and use their funding; interest groups have no such limits.

e. Political parties need interest groups in order to further their policies, but interest groups don't need political parties.

2. How do interest groups promote democracy?

a. They help officials get elected.

b. They help to make the president aware of items that were not previously part of his or her agenda.

c. They help to communicate the views of industry to staunch the regulatory direction of Congress.

d. They help to contribute funds and other means of support to public officials to gain their trust.

e. They help to convey the policy views of individuals and groups to public officials.

3. How does the American constitutional system encourage the participation of interest groups?

a. Because there are so many state and federal officials and political candidates, there are many opportunities for interest groups to influence government.

b. Individuals who see a need cannot begin their own interest groups because of their high cost of maintenance.

c. Interest groups have little power due to their lack of influence on the public.

d. Only one of the branches of the government, Congress, provides opportunities for interest groups to influence government.

e. The low frequency of elections results in almost no time for campaigning.

4. According to critics of pluralism, which of the following groups is most likely to take advantage of the American political system?

a. children
b. immigrants
c. minorities
d. the rich
e. the poor

5. Which of the following theories offers the most positive interpretation of the effect of interest groups on American democracy?

a. elite theory
b. free market theory
c. hyperelitist theory
d. hyperpluralism
e. pluralism

6. Why does the establishment of an iron triangle among lobbyists, a government agency, and a congressional committee often lead them to accomplish an important goal?

a. All three are motivated by their own self-interest, which is to improve the same aspect of American life.

b. The government officials would be too embarrassed to fail in front of the lobbyists.

c. The lobbyists bribe the other two groups.

d. The lobbyists threaten to expose the incompetence of the government officials.

e. They keep each other honest.

7. What advantages does an actual group have over a potential one?

a. The actual group can offer access to collective goods to its members, rather than offering potential access to everyone.

b. The actual group ensures selective benefits that are available only to active members, rather than to potential free-riders.

c. The actual group has government backing and funding regarding its policy preferences, rather than potential government support.

d. The actual group is made up of members with a narrow policy interest, which gives it more influence because the resources are not spread out.

e. The actual group is made up of people who are actively taking part in pursuing a policy interest, whereas the potential group consists of all the people who are affected, many of whom are inactive.

8. Why might a group that lobbies for an end to discrimination on the basis of gender have a free-rider problem?

a. Many people do not know that they have to pay dues to the group.

b. Other people try to take credit for the group's accomplishment.

c. So many people benefit from it that most members have little incentive to take an active role themselves.

d. The group does not get enough publicity.

e. Women, who will benefit the most, do not usually join interest groups.

9. Why might some large lobbying groups not register as lobbyists?

a. It is not a law that they register.

b. Lobbying is not their principal activity.

c. Their clients ask them not to register.

d. Their offices are not in Washington, D.C.

e. They wish to avoid certain tax regulations.

10. Why is the public image of an interest group important?

a. Public image determines whether an interest group can retain access to lawmakers regardless of public opinion on issues.

b. Public image is the most easily controlled aspect of an interest group's attempts to affect government decision making.

c. Public opinion of a candidate and an interest group tells an interest group if or where to practice electioneering.

d. Public opinions of interest groups and issues are eventually communicated to lawmakers through voting behavior.

e. Public opinion on issues informs the interest groups of their potential group size and their potential power.

11. When Richard Hall and Alan Deardorff called lobbying a form of "legislative subsidy," they were referring to the _____.

a. importance of political partisanship

b. legitimate services lobbyists often perform for their allies on Capitol Hill

c. means by which lobbyists pay congressmen for their support

d. power of professional politicians

e. power of think tanks in politics

12. Why do so many different interest groups exist among the business community?

a. Different industries have different financial concerns.

b. Geographical differences make combining difficult.

c. They cannot agree on anything.

d. They have not had a chance to consolidate.

e. They want to approach members of Congress from many different angles.

13. What is organized labor's main long-range problem in American politics?

a. its continued support for unpopular right-wing causes

b. its focus on bread-and-butter issues

c. its lack of funds

d. shrinking number of members in private sector jobs

e. the negative view of labor that most people hold

14. The large number and variety of interest groups in the United States generates a tension between _____.

a. a greater sense of unity and political division

b. freedom and anarchy

c. left and right

d. more efficient government and government waste

e. self-interest and the public good

15. Which of the following best characterizes James Madison's view of how government should deal with competing interests?

a. He believed American society would be best served by a relatively small number of powerful groups.

b. He believed that interest groups were dangerous because the common man was not qualified to speak for the public interest.

c. He favored a wide-open system in which many groups would participate and counterbalance one another.

d. He wanted the Constitution to prohibit groups and factions.

e. He was not worried about the dangers of interest groups and factions.

Explore Further

WEB SITES

www.aarp.org
The official site of AARP.

www.aflcio.org
The nation's largest labor association, the AFL–CIO, posts material at this site.

www.nea.org
The site of the National Education Association.

www.greenpeaceusa.org
The place to go to learn more about the activities of this environmental protection group.

www.commoncause.org
The official site of Common Cause, one of the nation's oldest and largest public affairs interest groups.

FURTHER READING

Baumgartner, Frank R., et al. *Lobbying and Policy Change.* Chicago: University of Chicago Press, 2008. A path-breaking study of who wins and loses in the lobbying game and why.

Berry, Jeffrey M. *The New Liberalism: The Rising Power of Citizen Groups.* Washington, D.C.: Brookings Institution, 1999. Berry argues that citizen groups have been strikingly successful in influencing the policy agenda in recent decades.

Berry, Jeffrey M., and Clyde Wilcox. *The Interest Group Society,* 6th ed. New York: Longman, 2013. One of the best contemporary textbooks on interest groups in American politics.

Cigler, Allan J., and Burdett A. Loomis, eds. *Interest Group Politics,* 8th ed. Washington, D.C.: Congressional Quarterly Press, 2012. An excellent collection of original articles on the modern interest group system.

Domhoff, G. William. *Who Rules America? Challenges to Corporate and Class Dominance.* New York: McGraw-Hill, 2010. A good summary of the elitist view of interest groups.

Herrnson, Paul S., Christopher J. Deering, and Clyde Wilcox, eds. *Interest Groups Unleashed.* Washington, D.C.: Congressional Quarterly, 2012. A set of interesting case studies of how interest groups have been participating in the electoral process.

Kollman, Ken. *Outside Lobbying: Public Opinion and Interest Group Strategies.* Princeton, NJ: Princeton University Press, 1998. An insightful study of how many interest groups use public opinion in the lobbying process.

Lowi, Theodore J. *The End of Liberalism,* 2nd ed. New York: Norton, 1979. A critique of the role of subgovernments and the excessive deference to interest groups in the American political system.

Olson, Mancur. *The Logic of Collective Action.* Cambridge, MA: Harvard University Press, 1965. Develops an economic theory of groups, showing how the cards are stacked against larger groups.

Rauch, Jonathan. *Demosclerosis: The Silent Killer of American Government.* New York: Random House, 1994. A good treatment of hyperpluralism in American politics.

11

Congress

Politics in Action: Governing in Congress

In the autumn of 2013, partisan polarization, the differences between the parties in Congress, was at an historic high. The federal government shut down for 16 days because legislators could not agree on a budget, even a temporary one. Republicans would not agree to increase the government's revenues, and Democrats would not accept cutting expenditures. In addition, many Republicans insisted the president agree to defund his signature health care reform policy before they would agree to spend funds for the rest of the government. Even in the face of widespread public criticism of the shutdown, Congress could not agree on anything more than pushing budgeting decisions three months down the road.

What happened in Congress in 2013 was extreme. Yet even under more ordinary circumstances, Congress usually moves slowly to pass legislation. The Madisonian system of the separation of powers and checks and balances complicates policymaking. Moreover, power is fragmented within Congress, and representatives and senators tend to be fiercely independent. One Senate leader declared that trying to move the Senate to act is like "trying to push a wet noodle": When Congress faces the great issues of the day, it often cannot arrive at any decision at all.

The inability to compromise and make important policy decisions—what we commonly refer to as *gridlock*—does not please the public. Its approval of Congress has been in the single digits, the lowest it had ever been. Nevertheless, most of the members of Congress who ran for reelection in 2014 won. It seems as though individual senators and representatives were doing what their constituents wanted them to do, although Congress as a whole was not.

Congress is both our central policymaking branch and our principal *representative* branch. As such, it lies at the heart of American democracy. How does Congress combine its roles of representing constituents *and* making effective public policy? Some critics argue that Congress is too responsive to constituents and, especially, to organized interest groups and is thus unable to make difficult choices regarding public policy, such as reining in spending. Others argue that

11.1
Characterize the backgrounds of members of Congress and assess their impact on the ability of members of Congress to represent average Americans, p. 342.

11.2
Identify the principal factors influencing the outcomes in congressional elections, p. 345.

11.3
Compare and contrast the House and Senate, and describe the roles of congressional leaders, committees, caucuses, and staff, p. 351.

11.4
Outline the path of bills to passage and explain the influences on congressional decision making, p. 362.

11.5
Assess Congress's role as a representative body and the impact of representation on the scope of government, p. 369.

Congress is the center of policymaking in the United States, but the decentralization of power within Congress and also between the three branches of the federal government makes it difficult to get things done. Here President Barack Obama delivers his 2014 State of the Union address before a joint session of Congress.

342

11.1

11.2

11.3

11.4

11.5

The Representatives and Senators

Characterize the backgrounds of members of Congress and assess their impact on the ability of members of Congress to represent average Americans.

Being a member of Congress is a difficult and unusual job. A person must be willing to spend considerable time, trouble, and money to obtain a crowded office on Capitol Hill. To nineteenth-century humorist Artemus Ward, such a quest was inexplicable: "It's easy to see why a man goes to the poorhouse or the penitentiary. It's because he can't help it. But why he should voluntarily go live in Washington is beyond my comprehension."[1]

☐ The Members

To many Americans, being a member of Congress may seem like a glamorous job. What citizens do not see are the 14-hour days spent dashing from one meeting to the next (members are often scheduled to be in two places at the same time),[2] the continuous travel between Washington and constituencies, the lack of time for reflection or exchange of ideas, the constant fund-raising, the partisan rancor that permeates Congress, and—perhaps most important of all—the feeling of many members that Congress is making little headway in solving the country's problems.

There are attractions to the job, however. First and foremost is power. Members of Congress make key decisions about important matters of public policy. In addition, members of Congress earn a salary of $174,000—about three times the income of the typical American family, although far below that of hundreds of corporate presidents—and they receive generous retirement and health benefits.

There are 535 members of Congress. An even 100—2 from each state—are members of the Senate. The other 435 are members of the House of Representatives. The Constitution specifies only that members of the House must be at least 25 years old and have been American citizens for 7 years, that senators must be at least 30 years old and have been American citizens for 9 years, and that each member of Congress must reside in the state from which he or she is elected.

Members of Congress are not typical or average Americans, however, as the figures in Table 11.1 reveal. Those who argue that the country is run by a power elite

The Framers of the Constitution conceived of the legislature as the center of policymaking in America. Their plan was for the great disputes over public policy to be resolved in Congress, not in the White House or the Supreme Court. Although the prominence of Congress has ebbed and flowed over the course of American history, as often as not, Congress has been the true center of power in Washington.

The tasks of Congress become more difficult each year. On any given day, a representative or senator can be required to make sensible judgments about missiles, nuclear waste dumps, abortion, trade competition with China, income tax rates, the soaring costs of Social Security and Medicare, or any number of other issues. The proposal for the 2010 health care reform bill was about 1,400 pages long and weighed 6 pounds. Just finding the time to think about the issues—much less debate them—has become increasingly difficult. Despite the many demands of being a senator or representative, there is no shortage of men and women running for congressional office. The following sections will introduce you to these people.

Congress is too insulated from ordinary citizens and makes policy to suit the few rather than the many. Yet other critics focus on Congress as the source of government expansion. Does Congress's responsiveness predispose the legislature to increase the size of government to please those in the public wanting more or larger government programs?

TABLE 11.1 A PORTRAIT OF THE 114TH CONGRESS

Characteristic	House (435 Total)	Senate (100 Total)
Party		
Democrat	187	46
Republican	248	54
Gender		
Men	351	80
Women	84	20
Race/Ethnicity		
Asian	11	1
African American	42	2
Hispanic	29	3
Native American	2	0
White and other	351	94
Average age†	57	62
Religion†	Percent	Percent
Protestant	57	52
Roman Catholic	31	27
Jewish	5	11
Other and unspecified	7	10
Most common prior occupation*†	Percent	Percent
Public service/politics	42	42
Law	36	61
Business	43	29
Education	18	12

†Data for 113th Congress.
*Some members specify more than one occupation.

SOURCE: 114th Congress data based on press reports available a week after the November 4, 2014 elections. 113th Congress data compiled from: Congressional Research Service, *Membership of the 113th Congress: A Profile* (Washington, D.C.), October 31, 2013; Norman J. Ornstein, Thomas E. Mann, Michael J. Malbin, and Andrew Rugg, Vital *Statistics on Congress* (Washington, D.C.: Brookings Institution and American Enterprise Institute, 2013).

are quick to point out that members come largely from occupations with high status and usually have substantial incomes. Although calling the Senate a "millionaire's club" is an exaggeration, the proportion of millionaires and near millionaires in Congress is much higher than it is in an average crowd of 535 people. Business and law are the dominant prior occupations; other elite occupations such as academia are also well represented.

The prominence of lawyers in Congress is not surprising. Law especially attracts persons interested in politics and provides the flexibility (and often the financial support of a law firm) to wage election campaigns. In addition, many government positions in which aspiring members of Congress can make their mark, such as district attorney, are reserved for lawyers.

Some prominent groups are underrepresented. African Americans make up about 10 percent of the members of the House (compared with about 13 percent of the total population), but there are only two African Americans in the Senate. There are 29 Hispanics in the House and 3 in the Senate, although Hispanics compose 17 percent of the population. Asian and Native Americans are also underrepresented. However, women may be the most underrepresented group; they account for more than half the population but for only 19 percent of members of the House of Representatives—84 voting representatives (as well as the nonvoting representative from Washington, D.C.)—and for 20 senators.

How important are the personal characteristics of members of Congress? Can a group of predominantly white, upper-middle-class, middle-aged, Protestant males adequately represent a much more diverse population? Would a group more typical of

344

11.1

11.2

11.3

11.4

11.5

Representation is at the heart of democracy, but members of Congress may have different backgrounds than many of their constituents. Here Representative Michael McMahon of New York talks with constituents at an Arab American Heritage festival.

the population be more effective in making major policy decisions? The backgrounds of representatives and senators can be important if they influence how they prioritize and vote on issues. There is evidence that African American members are more active than are white members in serving African American constituents.[3] and they appear to increase African American constituents' contact with and knowledge about Congress.[4] On the average, women legislators seem to be more active than are men in pursuing the interests of women.[5] By the same token, representatives with a business background are more pro-business (less supportive of regulations, for example) than are other members,[6] while members from working-class occupations are more liberal on economic matters.[7]

Obviously, few members of Congress can claim *descriptive* representation—that is, representing constituents by mirroring their personal, politically relevant characteristics. They may, however, engage in *substantive* representation and so speak for the interests of groups of which they themselves are not members.[8] For example, a member of Congress with a background of wealth and privilege may champion the interests of the poor, as did the late Senator Edward Kennedy. Moreover, most members of Congress have lived for many years in the constituencies they represent and share many of the beliefs and attitudes of their constituents, even if they do not share their demographic characteristics. If they do not share their constituents' perspectives, they may find it difficult to keep their seats come election time. At the same time, women and African Americans in Congress are achieving important positions on committees, increasing the chances of making descriptive representation effective.[9]

☐ Why Aren't There More Women in Congress?

Sarah Fulton, a scholar of women in politics, found that in the 2012 elections, women won 46 percent of the House races in which they competed and 61 percent of the Senate races.[10] Yet, despite this record, women constitute only about a fifth of Congress. If women have proven themselves capable of competing with and winning against men, why aren't there more women in Congress?

Part of the reason for women's underrepresentation is that fewer women than men become major party nominees for office. For example, in 2012 a female major-party

incumbents

Those individuals who already hold office. In congressional elections, incumbents usually win.

nominee contested only 38 percent of the 435 House races and 55 percent of the Senate races. In one article, Fulton and her coauthors found that women with children are significantly less ambitious about running for office than are their male counterparts, largely because of greater child care responsibilities; however, they found no gender disparity in ambition among women without children. The authors also suggest that women's decisions to run are more sensitive than are men's to their perceptions of the odds of winning: women are less likely than are men to run when they perceive their odds to be poor; however, they are more likely than are men to run when they detect a political opportunity.[11]

In addition to the supply of female candidates, there is the issue of the electorate's demand. Voters appraise women candidates higher than male candidates on non-policy characteristics such as integrity, competence, collaboration, and problem-solving skills. Once women's quality advantage is taken into account, women encounter a 3 percent vote deficit relative to their male counterparts. Male independent voters are equally supportive of male and female candidates when women have a quality advantage. But, when candidates have the same quality, male independents are 23 percent less likely to vote for female than male candidates. Thus, to win, women must be more qualified on average than their male opponents.[12]

Congressional Elections

11.2 Identify the principal factors influencing the outcomes in congressional elections.

ongressional elections are demanding, expensive,[13] and, as you will see, generally foregone conclusions—yet members of Congress are first and foremost politicians. Men and women may run for Congress to forge new policy initiatives, but they also enjoy politics and consider a position in Congress near the top of their chosen profession. Even if they dislike politics, unless they get reelected, they will not be around long enough to shape policy.

□ Who Wins Elections?

Incumbents are individuals who already hold office. Sometime during each term, the incumbent must decide whether to run again or to retire voluntarily. Most decide to run for reelection. They enter their party's primary, almost always emerge victorious, and typically win in the November general election too. Indeed, the most predictable aspect of congressional elections is this: *incumbents usually win* (see Figure 11.1). Even in a year of great political upheaval such as 2010, in which the Republicans gained 6 seats in the Senate and 63 seats in the House, 84 percent of incumbent senators and 85 percent of incumbent representatives won their bids for reelection.

In the case of the House, not only do more than 90 percent of incumbents seeking reelection usually win, but most of them win with more than 60 percent of the vote. Perhaps most astonishing is the fact that even when challengers' positions on the issues are closer to the voters' positions, incumbents still tend to win.[14]

Why It Matters to You
Incumbent Success

If congressional seats were more competitive, it would be easier to change Congress. There would be more turnover in the membership of Congress as districts and states voted in candidates of the other party. However, defeating incumbents would mean also losing their experience in lawmaking. Thus fewer members of Congress would have expertise on complex policy issues.

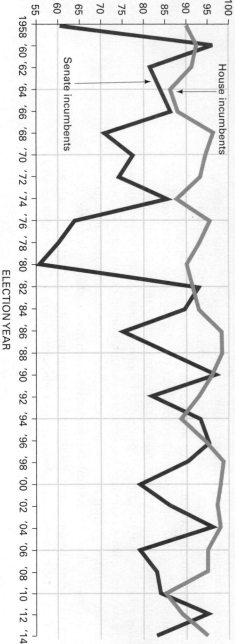

FIGURE 11.1 THE INCUMBENCY FACTOR IN CONGRESSIONAL ELECTIONS
It is not unusual for the public to disapprove of the performance of Congress as a whole, but it is unusual for incumbents to lose their bids for reelection. The many advantages of incumbency make it difficult to make substantial changes in the makeup of Congress in one election.

PERCENTAGE OF INCUMBENT CANDIDATES REELECTED

House incumbents

Senate incumbents

ELECTION YEAR

SOURCE: Data compiled by the authors. Figures reflect incumbents running in both primary and general elections.

The picture for the Senate is a little different. Even though senators still have a good chance of beating back challengers, the odds of reelection are often not as handsome as they are for House incumbents; senators typically win by narrower margins. Senators represent entire states, which are almost always more diverse than a congressional district within a state and thus provides a larger base for opposition to an incumbent. Inevitably, senators have less personal contact with their constituencies, which on average are about 10 times larger than those of members of the House of Representatives. Senators also receive more coverage in the media than representatives do and are more likely to be held accountable on controversial issues. Moreover, senators tend to draw more skilled and visible challengers, such as governors or members of the House, whom voters already know. Such challengers typically have substantial financial backing—another factor that lessens the advantages of incumbency.

Despite their chances of getting reelected, incumbents often feel quite vulnerable. As Thomas Mann put it, members of Congress perceive themselves to be "unsafe at any margin."[15] In recent years, they have been raising and spending more campaign funds, sending more mail to their constituents, visiting their states and districts more often, and staffing more local offices than ever before.[16]

☐ The Advantages of Incumbency

There are several possible explanations for the success of incumbents. One is that voters know how their elected representatives vote on important policy issues and agree with their stands, sending them back to Washington to keep up the good work. This, however, is usually not the case. Most citizens have trouble recalling the names of their congressional representatives (in one poll only 28 percent of the public could name their representatives in the House), let alone keeping up with their representatives' voting records. One study found that only about one-fifth of Americans could make an accurate guess about how their representatives voted on any issue in Congress,[17] in an American National Election Study, only 11 percent of the people even claimed to remember how their congressperson voted on a particular issue. The public's knowledge of congressional candidates declines precipitously once we look beyond simple recognition and generalized feelings.

Another possibility is that how voters feel about presidential candidates influences their choices in voting for Congress. However, most stories of the power of presidential "coattails" (voters supporting congressional candidates because those candidates belong to the president's party), seem to be just stories.[18] Bill Clinton, George W. Bush, and

Barack Obama won six presidential elections between them. Yet in each election they received a *smaller* percentage of the vote than did almost every winning member of their party in Congress. They had little in the way of coattails.

Journalists often claim that voters are motivated primarily by their pocketbooks. Yet members of Congress do not gain or lose many votes as a result of the ups and downs of the economy.[19]

What accounts for the success of congressional incumbents? Members of Congress engage in three primary activities that increase the probability of their being reelected: advertising, credit claiming, and position taking.[20] A lack of strong opponents and the high costs of campaigning further ensure their success.

ADVERTISING For members of Congress, advertising means much more than placing ads in the newspapers and on television. Most congressional advertising takes place between elections in the form of contact with constituents. The goal is *visibility*.

Members of Congress work hard to make themselves visible among their constituents, and they usually succeed. Not surprisingly, members concentrate on staying visible and make frequent trips home. In a typical week, members spend some time in their home states or districts, even though that may mean traveling far from Washington. Similarly, members use the franking privilege to mail newsletters to every household in their constituency.

In recent years, members of Congress have brought communication with their constituencies into the digital age. Congressional staffers track the interests of individual voters, file the information in a database, and then use e-mails or phone calls to engage directly with voters on issues they know they care about. Using taxpayers' money, legislators employ a technology that allows them to call thousands of households simultaneously and deliver a recorded message, inviting people in their districts to join in on a conference call. With the push of a button, a constituent can be on the line with the House member—and often with 1,000 or more fellow constituents. Equally important, lawmakers know from the phone numbers where the respondents live and, from what constituents say on the call, what issues interest them. Information gathered from these events, as well as from e-mails and phone calls from constituents, gets plugged into an electronic database, giving incumbents something challengers can only dream of: a detailed list of the specific interests of thousands of actual or potential voters. E-mail allows for personal interaction—and another reminder of why the incumbent should be reelected.

CREDIT CLAIMING Congresspersons seek to also engage in credit claiming, which involves enhancing their standing with constituents through service to individuals and the district. One member of Congress told Richard Fenno about the image he tried to cultivate among his constituents:

> [I have] a very high recognition factor. And of all the things [constituents] said about me, none of them said, "He's a conservative or a liberal," or "He votes this way on such and such an issue." "None of that at all. There were two things said. One, "He works hard." Two, "He works for us." Nothing more than that. So we made it our theme, "O'Connor gets things done"; and we emphasized the dams, the highways, the buildings, the casework.[21]

Morris Fiorina argues that when members of Congress go to their constituents and stress their policymaking record and their stands on new policy issues, they risk alienating at least some of those constituents. A member of Congress's vote for reducing government spending may win some friends, but it will make enemies of voters who link that vote with service cutbacks. Besides, a congressperson can almost never show that he or she alone was responsible for a major policy. Being only one of 435 members of the House or one of 100 senators, a person can hardly promise to end inflation, cut taxes, or achieve equal rights for women single-handedly.[22]

One thing, however, always wins congresspersons friends and almost never makes enemies: *servicing the constituency*. Members of Congress can do this in two ways: through casework and through obtaining federal funds. Doing **casework** means helping individual constituents—typically by cutting through some bureaucratic red tape to

casework
Activities of members of Congress that help constituents as individuals, particularly by cutting through bureaucratic red tape to get people what they think they have a right to get.

pork barrel

Federal projects, grants, and contracts available to state and local governments, businesses, colleges, and other institutions in a congressional district.

Because claiming credit may be important for reelection, members of Congress rarely pass up the opportunity to increase federal spending in their state or district. The early 2000s witnessed a surge in earmarks of expenditures for specific projects. The most expensive was the "Big Dig" in Boston, shown in progress in an aerial view here, which rerouted a principal highway so that it went through a 3.5-mile tunnel, rather than through the heart of the city.

give people what they think they have a right to get. Do you have trouble getting your check from the Social Security Administration on time? Call your congressperson; he or she can cut red tape. Does your town have trouble getting federal bureaucrats to respond to its request for federal construction money? Call your congressperson. Representatives and senators can single-handedly take credit for each of these favors.

The second way of servicing a constituency involves winning federal funds for states and districts. The so-called **pork barrel** is composed of federal projects, grants, and contracts available to state and local governments, businesses, colleges, and other institutions. Members of Congress love to take credit for federally-financed new highways, sewage treatment plants, or research institutes in their constituencies. Often they announce the awards through their offices. Moreover, the more often they claim credit, the more constituents support them.[23] In the past, members have worked hard to obtain appropriations earmarked for specific projects in their districts, and members who succeed have had an easier time in their reelection campaigns.[24]

As a result of the advantages of incumbents have in advertising and in credit claiming, incumbents, especially in the House, are usually much better known than their opponents and have a more favorable public image.[25] The opportunities to do casework and resort to the pork barrel provide incumbents with the basis for credit claiming. Yet casework and the pork barrel by themselves do not determine the outcome of congressional elections.[26]

POSITION TAKING Even if, in establishing their public images, members of Congress emphasize their experience, hard work, trustworthiness, and service to their constituencies—qualities unrelated to partisan or programmatic content—they must take positions on policies when they vote and when they respond to constituents' questions And the positions they take may affect the outcome of their elections, particularly if the relevant issues are salient to voters and the majority of voters disagree with the congressperson. This is especially true in elections for the Senate, in which issues are likely to play a greater role than in House elections.

WEAK OPPONENTS Another advantage for incumbents, particularly in the House, is that they are likely to face weak opponents.[27] In part because the advantages of incumbency scare off potentially effective opponents, those individuals who do run are usually not well known or well qualified and lack experience and organizational and financial backing.[28] The lack of adequate campaign funds is a special burden because challengers need money to compensate for the "free" recognition incumbents receive from their advertising and credit claiming.[29]

CAMPAIGN SPENDING It costs a great deal of money to get elected to Congress. In the 2011–2012 election cycle, congressional candidates and supporting party committees spent more than $2 billion to contest 435 House and 33 Senate seats. The average winner in the House spent about $1.6 million while the average Senate winner spent $11.5 million.[30]

Challengers have to raise large sums if they hope to defeat incumbents; the more they spend, the more votes they receive. Money buys them name recognition and a chance to be heard. Incumbents, by contrast, already have high levels of recognition among their constituents and benefit less (although they do benefit) from campaign spending; what matters most to the outcome of an election is how much their opponent spends. (In contests for open seats, discussed later in this chapter, the candidate who spends the most usually wins.[31]) In the end, however, challengers, especially those for House seats, are usually substantially outspent by incumbents. In both the Senate and House races in 2012, the typical incumbent outspent the typical challenger by a ratio of 2 to 1.[32]

The candidate spending the most money usually wins—but not always. In the 2012 Senate race in Connecticut, Republican Linda McMahon, the former chief executive of World Wrestling Entertainment, lost after spending more than $49 million, most from her own pocket. Her opponent, Christopher Murphy, spent only about one-fifth as much and won the seat.[33] Obviously, prolific spending in a campaign is no guarantee of success.

☐ The Role of Party Identification

At the base of every electoral coalition are the members of the candidate's party in the constituency. Most members of Congress represent constituencies in which their party is in the clear majority, which gives them yet another advantage when they run for reelection. Most people identify with a party, and most party identifiers reliably vote for their party's candidates. Indeed, about 90 percent of voters who identify with a party vote for the House candidates of their party. State legislatures have eagerly employed advances in technology to draw the boundaries of House districts so that there is a safe majority for one party. In addition, it is now more common for people to live in communities where their neighbors are likely to have political and other attitudes that are similar to their own,[34] which reduces the basis for party competition.

☐ Defeating Incumbents

In light of the advantages of incumbents, it is reasonable to ask why anyone challenges them at all. One of the main reasons is simply that challengers are often naïve about their chances of winning. Because few have the money for expensive polls, they rely on friends and local party leaders, who often tell them what they want to hear.

Sometimes challengers receive some unexpected help. An incumbent tarnished by scandal or corruption becomes instantly vulnerable. Voters do take out their anger at the polls. In a close election, negative publicity can turn victory into defeat.[35]

Incumbents can also lose many of their supporters when the boundaries of their districts change. After a federal census, which occurs every 10 years, Congress reapportions its membership. States that have gained significantly in population will be given more House seats; states that have lost substantial population will lose one or more of their seats. The state legislatures must then redraw their states' district lines; one incumbent may be moved into another's district, where the two must battle for one seat.[36] A state party in the majority is more likely to move two of the opposition party's representatives into a single district than two of its own. Or it may split the district of an incumbent of the minority party to make that district more competitive.

Finally, major political tidal waves occasionally roll across the country, leaving defeated incumbents in their wake. One such wave occurred in 1994, when the public mood turned especially sour and voters took out their frustration on Democratic incumbents, defeating two in the Senate and 34 in the House. In 2006 the tide turned and 6 Republican senators and 23 Republican representatives lost their seats. In 2010 it was again the Republicans' turn: they defeated 2 Democratic senators and 52 Democratic representatives in the general election.

Open Seats

When an incumbent is not running for reelection, and this or her seat is open, there is greater likelihood of real competition for the seat. If the party balance in a constituency is such that either party has a chance of winning, each side may offer a strong candidate who has name recognition among the voters or enough money to establish name recognition. Most of the turnover in the membership of Congress results when incumbents do not seek reelection.

Stability and Change

Because incumbents usually win reelection, there is some stability in the membership of Congress. This stability allows representatives and senators to gain some expertise in dealing with complex questions of public policy. At the same time, longevity in office may insulate members from the winds of political change. Safe seats make it more difficult for citizens to "send a message to Washington" with their votes. It takes a large shift in votes to affect the outcomes of most elections, particularly in the House. To increase turnover in the membership of Congress, some reformers have proposed *term limit* for representatives and senators[37] (see "You Are the Policymaker: Should We Impose Term Limits on Members of Congress?").

You Are the Policymaker

Should We Impose Term Limits on Members of Congress?

Many reformers are concerned that the incumbency advantage legislators enjoy creates, in effect, lifetime tenure, which serves as a roadblock to change and encourages ethics abuses. In recent years, the public has accorded Congress the lowest approval rates ever.

To increase turnover among legislators, reformers have proposed term limits that, generally restricted representatives to 6 or 12 consecutive years in office.

The movement to limit the terms of legislators spread rapidly across the country. Within a few years, 23 states enacted term limitations for members of their state legislatures. In 1994 the House Republicans made term limits for Congress part of their Contract with America.

Yet changing the terms of members of Congress is difficult to do: many members of Congress have fought term limits fiercely.

Opponents of term limits object to the loss of experienced legislators who know the issues and the legislative process. They object, too, that the American people should be able to vote for whomever they please.

In addition, they argue, there is plenty of new blood in the legislature: at the beginning of the 114th Congress (in 2015), most members of the House and Senate had served fewer than 10 years in Congress. Moreover, changes in the party makeup of the House appear to reflect changes in voters' preferences on public policy.*

Congress seems to be responsive to public opinion.

Proponents of term limits suffered two setbacks in 1995 when Congress failed to pass a constitutional amendment on term limits (it also failed in 1997) and when the Supreme Court, in *U.S. Term Limits, Inc. et al. v. Thornton et al.*, decided that state-imposed term limits on members of Congress were unconstitutional.

Here is the dilemma: Many Americans support a constitutional amendment to impose term limits on members of Congress. At the same time, most voters are comfortable with their own representatives and senators and appear content to reelect them again and again.

What do you think? If you were a policymaker, would you favor term limits?

*Suzanna De Boef and James A. Stimson, "The Dynamic Structure of Congressional Elections," *Journal of Politics* 57 (August 1995): 630–48.

How Congress Is Organized to Make Policy

11.3 Compare and contrast the House and Senate, and describe the roles of congressional leaders, committees, caucuses, and staff.

O f all the roles that senators and representatives play—including politician, fund-raiser, and constituency representative—policymaker is the most difficult. Congress is a collection of generalists, short on time, trying to make policy on specialized topics. As generalists on most subjects, they are surrounded by people who know (or claim to know) more than they do—lobbyists, agency administrators, even their own staffs. Even if they were specialists and had time to study all the issues thoroughly, making wise national policy would be difficult. If economists disagree about policies to fight unemployment, how are legislators supposed to know which policies will work better than others? Thus, the generalists must organize Congress to help them make specialized decisions. The Founders introduced just a hint of specialization into Congress when they split it into the House and the Senate.

☐ American Bicameralism

A **bicameral legislature** is a legislature divided into two houses. The U.S. Congress is bicameral, as is every American state legislature except Nebraska's, which has one house: it is unicameral. Our bicameral Congress is the result of the Connecticut Compromise at the Constitutional Convention. Each state is guaranteed two senators, and the number of representatives a state has is determined by its population—so California, for example, has 53 representatives while Alaska, Delaware, Montana, North Dakota, South Dakota, Vermont, and Wyoming each have just one). By creating a bicameral Congress, the Constitution set up yet another check and balance. No bill can be passed unless both House and Senate agree on it; each body can thus veto the policies of the other. Table 11.2 shows some of the basic differences between the two houses.

bicameral legislature
A legislature divided into two houses. The U.S. Congress and all state legislatures except Nebraska's are bicameral.

TABLE 11.2 HOUSE VERSUS SENATE: SOME KEY DIFFERENCES

Characteristic	House of Representatives	Senate
Constitutional powers	Initiates all revenue bills Passes all articles of impeachment	Confirms many presidential nominations Approves treaties Tries impeached officials
Membership	435 members	100 members
Term of office	2 years	6 years
Constituencies	Usually smaller	Usually larger
Centralization of power	More centralized; stronger leadership	Less centralized; weaker leadership
Political prestige	Less prestige	More prestige
Role in policymaking	More influential on budget; more specialized	More influential on foreign affairs; less specialized
Turnover	Small	Moderate
Role of seniority	More important in determining power	Less important in determining power
Procedures	Limited debate; limits on floor amendments allowed	Unlimited debate

352

11.1

11.2

11.3

11.4

11.5

House Rules Committee

The committee in the House of Representatives that reviews most bills coming from a House committee before they go to the full House.

filibuster

A strategy unique to the Senate whereby opponents of a piece of legislation use their right to unlimited debate to prevent the Senate from ever voting on a bill. Sixty members present and voting can halt a filibuster on legislation.

THE HOUSE More than four times as large as the Senate, the House is also more institutionalized—that is, more centralized, more hierarchical, and more disciplined.[38] Party loyalty to leadership and party-line voting are more common in the House than in the Senate. Partly because there are more members, leaders in the House do more leading than do leaders in the Senate. First-term House members have less power than senior representatives; they are more likely than first-term senators to be just seen and not heard.[39]

Both the House and the Senate set their own agendas. The **House Rules Committee**, which is responsive to the House leadership, reviews most bills coming from House committees before they go to the full House. The Rules Committee gives each bill a "rule," which schedules the bill on the calendar, allots time for debate, and usually limits the kinds and number of amendments, reducing the opportunities for the minority to propose changes. In recent years, House Republicans have operated under an informal rule when they have been in the majority. Known as the *Hastert Rule* for former Speaker Dennis Hastert, it holds that the Republicans will not allow the House to vote on a bill unless it has the support of a majority of the Republican caucus. As a result, representatives may be denied the opportunity to vote for a bill, even if a majority of Republicans and Democrats combined would support it.

THE SENATE The Framers thought the Senate would protect elite interests, counteracting the tendency of the House to protect the interests of the masses. They gave the House the power to initiate all revenue bills and to impeach officials; they gave the Senate the power to ratify all treaties, to confirm important presidential nominations (including nominations to the Supreme Court), and to try impeached officials. Despite the Framers' expectations, history shows that when the same party controls both chambers, the Senate is just as liberal as—and perhaps more liberal than—the House.[40] The real differences between the bodies lie in the Senate's organization and decentralized power.

Smaller than the House, the Senate is also less disciplined and less centralized. Today's senators are more nearly equal in power than representatives are. Even incoming senators sometimes get top committee assignments; they may even become chairs of key subcommittees.

The Filibuster. For a bill to pass, it must receive the support of at least a majority of each house of Congress. In the House, time for debate is tightly controlled. In the Senate, it may not be. The reason is a procedure unique to the Senate, the **filibuster.** The filibuster allows a senator who opposes a bill to engage in unlimited debate as a way to prevent the Senate from voting on that bill. In 1957 Strom Thurmond of South Carolina conducted the longest filibuster ever, holding forth for 24 hours and 18 minutes opposing a civil rights bill. Working together, like-minded senators can practically debate forever, tying up the legislative agenda until the proponents of a bill finally give up their battle. In essence, they literally talk the bill to death.

The power of the filibuster is not absolute, however. Sixty members present and voting can halt a filibuster by voting for *cloture* on debate. However, many senators are reluctant to vote for cloture for fear of setting a precedent to be used against them when *they* want to filibuster.

At its core, the filibuster raises profound questions about American democracy because it is used by a minority, sometimes a minority of one, to defeat a majority. While Southern senators like Strom Thurmond once used filibusters to try to prevent the passage of civil rights legislation,[41] more recently, senators have used the filibuster to oppose all types of legislation. Since the 1990s, filibusters have become the weapon of first resort for even the most trivial matters. Each senator has at least six opportunities to filibuster a single bill, and these opportunities can be used one after the other. In addition, the tactical uses of the filibuster have expanded. A senator may threaten to filibuster an unrelated measure in order to gain concessions on a bill he or she opposes.

Why has a majority not changed the rules to prevent filibusters? In 2013 it did: Frustrated by how often the Republican minority filibustered or threatened to filibuster presidential nominations to the executive branch and the judiciary, the majority Senate Democrats reduced the number of votes required to end debate on those types of nominations from two-thirds of the Senate to a simple majority. (They made one exception, nominations to the Supreme Court, which would still require approval of 60 senators to end debate.).

Until 2013, changing the rules required 67 votes. It is always difficult to obtain the agreement of two-thirds of the Senate on a controversial matter. Moreover, every senator knows that he or she might be in the minority on an issue at some time. A filibuster gives senators who are in the minority a powerful weapon for defending their (or their constituents') interests. Americans today commonly complain about gridlock in Congress. Nevertheless, senators have decided that they are more concerned with allowing senators to block legislation they oppose than with expediting the passage of legislation a majority favors.

Why It Matters to You

The Filibuster

Without the filibuster, the majority would be more likely to pass legislation; there would be less gridlock in Congress. However, minority interests would be more likely to lose.

Congressional Leadership

Leading 100 senators or 435 representatives in Congress—each jealous of his or her own power and responsible to no higher power than the constituency—is no easy task. Few members of Congress consider themselves followers. Much of the leadership in Congress is really party leadership. There are a few formal posts whose occupants are chosen by nonparty procedures, but those who have the real power in the congressional hierarchy are those whose party put them there.

THE HOUSE The **Speaker of the House** is the most important leader in the House of Representatives. The Speaker holds the only legislative office mandated by the Constitution. In practice, the majority party selects the Speaker. Before each Congress begins, the majority party presents its candidate for Speaker, who—because this person attracts the unanimous support of the majority party—is a shoo-in. Typically, the Speaker is a senior member of the party. John Boehner of Ohio, who has served in Congress since 1991, was elected Speaker in 2011. The Speaker is also two heartbeats away from the presidency, being second in line (after the vice president) to succeed a president who resigns, dies in office, or is convicted after impeachment.

Years ago, the Speaker was king of the congressional mountain. Autocrats such as "Uncle Joe Cannon" and "Czar Reed" ran the House like a fiefdom. A great revolt in 1910 whittled down the Speaker's powers and gave some of them to committees, but six decades later, members of the House restored some of the Speaker's powers. Today, the Speaker

- Presides over the House when it is in session
- Plays a major role in making committee assignments, which are coveted by all members to ensure their reelection
- Appoints or plays a key role in appointing the party's legislative leaders and the party leadership staff
- Exercises substantial control over assigning bills to committees

In addition to these formal powers, the Speaker has a great deal of informal clout inside and outside Congress. When the Speaker's party differs from the president's party, as it frequently does, the Speaker often serves as a national spokesperson for

---

Speaker of the House
An office mandated by the Constitution. The Speaker is chosen in practice by the majority party, has both formal and informal powers, and is second in line (after the Vice President) to succeed to the presidency should that office become vacant.

354

majority leader

The principal partisan ally of the Speaker of the House or the majority party's manager in the Senate.

whips

Party leaders who work with the majority leader or minority leader to count votes beforehand and lean on waverers whose votes are crucial to the passage of a bill favored by the party.

minority leader

The principal leader of the minority party in the House of Representatives or in the Senate.

John Boehner of Ohio (left) was elected Speaker in 2011. He is the most powerful member of the House of Representatives. Majority Leader Mitch McConnell of Kentucky (center) leads the Republicans in the Senate, which makes him the most powerful member of that body. Nevertheless, in the decentralized power structure of the upper chamber, even he must work and negotiate with Minority Leader Harry Reid of Nevada (right).

the party. A good Speaker knows the members of the House well—including their past improprieties, the ambitions they harbor, and the pressures they feel. He tries to keep his party unified and pass legislation that will create an attractive party record.

Leadership in the House, however, is not a one-person show. The Speaker's principal partisan ally is the **majority leader**—a job that has been the main stepping-stone to becoming Speaker. The majority leader is elected by his or her party and is responsible for scheduling bills and rounding up votes on behalf of the party's position on legislation. The current majority leader are the party's **whips**, whose job it is to convey the word party's position to rank-and-file congresspersons. Whips count votes before they are cast and lean on any waverers whose votes are crucial to the passage of a bill. Whips also report the views and complaints of the party rank and file back to the House leadership.

The minority party is also organized, poised to take over the Speakership and other key posts if it should win a majority in the House. It has a **minority leader**—currently Nancy Pelosi of California—as well as party whips who operate much like their counterparts in the majority party.

THE SENATE The vice president's only constitutionally defined job is to serve as president of the Senate. However, vice presidents usually slight their senatorial chores, except in the rare case when their vote can break a tie. Modern vice presidents are active in representing the president's views to senators, however.

It is the Senate majority leader—currently Republican Mitch McConnell of Kentucky—who, aided by the majority whip, serves as the workhorse of the party, corralling votes, scheduling floor action, and influencing committee assignments. The majority leader's counterpart in the opposition, the minority leader—currently Democrat Harry Reid of Nevada—has similar responsibilities and is supported by the minority whip. Power is widely dispersed in the contemporary Senate. Therefore, party leaders must appeal broadly for support, often speaking to the country directly or indirectly over television.

CONGRESSIONAL LEADERSHIP IN PERSPECTIVE Despite their stature and power, congressional leaders cannot always move their troops. Power in both houses of Congress, but especially the Senate, is decentralized. Leaders are elected by members of their own party and must remain responsive to them. Except in the most egregious cases (which rarely arise), leaders cannot administer severe punishments to those who do not support the party's stand, and no one expects members to vote against their constituents' interests. Senator Robert Dole nicely summed up any congressional leader's situation when he dubbed himself the "Majority Pleader."

standing committees
Committees in each house of Congress that handle bills in different policy areas.

joint committees
Congressional committees on a few subject-matter areas with membership drawn from both houses.

conference committees
Congressional committees formed when the Senate and the House pass a particular bill in different forms. Party leadership appoints members from each house to iron out the differences and bring back a single bill.

select committees
Congressional committees appointed for a specific purpose, such as the Watergate investigation.

Why It Matters to You

Party Strength

If congressional parties are strong, they can enforce strict party loyalty and thus are better able to keep their promises to voters. At the same time, strict party loyalty makes it more difficult for members of Congress to break with the party line to represent their constituents' special needs and interests.

Nevertheless, party leadership, at least in the House, has been more effective in recent years. Greater policy agreement within each party and greater differences between the parties have encouraged members to delegate power to their leaders. This delegation has made it easier for the Speaker to exercise his or her prerogatives regarding the assignment of bills and members to committees, the rules under which the House considers legislation on the floor, and the use of an expanded whip system. Thus it has become easier for a Speaker to advance an agenda that reflects the policy preferences of the majority party.[42]

☐ The Committees and Subcommittees

Will Rogers, the famous Oklahoman humorist, once remarked that "outside of traffic, there is nothing that has held this country back as much as committees."[43] Members of the Senate and the House would apparently disagree. Most of the real work of Congress goes on in committees, and committees are central to congressional policymaking.

Committees regularly hold hearings to investigate problems and possible wrongdoing and to oversee the executive branch. Most of all, *they control the congressional agenda and guide legislation* from its introduction to its send-off to the president for his signature, the first of which is by far the most important.

We can group committees into four types, the first of which is by far the most important.

1. **Standing committees** handle bills in different policy areas (see Table 11.3). Each house of Congress has its own standing committees. In Congress today, the typical representative serves on two committees and four subcommittees on those committees. (Subcommittees are smaller units of a committee created out of the committee membership). Senators average three committees and seven subcommittees.

2. **Joint committees** exist in a few policy areas, such as the economy and taxation, and draw their membership from both the Senate and the House.

3. **Conference committees** are formed when the Senate and the House pass different versions of the same bill (which they typically do). Appointed by the party leadership, a conference committee consists of members of each house chosen to iron out the differences between the Senate and the House bills and to report back a compromise bill.

4. **Select committees** may be temporary or permanent and usually have a specific focus. The House and Senate each have a permanent Select Committee on Intelligence, for example. In 2011 a Joint Select Committee on Deficit Reduction was given responsibility for developing a plan to cut the deficit.

THE COMMITTEES AT WORK: LEGISLATION With more than 11,000 bills submitted by members in the course of a two-year period, some winnowing is essential. Most

356

11.1
11.2
11.3
11.4
11.5

legislative oversight
Congress's monitoring of the executive branch bureaucracy and its administration of policy, performed mainly through committee hearings.

TABLE 11.3 STANDING COMMITTEES IN THE SENATE AND IN THE HOUSE

Senate Committees	House Committees
Agriculture, Nutrition, and Forestry	Agriculture
Appropriations	Appropriations
Armed Services	Armed Services
Banking, Housing, and Urban Affairs	Budget
Budget	Education and the Workforce
Commerce, Science, and Transportation	Energy and Commerce
Energy and Natural Resources	Ethics
Environment and Public Works	Financial Services
Finance	Foreign Affairs
Foreign Relations	Homeland Security
Health, Education, Labor, and Pensions	House Administration
Homeland Security and Governmental Affairs	Judiciary
Judiciary	Natural Resources
Rules and Administration	Oversight and Government Reform
Small Business and Entrepreneurship	Rules
Veterans' Affairs	Science and Technology
	Small Business
	Transportation and Infrastructure
	Veterans' Affairs
	Ways and Means

bills go first to a standing committee, which has virtually the power of life and death over it. The whole House or Senate usually considers only bills that obtain a favorable committee report.

A new bill that the Speaker sends to a committee typically goes directly to a subcommittee, which can hold hearings on the bill. Committee and subcommittee staffs conduct research, line up witnesses for hearings, and write and rewrite bills. Committees and their subcommittees produce reports on proposed legislation. A committee's most important output, however, is the "marked-up" (rewritten) bill itself, which it submits to the full House or Senate for debate and voting.

The work of committees does not stop when a bill leaves the committee room. Members of the committee usually serve as "floor managers" of the bill, helping party leaders hustle votes for it. They are also the "cue givers" to whom other members turn for advice.[44] When the Senate and the House pass different versions of the same bill, some committee members serve on the conference committee whose job it is to produce a compromise.

THE COMMITTEES AT WORK: OVERSIGHT The committees and subcommittees do not leave the scene even after legislation passes. They stay busy in **legislative oversight**, the process of monitoring the executive branch bureaucracy and its administration of policies, most of which Congress establishes by passing bills. Committees handle oversight mainly through hearings. When an agency wants a bigger budget, the relevant committee reviews its current budget. Even if no budgetary issues are involved, members of committees constantly monitor how the bureaucracy is implementing a law.[45] Agency heads and even cabinet secretaries testify, bringing graphs, charts, and data on the progress they have made and the problems they face. Committee staffs and committee members grill agency heads about particular problems. For example, a member may ask a Small Business Administration official why constituents who are applying for loans get the runaround; another member might focus on complaints from states regarding the No Child Left Behind law. In short, through oversight, Congress can pressure agencies and, in extreme cases, cut their budgets in order to secure compliance with congressional wishes.[46] Oversight also provides an opportunity to refine existing policies, such as reimbursements under Medicare, or respond to new problems, such as regulations regarding offshore drilling for oil.

Congress keeps tabs on more routine activities of the executive branch through its committee staff members. These members have specialized expertise in the fields and agencies that their committees oversee and maintain an extensive network of formal and informal contacts with the executive branch bureaucracy. By reading the voluminous reports that Congress requires of the executive branch and by receiving information from numerous sources—agencies, complaining citizens, members of Congress and their personal staff, state and local officials, interest groups, and professional organizations—staff members can keep track of the implementation of public policy.[47]

Congressional oversight grew as the size and complexity of the national government grew in the 1960s and in response to numerous charges that the executive branch had become too powerful. The tight budgets of recent years have provided additional incentives for oversight, as members of Congress have sought both to protect programs they favor from budget cuts and to get more value for the tax dollars spent on them. As the publicity value of receiving credit for controlling governmental spending has increased, so has the number of representatives and senators interested in oversight.[48]

Nevertheless, members of Congress have many competing responsibilities, and there are few political payoffs for carefully watching a government agency to see whether it is implementing policy properly. It is difficult to go to voters and say, "Vote for me. I oversaw the routine handling of road building." Because of this lack of incentives, Congress may overlook problems until it is too late to do much about them. For example, despite clear evidence that there were fundamental problems with how the Federal Emergency Management Agency responded to four hurricanes in 2004, when Hurricane Katrina hit the following year, Congress had still not held oversight hearings. Similarly, Congress missed the fact that various agencies with responsibility for overseeing the banking industry were negligent in identifying the looming problems in the financial sector that led to the recession of 2008–2009.

Another constraint on effective oversight is the fragmentation of committee jurisdictions, which inhibits Congress from taking a comprehensive view of complex issue areas. For example, a large number of committees and subcommittees have responsibility for oversight over homeland security (see Table 11.4). Committees resist giving

Most of the work of Congress occurs in committees. Here the Joint Select Committee on Deficit Reduction holds a hearing on the budget.

TABLE 11.4 SHARING OVERSIGHT OF HOMELAND SECURITY

The House created the Homeland Security Committee in 2002, but many other committees share jurisdiction over parts of the Department of Homeland Security and its agencies. This table shows this of fragmentation responsibility.

Homeland Security's Jurisdiction	Other Committees That Share Jurisdiction
Border and port security	Judiciary: Immigration policy and interior enforcement
	Agriculture: Animal and plant diseases
Customs	Ways and Means: Customs revenue
Homeland security information	Government Reform: Government-wide information management
Terrorism preparedness and domestic response	Armed Services: Any military response to terrorism
	Financial Services: Terrorist financing
	Select Intelligence: Intelligence-related activities at all agencies
	Transportation and Infrastructure: Emergency management and Coast Guard
Research and development	Science and Technology: Some research and development at DHS
Transportation security	Transportation and Infrastructure: Transportation safety, including the Federal Aviation Administration

SOURCE: Tim Starks, "Splintered Jurisdiction: GOP Won't Reorganize Homeland Panel," CCO Weekly, December 27, 2010, 2901.

up jurisdiction over parts of the bureaucracy, even when it is reorganized, as happened when the Department of Homeland Security was created in 2002.

In addition, the majority party largely determines if and when a committee will hold hearings. When the president's party has a majority in a house of Congress, that chamber is generally not aggressive in overseeing the administration because it does not wish to embarrass the president. During George W. Bush's presidency, when Republicans held the majority in the House, Democrats were critical of what they regarded as timid Republican oversight of the nation's intelligence establishment and the president's planning and implementation of the aftermath of the war in Iraq. Nevertheless, the president's partisans resisted holding the White House accountable, fearing that the Democrats would use hearings to discredit Bush. Critics charged that the failure to discern and make explicit the true costs of policy initiatives—from tax cuts to Medicare prescription drugs to the war in Iraq—made it impossible for Congress to do realistic cost–benefit analyses before it voted on those initiatives.[49] Once the Democrats gained majorities in Congress in the 2006 elections, the number of oversight hearings increased substantially. Significantly, the number of hearings diminished after the election of Democrat Barack Obama but then increased again in the House after the Republicans won a majority there in the 2010 elections.

Why It Matters to You
Inconsistent Oversight

Overseeing the executive branch is a major responsibility of Congress, yet the inconsistent performance in this area means that Congress is less likely either to anticipate or address important problems.

GETTING ON A COMMITTEE One of the primary objectives of an incoming member of Congress is to get on the right committee. A new member of the House from Iowa would probably prefer to be on the Agriculture Committee while a freshman senator from New York might seek membership on the Banking, Housing, and Urban Affairs Committee. Members seek committees that will help them achieve three goals: reelection, influence in Congress, and the opportunity to make policy in areas they think are important.[50]

Just after their election, new members communicate their committee preferences to their party's congressional leaders and members of their state delegation. Every committee includes members from both parties, but a majority of each committee's members (except for the House Ethics Committee), as well as its chair, come from the majority party in the chamber. Each party in each house has a slightly different way of picking its committee members. Party leaders almost always play a key role.

Those who have supported the leadership are favored in the committee selection process, but generally the parties try to grant members' requests for committee assignments whenever possible. They want their members to please their constituents and to develop expertise in an area of policy. (Being on the right committee helps members represent their constituencies more effectively and furthers their ability to engage in credit claiming). The parties also try to apportion the influence that comes with committee membership among the state delegations in order to accord representation to diverse components of the party.[51]

COMMITTEE CHAIRS AND THE SENIORITY SYSTEM Committee chairs are the most important influencers of their committees' agendas. Committee chairs play the dominant roles in scheduling hearings, hiring staff, appointing subcommittees, and managing committee bills when they are brought before the full house.

Until the 1970s, there was a simple way of picking committee chairs: the **seniority system.** If a committee member had served on a committee the longest and his or her party controlled the chamber, he or she got to be chair—regardless of his or her party loyalty, mental state, or competence.

The chairs were so powerful for most of the twentieth century that they could bully members or bottle up legislation at any time—and with the almost certain knowledge that they would be chairs for the rest of their careers in Congress. The more independent committee chairs are and the more power they have, the more difficult it can be to make coherent policy. Independent and powerful committee chairs can represent another obstacle to overcome in the complex legislative process.

In the 1970s younger members of Congress rebelled, and as a result both parties in both branches permitted members in both houses to vote on committee chairs. Today seniority remains the *general rule* for selecting chairs, especially in the Senate, but there are plenty of exceptions. In addition, new rules have limited both committee and subcommittee chairs to three consecutive, two-year terms; committee chairs have lost the power to cast proxy votes for those committee members not in attendance. In general, committee chairs are not as powerful as they were before the reform era. The party leadership in the House has much more control over legislation, often giving committees deadlines for reporting legislation and at times even bypassing committees to draft priority legislation.

committee chairs

Through their leadership of the committees, committee chairs have important influence on the congressional agenda. They play the dominant role in scheduling hearings, hiring staff, appointing subcommittees, and managing committee bills when they are brought before the full house.

seniority system

A simple rule for picking committee chairs, in effect until the 1970s. The member who had served on the committee the longest and whose party controlled the chamber became chair, regardless of party loyalty, mental state, or competence.

Why It *Matters* to You
The Committee System

The committee system in Congress is highly decentralized. As a result, it is open to the appeals of a wide range of "special" interests, especially those represented by highly paid lobbyists. If Congress were more *centralized* and only those interests cleared by the elected leadership received a hearing, special interests might be constrained. However, the danger would be that only those interests that reflected the views of the leadership would be heard.

caucus (congressional)
A group of members of Congress sharing some interest or characteristic. Many are composed of members from both parties and from both houses.

The proliferation of congressional caucuses gives member of Congress an informal yet powerful means of shaping policy. Composed of legislative insiders, caucuses—for example, the Hispanic Caucus—exert a much greater influence on policymaking than most citizen-based, outside interest groups can.

☐ Caucuses: The Informal Organization of Congress

Although the formal organization of Congress consists of its party leadership and its committee structures, the informal organization of Congress is also important. Informal networks of trust and mutual interest spring from numerous sources, including friendship, ideology, and geography.

Lately, the informal organization of Congress has been dominated by a growing number of caucuses. In this context, a **caucus** is a group of members of Congress who share some interest or characteristic. There are nearly 500 caucuses, most of them including members from both parties and some including members from both the House and the Senate. The goal of all caucuses is to promote the interests around which they are formed. Caucuses press for committees to hold hearings, push particular legislation, and pull together votes on bills they favor. They are somewhat like interest groups but with a difference: their members are members of Congress, not petitioners to Congress on the outside looking in. Thus caucuses—interest groups within Congress—are nicely situated to pack more punch.[52]

This explosion of informal groups in Congress has made the representation of interests in Congress more direct. Some caucuses, such as the Black Caucus, the Caucus for Women's Issues, and the Hispanic Caucus, focus on advancing the interests of demographic groups. Others, such as the Sunbelt Caucus, are based on regional interests. Still others, such as the Republican Study Committee, represent ideological groupings. Many caucuses are based on economic interests. For example, the Congressional Bourbon Caucus advocates for the bourbon industry by fighting proposals like a tax increase on liquor, while the Congressional Gaming Caucus deals with issues like reinvigorating the tourism industry and making sure regulations for Internet gambling are fair. Other caucuses focus, for instance, on health issues or on foreign policy matters dealing with specific countries.

☐ Congressional Staff

As noted earlier, members of Congress are overwhelmed with responsibilities. It is virtually impossible to master the details of the hundreds of bills about which they must make decisions each year or prepare their own legislation. They need help to meet their obligations, so they turn to their staff.

PERSONAL STAFF Most staff members work in the personal offices of individual members of Congress. The average representative has 17 assistants and the average senator has 41. In total, more than 11,000 individuals serve on the personal staffs of members of Congress. (Another 450 serve the congressional leaders.) In the summer, about 4,000 interns also work in members' offices on Capitol Hill (see "Young People and Politics: Are Opportunities to Intern Biased in Favor of the Wealthy?").

Most of these staffers spend their time on casework, providing services to constituents. They answer mail, communicate the members' views to voters, and help constituents solve problems. Nearly one-half of the House staffers and nearly one-third of the Senate personal staff work in members' offices in their home states or districts, not in Washington, which makes it easier for constituents to make contact with the staff. Other personal staff help members of Congress with legislative functions, including drafting legislation, meeting with lobbyists and administrators, negotiating agreements on behalf of their bosses, writing questions to ask witnesses at committee hearings, summarizing bills, and briefing legislators. Senators, who must cover a wider range of committee assignments than members of the House, are especially dependent on staff. Indeed, members of both houses are now more likely to deal with each other through staff intermediaries than directly.

COMMITTEE STAFF The committees of the House and Senate employ another 2,200 staff members. These staffers organize hearings, research legislative options, draft committee reports on bills, write legislation, and as we have seen, keep tabs on

Young People & Politics

Are Opportunities to Intern Biased in Favor of the Wealthy?

Many college students spend their summers working to pay for their studies during the rest of the year. Others, in contrast, serve as interns. Many of the interns have parents who support them financially during the summer. According to some experts, the focus on internships as a tool for professional success has never been greater, and about 80 percent of graduating college seniors have done a paid or unpaid internship. To some, an internship is an essential stepping-stone to career success.

Because Washington internships are in high demand, in most cases they do not pay, or they pay very little. The White House does not pay the interns who work there during the summer; in most cases the Supreme Court does not pay its undergraduate interns; and a vast majority of congressional offices do not pay the 4,000 summer interns who work on Capitol Hill, although a few, mostly on the Senate side, provide a limited stipend. To make matters worse, Washington is an expensive place to live. In some cases, universities or

other programs provide some financial help, but most interns are on their own.

As internships become increasingly important to career success, the concern has been raised that they may be creating a class system discriminating against students from less affluent families who must turn down unpaid internships to earn money for college expenses. To the extent that Washington internships serve as a pipeline for people to become policymakers in the nation's capital, critics fear that over time internships, like the rising costs of college tuition, will mean fewer working-class and even middle-class voices in high-level policy debates.

CRITICAL THINKING QUESTIONS

1. Is the internship system in Washington likely to bias policymaking in the future?
2. Should Congress appropriate funds so internships are more available to students from less wealthy backgrounds?

SOURCE: Jennifer 8. Lee, "Crucial Unpaid Internships Increasingly Separate the Haves from the Have-Nots," *New York Times,* August 10, 2004.

the activities of the executive branch. Committee staff members often possess high levels of expertise and can become very influential in policymaking. As a result, lobbyists spend a lot of time cultivating these staffers both to obtain information about likely legislative actions and to plant ideas for legislation.

STAFF AGENCIES Congress has three important staff agencies that aid it in its work. The first is the *Congressional Research Service (CRS)*, administered by the Library of Congress and composed of researchers, many with advanced degrees and highly developed expertise. Each year it responds to more than 250,000 congressional requests for information and provides members with nonpartisan studies. CRS also tracks the progress of major bills, prepares summaries of bills, and makes information about bills available electronically.

The *Government Accountability Office (GAO)*, with more than 3,100 employees, helps Congress perform its oversight functions by reviewing the activities of the executive branch to see if it is following the congressional intent of laws and by investigating the efficiency and effectiveness of policy implementation. The GAO also sets government standards for accounting, provides legal opinions, and settles claims against the government.

The *Congressional Budget Office (CBO)* focuses on analyzing the president's budget and making economic projections about the performance of the economy, the costs of proposed policies, and the economic effects of taxing and spending alternatives.

Committees, caucuses, and individual legislators follow bills from their introduction to their approval. The next section discusses this process, which is often termed "labyrinthine" since getting a bill through Congress is very much like navigating a difficult, intricate maze.

The Congressional Process and Decision Making

Outline the path of bills to passage and explain the influences on congressional decision making.

Congress's agenda is a crowded one—members introduce about 11,000 bills in each Congress, that is, in every two-year period. A **bill** is a proposed law, drafted in precise, legal language. Anyone can draft a bill. The White House and interest groups are common sources of bills.

However, only members of the House or the Senate can formally submit a bill for consideration. The traditional route for a bill as it works its way through the legislative labyrinth is depicted in Figure 11.2 on the next page. Most bills are quietly killed off early in the process. Members introduce some bills as a favor to a group or a constituent; others are private bills, granting citizenship to a constituent or paying a settlement to a person whose car was demolished by a postal service truck. Still other bills may alter the course of the nation.

Congress is typically a cumbersome decision-making body. Rules are piled on rules and procedures on procedures.[53] Moreover, legislating has been made more difficult by the polarized political climate that has prevailed since the 1980s.

Party leaders have sought to cope with these problems in various ways, including some already mentioned. What Barbara Sinclair has termed *unorthodox lawmaking* has become common in the congressional process, especially for the most significant legislation.[54] In both chambers on major legislation party leaders involve themselves in the legislative process much earlier and more deeply than they used to, using a variety of special procedures. For example, leaders in the House often refer bills to several

FIGURE 11.2 HOW A BILL BECOMES A LAW

Bills can come to Congress in two different ways:

- A bill can be introduced in either the House or the Senate by a member of that chamber. If the bill passes the chamber in which it originates, it is then sent to be introduced in the other chamber.
- A bill (in similar or identical versions) can be introduced in both chambers at the same time. (This type of bill is termed a companion bill.)

In either case, the bill follows parallel processes in the House and Senate, starting with committee action. If a committee gives a bill a favorable report, the whole chamber considers it. Many bills travel full circle, coming first from the White House as part of the presidential agenda and then, if the bill is passed by both chambers, returning to the president.

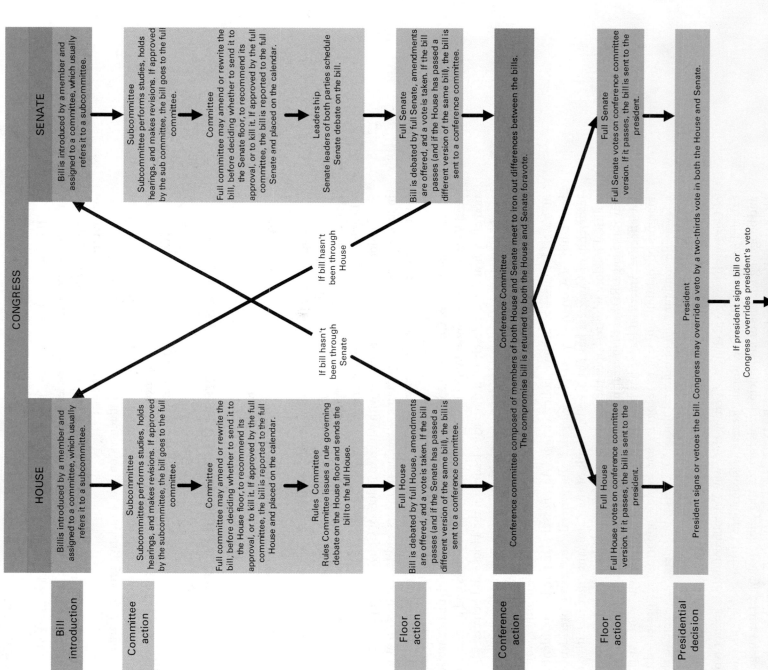

committees at the same time, bringing more interests to bear on an issue but at the same time complicating the process of passing the legislation. Since committee leaders cannot always negotiate compromises among committees, party leaders have accepted this responsibility; often they negotiate compromises and make adjustments to bills after a committee or committees report legislation. Sometimes for high-priority leg-islation party leaders simply bypass committees. In the House, special rules from the Rules Committee have become powerful tools for controlling floor consideration of bills and sometimes for shaping the outcomes of votes. Often party leaders from the two chambers negotiate among themselves instead of creating conference committees. Party leaders also use omnibus legislation that addresses numerous and sometimes unrelated subjects, issues, and programs to create winning coalitions, forcing members to support an entire bill to obtain passage of individual parts of it.

The new procedures are generally under the control of party leaders in the House, but in the Senate, leaders have less leverage. Individual senators have retained substan-tial opportunities for influence, such as using the filibuster. As a result, it is often more difficult to pass legislation in the Senate.

There are, of course, countless influences on this legislative process. Presidents, parties, constituents, interest groups, the congressional and committee leadership structure—these and other influences offer members cues for their decision making. So, too, do the ideologies of members.

☐ Presidents and Congress: Partners and Protagonists

Political scientists sometimes call the president the chief legislator, a phrase that might have appalled the Framers of the Constitution, with their insistence on the separation of powers. Presidents do, however, help create the congressional agenda. They are also their own best lobbyists.

Presidents have their own legislative agenda, based in part on their party's platform and their electoral coalition. Each president's task is to persuade Congress that his agenda should also be Congress's agenda; a president has a good chance that Congress will at least give his proposals a hearing.[55]

Presidents have many resources with which to influence Congress. They may try to influence members directly—by calling wavering members and telling them that the country's future hinges on their votes, for example—but they do not do this often. If a president was to pick just one key bill and spend 10 minutes on the telephone with each of the 535 members of Congress, he would spend 89 hours chatting with them. Instead, presidents wisely leave most White House lobbying to staff members and administra-tion officials and work closely with the party's leaders in the House and Senate.

It seems a wonder that presidents, even with all their power and prestige, can push and wheedle anything through the labyrinthine congressional process. The president must usually win at every stage shown in Figure 11.2—in other words, at least 11 times—to achieve policy change. As one scholar put it, presidential leadership of Congress is *at the margins*.[56] In general, successful presidential leadership of Congress has not been the result of the dominant chief executive of political folklore who reshapes the contours of the political landscape to pave the way for change. Rather than creating the conditions for major shifts in public policy, the effective American leader has been the less-heroic *facilitator* who works at the margins of coalition building to recognize and exploit opportunities presented by a favorable configuration of political forces. Of course, presidents can exercise the power of the veto to *stop* legislation they oppose.

Popular presidents and presidents with a large majority of their party in each house of Congress have a good chance of getting their way. Yet such conditions are not typi-cal, and presidents often lose. Ronald Reagan was considered a strong chief executive, and budgeting was one of his principal tools for affecting public policy. Yet the budgets he proposed to Congress were typically DOA, dead on arrival. Congress is truly an independent branch of government.

Party, Ideology, and Constituency

Presidents come and go; the parties endure. Presidents do not determine a congressional member's electoral fortunes; constituents do. Often more influential than presidents—on domestic policies especially—are party, ideology, and constituency.

PARTY INFLUENCE On some issues, members of the parties stick together like a marching band.[57] A vote for Speaker of the House is usually a straight party-line vote, with every Democrat on one side and every Republican on the other. On a few issues, however, a party coalition may come unglued, reflecting deep divisions within that party.

Differences between the parties are sharpest on questions of economic and social welfare policy.[58] On social welfare issues—for example, the minimum wage; aid to the poor, unemployed, or uninsured; and grants for education—Democrats are more supportive of government action than are Republicans. Democrats are also more supportive of government efforts to regulate the economy in an attempt to alleviate negative consequences of markets or to stimulate economic activity. Differences on national security policy have increased, with Republicans typically supporting greater expenditures on defense and a more aggressive foreign policy, especially regarding the use of force.

Party leaders in Congress help "whip" their members into line. Their power to do so is limited, of course. They cannot drum a recalcitrant member out of the party. Leaders can exert plenty of influence, however, for example, by making committee assignments or boosting a member's pet projects. They can exert the subtle but significant influence that comes from providing critical information to a member. Moreover, the congressional parties—that is, the party organizations within Congress—are a source of funding, as are political action committees (PACs) headed by members of the party leadership.

IDEOLOGY AND POLARIZED POLITICS Over the past three decades, the distance between the congressional parties has been growing steadily, as you can see in Figure 11.3. As the parties pulled apart ideologically, they also became more

FIGURE 11.3 INCREASING POLARIZATION IN CONGRESS

Differences between Democrats and Republicans in Congress have grown considerably since 1980. Polarized parties make for clear choices for the voters but also make compromise more difficult.

• *Is America best served by clear but sizeable differences between the parties in Congress? Why or why not?*

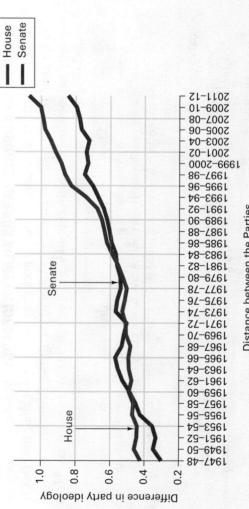

SOURCE: Authors' calculation of data from Keith Poole, posted at http://www.voteview.com/dwnl.htm.

homogeneous internally. In other words, Republicans in Congress became more consistently conservative, Democrats became more consistently liberal; the distance between those at the center of each of the two parties increased. As a result of the increased ideological differences between the parties in Congress, it has been more difficult to reach a compromises—and more difficult for the president to obtain policy support from the opposition party. Barack Obama received few Republican votes for any of his proposals; not a single Republican voted for his health care reform plan.

Why did this change happen? At the core of the increased ideological distance between the parties have been increasingly divergent electoral coalitions. The partisan makeup of House districts, sometimes aided by boundary drawing by state legislatures, became more one-sided. Because their own districts have a clearly Republican or Democratic majority, typical members of the House no longer have to worry about pleasing those at the center of their electorates. Instead, they have to please the center of their party. One result has been that members of Congress, especially in the House, hold more extreme political views than their constituents as a group.[59]

In addition, liberal and conservative voters have sorted themselves into the Democratic and Republican parties, respectively. There are many fewer liberal Republicans or conservative Democrats than there were a generation ago. Thus, conservatives have been more likely to support the more conservative party and liberals the more liberal party. As supporters of each party have linked their partisan and ideological views, they have made the differences between the parties more distinctive. Moreover, party loyalty among voters in congressional elections has also increased, so the relationship between ideology and voting has become notably stronger.

In short, what has happened is the following: changes in the preferences, behavior, and distribution of congressional voters gave the congressional parties constituencies that are more internally homogeneous, more divergent from one another, and thus more polarized. These constituencies in turn have elected more ideologically polarized representatives to Congress. The new members of Congress have adopted a polarized style that pays little heed to compromise.[60] Thus it is not surprising that Congress has a difficult time agreeing, for example, on taxation or spending.

The ideological differences between the parties have increased the incentives for each to win congressional seats and oppose the other party. Thus, members of Congress are more likely to support a president of their party and oppose one of the opposition party than in the past, and they are more likely to support efforts to discredit the opposition on grounds of its incompetence and lack of integrity. Similarly, there are more partisan battles over procedural issues that can affect the agenda on the floor of a chamber; and there are more efforts to steer the congressional agenda toward issues that allow a party to differentiate itself from the opposition and thus to promote itself as a party.[61]

CONSTITUENCY OPINION VERSUS MEMBER IDEOLOGY
Members of Congress are representatives; their constituents expect them to represent their interests in Washington. In 1714 Anthony Henry, a member of the British Parliament, received a letter from some of his constituents asking him to vote against an excise tax. He is reputed to have replied in part,

> Gentlemen: I have received your letter about the excise, and I am surprised at your insolence in writing to me at all ... may God's curse light upon you all, and may it make your homes as open and as free to the excise officers as your wives and daughters have always been to me while I have represented your rascally constituency.[62]

Needless to say, notions of representation have changed since Henry's time. Sometimes representation requires a balancing act. If some representatives favor more defense spending but suspect that their constituents do not, what are they to do?

The English politician and philosopher Edmund Burke advocated the concept of legislators as *trustees*, using their best judgment to make policy in the interests of the people. Others prefer the concept of representatives as *instructed delegates*, mirroring the preferences of their constituents. Actually, members of Congress are *politicos*, adopting both trustee and instructed delegate roles as they strive to be both representatives and policymakers.[63]

The best way constituents can influence congressional voting is also the most simple: elect a representative or senator who agrees with their views. Congressional candidates tend to take policy positions different from their opponents'. Moreover, the winners generally vote on roll calls as they said they would during their campaigns.[64] If voters use their good sense to elect candidates who share their policy positions, then constituents *can* influence congressional policy. If voters elect someone out of step with their thinking, it may be difficult to influence that person's votes.

It is a challenge for even well-intentioned legislators to know what people want. Some legislators pay careful attention to their mail, but the mail is a notoriously unreliable indicator of people's thinking; individuals with extreme opinions on an issue are more likely to write than those with moderate views. Some members send questionnaires to constituents, but the answers they receive are unreliable because few people respond. Some try public opinion polling, but it is expensive if professionally done and unreliable if not.

On some controversial issues, legislators ignore constituent opinion at great peril. For years, Southern members of Congress would not have dared to vote for a civil rights law. In recent decades, representatives and senators have been concerned about the many new single-issue groups. Such groups care little about a member's overall record; to them, a vote on one issue—gun control, abortion, gay marriage—is all that counts. Ready to pounce on one "wrong" vote and pour money into an opponent's campaign, these new forces in constituency politics make every legislator nervous. When issues are visible and salient to voters and easy for them to understand, their representatives are likely to be quite responsive to constituency opinion.[65]

Nevertheless, many issues are complex, obscure, and not salient to voters. On such issues legislators can safely ignore constituency opinion. Typically, ideology is the prime determinant on issues where ideological divisions between the parties are sharp and constituency preferences and knowledge are likely to be weak, such as defense and foreign policy.[66] However, the stronger constituency preferences are on issues and the weaker partisan ideology is, the more likely members are to deviate from their own positions and adopt those of their constituencies.[67] In short, when they have differences of opinion with their constituencies, members of Congress consider constituency preferences; however, they are not controlled by them.[68]

Lobbyists and Interest Groups

The nation's capital is crawling with lawyers, lobbyists, registered foreign agents, public relations consultants, and others—there are more than 12,000 registered lobbyists representing 12,000 organizations—all seeking to influence Congress. In 2013 lobbyists spent more than $3 billion on lobbying federal officials—plus millions more in campaign contributions and attempts to try to persuade members' constituents to send messages to Washington.[69] Many former members of Congress and staff members become lobbyists—at much higher pay. For example, more than 150 former lawmakers and congressional aides were working for financial firms as Congress considered new regulations in response to the financial crisis that hit in 2008. These lobbyists included two former Senate majority leaders, two former House majority leaders, and a former Speaker of the House.[70]

Point to Ponder

Interest groups play a central role in the legislative process. They provide valuable information and expertise to lawmakers and help build coalitions. Yet many people see them as "special interests" fighting for narrow interests.

Do organized interests play too great a role in policymaking?

"Mr. Speaker, will the gentleman from Small Firearms yield the floor to the gentleman from Big Tobacco?"

Lobbyists, some of them former members of Congress, can provide legislators with crucial policy information, political intelligence, and, often, assurances of financial aid in the next campaign—making those legislators with whom they agree more effective in the legislative process.[71] (In the debate regarding health care reform in 2009, statements by more than a dozen members of the House were ghostwritten by lobbyists.[72]) Lobbyists work closely with their legislative allies, especially at the committee level.[73] They also often coordinate their efforts at influencing members with party leaders who share their views. Grass-roots lobbying—such as computerized mailings to encourage citizens to pressure their representatives on particular issues—is a common activity. These days, interest groups coordinate their messages across multiple platforms, including television, Web sites, YouTube videos, and social media sites. Interest groups also distribute scorecards that show how members of Congress have voted on issues that are important to the groups; and they threaten members with electoral retaliation if they do not support the groups' stands.

There is some evidence that lobbying pays off,[74] but efforts to change policy usually meet with resistance (lobbying against change is more successful than lobbying for it),[75] and most efforts to change the status quo fail. Groups with the most money do not necessarily win.[76] Lobbyists usually make little headway with their opponents, so, for example, the lobbyist for General Motors who argues against automobile pollution controls will not have much influence with a legislator concerned about air pollution.

Concerned about lobbyists having inappropriate influence from lobbyists, Congress passed a law in 1995 requiring anyone hired to lobby members of Congress, congressional staff members, White House officials, and federal agencies to report what issues they were seeking to influence, how much they were spending on the effort, and the identities of their clients. Congress also placed severe restrictions on the gifts, meals, and expense-paid travel that public officials may accept from lobbyists. In theory, these reporting requirements and restrictions would not only prevent shady deals between lobbyists and members of Congress but also curb the influence of special interests. Nevertheless, slippage has occurred. In 2005 and 2006, for example, the country saw some congresspersons caught up in bribery scandals that involved lobbyists. Among those lobbyists was Jack Abramoff, who had been paid more than $80 million by six Native American tribes for his lobbying Congress on their behalf. He went to jail for corrupt practices that included extraordinary contributions to and expenditures on some representatives and senators. In response to the scandals, in 2007 Congress passed a new law and the House revised its ethics rules. Together, these measures strengthened public disclosure requirements concerning lobbying activity and funding, placed more restrictions on gifts and travel for members of Congress and their staff, provided for mandatory disclosure of earmarks in expenditure bills, and slowed the revolving door between Congress and the lobbying world.

There are many forces that affect senators and representatives as they decide how to vote on a bill. After his exhaustive study of influences on congressional decision making, John Kingdon concluded that none was important enough to suggest that members of Congress vote as they do because of one influence.[77] The process is as complex for individual legislators as it is for those who want to influence their votes.

Understanding Congress

11.5 | Assess Congress's role as a representative body and the impact of representation on the scope of government.

ongress is a complex institution. Its members want to make sound national policy, but they also want to return to Washington after the next election. How do these sometimes conflicting desires affect American democracy and the scope of American government?

Congress and Democracy

In a large nation, the success of democratic government depends on the quality of representation. Americans can hardly hold a national referendum on every policy issue on the government agenda; instead, they delegate decision-making power to representatives. If Congress is a successful democratic institution, it must be a successful representative institution.

Certainly, some aspects of Congress make it very *unrepresentative*. Its members are an American elite. Its leadership is chosen by its own members, not by any vote of the American people. Voters have little direct influence over the individuals who chair key committees or lead congressional parties. In addition, the Senate is apportioned to represent states, not population, a distribution of power that accords citizens in less populated states a greater say in key decisions. As you can see in "America in Perspective: Malapportionment in the Upper House," malapportionment is high in the U.S. Senate.

Nevertheless, the evidence demonstrates that Congress *does* try to listen to the American people. Whom voters elect makes a difference in how congressional votes turn out; which party is in power affects policies. Perhaps Congress could do a better job at representation than it does, but there are many obstacles to improved representation.

370

11.1
11.2
11.3
11.4
11.5

America in Perspective

Malapportionment in the Upper House

In a perfectly apportioned system, no citizen's vote weighs more than another's. In a malapportioned system, by contrast, the votes of some citizens weigh more than the votes of others. A number of democracies in developed countries have upper houses with significant powers. The U.S. Senate is the most malapportioned among them.

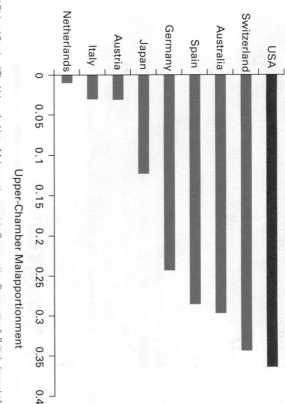

Upper-Chamber Malapportionment

SOURCE: David Samuels and Richard Snyder, "The Value of a Vote: Malapportionment in Comparative Perspective," *British Journal of Political Science* 31 (October 2001), p. 662.

CRITICAL THINKING QUESTION

In your opinion, is the high degree of malapportionment in the Senate a problem for American democracy? Why or why not?

Legislators find it difficult to know what constituents want. Groups may keep important issues off the legislative agenda. Members may spend so much time serving their constituents as individuals that they have little time left to represent their collective interests in the policymaking process.

Members of Congress are responsive to the people, if the people make clear what they want. For example, in response to popular demands, Congress established a program in 1988 to shield the elderly against the catastrophic costs associated with acute illness. In 1989, in response to complaints from the elderly that the program has led to increased Medicare premiums, Congress reversed itself and abolished most of what it had just created.

REPRESENTATIVENESS VERSUS EFFECTIVENESS The central legislative dilemma for Congress is how to faithfully represent constituents while, at the same time, making effective public policy. Supporters see Congress as a forum in which many interests compete for a spot on the policy agenda and over the form of a particular policy—just as the Framers intended.

Critics charge that Congress is too representative—so representative that it is incapable of taking decisive action to deal with difficult problems. The agricultural committees busily tend to the interests of farmers, while committees that focus on foreign trade worry about cutting agricultural subsidies. One committee wrestles with domestic unemployment, while another makes tax policy that encourages businesses to open new plants outside of the country. One reason why government spends too much, critics say, is that Congress is protecting the interests of too many people. As long as each interest tries to preserve the status quo, Congress cannot enact bold reforms.

On the other hand, defenders of Congress point out that, thanks to its being decentralized, there is no oligarchy in control to prevent the legislature from taking comprehensive action. In fact, Congress has enacted historic legislation such as the huge tax cuts of 1981 and 2001, the comprehensive (and complicated) tax reform of 1986, and various bills structuring the budgetary process designed to balance the budget.[78] In recent years, Congress has also passed health care reform, important trade bills, a prescription drug addition to Medicare, and a major program for elementary and secondary education.

There is no simple solution to Congress's dilemma. It tries to be both a representative and an objective policymaking institution. As long as this is true, it is unlikely that Congress will please all its critics.

☐ Congress and the Scope of Government

Congress is responsive to a multitude of interests, many of which desire government policies. Does this responsiveness predispose the legislature to increase the size of government to please the public? Does providing constituents with pork barrel spending and casework services create too much of an incentive for members of Congress to expand government programs? One can argue that big government helps members of Congress get reelected and gives them good reason to support making it bigger.

Members of Congress vigorously protect the interests of their constituents. At the same time, there are many members who agree with the conservative argument that government is not the answer to problems but rather *is* the problem. These individuals make careers out of fighting against government programs, although these same senators and representatives typically support programs aimed at aiding *their* constituents. In recent years, the Tea Party movement has helped elect many members of Congress who vigorously support scaling back the role of the federal government.

Americans have contradictory preferences regarding public policy. As we note in various chapters, they want to balance the budget and pay low taxes, but majorities also support most government programs. Congress does not impose programs on a reluctant public; instead, it responds to the public's demands for them.

Review the Chapter

The Representatives and Senators

11.1 Characterize the backgrounds of members of Congress and assess their impact on the ability of members of Congress to represent average Americans, p. 342.

Congress has proportionately more whites and males than the general population, and members of Congress are wealthier and better educated than the average American. Although they may not share their constituents' personal characteristics, they may represent their substantive political interests.

Congressional Elections

11.2 Identify the principal factors influencing the outcomes in congressional elections, p. 345.

Incumbents usually win reelection because they usually draw weak opponents, are usually better known and better funded than their opponents, typically represent constituencies where a clear majority share their party affiliation, and can claim credit for aiding their constituents. However, incumbents can lose if they are involved in a scandal, if their policy positions are substantially out of line with those of their constituents, or if the boundaries of their districts are redrawn to reduce the percentage of their constituents who identify with their party.

How Congress Is Organized to Make Policy

11.3 Compare and contrast the House and Senate, and describe the roles of congressional leaders, committees, caucuses, and staff, p. 351.

The House is much larger than the Senate and is also characterized by greater centralization of power in the party leadership and by more party discipline. Senators are more equal in power and may exercise the option of the filibuster to stop a majority from passing a bill. Congressional leaders are elected by their party members and must remain responsive to them. They cannot always depend on the votes of the members of their party. Committees do most of the work in Congress, considering legislation and overseeing the administration of policy. Although committees are now run more democratically than in the past, chairs have considerable

power to set their committees' agendas. Caucuses are part of the informal organization of Congress and are composed of representatives and senators who have a shared interest or characteristic. Personal, committee, and agency staff are crucial components of Congress, providing policy expertise and constituency service.

The Congressional Process and Decision Making

11.4 Outline the path of bills to passage and explain the influences on congressional decision making, p. 362.

Congress is typically a cumbersome decision-making body; the process for considering a bill has many stages. This complexity gives rise to unorthodox lawmaking, in which the congressional leadership bypasses some or all of those legislative stages. Presidents try to persuade Congress to support their policies, which usually earn space on the congressional agenda. Presidents' influence on congressional decision making is at the margins, however. Parties have become more homogeneous and more polarized in recent years and provide an important pull on their members on most issues. Constituencies have strong influence on congressional decision making on a few visible issues, while members' own ideologies exert more influence on less visible issues. Interest groups play a key role in informing Congress; sometimes the threat of their opposition influences how members vote.

Understanding Congress

11.5 Assess Congress's role as a representative body and the impact of representation on the scope of government, p. 369.

Although Congress is an elite institution, it is responsive to the public when the public makes its wishes clear. It is open to influence, which makes it responsive to many interests; its openness may also reduce its ability to make good public policy. Members of Congress often support expanding government to aid their constituents, generally in response to public demands for policy, but many also fight to limit the scope of government.

Learn the Terms

incumbents, p. 345
casework, p. 347
pork barrel, p. 348
bicameral legislature, p. 351
House Rules Committee, p. 352
filibuster, p. 352
Speaker of the House, p. 353

majority leader, p. 354
whips, p. 354
minority leader, p. 354
standing committees, p. 355
joint committees, p. 355
conference committees, p. 355
select committees, p. 355

legislative oversight, p. 356
committee chairs, p. 359
seniority system, p. 359
caucus (congressional), p. 360
bill, p. 362

Test Yourself

1. What is the main reason for women's underrepresentation in Congress?

a. Fewer women than men become major party nominees for office.
b. Male independent voters on average have a large bias against female candidates.
c. Male independent voters on average have a large bias toward male candidates.
d. Women are more likely than are men to run when they perceive their odds to be poor.
e. Women candidates usually rank lower than males with voters on non-policy characteristics.

2. What historical evidence is there to support the belief that members of Congress who are from predominantly wealthier and more advantaged backgrounds can effectively represent their constituents from less advantaged backgrounds?

a. Historically, there were many white members of Congress who fought against slavery and segregation.
b. The historical experience of predominantly male members of Congress voting against equal pay for women supports this belief.
c. The historical experience of predominantly wealthy members of Congress voting against raising the minimum wage supports this belief.
d. The historical experience of predominantly white members of Congress fighting to keep segregation in place supports this belief.
e. There is no historical evidence to support this belief.

3. Which of the following is most likely to hurt an incumbent legislator's chances for reelection?

a. The incumbent has been in office during an economic downturn.
b. The incumbent has gone through a scandalous and public divorce.
c. The incumbent has spent considerable time claiming credit for his voting record.
d. The incumbent has spent more money than his challenger on his reelection campaign.
e. The incumbent has supported the president's policy initiatives.

4. When redrawing state district lines, the state party in the majority is likely to _____.

a. allow the party in the minority to draw new district lines
b. ask the Supreme Court to draw new district lines
c. move two of the opposition party's representatives into a single district
d. move two of their own party's representatives into a single district
e. try to keep all existing district lines in place without letting any new ones be drawn

5. What would be the benefit of imposing term limits on Congress members?

a. It would ensure that Congress maintains descriptive representation of jurisdictions served by its members.
b. It would give incumbents a better chance at reelection.
c. It would give incumbents the opportunity to build expertise in complex policy areas.
d. It would make members less insulated from social and political change in their jurisdictions.
e. It would motivate members to work harder to maintain the favor of their constituencies.

6. Why may the filibuster be considered undemocratic?

a. It is used by the majority to defeat the minority.
b. It is used by the minority to defeat the majority.
c. It is used in the Senate but not in the House of Representatives.
d. It is used to prevent logrolling in Congress.
e. It is used to undermine the power of the Speaker of the House.

7. When the House and the Senate pass different versions of a bill, these versions are to be reconciled by which type of committee?

a. a conference committee
b. a joint committee
c. a reconciliation committee
d. a select committee
e. a standing committee

8. Committee oversight of the executive branch

a. helps the president with the public
b. is mostly reactive to problems
c. often preempts problems
d. relies heavily on interest groups
e. relies little on committee staff

9. Which of the following describes a noteworthy development in Congress in the past 20 years?

a. the increased importance of the House leadership
b. the increase in the power of subcommittee chairs
c. the increased strength of presidential leadership
d. the rise of the seniority system
e. the widespread dispersion of power in the House

10. Why are caucuses important to party alignment in Congress?

a. Party caucuses are the primary place for debates to take place about the merits and drawbacks of legislation.
b. Party caucuses provide opportunities to align interests of members in both houses to build support for legislation and lobby for hearings for particular bills.
c. Party caucuses reward those who vote the party line with party-funded annual bonuses.
d. The caucus leaders gather signatures from members as a commitment to vote a certain way.
e. When members do not vote with the party, they are required to explain their position in official testimony to their caucus.

11. The long series of decision points in the lawmaking process _____.

a. favors the status quo
b. limits the power of interest groups
c. makes it easier for majorities to rule
d. must be confronted by all legislation
e. prevents excessive executive influence

12. Party politics have become more polarized over the last three decades. What accounts for this shift?

a. Moderate policy positions do not make headlines, so more radical positions tend to gain more public favor.
b. Preferences, behavior, and distribution of congressional voters have changed.
c. Presidential politics have fueled bipartisanship in Congress.
d. The rise of the Internet and access to public records has led to the polarization of political views.
e. The voting electorate has aged and become more aligned with partisan politics.

13. The politico model of representation holds that representatives can alternately fulfill the role of trustee or delegate depending on the issue. Which of the following is an example of this model?

a. a representative who acts in the best interests of the people as a whole at all times
b. a representative who always mirrors the will of his or her constituents
c. a representative who refuses to make strategic plans and makes all decisions on a case-by-case basis
d. a senator who always follows her own conscience
e. a senator who follows his own judgment on a matter that does not attract much public interest, but mirrors his constituents' views on an issue of major public concern

14. Why are constituents in smaller states better represented in Congress than constituents in big states are?

a. Constituents in smaller states are more often demographically similar to their representatives, which is conducive to descriptive representation.
b. In small states, constituents have a shorter distance to travel to meet with representatives.
c. Senate seats are equally divided among the states.
d. Small states are more likely to be farming states, which for a long time have had a strong lobbying presence in Congress.
e. Smaller states are more likely to have shorter terms, so seats are open and are contested more often.

15. Some say the responsive nature of Congress's work predisposes it to increase the size of government. How can this be explained?

a. Congress is filled with "yes men" and "yes women" who need to please everyone in order to be reelected.
b. Congress must respond to needs of the electorate, and as the population grows, the needs of the electorate expand.
c. Congress responds to many different interests and influences and expanding government services helps members get reelected.
d. Congressional work is prestigious and most members of Congress want to keep their jobs and bring up their friends.
e. If Congress had the power to set the budgetary agenda, members would be incentivized to reduce government spending and programs.

Explore Further

WEB SITES

www.house.gov
The official House of Representatives Web site contains information on the organization, operations, schedule, and activities of the House and its committees. The site also contains links to the offices of members and committees and enables you to contact your representative directly.

www.senate.gov
The official Senate Web site contains information and links similar to those for the House.

congress.gov
Information on the activities of Congress, the status and text of legislation, the *Congressional Record*, committee reports, and historical documents.

www.fec.gov
Federal Election Commission data on campaign expenditures.

www.opensecrets.org
The Center for Responsive Politics Web site with data on the role of money in politics.

www.c-span.org
Video coverage of Congress in action.

www.congress.org
Nonpartisan news and information on Congress and policy.

www.rollcall.com
Roll Call, the online version of the Capitol Hill newspaper.

thehill.com
News about all aspects of Congress.

FURTHER READING

Baumgartner, Frank R., Jeffrey M. Berry, Marie Hohnacki, David C. Kimball, and Beth L. Leech. *Lobbying and Policy Change: Who Wins, Who Loses, and Why.* Chicago, IL: University of Chicago Press, 2009. Examines just how influential lobbyists are—and are not.

Binder, Sarah A. *Stalemate.* Washington, D.C.: Brookings Institution, 2003. Discusses the causes and consequences of legislative gridlock.

Jacobson, Gary C. *The Politics of Congressional Elections*, 9th ed. New York: Addison-Wesley Longman, 2013. An excellent review of congressional elections.

Koger, Gregory. *Filibustering.* Chicago: University of Chicago Press, 2010. Explains the development and uses of the filibuster.

Lee, Frances E. *Beyond Ideology: Politics, Principles, and Partisanship in the U. S. Senate.* Chicago: University of Chicago Press, 2009. Argues that many partisan battles are rooted in competition for power rather than disagreement over the proper role of government.

Lee, Frances E., and Bruce I. Oppenheimer. *Sizing Up the Senate: The Unequal Consequences of Equal Representation.* Chicago: University of Chicago Press, 1999. How representation in the Senate affects how people are represented, the distribution of government benefits, and the nature of election campaigns.

Loomis, Burdett A., ed. *The U.S. Senate: From Deliberation to Dysfunction.* Washington, D.C.: CQ Press, 2011. Explores issues of delay, gridlock, and polarization and how they are difficult to change.

Mann, Thomas E., and Norman J. Ornstein. *The Broken Branch.* New York: Oxford University Press, 2006. How Congress is failing America and how to get it back on track.

Mayhew, David R. *Congress: The Electoral Connection*, 2nd ed. New Haven, CT: Yale University Press, 2005. An analysis of Congress based on the premise that the principal motivation of congressional behavior is reelection.

Sinclair, Barbara. *Unorthodox Lawmaking*, 4th ed. Washington, D.C.: CQ Press, 2011. Explains how Congress tries to cope with decentralization and polarization.

12

The Presidency

Politics in Action: Presidential Power

s Barack Obama waited to deliver his State of the Union address in January 2015, he could reflect on his years as president. They had certainly been eventful. Winning an historic election in 2008, he had hoped to make rapid progress on his agenda for change. Once in office, however, he had to deal first with the greatest financial crisis since the Great Depression. Only then could he turn his attention to health care reform, climate change and energy legislation, immigration, and other crucial matters. Each of these issues presented challenges in forming winning coalitions, especially since Republicans adamantly opposed his proposals.

He was awarded the Nobel Peace Prize. Yet he also had to make critical and difficult decisions regarding the use of U.S. troops in Iraq and Afghanistan. Stopping the development of nuclear weapons in Iran and North Korea posed intractable problems. In addition, he had to deal with regime changes in the Middle East and a civil war in Syria.

The poor economy, the controversial nature of his proposals for reform, and the strident tone of the opposition all contributed to a decline in both his public approval and his party's chances in congressional midterm elections. He had campaigned as an agent of change, and he had proposed many reforms, but he faced the same challenges in accomplishing his goals as his predecessors. His frustrations only increased after the Republicans took control of the House in 2011.

12.1

Characterize the expectations for and the backgrounds of presidents and identify paths to the White House and how presidents may be removed, p. 378.

12.2

Evaluate the president's constitutional powers and the expansion of presidential power, p. 384.

12.3

Describe the roles of the vice president, cabinet, Executive Office of the President, White House staff, and First Lady, p. 387.

12.4

Assess the impact of various sources of presidential influence on the president's ability to win congressional support, p. 393.

12.5

Analyze the president's powers in making national security policy and the relationship between the president and Congress in this arena, p. 401.

12.6

Identify the factors that affect the president's ability to obtain public support, p. 407.

12.7

Characterize the president's relations with the press and power in the American democracy and the presidency, p. 412.

12.8

Assess the role of presidential power in the president's impact on the scope of government, p. 414.

The occupant of most powerful political position in the world but also highly constrained by the Madisonian system, the president must constantly seek support from the public, Congress, and even other nations. Here President Barack Obama speaks at Michigan State University.

378

12.1

12.2

12.3

12.4

12.5

12.6

12.7

12.8

Powerful, strong, leader of the free world, commander in chief—these are common images of the American president. The only place in the world where television networks assign permanent camera crews is the White House. The presidency is power, at least according to popular myth. Problems are brought to the president's desk, the president decides on the right courses of action and issues orders, and an army of aides and bureaucrats carries out these orders.

As Barack Obama and all other presidents soon discover, nothing could be further from the truth. The main reason why presidents have trouble getting things done is that other policymakers with whom they deal have their own agendas, their own interests, and their own sources of power. Presidents operate in an environment filled with checks and balances and competing centers of power. As one presidential aide put it, "Every time you turn around people resist you."[1] Congress is beholden not to the president, but to the individual constituencies of its members. Cabinet members often push on behalf of their departmental interests and constituencies (farmers in the case of the Department of Agriculture, for example). Rarely can presidents rely on unwavering support from their party, the public, or even their own appointees.

As the pivotal leader in American politics, the president is the subject of unending political analysis and speculation, especially about presidential power. World history is replete with examples of leaders who have exceeded the prescribed boundaries of their power. Is the Madisonian system strong enough to prevent the presidency from becoming too powerful and posing a threat to democracy? On the other hand, is the president *strong enough* to stand up to the diverse interests in the United States? Does the president have enough power to govern on behalf of the majority?

Another fundamental question regarding democratic leaders is the nature of their relationship with the public and its consequences for public policy. The president and vice president are the only officials elected by the entire nation. In their efforts to obtain public support from the broad spectrum of interests in the public, are presidents natural advocates of an expansion of government? Do they promise more than they should in order to please the voters? As they face the frustrations of governing, do presidents seek to centralize authority in the federal government, where they have greater influence, while reducing that of the states? Does the chief executive seek more power through increasing the role of government?

Because not everyone bends easily to even the most persuasive president, the president must be a *leader*. Richard Neustadt famously argued that presidents were generally in a weak position to command, so they had to rely on persuasion.[2] George Edwards found that presidents have a difficult time changing people's minds, however, so they have to recognize and exploit opportunities already in their environments.[3] To be effective, the president must have highly developed *political skills* to understand the political forces around him, mobilize influence, manage conflict, negotiate, and fashion compromises. Presidential leadership has varied over the years, depending in large part on the individual who holds our nation's highest office. The following sections explore who presidents are and how they try to lead those whose support they need to accomplish their goals.

The Presidents

12.1

Characterize the expectations for and the backgrounds of presidents and identify paths to the White House and how presidents may be removed.

he presidency is an institution composed of the roles presidents must play, the powers at their disposal, and the large bureaucracy at their command. It is also a highly personal office. The personality of the individual serving as president makes a difference.

Great Expectations

When a new president takes the oath of office, he faces many daunting tasks. Perhaps the most difficult is living up to the expectations of the American people. Americans expect the chief executive to ensure peace, prosperity, and security.[4] As President Carter remarked, "The President…is held to be responsible for the state of the economy…and for the inconveniences, or disappointments, or the concerns of the American people."[5] Americans want a good life, and they look to the president to provide it.

Americans are of two minds about the presidency. On the one hand, they want to believe in a powerful president, one who can do good. They look back longingly on the great presidents of the first American century—Washington, Jefferson, Lincoln—and some in the second century as well, especially Franklin D. Roosevelt.

On the other hand, Americans dislike a concentration of power. Although presidential responsibilities have increased substantially since the Great Depression and World War II, there has not been a corresponding increase in presidential authority or administrative resources to meet these new expectations. Americans are basically individualistic and skeptical of authority. According to Samuel Huntington, "The distinctive aspect of the American Creed is its antigovernment character. Opposition to power, and suspicion of government as the most dangerous embodiment of power, are the central themes of American political thought."[6]

Because Americans' expectations of the presidency are so high, who serves as president is especially important. Just who are the people who have occupied the Oval Office?

Who They Are

When Warren G. Harding, one of the least illustrious American presidents, was in office, attorney Clarence Darrow remarked, "When I was a boy, I was told that anybody could become president. Now I'm beginning to believe it."[7] The Constitution simply states that the president must be a natural-born citizen at least 35 years old and

Point to Ponder

The public holds high expectations for the president.

Do these expectations make the public prone to disappointment? Should we expect less from our presidents? Or should we make it easier for presidents to meet our expectations?

©1975 The Washington Post Writers Group, reprinted with permission.

'Okay, bring in the new guy….'

Twenty-second Amendment
Ratified in 1951, this amendment limits presidents to two terms of office.

Twenty-fifth Amendment
Ratified in 1967, this amendment permits the vice president to become acting president if the vice president and the president's cabinet determine that the president is disabled, and it outlines how a recuperated president can reclaim the job.

must have resided in the United States for at least 14 years. Before Barack Obama was inaugurated as the forty-fourth president in 2009, all American presidents had been white males and, except for John Kennedy, Protestant. This homogeneity conceals considerable variety. Over the years, all manner of men have occupied the Oval Office.

Thomas Jefferson was a scientist and scholar who assembled dinosaur bones when presidential business was slack. Woodrow Wilson, the only political scientist ever to become president, combined a Presbyterian moral fervor and righteousness with a professor's intimidating style of leadership and speech making. His successor, Warren G. Harding, became president because Republican leaders thought he looked like one. Poker was his pastime. Out of his element in the job, Harding is almost everyone's choice as the worst American president. His speech making, said opponent William G. McAdoo, sounded "like an army of pompous phrases marching across the landscape in search of an idea."[8] Harding's friends stole the government blind, prompting his brief assessment of the presidency: "God, what a job!"

Since 1953, the White House has been home to a war hero, a Boston-Irish politician, a small-town Texas boy who grew up to become the biggest wheeler-dealer in the Senate, a California lawyer described by his enemies as "Tricky Dick" and by his friends as a misunderstood master of national leadership, a former Rose Bowl player who had spent almost his entire political career in the House of Representatives, a former governor who had been a Georgia peanut wholesaler, a former governor of California, a CIA chief and ambassador who was the son of a U.S. senator, an ambitious governor from a small state, a former managing director of a Major League Baseball team who had won his first election only six years before becoming president, and a young black man who had served in national office for only four years before assuming the role of commander in chief (see Table 12.1).

So far, no woman has served as president. As social prejudices diminish and more women are elected to positions that serve as stepping stones to the presidency, it is likely that this situation will change.

☐ How They Got There

Regardless of their ability, background, or character, all presidents must come to the job through one of two basic routes.

ELECTIONS: THE TYPICAL ROAD TO THE WHITE HOUSE Most presidents take a familiar journey to 1600 Pennsylvania Avenue: they run for president through the electoral process. The Constitution guarantees a four-year term once in office (unless the president is convicted in an impeachment trial), but the **Twenty-second Amendment**, ratified in 1951, limits presidents to being elected to only two terms.

Only 13 presidents have actually served 2 or (in Franklin Roosevelt's case) more full terms in the White House: Washington, Jefferson, Madison, Monroe, Jackson, Grant, Cleveland (whose terms were not consecutive), Wilson, Franklin Roosevelt, Eisenhower, Reagan, Clinton, George W. Bush, and Obama. A few—Coolidge, Polk, Pierce, Buchanan, Hayes, and Lyndon Johnson—decided against a second term. Seven others—both the Adamses, Van Buren, Taft, Hoover, Carter, and George H. W. Bush—thought they had earned a second term but found that the voters did not concur.

SUCCESSION For more than 10 percent of American history, an individual who was not elected to the office has served as president. About one in five presidents succeeded to the job because they were vice president when the incumbent president either died or (in Nixon's case) resigned (see Table 12.2). In the twentieth century, almost one-third (5 of 18) of those who occupied the office were "accidental presidents."

The **Twenty-fifth Amendment**, ratified in 1967, created a means for selecting a new vice president when that office becomes vacant. The president nominates a new vice president, who assumes the office when both houses of Congress approve the nomination by majority vote. President Nixon chose Gerald Ford as vice president

TABLE 12.1 RECENT PRESIDENTS

President	Term	Party	Background	Presidency
Dwight D. Eisenhower	1953–1961	Republican	• Commander of Allied forces in Europe in World War II • Never voted until he ran for president	• Presided over relatively tranquil 1950s • Conservative domestic policies • Cool crisis management • Enjoyed strong public approval
John F. Kennedy	1961–1963	Democrat	• U.S. senator from Massachusetts • From very wealthy family • War hero	• Known for personal style • Presided over Cuban missile crisis • Ushered in era of liberal domestic policies • Assassinated in 1963
Lyndon B. Johnson	1963–1969	Democrat	• Senate majority leader • Chosen as Kennedy's running mate; succeeded him after the assassination	• Skilled legislative leader with a coarse public image • Launched the Great Society • Won passage of major civil rights laws • Escalated the Vietnam War • War policies proved unpopular; did not seek reelection
Richard M. Nixon	1969–1974	Republican	• U.S. senator from California • Served two terms as Eisenhower's vice president • Lost presidential election of 1960 to John F. Kennedy	• Presided over period of domestic policy innovation • Reopened relations with China • Ended Vietnam War • Resigned as a result of Watergate scandal
Gerald R. Ford	1974–1977	Republican	• House minority leader • First person ever nominated as vice president under Twenty-fifth Amendment	• Pardoned Richard Nixon • Helped heal the nation's wounds after Watergate • Lost election in 1976 to Jimmy Carter
Jimmy Carter	1977–1981	Democrat	• Governor of Georgia • Peanut farmer	• Viewed as honest but politically unskilled • Managed Iranian hostage crisis • Lost bid for reelection in 1980 • Brokered peace between Egypt and Israel
Ronald W. Reagan	1981–1989	Republican	• Governor of California • Well-known actor	• Won a substantial tax cut • Led fight for a large increase in defense spending • Hurt by Iran-Contra scandal • Known as the Great Communicator
George H. W. Bush	1989–1993	Republican	• U.S. representative from Texas • Director of CIA • Ambassador to UN • Served two terms as Reagan's vice president	• Led international coalition to victory in Gulf War • Presided over end of Cold War • Popular until economy stagnated • Lost reelection bid in 1992
William J. Clinton	1993–2001	Democrat	• Governor of Arkansas • Rhodes Scholar	• Moved Democrats to center • Presided over balanced budget • Benefited from strong economy • Tenure marred by Monica Lewinsky scandal • Impeached but not convicted
George W. Bush	2001–2009	Republican	• Governor of Texas • Son of President George Bush • Elected without plurality of the vote	• Launched war on terrorism • Won large tax cut • Established Department of Homeland Security • Began war with Iraq
Barack Obama	2009–	Democrat	• Senator from Illinois • First African American elected as president	• Dealt with financial crisis • Continued war on terrorism • Won health care reform

impeachment
The political equivalent of an indictment in criminal law, prescribed by the Constitution. The House of Representatives may impeach the president by a majority vote for "Treason, Bribery, or other high Crimes and Misdemeanors."

Watergate
The events and scandal surrounding a break-in at the Democratic National Committee headquarters in 1972 and the subsequent cover-up of White House involvement, leading to the eventual resignation of President Nixon under the threat of impeachment.

when Vice President Spiro Agnew resigned, and Ford then assumed the presidency when Nixon himself resigned. Thus, Ford did not run for either the vice presidency or the presidency before taking office.

Several times a president has become disabled, incapable of carrying out the job for weeks or even months at a time. After Woodrow Wilson suffered a stroke, his wife, Edith Wilson, became virtual acting president. The Twenty-fifth Amendment clarifies some of the Constitution's vagueness about disability. The amendment permits the vice president to become acting president if the vice president and the president's cabinet determine that the president is disabled or if the president declares his own disability, and it outlines how a recuperated president can reclaim the Oval Office. A law specifies the order of presidential succession—from the vice president, to the Speaker of the House, to the president pro tempore of the Senate and down through the cabinet members.

IMPEACHMENT Removing a discredited president before the end of a term is not easy. The Constitution prescribes the process of **impeachment**, which is roughly the political equivalent of an indictment in criminal law. The House of Representatives may, by majority vote, impeach the president for "Treason, Bribery, or other high Crimes and Misdemeanors." Once the House votes for impeachment, the case goes to the Senate, which tries the accused president, with the chief justice of the Supreme Court presiding. By a two-thirds vote, the Senate may convict and remove the president from office.

Why It Matters to You
Standards of Impeachment

It is not easy to impeach a president; the threshold for an impeachable offense is a high one. This standard makes it very difficult to remove a president Congress feels is performing poorly *between* elections. A lower threshold for impeachment would have the potential to turn the United States into a parliamentary system in which the legislature could change the chief executive at any time.

The House has impeached only two presidents. It impeached Andrew Johnson, Lincoln's successor, in 1868 on charges stemming from his disagreement with Radical Republicans over Civil War reconstruction policies. He narrowly escaped conviction. On July 31, 1974, the House Judiciary Committee voted to recommend that the full House impeach Richard Nixon as a result of the **Watergate** scandal. The three articles of impeachment charged that Nixon had (1) obstructed justice, (2) abused

---

TABLE 12.2 INCOMPLETE PRESIDENTIAL TERMS

President	Term	Succeeded by
William Henry Harrison	March 4, 1841–April 4, 1841	John Tyler
Zachary Taylor	March 4, 1849–July 9, 1850	Millard Fillmore
Abraham Lincoln	March 4, 1865–April 15, 1865ᵃ	Andrew Johnson
James A. Garfield	March 4, 1881–September 19, 1881	Chester A. Arthur
William McKinley	March 4, 1901–September 14, 1901ᵃ	Theodore Roosevelt
Warren G. Harding	March 4, 1921–August 2, 1923	Calvin Coolidge
Franklin D. Roosevelt	January 20, 1945–April 12, 1945ᵇ	Harry S. Truman
John F. Kennedy	January 20, 1961–November 22, 1963	Lyndon B. Johnson
Richard M. Nixon	January 20, 1973–August 9, 1974ᵃ	Gerald R. Ford

ᵃSecond term.
ᵇFourth term.

Richard Nixon was the only American president ever to resign his office. Nixon decided to resign rather than face impeachment for his role in the Watergate scandal, a series of illegal wiretaps, break-ins, and cover-ups.

his power, and (3) failed to comply with congressional subpoenas. Soon thereafter, a tape recording of White House conversations provided evidence that even Nixon's defenders found convincing, and Nixon resigned from the presidency rather than face certain impeachment and a Senate trial. In 1998, the House voted two articles of impeachment against President Bill Clinton on party-line votes. The public clearly opposed the idea, however, and in 1999 the Senate voted to acquit the president on both counts.

The Constitution provides only the most general guidelines as to the grounds for impeachment. Article II, Section 4, says, "The President, Vice President and all civil Officers of the United States, shall be removed from Office on Impeachment for, and Conviction of, Treason, Bribery, or other high Crimes and Misdemeanors."

There is agreement on at least four points regarding impeachable offenses:

1. *Impeachable behavior does not have to be a crime.* If, for example, the president refused to work or chose to invade a country solely to increase his public support, his actions could be grounds for impeachment, even though they would not violate the law.

2. *The offense should be grave.* A poker game in the White House, even though it may violate the law, would not constitute an impeachable offense.

3. *A matter of policy disagreement is not grounds for impeachment.* When Andrew Johnson was impeached in 1868 and survived conviction by only one vote, the real issue was his disagreement with Congress over the policy of Reconstruction following the Civil War. Johnson's impeachment is widely viewed as an abuse of impeachment power.

4. *Impeachment is an inherently political process.* The grounds for impeachment are ultimately whatever Congress decides they are because the Constitution assigns these calibrations to members' political judgment.

Beyond these points of agreement, we enter speculative territory. Thus, in Clinton's case, the question of what constituted an impeachable offense was hotly debated, as you can read in "You Are the Policymaker: What Should Be the Criteria for Impeaching the President?"

You Are the Policymaker

What Should Be the Criteria for Impeaching the President?

When the story of President Bill Clinton's sexual liaison with Monica Lewinsky first broke in January 1998, astute political observers immediately perceived that this was more than a lurid sex scandal involving the president. For although the sex angle attracted the most attention, there were also allegations of President Clinton committing perjury when questioned about the affair and obstructing justice by urging Lewinsky to lie under oath. These charges would clearly put any private citizen in danger of being indicted in a criminal court. For a president, who cannot be indicted while in office, it meant possible impeachment by the House of Representatives followed by a Senate trial.

After months of investigation into the allegations, Independent Counsel Kenneth Starr issued a report to Congress accusing President Clinton of 11 counts of possible impeachable offenses, including perjury, obstruction of justice, witness tampering, and abuse of power. The president's detractors used the report as a basis for charging that he had broken the law, failed in his primary constitutional duty to take care that the laws be faithfully executed, betrayed the public's trust, and dishonored the nation's highest office.

As a result, they argued, the president should be removed from office through the process of impeachment.

The White House fought back. First, the president apologized to the nation and engaged in a round of expressions of remorse before a variety of audiences. At the same time, the White House accused Starr of an intrusive investigation motivated by a political vendetta against the president. The White House argued that the president made a mistake in his private behavior, apologized for it, and should continue to do the job he was elected to do. Impeachment, the president's defenders said, was grossly disproportionate to the president's offense.

In December 1998, the House voted two articles of impeachment against President Clinton on nearly straight party-line votes. The articles charged him with lying to a grand jury and obstructing justice. In the Senate trial that followed, the standards for removing a president from office were hotly debated. Ultimately, neither article received support from even a bare majority of senators, much less the two-thirds threshold necessary to convict him of high crimes and misdemeanors.

What do you think? If you were a member of the House, would you have voted to impeach President Clinton?

Presidential Powers

12.2 Evaluate the president's constitutional powers and the expansion of presidential power.

The contemporary presidency hardly resembles the one the Constitution's Framers designed in 1787. The executive office they conceived had more limited authority, fewer responsibilities, and much less organizational structure than today's presidency. The Framers feared both anarchy and monarchy. They wanted an independent executive but disagreed about both the form the office should take and the powers it should exercise. In the end, they created an executive unlike any the world had ever seen[9] (see "America in Perspective: President or Prime Minister?").

☐ Constitutional Powers

The Constitution says remarkably little about presidential power. The discussion of the presidency begins with these general words: "The executive power shall be vested in a president of the United States of America." It goes on to list just a few powers (see Table 12.3). The Framers' invention fit nicely within the Madisonian system of shared power and checks and balances, forcing the president to obtain the support of officials in the other branches of government.

Institutional balance was essential to the convention delegates, who had in mind the abuses of past executives (including both the king and colonial governors) but also

America in Perspective

President or Prime Minister?

The Framers chose a presidential system of government for the United States. Most democracies in developed countries, however, have chosen a parliamentary system. In such a system, the chief executive, known as the prime minister, is selected by the members of the legislature from among themselves, rather than by the voters. More specifically, the majority party (or the largest bloc of votes in the legislature if there is no majority party) votes its party leader to be prime minister. The prime minister may remain in power for a long time—as long as his or her party or coalition has a majority of the seats and supports the leader.

Presidents and prime ministers govern quite differently. Prime ministers never face divided government, for example. Since they represent the majority party or coalition, they can almost always depend on winning votes in the legislature. In addition, party discipline is better in parliamentary systems than in the United States. Parties know that if the prime minister should lose on an important vote, he might have to call for an immediate election to try to obtain a working majority under unfavorable circumstances. As a result, members of parliament almost always support their leaders.

Prime ministers generally differ in background from presidents as well. They must be party leaders, as we have seen, and they are usually very effective communicators, with skills honed in the rough-and-tumble of parliamentary debate. In addition, they have had substantial experience dealing with national issues, unlike American governors who may move directly into the presidency. Cabinet members, who are usually senior members of parliament, have similar advantages.

So why does the United States maintain a presidential system? The Framers were concerned about the concentration of power and wanted to separate power so that the different branches could check each other. More concerned with the abuse of power than its effective use, they chose a presidential system—the first the world had ever known.

CRITICAL THINKING QUESTION

Would the United States be better off with a parliamentary system in which the majority party would have the power to govern and thus keep its electoral promises?

TABLE 12.3 CONSTITUTIONAL POWERS OF THE PRESIDENT

National Security Powers

Serve as commander in chief of the armed forces

Make treaties with other nations, subject to the agreement of two-thirds of the Senate

Nominate ambassadors, with the agreement of a majority of the Senate

Receive ambassadors of other nations, thereby conferring diplomatic recognition on other governments

Legislative Powers

Present information on the state of the union to Congress

Recommend legislation to Congress

Convene both houses of Congress on extraordinary occasions

Adjourn Congress if the House and Senate cannot agree on adjournment

Veto legislation (Congress may overrule with two-thirds vote of each house)

Administrative Powers

"Take care that the laws be faithfully executed"

Nominate officials as provided for by Congress and with the agreement of a majority of the Senate

Request written opinions of administrative officials

Fill administrative vacancies during congressional recesses

Judicial Powers

Grant reprieves and pardons for federal offenses (except impeachment)

Nominate federal judges, who are confirmed by a majority of the Senate

386

12.1
12.2
12.3
12.4
12.5
12.6
12.7
12.8

The Expansion of Power

Today there is more to presidential power than the Constitution alone suggests, and that power is derived from many sources. The role of the president has changed as America has increased in prominence on the world stage; technology has also reshaped the presidency. George Washington's ragtag militias (mostly disbanded by the time the first commander in chief took command) were much different from the mighty nuclear arsenal that today's president commands.

Presidents themselves have taken the initiative to develop new roles for the office. In fact, many presidents have enlarged the power of the presidency by expanding the president's responsibilities and political resources. Thomas Jefferson was the first leader of a mass political party. Andrew Jackson presented himself as the direct representative of the people. Abraham Lincoln mobilized the country for war. Theodore Roosevelt mobilized the public behind his policies. He and Woodrow Wilson set precedents for presidents to serve as world leaders; Wilson and Franklin D. Roosevelt developed the role of the president as manager of the economy.

Perspectives on Presidential Power

During the 1950s and 1960s, it was fashionable for political scientists, historians, and commentators to favor a powerful presidency. Historians rated presidents from strong to weak—and there was no question that "strong" meant good and "weak" meant bad. Political scientists waxed eloquent about the presidency as an institution epitomizing democratic government.[10] By the 1970s, many felt differently. Lyndon Johnson and the unpopular Vietnam War made people reassess the role of presidential power, and Richard Nixon and the Watergate scandal heightened public distrust. The Pentagon Papers, a secret history of the Vietnam War, revealed presidential duplicity. Nixon's "enemies list" and his avowed goal to "screw our enemies" by illegally auditing their taxes, tapping their phones, and using "surreptitious entry" (a euphemism for burglary) asserted that the president was above the law, possessing "inherent powers" that permitted presidents to order acts that otherwise would be illegal.

Early defenders of a strong presidency made sharp turnabouts in their position, arguing that the presidency had become too powerful for the nation's own good.[11] Whereas an older generation of scholars had written glowing accounts of the presidency, a newer generation wrote about "The Swelling of the Presidency" and "Making the Presidency Safe for Democracy."[12]

The Nixon era was followed by the presidencies of Gerald Ford and Jimmy Carter, whom many critics saw as weak leaders and failures. Once again, the country sought a strong leader, and in the 1980s many thought it found one in Ronald Reagan. Although Reagan experienced short periods of great influence, more typically he was frustrated in achieving his goals as the American political system settled back into its characteristic mode of stalemate and incremental policymaking. The Iran-Contra affair, in which some White House aides engaged in illegal activities, kept concern about a tyrannical

the excesses of state legislatures. The problem was how to preserve the balance without jeopardizing the independence of the separate branches or impeding the lawful exercise of their authority. The Framers resolved this problem by checking those powers they believed to be most dangerous, the ones that historically had been subject to the greatest abuse (for example, they gave Congress the power to declare war and the Senate the power to approve treaties and presidential appointments), while protecting the general spheres of authority from encroachment (the executive, for instance, was given a qualified veto).

Provisions for reelection and a short term of office also encouraged presidential responsibility. For those executives who flagrantly abused their authority, impeachment was the ultimate recourse.

presidency alive, while Reagan's inability, in most instances, to sway Congress evoked a desire on the part of some (mostly conservatives) for a stronger presidency. Reagan's immediate successors, George H. W. Bush and Bill Clinton, often found it difficult to get things done.

The presidencies of George W. Bush and Barack Obama raised anew the issue of presidential power. Bush asserted an expansive view of the president's constitutional powers, including withholding information from Congress under the doctrine of executive privilege, issuing statements asserting the right to disregard certain provisions of laws he signed, ordering without warrants electronic surveillance of individuals, and holding prisoners without trial for indefinite periods. Obama continued many of his predecessor's practices. He also actively used drones to kill terrorists, even American citizens, without trial and presided over a massive electronic surveillance effort. Once again, critics charged that presidential power threatened the constitutional balance of powers.

Running the Government: The Chief Executive

12.3 Describe the roles of the vice president, cabinet, Executive Office of the President, White House staff, and First Lady.

 lthough we often refer to the president as the "chief executive," it is easy to forget that one of the president's most important roles is presiding over the administration of government. This role receives less publicity than, for example, appealing to the public for support of policy initiatives, dealing with Congress, or negotiating with foreign powers, but it is of great importance nevertheless.

The Constitution exhorts the president to "take care that the laws be faithfully executed." In the early days of the republic, this clerical-sounding function was fairly easy. Today, the sprawling federal bureaucracy spends nearly $4 trillion a year and numbers more than 4 million civilian and military employees. Running such a large organization would be a full-time job for even the most talented of executives, yet it is only one of the president's many jobs.

One of the president's resources for controlling this bureaucracy is the power to appoint top-level administrators. New presidents have about 500 high-level positions available for appointment—cabinet and subcabinet jobs, agency heads, and other non–civil service posts—plus 2,500 lesser jobs. Since passage of the Budgeting and Accounting Act of 1921, presidents have had one other important executive tool: the power to recommend agency budgets to Congress.

The vastness of the executive branch, the complexity of public policy, and the desire to accomplish their policy goals have led presidents in recent years to pay even closer attention to appointing officials who will be responsive to the president's policies. Presidents have also taken more interest in the regulations issued by agencies. This trend toward centralizing decision making in the White House pleases those who think the bureaucracy should be more responsive to elected officials. On the other hand, it dismays those who believe that increased presidential involvement in policymaking will undermine the "neutral competence" of professional bureaucrats by encouraging them to follow the president's policy preferences rather than the intent of laws as passed by Congress.

Presidents also use **executive orders** to run the government. These orders carry the force of law and are used to implement statutes, treaties, and provisions of the Constitution.[13] Harry Truman desegregated the military, John F. Kennedy created the Peace Corps, Lyndon Johnson began affirmative action, Richard Nixon created the Environmental Protection Agency, Ronald Reagan centralized powers of regulatory review in the Office of Management and Budget, and George W. Bush established military tribunals for terrorists by executive order.

executive orders

Regulations originating with the executive branch. Executive orders are one method presidents can use to control the bureaucracy.

388

12.1
12.2
12.3
12.4
12.5
12.6
12.7
12.8

This section focuses on how presidents go about organizing and using the parts of the executive branch most under their control—the vice president, the cabinet, the Executive Office of the President, and the White House staff.

The Vice President

Once the choice of a vice president was an afterthought; it was often an effort to placate some important symbolic constituency. Jimmy Carter, a moderate southerner, selected as his running mate Walter Mondale, a well-known liberal from Minnesota, and conservative Ronald Reagan chose his chief rival, George H. W. Bush, in part to please Republican moderates.[14]

Vice presidents have rarely enjoyed the job. John Nance Garner of Texas, one of Franklin Roosevelt's vice presidents, declared that the job was "not worth a pitcher of warm spit."[15] Some have performed so poorly that they were deemed an embarrassment to the president. After Woodrow Wilson's debilitating stroke, almost everyone agreed that Vice President Thomas Marshall—a man who shirked all responsibility, including cabinet meetings—would be a disaster as acting president. Spiro Agnew, Richard Nixon's first vice president, had to resign and was convicted of evading taxes (on bribes he had accepted).

Before the mid-1970s, vice presidents usually found that their main job was waiting. The Constitution assigns them the minor tasks of presiding over the Senate and voting in case of a tie among the senators. As George H. W. Bush put it when he was vice president, "The buck doesn't stop here." Nonetheless, recent presidents have taken their vice presidents more seriously, involving them in policy discussions and important diplomacy.[16]

The relationship between Jimmy Carter and Walter Mondale marked a watershed in the vice presidency, as Mondale, an experienced senator, became a close advisor to the president, a Washington outsider. In choosing George H. W. Bush, Ronald Reagan also chose a vice president with extensive Washington experience. To become intimates of the president, both vice presidents had to be completely loyal, losing their political independence in the process. Although Bush himself chose as vice president Senator Dan Quayle of Indiana, considered by many a political lightweight, Albert Gore, Bill Clinton's vice president, was a Washington insider and played a prominent role in the administration. He met regularly with the president, represented him in discussions with the leaders of numerous countries, and chaired a prominent effort to "reinvent" government.

George W. Bush chose Richard Cheney, who had extensive experience in high-level positions in the national government, as his vice president and assigned him a central role in his administration. Cheney advised the president on a wide range of issues and chaired task forces dealing with major policy issues. He also was the focus of criticism, especially from those opposed to his support for the aggressive use of military power and an expansive view of presidential power. Barack Obama chose Senator Joseph Biden of Delaware as his vice president. Biden had substantial experience in government and became a close adviser to the president, especially on foreign policy. He also represented the president abroad and served as an important liaison with members of Congress.

The Cabinet

Although the Constitution does not mention the group of presidential advisers known as the **cabinet**, every president has had one. The cabinet is too large and too diverse, and its members (heads of the executive departments) are too concerned with representing the interests of their departments for it to serve as a collective board of directors, however. The major decisions remain in the president's hands. Legend has it that Abraham Lincoln asked his cabinet to vote on an issue, and the result was unanimity in opposition to his view. He announced the decision as "seven nays and one aye, the ayes have it."

cabinet
A group of presidential advisers not mentioned in the Constitution, although every president has had one. Today the cabinet is composed of 14 secretaries, the attorney general, and others designated by the president.

TABLE 12.4 THE CABINET DEPARTMENTS

Department	Year Created	Function
State	1789	Makes foreign policy, including treaty negotiations
Treasury	1789	Serves as the government's banker
Defense	1947	Formed by the consolidation of the former Departments of War and the Navy
Justice	1870	Serves as the government's attorney; headed by the attorney general
Interior	1849	Manages the nation's natural resources, including wildlife and public lands
Agriculture	1862	Administers farm and food stamp programs and aids farmers
Commerce	1903	Aids businesses and conducts the U.S. census
Labor	1913	Formed through separation from the Department of Commerce; runs programs and aids labor in various ways
Health and Human Services	1953	Originally created as the Department of Health, Education, and Welfare, it lost its education function in 1979 and Social Security in 1995
Housing and Urban Development	1966	Responsible for housing and urban programs
Transportation	1966	Responsible for mass transportation and highway programs
Energy	1977	Responsible for energy policy and research, including atomic energy
Education	1979	Responsible for the federal government's education programs
Veterans Affairs	1988	Responsible for programs aiding veterans
Homeland Security	2002	Responsible for protecting against terrorism and responding to natural disasters

George Washington's cabinet was small, consisting of just three secretaries (state, treasury, and war) and the attorney general. Presidents since Washington have increased the size of the cabinet by requesting Congress to establish new executive departments. Today 14 secretaries and the attorney general head executive departments and constitute the cabinet (see Table 12.4). In addition, presidents may designate other officials (the ambassador to the United Nations is a common choice) as cabinet members.[17]

Even in making his highest-level appointments, the president is subject to the constitutional system of checks and balances. For example, President Barack Obama nominated Tom Daschle, a former senator, as secretary of the Department of Health and Human Services. However, he had to withdraw the nomination after it became clear that Daschle's tax problems would create a barrier to his confirmation by the Senate.

The Executive Office

Next to the White House sits an ornate building called the EEOB, or Eisenhower Executive Office Building. It houses a collection of offices and organizations loosely grouped into the Executive Office of the President.[18] Congress has created some of these offices by legislation, and the president has simply organized the rest. The Executive Office started small in 1939, when President Roosevelt established it, but has grown with the rest of government. Three major policymaking bodies are housed in the Executive Office—the National Security Council, the Council of Economic Advisers, and the Office of Management and Budget—along with several other units that serve the president (see Figure 12.1).

12.1
12.2
12.3
12.4
12.5
12.6
12.7
12.8

National Security Council
The committee that links the president's foreign and military policy advisers. Its formal members are the president, vice president, secretary of state, and secretary of defense, and it is managed by the president's national security assistant.

Council of Economic Advisers
A three-member body appointed by the president to advise the president on economic policy.

Office of Management and Budget
An office that prepares the president's budget and also advises presidents on proposals from departments and agencies and helps review their proposed regulations.

FIGURE 12.1 EXECUTIVE OFFICE OF THE PRESIDENT

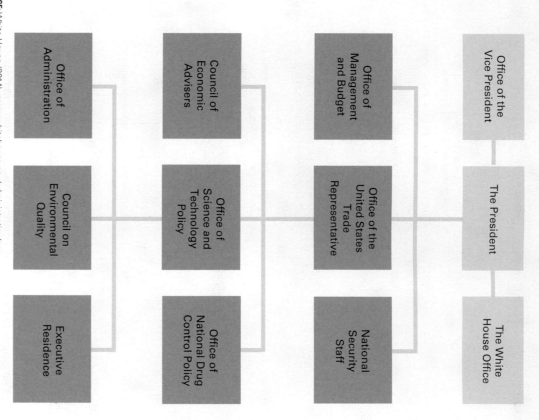

Office of the Vice President

The President

The White House Office

Office of Management and Budget

Office of the United States Trade Representative

National Security Staff

Council of Economic Advisers

Office of Science and Technology Policy

Office of National Drug Control Policy

Office of Administration

Council on Environmental Quality

Executive Residence

SOURCE: White House (2014), www.whitehouse.gov/administration/eop.

The **National Security Council** (NSC) is the committee that links the president's key foreign and military policy advisers. Its formal members include the president, vice president, and secretaries of state and defense, but its informal membership is broader. The president's special assistant for national security affairs plays a major role in the NSC, running a staff whose responsibilities include providing the president with information and policy recommendations on national security, aiding the president in national security crisis management, coordinating agency and departmental activities related to national security, and monitoring the implementation of national security policy.

The **Council of Economic Advisers** (CEA) has three members, each appointed by the president, who advise the president on economic policy. They prepare the annual *Economic Report of the President*, which includes data and analysis on the current state and future trends of the economy, and help the president make policy on inflation, unemployment, and other economic matters.

The **Office of Management and Budget** (OMB) originated as the Bureau of the Budget (BOB), which was created in 1921. The OMB is composed of a handful of political appointees and more than 600 career officials, many of whom are highly skilled professionals. Its major responsibility is to prepare the president's budget. President Nixon revamped the BOB in 1970 in an attempt to make it a managerial as well as a budgetary agency, changing its name in the process to stress its managerial functions.

Because each presidential appointee and department has an agenda, presidents need a clearinghouse—the OMB. Presidents use the OMB to review legislative

FIGURE 12.2 PRINCIPAL OFFICES IN THE WHITE HOUSE

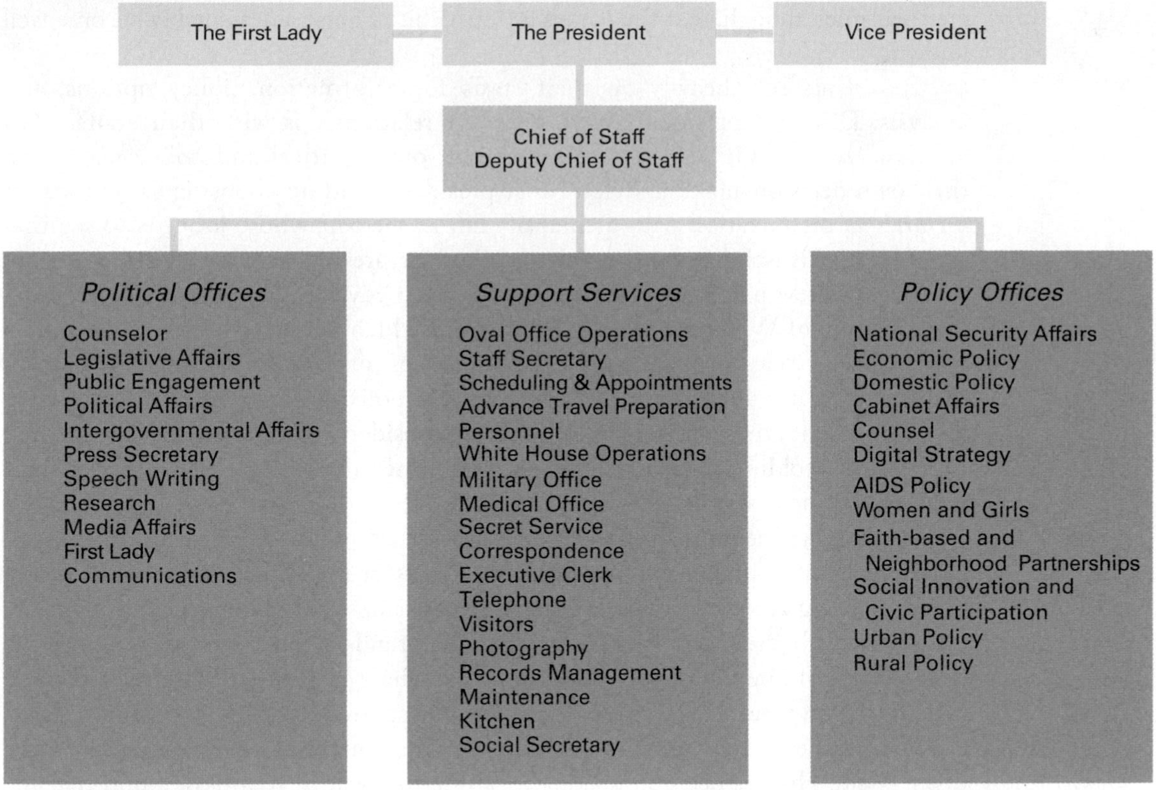

The First Lady — The President — Vice President

Chief of Staff
Deputy Chief of Staff

Political Offices

Counselor
Legislative Affairs
Public Engagement
Political Affairs
Intergovernmental Affairs
Press Secretary
Speech Writing
Research
Media Affairs
First Lady
Communications

Support Services

Oval Office Operations
Staff Secretary
Scheduling & Appointments
Advance Travel Preparation
Personnel
White House Operations
Military Office
Medical Office
Secret Service
Correspondence
Executive Clerk
Telephone
Visitors
Photography
Records Management
Maintenance
Kitchen
Social Secretary

Policy Offices

National Security Affairs
Economic Policy
Domestic Policy
Cabinet Affairs
Counsel
Digital Strategy
AIDS Policy
Women and Girls
Faith-based and Neighborhood Partnerships
Social Innovation and Civic Participation
Urban Policy
Rural Policy

SOURCE: White House (2014), www.whitehouse.gov/administration/eop.

proposals from the cabinet and other executive agencies so that they can determine whether they want an agency to propose these initiatives to Congress. The OMB assesses the proposals' budgetary implications and advises presidents on the proposals' consistency with their overall program. The OMB also plays an important role in reviewing regulations proposed by departments and agencies.

Although presidents find that the Executive Office is smaller and more manageable than the cabinet departments, it is still filled with people who often are performing jobs required by law. There is, however, one part of the presidential system that presidents can truly call their own: the White House staff.

☐ The White House Staff

Before Franklin D. Roosevelt, the president's personal staff resources were minimal. Only one messenger and one secretary served Thomas Jefferson. One hundred years later the president's staff had grown only to 13. Woodrow Wilson was in the habit of typing his own letters. As recently as the 1920s, the entire budget for the White House staff was no more than $80,000 per year.

Today, the White House staff includes about 600 people—many of whom the president rarely sees—who provide the chief executive with a wide variety of services ranging from making advance travel preparations to answering the avalanche of letters received each year (see Figure 12.2). At the top of the White House staff are the key aides the president sees daily: the chief of staff, congressional liaison aides, a press secretary, a national security assistant, and a few other administrative and political assistants.

The top aides in the White House hierarchy are people who are completely loyal to the president, and the president turns to them for advice on the most serious or mundane matters of governance. Good staff people are self-effacing, working only for the boss and shunning the limelight. The 1939 report of the Brownlow Committee, which served as the basis for the development of the modern White House staff, argued that presidential assistants should have a "passion for anonymity." So important are their roles, though, that the names of top White House aides quickly become well known.

Presidents rely heavily on their staffs for information, policy options, and analysis. Different presidents have different relationships with their staffs. They all organize the White House to serve their own political and policy needs and their own decision-making styles. Most presidents end up choosing some form of *hierarchical* organization with a chief of staff at the top, whose job it is to see that everyone else is doing his or her job and that the president's time and interests are protected. A few presidents, such as John F. Kennedy, have employed a *wheel-and-spokes* system of White House management in which many aides have equal status and are balanced against one another in the process of decision making.[19] Whatever the system, White House aides are central in the policymaking process—fashioning options, negotiating agreements, writing presidential statements, controlling paperwork, molding legislative details, and generally giving the president their opinions on most matters.

Recent presidents illustrate significant contrasts in decision-making styles. President Clinton immersed himself in the details of policy. He ran an open White House, dealing directly with a large number of aides and reading countless policy memoranda. His emphasis on deliberation and his fluid staffing system generated criticism that his White House was "indecisive" and "chaotic." George W. Bush took pride in being decisive and was more likely to delegate responsibility than was Clinton. Bush, however, was less likely to persist in asking probing questions. Investigations into the Bush White House's decision making regarding the war in Iraq have found that the president's aides sometimes failed to properly vet information and follow other appropriate procedures. Barack Obama has a deliberative decision-making style that is more orderly than Clinton's and more likely to challenge the premises of policy advocates than Bush's.

Despite presidents' reliance on their staffs, it is the president who sets the tone for the White House. Although it is common to blame presidential advisers for mistakes made in an administration, it is the president's responsibility to demand that staff members analyze a full range of options and their probable consequences before they offer the president their advice. If the chief executive does not demand quality staff work, then the work is less likely to be done, and disaster or embarrassment may follow.

☐ The First Lady

The First Lady has no official government position, yet she is often at the center of national attention. The media chronicles every word she speaks and every hairstyle she adopts. Although some people may think of First Ladies as well-dressed homemakers presiding over White House dinners, there is much more to the job.

Abigail Adams (an early feminist) and Dolley Madison counseled and lobbied their husbands. Edith Galt Wilson was the most powerful First Lady, virtually running the government when her husband, Woodrow, suffered a paralyzing stroke in 1919. Eleanor Roosevelt wrote a nationally syndicated newspaper column and tirelessly traveled and advocated New Deal policies. She became her crippled husband's eyes and ears around the country and urged him to adopt liberal social welfare policies. Lady Bird Johnson chose to focus on one issue, beautification, and most of her successors followed this single-issue pattern. Rosalyn Carter chose mental health, Nancy Reagan selected drug abuse prevention, and Barbara Bush advocated literacy, as did Laura Bush, a former librarian.

In what was perhaps a natural evolution in a society where women have moved into positions formerly held only by men, Hillary Rodham Clinton attained the most responsible and visible leadership position ever held by a First Lady. She was an influential adviser to the president, playing an active role in the selection of

Although the First Lady has no official government position, she is often at the center of national attention. In recent years, First Ladies have taken active roles in promoting policies ranging from highway beautification and mental health to literacy and health care. First Lady Michelle Obama gave high priority to supporting military families and veterans.

● *How would things change if a woman were elected president and her spouse was the First Man?*

nominees for cabinet and judicial posts, for example. Most publicly, she headed the planning for the president's massive health care reform plan in 1993 and became, along with her husband, its primary advocate. Michelle Obama has focused on a range of issues, which have included fighting childhood obesity, supporting military families, helping working women balance career and family, and encouraging national service.

Presidential Leadership of Congress: The Politics of Shared Powers

12.4   Assess the impact of various sources of presidential influence on the president's ability to win congressional support.

A long with their responsibility for running the executive branch, presidents must also deal intensively with the legislative branch. Near the top of any presidential job description would be "working with Congress." The American system of separation of powers is actually one of *shared* powers, so if presidents are to succeed in leaving their stamp on public policy, they must devote much of their time in office to leading the legislature in order to gain support for their initiatives. This effort requires wielding constitutional powers, building party coalitions, exploiting popular support, and exercising legislative skills.

veto

The constitutional power of the president to send a bill back to Congress with reasons for rejecting it. A two-thirds vote in each house can override a veto.

pocket veto

A type of veto occurring when Congress adjourns within 10 days of submitting a bill to the president and the president simply lets the bill die by neither signing nor vetoing it.

☐ Chief Legislator

Nowhere does the Constitution use the phrase *chief legislator*; it is strictly a phrase invented to emphasize the executive's importance in the legislative process. The Constitution simply requires that the president give a State of the Union report to Congress and instructs the president to bring other matters to Congress's attention "from time to time." But in actuality the president plays a major role in shaping the congressional agenda.

The Constitution also gives the president power to **veto** congressional legislation. Once Congress passes a bill, the president may (1) sign it, making it law; (2) veto it, sending it back to Congress with the reasons for rejecting it; or (3) let it become law after 10 working days by not doing anything. Congress can pass a vetoed law, however, if two-thirds of each house votes to override the president. In cases where Congress adjourns within 10 days of submitting a bill, the president can use a **pocket veto**, that is, simply let it die by neither signing nor vetoing it. Table 12.5 shows how frequently recent presidents have used the veto.

The presidential veto is usually effective; Congress has overridden only about 4 percent of all vetoed bills since the nation's founding. Thus, even the threat of a presidential veto can be an effective tool for persuading Congress to give more weight to the president's views. On the other hand, the veto is a blunt instrument. Presidents must accept or reject bills in their entirety; they cannot veto only the parts they do not like (in contrast, most governors have a *line-item veto*, allowing them to veto particular portions of a bill). As a result, the White House often must accept provisions of a bill it opposes in order to obtain provisions that it desires. In recent years, presidents have issued statements when they sign bills, saying they will not comply with certain provisions and, in effect, vetoing parts of bills.

Why It Matters to You
The President's Veto

Unlike most governors, the president does not have the power to veto parts of a bill. As a result, presidents cannot choose to delete, for example, items in the budget they perceive as wasteful. At the same time, the lack of a line-item veto helps to maintain the delicate balance of separate institutions sharing powers.

TABLE 12.5 PRESIDENTIAL VETOES

President	Regular Vetoes	Vetoes Overridden	Percentage of Vetoes Overridden	Pocket Vetoes	Total Vetoes
Eisenhower	73	2	3	108	181
Kennedy	12	0	0	9	21
Johnson	16	0	0	14	30
Nixon	26	7	27	17	43
Ford	48	12	25	18	66
Carter	13	2	15	18	31
Reagan	39	9	23	39	78
G. H. W. Bush	29	1	3	15	44
Clinton	37	2	5	1	38
G. W. Bush	12	4	33	0	12
Obama*	2	0	0	0	2

*as of January 2015

There are some bills, such as those appropriating funds for national defense, that *must* be passed. Knowing this, the president may veto a version containing provisions he opposes on the theory that Congress does not want to be held responsible for failing to defend the nation. Nevertheless, the presidential veto is an inherently negative resource. It is most useful for preventing legislation. Much of the time, however, presidents are more interested in passing their own legislation. To do so, they must marshal their political resources to obtain positive support for their programs. Presidents' three most useful resources are their party leadership, public support, and their own legislative skills.

Party Leadership

No matter what other resources presidents may have at their disposal, they remain highly dependent on their party to move their legislative programs. Representatives and senators of the president's party usually form the nucleus of coalitions supporting presidential proposals and provide considerably more support than do members of the opposition party. Thus, every president must provide party leadership in Congress, countering the natural tendency toward conflict between the executive and legislative branches that is inherent in the government's system of checks and balances.[20]

THE BONDS OF PARTY For most senators and representatives of the president's party, being in the same political party as the president creates a psychological bond. Personal loyalties or emotional commitments to their party and their party leader, a desire to avoid embarrassing "their" administration and thus hurting their chances for reelection, and a basic distrust of the opposition party are inclinations that produce support for the White House. Members of the same party also agree on many matters of public policy, and they are often supported by similar electoral coalitions, reinforcing the pull of party ties. These members also feel they have a collective stake in the president's success. Of course, the opposition party has incentives to resist the president. Thus, presidential leadership demarcates and deepens cleavages in Congress. The parties tend to be more cohesive on issues on which the president has taken a stand.[21]

If presidents could rely on their party members to vote for whatever the White House sent up to Capitol Hill, presidential leadership of Congress would be rather easy. All presidents would have to do is make sure members of their party showed up to vote. If their party had the majority, presidents would always win. If their party was in the minority, presidents would only have to concentrate on converting a few members of the other party.

SLIPPAGE IN PARTY SUPPORT Things are not so simple, however. Despite the pull of party ties, all presidents experience at least some slippage in the support of their party in Congress. Because presidents cannot always count on their own party members for support, even on key votes, they must be active party leaders and devote their efforts to conversion as much as to mobilization of members of their party.

The primary obstacle to party unity is the lack of consensus on policies among party members, especially in the Democratic Party. Jimmy Carter, a Democrat, remarked, "I learned the hard way that there was no party loyalty or discipline when a complicated or controversial issue was at stake—none."[22] When George W. Bush proposed reforming Social Security and immigration policy, many congressional Republicans refused to support him. Likewise, when Barack Obama negotiated deals with Republicans on taxes in 2010 and spending in 2011, many congressional Democrats voted against him.

This diversity of views often reflects the diversity of constituencies represented by party members. For decades, the defections of conservative and moderate Democrats from Democratic presidents was a prominent feature of American politics. When constituency opinion and the president's proposals conflict, members of Congress are more likely to vote with their constituents, whom they rely on for reelection. Moreover, if the president is not popular with their constituencies, congressional party members may avoid identifying too closely with the White House.

Presidents depend heavily on their party's leaders in Congress to pass their initiatives. Here, President Obama thanks House Speaker Nancy Pelosi after signing the Affordable Care Act. House Majority Leader Steny Hoyer and Senate Majority Leader Harry Reid are to her left.

LEADING THE PARTY

The president has some assets as party leader, including congressional party leaders, services, and amenities for party members, and campaign aid. Each asset is of limited utility, however.

The president's relationship with party leaders in Congress is a delicate one. Although the leaders are predisposed to support presidential policies and typically work closely with the White House, they are free to oppose the president or lend only symbolic support; some party leaders may be ineffective themselves. Moreover, party leaders, especially in the Senate, are not in strong positions to reward or discipline members of Congress.

To create goodwill with congressional party members, the White House provides them with many amenities, ranging from photographs with the president to rides on Air Force One. Perhaps more important, districts represented by members of the president's party receive more federal outlays than those represented by opposition party members.[23] Although this largesse may earn the president the benefit of the doubt on some policy initiatives, party members consider it their right to receive such favors from the White House and as a result are unlikely to be especially responsive to the president's largesse. In addition to offering a carrot, the president can, of course, wield a stick in the form of withholding favors, but this is rarely done.

If party members wish to oppose the White House, the president can do little to stop them. The parties are highly decentralized. National party leaders do not control those aspects of politics that are of vital concern to members of Congress—nominations and elections. Members of Congress are largely self-recruited, gain their party's nomination by their own efforts and not the party's, and provide most of the money and organizational support needed for their elections. Presidents can do little to influence the results of these activities.

One way for the president to improve the chances of obtaining support in Congress is to increase the number of fellow party members in the legislature. The phenomenon of **presidential coattails** occurs when voters cast their ballots for congressional candidates of the president's party because those candidates support the president. Most recent studies show that few races are determined by presidential coattails.[24] The change in party balance that usually emerges when the electoral dust has settled is strikingly small. In the 16 presidential elections between 1952 and 2012, the party of the winning presidential candidate averaged a net gain of 8 seats (out of 435) per election in the House and only 1 seat in the Senate, where the opposition party actually gained seats in 7 of the elections (see Table 12.6).

Recent presidents have campaigned actively for their party's candidates in midterm elections (those held between presidential elections), and there is evidence that they reap benefits from those members who win.[25] Nevertheless, the president's party typically *loses* seats, as you can see in Table 12.7. For example, in 1986, the Republicans lost 8 seats in the Senate, depriving President Reagan of a majority, and in 1994, the Democrats lost 8 Senate seats and 52 House seats, in the process losing control of both houses.[26] The president's party is especially likely to lose seats in the House when the president's approval rating is low and when the party gained a lot of seats in the previous election. Thus, the Democrats suffered large losses in the 2010 midterm elections, including 6 seats in the Senate and 63 in the House. In the 2014 midterms, Democrats lost 9 seats in the Senate and 16 seats in the House.

As this discussion suggests, the president's party often lacks a majority in one or both houses. Since 1953 there have been 30 years in which Republican presidents faced a Democratic House of Representatives and 22 years in which they faced a Democratic Senate. Democrat Bill Clinton faced both a House and a Senate with Republican majorities from 1995 through 2000. Barack Obama had to deal with a Republican majority in the House in 2011–2016 and in the Senate in 2015–2016.

presidential coattails
These occur when voters cast their ballots for congressional candidates of the president's party because they support the president. Research shows that few races are won this way.

TABLE 12.6 CONGRESSIONAL GAINS OR LOSSES FOR THE PRESIDENT'S PARTY IN PRESIDENTIAL ELECTION YEARS

Presidents cannot rely on their coattails to carry their party's legislators into office to help pass White House legislative programs. The president's party typically gains few, if any, seats when the president wins election. For instance, the Republicans lost seats in both houses when President George W. Bush was elected in 2000.

Year	President	House	Senate
1952	Eisenhower (R)	+22	+1
1956	Eisenhower (R)	−2	−1
1960	Kennedy (D)	−22	−2
1964	Johnson (D)	+37	+1
1968	Nixon (R)	+5	+6
1972	Nixon (R)	+12	−2
1976	Carter (D)	+1	0
1980	Reagan (R)	+34	+12
1984	Reagan (R)	+14	−2
1988	G. Bush (R)	−3	−1
1992	Clinton (D)	−10	0
1996	Clinton (D)	+9	−2
2000	G. W. Bush (R)	−2	−4
2004	G. W. Bush (R)	+3	+4
2008	Obama (D)	+21	+8
2012	Obama (D)	+8	+1
	Average	+7.9	+1.2

TABLE 12.7 CONGRESSIONAL GAINS OR LOSSES FOR THE PRESIDENT'S PARTY IN MIDTERM ELECTION YEARS

For decades, the president's party typically lost seats in midterm elections. Thus, presidents could not be certain of helping to elect members of their party once in office. The elections of 1998 and 2002 deviated from this pattern, and the president's party gained a few seats.

Year	President	House	Senate
1954	Eisenhower (R)	–18	–1
1958	Eisenhower (R)	–47	–13
1962	Kennedy (D)	–4	+3
1966	Johnson (D)	–47	–4
1970	Nixon (R)	–12	+2
1974	Ford (R)	–47	–5
1978	Carter (D)	–15	–3
1982	Reagan (R)	–26	0
1986	Reagan (R)	–5	–8
1990	G. Bush (R)	–9	–1
1994	Clinton (D)	–52	–8
1998	Clinton (D)	+5	0
2002	G. W. Bush (R)	+6	+2
2006	G. W. Bush (R)	–30	–6
2010	Obama (D)	–63	–6
2014*	Obama (D)	–16	–9
	Average	–24	–3

*Data available at press time.

Lacking majorities and/or dependable party support, the president usually has to solicit help from the opposition party. This is often a futile endeavor, however, since the opposition is generally not fertile ground for seeking support. Nevertheless, even a few votes may be enough to give the president the required majority.

Public Support

One of the president's most important resources for leading Congress is public support. Presidents who enjoy the backing of the public have an easier time influencing Congress. Said one top aide to Ronald Reagan, "Everything here is built on the idea that the president's success depends on grassroots support."[27] Presidents with low approval ratings in the polls find it difficult to influence Congress. As one of President Carter's aides put it when the president was low in the polls, "No president whose popularity is as low as this president's has much clout on the Hill."[28] Members of Congress and others in Washington closely watch two indicators of public support for the president: approval in the polls and mandates in presidential elections.

PUBLIC APPROVAL Members of Congress anticipate the public's reactions to their support for or opposition to presidents and their policies. They may choose to be close to or independent of the White House—depending on the president's standing with the public—to increase their chances for reelection. Representatives and senators may also use the president's standing in the polls as an indicator of presidential ability to mobilize public opinion against presidential opponents.

Public approval also makes the president's other leadership resources more efficacious. If the president is high in the public's esteem, the president's party is more likely to be responsive, the public is more easily moved, and legislative skills become more effective. Thus public approval is the political resource that has the most potential to turn a stalemate between the president and Congress into a situation supportive of the president's legislative proposals.

Widespread public support gives the president leeway and weakens resistance to presidential policies. It provides a cover for members of Congress to cast votes to which their constituents might otherwise object. They can defend their votes as support for the president rather than support for a certain policy alone.

Conversely, lack of public support narrows the range in which presidential policies receive the benefit of the doubt and strengthens the resolve of the president's opponents. Low ratings in the polls may also create incentives to attack the president, further eroding a weakened position. For example, after the U.S. occupation of Iraq turned sour and the country rejected his proposal to reform Social Security, it became more acceptable in Congress and in the press to raise questions about George W. Bush's capacities as president. Disillusionment is a difficult force for the White House to combat.

The impact of public approval or disapproval on the support the president receives in Congress is important, but it occurs at the margins of the effort to build coalitions behind proposed policies. No matter how low presidential standing dips, the president still receives support from a substantial number of senators and representatives. Similarly, no matter how high approval levels climb, a significant portion of Congress will still oppose certain presidential policies. Members of Congress are unlikely to vote against the clear interests of their constituencies or the firm tenets of their ideology out of deference to a widely supported chief executive. George W. Bush enjoyed very high public approval following the terrorist attacks of September 11, 2001, but Democrats did not support his domestic policy proposals. Public approval gives the president leverage, not command.[29]

In addition, presidents cannot depend on having the approval of the public, and it is not a resource over which they have much control, as we will see later. Once again, it is clear that presidents' leadership resources do not allow them to dominate Congress.

ELECTORAL MANDATES The results of presidential elections are another indicator of public opinion regarding presidents. An *electoral mandate*—the perception that the voters strongly support the president and his policies—can be a powerful symbol in American politics. It accords added legitimacy and credibility to the newly elected president's proposals. Moreover, concerns for both representation and political survival encourage members of Congress to support new presidents if they feel the people have spoken.[30]

More importantly, mandates change the premises of decisions. Following Roosevelt's decisive win in the 1932 election, the essential question became *how* government should act to fight the Depression rather than *whether* it should act. Similarly, following Johnson's overwhelming win in the 1964 election, the dominant question in Congress was not whether to pass new social programs but how many social programs to pass and how much to increase spending. In 1981, the tables were turned; Ronald Reagan's victory placed a stigma on big government and exalted the unregulated marketplace and large defense efforts. Reagan had won a major victory even before the first congressional vote.

Although presidential elections can structure choices for Congress, merely winning an election does not provide presidents with a mandate. Every election produces a winner, but mandates are much less common. Even large electoral victories, such as Richard Nixon's in 1972 and Ronald Reagan's in 1984, carry no guarantee that Congress will interpret the results as mandates from the people to support the president's programs. Perceptions of a mandate are weak if the winning candidate did not stress his policy plans in the campaign, as in 1972 and 1984, or if the voters also elected majorities in Congress from the other party, as in 1972 (of course, the winner may *claim* a mandate anyway).[31]

□ Legislative Skills

Presidential legislative skills include bargaining, making personal appeals, consulting with Congress, setting priorities, exploiting "honeymoon" periods, and structuring congressional votes. Of these skills, bargaining receives perhaps the most attention from commentators on the presidency.

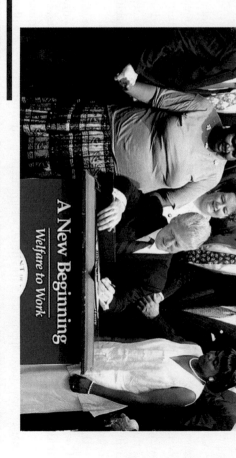

Presidents find the role of legislative leader a challenging one. Often they must compromise with opponents in Congress, as President Bill Clinton did in 1996 when he signed the welfare reform bill.

BARGAINING Reagan's budget director David Stockman recalled that "the last 10 or 20 percent of the votes needed for a majority of both houses on the 1981 tax cut had to be bought, period." The concessions for members of Congress included special breaks for oil-lease holders, real estate tax shelters, and generous loopholes that virtually eliminated the corporate income tax. "The hogs were really feeding," declared Stockman. "The greed level, the level of opportunities, just got out of control."[32]

Nevertheless, such bargaining—trading support on policies or providing specific benefits for representatives and senators—occurs less often and plays a less critical role in the creation of presidential coalitions in Congress than one might think. For obvious reasons, the White House does not want to encourage the type of bargaining Stockman describes, and there is a scarcity of resources with which to bargain, especially in an era where balancing the budget is a prominent goal for policymakers.

Moreover, the president does not have to bargain with every member of Congress to receive support. On controversial issues on which bargaining may be useful, the president usually starts with a sizable core of party supporters. To this group he may add those of the opposition party who provide support on ideological or policy grounds as well as those who provide support because of relevant constituency interests or strong public approval. The president needs to bargain only if this coalition does not provide a majority (or two-thirds on treaties and one-third on avoiding veto overrides).

MOVING FAST Presidents may improve their chances of success in Congress by making certain strategic moves. It is wise, for example, for a new president to be ready to send legislation to the Hill early during the first year in office in order to exploit the "honeymoon" atmosphere that typically characterizes this period. Lyndon Johnson, Ronald Reagan, and George W. Bush took advantage of this one-shot opportunity.

SETTING PRIORITIES An important aspect of presidential legislative strategy can be establishing priorities among legislative proposals. The goal of this effort is to set Congress's agenda. If presidents are unable to focus the attention of Congress on their priority programs, these programs may become lost in the complex and overloaded legislative process. Setting priorities is also important because presidents and their staffs can lobby effectively for only a few bills at a time. Moreover, each president's political capital is inevitably limited, and it is sensible to focus on a limited range of personally important issues; otherwise, this precious resource might be wasted.

The president is the nation's key agenda builder; what the administration wants strongly influences the parameters of Washington debate.[33] John Kingdon's careful study of the Washington agenda found that "no other single actor in the political system has quite the capability of the president to set agendas."[34] There are limits to what the president can do, however.

Although the White House can put off dealing with many national issues at the beginning of a new president's term in order to focus on its highest priority legislation, it cannot do so indefinitely. Eventually it must make decisions about a wide range of matters. Soon the legislative agenda is full and more policies are in the pipeline as the administration attempts to satisfy its constituents and responds to unanticipated or simply overlooked problems. Moreover, Congress is quite capable of setting its own agenda, providing competition for the president's proposals.

In general, presidential legislative skills must compete—as presidential public support does—with other, more stable factors that affect voting in Congress: party, ideology, personal views and commitments on specific policies, constituency interests, and so on. By the time a president tries to exercise influence on a vote, most members of Congress have made up their minds on the basis of these other factors.

After accounting for the status of the president's party in Congress and standing with the public, systematic studies have found that presidents known for their legislative skills (such as Lyndon Johnson) are no more successful in winning votes, even close ones, or obtaining congressional support than those considered less adept at dealing with Congress (such as Jimmy Carter).[35] The president's legislative skills are not at the core of presidential leadership of Congress. Even skilled presidents cannot reshape the contours of the political landscape and *create* opportunities for change. They can, however, recognize favorable configurations of political forces—such as existed in 1933, 1965, and 1981—and effectively exploit them to embark on major shifts in public policy.

Perhaps the most important role of presidents—and their heaviest burden—is their responsibility for national security. Dealing with Congress is only one of the many challenges presidents face in the realm of defense and foreign policy.

The President and National Security Policy

12.5 Analyze the president's powers in making national security policy and the relationship between the president and Congress in this arena.

onstitutionally, the president has the leading role in American defense and foreign policy (often termed *national security policy*). Such matters, ranging from foreign trade to war and peace, occupy much of the president's time. There are several dimensions to the president's national security responsibilities, including negotiating with other nations, commanding the armed forces, waging war, managing crises, and obtaining the necessary support in Congress.

☐ Chief Diplomat

The Constitution allocates certain powers in the realm of national security exclusively to the executive. The president alone extends diplomatic recognition to foreign governments—as Jimmy Carter did on December 14, 1978, when he announced the exchange of ambassadors with the People's Republic of China. The president can also terminate relations with other nations, as Carter did with Iran after Americans were taken hostage in Tehran.

The president also has the sole power to negotiate treaties with other nations, although the Constitution requires the Senate to approve them by a two-thirds vote. Sometimes

Presidents usually conduct diplomatic relations through envoys, but occasionally they engage in personal diplomacy. Here, President Carter celebrates a peace agreement he brokered between Israeli Prime Minister Menachem Begin and Egyptian President Anwar Sadat.

presidents win and sometimes they lose when presenting a treaty to the Senate. After extensive lobbying, Jimmy Carter persuaded the Senate to approve a treaty returning the Panama Canal to Panama (over objections such as those of one senator who declared, "We stole it fair and square"). Bill Clinton was not so lucky when he sought ratification of the Comprehensive Nuclear Test Ban Treaty. The Senate rejected it in 1999. At other times senators add "reservations" to the treaties they ratify, altering the treaty in the process.[36]

In addition to treaties, presidents also negotiate *executive agreements* with the heads of foreign governments. Executive agreements do not require Senate ratification (although the president is supposed to report them to Congress and they may require implementing legislation passed by majorities of each house.) Most executive agreements are routine and deal with noncontroversial subjects such as food deliveries or customs enforcement, but some, such as the Vietnam peace agreement and the SALT I agreement limiting offensive nuclear weapons, implement important and controversial policies.[37]

Occasionally presidential diplomacy involves more than negotiating on behalf of the United States. Theodore Roosevelt won the Nobel Peace Prize for his role in settling the war between Japan and Russia. One of Jimmy Carter's greatest achievements was forging a peace treaty between Egypt and Israel. For 13 days he mediated negotiations between the leaders of both countries at his presidential retreat, Camp David.

As the leader of the Western world, the president must try to lead America's allies on matters of both economics and defense. This is not an easy task, as Barack Obama experienced in dealing with the world financial crisis and George W. Bush found in his attempts to obtain support for invading Iraq. Given the natural independence of sovereign nations, the increasing economic might of other countries, and the many competing influences on policymaking in other nations, the president will continue to find such leadership challenging.

☐ Commander in Chief

Because the Constitution's Framers wanted civilian control of the military, they made the president the commander in chief of the armed forces. President George Washington actually led troops to crush the Whiskey Rebellion in 1794. Today, presidents do not take the task quite so literally, but their military decisions have changed the course of history.

When the Constitution was written, the United States did not have—nor did anyone expect it to have—a large standing or permanent army. Today the president is commander in chief of about 1.4 million uniformed men and women. In his farewell address, George Washington warned against permanent alliances, but today America has commitments to defend nations across the globe. Even more important, the president commands a vast nuclear arsenal. Never more than a few steps from the president is "the football," a briefcase with the codes needed to unleash nuclear war. The Constitution, of course, states that only Congress has the power to declare war, but it is unreasonable to believe that Congress can convene, debate, and vote on a declaration of war in the case of a nuclear attack.

☐ War Powers

Perhaps no issue of executive–legislative relations generates more controversy than the continuing dispute over war powers. Although charged by the Constitution with declaring war and voting on the military budget, Congress long ago accepted that presidents make short-term military commitments of troops, aircraft, or naval vessels. In recent decades, however, presidents have paid even less attention to constitutional details; for example, Congress never declared war during the conflicts in either Korea or Vietnam.

In 1973, Congress passed the **War Powers Resolution** (over President Nixon's veto). A reaction to disillusionment about American fighting in Vietnam and Cambodia, the law was intended to give Congress a greater voice in the introduction of American troops into hostilities. It required presidents to consult with Congress, whenever possible, before using military force, and it mandated the withdrawal of forces after 60 days unless Congress declared war or granted an extension. Congress could at any time pass a resolution that could not be vetoed, ending American participation in hostilities.

War Powers Resolution

A law passed in 1973, in reaction to American fighting in Vietnam and Cambodia, that requires presidents to consult with Congress whenever possible prior to using military force and to withdraw forces after 60 days unless Congress declares war or grants an extension. However, presidents have viewed the resolution as unconstitutional.

The president commands vast military resources, ranging from nuclear weapons and aircraft carriers to armies and special forces. Here, President Obama and his national security team watch the Navy Seals raid the compound of Osama bin Laden in 2011.

12.1

12.2

12.3

12.4

12.5

12.6

12.7

12.8

legislative veto

A vote in Congress to override a presidential decision. Although the War Powers Resolution asserts this authority, there is reason to believe that, if challenged, the Supreme Court would find the legislative veto in violation of the doctrine of separation of powers.

crisis

A sudden, unpredictable, and potentially dangerous event requiring the president to play the role of crisis manager.

Congress cannot regard the War Powers Resolution as a success, however. All presidents serving since 1973 have deemed the law an unconstitutional infringement on their powers as commander in chief, and there is reason to believe the Supreme Court would consider the law's use of the **legislative veto** (the ability of Congress to pass a resolution to override a presidential decision) to be a violation of the doctrine of separation of powers. Presidents have largely ignored the law and sent troops into hostilities, sometimes with heavy loss of life, without effectual consultation with Congress. The legislature has found it difficult to challenge the president, especially when American troops were endangered, and the courts have been reluctant to hear a congressional challenge on what would be construed as a political, rather than a legal, issue.[38]

For example, exercising his powers as commander in chief, George H. W. Bush on his own authority moved half a million troops to Saudi Arabia to liberate Kuwait after its invasion by Iraq in 1990. Congress averted a constitutional crisis when it passed (on a divided vote) a resolution authorizing the president to use force against Iraq. Bill Clinton in 1999 authorized the United States to take the leading role in a sustained air attack against Serbia to stop ethnic conflict there, but Congress could not agree on a resolution supporting the use of force. Barack Obama did not seek congressional authorization for U.S. support of NATO-led efforts to protect civilians in the Civil War in Libya and support efforts to overthrow that country's dictator.

George W. Bush faced little opposition to responding to the terrorist attacks of September 11, 2001. Congress immediately passed a resolution authorizing the use of force against the perpetrators of the attacks. The next year, Congress passed a resolution authorizing the president to use force against Iraq. However, Congress was less deferential to presidential war powers when the press revealed U.S. mistreatment of prisoners of war and the president's authorization (without a judicial warrant) of the National Security Agency to spy on persons residing within the United States.

Analysts continue to raise questions about the relevance of America's 200-year-old constitutional mechanisms for engaging in war. Some observers worry that the rapid response capabilities afforded the president by modern technology allow him to bypass congressional opposition, thus undermining the separation of powers. Others stress the importance of the commander in chief having the flexibility to meet America's global responsibilities and combat international terrorism without the hindrance of congressional checks and balances. All agree that the change in the nature of warfare brought about by nuclear weapons inevitably delegates to the president the ultimate decision to use such weapons.

Why It Matters to You

War Powers

The United States has never fully resolved the question of the president's war powers. The ambiguity about presidents' powers frees them from what some see as excessive constraints on their ability to conduct an effective foreign policy. On the other hand, if the president could only send troops into combat after a congressional resolution authorizing the use of force, it is possible that we would be less likely to go to war.

☐ **Crisis Manager**

The president's roles as chief diplomat and commander in chief are related to another presidential responsibility: crisis management. A **crisis** is a sudden, unpredictable, and potentially dangerous event. Most crises occur in the realm of foreign policy. They often involve hot tempers and high risks; quick judgments must be made on the basis of

Crisis management may be the most difficult of the president's many roles. By definition, crises are sudden, unpredictable, and dangerous. Here President George W. Bush meets with firefighters and rescue workers at the World Trade Center site three days after the terrorist attacks of September 11, 2001.

sketchy information. Be it American hostages held in Iran for Jimmy Carter or the discovery of Soviet missiles in Cuba for John F. Kennedy, a crisis challenges the president to make difficult decisions. Crises are rarely the president's doing, but handled incorrectly, they can be the president's undoing. On the other hand, handling a crisis well can remake a president's image, as George W. Bush found following the terrorist attacks of September 11, 2001.

Early in American history there were fewer immediate crises. By the time officials were aware of a problem, it often had resolved itself. Communications could take weeks or even months to reach Washington. Similarly, officials' decisions often took weeks or months to reach those who were to implement them. The most famous land battle of the War of 1812, the Battle of New Orleans, was fought *after* the United States had signed a peace treaty with Great Britain. Word of the treaty did not reach the battlefield; thus, General Andrew Jackson won a victory for the United States that contributed nothing toward ending the war, although it did help put him in the White House as the seventh president.

With modern communications, the president can instantly monitor events almost anywhere. Moreover, because situations develop more rapidly today, there is a premium on rapid action, secrecy, constant management, consistent judgment, and expert advice. Congress usually moves slowly (one might say deliberately), and it is large (making secrecy difficult), decentralized (requiring continual compromising), and composed of generalists. As a result, the president—who can come to quick and consistent decisions, confine information to a small group, carefully oversee developments, and call on experts in the executive branch—has become more prominent in handling crises.

406

12.1
12.2
12.3
12.4
12.5
12.6
12.7
12.8

Working with Congress

As America moves through its third century under the Constitution, presidents might wish the Framers had been less concerned with checks and balances in the area of national security. In recent years, Congress has challenged presidents on all fronts, including intelligence operations; the treatment of prisoners of war; foreign aid; arms sales; the development, procurement, and deployment of weapons systems; the negotiation and interpretation of treaties; the selection of diplomats; and the continuation of nuclear testing.

Congress has a central constitutional role in making national security policy, although this role is often misunderstood. The allocation of responsibilities for such matters is based on the Founders' apprehensions about the concentration of power and the potential for its abuse. They divided the powers of supply and command, for example, in order to thwart adventurism in national security affairs. Congress can thus refuse to provide the necessary authorizations and appropriations for presidential actions, whereas the chief executive can refuse to act (for example, by not sending troops into battle at the behest of the legislature).

Despite the constitutional role of Congress, the president is the driving force behind national security policy, providing energy and direction. Congress is well organized to deliberate openly on the discrete components of policy, but it is not well designed to take the lead on national security matters. Its role has typically been overseeing the executive rather than initiating policy.[39] Congress frequently originates proposals for domestic policy, but it is less involved in national security policy.[40]

The president has a more prominent role in foreign affairs as the country's sole representative in dealing with other nations and as commander in chief of the armed forces (functions that effectively preclude a wide range of congressional diplomatic and military initiatives). In addition, the nature of national security issues may make the failure to integrate the elements of policy more costly than in domestic policy. Thus, members of Congress typically prefer to encourage, criticize, or support the president rather than to initiate their own national security policy. If leadership occurs, it is usually centered in the White House.

Although Congress is typically reactive on national security policy, it can constrain the president, even on the initiation, scope, and duration of military actions. Members can introduce legislation to curtail the use of force, hold oversight hearings, and engage in debate over military policymaking in the public sphere. Such debate influences public opinion and thus raises the cost of military action for the president.[41]

Commentators on the presidency often refer to the "two presidencies"—one for domestic policy and the other for national security policy.[42] By this phrase they mean that the president has more success in leading Congress on matters of national security than on matters of domestic policy. The typical member of Congress, however, supports the president on roll-call votes about national security only slightly more than half the time. There is a significant gap between what the president requests and what members of Congress are willing to give. Certainly the legislature does not accord the president automatic support on national security policy.[43] Nevertheless, presidents do end up obtaining much, often most, of what they request from Congress on national security issues. Some of the support they receive is the result of agreement on policy; other support comes from the president's ability to act first, placing Congress in a reactive position and opening it to the charge that it is undermining U.S. foreign policy if it challenges the president's initiatives.

Presidents need resources to influence others to support their policies. One important presidential asset can be the support of the American people. The following sections will take a closer look at how the White House tries to increase and use public support.

Power from the People: The Public Presidency

"Public sentiment is everything. With public sentiment nothing can fail; without it nothing can succeed." These words, spoken by Abraham Lincoln, pose what is perhaps the greatest challenge to any president—to obtain and maintain the public's support. Because presidents are rarely in a position to command others to comply with their wishes, they must rely on persuasion. Public support is perhaps the greatest source of influence a president has, for it is more difficult for other power holders in a democracy to deny the legitimate demands of a president with popular backing.

☐ Going Public

Presidents are not passive followers of public opinion; they actively try to shape it. The White House is a virtual whirlwind of public relations activity.[44] Beginning with John Kennedy, the first "television president," presidents, with the notable exception of Richard Nixon, have been active in making public presentations. Indeed, they have averaged more than one appearance every weekday of the year in their attempts to obtain the public's support for themselves and their policies.

Often the White House stages the president's appearances purely to get the public's attention. George W. Bush chose to announce the end of major combat in Iraq on board the aircraft carrier the *Abraham Lincoln*. The White House's Office of Communications choreographed every aspect of the event, including positioning the aircraft carrier so the shoreline could not be seen by the camera when the president landed, arraying members of the crew in coordinated shirt colors over Bush's right shoulder, placing a banner reading "Mission Accomplished" to perfectly capture the president and the celebratory two words in a single camera shot, and timing the speech so the sun cast a golden glow on the president. In such a case, the president could have simply made an announcement, but the need for public support drives the

Presidents often use commercial public relations techniques to win support for their policy initiatives. President George W. Bush, for example, used the backdrop of an aircraft carrier to announce the end of the war in Iraq and obtain support for his stewardship.

White House to employ public relations techniques similar to those used to publicize commercial products.

In many democracies, different people occupy the jobs of head of state and head of government. For example, the queen is head of state in England, but she holds little power in government and politics. In America, these roles are fused. As head of state, the president is America's ceremonial leader and symbol of government. Trivial but time-consuming activities—tossing out the first baseball of the season, lighting the White House Christmas tree, meeting an extraordinary Boy or Girl Scout—are part of the ceremonial function of the presidency. Meeting foreign heads of state, receiving ambassadors' credentials, and making global goodwill tours represent the international side of this role. Presidents rarely shirk these duties, even when they are not inherently important. Ceremonial activities give them an important symbolic aura and a great deal of favorable press coverage, contributing to their efforts to build public support.

☐ Presidential Approval

The White House aims much of the energy it devotes to public relations at increasing the president's public approval. It believes that the higher the president stands in the polls, the easier it is to persuade others to support presidential initiatives. Because of the connection between public support and presidential influence, the press, members of Congress, and others in the Washington political community closely monitor the president's standing in the polls. For years, the Gallup Poll has asked Americans, "Do you approve or disapprove of the way [name of president] is handling his job as president?" You can see the results for presidents beginning with Eisenhower in Figure 12.3.

Presidents frequently do not have widespread public support, often failing to win even majority approval, as Figure 12.3 shows. For Presidents Nixon, Ford, Carter, George W. Bush, and Barack Obama, this average approval level was under 50 percent, and for Ronald Reagan it was only 52 percent. Although George H. W. Bush enjoyed much higher average approval levels for three years, in his fourth year his ratings dropped below 40 percent. Bill Clinton struggled to rise above the 50 percent mark in his first term.

FIGURE 12.3 PRESIDENTIAL APPROVAL

Most presidents seem to be most popular when they first enter office; later on, their popularity often erodes. Bill Clinton was an exception, enjoying higher approval in his second term than in his first. George W. Bush had high approval following 9/11, but public support diminished steadily after that.

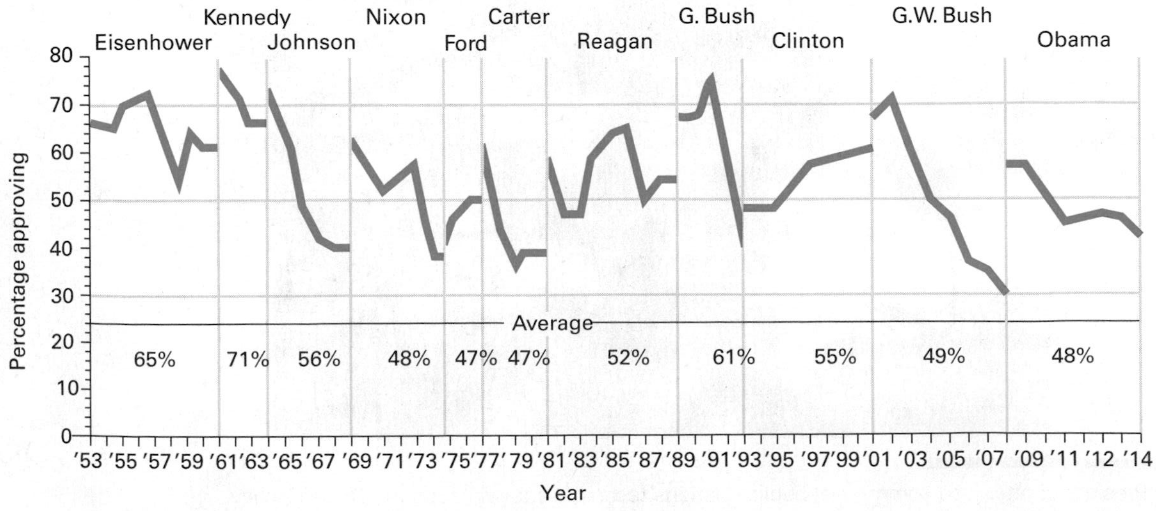

SOURCE: George C. Edwards III, *Presidential Approval* (Baltimore, MD: Johns Hopkins University Press, 1990); updated by the authors.

Presidential approval is the product of many factors.[45] Political party identification provides the basic underpinning of approval or disapproval and mediates the impact of other factors. Partisans are not inclined to approve presidents of the other party. Historically, those who identify with the president's party give the president approval more than 40 percentage points higher than do those who identify with the opposition party. In the more polarized times under George W. Bush and Barack Obama, this difference rose to more than 70 percentage points.

Presidents usually benefit from a "honeymoon" with the American people after taking office. Some observers believe that "honeymoons" are a fleeting phenomenon, with the public affording new occupants of the White House only a short grace period before they begin their inevitable descent in the polls. You can see in Figure 12.3 that declines do take place, but they are neither inevitable nor swift. Throughout his two terms in office, Ronald Reagan experienced considerable volatility in his relations with the public, but his record certainly shows that support can be revived; Bill Clinton enjoyed more approval in his second term than in his first.

Changes in approval levels appear to reflect the public's evaluation of how the president is handling policy areas such as the economy, war, and foreign affairs. Different policies are salient to the public at different times. For example, if international acts of terrorism on American interests are increasing, then foreign policy is likely to dominate the news and to be on the minds of Americans. If the economy turns sour, then people are going to be concerned about unemployment.

Contrary to conventional wisdom, citizens seem to focus on the president's efforts and stands on issues rather than on personality ("popularity") or simply how presidential policies affect them (the "pocketbook"). Job-related personal characteristics of the president, such as integrity and leadership skills, also play an important role in influencing presidential approval.

Sometimes public approval of the president takes sudden jumps. One popular explanation for these surges of support is "rally events," which John Mueller defined as events that are related to international relations, directly involve the United States and particularly the president, and are specific, dramatic, and sharply focused.[46] A classic example is the 18-percentage-point rise in President George H. W. Bush's approval ratings immediately after the Gulf War began in 1991. George W. Bush's approval shot up 39 percentage points in September 2001. Such occurrences are unusual and isolated events, however; they usually have little enduring impact on a president's public approval. George H. W. Bush, for example, dropped precipitously in the polls and lost his bid for reelection in 1992.

The criteria on which the public evaluates presidents—such as the way they are handling the economy, where they stand on complex issues, and whether they are "strong" leaders—are open to many interpretations. Different people see things differently (see "Young People & Politics: The Generation Gap in Presidential Approval"). The modern White House makes extraordinary efforts to control the context in which presidents appear in public and the way they are portrayed by the press in order to try to influence how the public views them. The fact that presidents are frequently low in the polls anyway is persuasive testimony to the limits of presidential leadership of the public. As one student of the public presidency put it, "The supply of popular support rests on opinion dynamics over which the president may exert little direct control."[47]

□ Policy Support

Commentators on the presidency often refer to it as a "bully pulpit," implying that presidents can persuade or even mobilize the public to support their policies if they are skilled communicators. Certainly presidents frequently do attempt to obtain public support for their policies with television or radio appearances and speeches to large groups.[48] All presidents since Truman have had media advice from experts on lighting, makeup, stage settings, camera angles, clothing, pacing of delivery, and other facets of making speeches.

Young People & Politics
The Generation Gap in Presidential Approval

P residential approval is not uniform across different groups in society. Young people approve of President Obama at higher rates than do other age groups, and especially more than those 65 or older. The higher approval could be because the younger generation is more liberal than are their elders, because it includes a higher percentage of minorities, because the president has made a special effort to reach out to young people via the Internet, or because of some other reasons.

Question: Do you approve or disapprove of the way Barack Obama is handling his job as president?

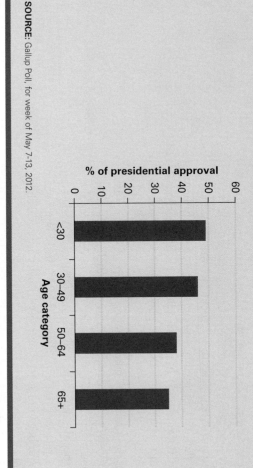

% of presidential approval

Age category

SOURCE: Gallup Poll, for week of May 7–13, 2012.

CRITICAL THINKING QUESTIONS

1. Why do you think young people are more supportive of President Obama than are their elders?

2. Do you think policymakers pay as much attention to the opinions of young people as to the opinions of those over 65?

Despite this aid and despite politicians' speaking experience, presidential speeches designed to lead public opinion have typically been rather unimpressive. In the modern era, experts consider only Franklin D. Roosevelt, John Kennedy, Ronald Reagan, Bill Clinton, and Barack Obama to have been especially effective speakers. Partly because of his limitations as a public speaker, George H. W. Bush waited until he had been in office for over seven months before making his first nationally televised address.

Moreover, the public is not always receptive to the president's message. For the most part, Americans are not especially interested in politics and government; thus, it is not easy to get their attention. Citizens also have predispositions about public policy (however ill informed) that filter presidential messages. When people encounter political information, they must balance two conflicting roles: as "updaters" who want to perceive the world objectively and as motivated reasoners who distort information to make it consistent with their political preferences. The more salient people's partisan identities—which are especially heightened during the long presidential campaigns and in an era of extreme partisan polarization—the more difficult it is for the president to get his message through.[49]

The public may miss the point of even the most colorful rhetoric or get its basic facts wrong, and thus may have difficulty evaluating policies sensibly. In his 2010 State of the Union address, President Obama declared that as part of its economic recovery plan, his administration had passed 25 different tax cuts. At about the same time in a Super Bowl Sunday interview, he touted the tax cuts in the stimulus package.

Ronald Reagan actively sought public support for his policies. Despite his skills as a communicator, he typically failed to move the public in his direction.

Nevertheless, shortly afterward, 24 percent of the public responded that the administration had *increased* taxes, and 53 percent said it kept taxes the same.[50] By the end of October, 52 percent of likely voters thought taxes had gone up for the middle class.[51]

Ronald Reagan, sometimes called the "Great Communicator," was certainly interested in policy change and went to unprecedented lengths to influence public opinion on behalf of such policies as deregulation, decreases in spending on domestic policy, and increases in the defense budget. Bill Clinton, also an extraordinarily able communicator, traveled widely and spoke out constantly on behalf of his policies, such as those dealing with the economy, health care reform, and free trade. Nevertheless, both presidents were typically unable to obtain the public's support for their initiatives.[52] More recently, George W. Bush made an extraordinary effort to obtain public backing for his stewardship of the war in Iraq and his proposal to reform Social Security. Like his predecessors, he was unsuccessful.[53] Similarly, Barack Obama was not able to rally the public behind his efforts to reform health care or for most of the elements of his economic policy. In the absence of national crises, most people are unreceptive to political appeals.

☐ Mobilizing the Public

Sometimes merely changing public opinion is not sufficient—the president wants the public to communicate its views directly to Congress. Mobilization of the public may be the ultimate weapon in the president's arsenal of resources with which to influence Congress. When the people speak, especially when they speak clearly, Congress listens.

Press coverage of the president is pervasive because of the importance of the presidency. At the same time, the press is the primary means by which the president communicates with the public. Here President Obama answers questions from the press in the White House briefing room.

The President and the Press

12.7 Characterize the president's relations with the press and news coverage of the presidency.

D espite all their efforts to lead public opinion, presidents do not directly reach the American people on a day-to-day basis. The mass media provide people with most of what they know about chief executives and their policies. The media also interpret and analyze presidential activities, even the president's direct appeals to the public. The press is thus the principal intermediary between the president and the public, and relations with the press are an important aspect of the president's efforts to lead public opinion.[54]

No matter who is in the White House or who reports on presidential activities, presidents and the press tend to be in conflict. George Washington complained that the "calumnies" against his administration were "outrages of common decency." Thomas Jefferson once declared that "nothing in a newspaper is to be believed." Presidents are policy advocates and thus want to control the amount and timing of information about their administration. The press, in contrast, wants all the information that exists without delay. As long as their goals are different, presidents and the media are likely to be adversaries.

Because of the importance of the press to the president, the White House monitors the media closely. The White House also goes to great lengths to encourage the media

However, the president is rarely able to mobilize the public because doing so involves overcoming formidable barriers. It entails the double burden of obtaining both opinion support and political action from a generally inattentive and apathetic public. In addition, the effort to mobilize the public is a risky strategy. If the president tries to mobilize the public and fails, the lack of response speaks clearly to members of Congress.

to project a positive image of the president's activities and policies. About one-third of the high-level White House staff members are directly involved in media relations and policy of one type or another, and most staff members are involved at some time in trying to influence the media's portrayal of the president.

The person who most often deals directly with the press is the president's *press secretary*, who serves as a conduit of information from the White House to the press. Press secretaries conduct daily press briefings, giving prepared announcements and answering questions. They and their staff also arrange private interviews with White House officials (often done on a background basis, in which the reporter may not attribute remarks to the person being interviewed), photo opportunities, and travel arrangements for reporters when the president leaves Washington.

The best-known direct interaction between the president and the press is the formal presidential press conference. Since the presidency of George H. W. Bush, however, prime-time televised press conferences have become relatively rare events. Presidents often travel around the country to gain television time to spread their messages. Barack Obama favors interviews with individual journalists as a means of reaching the public.

☐ Nature of News Coverage

Most of the news coverage of the White House comes under the heading "body watch." In other words, reporters focus on the most visible layer of the president's personal and official activities and provide the public with step-by-step accounts. They are interested in what presidents are going to do, how their actions will affect others, how they view policies and individuals, and how they present themselves, rather than in the substance of policies or the fundamental processes operating in the executive branch. Former ABC White House correspondent Sam Donaldson tells of covering a meeting of Western leaders on the island of Guadeloupe. It was a slow news day, so Donaldson did a story on the roasting of the pig the leaders would be eating that night, including "an exclusive look at the oven in which the pig would be roasted."[55] Because there are daily deadlines to meet and television reporters must squeeze their stories into sound bites measured in seconds, not minutes, there is little time for reflection, analysis, or comprehensive coverage.

Bias is the most politically charged issue in relations between the president and the press. A large number of studies have concluded that the news media, including the television networks and major newspapers, are not biased *systematically* toward a particular person, party, or ideology, as measured in the amount or favorability of coverage.[56] Cable news channels, especially Fox and MSNBC, are another story and have numerous commentators who approach the news from an ideological perspective.

To conclude that most news outlets contain little explicitly partisan or ideological bias is not to argue that the news does not distort reality in its coverage of the president. As the following excerpt from Jimmy Carter's diary regarding a visit to a U.S. Army base in Panama in 1978 illustrates, "objective" reporting can be misleading:

I told the Army troops that I was in the Navy for 11 years, and they booed. I told them that we depended on the Army to keep the Canal open, and they cheered. Later, the news reports said that there were boos and cheers during my speech.[57]

The news tends to be superficial, oversimplified, and often overblown, all of which means it provides the public with a distorted view of, among other things, presidential activities, statements, policies, and options. We also see that the press prefers to frame the news in themes, which both simplifies complex issues and events and provides continuity of persons, institutions, and issues. Once these themes are established, the press tends to maintain them in subsequent stories. Of necessity, themes emphasize some information at the expense of other information, often determining what is covered and the context in which it is presented. For example, once a stereotype of President Ford as a "bumbler" was established, his every stumble was magnified as the press emphasized behavior that fit the mold. He was repeatedly forced to defend his intelligence, and many of his acts and statements were reported as efforts to "act" presidential.[58]

News coverage of the presidency often tends to emphasize the negative (even if the presentation is seemingly neutral).[59] President Clinton received mostly negative coverage during his tenure in office, with a ratio of negative to positive comments on network television of about 2 to 1.[60] When the story broke regarding his affair with Monica Lewinsky, the press engaged in a feeding frenzy, providing an extraordinary amount of information on both the affair and the president's attempts to cover it up.[61] The trend of negative coverage continued in the George W. Bush[62] and Barack Obama presidencies.

In the past, most editors were reluctant to publish analyses sharply divergent from the president's position without direct confirmation from an authoritative source who would be willing to go on the record in opposition to the White House. This approach restrained media criticism of the president. During the famous investigation of the Watergate scandal, the *Washington Post* verified all information attributed to an unnamed source with at least one other independent source. It also did not print information from other media outlets unless its reporters could independently verify that information.[63] Things have changed, however.

The press relied on analysis, opinion, and speculation as much as on confirmed facts in its coverage of President Clinton's relations with Monica Lewinsky. Even the most prominent news outlets disseminated unsubstantiated reports of charges that those originally carrying the story had not independently verified. If one news outlet carried a charge, the rest, which did not wish to be scooped, soon picked it up. For example, the media widely reported unsubstantiated charges that members of the Secret Service had found the president and Ms. Lewinsky in a compromising position. Such reporting helped sensationalize the story, keeping it alive and undermining the president's efforts to focus the public's attention on matters of public policy.

Similarly, in 2004, the press gave immediate attention to a story on the CBS television program *60 Minutes* that revealed documents regarding President George W. Bush's service in the National Guard. The documents purported to show dissatisfaction with the president's performance—or nonperformance. On closer scrutiny, however, it turned out that the documents were forgeries.

On the other hand, the president has certain advantages in dealing with the press. The White House largely controls the environment in which the president meets the press—even going so far as to have the Marine helicopters revved as Ronald Reagan approached them so that he could not hear reporters' questions and give unrehearsed responses. The press typically portrays the president with an aura of dignity and treats him with deference.[64] According to Sam Donaldson, who was generally considered an aggressive White House reporter, "For every truly tough question I've put to officials, I've asked a dozen that were about as tough as Grandma's apple dumplings."[65]

Thus, when Larry Speakes left after serving as President Reagan's press secretary for six years, he told reporters they had given the Reagan administration "a fair shake."[66] Scott McClellan, a George W. Bush press secretary, concluded that media bias was not a problem and that any bias had minimal impact on the way the public was informed. The "Bush administration had no difficulty in getting our messages across to the American people," he declared.[67]

Understanding the American Presidency

Assess the role of presidential power in the American democracy and the president's impact on the scope of government.

Because the presidency is the single most important office in American politics, there has always been concern about whether the president, with all of his power, is a threat to democracy. The importance of the president has raised similar concerns about the scope of government in America.

The Presidency and Democracy

From the time the Constitution was written, there has been a fear that the presidency would degenerate into a monarchy or a dictatorship. Even America's greatest presidents have heightened these fears at times. Despite George Washington's well-deserved reputation for peacefully relinquishing power, he had certain regal tendencies that fanned the suspicions of the Jeffersonians. Abraham Lincoln, for all his humility, exercised extraordinary powers at the outbreak of the Civil War. Over the past century and a half, political commentators have alternated between extolling and fearing a strong presidency.

Concerns over presidential power are generally closely related to policy views. Those who oppose the president's policies are the most likely to be concerned about *too much* presidential power. As you have seen, however, aside from the possibility of a president's acting outside the law and the Constitution—as became a concern during the administrations of George W. Bush and Barack Obama with regard to the holding of prisoners and the interception of communications—there is little prospect that the presidency will be a threat to democracy. The Madisonian system of checks and balances remains intact.

This system is especially evident in an era characterized by divided government—government in which the president is of one party and a majority in one or both houses of Congress are of the other party. Some observers are concerned that there is too much checking and balancing and too little capacity to act on pressing national challenges. It is true that more potentially important legislation fails to pass under divided government than when one party controls both the presidency and Congress.[68] However, major policy change is possible under a divided government.[69]

The Presidency and the Scope of Government

Some of the most noteworthy presidents in the twentieth century (including Theodore Roosevelt, Woodrow Wilson, and Franklin Roosevelt) successfully advocated substantial increases in the role of the national government. Supporting an increased role for government is not inherent in the presidency, however; leadership can move in many directions. The presidents following Lyndon Johnson for the most part have championed constraints on government and limits on spending, especially in domestic policy. It is often said that the American people are ideologically conservative and operationally liberal. If so, for most of the past generation, it has been their will to choose presidents who reflected their ideology and a Congress that represented their appetite for public service. It has been the president more often than Congress who has said "no" to government growth.

Review the Chapter

The Presents

12.1

Characterize the expectations for and the backgrounds of presidents and identify paths to the White House and how presidents may be removed, p. 378.

Americans have high expectations of their presidents, who have come from a relatively wide range of backgrounds. Most presidents are elected by the public, but about one in five succeeded to the presidency when the president died or resigned. No president has been removed for disability, as provided by the Twenty-fifth Amendment, which also provides the mechanism for filling vacancies in the office of vice president, or by conviction of impeachment, although two presidents were impeached.

Presidential Powers

12.2

Evaluate the president's constitutional powers and the expansion of presidential power, p. 384.

The Constitution gives the president a few national security, legislative, administrative, and judicial powers, some of which are quite general. Presidential power has increased over time, through the actions of presidents and because of factors including technology and the increased prominence of the United States, and the assertion of presidential power has at times created controversy regarding the constitutional balance of powers.

Running the Government: The Chief Executive

12.3

Describe the roles of the vice president, cabinet, Executive Office of the President, White House staff, and First Lady, p. 387.

One of the president's principal responsibilities is to manage the executive branch. The vice president has played a central role in recent administrations. Cabinet members focus on running executive departments but play only a modest role as a unit. The Executive Office includes the Council of Economic Advisers; the National Security Council, which helps organize the president's national security decision making process; and the Office of Management and Budget, which prepares the budget and evaluates regulations and legislative proposals. Presidents rely heavily on the White House staff for information, policy options, and analysis. The First Lady has no official position but may play an important role in advocating on particular issues.

Presidential Leadership of Congress: The Politics of Shared Powers

12.4

Assess the impact of various sources of presidential influence on the president's ability to win congressional support, p. 393.

The veto is a powerful tool for stopping legislation the president opposes. The president's role as party leader is at the core of presidents' efforts to assemble a winning legislative coalition behind their proposals, but party members sometimes oppose the president, and presidents cannot do much to increase the number of fellow party members in the legislature in presidential or midterm election years. Moreover, the president frequently faces an opposition majority in Congress. Presidents rarely enjoy electoral mandates for their policies, but they can benefit from high levels of public approval. A variety of presidential legislative skills, ranging from bargaining to setting priorities, contribute only marginally to the president's success with Congress.

The President and National Security Policy

12.5

Analyze the president's powers in making national security policy and the relationship between the president and Congress in this arena, p. 401.

The president is the chief diplomat, commander in chief, and crisis manager. Presidents have substantial formal and informal powers regarding going to war, and these powers remain a matter of controversy. Congress has a central constitutional role in making national security policy, but leadership in this area is centered in the White House, and presidents usually receive the support they seek from Congress.

Power from the People: The Public Presidency

12.6

Identify the factors that affect the president's ability to obtain public support, p. 407.

Presidents invest heavily in efforts to win the public's support, but they often have low approval levels. Approval levels are affected by party identification; by evaluations of the president's performance on the economy, foreign affairs, and other policy areas; and by evaluations of the president's character and job-related skills. Presidents typically fail to obtain the public's support for their policy initiatives and rarely are able to mobilize the public to act on behalf of these initiatives.

The President and the Press

12.7 Characterize the president's relations with the press and news coverage of the presidency, p. 412.

The press is the principal intermediary between the president and the public. Presidents and the press are frequently in conflict over the amount, nature, and tone of the coverage of the presidency. Much of the coverage is superficial and without partisan or ideological bias, but there has been an increase in the negativity of coverage and there are an increasing number of ideologically biased sources of news.

Understanding the American Presidency

12.8 Assess the role of presidential power in the American democracy and the president's impact on the scope of government, p. 414.

The fear of a presidential power harmful to democracy is always present, but there are many checks on presidential power. Support of increasing the scope of government is not inherent in the presidency, and presidents have frequently been advocates of limiting government growth.

Learn the Terms

Twenty-second Amendment, p. 380
Twenty-fifth Amendment, p. 380
impeachment, p. 382
Watergate, p. 382
executive orders, p. 387
cabinet, p. 388
National Security Council, p. 390
Council of Economic Advisers, p. 390
Office of Management and Budget, p. 390
veto, p. 394
pocket veto, p. 394
presidential coattails, p. 397
War Powers Resolution, p. 403
legislative veto, p. 404
crisis, p. 404

Test Yourself

1. The president's great visibility also means that he _____.

a. will be held responsible for national disappointments

b. is always capable of winning reelection

c. can utilize his dominance in the media to overcome congressional opposition

d. can avoid responsibility for governmental failures

e. will have support for concentrating power

2. Which of the following is true concerning presidential selection and tenure?

a. Approximately half of the presidents in U.S. history have served two or more terms.

b. Impeachment has led to the removal of two presidents.

c. Nearly all presidents have won the office through election.

d. Several vice presidents have assumed the office when the president became incapacitated.

e. Presidents can serve up to 12 years in office.

3. The ability to nominate ambassadors, who are to be approved by a majority of the Senate, falls into what category of presidential powers?

a. administrative powers

b. judicial powers

c. legislative powers

d. national security powers

e. organizational powers

4. Which of the following statements best describes the role of the vice president today?

a. The vice president's main job is waiting.

b. The vice president's main job is casting tie-breaking votes in the Senate.

c. The vice president's main job is to balance the presidential ticket during the election.

d. The vice president's main job is to play a central role in administration policy and advising.

e. The vice president's main job is to negotiate treaties with other nations.

5. Each of the following works closely with the president. Who chooses a trademark policy issue to lobby for while in office?

a. chief of staff

b. director of the Office of Management and Budget

c. First Lady

d. policy overseer

e. secretary of the interior

6. In the period of 1952 through 2012 in presidential election years, the president's party typically _____.

a. makes significant gains in both houses of Congress

b. makes large gains in the House

c. loses seats in both houses

d. has averaged only a small net gain in the Senate

e. loses seats in the House

7. How can a bill still be passed after it has been vetoed by the president?

a. After "reconsidering" the bill, the sponsoring Congress members have the opportunity to convince the president to retract his veto.
b. Congress can override vote against the president's veto.
c. The Supreme Court must find the president's veto unconstitutional.
d. Two-thirds of the president's cabinet must disagree.
e. Vetoes issued during congressional recess do not have to be honored if a simple majority of Congress passes the bill.

8. What do executive agreements require?

a. ratification by the House of Representatives
b. ratification by the Senate
c. ratification by both houses of Congress
d. support of the cabinet
e. the agreement of neither Congress nor other officials

9. In what role of the office of the presidency might the president authorize sending troops to defend the national interest?

a. chief legislator
b. commander in chief
c. head of state
d. national intelligence overseer
e. party leader

10. What is the nature of presidential leadership?

a. persuading others to follow his lead
b. making unilateral decisions
c. recognizing and exploiting opportunities
d. convincing members of Congress to move in his direction
e. changing public opinion

11. Why have presidents found their ceremonial responsibilities instrumental in improving public opinion?

a. It adds to their prestige and standing with other government officials and the public.
b. It is a way to get more coverage of their office without the risk of negative press.
c. It is part of their role as leader of the United States and thus proves their leadership qualities.
d. It provides an alternative to showing the continual stress and demands of the office.
e. It unifies the country behind the president, often in times of division.

12. The investigation of President Clinton's relationship with Monica Lewinsky is an example of a presidential scandal that _____.

a. forced the majority of the president's cabinet to resign
b. included the invocation of executive privilege
c. led to the president's impeachment in the Senate
d. reflected a change in the way the media covered the president
e. required a presidential pardon

13. Who or what is most responsible for people's understanding of the president and his policies?

a. Congress
b. schools
c. the laws and policies that affect people on a daily basis
d. the mass media
e. the president himself

Explore Further

WEB SITES

www.whitehouse.gov/
Links to presidential speeches, documents, schedules, radio addresses, federal statistics, and White House press releases and briefings.

www.presidency.ucsb.edu/
Presidential papers, documents, and data.

www.whitehouse.gov/administration/eop
Information about the Executive Office of the President.

www.ipl.org/div/potus
Background on presidents and their administrations.

www.gpo.gov/fdsys/browse/collection. action?collectionCode=CPD
The Compilation of Presidential Documents, the official publication of presidential statements, messages, remarks, and other materials released by the White House Press Secretary.

www.youtube.com/whitehouse?gl=GB&user=whitehouse
White House YouTube channel.

www.presidentialrhetoric.com/
Presidential rhetoric, including videos of presidential speeches.

FURTHER READING

Burke, John P. *The Institutional Presidency*, 2nd ed. (Baltimore, MD: Johns Hopkins University Press, 2000). Examines the organization of the White House and presidential advising.

Cohen, Jeffrey E. *The Presidency in the Era of 24-Hour News* (Princeton, NJ: Princeton University Press, 2008). Explores how changes in the news media have affected the relationship between the president and the press.

Edwards, George C., III. *At the Margins: Presidential Leadership of Congress.* (New Haven, CT: Yale University Press, 1989). Examines the presidents' efforts to lead Congress and explains their limitations.

Edwards, George C., III. *On Deaf Ears: The Limits of the Bully Pulpit* (New Haven, CT: Yale University Press, 2003). The effect of presidents' efforts to change public opinion in the White House's pursuit of popular support.

Edwards, George C., III. *The Strategic President: Persuasion and Opportunity in Presidential Leadership* (Princeton, NJ: Princeton University Press, 2009). Argues that presidential power is not the power to persuade.

Edwards, George C., III. *Overreach: Leadership in the Obama Presidency* (Princeton, NJ: Princeton University Press, 2012). The challenges of presidential persuasion and the importance of understanding opportunities for change.

Fisher, Louis. *Constitutional Conflicts Between Congress and the President*, 5th ed. rev. (Lawrence, KS: University Press of Kansas, 2007). Presents the constitutional dimensions of the separation of powers.

Howell, William G. *Power Without Persuasion* (Princeton, NJ: Princeton University Press, 2003). Focuses on the use of the president's discretionary power.

Kumar, Martha. *Managing the President's Message: The White House Communications Operation* (Baltimore, MD: Johns Hopkins University Press, 2007). Explains White House communications and media operations.

Neustadt, Richard E. *Presidential Power and the Modern Presidents* (New York: Free Press, 1990). The most influential book on the American presidency; argues that presidential power is the power to persuade.

13

The Budget: The Politics of Taxing and Spending

Politics in Action: The Messy Politics of Budgeting

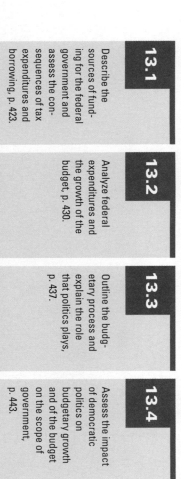

n 2011, the United States came perilously close to defaulting on its debts and throwing the world economy into a tailspin. Most analysts predicted interest rates would increase as lenders demanded more in compensation for taking greater risks in lending the government money. Because of the size of the U.S. economy, stock markets around the world would crash and the global economy would stagnate.

The United States had reached the debt limit—the limit of legally allowable debt set by Congress—and thus could not borrow more to cover interest payments it had to make on its debt. President Obama asked Congress to increase the debt limit, as many presidents have done before him. Republicans in Congress were reluctant to oblige. They insisted that before they agreed to increase the debt limit, the president and the Democrats would have to agree to reduce the debt over time through decreases in spending but not any increases in taxes. In the end, the parties could not agree and Congress passed a temporary solution that raised the debt limit but put off fashioning a long-term solution for two years. In the meantime, the large annual federal deficit was a serious constraint on the president, limiting

13.1

Describe the sources of funding for the federal government and assess the consequences of tax expenditures and borrowing, p. 423.

13.2

Analyze federal expenditures and the growth of the budget, p. 430.

13.3

Outline the budgetary process and explain the role that politics plays, p. 437.

13.4

Assess the impact of democratic politics on budgetary growth and of the budget on the scope of government, p. 443.

Dealing with the budget is one of the most intractable issues of American government, but also one of the most important. Here Wall Street traders watch as the stock market plunged after Standard and Poor's downgraded the U.S. credit rating in response to the inability of Congress and the president to agree on a plan to meet the government's financial obligations.

budget
A policy document allocating burdens (taxes) and benefits (expenditures).

expenditures
Government spending. Major areas of federal spending are social services and national defense.

revenues
The financial resources of the government. The individual income tax and Social Security tax are two major sources of the federal government's revenue.

his ability to pursue his "win the future" agenda by investing in education, job creation, and health care.

The budget, which determines taxing and spending for both domestic and national security policies, is almost invariably a key issue in national elections. In the election of 2012, Mitt Romney argued that we should make permanent large temporary tax cuts passed during the presidency of George W. Bush and that we should decrease the size of the federal government. Barack Obama, on the other hand, proposed increasing taxes on the wealthiest one percent of Americans and maintaining the services government provides. Both candidates knew that politicians who attempt to make tough decisions about the budget risk incurring voters' wrath.

In 1990 Republican President George H. W. Bush agreed to a budget deal that raised taxes and limited spending and substantially reduced the deficit. In 1992 he lost his bid for reelection. In 1993 democrat President Clinton also supported a program of higher taxes and spending constraints that ultimately helped balanced the budget. In the 1994 elections, however, republicans won majorities in both houses of Congress for the first time since 1952.

It is not surprising that the battle of the budget remains at the center of American politics. Two questions are central to public policy:

Who bears the burdens of paying for government?

Who receives the benefits?

Some observers who have considered these two questions are concerned that democracy could distort budgeting. Do politicians seek to "buy" votes by spending public funds on things voters will like and will remember on Election Day? Or is spending, instead, simply the rational response to demands made on government services by the many segments of American society? Do politicians pander to a perceived public desire to "soak the rich" with taxes that redistribute income?

Budgets are central to our theme of the scope of government. Indeed, for many programs, budgeting *is* policy: The amount of money spent on a program determines how many people are served, how well they are served, how much of something (weapons, vaccines, and so on) the government can purchase. The bigger the budget, the bigger the government. But is the growth of the government's budget inevitable? Or are the battles over the allocation of scarce public resources actually a *constraint* on government?

Every year the president and Congress must appropriate funds. If they fail to do so, the government will come to a standstill. The army will be idled, Social Security offices will close, and food stamps will not be distributed to low-income households. Obtaining funds and spending them is the essence of budgeting, and budgeting is central to policymaking. It is not surprising that the battle of the budget remains at the center of American politics.

A **budget** is a policy document allocating burdens (taxes) and benefits (**expenditures**). The president and Congress have often been caught in a budgetary squeeze: Americans want them to balance the budget, maintain or increase the level of government spending on most policies, and keep taxes low. As a result, the president and Congress are preoccupied with budgeting, trying to cope with these contradictory demands.

Figure 13.1 provides an overview of the federal budget for 2015. You can see that expenditures exceed **revenues** by a considerable margin and that the total national debt is roughly the size of the U.S. economy.

FIGURE 13.1 THE FEDERAL BUDGET: AN OVERVIEW

The federal budget consists of revenues and expenditures. When expenditures exceed revenues, the budget runs a deficit. The accumulation of debt over time composes the national debt.

Data are estimates for fiscal year 2015.

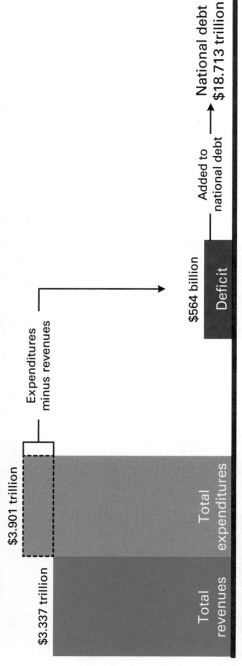

$3.901 trillion

Expenditures minus revenues

$3.337 trillion

Total revenues

Total expenditures

$564 billion

Deficit

Added to national debt → National debt $18.713 trillion

SOURCE: *Budget of the United States Government, Fiscal Year 2015: Historical Tables* (Washington, D.C.: U.S. Government Printing Office, 2014), Tables 1.1 and 7.1.

Federal Revenue and Borrowing

13.1 Describe the sources of funding for the federal government and assess the consequences of tax expenditures and borrowing.

upreme Court Justice Oliver Wendell Holmes, Jr. declared that "taxes are what we pay for civilization." Although he asserted, "I like to pay taxes," most taxpayers throughout history have not shared his sentiment. The art of taxation, said Jean-Baptiste Colbert, Louis XIV's finance minister, is in "so plucking the goose as to procure the largest quantity of feathers with the least possible amount of hissing."[1] In Figure 13.2, you can see where the federal government has been getting its feathers. The three major sources of federal revenue are personal income taxes, corporate income taxes, and social insurance taxes. A small share comes from receipts from such sources as excise taxes (a tax levied on the manufacture, transportation, sale, or consumption of a good—for example, taxes on gasoline).

□ Personal and Corporate Income Tax

Every April 15th, millions of bleary-eyed American taxpayers struggle to mail or submit online their income tax forms before midnight. Most individuals are required to pay the government a portion of the money they earn; this portion is an **income tax**. In the early years of the nation, long before the days of a large national defense, Social Security, and the like, fees collected on imported goods financed most of the federal government. Congress briefly adopted an income tax to pay for the Civil War, but the first peacetime income tax was enacted in 1894. Even though the tax was only 2 percent of income earned beyond the then-magnificent sum of $4,000, a lawyer opposing it called the tax the first step of a "communist march." The Supreme Court wasted little time in declaring the tax unconstitutional in *Pollock v. Farmer's Loan and Trust Co.* (1895). In 1913, the *Sixteenth Amendment* was added to the Constitution, explicitly permitting Congress to levy an income tax. Today, the Internal Revenue Service (IRS), established to collect income tax, receives about 140 million individual tax returns each year.[2]

The income tax is generally *progressive*, meaning that those with more taxable income not only pay more taxes but also pay higher *rates* of tax. The rates currently

income tax

Shares of individual wages and corporate revenues collected by the government. The Sixteenth Amendment explicitly authorized Congress to levy a tax on income.

Sixteenth Amendment

The constitutional amendment adopted in 1913 that explicitly permitted Congress to levy an income tax.

FIGURE 13.2 FEDERAL REVENUES

Individual income taxes make the largest contribution to federal revenues, but nearly a third of federal revenues comes from social insurance taxes. In bad economic times, tax revenues decrease as fewer people are working and paying taxes. Revenue from individual income taxes also decline after tax cuts, such as in 2001. In 2011–2012, there was a temporary decrease in social insurance taxes to help stimulate the economy. This is a stacked graph in which the *difference* between the lines indicates the revenues raised by each tax.

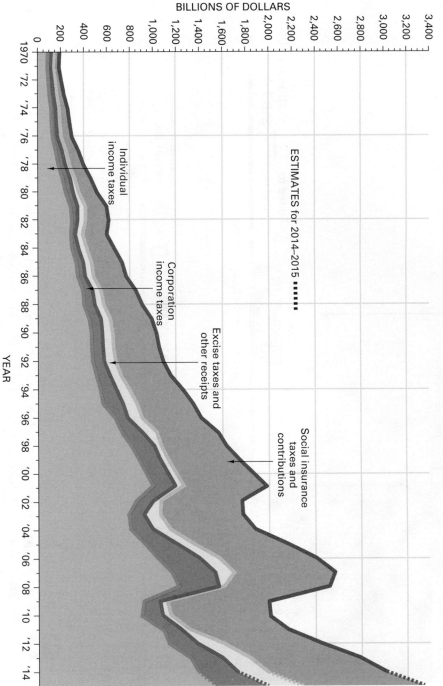

SOURCE: *Budget of the United States Government, Fiscal Year 2015: Historical Tables* (Washington, D.C.: U.S. Government Printing Office, 2014), Table 2.1.

Why It Matters to You
The Progressive Income Tax

The income tax is progressive in that those with higher incomes typically pay a higher rate of taxes. Most people would probably find it unfair to pay taxes at the same rate as a millionaire. If a uniform tax rate were set at a level that everyone could afford to pay, it would have to be set very low. In this case there may not be sufficient revenues to fund critical government programs.

range from 10 percent to 39.6 percent. In 2013, 43 percent of those filing income tax returns paid no income tax at all.[3] The 1 percent of taxpayers with the highest taxable incomes pay about 35 percent of all the federal income taxes, more than the bottom 95 percent of tax filers. The top 10 percent pay 68 percent of all federal income taxes, while those in the bottom 50 percent of taxable income pay about 3 percent.[4] Some people feel that a progressive tax is the fairest type of taxation because those who have the most pay higher rates. Others, however, have proposed a "flat" tax, with everyone taxed at the same rate; still others have suggested that we abandon the income tax and rely on a national sales tax, much like the sales taxes in most states. It is easy to criticize the income tax but difficult to obtain agreement on a replacement.

Corporations, like individuals, pay income taxes. Although corporate taxes once yielded more revenues than individual income taxes, this has not been true since 1943. In 2015, corporate taxes yielded about 13 cents of every federal revenue dollar, compared with 46 cents from individual income taxes.[5]

Social Insurance Taxes

Both employers and employees pay Social Security and Medicare taxes. Money for these social *insurance taxes* is deducted from employees' paychecks and matched by their employers. Unlike other taxes, these payments are earmarked for a specific purpose: the Social Security trust funds, which pay benefits to the elderly, the disabled, and the widowed and help support state unemployment programs; and the Medicare trust funds, which pay for medical care for seniors. In 2014, employees and employers each paid a Social Security tax equal to 6.2 percent of the first $117,000 of earnings, and for Medicare they paid another 1.45 percent on *all* earnings. Individuals earning more than $200,000 pay an additional 0.9 percent in Medicare taxes. As presidents and Congress have cut income taxes and as the large baby boomer generation has hit its peak work years, social insurance taxes have grown faster than any other source of federal revenue. In 1957, these taxes made up a mere 12 percent of federal revenues; today they account for more than a third.

Borrowing

Tax revenues normally do not cover the federal government's expenditures. The additional funds must come through borrowing. When the federal government wants to borrow money, the Treasury Department sells bonds, guaranteeing to pay interest to bondholders. Citizens, corporations, mutual funds, other financial institutions, and even foreign governments may purchase these bonds. In addition, the federal government has *intragovernmental debt* on its books. This debt is what the Treasury owes various Social Security and other trust funds because the government uses for its general purposes revenue collected from social insurance taxes designated to fund Social Security and other specific programs. Most government borrowing is not for capital needs (such as buildings and machinery) but for day-to-day expenses—farm subsidies, military pensions, aid to states and cities, and so on.

Over the past 30 years, with the exception of 1998–2001, the national government has run up large annual budget deficits. A budget **deficit** occurs when expenditures exceed revenues in a fiscal year, in other words, when the national government spends more money than it receives in taxes. Thus, as a result of this succession of annual deficits, the total **national debt** rose sharply during the 1980s and then again since 2001, increasing from less than $1 trillion in 1980 to about $18.7 trillion by 2015 (Figure 13.3). About seven percent of all current budget expenditures go to paying just the interest on this debt.[6]

Borrowing money shifts the burden to future taxpayers, who will have to service the debt, with every dollar the government borrows costing taxpayers many more dollars in interest. Dollars spent servicing the debt cannot be spent on health care, education, or infrastructure. Paying the interest on the debt is not optional.

Some believe that government borrowing may crowd out private borrowers, both individuals and businesses, from the loan marketplace. Over the past 70 years, a substantial percentage of all the net private savings in the country have gone to the federal government. Most economists believe that when the economy is strong the government's competing to borrow money may lead to increased interest rates, making it more difficult, for example, for businesses to invest in capital expenditures (such as new plants and equipment) that produce economic growth. Higher interest rates also raise the costs to individuals of financing homes or credit card purchases. Large deficits also make the American government dependent on foreign investors, including other governments, to fund its debt—not a favorable position for a superpower. Foreign investors currently hold a majority of the federal government's public debt. If they stop lending us money, perhaps to gain leverage in foreign policy, interest rates would rise and the economy would be depressed.

In bad economic times, when tax revenues decrease because fewer people are working, deficits are likely to increase. While revenues diminish, the demands for

deficit
An excess of federal expenditures over federal revenues.

national debt
All the money borrowed by the federal government over the years and still outstanding. Today the national debt is about $18.7 trillion.

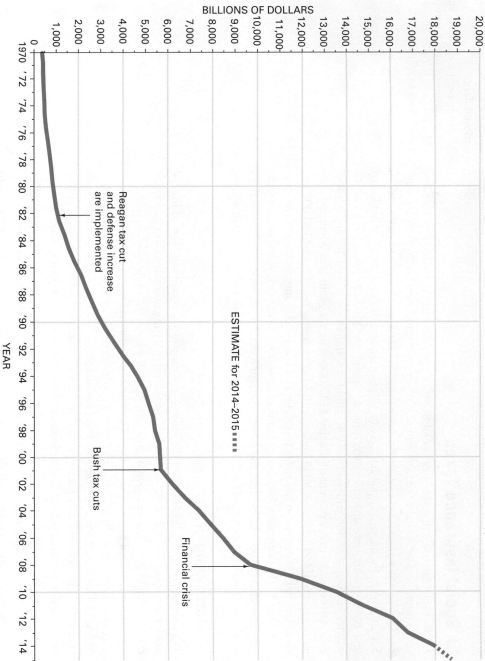

FIGURE 13.3 TOTAL NATIONAL DEBT

The national debt climbed steadily throughout the 1980s, leveled off in the 1990s, and has risen sharply since 2001 and especially after the financial crisis of 2008.

SOURCE: *Budget of the United States Government, Fiscal Year 2015: Historical Tables* (Washington, D.C.: U.S. Government Printing Office, 2014), Table 7.1.

unemployment insurance, food stamps, and other components of the social safety net increase. The president and Congress may also decide to cut taxes to stimulate the economy, or they may choose to spend money to create jobs, both of which occurred in 2009. All such decisions add to the deficit and increase the need to borrow.

The need to borrow, in turn, creates an issue in Congress, which legislates a limit on how much the federal government may borrow, often referred to as the *debt ceiling*. As we saw in the opener to this chapter, when Congress is faced with increasing the debt ceiling, the opposition party has an opportunity to criticize the president and use the need to borrow as leverage to extract concessions on other policies.

Sometimes politicians complain that, since families and businesses and even state and local governments balance their budgets, the federal government ought to be able to do the same. However, most families do *not* balance their budgets. They use credit cards to give themselves instant loans, and they go to the bank to borrow money for major purchases such as automobiles and, most important, homes, with mortgages on homes being debts they carry for years. And state and local governments and private businesses differ from the federal government in having a *capital budget*, a budget for expenditures on items that will serve for the long term, such as equipment, roads, and buildings. Thus, for example, when airlines purchase new airplanes or when school districts build new schools, they do not pay for them out of current income. Instead, they borrow money, often through issuing bonds, and these debts do not count against the operating budget. In contrast, when the federal government purchases new jets for the air force or new buildings for medical research, these purchases are counted as current expenditures and run up the deficit.

Why It Matters to You
Deficit Spending

The federal government can run a deficit and borrow money to pay its current expenses. States and cities can only borrow (by issuing bonds) for long-term capital expenses such as roads and schools. If the Constitution required a balanced budget, the federal government could not borrow money to provide increased services during an economic downturn, nor could it cut taxes to stimulate the economy in such a situation.

☐ Taxes and Public Policy

It's not surprising that tax policy provokes heated discussion—no other area of government policy affects as many Americans. In addition to raising revenues to finance its services, the government can use taxes to make citizens' incomes more-nearly or less-nearly equal, to encourage or discourage growth in the economy, and to promote specific interests.

TAX EXPENDITURES The 1974 Budget Act defines **tax expenditures** as "revenue losses attributable to provisions of the federal tax laws which allow a special exemption, exclusion, or deduction." These expenditures represent the difference between what the government actually collects in taxes and what it would have collected without special exemptions. Thus, tax expenditures amount to subsidies for different activities. Here are some examples:

- The government permits taxpayers to deduct their contributions to charities from their income, thus encouraging charitable contributions and in effect giving charities a subsidy.

- The government permits homeowners to deduct from their income the billions of dollars they collectively pay each year in mortgage interest, encouraging home ownership and in effect giving homeowners a subsidy.

- The government allows businesses that invest in new plants and equipment to deduct these expenses from their taxes at a more rapid rate than they deduct other expenses, encouraging investment in new plants and equipment. In effect, the owners of these businesses, including stockholders, get a subsidy that is unavailable to owners of other businesses.

Tax expenditures are among the most obscure aspects of a generally obscure budgetary process, partly because they receive no regular review by Congress—a great advantage for those who benefit from a tax expenditure.[7] Although few ordinary citizens seem to realize it, the magnitude of tax expenditures is enormous, as you can see in Table 13.1.

On the whole, tax expenditures benefit middle- and upper-income taxpayers and corporations. Poorer people, who tend not to own homes, can take little advantage of provisions that permit homeowners to deduct mortgage interest payments. Likewise, poorer people in general can take less advantage of the exclusion of taxes on contributions to individual retirement accounts or interest on state and local bonds. Students, however, are an exception to this generalization (see "Young People and Politics: Education and the Federal Tax Code").

To some, tax expenditures such as business-related deductions, tuition tax credits, and lower tax rates on profits on stock and real estate ("capital gains") are "loopholes." To others, they are public policy choices that support a social activity worth encouraging through tax subsidies. Sometimes, deductions can be abused. One billionaire made a charitable donation in her will of as much as $8 billion for the care and welfare of dogs. The estate tax on the $8 billion would have been $3.6 billion, but because she took a charitable deduction, her estate paid no tax. Thus, her deduction constituted a

TABLE 13.1 TAX EXPENDITURES: THE MONEY GOVERNMENT DOES NOT COLLECT

Tax expenditures are essentially money that government could collect but does not because they are exempted from taxation. The Office of Management and Budget estimated that the total tax expenditures in 2015 would be more than $1.1 trillion—an amount equal to more than one-third of the total federal receipts. Individuals receive most of the tax expenditures, and corporations get the rest. Here are some of the largest tax expenditures and their cost to the treasury:

Tax Expenditure	Cost
Exclusion of employer contributions to health care and insurance	$207 billion
Exclusion of net imputed rental income	$80 billion
Deduction of mortgage interest on owner-occupied houses	$74 billion
Deductions for state and local taxes	$67 billion
Capital gains (nonhome, agriculture, or mining)	$69 billion
Deferral of income from controlled foreign corporations	$76 billion
Deductions for charitable contributions	$58 billion
Exclusion of capital gains on home sales	$57 billion
Exclusion of Social Security and disability benefits	$39 billion
Exclusion for interest earned on state and local government bonds	$35 billion
Exclusion of capital gains on home sales	$57 billion
Capital gains at death	$32 billion
Treatment of qualified dividends	$27 billion
Child credit	$24 billion
Exclusion of interest on life insurance savings	$23 billion

SOURCE: *Budget of the United States Government, Fiscal Year 2015: Analytical Perspectives* (Washington, D.C.: U.S. Government Printing Office, 2014), Table 14.3. Data are estimates for fiscal year 2015.

Government could lower overall tax rates by taxing things it does not currently tax, such as Social Security benefits, pension fund contributions, charitable contributions, and the like. You can easily figure out, though, that these are not popular items to tax, and doing so would evoke strong opposition from powerful interest groups.

subsidy from the federal government, which means from all taxpayers. The money the treasury lost was approximately half what the government spends in a year on Head Start, a program that benefits 900,000 children.[8]

Regardless of how they are viewed, tax expenditures amount to the same thing: revenues that the government loses because certain items are exempted from normal taxation or are taxed at lower rates. If there were no tax expenditures, the federal government's total tax receipts in 2015 would be increased by about one-third.

TAX REDUCTION Perennially popular with the public, tax reduction tends to have different consequences for different groups. Early in his administration, President Reagan proposed a massive tax-cut bill, which Congress obligingly passed in July 1981. As a result of this legislation, the federal tax bills of Americans were reduced 25 percent, corporate income taxes were also reduced, new tax incentives were provided for personal savings and corporate investment, and taxes were *indexed* to the cost of living. With the indexing of taxes, beginning in 1985, inflation could no longer push income into higher brackets, and, since people in higher brackets pay a higher *percentage* of their incomes in taxes, tax revenues were less than they would have been without indexing.

Families with high incomes saved many thousands of dollars in taxes, but those at the lower end of the income ladder saw little change in their tax burden because of separate increases in social insurance and excise taxes (which fall disproportionately on those with lower incomes). Moreover, the massive deficits that began in the 1980s were at least in part a consequence of the 1981 tax cuts, as government continued to spend while reducing its revenues.

Young People & Politics

Education and the Federal Tax Code

If you think that the federal income tax is something that does not affect you much as a student, you are wrong. For example, if you are footing the costs of higher education, education tax credits can help offset these costs. But the rules for obtaining a tax credit are far from simple.

First, there is the American Opportunity Credit, which applies only for the first four years of postsecondary education, whether in a college or a vocational school. The American Opportunity Credit can be worth up to $2,500 per eligible student, per year to a family. It does not apply for education beyond these four years, however, and you must be enrolled at least half time to receive the credit. Up to $1,000 of the credit is refundable, meaning you can get it even if you owe no tax.

The Lifetime Learning Credit applies to undergraduate, graduate, and professional degree courses, including instruction to acquire or improve your job skills. If you qualify, your credit equals 20 percent of the first $10,000 of postsecondary tuition and fees you pay during the year for all eligible students in a family, for a maximum credit of $2,000 per tax return.

The American Opportunity Credit and the Lifetime Learning Credit are education credits you can subtract in full from your federal income tax, not just deduct from your taxable income.

Naturally, there are restrictions on claiming these credits. To qualify for either credit, you must pay postsecondary tuition and fees for yourself, your spouse, or your dependent. The credit may be claimed by the parent or the student but not by both. However, if the student was claimed as a dependent, the student cannot claim the credit. Moreover, you cannot claim both the American Opportunity Credit and the Lifetime Learning Credit for the same student (such as yourself) in the same year. Parents with children or attending school themselves can claim more than one American Opportunity Credit but only one Lifetime Learning Credit.

These credits are not for everyone. The American Opportunity Credit is gradually reduced for those with modified adjusted gross income (MAGI) between $80,000 and $90,000 ($160,000 and $180,000 for those married and filing jointly) and eliminated completely for those with MAGI exceeding those amounts. The comparable figures for the Lifetime Learning Credit are $54,000 and $64,000 for individuals and $108,000 and $128,000 for those who are married and filing jointly. If a taxpayer is married, the credit may be claimed only on a joint return. In addition, the American Opportunity Credit is not allowed for a student convicted of a felony drug offense while in school.

A taxpayer may also take a deduction for up to $4,000 of higher-education expenses, but only when opting not to use the education credits. A different deduction lets taxpayers recoup some of the cost of student loan interests. It and other deductions and credits also begin to diminish as taxpayers earn more.

Welcome to the federal tax code. As you can see, Congress has chosen to give students benefits in the tax code, but it has also been concerned that people do not abuse these benefits. Thus, even students have to face the intricacies of the federal tax code and work out the myriad tax credits and deductions that help defray the costs of a college education. In the end, however, most people agree that it is worth the effort.

CRITICAL THINKING QUESTIONS

1. Why doesn't Congress simply appropriate money for students and send them a check instead of relying on the tax code?
2. What are the obstacles to simplifying the tax code?

In 1993, President Clinton, seeking to deal with these deficits, persuaded Congress to raise the income tax rate on those in the top 2 percent of income and the top corporate income tax rate. However, when budget surpluses materialized (briefly) in the late 1990s, tax reduction once again became a popular rallying cry. In 2001, at the behest of George W. Bush, Congress enacted a tax cut that gradually lowered tax rates over the next 10 years; in 2003 Congress reduced the tax rates on capital gains and dividends.

Some claim that cutting taxes is a useful way to limit government expansion, or to "starve the beast." In reality, however, government often *grows* more rapidly following substantial tax cuts.[9] For example, the 2001 tax cuts were followed by the reappearance of massive deficits when the president asked Congress to fund two wars and an expensive prescription drug addition to the Social Security program. Moreover, despite the clamor for tax reduction, as you can see in "America in Perspective: How Big Is the Tax Burden?" among democracies with developed economies, America has one of the *smallest* tax burdens.

America in Perspective

How Big Is the Tax Burden?

Americans commonly complain that taxes are too high. Yet the figures in the graph show that the governments in the United States (national, state, and local) tax a smaller percentage of the resources of the country than do those in almost all other democracies with developed economies. Looked at in this perspective, the tax burden in the United States is rather modest. Sweden and Denmark, at the other extreme,

take nearly half the wealth of the country in taxes each year.

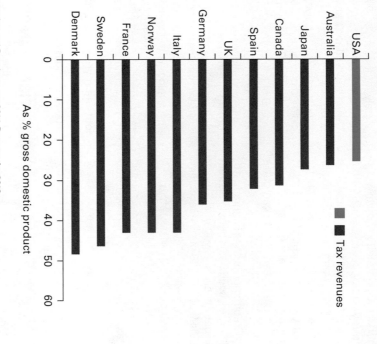

As % gross domestic product

■ Tax revenues

SOURCE: Organization for Economic Cooperation and Development 2014. Data are for 2012.

CRITICAL THINKING QUESTIONS

1. What is the appropriate level of taxation?
2. Is it possible to answer such a question in the abstract, without reference to the services we want from government?

Federal Expenditures

13.2

Analyze federal expenditures and the growth of the budget.

I
n 1932, when President Franklin D. Roosevelt took office in the midst of the Great Depression, the federal government was spending just over $3 billion a year. Today, the federal government spends that much in a single morning. Program costs once measured in the millions are now measured in billions. You can see in Figure 13.4 how the federal budget has grown in actual dollars in recent decades and how the various categories of expenditures have grown.

Figure 13.4 makes two interesting points. First, expenditures keep rising (although the rise would not look so steep if we controlled for the changes in the value of the dollar). Second, the policies and programs on which the government spends money change over time.

This section explores three important questions: Why are government budgets so big? Where does the money go? Why is it difficult to control federal expenditures?

FIGURE 13.4 FEDERAL EXPENDITURES

The biggest category of federal expenditures is payments to individuals, composing more than 60 percent of the budget. National defense accounts for about one-fifth of the budget. This is a stacked graph in which the *difference* between the lines indicates the amount spent on each category. The economic crisis of 2008–2009 led to a dramatic increase in the budget.

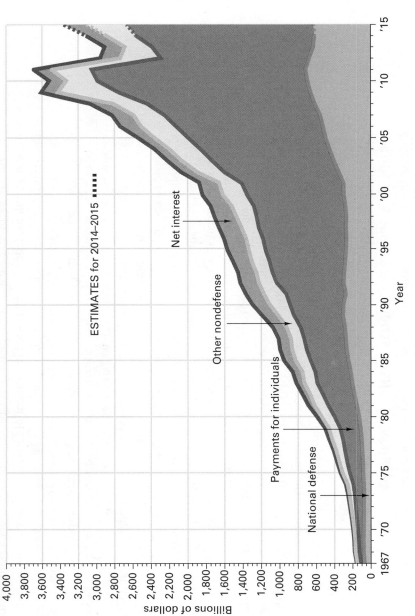

ESTIMATES for 2014–2015 ▪▪▪▪▪

Net interest

Other nondefense

Payments for individuals

National defense

Year

Billions of dollars

1967 '70 '75 '80 '85 '90 '95 '00 '05 '10 '15

SOURCE: *Budget of the United States Government, Fiscal Year 2015: Historical Tables* (Washington, D.C.: U.S. Government Printing Office, 2015), Table 6.1.

☐ Big Governments, Big Budgets

One answer to the question of why budgets are so large is simple: Big budgets are necessary to pay for big governments. Among the most important changes of the twentieth century was the rise of large governments.[10] As in other Western nations, the growth of government in the United States has been dramatic. American governments—national, state, and local—spend an amount equal to one-third of the gross domestic product (GDP). The national government's expenditures alone currently represent about one-fourth of the GDP.[11]

The public sector expands principally in response to the public's preferences and changes in economic and social conditions, such as economic downturns, urbanization, or pollution, that affect the public's level of demand for government activity.[12] As a result, the rise of big government has been strongly resistant to reversal: citizens like government services. Even Ronald Reagan, a strong leader with an antigovernment orientation, succeeded only in slowing the growth of government, not in actually trimming its size. When he left office, the federal government employed more people and spent more money than when he was inaugurated.

Two developments associated with government growth in America are the rise of the national security state and the rise of the social service state.

☐ The Rise of the National Security State

Before World War II, the United States had customarily disbanded a large part of its military forces at the end of a war. After World War II, however, the Cold War with the Soviet Union resulted in the growth of a permanent military establishment and increased acquisition of expensive military technology. Fueling this military machine greatly increased the cost of government. It was President Eisenhower, a five-star general, who coined the phrase *military-industrial complex* to characterize—and warn against—the close relationship between the military hierarchy and the defense industry that supplies its hardware needs.

In the 1950s and early 1960s, spending for past and present wars amounted to more than half the federal budget. The Department of Defense, in other words, received the majority of federal dollars. A common liberal complaint was that government was shortchanging the poor while lining the pockets of defense contractors. The situation soon changed, however. From the late 1960s through the 1970s, defense expenditures measured in constant dollars (dollars adjusted for inflation) crept downward (see Figure 13.5); meanwhile, as we shall see later, social welfare expenditures were rapidly increasing.

At President Reagan's urging, Congress increased the defense budget substantially, mostly during his first term. Although in the 1990s defense expenditures decreased in response to the end of the Cold War and reduced tensions in Europe, they increased again following the terrorist attacks of September 11th, 2001, and especially with the war in Iraq, substantially exceeding Cold War expenditures. Nevertheless, the budget of the Department of Defense, once the driving force in the expansion of the federal budget, now constitutes only about one-fifth of all federal expenditures.

Payrolls and pensions for the more than 7 million persons who work for the Pentagon, serve in the reserves, or receive military retirement pay, veterans' pensions, or disability compensation constitute a large component of the defense budget. So do the research, development, and *procurement* (purchasing) of military hardware. The costs of procurement are high, and advanced technology makes any weapon, fighter plane,

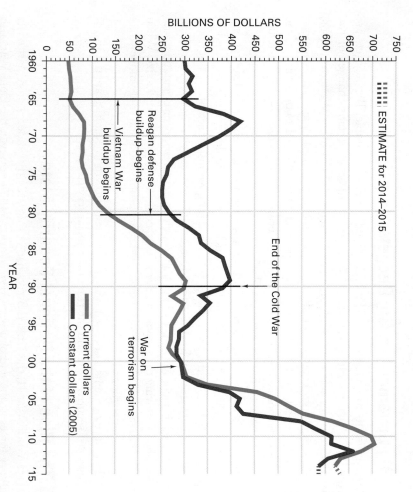

FIGURE 13.5 TRENDS IN NATIONAL DEFENSE SPENDING

Defense expenditures increased rapidly during the Reagan administration and declined with the end of the Cold War. They increased again after the September 11th, 2001, terrorist attacks and the invasion of Iraq in 2003, decreasing as the wars in Iraq and Afghanistan wound down.

SOURCE: *Budget of the United States Government, Fiscal Year 2015: Historical Tables* (Washington, D.C.: U.S. Government Printing Office, 2014), Table 6.1.

Social Security Act
A 1935 law intended to provide a minimal level of sustenance to older Americans and thus save them from poverty.

Medicare
A program added to the Social Security system in 1965 that provides health insurance for the elderly, covering hospitalization, doctor fees, and other health expenses.

The U.S. Air Force unveiled its new stealth bomber in 1989. The plane's unusual shape allows it to fly undetected by enemy radar, but such technology costs money—over $2 billion per plane. These huge expenditures contributed to substantial increases in the defense budget in the 1980s.

or component more expensive than its predecessors. Moreover, cost overruns are common. The American fleet of stealth bombers cost several times the original estimate—over $2 *billion* each.

The Rise of the Social Service State

The biggest slice of the budget pie, once reserved for defense, now belongs to *income security* expenditures, a bundle of policies extending direct and indirect aid to the elderly, the poor, and the needy. In 1935, during the Great Depression and the administration of President Franklin D. Roosevelt, Congress passed the **Social Security Act.** The act was intended to provide a minimal level of sustenance to older Americans, saving them from poverty. In January 1940, the treasurer of the United States sent the nation's first Social Security check to Ida Fuller of Brattleboro, Vermont—a payment of $22.54 for the month. In 2014, the average check for retired workers was $1,283 a month.

Over the years, Social Security has undergone various expansions. In the 1950s, disability insurance became a part of the Social Security program; thus, workers who were disabled could also collect benefits. In 1965, as part of President Lyndon Johnson's Great Society programs, Congress expanded the system to include **Medicare,** which provides both hospital and physician coverage to the elderly. Congress added a prescription drug benefit to Medicare in 2003. Today, about 57 million Americans receive payments from the Social Security system each month.

Social Security is less an insurance program than a kind of intergenerational contract. Essentially, money is taken from the working members of the population and spent on the retired members. Today, however, this intergenerational relationship is threatened by demographic and economic realities. Because of increased life expectancy and lower birthrates, the percentage of older people in the population has been increasing and there are proportionately fewer working members to support proportionately more retirees. In 1940, the entire Social Security system was financed with a 3 percent tax on payrolls, as there were approximately 50 workers to support each Social Security beneficiary. Today, that number has dropped to only 2.8 workers. By the year 2033, when the parents of today's college students will be receiving their checks, only 2.1 workers will be supporting each beneficiary.[13]

Not surprisingly, by the early 1980s the Social Security program faced a problem. In scholar Paul Light's candid phrasing, "It was going broke fast."[14] Congress responded by increasing social insurance taxes—hence the 15 percent rate—so that more would continue to come into the Social Security Trust Fund than would be being spent. The goal was to create a surplus to help finance payments when the baby boomers retired.

In 1999, with a budget surplus having materialized, President Clinton proposed allocating much of the surplus to Social Security and investing some of the Social Security funds in the stock market. Everyone agreed that saving Social Security was a high priority, but not everyone agreed with the president's solutions. As a result, no major changes occurred. George W. Bush faced similar resistance to his proposals for investing part of individuals' social insurance tax payments in the stock market. Nevertheless, the fiscal clock keeps ticking, and it will not be long before Social Security's costs will begin to exceed its income from tax collections. Medicare is in even greater fiscal jeopardy; its costs will exceed its income even sooner, and the trust fund for the hospital insurance part of Medicare will be depleted by the end of the next decade. In short, financing Social Security and Medicare remains a great challenge.

Social Security is the largest social policy of the federal government. In 2015, the total Social Security expenditures were $1.4 trillion, 36 percent of the federal expenditures of $3.9 trillion.[15] However, in the decades since the enactment of the Great Society programs, increasing expenditures in health, education, job training, and many other areas have also contributed significantly to the rise of the social service state and to America's growing budget. No brief list can do justice to the range of government social programs, which provide funds for the elderly, businesses run by minority entrepreneurs, consumer education, drug rehabilitation, environmental education, food subsidies for the poor, guaranteed loans to college students, housing allowances for the poor, inspections of hospitals, and so on. Liberals tend to favor these programs to assist individuals and groups in society, conservatives to see them as a drain. In any event, they cost money—a lot of it (see Figure 13.6).

The rise of the social service state and the rise of the national security state are linked with much of American governmental growth since the end of World War II. Although American social services expanded less than similar services in Western European nations, for most of the postwar period American military expenditures

Much of the federal budget goes to providing Social Security and Medicare for the elderly. These programs have been very successful in reducing poverty among the elderly but are the biggest contributors to rising deficits.

incrementalism
A description of the budget process in which the best predictor of this year's budget is last year's budget, plus a little bit more (an increment). According to Aaron Wildavsky, "Most of the budget is a product of previous decisions."

FIGURE 13.6 TRENDS IN SOCIAL SERVICE SPENDING

Social service spending, principally on health, education, and income security, has increased substantially since the 1960s and now makes up about two-thirds of the budget. With more people reaching retirement age in the last few years, spending on Social Security and Medicare has increased especially rapidly.

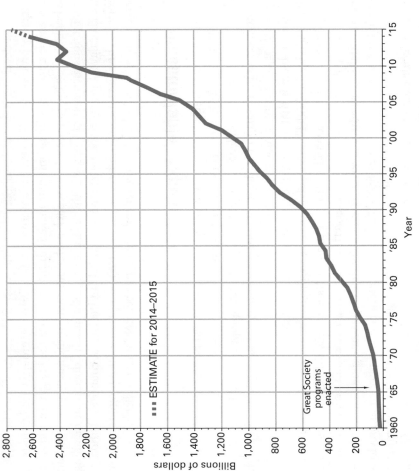

SOURCE: *Budget of the United States Government, Fiscal Year 2015: Historical Tables* (Washington, D.C.: U.S. Government Printing Office, 2014), Table 3.1.

expanded more rapidly than in other countries. Together, these factors help explain why the budget is the center of attention in American government today. Why is it so difficult to bring this increasing federal budget under control?

☐ Incrementalism

Sometimes political scientists use the term *incrementalism* to describe the spending and appropriations process. **Incrementalism** means simply that the best predictor of this year's budget is last year's budget plus a little bit more (an increment). According to Wildavsky and Caiden, "The largest determining factor of the size and content of this year's budget is last year's. Most of each budget is a product of previous decisions."16 Incremental budgeting has several features:

- Policymakers focus little attention on the budgetary base—the amounts agencies have had over the previous years.
- Usually, agencies can safely assume they will get at least the budget they had the previous year.
- Most of the debate and most of the attention of the budgetary process focus on the proposed increment.
- The budget for any given agency tends to grow by a little bit every year.

This picture of the federal budget is one of constant growth. Expenditures mandated by an existing law or obligation (such as Social Security) are particularly likely to follow a neat pattern of increase. There are exceptions, however. Paul Schulman

uncontrollable expenditures
Expenditures that are determined by how many eligible beneficiaries there are for a program or by previous obligations of the government and that Congress therefore cannot easily control.

entitlements
Policies for which Congress has obligated itself to pay X level of benefits to Y number of recipients. Social Security benefits are an example.

☐ "Uncontrollable" Expenditures

At first glance, it is hard to see how one could call the federal budget uncontrollable. After all, Congress has the constitutional authority to budget—to add or subtract money from an agency. Indeed, all recent presidents have proposed, and Congress has adopted, some proposals to cut the growth of government spending. How, then, can one speak of an uncontrollable budget?

The problem is that much of the government's budget does not fit what we might call the "allowance model" of the budget, in which Congress allocates a lump sum—say, $5.2 billion—to an agency and instructs it to meet its expenses throughout the fiscal year. Indeed, about two-thirds of the government's budget does not work this way. **Uncontrollable expenditures** result from policies that make some group automatically eligible for some benefit, such as Social Security or veterans' benefits, or from previous obligations of the government, such as interest on the national debt. The government does not decide each year, for example, whether it will pay the interest on the debt or send checks to Social Security recipients.

Many expenditures are uncontrollable because Congress has, in effect, obligated itself to pay X level of benefits to Y number of recipients. Congress writes the eligibility rules; the number of people eligible and their level of guaranteed benefits determine how much Congress must spend. Such policies are called **entitlements**, and they range from agricultural subsidies to veterans' aid. Each year, Congress's bill for these policies is a straightforward function of the X level of benefits times the Y beneficiaries. The biggest uncontrollable expenditure of all is the Social Security system, including Medicare, which in 2015 cost more than $1.4 *trillion* dollars for the year. Individuals who are eligible automatically receive Social Security payments. Of course, Congress can, if it desires, cut Social Security benefits or tighten eligibility restrictions. Doing so, however, would provoke a monumental outcry from millions of elderly voters.

observed that budgets for the National Aeronautics and Space Administration (NASA) were hardly incremental; they initially rose as fast as a NASA rocket but later plummeted to a fraction of their former size.[17] Incrementalism may be a general tendency of the budget, but it does not fully describe all budgetary politics.[18]

Because so much of the budgetary process looks incremental, there is a never-ending call for budgetary reform. The idea is always to make it easier to compare programs so that the "most deserving" ones can be supported and the "wasteful" ones cut. Nevertheless, the budgetary process, like all aspects of government, is affected by groups with interests in taxes and expenditures. These interests make it difficult to pare the budget. In addition, the budget is too big to review from scratch each year, even for the most systematic and conscientious members of Congress. The federal budget is a massive document, detailing annual outlays larger than the entire economies of all but the largest countries. Although efforts to check incrementalism have failed, so have attempts to reduce programs whose costs are rising rapidly. Much of the federal budget has become "uncontrollable."

Why It Matters to You
"Uncontrollable" Spending

Much of the federal budget is "uncontrollable" in the sense that it does not come up for reauthorization on a regular basis. If entitlement programs were subject to the same annual authorizations that most other programs receive, they would probably have less secure funding. We might spend less money on them and more on other services. This flexibility might please some people, especially those not receiving entitlement benefits, but those receiving Social Security and Medicare payments, for example, prefer more reliable funding.

Point to Ponder

Spending on national defense, interest on the debt, and, especially, Social Security and health care accounts for most of the federal budget, and these expenditures have grown rapidly in recent years.

Is there any way to bring these expenditures under control?

THE ACCELERATOR IS STUCK!!

NATIONAL DEFENSE

MEDICAID
MEDICARE
SOCIAL SECURITY
INTEREST ON DEBT

SPENDING

DEFICIT

MATSON
ST. LOUIS POST-DISPATCH

The Budgetary Process

13.3 Outline the budgetary process and explain the role that politics plays.

he distribution of the government's budget is the outcome of a very long, complex process that starts and ends with the president and has Congress squarely in the middle. Because budgets are so important to almost all other policies, the budgetary process is the center of political battles in Washington and involves nearly everyone in government. Nestled inside the tax and expenditures figures are thousands of policy choices, each prompting plenty of politics.

☐ Budgetary Politics

Public budgets are the supreme example of Harold Lasswell's definition of politics as "who gets what, when, and how." Budget battles are fought over contending interests, ideologies, programs, and agencies.

STAKES AND STRATEGIES Every political actor has a stake in the budget. Mayors want to keep federal grants-in-aid flowing in, defense contractors like a big defense budget, and scientists push for a large budget for the National Science Foundation. Agencies within the government also work to protect their interests. Individual members of Congress act as policy entrepreneurs for new ideas and support constituent benefits, both of which cost money. Presidents try to use budgets to manage the economy and leave their imprint on Congress's policy agenda.

Think of budgetary politics as resembling a game in which players adopt various strategies.[19] Agencies pushing their budgetary needs to Congress, for instance, try to link the benefits of their program to a senator's or representative's electoral needs. Often, agencies pad their requests a bit, hoping that the almost inevitable cuts will be bearable. President John Adams justified this now common budgetary gambit by saying to his cabinet, "If some superfluity not be given Congress to lop off, they will cut into the very flesh of the public necessities." Interest groups try to identify their favorite programs with the national interest. Mayors tell Congress not how much they like to receive federal aid but how crucial cities are to national survival. Farmers stress not that they like federal

House Ways and Means Committee

The House of Representatives committee that, along with the Senate Finance Committee, writes the tax codes, subject to the approval of Congress as a whole.

Senate Finance Committee

The Senate committee that, along with the House Ways and Means Committee, writes the tax codes, subject to the approval of Congress as a whole.

Congressional Budget Office

Advises Congress on the probable consequences of its decisions, forecasts revenues, and is a counterweight to the president's Office of Management and Budget.

Because budgetary policy is so important, decision makers may be reluctant to compromise. In 1995–1996, the inability of the president and Congress to reach agreement led to the shutdown of much of the federal government.

aid but that feeding a hungry nation and world is the main task of American agriculture. In the game of budgetary politics, there are plenty of players, all with their own strategies.

THE PLAYERS Deciding how to spend trillions of dollars is a process likely to attract plenty of interest—from those formally required to participate in the process as well as those whose stakes are too big to ignore it. Here are the main actors in the budgetary process (see Figure 13.7):

- *Interest groups.* No lobbyist worth his or her pay would ignore the budget. Lobbying for a group's needs takes place in the agencies, with presidents (if the lobbyist has access to them), and before congressional committees. A smart agency head will be sure to involve interest groups in defending the agency's budget request.

- *Agencies.* Convinced of the importance of their mission, the heads of agencies almost always push for higher budget requests. They send their requests to the Office of Management and Budget and later get a chance to present themselves before congressional committees as well.[20]

- *The Office of Management and Budget (OMB).* The OMB is responsible to the president, its boss, but no president has the time to understand and make decisions about the billions of dollars in the budget—parceled out to hundreds of agencies, some of which the chief executive knows little or nothing about. The director and staff of the OMB have considerable independence from the president, which makes them major actors in the budget process.

- *The president.* The president makes final decisions on what to propose to Congress. In early February, the president unveils the proposed budget; the president then spends many a day trying to ensure that Congress will stick close to the recommendations.

- *Tax committees in Congress.* The government cannot spend money it does not have (or cannot borrow). The **House Ways and Means Committee** and the **Senate Finance Committee** write the tax codes, subject to the approval of Congress as a whole.

- *Budget Committees and the Congressional Budget Office.* The **Congressional Budget Office,** which advises Congress on the probable consequences of its

FIGURE 13.7 THE PLAYERS IN THE BUDGETARY PROCESS

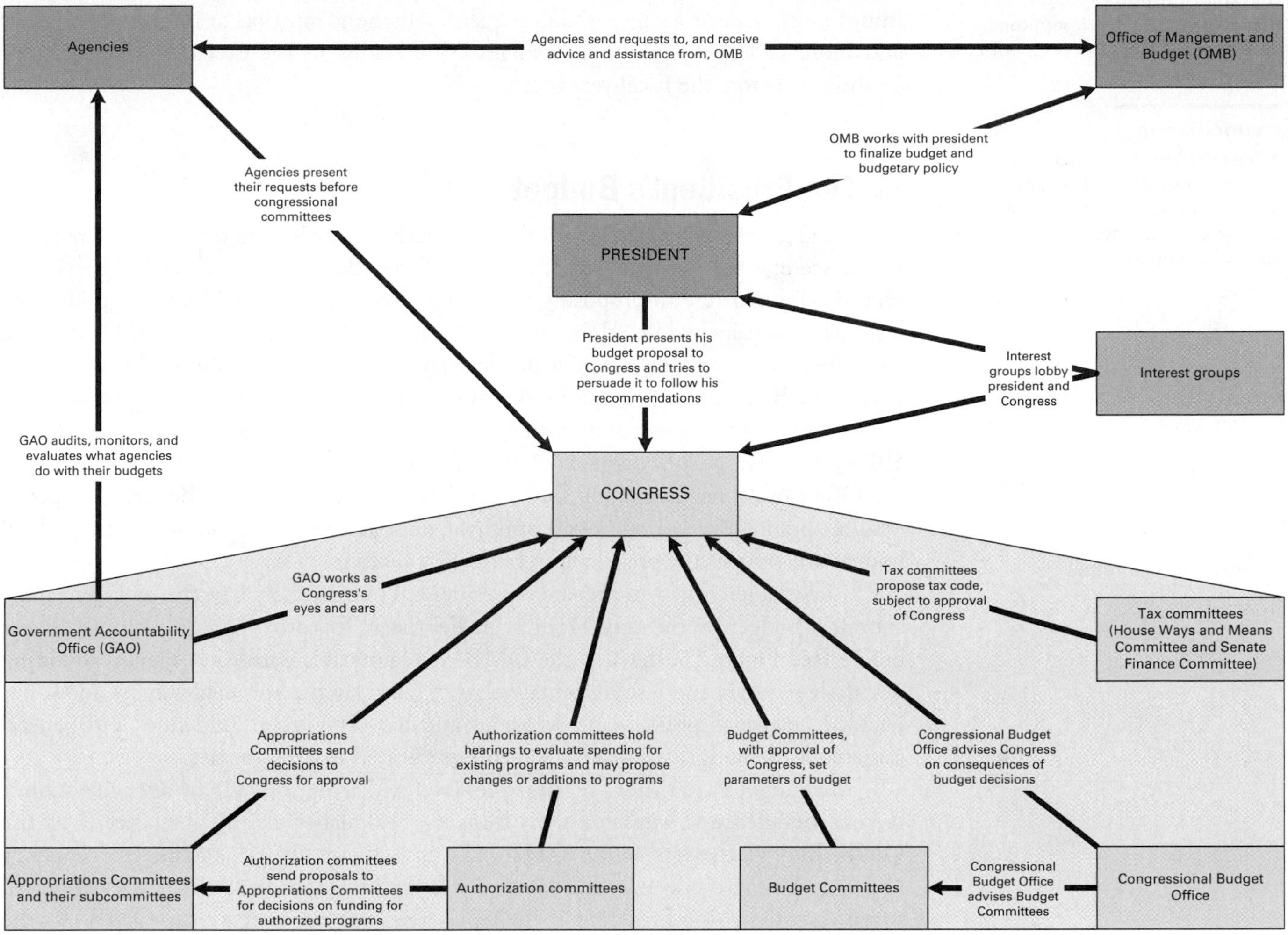

Office of Management and Budget (OMB)

Interest groups

Agencies

PRESIDENT

CONGRESS

Government Accountability Office (GAO)

Tax committees (House Ways and Means Committee and Senate Finance Committee)

Congressional Budget Office

Budget Committees

Authorization committees

Appropriations Committees and their subcommittees

Agencies send requests to, and receive advice and assistance from, OMB

OMB works with president to finalize budget and budgetary policy

Interest groups lobby president and Congress

President presents his budget proposal to Congress and tries to persuade it to follow his recommendations

Agencies present their requests before congressional committees

GAO works as Congress's eyes and ears

Appropriations Committees send decisions to Congress for approval

Authorization committees send proposals to Appropriations Committees for decisions on funding for authorized programs

GAO audits, monitors, and evaluates what agencies do with their budgets

Tax committees propose tax code, subject to approval of Congress

Congressional Budget Office advises Congress on consequences of budget decisions

Budget Committees, with approval of Congress, set parameters of budget

Authorization committees hold hearings to evaluate spending for existing programs and may propose changes or additions to programs

Congressional Budget Office advises Budget Committees

budget decisions, forecasts revenues, and is a counterweight to the president's OMB, and its parent committees, the Senate and House Budget Committees, set the parameters of the congressional budget process through examining revenues and expenditures in the aggregate and proposing resolutions that Congress may pass to bind itself within certain limits.

- *Authorization committees.* Committees of Congress, ranging from Agriculture to Veterans Affairs, propose new laws, which require new expenditures, for passage by the full Congress. Committee members may use hearings either to publicize the accomplishments of their pet agencies, thus supporting larger budgets for them, or to question agency heads about waste or overspending.

- *Appropriations Committees and their subcommittees.* The Appropriations Committees in each house make recommendations to the full Congress on who gets what. These committees take new or old policies coming from the subject-matter committees and decide how much to spend. Appropriations subcommittees hold hearings on specific agency requests.

- *Congress as a whole.* The Constitution requires that Congress as a whole approve taxes and appropriations, and senators and representatives have a strong interest in delivering federal dollars to their constituents. A dam here, a military base there, and a job-training program somewhere else—these are items that members look for in the budget.

- *The Government Accountability Office (GAO).* Congress's role does not end when it has passed the budget. The GAO works as Congress's eyes and ears, auditing, monitoring, and evaluating what agencies are doing with their budgets.

budget resolution

A resolution binding Congress to a total expenditure level, supposedly the bottom line of all federal spending for all programs.

reconciliation

A congressional process through which program authorizations are revised to achieve required savings. It usually also includes tax or other revenue adjustments.

Budgeting involves a cast of thousands. However, their roles are carefully scripted, and their time on stage is limited because budget making is both repetitive (the same things must be done each year) and sequential (actions must occur in the proper order and more or less on time). The budget cycle begins in the executive branch a full 19 months before the fiscal year begins.

☐ The President's Budget

Until 1921, the various agencies of the executive branch sent their budget requests to the secretary of the treasury, who in turn forwarded them to Congress. Presidents played a limited role in proposing the budget; sometimes they played a year before. Agencies basically peddled their own budget requests to Congress. In 1921 Congress, concerned about retiring the debt the country had accumulated during World War I, passed the Budget and Accounting Act, which required presidents to propose an executive budget to Congress, and created the Bureau of the Budget to help them. In the 1970s, President Nixon reorganized the Bureau of the Budget and gave it a new name, the Office of Management and Budget (OMB). The OMB, whose director is a presidential appointee requiring Senate approval, now supervises preparation of the federal budget and advises the president on budgetary matters.

It takes a long time to prepare a presidential budget.[21] By law, the president must submit a budget by the first Monday in February. The process begins almost a year before (see Figure 13.8), when the OMB communicates with each agency, sounding out their requests and issuing tentative guidelines. By the summer, the president has decided on overall policies and priorities and has established guidelines and general targets for the budget. These are then communicated to the agencies.

The budget makers now get down to details. During the fall, the agencies submit formal, detailed estimates for their budgets, zealously pushing their needs to the OMB. Budget analysts at the OMB pare, investigate, weigh, and meet on agency requests. Often, the agency heads ask for hefty increases; sometimes they threaten to go directly to the president if their priorities are not met by the OMB. As the Washington winter sets in, the budget document is readied for final presidential approval. There is usually some last-minute juggling—agencies may be asked to change their estimates to conform to the president's decisions, or cabinet members may make a last-ditch effort to bypass the OMB and convince the president to increase their funds. With only days—or hours—left before the submission deadline, the budget document is rushed to the printers. Then the president sends it to Capitol Hill. The next steps are up to Congress.

☐ Congress and the Budget

According to the Constitution, Congress must authorize all federal appropriations. Thus, Congress always holds one extremely powerful trump card in national policymaking: the power of the purse.[22] This year, Congress will decide how to spend nearly $4 trillion.

An important part of the process of establishing a budget is setting limits on expenditures on the basis of revenue projections. Thus, in April of each year, both houses are expected to agree on a **budget resolution**—thereby binding Congress to a total expenditure level that should form the bottom line of all federal spending for all programs. Only then is Congress supposed to begin acting on the individual appropriations. The congressional budget resolution often requests that certain changes be made in law, primarily to achieve savings incorporated into the spending totals and thus meet the budget resolution. These changes are legislated in two separate ways.

First is budget **reconciliation**, a process by which program authorizations are revised to achieve required savings; it frequently also includes tax or other revenue adjustments. Usually reconciliation comes near the end of the budgetary process,

FIGURE 13.8 THE BUDGET PROCESS

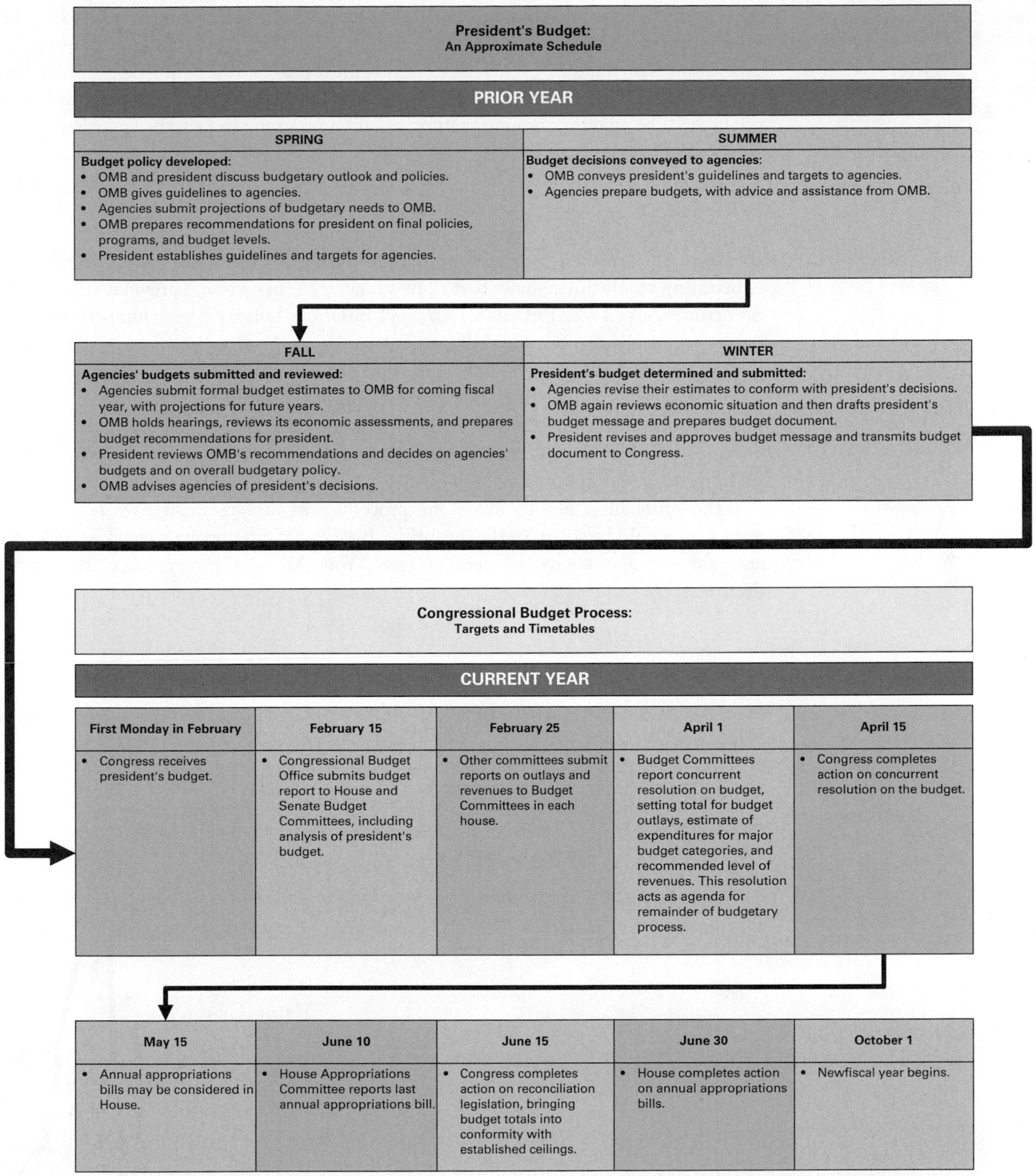

President's Budget:
An Approximate Schedule

PRIOR YEAR

SPRING	SUMMER
Budget policy developed: • OMB and president discuss budgetary outlook and policies. • OMB gives guidelines to agencies. • Agencies submit projections of budgetary needs to OMB. • OMB prepares recommendations for president on final policies, programs, and budget levels. • President establishes guidelines and targets for agencies.	**Budget decisions conveyed to agencies:** • OMB conveys president's guidelines and targets to agencies. • Agencies prepare budgets, with advice and assistance from OMB.

FALL	WINTER
Agencies' budgets submitted and reviewed: • Agencies submit formal budget estimates to OMB for coming fiscal year, with projections for future years. • OMB holds hearings, reviews its economic assessments, and prepares budget recommendations for president. • President reviews OMB's recommendations and decides on agencies' budgets and on overall budgetary policy. • OMB advises agencies of president's decisions.	**President's budget determined and submitted:** • Agencies revise their estimates to conform with president's decisions. • OMB again reviews economic situation and then drafts president's budget message and prepares budget document. • President revises and approves budget message and transmits budget document to Congress.

Congressional Budget Process:
Targets and Timetables

CURRENT YEAR

First Monday in February	February 15	February 25	April 1	April 15
• Congress receives president's budget.	• Congressional Budget Office submits budget report to House and Senate Budget Committees, including analysis of president's budget.	• Other committees submit reports on outlays and revenues to Budget Committees in each house.	• Budget Committees report concurrent resolution on budget, setting total for budget outlays, estimate of expenditures for major budget categories, and recommended level of revenues. This resolution acts as agenda for remainder of budgetary process.	• Congress completes action on concurrent resolution on the budget.

May 15	June 10	June 15	June 30	October 1
• Annual appropriations bills may be considered in House.	• House Appropriations Committee reports last annual appropriations bill.	• Congress completes action on reconciliation legislation, bringing budget totals into conformity with established ceilings.	• House completes action on annual appropriations bills.	• New fiscal year begins.

although occasionally the president and Congress have sought to use it in place of the regular lawmaking process.

The second way that laws are changed to meet the budget resolution (or to create or change programs for other reasons) involves more narrowly drawn legislation. An **authorization bill** is an act of Congress that establishes or changes a government program. Authorizations specify program goals and, for discretionary programs, set the maximum amount that they may spend. For entitlement programs, an authorization sets or changes eligibility standards and benefits that must be provided by the

authorization bill

An act of Congress that establishes, continues, or changes a discretionary government program or an entitlement. It specifies program goals and maximum expenditures for discretionary programs.

appropriations bill

An act of Congress that actually funds programs within limits established by authorization bills. Appropriations usually cover one year.

continuing resolutions

When Congress cannot reach agreement and pass appropriations bills, these resolutions allow agencies to spend at the level of the previous year.

program. Authorizations may be for one year, or they may run for a specified or indefinite number of years.

Congress must pass an additional measure, termed an **appropriations bill,** to fund programs established by authorization bills. For example, if Congress authorizes expenditures on building highways, Congress must pass another bill to appropriate the funds to build them. Appropriations bills usually fund programs for one year and cannot exceed the amount of money authorized for a program; in fact, they may appropriate *less* than was authorized.

Despite the elaborate rules for budgeting, Congress has often failed to meet its own budgetary timetable. There has been too much conflict over the budget for the system to work according to design. Moreover, in many instances Congress has not been able to reach agreement and pass appropriations bills at all and has instead resorted to **continuing resolutions**—laws that allow agencies to spend at the previous year's level. Sometimes, as in 1986, 1987, and 2007, appropriations bills have been lumped together in one enormous and complex bill (rather than in the 13 separate appropriations bills covering various components of the government that are supposed to pass), precluding adequate review by individual members of Congress and forcing the president either to accept unwanted provisions or to veto the funding for the entire government. These omnibus bills may also become magnets for unrelated and controversial pieces of legislation that could not pass on their own.

The problem is not so much the procedure as disagreement over how scarce resources should be spent. In the meantime, budget deficits continue (see Figure 13.9) and are a major source of conflict (see "You Are the Policymaker: Balancing the Budget").

FIGURE 13.9 FLUCTUATING DEFICITS

Annual federal deficits mushroomed during the Reagan administration (1981–1988), despite the president's oft-repeated commitment to a balanced budget. The deficit disappeared during the Clinton administration, and the nation began running a surplus in fiscal year 1998. By 2002, however, the United States was back in the red. Annual deficits grew even larger beginning in 2009 as the government dealt with the financial crisis that hit the United States in 2008, but they fell sharply as the economy recovered.

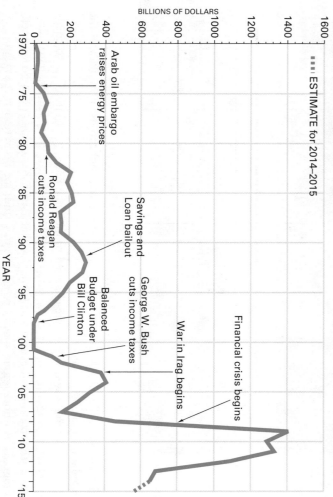

SOURCE: *Budget of the United States Government, Fiscal Year 2015: Historical Tables* (Washington, D.C.: U.S. Government Printing Office, 2014), Table 1.1.

You Are the Policymaker

Balancing the Budget

The national government is running large budget deficits and the national debt continues to grow. Here is the situation you would face as a budget decision maker: According to the OMB, in fiscal year 2015 the national government will have revenues (including Social Security taxes) of about $3.34 trillion. Mandatory expenditures for domestic policy (entitlements such as Social Security, Medicare, Medicaid, and other prior obligations) total about $2.46 trillion. Nondiscretionary payments on the national debt will cost another $252 billion, bringing you to a total of $2.71 trillion. National defense will cost an additional $631 billion.

Adding defense brings the budget total to an amount equal to the total revenue of the national government.

Moreover, you have yet to spend anything on discretionary domestic policy programs such as those for education, transportation, health, law enforcement, and natural resources and the environment. Maintaining current programs will take $563 billion. If you spend this amount, it will all be deficit spending—and you will not even have had a chance to fund any significant new programs. Moreover, you may have to ask Congress for additional funds to pay for a military action somewhere in the world.

What would you do? Would you drastically reduce defense expenditures? Or would you leave them alone and close down substantial portions of the rest of the government—the core programs that have broad public support? Would you show great political courage and seek a tax increase to pay for these programs?

SOURCE: *Budget of the United States Government, Fiscal Year 2015: Historical Tables* (Washington, D.C.: U.S. Government Printing Office, 2014), Tables 1.1, 8.5, and 8.7.

Understanding Budgeting

13.4   Assess the impact of democratic politics on budgetary growth and of the budget on scope of government.

C itizens and politicians alike fret about whether government is too big. There is agreement on the centrality of budgeting to modern government and politics, however.

□ Democracy and Budgeting

Almost all democracies have seen a substantial growth in government in the twentieth century. Economists Allan Meltzer and Scott Richard have argued that government grows in a democracy because of the equality of suffrage. Each voter has one vote, so those with less income have considerable clout. Parties must appeal to a majority of the voters. Hence, claim Meltzer and Richard, less-well-off voters will always use their votes to support public policies that redistribute benefits from the rich to the less-well-off.[23] Many politicians willingly cooperate with the desire of voters to expand their benefits because voters return the favor at election time. Not surprisingly, the most rapidly growing areas of expenditures are Social Security, Medicaid, Medicare, and social welfare programs, which benefit the working and middle classes more than the rich.

Many believe that elites, particularly corporate elites, oppose big government. However, large banks and financial institutions and corporations such as Lockheed, United Airlines, and General Motors have appealed to the government for large bailouts when times got rough. Corporations support a big government that offers them contracts, subsidies, and other benefits. A large procurement and research-and-development budget at the Department of Defense benefits defense contractors, their workers, and their shareholders.

Low-income and wealthy voters alike have voted for parties and politicians who promised them benefits. Citizens are not helpless victims of big government and its big taxes; they are at least coconspirators. When the air is foul, Americans expect government to help clean it up. When Americans get old, they expect a Social Security check. In a democracy, what people want affects what government does.

Government also grows by responding to groups and their demands. The parade of political action committees is one example of groups asking government for assistance. From agricultural lobbies supporting loans to zoologists pressing for aid from the National Science Foundation, groups seek to expand their favorite part of the budget. They are aided by committees and government agencies that work to fund projects favored by supportive groups.

However, a concern over tax rates and jobs has played a critical role in reining in the government.[24] Some politicians compete for votes by promising not to expand government—as was the case with Ronald Reagan and George W. Bush, both elected to the presidency twice, and with the Republicans who took control of Congress in 1995 and the House in 2011. No country has a more open system than the United States, but Americans have chosen to tax less and spend less on public services than almost all other democracies with developed economies. Interestingly, within the United States, most of the states with lower average incomes vote for candidates promising the least in the way of government benefits. In short, democracy may encourage government growth, but it does not compel it.

Among the most common criticisms of government is that it fails to balance the budget. Public officials are often criticized for lacking the will to deal with the problem, yet it is not lack of resolve that prevents a solution to large budget deficits. Instead, it

Americans are of two minds about the budget. They prefer low taxes, but they also desire public services, like the preservation of scenic areas such as Arches National Park. As long as voters have contradictory demands for public policy, their elected representatives are unlikely to easily resolve basic decisions about taxing and spending.

is a lack of consensus on policy. Americans want to spend money on programs but not pay taxes,[25] and, being a democracy, this is exactly what the government does. Similarly, voters reward members of Congress for bringing pork barrel projects to their states and districts.[26] The inevitable result is red ink.

☐ The Budget and the Scope of Government

Issues regarding the scope of government have pervaded this chapter. The bigger the budget, the more generous the benefit, the more rigorous the regulation, the bigger the government. When the country has seen a need, whether to defend itself or to provide for the elderly, it has found a way to do it. Even presidents, such as Ronald Reagan and George W. Bush, who led the fight to cut taxes, also wanted to substantially expand at least part of the government. It may seem, then, that there is no limit to government growth.

The budgetary process can also limit government, however. Because of the emphasis on tax cuts since 1980 as the "politics of scarcity"—scarcity of funds, that is. Thus, the budget can be a force for reining in the government as well as for expanding its role. For example, President Bill Clinton came into office hoping to make new investments in education, worker training, and the country's physical infrastructure, such as roads and bridges, and to expand health care coverage. He soon found, however, that there was no money to fund new programs. Instead, he had to emphasize cutting the budget deficit. Much of the opposition to Barack Obama's proposal for health care reform was inspired by a fear of increasing the national debt. Thus, America's large budget deficits have been as much a constraint on government as they have been evidence of a burgeoning public sector.

Review the Chapter

Federal Revenue and Borrowing

13.1 Describe the sources of funding for the federal government and assess the consequences of tax expenditures and borrowing, p. 423.

The personal income tax is the largest source of revenue for the federal government, with social insurance taxes a close second. Other revenue comes from the corporate income tax and excise taxes. Borrowing plays a major role in funding the government, and the national debt has grown rapidly in the past decade, as have government expenditures. Interest on this debt will eat up an increasing portion of future budgets. Tax expenditures represent an enormous drain on revenues but subsidize many popular activities.

Federal Expenditures

13.2 Analyze federal expenditures and the growth of the budget, p. 430.

Budgets have grown with the rise of the national security state and the social service state. National security and, especially, social services such as Social Security and Medicare, plus interest on the debt, make up most of the budget. Much of the budget represents uncontrollable expenditures, primarily entitlements to payments that the government has committed to make at a certain level and that are difficult to limit. Expenditures for most policies grow incrementally, with each year's budget building

on the previous year's, and many interests ask Congress and the president to spend more on their favorite policies.

The Budgetary Process

13.3 Outline the budgetary process and explain the role that politics plays, p. 437.

The budgetary process is a long and complex one that involves the president, agencies, Congress as a whole, and many important congressional committees. The president submits the budget to Congress, whose reformed budgetary process has nonetheless not brought spending in line with revenues. Because budgets are central for most policies, politics are pervasive in the budgetary process as players battle over contending interests, ideologies, programs, and agencies.

Understanding Budgeting

13.4 Assess the impact of democratic politics on budgetary growth and of the budget on scope of government, p. 443.

Budgets in democracies grow because the public and organized interests demand new and larger public services. However, some politicians compete for votes by promising to limit budgets. Increasing budgets increase the scope of government, but decreases in taxes and increases in debt make it more difficult to add or expand programs.

Learn the Terms

budget, p. 422
expenditures, p. 422
revenues, p. 422
income tax, p. 423
Sixteenth Amendment, p. 423
deficit, p. 425
national debt, p. 425
tax expenditures, p. 427

Social Security Act, p. 433
Medicare, p. 433
incrementalism, p. 435
uncontrollable expenditures, p. 436
entitlements, p. 436
House Ways and Means Committee, p. 438

Senate Finance Committee, p. 438
Congressional Budget Office, p. 438
budget resolution, p. 440
reconciliation, p. 440
authorization bill, p. 441
appropriations bill, p. 442
continuing resolutions, p. 442

Test Yourself

1. How do Social Security taxes differ from other forms of taxation?

a. They are earmarked for a specific purpose.

b. They are not counted as government revenue.

c. They are only taken out of capital gains income.

d. They are the only form of taxation to have decreased.

e. Their tax rate cannot be changed.

2. Why is the growing national debt such an important problem?

a. Each year the debt is not paid, it doubles due to interest.

b. Dollars spent servicing the debt cannot be spent on health care, education, or infrastructure.

c. Few foreign countries will be willing to trade with an America burdened by debt.

d. The debt caused the 2008 economic downturn and subsequent recession.

e. The debt is leading to a sharp increase in inflation of the American dollar.

3. Why do many economists believe that when the economy is strong, it can be difficult for businesses to invest in capital expenditures?

a. A significant portion of corporate profit is redirected to employees to adjust for inflation.

b. Businesses lose many tax exemptions during good economic times; limiting the money they can spend.

c. Government competition to borrow money can lead to increased interest rates.

d. Historically, the government imposes greater regulations on business spending during economic boom times.

e. In seeking to create a budget surplus, corporate tax rates are increased.

4. Which of the following is an example of a tax expenditure?

a. deduction for political campaign contribution

b. deferral of income from multinational companies

c. exclusion of capital gains from sales of publicly traded stock

d. exclusion of taxes on individual retirement and 401(k) account contributions and earnings

e. total national spending in compliance with the tax code

5. What is the primary reason that future defense procurements will be significantly more expensive than they are today?

a. advancements in technology

b. cost overruns

c. Department of Defense budget cuts

d. inflation

e. the rising price of oil

6. Why has the rise of big government been strongly resistant to reversal?

a. Dangers abroad necessitate an increasing defense budget.

b. Generally, citizens like receiving government services.

c. It is almost impossible to lay off existing government employees.

d. Legislation creating new agencies and programs cannot be overturned.

e. The concept of small government is un-American.

7. Why is it so difficult to control federal expenditures?

a. It is difficult to estimate future spending needs when population growth is so erratic.

b. Many expenditures are uncontrollable entitlements.

c. Technological advancements require significant increases in government expenditures.

d. The American budgetary process is rank with corruption.

e. The Department of Defense resists any attempts to limit its increasing funding.

8. The intergenerational contract nature of the Social Security program is threatened because _____.

a. both the Republican and Democratic parties are aiming to phase it out in coming years

b. Congress has yet to renew the program, which is set to expire in 2015

c. many believe that it will be voted down in a national referendum in 2013

d. the Social Security Trust Fund will be depleted by 2017

e. there are proportionally fewer workers to fund the program for the larger proportion of retirees

9. Carla owns a business that she runs out of her home. She is using her budget from last year to estimate her budget for this year and allowing some room for growth. What principle is Carla using?

a. Deficit reduction
b. Expenditure reduction
c. Expenditures and revenue
d. Incrementalism
e. Surplus calculation

10. What aspect of the Budget and Accounting Act of 1921 has had the most profound effect on U.S. politics today?

a. The act allowed Congress to apply for loans to begin rebuilding the postwar economy, a practice which Congress has continued, increasing the current national debt.
b. The act banned the president from cutting funding from agencies, which only led to greater national debts for later generations.
c. The act prevented the president from attending Congressional hearings regarding the budget, which now gives the president less direct control of the annual budget.
d. The act required the president to attend Congressional hearings regarding the budget, a process which continues today and takes most of the year.
e. The act required the president to present a budget to Congress, a process which continues today and is the center of great political contention.

11. Why do many government agencies pad their budget requests?

a. By padding budget requests, they can compensate for previous cost overruns.
b. Corruption is rampant in agency budgets, and it is a way to hide the disappearance of money.
c. Government agencies use budget requests to make the case for why they failed to accomplish goals in the previous year.
d. Money is a sign of importance, so agencies try to outdo each other.
e. They do so in the hope that the inevitable cuts will be bearable.

12. Why is the budgetary process the center of so many political battles in Washington?

a. Because the budget takes a relatively short time to produce compared to other issues, fighting is intense.
b. It concerns the salaries of federally elected officials and therefore is politically and personally important to them.
c. It is important to almost all other policies and involves nearly everyone in government.
d. It is the most polarizing social issue in America today.
e. It is the only issue in American government on which the president and Congress work together without the help of the Supreme Court.

13. Why might corporations support a big government?

a. Big governments have more opportunities to offer contracts, subsidies, and other benefits.
b. Large governments will not bail out companies that are struggling, which allows stronger companies to control larger portions of the market.
c. Larger governments rely more on privatized companies to provide benefits to citizens.
d. Smaller governments have more opportunities to offer contracts, subsidies, and other benefits but provide little challenge.
e. Small governments rely less on privatized companies to provide benefits to citizens.

Explore Further

WEB SITES

www.whitehouse.gov/administration/eop/cea/economic-report-of-the-President
The Economic Report of the President.

www.irs.ustreas.gov
The Internal Revenue Service home page, containing a wealth of information about taxes.

www.whitehouse.gov/omb
The Office of Management and Budget home page. Clicking on the current year's budget takes you to all the current budget documents.

www.cbo.gov
Congressional Budget Office home page, containing budgetary analyses and data.

www.taxpolicycenter.org
A joint venture of the Urban Institute and the Brookings Institution, containing many studies of budgets and taxes.

www.taxfoundation.org
The Tax Foundation site, with a wealth of tax information.

www.cbpp.org
The Center on Budget and Policy Priorities focuses on how fiscal policy and public programs affect low- and moderate-income families and individuals.

FURTHER READING

Bennett, Linda L. M., and Stephen Earl Bennett. *Living with Leviathan.* Lawrence: University Press of Kansas, 1990. Examines Americans' coming to terms with big government and their expectations of government largesse.

Berry, William D., and David Lowery. *Understanding United States Government Growth.* New York: Praeger, 1987. An empirical analysis of the causes of the growth of government in the period since World War II.

Jones, Bryan D., and Walter Williams. *The Politics of Bad Ideas.* New York: Pearson Longman, 2007. Shows that there are many bad ideas regarding budgetary policy and explains why they persist.

King, Ronald F. *Money, Taxes, and Politics.* New Haven, CT: Yale University Press, 1993. Explains why democratically elected officials approve tax policies that make rich people richer.

Rubin, Irene S. *The Politics of Public Budgeting: Getting and Spending, Borrowing and Balancing,* 7th ed. Washington, D.C.: CQ Press, 2013. Shows how politics pervades budgetary decisions at every stage.

14

The Federal Bureaucracy

Politics in Action: Regulating Food

Americans do not want to worry about the safety of the food they eat. Indeed, food safety is something we take for granted. But who assures this safety? Bureaucrats. It is their job to keep our food safe from contamination. Although we rarely think about food inspections, they represent one of the most important regulatory functions of government. The fact that we rarely think about food safety is testimony to the success of bureaucrats in carrying out their tasks.

Policing the food supply is not a straightforward task, however. It involves a complex web of federal agencies with overlapping jurisdictions. At least 15 agencies and 30 statutes regulate food safety. Eggs in the shell fall under the purview of the Food and Drug Administration (FDA), but once cracked and processed, they come under the jurisdiction of the U.S. Department of Agriculture (USDA). The USDA is responsible for regulating meat and poultry, while the FDA handles most other food products, including seafood and produce. Cheese pizzas are the FDA's responsibility, but if they have pepperoni on top, Agriculture inspectors step in.

Other parts of the government also play a prominent role in enforcing food safety laws. For example, the Environmental Protection Agency oversees pesticides applied to crops, the Centers for Disease Control and Prevention track food-related illnesses, and the Department of Homeland Security coordinates agencies' safety and security activities.

Is this complex system the result of bureaucratic maneuvering? No—Congress created the system layer on top of layer, with little regard to how it should work as a whole. Critics argue that the system is outdated and that it would be better to create a single food safety agency that could target inspections, streamline safety programs, and use resources more efficiently. However, such proposals have generated little enthusiasm in Congress, where committees are sensitive about

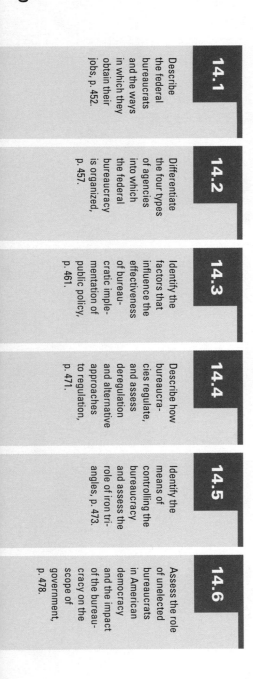

14.1
Describe the federal bureaucrats and the ways in which they obtain their jobs, p. 452.

14.2
Differentiate the four types of agencies into which the federal bureaucracy is organized, p. 457.

14.3
Identify the factors that influence the effectiveness of bureaucratic implementation of public policy, p. 461.

14.4
Describe how bureaucracies regulate, and assess deregulation and alternative approaches to regulation, p. 473.

14.5
Identify the means of controlling the bureaucracy and assess the role of iron triangles, p. 473.

14.6
Assess the role of unelected bureaucrats in American democracy and the impact of the bureaucracy on the scope of government, p. 478.

Government bureaucrats, such as this meat inspector, provide essential services and have important expertise. Although we often take bureaucrats for granted, the quality of our lives would be considerably diminished without them.

452

14.1
14.2
14.3
14.4
14.5
14.6

bureaucracy
According to Max Weber, a hierarchical authority structure that uses task specialization, operates on the merit principle, and behaves with impersonality.

losing jurisdiction over agencies. (For example, in the House, the Energy and Commerce Committee has oversight over the FDA while the Agriculture Committee has responsibility for the USDA.) Furthermore, growers and manufacturers fear a single agency would impose onerous new regulations, product recalls, and fines and could be used by empire-building bureaucrats to expand their budget and regulatory authority. So, little change occurs.

Bureaucracies face other challenges in insuring safe food. The FDA is so short of staff that it can inspect the average U.S. food company just once every 10 years. Nearly two-thirds of all fruits and vegetables and three-quarters of all seafood consumed in the United States in a year come from outside the country in 24 million separate shipments through more than 300 ports, but the FDA can inspect less than 1 percent of food imports—despite repeated problems with contaminated products.

Bureaucrats are central to our lives. They provide essential public services. They possess crucial information and expertise that make them partners with the president and Congress in decision making about public policy. Who knows more than bureaucrats about Social Security recipients or the military capabilities of China? Bureaucrats are also central to politics. They do much more than simply follow orders. Because of their expertise, bureaucrats inevitably have discretion in carrying out policy decisions, which is why congressional committees and interest groups take so much interest in what they do.

Bureaucratic power extends to every corner of American economic and social life, yet bureaucracies are scarcely hinted at in the Constitution. Congress creates each bureaucratic agency, sets its budget, and writes the policies it administers. Most agencies are responsible to the president, whose constitutional responsibility to "take care that the laws shall be faithfully executed" sheds only a dim light on the problems of managing so large a government. How to manage and control bureaucracies is a central problem of democratic government.

Reining in the power of bureaucracies is also a common theme in debates over the scope of government in America. Some political commentators see the bureaucracy as the prime example of a federal government growing out of control. They view the bureaucracy as acquisitive, constantly seeking to expand its size, budgets, and authority while entangling everything in red tape and spewing forth senseless regulations. Others see the bureaucracy as laboring valiantly against great odds to fulfill the missions elected officials have assigned it. Where does the truth lie? The answer is less obvious than you may think. Clearly, bureaucracies require closer examination.

The Bureaucrats

14.1
Describe the federal bureaucrats and the ways in which they obtain their jobs.

ureaucrats are typically much less visible than the president or members of Congress. As a result, Americans usually know little about them. This section examines some myths about bureaucrats and explains who they are and how they got their jobs.

The German sociologist Max Weber advanced his classic conception of bureaucracy, stressing that the bureaucracy was a "rational" way for a modern society to conduct its business.[1] According to Weber, a **bureaucracy** depends on certain elements: It has a *hierarchical authority structure*, in which power flows from the top down and responsibility flows from the bottom up; it uses *task specialization* so that experts instead of amateurs perform technical jobs; and it develops extensive *rules*, which may seem extreme at times, but which allow similar cases to be handled similarly instead of capriciously.

Bureaucracies operate on the *merit principle*, in which entrance and promotion are awarded on the basis of demonstrated abilities rather than on "who you know." Bureaucracies behave with *impersonality* so that they treat all their clients impartially. Weber's classic prototype of the bureaucratic organization depicts the bureaucracy as a well-constructed machine with plenty of (hierarchical) working parts.

☐ Some Bureaucratic Myths and Realities

Bureaucrat baiting is a popular American pastime. Even presidential candidates have climbed aboard the antibureaucracy bandwagon. Jimmy Carter complained about America's "complicated and confused and overlapping and wasteful" bureaucracies; Gerald Ford spoke of the "dead weight" of bureaucracies; and Ronald Reagan insisted that bureaucrats "overregulated" the American economy, causing a decline in productivity.

Any object of such unpopularity will spawn plenty of myths. The following are some of the most prevalent myths about bureaucracy:

- *Americans dislike bureaucrats.* Despite the rhetoric about bureaucracies, Americans are generally satisfied with bureaucrats and the treatment they get from them. Americans may dislike bureaucracies, but they like individual bureaucrats. Surveys have found that two-thirds or more of those who have had encounters with a bureaucrat evaluate these encounters positively. In most instances, people describe bureaucrats as helpful, efficient, fair, courteous, and working to serve their clients' interests.[2]

- *Bureaucracies are growing bigger each year.* This myth is half true and half false. The number of government employees has been expanding, but not the number of *federal* employees. Almost all the growth in the number of public employees has occurred in state and local governments; this number more than doubled in a 40-year period beginning in 1965 while the number of federal employees remained constant. Today, the approximately 20 million state and local public employees far outnumber the approximately 2.6 million civilian (including postal) and 1.3 million active duty military federal government employees. As a percentage of America's total workforce, *federal* government civilian employment has been shrinking, not growing; it now accounts for about 2 percent of all civilian jobs.[3]

  Of course, many state and local employees work on programs that are federally funded, and the federal government hires many private contractors to provide goods and services ranging from hot meals to weapons systems.[4] Such people provide services directly to the federal government or to citizens on its behalf.

- *Most federal bureaucrats work in Washington, D.C.* Fewer than one in seven federal civilian employees work in the Washington, D.C., metropolitan area. In addition, more than 43,000 federal civilian employees work in foreign countries and American territories.[5] If you look in your local phone book under "U.S. Government," you will probably find listings for the local offices of the Postal Service, the Social Security Administration, the FBI, the Department of Agriculture's county agents, recruiters for the armed services, air traffic controllers, the Internal Revenue Service (IRS), and many others.

- *Bureaucracies are ineffective, inefficient, and always mired in red tape.* No words describing bureaucratic behavior are better known than "red tape."[6] Bureaucracy, however, is simply a way of organizing people to perform work. General Motors, a college or university, the U.S. Army, the Department of Health and Human Services, and the Roman Catholic Church are all bureaucracies. Bureaucracies are a little like referees: When they work well, no one gives them much credit, but when they work poorly, everyone calls them unfair, incompetent, or inefficient. Bureaucracies may be inefficient at times, but no one has found a substitute for them, and no one has yet demonstrated that government bureaucracies are more or less inefficient, ineffective, or mired in red tape than private bureaucracies.[7]

Anyone who looks with disdain on American bureaucracies should contemplate life without them. Despite all the complaining about bureaucracies, the vast majority of tasks carried out by governments at all levels are noncontroversial. Bureaucrats deliver mail, test milk, issue Social Security and student loan checks, run national parks, and perform other routine governmental tasks in a perfectly acceptable manner.

Most federal civilian employees work for just a few of the agencies (see Table 14.1 and Figure 14.1). The Department of Defense employs about 28 percent of federal *civilian* workers in addition to the more than 1.3 million men and women in uniform.

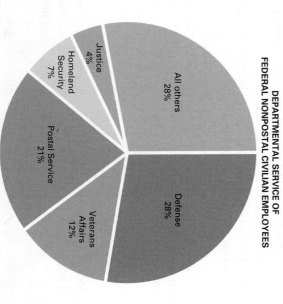

FIGURE 14.1 DEPARTMENTAL SERVICE OF FEDERAL NONPOSTAL CIVILIAN EMPLOYEES

DEPARTMENTAL SERVICE OF
FEDERAL NONPOSTAL CIVILIAN EMPLOYEES

- All others 28%
- Justice 4%
- Homeland Security 7%
- Postal Service 21%
- Veterans Affairs 12%
- Defense 28%

SOURCE: *Budget of the United States Government, Fiscal Year 2015: Analytical Perspectives* (Washington, D.C.: U.S. Government Printing Office, 2014), Tables 11.2 and 11.3.

Altogether, the department makes up more than half the federal bureaucracy. The Postal Service accounts for an additional 21 percent of the federal civilian employees, and the Department of Veterans Affairs, clearly related to national defense, accounts

TABLE 14.1 FEDERAL CIVILIAN EMPLOYMENT

Executive Departments

	Number of Employees[a]
Defense (military functions)	749,100
Veterans Affairs	321,400
Homeland Security	189,800
Justice	117,400
Treasury	108,800
Agriculture	90,800
Health and Human Services	74,600
Interior	69,900
Transportation	56,800
Commerce	45,100
State	33,300
Labor	17,800
Energy	15,900
Housing and Urban Development	8,900
Education	4,100

Larger Noncabinet Agencies

	Number of Employees[a]
U.S. Postal Service	559,265
Social Security Administration	64,100
Corps of Engineers	22,500
National Aeronautics and Space Administration	17,600
Environmental Protection Agency	15,400
Tennessee Valley Authority	12,900
General Services Administration	13,100

[a]Figures are for 2015.

SOURCE: *Budget of the United States Government, Fiscal Year 2015: Analytical Perspectives* (Washington, D.C.: U.S. Government Printing Office, 2014), Tables 8.2 and 8.3.

14.1
14.2
14.3
14.4
14.5
14.6

for about 12 percent of employees. The Departments of Homeland Security and Justice represent 7 and 4 percent of employees, respectively. All other functions of government are handled by the remaining quarter or so of federal employees.

Civil Servants

Given the size of the bureaucracy, it is difficult to imagine a statistically typical bureaucrat. As a whole, however, the permanent bureaucracy is more broadly representative of the American people than are legislators, judges, or presidential appointees in the executive branch[8] (see Figure 14.2).

The diversity of bureaucratic jobs mirrors the diversity of private-sector jobs, including occupations literally ranging from A to Z. Accountants, bakers, census analysts, defense procurement specialists, electricians, foreign service officers, guards in federal prisons, home economists, Indian Affairs agents, judges, kitchen workers, lawyers, missile technologists, narcotics agents, ophthalmologists, postal carriers, quarantine specialists, radiologists, stenographers, truck drivers, underwater demolition experts, virologists, wardens, X-ray technicians, youth counselors, and zoologists all work for the government.

Until little more than one hundred years ago, a person got a job with the government through the patronage system. **Patronage** is a hiring and promotion system based on political factors rather than on merit or competence. Working in a congressional campaign, making large donations, and having the right connections helped people secure jobs with the government. Nineteenth-century presidents staffed the government with their friends and allies, following the view of Andrew Jackson that "to the victors belong the spoils." Scores of office seekers would swarm the White House after Inauguration Day. It is said that during a bout with malaria, Lincoln told an aide to "send in the office seekers" because he finally had something to give them.

A disappointed office seeker named Charles Guiteau helped end this "spoils system" of federal appointments in 1881. Frustrated because President James A. Garfield would not give him a job, Guiteau shot and killed Garfield. Vice President Chester A. Arthur, who then became president, had been known as the Prince of Patronage; he had been collector of the customs for New York, a patronage-rich post. To the surprise of his critics, Arthur encouraged passage of the **Pendleton Civil Service Act** (1883), which created the federal civil service. Today, most federal agencies are covered by some sort of civil service system.

All **civil service** systems are designed to hire and promote members of the bureaucracy on the basis of merit and to create a nonpartisan government service. The **merit principle**—using entrance exams and promotion ratings to reward qualified

---

patronage
One of the key inducements used by party machines. A patronage job, promotion, or contract is one that is given for political reasons rather than for merit or competence alone.

Pendleton Civil Service Act
Passed in 1883, an act that created a federal civil service so that hiring and promotion would be based on merit rather than patronage.

civil service
A system of hiring and promotion based on the merit principle and the desire to create a nonpartisan government service.

merit principle
The idea that hiring should be based on entrance exams and promotion ratings to produce administration by people with talent and skill.

FIGURE 14.2 CHARACTERISTICS OF FEDERAL NONPOSTAL CIVILIAN EMPLOYEES

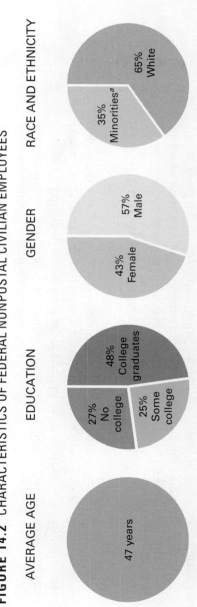

AVERAGE AGE — 47 years

EDUCATION — 27% No college, 25% Some college, 48% College graduates

GENDER — 43% Female, 57% Male

RACE AND ETHNICITY — 35% Minorities[a], 65% White

[a]Includes African Americans, Asian Americans, Native Americans, and Hispanics.

SOURCE: United States Office of Personnel Management, *Common Characteristics of the Government*, 2013.

Hatch Act
A federal law prohibiting government employees from active participation in partisan politics while on duty or for employees in sensitive positions at any time.

Office of Personnel Management
The office in charge of hiring for most agencies of the federal government, using elaborate rules in the process.

GS (General Schedule) rating
A schedule for federal employees, ranging from GS 1 to GS 18, by which salaries can be keyed to rating and experience.

Senior Executive Service
An elite cadre of about 9,000 federal government managers at the top of the civil service system.

---

individuals—is intended to produce an administration of people with talent and skill. Creating a nonpartisan civil service means insulating government workers from the risk of being fired when a new party comes to power. At the same time, the **Hatch Act**, originally passed in 1939 and amended most recently in 1993, prohibits civil service employees from actively participating in partisan politics while on duty. While off duty they may engage in political activities, but they cannot run for partisan elective offices or solicit contributions from the public. Employees with sensitive positions, such as those in the national security area, may not engage in political activities even while off duty.

Why It Matters to You
The Merit System

People obtain positions in the federal bureaucracy through a merit system and are protected against losing their jobs because of their political views. If the president could appoint a substantial percentage of bureaucrats, it is likely that they would be more responsive to the president but also likely that they would be less qualified to serve the public interest than today's bureaucrats.

The **Office of Personnel Management** (OPM) is in charge of hiring for most federal agencies. The president appoints its director, who is confirmed by the Senate. The OPM has elaborate rules about hiring, promotion, working conditions, and firing. To get a civil service job, usually candidates must first take a test. If they pass, their names are sent to agencies when jobs requiring their particular skills become available. For each open position, the OPM will send three names to the agency. Except under unusual circumstances, the agency must hire one of these three individuals. Each job is assigned a **GS (General Schedule) rating** ranging from GS 1 to GS 18. Salaries are keyed to rating and experience.

At the very top of the civil service system (GS 16–18) are about 9,000 members of the **Senior Executive Service**, the "cream of the crop" of the federal employees. These executives earn high salaries, and the president may move them from one agency to another as leadership needs change.

After a probationary period, civil servants are protected by the civil service system—overprotected, critics claim. Protecting all workers against political firings—a prerequisite for a nonpartisan civil service—may also protect a few from dismissal for good cause. Firing incompetents is hard work and is unusual. Employees are entitled to appeal, and these appeals can consume weeks, months, or even years. More than one agency has decided to tolerate incompetents, assigning them trivial or no duties, rather than invest its resources in the task of discharging them. In the case of female, minority, or older workers, appeals can also be based on antidiscrimination statutes, making dismissal potentially even more difficult.

Sometimes presidents seek more control over federal employees. President George W. Bush proposed to limit job protection for employees in the Department of Homeland Security. After a protracted battle, Congress agreed, although implementation of this change has been slow and opposed by employee unions.

☐ Political Appointees

As an incoming administration celebrates its victory and prepares to take control of the government, Congress publishes the *Plum Book*, which lists top federal jobs (that is, "plums") available for direct presidential appointment, often with Senate confirmation. There are about 500 of these top policymaking posts (mostly cabinet secretaries, undersecretaries, assistant secretaries, and bureau chiefs) and about 2,500 lesser positions.

All incoming presidents launch a nationwide talent search for qualified personnel. Presidents seek individuals who combine executive talent, political skills, and sympathy for policy positions similar to those of the administration. Often, the president tries to ensure some diversity and balance in terms of gender, ethnicity, region, and different interests within the party. Some positions, especially ambassadorships, go to large campaign contributors. A few of these appointees will be civil servants, temporarily elevated to a "political" status; most, however, will be political appointees, "in-and-outers" who stay for a while and then leave.

Once in office, these administrative policymakers constitute what Hugh Heclo has called a "government of strangers."[9] Their most important trait is their transience. The average assistant secretary or undersecretary lasts less than two years.[10] Few top officials stay long enough to know their own subordinates well, much less people in other agencies. Administrative routines, budget cycles, and legal complexities are often new to them. And although these *Plum Book* appointees may have the outward signs of power, many of them find it challenging to exercise real control over much of what their subordinates do and have difficulty leaving their mark on policy. They soon learn that they are dependent on senior civil servants, who know more, have been there longer, and will outlast them.

Analytical intelligence, substantive expertise, and managerial skills may be crucial to implementing policies effectively, but presidents usually place a premium on personal loyalty and commitment to their programs when evaluating candidates for positions in the bureaucracy. The White House wants bureaucratic responsiveness to its policies. Nonetheless, evidence indicates that bureaucratic resistance to change does not pose a substantial obstacle to presidents' achieving their goals and that career civil servants are more effective than political appointees at managing agencies.[11]

If policy loyalty can be problematic as a criterion for filling key positions, even more potentially problematic are the practices of using these positions to reward political associates and key campaign contributors and of satisfying the desire of high-level appointees to name their own subordinates. Such factors were, for example, behind George W. Bush's nomination of Michael Brown, the former president of the Arabian Horse Association, to head the Federal Emergency Management Agency—an appointment that came back to haunt him in the wake of the agency's performance in dealing with the destruction caused by Hurricane Katrina.

How the Federal Bureaucracy Is Organized

14.2 Differentiate the four types of agencies into which the federal bureaucracy is organized.

complete organizational chart of the American federal government would occupy a large wall. You could pore over this chart, trace the lines of responsibility and authority, and see how government is organized—at least on paper.

A very simplified organizational chart appears in Figure 14.3. A much easier way to look at how the federal executive branch is organized is to group agencies into four basic types: cabinet departments, independent regulatory commissions, government corporations, and independent executive agencies.

☐ Cabinet Departments

Each of the 15 cabinet departments is headed by a secretary (except the Department of Justice, which is headed by the attorney general), who has been chosen by the president and approved by the Senate. Undersecretaries, deputy undersecretaries, and assistant

458

14.1
14.2
14.3
14.4
14.5
14.6

FIGURE 14.3 ORGANIZATION OF THE EXECUTIVE BRANCH

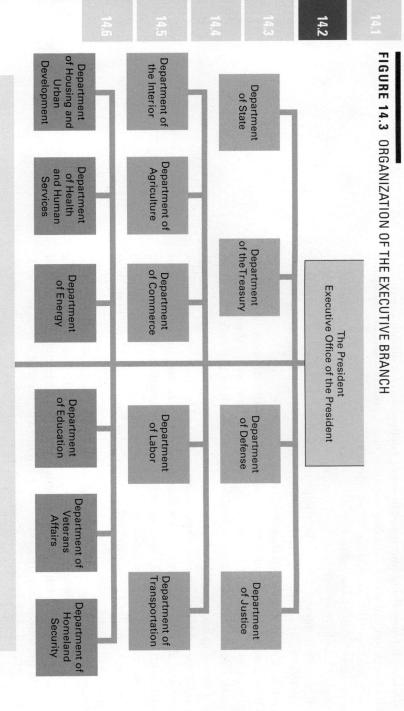

The President
Executive Office of the President

Department of State

Department of the Treasury

Department of Defense

Department of Justice

Department of the Interior

Department of Agriculture

Department of Commerce

Department of Labor

Department of Health and Human Services

Department of Housing and Urban Development

Department of Energy

Department of Education

Department of Veterans Affairs

Department of Transportation

Department of Homeland Security

INDEPENDENT ESTABLISHMENTS AND GOVERNMENT CORPORATIONS

Administrative Conference of the United States
African Development Foundation
Broadcasting Board of Governors
Central Intelligence Agency
Commodity Futures Trading Commission
Consumer Financial Protection Board
Consumer Product Safety Commission
Corporation for National and Community Service
Defense Nuclear Facilities Safety Board
Environmental Protection Agency
Equal Employment Opportunity Commission
Export-Import Bank of the United States
Farm Credit Administration
Federal Communications Commission
Federal Deposit Insurance Corporation
Federal Election Commission
Federal Housing Finance Board
Federal Labor Relations Authority
Federal Maritime Commission
Federal Mediation and Conciliation Service
Federal Mine Safety and Health Review Commission

Federal Reserve System
Federal Retirement Thrift Investment Board
Federal Trade Commission
General Services Administration
Inter-American Foundation
Merit Systems Protection Board
National Aeronautics and Space Administration
National Archives and Records Administration
National Capital Planning Commission
National Credit Union Administration
National Foundation on the Arts and Humanities
National Labor Relations Board
National Mediation Board
National Railroad Passenger Corporation (Amtrak)
National Science Foundation
National Transportation Safety Board
Nuclear Regulatory Commission
Occupational Safety and Health Review Commission

Office of the Director of National Intelligence
Office of Government Ethics
Office of Personnel Management
Office of Special Counsel
Overseas Private Investment Corporation
Peace Corps
Pension Benefit Guaranty Corporation
Postal Regulatory Commission
Railroad Retirement Board
Securities and Exchange Commission
Selective Service System
Small Business Administration
Social Security Administration
Tennessee Valley Authority
Trade and Development Agency
U.S. Agency for International Development
U.S. Commission on Civil Rights
U.S. International Trade Commission
U.S. Postal Service

SOURCE: Office of the Federal Register, *United States Government Manual 2014* (Washington, D.C.: U.S. Government Printing Office, 2014).

secretaries report to the secretary. Each department manages specific policy areas, and each has its own budget and its own staff. Each department has a unique mission and is organized somewhat differently. The real work of a department is done in the bureaus, which divide the work into more specialized areas (a bureau is sometimes called a *service, office, administration,* or other name).

Sometimes status as a cabinet department can be controversial. For several years, some Republicans have tried to disband the Education, Energy, and Commerce departments, arguing that they waste tax dollars and implement policies that should be terminated.

Independent Regulatory Commissions

Each **independent regulatory commission** has responsibility for making and enforcing rules to protect the public interest in a particular sector of the economy, as well as for judging disputes over these rules.[12] The independent regulatory commissions are sometimes called the alphabet soup of American government because most of them are known by their initials. Some examples follow:

- *FRB (Federal Reserve Board)*, charged with governing banks and, even more importantly, regulating the supply of money and thus interest rates

- *NLRB (National Labor Relations Board)*, created to regulate labor–management relations

- *FCC (Federal Communications Commission)*, charged with licensing radio and TV stations and regulating their programming in the public interest as well as with regulating interstate long-distance telephone rates, cable television, and the Internet

- *FTC (Federal Trade Commission)*, responsible for regulating business practices and controlling monopolistic behavior, and now involved in policing the accuracy of advertising

- *SEC (the Securities and Exchange Commission)*, created to police the stock market

Each of these independent regulatory commissions is governed by a small number of commissioners, usually 5 to 10 members appointed by the president and confirmed by the Senate for fixed terms. The president cannot fire regulatory commission members as easily as he can cabinet officers and members of the White House staff. The difference stems from a Supreme Court ruling in a case in which President Franklin Roosevelt fired a man named Humphrey from the FTC. Humphrey took the matter to court but died shortly afterward. When the executors of his estate sued for back pay, the Court held that presidents could not fire members of regulatory agencies without just cause (*Humphrey's Executor v. United States*, 1935). "Just cause" has never been defined clearly, and no member of a regulatory commission has been fired since.

Interest groups consider the rule making by independent regulatory commissions (and, of course, their membership) very important. The FCC can deny a multimillion-dollar TV station a license renewal—a power that certainly sparks the interest of the National Association of Broadcasters. The FTC regulates business practices, ranging from credit and loans to mergers—a power that prompts both business and consumers to pay careful attention to its activities and membership.

So concerned are interest groups with these regulatory bodies that some critics speak of the "capture" of the regulators by the regulatees.[13] It is common for members of commissions to be recruited from the ranks of the regulated. Sometimes, too, members of commissions or staffs of these agencies move on to jobs in the very industries they were regulating. Some lawyers among them use contacts and information gleaned

independent regulatory commission
A government agency with responsibility for making and enforcing rules to protect the public interest in some sector of the economy and for judging disputes over these rules.

460

14.1

14.2

14.3

14.4

14.5

14.6

government corporation
A government organization that, like business corporations, provides a service that could be delivered by the private sector and typically charges for its services. The U.S. Postal Service is an example.

at the commission when they leave and represent clients before their former employers at the commission.

For years the Minerals Management Service (now known as the Bureau of Ocean Energy Management, Regulation and Enforcement), which regulates offshore oil drilling, had the dual role of both fostering and policing the industry. The agency declared itself industry's partner and often adopted industry-generated standards as federal regulations, waived environmental reviews, and failed to pursue companies for equipment or safety failures. Agency employees also accepted gifts from oil and gas firms and partied with industry officials. The Nuclear Regulatory Commission is another agency that critics charge has been captured by those it regulates. A later section of this chapter discusses the bureaucracy's relationship with interest groups in more detail.

☐ Government Corporations

The federal government also has a handful of **government corporations.** These are not exactly like private corporations in which you can buy stock and collect dividends, but they are like private corporations—and different from other parts of the government—in two ways. First, they provide a service that could be handled by the private sector. Second, they typically charge for their services, though often at rates cheaper than those the consumer would pay to a private-sector producer.

The granddaddy of the government corporations is the Tennessee Valley Authority (TVA). Established in 1933 as part of the New Deal, it has controlled floods, improved navigation, protected the soil against erosion, and provided inexpensive electricity to millions of Americans in Tennessee, Kentucky, Alabama, and neighboring states. The post office, one of the original cabinet departments (first headed by Benjamin Franklin), has become the government's largest corporation: the U.S. Postal Service. Occasionally the government has taken over a "sick industry" and turned it into a government corporation. Amtrak, the railroad passenger service, is one example.

We depend on bureaucrats, such as those in the Environmental Protection Agency, to clean up our environment. They have had many successes, such as restoring Lake Erie to a state in which fish, and these fishermen, can thrive.

The Independent Executive Agencies

The **independent executive agencies** are essentially all the rest of the government—the agencies that are not cabinet departments, regulatory commissions, or government corporations. Their administrators typically are appointed by the president and serve at his will. Some 45 to 50 such agencies are listed in the current United States Government Manual. Among the biggest (in size of budget) are the following:

- *General Services Administration (GSA)*, the government's landlord, which handles buildings, supplies, and purchasing
- *National Science Foundation (NSF)*, the agency supporting scientific research
- *National Aeronautics and Space Administration (NASA)*, the agency that takes Americans to the moon and points beyond

Bureaucracies as Implementors

14.3 Identify the factors that influence the effectiveness of bureaucratic implementation of public policy.

Bureaucracies are essentially *implementors* of policy. They take congressional, presidential, and sometimes even judicial pronouncements and develop procedures and rules for implementing policy goals. They also manage the routines of government, from delivering mail to collecting taxes to training troops.

What Implementation Means

Public policies are rarely self-executing. Congress typically announces the goals of a policy in broad terms, sets up an administrative apparatus, and leaves the bureaucracy the task of working out the details of the program. In other words, the bureaucracy is left to implement the program. **Policy implementation** is the stage of policymaking between the establishment of a policy (such as the passage of a legislative act, the issuing of an executive order, the handing down of a judicial decision, or the promulgation of a regulatory rule) and the results of the policy for individuals.[14] In other words, implementation is a critical aspect of policymaking. At a minimum, implementation includes three elements:

1. Creation of a new agency or assignment of a new responsibility to an old agency
2. Translation of policy goals into operational rules and development of guidelines for the program
3. Coordination of resources and personnel to achieve the intended goals

Why the Best-Laid Plans Sometimes Flunk the Implementation Test

The Scottish poet Robert Burns once wrote, "The best laid schemes o' mice and men/ Gang aft a-gley [often go awry]." So, too, with the best intended public policies. Policies that people expect to work often fail. High expectations followed by dashed hopes are the frequent fate of well-intended public policies. Analysis reveals that implementation can break down for any of several reasons.

PROGRAM DESIGN One reason implementation can break down is faulty program design. Congress overwhelmingly passed a bill to guarantee health insurance to millions of Americans when they change or lose their jobs or lose coverage. Yet the law has been ineffective because insurance companies often charge these individuals premiums far higher than standard rates and thus they cannot afford the insurance.[15]

LACK OF CLARITY Congress is fond of stating a broad policy goal in legislation and then leaving implementation up to the bureaucracies. Members of Congress can thus escape messy details and place blame for the implementation decisions elsewhere (see "Young People and Politics: Drug Offenses and Financial Aid").

Such was the case with the controversial Title IX of the Education Act of 1972,[16] which declared, "No person in the United States shall, on the basis of sex, be excluded from participation in, be denied the benefits of, or be subjected to discrimination under any education program or activity receiving federal financial assistance." Because almost every college and university receives some federal financial assistance, the law forbade almost all colleges and universities from discriminating on the basis of gender. Interest groups supporting women's athletics convinced Congress to include a provision about college athletics. Congress directed the Secretary of Health, Education, and Welfare (today, Education) to publish regulations implementing the law, with "reasonable provisions considering the nature of the particular sports."

Young People & Politics

Drug Offenses and Financial Aid

In 1998, Congress included in a law governing financial aid for college students a provision that prohibited students convicted of drug offenses from receiving grants and loans from the federal government—even if the offense was relatively minor or the conviction happened years ago. A student convicted of a drug offense as an adult could be denied financial aid and from one year to life, depending on the number of offenses and severity of conviction. Not surprisingly, the provision became a matter of contention.

The provision itself might seem a bit severe, but there is more. Someone convicted of armed robbery, rape, or even murder, once out of prison, is entitled to government grants and loans with no questions asked. And yet drug offenses were enough to deny tens of thousands of would-be college students financial aid.

Members of Congress accused the Department of Education, under Clinton and Bush, of distorting the law's intent. They argued that the department, which administers financial aid programs, was being too strict in its interpretation. The department responded that Congress had written a vague law—one that simply referred to "a student who has been convicted," and that it was faithfully implementing the letter of the law. In effect, the department argued that it had no discretion in the matter and could not act on its own to make financial aid policy more just.

The George W. Bush administration suggested ending the prohibition on aid for those who violated

drug laws before entering college. However, it wanted to continue the aid ban for those who commit such crimes while enrolled in college. Its goal, the administration said, was to discourage students from using drugs. The problem, as others saw it, was that such a rule would still impose stiffer penalties for drug use than for any other crime. It would also have the effect of barring some first-time, minor offenders from getting financial aid while restoring it for more serious drug lawbreakers.

Eight years after passing the original ban on financial aid for drug use, Congress revised the law. The new statute allows students with past drug convictions to receive student aid, but current students who are convicted of drug offenses will still lose their federal aid—for a year for a first offense, two years for a second offense, and indefinitely for a third offense.

Anticipating implementation problems is difficult. Putting together coalitions within Congress is also difficult. One consequence of these difficulties is that laws are often vague—and often have unintended consequences as well.

CRITICAL THINKING QUESTIONS

1. How much discretion should a bureaucratic unit have to correct injustices in laws?

2. Why is it so difficult for Congress to anticipate problems implementing laws?

Just what does this part of the law mean? Proponents of women's athletics thought it meant that discrimination against women's sports was also prohibited. Some, with good reason, looked forward to seeing women's sports funded on an equal footing with men's. To colleges and universities with big-time athletic programs and to some alumni, however, the vague language called for equality in golf and swimming, not men's football and basketball programs, which could continue to have the lion's share of athletic budgets. The Department of Health, Education and Welfare developed a 30-page interpretation that recognized that football was "unique" among college sports. If football was unique, then the interpretation implied that male-dominated football programs could continue to outspend women's athletic programs.

Supporters of equal budgets for male and female athletics were outraged. A 100-word section in a congressional statute had prompted a 30-page interpretation by the bureaucracy, and the statute and its interpretation in turn prompted scores of court cases. Policy problems that Congress cannot resolve are not likely to be easily resolved by bureaucracies.

Bureaucrats receive not only unclear orders but also contradictory ones. James Q. Wilson points out that the Immigration and Naturalization Service (INS) was supposed to keep out illegal immigrants but let in necessary agricultural workers, to carefully screen foreigners seeking to enter the country but facilitate the entry of foreign tourists, and to find and expel undocumented aliens but not break up families, impose hardships, violate civil rights, or deprive employers of low-paid workers. "No organization can accomplish all of these goals well, especially when advocates of each have the power to mount newspaper and congressional investigations of the agency's 'failures.'"[17] Similarly, Congress has ordered the National Park Service to preserve the environmental quality of national parks *and* to keep the parks accessible to tourists. The Forest Service is supposed to help timber companies exploit the lumber potential in the national forests *and* to preserve the natural environment. The Bureau

Bureaucracies are often asked to implement unclear laws. When Congress prohibited gender discrimination in college athletics, for example, it left it to bureaucrats to create guidelines that would end discrimination while addressing the unique needs of different sports. It took years—and several lawsuits—to establish the law's meaning.

of Ocean Energy Management, Regulation and Enforcement is to meet the nation's energy needs by leasing tracts for exploration and collect the government's share of oil and gas revenue while also regulating the industry. It is not surprising that the former goal, supported by the energy industry, became the agency's primary objective.

LACK OF RESOURCES

As noted earlier, we often hear the charge that bureaucracies are bloated. The important issue, however, is not the size of the bureaucracy in the abstract but whether it is the appropriate size for the job the bureaucracy has been assigned to do.[18] As big as a bureaucracy may seem in the aggregate, it frequently lacks the staff—along with the necessary staff training, funding, supplies, and equipment—to carry out the tasks it has been assigned. In recent years, for example, the news has been filled with stories of serious problems, many of them ongoing, such as the following:

- U.S. troops in the war in Iraq had insufficient numbers of body armor and armored Humvees and trucks to protect them against roadside bombs.

- After the invasion of Iraq in March 2003, the United States had too few troops to devote to fighting the Taliban in Afghanistan.

- Although 80 percent of the nation's drug supply and half of its medical devices and food are imported, the Food and Drug Administration lacks the personnel and computer systems to identify, much less inspect, the plants producing these items.

- Because of a lack of funding, the popular Head Start program serves only about half the children who are eligible to participate.

- Because of a lack of personnel, the Social Security Administration takes well over a year to process claims for Disability Insurance.

- The Fish and Wildlife Service can only consider a very small fraction of the warranted petitions to protect endangered species.

- The U.S. Immigration and Customs Enforcement (ICE) lacks the personnel to track most of the millions of aliens who overstay their visas or engage in suspicious activities. The ICE also lacks the resources even to identify, much less deport, more than a small percentage of the 200,000 convicted criminal aliens in the United States.

- The FBI headquarters lacks computers that would allow the agency to search its own databases for multiple terms such as "aviation" and "schools," which would have helped in identifying the 9/11 terrorists. Only about 50 agents can converse in Arabic, and the agency has a serious shortage of translators for intercepted communications.

- National Guard units have only a third of the equipment they need to respond to domestic disasters and terrorist attacks.

- The Federal Aviation Administration (FAA) lacks the proper personnel and equipment to direct the nation's air traffic safely.

- The Department of Homeland Security could not deploy new machines for detecting smuggled nuclear bombs because the United States had run out of a crucial element, helium 3.

- A lack of skilled personnel, the use of outdated instruments, and aging facilities hamper the nation's ability to identify the source of a nuclear weapon used in a terrorist attack.

- The Bureau of Ocean Energy Management, Regulation and Enforcement lacks the resources and technically trained personnel to oversee ocean drilling and has to rely on the expertise of those it is supposed to regulate.

- There is a shortage of epidemiologists who are trained to recognize and investigate the outbreak of infectious disease.

standard operating procedures
Better known as SOPs, these procedures for everyday decision making enable bureaucrats to bring efficiency and uniformity to the running of complex organizations. Uniformity promotes fairness and makes personnel interchangeable.

Why It Matters to You

Bureaucratic Resources

A case can be made that some bureaucracies are too small. It is likely that a substantial increase in the resources available to those who implement policies would result in improved quality of government services and in the increased ability of agencies to appropriately implement the policies established by Congress and the president.

Why does Congress not simply give the bureaucracies more resources? Some well-organized interests fight against adding resources to particular agencies because they do not wish to be inspected or regulated and prefer an ineffective bureaucracy. Polluters, coal mine owners, and bankers, for example, rarely welcome inspections.

Equally important is the scarcity of budgetary resources. Pressures to allocate personnel to direct services—for example, to the provision of agricultural expertise to farmers—limit the staff available to implement other policies. In addition, the irresistible urge of policymakers to provide services to the public helps to ensure that the bureaucracies will have more programs than they have resources to adequately implement. In 2010, Congress expanded the FDA's mission for food safety, requiring more frequent inspections of food facilities. It did not expand the agency's budget commensurate with its new responsibilities, however. The budget for the agency overseeing offshore oil drilling was basically flat for four decades, even as drilling activity in deep water drastically increased and the technology grew more complicated.

Finally, in an age when "big government" is under attack, there are strong political incentives to downsize government bureaucracy.

LACK OF AUTHORITY Agencies may also lack the *authority* necessary to meet their responsibilities. In 2008, we learned that the Securities and Exchange Commission's supervision of Wall Street's largest investment banks was on a "voluntary" basis. The FDA, which has responsibility for protecting the public from prescription drugs that have dangerous side effects, does no testing of its own and must rely entirely on the test results submitted by manufacturers. Yet it lacks the subpoena power to obtain documents when it suspects that drug companies are withholding data about adverse drug reactions or misrepresenting test results. It often lacks access even to company documents used as evidence in private product-liability cases. Similarly, the Department of Agriculture lacks authority to close meat processing plants—even those with serious violations of food safety standards.

Some agencies not only lack authority but frequently fail to exercise the authority that they have. The Mine Safety and Health Administration can seek to close mines that it deems unsafe and to close repeat offenders, but it rarely does so. In addition, the fines it levies are relatively small and many go uncollected for years. It lacks subpoena power, a basic investigatory tool, and its criminal sanctions are weak.

Many policies are implemented by state and local governments. The federal government may try to influence elementary and secondary education, for example, but it is the state and local governments that provide the actual services. Federal influence over these governments is indirect, at best. Other policies, ranging from safety in the workplace to pollution control, are implemented by thousands of private individuals, groups, and businesses.[19] With such implementers, bureaucrats are more likely to request, educate, and negotiate than to issue orders and institute legal proceedings.

ADMINISTRATIVE ROUTINE For most bureaucrats, administration is a routine matter most of the time. They follow **standard operating procedures**, better known as SOPs, to help them make numerous everyday decisions. Standard rules save time. If a

466

14.1

14.2

14.3

14.4

14.5

14.6

administrative discretion
The authority of administrative actors to select among various responses to a given problem. Discretion is greatest when routines, or standard operating procedures, do not fit a case.

street-level bureaucrats
A phrase referring to those bureaucrats who are in constant contact with the public and have considerable administrative discretion.

Social Security caseworker had to take the time to invent a new rule for every potential client and clear it at higher levels, few clients would be served. Thus, agencies write detailed manuals to cover as many particular situations as officials can anticipate. The regulations elaborating the Internal Revenue Code compose an IRS agent's bible. Similarly, a customs agent has binders filled with rules and regulations about what can and cannot be brought into the United States duty free.

In addition, SOPs bring uniformity to complex organizations. Justice is better served when officials apply rules uniformly, as in the implementation of welfare policies that distribute benefits to the needy or in the levying of fines for underpayment of taxes. Uniformity also makes personnel interchangeable. The army, for example, can transfer soldiers to any spot in the world, and they can find out how to do their job by referring to the appropriate manual.

Routines are essential to bureaucracy. Yet, when not appropriate to a situation, they can become frustrating "red tape" or even potentially dangerous obstacles to action. An October 1983 terrorist attack on their barracks outside Beirut, Lebanon, killed 241 Marines while they slept. A presidential commission appointed to examine the causes of the tragedy concluded that, among other factors, the Marines in the peacekeeping force were "not trained, organized, staffed, or supported to deal effectively with the terrorist threat."[20] In other words, they had not altered their SOPs regarding security, which is basic to any military unit, to meet the unique challenges of a terrorist attack.

The FAA's protocols (routines) for hijackings assumed that the pilot of a hijacked aircraft would notify an air traffic controller that there had been a hijacking, that the FAA could identify the plane, that there would be time for the FAA and NORAD (North American Aerospace Defense Command) to address the issue, and that the hijacking would not be a suicide mission. As the 9/11 Commission put it, these SOPs were "unsuited in every respect" for the 9/11 terrorist hijackings.[21]

Sometimes an agency simply fails to establish routines that are necessary to complete its tasks. For example, the General Accounting Office found that the FAA failed to determine whether the violations its inspectors uncovered at aircraft repair stations were ever corrected. The FAA did not keep the proper paperwork for adequate follow-up activities.

ADMINISTRATORS' DISPOSITIONS Bureaucrats operate not only within the confines of routines, but often with considerable discretion to behave independently. **Administrative discretion** is the authority of administrative actors to select among various responses to a given problem.[22] Discretion is greatest when rules do not fit a particular case, and this situation is common—even in agencies with elaborate rules and regulations.

Some administrators exercise more discretion than others. Michael Lipsky coined the phrase **street-level bureaucrats** to refer to those bureaucrats who are in constant contact with the public (often a hostile one) and have considerable discretion; they include police officers, welfare workers, and lower-court judges.[23] No amount of rules, not even in thousands of pages as with IRS rules, will eliminate the need for bureaucratic discretion on some policies. It is up to the highway patrol officer who stops you to choose whether to issue you a warning or a ticket.

Ultimately, the way bureaucrats use discretion depends on their dispositions toward the policies and rules they administer. Some of these policies and rules may conflict with their views or their personal or organizational interests. When people are asked to execute orders with which they do not agree, slippage is likely to occur between policy decisions and performance. A great deal of mischief may occur as well.

On one occasion, President Nixon ordered Secretary of Defense Melvin Laird to bomb a Palestine Liberation Organization hideaway, a move Laird opposed. As Laird later said, "We had bad weather for forty-eight hours. The Secretary of Defense can always find a reason not to do something."[24] The president's order was stalled for days and eventually rescinded.

Controlling the exercise of discretion is a difficult task. It is not easy to fire bureaucrats in the civil service, and removing appointed officials may be politically embarrassing to the president, especially if those officials have strong support in

Point to Ponder

Bureaucracies are inherently hierarchical, have many rules, and accord bureaucrats discretion in the implementation of those rules. Sometimes the rules are inappropriate and frustrate those to whom they apply.

However, is there an alternative to providing services through bureaucracies?

"It's always cozy in here. We're insulated by layers of bureaucracy."

Congress and among interest groups. In the private sector, leaders of organizations provide incentives such as pay raises to encourage employees to perform their tasks in a certain way. In the public sector, however, special bonuses are rare, and pay raises tend to be small and across the board. Moreover, there is not necessarily room at the top for qualified bureaucrats. Unlike a typical private business, a government agency cannot expand just because it is performing a service effectively and efficiently.

In the absence of positive and negative incentives, the government relies heavily on rules to limit the discretion of implementors. As former vice president Al Gore put it in a report issued by the National Performance Review,

> Because we don't want politicians' families, friends, and supporters placed in "no-show" jobs, we have more than 100,000 pages of personnel rules and regulations defining in exquisite detail how to hire, promote, or fire federal employees. Because we don't want employees or private companies profiteering from federal contracts, we create procurement processes that require endless signatures and long months to buy almost anything. Because we don't want agencies using tax dollars for any unapproved purpose, we dictate precisely how much they can spend on everything from telephones to travel.[25]

Often these rules end up creating new obstacles to effective and efficient governing, however. As U.S. forces were streaming toward the Persian Gulf in the fall of 1990 to liberate Kuwait from Iraq, the air force placed an emergency order for 6,000 Motorola commercial radio receivers. But Motorola refused to do business with the air force because of a government requirement that the company set up separate accounting and cost-control systems to fill the order. The only way the U.S. Air Force could acquire the much-needed receivers was for Japan to buy them and donate them to the United States!

Bureaucrats typically apply thousands of pages of rules in the performance of routine tasks, but many bureaucrats—especially street-level bureaucrats—must use administrative discretion as well. These border patrol officers, shown arresting undocumented immigrants on the U.S.-Mexican border, must decide whom they will search carefully and whom they will let pass with a quick check.

FRAGMENTATION

Sometimes, as we saw in the regulation of food, responsibility for a policy is dispersed among several units within the bureaucracy. The federal government has had as many as 96 agencies involved with the issue of nuclear proliferation. Similarly, in the field of welfare, 10 different departments and agencies administer more than 100 federal human services programs. The Department of Health and Human Services has responsibility for basic welfare grants to the states to aid families, the Department of Housing and Urban Development provides housing assistance for the poor, the Department of Agriculture runs the food stamp program, and the Department of Labor administers training programs and provides assistance in obtaining employment.

The resources and authority necessary for the president to attack a problem comprehensively are often distributed among many bureaucratic units. In 2009, the National Security Agency, the State Department, and the CIA had separate bits of information that Umar Farouk Abdulmutallab was a potential threat to the United States. Nevertheless, on Christmas Day he was allowed to board a plane to the United States with explosives hidden in his underclothing. The agencies had failed to share and "connect the dots" among the various pieces of information.

More broadly, consider border security, an important element of homeland security. In 2002, prior to the establishment of the Department of Homeland Security, at least 33 departments and agencies had responsibility for protecting America's borders, focusing on threats ranging from illegal immigrants and chemical toxins to missiles and electronic sabotage. It is difficult to coordinate so many different agencies, especially when they lack a history of trust and cooperation. Moreover, there are often physical obstacles to cooperation, such as the largely incompatible computer systems of the ICE and the Coast Guard. Once the borders have been breached and an attack has occurred, many other offices get involved in homeland security, including hundreds of state and local agencies.

When the BP Deepwater Horizon spill occurred in the Gulf of Mexico, Americans learned that although the federal government owns the ocean up to 200 miles off U.S. shores, Washington had no central body directed with making decisions about how to explore, map, preserve, exploit, and manage it. Disaster struck, and the nation watched in dismay as the dozens of offices and agencies with jurisdiction over slices of ocean activity—environmental protection, offshore drilling, national security, science—scrambled to take control. But the bureaucrats were mostly at the mercy of the only people with the expertise to plumb the Gulf's depths, the BP engineers. At the height of the crisis, President Obama issued an executive order pulling together the 24 separate offices and agencies—housed in the Commerce, Defense, Energy, and Interior departments, the Environmental Protection Agency, the National Oceanic and Atmospheric Administration, and elsewhere—and required them all to report to a new umbrella entity, the White House's National Oceans Council.

If fragmentation is a problem, why not reorganize the government? The answer lies in hyperpluralism and the decentralization of power. Congressional committees recognize that they would lose jurisdiction over agencies if these agencies were merged with others. Interest groups do not want to give up the close relationships they have developed with "their" agencies. Agencies themselves do not want to be submerged within a broader bureaucratic unit. Moreover, most bureaucratic units have multiple responsibilities, making it difficult to subsume them under one organizational umbrella. All these forces fight reorganization, and they usually win.[26] President Clinton's proposal to merge the Drug Enforcement Administration and the Customs Service met with immediate opposition from the agencies and their congressional allies. Pursuing the merger became too costly for the president, who had to focus on higher-priority issues.

Nevertheless, under the right conditions, reorganization is possible. Following the attacks of September 11, 2001, President George W. Bush concluded, in the summer of 2002, that the only way to overcome the fragmentation of agencies involved in providing homeland security was to create a new department. Congress created the Department of Homeland Security at the end of 2002, the largest reorganization of the federal government in half a century.

Fragmentation not only disperses responsibility but also allows agencies to work at cross-purposes. For years, one agency supported tobacco farmers while another discouraged smoking. One agency encourages the redevelopment of inner cities while another helps build highways, making it easier for people to live in the suburbs. One agency helps farmers grow crops more efficiently while another pays them to produce less. As long as Congress refuses to make clear decisions about priorities, bureaucrats will implement contradictory policies.

☐ A Case Study of Successful Implementation: The Voting Rights Act of 1965

Even when a policy is controversial, implementation can be effective if goals are clear and there are adequate means to achieve them. In 1965, Congress, responding to generations of discrimination against prospective African American voters in the South, passed the Voting Rights Act. The act outlawed literacy tests and other tests previously used to discriminate against African American registrants. Congress singled out six states in the Deep South in which the number of registered African American voters was minuscule and ordered the Justice Department to send federal registrars to each county in those states to register qualified voters. Those who interfered with the work of federal registrars were to face stiff penalties.

Congress charged the attorney general, as the head of the Justice Department, with implementing the Voting Rights Act. He acted quickly and dispatched hundreds of registrars—some protected by U.S. marshals—to Southern counties. Within seven and a half months of the act's passage, more than 300,000 new African American voters were on the rolls. The proportion of African Americans in the South who were registered to vote increased from 43 percent in 1964 to 66 percent in 1970, partly because of the Voting Rights Act.[27]

Implementation of the 1965 Voting Rights Act was successful because its goal was clear: to register African Americans to vote in counties that had denied them their voting rights for years. In addition, implementors, such as this federal registrar, had the authority to do their jobs.

The Voting Rights Act was a successful case of implementation by any standard, but not because it was popular with everyone. Southern representatives and senators were outraged by the bill, and a filibuster had delayed its passage in the Senate. It was successful because its goal was clear (to register large numbers of African American voters), its implementation was straightforward (sending out people to register them), and the authority of the implementors was clear (they had the support of the attorney general and even U.S. marshals) and concentrated in the Justice Department, which was disposed to implementing the law vigorously.

☐ Privatization

A movement to "reinvent government" started in the 1980s. At the heart of this endeavor were efforts to decentralize authority within agencies to provide more room for innovation and to provide performance incentives for government bureaucracies through market competition with private contractors, which could bid to provide government services. Since that time private contractors have become a virtual fourth branch of the national government, which spends nearly half a trillion dollars a year on them. The war in Iraq, increased emphasis on domestic security, and the aftermath of Hurricane Katrina all gave this trend a further impetus.

Everyone seems to agree that the government cannot operate without contractors, which provide the surge capacity to handle crises without expanding the permanent bureaucracy. Moreover, contractors may provide specialized skills that the government lacks. Some government executives favor contractors because they find the federal bureaucracy slow, inflexible, or incompetent. Using contractors also allows officials to brag about cutting the federal work force while actually expanding the number of people working for the government.

The theory behind contracting for services is that competition in the private sector will result in better service at lower costs than that provided by public bureaucracies, who have traditionally had a monopoly on providing services. Although there is evidence that some local governments have saved money on services such as garbage collection, there is no evidence that private contractors have provided services more efficiently at the federal level. Moreover, competition is not always present. One study found that fewer than half of the new contracts and payments against existing contracts are now subject to full and open competition.[29] For example, the government has spent billions of dollars in no-bid contracts for companies such as Halliburton to rebuild Iraq.

Contracting also almost always leads to less public scrutiny, as government programs are hidden behind closed corporate doors. Companies, unlike agencies, are not subject to the Freedom of Information Act, which allows the public to gain access to government documents. Members of Congress have sought unsuccessfully for years to get the Army to explain the contracts for Blackwater USA security officers in Iraq, which involve several costly layers of subcontractors. Partly because of the relative lack of openness, efforts to privatize public services have been marked by extensive corruption and sometimes by extensive cost overruns.

Bureaucracies as Regulators

14.4 Describe how bureaucracies regulate, and assess deregulation and alternative approaches to regulation.

Government **regulation** is the use of governmental authority to control or change some practice in the private sector. Regulations by government, filling hundreds of volumes, pervade Americans' everyday lives and the lives of businesses, universities, hospitals, and other institutions. Regulation may be the most controversial role of the bureaucracies. Congress gives bureaucrats broad mandates to regulate activities as diverse as interest rates, the location of nuclear power plants, and food additives.

Regulation in the Economy and in Everyday Life

The notion that the American economy is largely a "free enterprise" system, unfettered by government intervention, is about as up to date as a Model T Ford. You can begin to understand the sweeping scope of governmental regulation by examining how the automobile industry is regulated:

- The Securities and Exchange Commission regulates buying and selling stock in an automobile corporation.

- Relations between the workers and managers of the company come under the scrutiny of the National Labor Relations Board.

- The Department of Labor and the Equal Employment Opportunity Commission mandate affirmative action in hiring workers in automobile production plants because automakers are major government contractors.

- The EPA, the National Highway Traffic Safety Administration, and the Department of Transportation require that cars include pollution-control, energy-saving, and safety devices.

- Unfair advertising and deceptive consumer practices in marketing cars come under the watchful eye of the FTC.

From the beginnings of the American republic until 1887, the federal government made almost no regulatory policies. The little regulation that was produced originated with state and local authorities, and opponents disputed even the minimal regulatory powers of state and local governments. In 1877, the Supreme Court upheld the right of government to regulate the business operations of a firm. The case, *Munn v. Illinois*, involved the right of the state of Illinois to regulate the charges and services of a Chicago warehouse. Farmers at this time were seething about alleged overcharging by railroads, grain elevator companies, and other business firms. In 1887—a decade after *Munn*—Congress created the first regulatory agency, the

regulation
The use of governmental authority to control or change some practice in the private sector.

472

14.1
14.2
14.3
14.4
14.5
14.6

deregulation
The lifting of government restrictions on business, industry, and professional activities.

Interstate Commerce Commission (ICC), and charged it with regulating the railroads, their prices, and their services to farmers; the ICC thus set the precedent for regulatory policymaking.

As regulators, bureaucratic agencies typically operate with a large grant of power from Congress, which may detail goals to be achieved but permit the agencies to sketch out the regulatory means. In 1935, for example, Congress created the National Labor Relations Board to control "unfair labor practices," but the NLRB had to play a major role in defining "fair" and "unfair." Most agencies charged with regulation must first develop a set of rules, often called *guidelines*. The appropriate agency may specify how much food coloring it will permit in a hot dog, how many contaminants it will allow an industry to dump into a stream, how much radiation from a nuclear reactor is too much, and so forth. Guidelines are developed in consultation with—and sometimes with the agreement of—the people or industries being regulated.

Next, the agency must apply and enforce its rules and guidelines, either in court or through its own administrative procedures. Sometimes it waits for complaints to come to it, as the Equal Employment Opportunity Commission does; sometimes it sends inspectors into the field, as OSHA does; and sometimes it requires application for a permit or license to demonstrate performance consistent with congressional goals and agency rules, as the FCC does. Often government agencies take violators to court, hoping to secure a judgment and fine against an offender (see "You Are the Policymaker: How Should We Regulate?"). Whatever strategy Congress permits a regulating agency to use, all regulation contains these elements: (1) *a grant of power and set of directions from Congress*, (2) *a set of rules and guidelines* by the regulatory agency itself, and (3) *some means of enforcing compliance* with congressional goals and agency regulations.

☐ Deregulation

With the growth of regulation, **deregulation**—the lifting of government restrictions on business, industry, and professional activities—became a fashionable term.[30] The idea behind deregulation is that the number and complexity of regulatory policies have made regulation too complicated and burdensome. To critics, regulation distorts market forces and has the following problems:

- *Raising prices.* If the producer is faced with expensive regulations, the cost will inevitably be passed on to the consumer in the form of higher prices.

- *Hurting America's competitive position abroad.* Other nations may have fewer regulations on pollution, worker safety, and other business practices than the United States. Thus, American products may cost more in the international marketplace, undermining sales in other countries.

- *Failing to work well.* Tales of failed regulatory policies are numerous. Regulations may be difficult or cumbersome to enforce. Critics charge that regulations sometimes do not achieve the results that Congress intended and maintain that they simply create massive regulatory bureaucracies.

Not everyone, however, believes that deregulation is in the nation's best interest.[31] For example, critics point to severe environmental damage resulting from lax enforcement of environmental protection standards during the Reagan administration. Similarly, many observers attribute much of the blame for the enormously expensive bailout of the savings and loan industry in 1989 to deregulation in the 1980s. Californians found that deregulation led to severe power shortages in 2001. The burst of the real estate bubble in 2007 and 2008 and the resulting financial crisis and bailouts led to demands for increased regulation of financial institutions.

You Are the Policymaker

How Should We Regulate?

Almost every regulatory policy was created to achieve some desirable social goal. When more than 6,000 people are killed annually in industrial accidents, who would disagree with the goal of a safer workplace? Who would dissent from greater highway safety, when more than 32,000 die each year in automobile accidents? Who would disagree with policies to promote equality in hiring, given the history of discrimination against women and minorities in the workplace? Who would disagree with policies to reduce industrial pollution, when pollution threatens health and lives? However, there may be more than one way to achieve these—and many other—desirable social goals.

One approach to regulation is **command-and-control policy**, in which the government tells business how to reach certain goals, checks that these commands are followed, and punishes offenders. An alternative approach is an **incentive system**, in which policymakers employ marketlike strategies to regulate industry. Advocates of using incentives argue that, instead of, for example, telling construction businesses how their ladders must be constructed, measuring the ladders, and charging a small fine for violators, it would be more efficient and effective to levy a high tax on firms with excessive worker injuries. Instead of trying to develop standards for about 100,000 pollution sources, it would be easier and more effective to levy a high tax on those who cause pollution. The government could even provide incentives in the form of rewards for such socially valuable behavior as developing technology to reduce pollution.

This second approach is evident in a proposal by President Obama to stem carbon dioxide emissions

through a market-based cap-and-trade system in which the government sets a mandatory cap on emissions and then issues companies or other groups credits for a certain amount of emissions. Companies that need to increase their emission allowance must buy credits from those who pollute less. In effect, the buyer is paying a charge for polluting, while the seller is being rewarded for having reduced emissions by more than was needed. Thus, in theory, those who can reduce emissions most cheaply will do so, achieving the pollution reduction at the lowest cost to society. The goal is to encourage the development of the most innovative and efficient means of limiting emissions without inhibiting economic growth.

Not everyone is keen on the use of incentives. Some argue that the command-and-control system of regulation is preferable because it works like preventive medicine—it is designed to minimize pollution or workplace accidents before they become too severe. They point out that penalties for excessive pollution or excessive workplace accidents would be imposed only after substantial damage had been done. They add that taxes on pollution or unsafe work environments could be passed along to consumers as higher prices, in which case they would not be much of a deterrent. Moreover, it would take a large bureaucracy to carefully monitor the level of pollution discharged and a complex calculation to determine the level of tax necessary to encourage businesses not to pollute.

What do you think? The issue of the manner of regulation is a complex one. Is the command-and-control system the best way of achieving regulatory goals, or might an incentive system be more effective?

In addition, many regulations have proved beneficial to Americans. To give just a few examples, as a result of government regulations, we breathe cleaner air,[32] we have lower levels of lead in our blood, miners are safer at work,[33] seacoasts have been preserved,[34] and children are more likely to survive infancy.[35]

Controlling the Bureaucracy

14.5 Identify the means of controlling the bureaucracy and assess the role of iron triangles.

A nything as large and powerful as the federal bureaucracy requires watching. Both the president and Congress have responsibility for making the bureaucracy responsive to elected officials (and presumably the public), and both have a set of tools for, and challenges in, doing so.

command-and-control policy
The typical system of regulation whereby government tells business how to reach certain goals, checks that these commands are followed, and punishes offenders.

incentive system
An alternative to command-and-control, with marketlike strategies such as rewards used to manage public policy.

executive orders
Regulations originating with the executive branch. Executive orders are one method presidents can use to control the bureaucracy.

□ Presidents Try to Control the Bureaucracy

Presidents try hard—not always with success—to impose their policy preferences on agencies (although their frustrations might be less than those of leaders in some other countries, as you can see from "America in Perspective: Influencing Independent Agencies"). Following are some of their tactics:

- *Appoint the right people to head the agency.* Normally, presidents control the appointments of agency heads and subheads. Putting their people in charge is one good way for presidents to influence agency policy.[36] The president does not have a completely free hand, however. President Clinton had no use for his FBI director, Louis Freeh, who would barely talk to him, but he did not fire Freeh, for fear of being denounced as purging an enemy.

- *Issue orders.* Presidents can issue **executive orders** to agencies. These orders carry the force of law and are used to implement statutes, treaties, and provisions of the Constitution.[37] For example, following the 9/11 terrorist attacks, George W. Bush issued executive orders creating a new cabinet position to coordinate homeland security and a Homeland Security Council, authorizing the secretaries of the navy, army, and air force to call up reservists for active duty, lifting a ban on the CIA engaging in political assassination, and establishing military tribunals to try terrorists. Sometimes presidential aides simply pass the word that the president wants something done. These messages usually suffice, although agency heads are reluctant to run afoul of Congress or the press on the basis of a broad presidential hint. The president's rhetoric in speeches outside the bureaucracy may also influence the priorities of bureaucrats.[38]

- *Alter an agency's budget.* The Office of Management and Budget (OMB) is the president's own final authority on any agency's budget. The OMB's threats to cut here or add there will usually get an agency's attention. Each agency, however, has

America in Perspective

Influencing Independent Agencies

We often think of the president as head of the executive branch, but there are agencies, such as the Federal Reserve Board, that are very powerful and are generally free from the chief executive's direction. This often leaves presidents frustrated, as when they wish the Federal Reserve Board to lower interest rates to stimulate the economy. There are even more autonomous agencies in Latin America, however—agencies removed from the direct control of the president and the legislature.

Why would Latin American governments create agencies they cannot control? The primary reason is to protect a new agency providing a new service from changes in policy made by future decision makers. Those who create an agency fear that its policies will be undone by a new administration or legislature, so they make it autonomous.

These autonomous agencies often have their own sources of revenue and thus can increase their

budgets without going through the public and controversial process of government budget debates. They are also freer from legislative oversight and formal presidential controls than are regular agencies, and conflict over their programs is less visible. Until recently, expenditures for autonomous agencies also allowed the government to engage in creative financing because when these agencies contracted debt, it did not count against the central government's debt (which is substantial in some Latin American countries).

Autonomy is decidedly a mixed blessing, however. Creative financing is not necessarily good for a nation, nor is the difficulty policymakers have in consolidating bureaucracies and increasing their efficiency. The lack of traditional means of influence also makes it difficult to alter the priorities of agencies, such as shifting the emphasis from building roads to building apartments.

SOURCES: Michelle M. Taylor, "When Are Juridically Autonomous Agencies Responsive to Elected Officials? A Simulation Based on the Costa Rican Case," *Journal of Politics* 57 (November 1995): 1070–92; Bruce M. Wilson, Juan Carlos Rodríguez Cordero, and Roger Handberg, "The Best Laid Schemes ... Gang Aft A-gley: Judicial Reform in Latin America—Evidence from Costa Rica," *Journal of Latin American Studies* 36 (August 2004).

its constituents within and outside of Congress, and Congress, not the president, does the appropriating.

- *Reorganize an agency.* Although President Reagan promised, proposed, and pressured to abolish the Department of Energy and the Department of Education, he never succeeded—largely because each department was in the hands of an entrenched bureaucracy backed by elements in Congress and strong constituent groups. Reorganizing an agency is hard to do if it is a large and strong agency, and reorganizing a small and weak agency is often not worth the trouble. Nevertheless, as we saw, a massive reorganization occurred in 2002 with the creation of the Department of Homeland Security.

☐ Congress Tries to Control the Bureaucracy

Congress exhibits a paradoxical relationship with the bureaucracies. On the one hand (as we have seen), members of Congress may find a big bureaucracy congenial.[39] Big government provides services to constituents, who may show their appreciation at the polls. Moreover, when Congress lacks the answers to policy problems, it hopes the bureaucracies will find them. Unable itself, for example, to resolve the touchy issue of equality in intercollegiate athletics, Congress passed the ball to the Department of Health, Education, and Welfare. Unable to decide how to make workplaces safer, Congress produced OSHA. Congress is typically the problem-identifying branch of government, setting the bureaucratic agenda but letting the agencies decide how to implement the goals it sets.

On the other hand, Congress has found it challenging to control the government it helped create. There are several measures Congress can take to oversee the bureaucracy:

- *Influence the appointment of agency heads.* Even when the law does not require senatorial approval of a presidential appointment, members of Congress are not shy in offering their opinions about who should and should not be running the agencies. When congressional approval is required, members are doubly influential. Committee hearings on proposed appointments are almost guaranteed to produce lively debates if some members find the nominee's probable orientations objectionable.

- *Alter an agency's budget.* With the congressional power of the purse comes a mighty weapon for controlling bureaucratic behavior. For example, cutting a budget will make it more difficult for an agency to regulate behavior. Congress can also pass limitation riders, which forbid agencies from spending money for specific purposes.[40] At the same time, Congress knows that many agencies perform services that its constituents demand. Too much budget cutting may make an agency more responsive—at the price of losing an interest group's support for a reelection campaign. Congress can also order the bureaucracy to spend money in certain ways through detailed provisions in laws or, more informally, through statements in reports on legislation.

- *Hold hearings.* Committees and subcommittees can hold periodic hearings as part of their oversight responsibilities, and in these hearings they may parade flagrant agency abuses of congressional intent in front of the press. However, the very committee that created a program usually has responsibility for oversight of it and thus has some stake in showing the agency in a favorable light. Furthermore, members of Congress have other disincentives for vigorous oversight, including a desire not to embarrass the chief executive.

- *Rewrite the legislation or make it more detailed.* Congress can overturn agency rules or limit an agency's authority to make them. In addition, every statute is filled with instructions to its administrators. To limit bureaucratic discretion and make its instructions clearer, Congress can write new or more detailed legislation. Still, even voluminous detail can never eliminate discretion.

476

14.1

14.2

14.3

14.4

14.5

14.6

iron triangles

Also known as *subgovernments*, a mutually dependent, mutually advantageous relationship between bureaucratic agencies, interest groups, and congressional committees or subcommittees. Iron triangles dominate some areas of domestic policymaking.

Sometimes these efforts are detrimental to bureaucratic performance. In 2008, about 80 House and Senate committees and subcommittees claimed jurisdiction over a portion of homeland security issues. Officials in the Department of Homeland Security have to spend a large percentage of their time testifying to these committees, and the balkanized jurisdiction has undermined the ability of Congress to perform comprehensive oversight. Moreover, different committees may send different signals to the same agency. One may press for stricter enforcement of regulations, for example, while another seeks more exemptions.

☐ Iron Triangles and Issue Networks

Agencies' strong ties to interest groups on the one hand and to congressional committees and subcommittees on the other further complicate efforts to control the bureaucracy. Bureaucracies often enjoy cozy relationships with interest groups and with committees or subcommittees of Congress. When agencies, groups, and committees all depend on one another and are in close, frequent contact, they form what are sometimes called **iron triangles** or *subgovernments*—triads that have advantages for all sides (see Figure 14.4). Thus, for example, a subcommittee on aging, senior citizens'

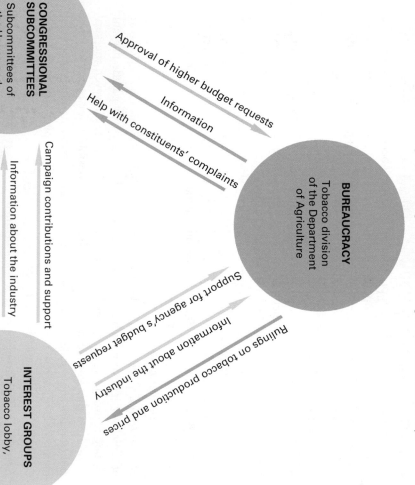

FIGURE 14.4 IRON TRIANGLES: ONE EXAMPLE

Iron triangles—composed of bureaucratic agencies, interest groups, and congressional committees or subcommittees—have dominated some areas of domestic policymaking by combining internal consensus with a virtual monopoly on information in their area. The tobacco triangle is one example; there are dozens more. Iron triangles are characterized by mutual dependency in which each element provides key services, information, or policy for the others. The arrows indicate some of these mutually helpful relationships. In recent years, a number of well-established iron triangles, including the tobacco triangle, have been broken up.

CONGRESSIONAL SUBCOMMITTEES
Subcommittees of the House and Senate agricultural committees

BUREAUCRACY
Tobacco division of the Department of Agriculture

INTEREST GROUPS
Tobacco lobby, including both farmers and manufacturers

Approval of higher budget requests

Information

Help with constituents' complaints

Campaign contributions and support

Information about the industry

Legislation affecting tobacco farmers and other members of the industry

Support for agency's budget requests

Information about the industry

Rulings on tobacco production and prices

interest groups, and the Social Security Administration are likely to agree on the need for more Social Security benefits. Richard Rettig has recounted how an alliance slowly jelled around the issue of fighting cancer. It rested on three pillars: cancer researchers, agencies within the National Institutes of Health, and members of congressional health subcommittees.[41]

When these iron triangles shape policies for senior citizens, the fight against cancer, tobacco, or any other interest, officials in the different triangles make each policy independently of the others, sometimes even in contradiction to other policies. For example, for years the government supported tobacco farmers in various ways while encouraging people not to smoke. Moreover, the iron triangles' decisions tend to bind larger institutions, such as Congress and the White House. Congress often defers to the decisions of committees and subcommittees, especially on less visible issues. The White House may be too busy wrestling with global concerns to fret over agricultural issues or cancer. Emboldened by this lack of involvement, subgovernments flourish and add a strong decentralizing and fragmenting element to the policymaking process.

There is often a cozy relationship—and even movement—between components of the three sides of a subgovernment. For example, in 2003, Congress added a massive prescription drug benefit under Medicare. Representative Billy Tauzin shepherded the drug bill through the House as chair of the Energy and Commerce Committee. He then retired from Congress to head the Pharmaceutical Research and Manufacturers of America, a powerful industry lobby group, for an estimated $2 million a year. Thomas Scully, the Medicare administrator and lead negotiator for the administration, resigned his position within weeks after the passage of the bill to join a lobbying firm that represented several health care industry companies significantly affected by the new law. He also announced he would be working part time for an investment firm with interests in several more companies affected by the new law.

In recent years, the system of subgovernments has become overlaid with an amorphous system of *issue networks*. These networks have led to more widespread participation in bureaucratic policymaking, including by many who have technical policy expertise and are drawn to issues because of intellectual or emotional commitments rather than material interests. Those concerned with environmental protection, for example, have challenged formerly closed subgovernments on numerous fronts. This opening of the policymaking process complicates the calculations and decreases the predictability of those involved in the stable and relatively narrow relationships of subgovernments.[42]

THE DEATH OF AN IRON TRIANGLE Although subgovernments are often able to dominate policymaking for decades, they are not indestructible.[43] For example, the subgovernment pictured in Figure 14.4 long dominated smoking and tobacco policy, focusing on crop subsidies to tobacco farmers. But increasingly, these policies came under fire from health authorities, who were not involved in tobacco policymaking in earlier years. Similarly, Congress no longer considers pesticide policy, once dominated by chemical companies and agricultural interests, separately from environmental and health concerns.

An especially vivid example of the death of an iron triangle is the case of nuclear power.[44] During the 1940s and 1950s, Americans were convinced that the technology that had ended World War II could also serve peaceful purposes. Nuclear scientists spoke enthusiastically about harnessing the atom to achieve all sorts of goals, eventually making electricity so inexpensive that it would be "too cheap to meter." Optimism in progress through science was the rule, and the federal government encouraged the development of nuclear power through a powerful iron triangle.

Congress established a special joint committee, the Joint Committee on Atomic Energy, with complete control over questions of nuclear power. It also created a new executive agency, the Atomic Energy Commission (AEC). The committee, the commission, and the private companies that built nuclear power plants, and the electrical utilities that operated them together formed a powerful subgovernment. America built more nuclear power plants than any other country in the world, and American technology was exported overseas to dozens of nations.

478

14.1
14.2
14.3
14.4
14.5
14.6

Nuclear power today—after the accidents at Three Mile Island and Chernobyl and the various cost overruns associated with the industry—bears almost no resemblance to nuclear power in the early 1960s when the iron triangle was at its peak. What happened? Before the 1960s had ended, the experts had begun to lose control. When critics raised questions concerning the safety of the plants and were able to get local officials to question the policies publicly, the issue grew into a major political debate, associated with the growth of environmentalism. Opposition to nuclear power destroyed two of the most powerful legs of the iron triangle. Congress disbanded the Joint Committee on Atomic Energy; a variety of congressional committees now claim some jurisdiction over nuclear power questions. Similarly, Congress replaced the AEC with two new agencies: the Nuclear Regulatory Commission and the Department of Energy.

The nuclear power industry was devastated: no new nuclear power plants have been started in the United States since 1978, and almost all those under construction at that time have been abandoned at huge financial loss. Nuclear power provides only about 12 percent of our total energy production. In sum, the wave of environmental concern that developed in the late 1960s swept away one of the most powerful iron triangles in recent American history.

This is not the end of the story, however. The extraordinarily high price of gasoline and heating fuel in much of this century and concerns over global warming have encouraged a reconsideration of nuclear power. The Gallup Poll has found, for example, that a majority of the public supports the use of nuclear energy to produce electricity.

If the nuclear power industry should revive, there will be renewed calls for strict regulation—from both the bureaucracy and Congress. Whether an iron triangle reemerges will depend on whether the public is attentive to the issue of nuclear power and whether it allows experts to define safety concerns as technical matters appropriate only for experts to decide.

Understanding Bureaucracies

14.6 Assess the role of unelected bureaucrats in American democracy and the impact of the bureaucracy on the scope of government.

s both implementors and regulators, bureaucracies are making public policy, not just administering someone else's decisions. The fact that bureaucrats, who are not elected, compose most of the government raises fundamental issues about who controls governing and about the proper role of bureaucracies.

☐ Bureaucracy and Democracy

Bureaucracies constitute one of America's two unelected policymaking institutions (courts being the other). In democratic theory, popular control of government depends on elections, but we could not possibly elect the millions of federal civilian and military employees, or even the few thousand top bureaucrats, although they spend about nearly $4 trillion. Furthermore, the fact that voters do not elect civil servants does not mean that bureaucracies cannot respond to and represent the public's interests. And as we saw earlier, in their backgrounds, bureaucrats are more representative of the American people than are elected officials. Much depends on whether bureaucracies are effectively controlled by the policymakers citizens do elect—the president and Congress.[45]

☐ Bureaucracy and the Scope of Government

To many, the huge American bureaucracy is the prime example of the federal government growing out of control. As this chapter discussed earlier, some observers view the bureaucracy as acquisitive, constantly seeking to expand its size, budgets, and authority. Much of the political rhetoric against big government also adopts this line of argument, along with complaints about red tape, senseless regulations, and the like. It is easy to take potshots at a faceless bureaucracy that usually cannot respond.

One should keep in mind, however, that the federal bureaucracy has not grown over the past 40 years. Moreover, since the population of the country has grown significantly during this period, the federal bureaucracy has actually *shrunk* in size relative to the population it serves.

Originally, the federal bureaucracy had the modest role of promoting the economy, defending the country, managing foreign affairs, providing justice, and delivering the mail. Its role gradually expanded to include providing services to farmers, businesses, and workers. With social and economic changes in the United States, a variety of interests placed additional demands on government. We now expect government—and the bureaucracy—to play an active role in dealing with social and economic problems. A good case can be made that the bureaucracy is actually too *small* for many of the tasks currently assigned to it—tasks ranging from the control of illicit drugs to protection of the environment.

In addition, it is important to remember that when the president and Congress have chosen to deregulate certain areas of the economy or cut taxes, the bureaucracy could not and did not prevent them from doing so. The question of what and how much the federal government should do—and thus how big the bureaucracy should be—is answered primarily at the polls and in Congress, the White House, and the courts—not by faceless bureaucrats.

Review the Chapter

The Bureaucrats

14.1 Describe the federal bureaucrats and the ways in which they obtain their jobs, p. 452.

Bureaucrats perform most of the vital services the federal government provides, although their number has not grown, even as the population has increased and the public has made additional demands on government. Bureaucrats shape policy as administrators, as implementors, and as regulators. Most federal bureaucrats get their jobs through the civil service system; as a group, these civil servants are broadly representative of the American people. The top policymaking posts, however, are filled through presidential appointments, often with Senate confirmation.

How the Federal Bureaucracy Is Organized

14.2 Differentiate the four types of agencies into which the federal bureaucracy is organized, p. 457.

The organization of the federal bureaucracy is most easily understood by categorizing agencies into four types: cabinet departments, independent regulatory commissions, government corporations, and independent executive agencies. The 15 cabinet departments each manage a specific policy area. Independent regulatory commissions make and enforce rules in a particular sector of the economy. Government corporations provide services that could be handled by the private sector and charge for their services. Independent executive agencies account for most of the rest of the federal bureaucracy.

Bureaucracies as Implementors

14.3 Identify the factors that influence the effectiveness of bureaucratic implementation of public policy, p. 461.

As policy implementors, bureaucrats translate legislative policy goals into programs. The effectiveness of policy implementation is influenced by various factors: the policy or program design, the clarity of the legislation or regulations being implemented, the resources available for implementation, the ability of administrators to depart from SOPs when

necessary, the disposition of administrators toward the policy they implement, and the extent to which responsibility for policy implementation is concentrated rather than dispersed across agencies.

Bureaucracies as Regulators

14.4 Describe how bureaucracies regulate, and assess deregulation and alternative approaches to regulation, p. 471.

Congress increasingly delegates large amounts of power to bureaucratic agencies to develop rules regulating practices in the private sector. Agencies apply and enforce their rules, in court or through administrative procedures. Regulation affects most areas of American society, and criticism that regulations are overly complicated and burdensome has led to a movement to deregulate. However, many regulations have proved beneficial, and deregulation has itself resulted in policy failures.

Controlling the Bureaucracy

14.5 Identify the means of controlling the bureaucracy and assess the role of iron triangles, p. 473.

The president and Congress have several means of controlling the bureaucracy, including appointments, budgets, reorganization, investigations, and direct orders and specific legislation. Nevertheless, the president and Congress face challenges to their control, among them iron triangles, which include agencies, congressional committees or subcommittees, and interest groups.

Understanding Bureaucracies

14.6 Assess the role of unelected bureaucrats in American democracy and the impact of the bureaucracy on the scope of government, p. 478.

Although bureaucrats are not elected, bureaucracies are not necessarily undemocratic. Bureaucrats are competent and reasonably representative of Americans. And they may be controlled by elected decision makers. The role of government and hence the size of the bureaucracy depends more on voters than on bureaucrats.

Learn the Terms

bureaucracy, p. 452
patronage, p. 455
Pendleton Civil Service Act, p. 455
civil service, p. 455
merit principle, p. 455
Hatch Act, p. 456
Office of Personnel Management, p. 456

GS (General Schedule) rating, p. 456
Senior Executive Service, p. 456
independent regulatory commission, p. 459
government corporations, p. 460
independent executive agency, p. 461
policy implementation, p. 461
standard operating procedures, p. 465

administrative discretion, p. 466
street-level bureaucrats, p. 466
regulation, p. 471
deregulation, p. 472
command-and-control policy, p. 473
incentive system, p. 473
executive orders, p. 474
iron triangles, p. 476

Test Yourself

1. Which of the following is a major change in American bureaucracy that occurred as a result of the Pendleton Civil Service Act?

a. elimination of merit testing as a means of federal hiring
b. introduction of unions into the federal workforce
c. requirement that all government employees sign loyalty oaths
d. transformation from a civil service to a patronage system
e. transformation from a patronage to a civil service system

2. Which of the following statements best characterizes the functioning of government corporations?

a. They help manage the government's many buildings, archives, and storage facilities.
b. They help regulate corporations and businesses in the private sector.
c. They help the government hire talented workers from the private sector.
d. They implement congressional policies in the economic domain.
e. They provide and charge for services that could be provided by the private sector.

3. What are the parts of the federal bureaucracy with responsibility for different sectors of the economy, and making and enforcing rules designed to protect the public interest?

a. Cabinet departments
b. Government corporations
c. Independent executive agencies
d. Independent regulatory commissions
e. Private sectors

4. What was the main obstacle to the successful implementation of the policy prohibiting sex discrimination in intercollegiate athletics?

a. opposition by the National Collegiate Athletic Association
b. public opinion concerning the appropriateness of women's participation in all sports
c. the exemption of revenue-producing sports
d. the lack of clarity and vague policy goals stated in Title IX
e. the lack of presidential willingness to take on the issue

5. When bureaucrats are asked to execute orders with which they do not agree, _____.

a. implementation follows standard operating procedures
b. slippage is likely to occur between policy decisions and performance
c. they are likely to lose their jobs if they do not follow through with the orders
d. they can file a Conflict of Interest Form and will be exempted from that duty by their boss
e. they usually ignore the orders

6. The administration hoped that the creation of the Department of Homeland Security in 2002 would help overcome problems of _____ involved in providing for security.

a. centralization
b. deregulation
c. fragmentation
d. lack of resources
e. standard operating procedures

7. Which of the following is true about bureaucracies as regulators?

a. Bureaucratic agencies have a grant of power and set of directions from Congress.

b. Bureaucratic agencies must adhere to strict guidelines mandated by Congress.

c. Bureaucratic agencies regulate products without consulting the industries being regulated.

d. Bureaucratic agencies' regulation of society has declined in recent decades.

e. Bureaucratic agencies' regulatory activity increases only during liberal administrations.

8. Which of the following statements about government regulation in America is accurate?

a. Regulatory agencies tended to be more popular in the early years of the nation's history, and then grew more controversial during the late-nineteenth century.

b. The Constitution organized only six regulatory agencies; the others have been created within the past year or so.

c. The Federal Communications Commission was the first independent regulatory agency.

d. The Supreme Court case of *Raich v. Gonzales* in 1877 first upheld the federal government's right to regulate business.

e. Until 1887, the federal government made almost no regulatory policies and had no regulatory agencies.

9. Which government policy allowed the combining of commercial and investment sectors in the banking industry beginning in the 1990s?

a. cap and trade

b. deregulation

c. fragmentation

d. privatization

e. regulation

10. The overlaying of subgovernments with a system of issue networks has ensured which of the following?

a. Participation in the policy process is more widespread.

b. Policymaking is stable and predictable.

c. Presidents are actively involved in most policy areas.

d. Subgovernments will be virtually impossible to dismantle.

e. The bureaucracy is more independent of elected branches of government.

11. The effort to control the federal bureaucracy through budgetary appropriation falls under the jurisdiction of which part of government?

a. Congress

b. Office of Management and Budget

c. the Internal Revenue Service

d. the president

e. the Supreme Court

12. The increased attention to environmental concerns that arose in the 1960s had what effect on nuclear power in the United States?

a. It devastated the industry and broke up one of the most powerful iron triangles in American history.

b. It led to an increase in the number of nuclear plants built in the United States.

c. It led to cleaner emissions and stricter regulations on nuclear waste and power production.

d. It weakened American confidence in its government, and led to the creation of most myths surrounding bureaucracy.

e. Public discussion led to a greater demand for nuclear power, but lack of funding meant demand could not be met.

13. Despite the popular impression that policy is decided by the president and Congress and merely implemented by the federal bureaucracy, policy is, in fact, _____.

a. also made by the bureaucracy

b. determined by the U.S. Supreme Court's actions

c. implemented by the executive branch

d. implemented by the legislative branch

e. often left to the recipients of social services

14. The vast majority of the federal government is made up of bureaucrats. How can such an enormous organization serve the interest of the citizenry?

a. through control by elected officials

b. through customer service representatives

c. through hiring based on patronage

d. through limiting bureaucratic budgets

e. through weekly newsletters mailed to the people

Explore Further

WEB SITES

*http://www.usgovernmentmanual.gov/?AspxAutoDetectCookie
Support=1*
U.S. Government Manual, which provides information on the organization of the U.S. government.

www.gpoaccess.gov/fr/index.html
The *Federal Register*, which provides information on U.S. laws and regulations.

www.whitehouse.gov/administration/cabinet
Information on federal cabinet departments.

www.usa.gov/Agencies/Federal/All_Agencies/index.shtml
Information on all federal departments, independent agencies, and commissions.

www.opm.gov/feddata/
Federal employment statistics.

www.opm.gov
Office of Personnel Management Web site, with information on federal jobs and personnel issues.

FURTHER READING

Aberbach, Joel D., and Bert A. Rockman. *In the Web of Politics.* Washington, D.C.: Brookings Institution, 2000. Examines federal executives and the degree to which they are representative of the country and responsive to elected officials.

Arnold, Peri E. *Making the Managerial Presidency,* 2nd ed. Princeton, NJ: Princeton University Press, 1996. A careful examination of efforts to reorganize the federal bureaucracy.

Derthick, Martha. *Up in Smoke,* 3rd ed. Washington, D.C.: CQ Press, 2011. Examines how Congress gave the FDA broad authority to regulate tobacco products.

Goodsell, Charles T. *The New Case for Bureaucracy,* Washington, D.C.: CQ Press, 2015. A strong case on behalf of the effectiveness of bureaucracy.

Gormley, William T., Jr., and Steven J. Balla. *Bureaucracy and Democracy: Accountability and Performance,* 3rd ed. Washington, D.C.: CQ Press, 2012. Discusses the accountability of unelected bureaucrats in a democracy.

Kerwin, Cornelius M., and Scott R. Furlong. *Rulemaking: How Government Agencies Write Law and Make Policy,* 4th ed. Washington, D.C.: CQ Press, 2010. Explains how agencies write regulations to implement laws.

Kettl, Donald F. *System Under Stress,* 3rd ed. Washington, D.C.: CQ Press, 2013. Evaluates the consequences of bureaucratic reorganization in response to crises.

Lewis, David E. *The Politics of Presidential Appointments.* Princeton, NJ: Princeton University Press, 2008. Analyzes how presidential appointments are made and what difference they make.

Osborne, David, and Peter Plastrik. *Banishing Bureaucracy,* 2nd ed. David Osborne, 2006. Five strategies for reinventing government.

Savas, E. S. *Privatization and Public-Private Partnerships.* Chatham, NJ: Chatham House, 1999. A conservative economist's argument that many public services performed by bureaucracies would be better handled by the private sector.

15

The Federal Courts

Politics in Action: Finding Justice in the Supreme Court

15.1	Identify the basic elements of the American judicial system and the major participants in it, p. 486.
15.2	Outline the structure of the federal court system and the major responsibilities of each component, p. 488.
15.3	Explain the process by which judges and justices are nominated and confirmed, p. 493.
15.4	Describe the backgrounds of judges and justices and assess the impact of background on their decisions, p. 498.
15.5	Outline the judicial process at the Supreme Court level and assess the major factors influencing decisions and their implementation, p. 502.
15.6	Trace the Supreme Court's use of judicial review in major policy battles in various eras of American history, p. 509.
15.7	Assess the role of unelected courts and the scope of judicial power in American democracy, p. 513.

J ason Pepper, a meth addict and drug dealer, got lucky after he was arrested in 2004. A sympathetic judge gave him a fraction of the prison time he could have received and, more importantly, sent him to a place where he got extensive drug treatment. He turned his life around, attended college, succeeded at a good job, and got married. Then his luck ran out. A federal appeals court held that his sentence was too lenient under federal sentencing rules and ordered him back to prison in 2009.

His luck turned again, however, as the U.S. Supreme Court chose his appeal from the thousands it receives each year. On December 6, 2010, the day of the oral argument on Pepper's case (there are no trials in the Supreme Court), his attorneys walked up the steep steps of the Supreme Court building, the impressive "Marble Palace" with the motto "Equal Justice Under Law" engraved over its imposing columns. The justices, clothed in black robes, took their seats at the bench in front of a red velvet curtain. The attorneys for each side had just 30 minutes to present their cases, including time for interruptions by justices with questions. When the attorneys' time was up, a discreet red light went on over their lectern, and they immediately stopped talking.

That was the end of the hearing, but not the end of the process. Months passed as the justices deliberated and negotiated an opinion. On March 2, 2011, the Court ruled that the appeals court had erred and that the sentencing guidelines were advisory, not mandatory. Moreover, it declared that judges should consider all available evidence, such as Pepper's exemplary change in lifestyle, to determine the appropriate punishment. Pepper had won his case (*Pepper v. United States*). Equally important, in clarifying the rules that guide judges as they try to set sentences

The United States has unusually powerful courts, and the Supreme Court sits atop the judicial hierarchy. Americans have never fully resolved the role of strong, unelected courts in a democracy and the appropriate extent of judicial power.

486

15.1

15.2

15.3

15.4

15.5

15.6

15.7

that both comport with national norms and ensure justice is done in individual cases, the Court's decision became a precedent that gave federal judges more leeway to provide second chances to the criminals who come before them.

In Pepper's case, the Supreme Court decided the meaning of an act of Congress, which had established the sentencing rules. In other cases, it may decide the meaning of the Constitution and even overrule the decisions of elected officials. Despite the trappings of tradition and majesty, however, the Court does not reach its decisions in a political vacuum. Instead, it and other courts work in a context of political influences and considerations, a circumstance that raises important questions about the role of the judiciary in the U.S. political system.

The federal courts pose a special challenge to American democracy. Although it is common to elect state judges, the president *nominates* federal judges to their positions—for life. The Framers of the Constitution purposefully insulated federal judges from the influence of public opinion. How can we reconcile powerful courts populated by unelected judges with American democracy? Do they pose a threat to majority rule? Or do the federal courts actually function to protect the rights of minorities and thus maintain the type of open system necessary for democracy to flourish?

The power of the federal courts also raises the issue of the appropriate scope of judicial power in our society. Federal courts are frequently in the thick of policymaking on issues ranging from affirmative action and abortion to physician-assisted suicide and health care policy. Numerous critics argue that judges should not be actively involved in determining public policy—that they should leave policy to elected officials, focusing instead on settlement of routine disputes. On the other hand, advocates of a more aggressive role for the courts emphasize that judicial decisions have often met pressing needs—especially needs of the politically or economically powerless—left unmet by the normal processes of policymaking. For example, we have already seen the leading role that the federal courts played in ending legally supported racial segregation in the United States. To determine the appropriate role of the courts in our democracy, we must first understand the nature of our judicial system.

However impressive the Supreme Court may be, it makes only the tiniest fraction of American judicial policy. The Court decides a handful of issues each year—albeit often key issues, with some decisions shaping people's lives and perhaps even determining matters of life and death. In addition to the Supreme Court, there are 12 federal courts of appeals plus a Court of Appeals for the Federal Circuit, 91 federal district courts, and thousands of state and local courts. This chapter focuses on federal courts and the judges who serve on them—the men and women in black robes who are important policymakers in the American political system.

The Nature of the Judicial System

15.1
Identify the basic elements of the American judicial system and the major participants in it.

he judicial system in the United States is, at least in principle, an adversarial one in which the courts provide an arena for two parties to bring their conflict before an impartial arbiter (a judge). The system is based on the theory that justice will emerge out of the struggle between two contending points of view. The task of the judge is to apply the law to the case, determining which party is legally correct. In reality, most cases never go to trial, because they are settled by agreements reached out of court.

There are two basic kinds of cases—criminal law and civil law cases:

- In a *criminal law* case, the government charges an individual with violating specific laws, such as those prohibiting robbery. The offense may be harmful to an

standing to sue
The requirement that plaintiffs have a serious interest in a case, which depends on whether they have sustained or are likely to sustain a direct and substantial injury from another party or from an action of government.

class action suits
Lawsuits in which a small number of people sue on behalf of all people in similar circumstances.

justiciable disputes
Issues capable of being settled as a matter of law.

individual or to society as a whole, but in either case it warrants punishment, such as imprisonment or a fine.

• A *civil law* case involves a dispute between two parties (one of whom may be the government itself) over a wide range of matters including contracts, property ownership, divorce, child custody, mergers of multinational companies, and personal and property damage. Civil law consists of both *statues* (laws passed by legislatures) and *common law* (the accumulation of judicial decisions about legal issues).

Just as it is important not to confuse criminal and civil law, it is important not to confuse state and federal courts. The vast majority of all criminal and civil cases involve state law and are tried in state courts. Criminal cases such as burglary and civil cases such as divorce normally begin and end in the state, not the federal, courts.

□ Participants in the Judicial System

Every case has certain components in common, including litigants, attorneys, and judges; in some cases organized groups also become directly involved. Judges are the policymakers of the American judicial system, and we examine them extensively in later sections of this chapter. Here we will discuss the other regular participants in the judicial process.

LITIGANTS The Constitution restricts federal judges to deciding "cases" or "controversies"—that is, actual disputes rather than hypothetical ones. Judges do not issue advisory opinions on what they think (in the abstract) may be the meaning or constitutionality of a law. The judiciary is essentially passive, dependent on others to take the initiative.

Thus, two parties must bring a case to the court before it may be heard. Every case is a dispute between a *plaintiff* and a *defendant*, in which the former brings some charge against the latter. Sometimes the plaintiff is the government, which may bring a charge against an individual or a corporation. The government may charge Smith with a brutal murder or charge the XYZ Corporation with illegal trade practices. All cases are identified with the name of the plaintiff first and the defendant second, for example, *State v. Smith* or *Anderson v. Baker*. In many (but not all) cases, a *jury*, a group of citizens (usually 12), is responsible for determining the outcome of a lawsuit.

Litigants end up in court for a variety of reasons. Some are reluctant participants—the defendant in a criminal case, for example. Others are eager for their day in court. For some, the courts can be a potent weapon in the search for a preferred policy.

Not everyone can challenge a law, however. Plaintiffs must have what is called **standing to sue**; that is, they must have serious interest in a case, which is typically determined by whether they have sustained or are in immediate danger of sustaining a direct and substantial injury from another party (such as a corporation) or an action of government. Merely being a taxpayer and being opposed to a law do not provide the standing necessary to challenge that law in court.

The courts have broadened the concept of standing to sue to include **class action suits**, which permit a small number of people to sue on behalf of all other people in similar circumstances. These suits may be useful in cases as varied as civil rights, in which a few persons seek an end to discriminatory practices on behalf of all who might be discriminated against, and environmental protection, in which a few persons may sue a polluting industry on behalf of all who are affected by the air or water that the industry pollutes. In recent years, the Supreme Court has placed some restrictions on such suits.

Conflicts must not only arise from actual cases between litigants with standing to sue, but they must also be **justiciable disputes**—issues that are capable of being settled by legal methods. For example, one would not go to court to determine whether Congress should fund missile defense, for the matter could not be resolved through legal methods or knowledge.

ATTORNEYS Lawyers are indispensable actors in the judicial system. Law is one of the nation's largest professions, with about 1.25 million attorneys practicing in the United States today.[1] Although lawyers were once available primarily to the rich, today the

488

15.1
15.2
15.3
15.4
15.5
15.6
15.7

amicus curiae ("friend of the court") briefs
Legal briefs submitted by a "friend of the court" for the purpose of influencing a court's decision by raising additional points of view and presenting information not contained in the briefs of the formal parties.

Linda Brown (left), shown here outside her segregated school, was the plaintiff challenging legal segregation in public education.

The Structure of the Federal Judicial System

Outline the structure of the federal court system and the major responsibilities of each component.

The Constitution is vague about the structure of the federal court system. Specifying only that there would be a Supreme Court, the Constitution left it to Congress's discretion to establish lower federal courts of general jurisdiction. In the Judiciary Act of 1789, Congress created these additional *constitutional courts*, and although the system has been altered over the years, the United States has never been without them. The current organization of the federal court system is displayed in Figure 15.1.

As you can see in the figure, Congress has also established *legislative courts* for specialized purposes. These courts include the Court of Military Appeals, the Court of Federal Claims, the Court of International Trade, and the Tax Court. Legislative courts

federally funded Legal Services Corporation employs lawyers to serve the legal needs of the poor, and state and local governments provide public defenders for people accused of crimes. Moreover, some employers and unions now provide legal insurance, through which individuals who have prepaid can secure legal aid when needed. That access to lawyers has become more equal does not, of course, mean that quality of representation is equal. The wealthy can afford high-powered attorneys who can invest many hours in their cases and arrange for testimony by expert witnesses. The poor are often served by overworked attorneys with few resources to devote to an individual case.

GROUPS Because they recognize the courts' ability to shape policy, interest groups often seek out litigants whose cases seem particularly strong. Few groups have been more successful in finding good cases and good litigants than the National Association for the Advancement of Colored People (NAACP), which decided to sue the school board of Topeka, Kansas, on behalf of a young schoolgirl named Linda Brown in *Brown v. Board of Education* (1954). The NAACP was seeking to end the policy of "separate but equal"—meaning racially segregated—public education, and NAACP legal counsel Thurgood Marshall believed that Topeka represented a stronger case than did other school districts because the city provided segregated facilities that were otherwise genuinely equal. The courts could not resolve the case simply by insisting that expenditures for schools for white and African American children be equalized.

The American Civil Liberties Union (ACLU) is another interest group that is always seeking cases and litigants to support in its defense of civil liberties. One ACLU attorney stressed that principle took priority over a particular client, saying that some of ACLU's clients are "pretty scurvy little creatures. It's the principle that we're going to be able to use these people for that's important."[2]

At other times groups do not directly argue the case for litigants, but support them instead with *amicus curiae ("friend of the court") briefs*, which attempt to influence the Court's decision, raise additional points of view, and present information not contained in the briefs of the attorneys for the official parties to the case. In controversial cases, many groups may submit such briefs to the Court: groups presented 136 briefs in the health care reform case in 2012.

All these participants—plaintiffs, defendants, lawyers, and interest groups—play a role in the judicial drama, as do, in many instances, the public and the press. Much of the drama takes place outside the courtroom. How these participants arrive in the courtroom and which court they go to reflect the structure of the court system.

FIGURE 15.1 ORGANIZATION OF THE FEDERAL COURT SYSTEM

The federal court system is composed of both constitutional courts (the Supreme Court, the courts of appeals, and the district courts) and legislative courts, which have specialized jurisdictions. Losers in cases before independent regulatory commissions may appeal to the courts of appeals.

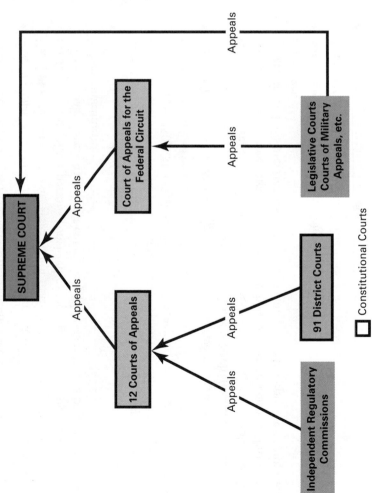

Constitutional Courts

original jurisdiction
The jurisdiction of courts that hear a case first, usually in a trial. These are the courts that determine the facts about a case.

appellate jurisdiction
The jurisdiction of courts that hear cases brought to them on appeal from lower courts. These courts do not review the factual record, only the legal issues involved.

district courts
The 91 federal courts of original jurisdiction. They are the only federal courts in which trials are held and in which juries may be impaneled.

are staffed by judges who have fixed terms of office and who lack the protections against removal or salary reductions that judges on constitutional courts enjoy. The judges apply a body of law within their area of jurisdiction but cannot exercise the power of judicial review (of finding the actions of the legislative or executive branch unconstitutional).

In this section, we focus on the constitutional courts, that is, on the courts of general jurisdiction—district courts, courts of appeals, and the Supreme Court—which hear a wide range of cases. First, we must clarify another difference among courts—that between courts with original jurisdiction and courts with appellate jurisdiction:

- Courts with **original jurisdiction** hear a case first, usually in a trial. These are the courts that determine the facts about a case, whether it is a criminal charge or a civil suit. More than 90 percent of court cases begin and end in the court of original jurisdiction. Lawyers can sometimes appeal an adverse decision to a higher court for another decision.

- Courts with **appellate jurisdiction** hear cases brought to them on appeal from a lower court. Appellate courts do not review the factual record, only the legal issues involved. At the state level, the appellate process normally ends with the state's highest court of appeal, which is usually called the state supreme court. Litigants may appeal decisions from a state high court only to the U.S. Supreme Court, and only if they meet certain conditions, discussed next.

☐ District Courts

The entry point for most litigation in the federal courts is one of the **district courts**, of which there are 91, with at least 1 in each state, in addition to 1 in Washington, D.C., and 1 in Puerto Rico (there are also 3 somewhat different territorial courts for Guam,

490

15.1
15.2
15.3
15.4
15.5
15.6
15.7

courts of appeals
Appellate courts empowered to review all final decisions of district courts, except in rare cases. In addition, they also hear appeals to orders of many federal regulatory agencies.

the Virgin Islands, and the Northern Mariana Islands). The district courts are courts of original jurisdiction; they hear no appeals. They are the only federal courts that hold trials and impanel juries. The 675 district court judges usually preside over cases alone, but certain rare cases require that 3 judges constitute the court. Each district court has between 2 and 28 judges, depending on the amount of judicial work within its territory. The jurisdiction of the district courts extends to the following:

- *Federal crimes.* Keep in mind that about 98 percent of all the criminal cases are heard in state and local court systems, not in the federal courts. Moreover, only a small percentage of the persons convicted of federal crimes in the federal district courts actually have a trial. Most enter guilty pleas as part of a bargain to receive lighter punishment.

- *Civil suits under federal law.* As with criminal cases, state and local courts handle most civil suits. Also as with criminal cases, only a small percentage of those civil cases that commence in the federal courts are decided by trial—about 1 percent of the more than 250,000 civil cases resolved each year;[3] in the vast majority of cases, litigants settle out of court.

- *Civil suits between citizens of different states, or between a citizen and a foreign national, where the amount in question exceeds $75,000.* Such *diversity of citizenship* cases may involve, say, a Californian suing a Texan. Congress established this jurisdiction to protect against the possible bias of a state court in favor of a citizen from that state. In these cases, federal judges are to apply the appropriate state laws.

- *Supervision of bankruptcy proceedings.*

- *Review of the actions of some federal administrative agencies.*

- *Admiralty and maritime law cases.*

- *Supervision of the naturalization of aliens.*

District judges rely on an elaborate supporting cast, including clerks, bailiffs, law clerks, stenographers, court reporters, and probation officers. U.S. marshals are assigned to each district to protect the judicial process and to serve the writs that the judges issue. Federal magistrates, appointed to eight-year terms, issue warrants for arrest, determine whether to hold arrested persons for action by a grand jury, and set bail. They also hear motions subject to review by their district judge and, with the consent of both parties in civil cases and of defendants in petty criminal cases, preside over some trials. As the workload for district judges increases (more than 372,000 cases commenced in 2012),[4] magistrates are becoming essential components of the federal judicial system.

Another important player at the district court level is the *U.S. attorney.* Each of the 91 regular districts has a U.S. attorney who is nominated by the president and confirmed by the Senate and who serves at the discretion of the president (U.S. attorneys do not have lifetime appointments). These attorneys and their staffs prosecute violations of federal law and represent the U.S. government in civil cases.

Most of the cases handled in the district courts are routine, and few result in policy innovations. Usually district court judges do not even publish their decisions. Although most federal litigation ends at this level, a large percentage of the cases that district court judges actually decide (as opposed to those settled out of court or by guilty pleas) go forward on appeal. A distinguishing feature of the American legal system is the relative ease of appeals. U.S. law gives everyone a right to an appeal to a higher court. The loser in a case only has to request an appeal to be granted one. Of course, the loser must pay a substantial legal bill to exercise this right.

☐ Courts of Appeals

Congress has empowered the U.S. **courts of appeals** to review all final decisions of district courts, except in rare instances in which the law provides for direct review by the Supreme Court (injunctive orders of special three-judge district courts and certain decisions holding acts of Congress unconstitutional). Courts of appeals also have authority to review and enforce the orders of many independent regulatory commissions, such as the Securities and Exchange Commission and the National Labor Relations Board. About 75 percent of the more than 57,000 cases filed in the courts of appeals each year come from the district courts.[5]

The United States is divided into 12 *judicial circuits*, including one for the District of Columbia (see Figure 15.2). Each circuit, except that for Washington, D.C., serves at least two states and has between 6 and 28 permanent circuit judgeships (179 in all), depending on the amount of judicial work in the circuit. Each court of appeals normally hears cases in rotating panels consisting of three judges but may sit *en banc* (with all judges present) in particularly important cases. Decisions in either arrangement are made by majority vote of the participating judges.

There is also a special appeals court called the *U.S. Court of Appeals for the Federal Circuit.* Congress established this court, composed of 12 judges, in 1982 to hear appeals in specialized cases, such as those regarding patents, claims against the United States, and international trade.

The courts of appeals focus on correcting errors of procedure and law that occurred in the original proceedings of legal cases, such as when a district court judge gave improper instructions to a jury or misinterpreted the rights provided under a law. These courts are appellate courts and therefore hold no trials and hear no testimony. Their decisions set precedent for all the courts and agencies within their jurisdictions.

The Supreme Court

Sitting at the pinnacle of the American judicial system is the U.S. **Supreme Court.** The Court does much more for the American political system than decide individual cases. Among its most important functions are resolving conflicts among the states and maintaining national supremacy in the law. The Supreme Court also plays an important role in ensuring uniformity in the interpretation of national laws. For example, in 1984 Congress created a federal sentencing commission to write guidelines aimed at reducing

Supreme Court
The pinnacle of the American judicial system. The Court ensures uniformity in interpreting national laws, resolves conflicts among states, and maintains national supremacy in law. It has both original jurisdiction and appellate jurisdiction.

FIGURE 15.2 THE FEDERAL JUDICIAL CIRCUITS

The 12 judicial circuits differ considerably in size. Not shown in the map are Puerto Rico (part of the First Circuit, the Virgin Islands (in the Third Circuit), and Guam and the Northern Mariana Islands (in the Ninth Circuit).

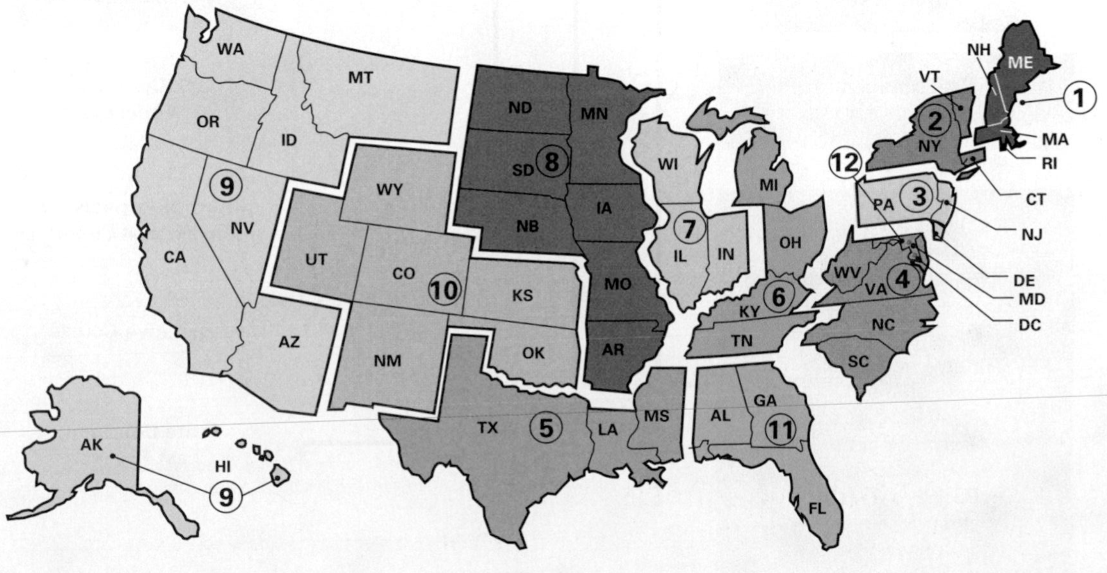

492

15.1
15.2
15.3
15.4
15.5
15.6
15.7

the wide disparities in punishment for similar crimes tried in federal courts. By 1989, more than 150 federal district judges had declared the law unconstitutional, and another 115 had ruled it valid. Only the Supreme Court could resolve this inconsistency in the administration of justice, which it did when it upheld the law.

There are nine justices on the Supreme Court: eight associates and one chief justice (only members of the Supreme Court are called *justices*; all others are called *judges*). The Constitution does not require this number, however, and there have been as few as 6 justices and as many as 10. Congress altered the size of the Supreme Court many times between 1801 and 1869. In 1866, it reduced the size of the Court from 10 to 7 members so that President Andrew Johnson could not nominate new justices to fill two vacancies. When Ulysses S. Grant took office, Congress increased the number of justices to nine because it was confident that he would nominate members to its liking. Since then, the number of justices has remained stable.

All nine justices sit together to hear cases and make decisions. But they must first decide which cases to hear. A familiar battle cry for losers in litigation in lower courts is "I'll appeal this all the way to the Supreme Court." In reality, this is unlikely to happen. Unlike other federal courts, the Supreme Court decides which cases it will hear.

You can see in Figure 15.3 that the Court does have an original jurisdiction, yet very few cases arise under it. The government does not usually wish to prosecute diplomats (it just sends them home), and there are not many legal disputes involving states as states (as opposed to, say, a prosecutor representing a state in criminal trial). Almost all the business of the Court comes from the appellate process. Litigants may appeal cases from both federal and state courts. However, as you can see in

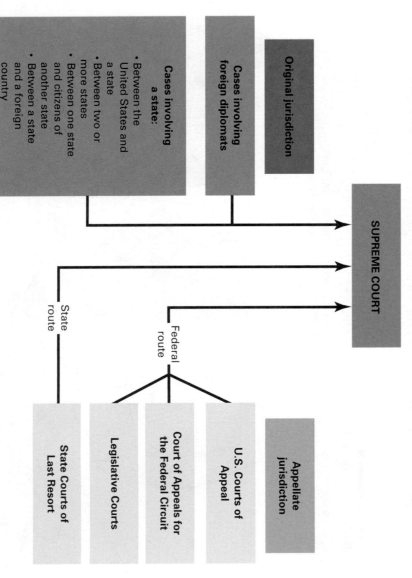

FIGURE 15.3 HOW CASES REACH THE SUPREME COURT

There are three routes to the U.S. Supreme Court. The first is through its original jurisdiction, where the Court hears a case in the first instance. Very few cases fall into this category, however. Most cases reach the Court through appeals from decisions in lower federal courts. Some cases also reach the Court as appeals from the highest state court that can hear a state case.

TABLE 15.1 SOURCES OF FULL OPINIONS IN THE SUPREME COURT, 2012–2013

Most cases that reach the Supreme Court are appeals from lower federal courts. Federal *habeas corpus* is a procedure under which a federal court may review the legality of an individual's incarceration.

Type of Case	Number of Cases
Original jurisdiction	0
Civil actions from lower federal courts	48
Criminal cases from lower federal courts	9
Federal *habeas corpus* cases	9
Civil actions from state courts	6
Criminal cases from state courts	6
Total	78

SOURCE: "The Supreme Court, 2012 Term: The Statistics," 127 (November 2013): 373–377.

Table 15.1, the vast majority of appeals heard by the Supreme Court are from the federal courts (i.e., from the federal system appellate courts shown in Figure 15.1).

Appeals from state courts must involve a "substantial federal question"; in deference to the states, the Supreme Court hears cases from state courts only if they involve federal law, and then only after the petitioner has exhausted all the potential remedies in the state court system. (Losers in a case in the state court system can appeal only to the Supreme Court, and not to any other federal court.) The Court will not try to settle matters of state law or determine guilt or innocence in state criminal proceedings. To obtain a hearing in the Supreme Court, a defendant convicted in a state court might demonstrate, for example, that the trial was not fair as required by the Bill of Rights, which was extended to cover state court proceedings by the due process clause of the Fourteenth Amendment.

The Politics of Judicial Selection

15.3 Explain the process by which judges and justices are nominated and confirmed.

udges are the central participants in the judicial system, and nominating federal judges and Supreme Court justices is a president's opportunity to leave an enduring mark on the American legal system. Guaranteed by the Constitution the right to serve "during good behavior," federal judges and justices enjoy, for all practical purposes, lifetime positions. They may be removed only by conviction of impeachment, which has occurred a mere seven times in over two centuries. Congress has never removed a Supreme Court justice from office, although it tried but did not convict Samuel Chase in 1805. Nor can Congress reduce the salaries of judges, a stipulation that further insulates them from political pressures. The president's discretion is actually less than it appears, however, since the Senate must confirm each nomination

Why It Matters to You
Judicial Election

The public directly elects most state and local judges. All federal judges and justices are nominated by the president and confirmed by the Senate for lifetime tenures. If we elected federal judges, their decisions on highly visible issues might be more responsive to the public—but less responsive to the Constitution.

senatorial courtesy

An unwritten tradition whereby nominations for state-level federal judicial posts are usually not confirmed if they are opposed by a senator of the president's party from the state in which the nominee will serve. The tradition also applies to courts of appeals when there is opposition from a senator of the president's party who is from the nominee's state.

by majority vote. Because the judiciary is a coequal branch, the upper house of the legislature sees no reason to be especially deferential to the executive's recommendations.

☐ The Lower Courts

Central to the Senate's consideration of state-level federal judicial nominations to the district courts and courts of appeals is the unwritten tradition of **senatorial courtesy:**[6]

- For district court positions, the Senate does not confirm nominees if they are opposed by a senator of the president's party from the state in which the nominee is to serve.

- For courts of appeals positions, the Senate does not confirm nominees opposed by a senator of the president's party from the state of the nominee's residence.

To invoke the right of senatorial courtesy, the relevant senator usually simply states a general reason for opposition. Other senators then honor their colleague's views and oppose the nomination, regardless of their personal evaluations of the candidate's merits.

Because of the strength of this informal practice, presidents usually check carefully with the relevant senator or senators ahead of time to avoid making a nomination that the Senate will not confirm. Moreover, typically when there is a vacancy for a federal district judgeship, the relevant senator or senators from the state where the judge will serve suggest one or more names to the attorney general and the president. If neither senator is of the president's party, then the party's state congresspersons or other state party leaders may make suggestions. Other interested senators may also try to influence a selection.[7]

In early 2009, Senate Republicans added a new element to senatorial courtesy when they sent President Obama a letter in which they vowed to prevent the confirmation of judicial nominees in instances where the White House did not properly consult Republican home-state senators. The implication of this letter is that members of the opposition party would have a de facto veto power, something without precedent in the history of judicial selection.[8] President Obama reached out to Republican senators, but they often refused to make recommendations for the district courts, delaying or obstructing the process.

The White House, the Department of Justice, and the Federal Bureau of Investigation conduct competency and background checks on persons suggested for judgeships, and the president usually selects a nominee from those who survive the screening process. If one of these survivors was recommended by a senator to whom senatorial courtesy is due, it is difficult for the president to reject the recommendation in favor of someone else who survived the process. Thus, senatorial courtesy turns the Constitution on its head, and, in effect, the Senate ends up making nominations and the president then approving them.

Why It Matters to You
Senatorial Courtesy

Because of the practice of senatorial courtesy, senators in effect end up nominating persons to be district court judges. If the Senate abolished this practice, it would give presidents greater freedom in making nominations and more opportunity to put their stamp on the judiciary.

Others have input in judicial selection as well. The Department of Justice may ask sitting judges, usually federal judges, to evaluate prospective nominees. Sitting judges may also initiate recommendations, advancing or retarding someone's chances of being nominated. In addition, candidates for the nomination are often active on their own behalf. They alert the relevant parties that they desire the position and may orchestrate a campaign of support. As one appellate judge observed, "People don't just get judgeships without seeking them."[9]

The president usually has more influence in the selection of judges to the federal courts of appeals than to federal district courts. The decisions of appeals courts are generally more significant than those of lower courts, so the president naturally takes a greater interest in appointing people to these courts. At the same time, individual senators are in a weaker position to determine who the nominee will be because the jurisdiction of an appeals court encompasses several states. Although custom and pragmatic politics require that these judgeships be apportioned among the states in a circuit, the president has some discretion in doing this and therefore has a greater role in recruiting appellate judges than in recruiting district court judges. Even here, however, senators of the president's party from the state in which the candidate resides may be able to veto a nomination.

Traditionally, the Senate confirmed lower federal court nominations swiftly and unanimously. However, the increasing polarization of partisan politics in recent years has affected judicial nominations, especially those for the courts of appeals. Increasingly, lower court confirmations have become lengthy and contentious proceedings. Interest groups opposed to nominations have become more active and encourage senators aligned with them to delay and block nominations.[10] As a result, there has been a dramatic increase in the time for confirmation,[11] which in turn has decreased the chances of confirmation. Since 1992, the Senate has confirmed only 60 percent of nominees to the courts of appeals.[12]

Senators of the opposition party filibustered or otherwise derailed the confirmations of a number of high-profile nominations of Presidents Clinton and George W. Bush. In response, the presidents appointed some judges to the courts of appeals as recess appointments. Such appointments are unusual and good only for the remainder of a congressional term. (In 2014 the Supreme Court tightly constrained the president's ability to make such appointments.)[13] After the Republicans nearly voted to end the possibility of filibustering judicial nominations, 14 senators from both parties forged a deal that allowed some—but not all—of Bush's stalled judicial nominees to receive floor votes. Nevertheless, conflict over nominations continued as the Republican minority used secret holds, threats of filibusters, and various Senate procedures to delay and often stymie Barack Obama's judicial nominations, even at the district court level. In response, in 2013 the Democrats prevailed in changing the Senate's rules to end filibusters for nominations to all but the Supreme Court.

☐ The Supreme Court

The president is vitally interested in the Supreme Court because of the importance of its work and is usually intimately involved in recruiting potential justices. Nominations to the Court may be a president's most important legacy to the nation.

A president cannot have much impact on the Court unless there are vacancies to fill. Although on the average there has been an opening on the Supreme Court every two years, there is a substantial variance around this mean.[14] Franklin D. Roosevelt had to wait five years before he could nominate a justice; in the meantime, he was faced with a Court that found much of his New Deal legislation unconstitutional. Jimmy Carter was never able to nominate a justice. Between 1972 and 1984, there were only two vacancies on the Court. Nevertheless, Richard Nixon was able to nominate four justices in his first three years in office, and Ronald Reagan had the opportunity to add three new members.

When the chief justice's position is vacant, the president may nominate either someone already on the Court or someone from outside to fill the position. Usually presidents choose the latter course to widen their range of options, but if they decide to elevate a sitting associate justice—as President Reagan did with William Rehnquist in 1986—the nominee must go through a new confirmation hearing by the Senate Judiciary Committee.

The president operates under fewer constraints in nominating persons to serve on the Supreme Court than in nominations for the lower courts. Although many of the same actors are present in the case of Supreme Court nominations, their influence is typically quite different. The president usually relies on White House aides, the attorney general, and the Department of Justice to identify and screen candidates for the

Court. Sitting justices often try to influence the nominations of their future colleagues, but presidents feel little obligation to follow their advice.

Senators also play a lesser role in the recruitment of Supreme Court justices than in the selection of lower-court judges, as the jurisdiction of the Court obviously goes beyond individual senators' states or regions. Thus presidents typically consult with senators from the state of residence of a nominee after they have decided whom to select. At this point, senators are unlikely to oppose a nomination, because they like having their state receive the honor and are well aware that the president can simply select someone from another state. Although home-state senators do not play prominent roles in the selection process for the Court, the Senate actively exercises its confirmation powers and, through its Judiciary Committee, may probe a nominee's judicial philosophy in great detail.

Candidates for nomination usually keep a low profile. They can accomplish little through aggressive politicking, and because of the Court's standing, actively pursuing the position might offend those who play important roles in selecting nominees. The American Bar Association's Standing Committee on the federal judiciary has played a varied but typically modest role at the Supreme Court level. Presidents have not generally been willing to allow the committee to prescreen candidates before their nominations are announced. George W. Bush chose not to seek its advice at all.

Through 2014, there have been 153 nominations to the Supreme Court, and 112 people have served on the Court. Four people were nominated and confirmed twice, 8 declined appointment or died before beginning service on the Court, and 29 failed to secure Senate confirmation. Presidents have failed 20 percent of the time to appoint the nominees of their choice to the Court—a percentage much higher than for any other federal position.

RECENT NOMINATIONS For most of the twentieth century, confirmations of Supreme Court nominees were routine affairs. Only one nominee failed to win confirmation in the first two-thirds of the century. But, as Table 15.2 shows, the situation changed beginning in the 1960s, tumultuous times that bred ideological conflict. Although John F. Kennedy had no trouble with his two nominations to the Court—Byron White and Arthur Goldberg—his successor, Lyndon Johnson, was less fortunate. In the face of strong opposition, Johnson had to withdraw his nomination of Abe Fortas (already serving on the Court) to serve as chief justice; as a result, the Senate never voted on Homer Thornberry, Johnson's nominee to replace Fortas as an associate justice. Richard Nixon, the next president, had two nominees in a row rejected after bruising battles in the Senate.

Two of President Reagan's nominees proved unsuccessful. In 1987, Reagan nominated Robert H. Bork to fill the vacancy created by the resignation of Justice Lewis Powell. Bork testified before the Senate Judiciary Committee for 23 hours. A wide range of interest groups entered the fray, mostly in opposition to the nominee, whose views they claimed were extremist. In the end, following a bitter floor debate, the Senate

TABLE 15.2 UNSUCCESSFUL SUPREME COURT NOMINEES SINCE 1900

Nominee	Year	President
John J. Parker	1930	Hoover
Abe Fortas[a]	1968	Johnson
Homer Thornberry[b]	1968	Johnson
Clement F. Haynesworth, Jr.	1969	Nixon
G. Harrold Carswell	1970	Nixon
Robert H. Bork	1987	Reagan
Douglas H. Ginsburg[a]	1987	Reagan
Harriet Miers[a]	2005	G. W. Bush

[a] Nomination withdrawn. Fortas was serving on the Court as an associate justice and was nominated to be chief justice.
[b] The Senate took no action on Thornberry's nomination.

rejected the president's nomination by a vote of 42 to 58. Six days after the Senate vote on Bork, the president nominated Judge Douglas H. Ginsburg to the high court. Just nine days later, however, Ginsburg withdrew his nomination after disclosures that he had used marijuana while a law professor at Harvard.

In June 1991, when Associate Justice Thurgood Marshall announced his retirement from the Court, President George H. W. Bush announced his nomination of another African American, federal appeals judge Clarence Thomas, to replace Marshall. Thomas was a conservative, so this decision was consistent with the Bush administration's emphasis on placing conservative judges on the federal bench. Liberals were placed in a dilemma. On the one hand, they favored a minority group member serving on the nation's highest court, and particularly an African American replacing the Court's only African American. On the other hand, Thomas was unlikely to vote the same way as Thurgood Marshall had voted, and was likely instead to strengthen the conservative trend in the Court's decisions. This ambivalence inhibited spirited opposition to Thomas, who was circumspect about his judicial philosophy in his appearances before the Senate Judiciary Committee. Thomas's confirmation was nearly derailed, however, by charges of sexual harassment leveled against him by University of Oklahoma law professor Anita Hill. Ultimately, following Hill's testimony and Thomas's denial of the charges, he was confirmed in a 52-to-48 vote—the closest margin by which a Supreme Court nomination had been confirmed in more than a century.

President Clinton's two nominees—Ruth Bader Ginsburg and Stephen Breyer—did not cause much controversy and were readily confirmed Similarly, the Senate easily confirmed George W. Bush's nomination of John Roberts as chief justice to succeed William Rehnquist. Indeed, he was not an easy target to oppose. His pleasing and professional personal demeanor and his disciplined and skilled testimony before the Senate Judicial Committee gave potential opponents little basis for opposition.

Ideological conflict returned to the fore, however, when Bush then nominated White House counsel Harriet Miers to replace Justice Sandra Day O'Connor. By settling on a loyalist with no experience as a judge and little substantive record on abortion, affirmative action, religion, and other socially divisive issues, the president shied away from a direct confrontation with liberals and in effect asked his base on the right to trust him on his nomination. However, many conservatives, having hoped and expected that he would make an unambiguously conservative choice to fulfill their goal of clearly altering the Court's balance, were bitterly disappointed and highly critical. They demanded a known conservative. The nomination also smacked of cronyism, with the president selecting a friend rather than someone of obvious merit, and the comparison with Roberts underscored the thinness of Miers's qualifications. In short order, Miers withdrew from consideration, and the president nominated Samuel Alito.

Alito was clearly a traditional conservative and had a less impressive public presence than Roberts. Response to him followed party lines, but he appeared too well qualified and unthreatening in his confirmation hearings to justify a filibuster, and without one, his confirmation was assured. The Senate confirmed Alito by a vote of 58 to 42.

President Obama made his first nomination to the Court in 2009, selecting Sonia Sotomayor. Although conservatives raised questions about some of her previous statements and decisions, she was confirmed by a vote of 68 to 31, largely along party lines. When she took the oath of office, she became the first Hispanic justice. In 2010, the president nominated Solicitor General Elena Kagan to the Court. She was confirmed by a vote of 63 to 37, once again largely along party lines.

It is difficult to predict the politics surrounding future nominations to the Supreme Court. One prediction seems safe, however: as long as Americans are polarized around social issues and as long as the Court makes critical decisions about these issues, the potential for conflict over the president's nominations is always present.

Nominations are most likely to run into trouble under certain conditions. Presidents whose parties are in the minority in the Senate or who make a nomination at the end of their terms face a greatly increased probability of substantial opposition.[15] Presidents whose views are more distant from the norm in the Senate or who are

498

15.1
15.2
15.3
15.4
15.5
15.6
15.7

Elena Kagan is the newest member of the Supreme Court. She is unusual among recent justices in not having been a judge prior to her nomination. Instead, she was solicitor general of the United States, arguing cases before the Court.

The Backgrounds of Judges and Justices

15.4 Describe the backgrounds of judges and justices and assess the impact of background on their decisions.

The Constitution sets no special requirements for judges or justices, but most observers conclude that the federal judiciary comprises a distinguished group of men and women. Competence and ethical behavior are important to presidents for reasons beyond merely obtaining Senate confirmation of their judicial nominees. Skilled and honorable judges and justices reflect well on the president and are likely to do so for many years, and, of course, they can more effectively represent the president's views. The criteria of competence and ethics, however, still leave a wide field from which to choose; other characteristics also carry considerable weight.

appointing a person who might alter the balance on the Court are also likely to face additional opposition. However, opponents of a nomination usually must be able to question a nominee's legal competence or ethics in order to defeat the nomination. Most people do not consider opposition to a nominee's ideology a valid reason to vote against confirmation. For example, liberals disagreed strongly with the views of William Rehnquist, but he was easily confirmed as chief justice. By raising questions about competence or ethics, opponents are able to attract moderate senators to their side and to make ideological protests seem less partisan.

Backgrounds

The judges serving on the federal district and circuit courts are not a representative sample of the American people. They are all lawyers (although this is not a constitutional requirement). They are also overwhelmingly white males. Jimmy Carter appointed more women and minorities to the federal bench, more than all previous presidents combined. Ronald Reagan did not continue this trend, although he was the first to appoint a woman to the Supreme Court. In screening candidates, his administration placed a higher priority on conservative ideology than on diversity, as did George H. W. Bush's administration. Bill Clinton's nominees were more liberal than were the nominees of Reagan and Bush, and a large percentage of them were women and minorities. George W. Bush's nominees were more diverse than those of his father although less so than those of Clinton and Carter, and they were uniformly conservative.[16] Barack Obama nominated mostly ideologically moderate judges and justices, and, for the first time in American history, the president nominated women and ethnic minorities to a majority of the judicial vacancies.[17]

Federal judges have typically held office as a judge or prosecutor, and often they have been involved in partisan politics. This involvement is generally what brings them to the attention of senators and the Department of Justice when they seek nominees for judgeships. As former U.S. attorney general and Circuit Court Judge Griffin Bell once remarked, "For me, becoming a federal judge wasn't very difficult. I managed John F. Kennedy's presidential campaign in Georgia. Two of my oldest and closest friends were senators from Georgia. And I was campaign manager and special unpaid counsel for the governor."[18]

Like their colleagues on the lower federal courts, Supreme Court justices are not a representative sample of the population (see Table 15.3 for the current justices). All have been lawyers, and all but six have been white males (Thurgood Marshall, nominated in 1967; Sandra Day O'Connor, nominated in 1981; and Clarence Thomas, Ruth Bader Ginsburg, Sonia Sotomayor, and Elena Kagan, all on the current Court). Most have been in their fifties and sixties when they took office, from the upper-middle or upper class, and Protestants.

Typically, justices have held high administrative or judicial positions before moving to the Supreme Court. Most have had some experience as a judge, often at the appellate level, and many have worked for the Department of Justice. Some have held elective office, and a few have had no government service but have been distinguished attorneys. The fact that many justices, including some of the most distinguished ones, have not had previous judicial experience may seem surprising, but the unique work of the Court renders this background much less important than it might be for other appellate courts.

TABLE 15.3 SUPREME COURT JUSTICES, 2013

Name	Year of Birth	Previous Position	Nominating President	Year of Confirmation
John G. Roberts, Jr.	1955	U.S. Court of Appeals	G. W. Bush	2005
Antonin Scalia	1936	U.S. Court of Appeals	Reagan	1986
Anthony M. Kennedy	1936	U.S. Court of Appeals	Reagan	1988
Clarence Thomas	1948	U.S. Court of Appeals	G. H. W. Bush	1991
Ruth Bader Ginsburg	1933	U.S. Court of Appeals	Clinton	1993
Stephen G. Breyer	1938	U.S. Court of Appeals	Clinton	1994
Samuel A. Alito, Jr.	1950	U.S. Court of Appeals	G. W. Bush	2006
Sonia Sotomayor	1954	U.S. Court of Appeals	Obama	2009
Elena Kagan	1960	U.S. Solicitor General	Obama	2010

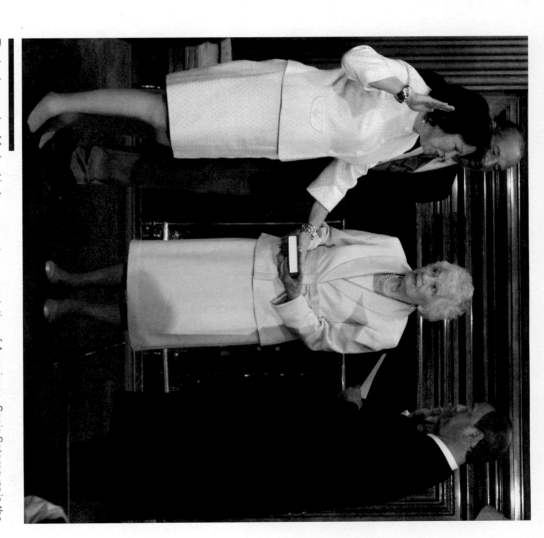

The backgrounds of federal judges are not representative of Americans. Sonia Sotomayor is the first Hispanic American to serve on the Supreme Court.

□ Criteria for Selection

Geography was once a prominent criterion for selection to the Court, but it is no longer very important. Presidents do like to spread the slots around, however, as when Richard Nixon decided that he wanted to nominate a Southerner. At various times there have been what some have termed a "Jewish seat" and a "Catholic seat" on the Court, but these guidelines are not binding on the president. For example, after a half-century of having a Jewish justice, the Court did not have one from 1969 to 1993. And although only 12 Catholics have served on the Court, 6 of the current justices are Catholic.

Partisanship has been and remains an important influence on the selection of judges and justices. Only 13 of 112 members of the Supreme Court have been nominated by presidents of a different party. Moreover, many of the 13 exceptions were actually close to the president in ideology, as was the case in Richard Nixon's appointment of Lewis Powell. Herbert Hoover's nomination of Benjamin Cardozo seems to be one of the few cases in which partisanship was completely dominated by merit as a criterion for selection.

The role of partisanship is really not surprising. Most of a president's acquaintances are made through the party, and there is usually a certain congruity between party and political views. Most judges and justices have at one time been active partisans—an experience that gave them visibility and helped them obtain the positions from which they moved to the courts. Moreover, judgeships are considered very prestigious patronage plums. Indeed, the decisions of Congress to create new judgeships—and thus new positions for party members—are closely related to whether the majority party in Congress is the same as the party of the president. Members of the majority party in the legislature want to avoid providing an opposition party president with new positions to fill with their opponents.

Ideology is as important as partisanship in the selection of judges and justices. Presidents want to appoint to the federal bench people who share their views. In effect, all presidents try to "pack" the courts. They want more than "justice"; they want policies with which they agree. Presidential aides survey candidates' decisions (if they have served on a lower court),[19] speeches, political stands, writings, and other expressions of opinion. They also glean information from people who know the candidates well. Although it is considered improper to question judicial candidates about upcoming court cases, it is appropriate to discuss broader questions of political and judicial philosophy. The Reagan administration was especially concerned about such matters and had each potential nominee fill out a lengthy questionnaire and be interviewed by a special committee in the Department of Justice. Both George H. W. Bush and George W. Bush were also attentive to appointing conservative judges. Bill Clinton was less concerned with appointing liberal judges, at least partly to avoid costly confirmation fights, and instead focused on identifying persons with strong legal credentials, especially women and minorities. Barack Obama approached judicial nominations much like Clinton.[20]

Members of the federal bench also play the game of politics, of course, and may try to time their retirements so that a president with compatible views will choose their successor and perhaps a like-minded Senate will vote on the nomination. For example, it appears that Justice David Souter timed his retirement in 2009 so that Barack Obama rather than George W. Bush would name a new justice. This concern about a successor is one reason why justices remain on the Supreme Court for so long, even when they are clearly infirm.[21]

☐ Background Characteristics and Policymaking

Presidents are typically pleased with the performance of their nominees to the Supreme Court and through them have slowed or reversed trends in the Court's decisions. Franklin D. Roosevelt's nominees substantially liberalized the Court, whereas Richard Nixon's turned it in a conservative direction, from which it has yet to move.

Nevertheless, it is not always easy to predict the policy inclinations of candidates, and presidents have been disappointed in their nominees about one-fourth of the

The U.S. Supreme Court, 2013: Front row, left to right: Clarence Thomas, Antonin Scalia, John G. Roberts, Anthony M. Kennedy, and Ruth Bader Ginsburg. Second row, left to right: Sonia Sotomayor, Stephen G. Breyer, Samuel Alito, and Elena Kagan.

time. President Eisenhower, for example, was displeased with the liberal decisions of both Earl Warren and William Brennan. Once, when asked whether he had made any mistakes as president, Eisenhower replied, "Yes, two, and they are both sitting on the Supreme Court."[22] George H. W. Bush was disappointed with David Souter, who ended up siding with the Court's liberal bloc on abortion rights and other issues.

Presidents influence policy through the values of their judicial nominees, but this impact is limited by numerous legal and "extralegal" factors beyond the chief executive's control. As Harry Truman put it, "Packing the Supreme Court can't be done. . . . I've tried it and it won't work. . . . Whenever you put a man on the Supreme Court, he ceases to be your friend. I'm sure of that."[23]

Although women and people of different ethnicities and religions may desire to have people in their group appointed to the federal bench—at the very least, judgeships have symbolic importance for them[24]—the real question is what, if any, policy differences result. There is some evidence that female judges on the courts of appeals are more likely than are male judges to support charges of sex discrimination and sexual harassment, and they seem to influence the male judges deciding the cases with them.[25] Similarly, racial and ethnic minority judges on these courts are more likely to find for minority plaintiffs in voting rights cases and also to influence the votes of white judges sitting with them.[26] At the level of the Supreme Court, conservative Justice Antonin Scalia has said that Justice Thurgood Marshall "could be a persuasive force just by sitting there. He wouldn't have to open his mouth to affect the nature of the conference and how seriously the conference would take matters of race."[27] It is true, of course, that Justice Clarence Thomas, the second African American justice, is one of the most conservative justices since the New Deal, illustrating that not everyone from a particular background has a particular point of view.

Many members of each party have been appointed, of course, and it appears that Republican judges in general are somewhat more conservative than are Democratic judges. Former prosecutors serving on the Supreme Court have tended to be less sympathetic toward defendants' rights than have other justices. It seems, then, that background does make some difference,[28] yet for reasons that we examine in the following sections, on many issues party affiliation and other characteristics are imperfect predictors of judicial behavior.

The Courts as Policymakers

15.5 Outline the judicial process at the Supreme Court level and assess the major factors influencing decisions and their implementation.

 "Judicial decision making," a former Supreme Court law clerk wrote in the *Harvard Law Review*, "involves, at bottom, a choice between competing values by fallible, pragmatic, and at times nonrational men and women in a highly complex process in a very human setting."[29] This is an apt description of policymaking in the Supreme Court and in other courts, too. The next sections look at how courts make policy, paying particular attention to the role of the U.S. Supreme Court. Although it is not the only court involved in policymaking and policy interpretation, its decisions have the widest implications for policy.

☐ Accepting Cases

Deciding what to decide about is the first step in all policymaking. Courts of original jurisdiction cannot very easily refuse to consider a case; the U.S. Supreme Court has much more control over its agenda. The approximately 8,000 cases submitted annually to the U.S. Supreme Court must be read, culled, and sifted. Figure 15.4 shows the stages of this process. At least once each week, the nine justices meet in conference.

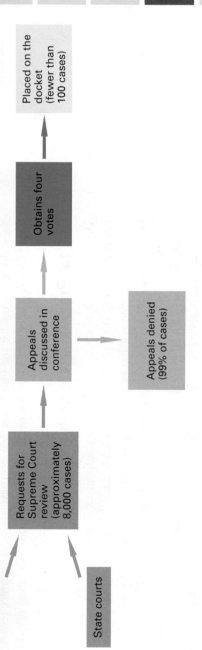

FIGURE 15.4 OBTAINING SPACE ON THE SUPREME COURT'S DOCKET

Federal courts → Requests for Supreme Court review (approximately 8,000 cases) ← State courts

Requests for Supreme Court review → Appeals discussed in conference

Appeals discussed in conference → Obtains four votes

Appeals discussed in conference → Appeals denied (99% of cases)

Obtains four votes → Placed on the docket (fewer than 100 cases)

With them in the conference room sit some 25 carts, each wheeled in from the office of one of the nine justices and each filled with petitions, briefs, memoranda, and every item the justices are likely to need during their discussions. These meetings operate under the strictest secrecy; only the justices themselves attend.

The first task of the justices at these weekly conferences is to establish an agenda for the Court. Before the meeting, the chief justice circulates a list of cases to discuss, and any justice may add other cases. Because few of the justices can take the time to read materials on every case submitted to the Court, most rely heavily on law clerks to screen each case.[30] If four justices agree to grant review of a case (in what is known as the "rule of four"), it is placed on the docket and scheduled for oral argument and the Court typically issues to the relevant lower federal or state court a *writ of certiorari*, a formal document calling up the case. In some instances, the Court will instead decide a case on the basis of the written record already on file with the Court.

The cases the Court is most likely to select are those that involve major issues—especially civil liberties, conflict between different lower courts on the interpretation of federal law (as when a court of appeals in Texas prohibits the use of affirmative action criteria in college admissions and a court of appeals in Michigan approves their use), or disagreement between a majority of the Supreme Court and lower-court decisions.[31]

Because getting into the Supreme Court is half the battle, it is important to remember this chapter's earlier discussion of standing to sue (litigants must have serious interest in a case, having sustained or being in immediate danger of sustaining a direct and substantial injury from another party or an action of government)—a criterion the Court often uses to decide whether to hear a case. As we discuss later in this chapter, the Court will sometimes avoid hearing cases that are too politically "hot" to handle or that divide the Court too sharply.[32]

Another important influence on the Supreme Court's decisions to accept cases is the solicitor general.[33] As a presidential appointee and the third-ranking official in the Department of Justice, the **solicitor general** is in charge of the appellate court litigation of the federal government. The solicitor general and a staff of about two dozen experienced attorneys have four key functions: (1) to decide whether to appeal cases the government has lost in the lower courts, (2) to review and modify the briefs presented in government appeals, (3) to represent the government before the Supreme Court, and (4) to submit an *amicus curiae* brief on behalf of a litigant in a case in which the government has an interest but is not directly involved.[34] The solicitors general are careful to seek Court review only of important cases. By avoiding frivolous appeals and displaying a high degree of competence, they typically earn the confidence of the Court, which in turn grants review of a large percentage of the cases they submit.[35] Often, the Court asks the solicitor general to provide the government's opinion on whether to accept a case.

solicitor general
A presidential appointee and the third-ranking official in the Department of Justice. The solicitor general is in charge of the appellate court litigation of the federal government.

opinion
A statement of legal reasoning behind a judicial decision. The content of an opinion may be as important as the decision itself.

Ultimately, the Supreme Court decides very few cases. In recent years, the Court has made about 80 formal written decisions per year in which their opinions could serve as precedent and thus as the basis of guidance for lower courts. In a few dozen additional cases, the Court reaches a *per curiam decision*—that is, a decision without explanation. Such decisions resolve the immediate case but have no value as precedent because the Court does not offer reasoning that would guide lower courts in future decisions.[36]

☐ The Process of Decision Making

The second task of the justices' weekly conferences is to discuss cases that the Court has heard. From the first Monday in October until June, the Court hears oral arguments in two-week cycles: two weeks of courtroom arguments followed by two weeks of reflecting on cases and writing opinions about them. Figure 15.5 shows the stages in this process.

Before the justices enter the courtroom to hear the lawyers for each side present their arguments, they have received elaborately prepared written briefs from each party involved. They have also probably received several *amicus curiae* briefs from parties (often groups) who are interested in the outcome of the case but who are not formal litigants. As already noted, *amicus curiae* briefs may be submitted by the government, under the direction of the solicitor general, in cases in which it has an interest. For instance, if a case between two parties involves the question of the constitutionality of a federal law, the federal government naturally wants to have its voice heard. Administrations also use these briefs to urge the Court to change established doctrine. For example, the Reagan administration frequently submitted *amicus curiae* briefs to the Court to try to change the law dealing with defendants' rights.

In most instances, the attorneys for each side have only a half-hour to address the Court. During this time they summarize their briefs, emphasizing their most compelling points.[37] The justices may listen attentively, interrupt with penetrating or helpful questions, request information, talk to one another, read (presumably briefs), or simply gaze at the ceiling. After 25 minutes, a white light comes on at the lectern from which the lawyer is speaking, and five minutes later a red light signals the end of that lawyer's presentation, even if he or she is in midsentence. Oral argument is over.[38]

Back in the conference room, the chief justice, who presides over the Court, raises a particular case and invites discussion, turning first to the senior associate justice. Discussion can range from perfunctory to profound and from courteous to caustic. If the votes are not clear from the individual discussions, the chief justice may ask each justice to vote. Once a tentative vote has been reached on a case, it is necessary to write an **opinion**, a statement of the legal reasoning behind the decision for the case.

Opinion writing is no mere formality. In fact, the content of an opinion may be as important as the decision itself. Broad and bold opinions have far-reaching implications for future cases; narrowly drawn opinions may have little impact beyond the case being decided. Tradition in the Supreme Court requires that the chief justice, if in the majority, write the opinion or assign it to another justice in the majority. The chief justice often writes the opinion in landmark cases, as Earl Warren did in *Brown v. Board of Education* and Warren Burger did in *United States v. Nixon*. If the chief justice is part of the minority, the senior associate justice in the majority assigns the opinion. The person assigned to write an opinion circulates drafts within the Court, justices make suggestions, and they all conduct negotiations among themselves.[39] The content of the opinion can win

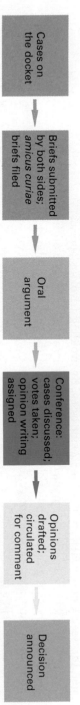

Cases on the docket → Briefs submitted by both sides; *amicus curiae* briefs filed → Oral argument → Conference: cases discussed; votes taken; opinion writing assigned → Opinions drafted; circulated for comment → Decision announced

FIGURE 15.5 THE SUPREME COURT'S DECISION-MAKING PROCESS

or lose votes. A justice must redraft an opinion that proves unacceptable to the majority of his or her colleagues on the Court.

Justices are free to write their own opinions, to join in other opinions, or to associate themselves with part of one opinion and part of another. Justices opposed to all or part of the majority's decision write *dissenting opinions*. *Concurring opinions* are those written not only to support a majority decision but also to stress a different constitutional or legal basis for the judgment.

When the justices have written their opinions and taken the final vote, they announce their decision. At least six justices must participate in a case, and decisions are made by majority vote. If there is a tie (because of a vacancy on the Court or because a justice chooses not to participate because of a conflict of interest), the decision of the lower court from which the case came is sustained. Five votes are necessary for the logic to serve as precedent for judges of lower courts.

☐ The Basis of Decisions

Judges and justices settle the vast majority of cases on the principle of *stare decisis* ("let the decision stand"), meaning that an earlier decision should hold for the case being considered. All courts rely heavily on **precedent**—the way similar cases were handled in the past—as a guide to current decisions. Lower courts, of course, are expected to follow the precedents of higher courts in their decision making. If the Supreme Court, for example, rules in favor of the right to abortion under certain conditions, it has established a precedent that lower courts are expected to follow. Lower courts have much less discretion than the Supreme Court.[40]

The Supreme Court is in a position to overrule its own precedents, and it has done so more than 200 times.[41] One of the most famous of such instances occurred with *Brown v. Board of Education* (1954), in which the court overruled *Plessy v. Ferguson* (1896) and found that segregation in the public schools violated the Constitution.

What happens when precedents are unclear? This is especially a problem for the Supreme Court, which is more likely than other courts to handle cases at the forefront of the law, where precedent is typically less firmly established. Moreover, the justices are often asked to apply to concrete situations the vague phrases of the Constitution ("due process of law," "equal protection," "unreasonable searches and seizures") or vague statutes passed by Congress. This ambiguity provides leeway for the justices to disagree (the Court decides unanimously only about one-third of the cases in which it issues full opinions) and for their values to influence their judgment. In contrast, when precedents are clear and legal doctrine is well established, legal factors are more likely to play a preeminent role in Supreme Court decision making.[42]

stare decisis
A Latin phrase meaning "let the decision stand." Most cases reaching appellate courts are settled on this principle.

precedent
How similar cases have been decided in the past.

The content of a Supreme Court opinion may be as important as the decision itself, and justices may spend months negotiating a majority opinion. Here, William Rehnquist prepares an opinion.

originalism
A view that the Constitution should be interpreted according to the original intentions or original meaning of the Framers. Many conservatives support this view.

The Constitution does not specify a set of rules by which justices are to interpret it. There are a number of approaches to decision making. One is **originalism**, which takes two principal forms:

- The *original intent theory* holds that interpretation of a written constitution or law should be consistent with what was meant by those who drafted and ratified it. Justice Clarence Thomas is the most prominent advocate of this view.

- The *original meaning theory* is the view that judges should base their interpretations of a written constitution or law on what reasonable persons living at the time of its adoption would have declared the ordinary meaning of the text to be. It is with this view that most originalists, such as Justice Antonin Scalia, are associated,[43] original meaning being more discernible than the often nebulous original intent.

Advocates of originalism view it as a means of constraining the exercise of judicial discretion, which they see as the foundation of the liberal Court decisions, especially on matters of civil liberties, civil rights, and defendants' rights. They also see following original intent or meaning as the only basis of interpretation consistent with democracy. Judges, they argue, should not dress up constitutional interpretations with *their* views on "contemporary needs," "today's conditions," or "what is right." It is the job of legislators, not judges, to make such judgments.

Both of these theories share the view that there is an authority, contemporaneous with a constitution's or statute's ratification, that should govern its interpretation. However, originalists do not propose to turn the clock back completely, as by, say, upholding a statute that imposed the punishment of flogging, of which the Constitution's Framers approved.

Of course, originalists often disagree among themselves about original meanings, and sometimes they agree about the founders' intentions but disagree about overturning deeply rooted precedents, such as bans on segregation and school prayers, that may clash with those intentions. Moreover, even when there is broad scholarly agreement about original understanding, originalists sometimes ignore it.

The primary alternative does not have a clear label, but those holding it view the Constitution as written in flexible terms, as a document whose meaning is dynamic and thus changes over time. Advocates of this approach to decision making, such as Justice Stephen Breyer, assert that the Constitution is subject to multiple meanings, to being given different interpretations by thoughtful people in different ages. Judges from different times and places will differ about what they think the Constitution means.[44] Thus, judicial discretion comes into play even if judges claim to be basing decisions on original intent. For advocates of this approach, originalism's apparent deference to the intentions of the Framers is simply a cover for making conservative decisions.

In addition, these jurists contend that trying to reconstruct or guess the Framers' intentions or meaning is very difficult. Recent key cases before the Supreme Court have concerned issues such as campaign financing, abortions, the Internet, and wiretapping that the Framers could not have imagined; there were no super-PACs, contraceptives or modern abortion techniques, or computers, electronic surveillance equipment, or telephones in 1787. When the Founders wrote the Constitution, they embraced not specific solutions but general principles, which frequently lacked discrete, discoverable meaning or intent. Moreover, there is often no record of their intentions, nor is it clear whose intentions should count—those of the writers of the Constitution, those of the more than 1,600 members who attended the ratifying conventions, or those of the voters who sent them there. This problem grows more complex when you consider the amendments to the Constitution, which involve thousands of additional "Framers." Moreover, historian Jack N. Rakove points out that there is little historical evidence that the Framers believed that their intentions should guide later interpretations of the Constitution.[45]

Given the discretion that justices often have in making decisions, it is not surprising that consistent patterns related to their values and ideology—to conservative versus liberal positions—are often evident in their decisions. A number of scholars have proposed an *attitudinal model* of decision making in which justices decide cases based largely on the outcomes they prefer rather than on precedent or the meaning or

judicial implementation

How and whether court decisions are translated into actual policy, thereby affecting the behavior of others. The courts rely on other units of government to enforce their decisions.

Point to Ponder

Supreme Court justices have substantial discretion in deciding constitutional issues.

Are you content with this judicial freedom? Is there any way to constrain Court decisions?

"Do you ever have one of those days when every-thing seems unconstitutional?"

intentions of the Constitution's framers or of legislators.[46] In other words, they argue, policy preferences matter in judicial decision making, especially on the nation's highest court. Although precedent, legal principles, and even political pressures from the public, Congress, and the White House constrain justices' discretion,[47] justices usually arrive at a decision consistent with their policy preferences.

Implementing Court Decisions

The Court conveys its decisions to the press and the public through formal announcements in open court. Media coverage of the Court remains primitive—short and shallow. Doris Graber reports that "much reporting on the courts—even at the Supreme Court level—is imprecise and sometimes even wrong."[48] More important to the legal community, the decisions are bound weekly and made available to every law library and lawyer in the United States. There is, of course, an air of finality to the public announcement of a decision. In fact, however, even Supreme Court decisions are not self-implementing; they are actually "remands" to lower courts, instructing them to act in accordance with the Court's decisions.

Reacting bitterly to one of Chief Justice Marshall's decisions, President Andrew Jackson is said to have grumbled, "John Marshall has made his decision; now let him enforce it." Court decisions carry legal, even moral, authority, but courts must rely on other units of government to enforce their decisions. **Judicial implementation** refers to how and whether court decisions are translated into actual policy, thereby affecting the behavior of others.

Judicial decision is the end of one process—the litigation process—and the beginning of another process—the process of judicial implementation. Sometimes delay and stalling follow even decisive court decisions. There is, for example, the story of the tortured efforts of a young African American named Virgil Hawkins to get himself admitted to the University of Florida Law School. Hawkins's efforts began in 1949, when he first applied for admission, and ended unsuccessfully in 1958, after a decade of

508

15.1
15.2
15.3
15.4
15.5
15.6
15.7

court decisions. Despite a 1956 order from the U.S. Supreme Court to admit Hawkins, legal skirmishing continued and eventually produced a 1958 decision by a U.S. district court in Florida ordering the admission of nonwhites but upholding the denial of admission to Hawkins. Thus, other courts and other institutions of government can be roadblocks in the way of judicial implementation.

Charles Johnson and Bradley Canon suggest that implementation of court decisions involves several elements:[49]

- First, there is an *interpreting population*, heavily composed of lawyers and judges. They must correctly understand and reflect the intent of the original decision in their subsequent actions. Usually lower-court judges do follow the Supreme Court, but sometimes they circumvent higher-court decisions to satisfy their own policy interests.[50]

- Second, there is an *implementing population*. Suppose the Supreme Court held (as it did) that prayers organized by school officials in the public schools are unconstitutional. The implementing population (school boards and school administrators whose schools are conducting prayers) must then actually abandon prayers. Police departments, hospitals, corporations, government agencies—all may be part of the implementing population. With so many implementors, many of whom may disagree with a decision, there is plenty of room for "slippage" between what the Supreme Court decides and what actually occurs (as has been evident with school prayers).[51] Judicial decisions are more likely to be implemented smoothly if implementation is concentrated in the hands of a few highly visible officials, such as the president or state legislators. Even then, the courts may face difficulties. Responding to the *Brown* decision ending legal segregation in the nation's public schools, in 1959 the Board of Supervisors for Prince Edward County, abetted by changes in Virginia laws, refused to appropriate *any* funds for the County School Board. This action effectively closed all public schools in the county to avoid integrating them. The schools remained closed for five years until the legal process finally forced them to reopen.

- Third, every decision involves a *consumer population*. For example, the consumer population of an abortion decision is those people who may want to have an abortion (and those who oppose them); the consumers of the *Miranda* decision on reading suspects their rights are criminal defendants and their attorneys. The consumer population must be aware of its newfound rights and stand up for them.

Virgil Hawkins' unsuccessful struggle to attend the all-white University of Florida Law School illustrates how judicial implementation can affect the impact of Court decisions. Despite the Court's order to admit Hawkins, he was never able to attend the university.

Congress and presidents can also help or hinder judicial implementation. When the Supreme Court, the year after its 1954 decision in *Brown v. Board of Education*, ordered public schools desegregated "with all deliberate speed," President Eisenhower refused to state clearly that Americans should comply, which may have encouraged local school boards to resist the decision. Congress was not much help either; only a decade later, in the wake of the civil rights movement, did it pass legislation denying federal aid to segregated schools. Different presidents have different commitments to a particular judicial policy. For example, the Obama administration decided not to defend the constitutionality of the 1996 Defense of Marriage Act.

Why It Matters to You

The Lack of a Judicial Bureaucracy

The federal courts lack a bureaucracy to implement their decisions. In fact, some of the Supreme Court's most controversial decisions, such as those dealing with school integration and school prayers, have been implemented only with great difficulty. If the courts had a bureaucracy to enforce their decisions, justice might be better served, but such a bureaucracy would have to be enormous to monitor, for example, every school or every police station.

The Courts and Public Policy: A Historical Review

15.6 Trace the Supreme Court's use of judicial review in major policy battles in various eras of American history.

L ike all policymakers, the courts are choice makers. Ultimately, the choices they make affect us all (see "Young People & Politics: The Supreme Court Is Closer Than You Think"). Confronted with controversial policies, they make controversial decisions that leave some people winners and others losers. The courts have made policy about slavery and segregation, corporate power and capital punishment, and dozens of other controversial matters.

Until the Civil War, the dominant questions before the Court concerned slavery and the strength and legitimacy of the federal government; these latter issues were resolved in favor of the supremacy of the federal government. From the Civil War until 1937, questions of the relationship between the federal government and the economy predominated. During this period, the Court restricted the power of the federal government to regulate the economy. From 1938 to the present, the paramount issues before the Court have concerned personal liberty and social and political equality. In this era, the Court has enlarged the scope of personal freedom and civil rights and has removed many of the constitutional restraints on the regulation of the economy.

Few justices played a more important role in making the Court a significant national agenda setter than John Marshall, chief justice from 1801 to 1835. His successors have continued not only to respond to the political agenda but also to shape discussion and debate about it.

☐ John Marshall and the Growth of Judicial Review

Scarcely was the government housed in its new capital when Federalists and Democratic-Republicans clashed over the courts. In the election of 1800, Democratic-Republican Thomas Jefferson beat Federalist incumbent John Adams. Determined to leave at least the judiciary in trusted hands, Adams tried to fill it with Federalists. He is alleged to have stayed at his desk signing commissions until 9:00 PM on his last day in the White House (March 3, 1801).

15.1
15.2
15.3
15.4
15.5
15.6
15.7

Young People & Politics

The Supreme Court Is Closer Than You Think

The Supreme Court of the United States may seem remote and not especially relevant to a college student. Yet a surprising number of its most important decisions have been brought by young adults seeking protection for their civil rights and liberties. For example, in *Rostker v. Goldberg* (1981) several young men filed a suit claiming that the Military Selective Service Act's requirement that only males register for the draft was unconstitutional. Although the Court held that the requirement was constitutional, draft registration was suspended temporarily during the suit.

In *Board of Regents of University of Wisconsin System v. Southworth* (2000), the Court upheld the University of Wisconsin's requirement of a fee to fund speakers on campus, even if the speakers advocated views that offended some students; in *Zurcher v. Stanford Daily* (1978), the Court decided against a campus newspaper that sought to shield its files from a police search. In 1992, the Supreme Court ruled that legislatures and universities may not single out racial, religious, or sexual insults or threats for prosecution as "hate speech" or "bias crimes" (*R.A.V. v. St. Paul*). In cases such as those stemming from Gregory Johnson's burning an American flag at the 1984 Republican National Convention to protest nuclear arms buildup (which the Court protected in *Texas v. Johnson* [1989]) and David O'Brien's burning a draft card (which the Court

did not protect in *United States v. O'Brien* [1968]), young adults have also been pioneers in the area of symbolic speech.

Issues of religious freedom have also prominently featured college students. In *Widmar v. Vincent* (1981), the Court decided that public universities that permit student groups to use their facilities must allow student religious groups on campus to use the facilities for religious worship. In 1995, the Court held that the University of Virginia was constitutionally required to subsidize a student religious magazine on the same basis as other student publications (*Rosenberger v. University of Virginia*). However, in 2004 the Court held that the state of Washington was within its rights when it excluded students pursuing a devotional theology degree from its general scholarship program (*Locke v. Davey*).

Thus, the Supreme Court has a long history of dealing with issues of importance to young adults. Often it is young adults themselves who initiate the cases—and who take them all the way to the nation's highest court.

CRITICAL THINKING QUESTIONS

1. Why do you think cases involving young people tend to involve civil liberties issues?
2. What other issues of particular importance to young people should the Supreme Court decide?

Marbury v. Madison
The 1803 case in which Chief Justice John Marshall and his associates first asserted the right of the Supreme Court to determine the meaning of the U.S. Constitution. The decision established the Court's power of judicial review over acts of Congress, in this case the Judiciary Act of 1789.

In the midst of this flurry, Adams appointed William Marbury to the minor post of justice of the peace in the District of Columbia. In the rush of last-minute business, however, Secretary of State John Marshall failed to deliver commissions to Marbury and 16 others. He left the commissions to be delivered by the incoming secretary of state, James Madison.

Madison and Jefferson were furious at Adams's actions and refused to deliver the commissions. Marbury and three others in the same situation sued Madison, asking the Supreme Court to order Madison to give them their commissions. They took their case directly to the Supreme Court under the Judiciary Act of 1789, which gave the Court original jurisdiction in such matters.

The new chief justice was none other than Adams's former secretary of state and arch-Federalist John Marshall, himself one of the "midnight appointments" (he took his seat on the Court barely three weeks before Adams's term ended). Marshall and his Federalist colleagues were in a tight spot. Threats of impeachment came from Jeffersonians fearful that the Court would vote for Marbury. Moreover, if the Court ordered Madison to deliver the commissions, he was likely to ignore the order, putting the prestige of the nation's highest court at risk over a minor issue. Marshall had no means of compelling Madison to act. The Court could also deny Marbury's claim. Taking that option, however, would concede the issue to the Jeffersonians and give the appearance of retreat in the face of opposition, thereby reducing the power of the Court.

Marshall devised a shrewd solution to the case of *Marbury v. Madison*. In February 1803, he delivered the unanimous opinion of the Court. First, Marshall and

judicial review

The power of the courts to determine whether acts of Congress and, by implication, the executive are in accord with the U.S. Constitution. Judicial review was established by John Marshall and his associates in *Marbury v. Madison.*

his colleagues argued that Madison was wrong to withhold Marbury's commission. The Court also found, however, that the Judiciary Act of 1789, under which Marbury had brought suit, contradicted the plain words of the Constitution about the Court's original jurisdiction. Thus, Marshall dismissed Marbury's claim, saying that the Court, according to the Constitution, had no power to require that the commission be delivered.

Conceding a small battle over Marbury's commission (he did not get it), Marshall won a much larger war, asserting for the courts the power to determine what is and what is not constitutional. As Marshall wrote, "An act of the legislature repugnant to the Constitution is void," and "it is emphatically the province and duty of the judicial department to say what the law is." The chief justice established the power of **judicial review**, the power of the courts to hold acts of Congress and, by implication, the executive in violation of the Constitution.

Marbury v. Madison was part of a skirmish between the Federalists on the Court and the Democratic-Republican–controlled Congress. Partly to rein in the Supreme Court, for example, the Jeffersonian Congress in 1801 abolished the lower federal appeals courts and made the Supreme Court judges return to the unpleasant task of "riding circuit"—serving as lower-court judges around the country. This was an act of studied harassment of the Court by its enemies.

After *Marbury*, angry members of Congress, together with other Jeffersonians, claimed that Marshall was a "usurper of power," setting himself above Congress and the president. This view, however, was unfair. State courts, before and after the Constitution, had declared acts of their legislatures unconstitutional. In the Federalist Papers, Alexander Hamilton had expressly assumed the power of the federal courts to review legislation. And in fact the federal courts had already used this power: *Marbury* was not even the first case to strike down an act of Congress, as a lower federal court had done so in 1792, and the Supreme Court itself had approved a law after a constitutional review in 1796. Marshall was neither inventing nor imagining his right to review laws for their constitutionality.

The case illustrates that the courts must be politically astute in exercising their power over the other branches. By in effect reducing its *own* power—the authority to hear cases such as Marbury's under its original jurisdiction—the Court was able to assert the right of judicial review in a fashion that the other branches could not easily rebuke.

More than any other power of the courts, judicial review has embroiled them in policy controversy. Before the Civil War, the Supreme Court, headed by Chief Justice Roger Taney, held the Missouri Compromise unconstitutional because it restricted slavery in the territories. The decision was one of many steps along the road to the Civil War. After the Civil War, the Court was again active, this time using judicial review to strike down dozens of state and federal laws curbing the growing might of business corporations.

☐ The "Nine Old Men"

Never was the Court as controversial as during the New Deal. At President Roosevelt's urging, Congress passed dozens of laws designed to end the Depression. However, conservatives (most nominated by Republican presidents), who viewed federal intervention in the economy as unconstitutional and tantamount to socialism, dominated the Court.

The Supreme Court began to dismantle New Deal policies one by one. The National Industrial Recovery Act was one of a string of anti-Depression measures. Although this act was never particularly popular, the Court sealed its doom in *Schechter Poultry Corporation v. United States* (1935), declaring it unconstitutional because it regulated purely local business that did not affect interstate commerce.

Incensed, Roosevelt in 1937 proposed what critics called a "court-packing plan." Noting that the average age of the Court was over 70, Roosevelt railed against those "nine old men." The Constitution gave the justices lifetime jobs (see "America in Perspective: The Tenure of Supreme Court Judges"), but Congress can determine the number of justices. Thus, FDR proposed that Congress expand the size of the Court, a move that would have allowed him to appoint additional justices sympathetic to the New Deal.

Congress objected and never passed the plan. It became irrelevant, however, when two justices, Chief Justice Charles Evans Hughes and Associate Justice Owen Roberts, began switching their votes in favor of New Deal legislation. (One wit called it the "switch in time that saved nine.") Shortly thereafter, Associate Justice William Van Devanter retired, and Roosevelt got to make the first of his many appointments to the Court.

☐ The Warren Court

Few eras of the Supreme Court have been as active in shaping public policy as that of the Warren Court (1953–1969), presided over by Chief Justice Earl Warren. Scarcely had President Eisenhower appointed Warren when the Court faced the issue of school segregation. In 1954, it held that laws requiring segregation of the public schools were unconstitutional. Later it expanded the rights of criminal defendants, extending the right to counsel and protections against unreasonable search and seizure and self-incrimination. It ordered states to reapportion both their legislatures and their congressional districts according to the principle of one person, one vote, and it prohibited organized prayer in public schools. So active was the Warren Court that right-wing groups, fearing that it was remaking the country, posted billboards all over the United States urging Congress to "Impeach Earl Warren."[52]

☐ The Burger Court

Warren's retirement in 1969 gave President Richard Nixon his hoped-for opportunity to appoint a "strict constructionist"—that is, one who interprets the Constitution

CRITICAL THINKING QUESTIONS

1. If a constitutional convention were reconvened today, would we still opt for life tenure?

2. Do you agree with Alexander Hamilton's argument in Federalist #78 that life tenure was an excellent means of securing "a steady, upright, and impartial administration of the laws"?

America in Perspective

The Tenure of Supreme Court Judges

The U.S. Supreme Court plays a crucial role in American government, and federal judges, including Supreme Court justices, have tenure for life. As a result, the average age of U.S. justices is high, and there are typically many justices who are over 75 years old. Life tenure also means that there are fewer changes of justices than there would be in a system with shorter terms.

Interestingly, every other established democracy provides for some limits on the tenure of judges on its highest constitutional court. Here are some examples:

Country	Term for Judges on Highest Constitutional Court
France	9-year, nonrenewable term
Italy	9-year, nonrenewable term
Portugal	9-year, nonrenewable term
Spain	9-year, nonrenewable term
Germany	12-year term, must retire at 68
Japan	10-year term, must retire at 70; voters vote to renew justices every 10 years
India	serve under good behavior up to age 65
Australia	serve under good behavior up to age 70
Canada	serve under good behavior up to age 75

SOURCE: Steven G. Calabresi and James Lindgren, "Term Limits for the Supreme Court: Life Tenure Reconsidered," *Harvard Journal of Law and Public Policy* 29 (Summer 2006), pp. 819–822.

narrowly—as chief justice. He chose Minnesotan Warren E. Burger, then a conservative judge on the District of Columbia Court of Appeals. As Nixon hoped, the Burger Court turned out to be more conservative than the liberal Warren Court. It narrowed defendants' rights, though it did not overturn the fundamental contours of the *Miranda* decision. The conservative Burger Court, however, also wrote the abortion decision in *Roe v. Wade*, required school busing in certain cases to eliminate historic segregation, and upheld affirmative action programs in the *Weber* case. One of the most notable decisions of the Burger Court weighed against Burger's appointer, Richard Nixon. At the height of the Watergate scandal, the Supreme Court was called on to decide whether Nixon had to turn his White House tapes over to the courts. It unanimously ordered him to do so in *United States v. Nixon* (1974), thus hastening the president's resignation.

☐ The Rehnquist and Roberts Courts

By the early 1990s, the conservative nominees of Republican presidents, led by Chief Justice William Rehnquist, composed a clear Supreme Court majority. In 2005, John Roberts replaced Rehnquist as chief justice, but the basic divisions on the Court have remained relatively stable. Like the Burger Court, the Supreme Court in recent years has been conservative, and like both the Warren and the Burger Courts, it has been neither deferential to Congress nor reluctant to enter the political fray. The Court's decision in *Bush v. Gore* (2000) that decided the 2000 presidential election certainly represents a high point of judicial activism.

However one evaluates the Court's direction, in most cases in recent years the Court has not created a revolution in constitutional law. Instead, it has limited, rather than reversed, rights established by liberal decisions such as those regarding defendants' rights and abortion. Although its protection of the First Amendment rights of free speech and free press has remained robust, the Court has tended no longer to see itself as the special protector of individual liberties and civil rights for minorities and has raised important obstacles to affirmative action programs. In the area of federalism, however, the Court has blazed new paths in constraining the federal government's power over the states.

Understanding the Courts

15.7	Assess the role of unelected courts and the scope of judicial power in American democracy.

 owerful courts are unusual; few nations have them. The power of American judges raises questions about the compatibility of unelected courts with a democracy and about the appropriate role for the judiciary in policymaking.

☐ The Courts and Democracy

Announcing his retirement in 1981, Justice Potter Stewart made a few remarks to the handful of reporters present. Embedded in his brief statement was this observation: "It seems to me that there's nothing more antithetical to the idea of what a good judge should be than to think it has something to do with representative democracy."[53] He meant that judges should not be subject to the whims of popular majorities. In a nation that insists so strongly that it is democratic, where do the courts fit in?

In some ways, the courts are not a very democratic institution. Federal judges are not elected and are almost impossible to remove. Indeed, their social backgrounds probably make the courts the most elite-dominated policymaking institution. If democracy requires that key policymakers always be elected or be continually responsible to those who are, then the courts diverge sharply from the requirements of democratic government.

The Supreme Court frequently makes controversial decisions regarding important matters of politics and public policy. Critics often argue that unelected judges are making decisions best left to elected officials. Here, demonstrators express their opinions about President Obama's health care reform bill.

The Constitution's Framers wanted it that way. Chief Justice Rehnquist, a judicial conservative, put the case as follows: "A mere change in public opinion since the adoption of the Constitution, unaccompanied by a constitutional amendment, should not change the meaning of the Constitution. A merely temporary majoritarian ground-swell should not abrogate some individual liberty protected by the Constitution."[54]

The courts are not entirely independent of popular preferences, however. Turn-of-the-twentieth-century Chicago humorist Finley Peter Dunne had his Irish saloon-keeper character "Mr. Dooley" quip that "th' Supreme Court follows th' iliction returns." Many years later, political scientists have found that the Court usually reflects popular majorities.[55] Even when the Court seems out of step with other policymakers, it eventually swings around to join the policy consensus,[56] as it did in the New Deal. A study of the period from 1937 to 1980 found that the Court was clearly out of line with public opinion only on the issue of prayers in public schools.[57] In addition, congressional Court-curbing proposals are typically driven by public discontent, and the Court usually responds to such proposals by engaging in self-restraint and moderating its decisions.[58] Similarly, the Court often moves toward the position articulated on behalf of the White House by the solicitor general.[59]

Despite the fact that the Supreme Court sits in a "marble palace," it is not as insulated from the normal forms of politics as one might think. For example, when the Court took up *Webster v. Reproductive Health Services* (1989), the two sides in the abortion debate flooded the Court with mail, targeted it with advertisements and protests, and bombarded it with 78 *amicus curiae* briefs. Members of the Supreme Court are unlikely to cave in to interest group pressures, but they are aware of the public's concern about issues, and this awareness becomes part of their consciousness as they decide cases. Political scientists have found that the Court is more likely to hear cases for which interest groups have filed *amicus curiae* briefs[60] and that such briefs may make a difference in the Court's decisions.[61]

Courts can also promote pluralism. When groups go to court, they use litigation to achieve their policy objectives.[62] Both civil rights groups and environmentalists, for example, have blazed a path to show how interest groups can effectively use the courts to achieve their policy goals. Thurgood Marshall, the legal wizard of the NAACP's litigation strategy, not only won most of his cases but also won for himself a seat on the Supreme Court. Almost every major policy decision these days ends up in court. Chances are good that some judge can be found who will rule in an interest group's favor. On the other hand, agencies and businesses commonly find themselves ordered

judicial restraint
An approach to decision making in which judges play minimal policy-making roles and defer to legislatures whenever possible.

judicial activism
An approach to decision making in which judges sometimes make bold policy decisions, even charting new constitutional ground.

Interest groups often use the judicial system to pursue their policy goals, forcing the courts to rule on important social issues. Some Hispanic parents, for example, have successfully sued local school districts to compel them to offer bilingual education.

by different courts to do opposite things. The habit of always turning to the courts as a last resort can add to policy delay, deadlock, and inconsistency.

☐ The Scope of Judicial Power

The courts, Alexander Hamilton wrote in the *Federalist Papers*, "will be least in capacity to annoy or injure" the people and their liberties.[63] Throughout American history, critics of judicial power have disagreed. They see the courts as too powerful for their own—or the nation's—good. Yesterday's critics focused on John Marshall's "usurpations" of power, on the proslavery decision in *Dred Scott*, or on the efforts of the "nine old men" to kill off Franklin D. Roosevelt's New Deal legislation. Today's critics are never short of arguments to show that courts go too far in making policy.[64]

Courts make policy on both large and small issues. In the past few decades, courts have made policies on major issues involving school busing, abortion, affirmative action, nuclear power, legislative redistricting, bilingual education, prison conditions, counting votes in the 2000 presidential election, and many other key issues.[65]

There are strong disagreements about the appropriateness of the courts playing a prominent policymaking role. Many scholars and judges favor a policy of **judicial restraint**, in which judges adhere closely to precedent and play minimal policymaking roles, deferring to legislatures by upholding laws whenever possible. These observers stress that the federal courts, composed of unelected judges, are the least democratic branch of government and question the qualifications of judges for making policy decisions and balancing interests. Advocates of judicial restraint believe that decisions such as those on abortion and prayer in public schools go well beyond the "referee" role they say is appropriate for courts in a democracy.

On the other side are proponents of **judicial activism**, in which judges are less deferential to elected officials and sometimes make bold policy decisions, even charting new constitutional ground. Advocates of judicial activism emphasize that the courts may alleviate pressing needs—especially needs of those who are politically or economically weak—left unmet by the majoritarian political process. Americans have never resolved the issue of judicial restraint versus judicial activism, as you can see in "You Are the Policymaker: The Debate over Judicial Activism."

It is important not to confuse judicial activism or restraint with liberalism or conservatism. In Table 15.4, you can see the varying levels of the Supreme Court's use of judicial review to void laws passed by Congress in different eras. In the early years of

516

15.1
15.2
15.3
15.4
15.5
15.6
15.7

You Are the Policymaker

The Debate over Judicial Activism

Just what role should the Supreme Court play in American politics? Should it simply provide technical interpretations of legislation and the Constitution, leaving all policy initiatives to the elected branches? Or should it take a more aggressive role in protecting rights, especially of those who fare less well in majoritarian political process?

Republicans, spurred by their opposition to the Supreme Court's liberal decisions on issues such as school prayer, defendants' rights, flag burning, and abortion, usually call for justices to exercise judicial restraint. However, the justices they nominate are often not

deferential to Congress and vote to strike down acts of Congress, furthering conservative goals in the process but undermining judicial restraint. Democrats often favor judicial activism but are highly critical of conservative courts undermining liberal policies, whether in the early years of the New Deal or in the past three decades.

What do you think? The choice here is at the very heart of the judicial process. If you were a justice sitting on the Supreme Court and were asked to interpret the meaning of the Constitution, would you defer to elected officials or would you approach your decisions as a co-equal policymaker? What would *you* do?

---

the New Deal (falling within the 1930–1936 period in the table), judicial activists were conservatives. During the tenure of Earl Warren as chief justice (1953–1969), activists made liberal decisions. The Courts under Chief Justices Warren Burger (1969–1986), William Rehnquist (1986–2005), and John Roberts (2005–), composed of mostly conservative nominees of Republican presidents, marked the most active use in the nation's history of judicial review to void congressional legislation.[66]

The problem remains of reconciling the American democratic heritage with an active policymaking role for the judiciary. The federal courts have developed a doctrine of **political questions** as a means to avoid deciding some cases, principally those that involve conflicts between the president and Congress. The courts have shown no willingness, for example, to settle disputes regarding the constitutionality of the War Powers Resolution, which Congress designed to constrain the president's use of force.

Similarly, judges typically attempt, whenever possible, to avoid deciding a case on the basis of the Constitution, preferring less contentious "technical" grounds. They also employ issues of jurisdiction, mootness (whether a case presents a real controversy in which a judicial decision can have a practical effect), standing, ripeness (whether the issues of a case are clear enough and evolved enough to serve as the basis of a decision), and other conditions to avoid adjudication of some politically charged cases.[67] The Supreme Court refused to decide, for example, whether it was legal to carry out the war in Vietnam without an explicit declaration of war from Congress.

As you saw in the discussion of *Marbury v. Madison*, from the earliest days of the Republic, federal judges have been politically astute in their efforts to maintain the legitimacy of the judiciary and to conserve their resources. (Remember that judges are typically recruited from political backgrounds.) They have tried not to take on too many politically controversial issues at one time. They have also been much more likely to find state and local laws unconstitutional (about 1,100) than federal laws (fewer than 200, as shown in Table 15.4).

Another factor that increases the acceptability of activist courts is the ability to overturn their decisions. First, the president and the Senate determine who sits on the federal bench. Second, Congress, with or without the president's urging, can begin the process of amending the Constitution to overcome a constitutional decision of the Supreme Court. Although this process does not occur rapidly, it is a safety valve. The Eleventh Amendment in 1795 reversed the decision in *Chisolm v. Georgia*, which permitted an

---

political questions

A doctrine developed by the federal courts and used as a means to avoid deciding some cases, principally those involving conflicts between the president and Congress.

statutory construction
The judicial interpretation of an act of Congress. In some cases where statutory construction is an issue, Congress passes new legislation to clarify existing laws.

TABLE 15.4 SUPREME COURT RULINGS IN WHICH FEDERAL STATUTES[a] HAVE BEEN FOUND UNCONSTITUTIONAL[b]

Period	Statutes Voided
1798–1864	2
1864–1900	21 (22)[c]
1901–1910	9
1911–1920	11
1921–1930	13
1931–1940	14
1941–1952	3
1953–1969	23
1970–1986	33
1987–2004	39
2005–present	12
Total	180

[a]In some cases, provisions of multiple statutes have been found unconstitutional. In other instances, decisions in several cases have found different parts of the same statutes unconstitutional.

[b]In whole or in part.

[c]An 1883 decision in the *Civil Rights Cases* consolidated five different cases into one opinion declaring one act of Congress void. In 1895, *Pollock v. Farmers Loan and Trust Co.* was heard twice, with the same result both times.

SOURCE: U.S. Senate, *The Constitution of the United States of America: Analysis and Interpretation* and biannual supplements. Updated by authors.

individual to sue a state in federal court; the Fourteenth Amendment in 1868 reversed the decision in *Dred Scott v. Sanford*, which held African Americans not to be citizens of the United States; the Sixteenth Amendment in 1913 reversed the decision in *Pollock v. Farmer's Loan and Trust Co*, which prohibited a federal income tax; and the Twenty-Sixth Amendment in 1971 reversed part of *Oregon v. Mitchell*, which voided a congressional act according 18- to 20-year-olds the right to vote in state elections.

Even more drastic options are available as well. Just before leaving office in 1801, the Federalists created a tier of circuit courts and populated them with Federalist judges; the Jeffersonian Democrats took over the reins of power and promptly abolished the entire level of courts. In 1869, the Radical Republicans in Congress altered the appellate jurisdiction of the Supreme Court to prevent it from hearing a case (*Ex parte McCardle*) that concerned the Reconstruction Acts. This kind of alteration is rare, but it occurred recently. The George W. Bush administration selected the naval base at Guantánamo as the site for a detention camp for terrorism suspects in the expectation that its actions would not be subject to review by federal courts. In June 2004, however, the Supreme Court ruled that the naval base fell within the jurisdiction of U.S. law and that the *habeas corpus* statute that allows prisoners to challenge their detentions was applicable. In 2005 and again in 2006, Congress stripped federal courts from hearing habeas corpus petitions from the detainees in an attempt to thwart prisoners from seeking judicial relief. In the end, however, the Supreme Court held Congress's actions to be unconstitutional.

Finally, if the issue is one of **statutory construction**, in which a court interprets an act of Congress, then the legislature routinely passes legislation that clarifies existing laws and, in effect, overturns the courts.[68] In 1984, for example, the Supreme Court ruled in *Grove City College v. Bell* that Congress had intended that when an institution receives federal aid, only the program or activity that actually gets the aid, not the entire institution, is covered by four federal civil rights laws. In 1988, Congress passed a law specifying that the entire institution is affected. Congress may also pass laws with detailed language to constrain judicial decision making.[69] The description of the judiciary as the "ultimate arbiter of the Constitution" is hyperbolic; all the branches of government help define and shape the Constitution.

Review the Chapter

The Nature of the Judicial System

15.1 Identify the basic elements of the American judicial system and the major participants in it, p. 486.

The vast majority of cases are tried in state, not federal, courts. Courts can only hear "cases" or "controversies" between plaintiffs and defendants. Plaintiffs must have standing to sue, and judges can only decide justiciable disputes. Attorneys also play a central role in the judicial system. Interest groups sometimes promote litigation and often file *amicus curiae* briefs in cases brought by others.

The Structure of the Federal Judicial System

15.2 Outline the structure of the federal court system and the major responsibilities of each component, p. 488.

The district courts are courts of original jurisdiction and hear most of the federal criminal and civil cases and diversity of citizenship cases, supervise bankruptcy proceedings, and handle naturalization and admiralty and maritime law, and review the actions of some federal administrative agencies. Circuit courts, or courts of appeals, hear appeals from the district courts and from many regulatory agencies. They focus on correcting errors of procedure and law that occurred in the original proceedings of legal cases. The Supreme Court sits at the pinnacle of the system, deciding individual cases, resolving conflicts among the states, maintaining national supremacy in the law, and ensuring uniformity in the interpretation of national laws. Most Supreme Court cases come from the lower federal courts, but some are appeals from state courts and a very few are cases for which the Court has original jurisdiction.

The Politics of Judicial Selection

15.3 Explain the process by which judges and justices are nominated and confirmed, p. 493.

The president nominates and the Senate confirms judges and justices. Senators from the relevant state play an important role in the selection of district court judges, as a result of senatorial courtesy, while the White House has more discretion with appellate judges and, especially, Supreme Court justices. Although the Senate confirms most judicial nominations, it has rejected or refused to act on many in recent years, especially for positions in the higher courts.

The Backgrounds of Judges and Justices

15.4 Describe the backgrounds of judges and justices and assess the impact of background on their decisions, p. 498.

Judges and justices are not a representative sample of the American people. They are all lawyers and are disproportionately white males. They usually share the partisan and ideological views of the president who nominated them, and these views are often reflected in their decisions, especially in the higher courts. Other characteristics such as race and gender are also seen to influence decisions.

The Courts as Policymakers

15.5 Outline the judicial process at the Supreme Court level and assess the major factors influencing decisions and their implementation, p. 502.

Accepting cases is a crucial stage in Supreme Court decision making, and the Court is most likely to hear cases on major issues, when it disagrees with lower court decisions, and when the federal government, as represented by the solicitor general, asks for a decision. Decisions, announced once justices have written opinions and taken a final vote, in most cases follow precedent, but the Court can overrule precedents, and decisions where the precedents are less clear often reflect the justices' values and ideologies. The implementation of Court decisions depends on an interpreting population of judges and lawyers, an implementing population ranging from police officers and school boards to state legislatures and the president, and a consumer population of citizens affected by the decision.

The Courts and Public Policy: A Historical Review

15.6 Trace the Supreme Court's use of judicial review in major policy battles in various eras of American history, p. 509.

Since its astute first overturning of a congressional statute in *Marbury v. Madison*, the Court has exercised judicial review to play a key role in many of the major policy battles in American history. Until the Civil War, the dominant questions before the Court concerned slavery and the strength and legitimacy of the federal government, with the latter questions resolved in favor of the supremacy of the federal government. From the Civil War until 1937, questions of the relationship between the federal government and the economy predominated, with the Court restricting the government's power to regulate the economy. From 1938 until the present, the paramount issues before the Court have concerned personal liberty and social and political equality. In this era, the Court has enlarged the scope of personal freedom and civil rights and has removed many of the constitutional restraints on the regulation of the economy. In recent years, the Court has been less aggressive in protecting civil rights for minorities but has constrained the federal government's power over the states.

Understanding the Courts

15.7 Assess the role of unelected courts and the scope of judicial power in American democracy, p. 513.

Judges and justices are not elected and are difficult to remove, but they are not completely insulated from politics and often have acted to promote openness in the political system. They also have a number of tools for avoiding making controversial decisions, which they often employ, and there are a number of means more democratically selected officials can use to overturn Court decisions.

Learn the Terms

standing to sue, p. 487
class action suits, p. 487
justiciable disputes, p. 487
amicus curiae ("friend of the court") briefs, p. 488
original jurisdiction, p. 489
appellate jurisdiction, p. 489
district courts, p. 489
courts of appeals, p. 490
Supreme Court, p. 491
senatorial courtesy, p. 494
solicitor general, p. 503
opinion, p. 504
stare decisis, p. 505
precedent, p. 505
originalism, p. 506
judicial implementation, p. 507
Marbury v. Madison, p. 510
judicial review, p. 511
judicial restraint, p. 515
judicial activism, p. 515
political questions, p. 516
statutory construction, p. 517

Test Yourself

1. Who can challenge a law in an American court?
a. Any citizen can challenge any law.
b. Any tax-paying citizen can challenge any law.
c. Only a lawyer can challenge a law.
d. Only a person who has a serious interest in a case can challenge a law.
e. Only a person who is included in a class action suit can challenge a law.

2. How could *amicus curiae* briefs have influenced the Supreme Court's 2012 health care reform ruling?
a. They could have addressed the states' standing to sue.
b. They could have addressed whether health care reform was a criminal or civil matter.
c. They could have presented additional information regarding how health care reform or a lack of it would affect the American people.
d. They could have shown that a few states can sue on behalf of all the states.
e. They could have shown that health care reform was a justiciable dispute that should be addressed by the Court.

3. Which of the following was actually specified in the U.S. Constitution?
a. constitutional courts
b. the federal courts system
c. the Court of Military Appeals
d. the Tax Court
e. the U.S. Supreme Court

4. Suppose a person commits murder in a national park. Where would this murder case first be heard?
a. a legislative court
b. a U.S. district court in the district where the crime took place
c. the U.S. Court of Appeals for the Federal Circuit
d. the U.S. Court of Appeals in the circuit where the crime took place
e. the U.S. Supreme Court

5. Which of the following is true about the norm of senatorial courtesy for district court nominees?
a. The Senate is less likely to invoke this courtesy for district court nominees than it is to invoke it for appellate court nominees.
b. The Senate invokes this courtesy if a nominee is opposed by a senator of the president's party from the state in which the nominee is to serve.
c. The Senate invokes this courtesy only when a majority of senators agrees to invoke it.
d. The Senate invokes this courtesy only when a majority of the Senate judiciary committee agrees to invoke it.
e. The Senate invokes this courtesy when the president encourages the Senate to do so.

6. What is one of the major impacts of the increasing polarization of partisan politics on the courts?

a. Judicial qualifications have become less relevant than party affiliation.
b. Nominees are always controversial.
c. The percentage of judicial confirmations has increased.
d. The president is less interested in filling judicial posts.
e. The time for confirmation has increased dramatically.

7. Which of the following is an example of a factor that plays a primary role in the selection of federal judges?

a. their sharing the ideology of the president
b. their affiliation with lobby groups
c. their experience in the legislative branch
d. their pattern of campaign donations
e. their stance on questions of international law

8. Under which of the following scenarios is the Court most likely to decide to accept a case?

a. when at least three justices decide the case has merit
b. when the attorneys for the parties in the case make a personal appeal for a hearing
c. when the case is appealed from a state supreme court
d. when the justices have additional clerks to help read numerous appeals
e. when the Solicitor General's Office decides to appeal a case the government has lost in lower court

9. Unlike the original intent theory, the original meaning theory considers _____.

a. how a law would have been seen by ordinary people at the time of its adoption
b. how the Constitution would be interpreted in a modern-day context
c. how the writers of the Constitution would interpret a law
d. legal precedent
e. the specific public policy implications of a law

10. When Andrew Jackson famously remarked, "John Marshall has made his decision. Now let him enforce it," he was referring to the _____.

a. ability of Congress to cut funds for particular programs
b. ability of the Court to order the military to undertake particular actions
c. capacity of the states to override the decisions of the federal government
d. inability of the Court to enforce its decisions outside of the Court
e. strength of the presidency relative to the courts and legislature

11. Compared to the Warren Court, the Burger Court _____.

a. adopted very similar rulings
b. maintained rulings of the Warren Court and extended their legal reach
c. took a more activist rather than conservative approach to the Constitution
d. took a more conservative, strict constructionist approach to the Constitution
e. took a more moderate approach with both activist and conservative rulings

12. Which of the following statements about judicial review is accurate?

a. Judicial review is a judicial system in which the court of law in a neutral arena where two parties argue their differences.
b. Judicial review is a system of laws that defines crimes against the public order.
c. Judicial review is derived from a ruling originally issued by the Roberts Court.
d. Judicial review is not specifically mentioned in the U.S. Constitution.
e. Judicial review is the investigation of the federal courts by Congress.

13. In which of the following did the Supreme Court employ the doctrine of political questions?

a. *Chisolm v. Georgia*
b. *Marbury v. Madison*
c. rulings regarding the president's war powers
d. rulings on FDR's New Deal policies
e. *Dred Scott v. Sandford*

14. Advocates of _____ insist that judges should almost never overturn past decisions, whereas advocates of _____ believe that judges should have more leeway.

a. *interpretari decisis; stare decisis*
b. judicial activism; judicial restraint
c. judicial restraint; judicial activism
d. judicial restraint; judicial review
e. judicial review; judicial activism

Explore Further

WEB SITES

www.supremecourt.gov
Official site of the U.S. Supreme Court, with information about its operations.

www.fjc.gov
Federal Judicial Center Web site, with information on all federal judges, landmark legislation, and other judicial matters.

www.oyez.org
Web site that allows you to hear oral arguments before the Supreme Court. Also provides information on the Supreme Court and its docket.

www.uscourts.gov
Explains the organization, operation, and administration of federal courts.

www.justice.gov/olp/judicialnominations114.htm
Information on current judicial nominations.

www.bjs.gov
Bureau of Justice Statistics provides data on all aspects of the U.S. judicial system.

FURTHER READING

Abraham, Henry J. *Justices, Presidents, and Senators: A History of the U.S. Supreme Court Appointments from Washington to Bush II*, 5th ed. Lanham, MD: Rowman & Littlefield, 2008. A readable history of the relationships between presidents and the justices they appointed.

Bailey, Michael A., and Forrest Maltzman. *The Constrained Court: Law, Politics, and the Decisions Justices Make*. Princeton, NJ: Princeton University Press, 2011. Shows how the Supreme Court is constrained by legal principles and other branches of government.

Baum, Lawrence. *The Supreme Court*, 11th ed. Washington, D.C.: CQ Press, 2012. An excellent work on the operations and impact of the Court.

Binder, Sarah A., and Forrest Maltzman. *Advice and Dissent: The Struggle to Shape the Federal Judiciary*. Washington, D.C.: Brookings Institution, 2009. The best work on the process of judicial confirmations.

Carp, Robert A., Ronald Stidham, and Kenneth L. Manning. *Judicial Process in America*, 9th ed. Washington, D.C.: CQ Press, 2013. An overview of federal and state courts.

Clark, Tom S. *The Limits of Judicial Independence*. New York: Cambridge University Press, 2011. Shows how the Supreme Court responds to public opposition.

Goldman, Sheldon. *Picking Federal Judges*. New Haven, CT: Yale University Press, 1997. The definitive work on backgrounds and the politics of recruiting lower-court judges.

Johnson, Charles A., and Bradley C. Canon. *Judicial Policies: Implementation and Impact*, 2nd ed. Washington, D.C.: CQ Press, 1999. One of the best overviews of judicial policy implementation.

Segal, Jeffrey A., and Harold J. Spaeth. *The Supreme Court and the Attitudinal Model*. Cambridge, MA: Cambridge University Press, 1993. Examines how the attitudes and values of justices affect their decisions.

Sunstein, Cass R., David Schkade, Lisa M. Ellman, and Andrews Sawicki. *Are Judges Political?* Washington, D.C.: Brookings Institution, 2006. An analysis of politics on the federal courts of appeals.

16

Economic and Social Welfare Policymaking

Politics in Action: The Debate over the Ryan Budget Plan

W hen Paul Ryan (R-WI), the chair of the House Budget Committee, introduced a budget plan for 2012–2013 that called for major cuts in social welfare spending, he caused a stir with his comments about the impact of economic aid to poor people in America. Too many Americans, Ryan said, are receiving more from the government than they pay in taxes. There is, an "insidious moral tipping point, and I think the president is accelerating this." After recalling his family's humble beginnings in America as poor Irish immigrants and his belief in the virtue of people who "pull themselves up by the bootstraps," Ryan warned that a generous safety net "lulls able-bodied people into lives of complacency and dependency, which drains them of their very will and incentive to make the most of their lives. It's demeaning." Hence his proposal to reduce the size of the federal budget deficit included substantial cuts in social welfare spending.

These comments by Representative Ryan were in line with a long tradition of skepticism among conservatives about the effectiveness of social welfare programs. Conservatives have long argued that the welfare programs instituted under Lyndon Johnson's Great Society program

16.1
Identify the main policy tools that American government can employ to address economic problems, and contrast Keynesian and supply-side economics, p. 525.

16.2
Compare and contrast entitlement and means-tested social welfare programs, p. 532.

16.3
Assess the extent of economic inequality in America and the role of government in lessening it, p. 533.

16.4
Trace the changes over time in major federal welfare programs, p. 540.

16.5
Outline how America's Social Security program works and the challenge of keeping it financially solvent in the coming years, p. 543.

16.6
Distinguish American social welfare policy from that of other established democracies, p. 545.

16.7
Assess the impact of economic and social welfare policies on democracy and the scope of government in America, p. 546.

Job seekers register and pick up open job fliers from potential employers at Los Angeles Mission's annual Skid Row Career Fair. In addition to help from nonprofit organizations such as the LA Mission, people who are unemployed are helped by governmental social welfare programs such as unemployment insurance.

social welfare policies
Policies that provide benefits, cash or in-kind, to individuals, based on either entitlement or means testing.

have done more harm than good. They see these programs as having created a culture of poverty that leaves too many struggling Americans dependent on government assistance. A safety net is one thing, a hammock is another, they argue. Because of this skepticism, Mitt Romney, for example, held that the Ryan budget "does not balance the budget on the backs of the poor."

Democrats could scarcely have disagreed more. President Obama characterized the Ryan proposal as promoting a "you're-on-your-own" approach to economic and social welfare policymaking. "If you're born into poverty, lift yourself up out of your own—with your own bootstraps, even if you don't have boots; you're on your own," Obama said in remarks directed at the Ryan budget. "Hey, they believe that's how America has advanced. That's the cramped, narrow conception they have of liberty." Obama and Democratic leaders in Congress argued that the current level of social welfare spending represented a necessary helping hand for those in need. In their view, the budget should not be balanced by cutting programs that lower-income Americans have relied on, such as Medicaid, food stamps, and Pell education grants.

The Ryan budget proposal also illustrated a basic difference between the parties with regard to economic policymaking. An integral part of the proposal was cuts in the rate of taxation for people at all income levels, including the wealthiest Americans. From the Republican point of view, lower tax rates combined with lower social welfare spending would increase economic growth and be better for everyone. Democrats disagreed strongly, responding that the rich shouldn't be getting tax cuts while social programs for the poor are being scaled back and that higher taxes on the wealthy were needed to help reduce the budget deficit.

As you will see in this chapter, questions of economic and social welfare policy involve not only matters of compassion but also matters of effectiveness. As with so many other public policies, there are those who believe the government should do more and others who believe the government only makes things worse. Everyone would like to see America on "The Path to Prosperity," as Ryan titled his budget proposal; they just disagree about how economic and social welfare policy can and should be used to achieve this goal.

Liberals and conservatives often disagree about how the government can best promote economic growth, as we will see in this chapter, but everyone agrees that the government must play an important role in guiding the economy. The United States has a capitalistic economic system, in which individuals and corporations own the principal means of production and compete in a free market to reap profits, with this competition determining the amount of production and prices. However, the American economic system was never one of pure capitalism. Instead, from the beginning, the country has had a *mixed economy*, in which capitalism coexists with and is tempered by government involvement in the economy. And few areas of public policy so directly touch on the fundamental questions of "who gets what, when, and how" as policies that attempt to guide the economy.

The United States is a diverse nation whose citizens and groups achieve quite different levels of economic success. The fact that such inequality exists in American democracy, however, raises important political questions: what are the economic differences among Americans, and why do they exist? are they acceptable? what role should the government play in helping those who are less fortunate? what are the most effective government policies? The answers that Americans provide to these questions determine the nation's approach to **social welfare policies.** Social welfare policies attempt to provide assistance and support to specific groups in society through cash and other benefits. Who gets these benefits and what level of support is provided are issues that must be resolved by the political system. How America resolves these issues depends on how its leaders, political parties, interest groups, and citizens view the nature and distribution of poverty, the role of government, and the effectiveness of various social welfare programs.

Economic Policymaking

16.1 Identify the main policy tools that American government can employ to address economic problems, and contrast Keynesian and supply-side economics.

P erhaps the most famous saying from any recent presidential campaign was the 1992 Clinton campaign's "It's the economy, stupid." In running against incumbent George H. W. Bush, Bill Clinton constantly hammered home his message that Bush wasn't using the power of the federal government to try to alleviate the economic pain of the middle class. Like most politicians, Clinton knew that voters pay attention to what President Truman called "the most sensitive part of their anatomies," their pocketbooks. Countless studies by political scientists have reaffirmed the wisdom of Truman's observations about voters and their pocketbooks. Summarizing a generation of research, two political scientists put it plainly: "There is little doubt that economic conditions profoundly affect voters' electoral decisions."[1] Economic conditions are the best single predictor of voters' evaluation of how the president is doing his job.[2]

With all the bad economic news in 2008, the presidential election of that year was no exception to the rule of the centrality of economic issues. As Lewis-Beck and Nadeau write, "Gloom over the American economy found no precedent in contemporary times. This gloomy view translated itself sharply into a vote against McCain, for many felt the incumbent Republican administration was responsible."[3] David Plouffe, Obama's 2008 campaign manager, resurrected the old slogan from the 1992 Clinton campaign, and even titled one chapter of his book about the campaign "It's the Economy, Stupid."[4] In 2012, the shoe was on the other foot, as Mitt Romney argued that the Obama administration had performed poorly in its attempts to revitalize the economy, and Obama was forced to respond that he had done as well as could be expected under circumstances.

The connection between economic conditions and voting is real but complex. Mary may lose her job, but she does not quickly jump to the conclusion that the president deserves to be thrown out. Rather, voters tend to engage in what political scientists call "sociotropic" voting, assessing the overall rate of employment and unemployment more than their individual circumstances.[5] Furthermore, as political scientists Suzanna De Boef and Paul M. Kellstedt have shown, the "pictures in their heads" that American voters have of the economy are shaped not only by real economic conditions but also by partisanship and by news coverage of the economy.[6]

Like voters, the parties are economic animals. The two parties have different economic centers of gravity. There is often a choice to be made between two basic aims of government economic policy—fighting unemployment and fighting inflation—and when there is, the two parties have different priorities. Democrats are more likely to stress the importance of keeping unemployment low whereas Republicans are more likely to prioritize the battle against inflation. This partisan difference reflects the concerns of the parties' major constituencies. Democrats appeal particularly to working-class voters concerned about employment, whereas Republicans appeal particularly to voters with more money to save and invest who worry that inflation will erode their savings. Let us look at the twin economic—and political—concerns of unemployment and inflation.

☐ Two Major Worries: Unemployment and Inflation

The **unemployment rate** is the percentage of Americans seeking work who are unable to find it. Measuring how many and what types of workers are unemployed is one of the major jobs of the Bureau of Labor Statistics (BLS) in the Department of Labor. To carry out this task, the BLS conducts a huge statistical survey of 60,000 households every month. It then announces the nation's unemployment rate. The number of U.S. jobs has to increase by about 125,000 every month just to keep up with new entrants into the labor force (college graduates, for example) and thus avoid an increase in the unemployment rate.

unemployment rate
As measured by the Bureau of Labor Statistics, the proportion of the labor force actively seeking work but unable to find jobs.

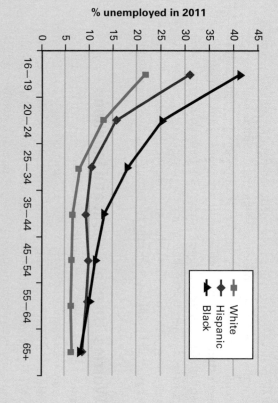

underemployment rate
As measured by the Bureau of Labor Statistics, a statistic that includes (1) people who aren't working and are actively seeking a job, (2) those who would like to work but have given up looking, and (3) those who are working part-time because they cannot find a full-time position.

inflation
A rise in price of goods and services.

Of course, the unemployment rate varies from time to time and group to group. For example, it rose to 10 percent in late 2009 with the economic recession, and it tends to be higher for young adults than for other groups (see "Young People & Politics: Unemployment Rates by Age and Race/Ethnicity, 2011"). The official unemployment rate that is reported on the first Friday of every month by the BLS actually underestimates how many Americans are suffering in the job market, because it leaves out those who have given up their job search or have only been able to obtain a part-time job. Thus, the BLS also reports on what is known as the **underemployment rate**, which takes into account not only people who aren't working and are actively seeking a job but also people who have become so discouraged that they have given up looking for employment and those who are working part-time because they cannot find a full-time job. As America headed to the polls in November 2012, the national unemployment rate was 7.9 percent, while the underemployment rate was 14.6 percent.

Inflation, the other major economic worry of policymakers, is a rise in prices for goods and services. For decades, the BLS has also kept tabs on inflation, using the

---

Young People & Politics

Unemployment Rates by Age and Race/Ethnicity, 2011

The unemployment rate is one of the nation's most important economic indicators and a political issue as well. Although Americans sometimes think of unemployment as mainly a problem for middle-aged people, in actuality unemployment rates are much higher for young Americans aged 16 to 24. This is especially true during recessions, as young entrants to the job market find that there are few new jobs available at a time when many companies are laying people off. Young blacks and Hispanics face a double whammy in their search for a job, as you can see by their very high unemployment rates during 2011, shown in the graph.

% unemployed in 2011

[graph with x-axis age groups: 16–19, 20–24, 25–34, 35–44, 45–54, 55–64, 65+; y-axis 0 to 45; legend: White, Hispanic, Black]

CRITICAL THINKING QUESTION

Some policymakers have suggested that the minimum wage should be reduced just for young people during recessions in order to give businesses a special incentive to hire them. Others oppose this step as likely to force many young people to accept extremely low wages. What do you think—would you favor a lower minimum wage for young Americans when jobs are scarce?

SOURCE: Bureau of Labor Statistics.

consumer price index
The key measure of inflation—the change in the cost of buying a fixed basket of goods and services.

laissez-faire
The principle that government should not meddle in the economy.

monetary policy
Government manipulation of the supply of money in private hands—one of two important tools by which the government can attempt to steer the economy.

consumer price index (CPI), which measures the change in the cost of buying a fixed "basket" of goods and services. Each month, BLS data gatherers fan out over the country looking at the prices of some 80,000 items from eggs to doctor visits. The goal of the CPI is to create a measure that reflects changes over time in the amount that consumers need to spend to achieve a certain standard of living.

Inflation has risen sharply during three periods since 1970, with each of these sharp rises tied to soaring prices for energy. The first inflationary shock occurred in 1973 and 1974, when Arab oil-producing nations cut off the flow of oil to the United States to protest American support for Israel during its war with Egypt and Syria. The second occurred when the Iranian Revolution of 1979 again disrupted the flow of oil from the Persian Gulf. Long lines and higher prices at the gas pumps were accompanied by an annual rate of inflation of 11 percent in 1979 and 14 percent during the election year of 1980. Finally, in 1991 when Iraq's invasion of Kuwait led to the Gulf War, there was a moderate surge in inflation as oil prices increased in anticipation of possible shortages (which actually never occurred). Since then, the annual inflation rate in the United States has consistently been below 4 percent. However, in the summer of 2008, the specter of high inflation suddenly loomed as the inflation rate briefly exceeded 5 percent due to a surge of worldwide oil prices to over $100 a barrel. At that point in the campaign, John McCain was planning to make this a major issue. Had oil prices and inflation proven to be the prime economic concern of the electorate in November rather than Wall Street's collapse and rising unemployment, McCain would probably have had a better chance to win in 2008.

Policies for Controlling the Economy

Voters take economic performance into account at the polling booth because they expect politicians to use the power of the federal government to try to control the economy. The time when government could assert that the private marketplace could handle economic problems has long passed, if it ever really existed. When the stock market crash of 1929 sent unemployment soaring, President Herbert Hoover clung to **laissez-faire**—the principle that government should not meddle at all with the economy. In the next presidential election, Hoover was handed a crushing defeat by Franklin D. Roosevelt, whose New Deal programs experimented with dozens of new federal policies to put the economy back on track. Since the New Deal, both Democratic and Republican policymakers have recognized that capitalism must be at least somewhat regulated by the federal government. The American political economy offers two important tools to steer the economy: monetary policy and fiscal policy.

MONETARY POLICY AND THE "FED" In February 2014, Janet Yellen took over as chairman of the Federal Reserve Board, thereby becoming the world's most important economist and one of the most powerful figures in American government. The chair of the Fed has more power over the U.S. economy than does any other person, including the president. A few choice words from her about the state of the economy can send financial markets either soaring or reeling. For example, long-time Fed chair Alan Greenspan once rhetorically asked in a speech whether the stock market might be displaying "irrational exuberance" and "unduly escalating asset values." An instant reaction was felt round the world, as the major stock markets immediately fell between 2 and 4 percent. All these markets interpreted Greenspan's remark to mean that he thought stocks were overvalued and that the Fed might raise American interest rates to cool down escalating stock prices and prevent an inflationary spiral.

Such is the power that the chair of the Fed can exercise at any time. Unlike the president, the Fed doesn't have to get congressional support for actions that are likely to impact the economy. And unlike Congress, the Fed deliberates in secret, making every public statement by its leader a potentially valuable clue as to how it might act. But what is the Fed, and what does it do?

The most important tool government has to manage the economy is its control over the money supply. The government's main economic policy is **monetary policy**, that is,

When the head of the Federal Reserve Board speaks, the financial industry listens intently for every clue as to how the Fed may act regarding interest rates. Here, traders on the floor of the Chicago Board of Trade monitor Fed chairman Janet Yellen's news conference following a Fed meeting.

monetarism

An economic theory holding that the supply of money is the key to a nation's economic health, with too much cash and credit in circulation producing inflation.

Federal Reserve System

The main instrument for making monetary policy in the United States. It was created by Congress in 1913 to regulate the lending practices of banks and thus the money supply.

manipulation of the supply of money and credit in private hands. An economic theory called **monetarism** holds that the supply of money is the key to the nation's economic health. Monetarists believe that having too much cash and credit in circulation generates inflation. Essentially, they advise that the rate of growth in the money supply should not exceed the rate of growth of the gross domestic product (GDP). Politicians worry constantly about the money supply because it affects the rate of interest that their constituents have to pay for home, car, business, and other loans. If there is too little money in circulation, credit tightens, economic growth is slowed, and employment levels fall.

The main agency for making monetary policy is the **Federal Reserve System**, commonly known as the Fed. Created by Congress in 1913 to regulate the lending practices of banks and thus the money supply, the Fed is intended to be formally beyond the control of the president and Congress. Its seven-member Board of Governors—appointed by the president and confirmed by the Senate—is expected to do its job without regard to partisan politics. Accordingly, members of the Fed's Board of Governors are given 14-year terms designed to insulate them from political pressures.

The Fed has several tools for affecting the supply of money and credit. Its policymaking body, the Federal Open Market Committee (FOMC), meets eight times a year and, taking into consideration a vast amount of economic data, sets a target for the "federal funds rate," the interest rate banks can charge each other for overnight loans. The Fed also buys and sells government bonds, and by doing this, it determines whether banks have more or less money to lend out. The more money banks have to lend, the cheaper borrowing is; if banks have less to lend, borrowing becomes more expensive, and interest rates rise.

Why It Matters to You

Interest Rates

Interest rates are the amount you pay to borrow money for a house or a car, for example. Banks or finance companies charge you these rates, but how high they are is strongly influenced by decisions of the Fed. Even a great credit rating cannot get you a low interest rate if the Federal Reserve Board is keeping the money supply tight.

fiscal policy

Use of the federal budget—taxes, spending, and borrowing—to influence the economy; along with monetary policy, a main tool by which the government can attempt to steer the economy. Fiscal policy is almost entirely determined by Congress and the president.

Keynesian economic theory

Named after English economist John Maynard Keynes, the theory emphasizing that government spending and deficits can help the economy deal with its ups and downs. Proponents of this theory advocate using the power of government to stimulate the economy when it is lagging.

In this way, the complicated financial dealings of the Fed affect the amount of money available and interest rates, which in turn impact inflation and the availability of jobs. In a 1977 amendment to the Federal Reserve Act, Congress imposed a dual mandate on the Fed: to promote maximum sustainable output and employment and to promote "stable" prices. This dual mandate involved a compromise between Democratic and Republican preferences. Today, some Republican leaders maintain that these goals are incompatible and that the tools at the disposal of the Fed are far better suited for fighting inflation. Congressman Mike Pence (R-IN), with the support of other influential Republicans, has proposed that the Fed should only be responsible for promoting a stable dollar.

Because the Fed can profoundly influence the state of the economy, it is no wonder that its every move attracts intense attention from the financial markets as well as politicians—and that presidents try to persuade the Fed to pursue policies in line with presidential plans for the country. For example, President Obama would not have wanted the Fed to raise interest rates in the months leading up to the November 2012 election, as higher interest rates probably would have weakened the nation's already anemic economic growth rate at that point.

In general, the Fed has been found to be fairly responsive to the White House, though not usually to the extent of trying to influence election outcomes.[7] Nevertheless, even the chief executive can be left frustrated by the politically insulated decisions of the Fed. Some have called for more openness in its decision-making process, whereas others have proposed more direct political control of the Fed through shorter terms for its Board of Governors.

FISCAL POLICY: KEYNESIAN VERSUS SUPPLY-SIDE ECONOMICS The second tool for steering the nation's economy is **fiscal policy**, or use of the federal budget—taxing, spending, and borrowing—to influence the economy. In contrast to monetary policy, fiscal policy is shaped mostly by Congress and the president. Moreover, the use of fiscal policy is influenced by political ideology and views of the appropriate scope of government.

One position on fiscal policy is that of **Keynesian economic theory**, named after English economist John Maynard Keynes. Keynes's landmark book, *The General Theory of Employment, Interest, and Money*, was published during the Depression of the 1930s, and Keynesianism soon became the dominant economic philosophy in America. His theory emphasized that government spending could help an economy weather the bad times that were part of the normal ups and downs of the business cycle. Keynes argued that government could spend its way out of the Depression by stimulating the economy through an infusion of money from government programs. If businesses were not able to expand, the government would need to pick up the slack, he claimed—even if it meant running up a substantial budget deficit. If there were no jobs available for people, the government should create some—building roads, dams, houses, or whatever seemed most appropriate. The key would be to get money back in the consumers' pockets, because if few people have money to buy goods, demand for goods will be weak. And if demand is lacking, the production of goods will be slowed, and the economic situation will worsen. Thus, the main goal of fiscal policy in the view of Keynesian economic theory is to increase demand. This is the tack that Franklin Roosevelt took during the New Deal, attacking the Great Depression through unprecedented federal spending that helped to create jobs. More recently, when President Obama took office in January 2009 in the midst of a severe recession, the first major bill that he signed was a $787 billion stimulus package that contained funding for numerous projects that the Democrats believed would combat the downturn and get millions of Americans back to work. In practice, this proved to be not so easy, as you can see in Figure 16.1.

Republicans have frequently criticized Keynesian economic policies as promoting the idea that the government can spend money more wisely than the people—a view they usually reject. For example, Republican House leader Eric Cantor summarized his party's response to the Obama stimulus package as follows: "We believed any bill designed to put Americans to work needed to take bold steps to encourage work,

supply-side economics
An economic theory, first applied during the Reagan administration, holding that the key task for fiscal policy is to stimulate the supply of goods, as by cutting tax rates.

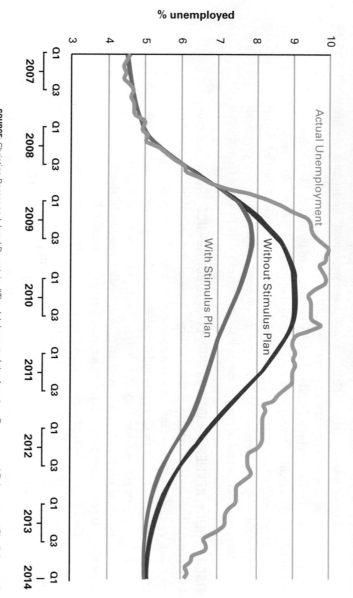

% unemployed

Actual Unemployment

Without Stimulus Plan

With Stimulus Plan

FIGURE 16.1 HOW THE OBAMA ADMINISTRATION'S PREDICTIONS OF THE IMPACT OF THE 2009 STIMULUS PLAN WENT AWRY

As Barack Obama prepared to be inaugurated president in January 2009, his staff prepared a massive economic stimulus bill to combat the rising tide of unemployment. Two of his economic advisors wrote a report detailing estimates of how job losses could be cut by pumping lots of federal money into the economy. They included the following graph, which offered a visual image of how much lower the unemployment rate would be if the stimulus plan were passed than without it.

As unemployment continued to rise unabated in 2009 and continued to be high through the 2010 and 2012 elections, this graph came back to haunt the Obama administration. Obviously, the predictions that were laid out in this graph were far off the mark. Conservatives argued strongly that the large discrepancy proved that the economic stimulus package had been a failure. The Obama administration responded that in January 2009 no one could have foreseen how dire the economic situation actually was and that unemployment would have risen even higher had the plan not been enacted. Ultimately, the voters sided with Obama in the 2012 election by reelecting him.

SOURCE: Christina Romer and Jared Bernstein, "The Job Impact of the American Recovery and Reinvestment Plan," January 9, 2009, p. 5; actual unemployment numbers from the Bureau of Labor Statistics.

investment, and business expansion, something that government spending under Keynesian economic theory too often fails to provide."[8] Instead of the Keynesian approach, Republican fiscal policy follows supply-side economics. The basic premise of **supply-side economics** is that the key task for fiscal policy is to stimulate the supply of goods, not their demand. First adopted during the presidency of Ronald Reagan,[9] supply-side economics maintains that big government soaks up too much of the GDP. By spending too freely and also taxing too heavily and regulating too tightly, government actually curtails economic growth. Supply-siders argue that lowering tax rates stimulates the supply of goods, as people are motivated to work longer, increase their savings and investments, and produce more. Economist Arthur Laffer proposed (legend says he did so on the back of a cocktail napkin) a curve suggesting that the more government taxed, the less people worked and thus the smaller the government's tax revenues. In its most extreme form, this theory held that by taking a smaller percentage of people's income, the government would actually get more total revenue as production increased. Thus, tax cuts, such as the $1.3 trillion tax cut that President George W. Bush signed into law in 2001, are a key tool of the supply-side approach.

Clearly, the Keynesian and supply-side approaches to fiscal policy make diametrically different assumptions about how the tools of fiscal policy should be used and, more generally, about the appropriate scope of government. Despite disagreements about approach, there is now clear agreement on one fundamental point: it is the government's responsibility to use fiscal policy to try to control the economy. But like controlling the weather, this is much easier said than done.

Why It Matters to You

Keynesian Versus Supply-Side Economics

Supply-side economic theory, as advocated by presidents Ronald Reagan and George W. Bush, represents a great departure from Keynesian economic theory, which has guided Democratic economic policymaking ever since the New Deal. Whereas Keynesian theory recommends government spending to combat economic downturns by increasing demand, supply-side economics advocates tax cuts in order to stimulate the supply of goods. The scope of government expands when Keynesian policies are enacted but contracts when supply-side economics is put into effect.

Point to Ponder

This cartoon portrays extreme versions of Keynesian and supply-side economic policies.

Do you think either of these approaches is fairly reasonable? If you think neither one is reasonable, can you envision a third way that falls somewhere in the middle?

© **Andy Singer**

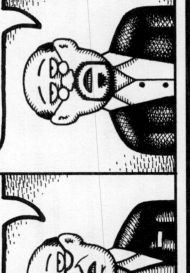

NO EXIT

CHOOSE ONE:

CONSERVATIVE ECONOMIC FANTASY

LIBERAL ECONOMIC FANTASY

IF WE KEEP CUTTING TAXES AND SPEND LESS, EVERYTHING WILL GET BETTER

IF WE RAISE TAXES AND SPEND MORE, EVERYTHING WILL GET BETTER

SINGER

Why It Is Hard to Control the Economy

Many politicians and voters—and even some political scientists—seem to believe that the economy can be easily controlled. Thus, some political scientists have argued that politicians manipulate the economy for short-run advantage to win elections, in a sort of "political business cycle."[10] Presidents, their argument goes, take special care to get the economy moving nicely just before elections, putting more money in voters' hands through either tax cuts or transfer payments such as Social Security and food stamps. A neat trick if you can do it—controlling economic conditions precisely in order to facilitate reelection. However, as economist Robert Samuelson points out, "If presidents could create jobs, the unemployment rate would rarely exceed 3.5 percent."[11]

The American free enterprise system makes it particularly difficult for elected officials to effectively control the economy. The billions of economic choices made by consumers and businesses are more important in their impact than are government policies. Because the private sector is much larger than the public sector, it dominates the economy. Big as the federal government is, it still spends only about a quarter of our GDP. Consumers and businesses make the vast majority of our economic decisions. Fiscal and monetary policy can influence these decisions—but not control them.

Another problem that policymakers face is that trying to control economic indicators like unemployment and inflation with precision is like attempting to stop on an economic dime. Government makes economic policy very slowly. Most policies must be decided on a considerable time before they can be implemented, let alone have their full impact on the economy. The federal budget, for example, is prepared many months in advance of its enactment into law, and once enacted, it is usually quite a while before new policies will have their full impact on the economy. Furthermore, the budgetary process is dominated by "uncontrollable expenditures," which are mandated by law. These expenditures include interest on the national debt, which must be paid, and benefits for which some groups are automatically eligible, such as Social Security. Not only do Social Security benefits go up automatically as the cost of living increases, but other programs like food stamps can become more expensive if more people become eligible for them due to an economic downturn. The remaining sections of this chapter will sketch out how the federal government impacts people's pocketbooks via a wide assortment of social welfare policies.

Types of Social Welfare Policies

Compare and contrast entitlement and means-tested social welfare programs.

O ur lives are affected by many government policies, but it is social welfare policies that most directly affect us as individuals. Such policies include hundreds of programs through which government provides support and assistance to specific groups of people—for example, Social Security checks for retired workers, food stamp benefits for poor families, and Medicare and Medicaid coverage of medical expenses for the elderly and the poor, respectively. Not surprisingly, social welfare policies are expensive. Expenditures on social programs dwarf what government spends on anything else, including national defense.

No area of public policy causes more confusion or stimulates more argument than does social welfare. One common misperception is to equate social welfare with government aid to the poor. In fact, these programs distribute far more money to the nonpoor than to people below the poverty line. Political scientist Martin Gilens notes that about five-sixths of all money for social programs goes to programs that people across all income levels are eligible for, such as Social Security and Medicare; only 17 percent of social spending goes to programs that target the poor.[12] Few Americans have qualms about assisting older Americans through government programs. However, government assistance to the poor is a different matter. As political scientists Stanley Feldman and Marco Steenbergen put it, Americans may be humanitarians, but they are not egalitarians.[13] To clarify the picture, it is useful to distinguish between two types of programs that social welfare policies consist of.

Entitlement programs provide benefits to individuals regardless of need. They are sometimes called "social insurance" programs because typically people (and their employers) pay into them and later get money from them. Thus, you don't have to be poor to get an entitlement, nor does being rich disqualify you. The two main entitlement programs, Social Security and Medicare, are the largest and most expensive social welfare programs in America. These programs have had a positive effect on the health and income of older Americans, who receive more and better medical treatment as a result of Medicare and in many cases are kept out of poverty by Social Security payments. Entitlement programs are rarely controversial and are often overwhelmingly popular (perhaps because everyone is *entitled* to them).

In contrast, **means-tested programs**, such as food stamps and Medicaid, provide benefits only to people with specific needs. To be eligible for means-tested programs, people have to prove that they qualify for them. Means-tested programs generate much political controversy, with the positions taken depending largely on how people see the poor and the causes of poverty. Poverty may be seen as largely a consequence of the individual's decisions and behaviors or as largely beyond the individual's control. When the poor are seen as victims of forces beyond their control (loss of a breadwinner, disabilities, poor economic opportunities), government programs are relatively uncontroversial, for liberals and conservatives alike. However, when the poor are seen as responsible for their poverty, by conservatives in particular, government programs tend to be seen as encouraging dependency. As Weil and Finegold summarize the situation, American welfare policy is frequently caught between two competing values: "the desire to help those who could not help themselves, and the concern that charity would create dependency."[14]

Let's look, therefore, at income and poverty and at what public policy has to do with each.

entitlement programs
Government programs providing benefits to qualified individuals regardless of need.

means-tested programs
Government programs providing benefits only to individuals who qualify based on specific needs.

Why It Matters to You
Perceptions of Poverty

Some people see the poor as lazy; others believe that most of the people who are poor are victims of circumstance. These perceptions of the poor affect the kinds of social welfare policies they favor. Conservatives tend to believe that means-tested welfare programs only discourage people from working. Liberals are more likely to see these programs as helping people weather difficult circumstances.

Income, Poverty, and Public Policy

16.3 Assess the extent of economic inequality in America and the role of government in lessening it.

he United States has one of the world's highest per capita incomes, and when cost of living and tax rates are taken into account, only a few small countries (for example, Norway, Brunei, and Luxembourg) rank ahead of the United States in terms of purchasing power. According to the Census Bureau, in 2013, the median American household income was $51,939—that is, half of American households made more than $51,939, and half made less. Thus, Americans are an affluent people.

Yet, no industrialized country has wider extremes of income than the United States—and the extremes in the United States have been widening. Timothy Smeeding,

One of the goals of the Occupy movement has been to draw attention to inequality in the distribution of income. Here, Occupy supporters gathered and formed a large "99%" in the middle of Freedom Plaza, in Washington, D.C. Chanting slogans like "We are the 99%," they tried to point out the growing income gap between the top 1 percent and the rest of Americans.

534

16.1
16.2
16.3
16.4
16.5
16.6
16.7

income distribution

The way the national income is divided into "shares" ranging from the poor to the rich.

relative deprivation

A perception by an individual that he or she is not doing well economically in comparison to others.

one of the leading researchers on poverty in America, points out that "over the last four decades, the United States has seen large increases in income inequality" and that "many developed countries have experienced at least modest increases in the inequality of ... income, but none so sustained as in the United States."[15] Americans like to think that theirs is the land of opportunity and that people who start off poor can work their way up the income ladder. But recent studies have come to the conclusion that social mobility is actually more limited in the United States than in most other established democracies.[16]

Income is important to politics, just as it is important to people. McCarty, Poole, and Rosenthal argue that American politics is becoming more polarized and that the main "conflict is basically over income redistribution."[17] Liberals and conservatives are divided about many things, but "who gets what" in terms of income is a major battleground.

☐ Who's Getting What?

In 2014, economist Thomas Piketty's book entitled *Capital in the Twenty-First Century*[18] rose to the top of the *New York Times* bestseller list with its compelling evidence that the rich had been getting richer for a long time. Like most social scientists, Piketty uses the concept of **income distribution** to describe how the national income is divided up. If we divide the population into groups based on income, say, into fifths, income distribution tells us what share goes to each group, from the bottom one-fifth to the top one-fifth. In the United States, the distribution of income across groups is quite uneven. The repercussions of different income distribution patterns can be considerable. Thomas B. Edsall remarks that "the distribution of income and wealth in a democratic country goes to the heart of its political ethic, defining the basic contours of a nation's sense of justice and equality."[19]

Income distribution in the United States has changed considerably in recent decades, as you can see in Figure 16.2. This change in income distribution has come about because the very rich have gotten much richer while others, especially the poor, have seen their incomes stagnate. Increasing inequality in the distribution of income can contribute to a situation known as **relative deprivation**, in which people believe

FIGURE 16.2 THE INCREASE IN INCOME INEQUALITY AND THE RISE OF THE TOP 1 PERCENT

The following graph demonstrates how much of the nation's income was received by people within each quintile (or fifth) of the population in 1979 and in 2007. Thus, in 2007, for example, people whose income placed them in the lowest 20 percent of households received just about 3 percent of the nation's income while those in the highest 20 percent took in 60 percent of the nation's income. In recent decades, the share of the highest fifth has grown while the shares of the other fifths have declined. Yet, not everyone in the top fifth has gained. The share of income received by people in the 81st through 99th percentiles has actually held steady at about 40 percent. It is only the people in the top 1 percentile of income who have gained, increasing their share of the nation's income from 10 percent in 1979 to a stunning 20 percent in 2007.

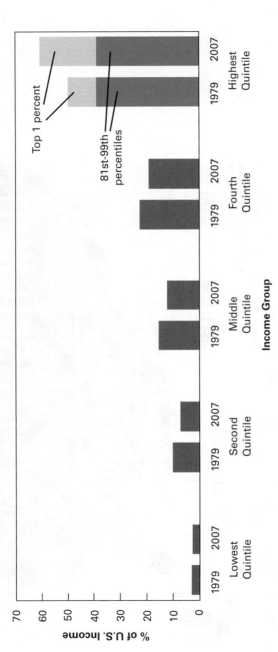

SOURCE: "Trends in the Distribution of Household Income Between 1979 and 2007." Congressional Budget Office, October 2011, p. xi. This report can be found online at http://www.cbo.gov/sites/default/files/10-25-HouseholdIncome_0.pdf.

they are not doing well compared to some reference group. For many observers, a sense of relative deprivation is becoming more common in America.

So far we have focused on **income**, the amount of money collected between two points in time. Income is different from **wealth**, the value of one's assets, including stocks, bonds, bank accounts, cars, houses, and so forth. Studies of wealth show even more inequality than those of income: one-third of America's wealth is held by the wealthiest 1 percent of the population, another one-third is held by the next 9 percent, and the remaining one-third is held by the other 90 percent.

☐ Who's Poor in America?

Counting the poor may seem easy, but it is not. First, one needs to define poverty. Compared with most people in Haiti, poor Americans seem almost prosperous. Russia is a poor country by American standards, but it is not afflicted with the poverty of rural Mexico. Mexico City may look poor to an American visitor, but many people come there from the Mexican countryside seeking prosperity—relatively speaking.

To define this inherently relative concept, the U.S. Census Bureau is charged with determining the **poverty line**, the income threshold below which an individual is considered impoverished. Whether the Census Bureau classifies a person as living in poverty depends on how his or her family's income falls with regard to the poverty threshold, which varies according to the number of adults and children in the family.

This official statistic was designed by Mollie Orshansky, a statistician with the Social Security Administration who realized that in order for politicians to do something about poverty, they first needed to have a way of measuring it. From her earlier work for the Department of Agriculture, Orshansky had learned that a family barely managing to make ends meet spent roughly one-third of its money on food. To set the poverty level,

income

The amount of money collected between any two points in time.

wealth

The value of assets owned.

poverty line

The income threshold below which people are considered poor, based on what a family must spend for an "austere" standard of living, traditionally set at three times the cost of a subsistence diet.

IF U.S. LAND MASS WERE DIVIDED LIKE U.S. WEALTH

1% WOULD OWN THIS

30% WOULD OWN THIS

9% WOULD OWN THIS

40% WOULD OWN THIS RED DOT

20% WOULD OWN THIS

OCCUPY

This graphic was designed and distributed by the Occupy movement as part of their campaign against the concentration of wealth in America. Others view inequality as inevitable in a system of capitalism and believe that it results in large part from individual variations in effort and talent.

she took the cost of the Department of Agriculture's subsistence diet and multiplied it by three. The federal government adopted this formula as its official measure of the poverty threshold in the mid-1960s and has continued to update the formula every year by factoring in inflation. In 2013, the poverty threshold for a single adult was $12,119, for two adults it was $15,600, and for a single parent with two children it was $18,222.

Orshansky never intended to create a permanent formula. She believed that if spending habits changed, then the measurement of poverty ought to be adjusted accordingly. Many scholars believe that today, because the cost of food has declined relative to the cost of other goods, an income equal to three times a subsistence food budget leaves a family in need of many necessities. For years, experts on the subject of poverty have called for a return to Mollie Orshansky's basic concept: what it really takes to maintain an austere standard of living. Moreover, in the decades since Orshansky's basic work was done, the Census Bureau has expanded its data collection efforts to assemble detailed information about spending patterns and income, thereby making a more complex and refined measurement of poverty possible. In 2010, the Obama administration announced that it had settled on an alternative measure, which takes into account a wide range of expenses, such as housing, utilities, child care, and medical treatment, as well as variations in the cost of living.[20] Because the traditional measure has been identified in much legislation as determining the eligibility for various government programs, it remains the official measure of poverty.

Officially, 45.3 million Americans, or about 14.5 percent of the population, were poor in 2013, according to the traditional measure employed by the Census Bureau. However, the official poverty counts tend to *underestimate* poverty in America, not only for the reasons discussed above but, more generally, because it is a snapshot in time rather than a moving picture. That is, a count of the poor at any one point in time can conceal millions who quickly drop into and out of poverty. Divorce, the loss of a breadwinner, job setbacks, and a new mouth to feed can precipitate a fall below the poverty line. Economic insecurity—the chance of suddenly falling into a much lower

feminization of poverty
The increasing concentration of poverty among women, especially unmarried women and their children.

FIGURE 16.3 POVERTY RATES FOR PERSONS WITH SELECTED CHARACTERISTICS: A COMPARISON OF THE OFFICIAL AND SUPPLEMENTAL MEASURES

In the following chart, you can see the poverty rates for various groups as determined by surveys conducted by the Census Bureau in 2012, based on both the traditional, official measure of poverty and the new, supplemental measure. The differences between the two measures are due to two extra considerations that the new measure takes into account. First, the new measure takes into account the benefits from government programs such as food stamps and the National School Lunch Program; this explains why it finds a significantly lower level of poverty among children. Second, it takes into account differences between groups in various cost of living factors, such as medical care; this explains why the new measure finds a much higher percentage of poverty among the elderly.

% in poverty

Legend: official measure, supplemental measure

Categories: Unmarried females, Unmarried males, Married couples, Central cities, Nonmetropolitan areas, Suburban areas, Under 18 years old, 18 to 64 years old, 65 years old and over, African American, Hispanic (any race), Asian, White, non-Hispanic

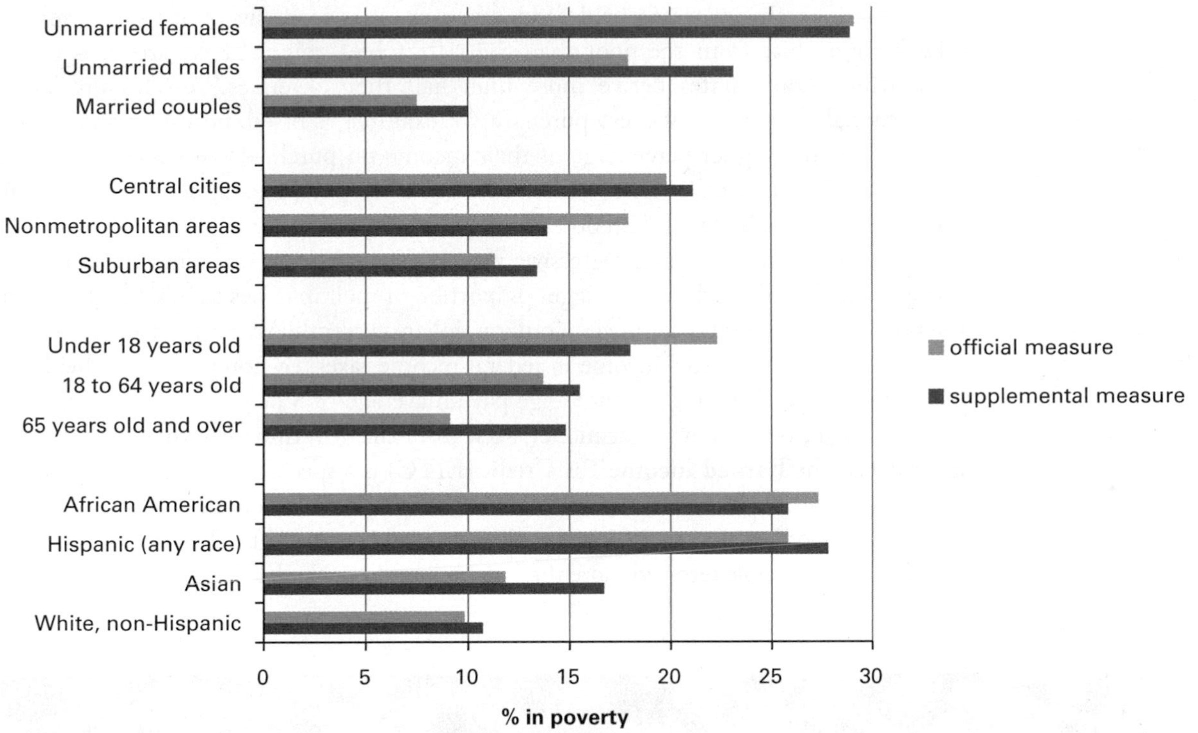

SOURCE: U.S. Census Bureau, "The Research Supplemental Poverty Measure: 2012." November 2013.

income bracket—is higher in the United States than in most industrialized countries. Over half of all Americans between the ages of 25 and 75 will spend at least one year in poverty during their lives, according to Jacob Hacker's analysis.[21]

Who's officially poor? Although the poor are a varied group, poverty is more associated with certain demographic characteristics, as you can see in Figure 16.3. Poverty rates are higher for African Americans, Hispanics, unmarried women, children, and inner-city residents. African Americans and Hispanics have a more than 20 percent chance of living in poverty, as opposed to roughly a 10 percent chance for white, non-Hispanics. Although poverty had long been a problem especially for the elderly, the creation of Social Security in 1935 and its expansion over time significantly reduced poverty among the elderly. Today, poverty is particularly a problem for unmarried women and their children. Experts often refer to the **feminization of poverty.** The poverty rate for female-headed families is almost 30 percent, as opposed to less than 10 percent for families with two parents.

How Public Policy Affects Income

To eradicate poverty, some people believe, the government should ensure that everyone has a minimal level of income, as well as adequate access to education and health care. But, of course, income is determined by many factors that are clearly not subject to governmental control—how hard people work, what opportunities are available in the area where they reside, and what kind of education parents could afford to provide. However, because government (national, state, and local) spends one of out every

538

16.1
16.2
16.3
16.4
16.5
16.6
16.7

progressive tax
A tax by which the government takes a greater share of the income of the rich than of the poor—for example, when a rich family pays 50 percent of its income in taxes, and a poor family pays 5 percent.

proportional tax
A tax by which the government takes the same share of income from everyone, rich and poor alike.

regressive tax
A tax in which the burden falls relatively more heavily on low-income groups than on wealthy taxpayers. The opposite of a progressive tax, in which tax rates increase as income increases.

Earned Income Tax Credit
Also known as the EITC, a refundable federal income tax credit for low- to moderate-income working individuals and families, even if they did not earn enough money to be required to file a tax return.

A sign at a farmers market in northern California announces the acceptance of Electronic Benefit Transfer (EBT) cards, which food stamp recipients can use to buy groceries. In 2012, fewer than a quarter of the nation's farmers markets were set up to use the EBT system. The federal government has allocated $4 million to provide wireless "point of sale" equipment, which will enable more of these markets to use EBT cards.

three dollars in the American economy, it is bound to have a major impact on citizens' income and wealth. There are two principal ways in which government affects a person's income. One is through its taxing powers; the other is through its expenditure policies.

TAXATION "Nothing," said Benjamin Franklin, "is certain in life but death and taxes." Taxes can be termed progressive, proportional, or regressive, depending on their effects on citizens' incomes. A **progressive tax** takes a bigger bite from the incomes of the rich than from those of the poor, for example, charging millionaires 50 percent of their income and the poor 5 percent of theirs. And, finally, a **regressive tax** takes a higher percentage from those at lower income levels than from the well-to-do.

A tax is rarely advocated or defended because it is regressive, but some taxes do take a bigger bite from the poor than the rich. Chief among these are sales taxes, from which many states derive more than half their revenues. A sales tax looks proportional—6 percent of every purchase, for example, is taxed. However, since poor families spend a higher percentage of their income on purchases—of food, clothing, school supplies, and other necessities—they wind up paying a higher percentage of their incomes in sales taxes than do the rich.

Federal income taxes are progressive; you only have to look at the rates on your tax forms to see this. The rich send a bigger proportion of their incomes to Washington than the poor. Americans who earn over a million dollars currently pay an average of 23 percent of their adjusted gross income in federal income taxes. By comparison, individuals in the $40,000 to $50,000 income range pay an average of 8 percent.[22] If your income is low enough, you can even get money back from the government rather than paying income tax. The **Earned Income Tax Credit** (EITC) is a special tax benefit for working people who earn low incomes. In 2013, a married couple who were raising two children on an income of less than $43,038 were eligible for this tax credit. The IRS reports that over 27 million people received more than $63 billion from the EITC program in 2013.[23]

GOVERNMENT EXPENDITURES

The second way in which government can affect personal income is through its expenditures. Each year millions of government checks are mailed to Social Security beneficiaries, retired government employees, veterans, and others. Unemployed workers receive payments through state-run unemployment insurance programs. The government also provides "in-kind" benefits, which give assistance in ways other than simply writing a check. Food stamps and low-interest college loans are both examples of in-kind benefits. These and other benefits—cash and in-kind—are called **transfer payments**; they transfer money from federal and state treasuries to individuals. In the case of state-run programs, such as unemployment insurance, benefits vary widely among the states. For example, as of 2014 maximum weekly unemployment benefits ranged from $674 in Massachusetts to $235 in Mississippi.

It is clear that many recipients are better off after these transfers than before, particularly the elderly, whose poverty rate declined from 35 percent in 1959 to 9 percent in 2013 primarily because of Social Security payments and Medicare. Many of the poor have been raised above the poverty line by these cash and in-kind transfers. In July 2014, 46.5 million Americans were receiving food stamps. The average monthly benefit of about $133 per person helped many families weather the worst of the recent economic downturn. A recent study by sociologists Mark Rank and Mark Hirschl startled some policymakers with its finding that half of Americans receive food stamps, at least briefly, by the time they turn 20. Among black children, the figure was 90 percent.[24]

Table 16.1 summarizes the major government social welfare programs that affect our incomes, both programs providing cash benefits and those providing in-kind benefits. We have already mentioned Social Security and Medicare as entitlement programs; notice that unemployment insurance is the other major entitlement program. The other programs are means-tested and are available only to the near-poor or the poor. In addition to Medicaid and food stamps, they include Temporary Assistance for Needy Families and Supplementary Security Income, providing cash to needy families and the needy with disabilities, and the Children's Health Insurance Program, subsidizing health care for children in poor families.

transfer payments
Benefits given by the government directly to individuals—either cash transfers, such as Social Security payments, or in-kind transfers, such as food stamps and low-interest college loans.

TABLE 16.1 THE MAJOR SOCIAL WELFARE PROGRAMS

Program	Description	Beneficiaries	Funding
Entitlement Programs—"Social Insurance"			
Social Security	Monthly payments	Retired or disabled people and surviving members of their families	Payroll tax on employees and employers
Medicare (Part A)	Partial payment of cost of hospital care	Retired and disabled people	Payroll taxes on employees and employers
Medicare (Part B)	Voluntary program of medical insurance (pays physicians)	Persons 65 or over and disabled Social Security beneficiaries	Beneficiaries pay premiums
Unemployment Insurance (UI)	Weekly payments; benefits vary by state	Workers who have been laid off and cannot find work	Taxes on employers; states determine benefits
The Means-Tested Programs			
Medicaid	Medical and hospital aid	The very poor	Federal grants to state health programs
Food stamps	Debit cards that can be used to buy food	People whose income falls below a certain level	General federal revenues
Temporary Assistance for Needy Families (TANF)	Payment	Families with children, either one-parent families or, in some states, two-parent families in which the breadwinner is unemployed	Paid partly by states and partly by the federal government
Supplemental Security Income (SSI)	Cash payments	Elderly, blind, or disabled people whose income is below a certain amount	General federal revenue
Children's Health Insurance Program (CHIPs)	Subsidies for insurance	Poor families with children	Federal and state revenues

540

16.1
16.2
16.3
16.4
16.5
16.6
16.7

Helping the Poor? Social Policy and the Needy

16.4 Trace the changes over time in major federal welfare programs.

H istorically, societies considered family welfare a private concern. Children were to be nurtured by their parents and, in turn, care for them in their old age. Governments took little responsibility for feeding and clothing the poor or anyone else. The life of the poor was grim almost beyond our imagining. In England, governments passed Poor Laws providing "relief" for the poor but intended, historians argue, to make the life of the poor so miserable that people would do almost anything to avoid the specter, disgrace, and agony of poverty.[25] It was scarcely better in the United States as late as the Great Depression, in the 1930s.

"Welfare" as We Knew It

The administration of Franklin D. Roosevelt implemented a host of policies to deal with the Depression, thus establishing a safety net for less fortunate Americans. The most important piece of this New Deal legislation was the **Social Security Act of 1935**. In addition to creating the Social Security entitlement program for the aged, this bill also created a program to assist some of the nation's poor. Known eventually as "Aid to Families with Dependent Children," this program brought various state programs together under a single federal umbrella to help poor families that had no breadwinner and had children to care for. The federal government established some uniform standards for the states and subsidized their efforts to help families. However, states were free to give generous or skimpy benefits, and payments ranged widely. For the first quarter-century of the program, enrollments remained small. Spurred in part by the civil rights movement, in 1964 President Lyndon Johnson declared a national "War on Poverty," and added food stamps and other programs to the arsenal of poverty-fighting policies. These programs—collectively called "welfare"—came to bitterly divide Republicans from Democrats and conservatives from liberals.

If Lyndon Johnson had declared war on poverty, President Ronald Reagan declared war on antipoverty programs. In 1981, he persuaded Congress to cut welfare benefits and lower the number of Americans on the welfare rolls, arguing that welfare had proved to be a failure. Conservative economist Charles Murray offered an influential and provocative argument that the social welfare programs that began with Johnson's War on Poverty not only failed to curb the advance of poverty but actually made the situation worse.[26] The problem, Murray maintained, was that these public policies discouraged the poor from solving their problems. He contended that welfare programs made it profitable to be poor and thus discouraged people from pursuing means by which they could rise out of poverty. For example, Murray claimed, since poor couples could obtain more benefits if they weren't married, most would not marry and the result would be further disintegration of the family. Many scholars disagreed,[27] but their arguments and interpretations of the data were overwhelmed by the public's extremely negative perception of welfare. "Deadbeat dads" who ran out on their families, leaving them on welfare, and "welfare queens" who collected money they didn't deserve became common images of a broken system.[28]

No one was clearer or blunter about American antipathy toward welfare than political scientist Martin Gilens.[29] He found that Americans tended to see welfare recipients as overwhelmingly African American. Whites' welfare attitudes were strongly influenced by whether they held negative stereotypes of African Americans, for example, perceiving them as "lazy."[30] Negative views of African American welfare mothers generated opposition to welfare in a way that views of white welfare mothers did not. Moreover, when Gilens counted magazine and newspaper stories about poor people over a period of several decades, he found that although only a third of all welfare recipients were African American, about three-quarters of these stories concerned African Americans.[31] Attitudes toward welfare, in short, became "race coded" and it was commonly concluded that many "undeserving poor" were on welfare.

The stage for a major welfare reform was set when Bill Clinton pledged to reform America's system of welfare in his successful bid for the presidency in 1992.

Ending Welfare as We Knew It: The Welfare Reform of 1996

Bill Clinton was determined to be a "centrist" president, fearing the "tax and spend" label Republicans applied to liberal Democrats. Clinton promised to "end welfare as we know it" by providing welfare recipients with two years of support—training, child care, and health care—in exchange for an agreement to find work. Republicans in Congress were even more enthusiastic about welfare reform than the new president. In August 1996, the president and congressional Republicans completed a welfare reform bill that received almost unanimous support from the Republicans but was opposed by about half of the congressional Democrats. Under the lofty name of the **Personal Responsibility and Work Opportunity Reconciliation Act (PRWORA)**, this bill provided that (1) each state would receive a *fixed* amount of money to run its own welfare programs, (2) people on welfare would have to find work within two years or lose all their benefits, and (3) there would be a lifetime maximum of five years for welfare. With the reform, the name of welfare was also changed, from Aid to Families with Dependent Children to **Temporary Assistance for Needy Families (TANF)**.

Today, the benefits from this means-tested program for the poorest of the poor are small and declining. Recipient families collect an average of about $363 monthly in TANF benefits. The number of families receiving aid has also declined: as you can see in Figure 16.4, the 1996 welfare reform bill has had its intended effect of dramatically reducing the percentage of the population receiving welfare benefits.

Personal Responsibility and Work Opportunity Reconciliation Act
The welfare reform law of 1996, which implemented the Temporary Assistance for Needy Families program.

Temporary Assistance for Needy Families
Replacing Aid to Families with Dependent Children as the program for public assistance to needy families, TANF requires people on welfare to find work within two years and sets a lifetime maximum of five years.

Since 1996, welfare reform policies have tried to reduce the welfare rolls and get recipients to work. The young single pictured here said that she had gained new hope from the Climb Wyoming job training program that she was enrolled in while temporarily receiving welfare payments. You can find out about this program for single mothers at www.climbwyoming.org.

FIGURE 16.4 HOW WELFARE REFORM DRASTICALLY REDUCED THE WELFARE ROLLS

Prior to the adoption of the welfare reform bill of 1996, the percentage of the population receiving welfare and food stamps fluctuated in sync with the poverty level. Whenever more people were in poverty, more people qualified for them and hence received benefits; the reverse was of course true whenever times were good and the poverty rate declined. However, once welfare reform was enacted the fact that states now had only a fixed amount of money to dole out under Temporary Aid to Needy Families (TANF) restricted their ability to expand the distribution of welfare benefits during economic hard times. Thus, even during the severe recession that began in 2008 the percentage of the population receiving welfare increased only slightly. In contrast, the percentage receiving food stamps went up markedly, as there were no such restrictions on this program.

% of the population

welfare reform
enacted 1996

—— in poverty   —— on food stamps   —— on welfare

SOURCE: " Indicators of Welfare Dependence," U.S. Department of Health and Human Services, *Annual Report to Congress*, 2008. Updated by the authors based on welfare caseload data reported by the U.S. Department of Health and Human Services' Administration for Children and Families, poverty statistics reported by the U.S. Census Bureau, and caseload data for food stamps as reported by the Department of Agriculture.

Why It Matters to You
The 1996 Reform of Welfare

Because, since the reform, the states have been faced with fixed amounts to spend on welfare and individuals limited in terms of how long they could receive benefits, the percentage of poor people who receive welfare assistance has declined markedly. Many liberals are concerned that a hole has been opened in the safety net; conservatives tend to be pleased that incentives for the poor to find gainful employment have been increased.

One reason that welfare remains unpopular may be that TANF, along with food stamps and health benefits, is seen as contributing to a flood of immigrants. In some states, controversial policies have been considered that would deny benefits to people who cannot prove that they are legal residents, as you can read about in "You Are the Policymaker: Should Government Benefits Be Denied to Illegal Immigrants?"

Today, welfare spending remains unpopular compared to most other governmental expenditures. The 2008 General Social Survey asked a random sample of the public whether spending should be increased or decreased in 22 categories. Education ranked as the American public's top priority for more spending; welfare ranked nineteenth with only aid to big cities, space exploration, and foreign aid ranking lower.[32]

You Are the Policymaker

Should Government Benefits Be Denied to Illegal Immigrants?

I n states such as Texas and California, which have experienced an influx of illegal immigrants particularly from Mexico and Central America, there is concern that providing public services to illegal immigrants is seriously draining state resources. The issue gained prominence as early as 1994, when Californians voted on Proposition 187, labeled by its proponents as the "Save Our State Initiative." This measure sought to cut illegal immigrants off from public services and benefits, such as education, and welfare benefits. Not only would Proposition 187 save the state treasury, its proponents argued, but it would discourage illegal immigrants, who came largely to take advantage of the free goods offered.

Opponents replied that although illegal immigration is surely a problem, the idea of cutting off public services could easily do more harm than good. They pointed out the public-health risks of denying illegal immigrants basic health care, such as immunizations that help control communicable diseases. If denied an education, some children of illegal immigrants, with nothing to do all day, they argued, would turn to crime. They also had a fairness argument: by paying sales taxes and rent, part of which goes to landlords' property taxes, illegal immigrants contribute to the tax base that pays for public services and thus should be entitled to make use of them.

The proponents of Proposition 187 won at the ballot box. However, they lost in their attempts to get the measure enforced. When Hispanic groups challenged the law, the courts ruled that the proposition violated the rights of illegal immigrants, as well as national laws concerning eligibility for federally funded benefits. Overall, the proposition was held to be an unconstitutional state scheme to regulate immigration.

California's experience with Proposition 187 has not stopped other states from trying to follow a similar course. In 2007, Oklahoma governor Brad Henry signed into law the "Taxpayer and Citizen Protection Act," which many advocates of cracking down on illegal immigration highly praised. Like California's Proposition 187, this act was designed to deny illegal immigrants the right to receive services and benefits such as welfare benefits, scholarships, and medical care other than emergency care. The act also made it a crime to transport or house illegal immigrants in Oklahoma. As with California's law, the Oklahoma law was successfully challenged in court by Hispanic groups on the grounds that responsibility for enforcing immigration laws belongs to the federal government, not the states.

What do you think? Should illegal immigrants be denied government benefits, such as welfare and in-state tuition? Or should illegal immigrants who have paid their fair share of taxes receive some or all of the benefits that American citizens do? What are the advantages and disadvantages of each approach?

Social Security: Living on Borrowed Time

16.5 Outline how America's Social Security program works and the challenge of keeping it financially solvent in the coming years.

E very year, the Social Security Administration sends out over 100 million letters titled "Your Social Security Statement" to Americans detailing their contributions to the **Social Security Trust Fund** and the likely benefits they can expect to receive from it when they retire. About 75 million baby boomers will be retiring between 2010 and 2030. Chances are that they will live longer and healthier lives than previous generations—and run up bigger costs for Social Security. Many experts, as well as politicians, believe that Social Security is badly in need of reform. They argue that it is moving inexorably toward a day, not very far off, when the income being paid into the program will not be enough for paying out benefits, at least not at the level that people have come to expect from their yearly Social Security statement. But what exactly is Social Security? Let's look at its history—and at its future.

Social Security Trust Fund
The "account" into which Social Security employee and employer contributions are "deposited" and used to pay out eligible recipients.

The Growth of Social Security

Social Security, officially called Old Age, Survivors and Disability Insurance (OASDI), has proved to be a highly successful and popular program. Year after year, more than 90 percent of people polled support Social Security. Although its benefits are relatively modest—the average monthly check for a retired worker in 2014 was $1,294—Social Security has lifted many elderly people out of poverty. Social Security taxes and benefits have both grown over the years because the program worked.

Social Security, now the most expensive public policy in the United States, began modestly enough, as part of Franklin Roosevelt's New Deal. President Roosevelt famously said that he wanted the fiscal basis to be so solid that "no damn politician can ever scrap my social security program." The fiscal soundness derived from the fact that, before money could go out to the beneficiaries, it would have to come into the federal treasury in payroll taxes. Indeed, over the years, Americans have tended to look on their Social Security benefits as getting back what they paid in. But from the start, taxes and benefits were not necessarily equivalent. The first Social Security recipient, a woman named Ida May Fuller from Brattleboro, Vermont, contributed a mere $22.54 and received benefits totaling $22,888.92, because she lived to an old age.[33] Today, however, a worker in his or her twenties may be facing the prospect of paying in more than he or she can expect to get back. To understand the problem, we have to look at how Social Security works.

Government taxes employees and their employers a percentage of each employee's income up to a maximum contribution. Both employee and employer contributions are paid into the Social Security Trust Fund, from which distributions are made to eligible retirees and those who are no longer able to work due to disability. Up until 2010, more money was paid in every year than paid out, with the consequence that a substantial sum was saved for the future. Since then, however, the Social Security Trust Fund has been running in the red, and unless some major changes are made to the program the surplus will be gradually depleted over the coming years. The reason is simple: there aren't enough workers paying in to the system to support all the people who are entitled to claim benefits from it. The ratio of workers to Social Security beneficiaries has been heading downward for quite some time and is projected to fall yet further. Thus, the Social Security program may be living on borrowed time.

Various demographic factors explain the changing ratio. When Social Security was established, average life expectancy for Americans was lower than the 65 years of age at which workers could begin to collect benefits. With medical advances, average life expectancy has soared to 78 years. The bottom line is that while the number of Social Security contributors (the workers) is growing slowly, the number of Social Security recipients (the retired) is growing rapidly.

In short, as the number of retirees grows (and their average benefit is increased to adjust for inflation, in what are called cost-of-living adjustments), Social Security payouts will exceed income, and within a number of years, the Trust Fund will be depleted. At that point, Congress will have to also use regular appropriations to pay out benefits to retirees—monies that thus would not be available for other purposes. There is no politically pleasant solution to this Social Security dilemma. Some experts say benefits must be cut, others say the rate of Social Security taxes must be increased, and yet others believe that both measures will be necessary.

Reforming Social Security

Politicians tread gingerly on the terrain of Social Security, fearing a backlash from older Americans,[34] a concern accentuated by the fact that older Americans are an age group with a high voting rate.[35] Nonetheless, the looming problems of Social Security are so serious that recent presidents have tried their hands at reform.

President George W. Bush proposed diverting about a third of individuals' Social Security contribution to private retirement funds. The idea was that individuals could reduce their contribution and put that part of the money into a private account, a stock, a bond, or another investment and then collect their gains—or perhaps face their losses—when they were eligible to collect Social Security. President Bush appointed a Commission to Strengthen Social Security, which advocated this idea of limited privatization of Social Security. The Commission argued that contributions put into the stock or bond market over the long haul would produce greater returns, making it possible for today's young people to receive more benefits when they retire. Critics countered that the problem was that permitting people to divert money from the system would merely hasten its bankruptcy. Moreover, the report couldn't have come at a worse time for advocates of privatization: stocks were slumping, and as their value declined, so did public support for President Bush's proposal.

In 2010, President Obama appointed a commission to draft a proposal for dealing with the nation's long-term fiscal problems, including the deficit that the Social Security Trust Fund will soon be facing. Unlike Bush, Obama has adamantly opposed any privatization of Social Security. Other than the privatization proposal, however, Obama insisted that all ideas should be on the table for the commission's consideration. The commission made four recommendations to put Social Security on a sound fiscal course for the future: (1) gradually increase the age by which people would be entitled to benefits; (2) revise the inflation adjustment formula for benefits so that recipients would receive less of a raise every year; (3) reduce benefits for retirees who have substantial income from other sources; and (4) raise the maximum contribution that workers pay in to the system, thereby taxing wealthy Americans more. Which option, or combination thereof, Congress and the president ultimately agree to implement will determine the future of America's most popular social welfare policy.

Social Welfare Policy Elsewhere

16.6 Distinguish American social welfare policy from that of other established democracies.

Most industrial nations tend to be far more generous with social welfare programs than is the United States. This greater generosity is evident in programs related to health, child care, unemployment compensation, and income maintenance for the elderly. Europeans often think of their countries as "welfare states," with all the generous benefits—and, by U.S. standards, staggering taxes—that this implies.[36] One example can be seen in "America in Perspective: Parental Leave Policies."

Most Americans would be amazed at the range of social benefits in the average European country. French parents, for example, are guaranteed the right to put their toddlers in *crèches* (day care centers), regardless of whether the parents are rich or poor, at work or at home. French unemployment benefits are generous by American standards, although French unemployment rates are considerably higher than ours. In many European countries, free or low-cost government health care policies even include treatments at health spas.

Europeans pay a high price for generous benefits. Tax rates in Western European nations far exceed those in the United States; in some cases, top tax rates exceed 50 percent of income. Moreover, the problems that the United States faces in funding Social Security occur to an even greater extent in many European countries, not only because of the level of benefits but also because their populations are shrinking due to very low birthrates, which compounds the issue of fewer taxpayers supporting an aging population.

Americans tend to see poverty and social welfare needs as individual concerns, whereas European nations tend to support greater governmental responsibility for these problems. For example, 71 percent of Americans believe that the poor could escape poverty if they worked hard enough, compared to just 40 percent of Europeans.[37] Also, Europeans often have a more positive attitude toward government, whereas Americans are more likely to distrust government action in areas such as social welfare policy.

546

16.1
16.2
16.3
16.4
16.5
16.6
16.7

America in Perspective

Parental Leave Policies

Since 1993, U.S. federal law has required employers with 50 or more employees to provide workers (both women and men) with up to 12 weeks of *unpaid* leave for the birth or adoption of a child or the illness of a close family member. When President Clinton signed this law he hailed this as a landmark piece of legislation, whereas the majority of Republicans denounced it as yet another example of intrusive government. Compared to all other advanced industrialized democracies, though, the provisions of the American Family and Medical Leave Act are relatively meager. As you can see in the accompanying chart, all of the other established democracies provide for at least 10 weeks of *paid* leave for a 2-parent family to care for a new child and most that allow *unpaid* leave that greatly exceeds what American law provides for.

Weeks of leave for a 2-parent family

- Paid leave
- Unpaid leave

France, Spain, Germany, Sweden, Norway, Austria, Australia, Britain, Ireland, Italy, Japan, NZ, Canada, Denmark, Finland, Belgium, Netherlands, USA, Switzerland

0 50 100 150 200 250 300 350
Weeks of leave for a 2-parent family

SOURCE: Rebecca Ray et al., "Parental Leave Policies: Assessing Generosity and Gender Equality," Report of the Center for Economic and Policy Research, June 2009, p. 6. Updated by the authors for Australia, which implemented its first *paid family leave* in 2011.

During the 2008 presidential campaign, Barack Obama proposed that *unpaid* family leave in America be extended to companies with at least 25 employees, and that the federal government provide grants to states to help them implement programs to provide *paid family* leave.

CRITICAL THINKING QUESTIONS

Would you favor or oppose these proposals? If you favor them, would you go even further and bring American family leave policy into line with the norm in other advanced industrialized democracies?

Understanding Economic and Social Welfare Policymaking

16.7 Assess the impact of economic and social welfare policies on democracy and the scope of government in America.

Economic and social welfare policies are bound to be controversial in a capitalist, democratic political system. Very few issues divide liberals and conservatives more sharply. Americans struggle to balance individual merit and the rewards of initiative with the reality of systemic inequalities and the need to provide economic support to those who need it. Citizens disagree on how much government can or should do to even out the competition and protect those who are less able or too old to compete. In short, Americans seek to retain a commitment to both competition and compassion. Sorting out the proper balance of these values is at the heart of policy disagreements about economic and social welfare programs.

Democracy and Economic and Social Welfare Policies

The solutions to many of the problems of the free enterprise economy were achieved in America through the democratic process. As the voting power of the ordinary worker grew, so did the potential for government regulation of the worst ravages of the free enterprise system. Political pressure grew for action to restrict unfair business practices and protect individual rights. Over time, the state assumed responsibility for setting the age at which one could work, determining the normal work week, establishing standards for safety on the job, protecting pension funds, and many other aspects of economic life. Just as the right of free speech is not interpreted so as to allow someone to shout "Fire!" in a crowded movie theater, so the right to free enterprise is no longer interpreted as a giving businesses the right to employ 10-year-olds or to have employees work in unsafe conditions. It is now generally agreed that such practices should be forbidden by the government. Through their choices at the ballot box, Americans essentially decided to give up certain economic freedoms for the good of society as a whole.

It would be an exaggeration, however, to say that democracy regularly facilitates an economic policy that looks after the general rather than specific interests. In a democracy, competing demands are resolved by government decision makers. But these policymakers do not act in a vacuum. They are aligned with and pay close attention to various groups in society. In the social welfare policy arena, the competing groups are often quite unequal in terms of political resources. For example, the elderly are relatively well organized and often have the resources needed to wield significant influence in support of programs they desire. As a result, they are usually successful in protecting and expanding their programs. For the poor, however, influencing political decisions is more difficult. They vote less frequently and lack strong, focused organizations and money. Larry Bartels finds that elected officials are often unresponsive to the policy preferences of low-income citizens.[38]

Although government benefits are difficult to obtain, especially for the poor, the nature of democratic politics also makes it difficult to withdraw benefits once they are established. Policymaking in the United States is very incremental in nature. Once put into place, policies develop a life of their own. They engage supporters in the public,

As American workers have gained more political power, they have demanded government action to improve working conditions and regulate business practices. No longer can children be found working in factories, as did this 11-year-old girl in a Tennessee textile mill around 1910.

in Congress, in the bureaucracy, and among key interest groups. Tremendous pressures come from these supporters to expand, or at least keep, existing programs. These pressures persist even when the size and costs of programs seem to have grown beyond anything originally envisioned, as has often been the case with social welfare programs.

□ Economic and Social Welfare Policies and the Scope of Government

Liberals and conservatives fundamentally disagree about the scope of government involvement in the economy. In general, liberals look to the writings of economists such as John Maynard Keynes and Robert Solow, whose work offers justification for an expanded role of government in stimulating the economy. Conservatives, on the other hand, rely on Friedrich Hayek's influential theories on the free market and on Milton Friedman's arguments against government intervention. Whereas liberals focus on the imperfections of the market and what government can do about them, conservatives focus on the imperfections of government. For example, while liberals often propose government spending to create new jobs, conservatives argue that businesses can create new jobs and prepare people for them if government will just get out of the way.

Ever since the New Deal and the creation of Social Security, the growth of government has been largely driven by the growth of social welfare policies. Conservatives complain about the "welfare state." Even if ours is small relative to those of other nations, the American social welfare system grows generation by generation. American attitudes toward the growth of social welfare often depend on their assessment of what Schneider and Ingram call "target groups."[39] The elderly and the "deserving poor"—groups viewed favorably—are one thing; the "undeserving poor" are quite another. The debate about the scope of social welfare policies is influenced by the controversy concerning how deserving various groups are, as well as by the political resources of the beneficiaries.

Review the Chapter

Economic Policymaking

16.1 Identify the main policy tools that American government can employ to address economic problems, and contrast Keynesian and supply-side economics, p. 525.

Two major instruments are available to government for managing the economy: monetary policy and fiscal policy. Republicans have become the party of supply-side economics, believing that tax cuts will lead to economic growth and jobs. Democrats disagree, sticking to Keynesian economic theory, which recommends government spending in order to stimulate demand for goods during economic downturns.

Types of Social Welfare Policies

16.2 Compare and contrast entitlement and means-tested social welfare programs, p. 532.

Means-tested social welfare programs provide benefits only to people who qualify for them based on specific needs. In contrast, entitlement programs provide benefits to individuals without regard to need. Because entitlement programs can provide benefits to everyone, they are generally more popular with the public than means-tested programs.

Income, Poverty, and Public Policy

16.3 Assess the extent of economic inequality in America and the role of government in lessening it, p. 533.

Despite America's affluence, the extent of inequality—the disparity between incomes—is quite substantial and has been increasing in recent decades. America's means-tested social welfare programs help to reduce inequality by helping the poorest individuals. Progressive taxes, such as the federal income tax, also alleviate inequality by taking a bigger bite out of the rich than the middle class.

Helping the Poor? Social Policy and the Needy

16.4 Trace the changes over time in major federal welfare programs, p. 540.

The Aid to Families with Dependent Children (AFDC) program was begun during FDR's New Deal, greatly expanded during the period of LBJ's Great Society, and then reduced in scope by the Reagan administration. When he ran for president in 1992, Bill Clinton promised to "end welfare as we know it." With the help of a Republican majority in Congress in 1996, the AFDC program was replaced by Temporary Assistance to Needy Families (TANF). The major innovation of the new law was that recipients of aid can only be on the welfare rolls for two consecutive years and five years during their lifetime.

Social Security: Living on Borrowed Time

16.5 Outline how America's Social Security program works and the challenge of keeping it financially solvent in the coming years, p. 543.

The Social Security program collects a payroll tax from workers and their employers each month and pays out monthly benefits to retirees. It has proved to be a highly successful and popular program. However, demographic trends have put the program in danger, as soon there will not be enough workers per beneficiary to keep the program solvent. The government will soon need to decide on and implement difficult changes such as raising Social Security taxes or reducing benefits.

Social Welfare Policy Elsewhere

16.6 Distinguish American social welfare policy from that of other established democracies, p. 545.

Most established democracies have more expensive and generous social welfare programs than does the United States. In particular, European governments provide citizens with benefits, such as paid parental leave upon the birth of a child, that are unheard of in the United States. Taxes in Europe have to be higher than taxes in the United States in order to pay for these benefits.

Understanding Economic and Social Welfare Policy

16.7 Assess the impact of economic and social welfare policies on democracy and the scope of government in America, p. 546.

As in most policy arenas, groups with ample political resources tend to get more of what they want in the battle over social welfare policies. Thus, the elderly have been very successful in preserving their Social Security and Medicare benefits, whereas the poor have faced difficulties in preserving welfare funding. Overall, the growth in social welfare spending, particularly for Social Security and Medicare, accounts for much of the increase in the scope of government in recent decades.

Learn the Terms

social welfare policies, p. 524
unemployment rate, p. 525
underemployment rate, p. 526
inflation, p. 526
consumer price index, p. 527
laissez-faire, p. 527
monetary policy, p. 527
monetarism, p. 528
Federal Reserve System, p. 528
fiscal policy, p. 529
Keynesian economic theory, p. 529

supply-side economics, p. 530
entitlement programs, p. 533
means-tested programs, p. 533
income distribution, p. 534
relative deprivation, p. 534
income, p. 535
wealth, p. 535
poverty line, p. 535
feminization of poverty, p. 535
progressive tax, p. 538
proportional tax, p. 538

regressive tax, p. 538
Earned Income Tax Credit, p. 538
transfer payments, p. 539
Social Security Act of 1935, p. 540
Personal Responsibility and Work
    Opportunity Reconciliation
    Act, p. 541
Temporary Assistance for Needy
    Families, p. 541
Social Security Trust Fund, p. 543

Test Yourself

1. What is the most important tool the government has for directing the economy?

a. control over government subsidies
b. control over investment practices
c. control over labor laws
d. control over the money supply
e. control over trade policy

2. Which of the following economic indicators would be most likely to have a significant effect on voting during an election year?

a. the unemployment rate
b. income equality between the classes
c. the wage gap between men and women
d. the federal reserve's discount rate for banks
e. the consumer price index (CPI)

3. What distinguishes Keynesian economic theory from supply-side economics?

a. regulation of the money supply
b. the appropriate actions of the Federal Reserve Board
c. the appropriate scope of government
d. the balance of economic power between Congress and the president
e. whether to use fiscal policy at all

4. Which of the following is characterized as an entitlement program?

a. Children's Health Insurance Program
b. food stamps
c. Medicaid
d. Medicare
e. Supplemental Security Income

5. A fiscally conservative political candidate is most likely to oppose which of the following?

a. cutting back environmental regulations that increase the costs of running a business
b. increasing funding for means-tested programs such as food stamps or welfare
c. increasing military spending to fund projects in their own state
d. increasing tax deductions for large corporations
e. paying Social Security benefits to retirees

6. Among which of the following groups is poverty most common?

a. Asian Americans
b. children
c. inner-city residents
d. older Americans
e. unmarried women with children

7. Which of the following statements accurately describes sales taxes?

a. Sales tax is progressive, because the tax is higher on higher-income people.
b. Sales tax is proportional, because it takes a greater percentage from the rich.
c. Sales tax is proportional, because it takes the same percentage from rich and poor alike.
d. Sales tax is regressive, because the poor spend more of their incomes on purchases.
e. Sales tax is regressive, because the tax is higher on lower-income people.

8. Why are conservatives more likely to support the Earned Income Tax Credit than other social welfare policies?

a. It has time limits.
b. It is an entitlement.
c. It is means-tested.
d. Only the unemployed benefit from it.
e. Only those who work can benefit from it.

9. Which of the following is one reason the Personal Responsibility and Work Opportunity Reconciliation Act has failed to affect welfare's unpopularity?

a. It encourages racist attitudes toward minorities.
b. It fails to curb the advance of poverty.
c. It is seen as contributing to increased immigration.
d. It is seen as encouraging people to remain poor.
e. It makes poverty worse, rather than assisting the poor.

10. A major study by conservative economist Charles Murray argued that the social programs of Johnson's War on Poverty _____.

a. did not eliminate poverty and it did reduce the number of poor
b. did not help the poor enough
c. enabled the poor to solve their own problems
d. failed to curb the advance of poverty and actually made the situation worse
e. were able to reduce poverty in America, but had no effect on racial discrimination

11. What do opponents of privatizing Social Security argue?

a. that losses in the stock market could spell disaster for retirement funds
b. that private accounts are more susceptible to inflation
c. that private accounts may outpace current benefits
d. that privatization puts citizens in charge of their own retirement
e. that privatization would automatically shift the retirement age

12. The most important ratio for Social Security is that of _____.

a. beneficiaries to tax rates
b. contributions to the number of contributors
c. contributions to workers
d. tax rates to workers
e. workers to beneficiaries

13. What is the fundamental difference between how Americans and Europeans see poverty and social welfare?

a. American government is more generous with social welfare programs.
b. American unemployment rates are considerably higher.
c. Americans have a more positive attitude toward government.
d. Americans see them as individual concerns.
e. Americans see them as the responsibility of government.

14. The solutions to many problems of free enterprise were achieved through the democratic process in America. From which of the following did political pressure on these issues grow?

a. action to restrict unfair business practices
b. the demands of the middle class seeking fair taxes
c. the desire for shorter work days
d. the need for tax reform
e. the work of special interest groups

15. What is the key difference between liberal and conservative approaches to job creation?

a. Liberals advocate a Keynesian approach, while conservatives advocate laissez-faire.
b. Liberals are more concerned with unemployment than conservatives.
c. Liberals argue for government-created jobs and conservatives for business-created jobs.
d. Liberals argue for more blue-collar jobs and conservatives for more white-collar jobs.
e. Liberals argue to raise the minimum wage, while conservatives argue that will stop job creation.

Explore Further

WEB SITES

www.whitehouse.gov/cea
Reports of the President's Council of Economic Advisers, such as the annual Economic Report of the President.

www.federalreserve.gov
Information about the activities of the Federal Reserve Board.

www.aspe.hhs.gov/hsp/indicators-rtc/index.shtml
The Department of Health and Human Services issues an annual report to Congress on indicators of welfare dependence, which it posts at this site.

www.equalitytrust.org.uk/
A good site for information about inequality in the United States and other countries.

www.feedingamerica.org/
Information on who is going hungry in America and what is being done about it.

FURTHER READING

Alesina, Alberto, and Edward L. Glaeser. *Fighting Poverty in the US and Europe: A World of Difference.* New York: Oxford University Press, 2005. A systematic analysis of different approaches to the problems of domestic inequality and poverty.

Bartels, Larry M. *Unequal Democracy: The Political Economy of the New Gilded Age.* Princeton, NJ: Princeton University Press, 2008. A very influential analysis of the political causes and consequences of America's growing income gap.

Eberstadt, Nicholas. *The Poverty of 'The Poverty Rate': Measure and Mismeasure of Want in Modern America.* Washington, D.C.: American Enterprise Institute, 2008. Eberstadt argues that the official measurement of poverty is flawed, consistently overestimating the true extent of people living in desperate straits in America.

Gilens, Martin. *Why Americans Hate Welfare: Race, Media, and the Politics of Antipoverty Policy.* Chicago, IL: University of Chicago Press, 1999. Gilens argues that public opposition to

welfare is fed by a combination of racial and media stereotyping about the true nature of America's poor.

Gosling, James J. *Economics, Politics, and American Public Policy.* New York: M.E. Sharpe, 2007. A brief introduction to the politics of economic policy.

Haskins, Ron. *Work over Welfare: The Inside Story of the 1996 Welfare Reform Law.* Washington, D.C.: Brookings Institution, 2007. The most authoritative account of the passage of the landmark reform of welfare.

Iceland, John. *Poverty in America: A Handbook, with a 2012 Preface.* Berkeley, CA: University of California Press, 2012. A comprehensive review of poverty in America, examining how poverty is measured and understood, as well as how public policies have dealt with it over time.

Mishel, Lawrence et al. *The State of Working America*, 12th ed. Ithaca, NY: ILR Press, 2013. Prepared biennially by the Economic Policy Institute, this book includes a wide variety of data on family incomes, wages, taxes, unemployment, and other aspects of the American economy.

Page, Benjamin I., and Lawrence R. Jacobs. *Class War?* Chicago, IL: University of Chicago Press, 2009. An examination of what Americans think about economic equality and what they think the government should do about it.

Sloan, John. *The Reagan Effect.* Lawrence, KS: University Press of Kansas, 1999. The enduring effect of Ronald Reagan's supply-side economics on the economy and political system.

Vavreck, Lynn. *The Message Matters: The Economy and Presidential Campaigns.* Princeton, NJ: Princeton University Press, 2009. An excellent analysis of how presidential candidates have dueled over the economy in recent campaigns.

Wilkinson Richard, and Kate Pickett. *The Spirit Level: Why Greater Equality Makes Societies Stronger.* New York: Bloomsbury Press, 2009. A thought-provoking examination of how economic inequality is related to a host of social problems, employing data from the 50 U.S. states as well as other democracies.

17

Policymaking for Health Care, the Environment, and Energy

Politics in Action: The President Tries to Reform Health Care

O n September 9, 2009, President Barack Obama addressed a joint session of Congress on health care. He pointed out that it had been nearly a century since Theodore Roosevelt had called for health care reform. John Dingell, Sr., introduced a bill for comprehensive reform in 1943 and his son, who replaced him in the House, had been introducing the same bill for half a century. The health care system, the president said, was at the breaking point. Too many people lacked access to health care, and the costs for everyone were out of control. "We are . . . the only advanced democracy on Earth," the president proclaimed, "that allows such hardship for millions of its people."

17.1

Outline the problems of health care in America and the role of government in health care, p. 554.

17.2

Analyze the conflicts between economic growth and environmental protection, and identify the major national environmental protection policies, p. 564.

17.3

Evaluate the advantages and disadvantages of each of the principal sources of energy in the United States, p. 572.

17.4

Assess the role of democratic politics in making health care, environmental, and energy policy and the effect of these policies on the scope of government, p. 575.

Many Americans enjoy perhaps the best health care in the world. However, not all Americans, such those pictured here waiting to register for medical treatment in a rural health clinic, have effective access to health care. Providing this access is one of the most complex, contentious, and expensive issues of public policy.

Health Care Policy

here are few things more important to people than their health. Americans tend to believe they enjoy the best health care in the world. But is this true? What are the measures of health care? Do Americans enjoy the best health? And just how much are Americans paying for their health care? To what extent does everyone have access to state-of-the-art medical technology? And what role does government play in the financing, delivery, and regulation of health care? How does it make policy regarding health care?

Although Americans are generally healthy, which is unsurprising given the country's wealth, they lag behind a number of other countries in some key health care categories, such as life expectancy and the infant mortality rate (see "America in Perspective: The Costs and Benefits of Health Care").[1] The average life expectancy of 79 years is slightly lower than that in Canada and most other developed nations. Experts consider a nation's *infant mortality rate*—the proportion of babies who do not survive the first five years of life—a key indicator of the nation's health. The chances of a baby born in the United States dying in the first five years of life are more than twice as great as those of a baby born in Japan. Yet the United States spends more per person on health care than any other country. If there is a gap between U.S. expenditures on health care and results in terms of health, this gap may be partly explained by the U.S. health care system.

The Cost of Health Care

American health care costs are staggering. Americans now spend more than $2.9 *trillion* a year on health care. Health expenditures are one of the largest components of America's economy, accounting in 2012 for 17 percent of the gross domestic product (GDP),[2] a higher proportion than in any other country. Other democracies with developed economies, including Canada, Japan, the United Kingdom, France, and Germany, spend much less of their wealth on health care while providing universal health care coverage for their citizens.

They came to power.

Dealing with the crucial area of health care has never been easy. Passage of major legislation in the areas of the environment and energy has also proved difficult. President Obama proposed a plan to deal with greenhouse emissions and global warming, but it failed to pass. And nothing like a comprehensive national energy policy has ever passed, either.

Health, the environment, and energy all are central to human well-being and thus highly salient to both the public and policymakers. These are also highly technical areas requiring complex policies that are difficult for most people to understand and evaluate. In addition, these policy areas cut across the rest of American society. For example, the environment and energy production affect health and also economic development. Equally important, these areas seem to call for government action to solve problems that appear intractable.

Yet government action is difficult on such complex matters that involve so many segments of American life so fundamentally. These policy areas thus raise profound questions. Is American democracy capable of resolving such complex matters? And just what should the government's role be in dealing with them?

The president proposed a solution to the problems he identified, but many in the Congress and the public were not convinced. After a protracted battle, and despite significant public opposition, the president prevailed. Obama and his party paid for their victory, however, losing heavily in the 2010 midterm elections, and Republicans vowed to repeal the bill when they came to power.

America in Perspective

The Costs and Benefits of Health Care

American health care presents a paradox: as a nation, we spend a far larger share of our national income on health than any other industrialized country, in terms of both per capita spending and percentage of gross domestic product (GDP) spent on health care, yet we are far from having the healthiest population, as indicated by both life expectancy and the infant mortality rate.

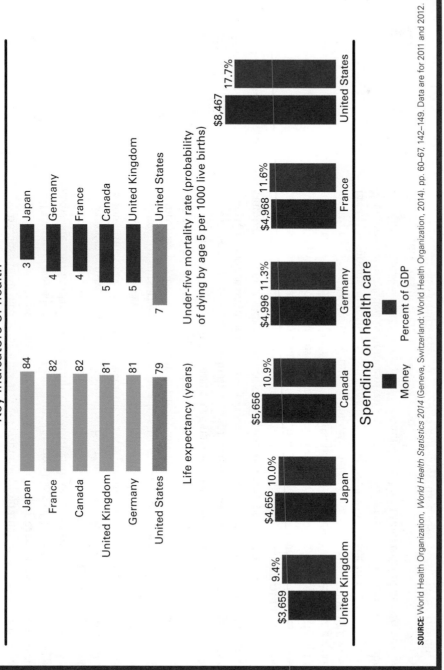

Key indicators of health

Life expectancy (years)

Japan	84
France	82
Canada	82
United Kingdom	81
Germany	81
United States	79

Under-five mortality rate (probability of dying by age 5 per 1000 live births)

Japan	3
Germany	4
France	4
Canada	5
United Kingdom	5
United States	7

Spending on health care

Money ■   Percent of GDP ■

Country	Money	Percent of GDP
United Kingdom	$3,659	9.4%
Japan	$4,656	10.0%
Canada	$5,656	10.9%
Germany	$4,996	11.3%
France	$4,968	11.6%
United States	$8,467	17.7%

SOURCE: World Health Organization, *World Health Statistics 2014* (Geneva, Switzerland: World Health Organization, 2014): pp. 60–67, 142–149. Data are for 2011 and 2012.

The costs of health care are a major obstacle to balancing the federal budget. Indeed, about one-fourth of all federal expenditures go for health care.[3] As President Clinton said shortly before taking office, "If I could wave a magic wand tomorrow and do one thing for this economy, I would bring health costs in line with inflation . . . because . . . that would free more money for people to invest in the plants and the production and the jobs of the future."[4]

Why are health care expenditures in the United States so high? Americans do not have more doctor visits or hospital stays than people in other countries. For example, Germans, the British, and others spend more nights in the hospital than Americans. And doctor visits per person have actually been declining in the United States.[5]

Other factors are behind the high cost of health care in America. American health providers have overbuilt medical care facilities (a substantial percentage of all hospital beds are vacant on any given day), and doctors and hospitals have few incentives to be more efficient. New technologies, drugs, and procedures often add to the cost of health care, including by addressing previously untreatable conditions and by providing better but more expensive care. Thus, much of the money that Americans pay for health care is spent on procedures and treatments, such as kidney dialysis and organ transplants, that may not be widely available in other countries and that may cost a lot—sometimes hundreds of thousands of dollars.

Part of the reason health care in the United States may rely excessively on expensive high-tech solutions is that medical bills are paid by a mixture of government funds, private insurance, and individuals' out-of-pocket payments; no one has primary responsibility for paying—or controlling—health care costs. In countries with national health care systems (or national health insurance), government policymakers have focused more on containing costs, especially administrative costs, as well as on ensuring equality of care. In the United States, cost containment and, as we will discuss, equality of care have taken a back seat to technological advances. To give one example, competition among urban hospitals to provide the most advanced care has led to duplication of expensive equipment and thus higher health costs.

Because insurance companies and government programs pay for most health care expenses, most patients have no reason to ask for cheaper care—they do not face the full financial consequences of their care. The providers of health care, such as physicians, are also insulated from competing with each other to offer less expensive care. In fact, with the rise in medical malpractice suits, doctors may be ordering extra tests, however expensive they may be, to ensure that they cannot be sued—an approach that is sometimes called "defensive medicine." Such practices drive up the costs of medical care for everyone. As doctors are hit with higher and higher costs for insurance against malpractice suits, they increase their fees to pay their premiums. Because insurance companies pay the bills, patients do not protest. However, increased costs associated with medical care are making insurance rates skyrocket.

Business groups are increasingly calling for relief from the high costs of health care. For example, they complain that their foreign competitors avoid the high costs of private insurance premiums because in many other countries governments, rather than employers, cover health insurance costs. And as many people who must seek medical care are uninsured or underinsured, employers complain that the rising insurance rates they must pay represent inflated premiums intended to cover the costs of care for the uninsured or underinsured. To combat rising rates, some employers attempt to reduce their burden by cutting out benefits, particularly benefits covered by government programs. At the same time, employers defend the more than $200 billion tax break, or subsidy, that they receive for providing health insurance to their employees. Yet employer-provided insurance often has high administrative costs, discourages labor mobility as employees fear losing their insurance, and continues to insulate people from the consequences of their health care costs.

Not only are health care costs high but they have also been rising rapidly, as Figure 17.1 shows. At this rate of increase, we will likely be spending 20 percent of our GDP for health care by 2020. The cost of premiums for family coverage for employer-based insurance has increased by 154 percent since 2000.[6] Because government is so deeply involved in health care, government's burden will soar as well. The two major government health care programs—Medicare and Medicaid—could amount to nearly a fourth of the GDP by 2050.

The inefficiencies of the U.S. health care system are part of the explanation for the gap between the high costs that Americans pay for health care and the health benefits they derive, a gap made clear by comparisons with other countries. Another part of the explanation can be found in Americans' unequal access to health care.

☐ Access to Health Care

Inequalities in health care and hence in health are a serious problem in America. Although the world's highest-quality care is available to some citizens, many poor and working-class Americans are relegated to an inferior health care system, because access to health insurance is not universal in the United States as it is in many countries.

Americans gain access to health care in a variety of ways. About two-thirds of Americans have private health insurance of some kind. The most common means of access is through private health insurance plans, generally obtained through employers

health maintenance organization
Organization contracted by individuals or insurance companies to provide health care for a yearly fee. Such network health plans limit the choice of doctors and treatments. More than half of Americans are enrolled in health maintenance organizations or similar programs.

FIGURE 17.1 THE RISING COSTS OF HEALTH CARE

The United States spends an enormous amount on health care, and these expenditures have risen rapidly over the past 50 years. Getting health care expenditures under control is one of the greatest challenges of both government and the health care industry.

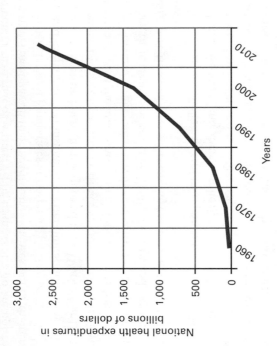

SOURCE: National Center for Health Statistics, *Health, United States, 2013* (Washington, D.C.: U.S. Government Printing Office, 2014), p. 331.

55 percent), sometimes obtained individually (9 percent). Individual policies are often significantly more expensive than policies obtained through employers, as employers are able to bargain for group rates with insurers.[7]

The traditional form of private insurance plans is the fee-for-service health insurance policy, in which a policyholder pays an annual premium and then is entitled to have the insurance company pay a certain amount of each medical service obtained during the year. This traditional system posed problems for cost containment in that it gave doctors incentives to provide additional, and perhaps unnecessary, services; in effect, the more treatments doctors provided, the more money they made. Moreover, doctors insisted that patients be able to choose their own physicians without restrictions, which made it impossible to contract with groups of doctors to provide services more economically.

In recent years, private market forces have changed the country's health care system dramatically, through the growth of managed care. Today, private insurance often takes the form of contracting with a **health maintenance organization** (HMO), a network of health care providers that directly provides all or most of a person's health care for a yearly fee. More than half of Americans are enrolled in HMOs or other forms of network health plans.

Managed care grew on the strength of its claims to provide better service at a lower cost. By focusing on prevention rather than treatment and by designating a single doctor as a patient's primary care provider, rather than having patients treated by different specialists with no central coordination or oversight, managed care was intended to improve health care and contain costs. Insurers negotiate with physician groups and hospitals on fees and costs and try to monitor care to control unnecessary use. At least three-fourths of all doctors have joined networks, signing contracts covering at least some of their patients to cut their fees and accept oversight of their medical decisions. Of course, HMOs have done nothing to ease the plight of those without health insurance.

Other Americans have access to health care through government programs. Nearly everyone 65 and older participates in Medicare, a government-subsidized program. Medicaid and the Children's Health Insurance Program, other government programs, cover more than 70 million people in families with low incomes.[8] (We discuss these programs later in this chapter.)

THE UNINSURED In 2012, 48 million people—15 percent of the public—were without health insurance coverage. The uninsured are disproportionately young, including more than 7 million children and nearly 15 million young adults. Minorities and those with low incomes are also more likely to lack health insurance,[9] and their health is likely to be poorer than that of whites.[10] The uninsured who are not covered by government programs must pay all their health care expenses out of their own pocket and are not able to benefit from group rates at hospitals.

Getting and keeping health insurance is often linked to having a job, especially a high-paying job. The reason is a historical quirk: during World War II, the federal government imposed a wage freeze, and to attract workers, many employers paid health benefits. Thus was forged the link between one's job and one's health insurance. Today, 55 percent of Americans get their health insurance from the workplace.[11] Often, the lack of health insurance is associated with short periods of unemployment—or with working part time, as part-time employees may not be eligible for employer insurance plans.

Although insurance is linked to employment, the majority of the nation's uninsured are full-time workers (and their families), most of whom work for companies with 100 or fewer employees and earn low wages. Small companies have to pay more for health insurance than larger companies do, mostly because health risks and marketing and administrative costs cannot be spread as broadly. Thus, many small companies have found providing health insurance too costly. In addition, some companies have cut back on benefits to dependents of workers. As a result, even if parents have coverage through their employers, their children may be uninsured.

Millions of Americans have inadequate insurance and receive less and poorer quality health care than do those with more comprehensive insurance. These individuals, much like those without insurance, often postpone treatment until illnesses worsen and require more expensive emergency treatment. Insurance can also be inadequate because of the share of the cost that people have to pay themselves, costs that can leave policyholders with significant debt should a medical crisis occur. In part because of such problems, many workers who are offered health insurance by their employers or unions do not take it.

As the foregoing discussion suggests, access to health insurance in the United States is closely tied to income. In 2012, 25 percent of those with household incomes of less than $25,000 per year lacked health insurance, despite the existence of government-subsidized programs such as Medicaid and Medicare. Among these low-income households are many single-mother households; the uninsured include 9 percent of all children, although the percentage of children who are uninsured varies considerably from state to state. Access to health insurance is also tied to race and ethnicity. Thus, 29 percent of Hispanics and 19 percent of African Americans lack health insurance, compared to 11 percent of non-Hispanic whites.[12]

For Americans who lack health insurance, the problem is not lack of access to the most up-to-date research and equipment but, rather, the more fundamental problem of lack of access to a family doctor or someone to administer prenatal and neonatal care. Americans without insurance tend not to see health care professionals regularly and are less likely to receive preventive care; children have less access to well-child care, immunizations, basic dental services, and prescription medication.[13] Studies have found that many Americans do without health care, postpone it, or resort to emergency rooms for minor illnesses (see "Young People & Politics: Health Insurance, Emergency Rooms, and Young Americans").[14] To an even greater extent than with the underinsured, when the uninsured receive care, the care is typically poorer quality, and medical problems can quickly lead to medical debt.[15] Some Americans who lack insurance and are confronted with serious illness have resorted to "medical migration," outsourcing their medical care to cheaper foreign hospitals, for example, in India.[16]

Young People & Politics

Health Insurance, Emergency Rooms, and Young Americans

Health insurance can be expensive, and young people often lack discretionary income. For this reason, and because they are less likely than their elders to have jobs with benefits and less likely to worry about health issues, Americans between 19 and 35 have been disproportionately uninsured; nearly 30 percent have lacked health insurance. The mandate in the Affordable Care Act to purchase health insurance may seem like an unfair burden. But was it?

Although young people are less likely to become seriously ill than older adults (chances of getting heart disease or cancer increase with age), they are more likely to be injured, particularly in traffic accidents—and these often require expensive emergency care. Teens are also twice as likely as adults to be hurt on the job. Except for the very old (those over 75), young adults are the biggest users of emergency rooms.

In response to charges that emergency rooms were denying service to patients unable to pay, Congress in 1986 passed the Emergency Medical Treatment and Labor Act (EMTALA). EMTALA makes it illegal for emergency rooms to turn people away. Still, as a patient in the emergency room, one of the first questions you are likely to be asked is, "What insurance do you have?" Because young adults have had a harder time answering that question than did any other age group, a trip to the emergency room could leave them with big medical debts at a time when they are trying to establish a good credit history.

Emergency rooms provide critical care, but they are the most expensive single component of the health care system. In addition, when people cannot pay their bills, often because they lack health insurance, the costs of providing emergency care are shifted to others using the hospital. In effect, many young adults shifted the burden of paying for their health care to older adults. One consequence of the mandate to have health insurance is that young adults will now be paying their own way.

CRITICAL THINKING QUESTIONS

1. Should young Americans—or all Americans—be required to purchase health insurance, just as they are required to purchase collision insurance on their cars?

2. Should emergency rooms be required by law to treat everyone who comes in?

SOURCES: Centers for Disease Control and Prevention, *National Health Interview Survey* (Washington, D.C.: U.S. Government Printing Office, 2014); National Center for Health Statistics, *Health, United States, 2013* (Washington, D.C.: U.S. Government Printing Office, 2014).

The uninsured are more likely to be hospitalized for conditions that could have been prevented, and more likely to die in the hospital than those with insurance.[17] Lack of health insurance has been estimated to cause tens of thousands of preventable deaths each year.[18] Long-term studies show that people without health insurance face a 25 percent higher risk of dying than those with insurance.[19] When poor people are given medical insurance, they not only find regular doctors and see doctors more often but they also feel better, are less depressed, and are better able to maintain financial stability.[20]

The racial and ethnic disparities in access to health care are reflected in differences between groups in measures of health. Average life expectancy is five years longer for whites than for African Americans. In fact, average life expectancy for African American males is lower than in many Eastern European and less developed countries. Not all of this difference can be explained by variances in lifestyles and nutrition. Similarly, African American infant mortality is twice as high as that for whites.[21] For both life expectancy and infant mortality, lack of insurance appears to play a significant role in explaining the differences.

Factors affecting health in early childhood and throughout life begin prenatally, but, as a result of lack of access to health care, many pregnant women, especially in the nation's inner cities, do not obtain the care needed to ensure that their babies will be born healthy. Lacking an obstetrician or family doctor (poor neighborhoods, urban and rural, have too few doctors), these women may not get prenatal care for most of their pregnancy. This is yet another example of the point made earlier: often, availability of family doctors and routine hospital services is more important in determining the quality of a nation's health care than is availability of high-tech medical equipment.

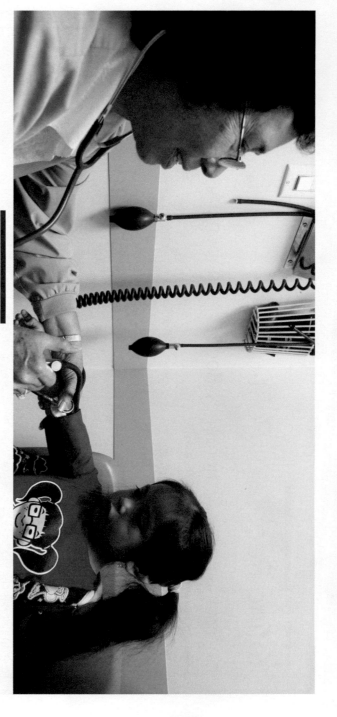

There are substantial disparities in access to health care in America. Those with less access, such as this child, are likely to live shorter and less healthy lives than those with more access.

RATIONING HEALTH CARE Disparities in access together with the great cost of many potentially lifesaving procedures of modern medicine raise important and complicated questions of public policy. Dollars spent on expensive procedures to save a few lives cannot be spent on other pressing health care needs. Thus, for example, when the government allows Medicare payments for certain procedures, less money may be available for rural hospitals or for health clinics in poor areas of the nation's cities.

Although many Americans vehemently oppose "rationing" of medical care, such rationing in effect goes on all the time in our system.[22] Much rationing is informal; physicians and families quietly agree not to provide further care to a loved one. Some of it is formal. Virtually every insurance plan sets limits to the services for which it will pay and for total payments. Medical boards have elaborate rules for allocating donated organs. Oregon has taken the lead on the issue of rationing health care, trying to set priorities for medical treatments under its Medicaid program. By not providing some costly treatments that might save or prolong people's lives, the Oregon program is able to use its resources to provide medical care for a larger pool of people. Evidence shows that Oregon's effort works well and that patient satisfaction is higher than before the plan was implemented.[23]

☐ The Role of Government in Health Care

Americans often think insurance companies pay most health care costs, but in fact the government pays more of the costs than does the private insurance industry. National, state, and local governments pay for 42 percent of the total cost of health services and supplies, mostly through Medicare and Medicaid. Moreover, the government subsidizes employer-provided health insurance with tax breaks worth nearly $200 billion per year. Many hospitals are connected to public universities, and much medical research is financed through the National Institutes of Health and other federal agencies. More than 20,000 physicians work for the federal government, most providing health care for the armed forces and veterans, and nearly all the rest receive payments from it. The government thus plays an important health care role in America, although less so than in other countries.

One-third of the public receive benefits from the government Medicaid or Medicare programs (some people have both Medicare and private insurance), and 14 million people receive government-provided health care through the military.[24]

Passed by Congress in 1965, **Medicare**, health care insurance for the elderly, is part of the Social Security system and covers nearly 51 million people, or about 16 percent

Medicare
A program added to the Social Security system in 1965 that provides hospitalization insurance for the elderly and permits older Americans to purchase inexpensive coverage for doctor fees and other medical expenses.

of the population.[25] As with Social Security, paycheck deductions include payments into Medicare and, when a person becomes eligible, he or she receives the benefits. Part A of Medicare provides hospitalization insurance and short-term nursing care; Part B, which is voluntary, permits older Americans to purchase inexpensive coverage for doctor fees and other nonhospital medical expenses. Part D, which went into effect in 2006, covers much of the cost of prescription drugs.

In another parallel with Social Security, Medicare costs are outrunning tax contributions to the Medicare Trust Fund. Medicare is the most rapidly increasing component of the federal budget. It currently costs about $529 billion in 2015, accounting for about 14 percent of the budget,[26] and without reform, this percentage will soar. To save money, Medicare has frequently cut back on the fees it pays doctors and hospitals. As a result, some doctors and hospitals do not accept Medicare patients, because Medicare payments for services do not cover their costs.

Despite such cuts, Medicare expenditures keep growing, in part because of Medicare's vocal constituency. The elderly are one of the most powerful voting and lobbying forces in American politics. AARP, formerly known as the American Association of Retired Persons, has grown from about 150,000 members in 1959 to about 40 million today, making it the largest voluntary association in the world. This single group now can claim to represent one American in eight. Not only does AARP relentlessly advocate increasing Medicare benefits but elderly Americans dependent on Social Security and Medicare actively participate in American elections.[27] In addition, powerful organizations representing hospitals and doctors lobby for Medicare to pay for the latest techniques and procedures. Health care policy that favors the elderly is one of the results of this interest group activity. When Congress, in 1989, passed a Social Security surtax designed to pay for new catastrophic illness coverage, the elderly objected, and the next year Congress repealed the tax.

For workers in low-paying service jobs that do not include health insurance, and for those who are unemployed and cannot afford private health insurance, there is no organization capable of exerting such influence in government. Because many of these people do not vote, the bias in representation is even greater. Nevertheless, the nation has spent substantial sums to provide health care for the poor.

Medicaid, the program designed to provide health care for the poor (including the elderly poor), also passed in 1965 and serves more than 62 million people, most of whom are children and adults in low-income families. The remainder is disabled or elderly, many of them requiring long-term care. Nine million people are covered by both Medicaid and Medicare.[28] The current cost of Medicaid to the federal government is $331 billion a year.[29] Medicaid is funded by both the states and the national government, and eligibility and services vary by state. The costs to states for Medicaid are about $183 billion,[30] and Medicaid expenditures compose nearly a quarter of state budgets. Medicaid covers 70 percent of nursing home residents, 60 percent of low-income children, 41 percent of all women giving birth, 27 percent of low-income adults, and 20 percent of people with severe disabilities.[31] The program now pays about one-fifth of the expenditures for health care in the United States and about half of expenditures for nursing-home care.[32]

Created in 1997, the *Children's Health Insurance Program* (CHIP) is a state and federal partnership that targets uninsured children and pregnant women in families with incomes too high to qualify for most state Medicaid programs but, often, too low to afford private coverage. It serves about 8 million children.[33] Within federal guidelines, each state determines the design of its CHIP, including eligibility parameters, benefit packages, payment levels for coverage, and administrative procedures.

Reform Efforts

More than 60 years ago, Harry S. Truman called for **national health insurance**, a compulsory insurance program to finance all Americans' medical care. The American Medical Association opposed the idea, disparaging it as "socialized medicine" because

Medicaid
A public assistance program designed to provide health care for poor Americans and funded by both the states and the national government.

national health insurance
A compulsory insurance program for all Americans that would have the government finance citizens' medical care. First proposed by President Harry S. Truman.

the program would be government run. Truman's proposal went nowhere. Although every other industrial nation in the world has adopted some form of national health insurance, the United States remained the exception.

Why It Matters to You
National Health Insurance

The United States, unlike all other developed nations, does not have national health insurance. Would Americans have more access to health care if we adopted such a system? Would they receive better or worse quality of care under a policy of national health insurance?

BILL CLINTON Nearly a half-century later, President Bill Clinton made health care reform the centerpiece of his first administration. His five-pound, 1,342-page Health Security Act proposal in 1993 was an effort to deal with the two great problems of health care policy: costs and access. The difficulties the president faced with this proposal reveal much about the challenge of reforming health care in America.[34]

Clinton's main concern was guaranteeing health care coverage for all Americans. His plan would particularly have benefited people without any health insurance, but it would also have extended coverage for millions of others with inadequate health insurance.

Paying for the plan would have necessitated either broad-based taxes, which were politically unpalatable, or a requirement that employers provide health insurance for their employees or pay a premium into a public fund (which would also cover Medicaid and Medicare recipients). The president chose the employer insurance option, but the small business community was adamantly opposed to bearing the cost of providing health insurance. The president also proposed raising taxes on cigarettes, which angered the tobacco industry, and imposing a small tax on other large companies.

Because the White House reform plan for health care was bureaucratic and complicated, it was easy for opponents to label it a government takeover of the health care system. An aggressive advertising campaign mounted by the health insurance industry characterized the president's plan as being expensive and experimental, as providing lower-quality and rationed care, and as killing jobs. The health insurance industry's famous "Harry and Louise" ads—in which Harry and Louise, sitting at their kitchen table, mull over the Clinton plan and conclude, "There's got to be a better way"—were one of the most effective policy-oriented campaigns in history.

In addition, the middle class felt its health care threatened. Gallup polls found that the public saw Clinton's health care reform proposal as a Democratic social welfare program that would help the poor, hurt the middle class, and create bigger government. In the end, there was more concern about too much government with the plan than there was about too little health insurance without it.[35] After a long and tortuous battle, the plan died in Congress.

BARACK OBAMA Early in his administration, Barack Obama made comprehensive health care reform a top priority in domestic policy. After a tumultuous battle in Congress, and without the support of public opinion, the Affordable Care Act passed in 2010. For those who already had health insurance, the new law

- ends discrimination by health insurance companies against people with preexisting conditions.

- prevents insurance companies from dropping coverage when people become sick and needed it most.

- allows young people to remain on their parents' insurance until the age of 26.

- caps out-of-pocket expenses for the insured.

17.1

17.2

17.3

17.4

563

- eliminate extra charges for preventive care like mammograms, flu shots, and diabetes tests.
- closes a gap in Medicare's coverage for prescription drugs.

The law also dealt with those who lacked health insurance by

- requiring large employers to provide health insurance for their employees.
- requiring everyone to have health insurance (so that everyone would contribute to the pool of resources for health care and contribute to the costs of their own health care).
- creating new insurance marketplace or exchanges that would allow people without insurance, as well as small businesses, to compare plans and buy insurance at competitive prices.
- providing tax credits to help people buy health insurance and to help small businesses cover their employees.
- expanding Medicaid eligibility.

Businesses complained about the costs of covering employees. Others criticized the requirement that everyone have health insurance limited individuals' freedom of choice. Although the president claimed that his reform proposal would not add to the budget deficit because it was possible to cut costs in the health care system and reform medical malpractice law, not everyone agreed.

Obama faced a strategic problem in attempting to reform the health care system without igniting fears that people could lose what they liked about their own health care. Most people were reasonably satisfied with the quality of their own medical care. They worried that if the government guaranteed health coverage, they would see declines in the quality of their own care, limits on their ability to choose doctors and get needed treatment, and increases in their out-of-pocket health costs and tax bills.[36]

An equally important obstacle to reforming health care was the general political climate. The president had to propose enormous expenditures to combat the economic crisis he inherited, running up record deficits in the process. These policies made the country risk averse. Moreover, comprehensive reform of such a large sector of the economy is inherently complex policy, making it difficult to explain and easy for opponents to caricature.

President Obama made reforming health care a top priority, but he faces widespread resistance. Here he speaks for reform shortly before the final congressional vote on his plan.

Despite all his and his administration's efforts, the president never obtained the support of a majority—or even plurality—of the public for health care reform. Nevertheless, the White House and the Democratic majorities in Congress pushed through an historic comprehensive health care reform bill, the Affordable Care Act, in 2010, with the potential to extend health insurance coverage to 32 million people.

This success cost the Democrats a number of seats in the 2010 congressional elections,[37] and Republicans in the House have voted to repeal all or part of the law numerous times. They also challenged the constitutionality of the mandate to have health insurance. In 2012, the Supreme Court upheld the mandate but allowed states to opt out of extending Medicaid coverage, and nearly half of them have done so.

The start-up of the new law further complicated matters. When people initially went to the relevant Web sites to sign up for health insurance, they found the sites did not work properly. It took several months to remedy the problem, irritating and confusing people in the process—and giving opponents additional opportunities to call for the law's repeal. By the summer of 2014, however, 13 million people had obtained new health insurance through the ACA.

Environmental Policy

17.2 Analyze the conflicts between economic growth and environmental protection, and identify the major national environmental protection policies.

T he natural environment might seem to be above politics. After all, public opinion analyst Louis Harris reported that "the American people's desire to battle pollution is one of the most overwhelming and clearest we have ever recorded"[38] Concern for the environment is further reflected in the rapid growth of environmental groups.

As in other areas, however, there is significant politically charged debate over the environment. Attempts to control air quality or limit water pollution often encounter political opposition because of their impact on business, economic growth, and jobs; hence, policymaking choices are involved. And although Americans may be generally in favor of "doing something" about the environment, specific proposals, for example, to limit suburban growth, encourage carpooling, increase taxes on gasoline, or limit access to national parks, have met with strong resistance.

☐ Economic Growth and the Environment

Nobody is against cleaning up and preserving the environment. Political questions arise because environmental concerns often conflict with equally legitimate concerns about economic growth and jobs. Pollution is generated in the course of making cars, producing electricity, and providing food and the consumer products that Americans take for granted. On federally owned land, including national parks and forests, there has long been a policy of multiple use whereby mining, lumbering, and grazing leases are awarded to private companies or ranchers at very low cost. Often the industries supported by these arrangements are important sources of jobs in otherwise depressed areas, and they may also help lessen the country's dependence on foreign sources of oil and minerals. For most of American history, pollution was seen simply as an inevitable byproduct of economic growth.

Although the conservation movement began in the nineteenth century, it was in the 1960s and 1970s that environmental interest groups exploded in both size and number. Today, for example, the National Wildlife Federation has nearly 4.5 million members; Greenpeace USA, the World Wildlife Fund, and the Conservation Foundation have more than a million members each; and the Sierra Club, the Clean

Water Action Project, the Nature Conservancy, and the National Audubon Society have more than a half-million members each. And there are numerous other environmental groups, ranging from the Wilderness Society to the Center for Health, Environment & Justice.

As science clarified the impact of environmental degradation and as old groups evolved into active political organizations and new groups formed and grew, the environment became a more important policymaking concern. If at first many politicians viewed these new lobbyists with skepticism, over time the environmental movement became more influential. Now politicians of both parties seek the support of environmental groups when they run for office. Issues once considered only from the standpoint of jobs and economic growth are now also considered from an environmental standpoint.

The fact that environmental considerations now come into play is apparent, for example, in debates about local and state economic development. In the federal system, states compete for economic advantage. States and cities push to attract large investments, such as automobile plants, as new business can be a boon to their economies. Business elites can argue that stringent pollution-control laws will prevent new businesses from coming and drive businesses away by driving up their costs. But states with lax pollution enforcement may find their citizens unhappy and residents of other states, including those who might relocate with new businesses, reluctant to move there. Moreover, costs to a state of enforcing pollution legislation may be offset by savings in health care costs achieved by reducing health risks to residents. Thus, state competition does not always work against pollution standards. In fact, sometimes states compete with each other to enforce tighter pollution and land use controls. Many states today—including California, which has the most stringent antipollution laws in the country—are betting that legislation designed to achieve environmental goals will not have a negative economic impact on the state.

Conflicts between economic growth and environmental goals are apparent in Alaska and the Northwest, with political battles pitting lumbering interests against national and local environmental groups. Lumbering provides jobs, but it decimates

Coastal states often desire the jobs provided by offshore drilling. Yet they may also find their coast lines covered with oily sludge, and their tourism and fishing industries adversely affected. Here workers try to protect the Louisiana coast line from the BP oil spill in 2010.

Environmental Protection Agency

The largest federal independent regulatory agency, created in 1970 to administer much of U.S. environmental protection policy.

National Environmental Policy Act

Passed in 1969, the centerpiece of federal environmental policy, which requires agencies to file environmental impact statements.

environmental impact statement

A detailing of a proposed policy's environmental effects, which agencies are required to file with the EPA every time they propose to undertake a policy that might be disruptive to the environment.

old-growth trees in Alaska's Tongass National Forest and on public lands in Oregon and Washington. Environmentalists complain that some of the few remaining large tracts of virgin forest are being felled by logging companies operating under generous lease agreements with the U.S. government. Similarly, oil exploration on public lands and offshore in coastal waters brings the goals of environmental protection and economic growth into conflict. The mammoth BP oil spill in the Gulf of Mexico in 2010, like the *Exxon Valdez* spill off the Alaskan coast in 1989, demonstrated the environmental risks of oil exploration. Yet Alaskans and Louisianans are keen on the jobs that oil provides and the revenues from oil that keeps their taxes low.

The very success of the environmental movement in passing laws designed to protect public health and to preserve or restore the environment has spawned a backlash. Opponents of strict environmental protection laws demand evidence that policies are accomplishing their goals. Arguing that the effects of environmental regulations on employment, economic growth, and international competitiveness must be part of the policymaking equation, they insist that Congress and the bureaucracy subject regulations to cost–benefit analysis to determine that they do not cost more than the benefits they create. Others, especially ranchers, miners, farmers, and the timber industry, demand inexpensive access to public land and the right to use their own property as they wish or else be compensated by government for being prohibited from doing so.

In arguing for a more cautious approach to environmental protection, opponents also point to mistakes that have been made. For example, in the early 1980s, government scientists argued that exposure to asbestos could cause thousands of cancer deaths. Because asbestos was used as insulation in schools and public buildings, parents and others reacted with alarm. In 1985, Congress approved a sweeping law that led cities and states to spend between $15 billion and $20 billion to remove asbestos from public buildings. But in 1990, Environmental Protection Agency officials admitted that ripping out the asbestos had been an expensive mistake; the removal often sent tiny asbestos fibers into the air. Now the agency's advice is that, unless asbestos is damaged or crumbling, it be left untouched.

☐ Environmental Policies in America

Until the early 1960s, what environmental policies existed focused largely on conservation and the national parks. Created in 1970, the **Environmental Protection Agency** (EPA) is now the nation's largest federal regulatory agency. The EPA has a wide-ranging mission; it is charged with administering policies dealing with land use, air and water quality, and wilderness and wildlife preservation.

ENVIRONMENTAL IMPACTS The centerpiece of federal environmental policy is the **National Environmental Policy Act (NEPA)**, passed in 1969.[39] This law requires government agencies to file an **environmental impact statement (EIS)** with the EPA every time they propose to undertake a policy that is potentially disruptive to the natural environment. The EIS details possible environmental effects of the proposed policy. Big dams and small post offices, major port construction and minor road widening—proposals for all these projects must include an EIS.

Strictly speaking, an environmental impact statement is merely a procedural requirement. In practice, the filing of impact statements alerts environmentalists to proposed projects. Environmentalists can then take agencies to court for violating the act's procedural requirements if the agencies file incomplete or inaccurate impact statements. Because environmental impacts are usually so complicated and difficult to predict, it is relatively easy to argue that the statements are either incomplete or inaccurate in some way. Agencies have often argued that the statements are either incomplete or inaccurate in some way. Agencies have often abandoned proposed projects to avoid prolonged court battles with environmental groups.

The law does not give the environmental groups the right to stop any environmentally unsound activities, but it does give them the opportunity to delay construction so much that agencies simply give up. Chances are that many of the biggest public works projects of the past century—including the Hoover Dam, Kennedy Airport, Cape Canaveral's space facility, and most Tennessee Valley Authority projects—would not have survived the environmental scrutiny to which they would have been subject had they been undertaken after the NEPA was enacted. In any case, the NEPA has been an effective tool in preventing environmental despoilation.

CLEAN AIR Another landmark piece of legislation affecting the environment is the **Clean Air Act of 1970**, which charges the EPA with protecting and improving the quality of the nation's air, to minimize people's exposure to airborne contaminants. Among its provisions is that the Department of Transportation (DOT) undertake to reduce automobile emissions. For years after the act's passage, fierce battles raged between the automakers and the DOT about how stringent the requirements had to be. Automakers claimed it was impossible to meet DOT standards; the DOT claimed that automakers were dragging their feet in the hope that Congress would delay or weaken the requirements. Although Congress did weaken the requirements, the smaller size of American cars, the use of unleaded gasoline, and the lower gas consumption of new cars are all due in large part to DOT regulations.

Over time, Congress has reauthorized the Clean Air Act and significantly increased the controls on cars, oil refineries, chemical plants, and coal-fired utility plants. In particular, the reauthorization in 1990 was the strongest step forward in the fight to clean the air since the bill's original passage. As a result of federal policies, air pollution from toxic organic compounds and sulfur dioxide has decreased substantially since 1970.

CLEAN WATER Congress acted to control pollution of the nation's lakes and rivers with the **Water Pollution Control Act of 1972**. This law was enacted in reaction to the tremendous pollution of Northeastern rivers and the Great Lakes. Since its passage, water quality has improved dramatically. In 1972, only one-third of U.S. lakes and rivers were safe for fishing and drinking. Today, the fraction has doubled to two-thirds. And with less polluted waters, the number of waterfowl has increased substantially.

Nevertheless, federal laws regulate only "point sources"—places where pollutants can be dumped in the water, such as a paper mill along a river. What is hard to regulate is the most important cause of water pollution, "runoff" from streets, roads, fertilized lawns, farms, and service stations.

WILDERNESS PRESERVATION One component of the environment that has received special attention is wilderness—those areas that are largely untouched by human activities. Wilderness preservation is important to biodiversity and for recreational purposes and symbolic reasons as well. The founding of the National Park System in 1916 put the United States in the forefront of wilderness preservation. Among the most consistently successful environmental campaigns have been those aimed at preserving wild lands,[40] and there are now 378 national parks and 155 national forests. Still, only about 4 percent of the land in the United States is designated as wilderness, and half of that is in Alaska. The strains of overuse may make it necessary to restrict the public's access to national parks so they may be preserved for future generations. And wilderness areas come under increasing pressure from those, such as logging and mining interests, who stress the economic benefits lost by keeping them intact.

ENDANGERED SPECIES Preserving wilderness areas indirectly helps protect wildlife. National policy protects wildlife in other, more direct ways as well. The **Endangered Species Act of 1973**, for example, created an endangered species protection program in the U.S. Fish and Wildlife Service. More important, the law required the government to actively protect each of the hundreds of species listed as endangered, regardless of the economic consequences for the areas that were the habitats of the species. During the Reagan administration, the act was amended to allow exceptions in cases of overriding national or regional interest. A cabinet-level

Clean Air Act of 1970
The law aimed at combating air pollution, by charging the EPA with protecting and improving the quality of the nation's air.

Water Pollution Control Act of 1972
A law intended to clean up the nation's rivers and lakes by enabling regulation of point sources of pollution.

Endangered Species Act of 1973
A law requiring the federal government to protect all species listed as endangered.

You Are the Policymaker

How Much Should We Do to Save a Species?
The Florida Manatee

The manatee is a plump, squinty-eyed, walrus-like freshwater mammal, 9 to 10 feet in length and weighing in at about 1,000 pounds. Manatees are friendly and intelligent animals that spend most of the day sleeping in the water, surfacing for air regularly at intervals no greater than 20 minutes and grazing in shallow waters at depths of 3 to 7 feet. They may live up to 60 years. Because manatees cannot survive very long in water below 68 degrees Fahrenheit, Florida is the manatee's natural winter range. They congregate around warm water springs and man-made sources of warm water such as power plant discharges.

One of the major killers of manatees is the propellers on the thousands of boats in Florida's lakes and rivers. Biologists even use scar patterns from the propellers to identify individual manatees. Another significant threat is loss of reliable warm water habitats that allow manatees to survive the cold in winter. Natural springs are threatened by increased demands for water supply, and aging power plants may need to be replaced. Sea grass and other aquatic foods that manatees depend on are affected by water pollution. Some people think the money could be better spent.

The manatee is one of the charter members of the endangered species list. They are also protected under the Federal Marine Mammal Protection Act. Thus, two federal laws make it illegal to harm, harass,

injure, or kill manatees. In addition, Florida passed laws, including the Florida Manatee Sanctuary Act, to protect its unique marine mammal.

If a species is on the endangered species list, both the federal and state governments must enact policies to protect its habitat. Nearly one-quarter of Florida's canals, rivers, and lakes were designated as manatee protection areas. Any construction project had to come to a halt if a manatee appeared within 100 feet and could resume only if the animal left—as the regulation put it—"of its own volition." Boating was curtailed. Fishing was limited. Canal locks were refitted at a substantial cost.

In this case, then, as often occurs, the Endangered Species Act collided with other interests—economic growth, property rights, and recreational activities. The Coastal Conservation Association of Florida, a pro-fishing group, produced data to show that the manatee population was increasing, and that regulations should be reduced and the habitat restrictions eased. (Environmentalists challenged the data.) Developers wanted more flexibility to develop property. The direct costs of protecting the manatee so far have been more than 10 million dollars. Some

What do you think? When have we done enough to save a species? How much should we sacrifice to save a species?

SOURCES: U.S. Fish and Wildlife Service, *Federal and State Endangered and Threatened Species Expenditures, Fiscal Year 2010*, Craig Pittman, "Fury over a Gentle Giant," *Smithsonian Magazine*, February 2004, 55–59.

committee, quickly labeled "The God Squad," was established to decide such cases. As EPA chief William Reilly explained, "The God Squad is a group of people, of which I am a minor divinity, which has the power to blow away a species."[41]

Because endangered species are increasingly threatened by expanding human populations and growing demands for development, implementation of the act has often been controversial. Bringing back the wolves in Yellowstone has a certain appeal to many Americans but not to neighboring ranchers. As of 2014, the endangered species list included 467 animal and 720 plant species in the United States.[42] (For a look at policy issues related to saving a particular species, see "You Are the Policymaker: How Much Should We Do to Save a Species? The Florida Manatee.")

TOXIC WASTES Long before the environmental movement began, polluters created problems that are still unresolved. For example, during the 1940s and 1950s, Hooker Chemical Company dumped toxic wastes near the shores of the Love Canal in New York. In 1953, the company generously donated a 16-acre plot next to the canal to build a school. In the 1970s, investigators discovered tons of chemicals, some in rotting barrels, and adults were later found to have developed liver, kidney, and other health problems linked to the chemicals. The level of contamination was high, and Hooker Chemical Company had gone out of business. With Love Canal, and the

Superfund
A fund created by Congress in 1980 to clean up hazardous waste sites.

identification of a huge number of other toxic waste dumps, popular outcry led to action from Washington.[43]

In 1980, Congress established a **Superfund**, a fund to clean up toxic waste sites, created by taxing chemical products. The law that established the fund specified that polluters were responsible for paying for cleanups; the fund was to be used when polluters could not be identified. A controversial retroactive liability provision held companies liable even for legal dumping prior to 1980. The law also contained strict provisions for liability, under which the government could hold a single party liable for cleaning up an entire site that had received waste from many sources.[44]

The Comprehensive Environmental Response, Compensation, and Liability Act (the formal name of the Superfund law) has virtually eliminated haphazard dumping of toxic wastes, including through prohibitions and requirements it established, but it has been less successful in cleaning up existing waste. In endless rounds of litigation that ensued, companies facing multimillion-dollar cleanup bills tried to recover some of their costs by suing smaller companies that had contributed to the hazardous waste, and companies fought with their insurers over whether policies written in the early 1980s covered Superfund-related costs.[45]

The EPA, which administers the Superfund law, has located and analyzed tens of thousands of hazardous waste sites. Cleaning up sites can take many years and cost millions of dollars each. The agency has cleaned more than 1,100 sites, and work is going on at more than 400 additional sites. Nevertheless, there are hundreds of additional sites requiring cleaning in 49 states and the District of Columbia. Originally, a tax on oil and chemical companies funded the Superfund, but the tax expired in 1995. The fund now depends on general revenues, which have been in short supply, slowing the rate of cleanup.

Policies in addition to the Superfund law also require monitoring and regulation of the use and disposal of hazardous wastes. Regulations mandated by the Resource Conservation and Recovery Act of 1977, for example, require "cradle-to-grave" tracking of many toxic chemicals, specify how these chemicals are to be handled while in use or in transit, and prescribe certain disposal techniques.

NUCLEAR WASTE Another serious environmental challenge is the disposal of nuclear waste, such as that from nuclear reactors and the production of nuclear weapons. Nuclear waste must be isolated to protect not only us but also people in the distant future, as these materials can take millennia to decay to the point at which they are safe. Tens of thousands of tons of highly radioactive nuclear waste are sitting in temporary sites around the country, most of them near nuclear power plants. Congress has studied, debated, and fretted for years over where to store the nation's nuclear waste. In the 1980s, Congress envisioned that spent nuclear fuel would be consolidated and permanently buried. It designated Yucca Mountain in Nevada as the provisional site in 1987. Questions about the safety and cost of the site and the vehement opposition from Nevada's congressional delegation have delayed the implementation of the plan. Although President Bush signed off on the plan in 2002, President Obama reversed the decision in 2009, and we still have no national storage site in the United States.

It is not surprising that no state is eager to have a storage area for nuclear wastes within its boundaries. Nevertheless, nuclear waste keeps accumulating. Widening opposition to potentially hazardous industrial facilities, such as toxic or nuclear waste dumps, has further complicated environmental policymaking in recent years. Local groups have often successfully organized resistance to planned development, rallying behind the cry, "Not In My Back Yard!"[46] The so-called NIMBY phenomenon highlights another difficult dilemma in environmental policy: how can government equitably distribute the costs associated with society's seemingly endless demand for new technologies, some of which turn out to be environmentally threatening? If, for example, we are to use nuclear power to keep our lights on, the waste it produces must go in someone's backyard. But whose?

global warming
The increase in the earth's temperatures that, according to most scientists, is occurring as a result of the carbon dioxide that is produced when fossil fuels are burned collecting in the atmosphere and trapping energy from the sun.

Why It *Matters* to You

"NIMBY"

Most Americans say "NIMBY"—not in my backyard—when government proposes locating unwanted waste dumps, toxic disposal sites, and other unhealthy land uses near their homes. Should government give every neighborhood a veto over having to house wastes? If every community, even sparsely populated areas, had a veto, where would society dispose of its hazardous materials?

☐ Global Warming

One of the most intractable and potentially serious environmental issues is **global warming.** When fossil fuels (coal, oil, and natural gas—the remnants of ancient plants and animals) are burned, they produce carbon dioxide. It, along with smaller quantities of methane and other gases, collects in the atmosphere, wrapping the earth in an added layer of insulation and heating the climate. The "greenhouse effect" occurs when energy from the sun is trapped under the atmosphere and warms the earth as a result, much as in a greenhouse. The deforestation of trees capable of absorbing pollutants, mainly carbon dioxide, reinforces this effect. [47]

Most scientists agree that the earth is warming at a rapid rate and will be between 2 and 6 degrees warmer by the year 2100. This may not seem like a major change, but the world is now only 5 to 9 degrees warmer than during the depths of the last ice age, 20,000 years ago. Scientists predict that if the warming trend is not reversed, seas will rise (gobbling up shorelines and displacing millions of people); severe droughts, rainstorms, heat waves, and floods will become more common; and broad shifts in climatic and agricultural zones will occur, bringing famine, disease, and pestilence to some areas. [48]

There is no technology to control carbon emissions, so the principal way to reduce greenhouse gases is to burn less fuel or find alternative sources of energy. In 1992, industrialized countries met in Rio de Janeiro and voluntarily agreed to cut greenhouse gas emissions to 1990 levels by the year 2000. None of the countries came close to meeting these goals. In 1997, 150 nations met in Kyoto, Japan, and agreed in principle to require 38 industrial nations to reduce their emissions of greenhouse gases below 1990 levels by about 2010. Few came close to meeting their goal. President Clinton

Global warming has many consequences, including the melting of polar ice. As a result, polar bears are losing their access to seals, a primary source of food.

never submitted the treaty to the Senate, and President George W. Bush renounced it. Meetings since then have not produced a binding treaty.

Opponents of cutting greenhouse gases fear it will cost a staggering sum. Industries that have to adjust their emissions may become less competitive and jobs may be lost as a result. Moreover, the costs of taking action are immediate, but carbon dioxide lingers in the atmosphere for over 100 years, so the benefits of reductions would not be felt for decades.

Disputes have arisen between industrialized and developing nations over distributing the burden of cutting greenhouse gas emissions. The former group argues that developing nations produce more emissions per dollar of gross domestic product than do developed countries. The latter counters that the rich countries got rich by burning coal and oil and still produce most of the emissions today. (The United States alone, with only 4 percent of the world's population, produces more than 20 percent of the gases that cause global warming.) Thus, the developing nations argue, developed nations should bear most of the burden of reducing global warming. The developing nations also point out that in many cases they are the ones who would be hurt most by climate changes and that they are hard-pressed enough as it is.

In addition, not everyone is convinced that the earth's warming is the result of greenhouse gases. Some politicians in the United States believe that scientific support for the global warming hypothesis is weak. Senator James Inhofe of Oklahoma has called global warming "the greatest hoax ever perpetrated on the American people." Scientific uncertainty in a technological age undermines efforts to deal with problems caused by technology.

President Obama proposed to stem carbon dioxide emissions through a market-based cap-and-trade system in which the government sets a mandatory cap on emissions and then issues companies or other groups credits for a certain amount of emissions. Companies that need to increase their emission allowance must buy credits from those who pollute less. In effect, the buyer is paying a charge for polluting, while the seller is being rewarded for having reduced emissions by more than was needed. Thus, in theory, those who can reduce emissions most cheaply will do so, achieving the pollution reduction at the lowest cost to society. The goal is to encourage the development of the most innovative and efficient means of limiting emissions without inhibiting economic growth. An early example of an emission trading system was the sulphur dioxide trading system under the framework of the Acid Rain Program of the 1990 Clean Air Act, which has reduced these emissions by 50 percent since 1980. Several states, led by California, have set up emissions trading systems.

The president's proposal did not pass Congress. Opponents argued that the costs of emissions controls would be passed on to consumers in the form of higher energy costs, amounting to a tax on all energy use. Such a tax increase, they claimed, could lead to a loss of jobs. In 2014, the president used his executive authority to place limits on the carbon emissions from power plants. These regulations were particularly significant for coal-burning plants, the most concentrated sources of greenhouse gases.

As a result of the conflicting views regarding global warming and the burden of reducing it, little progress has been made in the United States. The issues and problems become even more apparent when we look at energy policy.

Why It Matters to You
Global Warming

Many scientists believe that global warming will have dire consequences for the entire world. Because of its advanced economic system, the United States produces a larger quantity of greenhouse gases per person than does any other nation. At the same time, no one can force the United States to reduce its emissions. What are our responsibilities to other peoples? How much cost, if any, should the American people bear to benefit the rest of the world, as well as the United States?

Energy Policy

17.3

Evaluate the advantages and disadvantages of each of the principal sources of energy in the United States.

Modern American society depends on the availability of abundant energy. Yet energy use is tied to emission of pollutants and greenhouse gases, and America's energy resources are limited. The challenge of sustaining Americans' standard of living and accustomed patterns of life in the face of both these sets of issues presents policymakers with thorny problems to resolve.

Once Americans used wood, animals, water, and people power for energy. Today 80 percent of the nation's energy comes from coal, oil, and natural gas (see Figure 17.2). Americans search continually for new and more efficient sources of energy, both to increase supplies and to reduce pollution. Much of this research on new energy sources and efficiencies comes from the federal government.

☐ Coal

Coal is America's most abundant fuel. An estimated 90 percent of the country's energy resources are in coal deposits—enough to last hundreds of years. Coal accounts for 19 percent of the energy Americans use, and it produces 39 percent of America's electricity.[49] Although coal may be the nation's most plentiful fuel, unfortunately it is also the dirtiest. It contributes to global warming and smog, and it is responsible for the "black lung" health hazard to coal miners and for the soot-blackened cities of the Northeast. In addition, the burning of coal to produce electricity is largely responsible for acid rain.

☐ Petroleum and Natural Gas

In many ways the lifeblood of America's economy, petroleum, or oil, currently supplies 36 percent of our total energy needs and almost all the fuel we use in our cars and trucks.[50] Natural gas produces 25 percent of our electricity.[51] Natural gas and petroleum are somewhat cleaner than coal, but they both contribute to global warming. In addition, transporting oil can result in spills that cause serious environmental damage, and refining oil pollutes the air. Moreover, we import about a third of the oil we use (see Figure 17.3). In payment for imported oil, the United States sends enormous amounts of cash to other nations, increasing its balance of trade deficit,

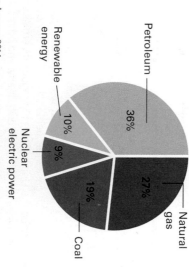

FIGURE 17.2 SOURCES OF AMERICA'S ENERGY

Despite the technological advances of society, America still relies on traditional sources for its energy: coal, oil, and natural gas. Coal generates nearly half of our electricity; oil fuels our cars, trucks, and planes. Only 10 percent of our energy comes from renewable sources, mainly hydroelectric and geothermal power.

SOURCE: Energy Information Agency, 2014.

FIGURE 17.3 IMPORTING PETROLEUM

In a single generation, the United States moved from supplying most of its petroleum needs to importing 60 percent and then back to importing less than half of its petroleum and petroleum products.

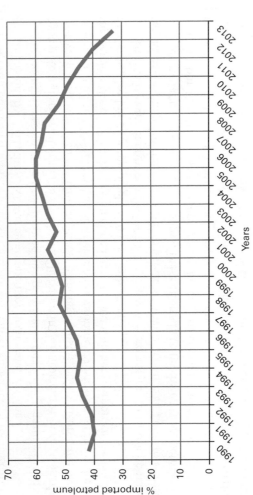

SOURCE: U.S. Energy Information Administration, *Monthly Energy Review, May 2012*, Table 3.3a.

and, as some of these nations are not too friendly to the United States, helping to fund potential adversaries. Finally, in today's world many countries compete for oil, and, in particular, surging economic growth in China and India is increasing demand and hence prices.

Dependence on foreign oil also places the United States at the mercy of actions of other nations. Much of the world's natural oil reserves are in Russia and in Middle Eastern countries—countries on which the United States cannot necessarily rely for dependable supplies of fuel. When the United States supported Israel in the Yom Kippur War in 1973, Arab nations proclaimed an embargo on oil shipments to the United States. High prices, which hurt the economy, also resulted in long lines at the gas pump. When Iraq invaded oil-rich Kuwait in 1990, the United States went to war to drive the Iraqis out and deny them the possibility of controlling another 10 percent of the world's oil supply.

In the event that the United States is confronted with a serious disruption in oil supplies today, the Strategic Petroleum Reserve, which was established following the embargo, can provide an emergency supply of crude oil. The reserve, maintained by the Department of Energy, consists of oil that is stockpiled in underground salt caverns along the Gulf of Mexico coastline. In addition, the Department of Energy maintains an emergency supply of heating oil for consumers in the Northeast, who depend on this fuel for much of their heating needs. Two million barrels of this heating oil are stored in commercial terminals and can be released quickly should severe weather or other emergencies create life-threatening shortages.

One way to minimize the effects of an oil supply disruption is to ensure that our domestic production of oil is maintained. Remaining U.S. oil fields are becoming increasingly costly to produce because much of the easy-to-find oil has already been recovered. Yet, for every barrel of oil that flows from U.S. fields, nearly two barrels remain in the ground. Higher oil prices encourage the development of technology to find and produce much of this "left-behind" oil.

Oil exploration on public lands and offshore in coastal waters also has potential to increase America's oil supplies. However, this drilling also raises issues of environmental protection. Energy companies and environmentalists have battled over Alaska's reserves for years, stalling drilling there. In 2010, President Obama announced opening large areas of the American coastline to offshore drilling.

Two months later, an offshore oil rig exploded in the Gulf of Mexico, setting off the largest oil spill in history. It is clear that regulators in the Department of Interior had failed to do their jobs and that BP, the operator of the well, had not followed industry standards. The Obama administration quickly reorganized the bureaucracy dealing with offshore drilling, but this could not prevent environmental damage from the spilled oil. By 2011, the Gulf was again open for deep water drilling.

In recent years controversy has focused on a proposal to build the Keystone Pipeline System to transport oil from the Athabasca Oil Sands in northeastern Alberta, Canada, to several destinations in the United States. Although most people welcome the prospect of new oil supplies, many land-owners and environmentalists oppose the route of the pipeline. As of 2014, the president had not decided whether to approve the federal permitting for building the pipeline in the United States.

In recent years, energy companies have employed a process called hydraulic fracturing, or "fracking," to create fractures in a rock layer with pressurized fluids to release petroleum, natural gas, and coal seam gas. These efforts have produced more petroleum and gas, but they have come under scrutiny because of concerns about the environment, health, and safety. Critics worry about the contamination of groundwater, risks to air quality, the potential migration of gases and hydraulic fracturing chemicals to the surface, and the potential mishandling of waste. Government at all levels is just starting to deal with the consequences of this new technology.

☐ Nuclear Energy

The most controversial energy source is nuclear power. During the 1940s and 1950s, Americans were convinced that the technology that had ended World War II could be

Do you think Americans will be willing to make such sacrifices?

sacrifices by every citizen.

Effectively conserving energy (and limiting greenhouse gas emissions) requires

Point to Ponder

HEY, NOBODY SAID
THAT ENERGY
INDEPENDENCE
WOULD BE PAIN-
FREE. NOW, SIT
BACK AND ENJOY
VACATION.

made to serve peaceful purposes. Nuclear scientists spoke enthusiastically about harnessing the atom to produce electricity that would be "too cheap to meter." These claims, however, were met with increasing skepticism in the light both of huge cost overruns in the construction of nuclear power plants and of the accidents at Three Mile Island and Chernobyl, in 1979 and 1986, respectively. Perhaps the most significant blow of all to the nuclear power industry was the wave of environmental concern that developed in the late 1960s.[52] Environmentalists opposed nuclear power because of radiation leaks in the mining, transportation, and use of atomic fuel; because of the enormous problem of nuclear waste disposal; and because of the inherent difficulty of regulating such complex technology. No new nuclear power plants have been started in the United States since 1978, and almost all those under construction at that time have been abandoned at huge financial loss.[53]

Nevertheless, defenders of nuclear energy continued to argue that burning coal and oil to generate electricity blackens miners lungs, causes acid rain that defoliates forests and kills lakes, adds to global warming, and creates other problems. And in recent years, the high price of gasoline and heating fuel and concerns over global warming have encouraged a reconsideration of nuclear power. Leaders of both political parties and the American public support an increase to the percentage of electricity produced by nuclear energy from the current 19 percent.[54]

Nuclear power received a setback in 2011, however, when an earthquake-generated tsunami damaged several nuclear reactors in Fukushima, Japan. At the very least, it will be years before the percentage of electricity in the United States produced by nuclear power increases substantially.

☐ Renewable Sources of Energy

Renewable energy sources include water, wind, the sun, geothermal sources, hydrogen, and biomass. Using water to drive turbines, hydroelectric power facilities in the United States generate about 6 percent of our electricity. Wind power, harnessed with modern windmills, generates about 1 percent of our electricity and is one of the nation's fastest-growing sources of energy. Biomass power is obtained from plants and plant-derived materials and can be used to produce electricity (biopower) and liquid fuels (biofuels). It also generates about 1 percent of the electricity in the United States.[55] However, although they may ultimately play a significant role, the contribution of renewable sources of energy to America's energy supply is likely to remain small for the foreseeable future.

Understanding Health Care, Environmental, and Energy Policy

17.4 Assess the role of democratic politics in making health care, environmental, and energy policy and the effect of these policies on the scope of government.

ealth care, environmental, and energy issues have at least three things in common. First, they involve human health and welfare and thus are highly salient to both the public and policymakers. Second, they are highly technical areas in which ordinary people are ill equipped to make policy. Finally, dealing with them requires expanding the scope of government.

☐ Democracy, Health Care, and Environmental Policy

High-tech issues, more than any others, strain the limits of public participation in a democracy. From ethical issues raised by machines and devices that can keep patients alive indefinitely to threats to public safety inherent in an accident at a nuclear power plant, governments are constantly called on to make decisions that involve tremendously complex technologies. Does unavoidable ignorance about complex technological issues involved in health care and environmental and energy policy mean that citizens cannot participate effectively in the public policy debates on these areas of policy?

Most Americans do not want to leave these issues to "experts" to decide, and they do not. When the president proposes complex health care reform, the public takes a stand. When there are tradeoffs to be made between economic growth and clean air, average citizens express their opinions. Sometimes these opinions are ill-informed, but democracy is often a messy business. In addition, the public often relies on group representation to help them out with technical issues. Interest groups—associations of professionals and citizens—play an active role in making the complicated decisions that will affect Americans for generations and thus help translate public opinion into policy.

☐ The Scope of Government and Health Care, Environmental, and Energy Policy

In the area of health care, the scope of the federal government has grown rapidly. Medicare for the elderly, Medicaid for the poor, and tax subsidies for employer-provided health insurance are large, expensive public policies. Adding prescription drug coverage for the elderly was a large increase in the cost of governmentally supported medicine. The health care reform bill passed in 2010 added yet further government responsibilities to ensure that all American have access to health care and to regulate private health insurance companies. Nonetheless, health care policy is the most important single policy difference between the United States and other industrialized democracies. We have a mixed, mostly private system; many other industrialized democracies have an almost entirely public one.

In the past three decades, concerns for environmental protection have placed additional demands on the federal government. Volumes of regulations and billions of dollars spent on environmental protection have enlarged the scope of government's environmental policy. Responding to the issue of global warming will require yet more regulations. Developing and protecting sources of energy also requires government subsidies, and sometimes even war. Moreover, pollution, a byproduct of energy use, raises issues of government protection of the nation's health and environment. It would be convenient to ignore these policy demands, but the public expects the government to act.

Review the Chapter

Health Care Policy

17.1 Outline the problems of health care in America and the role of government in health care, p. 554.

America's health costs are both extremely high and increasing at a rapid rate. The health care system provides few incentives for controlling costs, and Americans who can afford it demand the most advanced care. There are severe inequalities in health care and hence in health in America. Insurance has been mainly obtainable as a benefit from employers, and many poor and working-class Americans, uninsured or underinsured, have been relegated to an inferior health care system. The government provides health care for the elderly and the poor through Medicare and Medicaid, and since the reforms of 2010, intended to increase access and help control costs, it provides subsidies for health insurance to small businesses and individuals.

Environmental Policy

17.2 Analyze the conflicts between economic growth and environmental protection, and identify the major national environmental protection policies, p. 564.

Environmental concerns often conflict with equally legitimate concerns about economic growth and jobs. Interest groups advocating environmental protection now play a critical role in environmental policymaking. The Environmental Protection Agency is charged with administering policies dealing with land use, air and water quality, and wilderness and wildlife preservation. The National Environmental Policy Act requires the federal government to file an environmental impact statement with the EPA every time it proposes to undertake a policy that is potentially disruptive to the environment. The Clean Air Act charges the EPA with protecting and improving the quality of the nation's air, while the Water Pollution Control Act aims to clean the nation's water. Yet other policies, such as the Endangered Species Act, seek to preserve wilderness areas and wildlife. The disposal of toxic wastes, including nuclear waste, continues to challenge policymakers, although the Superfund has helped to clean up toxic waste sites. Global warming is another intractable issue, as there is disagreement over the role of carbon emissions in warming the earth and there is no agreed-upon approach to controlling them.

Energy Policy

17.3 Evaluate the advantages and disadvantages of each of the principal sources of energy in the United States, p. 572.

Coal is America's most abundant fuel and produces nearly half our electricity, but it is the dirtiest source of energy. Petroleum supplies most of our motor fuel, and natural gas produces over a fifth of our electricity. Although they are somewhat cleaner than coal, they both contribute to global warming, and drilling, transporting, and refining of oil and gas are also sources of pollution. Moreover, the United States is dependent on other nations to supply much of its oil and gas. Nuclear power is clean and provides more than a fifth of our electricity. However, many question its safety, and the storage of nuclear waste has proven to be an intractable problem. Renewable energy sources, including water, wind, solar, geothermal, hydrogen, and biomass, will probably play an important role at some point, but for the foreseeable future, their contribution to America's energy supply is likely to remain small.

Understanding Health Care, Environmental, and Energy Policy

17.4 Assess the role of democratic politics in making health care, environmental, and energy policy and the effect of these policies on the scope of government, p. 575.

High-tech issues strain the limits of public participation in a democracy, but most Americans do not leave these issues to "experts" to decide. The public often relies on group representation to help them out with technical issues.

The scope of the federal government has grown as it has provided health care for the elderly, the poor, and, more recently, those who simply cannot afford health insurance. Health is the most rapidly growing public policy and poses a long-term challenge for budgeters. Similarly, concerns for environmental protection have placed additional demands on the federal government, increasing its regulatory reach. The public also expects the government to ensure a sufficient supply of energy and to deal with its polluting by-products.

Learn the Terms

health maintenance organization, p. 557
Medicare, p. 560
Medicaid, p. 561
national health insurance, p. 561
Environmental Protection Agency, p. 566

National Environmental Policy Act, p. 566
environmental impact statements, p. 566
Clean Air Act of 1970, p. 567
Water Pollution Control Act of 1972, p. 567

Endangered Species Act of 1973, p. 567
Superfund, p. 567
global warming, p. 570

Test Yourself

1. Which of the following is a reason health care in the United States is so costly compared to health care in other countries?

a. Americans have access to fewer health facilities than do citizens of other nations.
b. Americans have coverage for a greater proportion of their population than do citizens of other nations.
c. Americans have fewer incentives to contain health costs care than do officials of other nations.
d. Americans spend more time in the hospital than do citizens of other nations.
e. Americans visit the doctor more frequently than do citizens of other nations.

2. What is one reason Medicare is often an issue in political campaigns?

a. Democrats and Republicans generally agree on how to reform Medicare.
b. Most media coverage is concerned with Medicare issues.
c. Politicians generally want to limit the influence of the elderly in elections.
d. The elderly are one of the most powerful voting and lobbying forces in American politics.
e. Young people are opposed to Medicare benefits for the elderly.

3. What is one result of President Obama's Affordable Care Act?

a. It allows health insurance companies to refuse coverage to people with preexisting conditions.
b. It opened a gap in Medicare's prescription drug coverage.
c. Out-of-pocket expenses for the insured are uncapped.
d. Preventative care costs more.
e. Young people can stay on their parents' insurance until age 26.

4. Which of the following twentieth century events forged a link between employment and health benefits in the United States?

a. the civil rights movement
b. the Vietnam War
c. the Watergate scandal
d. World War I
e. World War II

5. Unlike all other developed nations, the United States does not have _____.

a. federal health insurance
b. health insurance designated especially for children under the age of 18
c. health insurance designated especially for infants
d. local health insurance
e. national health insurance

6. Why would Louisianans and Alaskans be opposed to strict oil regulations or sanctions?

a. Many of them are not properly informed on oil's dangers to the environment.
b. Many of them do not agree that the environment should be the government's responsibility.
c. Many of them rely on oil for jobs and its revenues to reduce taxes.
d. They consume more gas and oil than the other 48 states.
e. They support the Environmental Protection Agency.

7. Why do developing nations argue against agreements to limit global warming?

a. Although they have growing economies that can afford to spend more, they contribute the least to global warming.

b. Rich nations should pay, because they are the only ones causing climate change.

c. They would be hurt most economically by programs to limit global warming.

d. They would be required to ensure that other countries comply as well.

e. They would rather fund programs to limit global warming directly.

8. Why is the National Environmental Policy Act of 1969 the centerpiece of federal environmental policy?

a. By requiring environmental impact statements, the act places responsibility on federal agencies.

b. The act bars all environmentally unsound proposals.

c. The act gained broad support for environmental protection from both political parties.

d. The act places responsibility for protecting the environment on the states.

e. The act shifts the burden of protecting the environment to private industry.

9. Why do many people oppose regulations and restrictions designed to cut greenhouse gas emissions?

a. Scientific uncertainty in a technological age undermines efforts to curb the effects of the technology.

b. The costs of taking action are immediate, but the benefits may not be felt for decades.

c. The technologies necessary to accomplish the cuts have not been invented yet.

d. They believe the Environmental Protection Agency standards are an example of government overreach.

e. They do not want to change the way they operate their businesses or industries.

10. Even when public opinion supports an issue, it may still be controversial. Many Americans may be generally in favor of "doing something" about the environment, however they _____.

a. disagree with the Endangered Species Act

b. do not believe it is the responsibility of the government

c. do not feel the government is doing a good enough job

d. feel the National Environmental Policy Act goes too far

e. may disagree with specific policy proposals

11. Marge is against the use of nuclear energy. What is one reason she may use to argue her position?

a. Nuclear energy causes mutations in living forms within a certain radius of nuclear energy plants, no matter how well the radioactive substances are contained.

b. Nuclear energy is so easy to harness that many private individuals will create technology to do so.

c. Nuclear energy is so expensive it is impractical for widespread use.

d. Nuclear waste will fill up landfills too quickly, which will create the need for more landfills.

e. Radiation leaks may occur when using atomic fuel.

12. Which of the following is one reason why, despite being America's most abundant energy source, coal is not the most used?

a. Burning coal contaminates ground water deposits.

b. Burning coal produces high amounts of greenhouse gases and acid rain.

c. Coal is the most controversial energy source.

d. Coal is difficult to mine.

e. Coal is the hardest fossil fuel to refine.

13. What is the chief problem with the United States' dependence on energy derived from oil?

a. Oil hampers the country's economic growth.

b. Oil must compete with renewable resources.

c. The United States buys its oil only from hostile nations.

d. The United States must import about a third of the oil it consumes.

e. The United States must import about two-thirds of the oil it consumes.

14. Which of the following statements describes what health care, environmental, and energy issues have in common?

a. They are not dealt with in the original Constitution, but are addressed in subsequent amendments, and are overseen by the Supreme Court.

b. They involve the public welfare; are highly technical; and require expansion of government scope to address.

c. They primarily impact the elderly; are largely ignored by Republican candidates; and disproportionally impact citizens from different socioeconomic backgrounds.

d. They strain the limits of public participation in democracy; the public does not want to leave them in the hands of "experts" or in the sole purview of the government.

e. They were originally the purview of the states but became linked to federal government during World War II, and are now expected by the public to be handled by the government.

15. Dr. Jones is a U.S. citizen with very strong opinions about how the recent health care reform will affect him and his fellow citizens. What is a major way that Dr. Jones is likely to get involved in the decision-making process regarding this policy?

a. He will join an interest group that represents doctors and other medical professionals.

b. He will leave the decision making to the "experts."

c. He will refuse to vote as a protest against uninformed decision making.

d. He will start an Occupy movement in front of the local hospital.

e. He will try to explain his opinions to all of his friends and family who have no familiarity with the medical profession.

Explore Further

WEB SITES

www.kff.org
Kaiser Family Foundation Web site, with excellent studies of health care–related issues.

www.cms.gov
Centers for Medicare and Medicaid Services Web site, with information on the two largest government health programs.

www.epa.gov
Official site for the Environmental Protection Agency, which provides information on policies and current environmental issues.

www.sierraclub.org
Web site for the Sierra Club, one of the most active environmental protection organizations.

www.epa.gov/superfund/
Environmental Protection Agency information about toxic waste sites and their cleanup.

www.epa.gov/climatechange/
Environmental Protection Agency information on climate change.

www.eia.doe.gov
The best source of information on energy sources, consumption, and policy.

www.fws.gov
U.S. Fish and Wildlife Service, the protector of endangered species.

energy.gov
U.S. Department of Energy Web site, featuring information on a wide range of energy-related topics.

www.api.org
American Petroleum Institute site, with information on many energy issues.

www.ncseonline.org/
National Council for Science and the Environment site dedicated to improving the scientific basis for environmental decision making.

www.who.int/whosis/en/
World Health Organization site with data on health care around the world.

FURTHER READING

Casamayou, Maureen Hogan. *The Politics of Breast Cancer.* Washington, D.C.: Georgetown University Press, 2001. How women's groups and others organized to elevate breast cancer research on the policy agenda.

Hillstrom, Kevin. *U.S. Health Policy and Politics: A Documentary History.* Washington, D.C.: CQ Press, 2012. Primary source documents on health policy.

Jacobs, Lawrence R., and Theda Skocpol. *Health Care Reform and American Politics: What Everyone Needs to Know,* rev. and updated ed. New York: Oxford University Press, 2012. The politics of health care reform.

Morone, James A., Theodor J. Litman, and Leonard S. Robins. *Health Politics and Policy,* 5th ed. Boston, MA: Cengage, 2014. The politics and policy of health care.

Patel, Kant, and Mark Rushefsky. *Health Care in America: Separate and Unequal.* Armonk, NY: M.E. Sharpe, 2008. Examines the causes of the inequalities of the American health care system and discusses various policy alternatives.

Rosenbaum, Walter A. *Environmental Politics and Policy,* 9th ed. Washington, D.C.: CQ Press, 2013. The actors, institutions, processes, and polices involved in environmental policymaking.

Rosenbaum, Walter A. *American Energy: The Politics of 21st Century Policy.* Washington, D.C.: CQ Press, 2014. Discusses how important actors, institutions, and issues impact American energy policymaking and the substance of energy policy.

Shaffer, Brenda. *Energy Politics.* Philadelphia: University of Pennsylvania Press, 2009. An excellent introduction to the international politics of energy.

Smith, Zachary A. *The Environmental Policy Paradox*, 6th ed. New York: Pearson, 2012. An introduction to environmental policymaking.

Vanderheiden, Steve. *Atmospheric Justice: A Political Theory of Climate Change*. New York: Oxford University Press, 2008. An incisive examination of the public policy challenges of global warming via the conceptual frameworks of justice, equality, and responsibility.

Vig, Norman J., and Michael E. Kraft, ed. *Environmental Policy*, 8th ed. Washington, D.C.: CQ Press, 2009. Useful articles on a range of environmental policy issues.

Weissert, William G. and Carol S. Weissert. *Governing Health: The Politics of Health Policy*, 4th ed. Baltimore, MD: Johns Hopkins University Press, 2012. Comprehensive treatment of health care policy with a focus on political strategy.

Yergin, Daniel. *The Prize: The Epic Quest for Oil, Money and Power*. New York: Simon and Schuster, 1991. The story of oil.

Yergin, Daniel. *The Quest: Energy, Security, and the Remaking of the Modern World*. New York: Penguin Press, 2011. A gripping account of the quest for sustainable sources of energy.

18

National Security Policymaking

Politics in Action: A New Threat

O n September 11, 2001, America trembled. Terrorist attacks on the World Trade Center in New York and the Pentagon in Washington killed thousands and exposed the nation's vulnerability to unconventional attacks.

Less than 12 years after the fall of the Berlin Wall and the diminishment of Communism as a threat, the United States could no longer take comfort in its status as the world's only superpower. Suddenly the world seemed a more threatening place, with dangers lurking around every corner.

Pursuing its new foreign policy emphasis on ending terrorism, the United States launched wars against Afghanistan and Iraq. The United States won the battles quite easily, but the aftermath of the wars led to more deaths than the fighting itself and forced America to invest tens of billions of dollars in reconstruction and military occupation. Particularly because Iraq had in fact little or no connection to Al Qaeda, the terrorist organization behind the September 11 attacks, debate rages as to whether U.S. actions dealt terrorists a severe blow or had the effect of radicalizing opponents and recruiting new terrorists to their cause. At the same time, "rogue" states like Iran and North Korea have continued their development of nuclear weapons, threatening to make the world even less stable.

18.1	**18.2**	**18.3**	**18.4**	**18.5**	**18.6**
Identify the major instruments and actors in making national security policy, p. 584.	Outline the evolution of and major issues in American foreign policy through the end of the Cold War, p. 591.	Explain the major obstacles to success in the war on terrorism, p. 597.	Identify the major elements of U.S. defense policy, p. 600.	Analyze the evolving challenges for U.S. national security policy, p. 603.	Assess the role of democratic politics in making national security policy and the role of national security policy in expanding government, p. 612.

Perhaps the most troublesome issue in national security is the spread of terrorism. The attacks on September 11, 2001, redirected U.S. foreign policy toward ending terrorism, including launching wars in Iraq and Afghanistan.

18.1

18.2

18.3

18.4

18.5

18.6

foreign policy

Policy that involves choice taking about relations with the rest of the world. The president is the chief initiator of U.S. foreign policy.

American Foreign Policy: Instruments, Actors, and Policymakers

Identify the major instruments and actors in making national security policy.

F oreign policy, like domestic policy, involves making choices—but the choices involved are about relations with the rest of the world. Because the president is the main force behind foreign policy, every morning the White House receives a highly confidential intelligence briefing that might cover monetary transactions in Shanghai, last night's events in some trouble spot on the globe, or Fidel Castro's health. The briefing is part of the massive informational arsenal the president uses to manage American foreign policy.

Answering the question of the appropriate role of the national government in the area of national security policy—an area encompassing foreign policy and national defense—has become more important and perhaps more difficult than ever. America's status in the world makes leadership unavoidable. What should be the role of the world's only remaining superpower? What should we do with our huge defense establishment? Should we go it alone, or should we work closely with our allies on issues ranging from fighting terrorism and stopping nuclear proliferation to protecting the environment and encouraging trade? At the same time, a number of critical areas of the world, most notably the Middle East, have a frightening potential for conflict. Should the United States get involved in trying to end conflicts resulting from ethnic and religious differences and regional issues? Does the United States have a choice about involvement when the conflict could affect its ability to fight terrorism or prevent the use of nuclear weapons?

And just how should we decide about national security policy? Should the American people and their representatives participate as fully in the policymaking process as they do for domestic policy? Or should they delegate discretion in this area to officials who seem at home with the complex and even exotic issues of defense and foreign policy? Can the public and its representatives in Congress or in interest groups even exert much influence on the elites who often deal in secrecy with national security policy?

National security is as important as ever. New and complex challenges have emerged to replace the conflict with communism. Some of these challenges, such as the fight against terrorism, are traceable to a malevolent enemy—but many others are not.

☐ Instruments of Foreign Policy

The instruments of foreign policy are different from those of domestic policy. Foreign policies depend ultimately on three types of tools: military, economic, and diplomatic.

MILITARY Among the oldest instruments of foreign policy are war and the threat of war. German general Karl von Clausewitz once called war a "continuation of politics by other means." The United States has been involved in only a few full-scale wars. It has often employed force to influence actions in other countries, however. Historically, most such uses of force have been close to home, in Central America and the Caribbean.

In recent years, the United States has used force to influence actions in a range of trouble spots around the world—not only to topple Saddam Hussein's regime in Iraq and the Taliban regime in Afghanistan but also, for example, to oppose ethnic cleansing in the Kosovo province of the former Yugoslavia, to prevent the toppling of the democratic government of the Philippines, to assist a UN peacekeeping mission in Somalia, to help overthrow Maummar Qaddafi's regime in Libya, and to rescue stranded foreigners and protect our embassy in Liberia. The United States also employed military force to aid the democratic transfer of power in Haiti and for humanitarian relief operations in Iraq, Somalia, Bangladesh, Russia, and Bosnia and elsewhere in the former Yugoslavia.

ECONOMIC Today, economic instruments are becoming weapons almost as potent as those of war. The control of oil can be as important as the control of guns. Trade regulations, tariff policies, monetary policies, and economic sanctions are other economic instruments of foreign policy. A number of studies have called attention to the importance of a country's economic vitality to its long-term national security.[1]

DIPLOMACY Diplomacy is the quietest instrument of influence. It is the process by which nations carry on relationships with each other. Although diplomacy often evokes images of ambassadors at chic cocktail parties, the diplomatic game is played for high stakes. Sometimes national leaders meet in summit talks. More often, less prominent negotiators work out treaties covering all kinds of national contracts, from economic relations to aid for stranded tourists.

Actors on the World Stage

If all the world's a stage, then there are more actors on it—governmental and otherwise—than ever before. More than 125 nations have emerged since 1945. Once foreign relations were almost exclusively transactions among nations, in which leaders used military, economic, or diplomatic methods to achieve foreign policy goals. Although nations remain the main actors, the cast has become more varied.

INTERNATIONAL ORGANIZATIONS Most of the challenges in international relations, ranging from peacekeeping and controlling weapons of mass destruction to protecting the environment and maintaining stable trade and financial networks, require the cooperation of many nations. It is not surprising that international organizations play an increasingly important role on the world stage.

The best-known international organization is the **United Nations** (UN). The UN was created in 1945 and has its headquarters in New York. Its members agree to renounce war and to respect certain human and economic freedoms (although they sometimes fail to keep these promises). In addition to its peacekeeping function, the UN runs programs in areas including economic development and health, education, and welfare.

The UN *General Assembly* is composed of 193 member nations, each with one vote. Although not legally binding, General Assembly resolutions can achieve a measure of collective legitimization when a broad international consensus is formed on some matter concerning relations among states. It is the *Security Council*, however, that is the seat of real power in the UN. Five of its 15 members (the United States, Great Britain, China, France, and Russia) are permanent members; the others are chosen from session to session by the General Assembly. Each permanent member has a veto over Security Council decisions, including any decisions that would commit the UN to a military peacekeeping operation. The *Secretariat* is the executive arm of the UN and directs the administration of UN programs. Composed of about 9,000 international civil servants, it is headed by the secretary-general.

Since 1948, there have been 63 UN peacekeeping operations, including 50 created by the Security Council since 1988. In 2014, there were 16 such operations under-way—in Abyei, South Sudan, Haiti, the Democratic Republic of the Congo, Western Sahara, Afghanistan, India and Pakistan, Syria, Ivory Coast, Liberia, Lebanon, Cyprus, Kosovo, Darfur, Mali, and the Middle East generally.

The United States often plays a critical role in implementing UN policies, although U.S. attitudes toward the UN have varied. President Clinton envisioned an expanded

United Nations

Created in 1945 and currently including 193 member nations, with a central peacekeeping mission and programs in areas including economic development and health, education, and welfare. The seat of real power in the UN is the Security Council.

586

18.1
18.2
18.3
18.4
18.5
18.6

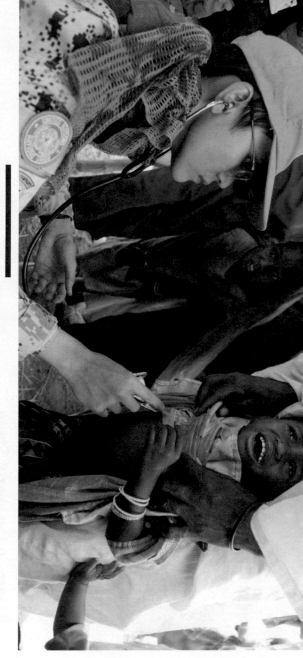

The most prominent international organization is the United Nations. In addition to its efforts to keep the peace, it supports important programs in economic development and health, education, and welfare.

role for UN peacekeeping operations at the beginning of his term but later concluded that the UN is often not capable of making and keeping peace, particularly when hostilities among parties still exist. He also backtracked on his willingness to place American troops under foreign commanders—always a controversial policy. George W. Bush sought but did not receive UN sanction for the war with Iraq. He, too, expressed skepticism of the organization's ability to enforce its own resolutions. Nevertheless, many countries feel the legitimacy of the UN is crucial for their participation in peacekeeping or other operations requiring the use of force.

The UN is only one of many international organizations. The International Monetary Fund, for example, helps regulate the chaotic world of international finance, the World Bank finances development projects in new nations, the World Trade Organization attempts to regulate international trade, and the Universal Postal Union helps get the mail from one country to another.

REGIONAL ORGANIZATIONS The post–World War II era has seen a proliferation of *regional organizations*—organizations of several nations bound by a treaty, often for military reasons. The **North Atlantic Treaty Organization** (NATO) was created in 1949. Its members—the United States, Canada, most Western European nations, and Turkey—agreed to combine military forces and to treat a war against one as a war against all. During the Cold War, more than a million NATO troops (including about 325,000 Americans) were spread from West Germany to Portugal as a deterrent to foreign aggression. To counter the NATO alliance, the Soviet Union and its Eastern European allies formed the Warsaw Pact. With the thawing of the Cold War, however, the Warsaw Pact was dissolved and the role of NATO changed dramatically. In 1999, Poland, Hungary, and the Czech Republic, former members of the Warsaw Pact, became members of NATO. Since then, eight additional Eastern European countries—Slovakia, Slovenia, Bulgaria, Romania, Latvia, Estonia, Lithuania, and Croatia—have joined the alliance.

Regional organizations can have economic as well as military and political functions. The **European Union** (EU) is a transnational government composed of most European nations. The EU coordinates monetary, trade, immigration, and labor

North Atlantic Treaty Organization

A regional organization that was created in 1949 by nations including the United States, Canada, and most Western European nations for mutual defense and has subsequently been expanded.

European Union

A transnational government composed of most European nations that coordinates monetary, trade, immigration, and labor policies, making its members one economic unit.

policies so that its members have become one economic unit, just as the 50 states of the United States are an economic unit. Most EU nations have adopted a common currency, the euro. Other economic federations exist in Latin America, Africa, and Asia, although none is as unified as the EU.

MULTINATIONAL CORPORATIONS A large portion of the world's industrial output comes from *multinational corporations* (MNCs), and they account for more than one-tenth of the global economy and one-third of world exports. Sometimes more powerful (and often much wealthier) than the governments under which they operate, MNCs have voiced strong opinions about governments, taxes, and business regulations. They have even linked forces with agencies such as the Central Intelligence Agency (CIA) to overturn governments they disliked. In the 1970s, for example, several U.S.-based multinationals worked with the CIA to "destabilize" the democratically elected Marxist government in Chile, which Chile's military then overthrew in 1973. Although rarely so heavy-handed, MNCs are forces to be reckoned with in nearly all nations.[2]

NONGOVERNMENTAL ORGANIZATIONS Groups that are not connected with governments, known as *nongovernmental organizations* (NGOs), are also actors on the global stage. Churches and labor unions have long had international interests and activities. Today, environmental and wildlife groups, such as Greenpeace, have also proliferated internationally, as have groups interested in protecting human rights, such as Amnesty International.

TERRORISTS Not all groups, however, are committed to saving whales, oceans, or even people. Some are committed to the overthrow of particular governments and operate as terrorists around the world. Airplane hijackings and assassinations, bombings, and similar terrorist attacks have made the world a more unsettled place. Conflicts within a nation or region may spill over into world politics. Terrorism in the Middle East, for example, affects the price of oil in Tokyo, New York, and Berlin. Terrorism sponsored by Iran may strain relations between the West and Russia.

INDIVIDUALS Finally, *individuals* are international actors. Tourism sends Americans everywhere and brings to America legions of tourists from around the world. Tourism creates its own costs and benefits and thus can affect international relations and the international economic system. It may enhance friendship and understanding among nations. However, more tourists traveling out of the country than arriving in the country can create problems with a country's balance of payments (discussed later in this chapter). In addition to tourists, growing numbers of students are going to and coming from other nations; they are carriers of ideas and ideologies. So are immigrants and refugees, who also place new demands on public services.

Just as there are more actors on the global stage than in the past, there are also more American decision makers involved in foreign policy problems.

☐ The Policymakers

There are many policymakers involved with national security policy, but any discussion of foreign policymaking must begin with the president.

THE PRESIDENT The president is the main force behind foreign policy. As chief diplomat, the president negotiates treaties; as commander in chief of the armed forces, the president deploys American troops abroad. The president also appoints U.S. ambassadors and the heads of executive departments (with the consent of the Senate) and has the sole power to accord official recognition to other countries and receive (or refuse to receive) their representatives.

Presidents make some foreign policy through the formal mechanisms of treaties or executive agreements. Both are written accords in which the parties agree to specific

588

18.1

18.2

18.3

18.4

18.5

18.6

secretary of state
The head of the Department of State and traditionally the key adviser to the president on foreign policy.

actions and both have legal standing, but only treaties require Senate ratification. Thus, presidents usually find it more convenient to use executive agreements. Since the end of World War II, presidents have negotiated thousands of executive agreements but only about 800 treaties. Most executive agreements deal with routine and noncontroversial matters, but they have also been used for matters of significance, as in the case of the agreement ending the Vietnam War and arms control agreements.

The president combines constitutional prerogatives with greater access to information than other policymakers and can act with speed and secrecy if necessary. The White House also has the advantages of the president's role as a leader of Congress and the public and of the president's ability to commit the nation to a course of action. Presidents do not act alone in foreign policy, however. They are aided (and sometimes thwarted) by a huge national security bureaucracy. In addition, they must contend with the views and desires of Congress, which also wields considerable clout in the foreign policy arena—sometimes in opposition to a president.

THE DIPLOMATS The State Department is the foreign policy arm of the U.S. government. Its head is the **secretary of state** (Thomas Jefferson was the first). Traditionally, the secretary of state has been the key adviser to the president on foreign policy matters. In countries from Albania to Zimbabwe, the State Department staffs over 300 U.S. embassies, consulates, and other posts, representing the interests of Americans. Once a dignified and genteel profession, diplomacy is becoming an increasingly dangerous job. The 1979 seizure of the American embassy in Tehran, Iran, the 1998 bombing of the American embassies in Nairobi, Kenya, and Dar es Salaam, Tanzania, and the 2012 attack on the U.S. mission in Benghazi, Libya, are extreme examples of the hostilities diplomats can face.

The approximately 34,000 State Department employees are organized into functional areas (such as economic and business affairs and human rights and

Point to Ponder

The president is at the center of national security policymaking, and juggling a wide range of international problems, often not of his making, is inevitably at the top of the White House's agenda.

Is it possible for one person, no matter how capable, to devote the necessary attention to such an array of issues?

SOURCE: Robert Ariail, *The State* (Columbia SC) May 28, 2009.

humanitarian affairs) and area specialties (a section on Middle Eastern affairs, one on European affairs, and so on), each nation being handled by a "country desk." The political appointees who occupy the top positions in the department and the highly select members of the Foreign Service who compose most of the department are heavily involved in formulating and executing American foreign policy.

Many recent presidents have found the State Department too bureaucratic and intransigent. Even its colloquial name of "Foggy Bottom," taken from the part of Washington where it is located, conjures up less than an image of proactive cooperation. Some presidents have bypassed institutional arrangements for foreign policy decision making and have instead established more personal systems for receiving policy advice. Presidents Nixon and Carter, for example, relied more heavily on their assistants for national security affairs than on their secretaries of state. Thus, in their administrations, foreign policy was centered in the White House and was often disconnected from what was occurring in the State Department. Critics, however, charged that this situation led to split-level government and chronic discontinuity in foreign policy.[3] In most recent presidencies, the secretary of state has played a lead role in foreign policy making.

THE NATIONAL SECURITY ESTABLISHMENT Foreign policy and defense policy are closely linked. Thus, a key foreign policy actor is the Department of Defense, often called "the Pentagon" after the five-sided building in which it is located. Created by Congress after World War II, the department collected together the U.S. Army, Navy, and Air Force. The services have never been thoroughly integrated, however, and critics contend that they continue to plan and operate too independently of one another, although reforms made under the Goldwater–Nichols Defense Reorganization Act of 1986 increased interservice cooperation and centralization of the military hierarchy. The **secretary of defense** manages a budget larger than the entire budget of most nations and is the president's main civilian adviser on national defense matters.

The **Joint Chiefs of Staff** is made up of the commanding officers of each of the services, along with a chairperson and vice chairperson. American military leaders are sometimes portrayed as aggressive hawks in policymaking. However, Richard Betts carefully examined the Joint Chiefs' advice to the president in many crises and found them to be no more likely than civilian advisers to push an aggressive military policy.[4]

High-ranking officials are supposed to coordinate American foreign and defense policies. Congress formed the *National Security Council* (NSC) in 1947 for this purpose.

secretary of defense
The head of the Department of Defense and the president's key adviser on military policy and, as such, a key foreign policy actor.

Joint Chiefs of Staff
A group that consists of the commanding officers of each of the armed services, a chairperson, and a vice chairperson, and advises the president on military policy.

Diplomatic, defense, and intelligence officials are key players in the national security establishment. Here President Obama meets with top military officials in the Oval Office.

18.1
18.2
18.3
18.4
18.5
18.6

Central Intelligence Agency
An agency created after World War II to coordinate American intelligence activities abroad and to collect, analyze, and evaluate intelligence.

The NSC is composed of the president, the vice president, the secretary of defense, and the secretary of state. The president's assistant for national security—a position that first gained public prominence with the flamboyant, globe-trotting Henry Kissinger during President Nixon's first term—manages the NSC staff. The chairman of the Joint Chiefs of Staff is the statutory military advisor to the Council, and the director of National Intelligence (discussed later) is the intelligence advisor to the NSC. In the Obama administration, the president's chief of staff, counsel, and assistant for economic policy attend NSC meetings. The attorney general and the director of the Office of Management and Budget are invited to attend meetings pertaining to their responsibilities. The heads of other executive departments and agencies, as well as other senior officials, are invited to attend meetings of the NSC when appropriate.

Despite the coordinating role assigned to the NSC, conflict within the national security establishment remains common. The NSC staff has sometimes competed with, rather than integrated policy advice from, cabinet departments—particularly State and Defense. It has also become involved in covert operations. In 1986, officials discovered that NSC staff members were secretly selling battlefield missiles to Iran in return for help in gaining the release of hostages held by Iranian-backed terrorists in Lebanon and then were secretly funneling some of the money from the sale to anticommunist rebels (called *Contras*) fighting the Nicaraguan government, despite a congressional ban on such aid. The scandal that erupted, termed the Iran-Contra affair, resulted in the resignation of the president's assistant for national security affairs, Vice Admiral John Poindexter, and the sacking of a number of lower-level NSC officials.

All policymakers require information to make good decisions. Information on the capabilities and intentions of other nations is often difficult to obtain. As a result, governments resort to intelligence agencies to obtain and interpret such information. Congress created the **Central Intelligence Agency (CIA)** after World War II to coordinate American information- and data-gathering intelligence activities abroad and to collect, analyze, and evaluate its own intelligence.

The CIA plays a vital role in providing information and analysis necessary for effective development and implementation of national security policy. Most of its activities are uncontroversial because the bulk of the material it collects and analyzes comes from readily available sources, such as government reports and newspapers. Also generally accepted is its use of espionage to collect information—when the espionage is directed against foreign adversaries. However, in the 1970s, Congress discovered that at times the agency had also engaged in wiretaps, interception of mail, and the infiltration of interest groups in the United States. These actions violated the CIA's charter, and revelations of spying on Americans who disagreed with the foreign policy of the administration badly damaged the agency's morale and external political support.

The CIA also has a long history of involvement in other nations' internal affairs. After the end of World War II, for example, the CIA provided aid to anticommunist parties in Italy and West Germany. It was no less busy in developing countries, where, for example, it nurtured coups in Iran in 1953 and in Guatemala in 1954. The CIA has also trained and supported armies—most notably, in Vietnam. In the 1980s, a major controversy surrounded the CIA's activities when congressional inquiries into the Iran-Contra affair, discussed earlier, suggested that the agency under Director William Casey, had been quietly involved in covert operations to assist the Contra rebels.[5]

Since the end of the Cold War, there has been substantial debate on the role of the CIA. The end of the Cold War reduced pressure for covert activities and brought a climate more conducive to focusing on conventional intelligence gathering. Currently, Congress requires the CIA to inform relevant congressional committees promptly of existing and anticipated covert operations. However, the failure to predict the terrorist attacks on September 11, 2001, changed the tenor of the debate, with many leaders calling for an increase in covert capabilities. Perhaps more disconcerting was the CIA's conclusion that Iraq possessed weapons of mass destruction. Destroying these weapons became the principal justification for the war, and their absence was a major embarrassment for the agency and the Bush administration.

There are numerous other components of America's intelligence community, which has a combined budget of about $55 billion per year. For example, the National Reconnaissance Office uses imagery satellites to monitor missile sites and other military activities around the world. The *National Security Agency* (NSA) is on the cutting edge of electronic eavesdropping capabilities and produces foreign signals intelligence. It also works to protect against foreign adversaries' gaining access to sensitive or classified national security information. In 2008, Congress allowed officials the use of broad warrants to eavesdrop on large groups of foreign targets at once rather than requiring individual warrants for wiretapping purely foreign communications.

In 2013, Edward Snowden, a former contractor for NSA, leaked documents revealing operational details of a global surveillance apparatus run by the NSA, along with numerous commercial and international partners. The surveillance programs included extensive Internet surveillance programs, as well as the interception of U.S. and European telephone metadata. Critics charged the NSA with violating Americans' privacy. The NSA responded that it was careful to protect civil liberties and that the program was necessary to protect Americans against terrorism. President Obama proposed some additional protections of civil liberties, but the core of the programs remain.

To better coordinate the nearly 100,000 people working in 16 agencies involved in intelligence and oversee the more than $50 billion intelligence budget, Congress in 2004 created a *director of national intelligence*. The person filling this position is to be the president's chief adviser on intelligence matters. It is not easy to manage such a large number of diverse agencies, spread across numerous departments, and there have been growing pains and slips in the process of improving coordination, as when the intelligence community failed to prevent a terrorist with explosives hidden in his clothing from boarding a plane to Detroit on Christmas Day in 2009.

CONGRESS The U.S. Congress shares with the president constitutional authority over foreign and defense policy. Congress has sole authority, for example, to declare war, raise and organize the armed forces, and appropriate funds for national security activities. The Senate determines whether treaties will be ratified and ambassadorial and cabinet nominations confirmed. The "power of the purse" and responsibilities for oversight of the executive branch give Congress considerable clout, and each year senators and representatives carefully examine defense budget authorizations.[6]

Congress's important constitutional role in foreign and defense policy is sometimes misunderstood. It is a common mistake among some journalists, executive officials, and even members of Congress to believe that the Constitution vests foreign policy decisions solely in the president. Sometimes this erroneous view leads to perverse results, such as the Iran-Contra affair, discussed earlier, in which officials at high levels in the executive branch "sought to protect the president's 'exclusive' prerogative by lying to Congress, to allies, to the public, and to one another" (apparently without the knowledge of the president). Louis Fisher suggests that such actions undermined the "mutual trust and close coordination by the two branches that are essential attributes in building a foreign policy that ensures continuity and stability."[7]

American Foreign Policy Through the Cold War

18.2 Outline the evolution of and major issues in American foreign policy through the end of the Cold War.

 ntil the mid-twentieth century, American foreign policy for the most part emphasized keeping a distance from the affairs of other countries, with the exception of neighbors to the south, in whose affairs

18.1
18.2
18.3
18.4
18.5
18.6

isolationism

The foreign policy course the United States followed throughout most of its history whereby it tried to stay out of other nations' conflicts, particularly European wars.

it intervened frequently. Following World War II, the United States, which had emerged as the dominant power, became locked in an ideological conflict with the Soviet Union.

☐ Isolationism

Throughout most of its history, the United States followed a foreign policy course called **isolationism**. This policy, articulated by George Washington in his farewell address, directed the country to stay out of other nations' conflicts, particularly European wars. The famous *Monroe Doctrine*, enunciated by President James Monroe, reaffirmed America's intention to stay out of Europe's affairs but warned European nations to stay out of Latin America. The United States—believing that its own political backyard included the Caribbean and Central and South America—did not hesitate to send marines, gunboats, or both to intervene in Central American and Caribbean affairs (for interventions since 1900, see Figure 18.1). When European nations were at war, however, Americans relished their distance from the conflicts. So it was until World War I (1914–1918).

In the wake of World War I, President Woodrow Wilson urged the United States to join the League of Nations, a forerunner to the UN. The U.S. Senate refused to ratify the League of Nations treaty, indicating that the country was not ready to abandon the long-standing American habit of isolationism, and that the Senate was not ready to relinquish any of its war-making authority to an international body. It was World War II, which forced the United States into a global conflict, that dealt a deathblow to American isolationism. Most nations signed a

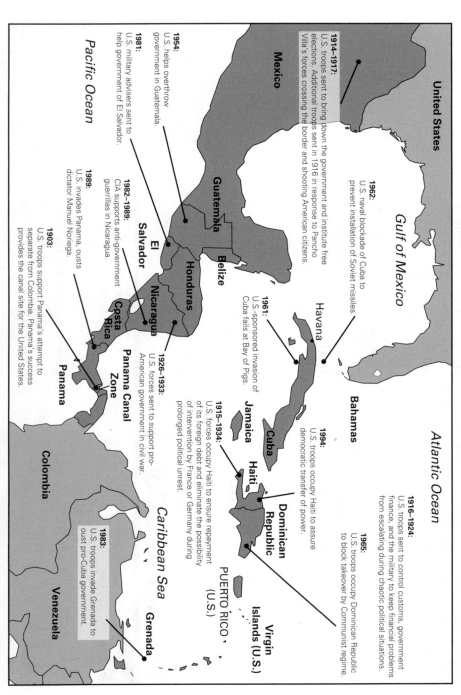

FIGURE 18.1 U.S. MILITARY INTERVENTIONS IN CENTRAL AMERICA AND THE CARIBBEAN SINCE 1900

United States

Gulf of Mexico

Atlantic Ocean

1916–1924:
U.S. troops sent to control customs, government finance, and the military to keep financial problems from escalating during chaotic political situations.

Bahamas

Havana

1962:
U.S. naval blockade of Cuba to prevent installation of Soviet missiles.

Mexico

1914–1917:
U.S. troops sent to bring down the government and institute free elections. Additional troops sent in 1916 in response to Pancho Villa's forces crossing the border and shooting American citizens.

1954:
U.S. helps overthrow government in Guatemala.

Guatemala

Belize

1961:
U.S.-sponsored invasion of Cuba fails at Bay of Pigs.

Cuba

Jamaica

1994:
U.S. troops occupy Haiti to assure democratic transfer of power.

1965:
U.S. troops occupy Dominican Republic to block takeover by Communist regime.

Honduras

1981:
U.S. military advisers sent to help government of El Salvador.

El Salvador

1926–1933:
U.S. forces sent to support pro-American government in civil war.

1915–1934:
U.S. forces occupy Haiti to ensure repayment of its foreign debt and eliminate the possibility of intervention by France or Germany during prolonged political unrest.

Haiti

Dominican Republic

PUERTO RICO (U.S.)

Virgin Islands (U.S.)

Pacific Ocean

1982–1989:
CIA supports anti-government guerrillas in Nicaragua.

Nicaragua

Costa Rica

1989:
U.S. invades Panama, ousts dictator Manuel Noriega.

1903:
U.S. troops support Panama's attempt to separate from Colombia; Panama's success provides the canal site for the United States.

Panama Canal Zone

Panama

Caribbean Sea

Grenada

1983:
U.S. troops invade Grenada to oust pro-Cuba government.

Colombia

Venezuela

charter for the UN at a conference in San Francisco in 1945. The United States was an original signatory and soon donated land to house the UN permanently in New York City.

The Cold War

At the end of World War II, the Allies had vanquished Germany and Japan, and much of Europe was strewn with rubble. The United States was unquestionably the dominant world power both economically and militarily. It not only had helped to bring the war to an end but also had inaugurated a new era in warfare by dropping the first atomic bombs on Japan in August 1945. Because only the United States possessed nuclear weapons, Americans looked forward to an era of peace secured by their nuclear umbrella.

After World War II, the United States forged strong alliances with the nations of Western Europe. To help them rebuild their economies, the United States poured billions of dollars into war-ravaged European nations through a program known as the Marshall Plan—named after its architect, Secretary of State George C. Marshall. A military alliance was also forged; the creation of NATO in 1949 affirmed the mutual military interests of the United States and Western Europe.

CONTAINMENT Although many Americans expected cooperative relations with the Soviet Union, their wartime ally, they soon abandoned these hopes. There is still much dispute about how the Cold War between the United States and the Soviet Union started.[8] Even before World War II ended, some American policymakers feared that the Soviets were intent on spreading communism not only to their neighbors but around the globe. All of Eastern Europe fell under Soviet domination as World War II ended. In 1946, Winston Churchill warned that the Russians had sealed off Eastern Europe with an "iron curtain."

Communist support of a revolt in Greece in 1946 compounded fears of Soviet aggression. Writing in *Foreign Affairs* in 1947, foreign policy strategist George F. Kennan proposed a policy of "containment."[9] His **containment doctrine** called for the United States to isolate the Soviet Union—to "contain" its advances and resist its encroachments—by peaceful means if possible but with force if necessary. When economic problems forced Great Britain to decrease its support of Greece, the United States stepped in based on the newly proclaimed Truman Doctrine, in which the United States declared it would help other nations oppose communism. The Soviet Union responded with the Berlin Blockade of 1948–1949, in which it closed off land access to West Berlin (which was surrounded by communist East Germany). The United States and its allies broke the blockade by airlifting food, fuel, and other necessities to the people of the beleaguered city.

The fall of China to Mao Zedong's communist-led forces in 1949 seemed to confirm American fears that communism was a cancer spreading over the "free world." In the same year, the Soviet Union exploded its first atomic bomb. The invasion of pro-American South Korea by communist North Korea in 1950 further fueled American fears of Soviet imperialism. President Truman said bluntly, "We've got to stop the Russians now," and sent American troops to Korea under UN auspices. The Korean War was a chance to put containment into practice. Involving China as well as North Korea, the war dragged on until July 27, 1953.

The 1950s were the height of the **Cold War**, though hostilities never quite erupted into armed battle between them, the United States and the Soviet Union were often on the brink of war. John Foster Dulles, secretary of state under Eisenhower, proclaimed a policy often referred to as "brinkmanship," in which the United States was to be prepared to use nuclear weapons in order to *deter* the Soviet Union and communist China from taking aggressive actions.

By the 1950s, the Soviet Union and the United States were engaged in an **arms race**. One side's weaponry goaded the other side to procure yet more weaponry,

---

containment doctrine
A foreign policy strategy advocated by George Kennan that called for the United States to isolate the Soviet Union, "contain" its advances, and resist its encroachments by peaceful means if possible but by force if necessary.

Cold War
The hostility between the United States and the Soviet Union, which often brought them to the brink of war and which spanned the period from the end of World War II until the collapse of the Soviet Union and Eastern European communist regimes in 1989 and the years following.

arms race
A tense relationship beginning in the 1950s between the Soviet Union and the United States whereby one side's weaponry became the other side's goad to procure more weaponry, and so on.

594

18.1
18.2
18.3
18.4
18.5
18.6

The Soviet Union built the Berlin Wall to separate communist East Berlin from the western sectors of the city. Here President John F. Kennedy looks over the wall in 1963 shortly before delivering a rousing anti-communist speech to the citizens of West Berlin.

as one missile led to another. By the mid-1960s, the result of the arms race was a point of *mutual assured destruction* (MAD), in which each side had the ability to annihilate the other even after absorbing a surprise attack. These nuclear capabilities also served to deter the use of nuclear weapons. Later sections of this chapter will examine efforts to control the arms race.

THE VIETNAM WAR The Korean War and the 1949 victory of communist forces in China fixed the U.S. government's attention on Asian communism. In 1950, President Truman decided to aid France's effort to retain its colonial possessions in Southeast Asia, but the Vietnamese communists finally defeated the French in a battle at Dien Bien Phu in 1954. The morning after the battle, peace talks among the participants and other major powers began in Geneva, Switzerland. Although a party to the resultant agreements, which stipulated that the country be temporarily divided into north and south regions and national elections be held throughout Vietnam in 1956, the United States never accepted them. Instead, it began supporting one noncommunist leader after another in South Vietnam, each seemingly more committed than the last to defeating communist forces in the North.[10]

Unable to contain the forces of the communist guerillas and the North Vietnamese army with American military advisers, President Lyndon Johnson sent in American troops—more than 500,000 at the peak of the undeclared war. He dropped more bombs on communist North Vietnam than the United States had dropped on Germany in all of World War II. These American troops and massive firepower failed to contain the North Vietnamese, however. At home, widespread protests against the war contributed to Johnson's decisions not to run for reelection in 1968 and to begin peace negotiations.

The new Nixon administration prosecuted the war vigorously, in Cambodia as well as in Vietnam, but also negotiated with the Vietnamese communists. A peace treaty was signed in 1973, but, as many expected, it did not hold. South Vietnam's capital, Saigon, finally fell to the North Vietnamese army in 1975. South and North Vietnam were reunited into a single nation, and Saigon was renamed Ho Chi Minh City in honor of the late leader of communist North Vietnam.

Looking back on the Vietnam War, many Americans question its worth. It divided the nation and made citizens painfully aware of the government's ability to lie to them—and (perhaps worse) to itself. It reminded Americans that even a "great power" cannot prevail in a protracted military conflict against a determined enemy unless there is a clear objective and unless the national will is sufficiently committed to expend vast resources on the task.

THE ERA OF DÉTENTE Even while the United States was waging the Vietnam War, Richard Nixon—a veteran fighter of the Cold War—supported a new policy that came to be called *détente*. The term was popularized by Nixon's national security adviser and later secretary of state, Henry Kissinger.

Détente represented a slow transformation from conflict thinking to cooperative thinking in foreign policy strategy. It sought a relaxation of tensions between the superpowers, coupled with firm guarantees of mutual security. The policy assumed that the United States and the Soviet Union had no permanent, immutable sources of conflict; that both had an interest in peace and world stability; and that a nuclear war was—and should be—unthinkable. Thus, foreign policy battles between the United States and the Soviet Union were to be waged with diplomatic, economic, and propaganda weapons; the threat of force was downplayed.

One major initiative emerging from détente was the *Strategic Arms Limitation Talks* (SALT). These talks represented a mutual effort by the United States and the Soviet Union to limit the growth of their nuclear capabilities, with each power maintaining sufficient nuclear weapons to deter a surprise attack by the other. Nixon signed the first SALT accord in 1972, and negotiations for a second agreement, SALT II, soon followed. After six years of laborious negotiations, President Carter finally signed the agreement and sent it to the Senate in 1979. The Soviet invasion of Afghanistan that year caused Carter to withdraw the treaty from Senate consideration, however, even though both he and Ronald Reagan insisted that they would remain committed to the agreement's limitations on nuclear weaponry.

The United States applied the philosophy of détente to the People's Republic of China as well as to the Soviet Union. After the fall of the pro-American government in 1949, the United States had refused to extend diplomatic recognition to the world's most populous nation, recognizing instead the government in exile on the nearby island of Taiwan. As a senator in the early 1950s, Richard Nixon had been an implacable foe of "Red China," even suggesting that the Democratic administration had traitorously "lost" China. Nevertheless, two decades later this same Richard Nixon became the first president to visit the People's Republic and sent an American mission there. President Jimmy Carter extended formal diplomatic recognition to China in 1979. Over time, cultural and economic ties between the United States and China increased greatly.

Not everyone favored détente, however. Even Carter called for a substantial increase in defense spending after the Soviet Union invaded Afghanistan in 1979. Few people saw more threats from the Soviet Union than did Ronald Reagan, who called it the "Evil Empire." He viewed the Soviet invasion of Afghanistan as typical Russian aggression that, if unchecked, could only grow more common. He hailed anticommunist governments everywhere and pledged to increase American defense spending.

THE REAGAN REARMAMENT From the mid-1950s to 1981 (with the exception of the Vietnam War), the defense budget had generally been declining as a percentage of both the total federal budget and the GDP. In 1955, during the Eisenhower administration, defense accounted for 61 percent of the federal budget and about 10 percent of the GDP. By the time President Reagan took office in 1981, the two numbers had dropped to 23 and 5.2 percent, respectively. These figures reflected a substantial cut indeed, although the decrease came about more because levels of social spending had increased than because military spending had declined.

According to Reagan, America faced a "window of vulnerability" because the Soviet Union was galloping ahead of the United States in military spending and, as a result, the United States had to build its defenses before it could negotiate arms control agreements. Reagan proposed the largest peacetime defense spending increase in American history: a five-year defense buildup costing $1.5 trillion. Defense officials

détente
A policy, beginning in the early 1970s, that sought a relaxation of tensions between the United States and the Soviet Union, coupled with firm guarantees of mutual security.

Beginning in 1989, communism in the Soviet Union and Eastern Europe suddenly began to crumble. The Berlin Wall fell, and the threat of nuclear war between the superpowers diminished. However, the thaw in the Cold War left a host of difficult new national security issues.

---

were ordered to find places to spend more money.[11] These heady days for the Pentagon lasted only through the first term of Reagan's presidency; however. In his second term, concern over huge budget deficits brought defense spending to a standstill. Once inflation is taken into account, Congress appropriated no increase in defense spending at all from 1985 to 1988.

In 1983 President Reagan added another element to his defense policy—a new plan for defense against missiles. He called it the Strategic Defense Initiative (SDI); critics quickly renamed it "Star Wars." Reagan's plans for SDI proposed creating a global umbrella in space wherein computers would scan the skies and use various high-tech devices to destroy invading missiles. The administration proposed a research program that would have cost tens of billions of dollars over the next decade.

In the face of an onslaught of criticism regarding the feasibility of SDI, its proponents reduced their expectations about the size and capabilities of any defensive shield that could be erected over the next generation. Talk of a smaller system—capable of protecting against an accidental launch of a few missiles or against a threat by some Third World country with nuclear weapons—replaced the dream of an impenetrable umbrella over the United States capable of defeating a massive Soviet nuclear strike.

THE FINAL THAW IN THE COLD WAR On May 12, 1989, in a commencement address at Texas A&M University, President George H. W. Bush announced a new era in American foreign policy. He termed this an era "beyond containment" and declared the goal of the United States would shift from containing Soviet expansion to seeking the integration of the Soviet Union into the community of nations.

The Cold War ended as few had anticipated—spontaneously. Suddenly, the elusive objective of 40 years of post–World War II U.S. foreign policy—freedom and self-determination for Eastern Europeans and Soviet peoples and the reduction of the military threat from the East—was achieved. Forces of change sparked by Soviet leader Mikhail Gorbachev led to a staggering wave of upheaval that shattered communist regimes and the postwar barriers between Eastern and Western Europe. The Berlin Wall, the most prominent symbol of oppression in Eastern Europe, came tumbling down on November 9, 1989, and East and West Germany formed a unified, democratic republic. The Soviet Union split into 15 separate nations, and noncommunist governments formed in most of them. Poland, Czechoslovakia (soon splitting into the Czech Republic and Slovakia), and Hungary established democratic governments, and reformers overthrew the old-line communist leaders in Bulgaria and Romania.

In 1989, reform seemed on the verge of occurring in China as well. That spring in Tiananmen Square, the central meeting place in Beijing, thousands of students held protests on behalf of democratization. Unable to tolerate challenges to their rule any longer, the aging Chinese leaders forcibly—and brutally—evacuated the square, crushing some protestors under armored tanks. It is still not clear how many students were killed and how many others arrested, but the reform movement in China received a serious setback. This suppression of efforts to develop democracy sent a chill through what had been a warming relationship between the United States and the People's Republic of China.

Reform continued elsewhere, however. On June 17, 1992, Boris Yeltsin addressed a joint session of the U.S. Congress. When the burly, silver-haired president of the new Russian republic entered the House chamber, members of Congress greeted him with chants of "Bo-ris, Bo-ris," and hailed him with numerous standing ovations.

Yeltsin proclaimed to thunderous applause,

> The idol of communism, which spread *everywhere* social strife, animosity and
> unparalleled brutality, which instilled fear in humanity, has collapsed … I am here
> to assure you that we will not let it rise again in our land.[12]

The Cold War that had been waged for two generations had ended, and the West, led by the United States, had won.

American Foreign Policy and the War on Terrorism

18.3 Explain the major obstacles to success in the war on terrorism.

he end of the Cold War raised hopes that a long era of relative tranquility would follow. Although in many parts of the world, conflicts continued and new conflicts arose, Americans experienced a sense of diminished danger. This sense was shattered by the events of September 11, 2001, however, and terrorism moved to the fore as a foreign policy concern.

☐ The Spread of Terrorism

Perhaps the most troublesome issue in the national security area is the spread of *terrorism*—the use of violence to demoralize and frighten a country's population or government. Terrorism takes many forms, including the bombing of buildings (such as the attacks on the World Trade Center and the Pentagon on September 11, 2001; on the American embassies in Kenya and Tanzania in 1998; and on the World Trade Center in 1993) and ships (such as the USS *Cole* in Yemen in 2000), the assassinations of political leaders (as when Iraq attempted to kill former president George Bush in 1993), and the kidnappings of diplomats and civilians (as when Iranians took Americans hostage in 1979).

It is difficult to defend against terrorism, especially in an open society. Terrorists have the advantage of stealth and surprise and, often, of a willingness to die for their cause. Improved security measures and better intelligence gathering can help. So, perhaps, can punishing governments and organizations that engage in terrorist activities. In 1986, the United States launched an air attack on Libya in response to Libyan-supported acts of terrorism; and in 1993, the United States struck at Iraq's intelligence center in response to a foiled plot to assassinate former president George Bush.

Terrorism takes many forms, including the bombing or other destruction of buildings and ships. Shown here are the results of terrorist attacks on the World Trade Center in New York in 2001, the American consulate in Benghazi, Libya, in 2012, and the USS *Cole* in Yemen in 2000.

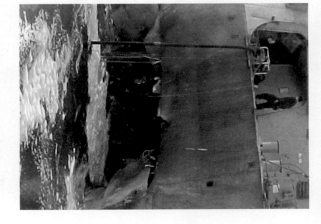

☐ Afghanistan and Iraq

Following the September 11, 2001, attacks, the United States declared war on terrorism. President George W. Bush made the war the highest priority of his administration, and the United States launched an attack on bin Laden and Al Qaeda and on the Taliban regime that had been harboring them. The Taliban fell in short order, although many suspected members of Al Qaeda escaped. In the meantime, the president declared that Iran, Iraq, and North Korea formed an "axis of evil" and began laying plans to remove Iraqi president Saddam Hussein from power. In 2003, a U.S.-led coalition toppled Hussein.

In the 2000 presidential campaign, George W. Bush had spoken of "humility" in foreign affairs and cautioned against overextending America's military. He had also warned against "nation building," which involves installing institutions of a national government in a country and often requires massive investment and military occupation. However, in the wake of the September, 11, 2001, attacks, the threat of terrorism caused the president to rethink these views, and the administration began talking about meeting America's "unparalleled responsibilities." With the invasion of Iraq, one of those responsibilities became to rebuild and democratize Iraq.

There is broad consensus that the planning for postwar Iraq was poor. The administration presumed that Americans would be welcomed as liberators, that Iraqi oil would pay for most (if not all) of the necessary reconstruction of the country, and that the Iraqis possessed the necessary skills and infrastructure to do the job. These premises proved to be faulty, and the United States faced first chaos and then a protracted insurrection, especially in the "Sunni triangle" around Baghdad. Five years after the end of the official fighting, 140,000 American troops were still stationed in Iraq, straining our defense resources. As both U.S. expenditures on reconstruction and American casualties mounted, the public's support for the effort declined substantially, and President Bush experienced a corresponding drop in his approval ratings.

Although President Bush often declared that postwar Iraq was the front line in the global war on terror, his critics responded that the war proved a boon for extremists. Muslims consider Iraq, the seat of Islamic power for five centuries, sacred ground. The presence of foreign, non-Muslim occupiers made the country a magnet for militants who opposed their presence and welcomed an opportunity to kill Americans and other Westerners.

Moreover, since the war in Afghanistan, Al Qaeda has transformed itself into an umbrella organization that provides an inspirational focal point for loosely affiliated terrorist groups in dozens of countries worldwide. Some view this transformed threat as potentially more dangerous than the one posed by the original Al Qaeda. A "decapitation" strategy, focusing on the elimination of a small group of senior figures in the original Al Qaeda network, may no longer be an adequate or appropriate strategy for dealing with a threat that has, in effect, metastasized.

Because of the increasingly decentralized nature of the terrorist threat, the military component of the global counterterrorism campaign is more likely to resemble a war of attrition on multiple fronts than a limited number of surgical strikes against a single adversary. One consequence is that the war on terrorism is likely to persist for many years. There were more than 9,700 terrorist attacks worldwide during 2013, resulting in nearly 18,000 deaths, 33,000 injuries, and 3,000 kidnappings. Most of the attacks and two-thirds of the deaths occurred in Iraq, Afghanistan, and Pakistan.[13]

Nor is it likely that the use of military force alone will suffice. Some observers argue that relying primarily on the use of force to combat terrorism is responding to a tactic (terrorism) rather than to the forces that generate it. Traditionally, winning a war involved defeating an enemy nation on the battlefield and forcing it to accept political terms. In contrast, winning the war on terror, involving as it does terrorist groups and not enemy states, will require political changes that erode and ultimately undermine support for the ideology and strategy of those determined to destroy the United States and its allies. The war will be won not when Washington and its allies kill or capture all terrorists or potential terrorists but when the ideology the terrorists espouse is discredited; when their tactics are seen to have failed; and when potential terrorists find more promising paths to the dignity, respect, and opportunities they crave.

In 2007, President Bush ordered a troop "surge" in Iraq. It was designed to quell violence and give Iraqis the opportunity to establish a democratic government, train forces to assume police and defense responsibilities, and engage in national reconciliation among the major religious and ethnic groups. The first goal was met, as violence was reduced. Progress on the other goals has been much slower, however. Nevertheless, President Obama followed Bush's timetable and removed the last American troops in 2011.

Obama turned America's attention to Afghanistan, which continued to be threatened by Taliban insurgents and religious extremists, some of whom were linked to Al Qaeda and to sponsors outside the country. Ensuring legitimate and effective governance in Afghanistan, delivering relief assistance, and countering the surge in narcotics cultivation remained major challenges for the international community. In 2009, President Obama announced an increase of 30,000 U.S. troops in Afghanistan. Success was elusive, however, although Navy Seals killed Osama bin Laden in 2011.

To compound the problem, a terrorist haven emerged in Pakistan's remote tribal belt. As Pakistan is understandably sensitive to another country's military operating within its borders, the U.S. military has been hampered in conducting the sort of missions that would disrupt terrorist activity there. In addition, it appears that there is substantial sympathy for the Taliban among many Pakistani military and intelligence officials, which constrains Pakistan's own efforts to fight the terrorists.

Whatever the current issues in the debate over the war on terrorism, there is no doubt that the need to fight terrorists has forced Americans to rethink some of the basic tenets of U.S. national security policy.

Defense Policy

18.4 Identify the major elements of U.S. defense policy.

T he politics of national defense involves high stakes—the nation's security, for example. Domestic political concerns, budgetary limitations, and ideology all influence decisions on the structure of defense (military) policy and negotiations with allies and adversaries. All public policies include budgets, people, and equipment. In the realm of national defense, these elements are especially critical because of the size of the budget and the bureaucracy as well as the destructive potential of modern weapons. The goals of American defense policy are to win the war on terrorism, defend American territory against new threats, and, if necessary, conduct a number of smaller military actions around the world. A large military infrastructure is necessary to meet these goals.

☐ Defense Spending

Defense spending now makes up about one-fifth of the federal budget. Although this is a much smaller percentage than in earlier years, vast sums of money and fundamental questions of public policy are still involved (see Figure 18.2). Some scholars have argued that America faces a trade-off between defense spending and social spending. A nation, they claim, must choose between guns and butter, and more guns means less butter. Evidence supporting the existence of such a trade-off is mixed, however. In general, defense and domestic policy expenditures appear to be independent of each other.[14]

Defense spending is a thorny political issue, entangled with ideological disputes. Conservatives advocate increases in defense spending and insist that America maintain

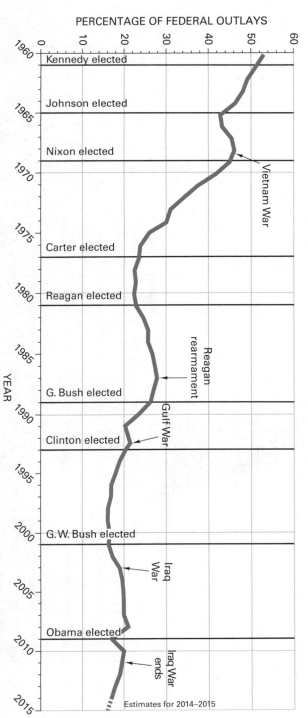

FIGURE 18.2 TRENDS IN DEFENSE SPENDING

John F. Kennedy took office in 1961 at the height of the Cold War. National defense was the dominant public policy for the U.S. government; it accounted for half of all the money that the government spent ("outlays") that year. Things have changed dramatically since then, however. Although defense spending continued to increase until the 1990s, spending on other policies increased even more. As a result, defense spending is now only about one-fifth of the budget. Still, at more than $600 billion per year through 2015, it remains a significant sum, one over which battles continue to be fought in Congress.

PERCENTAGE OF FEDERAL OUTLAYS

0 10 20 30 40 50 60

1960 — Kennedy elected

1965 — Johnson elected

Nixon elected

1970

Vietnam War

1975

Carter elected

1980 — Reagan elected

1985

Reagan rearmament

G. Bush elected

1990

Gulf War

Clinton elected

1995

2000 — G. W. Bush elected

Iraq War

2005

Obama elected

2010

Iraq War ends

2015

Estimates for 2014–2015

YEAR

SOURCE: Budget of the United States Government, Fiscal Year 2015: Historical Tables (Washington, D.C.: U.S. Government Printing Office, 2014), Table 3.1.

its readiness at a high level. They point out that many nations and terrorist organizations retain potent military capability and that wars on a significant scale are still possible. Liberals have supported increased defense spending for the war on terrorism but more generally are skeptical of defense spending. They maintain that the Pentagon wastes money and that the United States buys too many guns and too little butter. The most crucial aspect of national defense, they argue, is a strong economy, which is based on investments in "human capital" such as health and education.

Why It Matters to You
The Defense Budget

In the twenty-first century, the United States spends about one-fifth of its national budget on defense to support a large defense establishment. This expenditure contributes to large annual budget deficits, although some argue that we should spend even more to protect the country against terrorism.

In the 1990s, the lessening of East–West tensions gave momentum to significant reductions in defense spending, which some called the *peace dividend*. Changing spending patterns was not easy, however. For example, military hardware developed during the early 1980s has proven to be increasingly expensive to purchase and maintain. And when the assembly lines at weapons plants close down, submarine designers, welders, and many others lose their jobs. These programs become political footballs as candidates compete over promises to keep weapons systems in production.[15] Ideology plays a crucial role in the basic decisions members of Congress make regarding defense spending, but once these decisions are made, liberal as well as conservative representatives and senators fight hard to help constituencies win and keep defense contracts.[16]

The trend of reductions in defense spending reversed abruptly in 2001 following the September 11 terrorist attacks. Whatever the proper level of spending, there is no question that the United States spends more on defense than the next 15 or 20 biggest spenders combined. The United States has overwhelming nuclear superiority, the world's dominant air force, the only navy with worldwide operations (which also has impressive airpower), and a unique capability to project power around the globe. No other country in modern history has come close to this level of military predominance, and the gap between the United States and other nations is increasing. Moreover, the military advantages are even greater when one considers the quality as well as the quantity of U.S. defense capabilities. America has exploited the military applications of advanced communications and information technology and has developed the ability to coordinate and process information about the battlefield and to destroy targets from afar with extraordinary precision.

With America's withdrawal from Iraq and its huge budget deficits, pressures once again grew to reduce military spending. President Obama ordered the Pentagon to reduce its budget, and the United States cut back on both personnel and weapons.

Personnel

Crucial to the structure of America's defense is a large standing military force. Payrolls and pensions for the more than 7 million persons who work for the Pentagon, serve in the reserves, or receive military retirement pay, veterans' pensions, or disability compensation constitute a large component of the defense budget. The United States has about 1.3 million men and women on active duty and about 821,000 in the National Guard and reserves (see Figure 18.3). There are about 300,000 active-duty troops deployed abroad; many of these troops are serving in Afghanistan, although there is also a substantial U.S. presence in Europe, Japan, and South Korea.[17] Foreign deployment is a very costly enterprise, and the ongoing wars in particular frequently evoke calls to bring the troops home. As demands have increased on active-duty personnel, the military now relies much more

FIGURE 18.3 SIZE OF THE ARMED FORCES*

SIZE (IN THOUSANDS)

Marines	184
Air Force	311
Navy	324
Army	490
Reserves	821

*2015 estimates

SOURCE: Office of Management and Budget, *Budget of the United States Government, Fiscal Year 2015: Appendix* (Washington, D.C.: U.S. Government Printing Office, 2014), 233–234.

heavily on National Guard and reserve units to maintain national security; National Guard and reserve units have served for extended periods in Iraq and Afghanistan.

☐ Weapons

To deter an aggressor's attack, the United States has relied on possession of a triad of nuclear weapons: ground-based intercontinental ballistic missiles (ICBMs), submarine-launched ballistic missiles, and strategic bombers. Both the United States and Russia have thousands of large nuclear warheads. These weapons, like troops, are costly: each stealth bomber costs over $2 *billion*; the total cost of building and maintaining nuclear weapons has been $8.5 *trillion*.[18] Moreover, nuclear weapons pose obvious dangers to human survival.

The end of the Cold War led to a focus on arms reduction. In 1988, President Reagan and Soviet leader Mikhail Gorbachev agreed to eliminate *intermediate-range*

President Reagan and Soviet President Mikhail Gorbachev signed a treaty eliminating intermediate-range nuclear missiles from Europe. The INF treaty marked the first time an American president had agreed to reduce current levels of nuclear weapons.

nuclear forces (INF), marking the first time the two sides agreed to reduce current levels of nuclear weapons. Three years later, Presidents Gorbachev and George H. W. Bush signed the *Strategic Arms Reduction Treaty* (START). The treaty had the distinction of being the first accord mandating the elimination of strategic nuclear weaponry. In 1993, President Bush and President Boris Yeltsin of Russia signed an agreement (START II) to cut substantially the U.S. and Russian nuclear arsenals (with the latter including those of Ukraine, Belarus, and Kazakhstan). The agreement banned large, accurate ICBMs with multiple warheads altogether. President George W. Bush, in 2002, and President Obama, in 2010, signed agreements with Russia to further limit strategic weapons.

Even while negotiating reductions on nuclear arsenals, President George W. Bush stepped up efforts begun by Ronald Reagan to build a national missile defense. To pursue this system, in December 2001 the president withdrew the United States from the Anti-Ballistic Missile Treaty, part of the SALT accord that the United States and the Soviet Union had signed in 1972.

Nuclear weapons are the most destructive in America's arsenal, but they are by no means the only weapons. Jet fighters, aircraft carriers, and even tanks are extraordinarily complex as well as extraordinarily costly. The perception that space-age technology helped win the Gulf War in "100 hours" and topple the Taliban regime in Afghanistan and Saddam Hussein in Iraq with few American casualties, along with the fact that producing expensive weapons provides jobs for American workers, mean that high-tech weapons systems will continue to play an important role in America's defense posture.

☐ Reforming Defense Policy

The rethinking of national security policy prompted by the changing nature of threats to America's security has led to a reforming of the nation's military. Reevaluating weapons systems is part of this effort. So is changing the force structure to make the armed forces lighter, faster, and more flexible. Yet other changes include more effectively coupling intelligence with an increasingly agile military and a greater use of Special Forces, elite, highly trained tactical teams that conduct specialized operations such as reconnaissance, unconventional warfare, and counterterrorism actions. New approaches to military conflict inevitably follow from such transformations.

Although the United States has unsurpassed military strength, numerous international matters clamor for attention, and armed forces are not relevant to many of them. Even the mightiest nation can be mired in intractable issues.

The New National Security Agenda

18.5 Analyze the evolving challenges for U.S. national security policy.

T he national security agenda is changing rapidly. To begin with, the role of military power is changing, and more countries now possess nuclear weapons. Moreover, international economic issues are increasingly important. Dealing with China and India on trade and finance has become as crucial as negotiating arms reductions with Russia. Economic competition with other countries has increased, as has the economic vulnerability of the United States. Oil supply lines, for example, depend on a precarious Middle Eastern peace and on the safe passage of huge tankers through a sliver of water called the Strait of Hormuz. In an interdependent world, our dependence on trade places us at the mercy of interest rates in Germany, restrictive markets in Japan, currency values in China, and so on. In addition, determining policy regarding the global environment has taken on new prominence. Inevitably, the national security agenda is having ever-greater repercussions for domestic policymaking.

☐ The Changing Role of Military Power

Although the United States is the world's mightiest military power, there are limits to what military strength can achieve.[19] In the long and controversial Vietnam War, for example, 500,000 American troops were not enough. Our military might did not protect us from the deadly terrorist attacks on September 11, 2001. Moreover, force is often not an appropriate way of achieving other goals—such as economic and ecological welfare—that are becoming more important in world affairs.[20] Economic conflicts do not yield to high-tech weapons. America cannot persuade nations to sell it cheap oil, or prop up the textile industry's position in world trade, by resorting to military might. The United States is long on firepower at the very time when firepower is decreasing in its utility as an instrument of foreign policy.

Although the United States is militarily supreme, it is becoming increasingly dependent on other countries to defeat terrorism, protect the environment, control weapons of mass destruction, regulate trade, and deal with other problems that cross national boundaries. Even the effective use of U.S. military power requires military bases, ports, airfields, fuel supplies, and overflight rights that only its allies can provide.[21]

According to Joseph Nye, it is "soft power"—the ability of a country to persuade others to do what it wants without force or coercion—that is often crucial to national security. Countries need to be able to exert this soft power as well as hard power; that is, security hinges as much on winning hearts and minds as it does on winning wars.[22] Indeed, American culture, ideals, and values have been important to helping Washington attract partners and supporters, to shaping long-term attitudes and preferences in a way that is favorable to the United States.

Despite these changes, military power remains an important element in U.S. foreign policy. One reason is that the end of the Cold War emboldened local dictators and reignited age-old ethnic rivalries that had been held in check by the Soviet Union, resulting in a greatly increased number of regional crises posing a threat to peace. The status of the United States as the only superpower meant that people were more likely to look to it for help when trouble erupted, as in the case of the former Yugoslavia. More recently, uprisings in the Middle East have raised anew the difficult foreign policy problem of deciding when to involve U.S. troops.

HUMANITARIAN INTERVENTIONS On various occasions in recent decades, the United States and its allies have used military force to accomplish humanitarian ends. Notable examples include the efforts to distribute food and then oust a ruthless and unprincipled warlord in Somalia in 1992 and 1993; restore the elected leader of Haiti in 1994; stop the ethnic warfare in Bosnia by bombing the Serbs in 1995; protect ethnic Albanians in Kosovo by bombing Serbs in 1999; and provide food, housing, and medical care in the aftermath of a severe earthquake in Haiti in 2010.

Such interventions are often controversial because they may involve violating a nation's sovereignty with the use of force. And the United States is usually hesitant to intervene, as American lives may be lost and there may be no clear ending point for the mission. Nevertheless, demands for humanitarian intervention continue to arise. For example, in recent years, the crisis in Darfur in western Sudan—where, since February 2003, more than 250,000 people have been killed and nearly 3 million displaced—prompted new calls for international humanitarian intervention.

Why It *Matters* to You

The Only Superpower

The United States is the world's only superpower. This puts us in a strong position to defend ourselves against other nations. It also means, however, that the United States comes under more pressure to intervene in the world's hot spots. Furthermore, being a superpower does not protect us against attacks by nonstate actors, such as terrorists.

ECONOMIC SANCTIONS An ancient tool of diplomacy, sanctions are nonmilitary penalties imposed on a foreign government in an attempt to modify its behavior. A wide range of penalties are possible—for example, a cutoff of aid, a ban on military sales, restrictions on imports, or a total trade embargo. The implied power behind sanctions that the United States imposes is U.S. economic muscle and access to U.S. markets.

Economic sanctions are often a first resort in times of crises, as a less risky and extreme measure than sending in troops. In many cases, they are the outgrowth of pressure from well-organized domestic political groups concerned about another country's policies related to ethnic or religious groups, the environment, human rights, or economic or other issues. These groups and government officials, in seeking sanctions, may want to curb unfair trade practices, end human rights abuses and drug trafficking, promote environmental initiatives, or stop terrorism.

Some economic sanctions have accomplished their intended goals; for example, sanctions levied against South Africa in the mid-1980s contributed to the demise of apartheid. Most experts, however, view these tools as having limited effect. The economic sanctions on Iran have yet to prevent it from seeking to build nuclear weapons.

To succeed, sanctions generally must have broad international support, which is rare. Unilateral sanctions are doomed to failure. The real losers may be U.S. companies that are forced to cede lucrative markets to competitors around the globe. For example, when President Carter imposed a grain embargo on the Soviet Union in 1980 in retaliation for the Soviet invasion of Afghanistan, only U.S. farmers were hurt; the Soviet Union simply bought grain elsewhere.

In addition, critics argue that sanctions are counterproductive because they can provoke a nationalist backlash. The decades-old sanctions against Cuba did not oust Marxist dictator Fidel Castro, and threats of sanctions against China at various times typically resulted in a hardening of China's attitude regarding human rights and other matters.

☐ Nuclear Proliferation

The spread of technology has enabled more countries to build nuclear weapons and the missiles to deliver them. Policymakers in the United States and other countries have sought to halt the spread of nuclear weapons, notably through the framework of the Nuclear Non-Proliferation Treaty, signed in 1968. The primary means of accomplishing this goal has been to encourage nations to agree that they would not acquire—or, at least, would not test—nuclear weapons. As you can see in Figure 18.4, only eight countries have declared that they have nuclear weapons capacities: the United States, Russia, Britain, France, China, India, Pakistan, and North Korea. Israel certainly also has nuclear weapons. South Africa and three countries that used to be part of the Soviet Union—Belarus, Kazakhstan, and Ukraine—have given up nuclear weapons. Algeria, Argentina, Brazil, Libya, South Korea, Sweden, and Taiwan have ended their nuclear weapons programs.

Currently, policymakers are most concerned about North Korea and about Iran, which is actively developing nuclear weapons capabilities. These nations pose serious threats to their neighbors and perhaps to the United States as well. Over the last two decades, the United States has promised a range of aid and other benefits to North Korea in return for ending its nuclear weapons program. These incentives have not worked, as North Korea tested a nuclear weapon in 2006 and now possesses a few nuclear weapons. Iran does not yet possess nuclear weapons, although it has taken a defiant stance and refused to cooperate fully with international weapons inspectors. Iran is likely to occupy a prominent position on the foreign policy agenda for some time (see "You Are the Policymaker: Defanging a Nuclear Threat").

Other nations have serious security concerns when faced with hostile neighbors possessing nuclear weapons, concerns that can contribute to nuclear proliferation. When India resumed testing of nuclear weapons in 1998, neighboring Pakistan quickly tested its first nuclear weapons. The two nations' possession of nuclear weapons is a matter of special concern because of their history of conflict over Kashmir. In addition, political instability in Pakistan raises concern over the government's control of its nuclear weapons.

FIGURE 18.4 THE SPREAD OF NUCLEAR WEAPONS

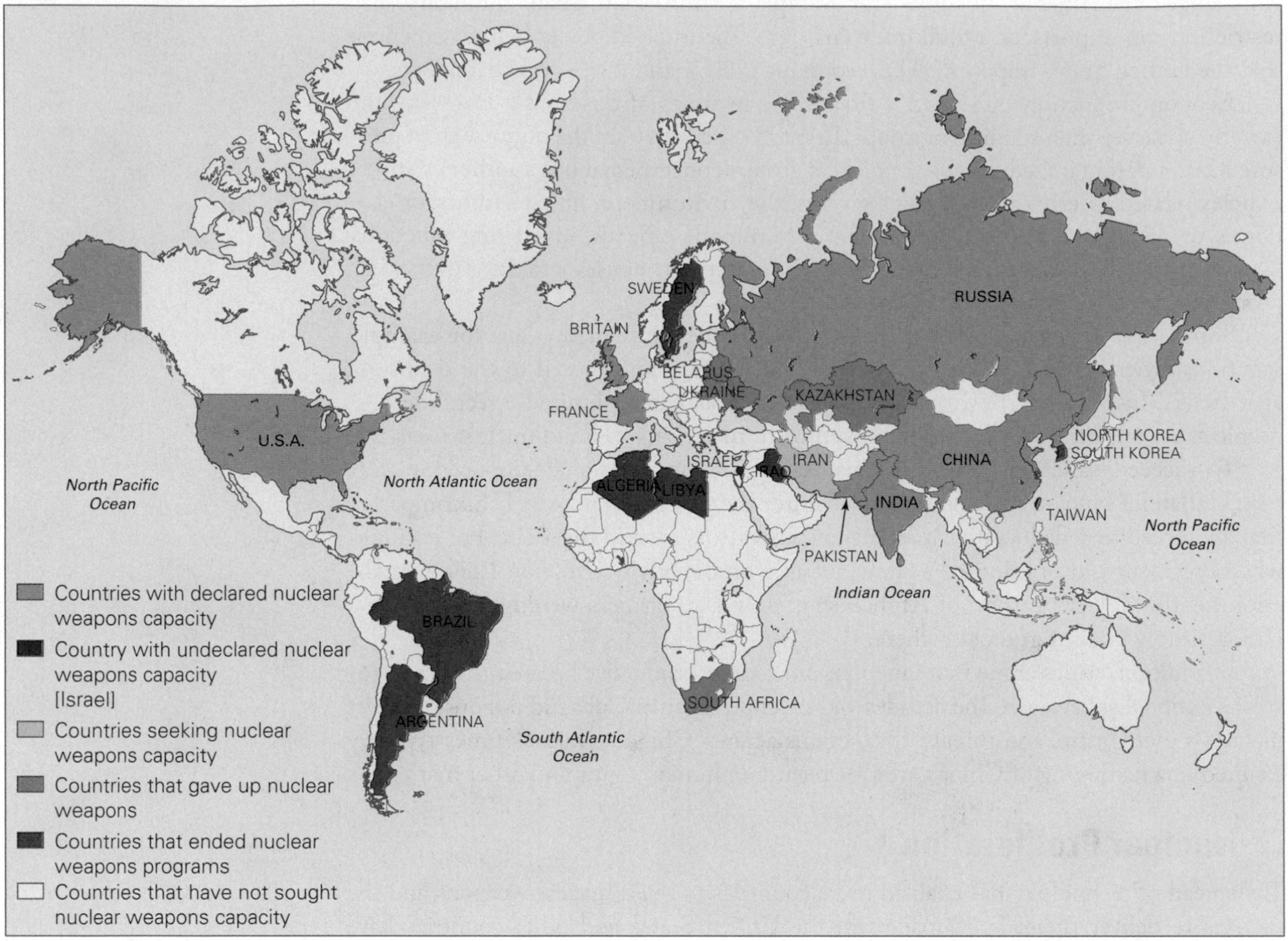

Countries with declared nuclear weapons capacity

Country with undeclared nuclear weapons capacity [Israel]

Countries seeking nuclear weapons capacity

Countries that gave up nuclear weapons

Countries that ended nuclear weapons programs

Countries that have not sought nuclear weapons capacity

interdependency
Mutual reliance, as in the economic realm, in which actions in nations reverberate and affect the economic well-being of people in other nations.

☐ The International Economy

At one time, nations' international economic policymaking centered largely on erecting high barriers to importing foreign products. Such economic isolationism is no longer feasible in today's international economy, characterized above all by **interdependency**, in which actions in a country reverberate and affect the economic well-being of people in other countries. The health of the American economy depends increasingly on the prosperity of its trading partners and on the smooth flow of trade and finance across borders (see "Young People & Politics: Embracing Globalization").

The *International Monetary Fund* (IMF) to which the United States is by far the largest contributor, is a cooperative international organization of 185 countries intended to stabilize the exchange of currencies and the world economy. In the late 1990s it provided loans and credits to a number of Asian countries, including South Korea, Thailand, Indonesia, and the Philippines, so they would not default on their debts—and in the process, throw the international economy into turmoil. In 2011, the IMF worked with European leaders to help debt-ridden countries such as Greece avoid defaulting on their debts.

INTERNATIONAL TRADE Since the end of World War II, trade among nations has grown rapidly. American exports and imports have increased 20-fold since 1970 alone. Among the largest U.S. exporters are grain farmers, producers of computer hardware and software, aircraft manufacturers, moviemakers, heavy construction companies, and purveyors of accounting and consulting services. Foreign tourist spending bolsters the U.S. travel, hotel, and recreation industries. American colleges and universities derive

You Are the Policymaker

Defanging a Nuclear Threat

One of the highest priorities of U.S. foreign policy is stopping the spread of nuclear weapons. Iran is close to building its first nuclear bomb. Nuclear weapons in Iranian hands is not a comforting thought. The State Department has designated Iran as the world's leading sponsor of terrorism, and it plays a disruptive role in sustaining violence in the region, particularly Syria. The former president, Mahmoud Ahmadinejad, has declared that Israel should be "wiped off the map." Iran has missiles that can now reach Israel and U.S. forces in Afghanistan and is developing missiles that can reach Western Europe and North America.

In addition, Iran's acquisition of nuclear weapons may set off an arms race in the volatile Middle East. If Iran gets the bomb, it may drive the Saudis, Turks, and others to develop their own nuclear weapons.

How should the U.S. deal with this threat? The first response was diplomacy. The United States and its Western European allies sought to convince Iran to stop its nuclear research, and the International Atomic Energy Agency sealed some nuclear research facilities. In 2006, however, Iran removed the seals and declared that it had every right to develop atomic energy.

Another option is economic sanctions. The United States and other countries imposed a matrix of economic sanctions to inhibit and discourage nuclear weapons development. Although the sanctions have made life less pleasant for Iranians, they have not stopped Iran's nuclear efforts. The United States could embargo Iran's main export, oil, but that would drive up energy prices everywhere and is unlikely to receive the international support necessary for economic sanctions to succeed. Curtailing foreign travel

will have little impact on a people who currently do not travel much outside their borders.

Another option is ordering the CIA and other agencies to encourage an overthrow of the government. The chances of succeeding in such a venture are small, however.

There are also military options. The United States could invade Iran, but the U.S. military is overstretched with its responsibilities around the world and is reducing the size of the armed forces to save money. In addition, invading Iran would mean occupying a large country of 80 million people. Such an effort would be very expensive and require an enormous military force. Moreover, there is no reason to think such an occupation would be over quickly, magnifying the cost.

A final option is air strikes by Israel or the United States, possibly accompanied by commando raids. It is doubtful that bombs could eradicate Iran's nuclear program (much of which is underground), but it is possible they could set it back for years, possibly long enough for the regime to implode.

Of course, Iran is not likely to react passively to such a strike; the mullahs running the country would almost certainly order terrorist retaliation against the United States and Israel and increase their efforts to sabotage our efforts in next-door Afghanistan and Iraq. Iran could also become a rallying point for the Islamic world, which is already deeply suspicious and often disdainful of American policy. One result could be a further radicalization of millions of Muslims and an increase in the pool of potential recruits to terrorism.

What do you think? President Obama faces a dilemma regarding Iran. If you were president, what would *you* do?

a significant portion of their revenue from educating foreign students. The globalization of finances has been even more dramatic than the growth of trade. Worldwide computer and communications networks link financial markets in all parts of the globe instantaneously, making it easier to move capital across national boundaries but also increasing the probability that, say, a steep decline on Wall Street will send the Japanese stock market plummeting.

Why It *Matters* to You

Economic Interdependence

The world economy is increasingly interdependent. This increased interdependence means, for example, that investments and markets in other countries provide economic opportunities for Americans but also that Americans are more dependent on the strength of other countries' economies and that U.S. products and workers face increased competition.

Young People & Politics

Embracing Globalization

The protests that regularly occur during economic summit meetings of the leaders of the world's most economically developed countries might lead you to conclude that young adults are in the forefront of opposition to globalization, the process by which national economies, societies, and cultures have become integrated through a globe-spanning network of communication, travel, and trade. Actually, the facts are quite different, according to the Pew *Global Attitudes Project* surveys.

In every country, globalization has produced some political tensions. However, strong majorities in all regions believe that increased global interconnectedness is a good thing, and in most regions young people are more likely than their elders to see advantages in increased global trade and communication, and they are more likely to support "globalization."

The hesitation among some older citizens to embrace the movement toward globalization may be due in part to national pride. Although people in all countries and of all ages are proud of their cultures, in North America and Western Europe in particular, that pride is markedly stronger among the older generations, with younger people tending to be less wedded to their cultural identities. In the United States, 68 percent of those aged 65 and older agree with the statement "our people are not perfect, but our culture is superior," while only 49 percent of those aged 18 to 29 agree. The generation gap in Western Europe is similar.

Despite the general attraction of globalization, solid majorities everywhere think their way of life needs to be protected against foreign influence. Again, that desire cuts across all age groups everywhere, but in the United States and Western Europe, there is a generation gap, with older people much more worried than are the young about protecting their country's way of life. In the

United States, 71 percent of people aged 65 and older agree that they want to shield their way of life from foreign influence, while just 55 percent of those aged 18 to 29 agree. This generation gap is even greater in France, Germany, and Britain, where older people are twice as likely as young people to be worried about erosion of their way of life.

Skepticism about foreign influence is evident in widespread, intense antipathy toward immigration. Majorities in nearly every country surveyed support tougher restrictions on people entering their countries. Again, however, age makes a difference. Immigrants are particularly unpopular across Europe, especially among the older generation, where half of those surveyed said they agreed completely with the statement that additional immigration controls were needed. In the United States, for example, 50 percent of those aged 65 and older indicate strong support for additional controls compared to only 40 percent of young people.

There are many reasons why young adults may be more supportive of globalization than are their elders. Better educated, more widely traveled, and more accustomed to the Internet, young adults seem to be less parochial, have less fear of change, and have more appreciation for the benefits of other cultures. Partially as a result of these attitudes, we should expect the trend toward globalization to accelerate over the coming decades.

CRITICAL THINKING QUESTIONS

1. Do you think young people fear foreign competition?

2. Do you agree that education and experience are the best explanations for the greater support of globalization among young people?

tariff
A tax added to imported goods to raise their price, thereby protecting businesses and workers from foreign competition.

Coping with foreign economic issues is becoming just as difficult—and, increasingly, just as important—as coping with domestic ones. In a simpler time, the main instrument of international economic policy was the **tariff**, a tax added to the cost of imported goods. Tariffs are intended to raise the price of imported goods and thereby protect the country's businesses and workers from foreign competition. Tariff making, though, is a game everyone can play. High U.S. tariffs encourage other nations to respond with high tariffs on American products. The high tariffs that the government enacted early in the Great Depression (and that some say aggravated this economic crisis) were the last of their kind. Since that time, the world economy has moved from high tariffs and protectionism to lower tariffs and freer trade. In recent decades, various agreements have lowered barriers to trade, including the 1993 *North American Free Trade Agreement* (*NAFTA*) with Canada and Mexico, the 1994 *General Agreement on Tariffs and Trade* (*GATT*), the 2005 Central American–Dominican Republic Free Trade Agreement, and the free trade agreements with South Korea, Columbia, and Panama in 2011.

International trade is a controversial subject. Opponents believe that it undermines U.S. laws that protect the environment and workers' rights, costs some employees their jobs, and encourages exploitation of foreign workers. Proponents argue that everyone benefits from increased trade. U.S. companies, such as McDonald's, aggressively seek to expand international sales.

However, nontariff barriers such as quotas, subsidies, and quality specifications for imported products are common means of limiting imports. In recent decades, for example, the United States has placed quotas on the amount of steel that could be imported and has negotiated voluntary limits on the importation of Japanese automobiles. Such policies do save American jobs involved in producing steel and automobiles, but they also raise the price of steel and automobiles that Americans buy, and, since increased steel prices raise the costs of making products that use steel, they also wind up costing American jobs. Both the United States and European countries provide significant subsidies for a range of agricultural products, subsidies that have sometimes proved to be obstacles to negotiating tariff reductions.

More foreign-owned companies are building factories in the United States—just as American companies have plants around the globe. Thus, many Hondas and Toyotas are made in the United States. Foreign-owned firms in the United States employ about 5 percent of the workforce and account for a significant percentage of research-and-development spending and investment in plants and equipment. These firms also pay more on average than do their counterparts in the rest of the U.S. economy.[23] As a result of the foreign investments in the United States, it is increasingly difficult to define "imports."

BALANCE OF TRADE When Americans purchase foreign products, they send dollars out of the country. Thus, for example, when a tanker of oil from Saudi Arabia arrives in Houston, dollars travel to Saudi Arabia. If other nations do not buy as much from us as we buy from them, then the United States is paying out more than it is taking in. A country's **balance of trade** is the ratio of what a country pays for imports to what it earns from exports. When a country imports more than it exports, it has a balance-of-trade *deficit.* Year after year, the American balance of trade has been preceded by a minus sign; in 2013, for example, the deficit for the balance of trade was $471 billion. Although the United States runs a surplus in exporting services (such as financial services), it runs a large deficit in manufactured goods.[24]

A balance of trade deficit can lead to a decline in the value of a nation's currency. If the dollar's buying power declines against other currencies, Americans pay more for goods that they buy from other nations. This decline in the value of the dollar, however, also makes American products cheaper abroad, thereby increasing our exports. Since

balance of trade
The ratio of what is paid for imports to what is earned from exports. When more is paid than earned, there is a balance-of-trade deficit.

18.1
18.2
18.3
18.4
18.5
18.6

Organization of Petroleum Exporting Countries

An economic organization consisting primarily of Middle Eastern nations that seeks to control the amount of oil its members produce and sell to other nations and hence the price of oil.

the late 1980s, the United States has experienced an export boom, reaching $2.3 trillion in 2011.[25] Exports account for more than 10 percent of the GDP. About 5 percent of all civilian employment in the United States is related to manufacturing exports. A substantial amount of white-collar employment—in the area of financial services, for example—is also directly tied to exports.

☐ Energy

In 1973, the **Organization of Petroleum Exporting Countries** (OPEC) responded to American support of Israel in its war against Egypt that year by embargoing oil shipments to the United States and Western European nations. The fuel shortages and long lines at gas stations that resulted from the 1973 oil embargo convincingly illustrated the growing interdependency of world politics.

More than half the world's recoverable reserves of oil lie in the Middle East; Saudi Arabia alone controls much of this resource. Within the United States, states such as Texas, Oklahoma, Louisiana, and Alaska produce considerable amounts of oil but far from enough to meet the country's needs. America imports nearly half of its annual consumption of oil from other countries, particularly from countries in the Middle East. The United States is less dependent on foreign sources of oil than are many European countries, like France or Italy, which have virtually no oil of their own, or Japan, which imports all its oil. On the other hand, America's dependence on foreign oil makes the United States vulnerable, especially because the Middle East remains unstable. The decision to respond to Iraq's invasion of Kuwait in 1990 was based in large part on the fact that Kuwait produces about 10 percent of the world's oil, and its neighbor, Saudi Arabia, also vulnerable to attack by Iraq, possesses about a quarter of the world's proven oil reserves.

☐ Foreign Aid

Presidents of both parties have pressed for aid to nations in the developing world. Aside from simple humanitarian concern, these requests have been motivated by, for example, a desire to stabilize nations that were friendly to the United States or that possessed supplies of vital raw materials. Sometimes aid has been given in the form of grants, but often it has taken the form of credits and loan guarantees to purchase American goods, loans at favorable interest rates, and forgiveness of previous loans. At other times, the United States has awarded preferential trade agreements for the sale of foreign goods in the United States.

A substantial percentage of foreign aid is in the form of military assistance and is targeted to a few countries the United States considers to be of vital strategic significance: Israel, Egypt, Turkey, and Greece have received the bulk of such assistance in recent years. Foreign aid programs have also assisted with goals, including agricultural modernization and irrigation as well as family planning in countries where high population growth rates are a problem. Food for Peace programs have subsidized the sale of American agricultural products to poor countries (and simultaneously given an economic boost to American farmers). Peace Corps volunteers have fanned out over the globe to provide medical care and other services in less developed nations.

Nevertheless, foreign aid has never been popular with Americans, who tend to greatly overestimate the extent of it. It is not surprising that Congress typically cuts the president's foreign aid requests; such requests lack an electoral constituency to support them, and many people believe that aid provided to developing nations serves only to further enrich their elites without helping the poor. Currently, Congress appropriates less than 1 percent of the federal budget for economic and humanitarian foreign aid. Although the United States donates more total aid (both for economic development and military assistance) than any other country, it devotes a smaller share of its GDP to foreign economic development than any other developed nation (see "America in Perspective: Ranking Largesse"). It is important to note, however, that the United States provides a great deal more aid through grants from private voluntary organizations, foundations, religious organizations, corporations, universities, and individuals.[26]

America in Perspective

Ranking Largesse

The United States is the largest donor of foreign aid, but it ranks lower than most industrialized nations in the percentage of its gross national income (GNI) it spends on economic development aid for needy nations. American private giving, which is not reflected in these figures, is substantial, however, and is typically much greater than private giving from other nations.

CRITICAL THINKING QUESTIONS

1. Which is the more informative measure of a nation's giving, total aid or percent of GNI?

2. Should the United States be giving more aid to underdeveloped nations?

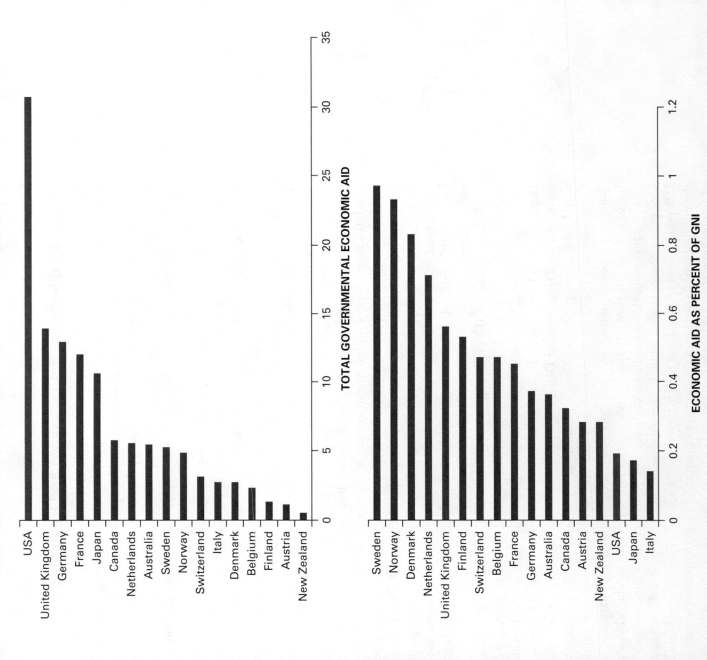

TOTAL GOVERNMENTAL ECONOMIC AID

ECONOMIC AID AS PERCENT OF GNI

SOURCE: Organization for Economic Cooperation and Development, *OECD Factbook 2014* (Paris: Organization for Economic Cooperation and Development, 2014).

612

18.1
18.2
18.3
18.4
18.5
18.6

Understanding National Security Policymaking

Although national security policy deals with issues and nations that are often far from America's shores, it is crucially important to all Americans. And the themes that have guided your understanding of American politics throughout *Government in America*—democracy and the scope of government—can also shed light on the topic of international relations.

☐ National Security Policymaking and Democracy

To some commentators, the conduct of America's international relations is undemocratic in the sense of having little to do with public opinion. Because domestic issues are closer to their daily lives and easier to understand, Americans are usually more interested in domestic policy than in foreign policy. This preference would seem to give public officials more discretion in making national security policy. In addition, some say, those with the discretion are elites in the State Department and unelected military officers in the Pentagon.

There is little evidence, however, that policies at odds with the wishes of the American people can be sustained; civilian control of the military is unquestionable. When the American people hold strong opinions regarding international relations—as when they first supported and later opposed the war in Vietnam—policymakers are usually responsive. Citizens in democracies do not choose to fight citizens in other democracies, and studies have found that well-established democracies rarely go to war against one another.[27]

In addition, the system of separation of powers plays a crucial role in foreign as well as domestic policy. The president takes the lead on national security matters, but Congress has a central role in matters of international relations. Whether treaties are ratified, defense budgets are appropriated, weapons systems are authorized, or foreign aid is awarded is ultimately at the discretion of Congress, the government's most representative policymaking body. Specific issues such as the proper funding for the Strategic Defense Initiative rarely determine congressional elections, but public demands for and objections to policies are likely to be heard in Washington.

When it comes to the increasingly important arena of American international economic policy, pluralism is pervasive. Agencies and members of Congress, as well as their constituents, all pursue their own policy goals. For example, the Treasury Department and the Federal Reserve Board worry about the negative balance of trade, and the Department of Defense spends billions in other countries to maintain American troops abroad. The Department of Agriculture and Department of Commerce and their constituents—farmers and businesspeople—want to peddle American products abroad and generally favor freer trade. The Department of Labor and the unions worry that the nation may export not only products but also jobs to other countries where labor costs are low. Jewish citizens closely monitor U.S. policy toward Israel, while Cuban Americans aggressively seek to influence U.S. policy toward Cuba. Even foreign governments hire lobbying firms and join in the political fray. As a result, a wide range of interests are represented in the making of foreign policy.

☐ National Security Policymaking and the Scope of Government

America's status and involvement as a superpower have many implications for how active the national government is in the realm of foreign policy and national defense. The war on terrorism, treaty obligations to defend allies around the world, the nation's economic interests in an interdependent global economy, and pressing new questions on the global agenda such as global warming all demand government action.

By any standard, the scope of government in these areas is large. The national defense consumes about a fifth of the federal government's budget and requires more than 2 million civilian and military employees for the Department of Defense. The United States has a wide range of political, economic, and other interests to defend around the world. As long as these interests remain, the scope of American government in foreign and defense policy will be substantial.

Review the Chapter

American Foreign Policy: Instruments, Actors, and Policymakers

18.1 Identify the major instruments and actors in making national security policy, p. 584.

The use and potential use of military force, economic policies, and diplomacy are the main instruments of national security policy. Nations, international and regional organizations, multinational corporations, nongovernmental organizations, terrorists, and individuals influence American national security policy. The president is the main force in national security policymaking, and he is assisted by the Departments of State and Defense and by the CIA and the rest of the intelligence establishment. Congress also plays an important role in national security policy.

American Foreign Policy Through the Cold War

18.2 Outline the evolution of and major issues in American foreign policy through the end of the Cold War, p. 591.

Until the mid-twentieth century, American foreign policy emphasized keeping a distance from the affairs of other countries, with the notable exception of countries in Latin America. Following World War II, the United States became locked in an ideological conflict with the Soviet Union and focused its foreign policy on containing communism and Soviet expansion. This competition came to include a nuclear arms race and U.S. involvement in wars in Korea and Vietnam against communist forces, but never war between the United States and the Soviet Union. There were efforts to relax tensions, but the Cold War did not end until the breakup of the Soviet Union and the liberalization of governments in Eastern Europe. Nevertheless, the United States maintained an enormous defense capability.

American Foreign Policy and the War on Terrorism

18.3 Explain major obstacles to success in the war on terrorism, p. 597.

The U.S. defense capability has been put to new use with the war on terrorism, the struggle that is at the top of America's national security priorities. It is difficult to defend against terrorism in an open society. Terrorists have the advantage of stealth and surprise and, often, of a willingness to die for their cause. They are also generally decentralized, so we cannot defeat them simply by attacking another nation. Moreover, winning the war on terrorism requires political as well as military successes. The United States' wars with

Iraq and Afghanistan were motivated by the fight against terrorists. However, ensuring legitimate, effective governance remains difficult, and a terrorist haven has emerged in remote regions of Pakistan.

Defense Policy

18.4 Identify the major elements of U.S. defense policy, p. 600.

The United States spends about one-fifth of its budget on national defense, and it has 1.4 million men and women in the active duty armed services and another 845,000 on the National Guard and reserves. Modern weapons systems are sophisticated, expensive, and dangerous, and the United States has entered a number of important agreements to reduce nuclear weapons. Recent reforms in defense policy, intended to reshape it for changed threats, have placed more emphasis on lighter, faster, and more flexible forces, the more effective use of intelligence, the use of Special Forces, and counterterrorism.

The New National Security Agenda

18.5 Analyze the evolving challenges for U.S. national security policy, p. 603.

Although the United States has great military power, many of the issues facing the world today are not military issues. Nuclear proliferation and terrorism present new challenges to national security, challenges not easily met by advanced weaponry alone. Global interdependency in economics, energy, the environment, and other areas has also become important, revealing new vulnerabilities and thus additional challenges for national security policy. The effective use of foreign aid is also a perennial policy concern.

Understanding National Security Policymaking

18.6 Assess the role of democratic politics in making national security policy and the role of national security policy in expanding government, p. 612.

Although there are different opinions over how much discretion to accord policymakers in national security policy, policies at odds with the public's wishes cannot be sustained, and Congress can be a crucial check on the executive. As long as the United States is fighting a war on terrorism, has treaty obligations to defend allies around the world, participates actively in an interdependent global economy, and must deal with pressing questions such as energy supplies, global warming, and nuclear proliferation, the scope of American government in foreign and defense policy will be substantial.

Learn the Terms

foreign policy, p. 584
United Nations, p. 585
North Atlantic Treaty
   Organization, p. 586
European Union, p. 586
secretary of state, p. 588
secretary of defense, p. 589

Joint Chiefs of Staff, p. 589
Central Intelligence Agency, p. 590
isolationism, p. 592
containment doctrine, p. 593
Cold War, p. 593
arms race, p. 593
détente, p. 595

interdependency, p. 606
tariff, p. 608
balance of trade, p. 609
Organization of Petroleum
   Exporting Countries, p. 610

Test Yourself

1. Why can it be said that American national interests exist around the world?

a. American interests can be found anywhere the military can access.

b. Many multinational corporations are based in the United States.

c. Other countries have forfeited their interests in favor of the United States.

d. Telecommunications have made the globe much smaller.

e. The reach of nuclear weapons is global.

2. An advantage the president has over Congress, with regard to foreign policy, is _____.

a. greater access to and control over information

b. the ability to confirm the appointments of nominees

c. the ability to draw money from the federal treasury without congressional consent during "times of great Crisis or Unrest"

d. the ability to enact treaties

e. the power to declare war

3. Which of the following federal agencies would you look to for information if you were asked to write about the U.S. history of espionage (the collection of confidential information about foreign governments)?

a. the Central Intelligence Agency

b. the Federal Bureau of Investigation

c. the Secret Service

d. the U.S. Customs Service

e. the U.S. Marshals Service

4. What was one of the lasting lessons of the Vietnam War?

a. that containment was a flawed policy

b. that coming out of isolationism was a mistake

c. that spending too much on the military could be economically disastrous for the United States in the short term

d. that the United States could not prevail in a conflict without public backing for the war

e. that the United States military was not trained to deal with the new type of warfare encountered in the war

5. Why did the United States pursue a policy of isolationism for most of its history?

a. A lackluster economy and rampant corruption prevented the country from turning its eyes elsewhere.

b. The country lacked the resources to engage itself in other parts of the world.

c. The country was rebuked several times early on when trying to engage foreign nations.

d. The Founders did not intend for the country to involve itself in the conflicts of foreign nations.

e. The U.S. government was intolerant of foreign peoples.

6. Which of the following supports George Kennan's foreign policy strategy?

a. allow the Soviet Union to spread communism

b. always use peaceful means to resolve disputes

c. contain Soviet advances into other countries

d. stay out of the affairs of other countries

e. use force before peaceful means

7. The threat posed by terrorist groups and hostile states supporting them caused America to _____.

a. emphasize the principles of deterrence and containment in foreign policy

b. make dramatic cuts in domestic expenditures to pay for the new war on terrorism

c. recall many of its senior diplomats from the Middle East

d. reconsider basic principles of its foreign policy

e. shift back to isolationism

8. Why is terrorism such a troublesome issue in national security today?

a. Few countries are willing to take the steps to combat terrorism.

b. Terrorism is difficult to defend against in an open society and to root out elsewhere.

c. Terrorists have and are willing to use weapons of mass destruction.

d. Terrorists have grown to be capable of far more destruction than foreign countries.

e. Throughout history, terrorists have proven themselves to be unbeatable.

9. Which of the following resulted from the effects of the 2007 troop "surge" in Iraq?

a. A democratic government was established.
b. Kurdistan was granted significant autonomy.
c. Reconciliation between the Shiites and Sunnis was achieved.
d. The execution of Saddam Hussein.
e. Violence against coalition forces came to a halt.

10. How is the United States reforming its defense policy today?

a. A massive drawdown is cutting the military in half.
b. Defense policy is shifting its focus toward Europe while becoming lighter.
c. More heavy equipment is designed for large conventional battles.
d. The armed forces are becoming lighter, faster, and more flexible.
e. The armed forces are becoming much more mobile and larger.

11. When military spending fell dramatically at the end of the Cold War, this was referred to as a(n) _____.

a. anomaly
b. cut-back
c. peace dividend
d. return to normalcy
e. temporary dip

12. Which of the following supports the use of economic sanctions?

a. a nationalist backlash in the country being sanctioned
b. sanctions against Cuba
c. the sanctions against South Africa in the mid-1980s
d. the U.S. grain embargo in 1980
e. threats of sanctions against China

13. Which of the following statements concerning international trade and the domestic economy is true?

a. Both businesses and individuals benefit and do not suffer from foreign trade.
b. Both businesses and individuals suffer and do not benefit from foreign trade.
c. Both individuals and businesses benefit and suffer from foreign trade.
d. Businesses suffer from foreign trade and individuals benefit from it.
e. Individuals suffer from foreign trade and businesses benefit from it.

14. Which of the following can happen as a result of a balance of trade deficit?

a. a country that exports more than it imports
b. a decline in the value of a nation's currency
c. an increase in the value of a nation's currency
d. a surplus in exporting services
e. stable prices on imported goods

15. Why do American citizens have little interest in foreign policy?

a. Domestic issues are closer to their daily lives and easier to understand.
b. It is widely accepted that foreign policy has little influence on their lives.
c. Most foreign policy is conducted behind closed doors.
d. The major news media rarely cover foreign policy.
e. They have little control over foreign policy.

Explore Further

WEB SITES

www.state.gov
Information about the Department of State and current foreign policy issues.

www.defense.gov
Information about the Department of Defense and current issues in national security policy.

https://www.cia.gov/library/publications/the-world-factbook/index.html
The CIA World Factbook.

www.oecd.org/home
The Organization for Economic Cooperation and Development provides a wealth of economic information on the world's nations.

www.nato.int/
Contains background and activities of NATO.

www.un.org/en
Background on the United Nations and its varied programs.

www.cfr.org
The Council on Foreign Relations is the most influential private organization in the area of foreign policy. Its Web site includes a wide range of information on foreign policy.

www.nctc.gov
The National Counterterrorism Center, with information on terrorism and on responses to terrorism.

FURTHER READING

Brzezinski, Zbigniew. *Strategic Vision: America and the Crisis of Global Power.* New York: Basic Books, 2012. Assesses the current state of world affairs as the center of gravity is shifting from the West to the East.

Easterly, William. *The White Man's Burden.* New York: Penguin, 2006. Why the West's efforts to aid the rest of the world have not been more effective.

Howell, William G., and Jon C. Pevehouse. *While Dangers Gather: Congressional Checks on Presidential War Powers.* Princeton, NJ: Princeton University Press, 2007. Shows how Congress can influence decisions on war.

Ikenberry, G. John. *Liberal Leviathan: The Origins, Crisis, and Transformation of the American World Order.* Princeton, NJ: Princeton University Press, 2011. The American-led liberal international order has brought peace and prosperity to millions around the globe, but the rise of the East and global interdependence challenge this order.

Mandelbaum, Michael. *The Case for Goliath: How America Acts as the World's Government in the Twenty-First Century.* New York: Public Affairs, 2006. Explains the ways in which the United States provides the world critical services, ranging from physical security to commercial regulation and financial stability.

Nye, Joseph S., Jr. *The Paradox of American Power: Why the World's Only Superpower Can't Go It Alone.* New York: Oxford University Press, 2002. Although the United States is militarily and economically supreme, it is increasingly dependent on other nations to accomplish its goals.

Nye, Joseph S., Jr. *Soft Power: The Means to Success in World Politics.* Cambridge, MA: Harvard University Press, 2004. Argues that national security hinges as much on winning hearts and minds as it does on winning wars.

Yergin, Daniel. *The Quest: Energy, Security, and the Remaking of the Modern World.* New York: Penguin Press, 2011. A gripping account of the quest for sustainable sources of energy.

Yergin, Daniel. *Shattered Peace: The Origins of the Cold War and the National Security State.* Boston, MA: Houghton Mifflin, 1977. An excellent political history of the early years of the Cold War and containment.

Zelizer, Julian. *Arsenal of Democracy: The Politics of National Security—From World War II to the War on Terrorism.* New York: Basic Books, 2009. Makes the case that domestic politics shapes foreign policies.

APPENDIX

The Declaration of Independence   619
The Federalist No. 10   621
The Federalist No. 51   624
The Constitution of the United States of America   626
Presidents of the United States   636
Party Control of the Presidency, Senate, and House of Representatives in the Twentieth and Twenty-first Centuries   639
Supreme Court Justices Serving in the Twentieth and Twenty-first Centuries   640

The Declaration of Independence*

In Congress, July 4, 1776

The Unanimous Declaration of the Thirteen United States of America

When in the Course of human events it becomes necessary for one people to dissolve the political bands which have connected them with another, and to assume among the powers of the earth, the separate and equal station to which the Laws of Nature and of Nature's God entitle them, a decent respect to the opinions of mankind requires that they should declare the causes which impel them to the separation.

We hold these truths to be self-evident, that all men are created equal, that they are endowed by their Creator with certain unalienable Rights, that among these are Life, Liberty and the pursuit of Happiness.—That to secure these rights, Governments are instituted among Men, deriving their just powers from the consent of the governed,—That whenever any Form of Government becomes destructive of these ends, it is the Right of the People to alter or to abolish it, and to institute new Government, laying its foundation on such principles and organizing its powers in such form, as to them shall seem most likely to effect their Safety and Happiness. Prudence, indeed, will dictate that Governments long established should not be changed for light and transient causes; and accordingly all experience hath shewn that mankind are more disposed to suffer, while evils are sufferable, than to right themselves by abolishing the forms to which they are accustomed. But when a long train of abuses and usurpations, pursuing invariably the same Object evinces a design to reduce them under absolute Despotism, it is their right, it is their duty, to throw off such Government, and to provide new Guards for their future security.

Such has been the patient sufferance of these Colonies; and such is now the necessity which constrains them to alter their former Systems of Government. The history of the present King of Great Britain is a history of repeated injuries and usurpations, all having in direct object the establishment of an absolute Tyranny over these States. To prove this, let Facts be submitted to a candid world.

He has refused his Assent to Laws, the most wholesome and necessary for the public good.

He has forbidden his Governors to pass Laws of immediate and pressing importance, unless suspended in their operation till his Assent should be obtained; and when so suspended, he has utterly neglected to attend to them.

He has refused to pass other Laws for the accommodation of large districts of people, unless those people would relinquish the right of Representation in the Legislature, a right inestimable to them and formidable to tyrants only.

He has called together legislative bodies at places unusual, uncomfortable, and distant from the depository of their Public Records, for the sole purpose of fatiguing them into compliance with his measures.

He has dissolved Representative Houses repeatedly, for opposing with manly firmness his invasions on the rights of the people.

He has refused for a long time, after such dissolutions, to cause others to be elected; whereby the Legislative Powers, incapable of Annihilation, have returned to the People at large for their exercise; the State remaining in the mean time exposed to all the dangers of invasion from without, and convulsions within.

He has endeavored to prevent the population of these States; for that purpose obstructing the Laws for

*This text retains the spelling, capitalization, and punctuation of the original.

Naturalization of Foreigners; refusing to pass others to encourage their migration hither, and raising the conditions of new Appropriations of Lands.

He has obstructed the Administration of Justice, by refusing his Assent to Laws for establishing Judiciary powers.

He has made Judges dependent on his Will alone, for the tenure of their offices, and the amount and payment of their salaries.

He has erected a multitude of New Offices, and sent hither swarms of Officers to harass our people, and eat out their substance.

He has kept among us, in times of peace, Standing Armies without the Consent of our legislatures.

He has affected to render the Military independent of and superior to the Civil power.

He has combined with others to subject us to a jurisdiction foreign to our constitution, and unacknowledged by our laws; giving his Assent to their Acts of pretended Legislation:

For quartering large bodies of armed troops among us:

For protecting them, by a mock Trial, from punishment for any Murders which they should commit on the Inhabitants of these States:

For cutting off our Trade with all parts of the world:

For imposing Taxes on us without our Consent:

For depriving us in many cases, of the benefits of Trial by Jury:

For transporting us beyond Seas to be tried for pretended offences:

For abolishing the free System of English Laws in a neighboring Province, establishing therein an Arbitrary government, and enlarging its Boundaries so as to render it at once an example and fit instrument for introducing the same absolute rule into these Colonies:

For taking away our Charters, abolishing our most valuable Laws, and altering fundamentally the Forms of our Governments:

For suspending our own Legislatures, and declaring themselves invested with power to legislate for us in all cases whatsoever.

He has abdicated Government here, by declaring us out of his Protection and waging War against us.

He has plundered our seas, ravaged our Coasts, burnt our towns, and destroyed the lives of our people.

He is at this time transporting large Armies of foreign Mercenaries to compleat the works of death, desolation and tyranny, already begun with circumstances of Cruelty & perfidy scarcely paralleled in the most

barbarous ages, and totally unworthy the Head of a civilized nation.

He has constrained our fellow Citizens taken Captive on the high Seas to bear Arms against their Country, to become the executioners of their friends and Brethren, or to fall themselves by their Hands.

He has excited domestic insurrections amongst us, and has endeavored to bring on the inhabitants of our frontiers, the merciless Indian Savages, whose known rule of warfare, is an undistinguished destruction of all ages, sexes and conditions.

In every stage of these Oppressions We have Petitioned for Redress in the most humble terms: Our repeated Petitions have been answered only by repeated injury. A Prince, whose character is thus marked by every act which may define a Tyrant, is unfit to be the ruler of a free people.

Nor have We been wanting in attention to our British brethren. We have warned them from time to time of attempts by their legislature to extend an unwarrantable jurisdiction over us. We have reminded them of the circumstances of our emigration and settlement here. We have appealed to their native justice and magnanimity, and we have conjured them by the ties of our common kindred to disavow these usurpations, which would inevitably interrupt our connections and correspondence. They too have been deaf to the voice of justice and consanguinity. We must, therefore, acquiesce in the necessity, which denounces our Separation, and hold them, as we hold the rest of mankind, Enemies in War, in Peace Friends.

We, therefore, the Representatives of the United States of America, in General Congress, Assembled, appealing to the Supreme Judge of the world for the rectitude of our intentions, do, in the Name, and by Authority of the good People of these Colonies, solemnly publish and declare, That these United Colonies are, and of Right ought to be Free and Independent States; that they are Absolved from all Allegiance to the British Crown, and that all political connection between them and the State of Great Britain, is and ought to be totally dissolved; and that as Free and Independent States, they have full Power to levy War, conclude Peace, contract Alliances, establish Commerce, and to do all other Acts and Things which Independent States may of right do. And for the support of this Declaration, with a firm reliance on the protection of divine Providence, we mutually pledge to each other our Lives, our Fortunes and our sacred Honor.

John Hancock

NEW HAMPSHIRE
Josiah Bartlett,
Wm. Whipple,
Matthew Thornton.

MASSACHUSETTS BAY
Saml. Adams,
John Adams,
Robt. Treat Paine,
Elbridge Gerry.

RHODE ISLAND
Step. Hopkins,
William Ellery.

CONNECTICUT
Roger Sherman,
Samuel Huntington,
Wm. Williams,
Oliver Wolcott.

NEW YORK
Wm. Floyd,
Phil. Livingston,
Frans. Lewis,
Lewis Morris.

NEW JERSEY
Richd. Stockton,
Jno. Witherspoon,
Fras. Hopkinson,
John Hart,
Abra. Clark.

PENNSYLVANIA
Robt. Morris,
Benjamin Rush,
Benjamin Franklin,
John Morton,
Geo. Clymer,
Jas. Smith,
Geo. Taylor,
James Wilson,
Geo. Ross.

DELAWARE
Caesar Rodney,
Geo. Read,
Tho. M'kean.

MARYLAND
Samuel Chase,
Wm. Paca,
Thos. Stone,
Charles Caroll of
 Carrollton.

VIRGINIA
George Wythe,
Richard Henry Lee,
Th. Jefferson,
Benjamin Harrison,
Thos. Nelson, jr.,
Francis Lightfoot Lee,
Carter Braxton.

NORTH CAROLINA
Wm. Hooper,
Joseph Hewes,
John Penn.

SOUTH CAROLINA
Edward Rutledge,
Thos. Heyward, Junr.,
Thomas Lynch, jnr.,
Arthur Middleton.

GEORGIA
Button Gwinnett,
Lyman Hall,
Geo. Walton.

The Federalist No. 10

James Madison

November 22, 1787

To the People of the State of New York.

Among the numerous advantages promised by a well constructed Union, none deserves to be more accurately developed than its tendency to break and control the violence of faction. The friend of popular governments, never finds himself so much alarmed for their character and fate, as when he contemplates their propensity to this dangerous vice. He will not fail therefore to set a due value on any plan which, without violating the principles to which he is attached, provides a proper cure for it. The instability, injustice and confusion introduced into the public councils, have in truth been the mortal diseases under which popular governments have every where perished; as they continue to be the favorite and fruitful topics from which the adversaries to liberty derive their most specious declamations. The valuable improvements made by the American Constitutions on the popular models, both ancient and modern, cannot certainly be too much admired; but it would be an unwarrantable partiality, to contend that they have as effectually obviated the danger on this side as was wished and expected. Complaints are every where heard from our most considerate and virtuous citizens, equally the friends of public and private faith, and of public and personal liberty; that our governments are too unstable; that the public good is disregarded in the conflicts of rival parties; and that measures are too often decided, not according to the rules of justice, and the rights of the minor party; but by the superior force of an interested and over-bearing majority. However anxiously we may wish that these complaints had no foundation, the evidence of known facts will not permit us to deny that they are in some degree true. It will be found indeed, on a candid review of our situation, that some of the distresses under which we labor, have been erroneously charged on the operation of our governments; but it will be found, at the same time, that other causes will not alone account for many of our heaviest misfortunes; and particularly, for that prevailing and increasing distrust of public engagements, and alarm for private rights, which are echoed from one end of the continent to the other. These must be chiefly, if not wholly, effects of the unsteadiness and injustice, with which a factious spirit has tainted our public administrations.

By a faction I understand a number of citizens, whether amounting to a majority or minority of the whole, who are united and actuated by some common impulse of passion, or of interest, adverse to the rights of other citizens, or to the permanent and aggregate interests of the community.

There are two methods of curing the mischiefs of faction: the one, by removing its causes; the other, by controlling its effects.

There are again two methods of removing the causes of faction: the one by destroying the liberty which is essential to its existence; the other, by giving to every citizen the same opinions, the same passions, and the same interests.

It could never be more truly said than of the first remedy, that it is worse than the disease. Liberty is to faction, what air is to fire, an aliment without which it instantly expires. But it could not be a less folly to abolish liberty, which is essential to political life, because it nourishes faction, than it would be to wish the annihilation of air, which is essential to animal life, because it imparts to fire its destructive agency.

The second expedient is as impracticable, as the first would be unwise. As long as the reason of man continues fallible, and he is at liberty to exercise it, different opinions will be formed. As long as the connection subsists between his reason and his self-love, his opinions and his passions will have a reciprocal influence on each other; and the former will be objects to which the latter will attach themselves. The diversity in the faculties of men from which the rights of property originate, is not less an insuperable obstacle to a uniformity of interests. The protection of these faculties is the first object of Government. From the protection of different and unequal faculties of acquiring property, the possession of different degrees and kinds of property immediately results; and from the influence of these on the sentiments and views of the respective proprietors, ensues a division of the society into different interests and parties.

The latent causes of faction are thus sown in the nature of man; and we see them every where brought into different degrees of activity, according to the different circumstances of civil society. A zeal for different opinions concerning religion, concerning Government and many other points, as well of speculation as of practice; an attachment to different leaders ambitiously contending for pre-eminence and power; or to persons of other descriptions whose fortunes have been interesting to the human passions, have in turn divided mankind into parties, inflamed them with mutual animosity, and rendered them much more disposed to vex and oppress each other, than to co-operate for their common good. So strong is this propensity of mankind to fall into mutual animosities, that where no substantial occasion presents itself, the most frivolous and fanciful distinctions have been sufficient to kindle their unfriendly passions, and excite their most violent conflicts. But the most common and durable source of factions, has been the various and unequal distribution of property. Those who hold, and those who are without property, have ever formed distinct interests in society. Those who are creditors, and those who are debtors, fall under a like discrimination. A landed interest, a manufacturing interest, a mercantile interest, a monied interest, with many lesser interests, grow up of necessity in civilized nations, and divide them into different classes, actuated by different sentiments and views. The regulation of these various and interfering interests forms the principal task of modern Legislation, and involves the spirit of party and faction in the necessary and ordinary operations of Government.

No man is allowed to be a judge in his own cause; because his interest would certainly bias his judgment, and, not improbably, corrupt his integrity. With equal, nay with greater reason, a body of men, are unfit to be both judges and parties, at the same time; yet, what are many of the most important acts of legislation, but so many judicial determinations, not indeed concerning the rights of single persons, but concerning the rights of large bodies of citizens, and what are the different classes of legislators, but advocates and parties to the causes which they determine? Is a law proposed concerning private debts? It is a question to which the creditors are parties on one side, and the debtors on the other. Justice ought to hold the balance between them. Yet the parties are and must be themselves the judges; and the most numerous party, or, in other words, the most powerful faction must be expected to prevail. Shall domestic manufactures be encouraged, and in what degree, by restrictions on foreign manufactures? are questions which would be differently decided by the landed and the manufacturing classes; and probably by neither, with a sole regard to justice and the public good. The apportionment of taxes on the various descriptions of property, is an act which seems to require the most exact impartiality; yet, there is perhaps no legislative act in which greater opportunity and temptation are given to a predominant party, to trample on the rules of justice. Every shilling with which they over-burden the inferior number, is a shilling saved to their own pockets.

It is in vain to say, that enlightened statesmen will be able to adjust these clashing interests, and render them all subservient to the public good. Enlightened statesmen will not always be at the helm: Nor, in many cases, can such an adjustment be made at all, without taking into view indirect and remote considerations, which will rarely prevail over the immediate interest which one party may find in disregarding the rights of another, or the good of the whole.

The inference to which we are brought, is, that the causes of faction cannot be removed; and that relief is only to be sought in the means of controlling its effects.

If a faction consists of less than a majority, relief is supplied by the republican principle, which enables the majority to defeat its sinister views by regular vote: It may clog the administration, it may convulse the society; but it will be unable to execute and mask its violence under the forms of the Constitution. When a majority is included in a faction, the form of popular government on the other hand enables it to sacrifice to its ruling passion or interest, both the public good and the rights of other citizens. To secure the public good, and private rights, against the danger of such a faction, and at the same time to preserve the spirit and the form of popular government, is then the great object to which our enquiries are directed: Let me add that it is the great desideratum, by which alone this form of government can be rescued from the opprobrium under which it has so long labored, and be recommended to the esteem and adoption of mankind.

By what means is this object attainable? Evidently by one of two only. Either the existence of the same passion or interest in a majority at the same time, must be prevented; or the majority, having such co-existent passion or interest, must be rendered, by their number and local situation, unable to concert and carry into effect schemes of oppression. If the impulse and the opportunity be suffered to coincide, we well know that neither moral nor religious motives can be relied on as an adequate control. They are not found to be such on the injustice and violence of individuals, and lose their efficacy in proportion to the number combined together; that is, in proportion as their efficacy becomes needful.

From this view of the subject, it may be concluded, that a pure Democracy, by which I mean, a Society, consisting of a small number of citizens, who assemble and administer the Government in person, can admit of no cure for the mischiefs of faction. A common passion or interest will, in almost every case, be felt by a majority of the whole; a communication and concert results from the form of Government itself; and there is nothing to check the inducements to sacrifice the weaker party, or an obnoxious individual. Hence it is, that such Democracies have ever been spectacles of turbulence and contention; have ever been found incompatible with personal security, or the rights of property; and have in general been as short in their lives, as they have been violent in their deaths. Theoretic politicians, who have patronized this species of Government, have erroneously supposed, that by reducing mankind to a perfect equality in their political rights, they would, at the same time, be perfectly equalized and assimilated in their possessions, their opinions, and their passions.

A republic, by which I mean a government in which the scheme of representation takes place, opens a different prospect, and promises the cure for which we are seeking. Let us examine the points in which it varies from pure democracy, and we shall comprehend both the nature of the cure and the efficacy which it must derive from the union.

The two great points of difference, between a democracy and a republic, are, first, the delegation of the government, in the latter, to a small number of citizens, elected by the rest; secondly, the greater number of citizens, and greater sphere of country, over which the latter may be extended.

The effect of the first difference is, on the one hand, to refine and enlarge the public views, by passing them through the medium of a chosen body of citizens, whose wisdom may best discern the true interest of their country, and whose patriotism and love of justice, will be least likely to sacrifice it to temporary or partial considerations. Under such a regulation, it may well happen, that the public voice, pronounced by the representatives of the people, will be more consonant to the public good, than if pronounced by the people themselves, convened for the purpose. On the other hand the effect may be inverted. Men of factious tempers, of local prejudices, or of sinister designs, may by intrigue, by corruption, or by other means, first obtain the suffrages, and then betray the interest of the people. The question resulting is, whether small or extensive republics are most favorable to the election of proper guardians of the public weal, and it is clearly decided in favor of the latter by two obvious considerations.

In the first place, it is to be remarked that, however small the republic may be, the representatives must be raised to a certain number, in order to guard against the cabals of a few; and that however large it may be, they must be limited to a certain number, in order to guard against the confusion of a multitude. Hence, the number of representatives in the two cases not being in proportion to that of the constituents, and being proportionally greatest in the small republic, it follows, that if the proportion of fit characters be not less in the large than in the small republic, the former will present a greater option, and consequently a greater probability of a fit choice.

In the next place, as each Representative will be chosen by a greater number of citizens in the large than in the small Republic, it will be more difficult for unworthy candidates to practise with success the vicious arts, by which elections are too often carried; and the suffrages of the people being more free, will be more likely to center on men who possess the most attractive merit, and the most diffusive and established characters.

It must be confessed, that in this, as in most other cases, there is a mean, on both sides of which inconveniences will be found to lie. By enlarging too much the number of electors, you render the representative too little acquainted with all their local circumstances and lesser interests; as by reducing it too much, you render him unduly attached to these, and too little fit to comprehend and pursue great and national objects. The Federal Constitution forms a happy combination in this respect; the great and aggregate interests being referred to the national, the local and particular, to the state legislatures.

The other point of difference is, the greater number of citizens and extent of territory which may be brought within the compass of Republican, than of Democratic Government; and it is this circumstance principally which renders factious combinations less to be dreaded in the former, than in the latter. The smaller the society, the fewer probably will be the distinct parties and interests composing it; the fewer the distinct parties and interests, the more frequently will a majority be found of the same party; and the smaller the number of individuals composing a majority, and the smaller the compass within which they are placed, the more easily will they concert and execute their plans of oppression. Extend the sphere, and you take in a greater variety of parties and interests; you make it less probable that a majority of the whole will have a common motive to invade the rights of other citizens; or if such a common motive exists, it will be more difficult for all who feel it to discover their own strength, and to act in unison with each other. Besides other impediments, it may be remarked, that where there is a consciousness of unjust or dishonorable purposes, communication is always checked by distrust, in proportion to the number whose concurrence is necessary.

Hence it clearly appears, that the same advantage, which a Republic has over a Democracy, in controlling the effects of faction, is enjoyed by a large over a small Republic—is enjoyed by the Union over the States composing it. Does this advantage consist in the substitution of Representatives, whose enlightened views and virtuous sentiments render them superior to local prejudices, and to schemes of injustice? It will not be denied, that the Representation of the Union will be most likely to possess these requisite endowments. Does it consist in the greater security afforded by a greater variety of parties, against the event of any one party being able to outnumber and oppress the rest? In an equal degree does the increased variety of parties, comprised within the Union, increase this security? Does it, in fine, consist in the greater obstacles opposed to the concert and accomplishment of the secret wishes of an unjust and interested majority? Here, again, the extent of the Union gives it the most palpable advantage.

The influence of factious leaders may kindle a flame within their particular States, but will be unable to spread a general conflagration through the other States: a religious sect may degenerate into a political faction in a part of the Confederacy but the variety of sects dispersed over the entire face of it, must secure the national Councils against any danger from that source: a rage for paper money, for an abolition of debts, for an equal division of property, or for any other improper or wicked project, will be less apt to pervade the whole body of the Union, than a particular member of it; in the same proportion as such a malady is more likely to taint a particular county or district, than an entire State.

In the extent and proper structure of the Union, therefore, we behold a Republican remedy for the diseases most incident to Republican Government. And according to the degree of pleasure and pride, we feel in being Republicans, ought to be our zeal in cherishing the spirit, and supporting the character of Federalists.

PUBLIUS

The Federalist No. 51

James Madison

February 6, 1788

To the People of the State of New York.

To what expedient then shall we finally resort for maintaining in practice the necessary partition of power among the several departments, as laid down in the constitution? The only answer that can be given is, that as all these exterior provisions are found to be inadequate, the defect must be supplied, by so contriving the interior structure of the government, as that its several constituent parts may, by their mutual relations, be the means of keeping each other in their proper places. Without presuming to undertake a full development of this important idea, I will hazard a few general observations, which may perhaps place it in a clearer light, and enable us to form a more correct judgment of the principles and structure of the government planned by the convention.

In order to lay a due foundation for that separate and distinct exercise of the different powers of government, which to a certain extent, is admitted on all hands to be essential to the preservation of liberty, it is evident that each department should have a will of its own; and consequently should be so constituted, that the members of each should have as little agency as possible in the appointment of the members of the others. Were this principle rigorously adhered to, it would require that all the appointments for the supreme executive, legislative, and judiciary magistracies, should be drawn from the same fountain of authority, the people, through channels, having no communication whatever with one another. Perhaps such a plan of constructing the several departments would be less difficult in practice than it may in contemplation appear. Some difficulties however, and some additional expense, would attend the execution of it. Some deviations therefore from the principle must be admitted. In the constitution of the judiciary department in particular, it might be inexpedient to insist rigorously on the principle; first, because peculiar qualifications being essential in the members, the primary consideration ought to be to select that mode of choice, which best secures these qualifications; secondly, because the permanent tenure by which the appointments are held in that department, must soon destroy all sense of dependence on the authority conferring them.

It is equally evident that the members of each department should be as little dependent as possible on those of the others, for the emoluments annexed to their offices. Were the executive magistrate, or the judges, not independent of the legislature in this particular, their independence in every other would be merely nominal.

But the great security against a gradual concentration of the several powers in the same department, consists in giving to those who administer each department, the necessary constitutional means, and personal motives, to resist encroachments of the others. The provision for defense must in this, as in all other cases, be made commensurate to the danger of attack. Ambition must be made to counteract ambition. The interest of the man must be connected with the constitutional right of the place. It may be a reflection on human nature, that such devices should be necessary to control the abuses of government. But what is government itself but the greatest of all reflections on human nature? If men were angels, no government would be necessary. If angels were to govern men, neither external nor internal controls on government would be necessary. In framing a government which is to be administered by men over men, the great difficulty lies in this: You must first enable the government to control the governed; and in the next place, oblige it to control itself. A dependence on the people is no doubt the primary control on the government; but experience has taught mankind the necessity of auxiliary precautions.

This policy of supplying by opposite and rival interests, the defect of better motives, might be traced through the whole system of human affairs, private as well as public. We see it particularly displayed in all the subordinate distributions of power; where the constant aim is to divide and arrange the several offices in such a manner as that each may be a check on the other; that the private interest of every individual, may be a sentinel over the public rights. These inventions of prudence cannot be less requisite in the distribution of the supreme powers of the state.

But it is not possible to give to each department an equal power of self defense. In republican government the legislative authority necessarily, predominates. The remedy for this inconveniency is, to divide the legislature into different branches; and to render them by different modes of election, and different principles of action, as little connected with each other, as the nature of their common functions, and their common dependence on the society, will admit. It may even be necessary to guard against dangerous encroachments by still further precautions. As the weight of the legislative authority requires that it should be thus divided, the weakness of the executive may require, on the other hand, that it should be fortified. An absolute negative, on the legislature, appears at first view to be the natural defense with which the executive magistrate should be armed. But perhaps it would be neither altogether safe, nor alone sufficient. On ordinary occasions, it might not be exerted with the requisite firmness; and on extraordinary occasions, it might be perfidiously abused. May not this defect of an absolute negative be supplied, by some qualified connection between this weaker department, and the stronger branch of the stronger department, by which the latter may be led to support the constitutional rights of the former, without being too much detached from the rights of its own department?

If the principles on which these observations are founded be just, as I persuade myself they are, and they be applied as a criterion, to the several state constitutions, and to the federal constitution, it will be found, that if the latter does not perfectly correspond with them, the former are infinitely less able to bear such a test.

There are moreover two considerations particularly applicable to the federal system of America, which place that system in a very interesting point of view.

First. In a single republic, all the power surrendered by the people, is submitted to the administration of a single government; and usurpations are guarded against by a division of the government into distinct and separate departments. In the compound republic of America, the power surrendered by the people, is first divided between two distinct governments, and then the portion allotted to each, subdivided among distinct and separate departments. Hence a double security arises to the rights of the people. The different governments will control each other; at the same time that each will be controlled by itself.

Second. It is of great importance in a republic, not only to guard the society against the oppression of its rulers; but to guard one part of the society against the injustice of the other part. Different interests necessarily exist in different classes of citizens. If a majority be united by a common interest, the rights of the minority will be insecure. There are but two methods of providing against this evil: The one by creating a will in the community independent of the majority, that is, of the society itself; the other by comprehending in the society so many separate descriptions of citizens, as will render an unjust combination of a majority of the whole, very improbable, if not impracticable. The first method prevails in all governments possessing an hereditary or self appointed authority. This at best is but a precarious security; because a power independent of the society may as well espouse the unjust views of the major, as the rightful interests, of the minor party, and may possibly be turned against both parties. The second method will be exemplified in the federal republic of the United States. While all authority in it will be derived from and dependent on the society, the society itself will be broken into so many parts, interests and classes of citizens, that the rights of individuals or of the minority, will be in little danger from interested combinations of the majority. In a free government, the security for civil rights must be the same as for religious rights. It consists in the one case in the multiplicity of interests, and in the other, in the multiplicity of sects. The degree of security in both cases will depend on the number of interests and sects; and this may be presumed to depend on the extent of country and number of people comprehended under the same government. This view of the subject must particularly recommend a proper federal system to all the sincere and considerate friends of republican government: Since it shows that in exact proportion as the territory of the union may be formed into more circumscribed confederacies or states, oppressive combinations of a majority will be facilitated, the best security under the republican form, for the rights of every class of citizens, will be diminished; and consequently, the stability and independence of some member of the government, the only other security, must be proportionally increased. Justice is the end of government. It is the end of civil society. It ever has been, and ever will be pursued, until it be obtained, or until liberty be lost in the pursuit. In a society under the forms of which the stronger faction can readily unite and oppress the weaker, anarchy may as truly be said to reign, as in a state of nature where the weaker individual is not secured against the violence of the stronger: And as in the latter state even the stronger individuals are prompted by the uncertainty of their condition, to submit to a government which may protect the weak as well as themselves: So in the former state, will the more powerful factions or parties be gradually induced by a like motive, to wish for a government which will protect all parties, the weaker as well as the more powerful. It can be little doubted, that if the state of Rhode Island was separated from the confederacy, and left to itself, the insecurity of rights under the popular form of government within such narrow limits, would be displayed by such reiterated oppressions of factious majorities, that some power altogether independent of the people would soon be called for by the voice of the very factions whose misrule had proved the necessity of it. In the extended republic of the United States, and among the great variety of interests, parties and sects which it embraces, a coalition of a majority of the whole society could seldom take place on any other principles than those of justice and the general good;

and there being thus less danger to a minor from the will of the major party, there must be less pretext also, to provide for the security of the former, by introducing into the government a will not dependent on the latter; or in other words, a will independent of the society itself. It is no less certain than it is important, notwithstanding the contrary opinions which have been entertained, that the larger the society, provided it lie within a practicable sphere, the more duly capable it will be of self government. And happily for the *republican cause*, the practicable sphere may be carried to a very great extent, by a judicious modification and mixture of the *federal principle*.

PUBLIUS

The Constitution of the United States of America*

(Preamble)

We the People of the United States, in Order to form a more perfect Union, establish Justice, insure domestic Tranquility, provide for the common defence, promote the general Welfare, and secure the Blessings of Liberty to ourselves and our Posterity, do ordain and establish this Constitution for the United States of America.

Article I.
(The Legislature)

Section 1. All legislative Powers herein granted shall be vested in a Congress of the United States, which shall consist of a Senate and House of Representatives.

Section 2. The House of Representatives shall be composed of Members chosen every second Year by the People of the several States, and the Electors in each State shall have the Qualifications requisite for Electors of the most numerous Branch of the State Legislature.

No person shall be a Representative who shall not have attained to the Age of twenty five Years, and been seven Years a Citizen of the United States, and who shall not, when elected, be an Inhabitant of that State in which he shall be chosen.

Representatives and direct [Taxes]¹ shall be apportioned among the several States which may be included within this Union, according to their respective Numbers [which shall be determined by adding to the whole Number of free Persons, including those bound to Service for a Term of Years, and excluding Indians not taxed, three fifths of all other Persons]² The actual Enumeration shall be made within three Years after the first Meeting of the Congress of the United States, and within every subsequent Term of ten Years, in such Manner as they shall by Law direct. The Number of Representatives shall not exceed one for every thirty Thousand, but each State shall have at Least one Representative; and until such enumeration shall be made, the State of New Hampshire shall be entitled to chuse three, Massachusetts eight, Rhode-Island and Providence Plantations one, Connecticut five, New-York six, New Jersey four, Pennsylvania eight, Delaware one, Maryland six, Virginia ten, North Carolina five, South Carolina five, and Georgia three.

When vacancies happen in the Representation from any State, the Executive Authority thereof shall issue Writs of Election to fill such Vacancies.

The House of Representatives shall chuse their speaker and other Officers; and shall have the sole Power of Impeachment.

Section 3. The Senate of the United States shall be composed of two Senators from each State [chosen by the Legislature thereof],³ for six Years; and each Senator shall have one Vote.

Immediately after they shall be assembled in Consequence of the first Election, they shall be divided as equally as may be into three Classes. The Seats of the Senators of the first Class shall be vacated at the Expiration of the second year, of the second Class at the Expiration of the fourth Year, and of the third Class at the Expiration of the sixth Year, so that one third may be chosen every second Year [and if Vacancies happen by Resignation, or otherwise, during the Recess of the Legislature of any

¹See Amendment XVI.

*This text retains the spelling, capitalization, and punctuation of the original. Brackets indicate passages that have been altered by amendments.

²See Amendment XIV.
³See Amendment XVII.

State, the Executive thereof may make temporary Appointments until the next Meeting of the Legislature, which shall then fill such Vacancies].[4]

No Person shall be a Senator who shall not have attained to the Age of thirty Years, and been nine Years a Citizen of the United States, and who shall not, when elected, be an Inhabitant of that State for which he shall be chosen.

The Vice President of the United States shall be President of the Senate, but shall have no Vote, unless they be equally divided.

The Senate shall chuse their other Officers, and also a President pro tempore, in the Absence of the Vice President, or when he shall exercise the Office of President of the United States.

The Senate shall have the sole Power to try all Impeachments. When sitting for that Purpose, they shall be on Oath or Affirmation. When the President of the United States is tried, the Chief Justice shall preside: And no Person shall be convicted without the Concurrence of two thirds of the Members present.

Judgment in Cases of Impeachment shall not extend further than to removal from Office, and disqualification to hold and enjoy any Office of honor, Trust or Profit under the United States; but the Party convicted shall nevertheless be liable and subject to Indictment, Trial, Judgment and Punishment, according to Law.

Section 4. The Times, Places and Manner of holding Elections for Senators and Representatives, shall be prescribed in each State by the Legislature thereof; but the Congress may at any time by Law make or alter such Regulations, except as to the Places of chusing Senators.

[The Congress shall assemble at least once in every Year, and such Meeting shall be on the first Monday in December, unless they shall by Law appoint a different Day.][5]

Section 5. Each House shall be the Judge of the Elections, Returns and Qualifications of its own Members, and a Majority of each shall constitute a Quorum to do Business; but a smaller Number may adjourn from day to day, and may be authorized to compel the Attendance of absent Members, in such Manner, and under such Penalties as each House may provide.

Each House may determine the Rules of its Proceedings, punish its Members for disorderly Behaviour, and, with the Concurrence of two thirds, expel a Member.

Each House shall keep a Journal of its Proceedings, and from time to time publish the same, excepting such Parts as may in their judgment require Secrecy; and the Yeas and Nays of the Members of either House on any

[4]See Amendment XVII.
[5]See Amendment XX.

question shall, at the Desire of one fifth of those present, be entered on the Journal.

Neither House, during the Session of Congress, shall, without the Consent of the other, adjourn for more than three days, nor to any other Place than that in which the two Houses shall be sitting.

Section 6. The Senators and Representatives shall receive a Compensation for their Services, to be ascertained by Law, and paid out of the Treasury of the United States. They shall in all Cases, except Treason, Felony and Breach of the Peace, be privileged from Arrest during their Attendance at the Session of their respective Houses, and in going to and returning from the same; and for any Speech or Debate in either House, they shall not be questioned in any other Place.

No Senator or Representative shall, during the Time for which he was elected, be appointed to any civil Office under the Authority of the United States, which shall have been created, or the Emoluments whereof shall have been encreased during such time; and no Person holding any Office under the United States, shall be a Member of either House during his Continuance in Office.

Section 7. All Bills for raising Revenue shall originate in the House of Representatives; but the Senate may propose or concur with Amendments as on other Bills.

Every Bill which shall have passed the House of Representatives and the Senate, shall, before it becomes a Law, be presented to the President of the United States; If he approves he shall sign it, but if not he shall return it, with his Objections to that House in which it shall have originated, who shall enter the Objections at large on their Journal, and proceed to reconsider it. If after such Reconsideration two thirds of that House shall agree to pass the Bill, it shall be sent, together with the Objections, to the other House, by which it shall likewise be reconsidered, and if approved by two thirds of that House, it shall become a Law. But in all such Cases the Votes of both Houses shall be determined by yeas and Nays, and the Names of the Persons voting for and against the Bill shall be entered on the Journal of each House respectively. If any Bill shall not be returned by the President within ten Days (Sundays excepted) after it shall have been presented to him, the Same shall be a Law, in like Manner as if he had signed it, unless the Congress by their Adjournment prevent its Return, in which Case it shall not be a Law.

Every Order, Resolution, or Vote to which the Concurrence of the Senate and House of Representatives may be necessary (except on a question of Adjournment) shall be presented to the President of the United States; and before the Same shall take Effect, shall be approved by him, or being disapproved by him, shall be repassed by two thirds of the Senate and House of Representatives, according to the Rules and Limitations prescribed in the Case of a Bill.

Section 8. The Congress shall have Power To lay and collect Taxes, Duties, Imposts and Excises, to pay the Debts and provide for the common Defence and general Welfare of the United States; but all Duties, Imposts and Excises shall be uniform throughout the United States;

To borrow Money on the credit of the United States;

To regulate Commerce with foreign Nations, and among the several States, and with the Indian Tribes;

To establish a uniform Rule of Naturalization, and uniform Laws on the subject of Bankruptcies throughout the United States;

To coin Money, regulate the Value thereof, and of foreign Coin, and fix the Standard of Weights and Measures;

To provide for the Punishment of counterfeiting the Securities and current Coin of the United States;

To establish Post Offices and post Roads;

To promote the Progress of Science and useful Arts, by securing for limited Times to Authors and Inventors the exclusive Right to their respective Writings and Discoveries;

To constitute Tribunals inferior to the supreme Court;

To define and punish Piracies and Felonies committed on the high Seas, and Offences against the Law of Nations;

To declare War, grant Letters of Marque and Reprisal, and make Rules concerning Captures on Land and Water;

To raise and support Armies, but no Appropriation of Money to that Use shall be for a longer Term than two Years;

To provide and maintain a Navy;

To make Rules for the Government and Regulation of the land and naval Forces;

To provide for calling forth the Militia to execute the Laws of the Union, suppress Insurrections and repel Invasions;

To provide for organizing, arming, and disciplining, the Militia, and for governing such Part of them as may be employed in the Service of the United States, reserving to the States respectively, the Appointment of the Officers, and the Authority of training the Militia according to the discipline prescribed by Congress;

To exercise exclusive Legislation in all Cases whatsoever, over such District (not exceeding ten Miles square) as may, by Cession of particular States, and the Acceptance of Congress, become the Seat of the Government of the United States, and to exercise like Authority over all Places purchased by the Consent of the Legislature of the State in which the Same shall be, for the Erection of Forts, Magazines, Arsenals, dock-Yards, and other needful Buildings;—And

To make all Laws which shall be necessary and proper for carrying into Execution the foregoing Powers, and all other Powers vested by this Constitution in the Government of the United States, or in any Department or Officer thereof.

Section 9. The Migration or Importation of such Persons as any of the States now existing shall think proper to admit, shall not be prohibited by the Congress prior to the Year one thousand eight hundred and eight, but a Tax or duty may be imposed on such Importation, not exceeding ten dollars for each Person.

The Privilege of the Writ of Habeas Corpus shall not be suspended, unless when in Cases of Rebellion or Invasion the public Safety may require it.

No Bill of Attainder or ex post facto Law shall be passed.

[No Capitation, or other direct, Tax shall be laid, unless in Proportion to the Census or Enumeration herein before directed to be taken.][6]

No Tax or Duty shall be laid on Articles exported from any State.

No Preference shall be given by any Regulation of Commerce or Revenue to the Ports of one State over those of another; nor shall Vessels bound to, or from, one State, be obliged to enter, clear, or pay Duties in another.

No Money shall be drawn from the Treasury, but in Consequence of Appropriations made by Law; and a regular Statement and Account of the Receipts and Expenditures of all public Money shall be published from time to time.

No Title of Nobility shall be granted by the United States: And no Person holding any Office of Profit or Trust under them, shall, without the Consent of the Congress, accept of any present, Emolument, Office, or Title, of any kind whatever, from any King, Prince, or foreign State.

Section 10. No State shall enter into any Treaty, Alliance, or Confederation; grant Letters of Marque and Reprisal; coin Money; emit Bills of Credit; make any Thing but gold and silver Coin a Tender in Payment of Debts; pass any Bill of Attainder, ex post facto Law, or Law impairing the Obligation of Contracts, or grant any Title of Nobility.

No State shall, without the Consent of the Congress, lay any Imposts or Duties on Imports or Exports, except what may be absolutely necessary for executing its inspection Laws: and the net Produce of all Duties and Imposts, laid by any State on Imports or Exports, shall be for the Use of the Treasury of the United States; and all such Laws shall be subject to the Revision and Controul of the Congress.

No State shall, without the Consent of Congress, lay any Duty of Tonnage, keep Troops, or Ships of War in time of Peace, enter into any Agreement or Compact with another State, or with a foreign Power, or engage in War, unless actually invaded, or in such imminent Danger as will not admit of delay.

[6]See Amendment XVI.

Article II.
(The Executive)

Section 1. The executive Power shall be vested in a President of the United States of America. He shall hold his Office during the Term of four Years, and, together with the Vice President, chosen for the same Term, be elected, as follows.

Each State shall appoint, in such Manner as the Legislature thereof may direct, a Number of Electors, equal to the whole Number of Senators and Representatives to which the State may be entitled in the Congress; but no Senator or Representative, or Person holding an Office of Trust or Profit under the United States, shall be appointed an Elector.

[The Electors shall meet in their respective States, and vote by Ballot for two Persons, of whom one at least shall not be an Inhabitant of the same State with themselves. And they shall make a List of all the Persons voted for, and of the Number of Votes for each; which List they shall sign and certify, and transmit sealed to the Seat of the Government of the United States, directed to the President of the Senate. The President of the Senate shall, in the Presence of the Senate and House of Representatives, open all the Certificates, and the Votes shall then be counted. The Person having the greatest Number of Votes shall be the President, if such Number be a Majority of the whole Number of Electors appointed; and if there be more than one who have such Majority, and have an equal Number of Votes, then the House of Representatives shall immediately chuse by Ballot one of them for President; and if no Person have a Majority, then from the five highest on the List the said House shall in like Manner chuse the President. But in chusing the President, the Votes shall be taken by States, the Representation from each State having one Vote; A quorum for this Purpose shall consist of a Member or Members from two thirds of the States, and a Majority of all the States shall be necessary to a Choice. In every Case, after the Choice of the President, the Person having the greatest Number of Votes of the Electors shall be the Vice President. But if there should remain two or more who have equal Votes, the Senate shall chuse from them by Ballot the Vice President.][7]

The Congress may determine the Time of chusing the Electors, and the Day on which they shall give their Votes; which Day shall be the same throughout the United States.

No Person except a natural born Citizen, or a Citizen of the United States, at the time of the Adoption of this Constitution, shall be eligible to the Office of President; neither shall any Person be eligible to that Office who shall not have attained to the Age of thirty five Years, and been fourteen Years a Resident within the United States.

[In Case of the Removal of the President from Office, or of his Death, Resignation, or Inability to discharge the Powers and Duties of the said Office, the Same shall devolve on the Vice President, and the Congress may by Law provide for the Case of Removal, Death, Resignation or Inability, both of the President and Vice President, declaring what Officer shall then act as President, and such Officer shall act accordingly, until the Disability be removed, or a President shall be elected.][8]

The President shall, at stated Times, receive for his Services, a Compensation, which shall neither be encreased nor diminished during the Period for which he shall have been elected, and he shall not receive within that Period any other Emolument from the United States, or any of them.

Before he enter on the Execution of his Office, he shall take the following Oath or Affirmation:—"I do solemnly swear (or affirm) that I will faithfully execute the Office of President of the United States, and will to the best of my Ability, preserve, protect and defend the Constitution of the United States."

Section 2. The President shall be Commander in Chief of the Army and Navy of the United States, and of the Militia of the several States, when called into the actual Service of the United States; he may require the Opinion, in writing, of the principal Officer in each of the executive Departments, upon any Subject relating to the Duties of their respective Offices, and he shall have Power to grant Reprieves and Pardons for Offences against the United States, except in Cases of Impeachment.

He shall have Power, by and with the Advice and Consent of the Senate, to make Treaties, provided two thirds of the Senators present concur; and he shall nominate, and by and with the Advice and Consent of the Senate, shall appoint Ambassadors, other public Ministers and Consuls, Judges of the supreme Court, and all other Officers of the United States, whose Appointments are not herein otherwise provided for, and which shall be established by Law: but the Congress may by Law vest the Appointment of such inferior Officers, as they think proper, in the President alone, in the Courts of Law, or in the Heads of Departments.

The President shall have Power to fill up all Vacancies that may happen during the Recess of the Senate, by granting Commissions which shall expire at the end of their next Session.

Section 3. He shall from time to time give to the Congress Information of the State of the Union, and recommend to their Consideration such Measures as he shall judge necessary and expedient; he may, on extraordinary Occasions, convene both Houses, or either of them, and in Case of Disagreement between them, with Respect to the Time of Adjournment, he may adjourn them to such Time as he shall think proper; he shall receive Ambassadors and other public Ministers; he shall take Care that the Laws be faithfully executed, and shall Commission all the Officers of the United States.

[7]See Amendment XII.

[8]See Amendment XXV.

Section 4. The President, Vice President and all civil Officers of the United States, shall be removed from Office on Impeachment for, and Conviction of, Treason, Bribery, or other high Crimes and Misdemeanors.

Article III.
(The Judiciary)

Section 1. The judicial Power of the United States, shall be vested in one supreme Court, and in such inferior Courts as the Congress may from time to time ordain and establish. The Judges, both of the supreme and inferior Courts, shall hold their Offices during good Behaviour, and shall, at stated Times, receive for their Services, a Compensation, which shall not be diminished during their Continuance in Office.

Section 2. The judicial Power shall extend to all Cases, in Law and Equity, arising under this Constitution, the Laws of the United States, and Treaties made, or which shall be made, under their Authority;—to all Cases affecting Ambassadors, other public Ministers and Consuls;—to all Cases of admiralty and maritime Jurisdiction;—to Controversies to which the United States shall be a Party;—to Controversies between two or more States;—[between a State and Citizens of another State;—][9] between Citizens of different States,—between Citizens of the same State claiming Lands under Grants of different States, [and between a State, or the Citizens thereof, and foreign States, Citizens or Subjects.][10]

In all Cases affecting Ambassadors, other public Ministers and Consuls, and those in which a State shall be Party, the supreme Court shall have original Jurisdiction. In all the other Cases before mentioned, the supreme Court shall have appellate Jurisdiction, both as to Law and Fact, with such Exceptions, and under such Regulations as the Congress shall make.

The Trial of all Crimes, except in Cases of Impeachment, shall be by Jury; and such Trial shall be held in the State where the said Crimes shall have been committed; but when not committed within any State, the Trial shall be at such Place or Places as the Congress may by Law have directed.

Section 3. Treason against the United States, shall consist only in levying War against them, or in adhering to their Enemies, giving them Aid and Comfort. No Person shall be convicted of Treason unless on the Testimony of two Witnesses to the same overt Act, or on Confession in open Court.

The Congress shall have Power to declare the Punishment of Treason, but no Attainder of Treason shall

[9]See Amendment XI.
[10]See Amendment XI.

work Corruption of Blood, or Forfeiture except during the Life of the Person attained.

Article IV.
(Interstate Relations)

Section 1. Full Faith and Credit shall be given in each State to the public Acts, Records, and judicial Proceedings of every other State. And the Congress may by general Laws prescribe the Manner in which such Acts, Records, and Proceedings shall be proved, and the Effect thereof.

Section 2. The Citizens of each State shall be entitled to all Privileges and Immunities of Citizens in the several States.

A Person charged in any State with Treason, Felony, or other Crime, who shall flee from Justice, and be found in another State, shall on Demand of the executive Authority of the State from which he fled, be delivered up, to be removed to the State having Jurisdiction of the Crime.

[No Person held to Service or Labour in one State, under the Laws thereof, escaping into another, shall, in Consequence of any Law or Regulation therein, be discharged from such Service or Labour, but shall be delivered up on Claim of the Party to whom such Service or Labour may be due.][11]

Section 3. New States may be admitted by the Congress into this Union; but no new State shall be formed or erected within the Jurisdiction of any other State; nor any State be formed by the Junction of two or more States, or Parts of States, without the Consent of the Legislatures of the States concerned as well as of the Congress.

The Congress shall have Power to dispose of and make all needful Rules and Regulations respecting the Territory or other Property belonging to the United States; and nothing in this Constitution shall be so construed as to Prejudice any Claims of the United States, or of any particular State.

Section 4. The United States shall guarantee to every State in this Union a Republican Form of Government, and shall protect each of them against Invasion, and on Application of the Legislature, or of the Executive (when the Legislature cannot be convened) against domestic Violence.

Article V.
(Amending the Constitution)

The Congress, whenever two thirds of both Houses shall deem it necessary, shall propose Amendments to this

[11]See Amendment XIII.

Constitution, or, on the Application of the Legislatures of two thirds of the several States, shall call a Convention for proposing Amendments, which, in either Case, shall be valid to all Intents and Purposes, as Part of this Constitution, when ratified by the Legislatures of three fourths of the several States, or by Conventions in three fourths thereof, as the one or the other Mode of Ratification may be proposed by the Congress; Provided that no Amendment which may be made prior to the Year One thousand eight hundred and eight shall in any Manner affect the first and fourth Clauses in the Ninth Section of the first Article; and that no State, without its Consent, shall be deprived of its equal Suffrage in the Senate.

Article VI.
(Debts, Supremacy, Oaths)

All Debts contracted and Engagements entered into, before the Adoption of this Constitution, shall be as valid against the United States under this Constitution, as under the Confederation.

This Constitution, and the laws of the United States which shall be made in Pursuance thereof; and all Treaties made, or which shall be made, under the Authority of the United States, shall be the supreme Law of the Land; and

the Judges in every State shall be bound thereby, any Thing in the Constitution or Laws of any State to the Contrary notwithstanding.

The Senators and Representatives before mentioned, and the Members of the several State Legislatures, and all executive and judicial Officers, both of the United States and of the several States, shall be bound by Oath or Affirmation, to support this Constitution; but no religious Test shall ever be required as a Qualification to any Office or public Trust under the United States.

Article VII.
(Ratifying the Constitution)

The Ratification of the Conventions of nine States, shall be sufficient for the Establishment of this Constitution between the States so ratifying the Same.

Done in Convention by the Unanimous Consent of the States present the Seventeenth Day of September in the Year of our Lord one thousand seven hundred and Eighty seven and of the Independence of the United States of America the Twelfth. IN WITNESS whereof we have hereunto subscribed our Names.

Go. WASHINGTON

Presid't. and deputy from Virginia

ATTTEST
William Jackson
Secretary

DELAWARE
Geo. Read
Gunning Bedford jun
John Dickinson
Richard Basset
Jaco. Broom

MASSACHUSETTS
Nathaniel Gorbam
Rufus King

CONNECTICUT
Wm. Saml. Johnson
Roger Sherman

NEW YORK
Alexander Hamilton

NEW JERSEY
Wh. Livingston
David Brearley
Wm. Paterson
Jona. Dayton

PENNSYLVANIA
B. Franklin
Thomas Mifflin
Robt. Morris
Geo. Clymer
Thos. FitzSimons
Jared Ingersoll
James Wilson
Gouv. Morris

NEW HAMPSHIRE
John Langdon
Nicholas Gilman

MARYLAND
James McHenry
Dan of St. Thos. Jenifer
Danl. Carroll

VIRGINIA
John Blair
James Madison Jr.

NORTH CAROLINA
Wm. Blount
Richd. Dobbs Spaight
Hu. Williamson

SOUTH CAROLINA
J. Rutledge
Charles Cotesworth
Pinckney
Charles Pinckney
Pierce Butler

GEORGIA
William Few

Abr. Baldwin addition to, and amendment of the Constitution of the United States of America, proposed by Congress and ratified by the Legislatures of the several states, pursuant to the Fifth Article of the original Constitution.

(The first ten amendments were passed by Congress on September 25, 1789, and were ratified on December 15, 1791.)

Amendment I—Religion, Speech, Assembly, Petition

Congress shall make no law respecting an establishment of religion, or prohibiting the free exercise thereof; or abridging the freedom of speech, or of the press; or the right

of the people peaceably to assemble, and to petition the Government for a redress of grievances.

Amendment II—Right to Bear Arms

A well regulated Militia, being necessary to the security of a free State, the right of the people to keep and bear Arms, shall not be infringed.

Amendment III—Quartering of Soldiers

No Soldier shall, in time of peace be quartered in any house, without the consent of the Owner, nor in time of war, but in a manner to be prescribed by law.

Amendment IV—Searches and Seizures

The right of the people to be secure in their persons, houses, papers, and effects, against unreasonable searches and seizures, shall not be violated, and no warrants shall issue, but upon probable cause, supported by Oath or affirmation, and particularly describing the place to be searched, and the persons or things to be seized.

Amendment V—Grand Juries, Double Jeopardy, Self-incrimination, Due Process, Eminent Domain

No person shall be held to answer for a capital, or otherwise infamous crime, unless on a presentment or indictment of a Grand Jury, except in cases arising in the land or naval forces, or in the Militia, when in actual service in time of War or public danger; nor shall any person be subject for the same offence to be twice put in jeopardy of life or limb; nor shall be compelled in any criminal case to be a witness against himself, nor be deprived of life, liberty, or property, without due process of law; nor shall private property be taken for public use, without just compensation.

Amendment VI—Criminal Court Procedures

In all criminal prosecutions, the accused shall enjoy the right to a speedy and public trial, by an impartial jury of the State and district wherein the crime shall have been committed, which district shall have been previously ascertained by law, and to be informed of the nature and cause of the accusation; to be confronted with the witnesses against him; to have compulsory process for obtaining witnesses in his favor, and to have the assistance of counsel for his defence.

Amendment VII—Trial by Jury in Common-law Cases

In Suits at common law, where the value in controversy shall exceed twenty dollars, the right of trial by jury shall be preserved, and no fact tried by a jury, shall be otherwise re-examined in any Court of the United States, than according to the rules of the common law.

Amendment VIII—Bails, Fines, and Punishment

Excessive bail shall not be required, nor excessive fines imposed, nor cruel and unusual punishments inflicted.

Amendment IX—Rights Retained by the People

The enumeration in the Constitution, of certain rights, shall not be construed to deny or disparage others retained by the people.

Amendment X—Rights Reserved to the States

The powers not delegated to the United States by the Constitution, nor prohibited by it to the States, are reserved to the States respectively, or to the people.

Amendment XI—Suits Against the States (Ratified February 7, 1795)

The Judicial power of the United States shall not be construed to extend to any suit in law or equity, commenced or prosecuted against one of the United States by Citizens of another State, or by Citizens or Subjects of any Foreign State.

Amendment XII—Election of the President and Vice-President (Ratified June 15, 1804)

The Electors shall meet in their respective states, and vote by ballot for President and Vice-President, one of whom, at least, shall not be an inhabitant of the same state with themselves; they shall name in their ballots the person voted for as President, and in distinct ballots the person voted for as Vice-President, and they shall make distinct lists of all persons voted for as President, and of all persons voted for as Vice-President, and of the number of votes for each, which lists they shall sign and certify, and transmit sealed to the seat of the government of the United States, directed to the President of the Senate;—The President of the Senate shall, in the presence of the Senate and House of Representatives, open all the certificates and the votes shall then be counted;—The person having the greatest number of votes for President, shall be the President, if such number be a majority of the whole number of Electors appointed; and if no person have such majority, then from the persons having the highest numbers not exceeding three on the list of those voted for as President, the House of Representatives shall choose immediately, by ballot, the President. But in choosing the President, the votes shall be taken by states, the representation from each state having one vote; a quorum for this purpose shall consist of a member or members from two-thirds of the states, and a majority of all the states shall be necessary to a Choice. [And if the House of Representatives shall not choose a President whenever the right of choice shall devolve upon them, before the fourth day of March next following, then the Vice-President shall act as President, as in the case of the death or other constitutional disability of the President.][12]—The person having the greatest number of votes as Vice-President, shall be the Vice-President, if such number be a majority of the whole number of Electors appointed, and if no person have a majority, then from the two highest numbers on the list, the Senate shall

[12]Amendment XX.

choose the Vice-President; a quorum for the purpose shall consist of two-thirds of the whole number of Senators, and a majority of the whole number shall be necessary to a choice. But no person constitutionally ineligible to the office of President shall be eligible to that of Vice-President of the United States.

Amendment XIII—Slavery (Ratified on December 6, 1865)

Section 1. Neither slavery nor involuntary servitude, except as a punishment for crime whereof the party shall have been duly convicted, shall exist within the United States, or any place subject to their jurisdiction.

Section 2. Congress shall have power to enforce this article by appropriate legislation.

Amendment XIV—Citizenship, Due Process, and Equal Protection of the Laws (Ratified on July 9, 1868)

Section 1. All persons born or naturalized in the United States, and subject to the jurisdiction thereof, are citizens of the United States and of the State wherein they reside. No State shall make or enforce any law which shall abridge the privileges or immunities of citizens of the United States; nor shall any State deprive any person of life, liberty, or property, without due process of law; nor deny to any person within its jurisdiction the equal protection of the laws.

Section 2. Representatives shall be apportioned among the several States according to their respective numbers, counting the whole number of persons in each State, excluding Indians not taxed. But when the right to vote at any election for the choice of electors for President and Vice President of the United States, Representatives in Congress, the Executive and Judicial officers of a State, or the members of the Legislature thereof, is denied to any of the male inhabitants of such State, being twenty-one years of age, and citizens of the United States, or in any way abridged, except for participation in rebellion, or other crime, the basis of representation therein shall be reduced in the proportion which the number of such male citizens shall bear to the whole number of male citizens twenty-one years of age in such State.

Section 3. No person shall be a Senator or Representative in Congress, or elector of President and Vice President, or hold any office, civil or military, under the United States, or under any State, who, having previously taken an oath, as a member of Congress, or as an officer of the United States, or as a member of any State legislature, or as an executive or judicial officer of any State, to support the Constitution of the United States, shall have engaged in insurrection or rebellion against the same, or given aid or comfort to the enemies thereof. But Congress may by a vote of two-thirds of each House, remove such disability.

Section 4. The validity of the public debt of the United States, authorized by law, including debts incurred for payment of pensions and bounties for services in suppressing insurrection or rebellion, shall not be questioned. But neither the United States nor any State shall assume or pay any debt or obligation incurred in aid of insurrection or rebellion against the United States, or any claim for the loss or emancipation of any slave, but all such debts, obligations and claims shall be held illegal and void.

Section 5. The Congress shall have power to enforce, by appropriate legislation, the provisions of this article.

Amendment XV—The Right To Vote (Ratified on February 3, 1870)

Section 1. The right of citizens of the United States to vote shall not be denied or abridged by the United States or by any State on account of race, color, or previous condition of servitude.

Section 2. The Congress shall have power to enforce this article by appropriate legislation.

Amendment XVI—Income Taxes (Ratified on February 3, 1913)

The Congress shall have power to lay and collect taxes on incomes, from whatever source derived, without apportionment among the several States, and without regard to any census or enumeration.

Amendment XVII—Election of Senators (Ratified on April 8, 1913)

The Senate of the United States shall be composed of two Senators from each State, elected by the people thereof, for six years; and each Senator shall have one vote. The electors in each State shall have the qualifications requisite for electors of the most numerous branch of the State legislatures.

When vacancies happen in the representation of any State in the Senate, the executive authority of such State shall issue writs of election to fill such vacancies: *Provided,* That the legislature of any State may empower the executive thereof to make temporary appointments until the people fill the vacancies by election as the legislature may direct.

This amendment shall not be so construed as to affect the election or term of any Senator chosen before it becomes valid as part of the Constitution.

Amendment XVIII—Prohibition (Ratified on January 16, 1919)

Section 1. After one year from the ratification of this article the manufacture, sale, or transportation of intoxicating liquors within, the importation thereof into, or the exportation thereof from the United States and all territory subject to the jurisdiction thereof for beverage purposes is hereby prohibited.

Section 2. The Congress and the several States shall have concurrent power to enforce this article by appropriate legislation.

Section 3. This article shall be inoperative unless it shall have been ratified as an amendment to the Constitution by the legislatures of the several States, as provided in the Constitution, within seven years from the date of the submission hereof to the States by the Congress.[13]

[13]Amendment XXI.

Amendment XIX—Women's Right To Vote (Ratified on August 18, 1920)

The right of citizens of the United States to vote shall not be denied or abridged by the United States or by any State on account of sex.

Congress shall have power to enforce this article by appropriate legislation.

Amendment XX—Terms of Office, Convening of Congress, and Succession (Ratified February 6, 1933)

Section 1. The terms of the President and Vice President shall end at noon on the 20th day of January, and the terms of Senators and Representatives at noon on the 3rd day of January, of the years in which such terms would have ended if this article had not been ratified; and the terms of their successors shall then begin.

Section 2. The Congress shall assemble at least once in every year, and such meeting shall begin at noon on the 3rd day of January, unless they shall by law appoint a different day.

Section 3. If, at the time fixed for the beginning of the term of the President, the President elect shall have died, the Vice President elect shall become President. If a President shall not have been chosen before the time fixed for the beginning of his term, or if the President elect shall have failed to qualify, then the Vice President elect shall act as President until a President shall have qualified; and the Congress may by law provide for the case wherein neither a President elect nor a Vice President elect shall have qualified, declaring who shall then act as President, or the manner in which one who is to act shall be selected, and such person shall act accordingly until a President or Vice President shall have qualified.

Section 4. The Congress may by law provide for the case of the death of any of the persons from whom the House of Representatives may choose a President whenever the right of choice shall have devolved upon them, and for the case of the death of any of the persons from whom the Senate may choose a Vice President whenever the right of choice shall have devolved upon them.

Section 5. Sections 1 and 2 shall take effect on the 15th day of October following the ratification of this article.

Section 6. This article shall be inoperative unless it shall have been ratified as an amendment to the Constitution by the legislatures of three-fourths of the several States within seven years from the date of its submission.

Amendment XXI—Repeal of Prohibition (Ratified on December 5, 1933)

Section 1. The eighteenth article of amendment to the Constitution of the United States is hereby repealed.

Section 2. The transportation or importation into any State, Territory, or possession of the United States for delivery or use therein of intoxicating liquors, in violation of the laws thereof, is hereby prohibited.

Section 3. This article shall be inoperative unless it shall have been ratified as an amendment to the Constitution by conventions in the several States, as provided in the Constitution, within seven years from the date of the submission hereof to the States by the Congress.

Amendment XXII—Number of Presidential Terms (Ratified on February 27, 1951)

No person shall be elected to the office of the President more than twice, and no person who has held the office of President, or acted as President, for more than two years of a term to which some other person was elected President shall be elected to the office of the President more than once. But this Article shall not apply to any person holding the office of President when this Article was proposed by the Congress, and shall not prevent any person who may be holding the office of President, or acting as President, during the term within which this Article becomes operative from holding the office of President or acting as President during the remainder of such term.

Amendment XXIII—Presidential Electors for the District of Columbia (Ratified on March 29, 1961)

Section 1. The District constituting the seat of Government of the United States shall appoint in such manner as the Congress may direct:

A number of electors of President and Vice President equal to the whole number of Senators and Representatives in Congress to which the District would be entitled if it were a State, but in no event more than the least populous State; they shall be in addition to those appointed by the States, but they shall be considered, for the purposes of the election of President and Vice President, to be electors appointed by a State; and they shall meet in the District and perform such duties as provided by the twelfth article of amendment.

Section 2. The Congress shall have power to enforce this article by appropriate legislation.

Amendment XXIV—Poll Tax (Ratified on January 23, 1964)

Section 1. The right of citizens of the United States to vote in any primary or other election for President or Vice President, for electors for President or Vice President, or for Senator or Representative in Congress, shall not be denied or abridged by the United States or any State by reason of failure to pay any poll tax or other tax.

Section 2. The Congress shall have power to enforce this article by appropriate legislation.

Amendment XXV—Presidential Disability and Vice Presidential Vacancies (Ratified on February 10, 1967)

Section 1. In case of the removal of the President from office or of his death or resignation, the Vice President shall become President.

Section 2. Whenever there is a vacancy in the office of the Vice President, the President shall nominate a Vice President who shall take office upon confirmation by a majority vote of both Houses of Congress.

Section 3. Whenever the President transmits to the President pro tempore of the Senate and the Speaker of the House of Representatives his written declaration that

he is unable to discharge the powers and duties of his office, and until he transmits to them a written declaration to the contrary, such powers and duties shall be discharged by the Vice President as Acting President.

Section 4. Whenever the Vice President and a majority of either the principal officers of the executive departments or of such other body as Congress may by law provide, transmit to the President pro tempore of the Senate and the Speaker of the House of Representatives their written declaration that the President is unable to discharge the powers and duties of his office, the Vice President shall immediately assume the powers and duties of the office as Acting President.

Thereafter, when the President transmits to the President pro tempore of the Senate and the Speaker of the House of Representatives his written declaration that no inability exists, he shall resume the powers and duties of his office unless the Vice President and a majority of either the principal officers of the executive department or of such other body as Congress may by law provide, transmit within four days to the President pro tempore of the Senate and the Speaker of the House of Representatives their written declaration that the President is unable to discharge the powers and duties of his office. Thereupon Congress shall decide the issue, assembling within forty-eight hours for that purpose if not in session. If the Congress, within twenty-one days after receipt of the latter written declaration, or, if Congress is not in session, within twenty-one days after Congress is required to assemble, determines by two-thirds vote of both Houses that the President is unable to discharge the powers and duties of his office, the Vice President shall continue to discharge the same as Acting President; otherwise, the President shall resume the powers and duties of his office.

Amendment XXVI—Eighteen-year-old Vote (Ratified on July 1, 1971)

Section 1. The right of citizens of the United States, who are eighteen years of age or older, to vote shall not be denied or abridged by the United States or by any State on account of age.

Section 2. The Congress shall have power to enforce this article by appropriate legislation.

Amendment XXVII—Congressional Salaries (Ratified on May 18, 1992)

Section 1. No law varying the compensation for the services of the Senators and Representatives, shall take effect, until an election of Representatives shall have intervened.

Presidents of the United States

YEAR	PRESIDENTIAL CANDIDATES	POLITICAL PARTY	ELECTORAL VOTE	PERCENTAGE OF POPULAR VOTE
1789	**George Washington**	—	69	—
	John Adams		34	
	Others		35	
1792	**George Washington**	—	132	—
	John Adams		77	
	Others		55	
1796	**John Adams**	Federalist	71	—
	Thomas Jefferson	Democratic-Republican	68	
	Thomas Pinckney	Federalist	59	
	Aaron Burr	Democratic-Republican	30	
	Others		48	
1800	**Thomas Jefferson**	Democratic-Republican	73	—
	Aaron Burr	Democratic-Republican	73	
	John Adams	Federalist	65	
	C. C. Pinckney	Federalist	64	
	John Jay	Federalist	1	
1804	**Thomas Jefferson**	Democratic-Republican	162	—
	C. C. Pinckney	Federalist	14	
1808	**James Madison**	Democratic-Republican	122	—
	C. C. Pinckney	Federalist	47	
	George Clinton	Independent-Republican	6	
1812	**James Madison**	Democratic-Republican	128	—
	De Witt Clinton	Federalist	89	
1816	**James Monroe**	Democratic-Republican	183	—
	Rufus King	Federalist	34	
1820	**James Monroe**	Democratic-Republican	231	—
	John Q. Adams	Independent-Republican	1	
1824	**John Q. Adams**	Democratic-Republican	84	30.9
	Andrew Jackson	Democratic-Republican	99	
	Henry Clay	Democratic-Republican	37	
	W. H. Crawford	Democratic-Republican	41	
1828	**Andrew Jackson**	Democratic	178	56.0
	John Q. Adams	National Republican	83	
1832	**Andrew Jackson**	Democratic	219	54.2
	Henry Clay	National Republican	49	
	William Wirt	Anti-Masonic	7	
	John Floyd	Independent Democrat	11	
1836	**Martin Van Buren**	Democratic	170	50.8
	William H. Harrison	Whig	73	
	Hugh L. White	Whig	26	
	Daniel Webster	Whig	14	
1840	**William H. Harrison***	Whig	234	52.9
	Martin Van Buren	Democratic	60	
	(John Tyler, 1841)			
1844	**James K. Polk**	Democratic	170	49.5
	Henry Clay	Whig	105	
1848	**Zachary Taylor***	Whig	163	47.3
	Lewis Cass	Democratic	127	
	(Millard Fillmore, 1850)			
1852	**Franklin Pierce**	Democratic	254	50.8
	Winfield Scott	Whig	42	
1856	**James Buchanan**	Democratic	174	45.3
	John C. Fremont	Republican	114	
	Millard Fillmore	American	8	
1860	**Abraham Lincoln**	Republican	180	39.8
	J. C. Breckinridge	Democratic	72	
	Stephen A. Douglas	Democratic	12	
	John Bell	Constitutional Union	39	
1864	**Abraham Lincoln***	Republican	212	55.1
	George B. McClellan	Democratic	21	
	(Andrew Johnson, 1865)			

Note: Presidents are shown in boldface.
*Died in office, succeeding vice president shown in parentheses.

636

YEAR	PRESIDENTIAL CANDIDATES	POLITICAL PARTY	ELECTORAL VOTE	PERCENTAGE OF POPULAR VOTE
1868	**Ulysses S. Grant**	Republican	214	52.7
	Horatio Seymour	Democratic	80	
1872	**Ulysses S. Grant**	Republican	286	55.6
	Horace Greeley	Democratic	**	
1876	**Rutherford B. Hayes**	Republican	185	48.0
	Samuel J. Tilden	Democratic	184	
1880	**James A. Garfield***	Republican	214	48.3
	Winfield S. Hancock	Democratic	155	
	(Chester A. Arthur, 1881)			
1884	**Grover Cleveland**	Democratic	219	48.5
	James G. Blaine	Republican	182	
1888	**Benjamin Harrison**	Republican	233	47.8
	Grover Cleveland	Democratic	168	
1892	**Grover Cleveland**	Democratic	277	46.0
	Benjamin Harrison	Republican	145	
	James B. Weaver	People's	22	
1896	**William McKinley**	Republican	271	51.1
	William J. Bryan	Democratic	176	
1900	**William McKinley***	Republican	292	51.7
	William J. Bryan	Democratic	155	
	(Theodore Roosevelt, 1901)			
1904	**Theodore Roosevelt**	Republican	336	56.4
	Alton B. Parker	Democratic	140	
1908	**William H. Taft**	Republican	321	51.6
	William J. Bryan	Democratic	162	
1912	**Woodrow Wilson**	Democratic	435	41.8
	Theodore Roosevelt	Progressive	88	
	William H. Taft	Republican	8	
1916	**Woodrow Wilson**	Democratic	277	49.2
	Charles E. Hughes	Republican	254	
1920	**Warren G. Harding***	Republican	404	60.3
	James M. Cox	Democratic	127	
	(Calvin Coolidge, 1923)			
1924	**Calvin Coolidge**	Republican	382	54.0
	John W. Davis	Democratic	136	
	Robert M. LaFollette	Progressive	13	
1928	**Herbert C. Hoover**	Republican	444	58.2
	Alfred E. Smith	Democratic	87	
1932	**Franklin D. Roosevelt**	Democratic	472	57.4
	Herbert C. Hoover	Republican	59	
1936	**Franklin D. Roosevelt**	Democratic	523	60.8
	Alfred M. Landon	Republican	8	
1940	**Franklin D. Roosevelt**	Democratic	449	54.7
	Wendell L. Willkie	Republican	82	
1944	**Franklin D. Roosevelt***	Democratic	432	53.4
	Thomas E. Dewey	Republican	99	
	(Harry S Truman, 1945)			
1948	**Harry S Truman**	Democratic	303	49.5
	Thomas E. Dewey	Republican	189	
	J. Strom Thurmond	States' Rights	39	
1952	**Dwight D. Eisenhower**	Republican	442	55.1
	Adlai E. Stevenson	Democratic	89	
1956	**Dwight D. Eisenhower**	Republican	457	57.4
	Adlai E. Stevenson	Democratic	73	
1960	**John F. Kennedy***	Democratic	303	49.7
	Richard M. Nixon	Republican	219	
	(Lyndon B. Johnson, 1963)			
1964	**Lyndon B. Johnson**	Democratic	486	61.1
	Barry M. Goldwater	Republican	52	

*Died in office, succeeding vice president shown in parentheses.

**Horace Greeley died between the popular vote and the meeting of the presidential electors.

Presidents of the United States (continued)

YEAR	PRESIDENTIAL CANDIDATES	POLITICAL PARTY	ELECTORAL VOTE	PERCENTAGE OF POPULAR VOTE
1968	**Richard M. Nixon**	Republican	301	43.4
	Hubert H. Humphrey	Democratic	191	
	George C. Wallace	American Independent	46	
1972	**Richard M. Nixon**†	Republican	520	60.7
	George S. McGovern	Democratic	17	
	(Gerald R. Ford, 1974)‡			
1976	**Jimmy Carter**	Democratic	297	50.1
	Gerald R. Ford	Republican	240	
1980	**Ronald Reagan**	Republican	489	50.7
	Jimmy Carter	Democratic	49	
	John B. Anderson	Independent	—	
1984	**Ronald Reagan**	Republican	525	58.8
	Walter Mondale	Democratic	13	
1988	**George Bush**	Republican	426	53.4
	Michael Dukakis	Democratic	112	
1992	**Bill Clinton**	Democratic	370	43.0
	George Bush	Republican	168	
	H. Ross Perot	Independent	—	
1996	**Bill Clinton**	Democratic	379	49.2
	Robert Dole	Republican	159	
	H. Ross Perot	Reform	—	
2000	**George W. Bush**	Republican	271	47.9
	Al Gore	Democratic	266	
	Ralph Nader	Green	—	
2004	**George W. Bush**	Republican	286	50.7
	John Kerry	Democratic	251	
	Patrick J. Buchanan	Reform	—	
2008	**Barack Obama**	Democratic	365	52.9
	John McCain	Republican	173	
	Ralph Nader	Independent	—	
2012	**Barack Obama**	Democratic	332	50.9
	Mitt Romney	Republican	206	

†Resigned
‡Appointed vice president

Party Control of the Presidency, Senate, and House of Representatives in the Twentieth and Twenty-first Centuries

CONGRESS	YEARS	PRESIDENT	SENATE* D	SENATE* R	SENATE* OTHER*	HOUSE D	HOUSE R	HOUSE OTHER*
57th	1901–03	McKinley	29	56	3	153	198	5
58th	1903–05	T. Roosevelt	32	58	—	178	207	—
59th	1905–07	T. Roosevelt	32	58	—	136	250	—
60th	1907–09	T. Roosevelt	29	61	—	164	222	—
61st	1909–11	Taft	32	59	—	172	219	—
62d	1911–13	Taft	42	49	—	228‡	162	1
63d	1913–15	Wilson	51	44	1	290	127	18
64th	1915–17	Wilson	56	39	1	230	193	8
65th	1917–19	Wilson	53	42	1	200	216	9
66th	1919–21	Wilson	48	48‡	1	191	237‡	7
67th	1921–23	Harding	37	59	—	132	300	1
68th	1923–25	Coolidge	43	51	2	207	225	3
69th	1925–27	Coolidge	40	54	1	183	247	5
70th	1927–29	Coolidge	47	48	1	195	237	3
71st	1929–31	Hoover	39	56	1	163	267	1
72d	1931–33	Hoover	47	48	1	216‡	218	1
73d	1933–35	F. Roosevelt	59	36	1	313	117	5
74th	1935–37	F. Roosevelt	69	25	2	322	103	10
75th	1937–39	F. Roosevelt	75	17	4	333	89	13
76th	1939–41	F. Roosevelt	69	23	4	262	169	4
77th	1941–43	F. Roosevelt	66	28	2	267	162	6
78th	1943–45	F. Roosevelt	57	38	1	222	209	4
79th	1945–47	Truman	57	38	1	243	190	2
80th	1947–49	Truman	45	51‡	—	188	246‡	1
81st	1949–51	Truman	54	42	—	263	171	1
82d	1951–53	Truman	48	47	1	234	199	2
83d	1953–55	Eisenhower	47	48	1	213	221	1
84th	1955–57	Eisenhower	48‡	47	1	232‡	203	—
85th	1957–59	Eisenhower	49‡	47	—	234‡	201	—
86th†	1959–61	Eisenhower	64‡	34	—	283‡	154	—
87th	1961–63	Kennedy	64	36	—	263	174	—
88th	1963–65	Kennedy/Johnson	67	33	—	258	176	—
89th	1965–67	Johnson	68	32	—	295	140	—
90th	1967–69	Johnson	64	36	—	248	187	—
91st	1969–71	Nixon	58‡	42	—	243‡	192	—
92d	1971–73	Nixon	55‡	45	—	255‡	180	—
93d	1973–75	Nixon	57‡	43	—	243‡	192	—
94th	1975–77	Ford	61‡	38	—	291‡	144	—
95th	1977–79	Carter	62	38	—	292	143	—
96th	1979–81	Carter	59	41	—	277	158	—
97th	1981–83	Reagan	47	53	—	243‡	192	—
98th	1983–85	Reagan	46	54	—	269‡	166	—
99th	1985–87	Reagan	47	53	—	253‡	182	—
100th	1987–89	Reagan	55‡	45	—	258‡	177	—
101st	1989–91	Bush	55‡	45	—	260‡	175	—
102d	1991–93	Bush	56‡	44	—	267‡	167	1
103d	1993–95	Clinton	57	43	—	258	176	1
104th	1995–97	Clinton	46	54‡	—	202	232‡	1
105th	1997–99	Clinton	45	55‡	—	206	228‡	1
106th	1999–01	Clinton	45	55‡	—	211	223‡	1
107th	2001–03	G. W. Bush	50	49	1	212	221	2
108th	2003–05	G. W. Bush	48	51	1	205	229	1
109th	2005–07	G. W. Bush	44	55	1	202	232	1
110th	2007–09	G. W. Bush	50‡	49	1	233‡	202	—
111th	2009–11	Obama	58	40	2	257	178	—
112th	2011–13	Obama	51	47	2	193	242‡	—
113th	2013–15	Obama	53	45	2	201	234‡	—
114th	2015–17a	Obama	44	54‡	2	187	248‡	—

*Excludes vacancies at beginning of each session. Party balance immediately following election.

†The 437 members of the House in the 86th and 87th Congresses are attributable to the at-large representative given to both Alaska (January 3, 1959) and Hawaii (August 21, 1959) prior to redistricting in 1962.

‡Chamber controlled by party other than that of the president.

aData available at press time.

D = Democrat R = Republican

Supreme Court Justices Serving in the Twentieth and Twenty-first Centuries

NAME	NOMINATED BY	SERVICE
John M. Harlan	Hayes	1877–1911
Horace Gray	Arthur	1882–1902
Melville W. Fuller*	Cleveland	1888–1910
David J. Brewer	Harrison	1890–1910
Henry B. Brown	Harrison	1890–1906
George Shiras, Jr.	Harrison	1892–1903
Edward D. White	Cleveland	1894–1910
Rufus W. Peckham	Cleveland	1895–1909
Joseph McKenna	McKinley	1898–1925
Oliver W. Holmes	T. Roosevelt	1902–1932
William R. Day	T. Roosevelt	1903–1922
William H. Moody	T. Roosevelt	1906–1910
Horace H. Lurton	Taft	1910–1914
Edward D. White	Taft	1910–1921
Charles E. Hughes	Taft	1910–1916
Willis Van Devanter	Taft	1911–1937
Joseph R. Lamar	Taft	1911–1916
Mahlon Pitney	Taft	1912–1922
James C. McReynolds	Wilson	1914–1941
Louis D. Brandeis	Wilson	1916–1939
John H. Clarke	Wilson	1916–1922
William H. Taft	Harding	1921–1930
George Sutherland	Harding	1922–1938
Pierce Butler	Harding	1923–1939
Edward T. Sanford	Harding	1923–1930
Harlan F. Stone	Coolidge	1925–1941
Charles E. Hughes	Hoover	1930–1941
Owen J. Roberts	Hoover	1930–1945
Benjamin N. Cardozo	Hoover	1932–1938
Hugo L. Black	F. Roosevelt	1937–1971
Stanley F. Reed	F. Roosevelt	1938–1957
Felix Frankfurter	F. Roosevelt	1939–1962
William O. Douglas	F. Roosevelt	1939–1975
Frank Murphy	F. Roosevelt	1940–1949
Harlan F. Stone	F. Roosevelt	1941–1946
James F. Byrnes	F. Roosevelt	1941–1942
Robert H. Jackson	F. Roosevelt	1941–1954
Wiley B. Rutledge	F. Roosevelt	1943–1949
Harold H. Burton	Truman	1945–1958
Fred M. Vinson	Truman	1946–1953
Tom C. Clark	Truman	1949–1967
Sherman Minton	Truman	1949–1956
Earl Warren	Eisenhower	1953–1969
John M. Harlan	Eisenhower	1955–1971
William J. Brennan, Jr.	Eisenhower	1956–1990
Charles E. Whittaker	Eisenhower	1957–1962
Potter Stewart	Eisenhower	1958–1981
Byron R. White	Kennedy	1962–1993
Arthur J. Goldberg	Kennedy	1962–1965
Abe Fortas	Johnson	1965–1969
Thurgood Marshall	Johnson	1967–1991
Warren E. Burger	Nixon	1969–1986
Harry A. Blackmun	Nixon	1970–1994
Lewis F. Powell, Jr.	Nixon	1971–1987
William H. Rehnquist	Nixon	1971–1986
John Paul Stevens	Ford	1975–2010
Sandra Day O'Connor	Reagan	1981–2006
William H. Rehnquist	Reagan	1986–2005
Antonin Scalia	Reagan	1986–
Anthony M. Kennedy	Reagan	1988–
David H. Souter	Bush	1990–2010
Clarence Thomas	Bush	1991–
Ruth Bader Ginsburg	Clinton	1993–
Stephen G. Breyer	Clinton	1994–
John G. Roberts, Jr.	G. W. Bush	2005–
Samuel A. Alito, Jr.	G. W. Bush	2006–
Sonia Sotomayor	Obama	2009–
Elena Kagan	Obama	2010–

*Boldface type indicates service as chief justice.

GLOSSARY

501(c) groups Groups that are exempted from reporting their contributions and can receive unlimited contributions. Section 501c of the tax code specifies that such groups cannot spend more than half their funds on political activities.

527 groups Independent political groups that are not subject to contribution restrictions because they do not directly seek the election of particular candidates. Section 527 of the tax code specifies that contributions to such groups must be reported to the IRS.

A

actual group The people in the potential group who actually join.

Adarand Constructors v. Pena A 1995 Supreme Court decision holding that federal programs that classify people by race, even for an ostensibly benign purpose such as expanding opportunities for minorities, should be presumed to be unconstitutional.

administrative discretion The authority of administrative actors to select among various responses to a given problem. Discretion is greatest when routines, or standard operating procedures, do not fit a case.

affirmative action A policy designed to give special attention to or compensatory treatment for members of some previously disadvantaged group.

Americans with Disabilities Act of 1990 A law passed in 1990 that requires employers and public facilities to make "reasonable accommodations" for people with disabilities and prohibits discrimination against these individuals in employment.

amicus curiae **("friend of the court") briefs** Legal briefs submitted by a "friend of the court" for the purpose of influencing a court's decision by raising additional points of view and presenting information not contained in the briefs of the formal parties.

Anti-Federalists Opponents of the U.S. Constitution at the time when the states were contemplating its adoption.

appellate jurisdiction The jurisdiction of courts that hear cases brought to them on appeal from lower courts. These courts do not review the factual record, only the legal issues involved.

appropriations bill An act of Congress that actually funds programs within limits established by authorization bills. Appropriations usually cover one year.

arms race A tense relationship beginning in the 1950s between the Soviet Union and the United States whereby one side's weaponry became the other side's goad to procure more weaponry, and so on.

Articles of Confederation The first constitution of the United States, adopted by Congress in 1777 and enacted in 1781. The Articles established a national legislature, the Continental Congress, but most authority rested with the state legislatures.

authorization bill An act of Congress that establishes, continues, or changes a discretionary government program or an entitlement. It specifies program goals and maximum expenditures for discretionary programs.

B

balance of trade The ratio of what is paid for imports to what is earned from exports. When more is paid than earned, there is a balance-of-trade deficit.

Barron v. Baltimore The 1833 Supreme Court decision holding that the Bill of Rights restrained only the national government, not the states and cities.

battleground states The key states that the presidential campaigns focus on because they are most likely to decide the outcome of the Electoral College vote.

beats Specific locations from which news frequently emanates, such as Congress or the White House. Most top reporters work a particular beat, thereby becoming specialists in what goes on at that location.

bicameral legislature A legislature divided into two houses. The U.S. Congress and all state legislatures except Nebraska's are bicameral.

bill A proposed law, drafted in legal language. Anyone can draft a bill, but only a member of the House of Representatives or the Senate can formally submit a bill for consideration.

Bill of Rights The first 10 amendments to the U.S. Constitution, drafted in response to some of the Anti-Federalist concerns. These amendments define such basic liberties as freedom of religion, speech, and press and guarantee defendants' rights.

block grants Federal grants given more or less automatically to states or communities to support broad programs in areas such as community development and social services.

Blue Dog Democrats Fiscally conservative Democrats who are mostly from the South and/or rural parts of the United States.

Brown v. Board of Education The 1954 Supreme Court decision holding that school segregation was inherently unconstitutional because it violated the Fourteenth Amendment's guarantee of equal protection. This case marked the end of legal segregation in the United States.

budget A policy document allocating burdens (taxes) and benefits (expenditures).

budget resolution A resolution binding Congress to a total expenditure level, supposedly the bottom line of all federal spending for all programs.

C

bureaucracy According to Max Weber, a hierarchical authority structure that uses task specialization, operates on the merit principle, and behaves with impersonality.

cabinet A group of presidential advisers not mentioned in the Constitution, although every president has had one. Today the cabinet is composed of 14 secretaries, the attorney general, and others designated by the president.

campaign contributions Donations that are made directly to a candidate or a party and that must be reported to the FEC. As of 2012, individuals were allowed to donate up to $2,500 per election to a candidate and up to $30,800 to a political party.

campaign strategy The master game plan candidates lay out to guide their electoral campaign.

casework Activities of members of Congress that help constituents as individuals, particularly by cutting through bureaucratic red tape to get people what they think they have a right to get.

categorical grants Federal grants that can be used only for specific purposes, or "categories," of state and local spending. They come with strings attached, such as non-discrimination provisions.

caucus A system for selecting convention delegates used in about a dozen states in which voters must attend an open meeting to express their presidential preference.

caucus (congressional) A group of members of Congress sharing some interest or characteristic. Many are composed of members from both parties and from both houses.

census An "actual enumeration" of the population, which the Constitution requires that the government conduct every 10 years. The census is a valuable tool for understanding demographic changes.

Central Intelligence Agency An agency created after World War II to coordinate American intelligence activities abroad and to collect, analyze, and evaluate intelligence.

chains Groups of newspapers published by media conglomerates and today accounting for over four-fifths of the nation's daily newspaper circulation.

checks and balances Features of the Constitution that limit government's power by requiring each branch to obtain the consent of the others for its actions, limiting and balancing power among the branches.

Citizens United v. Federal Election Commission A 2010 landmark Supreme Court case that ruled that individuals, corporations, and unions could donate unlimited amounts of money to groups that make independent political expenditures.

civic duty The belief that in order to support democratic government, a citizen should vote.

civil disobedience A form of political participation based on a conscious decision to break a law believed to be unjust and to suffer the consequences.

civil liberties The constitutional and other legal protections against government actions. Our civil liberties are formally set down in the Bill of Rights.

civil rights Policies designed to protect people against arbitrary or discriminatory treatment by government officials or individuals.

Civil Rights Act of 1964 The law making racial discrimination in hotels, motels, and restaurants illegal and forbidding many forms of job discrimination.

civil service A system of hiring and promotion based on the merit principle and the desire to create a nonpartisan government service.

class action suits Lawsuits in which a small number of people sue on behalf of all people in similar circumstances.

Clean Air Act of 1970 The law aimed at combating air pollution, by charging the EPA with protecting and improving the quality of the nation's air.

closed primaries Elections to select party nominees in which only people who have registered in advance with the party can vote for that party's candidates, thus encouraging greater party loyalty.

coalition A group of individuals with a common interest on which every political party depends.

coalition government When two or more parties join together to form a majority in a national legislature. This form of government is quite common in the multiparty systems of Europe.

Cold War The hostility between the United States and the Soviet Union, which often brought them to the brink of war and which spanned the period from the end of World War II until the collapse of the Soviet Union and Eastern European communist regimes in 1989 and the years following.

collective goods Goods and services, such as clean air and clean water, that by their nature cannot be denied to anyone.

command-and-control policy The typical system of regulation whereby government tells business how to reach certain goals, checks that these commands are followed, and punishes offenders.

commercial speech Communication in the form of advertising, which can be restricted more than many other types of speech.

committee chairs The most important influencers of the congressional agenda. They play dominant roles in scheduling hearings, hiring staff, appointing subcommittees, and managing committee bills when they are brought before the full house.

conference committees Congressional committees formed when the Senate and the House pass a particular bill in different forms. Party leadership appoints members from each house to iron out the differences and bring back a single bill.

Congressional Budget Office Advises Congress on the probable consequences of its decisions, forecasts revenues, and is a counterweight to the president's Office of Management and Budget.

Connecticut Compromise The compromise reached at the Constitutional Convention that established two houses of Congress: the House of Representatives, in which representation is based on a state's share of the U.S. population; and the Senate, in which each state has two representatives.

consent of the governed The idea that government derives its authority by sanction of the people.

constitution A nation's basic law. It creates political institutions, assigns or divides powers in government, and often provides certain guarantees to citizens. Constitutions can be either written or unwritten.

consumer price index The key measure of inflation—the change in the cost of buying a fixed basket of goods and services.

containment doctrine A foreign policy strategy advocated by George Kennan that called for the United States to isolate the Soviet Union, "contain" its advances, and resist its encroachments by peaceful means if possible but by force if necessary.

continuing resolutions When Congress cannot reach agreement and pass appropriations bills, these resolutions allow agencies to spend at the level of the previous year.

cooperative federalism A system of government in which powers and policy assignments are shared between states and the national government.

Council of Economic Advisers A three-member body appointed by the president to advise the president on economic policy.

courts of appeals Appellate courts empowered to review all final decisions of district courts, except in rare cases. In addition, they also hear appeals to orders of many federal regulatory agencies.

Craig v. Boren The 1976 ruling in which the Supreme Court established the "intermediate scrutiny" standard for determining gender discrimination.

crisis A sudden, unpredictable, and potentially dangerous event requiring the president to play the role of crisis manager.

critical election An electoral "earthquake" where new issues emerge, new coalitions replace old ones, and the majority party is often displaced by the minority party. Critical election periods are sometimes marked by a national crisis and may require more than one election to bring about a new party era.

cruel and unusual punishment Court sentences prohibited by the Eighth Amendment.

Declaration of Independence The document approved by representatives of the American colonies in 1776 that stated their grievances against the British monarch and declared their independence.

deficit An excess of federal expenditures over federal revenues.

democracy A system of selecting policymakers and of organizing government so that policy represents and responds to the public's preferences.

demography The science of population changes.

deregulation The lifting of government restrictions on business, industry, and professional activities.

détente A policy, beginning in the early 1970s, that sought a relaxation of tensions between the United States and the Soviet Union, coupled with firm guarantees of mutual security.

devolution Transferring responsibility for policies from the federal government to state and local governments.

direct mail A method of raising money for a political cause or candidate, in which information and requests for money are sent to people whose names appear on lists of those who have supported similar views or candidates in the past.

district courts The 91 federal courts of original jurisdiction. They are the only federal courts in which trials are held and in which juries may be impaneled.

dual federalism A system of government in which both the states and the national government remain supreme within their own spheres, each responsible for some policies.

due process clause Part of the Fourteenth Amendment guaranteeing that persons cannot be deprived of life, liberty, or property by the United States or state governments without due process of law.

E

Earned Income Tax Credit Also known as the EITC, a refundable federal income tax credit for low- to moderate-income working individuals and families, even if they did not earn enough money to be required to file a tax return.

Eighth Amendment The constitutional amendment that forbids cruel and unusual punishment.

elastic clause The final paragraph of Article I, Section 8, of the Constitution, which authorizes Congress to pass all laws "necessary and proper" to carry out the enumerated powers.

electioneering Direct group involvement in the electoral process, for example, by helping to fund campaigns, getting members to work for candidates, and forming political action committees.

Electoral College A unique American institution created by the Constitution, providing for the selection of the president by electors chosen by the state parties. Although the Electoral College vote usually reflects a popular majority, less populated states are overrepresented and the winner-take-all rule concentrates campaigns on close states.

electronic media Television, radio, and the Internet, as compared with print media.

elitism A theory of American democracy contending that an upper-class elite holds the power and makes policy, regardless of the formal governmental organization.

Endangered Species Act of 1973 A law requiring the federal government to protect all species listed as endangered.

Engel v. Vitale The 1962 Supreme Court decision holding that state officials violated the First Amendment when they wrote a prayer to be recited by New York's schoolchildren.

entitlement programs Government programs providing benefits to qualified individuals regardless of need.

entitlements Policies for which Congress has obligated itself to pay *X* level of benefits to *Y* number of recipients. Social Security benefits are an example.

enumerated powers Powers of the federal government that are specifically addressed in the Constitution; for Congress, including the powers listed in Article I, Section 8, for example, to coin money and regulate its value and impose taxes.

environmental impact statement A detailing of a proposed policy's environmental effects, which agencies are required to file with the EPA every time they propose to undertake a policy that might be disruptive to the environment.

Environmental Protection Agency The largest federal independent regulatory agency, created in 1970 to administer much of U.S. environmental protection policy.

equal protection of the laws Part of the Fourteenth Amendment emphasizing that the laws must provide equivalent "protection" to all people.

Equal Rights Amendment (ERA) A constitutional amendment passed by Congress in 1972 stating that "equality of rights under the law shall not be denied or abridged by the United States or by any state on account of sex." The amendment failed to acquire the necessary support from three-fourths of the state legislatures.

establishment clause Part of the First Amendment stating that "Congress shall make no law respecting an establishment of religion."

European Union A transnational government composed of most European nations that coordinates monetary, trade, immigration, and labor policies, making its members one economic unit.

exclusionary rule The rule that evidence cannot be introduced into a trial if it was not constitutionally obtained. The rule prohibits use of evidence obtained through unreasonable search and seizure.

executive orders Regulations originating with the executive branch. Executive orders are one method presidents can use to control the bureaucracy.

exit poll Public opinion surveys used by major media pollsters to predict electoral winners with speed and precision.

expenditures Government spending. Major areas of federal spending are social services and national defense.

extradition A legal process whereby a state surrenders a person charged with a crime to the state in which the crime is alleged to have been committed.

F

factions Groups such as parties or interest groups, which according to James Madison arose from the unequal distribution of property or wealth and had the potential to cause instability in government.

Federal Election Campaign Act A law passed in 1974 for reforming campaign finances. The act created the Federal Election Commission and provided for limits on and disclosure of campaign contributions.

Federal Election Commission A six-member bipartisan agency created by the Federal Election Campaign Act of 1974. The Federal Election Commission administers and enforces campaign finance laws.

federalism A way of organizing a nation so that two or more levels of government have formal authority over the same land and people. It is a system of shared power between units of government.

Federal Reserve System The main instrument for making monetary policy in the United States. It was created by Congress in 1913 to regulate the lending practices of banks and thus the money supply.

Federalist Papers A collection of 85 articles written by Alexander Hamilton, John Jay, and James Madison under the name "Publius" to defend the Constitution in detail.

Federalists Supporters of the U.S. Constitution at the time the states were contemplating its adoption.

feminization of poverty The increasing concentration of poverty among women, especially unmarried women and their children.

Fifteenth Amendment The constitutional amendment adopted in 1870 to extend suffrage to African Americans.

Fifth Amendment A constitutional amendment designed to protect the rights of persons accused of crimes, including protection against double jeopardy, self-incrimination, and punishment without due process of law.

filibuster A strategy unique to the Senate whereby opponents of a piece of legislation use their right to unlimited debate to prevent the Senate from ever voting on a bill. Sixty members present and voting can halt a filibuster.

First Amendment The constitutional amendment that establishes the four great liberties: freedom of the press, of speech, of religion, and of assembly.

fiscal federalism The pattern of spending, taxing, and providing grants in the federal system; it is the cornerstone of the national government's relations with state and local governments.

fiscal policy Use of the federal budget—taxes, spending, and borrowing—to influence the economy; along with monetary policy, a main tool by which the government can attempt to steer the economy. Fiscal policy is almost entirely determined by Congress and the president.

foreign policy Policy that involves choice taking about relations with the rest of the world. The president is the chief initiator of U.S. foreign policy.

formula grants Federal categorical grants distributed according to a formula specified in legislation or in administrative regulations.

Fourteenth Amendment The constitutional amendment adopted after the Civil War that declares "No State shall make or enforce any law which shall abridge the privileges or immunities of citizens of the United States; nor shall any state deprive any person of life, liberty, or property, without due process of law; nor deny to any person within its jurisdiction the equal protection of the laws."

free exercise clause A First Amendment provision that prohibits government from interfering with the practice of religion.

free-rider problem For a group, the problem of people not joining because they can benefit from the group's activities without joining.

frontloading The recent tendency of states to hold primaries early in the calendar in order to capitalize on media attention.

full faith and credit A clause in Article IV of the Constitution requiring each state to recognize the public acts, records, and judicial proceedings of all other states.

G

gender gap The regular pattern in which women are more likely to support Democratic candidates, in part because they tend to be less conservative than men and more likely to support spending on social services and to oppose higher levels of military spending.

Gibbons v. Ogden A landmark case decided in 1824 in which the Supreme Court interpreted very broadly the clause in Article I, Section 8, of the Constitution giving Congress the power to regulate interstate commerce as encompassing virtually every form of commercial activity.

Gideon v. Wainwright The 1963 Supreme Court decision holding that anyone, however poor, accused of a felony where imprisonment may be imposed has a right to a lawyer.

Gitlow v. New York The 1925 Supreme Court decision holding that freedoms of press and speech are "fundamental personal rights and liberties protected by the due process clause of the Fourteenth Amendment from impairment by the states" as well as by the federal government.

global warming The increase in the earth's temperatures that, according to most scientists, is occurring as a result of the carbon dioxide that is produced when fossil fuels are burned collecting in the atmosphere and trapping energy from the sun.

government The institutions through which public policies are made for a society.

government corporation A government organization that, like business corporations, provides a service that could be delivered by the private sector and typically charges for its services. The U.S. Postal Service is an example.

Gregg v. Georgia The 1976 Supreme Court decision that upheld the constitutionality of the death penalty, as "an extreme sanction, suitable to the most extreme of crimes."

gross domestic product (GDP) The sum total of the value of all the goods and services produced in a year in a nation.

GS (General Schedule) rating A schedule for federal employees, ranging from GS 1 to GS 18, by which salaries can be keyed to rating and experience.

H

Hatch Act A federal law prohibiting government employees from active participation in partisan politics while on duty or for employees in sensitive positions at any time.

health maintenance organization Organization contracted by individuals or insurance companies to provide health care for a yearly fee. Such network health plans limit the choice of doctors and treatments. More than half of Americans are enrolled in health maintenance organizations or similar programs.

Hernandez v. Texas A 1954 Supreme Court decision that extended protection against discrimination to Hispanics.

high-tech politics A politics in which the behavior of citizens and policymakers and the political agenda itself are increasingly shaped by technology.

House Rules Committee The committee in the House of Representatives that reviews most bills coming from a House committee before they go to the full House.

House Ways and Means Committee The House of Representatives committee that, along with the Senate Finance Committee, writes the tax codes, subject to the approval of Congress as a whole.

hyperpluralism A theory of American democracy contending that groups are so strong that government, which gives in to the many different groups, is thereby weakened.

I

impeachment The political equivalent of an indictment in criminal law, prescribed by the Constitution. The House of Representatives may impeach the president by a majority vote for "Treason, Bribery, or other high Crimes and Misdemeanors."

implied powers Powers of the federal government that go beyond those enumerated in the Constitution, in accordance with the statement in the Constitution that Congress has the power to "make all laws necessary and proper for carrying into execution" the powers enumerated in Article I.

incentive system An alternative to command-and-control, with marketlike strategies such as rewards used to manage public policy.

income The amount of money collected between any two points in time.

income distribution The way the national income is divided into "shares" ranging from the poor to the rich.

income tax Shares of individual wages and corporate revenues collected by the government. The Sixteenth Amendment explicitly authorized Congress to levy a tax on income.

incorporation doctrine The legal concept under which the Supreme Court has nationalized the Bill of Rights by making most of its provisions applicable to the states through the Fourteenth Amendment.

incrementalism A description of the budget process in which the best predictor of this year's budget is last year's budget, plus a little bit more (an increment). According to Aaron Wildavsky, "Most of the budget is a product of previous decisions."

incumbents Those already holding office. In congressional elections, incumbents usually win.

independent executive agencies The government agencies not accounted for by cabinet departments, independent regulatory commissions, and government corporations. Administrators are typically appointed by the president and serve at the president's pleasure. NASA is an example.

independent expenditures Expenses on behalf of a political message that are made by groups that are uncoordinated with any candidate's campaign.

independent regulatory commission A government agency with responsibility for making and enforcing rules to protect the public interest in some sector of the economy and for judging disputes over these rules.

independent regulatory agencies *[see independent regulatory commission]*

inflation A rise in price of goods and services.

interdependency Mutual reliance, as in the economic realm, in which actions in nations reverberate and affect the economic well-being of people in other nations.

interest group An organization of people with shared policy goals entering the policy process at several points to try to achieve those goals. Interest groups pursue their goals in many arenas.

intergovernmental relations The workings of the federal system—the entire set of interactions among national, state, and local governments, including regulations, transfers of funds, and the sharing of information.

investigative journalism The use of in-depth reporting to unearth scandals, scams, and schemes, at times putting reporters in adversarial relationships with political leaders.

invisible primary The period before any votes are cast when candidates compete to win early support from the elite of the party and to create a positive first impression of their leadership skills.

iron triangles Also known as *subgovernments,* a mutually dependent, mutually advantageous relationship between bureaucratic agencies, interest groups, and congressional committees or subcommittees. Iron triangles dominate some areas of domestic policymaking.

isolationism The foreign policy course the United States followed throughout most of its history whereby it tried to stay out of other nations' conflicts, particularly European wars.

J

Joint Chiefs of Staff A group that consists of the commanding officers of each of the armed services, a chairperson, and a vice chairperson, and advises the president on military policy.

joint committees Congressional committees on a few subject-matter areas with membership drawn from both houses.

judicial activism An approach to decision making in which judges sometimes make bold policy decisions, even charting new constitutional ground.

judicial implementation How and whether court decisions are translated into actual policy, thereby affecting the behavior of others. The courts rely on other units of government to enforce their decisions.

judicial restraint An approach to decision making in which judges play minimal policymaking roles and defer to legislatures whenever possible.

judicial review The power of the courts to determine whether acts of Congress and, by implication, the executive are in accord with the U.S. Constitution. Judicial review was established by *Marbury v. Madison.*

justiciable disputes Issues capable of being settled as a matter of law.

K

Keynesian economic theory Named after English economist John Maynard Keynes, the theory emphasizing that government spending and deficits can help the economy deal with its ups and downs. Proponents of this theory advocate using the power of government to stimulate the economy when it is lagging.

Korematsu v. United States A 1944 Supreme Court decision that upheld as constitutional the internment of more than 100,000 Americans of Japanese descent in encampments during World War II.

L

laissez-faire The principle that government should not meddle in the economy.

legislative oversight Congress's monitoring of the bureaucracy and its administration of policy, performed mainly through hearings.

legislative veto A vote in Congress to override a presidential decision. Although the War Powers Resolution asserts this authority, there is reason to believe that, if challenged, the Supreme Court would find the legislative veto in violation of the doctrine of separation of powers.

Lemon v. Kurtzman The 1971 Supreme Court decision that established that aid to church-related schools must (1) have a secular legislative purpose; (2) have a primary effect that neither advances nor inhibits religion; and (3) not foster excessive government entanglement with religion.

libel The publication of false and malicious statements that damage someone's reputation.

limited government The idea that certain restrictions should be placed on government to protect the natural rights of citizens.

linkage institutions The political channels through which people's concerns become political issues on the policy agenda. In the United States, linkage institutions include elections, political parties, interest groups, and the media.

lobbying According to Lester Milbrath, a "communication, by someone other than a citizen acting on his or her own behalf, directed to a governmental decision maker with the hope of influencing his or her decision."

M

majority leader The principal partisan ally of the Speaker of the House, or the party's manager in the Senate. The majority leader is responsible for scheduling bills, influencing committee assignments, and rounding up votes on behalf of the party's legislative positions.

majority rule A fundamental principle of traditional democratic theory. In a democracy, choosing among alternatives requires that the majority's desire be respected.

mandate theory of elections The idea that the winning candidate has a mandate from the people to carry out his or her platforms and politics. Politicians like the theory better than political scientists do.

Mapp v. Ohio The 1961 Supreme Court decision ruling that the Fourth Amendment's protection against unreasonable searches and seizures must be extended to the states.

Marbury v. Madison The 1803 case in which the Supreme Court asserted its right to determine the meaning of the U.S. Constitution. The decision established the Court's power of judicial review over acts of Congress.

mass media Television, radio, newspapers, magazines, the Internet, and other means of popular communication.

McCleskey v. Kemp The 1987 Supreme Court decision that upheld the constitutionality of the death penalty against charges that it violated the Fourteenth Amendment because minority defendants were more likely to receive the death penalty than were white defendants.

McCulloch v. Maryland An 1819 Supreme Court decision that established the supremacy of the national government over state governments. The Court, led by Chief Justice John Marshall, held that Congress had certain implied powers in addition to the powers enumerated in the Constitution.

McGovern-Fraser Commission A commission formed at the 1968 Democratic convention in response to demands for reform by minority groups and others who sought better representation.

means-tested programs Government programs providing benefits only to individuals who qualify based on specific needs.

media events Events that are purposely staged for the media and that are significant just because the media are there.

Medicaid A public assistance program designed to provide health care for poor Americans and funded by both the states and the national government.

Medicare A program added to the Social Security system in 1965 that provides hospitalization insurance for the elderly and permits older Americans to purchase inexpensive coverage for doctor fees and other medical expenses.

melting pot A term often used to characterize the United States, with its history of immigration and mixing of cultures, ideas, and peoples.

merit principle The idea that hiring should be based on entrance exams and promotion ratings to produce administration by people with talent and skill.

Miami Herald Publishing Company v. Tornillo A 1974 case in which the Supreme Court held that a state could not force a newspaper to print replies from candidates it had criticized, illustrating the limited power of government to restrict the print media.

Miller v. California A 1973 Supreme Court decision holding that community standards be used to determine whether material is obscene in terms of appealing to a "prurient interest" and being "patently offensive" and lacking in value.

minority leader The principal leader of the minority party in the House of Representatives or in the Senate.

minority majority The situation, likely beginning in the mid-twenty-first century, in which the non-Hispanic whites will represent a minority of the U.S. population and minority groups together will represent a majority.

minority rights A principle of traditional democratic theory that guarantees rights to those who do not belong to majorities.

Miranda v. Arizona The 1966 Supreme Court decision that sets guidelines for police questioning of accused persons to protect them against self-incrimination and to protect their right to counsel.

monetarism An economic theory holding that the supply of money is the key to a nation's economic health, with too much cash and credit in circulation producing inflation.

monetary policy Government manipulation of the supply of money in private hands—one of two important tools by which the government can attempt to steer the economy.

Motor Voter Act A 1993 act that requires states to permit people to register to vote when they apply for a driver's license.

N

NAACP v. Alabama The 1958 Supreme Court decision that the right to assemble meant Alabama could not require the state chapter of NAACP to reveal its membership list.

narrowcasting Media programming on cable TV (e.g., on MTV, ESPN, or C-SPAN) or the Internet that is focused on a particular interest and aimed at a particular audience, in contrast to broadcasting.

national chairperson The person responsible for the day-to-day activities of the party.

national committee One of the institutions that keeps the party operating between conventions. The national committee is composed of representatives from the states and territories.

national convention The supreme power within each of the parties. The convention meets every four years to nominate the party's presidential and vice-presidential candidates and to write the party's platform.

national debt All the money borrowed by the federal government over the years and still outstanding. Today the national debt is about $17.5 trillion.

National Environmental Policy Act Passed in 1969, the centerpiece of federal environmental policy, which requires agencies to file environmental impact statements.

national health insurance A compulsory insurance program for all Americans that would have the government finance citizens' medical care. First proposed by President Harry S. Truman.

National Security Council The committee that links the president's foreign and military policy advisers. Its formal members are the president, vice president, secretary of state, and secretary of defense, and it is managed by the president's national security assistant.

natural rights Rights inherent in human beings, not dependent on governments, which include life, liberty, and property. The concept of natural rights was central to English philosopher John Locke's theories about government and was widely accepted among America's Founders.

Near v. Minnesota The 1931 Supreme Court decision holding that the First Amendment protects newspapers from prior restraint.

New Deal coalition A coalition forged by the Democrats, who dominated American politics from the 1930s to the 1960s. Its basic elements were the urban working class, ethnic groups, Catholics and Jews, the poor, Southerners, African Americans, and intellectuals.

New Jersey Plan The proposal at the Constitutional Convention that called for equal representation of each state in Congress regardless of the state's population.

New York Times v. Sullivan A 1964 Supreme Court decision establishing that, to win damage suits for libel, public figures must prove that the defamatory statements were made with "actual malice" and reckless disregard for the truth.

Nineteenth Amendment The constitutional amendment adopted in 1920 that guarantees women the right to vote.

nomination The official endorsement of a candidate for office by a political party. Generally, success in the nomination game requires momentum, money, and media attention.

North Atlantic Treaty Organization A regional organization that was created in 1949 by nations including the United States, Canada, and most Western European nations for mutual defense and has subsequently been expanded.

O

Office of Management and Budget An office that prepares the president's budget and also advises presidents on proposals from departments and agencies and helps review their proposed regulations.

Office of Personnel Management The office in charge of hiring for most agencies of the federal government, using elaborate rules in the process.

open primaries Elections to select party nominees in which voters can decide on Election Day whether they want to participate in the Democratic or Republican contests.

opinion A statement of legal reasoning behind a judicial decision. The content of an opinion may be as important as the decision itself.

Organization of Petroleum Exporting Countries An economic organization consisting primarily of Middle Eastern nations that seeks to control the amount of oil its members produce and sell to other nations and hence the price of oil.

original jurisdiction The jurisdiction of courts that hear a case first, usually in a trial. These are the courts that determine the facts about a case.

originalism A view that the Constitution should be interpreted according to the original intentions or original meaning of the Framers. Many conservatives support this view.

P

party competition The battle of the parties for control of public offices. Ups and downs of the two major parties are one of the most important elements in American politics.

party dealignment The gradual disengagement of people from the parties, as seen in part by shrinking party identification.

party eras Historical periods in which a majority of voters cling to the party in power, which tends to win a majority of the elections.

party identification A citizen's self-proclaimed preference for one party or the other.

party image The voter's perception of what the Republicans or Democrats stand for, such as conservatism or liberalism.

party machines A type of political party organization that relies heavily on material inducements, such as patronage, to win votes and to govern.

party platform A political party's statement of its goals and policies for the next four years. The platform is drafted prior to the party convention by a committee whose members are chosen in rough proportion to each candidate's strength. It is the best formal statement of a party's beliefs.

party realignment The displacement of the majority party by the minority party, usually during a critical election period.

patronage One of the key inducements used by party machines. A patronage job, promotion, or contract is one that is given for political reasons rather than for merit or competence alone.

Pendleton Civil Service Act Passed in 1883, an act that created a federal civil service so that hiring and promotion would be based on merit rather than patronage.

Personal Responsibility and Work Opportunity Reconciliation Act The welfare reform law of 1996, which implemented the Temporary Assistance for Needy Families program.

Planned Parenthood v. Casey A 1992 case in which the Supreme Court loosened its standard for evaluating restrictions on abortion from one of "strict scrutiny" of any restraints on a "fundamental right" to one of "undue burden" that permits considerably more regulation.

plea bargaining A bargain struck between the defendant's lawyer and the prosecutor to the effect that the defendant will plead guilty to a lesser crime (or fewer crimes) in exchange for the state's promise not to prosecute the defendant for a more serious (or additional) crime.

Plessy v. Ferguson An 1896 Supreme Court decision that provided a constitutional justification for segregation by ruling that a Louisiana law requiring "equal but separate accommodations for the white and colored races" was constitutional.

pluralism A theory of American democracy emphasizing that the policymaking process is very open to the participation of all groups with shared interests, with no single group usually dominating. Pluralists tend to believe that as a result, public interest generally prevails.

pocket veto A type of veto occurring when Congress adjourns within 10 days of submitting a bill to the president and the president simply lets the bill die by neither signing nor vetoing it.

policy agenda The issues that attract the serious attention of public officials and other people actively involved in politics at the time.

policy entrepreneurs People who invest their political "capital" in an issue. According to John Kingdon, a policy entrepreneur "could be in or out of government, in elected or appointed positions, in interest groups or research organizations."

policy gridlock A condition that occurs when interests conflict and no coalition is strong enough to form a majority and establish policy, so nothing gets done.

policy impacts The effects a policy has on people and problems. Impacts are analyzed to see how well a policy has met its goal and at what cost.

policy implementation The stage of policymaking between the establishment of a policy and the consequences of the policy for the people affected. Implementation involves translating the goals and objectives of a policy into an operating, ongoing program.

policymaking institutions The branches of government charged with taking action on political issues. The U.S. Constitution established three policymaking institutions—Congress, the presidency, and the courts. Today, the power of the bureaucracy is so great that most political scientists consider it a fourth policymaking institution.

policymaking system The process by which policy comes into being and evolves. People's interests, problems, and concerns create political issues for government policymakers. These issues shape policy, which in turn impacts people, generating more interests, problems, and concerns.

policy voting Electoral choices that are made on the basis of the voters' policy preferences and where the candidates stand on policy issues.

political action committees (PACs) Groups that raise money from individuals and then distribute it in the form of contributions to candidates that the group supports. PACs must register with the FEC and report their donations and contributions to it. Individual contributions to a PAC are limited to $5,000 per year and a PAC may give up to $5,000 to a candidate for each election.

political culture An overall set of values widely shared within a society.

political efficacy The belief that one's political participation really matters—that one's vote can actually make a difference.

political ideology A coherent set of beliefs about politics, public policy, and public purpose, which helps give meaning to political events.

political issue An issue that arises when people disagree about a problem and how to fix it.

political participation All the activities used by citizens to influence the selection of political leaders or the policies they pursue. The most common means of political participation in a democracy is voting; other means include protest and civil disobedience.

political party According to Anthony Downs, a "team of men [and women] seeking to control the governing apparatus by gaining office in a duly constituted election."

political questions A doctrine developed by the federal courts and used as a means to avoid deciding some cases, principally those involving conflicts between the president and Congress.

political socialization The process through which individuals in a society acquire political attitudes, views, and knowledge, based on inputs from family, schools, the media, and others.

politics The process determining the leaders we select and the policies they pursue. Politics produces authoritative decisions about public issues.

poll taxes Small taxes levied on the right to vote. This method was used by most Southern states to exclude African Americans from voting. Poll taxes were declared void by the Twenty-fourth Amendment in 1964.

pork barrel Federal projects, grants, and contracts available to state and local governments, businesses, colleges, and other institutions in a congressional district.

potential group All the people who might be interest group members because they share some common interest.

poverty line The income threshold below which people are considered poor, based on what a family must spend for an "austere" standard of living, traditionally set at three times the cost of a subsistence diet.

precedent How similar cases have been decided in the past.

presidential coattails These occur when voters cast their ballots for congressional candidates of the president's party because they support the president. Recent studies show that few races are won this way.

presidential primaries Elections in which a state's voters go to the polls to express their preference for a party's nominee for president. Most delegates to the national party conventions are chosen this way.

press conferences Meetings of public officials with reporters.

print media Newspapers and magazines, as compared with electronic media.

prior restraint Government actions preventing material from being published. Prior restraint is usually prohibited by the First Amendment, as confirmed in *Near v. Minnesota*.

privileges and immunities The provision of the Constitution according citizens of each state the privileges of citizens of other states.

probable cause The situation in which the police have reasonable grounds to believe that a person should be arrested.

progressive tax A tax by which the government takes a greater share of the income of the rich than of the poor—for example, when a rich family pays 50 percent of its income in taxes, and a poor family pays 5 percent.

project grants Federal categorical grant given for specific purposes and awarded on the basis of the merits of applications.

proportional representation An electoral system used throughout most of Europe that awards legislative seats to political parties in proportion to the number of votes won in an election.

proportional tax A tax by which the government takes the same share of income from everyone, rich and poor alike.

protest A form of political participation designed to achieve policy change through dramatic and unconventional tactics.

public interest lobbies According to Jeffrey Berry, organizations that seek "a collective good, the achievement of which will not selectively and materially benefit the membership or activists of the organization."

public opinion The distribution of the population's beliefs about politics and policy issues.

public policy A choice that government makes in response to a political issue. A policy is a course of action taken with regard to some problem.

R

random-digit dialing A technique used by pollsters to place telephone calls randomly to both listed and unlisted numbers when conducting a survey.

random sampling The key technique employed by survey researchers, which operates on the principle that everyone should have an equal probability of being selected for the sample.

rational-choice theory A popular theory in political science to explain the actions of voters as well as politicians. It assumes that individuals act in their own best interest, carefully weighing the costs and benefits of possible alternatives.

reapportionment The process of reallocating seats in the House of Representatives every 10 years on the basis of the results of the census.

reconciliation A congressional process through which program authorizations are revised to achieve required savings. It usually also includes tax or other revenue adjustments.

Red Lion Broadcasting Company v. Federal Communications Commission A 1969 case in which the Supreme Court upheld restrictions on radio and television broadcasting similar to those it had overturned in *Miami Herald Publishing Company v. Tornillo*. It reasoned that such regulations are justified because there are only a limited number of broadcasting frequencies available.

Reed v. Reed The landmark case in 1971 in which the Supreme Court for the first time upheld a claim of gender discrimination.

Regents of the University of California v. Bakke A 1978 Supreme Court decision holding that a state university could weigh race or ethnic background as one element in admissions but could not set aside places for members of particular racial groups.

regressive tax A tax in which the burden falls relatively more heavily on low-income groups than on wealthy taxpayers. The opposite of a progressive tax, in which tax rates increase as income increases.

regulation The use of governmental authority to control or change some practice in the private sector.

relative deprivation A perception by an individual that he or she is not doing well economically in comparison to others.

representation A basic principle of traditional democratic theory that describes the relationship between the few leaders and the many followers.

republic A form of government in which the people select representatives to govern them and make laws.

responsible party model A view about how parties should work, held by some political scientists. According to the model, parties should offer clear choices to the voters and once in office, should carry out their campaign promises.

revenues The financial resources of the government. The individual income tax and Social Security tax are two major sources of the federal government's revenue.

right to privacy The right to a private personal life free from the intrusion of government.

right-to-work laws A state law forbidding requirements that workers must join a union to hold their jobs. State right-to-work laws were specifically permitted by the Taft-Hartley Act of 1947.

Roe v. Wade The 1973 Supreme Court decision holding that a state ban on abortions was unconstitutional. The decision forbade state control over abortions during the first trimester of pregnancy, permitted states to limit abortions to protect the mother's health in the second trimester, and permitted states to ban abortion during the third trimester.

Roth v. United States A 1957 Supreme Court decision ruling that "obscenity is not within the area of constitutionally protected speech or press."

S

sample A relatively small proportion of people who are chosen in a survey so as to be representative of the whole.

sampling error The level of confidence in the findings of a public opinion poll. The more people interviewed, the more confident one can be of the results.

Schenck v. United States A 1919 Supreme Court decision upholding the conviction of a socialist who had urged resistance to the draft during World War I. Justice Holmes declared that government can limit speech if the speech provokes a "clear and present danger" of substantive evils.

School District of Abington Township, Pennsylvania v. Schempp The 1963 Supreme Court decision holding that a Pennsylvania law requiring Bible reading in schools violated the establishment clause of the First Amendment.

Scott v. Sandford The 1857 Supreme Court decision ruling that a slave who had escaped to a free state enjoyed no rights as a citizen and that Congress had no authority to ban slavery in the territories.

search warrant A written authorization from a court specifying the area to be searched and what the police are searching for.

secretary of defense The head of the Department of Defense and the president's key adviser on military policy and, as such, a key foreign policy actor.

secretary of state The head of the Department of State and traditionally the key adviser to the president on foreign policy.

select committees Congressional committees appointed for a specific purpose, such as the Watergate investigation.

selective benefits Goods that a group can restrict to those who actually join.

selective exposure The process through which people consciously choose to get the news from information sources that have viewpoints compatible with their own.

selective perception The phenomenon that people's beliefs often guide what they pay the most attention to and how they interpret events.

self-incrimination The situation occurring when an individual accused of a crime is compelled to be a witness against himself or herself in court. The Fifth Amendment forbids involuntary self-incrimination.

Senate Finance Committee The Senate committee that, along with the House Ways and Means Committee, writes the tax codes, subject to the approval of Congress as a whole.

senatorial courtesy An unwritten tradition whereby nominations for state-level federal judicial posts are usually not confirmed if they are opposed by a senator of the president's party from the state in which the nominee will serve. The tradition also applies to courts of appeals when there is opposition from a senator of the president's party who is from the nominee's state.

Senior Executive Service An elite cadre of about 9,000 federal government managers at the top of the civil service system.

seniority system A simple rule for picking committee chairs, in effect until the 1970s. The member who had served on the committee the longest and whose party controlled the chamber became chair, regardless of party loyalty, mental state, or competence.

separation of powers A feature of the Constitution that requires each of the three branches of government—executive, legislative, and judicial—to be relatively independent of the others so that one cannot control the others. Power is shared among these three institutions.

Shays's Rebellion A series of attacks on courthouses by a small band of farmers led by Revolutionary War Captain Daniel Shays to block foreclosure proceedings.

single-issue groups Groups that have a narrow interest on which their members tend to take an uncompromising stance.

Sixteenth Amendment The constitutional amendment adopted in 1913 that explicitly permitted Congress to levy an income tax.

Sixth Amendment A constitutional amendment designed to protect individuals accused of crimes. It includes the right to counsel, the right to confront witnesses, and the right to a speedy and public trial.

Social Security Act A 1935 law intended to provide a minimal level of sustenance to older Americans and thus save them from poverty.

Social Security Act of 1935 Created both the Social Security program and a national assistance program for poor families, usually called Aid to Families with Dependent Children.

Social Security Trust Fund The "account" into which Social Security employee and employer contributions are "deposited" and used to pay out eligible recipients.

social welfare policies Policies that provide benefits, cash or in kind, to individuals, based on either entitlement or means testing.

soft money Political contributions earmarked for party-building expenses at the grassroots level or for generic party advertising. For a time, such contributions were unlimited, until they were banned by the McCain–Feingold Act.

solicitor general A presidential appointee and the third-ranking office in the Department of Justice. The solicitor general is in charge of the appellate court litigation of the federal government.

sound bites Short video clips of approximately 10 seconds. Typically, they are all that is shown from a politician's speech on the nightly television news.

Speaker of the House An office mandated by the Constitution. The Speaker is chosen in practice by the majority party, has both formal and informal powers, and is second in line to succeed to the presidency should that office become vacant.

standard operating procedures Better known as SOPs, these procedures for everyday decision making enable bureaucrats to bring efficiency and uniformity to the running of complex organizations. Uniformity promotes fairness and makes personnel interchangeable.

standing committees Separate subject-matter committees in each house of Congress that handle bills in different policy areas.

standing to sue The requirement that plaintiffs have a serious interest in a case, which depends on whether they have sustained or are likely to sustain a direct and substantial injury from another party or from an action of government.

stare decisis A Latin phrase meaning "let the decision stand." Most cases reaching appellate courts are settled on this principle.

statutory construction The judicial interpretation of an act of Congress. In some cases where statutory construction is an issue, Congress passes new legislation to clarify existing laws.

street-level bureaucrats A phrase coined by Michael Lipsky, referring to those bureaucrats who are in constant contact with the public and have considerable administrative discretion.

suffrage The legal right to vote in the United States, gradually extended to virtually all citizens over the age of 18.

Super PACs Independent expenditure-only PACs are known as Super PACs because they may accept donations of any size and can endorse candidates. Their contributions and expenditures must be periodically reported to the FEC.

superdelegates National party leaders who automatically get a delegate slot at the national party convention.

Superfund A fund created by Congress in 1980 to clean up hazardous waste sites. Money for the fund comes from taxing chemical products.

supremacy clause The clause in Article VI of the Constitution that makes the Constitution, national laws, and treaties supreme over state laws as long as the national government is acting within its constitutional limits.

supply-side economics An economic theory, first applied during the Reagan administration, holding that the key task for fiscal policy is to stimulate the supply of goods, as by cutting tax rates.

Supreme Court The pinnacle of the American judicial system. The Court ensures uniformity in interpreting national laws, resolves conflicts among states, and maintains national supremacy in law. It has both original jurisdiction and appellate jurisdiction.

symbolic speech Nonverbal communication, such as burning a flag or wearing an armband. The Supreme Court has accorded some symbolic speech protection under the First Amendment.

T

talking head A shot of a person's face talking directly to the camera. Because such shots are visually unstimulating, the major networks rarely show politicians talking for very long.

tariff A special tax added to imported goods to raise their price, thereby protecting businesses and workers from foreign competition.

tax expenditures Revenue losses that result from special exemptions, exclusions, or deductions allowed by federal tax law.

Temporary Assistance for Needy Families Replacing Aid to Families with Dependent Children as the program for public assistance to needy families, TANF requires people on welfare to find work within two years and sets a lifetime maximum of five years.

Tenth Amendment The constitutional amendment stating, "The powers not delegated to the United States by the Constitution, nor prohibited by it to the states, are reserved to the states respectively, or to the people."

Texas v. Johnson A 1989 case in which the Supreme Court struck down a law banning the burning of the American flag on the grounds that such action was symbolic speech protected by the First Amendment.

third parties Electoral contenders other than the two major parties. American third parties are not unusual, but they rarely win elections.

Thirteenth Amendment The constitutional amendment ratified after the Civil War that forbade slavery and involuntary servitude.

ticket splitting Voting with one party for one office and with another party for other offices. It has become the norm in American voting behavior.

transfer payments Benefits given by the government directly to individuals—either cash transfers, such as Social Security payments, or in-kind transfers, such as food stamps and low-interest college loans.

trial balloons Intentional news leaks for the purpose of assessing the political reaction.

Twenty-fifth Amendment   Ratified in 1967, this amendment permits the vice president to become acting president if the president and the president's cabinet determine that the president is disabled, and it outlines how a recuperated president can reclaim the job.

Twenty-fourth Amendment   The constitutional amendment passed in 1964 that declared poll taxes void in federal elections.

Twenty-second Amendment   Ratified in 1951, this amendment limits presidents to two terms of office.

U

U.S. Constitution   The document written in 1787 and ratified in 1788 that sets forth the institutional structure of U.S. government and the tasks these institutions perform. It replaced the Articles of Confederation.

uncontrollable expenditures   Expenditures that are determined by how many eligible beneficiaries there are for a program or by previous obligations of the government and that Congress therefore cannot easily control.

underemployment rate   As measured by the Bureau of Labor Statistics, a statistic that includes (1) people who aren't working and are actively seeking a job, (2) those who would like to work but have given up looking, and (3) and those who are working part-time because they cannot find a full-time position.

unemployment rate   As measured by the Bureau of Labor Statistics, the proportion of the labor force actively seeking work but unable to find jobs.

union shop   A provision found in some collective bargaining agreements requiring all employees of a business to join the union within a short period, usually 30 days, and to remain members as a condition of employment.

unitary governments   A way of organizing a nation so that all power resides in the central government. Most national governments today are unitary governments.

United Nations   Created in 1945 and currently including 193 member nations, with a central peacekeeping mission and programs in areas including economic development and health, education, and welfare. The seat of real power in the UN is the Security Council.

unreasonable searches and seizures   Obtaining evidence in a haphazard or random manner, a practice prohibited by the Fourth Amendment. Probable cause and/or a search warrant are required for a legal and proper search for and seizure of incriminating evidence.

V

veto   The constitutional power of the president to send a bill back to Congress with reasons for rejecting it. A two-thirds vote in each house can override a veto.

Virginia Plan   The proposal at the Constitutional Convention that called for representation of each state in Congress in proportion to that state's share of the U.S. population.

voter registration   A system adopted by the states that requires voters to register prior to voting. Some states require citizens to register as much as 30 days in advance, whereas others permit Election Day registration.

Voting Rights Act of 1965   A law designed to help end formal and informal barriers to African American suffrage. Under the law, hundreds of thousands of African Americans were registered, and the number of African American elected officials increased dramatically.

W

War Powers Resolution   A law passed in 1973, in reaction to American fighting in Vietnam and Cambodia, that requires presidents to consult with Congress whenever possible prior to using military force and to withdraw forces after 60 days unless Congress declares war or grants an extension. However, presidents have viewed the resolution as unconstitutional.

Water Pollution Control Act of 1972   A law intended to clean up the nation's rivers and lakes by enabling regulation of point sources of pollution.

Watergate   The events and scandal surrounding a break-in at the Democratic National Committee headquarters in 1972 and the subsequent cover-up of White House involvement, leading to the eventual resignation of President Nixon under the threat of impeachment.

wealth   The value of assets owned.

whips   Party leaders who work with the majority leader or minority leader to count votes beforehand and lean on waverers whose votes are crucial to a bill favored by the party.

white primary   Primary elections from which African Americans were excluded, an exclusion that, in the heavily Democratic South, deprived African Americans of a voice in the real contests. The Supreme Court declared white primaries unconstitutional in 1944.

winner-take-all system   An electoral system in which legislative seats are awarded only to the candidates who come in first in their constituencies.

writ of habeas corpus   A court order requiring jailers to explain to a judge why they are holding a prisoner in custody.

Z

Zelman v. Simmons–Harris   The 2002 Supreme Court decision that upheld a state program providing families with vouchers that could be used to pay for tuition at religious schools.

Zurcher v. Stanford Daily   A 1978 Supreme Court decision holding that a search warrant could be applied to a newspaper without necessarily violating the First Amendment rights to freedom of the press.

KEY TERMS IN SPANISH/
PALABRAS IMPORTANTES EN ESPAÑOL

501(c) groups—grupos 501(c)

527 groups—grupos 527

A

actual group—grupo actual

administrative discretion—discreción administrativa

affirmative action—acción afirmativa

Americans with Disabilities Act of 1990—
disposición legal de 1990 para ciudadanos americanos minusválidos

amicus curiae **("friend of the court") briefs**—instrucciones, informes, de la competencia de amigos del senado.

Anti-Federalists—anti-federalistas

appellate jurisdiction—jurisdicción apelatoria

appropriations bill—proyecto de ley de apropiación

arms race—carrera armamentista

Articles of Confederation—Artículos de la Confederación

authorization bill—estatuto de autorización

B

balance of trade—balance de intercambio comercial

beats—beats

battleground states—estados decisivos

bicameral legislature—legislatura bi-camaral

bill—proyecto de ley; moción; cuenta

Bill of Rights—proyecto de ley de derechos

block grants—otorgamientos en conjunto

Blue Dog Democrats—Democratas Perros Azules

budget—presupuesto

budget resolution—resolución de presupuesto

bureaucracy—burocracia

C

cabinet—gabinete

campaign contributions—contribuciones de campaña

campaign strategy—estrategia de campaña

casework—trabajo social

categorical grants—concesiones categorizadas

caucus—reunión del comité central o asamblea local de un partido

caucus (congressional)—Asamblea del Congreso

census—censo

Central Intelligence Agency—Agencia Central de Inteligencia

chains—cadena (cadenas periodísticas)

checks and balances—controles y contrapesos

civic duty—deber cívico

civil disobedience—desobediencia civil

civil liberties—libertades cíviles

civil rights—derechos civiles

Civil Rights Act of 1964—ley de Derechos Humanos de 1964

civil rights movement—movimiento de derechos civiles

civil service—administración pública

class action suits—demanda colectiva

Clean Air Act of 1970—ley contra la contaminación del aire de 1970

closed primaries—primarias cerradas

coalition—coalición

coalition government—coalición de gobierno

Cold War—Guerra Fría

collective goods—bien colectivos

command-and-control policy—política de ordenamiento y control

commercial speech—discurso comercial

committee chairs—presidentes de comité

conference committees—comités de conferencias

Congressional Budget Office—Oficina de Presupuesto del Congreso

Connecticut Compromise—Compromiso de Connecticut

consent of the governed—consentimiento del gobernado

constitution—constitución

consumer price index—índice de precios del consumidor

containment doctrine—doctrina o política de contención

continuing resolutions—resoluciones continuas

cooperative federalism—federalismo cooperativo

Council of Economic Advisers—Consejo de Asesores Económicos

courts of appeals—corte de apelación

crisis—crisis

critical election—elección crítica

cruel and unusual punishment—castigo cruel e inusual

D

Declaration of Independence—Declaración de Independencia

deficit—déficit

democracy—democracia

demography—demografía

deregulation—desregular, liberalizar

détente—relajación

devolution—descentralización

direct mail—correo directo

district courts—juzgado de distrito

dual federalism—federalismo dual

due process clause—cláusula del debido proceso

E

Earned Income Tax Credit—Crédito por Ingreso del Trabajo

Eighth Amendment—Octava Enmienda (constitucional)

elastic clause—cláusula flexible

electioneering—campaña electoral

Electoral College—colegio electoral

electronic media—medios electrónicos

elitism—teoría de la élite

Endangered Species Act of 1973—Ley de Especies en Peligro de Extinción de 1973

entitlement programs—programas de ayuda social

entitlements—derechos

enumerated powers—poderes enumerados

environmental impact statement—declaración de impacto sobre el ambiente

Environmental Protection Agency—Agencia de Protección al Ambiente

equal protection of the laws—igualdad de protección de la ley

Equal Rights Amendment (ERA)—enmienda de Igualdad de Derechos

establishment clause—cláusula de instauración

European Union—Unión Europea

exclusionary rule—regla de exclusión

executive orders—órdenes ejecutivas

exit poll—conteo de salida de votación

expenditures—gastos

extradition—extradición

F

factions—facciones

Federal Election Campaign Act—Ley de la Campaña Federal de Elección

Federal Election Commission—Comisión Federal Electoral

Federal Reserve System—Sistema Federal de Reserva

federalism—federalismo

Federalist Papers—Documentos Federalistas

Federalists—federalistas

feminization of poverty—feminizacion de la pobreza

Fifteenth Amendment—Quinceava Enmienda

Fifth Amendment—Enmienda Quinta

filibuster—intervención parlamentaria con objeto de impedir una votación

First Amendment—Enmienda Primera

fiscal federalism—federalismo fiscal

fiscal policy—política fiscal

foreign policy—política extranjera

formula grants—fórmula de concesión

Fourteenth Amendment—Catorceava Enmienda

free exercise clause—cláusula de ejercicio libre

free-rider problem—problema de polizón

frontloading—carga frontal

full faith and credit—fe y crédito completo

G

gender gap—disparidad de género

global warming—calentamiento global

government—gobierno

government corporations—corporación gubernamental

gross domestic product (GDP)—producto doméstico bruto

GS (General Schedule) rating—prorrateo programático general

H

Hatch Act—Ley Hatch

health maintenance organization—Organización para el Mantenimiento de la Salud

high-tech politics—política sobre alta tecnología

home rule—regla de casa (local)

House Rules Committee—Comité de Reglas de la Cámara

House Ways and Means Committee—Comité de Formas y Medios de la Cámara

hyperpluralism—hiperpluralismo; pluralismo en exceso

impeachment—juicio de impugnación
implied powers—poderes implícitos
incentive system—sistema de incentivos
income—ingresos
income distribution—distribución de ingresos
income tax—impuesto sobre ingresos
incorporation doctrine—doctrina de incorporación
incrementalism—incrementalismo
incumbents—titular en función
independent executive agencies—agencia ejecutiva independiente
independent expenditures—desembolsos independientes
independent regulatory commission—agencia regulatoria independiente
inflation—inflación
interdependency—interdependencia
interest group—grupos de interés
intergovernmental relations—relaciones intergubernamentales
investigative journalism—periodismo de investigación
invisible primary—primaria invisible
iron triangles—triángulos de acero
isolationism—aislacionismo

Joint Chiefs of Staff—Junta de Comandantes de las Fuerzas Armadas (Estado Mayor)
joint committees—comisiones
judicial activism—activismo judicial
judicial implementation—implementación judicial
judicial restraint—restricción judicial
judicial review—revisión judicial
justiciable disputes—conflictos enjuiciables

Keynesian economic theory—teoría económica keynesiana

laissez-faire—liberalismo económico
legislative oversight—supervisión legislativo
legislative veto—veto legislativo
libel—difamación, calumnia
limited government—gobierno limitado
linkage institutions—instituciones de enlace
lobbying—cabildeo

majority leader—líder de la mayoría
majority rule—gobierno de la mayoría
mandate theory of elections—mandato teórico de elecciones
mass media—medios de difusión (comunicación) masiva
McGovern–Fraser Commission—Comisión *McGovern–Fraser*
means–tested programs—programas basados en los ingresos de los beneficiarios
media events—evento de los medios de difusión (comunicación)
Medicaid—programa de asistencia médica estatal *Medicaid* para personas de bajos ingresos
Medicare—programa de asistencia médica estatal *Medicare* para personas mayores de 65 años
melting pot—crisol
merit principle—principio de mérito
minority leader—líder de la minoría parlamentaria
minority majority—mayoría de la minoría
minority rights—derechos de las minorías
monetarism—monetarismo
monetary policy—política monetaria
Motor Voter Act—Ley para promoción del voto

narrowcasting—transmisión cerrada; monitoreo cerrado
national chairperson—director/a de comité nacional
national committee—comité nacional
national debt—deuda nacional
National Environmental Policy Act—Ley de la Política Ambiental Nacional
national health insurance—seguro de salud nacional
national convention—convención nacional del partido
National Security Council—Consejo Nacional de Seguridad
natural rights—derechos naturales

658

policymaking system—sistema de normatividad política
policymaking institutions—instituciones de normatividad política
policy voting—política de votación
policy implementation—implementación política
policy impacts—impactos de las políticas
policy gridlock—parálisis política
policy entrepreneurs—política empresarial
policy agenda—agenda política
pocket veto—veto indirecto del presidente al no firmar dentro de los diez días establecidos
pluralism—teoría pluralista
plea bargaining—negociación de los cargos
Personal Responsibility and Work Opportunity Reconciliation Act—El Acto Personal de la Reconciliación de la Oportunidad de la Responsabilidad
Pendleton Civil Service Act—Ley del Servicio Público de Pendleton
patronage—patrocinio
party realignment—realinación del partido
party platform—plataforma del partido
party machines—maquinaria partidista
party image—imágen del partido
party identification—identificación partidista
party eras—épocas del partido
party dealignment—desalineamiento del partido
party competition—competencia de partido

P

original jurisdiction—jurisdicción original
originalism—originalismo
Organization of Petroleum Exporting Countries—Organización de Países Exportadores de Petróleo
opinion—opinión
open primaries—primarias abiertas
Office of Personnel Management—Oficina de Gestión de Personal
Office of Management and Budget—Oficina de Gestión y Presupuesto

O

North Atlantic Treaty Organization—Tratado de las Organizaciones del Atlántico Norte
nomination—nominación
Nineteenth Amendment—Enmienda Diecinueve
New Jersey Plan—Plan de New Jersey
New Deal coalition—coalición para el Nuevo Tratado

public policy—política pública
public opinion—opinión pública
public interest lobbies—cabildeo por intereses públicos
protest—protesta
proportional tax—impuesto proporcional
proportional representation—representación
project grants—proyecto de concesión
progressive tax—impuesto progresivo
probable cause—causa probable
privileges and immunities—privilegios e inmunidades
prior restraint—restricción anterior
print media—medios de comunicación impresos
press conferences—conferencias de prensa
presidential primaries—elecciones primarias presidenciales
presidential coattails—acción a la sombra presidencial
precedent—precedente
poverty line—límite económico mínimo para sobrevivencia
potential group—grupo potencial
pork barrel—asignación de impuestos estatales para el beneficio de una cierta zona o grupo
poll taxes—votación para impuestos
politics—política
political socialization—socialización política
political questions—cuestiones políticas
political party—partido político
political participation—participación política
political issue—asunto político
political ideology—ideología política
political efficacy—eficacia política
political culture—cultura política
political action committees (PACs)—comités de acción política

representation—representación
relative deprivation—privación relativa
regulation—norma, regla
regressive tax—impuesto regresivo
reconciliation—reconciliación
reapportionment—nueva distribución en la representación del congreso
rational-choice theory—teoría de selección racional
random sampling—muestreo aleatorio
random-digit dialing—llamadas con números aleatorios

R

republic—república
responsible party model—modelo de partido responsable
revenues—ingresos
right to privacy—derecho a la privacidad
right-to-work laws—leyes del derecho al trabajo

S

sample—muestra
sampling error—error de muestreo
search warrant—orden de cateo
secretary of defense—secretario de la defensa
secretary of state—secretario de estado
select committees—comités seleccionados
selective benefits—beneficios selectivos
selective exposure—percepción selectiva
selective perception—percepción selectiva
self-incrimination—auto incriminación
Senate Finance Committee—Comité Senatorial de Finanzas
senatorial courtesy—cortesía senatorial
Senior Executive Service—el de más alto rango en el servicio del ejecutivo
seniority system—sistema de antigüedad
separation of powers—separación de poderes
Shays's Rebellion—Rebelion de Shays
single-issue groups—grupos para una sola causa
Sixteenth Amendment—Enmienda Dieciséis
Sixth Amendment—Enmienda Sexta
Social Security Act—Ley de Seguro Social
Social Security Act of 1935—Ley de Seguro Social de 1935
Social Security Trust Fund—Fondo de Fideicomiso de Seguro Social
social welfare policies—políticas para el bien social
soft money—moneda débil, sin garantía
solicitor general—subsecretario de justicia
sound bites—segmentos de sonido
Speaker of the House—presidente de la cámara
standard operating procedures—procedimientos normales de operación
standing committees—comités permanentes
standing to sue—en posición de entablar demanda
stare decisis—variación de "decisión firme" o "decisión tomada"; la decisión se fundamenta en algo ya decidio.
statutory construction—construcción establecida por ley
street-level bureaucrats—burócratas de bajo nivel
suffrage—sufragio

Super PACs—Super PACs
superdelegates—superdelegados
Superfund—superfondo; fondo de proporciones mayores
supply-side economics—economía de la oferta
supremacy clause—cláusula de supremacía
Supreme Court—Suprema Corte
symbolic speech—discurso simbólico

T

talking head—busto parlante; presentador, entrevistador
tariff—tarifa
tax expenditures—gastos de impuesto
Temporary Assistance for Needy Families—Programa de Asistencia Temporal para las Familias Necesitadas
Tenth Amendment—Enmienda Décima
third parties—terceras personas
Thirteenth Amendment—Enmienda Treceava
ticket splitting—votación de candidatos de diferentes partidos para diferentes cargos
transfer payments—transferencia de pagos
trial balloons—globo de prueba; proponer algo para conocer la reacción de alguien
Twenty-fifth Amendment—Enmienda veinticincoava
Twenty-fourth Amendment—Enmienda veinticuatrava
Twenty-second Amendment—Enmienda veintidoava

U

U.S. Constitution—Constitución de los Estados Unidos
uncontrollable expenditures—gastos incontrolables
underemployment rate—nivel de subempleo, porcentaje de subempleo
unemployment rate—nivel de desempleo; porcentage de desempleo
union shop—empresa que emplea sólo trabajadores sindicalizados
unitary governments—estados/gobiernos unitarios
United Nations—Naciones Unidas
unreasonable searches and seizures—cateos y detenciones/embargos irrazonables
urban underclass—urbanita de clase baja

V

veto—veto
Virginia Plan—Plan Virginia

voter registration—registro de votantes

Voting Rights Act of 1965—Ley de Derechos del
    Elector de 1965

War Powers Resolution—Resolución de Poderes de
    Guerra

Water Pollution Control Act of 1972—Ley para el
    Control de la Contaminación de Aguas de 1972

Watergate—Watergate

wealth—riqueza

whips—miembro de un cuerpo legislativo encargado de
    hacer observar las consignas del partido

white primary—primaria blanca

winner-take-all system—sistema en el que el ganador
    toma todos los votos

writ of habeas corpus—un recurso de hábeas corpus

NOTES

1

1. John McCormick, "Lost Obama Interview Provides Portrait of Aspiring Politician," *Bloomberg News*, August 4, 2009. See http://www.bloomberg.com/apps/news?pid=washingtonstory &sid=aMI4WIBJTDA.

2. David Von Drehle, "The Year of the Youth Vote," *Time*, January 31, 2008. See http://www.time.com/time/politics /article/0,8599,1708570-2,00.html.

3. For example, younger people have consistently scored much lower than have senior citizens in the Pew Research Center's regular "News IQ" surveys. The reports from these surveys can be found at http://pewresearch.org/politicalquiz/.

4. Because the level of difficulty of the questions differed somewhat, one should only examine the differences within a year and not necessarily infer that political knowledge as a whole has decreased.

5. Stephen Earl Bennett and Eric W. Rademacher, "The Age of Indifference Revisited: Patterns of Political Interest, Media Exposure, and Knowledge Among Generation X," in Stephen C. Craig and Stephen Earl Bennett, eds., *After the Boom: The Politics of Generation X* (Lanham, MD: Rowman & Littlefield, 1997), 39.

6. Michael X. Delli Carpini and Scott Keeter, *What Americans Know About Politics and Why It Matters* (New Haven, CT: Yale University Press, 1996), chap. 6.

7. See Julia B. Isaacs et al., "Kids Share: Report on Federal Expenditures on Children Through 2010." Washington, D.C.: The Brookings Institution, July 2011, p. 18.

8. Data for Presidents Richard Nixon through George W. Bush can be found in Samuel Kernell, *Going Public: New Strategies of Presidential Leadership*, 4th ed. (Washington, DC: CQ Press, 2007), 140. We have compiled the data for Obama's Nielsen ratings from regular postings at http://blog .nielsen.com/nielsenwire/.

9. Anthony Corrado, "Elections in Cyberspace: Prospects and Problems," in Anthony Corrado and Charles M. Firestone, eds., *Elections in Cyberspace: Toward a New Era in American Politics* (Washington, DC: Aspen Institute, 1996), 29.

10. Jeremy D. Mayer, "Campaign Press Coverage—At the Speed of Light," In Richard J. Semiatin, ed., *Campaigns on the Cutting Edge* (Washington, DC: CQ Press, 2008), 152.

11. Ganesh Sitaraman and Previn Warren, *Invisible Citizens: Youth Politics After September 11* (New York: iUniverse, Inc., 2003), ix.

12. Harold D. Lasswell, *Politics: Who Gets What, When, and How* (New York: McGraw-Hill, 1938).

13. Robert A. Dahl, *Dilemmas of Pluralist Democracy* (New Haven, CT: Yale University Press, 1982), 6.

14. Robert A. Dahl, *A Preface to Democratic Theory* (Chicago: University of Chicago Press, 1956), 137.

15. Robert Putnam, *Bowling Alone: The Collapse and Revival of American Community* (New York: Simon & Schuster, 2000).

16. Jacob S. Hacker and Paul Pierson, *Off Center: The Republican Revolution and the Erosion of American Democracy* (New Haven, CT: Yale University Press, 2005), 16.

17. Ronald Inglehart and Christian Welzel, *Modernization, Cultural Change, and Democracy: The Human Development Sequence* (New York: Cambridge University Press, 2005), 2.

18. G. K. Chesterton, *What I Saw in America* (New York: Dodd, Mead & Co., 1922), 7.

19. Seymour Martin Lipset, *American Exceptionalism: A Double-Edged Sword* (New York: Norton, 1996), 31.

20. Ibid, 19

21. Louis Hartz, *The Liberal Tradition in America* (New York: Harcourt, Brace, 1955).

22. Frederick Jackson Turner, *The Significance of the Frontier in American History* (New York: Readex Microprint, 1966), 221.

23. John W. Kingdon, *America the Unusual* (New York: St. Martin's/Worth, 1999), 2.

24. Seymour Martin Lipset, *The First New Nation* (New York: Norton, 1979), 68.

25. James Q. Wilson, "How Divided Are We?" *Commentary*, February 2006, 15.

26. Ibid, 21.

27. Morris P. Fiorina, *Culture War? The Myth of a Polarized America*, 2nd ed. (New York: Longman, 2006), 165.

28. Wayne Baker, *America's Crisis of Values: Reality and Perception* (Princeton, NJ: Princeton University Press, 2005).

29. Dick Armey, *The Freedom Revolution* (Washington, DC: Regnery, 1995), 316.

2

1. Gordon S. Wood, *The Radicalism of the American Revolution* (New York: Vintage, 1993), 4.

2. Garry Wills, *Inventing America: Jefferson's Declaration of Independence* (New York: Doubleday, 1978), 13, 77.

3. Clinton Rossiter, *1787: The Grand Convention* (New York: Macmillan, 1966), 60.

4. On the Lockean influence on the Declaration of Independence, see Carl L. Becker, *The Declaration of Independence: A Study in the History of Political Ideas* (New York: Random House, 1942).

5. Seymour Martin Lipset, *The First New Nation* (New York: Basic Books, 1963).

6. Gordon S. Wood, *The Creation of the American Republic, 1776–1787* (Chapel Hill: University of North Carolina Press, 1969), 3.

7. On the Articles of Confederation, see Merrill Jensen, *The Articles of Confederation* (Madison: University of Wisconsin Press, 1940).

8. Wood, *The Radicalism of the American Revolution*, 6–7.

9. Calvin C. Jillson and Cecil L. Eubanks, "The Political Structure of Constitution-Making: The Federal Convention of 1787," *American Journal of Political Science* 28 (August 1984): 435–58. See also Calvin C. Jillson, *Constitution Making: Conflict and Consensus in the Federal Convention of 1787* (New York: Agathon, 1988).

10. See Arthur Lovejoy, *Reflections on Human Nature* (Baltimore: Johns Hopkins University Press, 1961), 57–63.

11. "Federalist #10," in Alexander Hamilton, James Madison, and John Jay, *The Federalist Papers*, 2nd ed, ed Roy P. Fairfield (Baltimore: Johns Hopkins University Press, 1981), 18.

12. This representation may have practical consequences. See Frances E. Lee, "Representation and Public Policy: The Consequences of Senate Apportionment for the Geographic Distribution of Federal Funds," *Journal of Politics* 60 (February1998): 34–62; and Daniel Wirls, "The Consequences of Equal Representation: The Bicameral Politics of NAFTA in the 103rd Congress," *Congress and the President* 25 (Autumn 1998): 129–45.

13. Cecelia M. Kenyon, ed., *The Antifederalists* (Indianapolis: Bobbs-Merrill, 1966), xxxv.

14. Rossiter, 1787.

15. See Charles A. Beard, *An Economic Interpretation of the Constitution of the United States* (New York: Macmillan, 1913); Robert E. Brown, *Charles Beard and the Constitution* (Princeton, NJ: Princeton University Press, 1956); Forrest B. McDonald, *We the People: The Economic Origins of the Constitution* (Chicago: University of Chicago Press, 1958); and Forrest B. McDonald, *Novus Ordo Seclorum: The Intellectual Origins of the Constitution* (Lawrence: University Press of Kansas, 1986).

16. A brilliant exposition of the Madisonian system is found in Robert A. Dahl, *A Preface to Democratic Theory* (Chicago: University of Chicago Press, 1956).

17. "Federalist #10," in Fairfield, *The Federalist Papers*.

18. "Federalist #51," in Fairfield, *The Federalist Papers*.

19. Quoted in Beard, *An Economic Interpretation of the Constitution of the United States*, 299.

20. See Kenyon, *The Antifederalists*.

21. Jackson Turner Main, *The Antifederalists* (Chapel Hill: University of North Carolina Press, 1961). For more on the Anti-Federalists, see Herbert J. Storing, *What the Anti-Federalists Were For* (Chicago: University of Chicago Press, 1981).

22. The early attempts to ratify the ERA are recounted in Janet Boles, *The Politics of the Equal Rights Amendment* (New York: Longman, 1978).

23. Jane J. Mansbridge, *Why We Lost the ERA* (Chicago: University of Chicago Press, 1986).

24. See "Federalist #10," in Fairfield, *The Federalist Papers*.

25. See, for example, James MacGregor Burns, *The Deadlock of Democracy* (Englewood Cliffs, NJ: Prentice Hall, 1963), 6.

3

1. *Ex parte Young* (1908).
2. *Alden v. Maine*, (1999). See also *College Savings Bank v. Florida Prepaid Postsecondary Education Expense Board* (1999); and *Florida Prepaid Postsecondary Education Expense Board v. College Savings Bank* (1999).
3. *Board of Trustees of University of Alabama, et al. v. Garrett, et al.* (2001).
4. *Fitzpatrick v. Bitzer* (1976).
5. *Central Virginia Community College v. Katz* (2006).
6. *Virginia Office for Protection and Advocacy v. Stewart* (2011).
7. *Monroe v. Pape* (1961); *Monell v. New York City Department of Social Welfare* (1978); *Owen v. Independence* (1980); *Maine v. Thiboutot*, (1980); *Oklahoma City v. Tuttle*, (1985); *Dennis v. Higgins* (1991).
8. *National Federation of Independent Business et al. v. Sebelius, Secretary of Health and Human Services, et al.* (2012).
9. *United States v. Windsor* (2013).
10. *Baldwin v. Fish and Game Commission of Montana* (1978).
11. The transformation from dual to cooperative federalism is described in Walker, *The Rebirth of Federalism*, chap. 4.
12. The classic discussion of cooperative federalism is found in Morton Grodzins, *The American System: A New View of Governments in the United States*, ed. Daniel J. Elazar (Chicago: Rand McNally, 1966).
13. For a study of how different states enforce federal child support enforcement, see Lael R. Keiser and Joe Soss, "With Good Cause: Bureaucratic Discretion and the Politics of Child Support Enforcement," *American Journal of Political Science* 42 (October 1998): 1133–56.
14. See Pew Research Center poll, September 25–October 31, 1997, and Craig Volden, "Intergovernmental Political Competition in American Federalism," *American Journal of Political Science* 49 (April 2005): 327–42.
15. Office of Management and Budget, *Budget of the United States Government, Fiscal Year 2015: Historical Tables* (Washington, DC: U.S. Government Printing Office, 2014), Tables 12.1 and 15.2.
16. On intergovernmental lobbying, see Donald H. Haider, *When Governments Go to Washington* (New York: Free Press, 1974) and Anne Marie Connisa, *Governments as Interest Groups: Intergovernmental Lobbying and the Federal System* (Westport, CT: Praeger, 1995).
17. *National Federation of Independent Business et al. v. Sebelius, Secretary of Health and Human Services, et al.* (2012).
18. On the states and cities as innovators, see Charles R. Shipan and Craig Volden, "The Mechanisms of Policy Diffusion," *American Journal of Political Science* 52 (October 2008): 840–57; Richard P. Nathan and Fred C. Doolittle, *Reagan and the States* (Princeton, NJ: Princeton University Press, 1987); Virginia Gray, "Innovation in the States: A Diffusion Study," *American Political Science Review* 67 (December 1973): 1174–85; and Jack L. Walker, "The Diffusion of Innovations in the American States," *American Political Science Review* 63 (September 1969): 880–99.
19. Michael A. Bailey, "Welfare and the Multifaceted Decision to Move," *American Political Science Review* 99 (February 2005): 125–35; Michael A. Bailey and Mark Carl Rom, "A Wider Race? Interstate Competition Across Health and Welfare Programs," *Journal of Politics* 66 (May 2004): 326–47; Craig Volden, "The Politics of Competitive Federalism: A Race to the Bottom in Welfare Benefits," *American Journal of Political Science* 46 (April 2002): 352–63; Paul E. Peterson and Mark Rom, "American Federalism, Welfare Policy, and Residential Choices," *American Political Science Review* 83 (September 1989): 711–28. But see William D. Berry, Richard C. Fording, and Russell L. Hanson, "Reassessing the 'Race to the Bottom' in State Welfare Policy," *Journal of Politics* 65 (May 2003): 327–49. Some states limit welfare payments to new residents. On environmental policy, see David M. Konisky, "Regulatory Competition and Environmental Enforcement: Is There a Race to the Bottom?" *American Journal of Political Science* 51 (October 2007): 853–72.
20. For an exception to the general pattern, see Lisa L. Miller, "The Representational Biases of Federalism: Scope and Bias in the Political Process, Revisited," *Perspectives on Politics* 5 (June 2007): 305–21.
21. See George C. Edwards III, *Why the Electoral College Is Bad for America*, 2nd ed (New Haven, CT: Yale University Press, 2011).
22. Office of Management and Budget, *Budget of the United States Government, Fiscal Year 2015: Historical Tables* (Washington, DC: US Government Printing Office, 2014), Table 15.3.

4

1. James W. Prothro and Charles M. Grigg, "Fundamental Principles of Democracy: Bases of Agreement and Disagreement," *Journal of Politics* 22 (1960): 276–94; John L. Sullivan et al., "The Sources of Political Tolerance: A Multivariate Analysis," *American Political Science Review* 75 (1981): 100–15.

2. Darren W. Davis and Brian D. Silver, "Civil Liberties vs. Security: Public Opinion in the Context of the Terrorist Attacks on America," *American Journal of Political Science* 48 (January 2004): 28–46.

3. See Kenneth D. Wald and Allison Calhoun-Brown, *Religion and Politics in the United States*, 6th ed. (Lanham, MD: Rowman & Littlefield, 2010).

4. *Widmar v. Vincent* (1981).

5. *Westside Community Schools v. Mergens* (1990).

6. *Good News Club v. Milford Central School* (2001).

7. *Lamb's Chapel v. Center Moriches Union Free School* (1993).

8. *Rosenberger v. University of Virginia* (1995).

9. *Locke v. Davey* (2004).

10. *Illinois ex rel McCollum v. Board of Education* (1948).

11. *Zorach v. Clauson* (1952).

12. *Stone v. Graham* (1980).

13. *Lee v. Weisman* (1992).

14. *Santa Fe School District v. Doe* (2000).

15. *Wallace v. Jaffree* (1985).

16. See, for example, Gallup poll of August 8–11, 2005.

17. *Edwards v. Aguillard* (1987).

18. *Epperson v. Arkansas* (1968).

19. *McCreary County v. American Civil Liberties Union of Kentucky* (2005).

20. *Van Orden v. Perry* (2005).

21. *Town of Greece, New York v. Galloway et al.* (2014).

22. *Lynch v. Donelly* (1984).

23. *County of Allegheny v. American Civil Liberties Union* (1989).

24. 2008 International Social Survey Program.

25. *Bob Jones University v. United States* (1983).

26. *Wisconsin v. Yoder* (1972).

27. *Hosanna-Tabor Evangelical Lutheran Church and School v. Equal Employment Opportunity Commission et al.* (2012).

28. *Burwell v. Hobby Lobby Stores, Inc.* (2014).

29. Denying people unemployment compensation is an exception to this rule.

30. *City of Boerne v. Flores* (1997).

31. *Gonzales v. O Centro Espirita Beneficente Uniao do Vegetal* (2006).

32. *Cutter v. Wilkinson* (2005).

33. Charles R. Lawrence III, "If He Hollers Let Him Go: Regulating Racist Speech on Campus," in *Words That Wound: Critical Race Theory, Assaultive Speech, and the First Amendment*, ed. Mari J. Matsuda, Charles R. Lawrence III, Richard Delgado, and Kimberle Crenshaw, (Boulder, CO: Westview, 1993), 67–68.

34. Ira Glasser, "Introduction," in *Speaking of Race, Speaking of Sex: Hate Speech, Civil Rights, and Civil Liberties*, ed. Henry Louis Gates Jr. (New York: New York University Press, 1994), 8.

35. *R.A.V. v. St. Paul* (1992). However, states may impose longer prison terms on people convicted of "hate crimes" (crimes motivated by racial, religious, or other prejudice) without violating their rights to free speech.

36. See Fred W. Friendly, *Minnesota Rag* (New York: Random House, 1981).

37. *Hazelwood School District v. Kuhlmeier* (1988).

38. *Morse v. Frederick* (2007).

39. The Supreme Court upheld the government's suit in *United States v. Snepp* (1980).

40. *McIntyre v. Ohio Elections Commission* (1995).

41. *Hudgens v. National Labor Relations Board* (1976).

42. *Pruneyard Shopping Center v. Robins* (1980).

43. *City of Ladue v. Gilleo* (1994).

44. *Jenkins v. Georgia* (1974).

45. *Schad v. Mount Ephraim* (1981).

46. *Barnes v. Glen Theater, Inc.* (1991); *Erie v. Pap's A.M.* (2000).

47. *Osborne v. Ohio* (1990).

48. *Reno v. ACLU* (1997).

49. *Ashcroft v. Free Speech Coalition* (2002).

50. *Brown v. Entertainment Merchants Association* (2011).

51. The story of this case is told in Anthony Lewis, *Make No Law: The Sullivan Case and the First Amendment* (New York: Random House, 1991).

52. Renata Adler, *Reckless Disregard* (New York: Knopf, 1986).

53. *Falwell v. Flynt* (1988).

54. *Tinker v. Des Moines Independent School District* (1969).

55. After Congress passed the Flag Protection Act of 1989 outlawing desecration of the American flag, the Supreme Court also found the act an impermissible infringement on free speech in *United States v. Eichman* (1990).

56. *United States v. O'Brien* (1968).

57. *Virginia v. Black* (2003).

58. *Nebraska Press Association v. Stuart* (1972).

59. *Richmond Newspapers v. Virginia* (1980).

60. *Greater New Orleans Broadcasting, Inc. v. United States* (1999).

61. *Central Hudson Gas & Electric Corporation v. Public Service Commission of N.Y.* (1980).

62. *FCC v. Pacifica Foundation* (1978).

63. *United States v. Playboy Entertainment Group* (2000).

64. *McConnell v. Federal Election Commission* (2003).

65. *Federal Election Commission v. Wisconsin Right to Life, Inc.* (2007).

66. *McCutcheon v. Federal Election Commission* (2014).

67. *Arizona Free Enterprise Club's Freedom Club PAC v. Bennett* (2011).

68. *Snyder v. Phelps* (2011).

69. *McCullen v. Coakley* (2014).

70. *Frisby v. Schultz* (1988).

71. *Rumsfeld v. Forum for Academic and Institutional Rights, Inc.* (2006).

72. *Kentucky v. King* (2011).

73. *Brigham City v. Stuart* (2006).

74. *Michigan v. Sitz* (1990).

75. *Illinois v. Caballes* (2005).

76. *Brendlin v. California* (2007). The police recognized the passenger as a parole violator.

77. *Safford Unified School District #1 v. Redding* (2009).

78. *Bell v. Wolfish* (2012).

79. *Maryland v. King* (2013).

80. *Knowles v. Iowa* (1998).

81. *Arizona v. Grant* (2009).

82. *City of Indianapolis v. Edmond* (2000).

83. *Florida v. J.L.* (2000).

84. *Kyllo v. U.S.* (2001).

85. *United States v. Jones* (2012).

86. *Riley v. California* (2014).

87. *Nix v. Williams* (1984).

88. *United States v. Leon* (1984).

89. *Arizona v. Evans* (1995).

90. *Hudson v. Michigan* (2006).

91. *United States v. Payner* (1980).

92. On the Miranda case, see Liva Baker, *Miranda: The Crime, the Law, the Politics* (New York: Atheneum, 1983).
93. *Arizona v. Fulminante* (1991).
94. *Berghuis v. Thompkins* (2010).
95. *Maryland v. Shatzer* (2010).
96. *J.D.B. v. North Carolina* (2011).
97. The story of Gideon is eloquently told by Anthony Lewis, *Gideon's Trumpet* (New York: Random House, 1964).
98. *United States v. Gonzalez-Lopez* (2006).
99. *Turner v. Rogers* (2011).
100. David Brereton and Jonathan D. Casper, "Does It Pay to Plead Guilty? Differential Sentencing and the Function of the Criminal Courts," *Law and Society Review* 16 (1981–1982): 45–70.
101. *Missouri v. Frye* (2012) and *Lafler v. Cooper* (2012).
102. *Batson v. Kentucky* (1986); *Miller-El v. Dretke* (2005).
103. *Apprendi v. New Jersey* (2000); *Blakely v. Washington* (2004); *United States v. Booker* (2005); *Cunningham v. California* (2007); *Southern Union Co. v. United States* (2012).
104. *Crawford v. Washington* (2004).
105. *Melendez-Diaz v. Massachusetts* (2009).
106. *Bullcoming v. New Mexico* (2011).
107. *Smith v. Cain* (2012).
108. *Brown v. Plata* (2011).
109. *Graham v. Florida* (2010); *Miller v. Alabama* (2012).
110. Joe Soss, Laura Langbein, and Alan R. Metelko, "Why Do White Americans Support the Death Penalty?" *Journal of Politics* 65 (May 2003): 397–421.
111. *Baze v. Rees* (2008).
112. Guttmacher Institute, 2011.
113. For example, *Madsen v. Women's Health Center* (1994) and *Hill v. Colorado* (2000).
114. *National Organization for Women v. Scheidler* (1994).
115. Although, as Chapter 15 on the judiciary will show, there is indirect accountability.

1. For opposing interpretations of the Fourteenth Amendment, see Judith A. Baer, *Equality Under the Constitution: Reclaiming the Fourteenth Amendment* (Ithaca, NY: Cornell University Press, 1983), and Raoul Berger, *Government by Judiciary: The Transformation of the Fourteenth Amendment* (Cambridge, MA: Harvard University Press, 1977).
2. Desmond King, *Separate but Unequal: Black Americans and the US Federal Government* (Oxford: Oxford University Press, 1995).
3. D. Garth Taylor, Paul B. Sheatsley, and Andrew M. Greeley, "Attitudes Toward Racial Integration," *Scientific American* 238 (June 1978): 42–49; Richard G. Niemi, John Mueller, and John W. Smith, *Trends in Public Opinion* (Westport, CT: Greenwood Press, 1989), 180.
4. There are a few exceptions. Religious institutions such as schools may use religious standards in employment. Gender, age, and disabilities may be considered in the few cases in which such occupational qualifications are absolutely essential to the normal operations of a business or enterprise, as in the case of a men's restroom attendant.
5. On the implementation of the Voting Rights Act, see Richard Scher and James Button, "Voting Rights Act: Implementation and Impact," in *Implementation of Civil Rights Policy*, ed. Charles Bullock III and Charles Lamb, (Monterey, CA: Brooks/Cole, 1984); Abigail M. Thernstrom, *Whose Votes Count?* (Cambridge, MA: Harvard University Press, 1987); and Chandler Davidson and Bernard Grofman, eds., *Quiet Revolution in the South: The Impact of the Voting Rights Act, 1965–1990* (Princeton, NJ: Princeton University Press, 1994).
6. *Shelby County, Alabama v. Holder, Attorney General, et al.* (2013).
7. U.S. Department of Commerce, *Statistical Abstract of the United States, 2010* (Washington, DC: U.S. Government Printing Office, 2010), Table 404. See David Lublin, *The Paradox of Representation: Racial Gerrymandering and Minority Interests in Congress* (Princeton, NJ: Princeton University Press, 1997), on how racial redistricting helped increase the number of minority representatives in Congress.
8. *Shaw v. Reno* (1993).
9. *Johnson v. DeGrandy* (1994).
10. *Miller v. Johnson* (1995).
11. *Bush v. Vera* (1996) and *Shaw v. Hunt* (1996).
12. *League of United Latin American Citizens v. Perry* (2006).
13. U.S. Census Bureau, 2014.
14. See Dee Brown, *Bury My Heart at Wounded Knee: An Indian History of the American West* (New York: Holt, Rinehart and Winston, 1970).
15. U.S. Census Bureau, 2012.
16. U.S. Department of Commerce, *Statistical Abstract of the United States, 2012*, Table 421.
17. *White v. Register* (1973).
18. U.S. Census Bureau, 2014.
19. U.S. Census Bureau, 2014.
20. See Eleanor Flexner, *Century of Struggle* (New York: Atheneum, 1971).
21. See J. Stanley Lemons, *The Woman Citizen: Social Feminism in the 1920s* (Urbana: University of Illinois Press, 1973).
22. *Kirchberg v. Feenstra* (1981).
23. *Arizona Governing Committee for Tax Deferred Annuity and Deferred Compensation Plans v. Norris* (1983).
24. *Michael M. v. Superior Court* (1981).
25. *Kahn v. Shevin* (1974).
26. U.S. Department of Labor, Bureau of Labor Statistics, *Women in the Labor Force: A Databook* (2010 Edition), 2011, Tables 1–7.
27. U.S. Department of Labor, Bureau of Labor Statistics, *Women in the Labor Force: A Databook* (2013 Edition), 2014, p. 2.
28. *Cleveland Board of Education v. LaFleur* (1974).
29. *United Automobile Workers v. Johnson Controls* (1991).
30. *Roberts v. United States Jaycees* (1984); *Board of Directors of Rotary International v. Rotary Club of Duarte* (1987); *New York State Club Association v. New York* (1988).
31. *United States v. Virginia et al.* (1996).
32. CNN, January 24, 2013.
33. *Rostker v. Goldberg* (1981).
34. American Association of University Women, *Crossing the Line: Sexual Harassment at School*, 2011.
35. www.eeoc.gov/laws/types/sexual_harassment.cfm.
36. *Meritor Savings Bank v. Vinson* (1986).
37. See also *Burlington Industries, Inc. v. Ellerth* (1998).
38. *University of Texas Southwestern Medical Center v. Nassar* (2013).
39. *Faragher v. City of Boca Raton* (1998); *Pennsylvania State Police v. Suders* (2004).
40. *Burlington Northern Santa Fe Railway Co. v. White* (2006).
41. U.S. Census Bureau, 2014.
42. *Massachusetts Board of Retirement v. Murgia* (1976).
43. *Smith v. City of Jackson* (2005).
44. *Olmstead v. L.C and E.W* (1999).
45. *Bregdon v. Abbott* (1998).
46. *Boy Scouts of America v. Dale* (2000).
47. Kenneth D. Wald, James W. Button, and Barbara A. Rienzo, "The Politics of Gay Rights in American Communities: Explaining Antidiscrimination Ordinances and Policies,"

American Journal of Political Science 40 (November 1996): 1152–78, examines why some communities adopt antidiscrimination ordinances and policies that include sexual orientation and others do not.

48. Gallup poll, May 8–11, 2014.

49. *United States v. Windsor* (2013).

50. Gallup poll, May 8–11, 2014.

51. On the affirmative action issues raised by *Bakke* and other cases, see Allan P. Sindler, *Bakke, De Funis and Minority Admissions* (New York: Longman, 1978).

52. *United Steelworkers of America, AFL-CIO v. Weber* (1979).

53. *Local Number 93 v. Cleveland* (1986); *United States v. Paradise* (1987).

54. *Local 28 of the Sheet Metal Workers v. EEOC* (1986).

55. *Fullilove v. Klutznick* (1980).

56. *Metro Broadcasting, Inc. v. Federal Communications Commission* (1990).

57. *Richmond v. J.A. Croson Co.* (1989).

58. *Firefighters v. Stotts* (1984).

59. *Wygant v. Jackson Board of Education* (1986).

60. Harry Holzer and David Newmark, "Assessing Affirmative Action," *Journal of Economic Literature* 38 (September 2000): 483–568.

61. See Barbara S. Gamble, "Putting Civil Rights to a Popular Vote," *American Journal of Political Science* 41 (January 1997): 245–69.

6

1. For details on this survey, see "Kaiser Tracking Poll: September 2013." This report is available online at: http://kff.org/report-section/kaiser-health-tracking-poll-september-2013/.

2. See http://2010.census.gov/2010census/why/index.php.

3. John F. Kennedy, *A Nation of Immigrants* (New York: Harper and Row, 1964).

4. Steven M. Gillon, *That's Not What We Meant to Do: Reform and Its Unintended Consequences in Twentieth-Century America* (New York: Norton, 2000), p. 178.

5. See *Statistical Abstract of the United States, 2007* (Washington, DC: U.S. Government Printing Office, 2007), 255.

6. Harold W. Stanley and Richard G. Niemi, *Vital Statistics on American Politics, 2009–2010* (Washington, DC: Congressional Quarterly Press, 2008), 53–54.

7. See Michael Hoefer et al., "Estimates of the Unauthorized Immigrant Population Residing in the United States: January 2011" (Washington, DC: Department of Homeland Security). This report is available online at https://www.dhs.gov/sites/default/files/publications/ois_ill_pe_2011.pdf.

8. Ronald T. Takaki, *Strangers from a Different Shore* (Boston: Little, Brown, 1989), chap. 11.

9. See http://www.census.gov/population/www/socdemo/education/cps2008.html.

10. Deborah J. Schildkraut, *Americanism in the Twenty-First Century: Public Opinion in the Age of Immigration* (New York: Cambridge University Press, 2011), p. 20.

11. Ellis Cose, *A Nation of Strangers: Prejudice, Politics, and the Populating of America* (New York: William Morrow and Company, 1992), 219.

12. Robert D. Putnam, "E Pluribus Unum: Diversity and Community in the 21st Century: the 2006 Johan Skytte Prize Lecture," *Scandinavian Political Studies*, Vol. 30, Issue 2 (2007): 150.

13. Richard Dawson et al., *Political Socialization*, 2nd ed. (Boston: Little, Brown, 1977), 33.

14. See M. Kent Jennings and Richard G. Niemi, *The Political Character of Adolescence: The Influence of Families and Schools* (Princeton, NJ: Princeton University Press, 1981), chap. 2.

15. See M. Kent Jennings and Richard G. Niemi, *Generations and Politics: A Panel Study of Young Adults and Their Parents* (Princeton, NJ: Princeton University Press, 1981).

16. John R. Alford, Carolyn L. Funk, and John R. Hibbing, "Are Political Orientations Genetically Transmitted?" *American Political Science Review* (May 2005): 153–67.

17. See Martin P. Wattenberg, *Is Voting for Young People?* (New York: Longman, 2008), chaps. 1–3.

18. David Easton and Jack Dennis, *Children in the Political System* (New York: McGraw-Hill, 1969), 106–7.

19. For an interesting analysis of public opinion data on the skepticism about polls amongst the public, see "Jibrum Kim et al., "Trends in Surveys on Surveys." *Public Opinion Quarterly* (Spring 2011): 165–191.

20. Jean M. Converse, *Survey Research in the United States: Roots and Emergence, 1890–1960* (Berkeley: University of California Press, 1987), 116. Converse's work is the definitive study on the origins of public opinion sampling.

21. Herbert Asher, *Polling and the Public: What Every Citizen Should Know* (Washington, DC: Congressional Quarterly Press, 1988), 59.

22. Mark S. Mellman, "Pollsters Cellphonobia Setting In," *The Hill*, May 23, 2007. See http://thehill.com/opinion/columnists/mark-mellman/8579-pollsters-cellphonobia.

23. Knowledge Networks, "Knowledge Networks Methodology, 1. See http://www.knowledgenetworks.com/ganp/docs/Knowledge%20Networks%20Methodology.pdf.

24. Kate Zernicke, "George Gallup Jr., of Polling Family, Dies at 81." *New York Times*, November 22, 2011.

25. Quoted in Norman M. Bradburn and Seymour Sudman, *Polls and Surveys: Understanding What They Tell Us* (San Francisco: Jossey-Bass, 1988), 39–40.

26. Lawrence R. Jacobs and Robert Y. Shapiro, *Politicians Don't Pander* (Chicago: University of Chicago Press, 2000), xiii.

27. Michael D. Shear, "Poll Results Drive Rhetoric of Obama's Health-Care Message." *Washington Post*, July 30, 2009.

28. W. Lance Bennett, *Public Opinion and American Politics* (New York: Harcourt Brace Jovanovich, 1980), 44.

29. E. D. Hirsch Jr., *Cultural Literacy* (Boston: Houghton Mifflin, 1986).

30. Michael X. Delli Carpini and Scott Keeter, *What Americans Know About Politics and Why It Matters* (New Haven, CT: Yale University Press, 1996), chap. 3. For an updated look at this topic, see "Public Knowledge of Current Affairs Little Changed by News and Information Revolutions: What Americans Know: 1989–2007" (report of the Pew Research Center for People & the Press, April 15, 2007). This report can be found online at http://people-press.org/reports/display.php3?ReportID=319.

31. W. Russell Neuman, *The Paradox of Mass Politics: Knowledge and Opinion in the American Electorate* (Cambridge, MA: Harvard University Press, 1986).

32. For a classic example of how voters rationally use group cues, see Arthur Lupia, "Shortcuts Versus Encyclopedias: Information and Voting Behavior in California Insurance Reform Elections," *American Political Science Review*, Vol. 88, Issue 1 (March 1994): 63–76.

33. Mark J. Hetherington, *Why Trust Matters* (Princeton, NJ: Princeton University Press, 2005), 4.

34. See, for example, Elaine C. Kamarck, "The Evolving American State: The Trust Challenge," *The Forum*, Vol. 7, Issue 4 (2010): Article 9.

35. See Ronald Inglehart, *Modernization and Postmodernization* (Princeton, NJ: Princeton University Press, 1997), 254–55.

Inglehart also shows that the decline of class voting is a general trend throughout Western democracies.

36. See Lydia Saad, "U.S. 1% is More Republican, but Not More Conservative," Gallup report, December 5, 2011. This report can be found online at http://www.gallup.com/poll/151310/U.S.-Republican-Not-Conservative.aspx.

37. See Seymour Martin Lipset and Earl Raab, *Jews and the New American Political Scene* (Cambridge, MA: Harvard University Press, 1995), chap. 6.

38. Angus Campbell et al., *The American Voter* (New York: Wiley, 1960), chap. 10.

39. Norman H. Nie, Sidney Verba, and John R. Petrocik, *The Changing American Voter* (Cambridge, MA: Harvard University Press, 1976), chap. 7.

40. See, for example, John L. Sullivan, James E. Pierson, and George E. Marcus, "Ideological Constraint in the Mass Public: A Methodological Critique and Some New Findings," *American Journal of Political Science* Vol.22 (May 1978): 233–49, and Eric R. A. N. Smith, *The Unchanging American Voter* (Berkeley: University of California Press, 1989).

41. Michael S. Lewis-Beck et al., *The American Voter Revisited* (Ann Arbor, MI: University of Michigan Press, 2008), 279.

42. Morris P. Fiorina, *Culture War? The Myth of a Polarized America*, 2nd ed. (New York: Longman, 2006), 127.

43. Ibid., 8.

44. This definition is a close paraphrase of that in Sidney Verba and Norman H. Nie, *Participation in America* (New York: Harper & Row, 1972), 2.

45. See Verba and Nie, *Participation in America*, and Sidney Verba, Kay Lehman Schlozman, and Henry E. Brady, *Voice and Equality: Civic Voluntarism in American Politics* (Cambridge, MA: Harvard University Press, 1995).

46. See Russell J. Dalton, *The Good Citizen* (Washington, DC: Congressional Quarterly Press, 2008), 60.

47. This letter can be found in Juan Williams, *Eyes on the Prize: America's Civil Rights Years, 1954–1965* (New York: Viking, 1987), 187–89.

48. Verba and Nie, *Participation in America*, 125.

49. Because registration procedures in Louisiana are regulated by the provisions of the Voting Rights Act, registration forms ask people to state their race and the registrars must keep track of this information. Thus, Louisiana can accurately report how many people of each race are registered and voted, which they regularly do.

50. See Verba and Nie, *Participation in America*, chap. 10.

51. See Lydia Saad, "Majorities in U.S. View Government as Too Intrusive and Powerful," Gallup report, October 13, 2010.

52. Tom W. Smith, "Trends in National Spending Priorities, 1973–2006," General Social Survey Report, 2007.

53. Campbell et al., *The American Voter*, 541.

54. Morris P. Fiorina, *Retrospective Voting in American National Elections* (New Haven: Yale University Press, 1981), 5.

7

1. See Frank Esser, "Dimensions of Political News Cultures: Sound Bite and Image Bite News in France, Germany, Great Britain, and the United States," *The International Journal of Press/Politics* (2008): 418.

2. See Darrell M. West, *Air Wars: Television Advertising in Election Campaigns, 1952–2008*, 5th ed. (Washington, DC: Congressional Quarterly Press, 2009), 67.

3. Stephen Ansolabehere and Shanto Iyengar, *Going Negative* (New York: Free Press, 1995). But for a different perspective, see John G. Geer, *In Defense of Negativity: Attack Ads in Presidential Campaigns* (Chicago: University of Chicago Press, 2006).

4. Mark Hertsgaard, *On Bended Knee: The Press and the Reagan Presidency* (New York: Farrar, Straus & Giroux, 1988), 34.

5. Bob Woodward, *The Agenda: Inside the Clinton White House* (New York: Simon and Schuster, 1994), 313.

6. Quoted in David Brinkley, *Washington Goes to War* (New York: Knopf, 1988), 171.

7. Sam Donaldson, *Hold On, Mr. President!* (New York: Random House, 1987), 54.

8. Marvin Kalb, *One Scandalous Story: Clinton, Lewinsky, and Thirteen Days That Tarnished American Journalism* (New York: Free Press, 2001), 6.

9. Donaldson, *Hold On, Mr President!*, 20.

10. Kalb, *One Scandalous Story*, 138.

11. See the classic report by Michael J. Robinson, "Public Affairs Television and the Growth of Political Malaise: The Case of 'The Selling of the Pentagon,'" *American Political Science Review* 70 (June 1976): 409–32. See also Joseph Cappella and Kathleen Hall Jamieson, *Spiral of Cynicism: The Press and the Public Good* (New York: Oxford University Press, 1997).

12. Quoted in Kathleen Hall Jamieson and Paul Waldman, *Electing the President 2000: The Insider's View* (Philadelphia: University of Pennsylvania Press, 2001), 6.

13. See, for example, Michael X. Delli Carpini and Scott Keeter, *What Americans Know About Politics and Why It Matters* (New Haven, CT: Yale University Press, 1996), and Ruy A. Teixeira, *The Disappearing American Voter* (Washington, DC: Brookings Institution, 1992).

14. Robert D. Putnam, *Bowling Alone: The Collapse and Revival of American Community* (New York: Simon & Schuster, 2000), 218.

15. Leonard Downie Jr. and Robert G. Kaiser, *The News About the News: American Journalism in Peril* (New York: Knopf, 2002), 65.

16. See the data posted by the Newspaper Association of America at: http://www.naa.org/Trends-and-Numbers/Newspaper-Revenue/Newspaper-Media-Industry-Revenue-Profile-2012.aspx.

17. Howard Kurtz, "The Press Loves a Hero, but ... Presidential Commission Won't Save Newspapers," *Washington Post*, August 17, 2009.

18. Russell Baker, *The Good Times* (New York: William Morrow, 1989), 326.

19. For some evidence that indicates Nixon was correct, see James N. Druckman, "The Power of Television Images: The First Kennedy–Nixon Debate Revisited," *Journal of Politics* (May 2003): 559–71.

20. See Walter Cronkite, *A Reporter's Life* (New York: Knopf, 1996), 257–58.

21. Frank Rich, "The Weight of an Anchor," *New York Times*, May 19, 2002.

22. Michael K. Bohn, *Nerve Center: Inside the White House Situation Room* (Dulles, VA: Brassey's, Inc., 2003), 59.

23. Project for Excellence in Journalism, *The State of the News Media, 2004*, www.stateofthenewsmedia.org/index.asp.

24. Sarah Sobieraj and Jeffrey M. Berry, *The Outrage Industry: Political Opinion and the New Incivility* (New York: Oxford University Press, 2014), 7.

25. Ibid., 40.

26. Shanto Iyengar and Kyu S. Hahn, "Red Media, Blue Media: Evidence of Ideological Selectivity in Media Use," *Journal of Communication* (2009): 19–39.

27. Two recent books that analyze various aspects of selective exposure are: Natalie Jomini Stroud, *Niche News: The Politics of News Choice* (New York: Oxford, 2011) and Jonathan M. Ladd, *Why Americans Hate the Media and How It Matters* (Princeton, NJ: Princeton University Press, 2012).

28. NBC News, "A Day in the Life of Obama's White House," June 3, 2009. See http://www.msnbc.msn.com/id/31050780/.

29. Thomas Rosenstiel, "The End of Network News," *Washington Post* (September 12, 2004).

30. Matthew Hindman, *The Myth of Digital Democracy* (Princeton, NJ: Princeton University Press, 2009), 61–63.

31. Bruce Bimber and Richard Davis, *Campaigning Online: The Internet in U.S. Elections* (New York: Oxford University Press, 2003), 145.

32. See "Brian Williams Weighs in on the News Media," http://journalism.nyu.edu/pubzone/wewantmedia/node/487.

33. Hindman, 103.

34. Doris A. Graber, *Mass Media and American Politics*, 8th ed. (Washington, DC: Congressional Quarterly Press, 2010), 32.

35. Priya Kumar, "Shrinking Foreign Coverage." *American Journalism Review*, January 2011.

36. Edward J. Epstein, *News from Nowhere: Television and the News* (New York: Random House, 1973).

37. Downie and Kaiser, *The News About the News*, 137.

38. This letter can be found in Hedrick Smith, ed., *The Media and the Gulf War: The Press and Democracy in Wartime* (Washington, DC: Seven Locks Press, 1992), 378–80. Smith's book contains an excellent set of readings on media coverage of the war.

39. Stephen J. Farnsworth and S. Robert Lichter, *The Mediated Presidency: Television News and Presidential Governance* (Lanham, MD: Rowman & Littlefield, 2006), 95–96.

40. A *Los Angeles Times* national poll conducted April 2–3, 2003, asked the following question: "Reporters have been assigned to U.S. military units in the region of Iraq and given unprecedented access to military action and personnel. Which of the following statements comes closer to your view: (1) Greater media coverage of the military action and U.S. personnel in Iraq is good for the country because it gives the American people an uncensored view of events as they unfold; or (2) Greater media coverage of the military action and U.S. personnel in Iraq is bad for the country because it provides too much information about military actions as they unfold?" The results were that 55 percent picked the first alternative, 37 percent picked the second, and 8 percent said they didn't know.

41. Jody Powell, "White House Flackery," in *Debating American Government*, 2nd ed., ed. Peter Woll (Glenview, IL: Scott, Foresman, 1988), 180.

42. Dan Rather, quoted in Hoyt Purvis, ed., *The Presidency and the Press* (Austin, TX: Lyndon B. Johnson School of Public Affairs, 1976), 56.

43. Kathleen Hall Jamieson and Joseph N. Capella, "The Role of the Press in the Health Care Reform Debate of 1993–1994," in *The Politics of News, the News of Politics*, ed. Doris Graber, Denis McQuail, and Pippa Norris (Washington, DC: Congressional Quarterly Press, 1998), 118–19.

44. This point is well argued in Kathleen Hall Jamieson, *Eloquence in an Electronic Age* (New York: Oxford University Press, 1988).

45. Daniel Hallin, "Sound Bite News: Television Coverage of Elections," *Journal of Communications* (Spring 1992); 1992–2008 data from studies by the Center for Media and Public Affairs.

46. Quoted in Austin Ranney, *Channels of Power* (New York: Basic Books, 1983), 116.

47. Walter Cronkite, *A Reporter's Life*, 376–77.

48. Stephen J. Farnsworth and S. Robert Lichter, *The Nightly News Nightmare: Media Coverage of U.S. Presidential Elections, 1988–2008* (Lanham, MD: Rowman & Littlefield, 2011), 163.

49. Michael Waldman, *POTUS Speaks: Finding the Words That Defined the Clinton Presidency* (New York: Simon and Schuster, 2000), 267.

50. David H. Weaver, et al., *The American Journalist in the 21st Century* (Mahwah, NJ: Lawrence Erlbaum, 2007), 17.

51. Bernard Goldberg, *Bias: A CBS Insider Exposes How the Media Distort the News* (Washington, DC: Regnery, 2002), 5.

52. Ibid, 119.

53. Ibid, 17.

54. Michael J. Robinson and Margaret Petrella, "Who Won the George Bush–Dan Rather Debate?" *Public Opinion* 10 (March/April 1988): 43.

55. Robinson, "Public Affairs Television, and the Growth of Political Malaise," 428.

56. W. Lance Bennett, *News: The Politics of Illusion*, 2nd ed. (New York: Longman, 1988), 46.

57. See Paul F. Lazarsfeld et al., *The People's Choice* (New York: Columbia University Press, 1944).

58. Shanto Iyengar and Donald R. Kinder, *News That Matters* (Chicago: University of Chicago Press, 1987).

59. Ibid, 118–19.

60. Joanne M. Miller and Jon A. Krosnick, "News Media Impact on the Ingredients of Presidential Evaluations: Politically Knowledgeable Citizens Are Guided by a Trusted Source," *American Journal of Political Science* (April 2000): 301–15.

61. Frederick T. Steeper, "Public Response to Gerald Ford's Statements on Eastern Europe in the Second Debate," in *The Presidential Debates: Media, Electoral, and Public Perspectives*, ed. George F. Bishop, Robert G. Meadow, and Marilyn Jackson-Beeck (New York: Praeger, 1978), 81–101.

62. Jamieson and Waldman, *Electing the President 2000*, 5–6.

63. John W. Kingdon, *Agendas, Alternatives, and Public Policies* (Boston: Little, Brown, 1984), 3.

64. Ibid.

65. Patrick Sellers, *Cycles of Spin: Strategic Communication in the U.S. Congress* (New York: Cambridge University Press, 2010), 224.

66. See the interview with Richard Valeriani in Juan Williams, *Eyes on the Prize* (New York: Viking, 1987), 270–71.

67. For an interesting study of how hiring a public relations firm can help a nation's TV image, see Jarol B. Manheim and Robert B. Albitton, "Changing National Images: International Public Relations and Media Agenda Setting," *American Political Science Review* 78 (September 1984): 641–57.

68. Bernard Cohen, *The Press and Foreign Policy* (Princeton, NJ: Princeton University Press, 1963), 13.

69. "Amid Criticism, Support for Media's 'Watchdog' Role Stands Out" (Pew Research Center for People & the Press, August 8, 2013.

70. Doris A. Graber, *Mass Media and American Politics*, 8th ed. (Washington, DC: Congressional Quarterly Press, 2010), 240.

71. Ronald W. Berkman and Laura W. Kitch, *Politics in the Media Age* (New York: McGraw-Hill, 1986), 311.

72. Ibid, 313.

73. Matthew Robert Kerbel, *Edited for Television: CNN, ABC, and the 1992 Presidential Campaign* (Boulder, CO: Westview, 1994), 196.

8

1. E. E. Schattschneider, *Party Government* (New York: Farrar and Rinehart, 1942), 1.

2. Anthony Downs, *An Economic Theory of Democracy* (New York: Harper & Row, 1957).

3. Marjorie Randon Hershey, *Party Politics in America*, 12th ed. (New York: Longman, 2007), 8.

4. Kay Lawson, ed., *Political Parties and Linkage: A Comparative Perspective* (New Haven, CT: Yale University Press, 1980), 3.

5. The major exception to this rule is nominations for the one-house state legislature in Nebraska, which is officially nonpartisan.

6. Downs, *An Economic Theory of Democracy.*

7. Morris P. Fiorina, *Congress: Keystone of the Washington Establishment*, 2nd ed. (New Haven, CT: Yale University Press, 1989), 101.

8. Frank Thorp, "Christie on GOP: I am going to do anything I need to do to win." NBC News, First Read, August 15, 2013.

9. See Adam Cohen and Elizabeth Taylor, *American Pharaoh* (Boston: Little, Brown, 2000), 155–63.

10. Melody Crowder-Meyer, "The Party's Still Going: Local Party Strength and Activity in 2008," in *The State of the Parties*, 6th ed., ed. John C. Green and Daniel J. Coffey (Lanham, MD: Rowman & Littlefield, 2011), 116.

11. John F. Bibby et al., "Parties in State Politics," in *Politics in the American States*, 4th ed., ed. Virginia Gray, Herbert Jacob, and Kenneth Vines (Boston: Little, Brown, 1983), 76–79.

12. John F. Bibby, "State Party Organizations: Coping and Adapting to Candidate-Centered Politics and Nationalization," in *The Parties Respond*, 3rd ed., ed. L. Sandy Maisel (Boulder, CO: Westview, 1998), 34.

13. Comments of Roy Romer and Jim Nicholson at the Bulen Symposium on American Politics, December 1, 1998, as noted by Martin Wattenberg.

14. Elizabeth N. Simas and Kevin A. Evans, "Linking Party Platforms to Perceptions of Presidential Candidates' Policy Positions, 1972–2000." *Political Research Quarterly* (December 2011): 837.

15. The term is from V. O. Key. The standard source on critical elections is Walter Dean Burnham, *Critical Elections and the Mainsprings of American Politics* (New York: Norton, 1970).

16. On the origins of the American party system, see William N. Chambers, *Political Parties in a New Nation* (New York: Oxford University Press, 1963).

17. See Richard Hofstadter, *The Idea of a Party System: The Rise of Legitimate Opposition in the United States, 1780–1840* (Berkeley: University of California Press, 1969).

18. James W. Ceaser, *Presidential Selection: Theory and Development* (Princeton, NJ: Princeton University Press, 1979), 130.

19. Quoted in James L. Sundquist, *Dynamics of the Party System*, rev. ed. (Washington, DC: Brookings Institution, 1983), 88. Sundquist's book is an excellent account of realignments in American party history.

20. Ibid, 1955.

21. On Boston, see Gerald H. Gamm, *The Making of New Deal Democrats: Voting Behavior and Realignment in Boston, 1920–1940* (Chicago: University of Chicago Press, 1989).

22. See Earl Black and Merle Black, *The Rise of Southern Republicans* (Cambridge, MA: Harvard University Press, 2002).

23. Steven J. Rosenstone, Roy L. Behr, and Edward H. Lazarus, *Third Parties in America* (Princeton, NJ: Princeton University Press, 1984).

24. The classic statement on responsible parties can be found in "Toward a More Responsible Two-Party System: A Report of the Committee on Political Parties," American Political Science Association, *American Political Science Review* 44 (1950): supplement, number 3, part 2.

25. See Marian Currinder, *Money in the House: Campaign Funds and Congressional Party Politics.* Boulder, CO: Westview Press, 2009.

26. See Evron M. Kirkpatrick, "Toward a More Responsible Party System: Political Science, Policy Science, or Pseudo-Science?" *American Political Science Review* 65 (1971): 965–90.

9

1. Karl Rove, "The Endless Campaign," *Wall Street Journal*, December 20, 2007, A17.

2. Anthony King, *Running Scared* (New York: Free Press, 1997).

3. Richard L. Fox and Jennifer L. Lawless, "Gaining and Losing Interest in Running for Public Office: The Concept of Dynamic Political Ambition," *Journal of Politics* (April 2011): 443.

4. R. W. Apple Jr., "Foley Assesses Presidential Elections and Tells Why He Wouldn't Run," *New York Times*, November 4, 1988, A12.

5. The McGovern–Fraser Commission report can be found online today at http://abacus.bates.edu/muskie-archives/ajcr/1971/McGovern%20Commission.shtml.

6. See Byron Shafer, *Quiet Revolution: The Struggle for the Democratic Party and the Shaping of Post-Reform Politics* (New York: Russell Sage Foundation, 1983).

7. William G. Mayer, "Superdelegates: Reforming the Reforms Revisited," in *Reforming the Presidential Nomination Process*, ed. Steven S. Smith and Melanie J. Springer (Washington, D.C.: Brookings, 2009), 103.

8. Marty Cohen et al., *The Party Decides: Presidential Nominations Before and After Reform* (Chicago: University of Chicago Press, 2008).

9. Thomas E. Mann, "Is This Any Way to Pick a President?," in *Reforming the Presidential Nomination Process*, ed. Steven S. Smith and Melanie J. Springer (Washington, D.C.: Brookings, 2009), 165.

10. David Plouffe, *The Audacity to Win: The Inside Story and Lessons of Barack Obama's Historic Victory* (New York: Viking, 2009), 176.

11. See Hugh Winebrenner, *The Iowa Precinct Caucuses: The Making of a Media Event* (Ames: Iowa State University Press, 1987).

12. *Des Moines Register*, "Iowans Should Challenge Presidential Contenders," March 4, 2011.

13. This tradition extends back to 1916. The early primary date was chosen then to coincide with the already existing town meetings. Town meetings were held in February prior to the thawing of the snow, which in the days of unpaved roads made traveling extremely difficult in the spring. In 1916 no one could have dreamed that by holding the state's primary so early they were creating a mass media extravaganza for New Hampshire.

14. Harold W. Stanley and Richard G. Niemi, *Vital Statistics on American Politics*, 6th ed. (Washington, D.C.: Congressional Quarterly Press, 1998), 173. The same research also showed that New Hampshire received just 3 percent of the TV coverage during the general election—a figure far more in line with its small population size.

15. The states of Iowa, New Hampshire, South Carolina, and Nevada were exempted from this requirement, as they were given special permission by the Republican National Committee to go early in the process.

16. Robert Farmer, quoted in Clifford W. Brown Jr., Lynda W. Powell, and Clyde Wilcox, *Serious Money: Fundraising and Contributing in Presidential Nomination Campaigns* (New York: Cambridge University Press, 1995), 1.

17. Frank Bruni, *Ambling into History: The Unlikely Odyssey of George W. Bush* (New York: HarperCollins, 2002), 5.

18. Larry M. Bartels, *Presidential Primaries and the Dynamics of Public Choice* (Princeton, NJ: Princeton University Press, 1988), 269.

19. Barack Obama, *The Audacity of Hope* (New York: Three Rivers Press, 2008), 358.

20. R. W. Apple, "No Decisions, No Drama," *New York Times*, August 1, 2000, A14.

21. Thomas E. Patterson, *The Mass Media Election* (New York: Praeger, 1980), 3.

22. Obama, *The Audacity of Hope*, 121.

23. "Cable Leads the Pack as Campaign News Source," Report of the Pew Research Center for the People & the Press, February 7, 2012.

24. Robert G. Boatright, "Fundraising—Present and Future," in *Campaigns on the Cutting Edge*, ed. Richard J. Semiatin (Washington, D.C.: Congressional Quarterly Press, 2008).

25. Thomas E. Patterson and Robert D. McClure, *The Unseeing Eye: The Myth of Television Power in National Elections* (New York: Putnam, 1976).

26. Jonathan S. Krasno and Daniel E. Seltz, "Buying Time: Television Advertising in the 1998 Congressional Elections," www.brennancenter.org/programs/cmag_temp/download.html.

27. David R. Runkel, ed., *Campaign for President: The Managers Look at '88* (Dover, MA: Auburn, 1989), 136.

28. Project for Excellence in Journalism, "Winning the Media Campaign: How the Press Reported the 2008 Presidential General Election," 33. This report can be found online at http://www.journalism.org/2008/10/22/winning-media-campaign/.

29. Frank J. Sorauf, *Inside Campaign Finance: Myths and Realities* (New Haven, CT: Yale University Press, 1992), 229.

30. For more information on the legal differences between 501c and 527 independent advocacy groups, see the summary information posted by the Center for Responsive Politics at: http://www.opensecrets.org/527s/types.php.

31. Kathleen Hall Jamieson, ed., *Electing the President 2012: The Insiders' View* (Philadelphia, PA: University of Pennsylvania Press, 2013), 161.

32. See http://www.opensecrets.org/news/2008/10/us-election-will-cost-53-billi.html.

33. Bradley A. Smith, *Unfree Speech: The Folly of Campaign Finance Reform* (Princeton, NJ: Princeton University Press, 2001), 173.

34. Shane Goldmacher, "Former Senate Leader Says Senators Spent Two-Thirds of Time Asking for Money." *National Journal*, January 16, 2014.

35. Gary C. Jacobson, "The Effects of Campaign Spending in House Elections: New Evidence for Old Arguments," *American Journal of Political Science* 34 (May 1990): 334–62.

36. Herbert E. Alexander, *Financing Politics: Money, Elections, and Political Reform*, 4th ed. (Washington, D.C.: Congressional Quarterly Press, 1992), 96.

37. See Dennis J. McGrath and Dane Smith, *Professor Wellstone Goes to Washington: The Inside Story of a Grassroots U.S. Senate Campaign* (Minneapolis: University of Minnesota Press, 1995).

38. Dan Nimmo, *The Political Persuaders: The Techniques of Modern Election Campaigns* (New York: Transaction, 1970), 5.

39. John Sides and Lynn Vavreck, *The Gamble: Choice and Chance in the 2012 Presidential Election* (Princeton, NJ: Princeton University Press, 2013), 103.

40. D. Sunshine Hillygus and Todd G. Shields, *The Persuadable Voter: Wedge Issues in Presidential Campaigns* (Princeton, NJ: Princeton University Press, 2008).

41. A summary of these survey results can be found at http://www.census.gov/hhes/www/socdemo/voting/index.html.

42. See Martin P. Wattenberg, "Should Election Day Be a Holiday?," *Atlantic Monthly*, October 1998, 42–46.

43. Anthony Downs, *An Economic Theory of Democracy* (New York: Harper & Row, 1957), chap. 14.

44. Gina Smith, "Haley Signs Voter ID Bill Into Law," *The State*, May 18, 2011.

45. See http://sos.iowa.gov/elections/pdf/2010/genstatestats.pdf.

46. The transcript for this debate can be found on the Web site for the Commission on Presidential Debates, at http://www.debates.org/index.php?page=october-19-1992-debate-transcript.

47. See George C. Edwards III, *At the Margins* (New Haven, CT: Yale University Press, 1989) , chap. 8.

48. Richard G. Niemi and Herbert F. Weisberg, eds., *Controversies in Voting Behavior*, 2nd ed. (Washington, D.C.: Congressional Quarterly Press, 1984), 164–65.

49. See Martin P. Wattenberg, *The Decline of American Political Parties, 1952–1996* (Cambridge, MA: Harvard University Press, 1998).

50. Russell J. Dalton, *The Apartisan American: Dealignment and Changing Electoral Politics* (Washington, D.C.: Congressional Quarterly Press, 2013), 190.

51. Shawn W. Rosenberg with Patrick McCafferty, "Image and Voter Preference," *Public Opinion Quarterly* 51 (Spring 1987): 44.

52. Arthur H. Miller, Martin P. Wattenberg, and Oksana Malanchuk, "Schematic Assessments of Presidential Candidates," *American Political Science Review* 80 (1986): 521–40.

53. Paul R. Abramson et al., *Change and Continuity in the 2012 Elections* (Washington, D.C.: Congressional Quarterly Press, 2014), 148.

54. Joan Shorenstein Center, "The Theodore H. White Lecture on Press and Politics with Maureen Dowd," 23. This lecture can be found online at http://www.hks.harvard.edu/presspol/prizes_lectures/th_white_lecture/transcripts/th_white_2007_dowd.pdf.

55. Abramson, Aldrich, and Rohde, chap. 6.

56. See Gary C. Jacobson, *A Divider, Not a Uniter: George W. Bush and the American People* (New York: Longman, 2007).

57. Jeffrey M. Jones, *Obama's Fifth Year Job Approval Rating Among Most Polarized*, Gallup Report, January 23, 2014.

58. Transcript, *Washington Week with Gwen Ifill*, PBS, September 30, 2011, http://www.pbs.org/weta/washingtonweek/watch/transcript/21890.

59. American Bar Association, *Electing the President* (Chicago: American Bar Association, 1967), 3.

60. The Twenty-third Amendment (1961) permits the District of Columbia to have three electors, even though it has no representatives in Congress.

61. David Plouffe, *The Audacity to Win: The Inside Story and Lessons of Barack Obama's Historic Victory* (New York: Viking, 2009), 247.

62. Sidney Blumenthal, *The Permanent Campaign* (New York: Simon & Schuster, 1982).

63. See Martin P. Wattenberg, *The Rise of Candidate-Centered Politics: Presidential Elections of the 1980s* (Cambridge, MA: Harvard University Press, 1991).

64. Benjamin Page, *Choices and Echoes in American Presidential Elections* (Chicago: University of Chicago Press, 1978), 153.

65. James W. Caeser, *Presidential Selection: Theory and Development* (Princeton, NJ: Princeton University Press, 1979), 83.

66. Benjamin Ginsberg, *Consequences of Consent* (Reading, MA: Addison-Wesley, 1982), 194.

67. Ibid., 198.

10

1. See: http://content.nejm.org/cgi/content/full/NEJMp0902392.

2. See: http://www.menshealth.com/health/sweet-soda-tax.

3. These figures can be found using the search feature on lobbying spending at the Center for Responsive Politics Web site. See http://www.opensecrets.org/lobby/index.php.

4. Alexis de Tocqueville, *Democracy in America*, vol. 2 (New York: Vintage, 1945), 114.

5. The 1959 figure is taken from Frank R. Baumgartner and Beth L. Leech, *Basic Interests: The Importance of Groups in Politics and in Political Science* (Princeton, NJ: Princeton University Press, 1998), 109; the 2012 figure is taken from the advertising posted for the most recent edition of Encyclopedia of Associations: National Organizations of the U.S.

6. The classic work is David B. Truman, *The Governmental Process*, 2nd ed. (New York, 1971).

7. Thomas R. Dye, *Who's Running America?* 5th ed. (Englewood Cliffs, NJ: Prentice Hall, 1990), 170.

8. Steve Coll, *Private Power: ExxonMobil and American Power* (New York: Penguin, 2012).

9. Theodore J. Lowi, *The End of Liberalism*, 2nd ed. (New York: Norton, 1979).

10. See Lee Fritschler, *Smoking and Politics: Policy Making and the Federal Bureaucracy* (Englewood Cliffs, NJ: Prentice Hall, 1983).

11. E. E. Schattschneider, *The Semisovereign People* (New York: Holt, Rinehart and Winston, 1960), 35.

12. Truman, *The Governmental Process*, 511.

13. Mancur Olson, *The Logic of Collective Action* (Cambridge, MA: Harvard University Press, 1965), especially 9–36.

14. Amy McKay, "Negative Lobbying and Policy Outcomes," *American Politics Research* (January 2012): 116–46.

15. Frank R. Baumgartner et al., *Lobbying and Policy Change: Who Wins, Who Loses, and Why* (Chicago: University of Chicago Press, 2009), 208–09.

16. Ibid., p. 210.

17. Lester W. Milbrath, *The Washington Lobbyists* (Chicago: Rand McNally, 1963), 8.

18. See Public Citizen, "Cashing In," November 19, 2009. This report can be found at http://www.citizen.org/documents/Ca$hing_in.pdf.

19. See https://www.columbiabooks.com/ProductDetail/the-18-0-1/Washington_Representatives_2009.

20. Norman Ornstein and Shirley Elder, *Interest Groups, Lobbying and Policymaking* (Washington, D.C.: Congressional Quarterly Press, 1978), 59–60.

21. "Is There Really a Lobbyist Problem?" May 5, 2009, press release from Common Cause.

22. Peter H. Stone, "Friends, After All," *National Journal*, October 22, 1994, 2440.

23. Rogan Kersh, "The Well-Informed Lobbyist: Information and Interest Group Lobbying," in *Interest Group Politics*, 7th ed., ed. Allan J. Cigler and Burdett A. Loomis (Washington, D.C.: Congressional Quarterly Press, 2007), 390.

24. Richard L. Hall and Alan V. Deardorff, "Lobbying as Legislative Subsidy," *American Political Science Review* 100 (February 2006): 69.

25. For a summary of recent studies on the influence of lobbying, see Baumgartner and Leech, *Basic Interests*, 130.

26. See Kelly Patterson and Matthew M. Singer, "Targeting Success: The Enduring Power of the NRA," in *Interest Group Politics*, 7th ed, ed. Allan J. Cigler and Burdett A. Loomis (Washington, D.C.: Congressional Quarterly Press, 2007): 37–64.

27. The data on spending by the baseball PAC, as well as many others, can be found at http://www.opensecrets.org/.

28. Frederic J. Frommer, "Baseball PAC Gives Thousands to Parties," Associated Press, May 13, 2003, http://www.fec.gov/press/cf_summaries.shtml.

29. The data on PAC spending in each year can be found at http://www.fec.gov/press/cf_summaries.shtml.

30. R. Kenneth Godwin and Barry J. Seldon, "What Corporations Really Want from Government: The Public Provision of Private Goods," in *Interest Group Politics*, 6th ed., ed. Allan

31. Archibald Cox and Fred Wertheimer, "The Choice Is Clear: It's People vs. the PACs," in *Debating American Government*, 2nd ed., ed. Peter Woll (Glenview, IL: Scott, Foresman, 1988), 125.

32. Karen Oren, "Standing to Sue: Interest Group Conflict in Federal Courts," *American Political Science Review* 70 (September 1976): 724.

33. Gregory A. Caldeira and John R. Wright, "Amici Curiae Before the Supreme Court: Who Participates, When, and How Much," *Journal of Politics* 52 (August 1990): 782–804.

34. Ronald J. Hrebenar and Ruth K. Scott, *Interest Group Politics in America*, 2nd ed. (Englewood Cliffs, NJ: Prentice Hall, 1990), 201.

35. Ken Kollman, *Outside Lobbying: Public Opinion and Interest Group Strategies* (Princeton, NJ: Princeton University Press, 1998), 33.

36. Quoted in Jeffrey M. Berry, *The Interest Group Society*, 2nd ed. (Glenview, IL: Scott Foresman, 1989), 103.

37. Paul Edward Johnson, "Organized Labor in an Era of Blue-Collar Decline," in *Interest Group Politics*, 3rd ed, ed. Allan J. Cigler and Burdett A. Loomis (Washington, D.C.: Congressional Quarterly Press, 1991), 33–62.

38. Christopher J. Bosso, "The Color of Money: Environmental Groups and the Pathologies of Fund Raising," in *Interest Group Politics*, 4th ed, ed. Allan J. Cigler and Burdett A. Loomis (Washington, D.C.: Congressional Quarterly Press, 1995), 102.

39. Russell J. Dalton, "The Greening of the Globe? Cross-National Levels of Environmental Group Membership," *Environmental Politics* (August 2005): 444.

40. For an interesting analysis of how changes in the regulatory environment, congressional oversight, and public opinion altered the debate on nuclear power, see Frank R. Baumgartner and Bryan D. Jones, *Agendas and Instability in American Politics* (Chicago: University of Chicago Press, 1993).

41. Dona C. Hamilton and Charles V. Hamilton, *The Dual Agenda: Race and Social Welfare Politics of Civil Rights Organizations* (New York: Columbia University Press, 1997), 2.

42. Jeffrey M. Berry, *Lobbying for the People* (Princeton, NJ: Princeton University Press, 1977), 7.

43. Robert H. Salisbury, "The Paradox of Interest Groups in Washington—More Groups, Less Clout," in *The New American Political System*, 2nd ed., ed. Anthony King (Washington, D.C.: American Enterprise Institute, 1990), 204.

44. Mark J. Rozell, Clyde Wilcox, and David Madland, *Interest Groups in American Campaigns: The New Face of Electioneering*, 2nd ed. (Washington, D.C.: Congressional Quarterly Press, 2006), 87.

45. Steven V. Roberts, "Angered President Blames Others for the Huge Deficit," *New York Times*, December 14, 1988, A16.

46. William M. Lunch, *The Nationalization of American Politics* (Berkeley: University of California Press, 1987), 206.

47. Salisbury, "The Paradox of Interest Groups in Washington," 229.

J. Cigler and Burdett A. Loomis, (Washington, D.C.: Congressional Quarterly Press, 2002) 219.

11

1. *Artemus Ward: His Book* (London: Ward, Bock, and Tyler, 1866), 83.

2. See Craig Schultz, ed., *Setting Course: A Congressional Management Guide* (Washington, D.C.: Congressional Management Foundation, 1994); and David E. Price, *The Congressional Experience: A View from the Hill* (Boulder, CO: Westview Press, 1999).

3. David T. Canon, *Race, Redistricting, and Representation: The Unintended Consequences of Black Majority Districts* (Chicago: University of Chicago Press, 1999).

4. Susan A. Banducci, Todd Donovan, and Jeffrey A. Karp, "Minority Representation, Empowerment, and Participation," *Journal of Politics* 66 (May 2004): 534–56.

5. On the impact of gender on representation, see Brian Frederick, "Are Female House Members Still More Liberal in a Polarized Era?" *Congress & the Presidency* 36 (Fall 2009): 181–202; Leslie A. Schwindt-Bayer and Renato Corbetta, "Gender Turnover and Roll-Call Voting in the U.S. House of Representatives," *Legislative Studies Quarterly* 29 (May 2004): 215–29; Arturo Vega and Juanita M. Firestone, "The Effects of Gender on Congressional Behavior and the Substantive Representation of Women," *Legislative Studies Quarterly* 20 (May 1995): 213–22; and Sue Thomas, "The Impact of Women on State Legislative Policies," *Journal of Politics* 53 (November 1991): 958–76; and John D. Griffin, Brian Newman, and Christina Wolbrecht, "A Gender Gap in Policy Representation in the U.S. Congress? *Legislative Studies Quarterly* 37 (February 2012): 35–66.

6. Christopher Witko and Sally Friedman, "Business Backgrounds and Congressional Behavior," *Congress and the Presidency* 35 (Spring 2008): 71–86.

7. Nicholas Carnes, "Does the Numerical Underrepresentation of the Working Class in Congress Matter?" *Legislative Studies Quarterly* 37 (February 2012): 5–34.

8. On various views of representation, see Hanna Pitkin, *The Concept of Representation* (Berkeley: University of California Press, 1967).

9. Sally Friedman, "House Committee Assignments of Women and Minority Newcomers, 1965–1994," *Legislative Studies Quarterly* 21 (February 1996): 73–81; Alan Gerber, "African Americans' Congressional Careers and the Democratic House Delegation," *Journal of Politics* 58 (August 1996): 831–45.

10. These data were calculated from www.cawp.rutgers.edu/fast_facts/elections/candidates_2012.php.

11. Sarah A. Fulton, Cherie D. Maestas, L. Sandy Maisel, and Walter J. Stone, "The Sense of a Woman: Gender, Ambition and the Decision to Run for Congress," *Political Research Quarterly* 59 (June 2006): 235–48.

12. Sarah A. Fulton, "Running Backwards and In High Heels: The Gendered Quality Gap and Incumbent Electoral Success" *Political Research Quarterly* 64 (December 2011); Sarah A. Fulton, "When Gender Matters: Macro-Dynamics and Micro-Mechanisms," *Political Behavior* 36 (September 2014).

13. A review of congressional campaign costs and spending can be found in Paul S. Herrnson, *Congressional Elections: Campaigning at Home and in Washington*, 6th ed. (Washington, D.C.: CQ Press, 2012).

14. John L. Sullivan and Eric Uslaner, "Congressional Behavior and Electoral Marginality," *American Journal of Political Science* 22 (August 1978): 536–53.

15. Thomas Mann, *Unsafe at Any Margin* (Washington, D.C.: American Enterprise Institute, 1978).

16. Glenn R. Parker, *Homeward Bound* (Pittsburgh: University of Pittsburgh Press, 1986); John R. Johannes, *To Serve the People* (Lincoln: University of Nebraska Press, 1984).

17. Patricia Hurley and Kim Q. Hill, "The Prospects for Issue Voting in Contemporary Congressional Elections," *American Politics Quarterly* 8 (October 1980): 446.

18. That presidential elections and congressional elections are not closely related is an argument made in Ray C. Fair, "Presidential and Congressional Vote-Share Equations," *American Journal of Political Science* 53 (January 2009): 55–72; and Lyn Ragsdale, "The Fiction of Congressional Elections as Presidential Events," *American Politics Quarterly* 8 (October 1980): 375–98. For evidence that voters' views of the president

affect their voting for senators, see Lonna Rae Atkeson and Randall W. Partin, "Economic and Referendum Voting: A Comparison of Gubernatorial and Senatorial Elections," *American Political Science Review* 89 (March 1995): 99–107. See, however, Fair, "Presidential and Congressional Vote-Share Equations."

19. James E. Campbell, *The Presidential Pulse of Congressional Elections* (Lexington: University Press of Kentucky, 1993), 119; Gary C. Jacobson, "Does the Economy Matter in Midterm Elections?" *American Journal of Political Science* 34 (May 1990): 400–404; Robert S. Erikson, "Economic Conditions and the Congressional Vote: A Review of the Macrolevel Evidence," *American Journal of Political Science* 34 (May 1990): 373–99; Benjamin Radcliff, "Solving a Puzzle: Aggregate Analysis and Economic Voting Revisited," *Journal of Politics* 50 (May 1988): 440–58; John R. Owens and Edward C. Olson, "Economic Fluctuations and Congressional Elections," *American Journal of Political Science* 24 (August 1980): 469–93.

20. David R. Mayhew, *Congress: The Electoral Connection* (New Haven, CT: Yale University Press, 1974).

21. Richard F. Fenno Jr., *Home Style* (Boston: Little, Brown, 1978), 106–107.

22. Morris P. Fiorina, *Congress: Keystone of the Washington Establishment*, 2nd ed. (New Haven, CT: Yale University Press, 1989). See also Glenn R. Parker, "The Advantages of Incumbency in Congressional Elections," *American Politics Quarterly* 8 (October 1980): 449–61.

23. Justin Grimmer, Solomon Messing, and Sean J. Westwood, "How Words and Money Cultivate a Personal Vote: The Effect of Legislator Credit Claiming on Constituent Credit Allocation," *American Political Science Review* 106 (November 2012): 703–719.

24. Jeffrey Lazarus, Jeffrey Glas, and Kyle T. Barbieri, "Earmarks and Elections to the U.S. House of Representatives," *Congress & the Presidency* 39 (September–December 2012): 254–69.

25. Gary C. Jacobson, *The Politics of Congressional Elections*, 8th ed. (New York: Longman, 2013), 130–142; Stephen Ansolabehere, James M. Snyder Jr., and Charles Stewart III, "Old Voters, New Voters, and the Personal Vote: Using Redistricting to Measure the Incumbency Advantage," *American Journal of Political Science* 44 (January 2000): 17–34.

26. See, for example, Glenn R. Parker and Suzanne L. Parker, "The Correlates and Effects of Attention to District by U.S. House Members," *Legislative Studies Quarterly* 10 (May 1985): 223–42; John C. McAdams and John R. Johannes, "Congressmen, Perquisites, and Elections," *Journal of Politics* 50 (May 1988): 412–39; and Paul Feldman and James Jondrow, "Congressional Elections and Local Federal Spending," *American Journal of Political Science* 28 (February 1984): 147–63.

27. On strategies of challengers, see Gary C. Jacobson and Samuel Kernell, *Strategy and Choice in Congressional Elections*, 2nd ed. (New Haven, CT: Yale University Press, 1983), and Gary C. Jacobson, "Strategic Politicians and the Dynamics of U.S. House Elections, 1946–1986," *American Political Science Review* 83 (September 1989): 773–94. See also Steven D. Levitt and Catherine D. Wolfram, "Decomposing the Sources of Incumbency Advantage in the U.S. House," *Legislative Studies Quarterly* 22 (February 1997): 45–60.

28. See Gary C. Jacobson, *Money in Congressional Elections* (New Haven, CT: Yale University Press, 1980).

29. On the importance of challenger quality and financing, see Alan I. Abramowitz, Brad Alexander, and Matthew Gunning, "Incumbency, Redistricting, and the Decline of Competition in U.S. House Elections," *Journal of Politics* 68 (February 2006): 75–88; Alan I. Abramowitz, "Explaining Senate Election Outcomes," *American Political Science*

Review 82 (June 1988): 385–403; and Donald Philip Green and Jonathan S. Krasno, "Salvation for the Spendthrift Incumbent," *American Journal of Political Science* 32 (November 1988): 884–907.

30. Center for Responsive Politics (www.opensecrets.org); Federal Election Commission (www.fec.gov).

31. Jacobson, *The Politics of Congressional Elections*, 51–59, 143–144. See also Alan Gerber, "Estimating the Effect of Campaign Spending on Senate Election Outcomes Using Instrumental Variables," *American Political Science Review* 92 (June 1998): 401–12; Robert S. Erikson and Thomas R. Palfrey, "Campaign Spending and Incumbency: An Alternative Simultaneous Equation Approach," *Journal of Politics* 60 (May 1998): 355–73; Christopher Kenny and Michael McBurnett, "An Individual-Level Multiequation Model of Expenditure Effects in Contested House Elections," *American Political Science Review* 88 (September 1994): 699–707; and Gary C. Jacobson, "The Effects of Campaign Spending in House Elections: New Evidence for Old Arguments," *American Journal of Political Science* 34 (May 1990): 334–62.

32. Center for Responsive Politics (www.opensecrets.org); Federal Election Commission (www.fec.gov).

33. Federal Election Commission, 2014.

34. Bill Bishop, *The Big Sort: Why the Clustering of Like-Minded America Is Tearing Us Apart* (Boston: Houghton Mifflin, 2008).

35. Susan Welch and John R. Hibbing, "The Effects of Charges of Corruption on Voting Behavior in Congressional Elections, 1982–1990," *Journal of Politics* 59 (February 1997): 226–39; and John G. Peters and Susan Welch, "The Effects of Corruption on Voting Behavior in Congressional Elections," *American Political Science Review* 74 (September 1980): 697–708; Gary C. Jacobson and Michael A. Dimock, "Checking Out: The Effects of Bank Overdrafts on the 1992 House Elections," *American Journal of Political Science* 38 (August 1994): 601–24. See also Marshal A. Dimock and Gary C. Jacobson, "Checks and Choices: The House Bank Scandal's Impact on Voters in 1992," *Journal of Politics* 57 (November 1995): 1143–59, and Carl McCurley and Jeffrey J. Mondak, "Inspected by #118406313: The Influence of Incumbents' Competence and Integrity in U.S. House Elections," *American Journal of Political Science* 39 (November 1995): 864–85.

36. For a discussion of the politics and process of reapportionment, see Thomas E. Mann, *Redistricting* (Washington, D.C.: Brookings Institution Press, 2008).

37. On term limits, see Gerald Benjamin and Michael J. Malbin, eds., *Limiting Our Legislative Terms* (Washington, D.C.: CQ Press, 1992).

38. Nelson W. Polsby et al., "Institutionalization of the House of Representatives," *American Political Science Review* 62 (1968): 144–68.

39. John R. Hibbing, "Contours of the Modern Congressional Career," *American Political Science Review* 85 (June 1991): 405–28.

40. See Bernard Grofman, Robert Griffin, and Amihai Glazer, "Is the Senate More Liberal than the House? Another Look," *Legislative Studies Quarterly* 16 (May 1991): 281–96.

41. See Sarah A. Binder and Steven S. Smith, *Politics or Principle? Filibustering in the United States Senate* (Washington, D.C.: Brookings Institution, 1997).

42. On the increasing importance of party leadership in the House, see David W. Rohde, *Parties and Leaders in the Postreform House* (Chicago: University of Chicago Press, 1991); Barbara Sinclair, "The Emergence of Strong Leadership in the 1980s House of Representatives," *Journal of Politics* 54 (August 1992): 657–84; and Gary W. Cox and Matthew D. McCubbins, *Legislative Leviathan* (Berkley: University of California Press, 1993).

43. Will Rogers Memorial Museums, www.willrogers.com/quotes.html

44. Said former House Speaker Jim Wright in *You and Your Congressman* (New York: Putnam, 1976), 190. See also Donald R. Matthews and James Stimson, *Yeas and Nays: Normal Decision-Making in the House of Representatives* (New York: Wiley, 1975), and John L. Sullivan et al., "The Dimensions of Cue-Taking in the House of Representatives: Variations by Issue Area," *Journal of Politics* 55 (November 1993): 975–97.

45. Steven Balla and Christopher J. Deering, "Police Patrols and Fire Alarms: An Empirical Examination of the Legislative Preference for Oversight," *Congress & the Presidency* 40 (January–April 2013): 27–40.

46. For more on congressional oversight, see Robert J. McGrath, "Congressional Oversight Hearings and Policy Control," *Legislative Studies Quarterly* 38 (August 2013): 349–76; Diana Evans, "Congressional Oversight and the Diversity of Members' Goals," *Political Science Quarterly* 109 (Fall 1994): 669–87; and Christopher H. Foreman Jr., *Signals from the Hill* (New Haven, CT: Yale University Press, 1988).

47. Joel D. Aberbach, *Keeping a Watchful Eye: The Politics of Congressional Oversight* (Washington, D.C.: Brookings Institution, 1990).

48. Ibid. See also Joel D. Aberbach, "What's Happened to the Watchful Eye?", *Congress and the Presidency* 29 (spring 2002): 3–23.

49. Thomas E. Mann and Norman J. Ornstein, *The Broken Branch* (New York: Oxford University Press, 2006).

50. Richard F. Fenno Jr., *Congressmen in Committees* (Boston: Little, Brown, 1973), 1.

51. Useful studies of committee assignments include Kenneth Shepsle, *The Giant Jigsaw Puzzle* (Chicago: University of Chicago Press, 1978), and Cox and McCubbins, *Legislative Leviathan*, chaps. 1, 7, and 8.

52. See Kristina C. Miler, "The Constituency Motivations of Caucus Membership," *American Politics Research* 39 (September 2011): 885–920; Jennifer Nicoll Victor and Nils Ringe, "The Social Utility of Informal Institutions," *American Politics Research* 37 (September 2009): 742–66; Susan Webb Hammond, *Congressional Caucuses in National Policy Making* (Baltimore: Johns Hopkins University Press, 1998).

53. For a thorough discussion of rule changes and the impact of procedures, see Steven S. Smith, *Call to Order: Floor Politics in the House and Senate* (Washington, D.C.: Brookings Institution, 1989). See also Walter J. Oleszek, *Congressional Procedures and the Policy Process*, 8th ed. (Washington, D.C.: CQ Press, 2010).

54. Barbara Sinclair, *Unorthodox Lawmaking*, 4th ed. (Washington, D.C.: CQ Press, 2011). See also Barbara Sinclair, "Orchestrators of Unorthodox Lawmaking: Pelosi and McConnell in the 110th Congress," *The Forum* 6 (2008).

55. George C. Edwards III and Andrew Barrett, "Presidential Agenda Setting in Congress," in *Polarized Politics: Congress and the President in a Partisan Era*, ed. Jon R. Bond and Richard Fleisher (Washington, D.C.: CQ Press, 2000).

56. George C. Edwards III, *At the Margins: Presidential Leadership of Congress* (New Haven, CT: Yale University Press, 1989).

57. For an excellent study of party influence in Congress, see Steven S. Smith, *Party Influence in Congress* (New York: Cambridge University Press, 2007).

58. James M. Snyder Jr. and Tim Groseclose, "Estimating Party Influence in Congressional Roll-Call Voting," *American Journal of Political Science* 44 (April 2000): 187–205; Aage Clausen, *How Congressmen Decide: A Policy Focus* (New York: St. Martin's Press, 1973).

59. Joseph Bafumi and Michael C. Herron, "Leapfrog Representation and Extremism: A Study of American Voters

and Their Members in Congress," *American Political Science Review* 104 (August 2010), 104: 519–542.

60. Sean M. Theriault, *The Gingrich Senators: The Roots of Partisan Warfare in Congress* (New York: Oxford University Press, 2013); and Sean M. Theriault, *Party Polarization in Congress* (Cambridge, UK: Cambridge University Press, 2008).

61. Frances E. Lee, *Beyond Ideology: Politics, Principles, and Partisanship in the U.S. Senate* (Chicago, IL: University of Chicago Press, 2009); Theriault, *Party Polarization in Congress*.

62. Quoted in Peter G. Richards, *Honourable Members* (London: Faber and Faber, 1959), 157.

63. See Roger H. Davidson, *The Role of the Congressman* (New York: Pegasus, 1969), and Thomas E. Cavanaugh, "Role Orientations of House Members: The Process of Representation" (paper delivered at the annual meeting of the American Political Science Association, Washington, D.C.: August 1979).

64. Tracy Sulkin, "Campaign Appeals and Legislative Action," *Journal of Politics* 71 (July 2009): 1093–1108; John L. Sullivan and Robert E. O'Connor, "Electoral Choice and Popular Control of Public Policy: The Case of the 1966 House Elections," *American Political Science Review* 66 (December 1972): 1256–68.

65. Stephen Ansolabehere and Philip Edward Jones, "Constituents' Responses to Congressional Roll-Call Voting," *American Journal of Political Science* 54 (July 2010): 583–97; Patricia A. Hurley and Kim Quaile Hill, "Beyond the Demand-Input Model: A Theory of Representational Linkages," *Journal of Politics* 65 (May 2003): 304–26; Christopher Wlezien, "Patterns of Representation: Dynamics of Public Preferences and Policy," *Journal of Politics* 66 (February 2004): 1–24.

66. Larry M. Bartels, however, found that members of Congress were responsive to constituency opinion in supporting the Reagan defense buildup. See his "Constituency Opinion and Congressional Policy Making: The Reagan Defense Buildup," *American Political Science Review* 85 (June 1991): 457–74.

67. Kim Quaile Hill and Patricia A. Hurley, "Dyadic Representation Reappraised," *American Journal of Political Science* 43 (January 1999): 109–37.

68. On the importance of ideology, see Keith T. Poole and Howard Rosenthal, *Ideology and Congress* (Piscataway, NJ: Transaction Press, 2007).

69. See data for 2013 on the Web site of the Center for Responsive Politics, *OpenSecrets.org*, at www.opensecrets. org, and the Web site *PoliticalMoneyLine*, at http://www. politicalmoneyline.com.

70. See "Cashing In," report by Public Citizen, available at www. citizen.org/congress/article_redirect.cfm?ID=19092, based on an analysis of data posted to OpenSecrets.org, the Website of the Center for Responsive Politics.

71. Richard L. Hall and Alan V. Deardorff, "Lobbying as Legislative Subsidy," *American Political Science Review* 100 (February 2006): 69–84; and Richard L. Hall and Kristina C. Miler, "What Happens After the Alarm? Interest Group Subsidies to Legislative Overseers," *Journal of Politics* 70 (October 2008): 990–1005.

72. Robert Pear, "In House, Many Spoke with One Voice: Lobbyists," *New York Times*, November 15, 2009.

73. See Frank R. Baumgartner, Jeffrey M. Berry, Marie Hojnacki, David C. Kimball, and Beth L. Leech, *Lobbying and Policy Change: Who Wins, Who Loses, and Why* (Chicago, IL: University of Chicago Press, 2009).

74. Brian K. Richter, Krislert Samphantharak, and Jeffrey F. Timmons, "Lobbying and Taxes," *American Journal of Political Science* 53 (October 2009): 893–909.

75. Amy McKay, "Negative Lobbying and Policy Outcomes," *American Politics Research* 40 (January 2012): 116–146.

76. Baumgartner, et al, *Lobbying and Policy Change*, chaps. 10–12.

77. John W. Kingdon, *Congressmen's Voting Decisions*, 3rd ed. (Ann Arbor: University of Michigan Press, 1989), 242.

78. See M. Darrell West, *Congress and Economic Policymaking* (Pittsburgh: University of Pittsburgh Press, 1987).

12

1. Quoted in Thomas E. Cronin, *The State of the Presidency*, 2nd ed. (Boston, MA: Little, Brown, 1980), 223.

2. Richard E. Neustadt, *Presidential Power and the Modern Presidents* (New York: Free Press, 1990).

3. George C. Edwards III, *The Strategic President: Persuasion and Opportunity in Presidential Leadership* (Princeton, NJ: Princeton University Press, 2009).

4. On the public's expectations of the president, see George C. Edwards III, *The Public Presidency* (New York: St. Martin's Press, 1983), chap. 5.

5. Office of the White House Press Secretary, *Remarks of the President at a Meeting with Non–Washington Editors and Broadcasters*, September 21, 1979, 12.

6. Samuel P. Huntington, *American Politics: The Promises of Disharmony* (Cambridge, MA: Belknap, 1981), 33.

7. Quoted in Irving Stone, *Clarence Darrow for the Defense* (Garden City, NY: Doubleday, Doran & Co., 1941), chap. 6.

8. Quoted in Warren G. Harding, *The White House, About the White House: Presidents*, www.whitehouse.gov/about/presidents/warrenharding/.

9. On the creation of the presidency, see Donald L. Robinson, *To the Best of My Ability* (New York: Norton, 1987), and Thomas E. Cronin, ed., *Inventing the American Presidency* (Lawrence, KS: University Press of Kansas, 1989).

10. A good example is Clinton Rossiter, *The American Presidency*, rev. ed. (New York: Harcourt, 1960).

11. Arthur Schlesinger, *The Imperial Presidency* (Boston, MA: Houghton Mifflin, 1973).

12. The titles of chapters 5 and 11 in Thomas E. Cronin, *The State of the Presidency*, 2nd ed. (Boston, MA: Little, Brown, 1980).

13. See Adam Warber, *Executive Orders and the Modern Presidency* (Boulder, CO: Lynne Rienner Publishers (2006); William G. Howell, *Power Without Persuasion* (Princeton, NJ: Princeton University Press, 2003); and Kenneth R. Mayer, *With the Stroke of a Pen, Executive Orders and Presidential Power* (Princeton, NJ: Princeton University Press, 2001).

14. On the factors important in the presidential nominee's choice of a running mate, see Lee Sigelman and Paul J. Wahlbeck, "The 'Veepstakes': Strategic Choice in Presidential Running Mate Selection," *American Political Science Review* 91 (December 1997): 855–64.

15. Patrick Cox, "John Nance Garner on the Vice Presidency—In search of the Proverbial Bucket," Briscoe Center for American History, University of Texas at Austin, www.cah.utexas.edu/news/press_release.php?press=press_bucket.

16. See Paul C. Light, *Vice Presidential Power* (Baltimore, MD: Johns Hopkins University Press, 1984).

17. For a study of the backgrounds of cabinet members, see Jeffrey E. Cohen, *The Politics of the U.S. Cabinet* (Pittsburgh, PA: University of Pittsburgh Press, 1988).

18. For background on the Executive Office, see John Hart, *The Presidential Branch*, 2nd ed. (Chatham, NJ: Chatham House, 1995).

19. Two useful books on the history and functions of the White House staff are Hart, *The Presidential Branch*, and Bradley H. Patterson Jr., *The White House Staff* (Washington, D.C.: Brookings Institution, 2000).

20. For a discussion of presidential party leadership in Congress, see George C. Edwards III, *At the Margins: Presidential Leadership of Congress* (New Haven, CT: Yale University Press, 1989), chaps. 3–5.

21. Frances E. Lee, *Beyond Ideology: Politics, Principles, and Partisanship in the U.S. Senate* (Chicago, IL: University of Chicago Press, 2009).

22. Jimmy Carter, *Keeping Faith* (New York: Bantam, 1982), 80.

23. Christopher R. Berry, Barry C. Burden, and William G. Howell, "The President and the Distribution of Federal Spending," *American Political Science Review* 104 (November 2010): 783–99.

24. For a review of these studies and an analysis showing the limited impact of presidential coattails on congressional election outcomes, see Edwards, *The Public Presidency*, 83–93.

25. Paul Herrnson, Irwin Morris, and John McTague, "The Impact of Presidential Campaigning for Congress on Presidential Support in the U.S. House of Representatives," *Legislative Studies Quarterly* 36 (February 2011): 99–122.

26. For evidence of the impact of the president's campaigning in midterm elections, see Jeffrey E. Cohen, Michael A. Krassa, and John A. Hamman, "The Impact of Presidential Campaigning on Midterm U.S. Senate Elections," *American Political Science Review* 85 (March 1991): 165–78. On the president's effect on congressional elections more broadly, see James E. Campbell, *The Presidential Pulse of Congressional Elections* (Lexington: University Press of Kentucky, 1993).

27. Quoted in Sidney Blumenthal, "Marketing the President," *New York Times Magazine*, September 13, 1981, 110.

28. Quoted in "Slings and Arrows," *Newsweek*, July 31, 1978, 20.

29. Edwards, *At the Margins*, chaps. 6–7.

30. Lawrence J. Grossback, David A. M. Peterson, and James A. Stimson, *Mandate Politics* (New York: Cambridge University Press, 2006).

31. For an analysis of the factors that affect perceptions of mandates, see Edwards, *At the Margins*, chap. 8.

32. David Stockman, *The Triumph of Politics* (New York: Harper & Row, 1986), 251–65; William Greider, "The Education of David Stockman," *Atlantic*, December 1981, 51.

33. George C. Edwards III and Andrew Barrett, "Presidential Agenda Setting in Congress," in *Polarized Politics*, ed. Jon R. Bond and Richard Fleisher (Washington, D.C.: Congressional Quarterly Press, 2000).

34. John Kingdon, *Agendas, Alternatives, and Public Policies* (Boston: Little, Brown, 1984), 25. On presidential agenda setting, see Paul C. Light, *The President's Agenda* (Baltimore, MD: Johns Hopkins University Press, 1991), and George C. Edwards III and B. Dan Wood, "Who Influences Whom? The President, Congress, and the Media," *American Political Science Review* 93 (June 1999): 327–44.

35. Edwards, *The Strategic President*, chap. 4; Edwards, *At the Margins*, chaps. 9–10; Jon R. Bond and Richard Fleisher, *The President in the Legislative Arena* (Chicago, IL: University of Chicago Press, 1990), chap. 8.

36. See David Auerswald and Forrest Maltzman, "Policymaking Through Advice and Consent: Treaty Considerations by the United States Senate," *Journal of Politics* 65 (November 2003): 1097–110.

37. On treaties and executive agreements, see Glen S. Krutz and Jeffrey S. Peake, *Treaty Politics and the Rise of Executive Agreements* (Ann Arbor, MI: University of Michigan Press, 2009).

38. For an analysis of war powers and other issues related to separation of powers, see Louis Fisher, *Constitutional Conflicts Between Congress and the President*, 5th ed. rev. (Lawrence, KS: University Press of Kansas, 2007), and Louis Fisher, *Presidential War Power*, 2nd ed. rev. (Lawrence, KS: University Press of Kansas, 2004).

39. See William G. Howell and Jon C. Pevehouse, *While Dangers Gather: Congressional Checks on Presidential War Powers* (Princeton, NJ: Princeton University Press, 2007).

40. See Barbara Hinckley, *Less than Meets the Eye* (Chicago, IL: University of Chicago Press, 1994).

41. Douglas L. Kriner, *After the Rubicon: Congress, Presidents, and the Politics of Waging War* (Chicago, IL: University of Chicago Press, 2010).

42. The phrase was originated by Aaron Wildavsky in "The Two Presidencies," *Trans-Action* 4 (December 1966): 7–14. He later determined that the two presidencies applied mostly to the 1950s. See Duane M. Oldfield and Aaron Wildavsky, "Reconsidering the Two Presidencies," in *The Two Presidencies: A Quarter Century Assessment*, ed. Steven A. Shull (Chicago, IL: Nelson-Hall, 1991), 181–90.

43. Edwards, *At the Margins*, chap. 4.

44. Samuel Kernell, *Going Public*, 4th ed. (Washington, D.C.: Congressional Quarterly Press, 2004).

45. Edwards, *The Public Presidency*, chap. 6; George C. Edwards III, *Presidential Approval* (Baltimore, MD: Johns Hopkins University Press, 1990).

46. Mueller also included the inaugural period of a president's term as a rally event. See John E. Mueller, *War, Presidents and Public Opinion* (New York: Wiley, 1973), 208–13.

47. Kernell, *Going Public*, 169.

48. On presidents' efforts to build policy support, see Jeffrey K. Tulis, *The Rhetorical Presidency* (Princeton, NJ: Princeton University Press, 1987).

49. Evan Parker-Stephen, "Campaigns, Motivation, and the Dynamics of Political Learning." *Working Paper*, 2008.

50. CBS News/*New York Times* poll, February 5–10, 2010.

51. Bloomberg News National Poll, October 24–26, 2010.

52. Useful comparisons over Reagan's and Clinton's tenures can be found in George C. Edwards III, *On Deaf Ears: The Limits of the Bully Pulpit* (New Haven, CT: Yale University Press, 2003), chaps. 2–3.

53. George C. Edwards III, *Governing by Campaigning: The Politics of the Bush Presidency*, 2nd ed. (New York: Longman, 2007).

54. The best source for the White House's relations with the press is Martha Kumar, *Managing the President's Message: The White House Communications Operation* (Baltimore, MD: Johns Hopkins University Press, 2007).

55. Sam Donaldson, *Hold On, Mr. President!* (New York: Random House, 1987), 196–97.

56. Three of the leading studies are Maria Elizabeth Grabe and Erik Page Bucy, *Image Bite Politics: News and the Visual Framing of Elections* (New York: Oxford University Press, 2009); Michael J. Robinson and Margaret A. Sheehan, *Over the Wire and on TV* (New York: Russell Sage Foundation, 1983), and Daniel C. Hallin, *The 'Uncensored War': the Media and Vietnam* (New York: Oxford University Press, 1986).

57. Carter, *Keeping Faith*, 179–80.

58. See Mark J. Rozell, *The Press and the Ford Presidency* (Ann Arbor, MI: University of Michigan Press, 1992).

59. Thomas E. Patterson, *Doing Well and Doing Good* (Cambridge, MA: Shorenstein Center, 2000), 10, 12; "Clinton's the One," *Media Monitor* 6 (November 1992): 3–5; S. Robert Lichter and Richard E. Noyes, *Good Intentions Make Bad News*, 2nd ed. (Lanham, MD: Rowman & Littlefield,1996), chaps. 6–7, esp. 288–99; "Campaign 2000 Final: How TV News Covered the General Election Campaign," *Media Monitor* 14 (November/December 2000); Thomas E. Patterson, *Out of Order* (New York: Knopf, 1993), 3–27, chap. 3.

60. *Media Monitor*, May/June 1995, 2–5; Thomas E. Patterson, "Legitimate Beef: The Presidency and a Carnivorous Press," *Media Studies Journal*, spring 1994, 21–26; "Sex, Lies, and

TV News," *Media Monitor* 12 (September/October 1998); "TV News Coverage of the 1998 Midterm Elections," *Media Monitor* 12 (November/December 1998). See also Andras Szanto, "In Our Opinion … : Editorial Page Views of Clinton's First Year," *Media Studies Journal*, spring 1994, 97–105; Lichter and Noyes, *Good Intentions Make Bad News*, 214.

61. See, for example, *Media Monitor*, June/July 1998.

62. Stephen J. Farnsworth and S. Robert Lichter, *The Mediated Presidency: Television News and Presidential Governance* (Lanham, MD: Rowman & Littlefield, 2006), 40–45, chap. 4; Stephen J. Farnsworth and S. Robert Lichter, *The Nightly News Nightmare: Television's Coverage of U.S. Presidential Elections, 1988–2004*, 2nd ed. (Lanham, MD: Rowman & Littlefield, 2007), chap. 4. See also Jeffrey E. Cohen, *The Presidency in the Era of 24-Hour News* (Princeton, NJ: Princeton University Press, 2008), chaps. 5–6.

63. Katherine Graham, *Personal History* (New York: Vintage, 1998).

64. Michael Baruch Grossman and Martha Joynt Kumar, *Portraying the President: The White House and the News Media* (Baltimore, MD: Johns Hopkins University Press, 1981), chaps. 10–11.

65. Donaldson, *Hold On, Mr. President?* 237–38.

66. Quoted in Eleanor Randolph, "Speakes Aims Final Salvo at White House Practices," *Washington Post*, January 31, 1987, A3.

67. Scott McClellan, *What Happened: Inside the Bush White House and Washington's Culture of Deception* (New York: Public Affairs, 2008), 156–58.

68. George C. Edwards III, Andrew Barrett, and Jeffrey S. Peake, "The Legislative Impact of Divided Government," *American Journal of Political Science* 41 (April 1997): 545–63.

69. David R. Mayhew, *Divided We Govern* (New Haven, CT: Yale University Press, 1991).

13

1. Quoted in Gerald Carson, *The Golden Egg: The Personal Income Tax, Where It Came From, How It Grew* (Boston: Houghton Mifflin, 1977), 12.

2. Tax Foundation, 2014.

3. Tax Policy Center, 2014.

4. Tax Foundation, 2014.

5. *Budget of the United States Government, Fiscal Year 2015: Historical Tables* (Washington, D.C.: U.S. Government Printing Office, 2014), Table 2.2.

6. *Budget of the United States Government, Fiscal Year 2015: Historical Tables* (Washington, D.C.: U.S. Government Printing Office, 2014), Tables 3.1 and 7.1.

7. Christopher Faricy and Christopher Ellis, "Public Attitudes Toward Social Spending and Tax Expenditures in the United States: The Differences Between Direct Spending and Tax Expenditures," *Political Behavior* 36 (March 2014): 53–76.

8. Ray D. Madoff, "Dog Eat Your Taxes?" *New York Times*, July 9, 2008.

9. An excellent discussion of such issues is Bryan D. Jones and Walter Williams, *The Politics of Bad Ideas* (New York: Pearson Longman, 2007).

10. For some perspectives on the rise of government expenditures, see David Cameron, "The Expansion of the Public Economy: A Comparative Analysis," *American Political Science Review* 72 (December 1978): 1243–61; and William D. Berry and David Lowery, *Understanding United States Government Growth* (New York: Praeger, 1987).

11. *Budget of the United States Government, Fiscal Year 2015: Historical Tables* (Washington, D.C.: U.S. Government Printing Office, 2014), Table 1.3.

12. Berry and Lowery, *Understanding United States Government Growth*.

13. Social Security Administration, 2014.

14. Paul Light, *Artful Work: The Politics of Social Security Reform* (New York: HarperCollins, 1985), 82.

15. *Budget of the United States Government, Fiscal Year 2013: Historical Tables* (Washington, D.C.: U.S. Government Printing Office, 2013), Tables 1.1 and 8.5.

16. Aaron Wildavsky and Naomi Caiden, *The New Politics of the Budgetary Process*, 3rd ed. (New York: Longman, 1997), 45.

17. Paul R. Schulman, "Nonincremental Policymaking: Notes Toward an Alternative Paradigm," *American Political Science Review* 69 (December 1975): 1354–70.

18. See Bryan D. Jones, Frank R. Baumgartner, et al., "A General Empirical Law of Public Budgets: A Comparative Analysis," *American Journal of Political Science* 53 (October 2009): 855–73; Bryan D. Jones and Frank R. Baumgartner, *The Politics of Attention* (Chicago: University of Chicago Press, 2005).

19. A good description of budgetary strategies is in Wildavsky and Caiden, *The New Politics of the Budgetary Process*, chap. 3.

20. For a discussion of the ways in which bureaucracies manipulate benefits to gain advantage with members of Congress, see Rebecca U. Thorpe, *The American Warfare State: The Domestic Politics of Military Spending* (Chicago, IL: University of Chicago Press, 2014).

21. A good review of the formation of the budget is Allen Schick, *The Federal Budget: Politics, Policy, Process*, 3rd ed. (Washington, D.C.: Brookings Institution, 2007).

22. An important work on congressional budget making is Wildavsky and Caiden, *The New Politics of the Budgetary Process*.

23. Allan Meltzer and Scott F. Richard, "Why the Government Grows (and Grows) in a Democracy," *The Public Interest* 52 (summer 1978): 117.

24. See James D. Savage, *Balanced Budgets and American Politics* (Ithaca, NY: Cornell University Press, 1988), for a study of the influence the principle of budget balancing has had on politics and public policy from the earliest days of U.S. history.

25. See, for example, CBS News/*New York Times* poll, January 15–19, 2011.

26. Pew Research Center for the People & the Press poll, July 29–August 1, 2010.

14

1. H. H. Gerth and C. Wright Mills, *From Max Weber: Essays in Sociology* (New York: Oxford University Press, 1958), chap. 8.

2. See Charles T. Goodsell, *The New Case for Bureaucracy* (Washington, D.C.: CQ Press, 2015), chap. 2. See also Daniel Katz et al., *Bureaucratic Encounters* (Ann Arbor: Institute for Social Research, University of Michigan, 1975).

3. U.S. Census Bureau, *U.S. Annual Survey of Public Employment & Payroll Summary Report: 2011* (Washington, D.C.: 2012); U.S. Office of Personnel Management, *Sizing Up the Executive Branch* (Washington, D.C.: 2013).

4. See Paul C. Light, *The True Size of Government* (Washington, D.C.: Brookings Institution, 1999), 1, 44.

5. Office of Personnel Management, *Major Work Locations of the Executive Branch* (Washington, D.C.: 2013).

6. See Herbert Kaufman, *Red Tape* (Washington, D.C.: Brookings Institution, 1977).

7. See Goodsell, *The Case for Bureaucracy*, 50–65.

8. Ibid., chap. 3.

9. Hugh M. Heclo, *A Government of Strangers: Executive Politics in Washington* (Washington, D.C.: Brookings Institution, 1977).

10. On the transient nature of presidential appointees, see G. Calvin Mackenzie, ed., *The In-and-Outers* (Baltimore: Johns Hopkins University Press, 1987).

11. David E. Lewis, *The Politics of Presidential Appointments* (Princeton, NJ: Princeton University Press, 2008); George C. Edwards III, "Why Not the Best? The Loyalty-Competence Trade-Off in Presidential Appointments," in *Innocent Until Nominated*, ed. G. Calvin Mackenzie (Brookings Institution, 2000).

12. On the independent regulatory agencies, see the classic work by Marver Bernstein, *Regulating Business by Independent Commission* (Princeton, NJ: Princeton University Press, 1955). See also, on regulation, James Q. Wilson, ed., *The Politics of Regulation* (New York: Basic Books, 1980), and A. Lee Fritschler and Bernard H. Ross, *Business Regulation and Government Decision-Making* (Cambridge, MA: Winthrop, 1980).

13. Bernstein, *Regulating Business by Independent Commission*, 90. For a partial test of the capture theory that finds the theory not altogether accurate, see John P. Plumlee and Kenneth J. Meier, "Capture and Rigidity in Regulatory Administration," in *The Policy Cycle*, ed. Judith May and Aaron Wildavsky (Beverly Hills, CA: Russell Sage Foundation, 1978). Another critique of the capture theory is Paul J. Quirk, *Industry Influence in Federal Regulatory Agencies* (Princeton, NJ: Princeton University Press, 1981).

14. George C. Edwards III, *Implementing Public Policy* (Washington, D.C.: Congressional Quarterly Press, 1980), 1.

15. For another dramatic example, see Martha Derthick, *New Towns In-Town* (Washington, D.C.: Urban Institute Press, 1972).

16. The implementation of the athletics policy is well documented in two articles by Cheryl M. Fields in the *Chronicle of Higher Education*, December 11 and 18, 1978, on which this account relies.

17. James Q. Wilson, *Bureaucracy* (New York: Basic Books, 1989), 158.

18. A good discussion of how policymakers ignored the administrative capacity of one important agency when assigning it new responsibilities can be found in Martha Derthick, *Agency Under Stress* (Washington, D.C.: Brookings Institution, 1990).

19. Kenneth J. Meier and Laurence J. O'Toole, *Bureaucracy in a Democratic State* (Baltimore, MD: Johns Hopkins University Press, 2006).

20. Report of the DOD Commission on Beirut International Airport Terrorist Act, October 23, 1983, December 20, 1983, 133.

21. *The 9/11 Commission Report* (New York: Norton, 2004), 17–18.

22. On administrative discretion, see Gary S. Bryner, *Bureaucratic Discretion* (New York: Pergamon Press, 1987).

23. Michael Lipsky, *Street-Level Bureaucracy* (New York: Russell Sage Foundation, 1980).

24. Quoted in Seymour Hersh, *The Price of Power: Kissinger in the Nixon White House* (New York: Summit, 1983), 235–36.

25. Albert Gore, *From Red Tape to Results: Creating a Government That Works Better and Costs Less* (New York: Times Books, 1993), 11.

26. For a careful analysis of efforts to reorganize the federal bureaucracy, see Peri E. Arnold, *Making the Managerial Presidency*, 2nd ed. (Princeton, NJ: Princeton University Press, 1996).

27. On the implementation and impact of the Voting Rights Act, see Charles S. Bullock III and Harrell R. Rodgers, Jr., *Law and Social Change: Civil Rights Laws and Their Consequences* (New York: McGraw-Hill, 1972), chap. 2; Richard Scher and James Button, "Voting Rights Act:

28. Light, *The True Size of Government*.

29. Scott Shane and Ron Nixon, "In Washington, Contractors Take on Biggest Role Ever," *New York Times*, February 4, 2007.

30. See Martha Derthick and Paul J. Quirk, *The Politics of Deregulation* (Washington, D.C.: Brookings Institution, 1985).

31. See, for example, Susan J. Tolchin and Martin J. Tolchin, *Dismantling America: The Rush to Deregulate* (New York: Oxford University Press, 1983).

32. Evan J. Ringquist, "Does Regulation Matter? Evaluating the Effects of State Air Pollution Control Programs," *Journal of Politics* 55 (November 1993): 1022–45.

33. Michael Lewis-Beck and John Alford, "Can Government Regulate Safety? The Coal Mine Example," *American Political Science Review* 74 (September 1980): 745–56.

34. Paul Sabatier and Dan Mazmanian, *Can Regulation Work? Implementation of the 1972 California Coastal Initiative* (New York: Plenum, 1983).

35. Gary Copeland and Kenneth J. Meier, "Gaining Ground: The Impact of Medicaid and WIC on Infant Mortality," *American Politics Quarterly* 15 (April 1987): 254–73.

36. See Lewis, *The Politics of Presidential Appointments*; Joel D. Aberbach and Bert A. Rockman, *In the Web of Politics* (Washington, D.C.: Brookings Institution, 2000); Richard P. Nathan, *The Administrative Presidency* (New York: Wiley, 1983).

37. See Adam Warber, *Executive Orders and the Modern Presidency* (Boulder, CO: Lynne Rienner Publishers, 2006); William G. Howell, *Power Without Persuasion* (Princeton, NJ: Princeton University Press, 2003); and Kenneth R. Mayer, *With the Stroke of a Pen, Executive Orders and Presidential Power* (Princeton, NJ: Princeton University Press, 2001).

38. Matthew Eshbaugh-Soha, *The President's Speeches: Beyond Going Public* (Boulder, CO: Lynne Rienner, 2006); and Andrew B. Whitford and Jeff Yates, "Policy Signals and Executive Governance: Presidential Rhetoric in the War on Drugs," *Journal of Politics* 65 (November 2003): 995–1012.

39. Morris Fiorina, *Congress: Keystone of the Washington Establishment*, 2nd ed. (New Haven, CT: Yale University Press, 1989).

40. Jason A. MacDonald, "Limitation Riders and Congressional Influence over Bureaucratic Policy Decisions," *American Political Science Review* 104 (November 2010): 766–82.

41. Richard A. Rettig, *Cancer Crusade: The Story of the National Cancer Act of 1971* (Princeton, NJ: Princeton University Press, 1978).

42. Hugh M. Heclo, "Issue Networks and the Executive Establishment," in *The New American Political System*, ed. Anthony King (Washington, D.C.: American Enterprise Institute, 1978), 87–124. See also William P. Browne and Won K. Paik, "Beyond the Domain: Recasting Network Politics in the Postreform Congress," *American Journal of Political Science* 37 (November 1993): 1054–78; and John P. Heinz, Edward O. Laumann, Robert L. Nelson, and Robert L. Salisbury, *The Hollow Core: Private Interests in National Policy Making* (Cambridge, MA: Harvard University Press, 1993).

43. Frank R. Baumgartner and Bryan D. Jones, *Agendas and Instability in American Politics* (Chicago: University of Chicago Press, 1993).

Implementation and Impact," in *Implementation of Civil Rights Policy*, ed. C. S. Bullock and C. M. Lamb (Monterey, CA: Brooks/Cole, 1984), chap. 2; and Abigail M. Thernstrom, *Whose Votes Count?* (Cambridge, MA: Harvard University Press, 1987).

44. Ibid.

45. See B. Dan Wood and Richard W. Waterman, *Bureaucratic Dynamics: The Role of Bureaucracy in a Democracy* (Boulder, CO: Westview, 1994).

15

1. American Bar Association.

2. Quoted in Lawrence C. Baum, *The Supreme Court*, 4th ed. (Washington, D.C.: CQ Press, 1992), 72.

3. Administrative Office of the United States Courts.

4. Administrative Office of the United States Courts.

5. Administrative Office of the United States Courts.

6. See Sarah A. Binder and Forrest Maltzman, *Advice and Dissent: The Struggle to Shape the Federal Judiciary* (Washington, D.C.: Brookings Institution, 2009) on the history and procedures regarding judicial nominations.

7. Sarah Binder and Forrest Maltzman, "The Limits of Senatorial Courtesy," *Legislative Studies Quarterly* 29 (February 2004): 5–22; Michael A. Sollenberger, "The Blue Slip: A Theory of Unified and Divided Government, 1979–2009," *Congress & the Presidency* 37 (May–August 2010): 125–56; and Brandon Rottinghaus and Chris Nicholson, "Counting Congress In: Patterns of Success in Judicial Nomination Requests by Members of Congress to Presidents Eisenhower and Ford," *American Politics Research* 38 (July 2010): 691–717.

8. Sheldon Goldman, Elliot Slotnick, and Sara Schiavoni, "Obama's Judiciary at Midterm," *Judicature* 94 (May–June 2011): 262–303.

9. Quoted in J. Woodford Howard Jr., *Courts of Appeals in the Federal Judicial System: A Study of the Second, Fifth, and District of Columbia Circuits* (Princeton, NJ: Princeton University Press, 1981), 101.

10. Nancy Scherer, Brandon L. Bartels, and Amy Steigerwalt, "Sounding the Fire Alarm: The Role of Interest Groups in the Lower Federal Court Confirmation Process," *Journal of Politics* 70 (October 2008): 1026–39.

11. Binder and Maltzman, *Advice and Dissent*, 4–6, chaps. 2, 4; Jon R. Bond, Richard Fleisher, and Glen S. Krutz, "Malign Neglect: Evidence That Delay Has Become the Primary Method of Defeating Presidential Appointment," *Congress & the Presidency* (Fall 2009): 226–43; and Lauren Cohen Bell, "Senatorial Discourtesy: The Senate's Use of Delay to Shape the Federal Judiciary," *Political Research Quarterly* 55 (September 2002): 589–607.

12. Binder and Maltzman, *Advice and Dissent*, 2–4, chap. 4.

13. *National Labor Relations Board v. Noel Canning et al* (2014).

14. See Gary King, "Presidential Appointments to the Supreme Court: Adding Systematic Explanation to Probabilistic Description," *American Politics Quarterly* 15 (July 1987): 373–86.

15. Charles R. Shipan and Megan L. Shannon, "Delaying Justice(s): A Duration Analysis of Supreme Court Confirmations," *American Journal of Political Science* 47 (October 2003): 654–68.

16. Sheldon Goldman, Sara Schiavoni, and Elliot Slotnick, "W. Bush's Judicial Legacy," *Judicature* 92 (May–June 2009): 258–88.

17. Sheldon Goldman, Elliot Slotnick, and Sara Schiavoni, "Obama's First Term Judiciary," *Judicature* 96 (July/August 2013): 7–47.

18. Quoted in Nina Totenberg, "Will Judges Be Chosen Rationally?," *Judicature* 60 (August/September 1976): 93.

19. One study found, however, that judicial experience does not help presidents predict justices' decisions on racial equality

cases. See John Gates and Jeffrey Cohen, "Presidents, Supreme Court Justices, and Racial Equality Cases: 1954–1984," *Political Behavior* 10 (November 1, 1988): 22–35.

20. Goldman, Slotnick, and Schiavoni, "Obama's Judiciary at Midterm."

21. On the importance of ideology and partisanship considerations in judicial retirement and resignation decisions, see Kjersten R. Nelson and Eve M. Ringsmuth, "Departures from the Court: The Political Landscape and Institutional Constraints," *American Politics Research* 37 (May 2009): 486–507; Deborah J. Barrow and Gary Zuk, "An Institutional Analysis of Turnover in the Lower Federal Courts, 1900–1987," *Journal of Politics* 52 (May 1990): 457–76.

22. Quoted in Henry J. Abraham, *Justices and Presidents: A Political History of Appointments to the Supreme Court*, 3rd ed. (New York: Oxford University Press, 1992), 266.

23. Ibid., 70.

24. See, for example, the important role that African American support played in the confirmation of Clarence Thomas even though he was likely to vote against the wishes of leading civil rights organizations. L. Marvin Overby, Beth M. Henschen, Julie Walsh, and Michael H. Strauss, "Courting Constituents: An Analysis of the Senate Confirmation Vote on Justice Clarence Thomas," *American Political Science Review* 86 (December 1992): 997–1003.

25. Jennifer L. Peresie, "Female Judges Matter: Gender and Collegial Decisionmaking in the Federal Appellate Courts," *Yale Law Journal* 114 (May 2005): 1759–90.

26. Adam B. Cox and Thomas J. Miles, "Judging the Voting Rights Act," *Columbia Law Review* 108 (January 2008): 1–54. But see Jason L. Morin, "The Voting Behavior of Minority Judges in the U.S. Courts of Appeals Does the Race of the Claimant Matter?" *American Politics Research* 42 (January 2014): 134–164.

27. Quoted in Adam Liptak, "The Waves Minority Judges Always Make," *New York Times*, May 1, 2009.

28. On the impact of the background of members of the judiciary, see Robert A. Carp and C. K. Rowland, *Policymaking and Politics in the Federal District Courts* (Knoxville, TN: University of Tennessee Press, 1983); Thomas G. Walker and Deborah J. Barrow, "The Diversification of the Federal Bench: Policy and Process Ramifications," *Journal of Politics* 47 (May 1985): 596–617; and C. Neal Tate, "Personal Attribute Models of the Voting Behavior of United States Supreme Court Justices: Liberalism in Civil Liberties and Economics Decisions, 1946–1978," *American Political Science Review* 75 (June 1981): 355–67.

29. Quoted in Nina Totenberg, "Behind the Marble, Beneath the Robes," *New York Times Magazine*, March 16, 1975, 37.

30. Ryan C. Black and Christina L. Boyd, "The Role of Law Clerks in the U.S. Supreme Court's Agenda-Setting Process," *American Politics Research* 40 (January 2012): 147–173.

31. Ryan C. Black and Ryan J. Owens, "Agenda Setting in the Supreme Court: The Collision of Policy and Jurisprudence," *Journal of Politics* 71 (July 2009): 1062–75; H. W. Perry Jr., *Deciding to Decide: Agenda Setting in the United States Supreme Court* (Cambridge, MA: Harvard University Press, 1991); Doris Marie Provine, *Case Selection in the United States Supreme Court* (Chicago, IL: University of Chicago Press, 1980); and Stuart H. Teger and Douglas Kosinski, "The Cue Theory of Supreme Court Certiorari Jurisdiction: A Reconsideration," *Journal of Politics* 42 (August 1980): 834–46.

32. Sidney Ulmer, "The Supreme Court's Certiorari Decisions: Conflict as a Predictive Variable," *American Political Science Review* (December 1984): 901–11.

33. Ryan C. Black and Ryan J. Owens, *The Solicitor General and the United States Supreme Court* (New York: Cambridge University Press, 2012).

34. On the solicitor general's *amicus* briefs, see Rebecca E. Deen, Joseph Ignagni and James Meernik, "Executive Influence on the U.S. Supreme Court: Solicitor General *Amicus* Cases, 1953–1997," *American Review of Politics* 22 (spring 2001): 3–26; and Timothy R. Johnson, "The Supreme Court, the Solicitor General, and the Separation of Powers," *American Politics Research* 31 (July 2001): 426–51.

35. See Rebecca Mae Salokar, *The Solicitor General* (Philadelphia, PA: Temple University Press, 1992).

36. Each year, data on Supreme Court decisions can be found in the November issue of the *Harvard Law Review*.

37. On the influence of oral arguments on the Supreme Court, see Timothy R. Johnson, Paul J. Wahlbeck, and James F. Spriggs II, "The Influence of Oral Arguments on the U.S. Supreme Court," *American Political Science Review* 100 (February 2006): 99–113.

38. A useful look at attorneys practicing before the Supreme Court is Kevin McGuire, *The Supreme Court Bar: Legal Elites in the Washington Community* (Charlottesville, VA: University Press of Virginia, 1993).

39. See, for example, Forrest Maltzman and Paul J. Wahlbeck, "Strategic Policy Considerations and Voting Fluidity on the Burger Court," *American Political Science Review* 90 (September 1996): 581–92; Paul J. Wahlbeck, James F. Spriggs II, and Forrest Maltzman, "Marshalling the Court: Bargaining and Accommodation on the United States Supreme Court," *American Journal of Political Science* 42 (January 1998): 294–315; and James F. Spriggs II, Forrest Maltzman, and Paul J. Wahlbeck, "Bargaining on the U.S. Supreme Court: Justices' Responses to Majority Opinion Drafts," *Journal of Politics* 61 (May 1999): 485–506.

40. See Chad Westerland, Jeffrey A. Segal, Lee Epstein, Charles M. Cameron, and Scott Comparato, "Strategic Defiance and Compliance in the U.S. Courts of Appeals," *American Journal of Political Science* 54 (October 2010): 891–905; Richard L. Pacelle Jr. and Lawrence Baum, "Supreme Court Authority in the Judiciary," *American Politics Quarterly* 20 (April 1992): 169–91; and Donald R. Songer, Jeffrey A. Segal, and Charles M. Cameron, "The Hierarchy of Justice: Testing a Principal-Agent Model of Supreme Court-Circuit Court Interactions," *American Journal of Political Science* 38 (August 1994): 673–96.

41. A. P. Blaustein and A. H. Field, "Overruling Opinions in the Supreme Court," *Michigan Law Review* 57, no. 2 (1957): 151; David H. O'Brien, *Constitutional Law and Politics*, 3rd ed. (New York: Norton, 1997), 38.

42. See, for example, Michael A. Bailey and Forrest Maltzman, *The Constrained Court: Law, Politics, and the Decisions Justices Make* (Princeton, NJ: Princeton University Press, 2011); Brandon L. Bartels, "The Constraining Capacity of Legal Doctrine on the U.S. Supreme Court," *American Political Science Review* 103 (August 2009): 474–95.

43. Antonin Scalia, *A Matter of Interpretation: Federal Courts and the Law* (Princeton, NJ: Princeton University Press, 1998).

44. See Stephen Breyer, *Active Liberty: Interpreting Our Democratic Constitution* (New York: Knopf, 2005).

45. Jack N. Rakove, *Original Meanings: Politics and Ideas in the Making of the Constitution* (New York: Vintage Books, 1996).

46. See, for example, Benjamin E. Lauderdale and Tom S. Clark, "The Supreme Court's Many Median Justices," *American Political Science Review* 106 (November 2012): 847–66; Lee Epstein, William M. Landes, and Richard A. Posner, *The Behavior of Federal Judges: A Theoretical and Empirical Study of Rational Choice* (Cambridge, MA: Harvard University Press, 2013); Jeffrey A. Segal and Harold J. Spaeth, *The Supreme Court and the Attitudinal Model* (Cambridge: Cambridge

University Press, 1993); Jeffrey A. Segal and Albert O. Cover, "Ideological Values and the Votes of U.S. Supreme Court Justices," *American Political Science Review* 83 (June 1989): 557–66; Tracey E. George and Lee Epstein, "On the Nature of Supreme Court Decision Making," *American Political Science Review* 86 (June 1992): 323–37; and Jeffrey A. Segal and Harold J. Spaeth, "The Influence of *Stare Decisis* on the Votes of United States Supreme Court Justices," *American Journal of Political Science* 40 (November 1996): 971–1003.

47. Brandon L. Bartels, "Choices in Context: How Case-Level Factors Influence the Magnitude of Ideological Voting on the U.S. Supreme Court," *American Politics Research* 39 (January 2011): 142–75; Bailey and Maltzman, *The Constrained Court*, Bartels, "The Constraining Capacity of Legal Doctrine on the U.S. Supreme Court."

48. Doris Graber, *Mass Media and American Politics*, 6th ed. (Washington, D.C.: CQ Press, 2002), 312–13. See also Richard Davis, *Justices and Journalists* (New York: Cambridge University Press, 2011).

49. Charles A. Johnson and Bradley C. Canon, *Judicial Politics: Implementation and Impact*, 2nd ed. (Washington, D.C.: CQ Press, 1999), chap. 1. See also James F. Spriggs II, "The Supreme Court and Federal Administrative Agencies: A Resource-Based Theory and Analysis of Judicial Impact," *American Journal of Political Science* 40 (November 1996): 1122–51.

50. See Westerland, Segal, Epstein, Cameron, and Comparato, "Strategic Defiance and Compliance in the U.S. Courts of Appeals"; Pacelle and Baum, "Supreme Court Authority in the Judiciary"; and Songer, Segal, and Cameron, "The Hierarchy of Justice: Testing a Principal-Agent Model of Supreme Court-Circuit Court Interactions."

51. Kevin T. McGuire, "Public Schools, Religious Establishments, and the U.S. Supreme Court: An Examination of Policy Compliance," *American Politics Research* 37 (January 2009): 50–74.

52. For an excellent overview of the Warren period by former Watergate special prosecutor and Harvard law professor Archibald Cox, see *The Warren Court* (Cambridge, MA: Harvard University Press, 1968).

53. "Excerpts from Stewart's Session with Reporters," *New York Times*, June 20, 1981.

54. William Rehnquist, "The Notion of a Living Constitution," in *Views from the Bench*, ed. Mark W. Cannon and David M. O'Brien (Chatham, NJ: Chatham House, 1985), 129. One study found, however, that judicial experience is not related to the congruence of presidential preferences and the justices' decisions on racial equality cases. See John Gates and Jeffrey Cohen, "Presidents, Supreme Court Justices, and Racial Equality Cases: 1954–1984," *Political Behavior* 10 (November 1, 1988): 22–35.

55. Richard Funston, "The Supreme Court and Critical Elections," *American Political Science Review* 69 (1975): 810; John B. Gates, *The Supreme Court and Partisan Realignment* (Boulder, CO: Westview, 1992); Thomas R. Marshall, "Public Opinion, Representation, and the Modern Supreme Court," *American Politics Quarterly* 16 (July 1988): 296–316; William Mishler and Reginald S. Sheehan, "The Supreme Court as a Countermajoritarian Institution? The Impact of Public Opinion on Supreme Court Decisions," *American Political Science Review* 87 (March 1993): 87–101; William Mishler and Reginald S. Sheehan, "Public Opinion, the Attitudinal Model, and Supreme Court Decision Making: A Micro-Analytic Perspective," *Journal of Politics* 58 (February 1996): 169–200; Roy B. Flemming and B. Dan Wood, "The Public and the Supreme Court: Individual Justice Responsiveness to American Policy Moods," *American Journal of Political Science* 41 (April 1997): 468–98; and Kevin T. McGuire and James

2. Robert S. Erikson, Matthew MacKuen, and James L. Stimson, *The Macro Polity* (New York: Cambridge University Press, 2002), 59.

3. Michael S. Lewis-Beck and Richard Nadeau (2009). Obama and the Economy in 2008. *PS: Political Science & Politics*, 42, 479–483. doi:10.1017/S1049096509090775.

4. See David Plouffe, *The Audacity to Win: The Inside Story and Lessons of Barack Obama's Historic Victory* (New York: Viking, 2009), chap. 15.

5. For a summary of economic conditions and voting choice, see Michael S. Lewis-Beck and Mary Stegmaier, "Economic Determinants of Electoral Outcomes," *Annual Review of Political Science* (Palo Alto, CA: Annual Reviews, 2000): 183–219.

6. Suzzana DeBoef and Paul M. Kellstedt, "The Political (and Economic) Origins of Consumer Confidence," *American Journal of Political Science* 48 (October 2004): 633–49.

7. See William Greider, *Secrets of the Temple: How the Federal Reserve Runs the Country* (New York: Simon and Schuster, 1987); Nathaniel Beck, "Elections and the Fed: Is There a Political Monetary Cycle?" *American Journal of Political Science* 20 (February 1987): 194–216; and Manabu Saeki, "Explaining Federal Reserve Monetary Policy," *Review of Policy Research* 19 (Summer 2002): 129–50.

8. Paul Ryan, Eric Cantor, and Kevin McCarthy, *Young Guns: A New Generation of Conservative Leaders* (New York: Threshold, 2010), 47.

9. The classic supply-side theory can be found in George Gilder, *Wealth and Poverty* (New York: Basic Books, 1981).

10. The most ardent proponent of this view is Edward Tufte. See his *Political Control of the Economy* (Princeton, NJ: Princeton University Press, 1978).

11. Robert Samuelson, "A Phony Jobs Debate," *Washington Post*, February 25, 2004, A25.

12. Martin Gilens, *Why Americans Hate Welfare* (Chicago: University of Chicago Press, 1999).

13. Stanley Feldman and Marco R. Steenbergen, "The Humanitarian Foundation of Public Support for Social Welfare," *American Journal of Political Science* 45 (July 2001): 658–77.

14. Alan Weil and Kenneth Finegold, "Introduction," in *Welfare Reform: The Next Act*, ed. Alan Weil and Kenneth Finegold (Washington, D.C.: Urban Institute Press, 2002), xiii.

15. Timothy M. Smeeding, "Public Policy, Income Inequality, and Poverty: The United States in Comparative Perspective," *Social Science Quarterly* 86 (2005): 955. See also Lane Kenworthy and Jonas Pontusson, "Rising Inequality and the Politics of Redistribution in Affluent Countries," *Perspectives on Politics* 3 (September 2005): 449–72.

16. See Jason DeParle, "Harder for Americans to Rise From Lower Rungs," *New York Times*, January 4, 2012.

17. Nolan McCarty, Keith T. Poole, and Howard Rosenthal, *Income Distribution and the Realignment of American Politics* (Washington, D.C.: American Enterprise Institute, 1977), 1. See also their *Polarized America: The Dance of Ideology and Unequal Riches* (Cambridge, MA: MIT Press, 2006).

18. Thomas Piketty, *Capital in the Twenty-First Century* (Cambridge, MA; Belknap Press, 2014).

19. Thomas B. Edsall, *The New Politics of Inequality* (New York: Norton, 1984), 18.

20. For more information on this new measure of poverty, see http://www.census.gov/hhes/povmeas/.

21. Jacob S. Hacker, *The Great Risk Shift* (New York: Oxford University Press, 2008), 24, 32.

22. See the *Statistical Abstract of the United States, 2012*, table 488. This information can be found online at http://www.census.gov/compendia/statab/2012/tables/12s0488.pdf.

23. See: http://www.irs.gov/uac/Newsroom/Earned-Income-Tax-Credit-Do-I-Qualify

A. Stimson, "The Least Dangerous Branch: New Evidence on Supreme Court Responsiveness to Public Preferences," *Journal of Politics* 66 (November 2004): 1018–35.

56. Bailey and Maltzman, *The Constrained Court*; Mario Bergara, Barak Richman, and Pablo T. Spiller, "Modeling Supreme Court Strategic Decision Making: The Congressional Constraint," *Legislative Studies Quarterly* 28 (May 2003): 247–80.

57. David G. Barnum, "The Supreme Court and Public Opinion: Judicial Decision Making in the Post–New Deal Period," *Journal of Politics* 47 (May 1985): 652–62.

58. Tom S. Clark, *The Limits of Judicial Independence* (New York: Cambridge University Press, 2011).

59. James F. Spriggs and Paul J. Wahlbeck, "Amicus Curiae and the Role of Information in the Supreme Court," *Political Research Quarterly* 50 (June 1997): 365–86.

60. Gregory A. Caldeira and John R. Wright, "Organized Interests and Agenda Setting in the U.S. Supreme Court," *American Political Science Review* 82 (December 1988): 1109–28.

61. Janet M. Box-Steffensmeier, Dino P. Christenson, and Matthew P. Hitt, "Quality Over Quantity: Amici Influence and Decision Making," *American Political Science Review* 107 (August 2013): 446–60.

62. On group use of the litigation process, see Karen Orren, "Standing to Sue: Interest Group Conflict in the Federal Courts," *American Political Science Review* 70 (September 1976): 723–42; Karen O'Connor and Lee Epstein, "The Rise of Conservative Interest Group Litigation," *Journal of Politics* 45 (May 1983): 479–89; and Lee Epstein and C. K. Rowland, "Debunking the Myth of Interest Group Invincibility in the Courts," *American Political Science Review* 85 (March 1991): 205–17.

63. "Federalist #78," in Hamilton, Madison, and Jay, *The Federalist Papers*.

64. However, see Gerald N. Rosenberg, *The Hollow Hope: Can Courts Bring About Social Change?* (Chicago, IL: University of Chicago Press, 1991). Rosenberg questions whether courts have brought about much social change.

65. Examples of judicial activism are reported in a critical assessment of judicial intervention by Donald Horowitz, *The Courts and Social Policy* (Washington, D.C.: Brookings Institution, 1977).

66. Paul Gerwitz and Chad Golder, "So Who Are the Activists?" *New York Times*, July 6, 2005.

67. Greg Goelzhauser, "Avoiding Constitutional Cases," *American Politics Research* 39 (May 2011): 483–511.

68. William N. Eskridge, "Overriding Supreme Court Statutory Interpretation Decisions," *Yale Law Journal* 101 (1991): 331–455; Joseph Ignagni and James Meernik, "Explaining Congressional Attempts to Reverse Supreme Court Decisions," *Political Research Quarterly* 10 (June 1994): 353–72. See also R. Chep Melnick, *Between the Lines: Interpreting Welfare Rights* (Washington, D.C.: Brookings Institution, 1994).

69. Kirk A Randazzo, Richard W. Waterman, and Jeffrey A. Fine, "Checking the Federal Courts: The Impact of Congressional Statutes on Judicial Behavior," *Journal of Politics* 68 (November 2006): 1006–17.

16

1. Brad T. Gomez and J. Matthew Wilson, "Political Sophistication and Economic Voting in the American Electorate: A Theory of Heterogeneous Attribution," *American Journal of Political Science* 45 (October 2001): 899.

24. Mark R. Rank and Thomas A. Hirschl, "Estimating the Risk of Food Stamp Use and Impoverishment During Childhood," *Archives of American Pediatrics and Adolescent Medicine* (November 2009): 994–99.

25. See, for example, Francis Fox Piven and Richard Cloward, *Regulating the Poor* (New York: Pantheon, 1971). For an empirical analysis of theories of the rise of welfare that finds some support for the Piven and Cloward thesis, see Richard Fording, "The Political Response to Black Insurgency: A Critical Test of Competing Theories of the State," *American Political Science Review* 95 (March 2001): 115–30.

26. Charles Murray, *Losing Ground: American Social Policy, 1950–1980* (New York: Basic Books, 1984). Marvin Olasky, the guru of "compassionate conservatism," makes a similar argument in his *Tragedy of Human Compassion* (Chicago, IL: Regnery, 1992). Doing good for people, especially through government, Olasky argues, is bad for them. For a contrary argument, see Benjamin Page and James R. Simmons, *What Government Can Do: Dealing with Poverty and Inequality* (Chicago, IL: University of Chicago Press, 2000).

27. See, for example, David T. Ellwood and Lawrence H. Summers, "Is Welfare Really the Problem?" *Public Interest* 83 (Spring 1986): 57–78.

28. See Ange-Marie Hancock, *The Politics of Disgust: The Public Identity of the Welfare Queen* (New York: New York University Press, 2004).

29. Martin Gilens, *Why Americans Hate Welfare: Race, Media, and the Politics of Antipoverty Policy* (Chicago, IL: University of Chicago Press, 1999).

30. Ibid, 140.

31. Ibid, chap. 5.

32. Tom Smith, *"Trends in National Spending Priorities, 1973–2008"* (Chicago, IL: National Opinion Research Center, 2009), 31. This report can be found online at http://news.uchicago.edu/images/pdf/090210.SPEND08.pdf.

33. For a good history of the Social Security system, see Sylvester J. Schieber and John B. Shoven, *The Real Deal: The History and Future of Social Security* (New Haven, CT: Yale University Press, 1999).

34. Andrea Louise Campbell explains how Social Security has energized one of America's most important interest groups in her *How Policies Make Citizens* (Princeton, NJ: Princeton University Press, 2002).

35. Martin Wattenberg, *Is Voting for Young People?* (New York: Pearson Longman, 2006), 4.

36. Political scientist Benjamin Ra.D.C.liff developed some empirical data to show that the extent of government welfare provisions is in fact positively related to people's sense of well-being from country to country. See his "Politics, Markets and Life Satisfaction: The Political Economy of Human Happiness," *American Political Science Review* 95 (December 2001): 939–52.

37. See Alberto Alesina and Edward L. Glaeser, *Fighting Poverty in the US and Europe: A World of Difference* (New York: Oxford, 2005), 4.

38. See Larry M. Bartels, *Unequal Democracy: The Political Economy of the New Gilded Age* (Princeton, NJ: Princeton University Press, 2008), chap. 9.

39. Anne Schneider and Helen Ingram, "The Social Construction of Target Populations," *American Political Science Review* 87 (1993): 334–47.

17

1. World Health Organization, 2014.

2. Centers for Medicare and Medicaid Services, 2014.

3. *Budget of the United States Government, Fiscal Year 2015: Historical Tables* (Washington, D.C.: U.S. Government Printing Office, 2014), Table 3.1.

4. Quoted in Richard L. Berke, "Clinton Warns That Economy May Still Be Bad," *New York Times*, December 8, 1992, A13.

5. Council of Economic Advisers, *Annual Report 2006*, 88.

6. Kaiser Family Foundation and Health Research and Educational Trust, *Employer Health Benefits 2013*, p. 24.

7. U.S. Census Bureau, *Income, Poverty, and Health Insurance Coverage in the United States: 2012*.

8. Centers for Medicare and Medicaid Services, 2014.

9. U.S. Census Bureau, *Income, Poverty, and Health Insurance Coverage in the United States: 2012*.

10. See, for example, U.S. Department of Commerce, *Statistical Abstract of the United States, 2010* (Washington, D.C.: U.S. Government Printing Office, 2012), Tables 104 and 116.

11. U.S. Census Bureau, *Income, Poverty, and Health Insurance Coverage in the United States: 2012*.

12. U.S. Census Bureau, *Income, Poverty, and Health Insurance Coverage in the United States: 2012*.

13. Institute of Medicine, *America's Uninsured Crisis: Consequences for Health and Health Care.* National Academies Press, February 2009.

14. Sara R. Collins, Jennifer L. Kriss, Michelle M. Doty, and Sheila D. Rustgi, *"Losing Ground: How the Loss of Adequate Health Insurance Is Burdening Working Families,"* Commonwealth Fund, August 2008.

15. Kaiser Family Foundation, *The Uninsured: A Primer, Key Facts about Americans Without Health Insurance.* Kaiser Family Foundation, 2011.

16. John Lancaster, "Surgeries, Side Trips for 'Medical Tourists,'" *Washington Post*, October 21, 2004, A1.

17. Kaiser Family Foundation, *The Uninsured: A Primer, Key Facts About Americans Without Health Insurance.* Kaiser Family Foundation, 2011.

18. Institute of Medicine, *Care Without Coverage: Too Little, Too Late* (Washington, D.C.: National Academy Press, 2002).

19. "Care Without Coverage," Institute of Medicine, May 2002, 6.

20. Amy Finkelstein, et al., "The Oregon Health Insurance Experiment," National Bureau of Economic Research Working Paper No. 17190, July 2011.

21. Centers for Disease Control and Prevention, *National Vital Statistics Reports*, Vol. 61, No. 6, October 10, 2012.

22. Robert Blank, *Rationing Medicine* (New York: Columbia University Press, 1988).

23. Howard M. Leichter, "The Poor and Managed Care in the Oregon Experience," *Journal of Health Politics, Policy and Law* 24 (October 1999): 1172–84.

24. U.S. Census Bureau, *Income, Poverty, and Health Insurance Coverage in the United States: 2012*.

25. Centers for Medicare and Medicaid Services, 2014.

26. *Budget of the United States Government, Fiscal Year 2015: Historical Tables* (Washington, D.C.: U.S. Government Printing Office, 2014), Table 16.1.

27. Andrea Louise Campbell, "Self-Interest, Social Security, and the Distinctive Political Participation Patterns of Senior Citizens," *American Political Science Review* 96 (September 2002): 565–74.

28. Kaiser Family Foundation, 2014.

29. *Budget of the United States Government, Fiscal Year 2015: Historical Tables* (Washington, D.C.: U.S. Government Printing Office, 2014), Table 16.1.

30. Centers for Medicare and Medicaid Services, 2014.

31. Kaiser Commission on Medicaid and the Uninsured and the Urban Institute, cited in *CQ Weekly*, May 16, 2011, p. 1046.
32. Kaiser Family Foundation, 2012.
33. Centers for Medicare and Medicaid Services, 2014.
34. The story of the Clinton health care plan is told in Theda Skocpol, *Boomerang: Health Care Reform and the Turn Against Government* (New York: Norton, 1996).
35. Polls of August 8–9, 1994, and August 15–16, 1994.
36. See George C. Edwards III, *Overreach: Leadership on the Obama Presidency* (Princeton, NJ: Princeton University Press, 2012), chap. 3.
37. Edwards, *Overreach*, chaps. 3 and 7.
38. Cited in Judith A. Layzer, *Open for Business: Conservatives' Opposition to Environmental Regulation* (Cambridge, MA: MIT Press, 2012), 95.
39. For a legislative and administrative discussion and evaluation of the NEPA, see Richard A. Loroff, *A National Policy for the Environment: NEPA and Its Aftermath* (Bloomington, IN: Indiana University Press, 1976).
40. Samuel Hays, *Beauty, Health, Permanence* (New York: Cambridge University Press, 1987), 99.
41. Charles P. Alexander, "On the Defensive," *Time*, June 15, 1992, 35.
42. U.S. Fish and Wildlife Service, 2014.
43. On toxic waste and its politics, see Robert Nakamura and Thomas Church, *Taming Regulation* (Washington, D.C.: Brookings Institution, 2003).
44. A good source of information on this policy is http://www.epa.gov/superfund/.
45. On implementing the Superfund law, see Thomas W. Church and Robert T. Nakamura, *Cleaning Up the Mess: Implementation Strategies in Superfund* (Washington, D.C.: Brookings Institution, 1993).
46. Denis J. Brion, *Essential Industry and the NIMBY Phenomenon* (New York: Quorum Books, 1991); Charles Piller, *The Fail-Safe Society* (New York: Basic Books, 1991); Daniel Mazmanian and David Morell, "The 'NIMBY' Syndrome: Facility Siting and the Failure of Democratic Discourse," in *Environmental Policy in the 1990s*, ed. Norman J. Vig and Michael E. Kraft (Washington, D.C.: Congressional Quarterly Press, 1990), chap. 6.
47. A good source of information on climate change is the Environmental Protection Agency's Climate Change site at www.epa.gov/climatechange/.
48. Royal Society and U.S. National Academy of Sciences, *Climate Change: Evidence and Causes*, 2014; Intergovernmental Panel on Climate Change *Climate Change 2014: Impacts, Adaptation, and Vulnerability*, 2014; National Academy of Sciences, *National Climate Assessment*, 2014; American Academy for the Advancement of Science Climate Science Panel, *What We Know: The Reality, Risks and Response to Climate Change*, 2014.
49. U.S. Energy Information Administration, 2014.
50. A classic study of oil is Daniel Yergin, *The Prize: The Epic Quest for Oil, Money and Power* (New York: Simon and Schuster, 1991).
51. U.S. Energy Information Administration, 2014.
52. Frank R. Baumgartner and Bryan D. Jones, *Agendas and Instability in American Politics* (Chicago, IL: University of Chicago Press, 1993).
53. See John L. Campbell, *Collapse of an Industry: Nuclear Power and the Contradictions of U.S. Policy* (Ithaca, NY: Cornell University Press, 1988).
54. U.S. Energy Information Administration, 2014.
55. U.S. Energy Information Administration, 2014.

1. See, for example, Paul Kennedy, *The Rise and Fall of the Great Powers* (New York: Random House, 1987).
2. Raymond Vernon, *In the Hurricane's Eye: The Troubled Prospects of Multinational Enterprises* (Cambridge, MA: Harvard University Press, 1998); United Nations, *World Investment Report, 2005* (New York: United Nations, 2005).
3. I. M. Destler, "National Security Management: What Presidents Have Wrought," *Political Science Quarterly* 95 (Winter 1980–1981): 573–88.
4. Richard Betts, *Soldiers, Statesmen, and Cold War Crises* (Cambridge, MA: Harvard University Press, 1977), 216, Table A.
5. See Bob Woodward, *Veil: The Secret Wars of the CIA, 1981–1987* (New York: Simon and Schuster, 1987).
6. A good study of the role of Congress in setting U.S. foreign policy is James M. Lindsay, *Congress and the Politics of U.S. Foreign Policy* (Baltimore: Johns Hopkins University Press, 1994). Congress's role in the defense budget process is discussed in Ralph G. Carter, "Budgeting for Defense," in *The President, Congress, and the Making of Foreign Policy*, ed. Paul E. Peterson (Norman: University of Oklahoma Press, 1994).
7. Louis Fisher, "Executive-Legislative Revelations in Foreign Policy" (paper presented at the United States–Mexico Comparative Constitutional Law Conference, Mexico City, June 17, 1998), 1.
8. An excellent treatment of the origins of the Cold War is Daniel Yergin, *Shattered Peace: The Origins of the Cold War and the National Security State* (Boston: Houghton Mifflin, 1977).
9. The article was titled "Sources of Soviet Conduct" and appeared in *Foreign Affairs* (July 1947) under the pseudonym X.
10. Stanley Karnow, *Vietnam: A History* (New York: Penguin Books, 1983), 43. Karnow's book is one of the best of many excellent books on Vietnam. See also Frances Fitzgerald, *Fire in the Lake* (Boston: Little, Brown, 1972) and David Halberstam, *The Best and the Brightest* (New York: Random House, 1972).
11. Nicholas Lemann, "The Peacetime War," *Atlantic Monthly*, October 1984, 72.
12. President Boris Yeltsin of Russia, Address to Joint Session of Congress, June 17, 1992. Quoted in "Summit in Washington: Excerpts from Yeltsin's Speech," *New York Times*, June 18, 1992.
13. Bureau of Counterterrorism, U.S. Department of State, *Country Reports on Terrorism 2013*, April 2014.
14. See, for example, Bruce Russett, "Defense Expenditures and National Well-Being," *American Political Science Review* 76 (December 1982): 767–77; William K. Domke, Richard C. Eichenberg, and Catherine M. Kelleher, "The Illusion of Choice: Defense and Welfare in Advanced Industrial Democracies, 1948–78," *American Political Science Review* 77 (March 1983): 19–35; and Alex Mintz, "Guns Versus Butter: A Disaggregated Analysis," *American Political Science Review* 83 (December 1989): 1285–96.
15. Rebecca U. Thorpe, *The American Warfare State: The Domestic Politics of Military Spending* (Chicago, IL: University of Chicago Press, 2014).
16. On the importance of ideology, see studies discussed in Robert A. Bernstein, *Elections, Representation, and Congressional Voting Behavior* (Englewood Cliffs, NJ: Prentice Hall, 1989), 70–76.
17. U.S. Department of Defense, Defense Manpower Data Center 2014.
18. Stephen I. Schwartz, ed., *Atomic Audit: The Costs and Consequences of U.S. Nuclear Weapons Since 1940* (Washington, D.C.: Brookings Institution, 1998); "Nuclear Testing," *RealClearScience*, June 3, 2013; Center for Nonproliferation Studies, 2014.

682

19. See, for example, Stanley Hoffman, *Gulliver's Troubles, or the Setting of American Foreign Policy* (New York: McGraw-Hill, 1968).

20. Robert O. Keohane and Joseph S. Nye Jr., *Power and Independence*, 4th ed. (New York: Longman, 2011).

21. Joseph S. Nye Jr., *The Paradox of American Power: Why the World's Only Superpower Can't Go It Alone* (New York: Oxford University Press, 2002).

22. Joseph S. Nye Jr., *Soft Power: The Means to Success in World Politics* (Cambridge, MA: Harvard University Press, 2004).

23. Robert M. Kimmit, "Public Footprints in Private Markets," *Foreign Affairs* 87 (January/February 2008): 126.

24. U.S. Census Bureau, Foreign Trade Division, 2014.

25. Ibid.

26. Carol C. Adelman, "The Privatization of Foreign Aid," *Foreign Affairs* 82 (November/ December 2003): 9–14.

27. See Bruce M. Russett, *Controlling the Sword* (Cambridge, MA: Harvard University Press, 1990), chap. 5; Thomas Hartley and Bruce M. Russett, "Public Opinion and the Common Defense: Who Governs Military Spending in the United States?" *American Political Science Review* 86 (December 1992): 905–15; Bruce M. Russett, *Grasping the Democratic Peace* (Princeton, NJ: Princeton University Press, 1993); Spencer R. Weart, *Never at War* (New Haven, CT: Yale University Press, 1998); Michael D. Ward and Kristian S. Gleditsch, "Democratizing Peace," *American Political Science Review* 92 (March 1998): 51–62; and Paul R. Hensel, Gary Foertz, and Paul F. Diehl, "The Democratic Peace and Rivalries," *Journal of Politics* 62 (November 2000): 1173–88.

CREDITS

Text and Photo

CHAPTER 1

Page 3: Theana Breugem/Foto24/Gallo Images/Getty Images; 7: Rhona Wise/AFP/Getty Images; 8: KEVIN LAMARQUE/Reuters/Corbis; 9: Romeo Gacad/AFP/Getty Images; 12: Rawpixel/Fotolia LLC; 14: Abraham Lincoln, *Gettysburg Address*, Thursday, November 19, 1863; 18: Roslan Rahmna/AFP/Getty Images; 19: Joseph Sohm/Visions of America/Corbis; 19: William Wirt(1817), *Sketches of the life and character of Patrick Henry;* 19: New Hampshire's official state motto; 20: Declaration of Independence; 21: James Q.Wilson, "How Divided Are We?" *Commentary,* February 2006, 21; 22: David Horsey, seattle-post intelligencer, 2002; 23: AureliaVentura/La Opinion/Newscom; 24: Ronald Reagan, farewell presidential address.

CHAPTER 2

Page 19: North Wind/North Wind Picture Archives; 19: Carol M. Highsmith Archive/Library of Congress, Prints and Photographs Division [LC-DIG-highsm−01908]; 19: Carol M. Highsmith Archive/Library of Congress, Prints and Photographs Division [LC-DIG-highsm−11889]; 19: Carol M. Highsmith Archive/Library of Congress, Prints and Photographs Division [LC-DIG-highsm−04961]; 31: Bettmann/CORBIS; 34: Joe Griffin/Hulton Archive/Getty Images; 34: U.S. Capitol Historical Society; 34: From The Story of the Thirteen Colonies. Copyright, 1898, by H. A. Guerber. American Book Company, publishers; 34: From The Story of the Thirteen Colonies. Copyright, 1898, by H. A. Guerber. American Book Company, publishers; 35: Declaration of Independence; 40: Scribner's Popular History of the US, 1897/Pearson Education; 44: G.B. Trudeau/Universal Uclick; 47: North Wind Picture Archives/The Image Works; 51: United States Capitol Historical Society; 51: George Washington's Diary, September 13–18, 1787; 55: Federalist #43," in Alexander Hamilton, James Madison, and John Jay, *The Federalist Papers,* 2nd ed, ed Roy P. Fairfield (Baltimore: Johns Hopkins University Press, 1981); 57: Paul Thompson/Topical Press Agency/Getty Images; 59: Mike Luckovich/Creators Syndicate; 61: Senator Jennings Randolph, 1971; 62: Carolyn Kaster/AP Images.

CHAPTER 3

Page 69: Rich Pedroncelli/AP Images; 71: Central Intelligence Agency, The World Factbook, 2014; 74: Hulton Archive/ Getty Images; 74: The Tenth Amendment; 76: John Moore/Getty Images News/Getty Images; 76: Article I, Section 8; 77: *Mack and Printz v. United States,* 521 U.S. 898 (1997); 79: *Baldwin v. Fish and Game Commission of Montana* (1978); 79: Andrew Burton/Reuters; 82: Edwin Beckenbach/Getty Images; 84: Office of Management and Budget, Budget of the United States Government, Fiscal Year 2015: Historical Tables (Washington, DC: U.S. Government Printing Office, 2014), Tables 12.1 and 12.2; 86: The Herb Block Foundation; 87: Jeff Greenberg/Peter Arnold/ Getty Images; 90: U.S. Department of Commerce, United States Census Bureau, Public Education Finances Report,

2013. The data are for 2011; 93: Office of Management and Budget, Budget of the United States Government, Fiscal Year 2015: Historical Tables (Washington, DC: U.S. Government Printing Office, 2014), Table 15.3.

CHAPTER 4

Page 99. Reed Saxon/Associated Press/Corbis; 100: Brandi Simons/AP Images; 101: U.S Constitution, The Ten Amendments; 102: U.S Constitution, The Fourteenth Amendment; 102: *Gitlow v. New York*, 268 U.S. 652 (1925); 102: U.S. Constitution, Establishment Clause; 104: Thomas Jefferson, *Jefferson's Letter to the Danbury Baptists*, Jan.1.1802; 104: *Lemon v. Kurtzman*, 403 U.S. 602 (1971); 105: *School District of Abington Township, Pennsylvania v. Schempp*, 374 U.S. 203 (1963); 105: Annie Griffiths Belt/Corbis; 108: AP Images; 110: Charles R. Lawrence III, "If He Hollers Let Him Go: Regulating Racist Speech on Campus," in *Words That Wound: Critical Race Theory, Assaultive Speech, and the First Amendment*, ed. Mari J. Matsuda, Charles R. Lawrence III, Richard Delgado, and Kimberle Crenshaw, (Boulder, CO: Westview, 1993), 67–68; 110: Ira Glasser, "Introduction," in *Speaking of Race, Speaking of Sex: Hate Speech, Civil Rights, and Civil Liberties*, ed. Henry Louis Gates Jr. (New York: New York University Press, 1994), 8; 112: *Roth v. United States*, 1957; 112: Bob Schutz/AP Images; 113: Warren Burger, *Miller v. California*, 1973; 113: *Erznoznik v. City of Jacksonville*, 422 U.S. 205 (1975); 114: Larry Downing/Reuters; 116: *Richmond Newspapers v. Virginia* (1980); 118: Getty Images Entertainment/ Getty Images; 120: Jean-Yves Rabeuf/The Image Works; 122: Robert Mankoff/ Cartoon Bank; 123: Chris Keane/ Reuters; 126: Justice William Rehnquist, *United States v. Montoya de Hernandez*, 473 U.S. 531 (1985); 127: The Fifth Amendment; 128: Kim Kulish/Corbis; 131: Tomas van Houtryve/AP Images; 131: *Boumediene v. Bush*, 2008; 132: *Gregg v. Georgia* (1976); 133: *Callins v. Collins* [1994]; 133: Death Penalty Information Center; Texas Execution Information Center; 134: *Baze v. Rees* (2008); 134: In Ryan's Words: 'I Must Act', January 11, 2003. *The New York Times*; 134: http://www.law.northwestern.edu/wrongfulconvictions/; 135: Justice Louis Brandeis, *Olmstead v. United States*, 277 U.S. 438 (1928); 136: Brendan McDermid/ Reuters; 137: Gallup Poll, May 8–11, 2014.

CHAPTER 5

Page 148: AP Images; 150: Bettmann/Corbis; 151: *Alexander v. Holmes County Board of Education*; 152: Data from Lawrence Baum; 153: James Zwerg, in an interview to Boston's Public Broadcasting Station WGBH; 154: The Fifteenth Amendment; 155: Chuck Burton/AP Images; 157: U.S. Census Bureau, 2014; 158: Alison Wright/Encyclopedia/Corbis; 159: Reuters/Adrees Latif/Corbis; 159: *Hernandez v. Texas* (1954); 159: *Plyler v. Doe* (1982); 160: Historical/ Corbis; 161: Declaration of Sentiments, July 19, 1848; 163: NASA/AP Images; 165: Mohammed Aneen/Reuters; 166: www.eeoc.gov/laws/types/sexual_ harassment.cfm; 166: *Harris v. Forklift Systems*, 1993; 168: ADA Amendments Act of 2008, 42 U.S. Code § 12102 – Definition of disability; 168: Chris O'Meara/ AP Images; 170: Tom Cheney/ Cartoon Bank; 171: Regents of the University of California v. Bakke (1978).

CHAPTER 6

Page 181: Jason Reed/Reuters; 183: Jason Smith/Getty Images Sport/Getty Images; 184: Steven M. Gillon, *That's Not What We Meant to Do: Reform and Its Unintended Consequences in Twentieth-Century America* (New York: Norton, 2000), p. 178; 185: "U.S. Legal Permanent Residents: 2013," Department of Homeland Security, May 2014; 186: U.S. Census Bureau estimates http://www.census.gov/population/ projections/data/national/2012/summarytables.html; 186: Matt York/AP Images;

187: Courtesy of Marty Wattenberg; 191: Albert Einstein, *The Survey*, Volume 76, Survey Associates, 1940; 195: David Kennedy, Thomas Bailey, 2009, *The American Spirit: United States History as Seen by Contemporaries*, Volume 1. Cengage Learning; 195: Chris Fitzgerald/CandidatePhotos/The Image Works; 196: Lindsay Foyle/Cartoon Stock; 198: Authors' analysis of 1958–2012 American National Election Study data. As there were no election studies for 2006 and 2010 we have used the following sources for those years: December 2006 Pew Research Center poll; February 5–10, 2010 *New York Times/CBS News Poll*; 198: Mark J. Hetherington, *Why Trust Matters* (Princeton, NJ: Princeton University Press, 2005), 4; 199: Obama, Remarks by the President in State of the Union Address, January 27, 2010; 200: Authors' analysis of the 2008 American National Election Study; 202: Michael S. Lewis-Beck et al., *The American Voter Revisited* (Ann Arbor, MI: University of Michigan Press, 2008), 279; 202: Morris P. Fiorina, *Culture War? The Myth of a Polarized America*, 2nd ed. (New York: Longman, 2006), 8; 204: Bettmann/Corbis; 205: John Filo/Premium Archive/Getty Images; 207: Verba and Nie, *Participation in America*, 125; 208: Campbell et al., *The American Voter*, 541; 209: Morris P. Fiorina, *Retrospective Voting in American National Elections* (New Haven: Yale University Press, 1981), 5.

CHAPTER 7

Page 215: Patrick Semansky/AP Images; 217: Chip Somodevilla/ Getty Images; 219: Chip Somodevilla/Getty Images News/Getty Images; 221: Dave Murray, "Obama concerned about newspapers" September 20, 2009 The Blade of Toledo; 223: Barry A. Hollander, "Late-Night Learning: Do Entertainment Programs Increase Political Campaign Knowledge for Young Viewers?" *Journal of Broadcasting and Electronic Media* (Decemer 2005): 412; 224: Project for Excellence in Journalism, The State of the News Media, 2004, www.stateofthenewsmedia.org/index.asp; 224: Paul Drinkwater/NBC/NBCU Photo Bank/Getty Images; 224–225: Sarah Sobieraj and Jeffrey M. Berry, *The Outrage Industry: Political Opinion and the New Incivility* (New York: Oxford University Press, 2014) 7; 225: Pew Research Center Surveys; 226: NBC News, "A Day in the Life of Obama's White House," June 3, 2009. See http://www.msnbc.msn.com/id/31050780/; 228: Chip Somodevilla/Getty Images; 229: Marshall McLuhan, Understanding Media; 232: Samuel Morse, First Telegraph Messages from the Capitol; 234: Gary Cameron/Reuters; 238: Bernard Cohen, *The Press and Foreign Policy* (Princeton, NJ: Princeton University Press, 1963), 13; 239: CSL, CartoonStock Ltd.

CHAPTER 8

Page 245: Shannon Stapleton/Reuters; 248: Frank Thorp, "Christie on GOP: I am going to do anything I need to do to win." *NBC News*, First Read, August 15, 2013; 249: Author's analysis of combined 2008 and 2010 General Social Survey data; 250: Kevin Lamarque/Reuters; 251: American National Election Studies, 1952–2012; 252: Authors' analysis of the 2008 American National Election Study; 253: Walter Bennett/Time & Life Pictures/Getty Images; 256: http://www.politifact.com/truth-o-meter/promises/; 257: Excerpts from party platforms as posted on the Web sites of each organization; 259: The Granger Collection, NYC; 260: Authors' analysis of two Pew Research Center polls conducted in January 2012; 263: Neno Images/PhotoEdit; 266: Kevin Spacey, "House of Cards," Season 1 Episode 9; 267: Daryl Cagle/Cagle Cartoons.

CHAPTER 9

Page 275: Alex Brandon/AP Images; 278: Michael Boyer/AP Images; 280: Robyn Beck/Getty Images; 281: John Cole/Cagle Cartoons; 284: Pew Research Center for the People & the Press. See http://www.pewresearch.org/fact-tank/2013/10/16/12-trendsshaping-digital-news/; 288: *McConnell v. Federal Election Commission*; 290: Kathleen Hall Jamieson, ed., *Electing the President 2012: The Insiders' View.* (Philadelphia, PA: University of Pennsylvania Press, 2013), p. 161; 291: Shane Goldmacher, "Former Senate Leader Says Senators Spent Two-Thirds of Time Asking for Money." *National Journal*, January 16, 2014; 291: Evan Vucci, FILE/AP Images; 292: John Sides and Lynn Vavreck, *The Gamble: Choice and Chance in the 2012 Presidential Election.* (Princeton, NJ: Princeton University Press, 2013), p. 103; 294: Governor Nikki Haley; 295: In all countries except for the United States, official reports of the percentage of registered voters casting valid votes. For the United States, the percentage of citizens participating was calculated based on Census Bureau reports of the number of citizens of voting age and reports from the states regarding how many people voted. 295: John Cross/Mankato Free Press/AP Images; 298: The Joplin Globe, T. Rob Brown/AP Images; 298: The transcript for this debate can be found on the Web site for the Commission on Presidential Debates, at http://www.debates.org/index.php?page=october-19-1992-debate-transcript; 299: George W. Bush; 299: Barack Obama's president-elect press conference - 25 November 2008; 299: Russell J. Dalton, *The Apartisan American: Dealignment and Changing Electoral Politics* (Washington, D.C.: Congressional Quarterly Press, 2013), p. 190; 300: Jason Squires/WireImage/Getty Images; 301: Transcript, Washington Week with Gwen Ifill, PBS, September 30, 2011, http://www.pbs.org/weta/washingtonweek/watch/transcript/21890; 304: Scott Olson/Getty Images; 307: James W. Caeser, *Presidential Selection: Theory and Development* (Princeton, NJ: Princeton University Press, 1979), 83; 308: The Washington Post/Contributor/Getty Images.

CHAPTER 10

Page 312: Rodale Press - http://www.menshealth.com/health/sweet-soda-tax; 314: Alexis de Tocqueville, *Democracy in America*, vol. 2 (New York: Vintage, 1945), 114; 315: Authors' analysis of the 2007 International Social Survey Program survey for civic-associations and the Comparative Study of Electoral Systems, module 2 (2001–2006) for working with others; 315: Leigh Vogel/Getty Images; 320: Universal Uclick; 323: See https://www.columbiabooks.com/ProductDetail/the-18-0-1/Washington_Representatives_2009; 324: Compiled by the author from 2009, 2010, 2011, 2012, and 2013 data from the Center for Responsive Politics. See www.opensecrets.org/lobby/top.php?index?Type=i&showYear=a; 327: Karen Bleier/AFP/Getty Images; 331: Jeffrey Markowitz/Sygma/Corbis; 332: Federal Election Commission; 333: Justin Sullivan/Getty Images; 335: Paul J. Richards/Staff/AFP/Getty Images.

CHAPTER 11

Page 7–8: 114th Congress data based on press reports available a week after the November 4, 2014 elections. 113th Congress data compiled from: Congressional Research Service, Membership of the 113th Congress: A Profile (Washington, D.C.), October 31, 2013; Norman J. Ornstein, Thomas E. Mann, Michael J. Malbin, and Andrew Rugg, Vital Statistics on Congress (Washington, D.C.: Brookings Institution and American Enterprise Institute, 2013); 342: *Artemus Ward: His book*, (London: Ward, Bock, and Tyler), 1866, p. 83; 343: Ken Cedeno/Corbis; 346: Robert Nickelsberg/Getty Images News/Getty Images; 350: David L Ryan/The Boston Globe/Getty Images; 355: Will Rogers Memorial Museums, www.willrogers.com/quotes.html; 356: Alex Wong/Getty Images News/Getty Images; 356: J. Scott Applewhite/AP Images; 356: Chip Somodevilla/Getty Images News/Getty Images; 359: Jonathan Ernst/Reuters; 361: Jennifer 8. Lee, "Crucial Unpaid Internships Increasingly Separate the Haves from the Have-Nots," *New York Times*, August 10, 2004; 362: Lauren Victoria Burke /AP Images; 370: J.B. Handelsman/Cartoonbank.

CHAPTER 12

Page 31: White House (www.whitehouse.gov/administration/eop), 2014; 379: Quoted in Irving Stone, *Clarence Darrow for the Defense* (Garden City, NY: Doubleday, Doran & Co., 1941), chap. 6; 379: Bill Pugliano/Getty Images; 380: Quoted in "Warren G. Harding," "The White House, About the White House: Presidents, www.whitehouse.gov/about/presidents/warrenharding/; 381: Universal Uclick; 383: Article II, Section 4; 385: Alex Webb/Magnum Photos New York; 386: The titles of chapters 5 and 11 in Thomas E. Cronin, *The State of the Presidency*, 2nd ed. (Boston: Little, Brown, 1980); 388: Patrick Cox, "John Nance Garner on the Vice Presidency—In search of the Proverbial Bucket," Briscoe Center for American History, University of Texas at Austin, www.cah.utexas.edu/news/press_release.php?press=press_bucket; 388: George W. Bush; 390: White House (www.whitehouse.gov/administration/eop), 2014; 395: Mary Ann Chastain / Reuters; 398: Chip Somodevilla/Getty Images News/Getty Images; 402: Stephen Jaffe /REUTERS; 404: Corbis; 405: Pete Souza/The White House/AP Images; 407: Abraham Lincoln; 407: Doug Mills/AP Images; 408: George C. Edwards III, *Presidential Approval* (Baltimore, MD: Johns Hopkins University Press, 1990); updated by the authors; 409: J. Scott Applewhite/AP Images; 410: Gallup Poll, for week of May 7–13, 2012; 413: Jimmy Carter, *Keeping Faith* (New York: Bantam, 1982). 179–80; 413: AP Images; 414: Alex Wong/Getty Images News/Getty Images.

CHAPTER 13

Page 423: Mario Tama/Getty Images; 424: Budget of the United States Government, Fiscal Year 2015: Historical Tables (Washington, DC: U.S. Government Printing Office, 2014), Table 2.1; 426: Budget of the United States Government, Fiscal Year 2015: Historical Tables (Washington, DC: U.S. Government Printing Office, 2014), Table 7.1; 427: 1974 Budget Act; 428: Budget of the United States Government, Fiscal Year 2015: Analytical Perspectives (Washington, DC: U.S. Government Printing Office, 2014), Table 14.3. Data are estimates for fiscal year 2015; 430: Organization for Economic Cooperation and Development 2014. Data are for 2012; 431: Budget of the United States Government, Fiscal Year 2015: Historical Tables (Washington, DC: U.S. Government Printing Office, 2015), Table 6.1; 432: Budget of the United States Government, Fiscal Year 2015: Historical Tables (Washington, DC: U.S. Government Printing Office, 2014), Table 6.1; 435: Budget of the United States Government, Fiscal Year 2015: Historical Tables (Washington, DC: U.S. Government Printing Office, 2014), Table 3.1; 435: Philip Wallick; 436: Lisa DeJong/AP Images; 437: President John Adams; 439: Robert Matson/Cagle Cartoons; 440: Doug Mills/AP Images; 442: Budget of the United States Government, Fiscal Year 2015: Historical Tables (Washington, DC: U.S. Government Printing Office, 2014), Table 1.1; 443: Budget of the United States Government, Fiscal Year 2015: Historical Tables (Washington, DC: U.S. Government Printing Office, 2014), Tables 1.1, 8.5, and 8.7; 444: Mike Theiss/National Geographic/Getty Images.

CHAPTER 14

Page 453: Montes De Oca Art/Taxi/Getty Images; 454: Budget of the United States Government, Fiscal Year 2015: Budget of the United States Government, Fiscal Year 2015: Analytical Perspectives (Washington, DC: U.S. Government Printing Office, 2014), Tables 11-2 and 11-3; 454: Budget of the United States Government, Fiscal Year 2015: Analytical Perspectives (Washington, DC: U.S. Government Printing Office, 2014), Tables 8-2 and 8-3; 458: Office of the Federal Register, United States Government Manual 2014 Washington, DC: U.S. Government Printing Office, 2014); 461: Robert Burns; 462: Ty Wright/Bloomberg/Getty Images; 462: Title IX of the Education Act of 1972; 465: Brian Pohorylo/Icon SMI/Corbis; 469: Frank Cotham/The Cartoon Bank; 470: Jack Kurtz/The Image

CHAPTER 15

Page 487: Jon Elswick /AP Images; 490: Time & Life Pictures/Getty Images; 493: "The Supreme Court, 2012 Term: The Statistics," 127 (November 2013): 373–377; 494: Quoted in J. Woodford Howard Jr., *Courts of Appeals in the Federal Judicial System: A Study of the Second, Fifth, and District of Columbia Circuits* (Princeton, NJ: Princeton University Press, 1981), p. 101; 499: Quoted in Nina Totenberg, "Will Judges Be Chosen Rationally?," *Judicature* 60 (August/September 1976): 93; 500: Larry Downing/Reuters; 502: Jim Young/Reuters; 502: Quoted in Henry J. Abraham, *Justices and Presidents: A Political History of Appointments to the Supreme Court*, 3rd ed. (New York: Oxford University Press, 1992), 266; 502: Quoted in Henry J. Abraham, *Justices and Presidents: A Political History of Appointments to the Supreme Court*, 3rd ed. (New York: Oxford University Press, 1992), 70; 502: Quoted in Adam Liptak, "The Waves Minority Judges Always Make," *New York Times*, May 1, 2009; 502: Quoted in Nina Totenberg, "Behind the Marble, Beneath the Robes," *New York Times Magazine*, March 16, 1975, 37; 503: Pablo Martinez Monsivais/ AP Images; 507: David Hume Kennerly/Getty Images; 507: Doris Graber, *Mass Media and American Politics*, 6th ed. (Washington, DC: CQ Press, 2002), 312–13. See also Richard Davis, *Justices and Journalists* (New York: Cambridge University Press, 2011); 509: Joseph Mirachi/Cartoonbank; 510: Bettmann/Corbis; 512: For an excellent overview of the Warren period by former Watergate special prosecutor and Harvard law professor Archibald Cox, see *The Warren Court* (Cambridge, MA: Harvard University Press, 1968); 512: Steven G. Calabresi and James Lindgren, "Term Limits for the Supreme Court: Life Tenure Reconsidered," *Harvard Journal of Law and Public Policy* 29 (Summer 2006), pp. 819–822; 513: "Excerpts from Stewart's Session with Reporters," *New York Times*, June 20, 1981; 514: William Rehnquist, "The Notion of a Living Constitution," in *Views from the Bench*, ed. Mark W. Cannon and David M. O'Brien (Chatham, NJ: Chatham House, 1985), 129. One study found, however, that judicial experience is not related to the congruence of presidential preferences and the justices' decisions on racial equality cases. See John Gates and Jeffrey Cohen, "Presidents, Supreme Court Justices, and Racial Equality Cases: 1954–1984," *Political Behavior* 10 (November 1, 1988): 22–35; 515: "Federalist #78," in Hamilton, Madison, and Jay, *The Federalist Papers*; 516: Yuri Gripas/ Reuters; 517: Paul Conklin/PhotoEdit; 517: U.S. Senate, The Constitution of the United States of America: Analysis and Interpretation and biannual supplements. Updated by authors

CHAPTER 16

Page 525: Kevork Djansezian/Getty Images News/Getty Images; 525: Brad T. Gomez and J. Matthew Wilson, "Political Sophistication and Economic Voting in the American Electorate: A Theory of Heterogeneous Attribution," *American Journal of Political Science* 45 (October 2001): 899; 526: Bureau of Labor Statistics; 530: Bloomberg/Getty Images; 532: The most ardent proponent of this view is Edward Tufte. See his *Political Control of the Economy* (Princeton, NJ: Princeton University Press, 1978); 533: Paul Singer/Andy Singer; 535: "Trends in the Distribution of Household Income Between 1979 and 2007." Congressional Budget Office, October 2011, p. xi. This report can be found online at http://www.cbo.gov/sites/default/files/10-25-HouseholdIncome_0.pdf; 536: Chip

Works; 472: Bettmann/Corbis; 474: Michelle M. Taylor, "When Are Juridically Autonomous Agencies Responsive to Elected Officials? A Simulation Based on the Costa Rican Case," *Journal of Politics* 57 (November 1995): 1070–92; Bruce M. Wilson, Juan Carlos Rodriguez Cordero, and Roger Handberg, "The Best Laid Schemes ... Gang Aft A-gley: Judicial Reform in Latin America—Evidence from Costa Rica," *Journal of Latin American Studies* 36 (August 2004).

Somodevilla/Getty Images News/Getty Images; 538: Stephen Ewen via owsposters.tumblr.com; 540: Rich Pedroncelli/AP Images; 543: Carmel Zucker/The New York Times/Redux; 549: Lewis W. Hine/Archive Photos/Getty Images.

CHAPTER 17

Page 555: Shannon Stapleton/Reuters; 555: World Health Organization, World Health Statistics 2014 (Geneva, Switzerland: World Health Organization, 2014). pp. 60–67, 142–149. Data are for 2011 and 2012; 557: National Center for Health Statistics, Health, United States, 2013 (Washington, DC: U.S. Government Printing Office, 2014), p. 331; 559: Centers for Disease Control and Prevention, National Health Interview Survey (Washington, DC: U.S. Government Printing Office, 2014); National Center for Health Statistics, Health, United States, 2013 (Washington, DC: U.S. Government Printing Office, 2014); 562: Lucy Nicholson/Reuters; 565: Jason Reed/Reuters; 567: Rick Wilking/Reuters; 568: U.S. Fish and Wildlife Service, Federal and State Endangered and Threatened Species Expenditures, Fiscal Year 2010; Craig Pittman, "Fury over a Gentle Giant," *Smithsonian Magazine*, February 2004, 55–59; 572: Joanna McCarthy/The Image Bank/Getty Images; 576: Creators Syndicate.

CHAPTER 18

Page 585: Chao Soi Cheong/AP Photo; 588: Albert Gonzalez Farran/UNAMID/Handout/Reuters; 590: United Media/United Feature Syndicate; 591: SIPA USA/SIPA/Newscom; 596: Corbis; 597: President Boris Yeltsin of Russia, Address to Joint Session of Congress, June 17, 1992. Quoted in "Summit in Washington: Excerpts from Yeltsin's Speech," *New York Times*, June 18, 1992; 598: Lionel Cironneau / AP Images; 600: Reuters; 600: Esam Al-Fetori/Reuters; 600: U.S. Navy/Getty Images; 604: Bettmann/Corbis; 611: Organization for Economic Cooperation and Development, OECD Factbook 2014 (Paris: Organization for Economic Development, 2014); 611: Liu zhanjun – Imaginechina/AP Images.

A

AARP, 320, 561
Abdulmutallab, Umar Farouk, 468
abortion
  interest groups and, 315, 321–322
  privacy rights and, 135–137
  protests over, 120
ACLU (American Civil Liberties Union), 121, 488
activism, judicial, 515, 516. *See also* interest groups; protests
actual group, 320
Adams, Abigail, 392
Adams, John
  on budgetary process, 437
  Declaration of Independence and, 33, 34
  Federalists candidate, 258
  Revolutionary War role of, 36
  vice presidency of, 53
Adams, Sherman, 392
Adarand Constructors v. Pena, 171
Adelson, Sheldon and Miriam, 18
administrative discretion, 466–467
advertising
  congressional, 347
  revenues, 220, 229
affirmative action, 170–173
Affordable Care Act, 180, 197
  challenges to, 78
  cooperative federalism and, 81
  Medicaid in, 87
  passage of, 21, 396, 562–564
  proposal for, 342
  state challenges to, 73
Afghanistan, U.S. war in, 9, 165, 598–599
AFL-CIO, 320, 330
African Americans
  civil rights for, 144, 146, 149–156
  in Congress, 343–344
  demographics of, 184
  equality interests, 333
  pluralism theory of, 317
  political ideology, 201
  political participation, 207
  social welfare for, 540–541
  voting rights of, 154–156, 469–470
  voting turnout, 297
age
  discrimination, 167
  political knowledge and, 4–6
  political participation, 191
Age Discrimination in Employment Act (1967), 167

agencies. *See also* bureaucracy; *departments by name*
  autonomous and independent, 474
  in budgetary process, 438
  iron triangles including, 476–478
  regulation by, 471–473
agenda-setting effect of media, 237–238
Agnew, Spiro, 382, 388
Agostini v. Felton, 104
Agriculture Department, 450, 465
Ahmadinejad, Mahmoud, 607
Aid to Families with Dependent Children, 540, 541
Aiken, Clay, 227
Ailes, Roger, 285
Alaska's Arctic National Wildlife Refuge, 332
Alexander v. Holmes County Board of Education, 151
Ali, Muhammad, 107, 108
Alito, Samuel, 497, 501
Al Qaeda, 598–599
Amendment. *See* specific amendment
American Association of Retired Persons, 319
American Bankers Association, 328
American Bar Association, 303
American Beverage Association, 314
American Civil Liberties Union (ACLU), 121, 488
American creed, 35–36
American flag, burning of, 30, 32, 116
American GI Forum, 158, 159
American Hospital Association, 320
American Indian Movement, 157
American labor movement, 330
American Medical Association, 328
American National Election Study, 317
American Nazi Party, 121
American Opportunity Credit, 429
American people. *See also* children; minorities; senior
    citizens; young people
  as constituents, 347–348
  demographics of, 182–183
  diversity of, 182
  graying of, 188–189
  as immigrant society, 183–184
  melting pot, 184–188
  regional shift, 188
American Revolution, 32–37
Americans Against Food Taxes, 314
Americans with Disabilities Act (1990), 87, 168
amicus curiae briefs, 328, 488, 503, 504, 514
Anthony, Susan B., 161
Anti-Federalists, 51–52
appellate jurisdiction, 489
Apple, R. W., 218
appropriations bills, 441

Arab Americans, civil rights of, 160–161
Argersinger v. Hamlin, 129
Arizona et al. v. United States, 76
Armey, Richard, 244
Armey, Richard "Dick,", 24
arms race, 593, 594. *See also* Cold War
Arthur, Chester A., 455
Articles of Confederation, 37–38, 40
Ashcroft, John, 127
Asian Americans
  civil rights of, 159–160
  demographics of, 184
  in voting, 297
Assange, Julian, 110
assembly, freedom of, 119–121
association, right to, 120–121
Atkins v. Virginia, 134
Atomic Energy Commission, 477
attorneys, 487–488
AT&T, 328
Audubon Society, 332

B

Baker, Russell, 221
Baker, Wayne, 22
Balke, Allan, 171
balance of trade, 609–610
bandwagon effect, 194
Barbour, Haley, 255
bargaining, 400
Barron v. Baltimore, 102
Bartels, Larry, 547
baseball industry political action committee, 325–326
battleground states, 304
Baum, Frank, 259
Baumgartner, Frank, 322
Beard, Charles A., 45
beats, 230
Bell, Griffin, 499
Benenson, Joel, 194
Bennett, Lance, 236
Bennett, Stephen, 4
Berke, Richard, 230
Berkman, Ronald, 239
Berlin Wall, 594, 596
Bernstein, Carl, 231
Berry, Jeffrey, 224, 334
Betts, Richard, 589
bias crimes, 110, 510
bias in news, 234–236, 413
Bibby, John, 255
bicameral legislature, 351–353
Biden, Joseph "Joe," 388
Bill of Rights
  civil liberties and, 101
  creation of, 52
  equality and, 147
  incorporation of, 103
  rights protected under, 53, 100–101
  states adhering to, 102
bills
  congressional, 362–364
  vetoing, 394–395, 404
Bimber, Bruce, 226
bin Laden, Osama, 403, 598–599
Bipartisan Campaign Reform Act (2002), 119
Blackmun, Harry, 133
Blake, J. F., 144
block grants, 85
blogs, 227–228
Blue Dog Democrats, 266
Board of Regents of the University of Wisconsin System v. Southworth, 98, 100, 510
Boatright, Robert, 284
Boehner, John, 8, 23, 62, 353, 354
Bohn, Michael, 224
Bond v. United States, 75
border security, 468
Bork, Robert H., 496–497
Bossie, David, 289
Boston Tea Party, 204
Boumediene v. Bush, 131
Bowers v. Hardwick, 169
BP Deepwater Horizon oil spill, 468, 566, 574
Brady Handgun Violence Prevention Act, 77
Brandeis, Louis, 135
Brandenburg v. Ohio, 112
Branzburg v. Hayes, 117
Brazil, government structure in, 62–63
Brennan, William, 502
Breyer, Stephen, 497, 501, 506
Britain, Revolutionary War with, 32–37
Brown, Dee, 157
Brown, Jerry, 291
Brown, Linda, 151, 488
Brown, Michael, 457
Brown v. Board of Education, 74, 151, 153, 333, 488, 504, 505, 509
Bryan, William Jennings, 259
Buckley v. Valeo, 119, 288
Budget Act (1974), 427
Budget and Accounting Act (1921), 387, 440
budgets, federal
  battles over, 420, 422
  budgetary process, 437–443
  congressional involvement with, 440
  defense, 431–433, 600–601
  deficits in, 422, 425, 427, 442
  democracy and, 443–445
  expenditures in, 422, 430–437, 539
  incrementalism in, 435–436
  Medicare, 84
  overview of, 422–423
  politics impact on, 437–443
  presidential involvement with, 464
  reconciliation, 464–465
  resolutions, 440
  revenue and borrowing in, 423–430

Ryan plan, 522, 524
scope of government and, 445
Social Security, 433–435
tax revenue for, 427–430
bureaucracy
administrators' dispositions in, 466–467
authority of, 465
cabinet departments in, 457–458
civil servants in, 455–456
congressional control of, 475–476
democracy and, 478, 479
deregulation and, 472–473
for food safety, 450–451, 452
fragmentation within, 468–469
government corporations in, 460
independent executive agencies in, 461
independent regulatory commissions in, 459–460
iron triangles including, 476–478
myths and realities of, 453–455
policy implementation role of, 461–471
political appointees in, 456–457
power of, 452
presidential control of, 474–475
privatization of, 470–471
regulatory role of, 471–473
resources of, 464–465
scope of government and, 452, 478–479
standard operating procedures of, 465
Bureau of Labor Statistics, 525
Bureau of Ocean Energy Management, Regulation and Enforcement, 460, 464
Bureau of the Budget, 390, 440
Burger, Warren, 113, 504, 513, 516
Burke, Edmund, 367
Burns, Robert, 461
Bush, Barbara, 392
Bush, George H. W.
approval ratings of, 409
campaigns, 256
flag protection support from, 30
foreign policy of, 596
media coverage, 219, 236
national security policies of, 404, 596, 603
presidency of, 266, 381
Republican Party, 255
vice presidency of, 388, 392
Bush, George W.
approval ratings of, 397, 409, 411
congressional elections and, 344–350
domestic spying under, 127
economic policy of, 24–25, 530
election of, 7, 185
executive orders of, 474
federal vs. state authority under, 83
Iraq war involvement of, 358
media coverage of, 407
military service of, 415
national security policies of, 404, 405, 598–599, 603
policy stances, 301
policy stances of, 395

presidency of, 16–17, 381
public approval, 408
on same-sex marriage, 169
Social Security and, 570–571
tax policy of, 429
UN and, 586
Bush, Laura, 392
Bush v. Gore, 513
business, interest group power of, 331–332

C

cabinet, 388–389, 457–458
cable television media, 222–226
California, 68, 171, 543
Callins v. Collins, 133
campaign costs
congressional, 349
democracy challenged by, 18
campaign finance, limitations on, 119
campaigns
campaigns for Congress, 345–350
comedy shows and, 223
congressional, 344–350, 397
contributions, regulation on, 287–288
democracy and, 306–307
direct mail, 284
economy in, 525
election, 274, 344–350
expensive, 291
freedom of speech and, 119
high-tech media, 283–285
incumbents in, 344–350
independent political expenditures, regulation on, 289–291
Internet usage, 226–228
marathon, 280–282
media coverage, 285
money and, 286–291
nomination, 274
organizing, 285–286
political parties, 247
polling and, 195
scope of government, 307
selective perception, 292
types of, 274
campaign strategy, 275
Canon, Bradley, 508
Cantor, Eric, 529
cap-and-trade system, 473, 571
capital budgets, 426
Capital in the Twenty-First Century (Piketty), 534
capital punishment, 132–134
Cardozo, Benjamin, 500
Carlin, George, 118
Carter, Jimmy
on bureaucracy, 453
on draft registration, 165
on expectations of presidency, 379
foreign policy of, 595

Carter, Jimmy (*continued*)
  on media, 232, 413
  on party on party loyalty, 395
  presidency of, 381, 388, 401, 402
  public approval, 408
Carter, Rosalyn, 392
casework, 347
Casey, William, 590
categorical grants, 83–85
caucuses
  congressional, 360
  presidential, 277–280
CBS News, 194
Census Bureau
  census taken by, 182–183
  on poverty line, 535–536
Center for Responsive Politics, 291
Center on Wrongful Convictions, Northwestern
  University, 134
Central America, military interventions in, 592
Central American-Dominican Republic Free Trade
  Agreement (2005), 608
Central Intelligence Agency (CIA), 587, 590
Chafee, Lincoln, 263
chains of newspapers, 229
chairpersons, congressional committee, 359
Chamber of Commerce, 331
Chase, Samuel, 493
Chávez, César, 159
checks and balances, 49, 50, 61–62
Cheney, Richard "Dick," 388
Chesterton, G. K., 19
Chicago Tribune, 231
children
  child labor, 547
  infant mortality rate, 554
Children's Health Insurance Program,
    539, 561
China, 593, 595, 597
Chinese Exclusion Act, 183
Chisolm v. Georgia, 516–517
Christie, Chris, 248
Churchill, Winston, 194, 593
*Church of the Lukumi Babalu Aye, Inc. v. City of
  Hialeah,* 109
CIA (Central Intelligence Agency), 587, 590
Citizens United v. Federal Election Commission,
    119, 290
civic duty, 294
civil disobedience, 205. *See also* protests
civil law cases, 487
civil liberties
  Bill of Rights protecting, 100–101, 102, 103
  controversies about, 98, 100
  defendants' rights as, 123–134
  democracy and, 138
  freedom of assembly as, 119–121
  freedom of religion as, 102–109
  freedom of speech/expression as, 30, 32, 109–119
  right to bear arms as, 121–123

right to privacy as, 135–137
  scope of government and, 138
civil rights. *See also* voting rights
  affirmative action and, 170–173
  of African Americans, 144, 146, 149–156
  of Arab Americans and Muslims, 160–161
  of Asian-Americans, 159–160
  civil rights movement, 144, 146, 152–154
  democracy and, 173–174
  federalism and, 91
  of Hispanic-Americans, 158
  of LGBT, 168–169
  of Native Americans, 156–158
  people with disabilities, 167–168
  scope of government and, 174–175
  of senior citizens, 167
  of women, 161–166
Civil Rights Act (1964), 85, 153–154, 163, 164, 172
Civil Rights Act (1968), 157
Civil Rights and Women's Equity in Employment Act
  (1991), 163, 164
civil servants, 455–456
Civil War, 73–74, 149–150
class action lawsuits, 487
Clay, Henry, 258
Clean Air Act, 87, 327, 567, 571
climate change, global, 570–571
Clinton, Hillary
  First Lady role of, 392–393
  superdelegates, 277
Clinton, William "Bill," 346
  approval ratings of, 411
  congressional elections and, 346–347
  election of, 201
  health care, 268, 555, 562
  impeachment attempt on, 383, 384
  media coverage, 232, 414
  nomination campaign, 281
  presidency of, 381, 392
  presidential campaign of, 525
  scandal involving, 218
  social welfare policy of, 541
  tax policy of, 429
  UN and, 429
  U.S.–China relations, 233
  welfare reform bill of, 404
closed primaries, 254
coal, as fuel, 572
coalition, 256
  government, 264
Coca-Cola, 314
Cohen, Bernard, 238
Coker v. Georgia, 134
Colbert, Jean-Baptiste, 423
Cold War, 586, 590, 591–597
Coleman, Norm, 293
Coll, Steve, 317
collective good, 320
collective goods, 10
colleges, federal support for, 81

Collins v. Smith, 121
command-and-control policy, 473
commerce power, 77–78
commercial speech, 117
committee chairs, 359
committees
  congressional, 355–359, 476
  iron triangles including, 476–478
  staff for, 361–362
Common Cause, 316, 323, 327, 334
Common Sense (Paine), 33
Communications Decency Act (1996), 114
Comprehensive Environmental Response, Compensation, and Liability Act (1980), 569
confederations, 70
conference committees, 355
Congress, 244. *See also* House of Representatives; Senate
  advertising for, 347
  approval ratings of, 340
  as bicameral legislature, 351–353
  bills in, 362–364
  budgetary role of, 438–439, 440–441
  bureaucratic oversight by/interaction with, 475–476
  caucuses in, 360
  "coattail" riding in, 346–347, 397
  committees in, 355–359
  committees of, 366–367
  constituents of, 366–367
  Continental, 33, 37–38
  credit claiming in, 347–348
  democracy and, 340, 342, 369–371
  demographics of, 342–344
  economic policy involvement of, 45–46
  gridlock in, 62–63, 340
  interest groups and, 314–316
  interns in, 361
  leadership of, 353–355
  legislative oversight by, 356–358
  national security role of, 406, 591
  party identification, 349
  polarization in, 21–22, 340, 365–366, 409
  policymaking role of, 340–342, 350, 351–362
  political ideologies influencing, 349, 365–369
  political party influence in, 365–366
  position taking in, 348
  presidents, relationship with, 364, 393–401
  scope of government and, 371
  staff of, 360–362
  term limits for, 350
  women employment and, 164
  women in, 344–345
Congressional Budget Office, 362, 438–439
Congressional Research Service, 362
congressional staff, 360–362
Congress of Racial Equality, 153
Connecticut Compromise, 43
consent of the governed, 35
conservatives, political ideology of, 199–201. *See also* Republican Party
constituents, congressional, 347–348

constitution
  defined, 32
  democracy and, 60–63
  state, 39, 100
Constitution, U.S.
  amendments to, 30, 52. (*See also* Bill of Rights; *specific amendments*), 53–59
  commerce clause, 68
  creation of, 41–51
  on economic issues, 44–46
  on equality, 42–44, 147–148
  on federalism, 72–79
  Federalists *vs.* Anti-Federalists on, 51–52
  flexibility of, 59
  on government structure, 47–50
  on individual rights, 46–47
  Madisonian system of government in, 47–50
  origins of, 32–37
  on presidency, 384–386
  ratification of, 51–53
  scope of government and, 61–63
  supremacy clause of, 73–78
Constitutional Convention, 35, 41–51, 193
consumer interest groups, 334
consumer price index, 527
Consumer Product Safety Commission, 334
containment doctrine, 593
Continental Congress, 33, 37, 38
continuing resolutions, 442
contraception, insurance coverage for, 108
Controlled Substances Act (1970), 68
convention, national party, 255
conventional participation, 204, 206
cooperative federalism, 80–82
corporate political action committees, 332
corporations, multinational, 587
Cose, Ellis, 188
Council of Economic Advisors, 390
courts
  activist, 516–517
  appellate, 490–491
  constitutional, 488
  democracy and, 513–515
  district, 489–490
  federal. (*See* federal courts)
  judges of. (*See* judges/justices)
  legislative, 488–489
  as policymaking institutions, 502–509
  public policy and, 509–513
  scope of judicial power, 515–517
  selection of judges for, 493–498
courts of appeals, 490–491
coverture, 161
Craig v. Boren, 162
Crawford v. Marion County Election Board, 294
credit claiming, 347–348
credit rating of U.S., 421
criminal law cases, 486–487
crisis management, 404–405
critical election, 258

Cronkite, Walter, 221, 232
crosscutting requirements, 85
crossover sanctions, 85
Crowder-Meyer, Melody, 255
cruel and unusual punishment, 132–134
Curley, James Michael, 253

D

Dahl, Robert, 14, 15
Daley, Richard, 253, 276
Dalton, Russell, 332
    political participation, 204
Darby, United States v., 74
Darrow, Clarence, 379
Daschle, Tom, 291, 389
Davis, Richard, 226
Dawes Act (1887), 156
Dean, Howard, 230, 255
Deardorff, Alan, 324
death penalty, 132–134
De Boef, Suzanna, 525
debt
    interest on, 420
    national, 420
    national debt limit or ceiling, 420, 426
    post-Revolutionary, 39–40
Declaration of Independence, 19, 21, 32–34, 35–36, 147
defendants, defined, 487
defendants, rights of
    as civil liberty, 123–134
    against cruel and unusual punishment, 132–134
    right to counsel, 129
    against searches and seizures, 125–127
    against self-incrimination, 127–129
    stages of criminal justice system, 124
    in trials, 129–132
Defense of Marriage Act (1996), 169, 509
    war on terrorism impacting, 127, 131
Defense Reorganization Act (1986), 589
deficits
    budget, 422, 425, 427, 442. *See also* national debt
    trade, 609–610
Delaware, Constitutional ratification by, 53
delegates, competing for, 275–282
Delli Carpini, Michael, 4–6
Deloria, Vine, 157
democracy
    budgets and, 443–445
    bureaucracy and, 478
    campaigns and, 306–307
    challenges to, 17–18
    civil liberties and, 138
    civil rights and, 173–174
    Congress and, 340–342, 369–371
    Constitution and, 60–63
    courts and, 486, 513–515
    defined, 14
    elite and class theory of, 16–17

    elite theorists, 335
    energy policy and, 575–576
    environmental policy and, 575–576
    federalism and, 90–92
    health care policy and, 575–576
    hyperpluralism theory of, 17
    hyperpluralist theorists, 335
    interest groups and, 334–335
    media and, 239
    national security policy and, 612
    pluralist theorists, 334–335
    pluralist theory on, 15–16
    political culture and, 19–22
    polling role of, 193–195
    presidency and, 415
    presidential *vs.* parliamentary systems of, 385
    public opinion and, 208–209
    responsible party government, 265–266
    traditional democratic theory on, 14–15
Democratic National Committee, 329
Democratic Party
    Blue Dog Democrats, 266
    McGovern–Fraser Commission, 276
    national convention, 255
    party identification, 250–251
Democratic–Republican Party, 258
demographics
    of American people, 182–183
    of civil servants, 455
    of Congress, 342–344
    factors for voting, 296–297
    of judges/justices, 498–502
    of poor people, 535–537
    of presidents, 379, 381
    of Social Security, 544
Dennis, Jack, 190
Dennis v. United States, 111–112
Department of Agriculture, 450, 465
Department of Commerce, 465
Department of Defense. *See also* military; national defense
    budget for, 432, 443–445
    employees of, 453–455
    foreign policy role of, 589–591
Department of Energy, 479, 573
Department of Homeland Security
    border security and, 468
    creation of, 358, 468
    employees of, 455, 456
    illegal immigrants, 186–187
    resources for, 464
Department of Interior, 574
Department of Justice
    judicial appointment/nomination involvement of, 494, 495
    judicial nominations by, 494–495
    solicitor general of, 503
Department of Labor, 468, 471, 525
Department of State, 588–589
Department of Transportation, 471, 567
Department of Veterans Affairs, 454
deregulation, 494–496

desegration, 150, 151, 509, 512. *See also Brown v. Board of Education*

détente, era of, 595

de Tocqueville, Alexis, 314

devolution, 82–83

Dickerson v. United States, 128

Dingell, John, 552

diplomacy, 585, 588–589, 605

direct mail, 284

director of national intelligence, 591

disabilities, people with
civil rights of, 167–168
disability insurance for, 464
Supplemental Security Income for, 539

discrimination
age, 167
reverse, 171

district courts, 489–490

District of Columbia v. Heller, 122

diversity. *See also* minorities
of American people, 182
policy gridlock due to, 18

divided party government, 261–262

Dole, Robert "Bob," 201, 255, 322, 354

"Don't ask, don't tell" policy, 169

Donaldson, Sam, 218, 413, 414

Dothard v. Rawlinson, 163, 164

Downie, Leonard, 230

Downs, Anthony, 246, 248

Downs model, 248–250

draft, military, 165

Dred Scott v. Sandford, 259, 517

drinking age, 82

drugs, use of in religious rituals, 108–109

dual federalism, 80

due process clause, 102

Dulles, John Foster, 593

Dunne, Finley Peter, 514

E

Earned Income Tax Credit, 538

Easton, David, 190

EBT (Electronic Benefit Transfer) cards, 538

economic interests, 330–332

economic issues. *See also* economic policy; money; wealth
in budgets. (*See* budgets, federal)
in campaigns, 525
Constitution addressing, 44–46
environment and, 564–566
in foreign policy, 585
inflation as, 526–527
in national security agenda, 603
post-Revolutionary, 39–40
unemployment as, 525, 526, 530

economic policy
budgets reflecting. (*See* budgets, federal)
control of economy, 532
democracy and, 547–548
fiscal policy as, 529–531
laissez-faire, 21, 527
monetary policy as, 527–529
national security policy and, 606–610
political party stances on, 524
regulation, 471–472
sanctions as, 605
scope of government and, 548
stimulus bill, 530

Edsall, Thomas B., 534

education. *See also Brown v. Board of Education*
affirmative action in, 170–172
church-related, 104
cooperative federalism in, 80–81
equality of, 150–152
financial aid for, 462
No Child Left Behind Act, 80, 83
segregation of, 509, 512
state and local spending on, 90
tax credits for, 429
women, 164

Education Act (1972), 163, 462

Education of All Handicapped Children Act (1975), 168

Edwards, George, 378

EEOC (Equal Employment Opportunity Commission), 153, 163, 164, 471

egalitarianism, 20. *See also* equality

Ehrlichman, John, 111

Eighteenth Amendment, 54

Eighth Amendment, 102, 123, 132

Eisenhower, Dwight D.
desegregation under, 151
judicial nominations by, 502, 512
on military-industrial complex, 432
presidency of, 381, 509

elastic clause, 76–77

elderly people. *See* senior citizens

election campaigns, 274. *See also* campaigns

electioneering, 325–327

elections, generally. *See also* elections, specifically
campaigns. *See* campaign costs; campaigns
congressional, 344–350
critical election, 258
Electoral College in, 302–305
judicial, 493
mandate theory of, 298
presidential, 380
presidential coattails, 346–347, 397
primary elections. *See* primaries
voting in. *See* voting

elections, specifically
of 1860, 259
of 1968, 261–262
of 1992, 230, 262, 525
of 1994, 349–350
of 2000, 5, 7, 91, 219
of 2006, 350
of 2008, 4, 226, 525
of 2010, 350, 554
of 2012, 525

Electoral College, 57, 302–305
electoral mandates, 399
electoral process, 48
Electronic Benefit Transfer (EBT) cards, 538
electronic surveillance, 110
electronic media, 222. *See also* Internet; television media
Elementary and Secondary Education Act (1965), 80
Eleventh Amendment, 75, 516
elitism, 317
congressional, 342–343
elite and class theory of democracy, 16–17
Ellsberg, Daniel, 111
Emergency Medical Treatment and Labor Act (1986), 559
Emerson, Ralph Waldo, 205
employees of government, 453–455
employment, women, 163–164
Employment Division v. Smith, 108
Encyclopedia of Associations, 316
Endangered Species Act (1973), 567–568
Energy Department, 479, 573
energy policy
coal, 572
democracy and, 575–576
national security policy and, 610
nuclear energy, 574–575
petroleum and natural gas, 572–574
renewable energy, 575
scope of government and, 576
sources of energy, 572
Engel v. Vitale, 105
entitlement programs, 533, 539. *See also* Medicare; Social Security
entitlements, 436, 539
entrapment, 129
enumerated powers, 76
environmental impact statements, 566–567
environmental interests, 332–333
environmental legislation, 327
environmental policy
clean air, 567
clean water, 567
democracy and, 575–576
economic growth and, 564–566
endangered species protection as, 567–568
global warming, 570–571
impact statements, 566–567
interest groups and, 332–333
nuclear waste disposal, 569
scope of government and, 576
toxic waste disposal, 568–569
wilderness preservation, 567
Environmental Protection Agency (EPA)
bureaucratic role of, 471
establishment of, 566
food safety regulation by, 450
Superfund law, 569
Epstein, Edward J., 230
Equal Employment Opportunity Commission (EEOC), 153, 163, 164, 471, 472

equality
conceptions of, 147
Constitution addressing, 42–44, 147–148
Declaration of Independence on, 147
egalitarianism, 20
of income, 533–539
interest groups, 333–334
liberty *vs.*, 146
political party stances on, 524
Equal Opportunity Act (1982), 84
equal protection of laws, 147
Equal Rights Amendment (ERA), 55–56, 162–163, 333
ERA (Equal Rights Amendment), 333
Erznoznik v. Jacksonville, 113
establishment clause, 102, 103–107
European Union, 586–587
evolution, teaching of, 106
exclusionary rule, 125–127
executive agreements, 402, 587
Executive Office of the President, 389–391, 458
executive orders, 387, 474
exit poll, 194, 303
Ex parte McCardle, 517
expenditures, 422, 427–428, 430–437, 539
extradition, 78
ExxonMobil, 317

F

FAA (Federal Aviation Administration), 464, 466
factions, 42, 47, 258
Falwell, Jerry, 116
families, political socialization through, 189–190
Family and Medical Leave Act (1993), 546
Farmer, James, 148
farmers, political participation of, 39–40
FCC (Federal Communication Commission), 117–118, 222, 459
FEC (Federal Election Commission), 287, 325
Federal Aviation Administration (FAA), 464, 466
Federal Bureau of Investigation (FBI), 464
Federal Communication Commission (FCC), 117–118, 222, 459
federal courts. *See also* judicial system; Supreme Court
appellate, 490–491
appellate jurisdiction of, 489
case acceptance by, 502–504
courts and, 513–515
decision making in, 504–509
democracy and, 486
district, 489–490
implementation of decisions of, 507–509
judicial circuits of, 491
judicial review in, 509–511
mandates from, 88
original jurisdiction of, 489
policymaking by, 502–509, 509–513
political questions doctrine of, 516
scope of judicial power, 486, 515–517
structure of, 488–493

Federal Election Campaign Act, 287
Federal Election Commission (FEC), 287, 325
Federal Emergency Management Agency, 357, 457
federal government. *See also departments by name*
    post-Revolutionary weakness of, 37–40
    size of, 93
federalism
    constitutional basis of, 72–79
    defining, 70–71
    democracy and, 90–92
    diversity in policy, 88–89
    intergovernmental relations under, 79–88
    scope of government and, 92–93
Federalist 10, 314
Federalist Papers, 41–42, 47, 51, 55, 258, 511, 515
Federalists, 51–52, 509–511, 517
Federal Marine Mammal Protection Act, 568
Federal Open Market Committee (FOMC), 528
Federal Reserve Act, 529
Federal Reserve Board, 458, 459, 474, 527–529
Federal Reserve System, 528
Federal Trade Commission (FTC), 117, 459
Feingold, Russell, 288
Feinstein, Dianne, 325
Feldman, Stanley, 533
feminist movement, 161–163
feminization of poverty, 537
Fenno, Richard, 347
Fifteenth Amendment, 60, 154
Fifth Amendment, 102, 127
filibusters, 352–353
Fiorina, Morris, 22, 209, 347
First Amendment, 98, 100, 101, 220, 229, 315
First Lady, 392–393. *See also First Ladies by name*
fiscal federalism, 83–88
fiscal policy, 529–531
Fish and Wildlife Service, 464
501(c) groups, 290
527 groups, 289
flag burning, 30, 32, 116
Flag Protection Act, 32
Florida Manatee Sanctuary Act, 568
Foley, Thomas, 275
Food and Drug Administration, 450, 452, 464
food safety, 450–451, 452
food stamps, 538, 539
Ford, Gerald
    on bureaucracy, 453
    media coverage of, 413
    presidency of, 380, 381, 382
    public approval, 408
Ford v. Wainwright, 134
foreign aid, 610, 611
Foreign Intelligence Surveillance Act (2008), 127
foreign policy
    Cold War and, 586, 590, 591–597
    congressional role in, 369–371, 372
    defined, 584
    diplomatic relations in, 585, 588–589
    economic instruments of, 585

    foreign aid as, 610, 611
    individual's role in, 587
    international organization role in, 585–586
    isolationism as, 592–593
    military role in, 584–585
    multinational corporation role in, 587
    national security establishment and, 51, 173, 368–369, 562, 564–571
    nongovernmental organization role in, 587
    presidential role in, 587–588
    regional organization role in, 586–587
    terrorism role in, 582, 584, 587, 597–599
Forest Service, 463
formula grants, 85
Fortas, Abe, 496
Fortune magazine, 319
Fourteenth Amendment, 75, 79, 102, 147, 333, 517
Fourth Amendment, 125, 126, 127, 135
Fox, Richard, 275
France, 34, 37
Franklin, Benjamin
    Constitutional Convention role of, 41, 44, 50
    on constitutional republic, 49, 50
    Declaration of Independence role of, 33, 34
    on Washington, 53
freedom
    of assembly, 119–121
    of religion, 102–109
Freedom of Access to Clinic Entrances Act (1994), 137
freedom of speech/expression
    campaigning, 119
    as civil liberty, 30, 109–119
    commercial speech and, 117
    flag burning as, 30
    FTC (Federal Trade Commission), 117
    libel and slander in, 115–116
    media and, 116–118
    obscenity and, 112–115
    prior restraint of, 110–111
    public order and, 111–112
    symbolic speech as, 116
Freedom Riders, 153
free exercise clause, 103, 107–109
Freeh, Louis, 474
free-rider problem, 320
Friedan, Betty, 162
frontloading, 279
FTC (Federal Trade Commission), 459
Fuller, Ida, 433, 544
full faith and credit, 78
Fulton, Sarah, 344–345
Furman v. Georgia, 132

G

Gallup, George
    election of, 192
    scope of government, 208
Gandhi, Mahatma, 205

Garcia, Hector P., 158
Garcia v. San Antonio Metro, 74
Garfield, James A., 382, 455
Garner, John Nance, 388
GATT (General Agreement on Tariffs and Trade, 1994), 608
gender discrimination/equality
affirmative action against, 170–173
civil rights in response to, 161–166
Equal Rights Amendment on, 55–56, 162–163
in military, 164–165
sexual harassment as, 166
Title IX addressing, 163, 462
wage discrimination based on, 163
in workplace, 163–164
gender gap
in Congress, 343, 344–345
political ideology, 201
General Agreement on Tariffs and Trade (GATT, 1994), 608
General Services Administration (GSA), 461
generation gap. *See also* age; senior citizens; young people
in globalization attitudes, 608
in presidential approval, 410
geography, knowledge of, 197
Germany, Revolutionary War role of, 36
Gerry, Elbridge, 50
Gibbons v. Ogden, 77
Gideon v. Wainwright, 129
Gilens, Martin, 532, 540–541
Gillon, Steven, 183
Gingrich, Newt, 244
Ginsburg, Douglas H., 496, 497
Ginsburg, Ruth Bader, 497, 499, 501
Gitlow v. New York, 102
globalization, 606–610
global warming, 570–571
Godwin, R. Kenneth, 326
Goldberg, Arthur, 496
Goldberg, Bernard, 235
Gonzales v. Carhart, 137
Gonzales v. Raich, 68
Gorbachev, Mikhail, 596, 602–603
Gore, Albert, Jr.
in 2000 election, 16–17
on bureaucracy, 467
vice presidency of, 388
government. *See also* departments by name; federalism
Articles of Confederation on structure of, 37–38
budgets for, 431
conflict between levels of, 68, 70
divided party, 261–262
growth of, 548
importance of, 2, 5
intergovernmental relations, 71, 79–88
key functions of, 8–10
local, 565
nature of, 42
number of, in U.S., 91–92
political parties, 247, 255–256
presidents and, 387–393
purpose of, 42
regulation of electronic media, 222
separation of church and state, 100, 104
separation of powers in, 42, 48–49, 50, 61–62
shutdown of, 438
trust in, 197–199
Government Accountability Office, 362, 439
government corporations, 460
Graber, Doris, 239, 507
Grant, Ulysses S., 492
grants, federal, 83–85
Gratz v. Bollinger, 172
Great Britain, Revolutionary War with, 32–37
Great Depression, New Deal programs during, 77, 511–512, 540
Great Society programs, 261, 433, 434, 522, 524, 540
Greenpeace, 333
Greenspan, Alan, 527
Gregg v. Georgia, 132, 133
gridlock in, 62–63
gridlock in Congress, 18, 340
Griswold v. Connecticut, 135
gross domestic product (GDP)
foreign economic development as percentage of, 611
government spending in relation to, 24–25, 431
size of, 93
tax burden as percentage of, 431
group theory of politics, 316–317
Grove City College v. Bell, 517
Grutter v. Bollinger, 171–172
GS (General Schedule) rating, 456
Guantánamo Bay, Cuba, 131, 517
Guinn v. United States, 154
Guiteau, Charles, 455
Gun-Free School Zones Act (1990), 77
guns, 77, 121–123. *See also* weapons

H

Hacker, Jacob, 16
Haley, Nikki, 187, 294
Hamdan v. Rumsfeld, 131
Hamdi v. Rumsfeld, 131
Hamilton, Dona and Charles, 333
Hamilton, Alexander
Constitution role of, 60
economic policies of, 75
Federalist Papers, 41–42, 47, 51, 55, 258, 511, 515
Revolutionary War role of, 34
wisdom of common people, 195
Hancock, John, 34
Harding, Warren G., 379, 380, 382
Harmelin v. Michigan, 132
Harper v. Virginia State Board of Elections, 154
Harris, Louis, 564
Harrison, William Henry, 259, 382
Harris v. Forklift Systems, 166

Hart-Celler Immigration and Nationality Act, 183
Hartz, Louis, 20
Hastert, Dennis, 352
Hastert Rule, 352
Hatch Act (1939), 456
hate speech, 110, 510
Hawkins, Virgil, 507–508
Hayes, Rutherford B., 150
Head Start program, 464
health care policy
    access to health care, 553, 556–560
    cost of health care, 554–556, 557
    democracy and, 575–576
    government role in health care, 560–561
    rationing, 465
    reform of, 180, 552, 554, 561–564
    scope of government and, 576
    uninsured population, 558–559
health insurance, 556–564, 576. *See also* Medicaid; Medicare
health maintenance organizations (HMOs), 557
Heclo, Hugh, 457
Henry, Anthony, 366
Henry, Brad, 543
Henry, Patrick, 19, 41, 52
Hernandez v. Texas, 159
Herring v. United States, 127
Hertsgaard, Mark, 217
Hetherington, Mark, 198
Hewitt, Hugh, 228
high-priced lobbyists, 324
high-tech media campaigns, 283–285
high-tech politics, 216
highways, government responsibility for, 80–81
Hill, Anita, 497
Hilton, Paris, 227
Hindman, Matthew, 226
Hirsch, E. D., 197
Hirschl, Mark, 539
Hispanic Americans
    civil rights of, 158–159
    demographics of, 185–187
    political ideology, 201
    in voting, 297
HMOs (health maintenance organizations), 557
Hobbes, Thomas, *Leviathan,* 41
Holmes, Oliver Wendell, 109, 423
homeland security, oversight of, 357–358
Hoover, Herbert, 218, 259, 527
House of Representatives. *See also* Congress
    characteristics of, 351–352
    committees in, 356
    Constitution on structure of, 43
    demographics of, 342–344
    Electoral College, 304
    homeland security oversight by, 358
    incumbents in, 344
    leadership of, 353–355
    Obama, Barack, 244
    political action committees, 326
    reapportionment, 188

Republican-controlled, 244
Rules Committee, 352, 364
Ways and Means Committee, 438
House Rules Committee, 352
Hoyer, Steny, 396
Huckabee, Mike, 280
Hughes, Charles Evans, 512
humanitarian interventions, 604, 610
human nature, 41, 47
Humphrey's Executor v. United States, 459
Huntington, Samuel, 379
Hunt v. Cromartie, 156
Hurricane Katrina, 207, 357, 457
Hussein, Saddam, 231, 584, 598, 603
hydraulic fracturing (fracking), 574
hyperpluralism, 317–319
hyperpluralist theories, of democracy, 17

ICBMs (intercontinental ballistic missiles), 602
immigrants/immigration
    American as immigrant society, 183–184
    globalization and, 608
    illegal, 159, 183, 186–187
    melting pot society of, 184–188
    policymaking, 185
    welfare programs and, 542, 543
Immigration and Customs Enforcement, 464
Immigration and Naturalization Service, 463
impeachment, 382–383
implied powers, 75–77
incentive systems, 473
income
    defined, 535
    distribution of, 533–534
    government expenditures and, 539
    public policy impacting, 537–539
    of state legislators, 39
    taxes on, 423–425, 538
incorporation doctrine, 102
incrementalism, budgetary, 435–436
incumbents, congressional, 344–350
independence, Revolutionary War battle for, 32–37. *See also*
    Declaration of Independence
independent executive agencies, 461
independent expenditures, 287
independent regulatory commissions, 459–460
Indian Bill of Rights, 157
Indian Claims Act (1946), 157
individualism
    media and, 238–239
    political culture based on, 20–21
individual rights, 46–47
industrialization, 92
inequality, political participation, 207
infant mortality rate, 554
inflation, 526–527
Inglehart, Ronald, 19

Inhofe, James, 571
insurance
  Children's Health Insurance Program, 539, 561
    Congress and, 360
    disability, 464, 539
    health, 556–564, 576. *See also* Medicaid; Medicare
    unemployment, 539
  insurance coverage for contraception, 108
intercontinental ballistic missiles (ICBMs), 602
interdependency of international economy, 606
interest groups. *See also* specific interest groups
  amicus curiae briefs, 328, 488, 504, 514
  budgetary process role of, 438
  bureaucratic interaction with, 459
  Congress and, 314–316, 367–369
  consumer, 334
  definition, 315
  democracy and, 334–335
  economic, 330–332
  electioneering, 325–327
  elitism theory of, 317
  environmental, 332–333, 564–565
  equality, 333–334
  financial resources, 322
  527 groups, 289
  foreign policy, 612–613
  health care, 561–562
  hyperpluralism theory of, 317–319
  implementation of court decisions and, 507
  ineffectiveness, large groups, 319–320
  intensity of, 321–322
  iron triangles, 318, 476–478
  liberalism, 317
  litigation, 327–328, 488
  lobbying, 323–325
  participation, 315
  pluralism theory of, 15–16, 316–317
  public appeals of, 328–329
  public interest lobbies, 334
  scope of government and, 335
  single-issue, 11, 321, 367
  strategies, 322–329
  success factors for, 319–322
  theories of, 316–319
  types of, 329–334
interest rates, 528
intergovernmental relations, 71, 79–88. *See also* federalism
interlocking directorates, 317
intermediate-range nuclear forces (INF) treaty, 602–603
Internal Revenue Service, 423
international economy, 606–610
International Monetary Fund, 606
international organizations and foreign policy, 585–586
international trade, national security policy impacted by, 606–610
Internet
  in campaigns, 226–228
  impact of, 226–228
  impact on media, 226–228
  political campaigns, 283

Internet pollsters, 193
internment camps, 160
internships, 361
Interstate Commerce Commission, 153, 472
investigative journalism, 218–219
invisible primary, 277
Iran
  Iran-Contra affair, 386, 590
  nuclear weapons in, 605
Iran-Contra affair, 235
Iraq war. *See also* Persian Gulf War
  CIA and, 590
  foreign policy and, 598–599
  legislative oversight of, 358
  presidential powers in, 59
iron triangles, 318, 476–478
  resources for, 464
isolationism, 592–593
issue networks, 476–477
Iyengar, Shanto, 236

J

Jackson, Andrew, 405, 507
Jackson, Michael, 116
Jackson State, 205
Jacobson, Gary, 291
Jacobson v. United States, 129
Jay, John, 51, 60
Jefferson, Thomas
  on Constitution, 53
  on Constitutional Convention, 41
  Declaration of Independence, 19, 34, 35–36, 147
  economic policy opposition by, 75
  judicial appointments impacting, 509–511
  on media, 412
  on political knowledge, 5
  Secretary of State role of, 588
  wisdom of common people, 195
Jim Crow laws, 149–150
Jindal, Bobby, 187
Johnson, Andrew, 382, 492
Johnson, Charles, 508
Johnson, Gregory Lee, 30, 32
Johnson, Lady Bird, 392
Johnson, Lyndon B.
  civil rights role of, 148, 158, 170
  educational policy of, 104
  Great Society program, 261, 433, 434, 522, 524, 540
  presidency of, 381
  social welfare policies of, 540
  Vietnam War, 261, 594
Johnson, William, 43
Johnson-Reid Immigration Act, 183
Joint Chiefs of Staff, 589
joint committees, 355
Jones v. Mayer, 154
journalism
  investigative, 218–219
  news reporting, 230–236

judges/justices
  demographics of, 498–502
  judicial review by, 49, 50, 57
  selection of, 493–498
  sentencing guidelines for, 484, 486
  supremacy clause and, 73
  of Supreme Court, 492, 497, 498, 499
  tenure of, 512
judicial activism, 515, 516
  defined, 511
judicial implementation, 507
judicial restraint, 515, 516
  defined, 511
judicial review, 509–511
judicial system. *See also* courts; federal courts; judges/justices
  judicial review in, 57, 509–511
  nature of, 486–488
  participants in, 487–488
  power of, 515–517
  structure of, 488–493
Judiciary Act (1789), 488, 510–511
juries, 130
justiciable disputes, 487

K

Kagan, Elena, 497, 498
Kaine, Tim, 255
Kaiser, Robert, 230
Keating, Charles, 322
Kellstedt, Paul M., 525
Kennan, George F., 593
Kennedy, Anthony M., 501
Kennedy, Edward, 344
Kennedy, John F.
  election of, 261
  on immigration, 183
  media coverage of, 407
  presidency of, 381, 382
Kennedy, Robert, 153
Kennedy v. Louisiana, 134
Kent State, 205
Kerbel Matthew, 239
Kerry, John, 282
Kersh, Rogan, 324
Keynes, John Maynard, 529, 548
Keynesian economic theory, 529–530
Keystone Pipeline System, 574
Kinder, Donald, 236
King, Martin Luther, Jr., 146, 148, 205
Kingdon, John, 21, 237, 369, 401
Kissinger, Henry, 590, 595
Kitch, Laura, 239
Knowledge Networks, 193
Kollman, Ken, 328
Korematsu v. United States, 160
Ku Klux Klan, 150, 153
Kumar, Priya, 229

L

labor, interest group power of, 330–331
Labor Department, 458, 525
labor union membership, 330
Labour Party, 267
Laffer, Arthur, 530
Laird, Melvin, 466
laissez-faire economic policy, 21, 527
Landon, Alf, 192
Lasswell, Harold D., 10, 437
Lawless, Jennifer, 275
Lawrence v. Texas, 169
Lawson, Kay, 247
lawyers, 487–488
leadership
  congressional, 353–355
  party, 395–398
  presidential, 378
League of Nations, 592
League of United Latin American Citizens, 159
Lee, Richard Henry, 33
Legal Defense Fund (NAACP), 151, 159
Legal Services Corporation, 488
legislative courts, 488–489
legislative oversight, 356–358
legislative vetoes, 404
Lemon v. Kurtzman, 104
Lennon, John, 306
lesbians/gays/bisexual/transgendered (LGBT) Americans
  attitudes toward, 203
  civil rights of, 168–169
Leviathan (Hobbes), 41
Lewinsky, Monica, 230, 384, 414
libel, 115–116
liberals, political ideology of, 199–201. *See also* Democratic Party
liberty. *See also* civil liberties; freedom
  equality *vs.*, 146
  political culture based on, 19
Lifetime Learning Credit, 429
Light, Paul, 433
Lightner, Candy, 82
limited government, 35
Lincoln, Abraham, 259
  on democracy, 14, 21
  presidency of, 382
  on public support, 407
  on slavery, 73–74
line-item vetoes, 394
linkage institutions, 12, 247
Lipset, Seymour Martin, 19, 36
Lipsky, Michael, 466
Literary Digest, 192
litigants, 487
litigation, 327–328
Livingston, Robert, 33
lobbying, 323–325, 367–369. *See also* interest groups
Lobbying Disclosure Act, 323

local government, 565
local parties, 253–254
Locke, Gary, 187
Locke, John, 35–36
Locke v. Davey, 510
Longoria, Felix, 158
Lopez, United States v., 77
Love Canal, 568
Lowi, Theodore, 317
Lunch, William, 335

M

Mack v. United States, 77
Madison, Dolley, 392
Madison, James, 258
   Bill of Rights by, 52
   factions, 334
   on factions/political parties/interest groups,
      Federalist Papers by, 41–42, 47, 51, 55, 511, 515
   interest groups, 314
   judicial appointment involvement of, 510–511
   Madisonian system of government by, 47–50
   pluralism and, 90
   political action committees, 327
   presidency of, 75
   property rights views of, 35
   Revolutionary War role of, 34
majority rule, 15, 47–48
majority leaders, congressional, 354
malapportionment in Senate, 369–370
manatees, protection of, 568
mandates
   electoral, 399
   federal grants and, 86–88
mandate theory of elections, 298
Mann, Thomas, 346
Mapp v. Ohio, 125–126
marathon campaign, 280–282
Marbury v. Madison, 49, 50, 57, 510–511, 516
marijuana for medical needs, 68, 70
marriage, same-sex, 169
Marshall, George C., 593
Marshall, John, 51, 75–76, 507, 509–511, 515
Marshall, Thomas, 388
Marshall, Thurgood, 488, 497, 499, 502
Marshall Plan, 593
Martin, Luther, 75–76
Mason, George, 50
Mayer, Jeremy, 8
Mayer, William, 277
McAdoo, William G., 380
McCafferty, Patrick, 299
McCain, John
   campaign finance reform initiatives of, 288
   presidential campaign of, 195, 280, 304, 525, 527
McCain-Feingold Act, 119, 289, 290
McCarthy, Joseph, 111, 112
McCarthy, Kevin, 266

McClellan, Scott, 414
McCleskey v. Kemp, 133
McMahon, Linda, 349
McLaurin v. Oklahoma State Regents, 151
McLuhan, Marshal, 229
Meacham v. Knolls Atomic Power Laboratory, 167
Means, Dennis, 157
means-tested programs, 533, 539
media, Internet, print media, television media.
   See also Internet; print media; television media
   bias, 413
   bias of, 234–236
   broadcasting to narrowcasting, 222–226
   in campaigns, 285
   democracy and, 239
   development of media politics, 218–229
   electronic, 222
   events, 217
   fair trials impacted by free press, 116–117
   impact of, 238–239
   individualism and, 238–239
   Internet impact, 226–228
   investigative journalism, 218–219
   news reporting via, 230–236
   policy agenda and, 237–238
   policy entrepreneurs and, 237–238
   political coverage by, 7
   political culture, 202
   political socialization through, 190
   presidential coverage by, 378, 412–414
   press conferences, 218
   print, 219–220
   private control of, 228–229
   public opinion influenced by, 236–237
   radio, 220–222
   scope of government and, 238
   shield laws protecting sources in, 117
   Supreme Court coverage by, 507
   television, 220–222
Medicaid
   budget for, 84, 561
   federal grants and mandates for, 86–87
   health care access through, 560, 561–562
   as means-tested programs, 539
   states opting out of extending coverage for, 564
Medicare, 302
   budget for, 433
   creation and expansion, 433
   as entitlement program, 539
   political participation and, 6
McCorvey, Norma, 135
McConnell, Mitch, 354
McConnell v. Federal Election Commission, 288
McGovern-Fraser Commission, 276
McGovern, George, 276
McDonald v. Chicago, 122
McCullough v. Maryland, 75–76
McClure, Robert, 285
McKinley, William, 382
McKay, Amy, 321

prescription drug benefit, 476
taxes paid toward, 425
Mellman, Mark, 193
Melroy, Pam, 163
melting pot, America as, 184–188
Meltzer, Allan, 443
Men's Health magazine, 312
merit principle, 452, 455
Mexican American Legal Defense and Education Fund, 159
Miami Herald Publishing Company v. Tornillo, 118
middle-class voting, 301–302
Miers, Harriet, 497
Milbrath, Lester, 323
military. *See also* Department of Defense; national defense; wars/wartime
Central American intervention by, 592
changing role of, 604–605
draft, 165
foreign policy role of, 584–585
humanitarian interventions, 610
humanitarian interventions by, 30
Joint Chiefs of Staff, 589
LGBT in, 169
military-industrial complex, 432
national security policy and, 604–605
personnel in, 601–602
president as commander in chief of, 402–403
sexual harassment in, 166
on wage discrimination, 163
weapons for, 602–603, 605
women in, 164–165
Military Commissions Act (2006), 131–132
Miller v. California, 113, 114
Minerals Management Service, 460
Mine Safety and Health Administration, 465
Mineta, Norman, 187
minorities. *See also specific minorities*
affirmative action for, 170–173
in Congress, 343, 344
demographics of, 157
health care access for, 558–559
judicial appointments of, 502
minority majority, 184
minority majority of, 156
poverty of, 537
rights of, 15, 174
unemployment rates of, 526
minority leaders, congressional, 354
Miranda v. Arizona, 127–128, 513
Missouri Compromise, 149, 511
mixed economy, 524
Mondale, Walter, 388
monetarism, 528
monetary policy, 527–529
money
campaigns and, 286–291
for constituents, 348
elections and, 291
interest groups with, 367

soft, 288
victory, 291
Monroe, James, 592
Monroe Doctrine, 592
Montesquieu, Baron, 42
Montoya de Hernandez, Rosa Elvira, 126
Morris, Robert, 34, 42
Morrison, United States v., 77
Morse, Samuel, 232
Motion Picture Association of America, 320
Motor Votor Act, 294
Mott, Lucretia, 161
Mueller, John, 409
multinational corporations, 587
multiparty systems, 264
Munn v. Illinois, 471
Muslims, civil rights of, 160–161

N

NAACP (National Association for the Advancement of Colored People), 120, 144, 150, 151, 333, 488, 514
NAACP v. Alabama, 121
Nader, Ralph, 264, 334
NAFTA (North American Free Trade Agreement, 1993), 608
narrowcasting, 222–226
National Aeronautics and Space Administration (NASA), 436, 461
National Annenberg Election Survey, 195
National Association for the Advancement of Colored People (NAACP), 333
National Beer Wholesalers Association, 319, 320
national chairperson, 255
national committee, 255
national convention, 255
national debt, 420, 425–427
national defense. *See also* Department of Defense; military; national security policy; wars/wartime
budget for, 431–433, 600–601
government role in providing, 9
policy on, 600–603
National Defense Education Act (1958), 80
National Education Association, 330
National Election Study on political participation, 4, 5
National Environmental Policy Act (1969), 566–567
National Guard, 464, 601–602
National Highway Traffic Safety Administration, 471
National Industrial Recovery Act, 511
National Labor Relations Board, 459, 471
National League of Cities v. Usery, 74
National Organization for Women (NOW), 162
National Park Service, 463
National Park System, 567
national party convention, 275
national party organizations, 255
National Reconnaissance Office, 591
National Restaurant Association, 319
National Rifle Association (NRA), 122, 246, 316

National Science Foundation, 461
National Security Agency, 127, 404, 591
National Security Council, 390, 589–590
national security policy
  budgets for, 431–433
  censorship in name of, 110
  congressional role in, 591
  defense policy and, 600–603. (*See also* national defense*)
  democracy and, 612
  electronic surveillance, 110
  energy policy and, 610
    as evolving, 603
  foreign aid and, 610, 611
  foreign policy and, 589–591
  international economy and, 606–610
  military in. (*See* military)
  presidential role in, 401–406
  scope of government and, 613
National Wildlife Federation, 332, 564
National Women's Political Caucus, 162
Native American Rights Fund, 157
Native Americans, civil rights of, 156–158
NATO (North Atlantic Treaty Organization), 586, 593
natural gas, as fuel, 572–574
natural rights, 35
Nature Conservancy, 332
Nazi party, 121
Near v. Minnesota, 110
Neuman, Russell, 197
Neustadt, Richard, 378
New Deal
  coalition, 259–261
  social welfare policies of, 77, 511–512. (*See also* Social Security)
New England Journal of Medicine, 312
New Hampshire
  Constitutional ratification by, 53
  motto of, 19
New Jersey Plan, 43
NewsHour, 239
New York, Constitutional ratification by, 53
New York Times, 194, 329
New York Times v. Sullivan, 115
New York Times v. United States, 111
New York Tribune, 259
NIMBY phenomenon, 569–570
Nimmo, Dan, 292
Nineteenth Amendment, 60, 161
Nixon, Richard
  détente and, 595
  impeachment of, 380
  judicial nominations by, 512–513
  media coverage, 221
  national security policy of, 466
  Pentagon papers and, 111
  presidency of, 386
  presidential election, 261
  public approval, 408
  resignation of, 380
  Watergate scandal involving, 382–383, 414

No Child Left Behind Act, 73, 87
No Child Left Behind Act (2002), 73, 80, 83, 87
Noll, Roger, 326
nomination, 247
  definition, 275
  judicial, 493–498
nomination campaigns
  caucus system, 277–282
  delegates, competing for, 275–282
  invisible primary, 277
  primary system, 277–282
  strategy, 275
nongovernmental organizations and foreign policy, 587
North American Free Trade Agreement (NAFTA, 1993), 608
North Atlantic Treaty Organization (NATO), 586, 593
North Carolina, Constitutional ratification by, 53
Northwest Ordinance (1787), 38
NOW (National Organization for Women), 162, 333
NRA (National Rifle Association), 246, 316
Nuclear Non-Proliferation Treaty (1968), 605
nuclear power
  energy policy on, 574–575
  iron triangles on, 477–478
  waste from, 569
Nuclear Regulatory Commission, 460, 478
nuclear weapons, 403, 603, 605
Nye, Joseph, 604

O

Obama, Barack
  BP Deepwater Horizon oil spill and, 468
  budget of, 420
  Congress and, 396
  economic policy of, 23, 24, 410–411, 529, 530
    election of, 185
  energy policy of, 573
  environmental policy of, 571
  health care policy, 180, 552, 554, 562–564
  House of Representatives, 244
  immigration policy, 187
  judicial nominations by, 497, 498
  media coverage of, 412
  national security policies of, 403, 404, 589, 599, 603
  nomination campaign, 281
  political parties and, 395
  on politics, 4
  presidency of, 378, 381, 392
  presidential campaign, 4, 272, 306
  presidential elections, 347
  presidential power of, 62
  public approval, 408
  on Ryan budget, 524
  Social Security and, 545
  speech at Michigan, 3
  superdelegates, 277
  trust in government, 199
Obama, Michelle, 313, 393

obscenity, 112–115
Occupy Wall Street, 16, 205, 534, 536
O'Connor, Sandra Day, 497, 499
Office of Management and Budget
  budgetary process role of, 438, 440, 474–475
  Executive Office role of, 389–391
Office of Personnel Management, 456
offshore drilling, 565, 573–574
oil industry, 468, 565–566, 572–574, 610
Olson, Mancur, 320
Open Housing Act (1968), 154
open primaries, 254
opinion. *See also* public opinion
  defined, 504
Oregon v. Mitchell, 517
Organization of Petroleum Exporting Countries, 610
originalism, 506
original jurisdiction, 489
Orren, Karen, 327
Orshansky, Mollie, 535–536

P

PACs (political action committees), 287
Paine, Thomas, *Common Sense*, 33
Pakistan and terrorism, 599
parental leave policies, 546
*Parents Involved in Community Schools v. Seattle School
  District No. 1*, 172
Parks, Rosa, 144, 146
parliamentary system of government, 385
party dealignment, 262
party era, 256–262
party machines, 253
party realignment, 258
patronage, 253, 455
Patterson, Thomas
  media coverage, 219
  study on candidates, 285
Paul, Alice, 162
peace dividend, 601
Pelosi, Nancy, 8, 396
Pence, Mike, 529
Pendleton Civil Service Act (1883), 455
Pentagon Papers, 111, 386
Pepper v. United States, 484, 486
PepsiCo, 314
Perot, Ross, 264, 288
Persian Gulf War, 467, 610
Personal Responsibility and Work Opportunity
  Reconciliation Act (1996), 541
personal staff, 361
Pew Research Center, 238, 283
Pierson, Paul, 16
Piketty, Thomas, 534
Pinckney, Charles C., 43
plaintiffs, 487
Planned Parenthood v. Casey, 136
plea bargaining, 130

Pledge of Allegiance, 190
Plessy v. Ferguson, 150, 505
Plouffe, David, 525
Plum Book, 456–457
Plunkett, George Washington, 253
pluralism, 316–317
pluralist theories, of democracy, 15–16
Plyler v. Doe, 159
pocket vetoes, 394
polarized politics, 21–22, 340, 365–366, 409
police riot, 276
policy agenda, 12–13, 237, 400–401
policy entrepreneurs, 237
policy gridlock, 18, 340
policy impacts, 13–14
policy implementation, bureaucratic, 461–471
policymaking institutions, 13
policymaking system, 11–14
policy voting, 300–301
political action committees (PACs), 287
  corporate, 332
  House of Representatives, 326
  interest groups, 325
political campaigns. *See* campaigns
political culture
  American creed of, 19–22, 35–36
  of American people, 188
  in media, 202
political efficacy, 294
political ideologies, 199–203, 500–501
political issues, 13, 17
political knowledge, generation gap in, 4–8
political participation
  age impacting, 4–8, 191
  class and, 207
  conventional, 204, 206
  defined, 10
  democracy and, 17–18
  inequality and, 207
  liberalization of requirements, 38–39
  protests as, 204–207
  of senior citizens, 4–6
  types, 203
  unconventional, 204, 206
  voting as, 6, 10–11
  of young people, 4–8
political parties. *See also specific parties*
  advantages, 265–266
  articulate policies, 247
  bills and, 362–364
  campaigns, 247
  in candidates selection, 246
  congressional influence of, 340, 349, 353–355, 358
  conservatives, 199–201. *See also* Republican Party
  coordinate policymaking, 248
  cues to voters, 247
  dealignment, 262
  definition, 246
  disadvantages, 265–266
  Downs model, 248–250

political parties (continued)
economic stances of, 524, 525
in electorate, 246
in government, 247, 255–256
identification with, 409
image of, 250
in judicial selection, 500–501
liberals, 199–201. See also Democratic Party
linkage institutions, 247
local parties, 253–254
national chairperson, 255
national committee, 255
national convention, 255
national party organizations, 255
organizations, 252–255
party machines, 253
patronage by, 253, 454
platform of, 257
polarization of, 21–22, 340, 365–366, 409
politics, 2
presidency and, 395–398
primaries, 254
proportional representation, 265
rational-choice theory, 248
realignment, 258
responsible party model, 265–266
scope of government and, 267–268
social welfare stances of, 522, 524
third parties, 246–247, 263–264
young people and, 252
political questions, 516
political questions doctrine, 516
political socialization
learning over lifetime, 191
process of, 189–191
politicos, 367
politics, 10–11
poll
conducting method, 192–193
decline of trust in government tracked via, 197–199
democratic role of, 193–195
exit, 194, 303
Pew Research Center, 238
random sampling, 192
results of, 195–197
sampling in, 192
Pollock v. Farmer's Loan and Trust Co., 423, 517
poll taxes, 60, 154
populism, 21
pork barrel, 348, 445
pornography, 113, 114, 115
position taking, 348
Postal Service, 454, 460
potential group, 320
poverty
demographics of, 537
feminization of, 537
health care access and, 558–559
measurement of, 535–536

poverty line, 535–536
Powell, Colin, 185
Powell, Jody, 231
Powell, Lewis, 496, 500
Powell v. Alabama, 129
power
bureaucratic, 452
chief legislator role of, 394–395
commerce, 77–78
congressional, 340, 342, 352
division of, 72–73
enumerated, 76
implied, 75–77
judicial, 515–517
presidential, 59, 379, 384–387, 394–395, 403–404, 415
separation of, 42, 48–49, 50, 61–62
war, 403–404
prayer in schools, 105–106
precedent, 505
Pregnancy Discrimination Act (1978), 163, 164
presidency. See also Presidents by name; Presidents by name
approval ratings for, 397–398
audience for speeches of, 7
budgetary role of, 438, 440, 441
as "bully pulpit," 409
bureaucratic interaction with, 474
cabinet appointed by, 388–389
chief diplomat role of, 401–402
chief executive role of, 387–393
coattails of, 346–347, 397
commander in chief role of, 402–403
Congress relationship with, 345–346, 364, 393–401
crisis management role of, 403–404
democracy and, 415
demographics of, 379
election to, 380. See also elections, specifically
executive agreements by, 402, 587
Executive Office of, 389–391, 458
executive orders by, 474
expectations for, 379
foreign policy role of, 587–588
impeachment of, 382–384
judicial nominations by, 496–498, 499, 501–502
leadership role of, 378
legislative skills of, 399–401
media coverage of, 378, 412–414
national security role of, 401–406
party leadership role of, 395–398
policymaking role of, 378
political appointments by, 378
powers of, 59, 379, 384–387, 394–395, 403–404, 415
public appointments by, 456–457
public approval, 408–409
public opinion and, 407–412
scope of government and, 415
staff of, 391–392, 413
succession to, 380–382

perceptions of, 533
public policy and, 533–539
underestimation of, 536–537
war on, 540

vetoes of, 394–395
vice presidency and, 388
war powers of, 403–404
presidential primaries, 278–279
press conferences, 218, 412, 413
press secretary, White House, 219, 231, 413
primaries, 277–280
  invisible, 277
  presidential, 278–279
print media
  bias of, 234–236, 413
  nonprofit organizations, 221
  online editions, 220
  politics and, 219–220
Printz v. United States, 77
priorities, setting, 400–401
prior restraint, 110–111
privacy rights as civil liberty, 135
privatization, bureaucratic, 470–471
privileges and immunities clause, 78–79, 102
probable cause, 125
progressive taxes, 538
project grants, 85
property rights, government preservation of, 35, 40, 45, 47
proportional representation, 265
proportional taxes, 538
protests
  abortion, 120
  antiwar, 116
  civil rights movement, 154–155, 157
  flag burning at, 30, 116
  freedom of assembly for, 119–121, 121–123
  health care reform, 514
  political participation, 204–207
public approval, 408–409
public displays of religious symbols, 106
public goods and services, government role in providing, 9–10
public housing, 88
public interest lobbies, 334
public opinion
  democracy and, 208–209
  health care reform, 180, 514
  measuring, 191–198
  presidency and, 407–412
  scope of government, 208–209
public order, 10, 111–112
public policies
  agenda for, 12–13, 400–401
  approval of and support for, 409–411
  civil rights movement and, 152–154
  Congress role in creating, 13, 340, 342, 351–362
  courts and, 509–513
  diversity among states, 88–89
  elections and, 307
  gridlock on, 18, 62–63, 340
  impact of, 13–14
  policymaking institutions creating, 13
  policymaking system for, 11–14
  presidential role in, 378
  representativeness vs. effectiveness, 370–371
  taxes and, 427–430
  types of, 13
public schools. *See also Brown v. Board of Education*
  Pledge of Allegiance, 190
  political socialization through, 190–191
  religious activities in, 104–106
  segregation of, 509, 512
  teaching evolution in, 106
Putnam, Robert, 16, 188

Q

Quayle, Dan, 388

R

racial discrimination/equality
  affirmative action against, 170–173
  federalism impacting, 74
  segregation/desegregation and, 77, 149–150
Rademacher, Eric, 4
radio media, 220–222
Rakove, Jack N., 506
Randall, Gene, 329
Randolph, Edmund, 43, 50
Randolph, Jennings, 61
random-digit dialing, 193
random sampling, 192
Rank, Mark, 539
Rasul v. Bush, 131
Rather, Dan, 228
rational-choice theory, 248
R.A.V. v. St. Paul, 510
Reagan, Nancy, 378, 392
Reagan, Ronald
  approval ratings of, 411
  on bureaucracy, 453
  bureaucratic interaction with, 474
  economic policy of, 530
  election of, 201
  federal *vs.* state authority under, 82–83
  foreign policy of, 595–596
  interest groups, 335
  international trade policy of, 92
  Iran-Contra affair, 235, 387
  media coverage, 214, 217, 414
  national security policies of, 602–603
  presidency of, 381, 386–387
  public relation, 409
  scope of government, 24–25, 208, 431
  tax policy of, 428
reapportionment, 349
reapportionment process, 188
reconciliation, 440
Reconstruction, 149–150
Red Lion Broadcasting Company v. Federal Communications Commission, 118
Reed v. Reed, 162

Reeves v. Sanderson, 167
Regents of the University of California v. Bakke, 171, 172, 328
regional organizations and foreign policy, 586–587
regressive taxes, 538
regulation, 470–471. *See also* environmental policy
Rehabilitation Act (1973), 167
Rehnquist, William, 126, 495, 497, 498, 513, 514, 516
Reid, Harry, 354, 396
Reilly, William, 568
relative deprivation, 534–535
religion
  animal sacrifices in, 109
  congressional, 366–367
  establishment clause on, 103–107
  freedom of, 102–109
  free exercise clause on, 107–109
  insurance coverage for contraception, 108
  in nominations to Supreme Court, 500
  political ideology, 201
  religious extremists, 107
  separation of church and state, 100, 104, 106
Religious Freedom Restoration Act (1993), 108–109
Rendell, Ed, 255
renewable sources of energy, 575
representation
  colonists', in British Parliament, 33
  congressional, 369–371
  descriptive *vs.* substantive, 344
  democratic theory on, 15
republic, 49–50
Republican National Committee, 248
Republican Party
  federalism stance of, 82–83
  scope of government, 208
Resource Conservation and Recovery Act (1977), 569
responsible party model, 265–266
Rettig, Richard, 477
revenues, 422, 423–430
reverse discrimination, 171
Revolutionary War, 32–37
Rhode Island, 39–40, 39–40f, 41, 53
Rice, Condoleezza, 185
Ricci v. DeStefano, 172
Richard, Scott, 443
Richardson, Bill, 272
rights
  to bear arms, 121–123
  to counsel, 129
  of defendants, 123–134
  individual, 46–47
  minority, 15, 174
  natural, 35
  privacy, 135–137
  property, 35, 40, 45, 47
right-to-work laws, 330
Ring v. Arizona, 134
Roberts, John G., 497, 501, 513, 516
Roberts, Owen, 512
Roe v. Wade, 135–136, 513

Rogers, Will, 355
Romer v. Evans, 169
Romney, Mitt
Rompilla v. Beard, 134
Roosevelt, Eleanor, 392
Roosevelt, Franklin D.
  election of, 192
  economic policy of, 422, 524
  media coverage, 236
  presidential campaign, 219
  in shows, 224
  media politics, 218
  New Deal of, 77, 511–512, 540
  presidency of, 382
  on racial discrimination, 150
  on Social Security, 544
Roosevelt, Teddy, 263
Roper v. Simmons, 134
Rosenberg, Shawn, 299
Rosenberger v. University of Virginia, 510
Rostker v. Goldberg, 165, 510
Roth v. United States, 112
Rosensteil, Thomas, 226
Rove, Karl, 219, 274
Russia, 37. *See also* Soviet Union (former)
Ryan, George, 133, 134
Ryan, Paul, 522, 524

S

Saenz v. Roe, 79
Salisbury, Robert, 335
SALT (Strategic Arms Limitation Talks), 595, 603
same-sex marriage/union, 169
sampling error, 192
Samuelson, Robert, 532
Sanchez, Linda, 159
Sanchez, Loretta, 159
Sandusky, Jerry, 234
Santa Clara Pueblo v. Martinez, 157
Santorum, Rick, 280
Scalia, Antonin, 501, 502, 506
scandals
  Clinton-Lewinsky, 218, 384, 414
  Iran-Contra, 235, 387, 590
  Watergate, 218, 231, 382–383, 414
Schattschneider, E. E., 246
  interest groups, 319
Schechter Poultry Corporation v. United States, 511
Schenck v. United States, 111
Schildkraut, Debra, 188
School District of Abington Township, Pennsylvania v. Schempp, 105
schools
  church-related, 104
  Pledge of Allegiance, 190
  political socialization through, 190–191
  single-gender, 163–164
Schulman, Paul, 435–436

scope of government
  budgets and, 445
  bureaucracy and, 452, 478–479
  campaigns and, 307
  civil liberties and, 138
  civil rights and, 174–175
  Congress and, 371
  Constitution and, 61–62
  federalism and, 92–93
  health care, environmental, energy policy and, 576
  interest groups and, 335
  judicial power, 486, 515–517
  media and, 238
  national security policy and, 613
  political divisions on, 23–24
  political parties and, 267–268
  presidency and, 415
  public opinion, 208–209
Scott v. Sandford, 149, 517
searches and seizures, 125–127
search warrant, 125
Second Amendment, 121–122
secretary of defense, 589
secretary of state, 588
Securities and Exchange Commission (SEC), 459, 465, 471
segregation/desegregation, 77, 150, 151, 509, 512. *See also*
  Brown v. Board of Education
Seldon, Barry J., 326
select committees, 355
selective benefits, 320
selective exposure, 225
selective perception, 292
self-incrimination, 127–129
Sellers, Patrick, 237
Senate. *See also* Congress
  African Americans, 343
  characteristics, 351, 352–353
  committees in, 356
  Constitution on structure of, 43
  demographics of, 342–344
  election to, 60
  filibusters in, 346–347
  Finance Committee, 438
  incumbents in, 346–347
  judicial system involvement of, 494–495, 496
  leadership of, 352, 354
  malapportionment in, 369–370
  states' representation in, 43
  senatorial courtesy, 494
Seneca Falls Declaration of Sentiments and Resolutions, 161
senior citizens. *See also* generation gap
  civil rights of, 167
  demographics of
  political participation of, 4–6
Senior Executive Service, 456
seniority system for congressional committee chairs, 359
separation of church and state, 100, 104, 106
separation of powers, 42, 48–49, 50, 61–62
September 11, 2001 terrorist attacks, 58–59, 87, 131, 161, 405, 582–583

Seventeenth Amendment, 60
sexual harassment, 166
Shays's Rebellion/Daniel Shays, 40, 45
Shepard, Matthew, 169
Sherman, Roger, 14, 34, 37, 43
Sides, John, 292
Sierra Club, 332
Simpson-Mazzoli Act, 187
Sinclair, Barbara, 362
single-issue group, 321
single-issue groups, 12, 367
Sitaraman, Ganesh, 8
Sixteenth Amendment, 55, 423, 517
Sixth Amendment, 129
slander, 115–116
Slaughterhouse Cases, 102
slavery
  Constitution on, 43–44
  era of, 149
  three-fifths compromise on, 44
Smith, Bradley, 291
Smith Act (1940), 111–112
Smith v. Allwright, 154
Snowden, Edward, 110, 591
Sobieraj, Sarah, 224
social class
  political ideology, 201
  political participation, 207
social insurance taxes, 425
socialized medicine, 328
Social Security. *See also* Medicare
  budget for/funding of, 433–434
  definition, 188
  Disability Insurance, 464
  as entitlement program, 539
  growth of, 544
  political participation and, 6
  reform of, 544–545
  retirement age, 167
  taxes paid toward, 425
  trust fund for, 543
Social Security Act (1935), 433, 540
Social Security Trust Fund, 543
social welfare policy. *See also* Social Security
  changes in over time, 540–542
  defined, 524
  democracy and, 547–548
  entitlement program, 539
  entitlement programs, 436, 533
  European *vs.* U.S, 545
  Great Society programs, 433, 434, 522, 524, 540
  illegal immigrants and, 542–543
  means-tested programs, 533, 539
  New Deal programs, 77, 511–512, 540
  parental leave, 546
  political party stances on, 522, 524
  Ryan budget plan and, 522, 524
  scope of government and, 548
  solicitor general, 503
  types of, 532–533

712

soft money, 288
soft power, 604
solicitor general, 503
Solow, Robert, 548
Sorauf, Frank, 287
Sotomayor, Sonia, 497, 499, 500, 501
sound bites, 232
Souter, David, 501, 502
South
  Blue Dog Democrats, 266
  political parties in, 261
Soviet Union (former). See also Russia
  Cold War against, 586, 590, 591–597
  political socialization, 189
Spacey, Kevin, 266
Speaker of the House, 353–355, 365. See also Speakers by name
Speakes, Larry, 414
SpeechNow.org v. FEC, 290
staff
  committee, 361–362
  congressional, 360–362
  personal, 361
standard operating procedures, bureaucratic, 465
  White House, 391–392, 413
standards of review, 147–148
standing committees, 355
standing to sue, 487
Stanton, Elizabeth Cady, 161
stare decisis, 505
Starr, Kenneth, 384
Star Wars (Strategic Defense Initiative), 596
State Department, 588–589
state government. See also states
  Articles of Confederation reliance on, 37–39
  as bicameral, 370
  Constitutional amendment role of, 54–56
  governors' role in, 39
  legislature of, 39
  liberalization of participation requirements in, 38–39
  mandates for, 86–88
  as unitary, 70
state legislators, economic status of, 39
states. See also specific states
  Bill of Rights applied to, 102
  Constitution ratification by, 51
  constitutions of, 39
  environmental policy implementation in, 565
  grants to, 83–86
  interstate obligations, 78–79
  minority demographics in, 157
  policy diversity among, 88–89
  powers denied by Constitution, 72
  representation of, 43
statutory construction, 517
Steenbergen, Marco, 533
Stern, Howard, 118
Sternberg v. Carhart, 136
Stevens, Stuart, 290
Stewart, Potter, 513
Stockman, David, 400

Strategic Arms Limitation Talks (SALT), 595, 603
Strategic Arms Reduction Treaty (START), 603
Strategic Defense Initiative (Star Wars), 596
Strategic Petroleum Reserve, 573
Strauder v. West Virginia, 150
street-level bureaucrats, 466
subgovernments, 476–478
succession to presidency, 380–382
suffrage, 154, 292
superdelegates, 277
Superfund law, 569
Super PACs, 18
Supplemental Security Income, 539
supply-side economics, 530, 531
supremacy clause, 73–78
Supreme Court. See also specific cases
  Bill of Rights and, 123–124
  case acceptance by, 502–504
  Constitutional interpretation by, 74–75, 76, 77–78
  decision making in, 504–509
  defined, 491
  implementation of decisions of, 507–509
  judicial review by, 49, 50, 57
  justices of, 492, 497, 498, 499, 501
  media coverage of, 507
  opinions of, 504–505
  presidency and, 495–498
  routing of cases to, 492
  sources of full opinions in, 493
  on standards of review, 147–148
  structure of, 491–493
Swann v. Charlotte-Mecklenburg County Schools, 151
Sweatt v. Painter, 151
symbolic speech, 116

T

Taft-Hartley Act, 330
Taliban, 584, 598–599, 603
talking head, 235
Taney, Roger, 511
tariffs, 608
Tauzin, Billy, 477
tax burden, 430
taxes
  British taxing colonists, 33
  budgets including tax revenue, 427–430
  economic policy and, 530
  education tax credits, 429
  Europe vs. U.S., 545
  government role in collecting, 10
  income, 423–425, 538
  poll, 60, 154
  public policy and, 427–430
  reductions in, 428–430
Taylor, Zachary, 259, 382
Teamsters Union, 328
Tea Party movement, 83, 371
technology. See also Internet

in campaigns, 284
congressional advertising and, 347
Constitutional change due to, 58
in health care, 555–556
political contact through, 61
polling methods changed by, 192–193
television media, 220–222
bias of, 234–236
cable, 222–236
comedy shows and, 223
FCC regulation, 222
narrowcasting, 222–236
Temporary Assistance for Needy Families, 539, 541, 542
Ten Commandments, public displays of, 106
Tennessee Valley Authority, 460
Tenth Amendment, 74–75
term of service, congressional, 350
terrorism
by Abdulmutallab, 468
in Beirut, Lebanon, 466
foreign policy response to, 582, 584, 587, 597–599
Guantánamo Bay detention camp, 131, 517
September 11, 2001 terrorist attacks, 58–59, 87, 131, 161, 405, 582–583
war on, 58–59, 127, 131
Texas v. Gregory Lee Johnson, 30, 116, 510
third political parties, 246–247, 263–264
Thirteenth Amendment, 55, 149
Thomas, Clarence, 497, 499, 501, 502, 506
Thoreau, Henry David, 205
Thornberry, Homer, 496
Thornburg v. Gingles, 155
three-fifths compromise, 44
ticket splitting, 251
Tinker, Mary Beth and John, 116
Title IX, 163, 462
Tocqueville, Alexis de, 15, 20
tourism and foreign policy, 587
toxic wastes, 568–569
trade, international, 606–609
transfer payments, 539
Transportation Department, 458, 567
treaties, 402, 587–588, 591, 612. *See also specific treaties; specific treaties*
trial balloons, 230
trials, 129–132
Truman, Harry S.
on desegregation, 150
on economic policy, 525
health care policy of, 561–562
on judicial nominations, 502
national security policies of, 593
Truman Doctrine, 593
Turner, Frederick Jackson, 21
Tweed, William, 253
Twenty-fifth Amendment, 380
Twenty-first Amendment, 54
Twenty-fourth Amendment, 60, 154
Twenty-second Amendment, 380
Twenty-seventh Amendment, 52

Twenty-sixth Amendment, 60, 61, 517
Twenty-third Amendment, 60

U

uncontrollable expenditures, 436
unconventional participation, 204, 206
underemployment rate, 526
unemployment, 525, 526, 530
unemployment insurance, 539
uninsured population, 558–559
union shop, 330
unitary government, 70
United Auto Workers, 330
United Farm Workers, 159
United Nations, 585–586
United States v. Darby, 74
United States v. Eichman, 32
United States v. Lopez, 77
United States v. Morrison, 77
United States v. Nixon, 504, 513
United States v. O'Brien, 510
universities, federal support for, 81
unorthodox lawmaking, 362
unreasonable searches and seizures, 125
urban party organizations, 253
USA Patriot Act, 59, 127
U.S. Postal Service, 454, 460
U.S. Term Limits, Inc. et al. v. Thornton et al., 350

V

Van Buren, Martin, 258
Van Devanter, William, 512
Vavreck, Lynn, 292
Verba, Sidney, 204
vetoes
legislative, 403
line-item, 394
presidential, 394–395
vice presidency. *See also Vice presidents by name*
presidency and, 388
presidential succession by, 380–382
Vietnam War
foreign policy and, 594–595
media coverage, 221
Pentagon Papers about, 111, 386
protests against, 205
Viguerie, Richard, 284
Violence Against Women Act (1994), 77
Virginia, Constitutional ratification by, 53
Virginia Military Institute (VMI), 164
Virginia Plan, 43
Virginia 21 Coalition, 321
VMI (Virginia Military Institute), 164
von Clausewitz, Karl, 584
voting
candidates, 299–300

voting (continued)
demographic factors, 296–297
Downs model, 248–250
elements of decisions, 299
middle-class, 301–302
party identifications, 299
policy, 300–301
political ideologies influencing, 366–367
political parties, 247
registration, 294
suffrage, 292
ticket splitting, 251
turnout rate, 6, 10–11, 191
turnout rates, 295

voting rights
as civil rights, 154–156
Constitution on, 53, 60
of minorities, 60
voting age, 60, 61
of women, 57, 60, 161
Voting Rights Act (1970), 60, 61, 154–156, 469–470

W

wage discrimination, 163
Wainwright v. Witt, 133
Wallace, George, 74, 263
Ward, Artemus, 342
War of 1812, 405
war on terrorism, 127
War Powers Resolution (1973), 403, 516
Warren, Earl, 151, 504, 512, 516
Warren, Previn, 8
wars/wartime
Afghanistan war, 9, 165
censorship during, 110
Civil War, 73–74, 149–150
Cold War, 586, 590, 591–597
conscientious objection to, 108
Iraq. See Iraq war
Persian Gulf War, 467, 610
Revolutionary War, 32–37
Vietnam War, 111, 205, 594–595
War of 1812, 405
war on terrorism, 58–59, 131
World War II, 160–161, 164, 593
Washington, George
Constitutional Convention role of, 51
foreign policy of, 592
on media, 412
on political parties, 246
presidency of, 53, 402, 415
Watergate scandal, 218, 231, 382–383, 414
Water Pollution Control Act (1972), 567
wealth
Constitutional Convention and, 45
defined, 535
influence on politics due to, 18
internships influenced by, 361

weapons
for military, 602–603, 605
nuclear, 403, 603, 605
right to bear arms, 121–123
Weaver, David, 234
Weber, Max, 452
Webster, Daniel, 75–76, 258
Webster v. Reproductive Health Services, 136, 322, 514
welfare reform, 541–542
Welzel, Christian, 19
Westmoreland, William, 115
Whig Party, 258–259
whips, congressional, 354, 365
White, Byron, 496
White House, 342
staff, 391–392, 413
White House press secretary, 413
white primaries, 154
Whitman, Meg, 291
Widmar v. Vincent, 510
WikiLeaks, 110
Wildavsky, Aaron, 435
wilderness preservation, 567
Wilkins, Roy, 148
Williams, Brain, 227
Wilson, Edith, 382, 392
Wilson, James, 50
Wilson, James Q., 21, 463
Wilson, Peggy, 163
Wilson, Woodrow, 262, 380, 382, 386, 388, 592
winner-take-all system, 264
women. See also gender discrimination/equality; gender
discrimination/ equality
civil rights of, 161–166
in Congress, 343, 344–345
education, 164
employment, 163–164
Equal Rights Amendment, 55–56, 162–163
judicial appointments of, 502
military service of, 164–165
pluralism theory of, 317
political ideology, 201
poverty of, 537
presidency and, 380
Title IX impacting, 163, 462–463
voting rights for, 161
in workplace, 163–164
Women, Infants, and Children (WIC) program, 23
Woodson v. North Carolina, 132
Woodward, Bob, 218
Woodward, Charlotte, 161
workplace issues
affirmative action, 170–173
age discrimination, 167
child labor as, 547
health insurance benefits, 556–558
homosexuality, 169
immigrant documentation, 159
international trade, 609
people with disabilities, 168

sexual harassment, 166
wages, 163
  for women, 163–164
World War II, 160, 164, 593
World Wildlife Fund, 332
writ of certiorari, 503
writ of habeas corpus, 46, 129

Y

Yates v. United States, 112
Yellen, Janet, 527, 528
Yeltsin, Boris, 597, 603
Young, Whitney, 148
young people. *See also* children; generation gap
  drug convictions and financial aid of, 462
  globalization and, 608
  health care access for, 559
  internship system for, 361
  judicial decisions impacting, 510

Obama presidential campaign and, 4
political campaigns, 284
political ideology, 200
political participation, 4–8, 207
political parties and, 252
political socialization, 189
presidential approval by, 410
socialization of, government role in, 10
turnout rates, 297
unemployment rates of, 526
voting by, 8
Yucca Mountain, Nevada, 569

Z

Zelman v. Simmons-Harris, 104
Zuniga, Markos Moulitsas, 228
Zurcher v. Stanford Daily, 117, 510
Zwerg, James, 153

1
1. d
2. a
3. d
4. d
5. e
6. a
7. a
8. a
9. a
10. d
11. d
12. e
13. a
14. b
15. c

2
1. a
2. b
3. c
4. d
5. e
6. e
7. a
8. e
9. e
10. a
11. c
12. c
13. b
14. a
15. b

3
1. b
2. b
3. d
4. b
5. c
6. a
7. a
8. b
9. e
10. d
11. a
12. e
13. a
14. d
15. c
16. e

4
1. c
2. c
3. d
4. c
5. b
6. c
7. e
8. c
9. a
10. d
11. e
12. d
13. c
14. e
15. d
16. e

5
1. a
2. e
3. a
4. d
5. c
6. a
7. e
8. e
9. d
10. b
11. c
12. d
13. b
14. a
15. d

6
1. a
2. d
3. e
4. c
5. c
6. d
7. b
8. b
9. e
10. e
11. b
12. c
13. b
14. c
15. c

7
1. d
2. b
3. d
4. d
5. b
6. d
7. a
8. d
9. b
10. a
11. a
12. b
13. e
14. b
15. e
16. d
17. d
18. d

8
1. c
2. b
3. e
4. d
5. a
6. a
7. a
8. c
9. d
10. a
11. b
12. a
13. e
14. e
15. b

9
1. e
2. c
3. d
4. e
5. a
6. b
7. d
8. d
9. d
10. c
11. d
12. a
13. e
14. a
15. b

10
1. c
2. e
3. a
4. d
5. e
6. a
7. e
8. c
9. b
10. d
11. b
12. a
13. d
14. e
15. c

11
1. a
2. a
3. b
4. c
5. d
6. b
7. a
8. b
9. a
10. b
11. a
12. b
13. e
14. c
15. c

12
1. a
2. c
3. d
4. d
5. c
6. d
7. b
8. e
9. b
10. c
11. a
12. d
13. d

13
1. a
2. b
3. c
4. d
5. a
6. b
7. b
8. e
9. d
10. e
11. e
12. c
13. a

14
1. e
2. e
3. d
4. d
5. b
6. c
7. a
8. e
9. b
10. a
11. a
12. a
13. a
14. a

15
1. d
2. c
3. e
4. b
5. b
6. e
7. a
8. e
9. a
10. d
11. d
12. d
13. c
14. c

16
1. d
2. a
3. c
4. d
5. b
6. e
7. d
8. e
9. c
10. d
11. a
12. e
13. d
14. a
15. c

17
1. c
2. d
3. e
4. e
5. e
6. c
7. c
8. a
9. b
10. e
11. e
12. b
13. d
14. b

18
1. b
2. a
3. a
4. d
5. d
6. c
7. d
8. b
9. a
10. d
11. c
12. c
13. c
14. b
15. a